i CLASSZONE.COM

Looking ~~for~~ ~~ways~~ ~~to~~ ~~inte~~grate the We~~b~~ ~~into~~ ~~your~~ ~~curri~~culum?

ClassZone, McDougal Littell's
textbook-companion Web site,
Online teaching support for you~~r~~
interactive content for your stu~~dents.~~

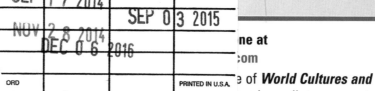

DATE DUE

APR 2 3 2007		
NOV 2 5 2007	JAN 1 1 2011	
OCT 0 5 2008		
	JAN 1 1 2012	
MAY 3 1 2011		
DEC 1 3 2011	JUL 3 0 2012	
	MAY 2 7 2014	
MAR 1 1 2014	MAY 2 8 2015	
SEP 1 7 2014		
	SEP 0 3 2015	
NOV 2 8 2014		
DEC 0 6 2016		

ORD   PRINTED IN U.S.A.

ClassZone is your online guide to *World Cultures and Geography*

- Links provide updated connections to relevant Web sites.
- Quizzes check comprehension with self-scoring assessment.
- Activities offer students a fun and engaging way to study world cultures and geography.
- Current Events check students' knowledge of the weekly news.
- Teacher Center provides lesson planning support and teaching ideas.

~~...~~ne at
~~...~~com
~~...~~e of *World Cultures and Geography, you have* immediate access to ClassZone.

Teacher Access Code

MCDYJQ49FDTCF

Use this code to create your own user name and password. Then access both teacher and student resources.

TEACHER'S EDITION

World Cultures
AND
GEOGRAPHY
Eastern Hemisphere

ONLINE EDITION@
CLASSZONE.COM

McDOUGAL LITTELL

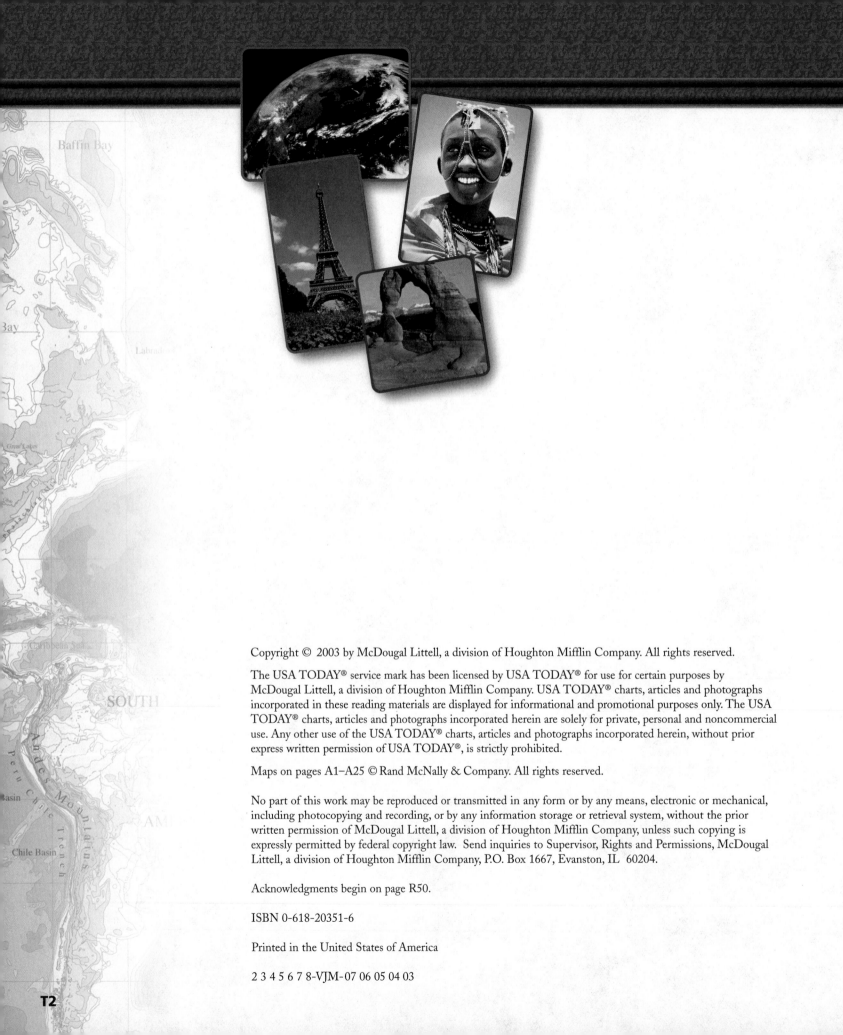

Acknowledgments begin on page R50.

ISBN 0-618-20351-6

Printed in the United States of America

2 3 4 5 6 7 8-VJM-07 06 05 04 03

Contents

Motivation

McDougal Littell's *World Cultures and Geography* offers a vibrant visual approach that motivates students to gain a greater appreciation of the diversity of peoples around the world.

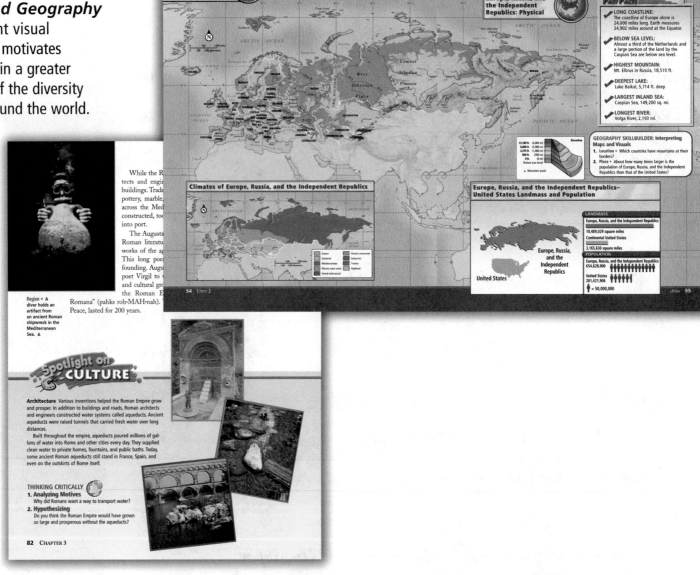

① Unit Atlas

A **Unit Atlas** introduces each unit with state-of-the-art maps and up-to-date charts and graphs—giving a colorful overview of each region. Every **Unit Atlas** includes a full-page physical map, a full-page political map, and several thematic maps.

② Spotlight on Culture

High-interest features like **Spotlight on Culture** provide a comprehensive look at cultural activities around the world, including dance, food, music, and art.

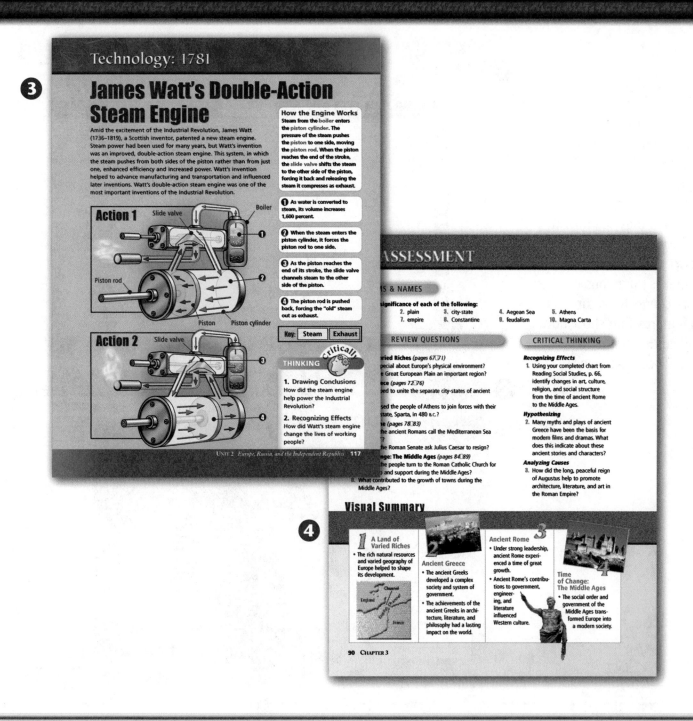

Technology: 1781

James Watt's Double-Action Steam Engine

Amid the excitement of the Industrial Revolution, James Watt (1736–1819), a Scottish inventor, patented a new steam engine. Steam power had been used for many years, but Watt's invention was an improved, double-action steam engine. This system, in which the steam pushes from both sides of the piston rather than from just one, enhanced efficiency and increased power. Watt's invention helped to advance manufacturing and transportation and influenced later inventions. Watt's double-action steam engine was one of the most important inventions of the Industrial Revolution.

How the Engine Works
Steam from the boiler enters the piston cylinder. The pressure of the steam pushes the piston to one side, moving the piston rod. When the piston reaches the end of the stroke, the slide valve shifts the steam to the other side of the piston, forcing it back and releasing the steam it compresses as exhaust.

1 As water is converted to steam, its volume increases 1,600 percent.

2 When the steam enters the piston cylinder, it forces the piston rod to one side.

3 As the piston reaches the end of its stroke, the slide valve channels steam to the other side of the piston.

4 The piston rod is pushed back, forcing the "old" steam out as exhaust.

Action 1 — Slide valve, Boiler, Piston rod, Piston, Piston cylinder

Action 2 — Slide valve

Key: Steam | Exhaust

THINKING Critically

1. Drawing Conclusions
How did the steam engine help power the Industrial Revolution?

2. Recognizing Effects
How did Watt's steam engine change the lives of working people?

UNIT 2 Europe, Russia, and the Independent Republics **117**

ASSESSMENT

TERMS & NAMES

Explain the significance of each of the following:

1. 2. plain 3. city-state 4. Aegean Sea 5. Athens
6. 7. empire 8. Constantine 9. feudalism 10. Magna Carta

REVIEW QUESTIONS

A Land of Varied Riches (pages 67–71)

1. What is special about Europe's physical environment?
2. Why is the Great European Plain an important region?

Ancient Greece (pages 72–76)

3. Who helped to unite the separate city-states of ancient Greece?
4. What caused the people of Athens to join forces with their rival city-state, Sparta, in 480 B.C.?

Ancient Rome (pages 78–83)

5. What did the ancient Romans call the Mediterranean Sea and why?
6. Why did the Roman Senate ask Julius Caesar to resign?

Time of Change: The Middle Ages (pages 84–89)

7. Why did the people turn to the Roman Catholic Church for help and support during the Middle Ages?
8. What contributed to the growth of towns during the Middle Ages?

CRITICAL THINKING

Recognizing Effects

1. Using your completed chart from Reading Social Studies, p. 66, identify changes in art, culture, religion, and social structure from the time of ancient Rome to the Middle Ages.

Hypothesizing

2. Many myths and plays of ancient Greece have been the basis for modern films and dramas. What does this indicate about these ancient stories and characters?

Analyzing Causes

3. How did the long, peaceful reign of Augustus help to promote architecture, literature, and art in the Roman Empire?

Visual Summary

1 A Land of Varied Riches
• The rich natural resources and varied geography of Europe helped to shape its development.

2 Ancient Greece
• The ancient Greeks developed a complex society and system of government.
• The achievements of the ancient Greeks in architecture, literature, and philosophy had a lasting impact on the world.

3 Ancient Rome
• Under strong leadership, ancient Rome experienced a time of great growth.
• Ancient Rome's contributions to government, engineering, and literature influenced Western culture.

4 Time of Change: The Middle Ages
• The social order and government of the Middle Ages transformed Europe into a modern society.

90 CHAPTER 3

---

3 Technology

Cross-curricular features such as **Technology** involve students in learning about the steam engine, China's Three Gorges Dam, and The Great Zimbabwe. Students learn about the impact of technology on culture through the combination of pictures and words in these engaging and interactive features.

4 Visual Summary

A **Visual Summary** at the end of each chapter summarizes the key ideas of that chapter. The key ideas are organized in easy-to-read charts that give visual learners and others another path to understanding.

Relevance

World Cultures and Geography offers interactive lessons that help students make the connection between geography and current events. Students see geography as more relevant when they see how it connects to other subjects they are studying. ***World Cultures and Geography*** makes numerous interdisciplinary connections through activities and features that show how geography and culture relate to literature, art, science, math, and other subjects.

❶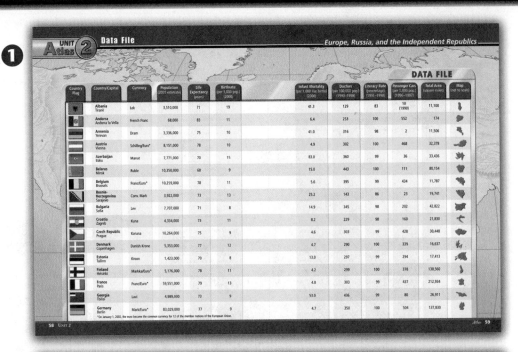

❷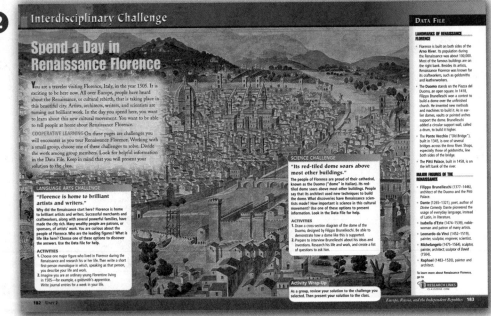

❶ Data File

Every unit contains a **Data File** as part of the **Unit Atlas.** This comprehensive, easy-to-read chart contains detailed demographic data on each region to help students make comparisons and connections. For regular data updates, go to **classzone.com**, the companion Web site for ***World Cultures and Geography.***

❷ Interdisciplinary Challenge

These interactive features place students in situations that challenge them to solve problems by making connections to other disciplines. Every **Interdisciplinary Challenge** includes a **Data File** of information that students use in solving the problems.

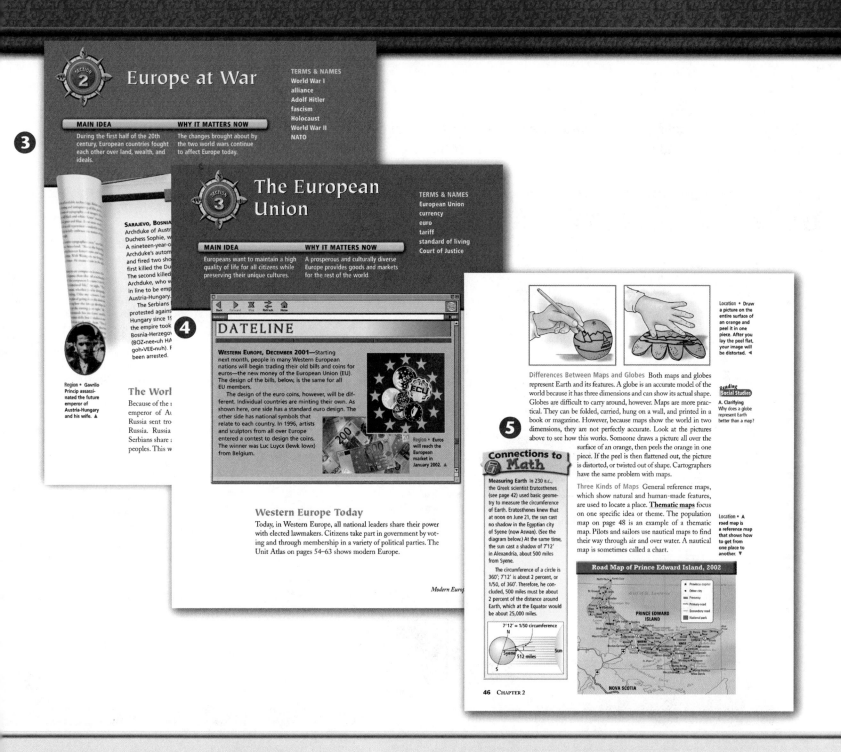

Skills

McDougal Littell's *World Cultures and Geography* places special emphasis on critical thinking, content-area reading, and map skills to provide continual social studies skill development.

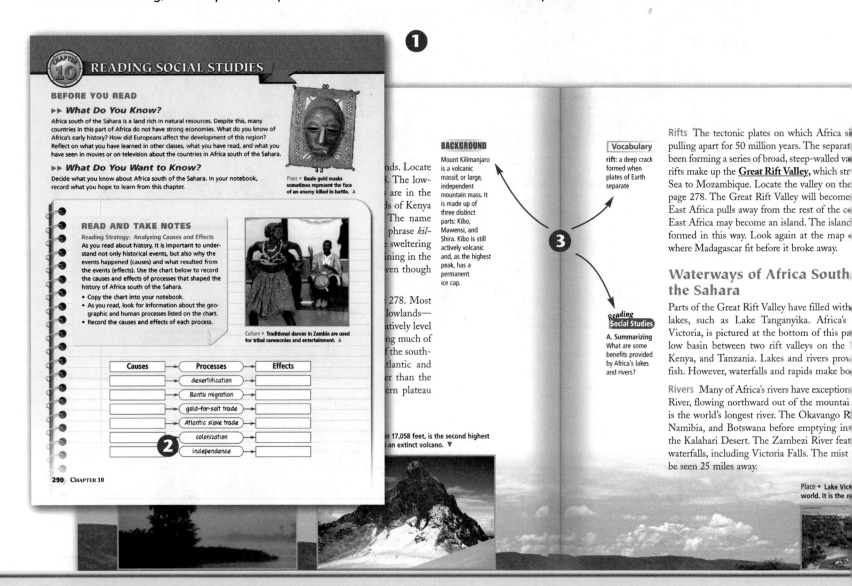

❶

CHAPTER 10 READING SOCIAL STUDIES

BEFORE YOU READ

▶▶ *What Do You Know?*

Africa south of the Sahara is a land rich in natural resources. Despite this, many countries in this part of Africa do not have strong economies. What do you know of Africa's early history? How did Europeans affect the development of this region? Reflect on what you have learned in other classes, what you have read, and what you have seen in movies or on television about the countries in Africa south of the Sahara.

▶▶ *What Do You Want to Know?*

Decide what you know about Africa south of the Sahara. In your notebook, record what you hope to learn from this chapter.

Place • **Baule gold masks sometimes represent the face of an enemy killed in battle.** ▲

READ AND TAKE NOTES

Reading Strategy: Analyzing Causes and Effects
As you read about history, it is important to understand not only historical events, but also why the events happened (causes) and what resulted from the events (effects). Use the chart below to record the causes and effects of processes that shaped the history of Africa south of the Sahara.

• Copy the chart into your notebook.
• As you read, look for information about the geographic and human processes listed on the chart.
• Record the causes and effects of each process.

Culture • **Traditional dances in Zambia are used for tribal ceremonies and entertainment.** ▲

Causes	Processes	Effects
	desertification	
	Bantu migration	
	gold-for-salt trade	
	Atlantic slave trade	
	colonization	
	independence	

❷

290 CHAPTER 10

BACKGROUND

Mount Kilimanjaro is a volcanic massif, or large, independent mountain mass. It is made up of three distinct parts: Kibo, Mawensi, and Shira. Kibo is still actively volcanic and, as the highest peak, has a permanent ice cap.

❸

nds. Locate
8. The low-
s are in the
ds of Kenya
The name
phrase *kil-*
e sweltering
ining in the
ven though

278. Most
lowlands—
atively level
g much of
f the south-
tlantic and
er than the
ern plateau

t 17,058 feet, is the second highest
s an extinct volcano. ▼

Vocabulary

rift: a deep crack formed when plates of Earth separate

Reading **Social Studies**

A. Summarizing What are some benefits provided by Africa's lakes and rivers?

Rifts The tectonic plates on which Africa si pulling apart for 50 million years. The separat been forming a series of broad, steep-walled va rifts make up the **Great Rift Valley,** which str Sea to Mozambique. Locate the valley on the page 278. The Great Rift Valley will become East Africa pulls away from the rest of the c East Africa may become an island. The island formed in this way. Look again at the map where Madagascar fit before it broke away.

Waterways of Africa South the Sahara

Parts of the Great Rift Valley have filled with lakes, such as Lake Tanganyika. Africa's Victoria, is pictured at the bottom of this pa low basin between two rift valleys on the Kenya, and Tanzania. Lakes and rivers prov fish. However, waterfalls and rapids make bo

Rivers Many of Africa's rivers have exception River, flowing northward out of the mountai is the world's longest river. The Okavango R Namibia, and Botswana before emptying in the Kalahari Desert. The Zambezi River feat waterfalls, including Victoria Falls. The mist be seen 25 miles away.

Place • **Lake Vic** world. It is the n

---

❶ Reading Social Studies

Every chapter begins with **Reading Social Studies.** The page features the widely used K-W-L strategy, asking students what they know about the region and what they would like to know.

❷ Graphic Organizers

The "Read and Take Notes" graphic organizer helps students determine the main ideas and other important information as they work their way through the text.

❸ Reading Social Studies, Vocabulary, and Background Notes

World Cultures and Geography provides reading support for students as they read. Side-column notes on every page support student comprehension at point of use. **Reading Social Studies** notes ask student-comprehension and critical-thinking questions. **Vocabulary** notes define important vocabulary words at point of use. **Background** notes provide vital historical information that helps to clarify events for students.

SKILLBUILDER

Reading Latitude and Longitude

▶▶ Defining the Skill

To locate places, geographers use a global grid system. Imaginary lines of latitude, called parallels, circle the globe. The Equator circles the middle of the globe at 0°. Parallels measure distance in degrees north and south of the Equator.

Lines of longitude, called meridians, circle the globe from pole to pole. Meridians measure distance in degrees east and west of the Prime Meridian. The Prime Meridian is at 0°. It passes through Greenwich, England.

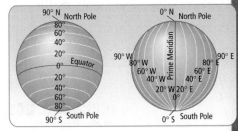

▶▶ Applying the Skill

The world map below shows lines of latitude and longitude. Use the strategies listed below to help you locate places on Earth.

How to Read Latitude and Longitude

Strategy ❶ Place a finger on the place you want to locate. With a finger from your other hand, find the nearest parallel. Write down its number. Be sure to include north or south. (You may have to "guesstimate" the actual number.)

Strategy ❷ Keep your finger on the place you want to locate. Now find the nearest meridian. Write down its number. Be sure to include east or west. (You may have to "guesstimate" the actual number.)

Strategy ❸ If you know the longitude and latitude of a place and want to find it on a map, put one finger on the line of longitude and another on the line of latitude. Bring your fingers together until they meet.

Write a Summary

Writing a summary will help you understand latitude and longitude. The paragraph to the right summarizes the information you have learned.

Use latitude and longitude to locate a place on a globe or map. Lines of latitude circle Earth. Lines of longitude run through the poles. The numbers of the lines at the place where two lines cross is the location of that place.

▶▶ Practicing the Skill

Turn to page 36 in Chapter 2, Section 1, "The Five Themes of Geography." Look at the map of Australia and write a paragraph summarizing how you located the city of Adelaide.

❹ Social Studies Skillbuilder

A one-page **Skillbuilder** feature in each chapter focuses on a specific skill related to social studies, such as sequencing events, reading a time line, or identifying cause and effect. Students work through a set of strategies in order to master each skill. There is also one **Skillbuilder Mini-Lesson** in each chapter, which provides additional practice with the skill from the previous chapter.

Interact with the World

World Cultures and Geography offers a wide variety of resources to help teachers manage their classroom and support students as they interact with the world.

Teacher's Resource Package

In-Depth Resources
Resources organized by unit, chapter, and section include:

- Unit Atlas Activities
- Data File Activities
- Guided Reading Worksheets
- Map Skills
- Skillbuilder Practice
- Vocabulary Worksheets
- Geography Workshops
- Reteaching Activities

Outline Map Activities
Outline maps and blackline masters for geography skills development

Cultures Around the World
60 articles and transparencies on a variety of cultural topics such as food, music, dance, art, literature, architecture, and cultural artifacts

Reading Study Guides
With Answer Key
For low-level readers, with an interactive summary and study guide for each section of the textbook

Access for Students Acquiring English: Spanish Translations
Strategies for teaching ESL students and Spanish translations of Chapter Summaries and selected In-Depth Resources

Block Scheduling Strategies
A pacing guide, chapter teaching models, organization charts, and suggestions for addressing multiple learning styles

Formal Assessment
Three levels of tests for each chapter, section quizzes, and rubrics for assessing writing

Integrated Assessment
Provides explanations and forms for a variety of assessment options, including cooperative learning, group discussion, role-playing, oral presentations, peer assessment, self-assessment, and portfolio assessment

Strategies for Test Preparation
Strategies and exercises to help prepare students for a variety of test-taking experiences

Strategies for Test Preparation Teacher's Edition

Rand McNally Classroom Atlas of World Geography

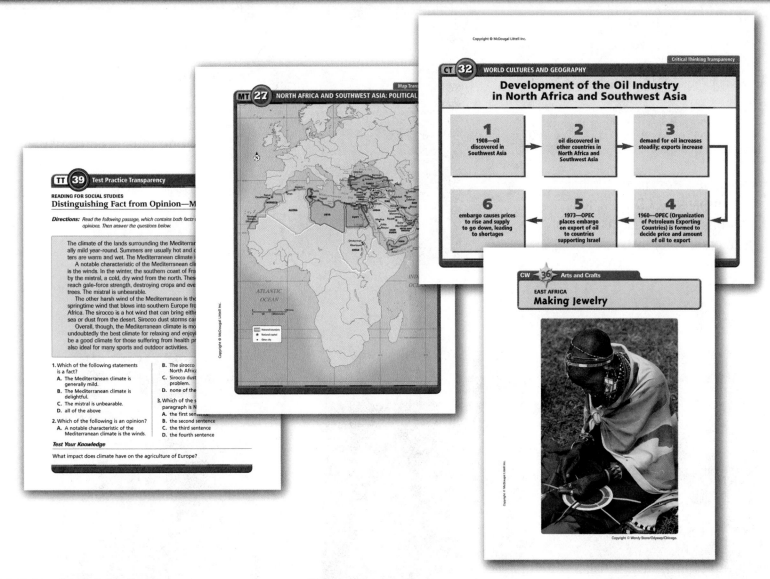

Additional Resources

World Cultures and Geography Workbook
Features note-taking strategies and graphic organizers for enhancing reading comprehension

Geography Posters
Two colorful posters for each unit

Houghton Mifflin Dictionary of Geography

Writing for Social Studies
Provides extra content-area writing support for writing research projects, historical narratives, essays, interviews, oral histories, book reviews, and short reports

Transparencies

Map Transparencies
Overlays and transparencies provide more than 70 maps for in-depth coverage of regions and locations

Critical Thinking Transparencies
Transparencies provide graphic organizers, cause-and-effect charts, and visual summaries

Cultures Around the World Transparencies
60 articles and transparencies on a variety of cultural topics such as food, music, dance, art, literature, architecture, and cultural artifacts

Test Practice Transparencies
One transparency for each section of the textbook reviews content and familiarizes students with a variety of testing items

Comprehensive Assessment Support

Comprehensive assessment materials in print, transparency, CD-ROM, and Internet formats offer students a variety of ways to prepare for tests.

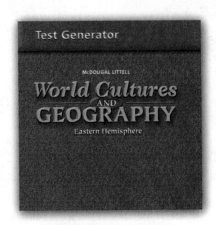

Test Generator CD-ROM

This CD-ROM contains a variety of pre-made tests and a test bank of items for creating customized tests. Questions are provided in three levels: basic, average, and advanced. Tools walk the user through the searching and editing steps and help teachers correlate tests to national and state standards.

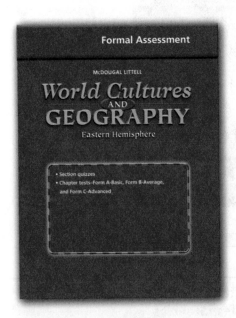

Formal Assessment

This Assessment book contains a variety of testing materials, including three levels of tests for each chapter, as well as section quizzes.

Integrated Assessment

This booklet includes rubrics for evaluating alternative assessments, including portfolios, cooperative learning activities, group discussions, and presentations.

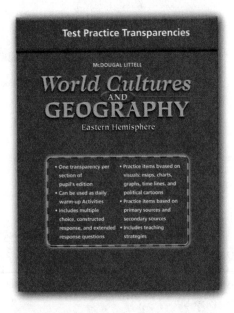

Test Practice Transparencies

Each transparency corresponds to one section of the textbook and reviews the content. The transparencies help students gain familiarity with a variety of testing items.

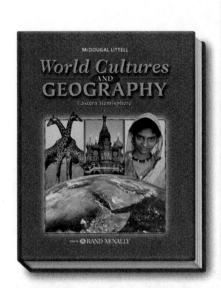

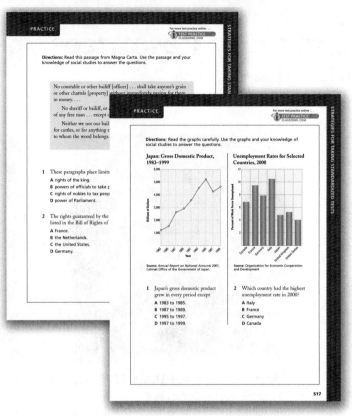

Strategies for Taking Tests

Strategies and exercises in the Pupil's Edition help prepare students for a variety of test-taking experiences. It includes strategies for multiple choice, constructed response, extended response, and document-based questions.

Online Test Practice

This student **Online Test Practice** feature can be accessed through **classzone.com**. The test practice includes test-taking tips, diagnostic tests, skill-based tutorials, and skills and strategies help.

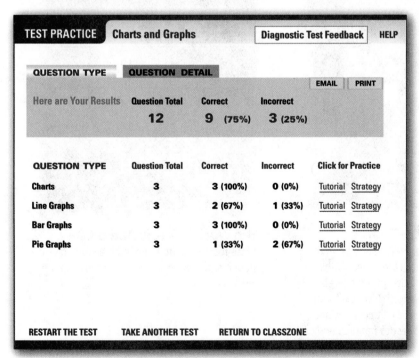

Integrated Technology Resources

Audio, video, online, and computer resources provide students
with additional opportunities to explore graphic information.

Power Presentations CD-ROM
These electronic presentations are a valuable
tool for use in classroom instruction.
Presentations contain outlines of each
chapter, maps, and slides for key concepts
and terms.

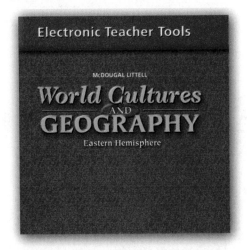

Electronic Teacher Tools CD-ROM
All of the teacher resources in the print
ancillaries are located on this convenient
CD-ROM. View, search, and print the
ancillaries, which are organized by resource
and chapter.

Chapter Summaries CD-ROM
Reinforce learning with recorded readings of
each chapter summary. Available in English
and Spanish.

There Is No Food Like My Food
These enjoyable videos give students the opportunity
to learn about foods from the United States, Mexico,
France, Israel, Senegal, India, and Japan.

Test Generator CD-ROM
Print pre-made tests or create your own from
a test bank of items that correspond to the
text. Questions are provided in three levels:
basic, average, and advanced. Tools walk you
through the searching and editing steps and
help you correlate your test to national and
state standards.

The World's Music Audio CD
These recordings from around the world give
students the opportunity to hear music that
reflects a variety of cultures.

World Cultures and Geography Online Edition

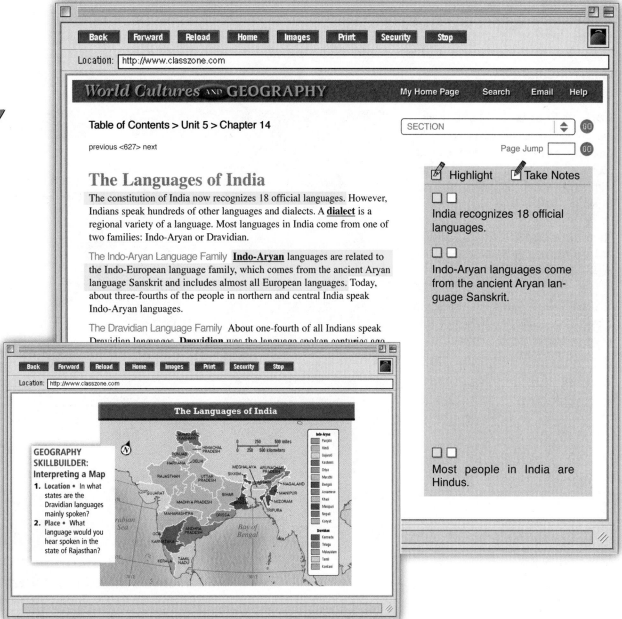

Back Forward Reload Home Images Print Security Stop

Location: http://www.classzone.com

World Cultures AND GEOGRAPHY

My Home Page   Search   Email   Help

Table of Contents > Unit 5 > Chapter 14

SECTION [ ] GO

previous <627> next

Page Jump [   ] GO

The Languages of India

The constitution of India now recognizes 18 official languages. However, Indians speak hundreds of other languages and dialects. A **dialect** is a regional variety of a language. Most languages in India come from one of two families: Indo-Aryan or Dravidian.

The Indo-Aryan Language Family **Indo-Aryan** languages are related to the Indo-European language family, which comes from the ancient Aryan language Sanskrit and includes almost all European languages. Today, about three-fourths of the people in northern and central India speak Indo-Aryan languages.

The Dravidian Language Family About one-fourth of all Indians speak Dravidian languages. **Dravidian** was the language spoken centuries ago

✎ Highlight   ✎ Take Notes

☐ ☐
India recognizes 18 official languages.

☐ ☐
Indo-Aryan languages come from the ancient Aryan language Sanskrit.

☐ ☐
Most people in India are Hindus.

Back Forward Reload Home Images Print Security Stop

Location: http://www.classzone.com

The Languages of India

GEOGRAPHY SKILLBUILDER:
Interpreting a Map
1. Location • In what states are the Dravidian languages mainly spoken?
2. Place • What language would you hear spoken in the state of Rajasthan?

Students enhance comprehension:
- Highlight text.
- Make notes in the margins.
- Look up key glossary words.
- Connect to relevant Web sites.
- Use interactive maps and illustrations.
- Take assessments online.
- Listen to section audio summaries.
- Participate in opinion polls.

Teachers enrich instruction:
- Create margin notes to guide student reading and activities.
- Post homework assignments.
- Place online worksheets at point of use.
- Receive assessment results via e-mail.
- Use animated maps and illustrations for presentations and lectures.

Internet Resources

The online guide to *World Cultures and Geography,* **classzone.com** offers:

Current Events Geographic issues that are spotlighted in each unit are expanded in **classzone.com**. Current Events contains links that provide students with current information related to these issues.

Research Links Links to a variety of Web sites to support student research and extend the content of each chapter.

Internet Activities Pre-selected Web sites engage students in a variety of activities correlated to chapter content.

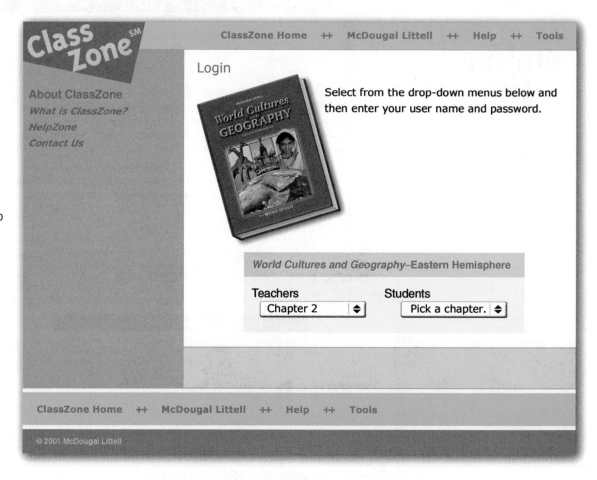

Interactive Self-Scoring Quizzes Quizzes for each chapter allow students to check their progress in geographic knowledge.

Online Test Practice Test practice is provided online to help students prepare for standardized tests. Included are test-taking tips, diagnostic tests, skill-based tutorials, and skills and strategies help.

Internet Research Tutorial A tutorial helps students learn to use the Internet as a research tool.

Online Lesson Planner This convenient planner lets you create customized lesson plans that use components of *World Cultures and Geography* to meet the needs of your students.

Focus on the World

A two-page **Planning Guide** at the beginning of every chapter of the *World Cultures and Geography* Teacher's Edition provides a chapter overview at a glance. It also outlines program resources section by section.

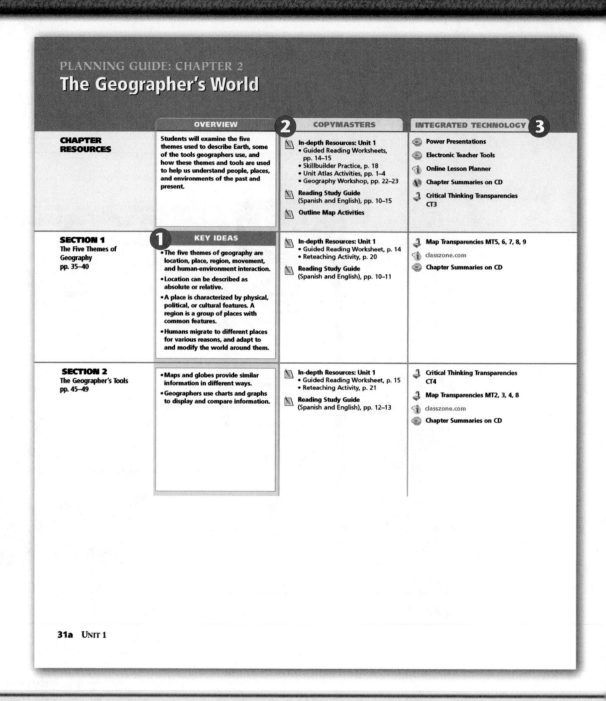

PLANNING GUIDE: CHAPTER 2
The Geographer's World

	OVERVIEW	**COPYMASTERS** ②	**INTEGRATED TECHNOLOGY** ③
CHAPTER RESOURCES	Students will examine the five themes used to describe Earth, some of the tools geographers use, and how these themes and tools are used to help us understand people, places, and environments of the past and present.	**In-depth Resources: Unit 1** • Guided Reading Worksheets, pp. 14–15 • Skillbuilder Practice, p. 18 • Unit Atlas Activities, pp. 1–4 • Geography Workshop, pp. 22–23 **Reading Study Guide** (Spanish and English), pp. 10–15 **Outline Map Activities**	Power Presentations Electronic Teacher Tools Online Lesson Planner Chapter Summaries on CD Critical Thinking Transparencies CT3
SECTION 1 ① The Five Themes of Geography pp. 35–40	**KEY IDEAS** • The five themes of geography are location, place, region, movement, and human-environment interaction. • Location can be described as absolute or relative. • A place is characterized by physical, political, or cultural features. A region is a group of places with common features. • Humans migrate to different places for various reasons, and adapt to and modify the world around them.	**In-depth Resources: Unit 1** • Guided Reading Worksheet, p. 14 • Reteaching Activity, p. 20 **Reading Study Guide** (Spanish and English), pp. 10–11	Map Transparencies MT5, 6, 7, 8, 9 classzone.com Chapter Summaries on CD
SECTION 2 The Geographer's Tools pp. 45–49	• Maps and globes provide similar information in different ways. • Geographers use charts and graphs to display and compare information.	**In-depth Resources: Unit 1** • Guided Reading Worksheet, p. 15 • Reteaching Activity, p. 21 **Reading Study Guide** (Spanish and English), pp. 12–13	Critical Thinking Transparencies CT4 Map Transparencies MT2, 3, 4, 8 classzone.com Chapter Summaries on CD

31a UNIT 1

① Key Ideas and Chapter Overview

A brief summary of each section and a **Chapter Overview** show how the content is structured to present a unifying chapter theme.

② CopyMasters

A complete listing of reproducible materials for each section reveals the depth of resource material that is available.

③ Integrated Technology

Technology is listed for each section and includes resources for audio and visual learners, electronic and online teacher tools, and Internet resources. Selected chapters also include the video resource **There Is No Food Like My Food,** which features foods from different cultures.

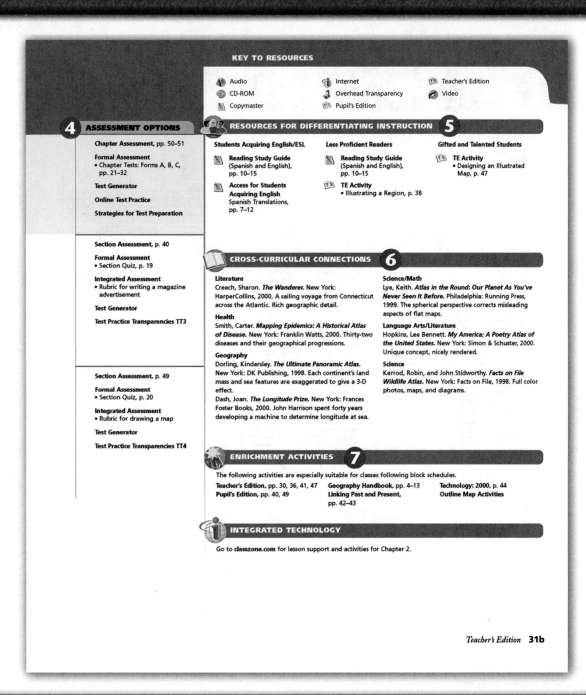

KEY TO RESOURCES

- 🎧 Audio
- 💿 CD-ROM
- 📋 Copymaster
- 🌐 Internet
- 📑 Overhead Transparency
- 📖 Pupil's Edition
- 📘 Teacher's Edition
- 📹 Video

④ ASSESSMENT OPTIONS

Chapter Assessment, pp. 50–51

Formal Assessment
• Chapter Tests: Forms A, B, C, pp. 21–32

Test Generator

Online Test Practice

Strategies for Test Preparation

Section Assessment, p. 40

Formal Assessment
• Section Quiz, p. 19

Integrated Assessment
• Rubric for writing a magazine advertisement

Test Generator

Test Practice Transparencies TT3

Section Assessment, p. 49

Formal Assessment
• Section Quiz, p. 20

Integrated Assessment
• Rubric for drawing a map

Test Generator

Test Practice Transparencies TT4

⑤ RESOURCES FOR DIFFERENTIATING INSTRUCTION

Students Acquiring English/ESL

📘 **Reading Study Guide** (Spanish and English), pp. 10–15

📘 **Access for Students Acquiring English** Spanish Translations, pp. 7–12

Less Proficient Readers

📘 **Reading Study Guide** (Spanish and English), pp. 10–15

📘 **TE Activity**
• Illustrating a Region, p. 38

Gifted and Talented Students

📘 **TE Activity**
• Designing an Illustrated Map, p. 47

📖 CROSS-CURRICULAR CONNECTIONS ⑥

Literature
Creech, Sharon. *The Wanderer.* New York: HarperCollins, 2000. A sailing voyage from Connecticut across the Atlantic. Rich geographic detail.

Health
Smith, Carter. *Mapping Epidemics: A Historical Atlas of Disease.* New York: Franklin Watts, 2000. Thirty-two diseases and their geographical progressions.

Geography
Dorling, Kindersley. *The Ultimate Panoramic Atlas.* New York: DK Publishing, 1998. Each continent's land mass and sea features are exaggerated to give a 3-D effect.
Dash, Joan. *The Longitude Prize.* New York: Frances Foster Books, 2000. John Harrison spent forty years developing a machine to determine longitude at sea.

Science/Math
Lye, Keith. *Atlas in the Round: Our Planet As You've Never Seen It Before.* Philadelphia: Running Press, 1999. The spherical perspective corrects misleading aspects of flat maps.

Language Arts/Literature
Hopkins, Lee Bennett. *My America: A Poetry Atlas of the United States.* New York: Simon & Schuster, 2000. Unique concept, nicely rendered.

Science
Kerrod, Robin, and John Stidworthy. *Facts on File Wildlife Atlas.* New York: Facts on File, 1998. Full color photos, maps, and diagrams.

🎆 ENRICHMENT ACTIVITIES ⑦

The following activities are especially suitable for classes following block schedules.

Teacher's Edition, pp. 30, 36, 41, 47
Pupil's Edition, pp. 40, 49

Geography Handbook, pp. 4–13
Linking Past and Present, pp. 42–43

Technology: 2000, p. 44
Outline Map Activities

🌐 INTEGRATED TECHNOLOGY

Go to **classzone.com** for lesson support and activities for Chapter 2.

Teacher's Edition **31b**

④ Assessment Options
This column lists the variety of **Assessment Options;** page numbers make chapter and section assessments quick to find.

⑤ Resources for Differentiating Instruction
Page references for the Teacher's Edition and ancillary activities for teaching students acquiring English, less proficient readers, and gifted and talented students are provided, as are Spanish language resources.

⑥ Cross-Curricular Connections
Resources for interdisciplinary teaching are listed. Books are categorized for literature, popular culture, history, science, and other disciplines.

⑦ Enrichment Activities
This listing highlights appropriate activities for block scheduling.

Chapter Pacing for Block Schedules

Teachers who teach in blocks will appreciate a special **Pacing Guide.** This easy-to-use guide is a valuable aid in planning lessons.

PACING GUIDE: CHAPTER 2

BLOCK SCHEDULE LESSON PLAN OPTIONS: 90-MINUTE PERIOD

DAY 1

CHAPTER PREVIEW, pp. 32–33
Class Time 20 minutes

- **Hypothesize** Use "What do you think?" questions in Focus on Geography on PE p. 33 to help students hypothesize about the uses of geography in exploring and understanding the world.

SECTION 1, pp. 35–40
Class Time 70 minutes

- **Summarizing** Have students write a brief description of a place they know well. Ask them to imagine they are describing it to someone who has never seen it. Write the five geography themes (location, place, region, movement, human-environment interaction) on the chalkboard. Have students share their descriptions, and ask them to decide into which geographical theme their description best fits. Review the themes as you discuss.
Class Time 30 minutes

- **Comparing** To compare the ideas of absolute location and relative location, have a student stand somewhere in the room. Ask students to describe his/her location first in an absolute way, then in a relative way. Have students explain the differences.
Class Time 10 minutes

- **Internet** Divide students into groups and have them visit **classzone.com** to learn more about Pangaea and changes in the locations of Earth's continents.
Class Time 30 minutes

DAY 2

SECTION 1, continued
Class Time 60 minutes

- **Reading a Map** Divide students into teams. Have them use the Rand McNally World Physical map on PE pp. A2–3 to find two location examples of each region shown in the Natural Regions of the World chart, on PE p. 38. Have groups present their examples to the class; they can point them out on a map.
Class Time 30 minutes

- **Analyzing Causes** Have students review the Human Migration map on PE p. 39. Lead a discussion about what natural features may have influenced or affected these movement patterns.
Class Time 10 minutes

- **Peer Review** To practice using longitude and latitude, ask students to choose a place in the world they would like to visit. Have students use the Skillbuilder on PE p. 41 to plot the longitude and latitude of their choice, keeping the location a secret. Then have students exchange coordinates, figure out the location, and check their answer with their partner.
Class Time 20 minutes

SECTION 2, pp. 45–49
Class Time 30 minutes

- **Making a Map** Review the concept of thematic maps, then ask students to make a thematic map of the school. They should clearly indicate the theme in the map's legend. Some possible themes: the locations of student activities, or the places where one can get food in the school.

DAY 3

SECTION 2, continued
Class Time 35 minutes

- **Cartographer** Have students use PE pp. 42–44 to review the skills cartographers use to construct maps. Encourage them to make an illustrated map of their town or neighborhood. Display the finished maps.

CHAPTER 2 REVIEW AND ASSESSMENT, pp. 50–51
Class Time 55 minutes

- **Review** Have students use the charts they created for Reading Social Studies on PE p. 34 to review the five geography themes.
Class Time 20 minutes

- **Assessment** Have students complete the Chapter 2 Assessment.
Class Time 35 minutes

❶ Comprehensive Planning
From the **Chapter Preview** to **Review and Assessment,** suggestions for content and pacing are all here.

❷ Estimated Times
Estimated times needed for each activity are provided to help teachers make efficient use of the block period.

❸ Teaching Options
Numerous teaching options are presented so teachers can vary the pacing of the class as well as the types of activities in which students are engaged.

TECHNOLOGY IN THE CLASSROOM

 DESIGNING WEB SITES

Students can design their own Web sites to organize information and to share their knowledge with other students at school and around the world. By creating a Web site, students gain experience in organizing information in a nonlinear fashion and get a behind-the-scenes look at what goes into developing materials for the Internet. Their Web sites can be kept on the classroom computer, uploaded to the school district's server, or uploaded to the Internet for students at other schools to view. The Web site at **classzone.com** is a helpful resource for students to learn about designing their own Web pages.

❶ ACTIVITY OUTLINE

Objective Students will design Web pages to teach other students about the Five Themes of Geography.

Task Have students work in groups to create a Web site that provides examples of the Five Themes of Geography and that teaches other students about each of the themes.

Class Time Three class periods

❷ DIRECTIONS

1. Hold a class discussion reviewing the Five Themes of Geography, as discussed in Chapter 2. Ask students to provide examples to explain each theme, and ask them to describe the reasons why it is important to be familiar with the concepts covered by each of these themes. For example, why is it important to identify your location (Theme 1) or to understand the impact of migration and transportation (Theme 4)?

2. Divide the class into small groups of about four students each. Assign one of the Five Themes. It may be necessary to assign some themes to more than one group.

3. Ask groups to create Web pages that will teach students in their grade or the grade below them about their assigned theme. They will need to provide text and images to help students learn the concepts of the theme. For example, for place (Theme 2), they might provide a brief description of what *place* means and then create a Web page that shows pictures of the landscape and people in their home town. They could then ask the audience to think about the special characteristics of their own home and to compare and contrast those features to the things they see on the Web page.

4. Suggest that students use the following criteria for completing their Web pages:

   - They must provide a two- to four-sentence description of what their theme is about.

   - They must include at least one example of how this theme relates to things they already know about (e.g., their home town, transportation, world regions).

   - They must include at least one image, and they must cite the source of the image if they have taken it from a book or another Web site.

5. Help several students design an overall home page that will link to each group's Web page. This main home page should contain a list of the Five Themes. As an option, upload this page and each group's site onto the school district's server, and register it with a search engine.

Teacher's Edition **31d**

Technology in the Classroom

Every chapter in the ***World Cultures and Geography*** Teacher's Edition includes a page providing an innovative strategy for using the Internet and other technologies in the classroom.

 Activity Outline
An overview introduces the strategy, presents an instructional rationale for using it with students, states the objective, and summarizes the task in direct, easy-to-understand terms. Recommended class time is also provided.

❷ Directions
The directions spell out, step-by-step, what students need to do to complete the activity. These straightforward directions ensure that students can incorporate technology into their daily lives.

Open Up the World

Teacher's Edition Lesson Support

The *World Cultures and Geography* Teacher's Edition provides a wealth of information and practical teaching suggestions to meet the needs of each student, link geography and culture to other subjects, develop critical thinking skills, and more.

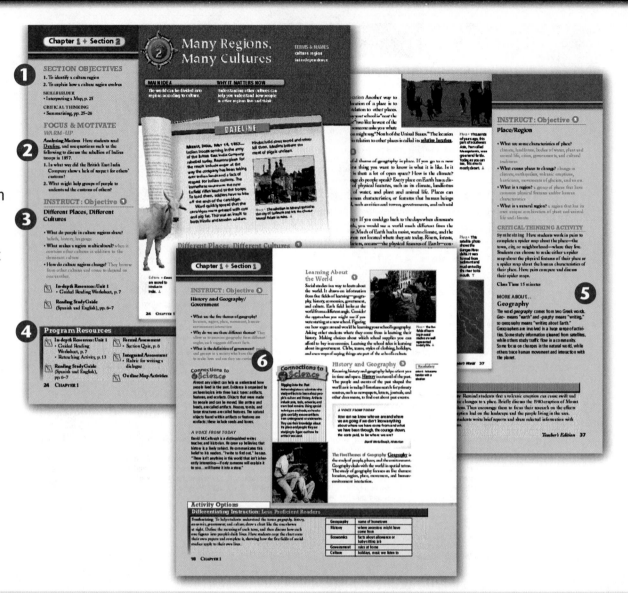

1 Section Objectives
The **Objectives** for the section are clearly spelled out. **Skillbuilder** and **Critical Thinking** skills covered in the section are also listed.

2 Focus & Motivate
Focus questions to stimulate students' thinking about the content of the section begin every lesson plan.

3 Instruct
Questions for every boldface heading in the body of the text help teachers review content and determine comprehension. Answers appear in blue type.

4 Program Resource References at Point of Use
Throughout the Teacher's Edition, references to the **Program Resources** at their point of use will help teachers plan and teach every lesson.

5 More About . . .
These short features provide additional information, often little-known facts, to supplement the text.

6 Enrichment
Additional content is often provided for these Pupil's Edition features: **A Voice from** (the country or region), **Biography, Connections to Citizenship** (and content area subjects), **Spotlight on Culture, Strange but True,** and **Citizenship in Action.**

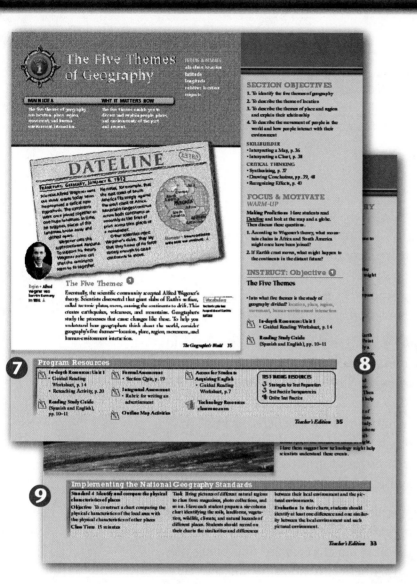

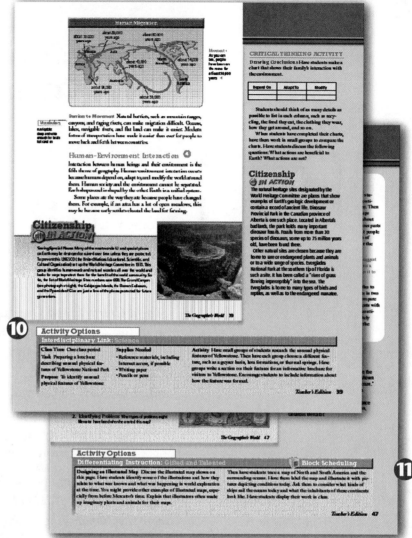

7 Program Resources
This listing of specific ancillaries for **World Cultures and Geography** will help teachers select appropriate support items to reinforce lessons.

8 Test-Taking Resources
Test-Taking Resources include Strategies for Test Preparation, Test Practice Transparencies, and Online Test Practice.

9 Implementing the National Geography Standards
World Cultures and Geography has 6 Unit Activities and 18 Chapter Activities that correlate to the *National Geography Standards*.

10 Activity Options
The bottom column of the Teacher's Edition pages contains a variety of activities for enriching teaching, including critical thinking activities, links to other subjects, activities for students acquiring English, plus activities for less proficient readers and gifted and talented students.

11 Block Scheduling
The **Block Scheduling** logo appears wherever an Activity Option is appropriate for block scheduling situations.

And there is more, including:

- **Recommended Resources**
- **Focus on Visuals**
- **Critical Thinking Activities**
- **Assess & Reteach**
- **Reteaching Activities**

The National Standards and *World Cultures and Geography*

Dear Educator:

As a geographer and former social studies teacher, I am pleased to welcome you to the exciting opportunity to teach young learners about the world in which we live. I hope you share my enthusiasm for teaching geography and helping students see the role that geography plays in understanding contemporary world cultures.

World Cultures and Geography organizes the study of today's world around five key geographic themes: *location, place, region, human-environment interaction,* and *movement.* The themes, which were first introduced in 1984 in the *Guidelines for Geographic Education,* are familiar to many social studies educators. This teacher-centered framework to organize geography instruction was developed two decades ago as an easy and accessible tool for introducing geographic concepts that go beyond map and globe skills and place names.

The themes were updated and enhanced with the publication of the *Geography for Life: National Geography Standards 1994.* The *National Geography Standards* represent the next big step toward improving the quality of geographic education in American schools. While the five themes help teachers plan opportunities for students to learn geography, the *National Geography Standards,* arranged in six essential elements, are student-centered. The standards present what students should know and be able to do in order to understand our world's people, places, and environments.

The essential elements of the national standards expand upon and deepen the five themes. For example, the theme *location* is the pivotal point of geography. If history is about time and chronology (when), geography is about space and location (where). The parallel element in the national standards is *Seeing the World in Spatial Terms.* For Grades 5–8, Standards 1, 2, and 3 implement this essential element by identifying specific knowledge and expectations that will help students to view the world in spatial terms.

The themes of *place* and *region* are also expanded upon and made more explicit in the national standards. The essential element *Places and Regions* introduces the theme of *place* in Standard 4 and *region* in Standard 5. Standard 6 examines how culture and experience influence people's perceptions of both place and region. The physical characteristics of place, and the processes that produce those characteristics, are explored in the essential element *Physical Systems* (Standards 7 and 8). The human characteristics of places, such as population, culture, settlement patterns, and migration, are described in greater detail in *Human Systems* (Standards 9, 10, 11, 12, and 13).

The theme *human-environment interaction* is elaborated upon in the essential element *Environment and Society,* with three related standards. Standard 14 looks at how human actions modify the physical environment, Standard 15 examines how physical systems affect human systems, and Standard 16 focuses on changes in resources.

The theme of *movement,* again a fundamental of geography, is a component of all the essential elements. It includes the movement of weather fronts, landslides, and other natural phenomena (*Physical Systems*) and the movement of people, goods, and ideas (*Human Systems*).

However, the five themes do not address one of the most important and beloved topics of the social studies—the link between history and geography. The essential element *The Uses of Geography* and Standards 17 and 18 give teachers clear guidelines and suggestions for teaching about the geography-history relationship. In summary, the *National Geography Standards* encompass the five themes, expand upon them, and transform them into student expectations.

As you will see in the pages of **World Cultures and Geography** and in suggested student activities, the program incorporates key aspects of the *National Geography Standards* to promote innovative practices in geography and to reflect current understandings about effective learning and teaching strategies. We hope that by presenting both the themes and the national standards, we will support teachers making the transition from the themes to the standards, benefiting students in the process.

Sarah W. Bednarz, Ph.D.
Texas A&M University
College Station, Texas

Correlation to the *National Geography Standards*

World Cultures and Geography correlates to the *National Geography Standards* through the Pupil's Edition and the Teacher's Edition. The following page references are representative of the many ways the textbook meets the national standards.

	Pupil's Edition	Teacher's Edition
GEOGRAPHY STANDARD 1 • THE WORLD IN SPATIAL TERMS		
How to use maps and other geographic representations, tools, and technologies to acquire, process, and report information from a spatial perspective	A1–A25, 19, 25, 27, 30–31, 35–39, 41–43, 45–51, 54–63, 67, 71, 73, 80–81, 91, 96, 102, 105, 114, 119, 124, 126, 129, 132, 138–139, 143, 149, 155, 157, 159, 169, 174, 179, 185, 189, 194, 199, 202–209, 216, 218, 222, 229, 233, 239, 245, 247–248, 250, 256–257, 259, 270, 273, 275, 278–287, 291, 297, 299, 302, 304, 308, 313, 318, 326, 331, 335, 340, 347, 351, 356, 359, 363, 366–373, 377–378, 384, 387, 390, 391, 393, 396, 399, 405, 419, 421, 427, 431, 440, 451, 455, 458–465, 470, 472–473, 479, 491, 498, 504, 509, 512, 519, 521, 523, 529, 532, 539	22, 23, 27, 32, 36, 41, 44, 45, 46, 47, 49, 50, 51, 54, 56, 63, 68, 71, 73, 80, 81, 124, 138, 159, 164, 174, 179, 186, 194, 202, 203, 204, 209, 215, 248, 250, 257, 278, 284, 286, 294, 295, 303, 348, 351, 354, 366, 372, 373, 376, 378, 382, 388, 391, 393, 404, 411, 417, 418, 419, 427, 440, 458, 459, 460, 462, 463, 464, 465, 467, 474, 479, 510, 523, 524
GEOGRAPHY STANDARD 2 • THE WORLD IN SPATIAL TERMS		
How to use mental maps to organize information about people, places, and environments in a spatial context	29, 51, 65, 75, 80, 83, 91, 119, 141, 143, 164, 199, 212, 216, 218, 221–222, 223–227, 238, 262–263, 273, 275, 292–295, 312, 335, 344–345, 352–353, 363, 376, 385–386, 398–399, 425, 431, 441–443, 467, 472, 474, 488, 491, 498–499, 507, 523, 526, 539	28, 29, 47, 54, 70, 103, 125, 128, 144, 172, 189, 191, 195, 241, 244, 246, 274, 280, 318, 366, 381, 385, 392, 443, 453, 516, 525

	Pupil's Edition	Teacher's Edition
GEOGRAPHY STANDARD 3 • THE WORLD IN SPATIAL TERMS		
How to analyze the spatial organization of people, places, and environments on Earth's surface	19, 38, 39, 48, 68, 71, 93, 104, 119, 159, 169, 250, 259, 275, 363, 378, 399, 419, 431, 509, 532	24, 25, 48, 49, 50, 51, 55, 59, 65, 69, 72, 73, 74, 83, 85, 88, 89, 90, 109, 126, 129, 131, 132, 134, 149, 155, 157, 185, 190, 195, 222, 230, 232, 237, 240, 245, 264, 266, 300, 302, 306, 309, 314, 332, 340, 355, 369, 387, 394, 395, 396, 397, 398, 402, 405, 421, 426, 439, 441, 442, 445, 446, 447, 449, 451, 456, 464, 473, 476, 484, 488, 501, 520, 529, 533, 534, 537, 539
GEOGRAPHY STANDARD 4 • PLACES AND REGIONS		
The physical and human characteristics of places	4–13, 19, 21, 24–26, 31, 35, 38, 48, 68–69, 72, 78, 107–108, 256–257, 259, 349, 379, 470, 473, 485–487, 490–491, 510–515, 522	24, 25, 33, 37, 42, 43, 57, 83, 92, 102, 104, 105, 114, 115, 116, 119, 173, 188, 211, 212, 213, 215, 216, 221, 225, 236, 237, 238, 242, 247, 252, 253, 256, 258, 268, 269, 270, 271, 272, 274, 291, 294, 298, 300, 306, 310, 312, 341, 345, 359, 361, 380, 386, 390, 428, 475, 477, 480, 490, 528
GEOGRAPHY STANDARD 5 • PLACES AND REGIONS		
That people create regions to interpret Earth's complexity	19, 24–25, 96, 138–139, 149, 155, 162, 173–174, 229, 233, 245, 304, 313, 356, 378, 381–382, 396, 407, 427, 438, 455, 469, 504, 529	15, 62, 172, 182, 183, 315, 420, 421, 423, 500
GEOGRAPHY STANDARD 6 • PLACES AND REGIONS		
How culture and experience influence people's perception of places and regions	52–53, 166–167, 174–175, 200–201, 228, 254–255, 268–269, 299, 344–345, 352–353, 364–365, 376–377, 408, 414–415, 438, 442–443, 456–457, 498–499, 536–537	121, 124, 182, 183, 204, 208, 254, 255, 285, 322, 349, 414, 422, 424, 437, 459, 480, 483, 485, 493
GEOGRAPHY STANDARD 7 • PHYSICAL SYSTEMS		
The physical processes that shape the patterns of Earth's surface	33, 35, 51, 65, 69, 71, 91, 213–216, 222, 224, 239, 292–295, 312, 363, 375, 379–380, 382–383, 417, 471–472, 474, 490–491	29, 35, 37, 39, 65, 70, 71, 135, 180, 203, 212, 213, 214, 216, 221, 239, 275, 279, 287, 291, 292, 293, 295, 312, 367, 372, 377, 378, 381, 383, 398, 417, 434, 461, 466, 468, 469, 470, 471, 472, 474, 490, 491, 523
GEOGRAPHY STANDARD 8 • PHYSICAL SYSTEMS		
The characteristics and spatial distribution of ecosystems on Earth's surface	19, 33, 38, 51, 213–216, 222, 224, 239, 312, 375, 525, 539	346, 347, 358, 369, 382, 383

	Pupil's Edition	Teacher's Edition
GEOGRAPHY STANDARD 9 • HUMAN SYSTEMS		
The characteristics, distribution, and migration of human populations on Earth's surface	19, 25, 38, 39, 48, 49, 109, 143, 259, 431, 467, 491, 519, 521, 523	14, 38, 61, 139, 277, 296, 326, 342, 389, 390, 393, 398, 401, 435, 445, 447, 525, 526
GEOGRAPHY STANDARD 10 • HUMAN SYSTEMS		
The characteristics, distribution, and complexity of Earth's cultural mosaics	21, 24–26, 30–31, 96–98, 100, 104–105, 118, 158, 164–165, 176–177, 180–181, 253, 259, 261, 275, 297–300, 312, 333, 349–350, 357, 363, 392–398, 420–423, 430, 445–447, 453–454, 510–515, 519–520, 522, 533–534, 538–539	164, 167, 281, 297, 400, 401, 414
GEOGRAPHY STANDARD 11 • HUMAN SYSTEMS		
The patterns and networks of economic interdependence on Earth's surface	20, 26, 30, 88, 102–104, 124, 145, 149–150, 156, 159–160, 163, 171, 177, 179–180, 195–196, 241, 298–299, 302–303, 312, 316, 324–326, 328, 332–333, 340, 346–348, 360, 392–394, 403, 405, 416–419, 430, 439–440, 444–445, 450, 452, 454, 479, 496, 498, 506–509, 518, 522, 531–533, 538	14, 70, 88, 93, 98, 100, 101, 107, 108, 110, 111, 118, 119, 156, 158, 161, 162, 163, 165, 166, 168, 169, 171, 176, 177, 178, 181, 185, 186, 198, 205, 218, 228, 241, 298, 300, 324, 325, 328, 339, 343, 348, 360, 416, 430, 431, 438, 441, 444, 449, 452, 456, 475, 477, 479, 480, 506, 507, 508, 509, 522, 531, 532, 534, 538
GEOGRAPHY STANDARD 12 • HUMAN SYSTEMS		
The processes, patterns, and functions of human settlement	12, 15, 40, 82, 88, 260, 264–267, 273, 297, 528	88, 90, 109, 113, 175, 311, 415, 435, 524
GEOGRAPHY STANDARD 13 • HUMAN SYSTEMS		
How the forces of cooperation and conflict among people influence the division and control of Earth's surface	24, 57, 121, 188–191, 241, 264–267, 317–321, 331, 342–343, 407, 409–413, 426	20, 31, 93, 121, 125, 128, 136, 142, 151, 174, 175, 177, 192, 193, 197, 198, 217, 218, 229, 230, 232, 234, 243, 244, 246, 247, 280, 307, 308, 309, 407, 410, 429, 430, 440, 441, 450, 451, 453, 482, 504, 522

	Pupil's Edition	Teacher's Edition
GEOGRAPHY STANDARD 14 • ENVIRONMENT AND SOCIETY		
How human actions modify the physical environment	19, 33, 40, 117, 157, 180, 211, 258, 291, 294, 337, 360, 386–387, 401, 408, 417, 428, 449, 489, 525, 539	40, 211, 408, 427, 467, 489, 525, 532
GEOGRAPHY STANDARD 15 • ENVIRONMENT AND SOCIETY		
How physical systems affect human systems	12, 19, 51, 181, 213–216, 382–383, 399	19, 39, 64, 65, 67, 126, 210, 213, 223, 224, 227, 254, 255, 259, 288, 337, 344, 432, 433, 443, 445, 447, 456, 469, 472, 473, 474, 528, 538
GEOGRAPHY STANDARD 16 • ENVIRONMENT AND SOCIETY		
The changes that occur in the meaning, use, distribution, and importance of resources	19, 44, 145, 186–187, 241, 249–251, 275, 332–333, 354–355	26, 38, 63, 145, 159, 171, 180, 209, 241, 279, 289, 295, 303, 306, 317, 322, 323, 334, 335, 352, 353, 371, 384, 403, 406, 407, 418, 419, 429, 444, 459, 489
GEOGRAPHY STANDARD 17 • THE USES OF GEOGRAPHY		
How to apply geography to interpret the past	39–40, 42, 45, 47, 69, 78–84, 88, 90, 105, 109, 111, 145, 148–150, 164–165, 224, 233, 235–238, 245–246, 248, 253, 259–260, 265–266, 275, 296–305, 307–313, 317–335, 340–343, 350, 355, 361–362, 379–380, 389–390, 404–407, 439–441, 445, 479–480, 528–530, 534, 538–539	44, 59, 60, 61, 62, 64, 66, 72, 75, 76, 78, 79, 80, 82, 83, 84, 85, 86, 87, 94, 95, 96, 97, 99, 100, 105, 112, 113, 114, 116, 118, 122, 123, 127, 129, 130, 131, 132, 133, 137, 138, 140, 141, 142, 143, 146, 147, 148, 149, 150, 151, 152, 154, 158, 160, 163, 168, 170, 182, 183, 184, 185, 187, 194, 196, 197, 198, 205, 207, 287, 290, 299, 301, 302, 310, 312, 316, 318, 319, 330, 331, 332, 333, 338, 339, 340, 343, 355, 356, 357, 368, 379, 387, 399, 404, 405, 412, 413, 436, 460, 461, 480, 482, 485, 486, 487, 488, 490, 493, 494, 495, 496, 497, 498, 499, 503, 504, 505, 508, 511, 512, 514, 515, 516, 518, 519, 521, 522, 527, 530, 533, 535, 539
GEOGRAPHY STANDARD 18 • THE USES OF GEOGRAPHY		
How to apply geography to interpret the present and plan for the future	44, 48, 49, 51, 67, 157, 163, 171, 180, 186, 198, 211, 241, 258, 291, 294–295, 337, 347, 375, 401, 431, 489, 515, 525	31, 34, 48, 57, 58, 77, 120, 162, 169, 206, 219, 262, 263, 282, 283, 285, 320, 321, 324, 327, 328, 329, 370, 371, 409, 417, 424, 425, 428, 463, 502, 517, 536

World Cultures AND GEOGRAPHY

Eastern Hemisphere

McDOUGAL LITTELL

McDOUGAL LITTELL

World Cultures
AND
GEOGRAPHY

Eastern Hemisphere

Sarah Witham Bednarz

Inés M. Miyares

Mark C. Schug

Charles S. White

McDougal Littell

Evanston, Illinois • Boston • Dallas

Senior Consultants

Sarah Witham Bednarz is Associate Professor of Geography at Texas A&M University, where she has taught since 1988. She earned a Ph.D. in educational curriculum and instruction from Texas A&M University in 1992 and has written extensively about geography literacy and education. Dr. Bednarz was an author of *Geography for Life: National Geography Standards*, 1994. In 1997, she received the International Excellence Award from the Texas A&M University International Programs Office.

Inés M. Miyares is Associate Professor of Geography at Hunter College–City University of New York. Born in Havana, Cuba, and fluent in Spanish, Dr. Miyares has focused much of her scholarship on Latin America, immigration and refugee policy, and urban ethnic geography. She holds a Ph.D. in geography from Arizona State University. In 1999, Dr. Miyares was the recipient of the Hunter College Performance Excellence Award for excellence in teaching, research, scholarly writing, and service.

Mark C. Schug is Director of the University of Wisconsin–Milwaukee Center for Economic Education. A 30-year veteran of middle school, high school, and university classrooms, Dr. Schug has been cited for excellence in teaching by the University of Wisconsin–Milwaukee and the Minnesota Council on Economic Education. In addition to coauthoring eight national economics curriculum programs, Dr. Schug has spoken on economic issues to audiences throughout the world. Dr. Schug edited *The Senior Economist* for the National Council for Economics Education from 1986 to 1996.

Charles S. White is Associate Professor in the School of Education at Boston University, where he teaches methods of instruction in social studies. Dr. White has written and spoken extensively on the role of technology in social studies education. He has received numerous awards for his scholarship, including the 1995 Federal Design Achievement Award from the National Endowment for the Arts, for the Teaching with Historic Places project. In 1997, Dr. White taught his Models of Teaching doctoral course at the Universidad San Francisco de Quito, Ecuador.

Acknowledgments begin on page R38.

ISBN 0-618-20350-8

Printed in the United States of America
1 2 3 4 5 6 7 8 9 – VJM – 07 06 05 04 03 02 01

Consultants and Reviewers

Content Consultants

Charmarie Blaisdell
Department of History
Northeastern University
Boston, Massachusetts

David Buck, Ph.D.
Department of History
University of Wisconsin–Milwaukee
Milwaukee, Wisconsin

Erich Gruen, Ph.D.
Departments of Classics and History
University of California, Berkeley
Berkeley, California

Charles Haynes, Ph.D.
Senior Scholar for Religious Freedom
The Freedom Forum First
    Amendment Center
Arlington, Virginia

Alusine Jalloh, Ph.D.
The Africa Program
University of Texas at Arlington
Arlington, Texas

Shabbir Mansuri
Council on Islamic Education
Fountain Valley, California

Michelle Maskiell, Ph.D.
Department of History
Montana State University
Bozeman, Montana

Vasudha Narayanan, Ph.D.
Department of Religion
University of Florida
Gainesville, Florida

Amanda Porterfield, Ph.D.
Department of Religious Studies
University of Wyoming
Laramie, Wyoming

Mark Wasserman, Ph.D.
Department of History
Rutgers University
New Brunswick, New Jersey

Multicultural Advisory Board

Dr. Munir Bashshur
Education Department
American University of Beirut
Beirut, Lebanon

Stephen Fugita
Ethnic Studies Program
Santa Clara University
Santa Clara, California

Sharon Harley
Afro-American Studies Program
University of Maryland at
    College Park
College Park, Maryland

Doug Monroy
Department of Southwest Studies
Colorado College
Colorado Springs, Colorado

Cliff Trafzer
Departments of History and
    Ethnic Studies
University of California, Riverside
Riverside, California

UNIT 1 Introduction to World Cultures and Geography

Asia
Europe
North America
PANGAEA
Africa
South America
Australia
Antarctica

 **UNIT 2** *continued from page vii*

UNIT 3 North Africa and Southwest Asia

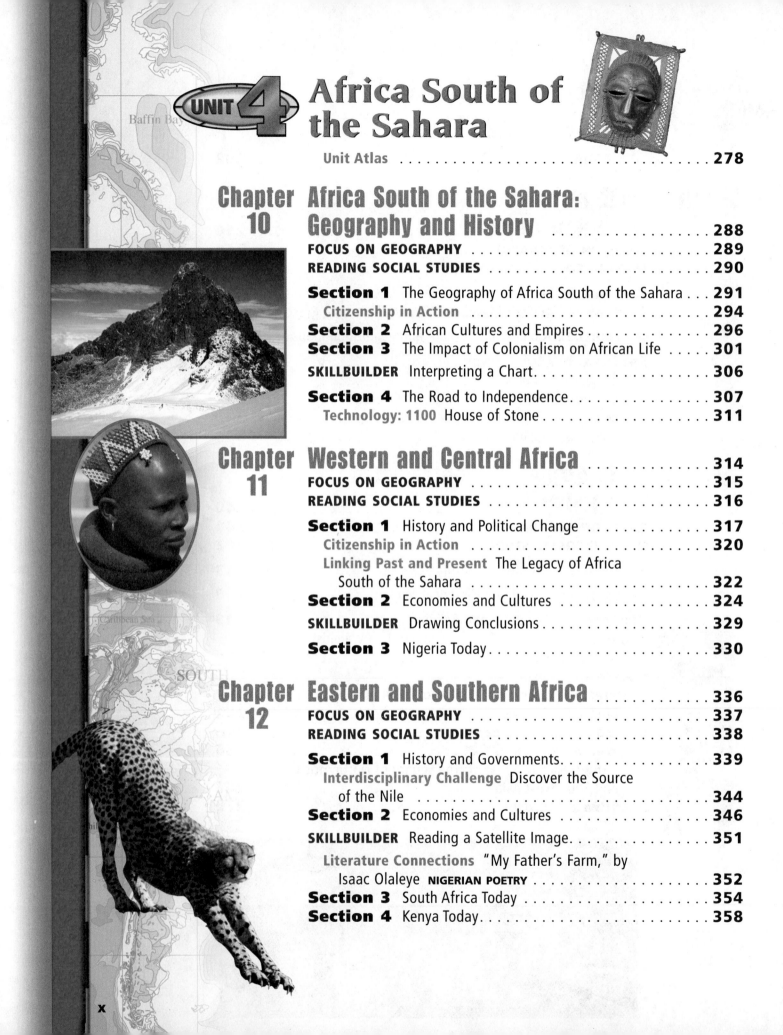

UNIT 4 Africa South of the Sahara

Unit 6
East Asia, Australia, and the Pacific Islands

Features

SKILLBUILDER

Citizenship IN ACTION

Strange but TRUE

Connections To...

Spotlight on CULTURE

Biography

FOCUS ON GEOGRAPHY

CHARTS AND GRAPHS

This section will help you develop and practice the skills you need to study social studies and to take standardized tests. Part 1, **Strategies for Studying Social Studies,** shows you the features of this book. It also shows you how to improve your reading and study skills.

Part 2, **Test-Taking Strategies and Practice,** gives you strategies to help you answer the different kinds of questions that appear on standardized tests. Each strategy is followed by a set of questions you can use for practice.

CONTENTS

Part 1: Strategies for Studying Social Studies

Reading is important in the study of social studies or any other subject. You can improve your reading skills by practicing certain strategies. Good reading skills help you remember more when you read. The next four pages show how some of the features of *World Cultures and Geography: Eastern Hemisphere* can help you learn and understand social studies.

Preview Chapters Before You Read

Each chapter begins with a two-page chapter opener. Study these pages to help you get ready to read.

1 Read the chapter title. Read the section titles. These tell what topics will be covered in the chapter.

2 Look at the art and photographs. Use the illustrations to help you identify themes or messages of the chapter.

3 Study the **Focus on Geography** feature. Use the questions to help you think about the information you might find in the chapter.

Preview Sections Before You Read

Each chapter has three, four, or five sections. These sections cover shorter time periods or certain themes.

1 Study the sentences under the headings **Main Idea** and **Why It Matters Now.** These headings tell what's important in the material you're about to read.

2 Look at the **Terms & Names** list. This list tells you what people and issues will be covered in the section.

3 Read the feature titled **Dateline.** It tells about a historical event as if it were happening today.

4 Skim the pages to see how the section is organized. Red headings are major topics. Blue headings are smaller topics or subtopics. The headings provide an outline of the section.

5 Skim the pages of the section to find key words. These words will often be in **boldface** type. Use the **Vocabulary** notes in the margin to help you with unfamiliar terms.

TERMS & NAMES
Mikhail Gorbachev
parliamentary republic
coalition government
ethnic cleansing
Duma

SECTION 2

Eastern Europe and Russia

TERMS & NAMES
Mikhail Gorbachev
parliamentary republic
coalition government
ethnic cleansing
Duma

MAIN IDEA
After the breakup of the Soviet Union, many former Soviet republics and countries of Eastern Europe became independent.

WHY IT MATTERS NOW
Nations once under Soviet rule are taking steps toward new economies and democratic governments.

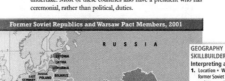

THE KREMLIN, MOSCOW, 1988—To reduce military spending, the Soviet Union has begun removing large numbers of troops and arms from Eastern Europe. This latest news is just one of many changes in the Soviet government since Mikhail Gorbachev (GORE-buh-chawf) came to power three years ago.

Although Gorbachev believes in the ideals of the Soviet system, he thinks that change is necessary to help solve the country's economic and political problems. Since 1985, Gorbachev has reduced Cold War tensions with the United States. At home in the Soviet Union, he has allowed more political and economic freedom.

Region • Mikhail Gorbachev leads the Soviet Union toward a freer society. ▲

The Breakup of the Soviet Union
Mikhail Gorbachev's reforms did not solve the problems of the Soviet Union. The economy continued to get worse. When Gorbachev did not force the countries of Eastern Europe to remain Communist, this further displeased many Communists.

Vocabulary
coup d'état: the overthrow of a government, usually by a small group in a position of power; often shortened to *coup*

In 1991, a group of more traditional Soviet leaders tried to take over the Soviet government. Thousands of people opposed this *coup d'état* (koo-day-TAH), and the coup failed. Then, one by one, the Soviet republics declared independence. The Warsaw Pact was dissolved. By the end of 1991, the Soviet Union no longer existed. The huge country had become 15 different nations.

Modern Eastern Europe

Each former Soviet republic set up its own non-Communist government. The countries of Eastern Europe that had been under Soviet control held democratic elections, and many wrote or revised their constitutions.

In some countries, such as the Czech Republic, former Communists were banned from important government posts. In other countries, such as Bulgaria, the former Communists reorganized themselves into a new political party and have won elections. Many different ethnic groups also tried to create new states within a nation or to re-establish old states that had not existed in many years.

BACKGROUND
The Central Asian Soviet republics were mostly Muslim. These republics are now the countries of Kazakhstan, Turkmenistan, Uzbekistan, Kyrgyzstan, and Tajikistan.

Parliamentary Republics Today, most of the countries of Eastern Europe are parliamentary republics. A **parliamentary republic** is a form of government led by the head of the political party with the most members in parliament. The head of government, usually a prime minister, proposes the programs that the government will undertake. Most of these countries also have a president who has ceremonial, rather than political, duties.

Former Soviet Republics and Warsaw Pact Members, 2001

RUSSIA

ESTONIA
LATVIA
LITHUANIA
RUSSIA BELARUS
EAST POLAND
GERMANY
CZECH REP.
SLOVAKIA UKRAINE
AUSTRIA HUNGARY MOLDOVA
SLOVENIA ROMANIA GEORGIA
CROATIA
BOSNIA HERZEGOVINA YUGOSLAVIA
BULGARIA KAZAKHSTAN
ALBANIA MACEDONIA ARMENIA UZBEKISTAN
AZERBAIJAN TURKMENISTAN KYRGYZSTAN
TAJIKISTAN

GEOGRAPHY SKILLBUILDER: Interpreting a Map
1. **Location** • Which former Soviet republics and Warsaw Pact members border Russia?
2. **Region** • On which continent are most of these countries located?

Use Active Reading Strategies As You Read

Now you're ready to read the chapter. Read one section at a time, from beginning to end.

1 Begin by looking at the **Reading Social Studies** page. Consider the questions under the **Before You Read** heading. Think about what you know already about the chapter topic and what you'd like to learn.

2 Review the suggestions in the **Read and Take Notes** section. These will help you understand and remember the information in the chapter.

3 Ask and answer questions as you read. Look for the **Reading Social Studies** questions in the margin. Answering these questions will show whether you understand what you've just read.

4 Study the **Background** notes in the margin for additional information on people, places, events, or ideas discussed in the chapter.

Reading Social Studies

B. Identifying Problems What are the main problems that face Russia today?

1

READING SOCIAL STUDIES
CHAPTER 6

BEFORE YOU READ

>> *What Do You Know?*

Before you read the chapter, think about what you already know about Europe. Do you have family, friends, or neighbors who were born in Europe? Have you read books, such as the Harry Potter series, that take place in Europe? Think about what you have seen or heard about Italy, England, France, or Germany in the news, during sporting events, and in your other classes.

>> *What Do You Want to Know?*

Decide what you know about Europe today. Then, in your notebook, record what you hope to learn from this chapter.

Region ● Euros are the most visible symbol of economic unity in Europe. ▲

2

READ AND TAKE NOTES

Reading Strategy: Comparing Comparing is a useful strategy for understanding how events change societies. As you read this chapter, compare Eastern Europe under communism with Eastern Europe after communism. Use the chart below to take notes.

• Copy the chart into your notebook.
• As you read, notice how government, economics, and culture differ under the old and new systems.
• After you read each section, record key ideas on your chart.

Place ● Some Christians in Ukraine dye Easter eggs brilliant colors. ▲

Aspect	Under Communism	After Communism
Government		
Economy		
Culture		

In 1995, the Serbs, Croats, and Muslims of Bosnia signed a peace treaty. In 1999, Milosevic began using ethnic cleansing against the Albanians in Kosovo, a region of Serbia. NATO peace-keepers tried to get the Serbs and Albanians of Kosovo to live together in peace. In 2000, public protests led to Milosevic's removal. He was subsequently arrested and tried for war crimes by the United Nations

Modern Russia

Life in Russia has improved since the breakup of the Soviet Un... Russian citizens can elect their own leaders. They enjoy m... freedom of speech. New businesses have sprung up. And some Russians have become wealthy.

Unfortunately, Russia still faces serious prob-lems. Many leaders are dishonest. The nation has been slow to reform its economic system. Most of the nation's new wealth has gone to a small number of people, so that many Russians remain poor. The crime rate has grown tremen-dously. The government has also fought a war against Chechnya (CHECH-nee-yah), a region of Russia that wants to become independent.

Russian Culture The fall of communism helped most Russians to more freely follow their cul-tural practices. Russians gained the freedom to practice the religion of their choice. They can also buy and read the great works of Russian lit-erature that once were banned. At the beginning of the 21st century, writers and other artists also have far more freedom to express themselves.

New magazines and newspapers are published. Even new history books are b... written. For the first time in decades, these publications are telling more of the truth about the Soviet Union.

Russia's Government Russia has a demo-cratic form of government. The president is elected by the people. The people also elect members of the **Duma** (DOO-muh), which is part of the legislature.

3 Reading Social Studies
B. Identifying Problems What are the main problems that face Russia today?

The WORLD'S HERITAGE

Russian Icons A special feature of Russian Orthodox churches are beautiful religious paintings called icons (EYE-kons). Russian icons usually depict biblical figures and scenes. They often decorate every corner of a church.

The greatest Russian icon painter was Andrei Rublev (AHN-dray ROO-blawl). He worked in the late 1300s and early 1400s. Rublev's paintings, one of which is shown below, are brightly colored and highlighted in gold. His work influenced many later painters, and today he is con-sidered one of the world's great religious artists.

4 BACKGROUND

One of the most popular pastimes in Russia is the game of chess. In fact, many of the world's greatest chess players, such as Boris Spassky, have been Russian.

BACKGROUND

One of the most popular pastimes in Russia is the game of chess. In fact, many of the world's greatest chess players, such as Boris Spassky, have been Russian.

Review and Summarize What You Have Read

When you finish reading a section, review and summarize the information you have learned. Reread any information that is still unclear.

1 Look again at the red and blue headings for a quick summary of the section.

2 Study the photographs, maps, charts, graphs, and illustrated features in the section. Think about how these visuals relate to the information you've learned.

3 Answer the questions in the **Assessment** section. This will help you think critically about what you've just read.

In 1999, three new members joined NATO: Poland, Hungary, and the Czech Republic. In 2001, Bulgaria, Romania, Slovakia, Slovenia, and the Baltic States were also working to become NATO members.

Vocabulary

Baltic States: Estonia, Latvia, and Lithuania—former Soviet republics th... on the Baltic...

War in the Balkan Peninsula

Since the late 1980s, much of Eastern Europe has been a place of turmoil and struggle. Yugoslavia, one of the countries located on Europe's Balkan Peninsula, has experienced terrible wars, extreme hardships, and great change.

Under Tito After World War II, Yugoslavia came under Marshal Tito's (TEE·toe) dictatorship. Tito controlled all the country's many different ethnic groups, which included Serbs, Croats, and Muslims. His rule continued until his death in 1980. Slobodan Milosevic (slow-boe-DON muh-LOW·suh-vitch) became Yugoslavia's president in 1989, after years of political turmoil.

BACKGROUND

By 1991, Croatia, Slovenia, Macedonia, and Bosnia-Herzegovina had gained independence from Yugoslavia. Only Serbia and Montenegro were still part of the Yugoslavian federation.

Milosevic Slobodan Milosevic, a Serb, wanted the Serbs to rule Yugoslavia. The Serbs in Bosnia began fighting the Croats and Muslims living there. The Bosnian Serbs murdered many Muslims so that Serbs would be in the majority. The Serbs called these killings of members of minority ethnic groups **ethnic cleansing**. Finally, NATO attacked the Bosnian Serbs and ended the war.

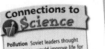

Connections to Science

Pollution Soviet leaders thought that industry would improve life for everyone. Developing industry was so important that the Soviet government did not worry about pollution. Few laws were passed to protect the environment.

In the 1970s and 1980s, there was not enough money to modernize industry or to reduce pollution. Some areas also could not afford proper sewage systems or recycling plants. Today, Eastern Europe has some of the worst pollution problems on the continent.

Place • Forestry is a major industry in Russia. These harvested logs are being floated downriver to be processed. ▷

Prices are no longer controlled by the government. This means that companies can charge a price that is high enough for them to make a profit. At the beginning of the 21st century, however, people's wages have not risen as fast as prices. Many people cannot afford to buy new products.

Some Russians have done well in the new economy. On the other hand, people with less education and less access to power have not done as well. Also, today most new businesses and jobs were in the cities, which meant that people in small towns had fewer job opportunities.

BACKGROUND

The Russian government is unable to enforce tax laws. Many people don't pay their taxes. Without that money, the government cannot provide basic services, such as health care.

The Balkan States, 1991 and 2001

National boundaries, 2...
Yugoslavia, 1991
Autonomous provin... boundaries, 2001
★ National capital

AUSTRIA   HUNGARY
Slovenia   Croatia   Vojvodina
Belgrade
Bosnia and   Serbia   ROMAN...
Herzegovina
SAN MARINO
Montenegro   Kosovo   BULG...
ITALY
Macedonia
ALBANIA   GREECE

GEOGRAPHY SKILLBUILDER: Interpreting a Map

1. Location • Which Balkan state borders Greece?

2. Region • How many countries developed from Yugoslavia?

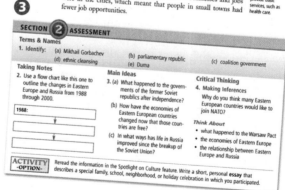

3

SECTION 2 ASSESSMENT

Terms & Names

1. Identify: (a) Mikhail Gorbachev   (b) parliamentary republic   (c) coalition government
(d) ethnic cleansing   (e) Duma

Taking Notes

2. Use a flow chart like this one to outline the changes in Eastern Europe and Russia from 1988 through 2000.

1988:
↓
↓

Main Ideas

3. (a) What happened to the governments of the former Soviet republics after independence?

(b) How have the economies of Eastern European countries changed now that those countries are free?

(c) In what ways has life in Russia improved since the breakup of the Soviet Union?

Critical Thinking

4. Making Inferences

Why do you think many Eastern European countries would like to join NATO?

Think About

• what happened to the Warsaw Pact
• the economies of Eastern Europe
• the relationship between Eastern Europe and Russia

ACTIVITY -OPTION- Reread the information in the Spotlight on Culture feature. Write a short, personal **essay** that describes a special family, school, neighborhood, or holiday celebration in which you participated.

USING STRATEGIES FOR . . .

Multiple Choice Explain to students that they will do best on test questions by thinking them through carefully and by applying test-taking strategies, such as the following.

1. It is important to read the incomplete sentence and evaluate each choice to find the best answer. In question 1, (B) could be a correct answer, because there is sand in the Sahara. However, the Sahara is not mostly made up of sand and boulders. It is mostly made up of scattered rock and gravel, making (A) the best and correct answer.

2. In question 2, you can rule out choices (B) and (D) for using the absolute words *every* and *all*. Then you can choose between (A) and (C). If you know that the Bantu are now an African people, you will choose the correct answer, (C).

3. In question 3 the last choice is *All of the above.* Make sure that the other choices are all correct if you pick this answer. Since (A), (B), and (C) are all correct, (D) is the correct answer.

4. Be careful when reading questions that have the phrase *is not.* First rule out all the nations that are in southern Africa—(A), (C), and (D). The one that remains, (B), is in western Africa. So (B) is the correct choice.

GENERAL TEST-TAKING TIPS

Share these tips with your students.

- The night before a test, make sure you get at least eight hours of sleep.
- Have a healthy breakfast or lunch before taking your test.
- Wear clothes that make you comfortable.
- Relax and enjoy the challenge!

Part 2: Test-Taking Strategies and Practice

Use the strategies in this section to improve your test-taking skills. First read the tips on the left page. Then use them to help you with the practice items on the right page.

Multiple Choice

A multiple-choice question is a question or incomplete sentence and a set of choices. One of the choices correctly answers the question or completes the sentence.

❶ Read the question or incomplete sentence carefully. Try to answer the question before looking at the choices.

❷ Look for key words in the question. They may help you figure out the correct answer.

❸ Read each choice with the question. Don't decide on your final answer until you have read all the choices.

❹ Rule out any choices that you know are wrong.

❺ Watch answers with words like *all, never,* and *only.* These answers are often incorrect.

❻ Sometimes the last choice is *All of the above.* Make sure that the other choices are all correct if you pick this answer.

❼ Be careful with questions that include the word *not.*

---

❶ **1** The Sahara is ⟨mostly⟩ ❷

   A sand, rocks, and gravel.

   B boulders and sand.

❸ choices **C** cliffs and gulleys.

   D grasses and bushes. ❹

> Words like *mostly* or *partly* are key words in multiple choice. Look for answers that are mostly true or partly true about the subject.

> You know that if the Sahara is a desert, **D** is incorrect. A desert cannot be mostly covered with grass and bushes.

2 Over hundreds of years, Bantu people migrated from West Africa to

   A South and Southwest Asia.

   B ⟨every⟩ continent on earth. ❺

   C East and South Africa.

   D ⟨all⟩ of North Africa and Arabia.

> Watch for answers that have words like *all, never, always, every,* and *only.* These answers are often incorrect.

3 The people of West Africa passed on their history by

   A painting pictures.

   B telling stories.

   C creating dances.

❻ **D** All of the above

4 Which of the following is ⟨not⟩ one of the nations in southern Africa?

   A Zimbabwe

   B Nigeria

   C Mozambique

   D Namibia

> First rule out all the answers that name southern African countries. The answer that remains is the correct choice. ❼

answers: 1 (A); 2 (C); 3 (D); 4 (B)

S6

Activity Options

Individual Needs: Students Acquiring English

Word Meaning Make sure students understand the following terms and concepts on these pages.

Strategy Page
   Question 1 *Sahara:* a desert
   Question 2 *migrated:* moved
      continent: one of the seven large land masses in the world

Practice Page

Be sure that students have studied the following topics:
   Black Death
   Reformation
   Ottoman Empire
   Atlantic slave trade

Directions: Read each question carefully. Choose the *best* answer from the four choices.

1 Which of the following was *not* a result of the Black Death?

  A Cities worked together during the plague.
  B Europe lost one-third of its population.
  C The Church lost its prestige among the people.
  D The economies of many countries were ruined.

2 Martin Luther started a reform movement when he

  A published the New Testament in German.
  B criticized some of the Church's practices.
  C wrote his 95 Theses and made them public.
  D All of the above

3 The Ottoman Empire reached its greatest size and glory under the rule of

  A Mehmet II.
  B Selim the Grim.
  C Suleiman the Lawgiver.
  D Timur the Lame.

4 During the 1700s, England controlled which of the following?

  A the sugar trade
  B the Atlantic slave trade
  C the cotton trade
  D the coconut trade

S7

PRACTICE QUESTIONS

Thinking It Through Share the following explanations with students as they discuss the strategies they used to answer the practice questions.

1. This is an example of a question that includes the phrase *was NOT*. First rule out all the answers that were results of the Black Death—(B), (C), and (D). Cities did not work together during the plague, so (A) is the correct answer.

2. In this question, the last choice is *All of the above*. So make sure that the other choices are all correct if you pick this answer. The correct answer is (D), since all of the choices are correct.

3. The key words in this question are *greatest size* and *glory*. Look for the ruler of the Ottoman Empire when it was at its greatest size and glory. The correct answer is (C).

4. *1700s* and *England* are key words in this question. In 1700 the English controlled the Atlantic slave trade, so the correct answer is (B).

Skills Tested in the Items

STRATEGY ITEMS		PRACTICE ITEMS	
Item Number	Skill Tested	Item Number	Skill Tested
1.	Categorizing	1.	Recognizing Effects
2.	Sequencing Events	2.	Analyzing Causes
3.	Summarizing	3.	Making Generalizations
4.	Clarifying	4.	Sequencing Events

USING STRATEGIES FOR . . .

Primary Sources Explain to students that they will do best on test questions by thinking them through carefully and by applying test-taking strategies, such as the following.

1. Review the question. Then reread the primary source to answer the question. Question 1 asks you to identify the kind of advice that Confucius is giving in the primary source. Look for key words such as *people*, *government*, and *officials*. The primary source gives advice on good government that would apply to rulers and their advisers, so (B) is the correct answer.

2. Question 2 asks you to identify the idea of the primary source. Skim the article to find information to help identify this idea. Confucius writes about *dignity*, *respect*, and inspiring *loyalty*. Then review the choices to find the sentence that best expresses that idea. Eliminate choices (A), (B), and (C). The correct answer is (D).

GENERAL TEST-TAKING TIPS

Share these tips with your students.

• Read the directions carefully before you begin to answer the questions.

• Plan the time you are given to take the test.

• Check your answers.

• Believe in yourself.

Primary Sources

Sometimes you will need to look at a document to answer a question. Some documents are primary sources. Primary sources are written or made by people who either saw an event or were actually part of the event. A primary source can be a photograph, letter, diary, speech, or autobiography.

❶ Look at the source line to learn about the document and its author. If the author is well known and has been quoted a lot, the information is probably true.

❷ Skim the article to get an idea of what it is about.

❸ Note any special punctuation. For example, ellipses (. . .) indicate that words and sentences have been left out.

❹ Ask yourself questions about the document as you read.

❺ Review the questions. This will give your reading a purpose and also help you find the answers more easily. Then reread the document.

Good Government

Chap 2.20 Lord Ji Kang asked, "What should I do in order to make the people respectful, loyal, and zealous [hard-working]?" The Master said: "Approach them with dignity and they will be respectful. Be yourself a good son and kind father, and they will be loyal. Raise the good and train the incompetent, and they will be zealous."

❷
❹

Chap. 13.2 Ran Yong (. . .) asked about government. The ❸ Master said: "Guide the officials. Forgive small mistakes. Promote [people] of talent." "How does one recognize that a [person] has talent and deserves to be promoted?" The Master said: "Promote those you know. Those whom you do not know will hardly remain ignored."

—*The Analects of Confucius*

> The *Analects* is a book of thoughts and ideas by Confucius. He was a scholar and teacher in ancient China. ❶

1 Confucius is giving advice on

  A how to be a gentleman.

  B how to be a good ruler.

  C how to become wealthy.

  D how to raise a good family.

❺

2 Which sentence *best* expresses the idea of these paragraphs?

  A The wise ruler governs people through fear.

  B People should obey their rulers no matter what.

  C A good ruler gives a lot of orders to people.

  D If rulers do things well, people will follow them.

answers: 1 (B); 2 (D)

S8

Activity Options

Individual Needs: Students Acquiring English

Word Meaning Make sure students understand the following terms and concepts on these pages.

Strategy Page: Primary Source
  dignity: being worthy
  incompetent: not having the ability to do what is necessary
  promote: advance; move up

Practice Page: Primary Source
  constable: a high public official
  Question 1 *nobles:* people of high rank or birth
  Question 2 *guaranteed:* promised
  Magna Carta: charter listing English liberties
  Bill of Rights: first ten amendments to the Constitution

For more test practice online . . .

TEST PRACTICE
CLASSZONE.COM

Directions: Read this passage from Magna Carta. Use the passage and your knowledge of social studies to answer the questions.

> No constable or other bailiff [officer] . . . shall take anyone's grain or other chattels [property] without immediately paying for them in money. . . .
>
> No sheriff or bailiff, or any one else, shall take horses or wagons of any free man . . . except on the permission of that free man.
>
> Neither we nor our bailiffs will take the wood of another man for castles, or for anything else . . . except by the permission of him to whom the wood belongs. . . .
>
> —Magna Carta (1215)

1   These paragraphs place limits on the

   A rights of the king.

   B powers of officials to take property.

   C rights of nobles to tax people.

   D power of Parliament.

2   The rights guaranteed by the Magna Carta are similar to those listed in the Bill of Rights of

   A France.

   B the Netherlands.

   C the United States.

   D Germany.

S9

PRACTICE QUESTIONS

Thinking It Through Share the following explanations with students as they discuss the strategies they used to answer the practice questions.

1. You need to skim the article to get an idea of what these paragraphs place limits on. Since the primary source describes the limits on the powers of officials to take property, the correct answer is (B).

2. This item is an example of using inference and your knowledge of world history to decide the correct answer. The correct answer is (C).

Skills Tested in the Items

STRATEGY ITEMS		PRACTICE ITEMS	
Item Number	**Skill Tested**	**Item Number**	**Skill Tested**
1.	Analyzing Primary Sources	1.	Analyzing Primary Sources
2.	Finding Main Ideas	2.	Making Comparisons

USING STRATEGIES FOR . . .

Secondary Sources Explain to students that they will do best on test questions by thinking them through carefully and by applying test-taking strategies, such as the following.

1. *First* is a key word. Skim the passage to find the first Pillar of Islam. The correct answer is (D).

2. Remember to review the question to see what information you will need to find. Then skim the passage for information about the duty Muslims must perform during Ramadan. The correct answer is (A).

GENERAL TEST-TAKING TIPS

Share these tips with your students.

• Glance over the test to determine the types and numbers of questions.

• Estimate the amount of time you have to spend on each type of question.

Secondary Sources

A secondary source is an account of events by a person who did not actually experience them. The author often uses information from several primary sources to write about a person or an event. Biographies, many newspaper articles, and history books are examples of secondary sources.

1 Read the title to get an idea of what the passage is about. (The title here indicates that the passage is about the religion of Islam.)

2 Skim the paragraphs to find the main idea of the passage.

3 Look for key words that help you understand the passage.

4 Ask yourself questions as you read. (You might ask yourself: Why are poor and physically challenged people excused from making the pilgrimage to Mecca?)

5 Review the questions to see what information you will need to find. Then reread the passage.

1 **The Five Pillars of Islam**

Muslims—people who follow Islam—have five duties. These are called the "Pillars of Islam" because the faith is based on them. **2**

The first duty is to profess faith in God. Muslims must say the sentence, "There is no God but Allah, and Muhammad is his prophet." They must say this in public at least once during their lives.

3 Note that each paragraph describes one of the five duties.

The (second) pillar is to pray five times a day. These prayers must be said while facing toward the holy city of Mecca in Saudi Arabia.

The third is to give support to the poor and needy. Charity to those in need has been an important part of Islam from the beginning.

The fourth duty is to fast—to not eat or drink—from dawn to sunset during the holy month of *Ramadan*.

The final duty is the *hajj*, or pilgrimage to Mecca. Every Muslim who can do so is expected to travel to (Mecca) at least once in his or her life. People who are physically unable or too poor to do so are excused from this requirement. **4**

Recall that Me is the holiest c of Islam.

1 What is the first Pillar of Islam?

A making the *hajj*

B giving charity to the poor

5 **C** praying five times a day

D professing faith in God

2 What particular duty must Muslims perform during the holy month of *Ramadan?*

A fasting from dawn to sunset

B praying five times a day

C giving charity to the poor

D professing faith in God

answers: 1 (D); 2 (A)

Activity Options

Individual Needs: Students Acquiring English

WORD MEANING Make sure students understand the following terms and concepts on these pages.

Strategy Page: Secondary Source

Prophet: a human messenger of a god
Ramadan: the ninth month of the Islamic calendar, observed by Muslims as sacred

Practice Page: Secondary Source

allies: countries that agree to help one another
neutral: not siding with one country or another

For more test practice online . . .

TEST PRACTICE

CLASSZONE.COM

Directions: Read this passage. Use the passage and your knowledge of social studies to answer the questions.

Before World War I

In 1892, France and Russia had become military allies. Later, Germany signed an agreement to protect Austria. If any nation attacked Austria, Germany would fight on its side. France and Russia had to support each other as well. For instance, if France got into a war with Germany, Russia had to fight Germany, too. This meant that in any war, Germany would have to fight on two fronts: France on the west and Russia on the east.

If a war broke out, what part would England play? No one knew. It might remain neutral, like Belgium. It might, if given a reason, fight against Germany.

---

1 If Russia and Germany went to war, which country had to help Russia?

A England

B Belgium

C Austria

D France

2 When World War I broke out, what part did England play?

A It remained neutral, like Belgium.

B It sided with Germany and Austria.

C It joined France in fighting Germany.

D It fought Russia after its revolution.

S11

PRACTICE QUESTIONS

Thinking It Through Share the following explanations with students as they discuss the strategies they used to answer the practice questions.

1. You may recall the answer to this question without needing to reread the passage. If not, you should skim the passage to identify the country which had to help Russia in a war against Germany. The first paragraph identifies (D) as the correct answer.

2. The secondary source gives information about military allies before World War I. So you need to use your knowledge of social studies to answer this question. The correct answer is (C).

Skills Tested in the Items

STRATEGY ITEMS		PRACTICE ITEMS	
Item Number	Skill Tested	Item Number	Skill Tested
1.	Clarifying; Summarizing	1.	Recognizing Effect
2.	Clarifying; Summarizing	2.	Summarizing

USING STRATEGIES FOR . . .

Political Cartoons Political cartoons are one kind of primary source. Remind students to analyze the political cartoon before reading the questions. They should identify the subject, note important symbols and details, interpret the message, and analyze the point of view. Then they will read the questions to identify the information they need to find.

Explain to students that they will do best on test questions by thinking them through carefully and by applying test-taking strategies, such as the following.

1. Since the swastika was the symbol of Nazi Germany, the correct answer for question 1 is (B).
2. To answer question 2, analyze the cartoonist's message. Look at how the cartoonist exaggerates the main object in the cartoon. The swastika, which represents Nazi Germany, is huge and appears to be turning like a wheel, about to roll down onto Poland and crush it. The label "Poland" tells what country is the subject of the cartoon's title, "Next!" Therefore, (A) is the correct answer.

GENERAL TEST-TAKING TIPS

Share these tips with your students.

- Ask questions before the test begins.
- Know how to fill in the answer form.
- Read and listen to directions carefully.

STRATEGIES

Political Cartoons

Cartoonists who draw political cartoons use both words and art to express opinions about political issues.

1 Try to figure out what the cartoon is about. Titles and captions may give clues.

2 Use labels to help identify the people, places, and events represented in the cartoon.

3 Note when and where the cartoon was published.

4 Look for symbols—that is, people, places, or objects that stand for something else.

5 The cartoonist often exaggerates the physical features of people and objects. This technique will give you clues as to how the cartoonist feels about the subject.

6 Try to figure out the cartoonist's message and summarize it in a sentence.

1 NEXT!

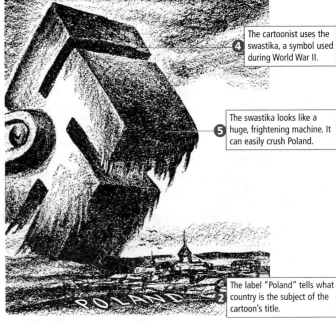

4 The cartoonist uses the swastika, a symbol used during World War II.

5 The swastika looks like a huge, frightening machine. It can easily crush Poland.

2 The label "Poland" tells what country is the subject of the cartoon's title.

Daniel Fitzpatrick / *St. Louis Post-Dispatch,* August 24, 1939.

3 The date is a clue that the cartoon refers to the beginning of World War II.

1 What does the swastika in the cartoon stand for?
A the Soviet Union
B Nazi Germany
C the Polish army
D the Austrian military

6 2 Which sentence *best* summarizes the cartoonist's message?
A Germany will attack Poland next.
B Poland should stop Germany.
C Germany will lose this battle.
D Poland will fight a civil war.

answers: 1 (B); 2 (A)

S12

Activity Options

Individual Needs: Students Acquiring English

WORD MEANING Make sure students understand the following terms and concepts.

Strategy Page
swastika: cross with the ends at right angles; symbol of Nazi Germany

Practice Page
Question 1 *westernization:* to adopt traditions of western countries

nationalization: to give the government control or ownership
modernization: to adopt modern ways
democratization: to adopt democratic ideas and beliefs
Question 2 *absolute monarchy:* government in which a king or queen has unlimited power
constitutional monarchy: government in which a king or queen's power is limited by law
plutocracy: government by the wealthy

For more test practice online . . .

TEST PRACTICE
CLASSZONE.COM

Directions: Study this cartoon. Use the cartoon and your knowledge of social studies to answer the questions.

The Barber Wants to Cut Off an Old Believer's Beard

The Granger Collection, New York

1 This cartoon shows Peter the Great of Russia as a barber. He is cutting off the beard of a Russian nobleman. The shaving of beards was part of Peter's program of

A westernization.

B nationalization.

C modernization.

D democratization.

2 This cartoon shows Peter forcing change on his subjects. What kind of government does this represent?

A absolute monarchy

B constitutional monarchy

C democracy

D plutocracy

S13

PRACTICE QUESTIONS

Thinking It Through Share the following explanations with students as they discuss the strategies they used to answer the practice questions.

1. Use the title and the cartoon to figure out what the cartoon is about. Also, the first two sentences of the question give you information to help you learn about the cartoon. Peter the Great is famous for "westernizing" Russian customs. Having no beard was a custom of western countries at the time of Peter the Great. The correct answer is (A).

2. Use information from the cartoon and from the first sentence in the question, as well as your knowledge of social studies to eliminate incorrect choices. Peter the Great was a monarch, so you can eliminate (C) and (D). Since Peter forced changes on his subjects, this implies that his powers were not limited by law and that he had absolute power over his subjects. The correct answer is (A).

Skills Tested in the Items

STRATEGY ITEMS		PRACTICE ITEMS	
Item Number	Skill Tested	Item Number	Skill Tested
1.	Clarifying	1.	Interpreting Political Cartoons; Analyzing Motives
2.	Summarizing; Analyzing Point of View	2.	Clarifying; Summarizing

USING STRATEGIES FOR . . .

Charts Explain to students that they will do best on test questions that they think through carefully by applying test-taking strategies, such as the following.

1. Question 1 asks you to compare the production of steel between 1980 and 1995 from column to column and row to row for the countries listed in the answer choices and shown in the chart. The correct answer is (D) because Russia/USSR produced the most steel between 1980 and 1995.

2. The key word in this question is *1995*. Read the row headed "1995" to find the continent that produced the most steel in that year. As the hint for Question 2 suggests, you can eliminate (A) and (D) because no African or North American countries are listed in the chart. Germany and the United Kingdom are in Europe, but these two countries produced far less steel than China, Japan, and Korea, which are located in Asia. The correct answer is (B).

GENERAL TEST-TAKING TIPS

Share these tips with your students.

- Use practice tests, such as the one you are taking now, to learn about your test-taking habits and weaknesses.
- Use this information to practice strategies that will help you be a successful test-taker.

Charts

Charts present facts in a visual form. History textbooks use several different types of charts. The chart that is most often found on standardized tests is the table. A table organizes information in columns and rows.

1 Read the title of the chart to find out what information is represented.

2 Read the column and row headings. Sometimes further information on headings is provided in footnotes.

3 Notice how the information in the chart is organized.

4 Compare the information from column to column and row to row.

5 Try to draw conclusions from the information in the chart.

6 Read the questions and then study the chart again.

3 This chart lists countries in alphabetical order. Other charts might organize countries according to region.

1 Steel Production for Selected Countries (in Thousands of Metric Tons)

Year	China	Germany*	Japan	Korea	Russia/ USSR	United Kingdom
1900	—	6,646	1	—	2,214	4,979
1910	—	13,699	250	—	3,444	6,476
1920	—	8,538	845	—	162	9,212
1930	—	11,511	2,289	—	5,761	7,443
1940	—	19,141	7,528	—	19,000	13,183
1950	61	12,121	4,839	—	27,300	16,553
1960	1,866	34,100	22,138	—	65,292	24,695
1970	1,779	45,041	93,322	—	115,886	28,314
1980	3,712	43,838	111,935	8,558	148,000	11,278
1990	6,535	44,022	110,339	23,125	154,414	17,896
1995	92,968	42,051	101,640	36,772	51,323	17,655

* Figures from 1950 through 1990 are for West Germany only.

Source: Japan Iron and Steel Federation

5 Information in the chart suggests that Asian countries are rapidly becoming the world's leading steel producers.

4 You might trace the change in steel production over the years for each country.

1 Which country produced the most steel between 1980 and 1995?

A China
B Germany
C Japan
D Russia/USSR

2 According to information in the chart, in 1995 the largest share of steel was being produced in

A Africa.
B Asia.
C Europe.
D North America.

You can eliminate **A** and **D** because no African or North American countries are listed in the chart.

answers: 1 (D); 2 (B)

S14

WORD MEANING

Make sure students understand the following terms and concepts on these pages.

Strategy Page

produced: made; manufactured

United Kingdom: Great Britain or Britain; includes England, Scotland, Wales, and Northern Ireland

Practice Page: Chart

oracle-bone reading: interpreting animal bones by priests

hieroglyphic writing: ancient Egyptian writing system

cuneiform writing: writing system using wedge-shaped symbols

papyrus: a tall reed used to make a material like paper

mummification: a process of embalming dead bodies

scribes: people who keep records

For more test practice online . . .

TEST PRACTICE
CLASSZONE.COM

Directions: Read the chart carefully. Use the chart and your knowledge of social studies to answer the questions.

Ancient Civilizations				
Feature	China	Egypt	Indus Valley	Mesopotamia
Location	River valley	River valley	River valley	River valley
Period	2000 B.C.-400 B.C.	3200 B.C.-600 B.C.	2500 B.C.-1500 B.C.	3500 B.C.-2000 B.C.
Specialized workers	Priests; government workers, soldiers; craft workers in bronze and silk; farmers	Priests; government workers, scribes, soldiers; workers in pottery, stone; farmers	Government officials; priests; workers in pottery, bricks; farmers	Priests; government officials, scribes, and soldiers; workers in pottery, textiles; farmers
Institutions	Walled cities; oracle-bone reading	Ruling class of priests, nobles; education system	Strong central government	Ruling class of priests and nobles; education for scribes
Record keeping	Pictographic writing	Hieroglyphic writing	Pictographic writing	Cuneiform writing
Advanced technology and artifacts	Writing; making bronze and silk; irrigation systems	Papyrus; mathematics; astronomy; engineering; pyramids; mummification; medicine	Irrigation systems; indoor plumbing; seals	Wheel; plow; sailboat; bronze weapons

1 Which civilization appeared first?

A China

B Egypt

C Indus Valley

D Mesopotamia

2 The Indus Valley civilization did *not* have

A an irrigation system.

B walled cities.

C government officials.

D indoor plumbing.

PRACTICE QUESTIONS

Thinking It Through Share the following explanations with students as they discuss the strategies they used to answer the practice questions.

1. The key word in this question is *first*. Read across the row with the heading "Period" to find the earliest date that a civilization first appeared—3500 B.C. Next move your eyes up the column to find the name of the civilization. The correct answer is (D).

2. Be careful with this question since it has the phrase *did NOT*. You need to find the three features that the Indus Valley civilization did have. The remaining feature in the choices will then be the correct answer. Look at the column with the heading "Indus Valley." Find the three features listed as choices. Since the Indus Valley civilization had an irrigation system, government officials, and indoor plumbing, (A), (C), and (D) are things the civilization did have. So the correct answer is (B), the Indus Valley civilization *did not* have walled cities.

S15

Skills Tested in the Items

STRATEGY ITEMS		PRACTICE ITEMS	
Item Number	Skill Tested	Item Number	Skill Tested
1.	Interpreting Charts	1.	Interpreting Charts: Sequencing Events
2.	Drawing Conclusions	2.	Interpreting Charts: Identifying Details

USING STRATEGIES FOR . . .

Line and Bar Graphs Remind students that the vertical axis goes up and down and is on the left side of the graph. The horizontal axis runs from left to right across the bottom of the graph.

Explain to students that they will do best on test questions by thinking them through carefully and by applying test-taking strategies, such as the following.

1. To answer question 1, you need to read each answer choice and compare the statement to the information in the chart to find the true statement. Notice that the trend of both total and Atlantic exports is to grow over time, so (A), (B), and (D) are false statements. The correct answer is (C).

2. *Most* is a key word. To answer question 2, you need to study the information in the bar graph to find the country with the tallest bar, which represents the country with the most automobiles per 1,000 people. The correct answer is (B).

GENERAL TEST-TAKING TIPS

Share these tips with your students.

- Do not spend too much time on one question.
- Skip a question you are having problems with. Go back to it later, if you have time.
- If you skip a question, be sure to skip the same number on your answer sheet.

Line and Bar Graphs

Graphs are often used to show numbers. Line graphs often show changes over time. Bar graphs make it easy to compare numbers.

1 Read the title of the chart to find out what information is represented.

2 Study the labels on the graph.

3 Look at the source line that tells where the graph is from. Decide whether you can depend on the source to provide reliable information.

4 See if you can make any generalizations about the information in the graph. If the graph shows information over time, note how the numbers change.

5 Read the questions carefully and then study the graph again.

1 Exports of English Manufactured Goods, 1699–1774

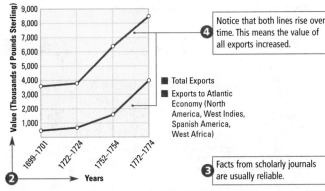

4 Notice that both lines rise over time. This means the value of all exports increased.

■ Total Exports
■ Exports to Atlantic Economy (North America, West Indies, Spanish America, West Africa)

3 Facts from scholarly journals are usually reliable.

Source: R. Davis, "English Foreign Trade, 1700–1774," *Economic History Review* (1962)

5 1 Which of the following is a true statement?

   A Exports to the New World declined over time.

   B Total exports stayed the same over time.

   C Total exports rose sharply after 1724.

   D Exports to the New World fell sharply after 1754.

1 Automobiles per 1,000 People for Selected Countries, 1997

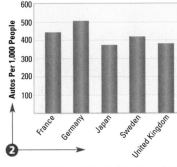

3 Facts from government agencies usually are reliable.

Source: *Statistical Abstract of the United States*

5 2 Which country had the most automobiles per 1,000 people in 1997?

   A France

   B Germany

   C Sweden

   D United Kingdom

answers: 1 (C); 2 (B)

Activity Options

Individual Needs: Students Acquiring English

WORD MEANING

Make sure students understand the following terms and concepts on these pages.

Strategy Page: Line Graph

Point out that the line graph covers the years 1699–1774, which is why one land is called "Spanish America."

Question 1 *declined:* downward movement

Practice Page: Line Graph

   gross domestic product: the value of goods and services created within a country in a year

Bar Graph

   unemployment rate: number of workers without jobs

For more test practice online . . .

TEST PRACTICE
CLASSZONE.COM

STRATEGIES FOR TAKING STANDARDIZED TESTS

Directions: Read the graphs carefully. Use the graphs and your knowledge of social studies to answer the questions.

Japan: Gross Domestic Product, 1983–1999

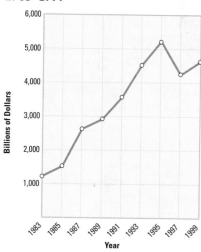

Source: *Annual Report on National Accounts 2001,* Cabinet Office of the Government of Japan

Unemployment Rates for Selected Countries, 2000

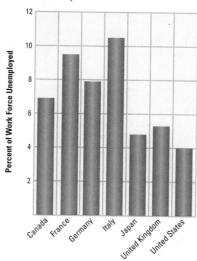

Source: Organization for Economic Cooperation and Development

1 Japan's gross domestic product grew in every period except

  A 1983 to 1985.

  B 1987 to 1989.

  C 1995 to 1997.

  D 1997 to 1999.

2 Which country had the highest unemployment rate in 2000?

  A Italy

  B France

  C Germany

  D Canada

PRACTICE QUESTIONS

Thinking It Through Share the following explanations with students as they discuss the strategies they used to answer the practice questions.

1. This is an example of an item in which you need to note the intervals between amounts and between dates. Since the gross domestic product of Japan declined from 1995 to 1997, the correct answer is (C).

2. To answer this item, you need to study the information in the bar graph to find the country with the highest bar, or highest unemployment rate. The correct answer is (A).

Skills Tested in the Items

STRATEGY ITEMS		PRACTICE ITEMS	
Item Number	**Skill Tested**	**Item Number**	**Skill Tested**
1.	Interpreting Charts; Making Generalizations	**1.**	Interpreting Graphs: Summarizing
2.	Interpreting Charts	**2.**	Interpreting Graphs: Summarizing

USING STRATEGIES FOR . . .

Pie Graphs Explain to students that they will do best on test questions by thinking them through carefully and by applying test-taking strategies, such as the following.

1. The key word is *two-thirds*. To answer question 1, you should compare the slices of the pie graph and read their percentages to find the slice that is nearly two-thirds or 66% of the entire world's population. Then read the legend to see which region is represented by that slice. The correct answer is (D).

2. The key words are *nearly the same*. Be sure to look at the pie graph and legend to find the answer. Compare the population percent for each region in each answer choice to find the two regions that have nearly the same proportion of the world's population. Since Europe has 12% and Africa has 13.3%, these two regions have nearly the same percentage of the world's population, so the correct answer is (B).

GENERAL TEST-TAKING TIPS

Share these tips with your students.

• Read the question and each answer choice before answering.

• Many items include choices that may seem right at first glance, but are actually wrong.

Pie Graphs

A pie, or circle, graph shows the relationship among parts of a whole. These parts look like slices of a pie. Each slice is shown as a percent of the whole pie.

1. Read the title of the chart to find out what information is represented.

2. The graph may provide a legend, or key, that tells you what different slices represent.

3. The size of the slice is related to the percentage. The larger the percentage, the larger the slice.

4. Look at the source line that tells where the graph is from. Ask yourself if you can depend on this source to provide reliable information.

5. Read the questions carefully, and study the graph again.

1 World Population by Region, 2000

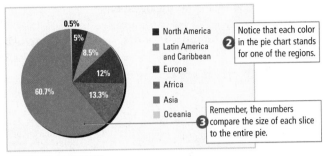

2 Notice that each color in the pie chart stands for one of the regions.

3 Remember, the numbers compare the size of each slice to the entire pie.

The Population Reference Bureau studies population data for the United States and other countries.

4 **Source:** Population Reference Bureau

1 Which region accounts for nearly two-thirds of the world's population?

A Africa

B North America

C Europe

D Asia

2 Two regions have nearly the same percentage of the world's population. They are

A Africa; Latin America and Caribbean.

B Europe; Africa.

C Latin America and Caribbean; Europe.

D North America; Europe.

To answer this question, find the two percentages in the pie graph that are almost the same.

answers: 1 (D); 2 (B)

S18

Activity Options

Individual Needs: Students Acquiring English

WORD MEANING

Make sure students understand the following terms and concepts on these pages.

Strategy Page

Question 1 *accounts for:* has

Practice Page: Pie Graph

energy consumption: energy use

Developing Asia: refers to countries in Asia that are in the process of industrializing

Directions: Read the pie graph. Use the graph and your knowledge of social studies to answer the questions.

World Energy Consumption by Region

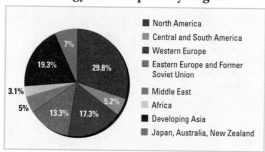

North America
Central and South America
Western Europe
Eastern Europe and Former Soviet Union
Middle East
Africa
Developing Asia
Japan, Australia, New Zealand

Source: "Earth Pulse," *National Geographic* (March 2001)

1 Which region uses the least energy?

A Western Europe
B Developing Asia
C Africa
D Eastern Europe and Former Soviet Union

2 Japan, Australia, and New Zealand are grouped together because they

A are in the same part of the world.
B have about the same number of people.
C are roughly the same size.
D use the same power sources.

PRACTICE QUESTIONS

Thinking It Through Share the following explanations with students as they discuss the strategies they used to answer the practice questions.

1. The key word is *least*. Compare the sizes of the slices of the pie to find the smallest slice. At 3.1 percent, Africa uses the least energy. The correct answer is (C).

2. You should use your knowledge of social studies to rule out choices you know are wrong. The population of Japan is much greater than Australia and New Zealand, so (B) is incorrect. Australia is a continent and therefore much larger than the islands of New Zealand and Japan, so (C) is incorrect. It is not likely that Japan, Australia, and New Zealand use the same power sources since Japan is a highly industrialized country and the other two greatly rely on agriculture for their economy, so (D) is incorrect. Japan, Australia, and New Zealand are grouped together because they are located in the Pacific Ocean along the same longitude, so the correct answer is (A).

S19

Skills Tested in the Items

STRATEGY ITEMS		PRACTICE ITEMS	
Item Number	**Skill Tested**	**Item Number**	**Skill Tested**
1.	Interpreting Graphs: Making Comparisons	1.	Interpreting Pie Graphs
2.	Interpreting Graphs: Making Comparisons	2.	Drawing Conclusions

USING STRATEGIES FOR . . .

Political Maps Explain to students that they will do best on test questions by thinking them through carefully and by applying test-taking strategies, such as the following.

1. This question asks you to find the city that was within the Mughal Empire by 1530. First, study the legend to find the color that stands for the Mughal Empire, 1530. Next, find the city listed in the answer choices that is within the Mughal Empire, 1530. The correct answer is (B).

2. This is an example of a question with *All of the above*. Make sure that all the choices are correct, if you choose (D) *All of the above*. To answer this question, you need to use your knowledge of world history to know where Europe is located. Since only the Ottoman Empire was within part of Europe, the correct answer is (A).

GENERAL TEST-TAKING TIPS

Share these tips with your students.

• Try to answer every question on the test.

• If you are not sure of an answer, make an educated guess.

• First eliminate the choices you are sure are *not* correct. Then choose from the choices that remain.

Political Maps

Political maps show the divisions within countries. A country may be divided into states, provinces, etc. The maps also show where major cities are. They may also show mountains, oceans, seas, lakes, and rivers.

1 Read the title of the map. This will give you the subject and purpose of the map.

2 Read the labels on the map. They also give information about the map's subject and purpose.

3 Study the key or legend to help you understand the symbols and/or colors on the map. (The legend shows the colors that indicate the three empires.)

4 Use the scale to estimate distances between places shown on the map. Maps usually show the distance in both miles and kilometers.

5 Use the North arrow to figure out the direction of places on the map.

6 Read the questions. Carefully study the map to find the answers.

1 Empires in South and Southwest Asia, 1500–1660

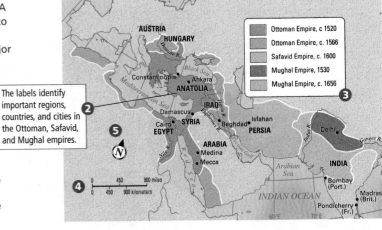

The labels identify important regions, countries, and cities in the Ottoman, Safavid, and Mughal empires.

1 Which city was within the Mughal Empire by 1530?

A Bombay

B Delhi

C Madras

D Pondicherry

2 Which empire controlled part of Europe?

A Ottoman

B Safavid

C Mughal

D All of the above

answers: 1 (B); 2 (A)

S20

Activity Options

Individual Needs: Students Acquiring English

WORD MEANING

Make sure students understand the following terms and concepts on these pages.

Strategy Page

political maps: maps not referring to politics, but showing borders of countries, states, and the like

Be sure students have studied the following empires in South and Southwest Asia:

Ottoman

Safavid

Mughal

For more test practice online . . .

TEST PRACTICE
CLASSZONE.COM

Directions: Study the map carefully. Use the map and your knowledge of social studies to answer the questions.

The Roman Empire, A.D. **400**

Legend:
- Eastern Roman Empire
- Western Roman Empire

0   250   500 miles
0   250   500 kilometers

1 Which area was part of the Eastern Roman Empire?

A Spain

B Gaul

C Anatolia

D All of the above

2 The most northern country in the Western Roman Empire was

A Syria.

B Gaul.

C Spain.

D Britain.

PRACTICE QUESTIONS

Thinking It Through Share the following explanations with students as they discuss the strategies they used to answer the practice questions.

1. *Eastern Roman Empire* are key words. Study the legend and the map to find the Eastern Roman Empire. Compare the answer choices with this area. The correct answer is (C).

2. *Most northern* are key words. To answer this question, use the legend and the map to find the Western Roman Empire. Next, use the North arrow to help you figure out which of the choices is the most northern country in the Western Roman Empire. The correct answer is (D).

S21

Skills Tested in the Items

STRATEGY ITEMS		PRACTICE ITEMS	
Item Number	Skill Tested	Item Number	Skill Tested
1.	Using Political Maps: Legends	1.	Reading a Map: Legend
2.	Interpreting Political Maps	2.	Reading a Map: Legend and Compass Direction

USING STRATEGIES FOR . . .

Thematic Maps Explain to students that they will do best on test questions by thinking them through carefully and by applying test-taking strategies, such as the following.

1. To answer question 1, use the map labels and the legend. The arrows and dates tell you where and when Buddhism spread. Find the arrow with the earliest date. This will tell you where Buddhism started. The correct answer is (B).

2. To answer question 2, use the map labels and the legend to find the routes tracing the spread of Buddhism. The correct answer is (C) because Buddhism spread from China to Korea and Japan.

GENERAL TEST-TAKING TIPS

Share these tips with your students.

• Think positively.

• Tell yourself that you can do it!

• If you have studied for the test, you are prepared to succeed.

Thematic Maps

Thematic maps focus on special topics. For example, a thematic map might show a country's natural resources or major battles in a war.

❶ Read the title of the map. This will give you the subject and purpose of the map.

❷ Read the labels on the map. They give information about the map's subject and purpose.

❸ Study the key or legend to help you understand the symbols on the map. (The arrows show where Buddhism started and where it spread.)

❹ Ask yourself whether the symbols show a pattern.

❺ Read the questions. Carefully study the map to find the answers.

❶ **The Spread of Buddhism**

❷ The labels name the major areas of South and East Asia. The dates show when Buddhism first came to each area.

❸ ▇ Area where Buddhism originated
← Spread of Buddhism

❹ Notice that the spread of Buddhism took several centuries.

❺ 1 Where did Buddhism start?
 A Japan
 B India
 C Borneo
 D Afghanistan

2 Buddhism spread from China to
 A Japan and Tibet.
 B Tibet and Korea.
 C Korea and Japan.
 D All of the above

answers: 1 (B); 2 (C)

Activity Options

Individual Needs: Students Acquiring English

Word Meaning Make sure students understand the following terms and concepts on these pages.

Strategy Page: Map
Buddhism: one of the major religions of the world

Practice Page: Map
conquest: the conquering; the capture of
Christian: referring to one of the major religions of the world
Muslim: referring to one of the major religions of the world

Directions: Read the map carefully. Use the map and your knowledge of social studies to answer the questions.

The Christian Conquest of Muslim Spain

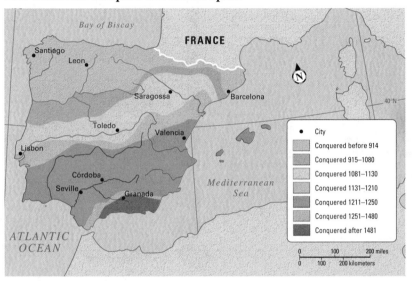

1 By A.D. 1250, how much of Spain did Christians control?

A Only a small portion

B About one third

C About one half

D Almost all the land

2 When did Spain recover Granada?

A 1000

B 1150

C 1450

D 1492

S23

PRACTICE QUESTIONS

Thinking It Through Share the following explanations with students as they discuss the strategies they used to answer the practice questions.

1. *A.D. 1250* are key words in the question. Use the map labels and the legend to determine how much of Spain the Christians controlled by A.D. 1250. The conquered areas cover all but a small part around Granada, so the answer is (D).

2. According to the legend, Granada is located within the area that was not conquered until after 1480, so the correct answer is (D).

Skills Tested in the Items

STRATEGY ITEMS		PRACTICE ITEMS	
Item Number	**Skill Tested**	**Item Number**	**Skill Tested**
1.	Reading a Map: Making Inferences	1.	Reading a Map:
		2.	Making Comparisons
2.	Reading a Map: Labels and Legend	3.	Reading a Map: Legend

USING STRATEGIES FOR . . .

Time Lines Explain to students that they will do best on test questions by thinking them through carefully and by applying test-taking strategies, such as the following.

1. To answer question 1, you need to read the question and then study the time line to find the answer. Find 1961 and 1966 on the time line and count how many countries became independent during this time. The correct answer is (C).

2. To answer question 2, you need to use your knowledge of social studies. You can eliminate (B) because the answer has *all* in it— some Europeans stayed in Africa after World War II. Eliminate (C) and (D) because these statements are not true. The correct answer is (A) because European nations suffered great devastation during World War II making it difficult to maintain colonies in Africa.

GENERAL TEST-TAKING TIPS

Share these tips with your students.

- Relax during the test.
- Several times during the test, take a few seconds to relax and breathe deeply.
- Occasional deep breaths will help relieve anxiety and keep you focused.

Time Lines

A time line is a chart that lists events in the order in which they occurred. Time lines can be vertical or horizontal.

1 Read the title to learn what period of time the time line covers.

2 Note the dates when the time line begins and ends.

3 Read the events in the order they occurred.

4 Think about what else was going on in the world on these dates. Try to make connections.

5 Read the questions. Then carefully study the time line to find the answers.

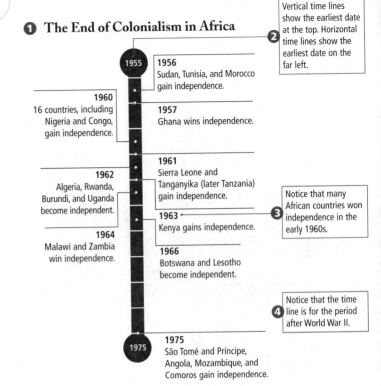

1 The End of Colonialism in Africa

Vertical time lines show the earliest date at the top. Horizontal time lines show the earliest date on the far left.

1955
1956 Sudan, Tunisia, and Morocco gain independence.

1960 16 countries, including Nigeria and Congo, gain independence.

1957 Ghana wins independence.

1961 Sierra Leone and Tanganyika (later Tanzania) gain independence.

1962 Algeria, Rwanda, Burundi, and Uganda become independent.

Notice that many African countries won independence in the early 1960s.

1963 Kenya gains independence.

1964 Malawi and Zambia win independence.

1966 Botswana and Lesotho become independent.

Notice that the time line is for the period after World War II.

1975 São Tomé and Príncipe, Angola, Mozambique, and Comoros gain independence.

1 Which correctly states the countries' rank from first to last in gaining independence?

A Algeria, Botswana, Ghana

B Malawi, Nigeria, Uganda

C Congo, Kenya, Mozambique

D Morocco, Rwanda, Sudan

2 Why do you think so many countries won their independence after World War II?

A European nations were weaker after the war.

B All Europeans in Africa moved back to Europe.

C Europe no longer wanted to own colonies.

D Europe gave each colony its own army after the war.

answers: 1 (C); 2 (A)

Activity Options

Individual Needs: Students Acquiring English

Word Meaning Make sure students understand the following terms and concepts on these pages.

Practice Page: Time Line
reforms: changes

constitution: plan of government
hardliners: uncompromising

For more test practice online . . .

TEST PRACTICE
CLASSZONE.COM

Directions: Read the time line. Use the information shown and your knowledge of social studies to answer the questions.

The Breakup of the Soviet Union

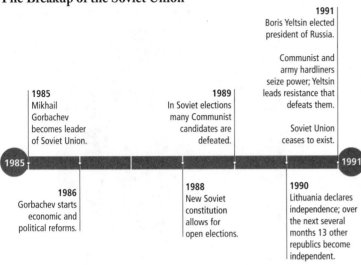

1985
Mikhail Gorbachev becomes leader of Soviet Union.

1986
Gorbachev starts economic and political reforms.

1988
New Soviet constitution allows for open elections.

1989
In Soviet elections many Communist candidates are defeated.

1990
Lithuania declares independence; over the next several months 13 other republics become independent.

1991
Boris Yeltsin elected president of Russia.

Communist and army hardliners seize power; Yeltsin leads resistance that defeats them.

Soviet Union ceases to exist.

1 What happened after Lithuania became independent?

   A Gorbachev started economic and political reforms.

   B Many other republics became independent.

   C A new constitution allowed for open elections.

   D Gorbachev defeated Yeltsin in a new election.

2 In which year did Communist and army hardliners try to seize power?

   A 1985

   B 1988

   C 1990

   D 1991

S25

PRACTICE QUESTIONS

Thinking It Through Share the following explanations with students as they discuss the strategies they used to answer the practice questions.

1. *After* is a key word. Find the name *Lithuania* on the time line, and read what happened after Lithuania became independent. The correct answer is (B).

2. To answer question 2, skim the time line to find the date when Communist and army hardliners tried to seize power. The correct answer is (D).

Skills Tested in the Items

STRATEGY ITEMS		PRACTICE ITEMS	
Item Number	**Skill Tested**	**Item Number**	**Skill Tested**
1.	Interpreting Time Lines	1.	Sequencing Events
2.	Analyzing Causes	2.	Interpreting Time Lines

USING STRATEGIES FOR . . .

Constructed Response Remind students of the following:

- To answer the constructed-response questions on this page, you need to use the document and your knowledge of world cultures.

- Some constructed-response questions do not include a document. Instead, all the questions may require you to use only your knowledge of world cultures to answer the questions.

- Sometimes constructed-response questions start with short answer questions and build up to a short essay. The short answers may help you write the short essay, so try to answer the questions in the order they are asked. When your responses are scored, each part will be worth some points, but the short essay will probably be worth more than the short-answer questions.

- Useful information may be found in a title, a caption, or a source line as well as in the document itself.

GENERAL TEST-TAKING TIPS

Share these tips with your students.

- Be sure to answer all parts of constructed-response questions or as many parts as you can. Each part is worth points.

- As you answer each question, make sure that the number of the answer and the number of the question are the same.

Constructed Response

Constructed-response questions focus on a document, such as a photograph, cartoon, chart, graph, or time line. Instead of picking one answer from a set of choices, you write a short response. Sometimes, you can find the answer in the document. Other times, you will use what you already know about a subject to answer the question.

1 Read the title of the document to get an idea of what it is about.

2 Study the document.

3 Read the questions carefully. Study the document again to find the answers.

4 Write your answers. You don't need to use complete sentences unless the directions say so.

1 The Salt March

2 This document is a photograph showing Mohandas K. Gandhi leading a demonstration.

Copyright © Hulton Archive

Mohandas Gandhi and poet Sarojini Naidu lead Indians in a march down the west coast of India. They are protesting the Salt Acts of 1930.

1 Mohandas Gandhi was an important leader in what country?

4 _India_

2 Read the title of the photograph. What was the Salt March?

It was a protest against the Salt Acts. These acts said that Indians could buy salt only from the British. They also had to pay sales taxes when they bought salt.

3 The question uses the plural "ways." Your answer must include more than one way.

3 What principle did Gandhi follow to win independence for India? Describe the (ways) he put this principle into action.

passive resistance, civil disobedience, or nonviolence. He led peaceful marches against unjust laws. He organized boycotts of British goods. He also told people not to cooperate with the British government.

S26

Activity Options

Individual Needs: Students Acquiring English

Word Meaning Make sure students understand the following terms and concepts on these pages.

Strategy Page: Document
   Salt Acts: sales tax imposed by the British government on salt purchased by Indians
   Question 3 *principle:* a rule or code of conduct

Practice Page: Document
   Zlata Filipovic: Make sure students know that Zlata Filipovic was a young girl when she wrote this diary entry.
   Sarajevo: the capital city of Bosnia and Herzegovina
   Question 1 *Balkans:* the countries occupying the Balkan Peninsula

For more test practice online . . .

TEST PRACTICE
CLASSZONE.COM

Directions: Read the following passage from *Zlata's Diary*. Use the passage and your knowledge of social studies to answer the questions. You do not need to use complete sentences

Saturday, May 2, 1992

Dear Mimmy,

Today was truly, absolutely the worst day ever in Sarajevo. The shooting started around noon. Mommy and I moved into the hall. Daddy was in his office, under our apartment, at the time. We told him on the intercom to run quickly to the downstairs lobby where we'd meet him. . . . The gunfire was getting worse, and we couldn't get over the wall to the Bobars', so we ran down to our own cellar.

The cellar is ugly, dark, smelly. Mommy, who's terrified of mice, had two fears to cope with. The three of us were in the same corner as the other day. We listened to the pounding shells, the shooting, the thundering noise overhead. We even heard planes. At one moment I realized that this awful cellar was the only place that could save our lives. Suddenly, it started to look almost warm and nice. It was the only way we could defend ourselves against all this terrible shooting. We heard glass shattering in our street. Horrible. I put my fingers in my ears to block out the terrible sounds. I was worried about Cicko. We had left him behind in the lobby. Would he catch cold there? Would something hit him? I was terribly hungry and thirsty. We had left our half-cooked lunch in the kitchen.

—Zlata Filipovic, *Zlata's Diary: A Child's Life in Sarajevo* (1994)

1 In the early 1990s, war broke out in the Balkans. Why were people fighting in Bosnia and Herzegovina?

2 What does Zlata say is happening in the city of Sarajevo?

3 How does the war affect Zlata and her family?

rpt from *Zlata's Diary* by Zlata Filipovic. Copyright © 1994 Editions Robert Laffont/Fixot.
by permission of Viking Penguin, a division of Penguin Putnam Inc.

S27

PRACTICE QUESTIONS

Thinking It Through Share the following explanations with students as they discuss the strategies they used to answer the practice questions.

1. Use your knowledge of world cultures to answer the question. The answer is that Serbs in Bosnia wanted to rid the country of Muslims.
2. Read the question and then study the document to find the answer. The answer is that Zlata says the city is being bombed and there is shooting in the streets.
3. You need to study the document to answer this question. The answer is that the family lives in fear of being killed. They must be ready to drop everything to find shelter when the bombing and shooting starts. Things are so bad that even the ugly, dark, smelly cellar starts to look almost warm and nice because hiding in it is the only way to save themselves.

Scoring Constructed-Response Questions

Constructed-response questions usually are scored using a rubric, or scoring guide. The questions on this page might be scored by giving 1 point for each question—a total score of 3 points. Another way of scoring these questions might be to give 1 point for each correct answer for questions 1 and 2, and 2 points for question 3 (1 point for knowing that the family lives in fear of being killed and 1 point for knowing that the family must be ready to drop everything to seek shelter in the cellar)—a total score of 4 points.

Skills Tested in the Items

STRATEGY ITEMS		PRACTICE ITEMS	
Item Number	**Skill Tested**	**Item Number**	**Skill Tested**
1.	Using Visual Sources: Identifying Details	1.	Analyzing Causes
2.	Finding Main Ideas	2.	Using Primary Sources
3.	Summarizing	3.	Recognizing Effects

USING STRATEGIES FOR . . .

Extended Response Remind students of the following:

- Read the extended-response questions that go with one document before beginning to answer any questions. Look for words that tell you how to organize your answer.

- In question 1, you are asked to complete a chart. You need to apply your knowledge of world cultures to complete the chart.

- In question 2, you need to apply your knowledge of the Industrial Revolution to write the essay. Key words are *changed people's lives.* Jot down your ideas and create an outline on a separate piece of paper. Use this outline to write a short essay to answer the question. Support your main ideas with details and examples.

GENERAL TEST-TAKING TIPS

Share these tips with your students.

- Write in complete sentences whenever appropriate. Extended-response essays require complete sentences.

- Remember, neatness counts! If the scorer cannot read your answer, you will not get credit for it.

- Use correct grammar, punctuation, and spelling to help the scorer understand your answer.

Extended Response

Extended-response questions, like constructed-response questions, focus on a document of some kind. However, they are more complicated and require more time to complete. Some extended-response questions ask you to present the information in the document in a different form. You might be asked to present the information in a chart in graph-form, for example. Other questions ask you to complete a document such as a chart or graph. Still others require you to apply your knowledge to information in the document to write an essay.

1 Read the title of the document to get an idea of what it is about.

2 Carefully read directions and questions.

3 Study the document.

4 Sometimes the question may give you part of the answer. (The answer given tells how inventions were used and what effects they had on society. Your answers should have the same kind of information.)

5 The question may require you to write an essay. Write down some ideas to use in an outline. Then use your outline to write the essay. (A good essay will contain the ideas shown in the sample response to the right.)

Read the column heads carefully. They offer important clues about the subject of the chart. For instance, the column head "Impact" is a clue about why these inventions were so important.

1 **Inventions of the Industrial Revolution** 3

Invention	Impact
Flying shuttle, spinning jenny, water frame, spinning mule, power loom	Spun thread and wove cloth faster; 4 more factories were built and more people hired
Cotton gin	Cleaned seeds faster from cotton; companies produced more cotton
Macadam road, steamboat, locomotive	Made travel over land and water faster; could carry larger, heavier loads; railroads needed more coal and iron
Mechanical reaper	Made harvesting easier; increased wheat production

2 1 Read the list of inventions in the left-hand column. Then in the right-hand column briefly state what the inventions meant to industry. The first item has been filled in for you.

2 The chart shows how some inventions helped create the Industrial Revolution. Write a short essay describing how the Industrial Revolution changed people's lives.

5 **Sample Response** The best essays will point out that progress in agriculture meant that fewer people were needed to work the farms. As a result, many farm workers went to the city looking for work in factories. As cities grew, poor sanitation and poor housing made them unhealthy and dangerous places to live. Life for factory workers was hard. They worked long hours under very bad conditions. At first, the Industrial Revolution produced three classes of people: an upper class of landowners and aristocrats; a middle class of merchants and factory owners; and a large lower class of poor people. Over the long term, though, working and living conditions improved even for the lower class. This was partly because factory goods could be sold at a lower cost. In time, even lower classes could afford to buy many goods and services.

S28

Activity Options

Individual Needs: Students Acquiring English

WORD MEANING

Make sure students understand the following terms and concepts on these pages.

Strategy Page: Document
  Industrial Revolution: radical changes needed to mechanize the making of products and farming
  impact: effect

Practice Page: Document
populous: highly populated

For more test practice online . . .

TEST PRACTICE
CLASSZONE.COM

Directions: Use the graph and caption below and your knowledge of social studies to answer the following question.

The World's Ten Most Populous Countries

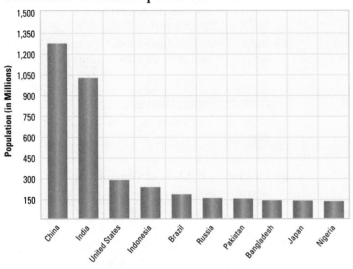

Source: *World Almanac and Book of Facts* (2001)

Six of the top ten most populous countries in the world—China, India, Indonesia, Pakistan, Bangladesh, and Japan—are located in Asia.

1 Write a brief essay about the impact of high population on the countries of Asia. Focus on the conditions that are found in these countries and the challenges that these countries face.

S29

PRACTICE QUESTIONS

Thinking It Through Share the following explanations with students as they discuss the strategies they used to answer the practice question.

• Study the graph and the extended-response question. Note that the question asks you to write about the impact of high population on the countries of Asia with a focus on the conditions and the challenges that these countries face.

• Apply your knowledge of world cultures to write a short essay to answer this question.

The best essays should include the following information:

The impact of high population on the countries of Asia

• High population in Asia causes a severe strain on natural resources, such as clean water. Many illnesses in Asia can be traced to inadequate supplies of clean water. This causes low life expectancy and high infant mortality in these countries.

• High population in Asia leads to shortages of such things as land, food, housing, jobs, and educational opportunities. These shortages cause the standard of living to be low in these countries.

• High population leads to deforestation as people cut down forests for fuel and shelter, and for land for farming and grazing. Deforestation can cause flooding, landslides, loss of topsoil, loss of animal homes, and climate change.

Scoring Extended-Response Questions

Extended-response questions usually are scored using a rubric, or scoring guide. The question on this page might be scored by giving each part 2 points, for a total score of 6 points.

Skills Tested in the Items

STRATEGY ITEMS		PRACTICE ITEMS	
Item Number	Skill Tested	Item Number	Skill Tested
1.	Analyzing Causes: Recognizing Effects	1.	Analyzing Issues; Developing Historical Perspective
2.	Identifying Consequences		

USING STRATEGIES FOR . . .

Document-Based Questions Remind students of the following:

- Document-based questions are designed to help you work like a historian. You are given several documents from a variety of sources that you must analyze, evaluate, and synthesize in order to write an essay, much the way a historian would proceed.

- Use the "Introduction" to help you organize your essay. The "Historical Context" gives you the focus of the document-based question. The document-based question shown here focuses on the Mongol Empire under Genghis Khan.

- Use the "Task" section to help you make a graphic organizer such as an outline, chart, or concept web to organize the information for your essay. This "Task" section explains that the essay must discuss two things: (1) how the Mongols conquered Central and East Asia; (2) how Mongol rule affected European lives. Make a two-column chart on a piece of scratch paper. Label the columns "Mongol Conquest of Central and East Asia" and "Effects of Mongol Rule on Europeans"

- As you answer the "Part 1: Short Answer" questions, also complete the chart.

- To answer the "Part 2: Essay" question, use the documents, the answers to the short-answer questions, the notes in your graphic organizer, and your knowledge of social studies to help you write the essay.

GENERAL TEST-TAKING TIPS

Share these tips with your students.

- Write legibly.

- Write dark enough for electronic scanners to read.

Document-Based Questions

To answer a document-based question, you have to study more than one document. First you answer questions about each document. Then you use those answers and information from the documents as well as your own knowledge of history to write an essay.

❶ Read the "Historical Context" section. It will give you an idea of the topic that will be covered in the question.

❷ Read the "Task" section carefully. It tells you what you will need to write about in your essay.

❸ Study each document. Think about the connection the documents have to the topic in the "Task" section.

❹ Read and answer the questions about each document. Think about how your answers connect to the "Task" section.

Introduction

❶ **Historical Context:** For hundreds of years, Mongol nomads lived in different tribes. They sometimes fought among themselves. In the late 1100s, a new leader—Genghis Khan—united these tribes. He turned the Mongols into a powerful fighting army.

❷ **Task:** Discuss how the Mongols conquered Central and East Asia and how their rule affected Europeans' lives.

Part 1: Short Answer

Study each document carefully. Answer the questions that follow.

❸ **Document 1: Mongol Warrior**

Victoria & Albert Museum, London/Art Resource, New York.

❹ **What were the characteristics of a Mongol Warrior?**

The Mongols were great horsemen who could ride a long way without rest. They attacked without warning, and showed no mercy. They used clever tricks to frighten their enemies. Also, they borrowed or invented new weapons of war.

S30

Document 2: The Mongol Empire

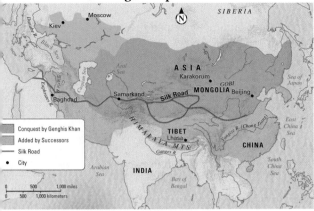

What route linked the Mongol Empire to Europe? What was the main purpose of this route?

Silk Road; as a trade route between Asia and Europe

Document 3: The Great Khan's Wealth

. . . All those who have gems and pearls and gold and silver must bring them to the Great Khan's mint. . . . By this means the Great Khan acquires all the gold and silver and pearls and precious stones of all his territories [lands]. . . .

. . . The Great Khan must have, as indeed he has, more treasure than anyone else in the world. . . . All the world's great [rulers] put together have not such riches as belong to the Great Khan alone.

—Marco Polo, *The Travels of Marco Polo* (c. 1300)

Why do you think Marco Polo's travels made Europeans want to see East Asia?

Europeans were interested in the treasure of the Great Khan and East Asia.

Part 2: Essay

Write an essay discussing how the Mongols conquered Central and East Asia and how their rule affected Europeans' lives. Use information from the documents, your short answers, and your knowledge of social studies. **6**

5 Read the essay question carefully. Then write a brief outline for your essay.

6 Write your essay. The first paragraph should introduce your topic. The middle paragraphs should explain it. The closing paragraph should restate the topic and your conclusion. Support your ideas with quotations or details from the documents. Add other supporting facts or details from your knowledge of world history.

7 A good essay will contain the ideas in the sample reponse below.

7 **Sample Response** The best essays will describe how the Mongols' tactics, fierce will, and strong military organization enabled them to conquer Central and East Asia. (Documents 1 and 2). The essays will also state that Mongol rule brought a period of peace and unity to regions that had been divided. This peace allowed trade to start again along the Silk Road (Document 2). This trade brought new ideas and products to Europe. Stories of the immense wealth in Mongol lands made Europeans want to tap into those riches (Document 3).

S31

Rubric for DBQ Essay

This sample rubric might be used to score a DBQ essay.

To score a 5, the DBQ essay:
•thoroughly answers all parts of Task.
•uses data from all documents.
•is supported with relevant facts.
•has outside knowledge.
•is well developed and organized.
•has a strong introduction and conclusion.

To score a 4, the DBQ essay:
•answers all parts of Task.
•uses data from most documents.
•is supported with relevant facts.
•has outside knowledge.
•is well developed and organized.
•has a good introduction and conclusion.

To score a 3, the DBQ essay:
•answers most parts of Task.
•uses data from some documents.
•is supported by some relevant facts.
•has little outside knowledge.
•is satisfactorily developed and organized.
•restates the essay theme.

To score a 2, the DBQ essay:
•answers some parts of the Task or all parts in a limited way.
•uses limited data from documents.
•uses few facts to support the essay.
•has little or no outside knowledge.
•is poorly organized.
•has limited or missing intro or conclusion.

To score a 1, the DBQ essay:
•shows limited understanding of the Task.
•uses limited data from documents.
•uses few or no facts or details to support essay.
•has no outside knowledge; is poorly organized.
•has limited or missing intro or conclusion.

To score a 0, the DBQ essay:
•does not answer the Task.
•is illegible; is blank or missing.

Skills Tested in the Items

STRATEGY ITEMS	
Item Number	**Skill Tested**
Documents 1. 2. 3.	Using Visual Sources: Summarizing Reading a Map: Legend Identifying Details and Making Inferences Using Primary Sources: Drawing Conclusions
Part 2: Essay	Recognizing Effects Synthesizing Information

PRACTICE QUESTIONS

Thinking It Through Share the following explanations with students as they discuss the strategies they used to answer the practice questions.

Part 1: Short Answer

Document 1. Analyze the picture and the caption (*abus:* "injustice"). French poor paid most of the taxes and, therefore, "carried" the nobles and clergy.

Document 2. Skim the source: Natural rights, such as liberty, property, security, and resistance to oppression.

Document 3. Read the timeline: Except for the Bastille, early events were fairly moderate. Nobles lost feudal rights and priests lost land. Later, the king's power was limited. Events became more violent after a mob captured the king and arrested the royal family. After Robespierre gained power, thousands were put to death. This Reign of Terror lasted from 1793–1794.

Part 2: Essay. Share the sample rubric on page S31 with students so they know the criteria they must meet to earn the maximum amount of points for this essay. Tell students the following:

• Use the "Introduction" to help you organize your essay. Jot down things you know about the time period or question theme. Use the "Task" to help you make a graphic organizer, such as an outline with three sections: "I. Social Classes," "II. Declaration of Rights," and "III. Revolution Turns Violent." As you answer the short-answer questions, also complete this outline.

• Use the documents, the answers to the short-answer questions, the notes in your graphic organizer, and your knowledge of social studies to help you write the essay.

Introduction

Historical Context: For many centuries, kings and queens ruled the countries of Europe. Their power was supported by nobles and armies. European society began to change. In the late 1700s, those changes produced a violent revolution in France.

Task: Discuss how social conflict and new ideas contributed to the French Revolution and why the Revolution turned radical.

Part 1: Short Answer

Study each document carefully. Answer the questions that follow.

Document 1: Social Classes in Pre-Revolutionary France

This cartoon shows a peasant woman carrying women of nobility and the Church. What does the cartoon say about the lives of the poor before the revolution?

Engraving: *Le Grand Abus*. Engraving of a cartoon held in the collection of M. de baron de Vinck d'Orp of Brussels/Mary Evans Picture Library, London.

Activity Options

Individual Needs: Students Acquiring English

Word Meaning Make sure students understand the following terms and concepts on these pages.

Practice Pages

Document 1 *social classes:* social levels
peasant: person in the lowest social level 200 years ago in France

Document 2 *preservation:* protection
resistance to oppression: fighting against the loss of freedoms

Document 2: A Declaration of Rights

> 1. Men are born and remain free and equal in rights. . . .
>
> 2. The aim of all political association is the preservation of the natural and [unlimited] rights of man. These rights are liberty, property, security, and resistance to oppression. . . .
>
> — *Declaration of the Rights of Man and of the Citizen* (1789)

According to this document, what rights belong to all people?

Document 3: The French Revolution — Major Events

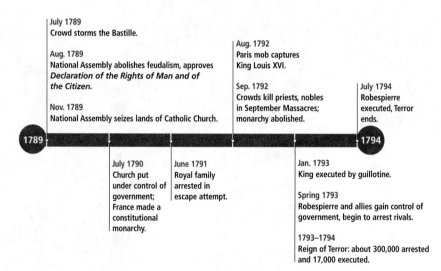

July 1789
Crowd storms the Bastille.

Aug. 1789
National Assembly abolishes feudalism, approves *Declaration of the Rights of Man and of the Citizen.*

Nov. 1789
National Assembly seizes lands of Catholic Church.

Aug. 1792
Paris mob captures King Louis XVI.

Sep. 1792
Crowds kill priests, nobles in September Massacres; monarchy abolished.

July 1794
Robespierre executed, Terror ends.

1789

July 1790
Church put under control of government; France made a constitutional monarchy.

June 1791
Royal family arrested in escape attempt.

Jan. 1793
King executed by guillotine.

Spring 1793
Robespierre and allies gain control of government, begin to arrest rivals.

1793–1794
Reign of Terror: about 300,000 arrested and 17,000 executed.

1794

Over time, the revolution became more violent. How does the information in the timeline show this?

Part 2: Essay

Write an essay discussing how social conflict and new ideas led to the French Revolution and why it became so violent. Use information from the documents, your short answers, and your knowledge of social studies to write your essay.

S33

Rubric for Essay

The best essays will address all three parts of the question—how social conflict contributed to the French Revolution, how new ideas led to the French Revolution, and why the Revolution became so violent.

Social Conflict
- Food shortages (outside knowledge)
- Resentment felt by the peasants and members of the Third Estate
  - toward the high taxes they paid
  - toward the privileges of the nobles, the clergy, and the king.

(Documents 1 and 3)

New Ideas
The spread of new ideas promoted rights for all people such as
- Equality
- Natural rights
- Liberty

(Document 2)

Reasons for Increased Violence
- Rumors of conservative reaction against revolutionary advances
- France's war with Austria and Prussia
- The radicalism of the Paris *sansculottes*
- Internal struggles among the revolutionaries

(outside knowledge)

Skills Tested in the Items

PRACTICE ITEMS	
Item Number	**Skill Tested**
Documents 1. 2. 3.	Interpreting Political Cartoon: Making Inferences Using Primary Sources: Identifying Details Interpreting Time Lines: Analyzing Causes; Recognizing Effects
Part 2: Essay	Essay Analyzing Issues Synthesizing Information

RAND McNALLY
World Atlas

Contents

Complete Legend for Physical and Political Maps

Symbols

 Lake

 Salt Lake

 Seasonal Lake

 River

\ Waterfall

— Canal

△ Mountain Peak

▲ Highest Mountain Peak

Cities

■ Los Angeles — City over 1,000,000 population

▣ Calgary — City of 250,000 to 1,000,000 population

• Haifa — City under 250,000 population

✸ Paris — National Capital

★ Vancouver — Secondary Capital (State, Province, or Territory)

Type Styles Used to Name Features

CHINA — Country

O N T A R I O — State, Province, or Territory

PUERTO RICO (U.S.) — Possession

A T L A N T I C O C E A N — Ocean or Sea

A l p s — Physical Feature

Borneo — Island

Boundaries

 International Boundary

 Secondary Boundary

Land Elevation and Water Depths

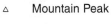

Land Elevation

Meters		Feet
3,000 and over	--	-- 9,840 and over
2,000 - 3,000	--	-- 6,560 - 9,840
500 - 2,000	--	-- 1,640 - 6,560
200 - 500	--	-- 656 - 1,640
0 - 200	--	-- 0 - 656

Water Depth

Less than 200	--	-- Less than 656
200 - 2,000	--	-- 656 - 6,560
Over 2,000	--	-- Over 6,560

ATLAS

ARCTIC OCEAN

Greenland

Baffin
Island

Baffin
Bay

Ja

Arctic

Iceland

Faroe

Mt. McKinley △
20,320 Ft
6,194m

Yukon

Mackenzie

Canadian Shield

Hudson
Bay

NORTH

Aleutian Islands

Vancouver

AMERICA

Rocky Mountains

Great Plains

St. Lawrence

Newfoundland

Los Angeles

Colorado

Mississippi

Appalachian Mts.

Washington D.C.

Cape Hatteras

Azores

ATLANTIC

Canary
Islands

Midway Is.

Tropic of Cancer

Baja
California

Gulf of Mexico

Yucatan
Peninsula

Cuba

Hispaniola

Puerto Rico

Cape
Verde
Islands

Hawaiian
Islands

Jamaica

Caribbean
Sea

Cape Verde

PACIFIC

Orinoco

Trinidad

OCEAN

Palmyra

Galapagos Islands

Amazon

Amazon

SOUTH

Equator

Kiribati

Basin

OCEAN

Marquesas Is.

Andes

AMERICA

Samoa
Islands

Mato Grosso
Plateau

St. Helena

Tonga
Is.

Cook
Islands

Tahiti

Andes

Tropic of Capricorn

Rio de Janeiro

Easter Island

Paraná

△ Mt. Aconcagua
22,831 Ft.
6,959m

Archipiélago
Juan Fernández

Buenos Aires

N

Chatham Is.

Patagonia

Falkland Is.

South
Georgia

0   1000   2000 Miles

South
Sandwich Is.

0   1000   2000   3000 Kilometers

Tierra del Fuego

Copyright by Rand McNally & Co.
Robinson Projection

Cape Horn

South
Orkney Is.

South
Shetland Is.

Antarctic Circle

Antarctic
Peninsula

Weddell
Sea

75

Ross
Sea

Marie
Byrd
Land

△ Vinson Massif
16,066 Ft
4,897m

ARCTIC OCEAN

Spitsbergen
Franz Josef
Land
North Cape
Novaya
Zemlya
75°
Scandinavian
Peninsula
Siberia
Lena
EUROPE
Ural Mts.
Ob'
Volga
Moscow
60°
Bering
Sea of Okhotsk
Sea
Don
Amur
Kamchatka
Peninsula
Sakhalin
Alps
Caucasus
Aral
Sea
ASIA
45°
dnia
Balkan
Peninsula
Black Sea
Mt. Elbrus
18,510 Ft.
5,642m
Pamir
Altai Mts.
Gobi Desert
Beijing
Sea of Japan
Hokkaidō
Honshū
Sicily
Mediterranean Sea
Crete
Cyprus
Plateau
of
Tibet
Himalayas
Huang
Yangtze
30°
Cairo
Zagros Mts.
India
Mt. Everest
29,035 Ft.
8,850m
Ganges
Mekong
East
China
Sea
Kyūshū
ra Desert
Arabian
Peninsula
Red Sea
Nile
Taiwan
PACIFIC
Tropic of Cancer
ahel
Mumbai
(Bombay)
Deccan
Plateau
Hainan
Island
South China
Sea
Mariana
Islands
Wake
Island
15°
FRICA
Arabian
Sea
Bay of
Bengal
Luzon
Socotra
Lakshadweep
Sri Lanka
Guam
OCEAN
Ethiopian
Plateau
Mindanao
Palau
Islands
Caroline
Islands
Marshall
Islands
Congo
Maldive
Islands
Borneo
Celebes
ba
Congo
Basin
Kilimanjaro
19,340 Ft.
5,895m
Rift Valley
Sumatra
New Guinea
Solomon
Islands
0°
Equator
Seychelles
Java
Timor
INDIAN
Cocos
Island
Zambezi
Madagascar
New
Hebrides
15°
Coral Sea
New Caledonia
Fiji
Is.
Mauritius
Reunion
Great
Sandy
Desert
Tropic of Capricorn
Kalahari
Desert
OCEAN
AUSTRALIA
Cape Town
Cape Leeuwin
Darling
Great Dividing Range
Sydney
30°
of Good Hope
North Island
Aoraki
(Mt. Cook)
12,316 Ft.
3,754m
Tasmania
South Island
45°
Kerguelen
Islands
60°
Antarctic Circle
en Maud
and
Enderby
Land
Wilkes Land
Victoria Land
75°
ANTARCTICA
15° 30° 45° 60° 75° 90° 105° 120° 135° 150° 165° 180°

RAND McNALLY

ARCTIC OCEAN

GREENLAND
(Den.)

Baffin
Bay

Arctic Circle

ICELAND

FAROE IS.
(Den.)

RUSSIA

ALASKA

Yukon (U.S.)

Anchorage

CANADA

Hudson
Bay

IRELAND

Aleutian Islands

Vancouver

Missouri

Montréal
Ottawa

Newfoundland

Azores
(Port.)

PORTUGAL

Chicago

New York
Washington D.C.

UNITED STATES

Casablanca

Los Angeles

Colorado

Houston

Mississippi

ATLANTIC

Canary
Islands
(Sp.)

MIDWAY IS.
(U.S.)

Tropic of Cancer

Gulf of Mexico

MEXICO

BAHAMAS

MAURITANIA

Hawaiian
Islands
(U.S)

Mexico City

CUBA

DOM. REP.

HAITI

PUERTO RICO (U.S.)

CAPE
VERDE

PACIFIC

BELIZE
GUAT. HOND.

JAMAICA

Caribbean
Sea

SENEGAL

GAMBIA

GUINEA-BISSAU

GUINEA

EL. SAL. NIC.

Caracas

TRINIDAD AND TOBAGO

SIERRA LEONE

COSTA
RICA

VENEZUELA

GUYANA

LIBERIA

PANAMA

SURINAME
FRENCH GUIANA

COLOMBIA

Equator

Galapagos Islands
(Ecuador)

ECUADOR

Amazon

KIRIBATI

OCEAN

PERU

BRAZIL

OCEAN

Lima

SAMOA

AMERICAN
SAMOA

COOK
ISLANDS (N.Z.)

BOLIVIA

ST. HELENA
(U.K.)

TONGA

FRENCH POLYNESIA

PARAGUAY

Rio de Janeiro

Tropic of Capricorn

Easter Island
(Chile)

ARGENTINA

Santiago

URUGUAY

N

Buenos
Aires

C
H
I
L
E

0   1000   2000 Miles

0   1000   2000   3000 Kilometers

Copyright by Rand McNally & Co.
Robinson Projection

FALKLAND IS.
(U.K.)

South
Georgia
(U.K.)

South
Orkney Is.
(U.K.)

Antarctic Circle

South
Shetland Is.
(U.K.)

Weddell
Sea

ARCTIC OCEAN

Franz Josef
Land

Novaya
Zemlya

FINLAND

SWEDEN   EST.
LAT.
LITH.
BELARUS

RUSSIA

Volga
Moscow

Novosibirsk

Bering

Sea

Sea of Okhotsk

60°

45°

GERMANY
POLAND

UKRAINE

KAZAKHSTAN

MONGOLIA

NORTH
KOREA

AUS. HUNG.
CZ.
SLVK.
CRO.
BOS.
SRB.
MLD.
ROM.

ITALY
Rome

ALB. MA.
GREECE
TURKEY

Black Sea

GEO.
ARM. AZER.

UZBEKISTAN

KYRG.

SOUTH
KOREA

JAPAN
Tokyo

Sea of Japan

CYPRUS LEB.
ISRAEL
SYRIA
IRAQ

TURKMENISTAN

TAJIK.

CHINA

Beijing

30°

Crete

TUNISIA
Mediterranean Sea

IRAN
AFGHANISTAN

Chang Jiang
(Yangtze)

Shanghai

PACIFIC

Cairo
JORDAN
KUWAIT

PAKISTAN

NEPAL
Ganges
BHU.

Tropic of Cancer

LIBYA
EGYPT

SAUDI
ARABIA
QATAR
U.A.E.

Kolkata
(Calcutta)
BNGL.

Guangzhou

TAIWAN

NORTHERN
MARIANA ISLANDS
(U.S.)

WAKE ISLAND
(U.S.)

NIGER

OMAN
Mumbai
(Bombay)

INDIA

MYANMAR
LAOS

South China

15°

CHAD
SUDAN
Red Sea
YEMEN

Arabian
Sea

Bay of
Bengal

THAILAND
Bangkok
VIETNAM
CAMBODIA

Sea

PHILIPPINES

GUAM (U.S.)

OCEAN

Addis
Ababa
DJIBOUTI

SRI LANKA

PALAU

NIGERIA
Lagos

CENTRAL
AFRICAN
REPUBLIC
ETHIOPIA

SOMALIA

MALDIVES

BRUNEI

FED. STATES OF
MICRONESIA

MARSHALL
ISLANDS

CAMEROON

Congo
UGANDA
KENYA

MALAYSIA

SINGAPORE

EQUATORIAL
GUINEA
GABON

RWANDA

Sumatra

Borneo

New Guinea

Equator   0°

REP. OF
CONGO
DEM. REP.
OF CONGO
BURUNDI

TANZANIA

SEYCHELLES

Java

Jakarta
INDONESIA

PAPUA
NEW GUINEA

SOLOMON
ISLANDS

EAST TIMOR

ANGOLA
ZAMBIA

COMOROS

INDIAN

Darwin

Coral Sea

VANUATU

15°

NAMIBIA

ZIMBABWE

MADAGASCAR
MAURITIUS

NEW CALEDONIA
(Fr.)

FIJI

BOTSWANA
MOZAMBIQUE
REUNION
(Fr.)

OCEAN

Tropic of Capricorn

SOUTH
AFRICA
SWAZILAND
LESOTHO

AUSTRALIA

Cape Town

Perth

Darling

30°
Sydney

Melbourne

NEW ZEALAND
Wellington

Tasmania

Kerguelen
Islands
(Fr.)

45°

60°

Antarctic Circle

ANTARCTICA

75°

15°   30°   45°   75°   90°   105°   120°   135°   150°   165°   180°

PACIFIC OCEAN

BRITISH COLUMBIA
ALBERTA
SASKATCHEWAN
MANITO
CA

WASHINGTON
Cape Flattery
Olympic Mts.
Mt. Olympus 7,965 Ft. 2,428m
Seattle
Puget Sound
Mt. Rainier 14,410 Ft. 4,392m
Columbia
Mt. Saint Helens 8,364 Ft. 2,549m
Columbia

MONTANA
ROCKY MOUNTAINS
Clark Fork
Flathead Lake
Marias
Milk
Missouri
Fort Peck Lake
Bitterroot Range
Blue Mts.
Salmon River Mountains
Salmon River
Snake
Yellowstone
Lake Sakakawea
NORTH DAKOT
Sheyenne
Jame

OREGON
Cape Blanco
Mt. McLoughlin 9,495 Ft. 2,894m
Deschutes
Mt. Hood 11,239 Ft. 3,426m
Willamette
Cascade Range
Coast Ranges

IDAHO
Borah Peak 12,662 Ft. 3,859m
Grand Teton 13,770 Ft. 4,197m
American Falls Res.
Snake
Granite Peak 12,799 Ft. 3,901m
Absaroka Range
Yellowstone Lake
Bighorn
Cloud Peak 13,167 Ft. 4,013m
Powder
Tongue
Bighorn Mts.
WYOMING
Great Divide Basin
Moreau
Lake Oahe
Cheyenne
Black Hills
Harney Peak 7,242 Ft. 2,207m
SOUTH DAKOTA
White Lake Francis Case
Niobrara
North Loup
NEBRASKA
Mi

Harney Basin
Goose Lake
Mt. Shasta 14,162 Ft. 4,317m
Cape Mendocino
Shasta Lake
Sacramento
Pyramid Lake
Lake Tahoe
Humboldt
Great NEVADA Basin
Great Salt Lake
Utah Lake
Wasatch Range
Flaming Gorge Res.
Kings Peak 13,528 Ft. 4,123m
Uinta Mts.
Green
Wheeler Peak 13,064 Ft. 3,982m

San Francisco
Sierra Nevada
Central Valley
San Joaquin
Mt. Whitney 14,494 Ft. 4,418m
Death Valley
CALIFORNIA
Coast Ranges
Point Arguello
Telescope Peak 11,050 Ft. 3,368m
Lake Powell
Colorado Plateau
San Juan
Longs Peak 14,255 Ft. 4,345m
Front Range
COLORADO
Denver
Mt. Elbert 14,433 Ft. 4,399m
Pikes Pk. 14,110 Ft. 4,301m
Sangre de Cristo Mountains
San Juan Mts.
UNITE
South Platte
North Platte
Platte
Republican
Smoky Hill
KANSAS
Arkansas

Mojave Desert
Los Angeles
Channel Islands
Lake Mead
Grand Canyon
Humphreys Peak 12,633 Ft. 3,851m
Little Colorado
ARIZONA
Salton Sea
Colorado
Gila
Phoenix
Salt
Baldy Peak 11,404 Ft. 3,476m
Peloncillo Mts.
Mt. Taylor 11,301 Ft. 3,445m
NEW MEXICO
Sacramento Mts.
Rio Grande
Wheeler Peak 13,161 Ft. 4,011m
Canadian
Red
OKLAHO
Llano Estacado
Cimarron

PACIFIC OCEAN

Guadalupe Pk. 8,749 Ft. 2,667m
Pecos
Emory Peak 7,825 Ft. 2,385m
Stockton Plateau
Edwards Plateau
TEXAS
Dall
Nueces
Rio Grande
MEXICO
Rio Grande

HAWAII inset:
Niihau
Kauai
Kalaheo
Oahu
Wahiawa
Honolulu
Lanai
Molokai
Maui
Kahoolawe
Hawaiian Islands
Kauai Channel
Mauna Kea 13,796 Ft. 4,205m
Mauna Loa 13,679 Ft. 4,169m
Hawaii
Hilo
HAWAII
PACIFIC OCEAN
0 50 Miles
0 50 Kilometers
N
© RMN.

ALASKA inset:
ARCTIC OCEAN
Point Barrow
Prudhoe Bay
Beaufort Sea
Chukchi Sea
Arctic Circle
RUSSIA
Brooks Range
Bering Strait
NORTHWEST TERRITORIES
Saint Lawrence Island
Nome
Yukon
Fairbanks
Mt. McKinley 20,320 Ft. 6,194m
Alaska Range
Tanana
Yukon
Kuskokwim
Anchorage
Valdez
Kenai Pen.
Gulf of Alaska
YUKON
CANADA
BRITISH COLUMBIA
Juneau
Bristol Bay
Bering Sea
Aleutian Islands
Kodiak Island
Alaska Peninsula
PACIFIC OCEAN
0 100 200 300 Miles
0 200 400 Kilometers
N
© RMN.

ATLAS

CANADA

ONTARIO

QUEBEC

NEW BRUNSWICK

St. Lawrence

Lake Nipigon

Lake of the Woods

Isle Royale

Keweenaw Peninsula

Whitefish Point

Great Lakes

Lake Superior

MAINE

Mt. Katahdin
5,268 Ft.
△ 1,606 m

Moosehead Lake

Kennebec

MINNESOTA

Upper Peninsula

MICHIGAN

Bruce Peninsula

Georgian Bay

Lake Huron

Green Bay

Lake Champlain

VERMONT

White Mts.

Mt. Washington
△ 6,288 Ft.
1,917 m

NEW HAMPSHIRE

Gulf of Maine

Minneapolis

Chippewa

WISCONSIN

Lake Winnebago

Wisconsin

Lower Peninsula

Saginaw Bay

Muskegon

Grand

Montréal

Adirondack Mountains

NEW YORK

Green Mts.

Connecticut

MASS. ★Boston

Cape Cod

IOWA

Iowa

Des Moines

Lake Michigan

Detroit

Lake Erie

Toronto ★

Lake Ontario

Niagara Falls

Allegheny Plateau

PENNSYLVANIA

Catskill Mts.

Hudson

CONNECTICUT R.I.

Nantucket Island

Chicago

Maumee

OHIO

Scioto

Appalachian Mountains

Susquehanna

Long Island

New York

Philadelphia

NEW JERSEY

UNITED STATES

INDIANA

Illinois

ILLINOIS

White

WEST VIRGINIA

Washington D.C.

DELAWARE

MARYLAND

Delaware Bay

Mississippi

Lake of the Ozarks

Missouri

St. Louis

Wabash

Ohio

Ohio

James

VIRGINIA

Chesapeake Bay

MISSOURI

Green

KENTUCKY

Lake Cumberland

Cumberland

Cumberland Plateau

Blue Ridge

Piedmont

Roanoke

Albemarle Sound

Cape Hatteras

Ozark Plateau

Boston Mts.

White

Kentucky Lake

Mt. Mitchell
6,684 Ft.
△ 2,037 m

NORTH CAROLINA

Pamlico Sound

TENNESSEE

Tennessee

Appalachian

Cape Lookout

Ouachita Mts.

ARKANSAS

Arkansas

Clarks Hill Lake

SOUTH CAROLINA

Pee Dee

Cape Fear

Cape Fear

ATLANTIC OCEAN

Yazoo

Atlanta ★

Santee

Coastal Plain

Ouachita

Tombigbee

MISSISSIPPI

ALABAMA

GEORGIA

Savannah

Sea Islands

Pearl

Alabama

Altamaha

Toledo Bend Res.

Red

Chattahoochee

Flint

N

LOUISIANA

Suwannee

Houston

New Orleans

Atchafalaya Bay

Mississippi Delta

Cape San Blas

Apalachee Bay

Cape Canaveral

GULF OF MEXICO

Tampa Bay

FLORIDA

Lake Okeechobee

The Everglades

Miami

Cape Sable

Florida Keys

0   100   200   300 Miles

0   100   200   300   400 Kilometers

Copyright by Rand McNally & Co.
Alber's Conic Equal Area Projection

19°   67°   66°

ATLANTIC OCEAN

N

Arecibo   San Juan ★

Mayagüez   Caguas

Ponce

18°

PUERTO RICO (U.S.)

0   25   50 Miles

0   25   50 Kilometers

Caribbean Sea

©RMN

25°

RAND McNALLY

A9

RAND McNALLY

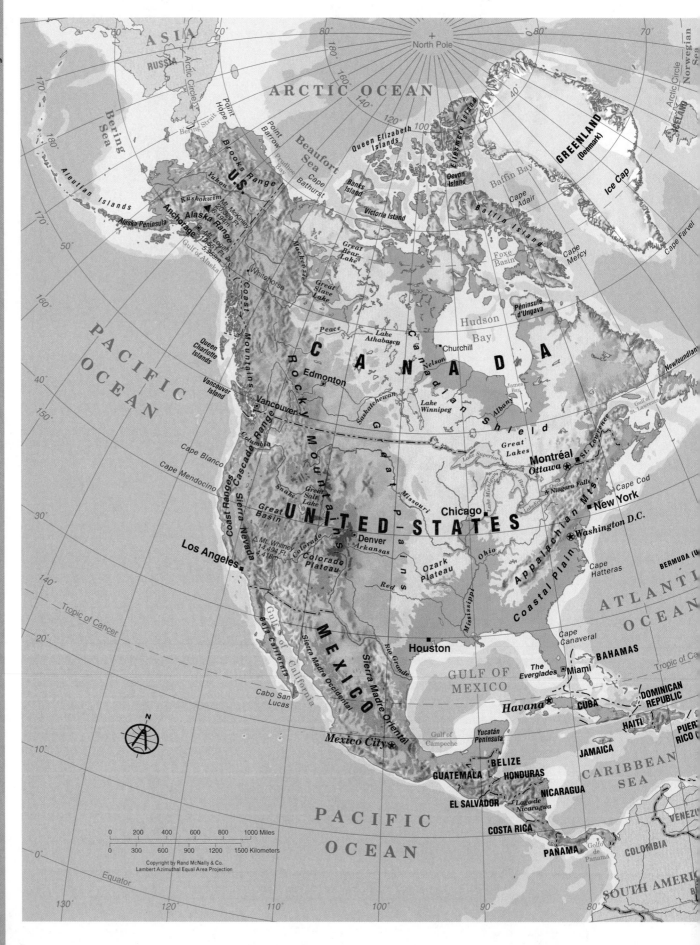

ASIA
RUSSIA
Arctic Circle

ARCTIC OCEAN

North Pole

Point Hope
Point Barrow
Prudhoe Bay
Bering Strait
Beaufort Sea
Cape Bathurst

Queen Elizabeth Islands
Ellesmere Island
Devon Island
Baffin Bay

GREENLAND
(Denmark)
Ice Cap

Bering Sea

Aleutian Islands

Brooks Range
U.S.
Yukon
Kuskokwim
Mt. McKinley 20,320 Ft. 6,194 m.
Alaska Range
Anchorage
Mt. Logan 19,551 Ft. 5,959 m.
Gulf of Alaska
Alaska Peninsula

Whitehorse

Banks Island
Victoria Island

Great Bear Lake

Mackenzie

Great Slave Lake

Foxe Basin
Cape Mercy
Cape Adair
Baffin Island

Cape Farvel

Coast Mountains

Queen Charlotte Islands

Vancouver Island

Peace
Lake Athabasca

CANADA

Churchill
Nelson

Hudson Bay

Canadian Shield

James Bay
Péninsule d'Ungava

Newfoundland

PACIFIC OCEAN

Edmonton

Rocky Mountains

Saskatchewan
Lake Winnipeg

Great Lakes
Lake Superior

Great Plains

Albany

Gulf of St. Lawrence

Vancouver

Cape Blanco
Cape Mendocino

Cascade Range
Columbia
Coast Ranges
Sierra Nevada

Snake
Great Salt Lake
Great Basin

Mt. Whitney 14,494 Ft. 4,418m.
Los Angeles

Tropic of Cancer

UNITED STATES

Denver
Colorado
Colorado Plateau

Missouri

Arkansas

Red

Ozark Plateau

Mississippi

Chicago

Lake Michigan

Ohio

Niagara Falls
Lake Erie
Lake Ontario

Montréal
Ottawa
St. Lawrence

Appalachian Mts.

Cape Cod
New York
Washington D.C.

Coastal Plain
Cape Hatteras

BERMUDA (U.)

ATLANTIC OCEAN

Gulf of California

Cabo San Lucas

Sierra Madre Occidental

MEXICO

Rio Grande

Houston

Cape Canaveral

GULF OF MEXICO

The Everglades
Miami

BAHAMAS

Tropic of Ca

Sierra Madre Oriental

Mexico City

Gulf of Campeche
Yucatán Peninsula

Havana
CUBA

HAITI

DOMINICAN REPUBLIC

PUERTO RICO (

JAMAICA

CARIBBEAN SEA

GUATEMALA
BELIZE
HONDURAS
EL SALVADOR
Lago de Nicaragua
NICARAGUA

COSTA RICA

PANAMA
Golfo de Panamá

VENEZU

COLOMBIA

SOUTH AMERI

PACIFIC OCEAN

N

0 200 400 600 800 1000 Miles
0 300 600 900 1200 1500 Kilometers

Copyright by Rand McNally & Co.
Lambert Azimuthal Equal Area Projection

Equator

ATLAS

RAND McNALLY

ASIA

RUSSIA

Bering
Sea

Aleutian Islands

ARCTIC OCEAN

North Pole

Arctic Circle

Queen Elizabeth
Islands

Beaufort
Sea

Prudhoe
Bay

U.S.

Anchorage

Fairbanks

Yukon

Valdez

Gulf of Alaska

Whitehorse

Juneau

PACIFIC
OCEAN

Columbia

Seattle

Victoria
Vancouver

Portland

Spokane

Sacramento

San Francisco

Las Vegas

Los Angeles

San Diego
Tijuana

Banks
Island

Victoria Island

Mackenzie

Great
Bear
Lake

Great
Slave
Lake

Yellowknife

Peace

Edmonton

Calgary

Saskatoon

Saskatchewan

Regina

Billings

Great
Salt
Lake

Denver

Colorado

Albuquerque

Phoenix

Devon
Island

CANADA

Nelson

Lake
Winnipeg

Winnipeg

Missouri

Minneapolis

Omaha

UNITED STATES

Kansas City

Arkansas

St. Louis

Oklahoma
City

Red

Ellesmere Island

Baffin Bay

Baffin Island

Hudson
Bay

Thunder Bay

Lake Superior

Milwaukee

Chicago

Indianapolis

Ohio

Memphis

Nashville

GREENLAND
(Denmark)

Godthåb

Arctic Circle

ICELAND
Reykjavik

Newfoundland

Quebec

Montréal
Ottawa
Toronto

Lake Ontario

Detroit
Cleveland

Cincinnati

Charlotte

Atlanta

St. Lawrence

Gulf of
St. Lawrence

Saint John

Halifax

Boston

New York

Philadelphia
Washington D.C.

Norfolk

Saint John's

ATLANTIC

OCEAN

BERMUDA (U.K.)

Mississippi

Dallas

Houston

San Antonio

Rio Grande

Chihuahua

Ciudad
Juárez

Hermosillo

Gulf of California

MEXICO

Culiacán

Torreón
Monterrey

San Luis Potosí

Guadalajara

León

Mexico City
Puebla

Acapulco

New Orleans

Jacksonville

Tampa

GULF OF
MEXICO

Miami

Mérida

Cancún

Veracruz

BELIZE
Belmopan

GUATEMALA

Guatemala City

San Salvador
EL SALVADOR

Managua

COSTA RICA
San José

PANAMA

HONDURAS

Tegucigalpa

Lago de
Nicaragua

NICARAGUA

Havana

CUBA

JAMAICA

Kingston

BAHAMAS

Nassau

Tropic of Cancer

HAITI

Port-au-
Prince

DOMINICAN
REPUBLIC

Santo
Domingo

PUERTO
RICO
(U.S.)

CARIBBEAN

SEA

Panama
City

Golfo
de
Panamá

Caracas

VENEZUELA

COLOMBIA

Bogotá

SOUTH AMERICA

BRAZIL

PACIFIC

OCEAN

N

0 200 400 600 800 1000 Miles

0 300 600 900 1200 1500 Kilometers

Copyright by Rand McNally & Co.
Lambert Azimuthal Equal Area Projection

Tropic of Cancer

Equator

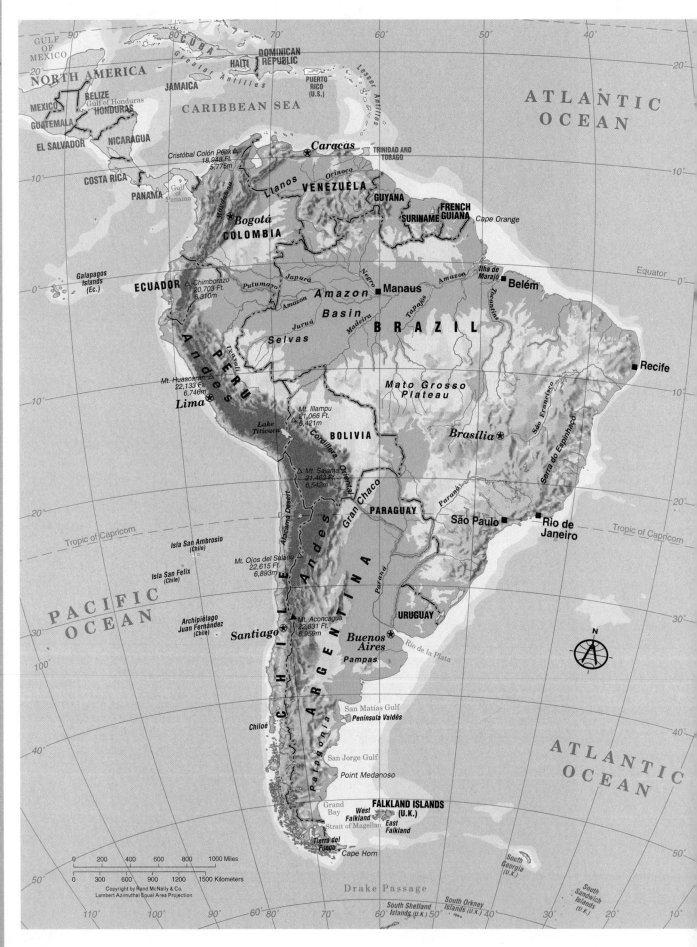

RAND MCNALLY

ATLAS

RAND McNALLY

GULF OF MEXICO
Havana
CUBA
80°
90°
70°
60°
50°
40°
20°
20°
DOMINICAN REPUBLIC
HAITI
PUERTO RICO (U.S.)
NORTH AMERICA
BELIZE
JAMAICA
Lesser Antilles
ATLANTIC OCEAN
MEXICO
HONDURAS
CARIBBEAN SEA
GUATEMALA
EL SALVADOR
NICARAGUA
COSTA RICA
10°
10°
PANAMA
Barranquilla
Maracaibo
Caracas
TRINIDAD AND TOBAGO
Cartagena
Barquisimeto
Valencia
Cúcuta
Orinoco
Ciudad Guayana
Bucaramanga
VENEZUELA
Georgetown
Medellín
GUYANA
Paramaribo
Bogotá
SURINAME
Cayenne
Cali
COLOMBIA
FRENCH GUIANA
Macapá
Equator
0°
0°
Quito
ECUADOR
Japurá
Putumayo
Negro
Amazon
Belém
São Luís
Guayaquil
Manaus
Santarém
Iquitos
Amazon
Tapajós
Tocantins
Fortaleza
Madeira
Imperatriz
Teresina
Juruá
B R A Z I L
Chiclayo
Ucayali
Natal
Trujillo
Pôrto Velho
Recife
PERU
Maceió
10°
10°
Lima
Feira de Santana
Aracaju
Cusco
BOLIVIA
Cuiabá
Salvador
Lake Titicaca
La Paz
Cochabamba
Goiânia
Brasília
Arequipa
Santa Cruz
Montes Claros
Sucre
Uberlândia
Campo Grande
Belo Horizonte
Vitória
Antofagasta
PARAGUAY
Campinas
Rio de Janeiro
20°
20°
Tropic of Capricorn
Salta
Asunción
São Paulo
Isla San Ambrosio (Chile)
San Miguel de Tucumán
Curitiba
Paraná
Caxias do Sul
Isla San Félix (Chile)
Pôrto Alegre
A R G E N T I N A
Córdoba
Santa Fe
Valparaíso
Rosario
URUGUAY
Archipiélago Juan Fernández (Chile)
Santiago
Mendoza
Buenos Aires
Montevideo
30°
30°
C H I L E
La Plata
Río de la Plata
Concepción
Bahía Blanca
Mar del Plata
PACIFIC OCEAN
100°
Chiloé
40°
40°
Archipiélago de los Chonos
Comodoro Rivadavia
ATLANTIC OCEAN
FALKLAND ISLANDS (U.K.)
West Falkland
N
East Falkland
Punta Arenas
Strait of Magellan
Tierra del Fuego
South Georgia (U.K.)
50°
50°
Drake Passage
South Shetland Islands (U.K.)
South Orkney Islands (U.K.)
South Sandwich Islands (U.K.)
110°
100°
90°
80°
70°
60°
50°
40°
30°
20°
10°

0   200   400   600   800   1000 Miles
0   300   600   900   1200   1500 Kilometers
Copyright by Rand McNally & Co.
Lambert Azimuthal Equal Area Projection

ICELAND

Surtsey

Horn   Fontur

Arctic Circle

NORWEGIAN
SEA

Lofoten Islands

Kebnekaise
6,926 Ft.
2,111m

ATLANTIC

OCEAN

FAROE ISLANDS
(Den.)

Scandinavian
Peninsula

NORWAY   SWEDEN

Galdhøpiggen △
8,100 Ft.
2,469m

Umeälven

Klarälven

Dalälven

Hebrides

Orkney
Islands

Grampian
Mts.

UNITED

NORTH

SEA

DENMARK

Stockholm

Vänern   Vättern

Öland

BALTIC

Skagerrak

Cheviot
Hills

KINGDOM

IRELAND

Irish
Sea

Great
Britain

St. George's Channel

Thames   London

NETHERLANDS

Elbe   Berlin

Oder

Bornholm
(Den.)

Northern   Eu

GERMANY   POLAND

English Channel   Strait of Dover

BELGIUM   Rhine

Bohemian
Forest

CZECH
REPUBLIC

Paris
Paris   LUX.
Basin

Seine

Black
Forest

SLOVAK

0   100   200   300   400 Miles

0   200   400   600 Kilometers

Copyright by Rand McNally & Co.
Lambert Conformal Conic Projection

Loire

FRANCE

Saône   Jura
SWITZERLAND   LIECH.   AUSTRIA   HUNGARY

Danube   Great Hun
Pl

Bay of Biscay

Dordogne

Massif
Central

Mt. Blanc
15,771 Ft.
4,808m

Rhône

A   l   p   s

Drava

SLOVENIA

CROATIA

Po

Apennines

BOSNIA AND
HERZEGOVINA

Ba

Cantabrian Mts.

Pyrenees

ANDORRA

MONACO

Corsica
(Fr.)

SAN
MARINO

Dinaric Alps

YUGOS

Douro

Iberian Mts.

Ebro

Rome

ADRIATIC SEA

Iberian
Peninsula

Lisbon

PORTUGAL

Tagus

SPAIN

ITALY   ALBANIA

Sierra Morena

Balearic Islands   Minorca

Sardinia
(It.)

△Vesuvius
4,190 Ft.
1,277m

Strait of Gibraltar

Ibiza   Majorca

TYRRHENIAN
SEA

GIBRALTAR
(U.K.)

MEDITERRAN

Algiers

Mt. Etna
10,902 Ft.
3,323m △
Sicily

IONIAN
SEA

MOROCCO   AFRICA   ALGERIA   TUNISIA

MALTA

■ Murmansk

Kola
Peninsula
Ponoy

WHITE SEA

Timan Ridge

Pechora

Ob'

URAL Mountains

Mezen

Northern Dvina

Onega

Northern Uvals
(Uplands)

Sukhona

Kama

Irtysh

LAND

Lake
Onega

Lake
Ladoga

elsinki

Finland

Rybinsk
Res.

R U S S I A

A S I A

NIA

Lake
Peipus

LATVIA

Valdai
Hills

✺ Moscow

Oka

Khoper

UANIA

Plain

Central
Russian
Upland

Don

Ural

KAZAKHSTAN

Caspian Depression

Aral Sea

Neman

BELARUS

Pripyat

Dnieper

Dnieper
Lowland

Donets Basin

Volga

UZBEKISTAN

Amu Darya

Syr Darya

Kiev ✺

UKRAINE

Dnieper

iester

MOLDOVA

C A S P I A N

S E A

TURKMENISTAN

MANIA

vanian Alps

Sea of Azov

Crimean
Peninsula

C a u c a s u s

▲ Mt. Elbrus
18,510 Ft.
5,642m

GEORGIA

Baku ✺

Danube

insula

B L A C K   S E A

ARMENIA

AZERBAIJAN

AZER.

BULGARIA

■ Istanbul

Olympus
Ft
7m

GEECE

T U R K E Y

IRAQ

IRAN

✺ Tehran

A E G E A N

S E A

SYRIA

Euphrates

North
Cyprus

Rhodes

CYPRUS

LEBANON

Tigris

Crete

ICELAND
Reykjavík

Arctic Circle

NORWEGIAN
SEA

A T L A N T I C

O C E A N

FAROE ISLANDS
(Den.)

Trondheim

Umeå

NORWAY   SWEDEN

Bergen

Oslo

Göteborg

Vänern   Vättern

Stockholm

DENMARK

Copenhagen

BALTIC

Skagerrak

LITHU

Kaliningrad

Gdańsk

POLAND

Szczecin

N   Hamburg

Elbe

Berlin

Oder

GERMANY   Warsaw

Wisla

SCOTLAND   Aberdeen

Glasgow

Edinburgh

UNITED

NORTHERN
IRELAND

Belfast

Irish
Sea

KINGDOM

NORTH
SEA

Dublin

IRELAND

Cork

Liverpool   Manchester

WALES

Birmingham   ENGLAND

Cardiff   Thames

NETHERLANDS

Amsterdam

The Hague

London

Plymouth

St. George's Channel

English Channel   Strait of Dover

Le Havre

Brussels

BELGIUM   Cologne

Bonn

Dresden   Wroclaw

Rhine

LUX.

Frankfurt

Prague

CZECH
REPUBLIC

Kra

Luxembourg

Paris

Strasbourg

Stuttgart

Munich

SLOVAK

Zürich   Vienna

Bern   LIECH.   AUSTRIA

SWITZERLAND

Bratislava

Budapest

HUNGARY

Nantes

Loire

Seine

FRANCE

Geneva

Lyon

SLOVENIA   Ljubljana

Milan   Venice   Zagreb   Belgr

Danube

0   100   200   300   400 Miles
0   200   400   600 Kilometers
Copyright by Rand McNally & Co.
Lambert Conformal Conic Projection

Bay of Biscay

A Coruña

Gijón

Bilbao

Bordeaux

Toulouse

Turin   Po

Genoa

Nice

CROATIA

BOSNIA AND
HERZEGOVINA

Sarajevo

YUGOS

Marseille

MONACO

SAN
MARINO

Florence

Porto

Valladolid

Ebro

ANDORRA

Zaragoza

Corsica
(Fr.)

ADRIATIC SEA

Lisbon

PORTUGAL

Tagus

Madrid

SPAIN

Barcelona

Valencia

Córdoba

Sardinia
(It.)

Rome

VATICAN CITY

ITALY

ALBANIA

Sko

Tiranë

Naples   Bari

Seville

Palma

Strait of Gibraltar

Málaga

GIBRALTAR
(U.K.)

Cagliari

TYRRHENIAN
SEA

Rabat

Palermo

Algiers

Sicily   Catania

IONIAN
SEA

AFRICA

MOROCCO   ALGERIA   TUNISIA

M E D I T E R R A N

Valletta   MALTA

RUSSIA

ASIA

WHITE SEA

Murmansk

Arkhangel'sk

Northern Dvina

Pechora

Ob'

Irtysh

Syktyvkar

Petrozavodsk
Lake Onega

Perm'

Kirov

Lake Ladoga

St. Petersburg

Izhevsk

Ufa

Cherepovets
Rybinsk Res.

Nizhniy Novgorod

Kazan'

Helsinki

Finland

Yaroslavl'

Tallinn

Lake Peipus

Tver'

Oka

ESTONIA

LATVIA

Samara

Moscow

Vilnius

Ryazan'

Penza

Syr Darya

Vitsyebsk

Tula

Saratov

Ural

Minsk

Bryansk

Lipetsk

Don

KAZAKHSTAN

Aral Sea

BELARUS

Homyel'

Voronezh

Volga

Volgograd

UZBEKISTAN

Chernobyl

Kiev

Kharkiv

Luhans'k

Astrakhan'

Amu Darya

Lviv

Vinnytsya

UKRAINE

Dnipro-
petrovs'k

Dnieper

Donets'k

Rostov

Dniester

Kryvyy Rih

Zaporizhzhya

Mariupol'

C
A
S
P
I
A
N
S
E
A

TURKMENISTAN

MOLDOVA

Iaşi

Chişinău

Stavropol'

40°

60°

Ashgabat

Cluj-Napoca

Odesa

Sea of Azov

Krasnodar

ROMANIA

Galaţi

Simferopol'

Groznyy

Sevastopol'

GEORGIA

Tbilisi

Baku

Craiova

Bucharest

BLACK SEA

Tehran

BULGARIA

Varna

AZERBAIJAN

Sofia

ARMENIA

AZER.

Plovdiv

Yerevan

Istanbul

IRAN

Thessaloniki

Ankara

TURKEY

GREECE

Athens

AEGEAN SEA

Crete

SEA

NORTH CYPRUS

Nicosia

CYPRUS

Beirut LEBANON

SYRIA

Euphrates

Baghdad

IRAQ

Tigris

30°

40°

50°

60°

70°

80°

RAND McNALLY

A17

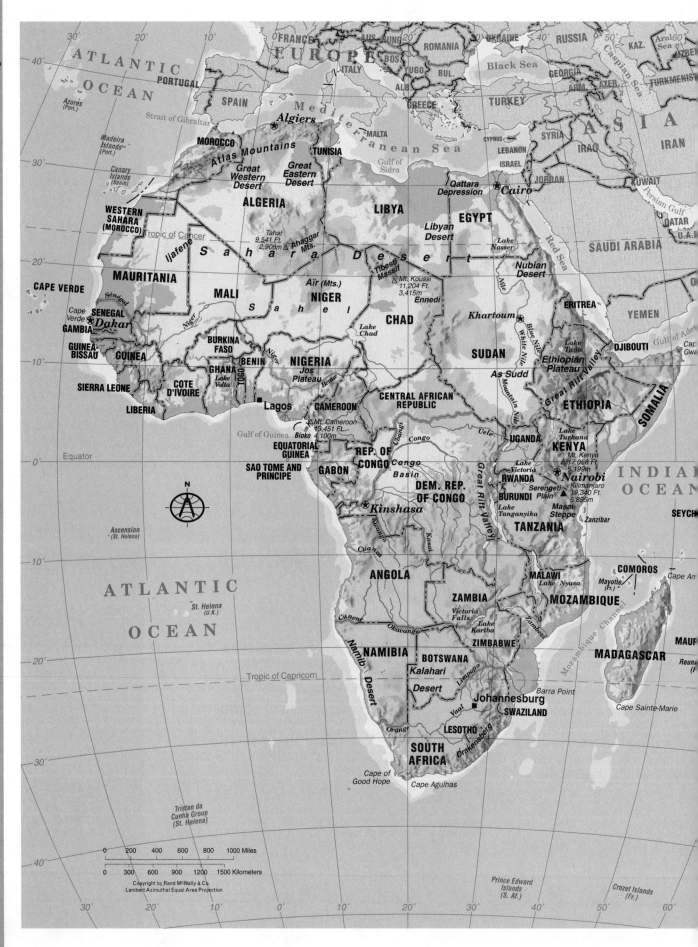

ATLANTIC
OCEAN

EUROPE

FRANCE
AUS. HUNG.
ROMANIA
RUSSIA
KAZ.
Aral Sea

PORTUGAL
ITALY
YUGO.
BUL.
Black Sea
GEORGIA
Caspian Sea
TURKMENISTAN

SPAIN
BOS.
ALB.
GREECE
TURKEY
ARM.
AZER.

Strait of Gibraltar
MALTA
Mediterranean Sea
CYPRUS
SYRIA
ASIA
IRAN

Azores
(Port.)
Algiers
LEBANON
ISRAEL
IRAQ

Madeira
Islands
(Port.)
MOROCCO
Atlas Mountains
TUNISIA
Gulf of
Sidra
Qattara
Depression
Cairo
JORDAN
KUWAIT
Persian Gulf
QATAR

Canary
Islands
(Spain)
Great
Western
Desert
Great
Eastern
Desert
ALGERIA
LIBYA
EGYPT
SAUDI ARABIA
U.A.E.

WESTERN
SAHARA
(MOROCCO)
Tropic of Cancer
Tahat
9,541 Ft.
2,908m
Ahaggar
Mts.
Libyan
Desert
Lake
Nasser
Red Sea

Ijafene
Sahara
Desert
Tibesti
Massif
Mt. Koussi
11,204 Ft.
3,415m
Nubian
Desert
Nile

MAURITANIA
Aïr (Mts.)
Ennedi
ERITREA
YEMEN
Gulf of Aden

CAPE VERDE
MALI
NIGER
CHAD
Khartoum
Blue Nile
DJIBOUTI
Cape
Gwa

Senegal
Sahel
Lake
Chad
SUDAN
White Nile
Lake
Tana
Ethiopian
Plateau

Cape
Verde
SENEGAL
Dakar
Niger
BURKINA
FASO
NIGERIA
As Sudd
Mountain Nile
Great Rift Valley

GAMBIA
GUINEA-
BISSAU
GUINEA
BENIN
Jos
Plateau
Benue
CENTRAL AFRICAN
REPUBLIC
ETHIOPIA
SOMALIA

GHANA
TOGO
Lake
Volta
CAMEROON
Lake
Turkana

SIERRA LEONE
COTE
D'IVOIRE
Lagos
Mt. Cameroon
13,451 Ft.
4,100m
Ubangi
UGANDA
KENYA
Mt. Kenya
17,058 Ft.
5,199m

LIBERIA
Gulf of Guinea
Bioko
EQUATORIAL
GUINEA
REP. OF
CONGO
Congo
Uele
Lake
Victoria
Nairobi

Equator
SAO TOME AND
PRINCIPE
GABON
Congo
Basin
RWANDA
Kilimanjaro
19,340 Ft.
5,895m
INDIAN
OCEAN

DEM. REP.
OF CONGO
BURUNDI
Serengeti
Plain
Masai
Steppe

Ascension
(St. Helena)
Kinshasa
Kwango
Kasai
Lake
Tanganyika
TANZANIA
Zanzibar
SEYCH

Cuanza
Great Rift Valley

ATLANTIC
ANGOLA
MALAWI
Lake Nyasa
COMOROS
Mayotte
(Fr.)
Cape Am

St. Helena
(U.K.)
Cunene
ZAMBIA
MOZAMBIQUE

OCEAN
Victoria
Falls
Lake
Kariba
Zambezi
Mozambique Channel
MADAGASCAR

Okavango
ZIMBABWE
MAUR

Namib
Desert
NAMIBIA
BOTSWANA
Limpopo
Reun
(F

Tropic of Capricorn
Kalahari
Desert
Barra Point

Johannesburg
SWAZILAND
Cape Sainte-Marie

Vaal
Drakensberg

Orange
LESOTHO

SOUTH
AFRICA

Cape of
Good Hope
Cape Agulhas

Tristan da
Cunha Group
(St. Helena)

0   200   400   600   800   1000 Miles

0   300   600   900   1200   1500 Kilometers

Copyright by Rand McNally & Co.
Lambert Azimuthal Equal Area Projection

Prince Edward
Islands
(S. Af.)

Crozet Islands
(Fr.)

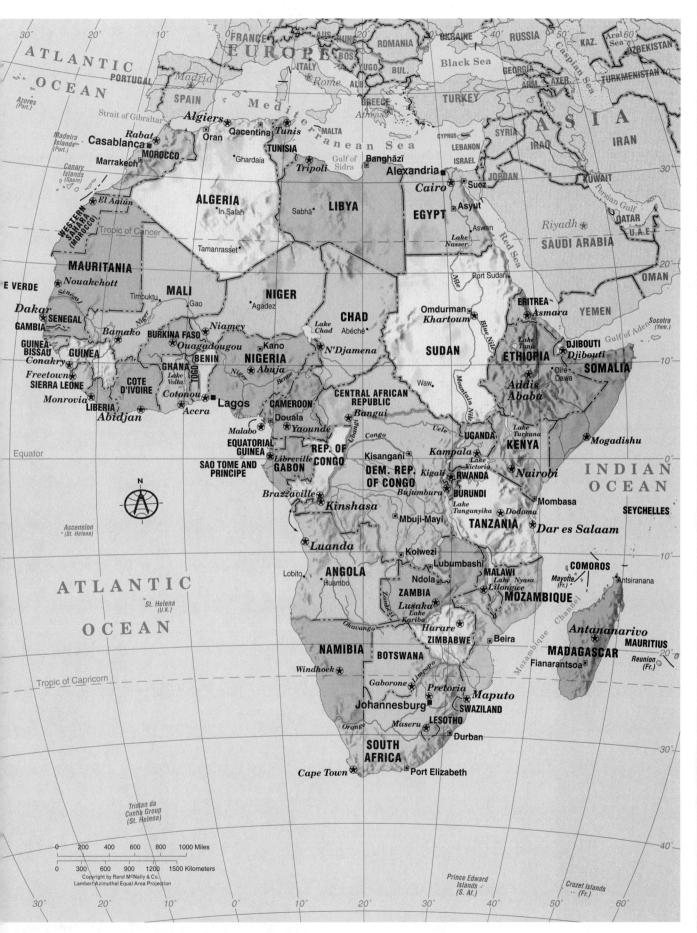

ATLAS

RAND McNALLY

ATLANTIC OCEAN

ARCTIC OCEAN

ICELAND

FAROE ISLANDS (Den.)

IRELAND

UNITED KINGDOM

London

NORWAY

SWEDEN

FINLAND

Barents Sea

Novaya Zemlya

Yamal Pen.

Kara Sea

PORTUGAL

SPAIN

DENMARK

NETH.

GERMANY

POLAND

ESTONIA

LATVIA

LITH.

BELARUS

Moscow

Volga

Ural Mountains

West

Siberian

Lowland

Novosib

Ob

MOROCCO

ALGERIA

TUNISIA

GIBRALTAR (U.K.)

ANDORRA

FRANCE

MONACO

SWITZ.

ITALY

AUSTRIA

CZECH

SLOVAKIA

HUNGARY

SLOV.

CRO.

BOS.

YUGO.

ALB.

MAC.

ROMANIA

BULGARIA

GREECE

UKRAINE

MOLD.

Black Sea

Caucasus

Caspian Depression

Astana

KAZAKHSTAN

Irtysh

Ishim

Mediterranean Sea

LIBYA

EGYPT

Cairo

Nile

CYPRUS

N. CYPRUS

LEBANON

ISRAEL

Sinai Pen.

JORDAN

SYRIA

TURKEY

Ararat

Mt. Ararat 16,940 Ft. 5,165m

GEORGIA

ARM.

AZER.

Caspian Sea

Ust-Urt Plateau

Aral Sea

UZBEKISTAN

Syr Darya

Amu Darya

Kara Kum (Desert)

TURKMENISTAN

TAJIKISTAN

KYRGYZSTAN

Tian Shan

Lake Balkhash

CHAD

SUDAN

Red Sea

An-Nafud

SAUDI ARABIA

Arabian Peninsula

IRAQ

Euphrates

Tigris

KUWAIT

Tehran

Zagros Mts.

Dasht-e Kavir

IRAN

Persian Gulf

BAHRAIN

QATAR

U.A.E.

AFGHANISTAN

Pamirs

Hindu Kush

Tarim Basin

K2 (Qogir Feng) 28,250 Ft. 8,611m

Kunlun

Altu

PAKISTAN

Indus

New Delhi

Ganges

Great Indian Desert

HIMALAYA M

NEPAL

Mt. Ev 29,03 8,8

Rub Al-Khali

OMAN

Gulf of Oman

ERITREA

YEMEN

DJIBOUTI

ETHIOPIA

DEM. REP. OF THE CONGO (ZAIRE)

UGANDA

RWANDA

BURUNDI

KENYA

SOMALIA

Gulf of Aden

Socotra (Yem.)

Arabian Sea

Mumbai (Bombay)

Godavari

Deccan Plateau

Western Ghats

Eastern Ghats

Ba

Be

INDIA

TANZANIA

ZAMBIA

MALAWI

MOZAMBIQUE

N

Lakshadweep (India)

SRI LANKA

MALDIVES

INDIAN OCEAN

0   200   400   600   800 Miles

0   200   400   600   800   1000 Kilometers

Copyright by Rand McNally & Co.
Lambert Azimuthal Equal Area Projection

ATLAS

RAND McNALLY

ATLANTIC OCEAN

ICELAND
IRELAND
London
United Kingdom
FAROE ISLANDS (Den.)
Norwegian Sea
Arctic Circle
NORWAY
SWEDEN
FINLAND
DENMARK
GERMANY
POLAND
ESTONIA
LATVIA
LITH.
BELARUS
UKRAINE
Kiev
Moscow
PORTUGAL
SPAIN
FRANCE
Paris
ANDORRA
MONACO
ITALY
Adriatic Sea
AUSTRIA
HUNGARY
ROMANIA
BULGARIA
GREECE
Black Sea
MOROCCO
GIBRALTAR
ALGERIA
TUNISIA
Mediterranean Sea
LIBYA
EGYPT
Cairo
Nile
SUDAN
CHAD
Red Sea
Blue Nile
ERITREA
ETHIOPIA
DJIBOUTI
Gulf of Aden
SOMALIA
KENYA
UGANDA
RWANDA
BURUNDI
TANZANIA
DEM. REP. OF THE CONGO (ZAIRE)
ZAMBIA
MALAWI
MOZAMBIQUE

ARCTIC OCEAN
Barents Sea
Svalbard (Nor.)
Spitsbergen
Franz Josef Land
Novaya Zemlya
Kara Sea
Severnaya Zemlya
Noril'sk

RUSSIA
Yekaterinburg
Chelyabinsk
Omsk
Novosibirsk
Barnaul
Semipalatinsk
Öskemen
Ob'
Irtysh
Ishim
Tobol

KAZAKHSTAN
Astana
Karaganda
Aral Sea
Lake Balkhash
Syr Darya
Almaty
Ürümqi

istanbul
Izmir
Ankara
TURKEY
N. CYPRUS
CYPRUS
LEBANON
SYRIA
Damascus
ISRAEL
JORDAN
Amman
GEORGIA
Tbilisi
ARM.
Yerevan
AZER.
Baku
Caspian Sea
Tabriz
Tehran
Mashhad
Esfahan
IRAN
Kabul
AFGHANISTAN
TURKMENISTAN
Ashgabat
UZBEKISTAN
Tashkent
Bishkek
KYRGYZSTAN
Dushanbe
TAJIKISTAN

IRAQ
Baghdad
Kuwait
KUWAIT
SAUDI ARABIA
Riyadh
Jiddah
Persian Gulf
BAHRAIN
QATAR
Abu Dhabi
U.A.E.
Gulf of Oman
Muscat
OMAN
YEMEN
Sanaa
Socotra (Yem.)

Islamabad
Amritsar
Lahore
PAKISTAN
Karachi
Delhi
New Delhi
NEPAL
Kathmandu
Hyderabad
Kanpur
Ahmadabad
INDIA
Nagpur
Mumbai (Bombay)
Hyderabad
Bangalore
Chennai (Madras)
Kolkata (Calcutta)
Lakshadweep (India)
MALDIVES
Colombo
SRI LANKA
Bay of Bengal
Arabian Sea
INDIAN OCEAN
Godavari
Ganges
Brahmaputra
Indus

N

0   200   400   600   800 Miles
0   200 400 600 800 1000 Kilometers
Copyright by Rand McNally & Co.
Lambert Azimuthal Equal Area Projection

ATLAS

RAND M^cNALLY

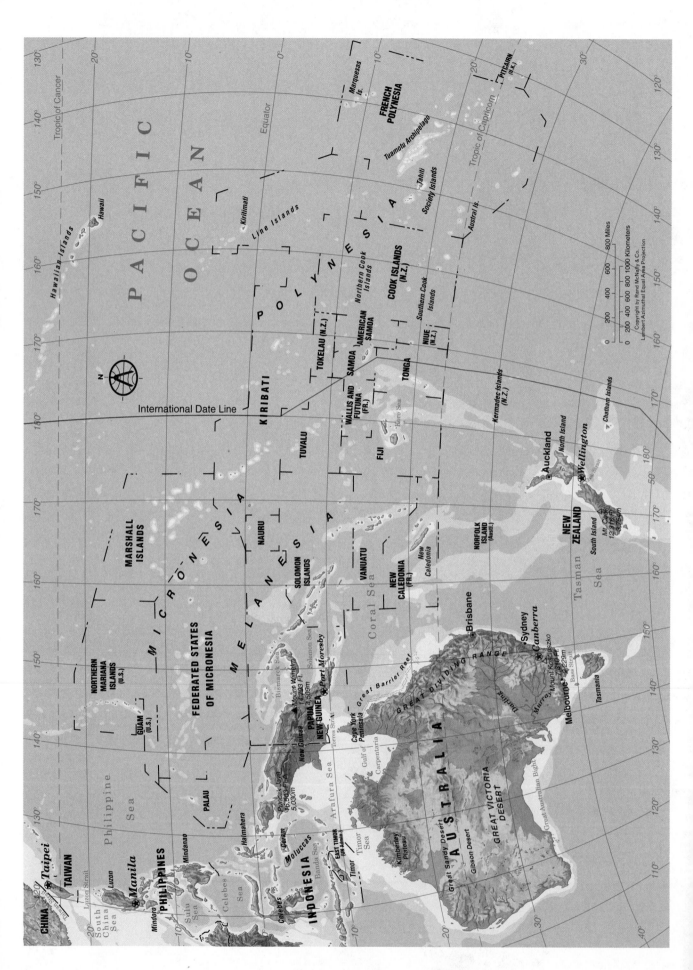

RAND M*NALLY

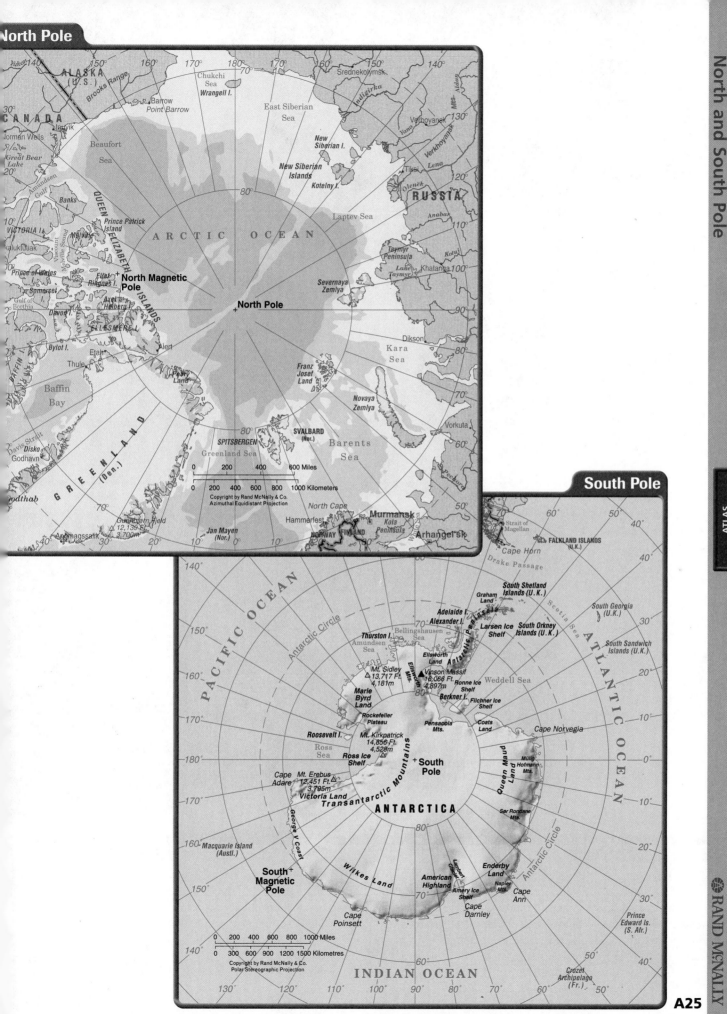

South Pole

North Pole map labels

ALASKA (U.S.)
Brooks Range
Barrow
Point Barrow
Chukchi Sea
Wrangell I.
Srednekolymsk
CANADA
Inuvik
Norman Wells
Great Bear Lake
Amundsen Gulf
Banks
Beaufort Sea
East Siberian Sea
New Siberian I.
Indigirka
Yana
Verkhoyansk
Verkhoyansk Mts.
VICTORIA I.
Prince Patrick Island
QUEEN ELIZABETH ISLANDS
New Siberian Islands
Kotelny I.
Tiksi
Lena
Oleněk
RUSSIA
Prince of Wales
Melville
Aldan
ARCTIC OCEAN
North Magnetic Pole
North Pole
Anabar
Kaluktuluak
Ellef Ringnes I.
Axel Heiberg I.
Somerset
Gulf of Boothia
Devon I.
ELLESMERE I.
Taymyr Peninsula
Lake Taymyr
Khatanga
Severnaya Zemlya
Bylot I.
BAFFIN I.
Etah
Alert
Peary Land
Dikson
Kara Sea
Baffin Bay
Thule
Franz Josef Land
Novaya Zemlya
Vorkuta
GREENLAND (Den.)
Davis Strait
Disko
Godhavn
SVALBARD (Nor.)
SPITSBERGEN
Greenland Sea
Barents Sea
Godthåb
Angmagssalik
Gunnbjørn Fjeld △ 12,139 Ft. 3,700m
Jan Mayen (Nor.)
North Cape
Hammerfest
Murmansk
Kola Peninsula
NORWAY
FINLAND
Arhangel'sk

0   200   400   600 Miles
0   200   400   600   800   1000 Kilometers
Copyright by Rand McNally & Co.
Azimuthal Equidistant Projection

South Pole map labels

Strait of Magellan
Cape Horn
FALKLAND ISLANDS (U.K.)
Drake Passage
South Shetland Islands (U.K.)
Graham Land
South Georgia (U.K.)
PACIFIC OCEAN
Antarctic Circle
Adelaide I.
Alexander I.
Bellingshausen Sea
Larsen Ice Shelf
South Orkney Islands (U.K.)
ATLANTIC OCEAN
Scotia Sea
South Sandwich Islands (U.K.)
Thurston I.
Amundsen Sea
Antarctic Peninsula
Ellsworth Land
Mt. Sidley △ 13,717 Ft. 4,181m
Ellsworth Mts.
Vinson Massif △ 16,066 Ft. 4,897m
Ronne Ice Shelf
Weddell Sea
Marie Byrd Land
Berkner I.
Filchner Ice Shelf
Rockefeller Plateau
Pensacola Mts.
Coats Land
Roosevelt I.
Mt. Kirkpatrick 14,856 Ft. 4,528m △
Cape Norvegia
Ross Sea
Ross Ice Shelf
South Pole
Queen Maud Land
Müllg Hofmann Mts.
Cape Adare
Mt. Erebus 12,451 Ft. 3,795m △
Victoria Land
Transantarctic Mountains
ANTARCTICA
Sør Rondane Mts.
George V Coast
Macquarie Island (Austl.)
South Magnetic Pole
Wilkes Land
American Highland
Lambert Glacier
Enderby Land
Napier Mts.
Cape Ann
Antarctic Circle
Cape Poinsett
Amery Ice Shelf
Cape Darnley
Prince Edward Is. (S. Afr.)
INDIAN OCEAN
Crozet Archipelago (Fr.)

0   200   400   600   800   1000 Miles
0   300   600   900   1200   1500 Kilometres
Copyright by Rand McNally & Co.
Polar Stereographic Projection

A25

UNIT 1

Introduction to World Cultures and Geography

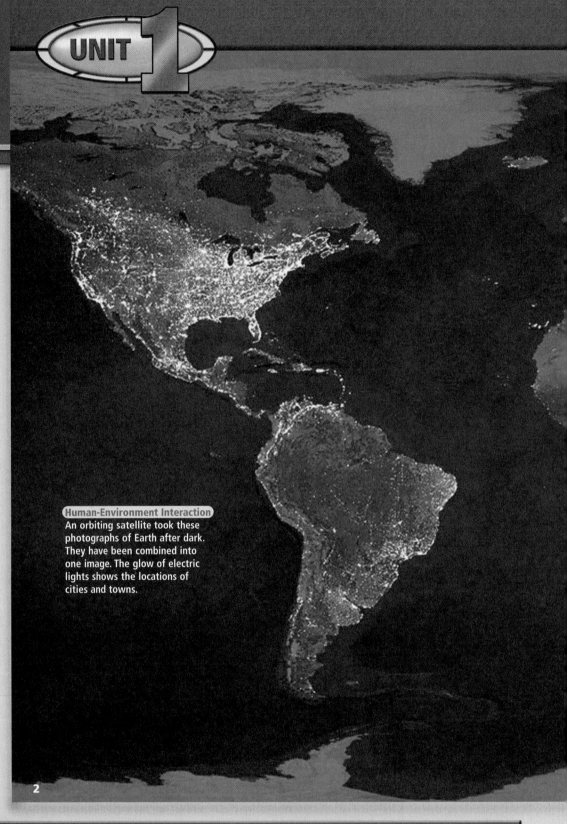

Before You Read

Previewing Unit 1

Unit 1 introduces the term *social studies* and identifies and describes the five fields of learning that contribute to social studies—geography, history, economics, government, and culture. The unit also explains the five themes of geography. It concludes with an explanation of how culture regions are grouped, how they change, and how they evolve. The importance of social studies as a way to understand Earth and its people is examined throughout the unit.

Human-Environment Interaction
An orbiting satellite took these photographs of Earth after dark. They have been combined into one image. The glow of electric lights shows the locations of cities and towns.

2

Unit Level Activities

1. Write an Editorial

After students read about culture regions, ask them to imagine that a historic site in their area is about to be destroyed due to highway construction. Have students decide whether they support or oppose the highway, citing reasons why the history of a people is a vital part of their culture, why the current needs of a people are important, and so on.

2. Write Interview Questions

Have students write questions they might ask a visitor from another country. Remind them to include questions about the five fields of social studies—geography, history, economics, government, and culture. Then have students trade questions with a partner and choose a foreign country about which they will answer the questions they have received. Have students interview each other using the questions and answers.

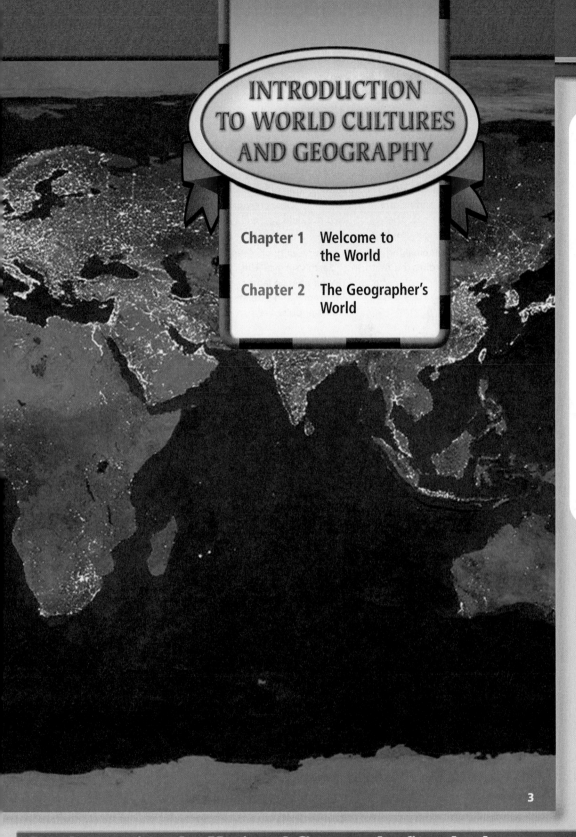

INTRODUCTION TO WORLD CULTURES AND GEOGRAPHY

FOCUS ON VISUALS

Interpreting the Photograph Have students examine the photograph. Ask a volunteer to read the caption aloud. Explain that satellites are human-made objects that orbit Earth. Ask students to identify the continents and major bodies of water in the photograph. Then ask them to locate the area in which they live. Guide students to think about what insights seeing Earth from the perspective of outer space can provide.

Possible Responses Only a camera many miles above Earth can capture these photographs. From this perspective, the continents seem close together despite the great distances between them. Combining photographs taken from this perspective creates an image of how Earth looks as a whole.

Extension Ask students to write a short radio broadcast in which a passenger in a manned satellite describes what Earth looks like from outer space.

Implementing the National Geography Standards

Standard 10 Describe visible cultural elements in the student's own community

Objective To identify various cultural elements in the student's environment

Class Time 25 minutes

Task Students work in groups to find examples of the different cultures represented in their communities. Assign each group one of these topics: religious institutions, restaurants, specialty stores, distinctive buildings, and media. Each group should list local examples of their topic. Have the groups share their examples.

Evaluation Groups should identify at least two foreign and two domestic examples of cultural elements in the community.

OBJECTIVES

1. To understand the methods for determining location
2. To interpret the different elements of a map
3. To understand the elements and purpose of the geographic grid
4. To examine different types of projections
5. To understand and interpret the different types of maps

FOCUS & MOTIVATE

WARM-UP

Using Maps Ask students to create a class list of the types of information that can be found on a map. Use the following questions to help them understand what is on a map.

1. Why would you look at a map?
2. What information would you expect to find on a map?

INSTRUCT: Objective ❶

Map Basics

- Where can you find the subject and basic information contained on a map? in its title
- What is the function of a compass rose? to show direction
- What is a legend? the explanation of symbols and colors used on a map
- What map features would you use to determine the distance between two places? scale

MORE ABOUT...

Magnetic Compasses

A compass consists of a small, lightweight magnet balanced atop a nearly frictionless pivot point. The magnet is sometimes called a needle. In response to Earth's magnetic field, the needle points toward the north. In the photograph on page 4 the needle is in the shape of an arrow.

Map Basics

Maps are an important tool for studying the use of space on Earth. This handbook covers the basic map skills and information that geographers rely on as they investigate the world—and the skills you will need as you study geography.

Mapmaking depends on surveying, or measuring and recording the features of Earth's surface. Until recently, this could be undertaken only on land or sea. Today, aerial photography and satellite imaging are the most popular ways to gather data.

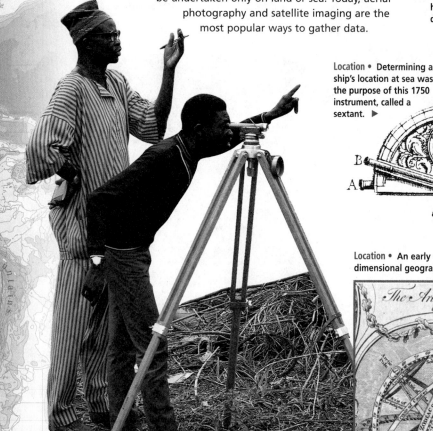

Location • Magnetic compasses, introduced by the Chinese in the 1100s, help people accurately determine directions. ▲

Location • Determining a ship's location at sea was the purpose of this 1750 instrument, called a sextant. ▶

Location • An early example of a three-dimensional geographic grid. ▼

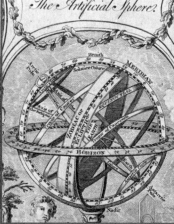

Human-Environment Interaction • Nigerian surveyors use a theodolite, which measures angles and distances on Earth. ▲

4 UNIT 1

Recommended Resources

BOOKS FOR THE TEACHER
The National Geographic Desk Reference. Washington, D.C., 1999. A geographic reference with hundreds of maps, charts, and graphs.
Erickson, Jon. *Making of the Earth:*
Geologic Forces That Shape Our Planet. Facts on File, Inc., NY, 2000. Discussion of formation of landforms.
VanCleave, Janice. *Janice VanCleave's Geography for Every Kid.* John Wiley and Sons, Inc., NY, 1993. Book of activities to help children understand geographic concepts such as how early explorers used maps, latitude and longitude, scale, grid, geographic versus magnetic north, compass rose, and time zones.

INTERNET
For more about geography skills, visit **classzone.com.**

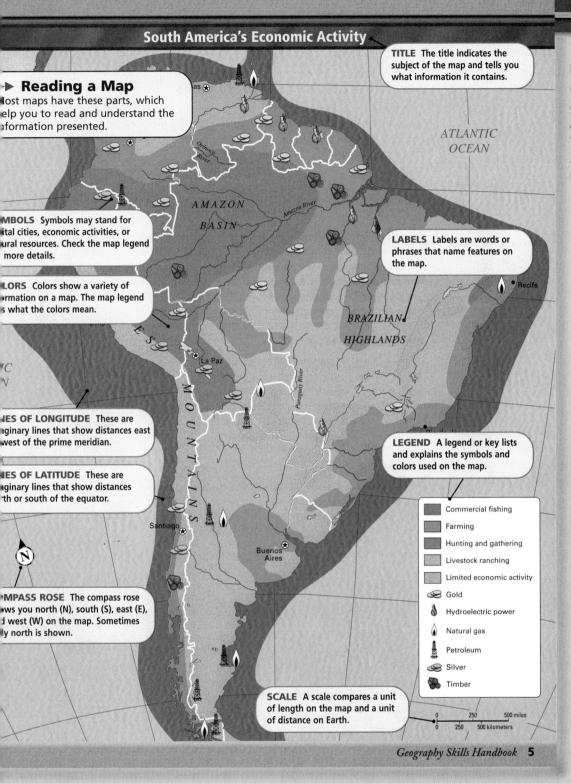

South America's Economic Activity

TITLE The title indicates the subject of the map and tells you what information it contains.

ATLANTIC OCEAN

▶ Reading a Map
Most maps have these parts, which help you to read and understand the information presented.

Orinoco River

AMAZON BASIN

Amazon River

SYMBOLS Symbols may stand for capital cities, economic activities, or natural resources. Check the map legend for more details.

LABELS Labels are words or phrases that name features on the map.

COLORS Colors show a variety of information on a map. The map legend tells what the colors mean.

Recife

BRAZILIAN HIGHLANDS

La Paz

ANDES MOUNTAINS

LINES OF LONGITUDE These are imaginary lines that show distances east and west of the prime meridian.

Paraguay River

LINES OF LATITUDE These are imaginary lines that show distances north or south of the equator.

LEGEND A legend or key lists and explains the symbols and colors used on the map.

N

Santiago

Buenos Aires

COMPASS ROSE The compass rose shows you north (N), south (S), east (E), and west (W) on the map. Sometimes only north is shown.

	Commercial fishing
	Farming
	Hunting and gathering
	Livestock ranching
	Limited economic activity
	Gold
	Hydroelectric power
	Natural gas
	Petroleum
	Silver
	Timber

SCALE A scale compares a unit of length on the map and a unit of distance on Earth.

0   250   500 miles
0   250   500 kilometers

Geography Skills Handbook **5**

Activity Options

Multiple Learning Styles: Spatial

Time One class period

Task Creating a map to use the basic features of mapmaking

Purpose To explore how the basic features of a map work

Supplies Needed
• Paper
• Colored pens and markers
• Large sheets of paper

Activity Have students create maps of the areas around their homes or school. Encourage them to make imaginative use of the basic features examined above. Students might create a scale using the length of their footsteps or design symbols to designate the location of favorite stores or homes of friends and relatives. With colors, they might show areas where they play. Display and discuss the maps in class.

INSTRUCT: Objective ❷

Longitude and Latitude Lines/Hemisphere/Scale

- What features of a map will help you find absolute locations? lines of longitude and latitude

- What is the term for half of the globe? hemisphere

- What determines the scale of a map? how much detail is to be shown on the map

MORE ABOUT...
Scale

Ratio scales, also called representative fraction scales or fractional scales, are the most accurate of all scale statements. Since they are presented numerically, they can be understood in any language.

Map Basics, cont.

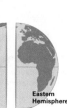

Longitude Lines (Meridians)

150°W 180° 150°E
120°W North 120°E
Pole
90°W 90°E

Prime Meridian

60°W 60°E

30°W 30°E
West Longitude 0° East Longitude

Latitude Lines (Parallels)

North Pole
90°N

60°N

30°N
Tropic of Cancer

Equator 0°

Tropic of Capricorn
30°S

60°S
90°S
South Pole

▶▶ Longitude and Latitude Lines

Longitude and latitude lines appear together on a map and allow you to pinpoint the absolute locations of cities and other geographic features. You express these locations as coordinates of intersecting lines. These are measured in degrees.

Longitude lines are imaginary lines that run north and south; they are also known as meridians. They show distances in degrees east or west of the prime meridian. The prime meridian is a longitude line that runs from the North Pole to the South Pole through Greenwich, England. It marks 0° longitude.

Latitude lines are imaginary lines that run east to west around the globe; they are also known as parallels. They show distances in degrees north or south of the equator. The equator is a latitude line that circles Earth halfway between the north and south poles. It marks 0° latitude. The tropics of Cancer and Capricorn are parallels that form the boundaries of the tropical zone, a region that stays warm all year.

▶▶ Hemisphere

Hemisphere is a term for half the globe. The globe can be divided into northern and southern hemispheres (separated by the equator) or into eastern and western hemispheres. The United States is located in the northern and western hemispheres.

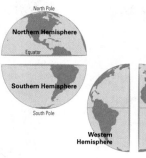

North Pole

Northern Hemisphere

Equator

Southern Hemisphere

South Pole

Western Hemisphere   Eastern Hemisphere

▶▶ Scale

A geographer decides what scale to use by determining how much detail to show. If many details are needed, a large scale is used. If fewer details are needed, a small scale is used.

Small scale used, without a lot of detail. ▼
WASHINGTON, D.C., METRO AREA
Scale: 1:4,500,000
1 inch = 70 miles

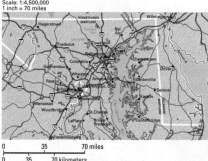

0   35   70 miles
0   35   70 kilometers

Larger scale used, with a lot of detail. ▼
WASHINGTON, D.C.
Scale: 1:88,700
1 inch = 1.4 miles

0   0.7   1.4 miles
0   0.7   1.4 kilometers

Activity Options

Interdisciplinary Link: Mathematics

Time 30 minutes

Task Creating a map and scale for the classroom

Purpose To understand how to use scale to represent distance and detail on a map

Supplies Needed
- Tape measures
- Rulers
- Grid paper
- Colored pencils

Activity Divide students into groups. Have one group measure the dimensions of the classroom. Have another group measure the sizes of the room's larger furnishings. A third group could measure the distance of these furnishings from the walls. After students finish collecting this data, have them draw a map that shows the classroom and its dimensions on the chalkboard. Next, provide students with a ratio (for example, 5 inches = 1 foot) and have them redraw the map of the room on their grid paper using this ratio.

▶▶ Projections

A projection is a way of showing the curved surface of Earth on a flat map. Flat maps cannot show sizes, shapes, and directions with total accuracy. As a result, all projections distort some aspect of Earth's surface. Below are four projections.

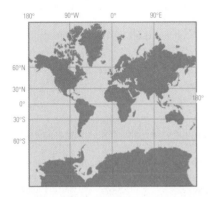

Mercator Projection • The Mercator projection shows most of the continents as they look on a globe. However, the projection stretches out the lands near the north and south poles. The Mercator projection is used for all kinds of navigation. ▲

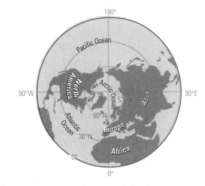

Azimuthal Projection • An azimuthal projection shows Earth so that a straight line from the central point to any other point on the map corresponds to the shortest distance between the two points. Sizes and shapes of the continents are distorted. ▲

Homolosine Projection • This projection shows landmasses shapes, and sizes accurately, but distances are not correct. ▲

Robinson Projection • For textbook maps, the Robinson projection is commonly used. It shows the entire Earth, with continents and oceans having nearly their true sizes and shapes. However, the landmasses near the poles appear flattened. ▲

MAP PRACTICE

MAIN IDEAS

1. (a) What is the longitude and latitude of your city or town?

(b) What information is provided by the legend in the map on page 5?

(c) What is a projection? Compare and contrast the depictons of Antarctica in the Mercator and Robinson projections.

CRITICAL THINKING

2. **Making Inferences** Why do you think latitude and longitude are important to sailors?

Think About

• the landmarks you use to find your way around

• the landmarks available to sailors on the ocean

INSTRUCT: Objective ④

Different Types of Maps

- **What is the purpose of a physical map?** to show landforms and bodies of water in a specific area

- **How does a physical map represent relief?** with color, shading, or contour lines

- **What is the purpose of a political map?** to show features on Earth's surface that are created by humans, such as countries, states, cities, and other political entities

MORE ABOUT...
Sea Level

Elevations are based on a landform's distance above or below sea level. But what if one sea is higher than another? And what happens when the level of the sea changes, for example, with the change of the tides? Because of these questions, geographers measure elevation using global mean sea level—the height of the surface of the sea averaged over all tide stages and over long periods of time.

Different Types of Maps

▶▶ Physical Maps

Physical maps help you see the landforms and bodies of water in specific areas. By studying a physical map, you can learn the relative locations and characteristics of places in a region.

On a physical map, color, shading, or contour lines are used to show elevations or altitudes, also called relief.

Ask these questions about the physical features shown on a physical map:

- Where on Earth's surface is this area located?
- What is its relative location?
- What is the shape of the region?
- In which directions do the rivers flow? How might the directions of flow affect travel and transportation in the region?
- Are there mountains or deserts? How might they affect the people living in the area?

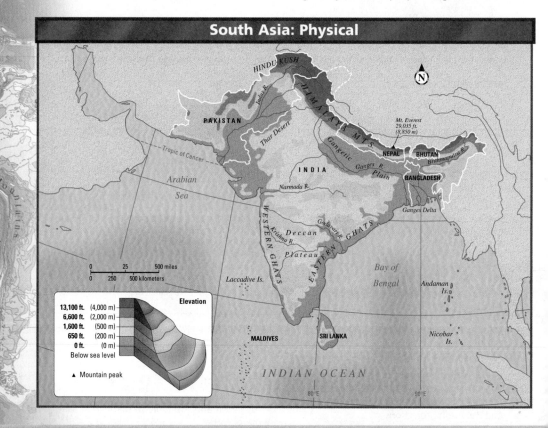

South Asia: Physical

8   UNIT 1

Activity Options

Differentiating Instruction: Less Proficient Readers

Class Time 10 minutes

Task Using mnemonic devices to help remember key terms

Purpose To help students differentiate between and remember longitude and latitude

Activity Some students may have difficulty remembering the difference between latitude and longitude. Have them use the following mnemonic device to differentiate the two terms and to remember them.

Latitude goes **a**round Earth. L**o**ngitude goes **o**ver Earth.

Help students devise a simple quiz game in which the answers to the questions are latitude or longitude.

▶▶ Political Maps

Political maps show features that humans have created on Earth's surface. Included on a political map may be cities, states, provinces, territories, and countries.

Ask these questions about the political features shown on a political map:

♦ Where on Earth's surface is this area located?

♦ What is its relative location? How might a country's location affect its economy and its relationships with other countries?

♦ What is the shape and size of the country? How might its shape and size affect the people living in the country?

♦ Who are the region's, country's, state's, or city's neighbors?

♦ How populated does the area seem to be? How might that affect activities there?

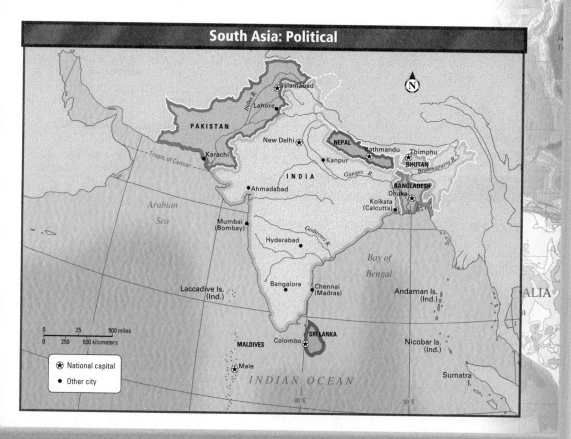

South Asia: Political

Geography Skills Handbook **9**

MORE ABOUT...
Political Boundaries

The boundaries we see on political maps are not always as fixed as they seem. Boundary disputes occur even in the United States. Recently the U.S. Supreme Court had to settle a dispute between New York and New Jersey. Leaders from each state argued that Ellis Island, the historic entry point for millions of immigrants to the United States, fell within their borders. In May 1998, the Supreme Court decided in favor of New Jersey.

Population

A population is the total number of people living in a defined area. That area may be as small as a neighborhood school or as large as the world. Births, deaths, and migration—the movement of people—determine the size of a population.

The study of population is called demography. Demographics are critical in making plans for the future. Demographers ask questions about where people are being born, how long they will live, and whether their basic needs can be met.

Activity Options

Multiple Learning Styles: Intrapersonal

Class Time 30 minutes

Task Creating a chart with maps and descriptions of border disputes

Purpose To have students examine contested political boundaries

Supplies Needed
• Magazines, newspapers
• Internet access

Activity Divide students into small groups. Ask them to use newspapers, magazines, or the Internet to find stories about disputed political borders. Encourage students to collect articles discussing various conflicts. Then have them create a large chart summarizing the conflicts.

| map showing labeled contested border | origin of dispute and current status |

Different Types of Maps, cont.

INSTRUCT: Objective ⑤

Thematic Maps

- What are thematic maps? maps that focus on specific themes or types of information
- What are some examples of types of thematic maps? maps that show climate, population density, vegetation
- What are some of the ways in which thematic maps are presented? as qualitative and flow-line maps and as cartograms

MORE ABOUT...
Cartographers

Cartography is the art of making maps or charts. People who draw maps are called cartographers. The word comes from the French *carte*, meaning "map" and the Greek *graph* meaning "writing."

▶▶ **Thematic Maps**

Geographers also rely on thematic maps, which focus on specific ideas. For example, in this textbook you will see thematic maps that show climates, types of vegetation, natural resources, population densities, and economic activities. Some thematic maps show historical trends; others may focus on movements of people or ideas. Thematic maps may be presented in a variety of ways.

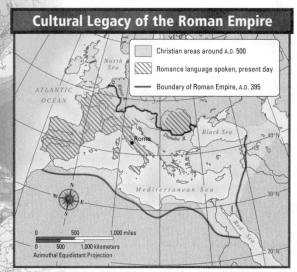

Cultural Legacy of the Roman Empire

Christian areas around A.D. 500
Romance language spoken, present day
Boundary of Roman Empire, A.D. 395

0   500   1,000 miles
0   500   1,000 kilometers
Azimuthal Equidistant Projection

Qualitative Maps On a qualitative map, colors, symbols, dots, or lines are used to help you see patterns related to a specific idea. The map shown here depicts the influence of the Roman Empire on Europe, North Africa, and Southwest Asia.

Use the suggestions below to help you interpret the map.
- Check the title to identify the theme and the data being presented.
- Carefully study the legend to understand the theme and the information presented.
- Look at the physical or political features of the area. How might the theme of the map affect them?
- What are the relationships among the data?

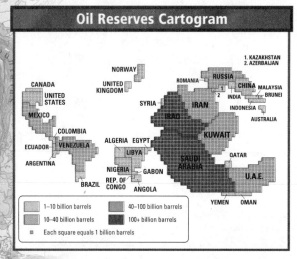

Oil Reserves Cartogram

1–10 billion barrels   40–100 billion barrels
10–40 billion barrels   100+ billion barrels
Each square equals 1 billion barrels

Cartograms A cartogram presents information about countries other than their shapes and sizes. The size of each country is determined by the data being presented, not its actual land size. On the cartogram shown here, the countries, sizes show the amounts of their oil reserves.

Use the suggestions below to help you interpret the map.
- Check the title and the legend to identify the data being presented.
- Look at the relative sizes of the countries shown. Which is the largest?
- Which countries are smallest?
- How do the sizes of these countries on a physical map differ from their sizes in the cartogram?
- What are the relationships among the data?

Activity Options

Multiple Learning Styles: Logical

Class Time 30 minutes

Task Locating different thematic maps

Purpose To familiarize students with different thematic maps

Supplies Needed
- Atlases
- Internet access
- Road maps, satellite maps, etc.

Activity Divide students into groups of four or more students. Provide each group with a list of different types of thematic maps. Within each group, have individual students pick one type of map from the list.

Students will be responsible for finding maps that focus on the theme they have chosen. When they have located their maps, have them interpret the information given on the map and prepare a presentation to the class that explains the information and its uses.

Flow-Line Maps Flow-line maps illustrate movements of people, goods, or ideas. The movements are usually shown by series of arrows. Locations, directions, and scopes of movement can be seen. The width of an arrow may show how extensive a flow is. Often the information is related to a period of time. The map shown here portrays the movement of the Bantu peoples in Africa.

Use the suggestions below to help you interpret the map.

♦ Check the title and the legend to identify the data being presented.

♦ Over what period of time did the movement occur?

♦ In what directions did the movement occur?

♦ How extensive was the movement?

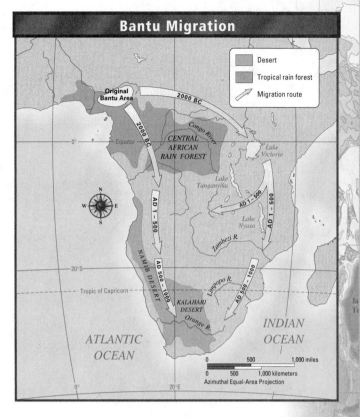

Bantu Migration

Desert
Tropical rain forest
→ Migration route

Original Bantu Area
2000 BC
2000 BC
CENTRAL AFRICAN RAIN FOREST
Congo River
Equator
0°
Lake Victoria
Lake Tanganyika
AD 1 – 500
AD 1 – 500
AD 1 – 500
Lake Nyasa
Zambezi R.
NAMIB DESERT
20°S
AD 500 – 1000
Tropic of Capricorn
Limpopo R.
AD 500 – 1000
KALAHARI DESERT
Orange R.
ATLANTIC OCEAN
INDIAN OCEAN
0 500 1,000 miles
0 500 1,000 kilometers
Azimuthal Equal-Area Projection
0°
20°E

Interpreting Maps Have students examine the Bantu migration map. Use the following questions to help them interpret the map: When did the Bantu migrations begin? The migrations began around 2000 B.C. When did the Bantu arrive at the Orange River in southern Africa? The Bantu arrived at the Orange River between A.D. 500 and 1000.

Class Time 10 minutes

MAP PRACTICE

Use pages 8–11 to help you answer these questions. Use the maps on pages 8–9 to answer questions 1–3.

1. In what direction does the Ganges River flow?

2. Kathmandu is the capital of which South Asian nation?

3. Which city is closer to the Thar Desert—Lahore, Pakistan, or New Delhi, India?

4. Why are only a few nations shown in the cartogram?

5. Which kind of thematic map would be best for showing the locations of climate zones?

Exploring Local Geography Obtain a physical-political map of your state. Use the data on it to create **two separate maps.** One should show physical features only, and the other should show political features only.

GeoActivity

Geography Skills Handbook **11**

Map Practice

Responses

1. The Ganges River flows southeast.
2. Nepal.
3. Lahore, Pakistan, is closer to the Thar Desert.
4. Only nations with oil reserves are shown. Most nations do not have oil reserves.
5. A qualitative map would be best for showing the location of climate zones.

GeoActivity

Integrated Assessment
• Rubric for creating a map

MORE ABOUT...

Deserts

Deserts are regions where the land is covered in sand or bare soil. Precipitation totals are always small, usually less than ten inches a year. Deserts are not always hot though. Temperatures can vary from extremely hot days to cold, even freezing, nights. The plants and animals that survive in the desert do so because they have adapted to the environment. Succulents, for example, store water in their leaves and stems. Many desert animals are nocturnal, taking advantage of the cool evenings to be active, while burrowing in the earth during the day.

Volcanoes

Most volcanoes form when molten rock from deep inside the earth rises to the surface at a fault line or soft spot in a tectonic plate. The molten rock that spurts out of the top of the volcano is known as lava.

Geographic Dictionary

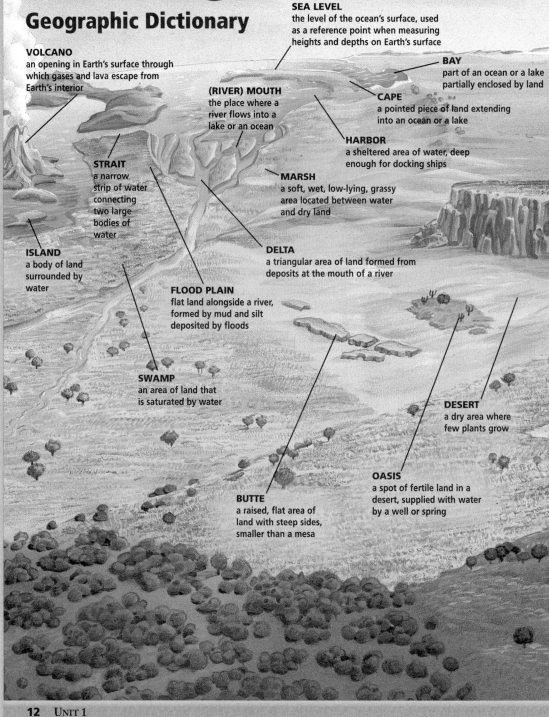

SEA LEVEL
the level of the ocean's surface, used as a reference point when measuring heights and depths on Earth's surface

VOLCANO
an opening in Earth's surface through which gases and lava escape from Earth's interior

BAY
part of an ocean or a lake partially enclosed by land

(RIVER) MOUTH
the place where a river flows into a lake or an ocean

CAPE
a pointed piece of land extending into an ocean or a lake

HARBOR
a sheltered area of water, deep enough for docking ships

STRAIT
a narrow strip of water connecting two large bodies of water

MARSH
a soft, wet, low-lying, grassy area located between water and dry land

ISLAND
a body of land surrounded by water

DELTA
a triangular area of land formed from deposits at the mouth of a river

FLOOD PLAIN
flat land alongside a river, formed by mud and silt deposited by floods

SWAMP
an area of land that is saturated by water

DESERT
a dry area where few plants grow

OASIS
a spot of fertile land in a desert, supplied with water by a well or spring

BUTTE
a raised, flat area of land with steep sides, smaller than a mesa

Activity Options

Differentiating Instruction: Gifted and Talented

Class Time one hour

Task Writing a report on the measurement of sea level using information gathered on the Internet or from library resources

Purpose To learn more about the use of sea level as a basis for determining elevation

Supplies Needed
- Internet access
- Library resource material

Activity Challenge gifted and interested students to use the Internet or library to investigate sea level as a basis for determining elevation.

They might examine the history of sea level measurement, the causes of fluctuations in sea levels, how these fluctuations are measured, and how global mean sea level is defined and measured.

Ask students to use their research to write a short report that includes a visual component to clarify difficult ideas and concepts. They should use this visual in a presentation to the class.

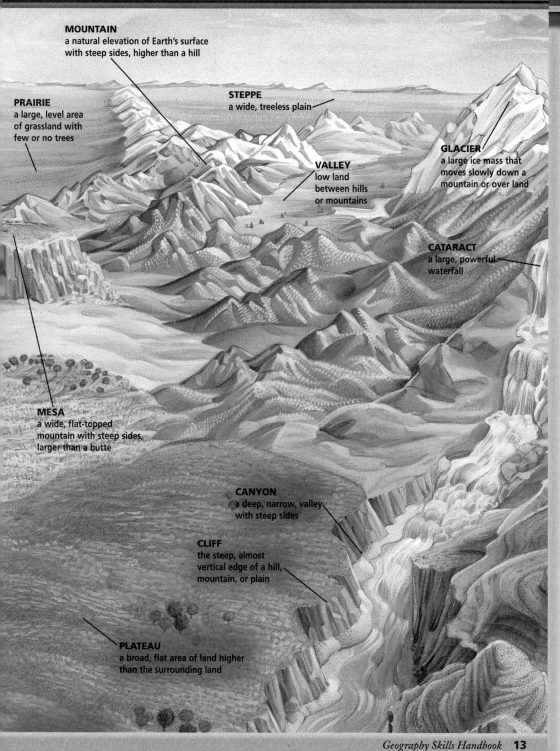

MOUNTAIN
a natural elevation of Earth's surface with steep sides, higher than a hill

STEPPE
a wide, treeless plain

PRAIRIE
a large, level area of grassland with few or no trees

GLACIER
a large ice mass that moves slowly down a mountain or over land

VALLEY
low land between hills or mountains

CATARACT
a large, powerful waterfall

MESA
a wide, flat-topped mountain with steep sides, larger than a butte

CANYON
a deep, narrow, valley, with steep sides

CLIFF
the steep, almost vertical edge of a hill, mountain, or plain

PLATEAU
a broad, flat area of land higher than the surrounding land

Geography Skills Handbook **13**

MORE ABOUT...
Glaciers

Glaciers cover about 6 million square miles or 3 percent of Earth's surface. They form at high elevations where it is cold enough for more snow to fall each year than melts. Over the years the snow gets deeper and deeper, and pressure from the weight of the snow turns it into huge sheets of ice. These sheets of ice flow, like slow-moving rivers, down the mountainside until they reach the warmer air along the ocean. When they break off, they form floating icebergs.

Steppes

A steppe is an area mainly covered with grassland. A steppe usually receives about 10 to 20 inches of rain a year. That is enough rain to support short grasses, but not enough for tall grass or trees. The Eurasian steppe, which extends from Hungary to China, is the largest grassland in the world.

Canyons

A deep, narrow valley with steep sides is called a canyon, from the Spanish word *cañon*, which means "tube" or "pipe." Most canyons develop in areas with arid climates, hard rocks, and streams that cascade down steep slopes. Scientists estimate that it took millions of years for the Grand Canyon in Arizona to form. Carved by the Colorado River the canyon is 18 miles wide in some places; at one point it is 1 mile deep from rim to river.

Welcome to the World

	OVERVIEW	COPYMASTERS	INTEGRATED TECHNOLOGY
CHAPTER RESOURCES	The student will examine the fields of learning that contribute to social studies and develop an understanding of culture and culture traits.	**In-depth Resources: Unit 1** • Guided Reading Worksheets, pp. 6–7 • Skillbuilder Practice, p. 10 • Unit Atlas Activities, pp. 1–4 • Geography Workshop, pp. 22–23 **Reading Study Guide** (Spanish and English), pp. 4–9 **Outline Map Activities**	Power Presentations Electronic Teacher Tools Online Lesson Planner Chapter Summaries on CD Critical Thinking Transparencies CT1

	KEY IDEAS		
SECTION 1 The World at Your Fingertips pp. 17–21	• Social studies draws from five fields of learning: geography, history, economics, government, and culture. • The five themes of geography are location, region, place, movement, and human-environment interaction. • Culture is the shared beliefs, customs, laws, and ways of living of a people. • A culture trait is any food, clothing, technology, language, tool, or belief shared by a cultural group.	**In-depth Resources: Unit 1** • Guided Reading Worksheet, p. 6 • Reteaching Activity, p. 12 **Reading Study Guide** (Spanish and English), pp. 4–5	Critical Thinking Transparencies CT2 Map Transparencies MT10 classzone.com Chapter Summaries on CD
SECTION 2 Many Regions, Many Cultures pp. 24–26	• People in culture regions share beliefs, history, and language. • Culture regions borrow from other cultures and depend on one another; many regions are multicultural.	**In-depth Resources: Unit 1** • Guided Reading Worksheet, p. 7 • Reteaching Activity, p. 13 **Reading Study Guide** (Spanish and English), pp. 6–7	Map Transparencies MT1 classzone.com Chapter Summaries on CD

KEY TO RESOURCES

))) Audio	Internet	TE Teacher's Edition
CD-ROM	Overhead Transparency	Video
Copymaster	PE Pupil's Edition	

ASSESSMENT OPTIONS

PE **Chapter Assessment,** pp. 30–31

Formal Assessment
• Chapter Tests: Forms A, B, C, pp. 17–18

Test Generator

Online Test Practice

Strategies for Test Preparation

PE **Section Assessment,** p. 21

Formal Assessment
• Section Quiz, p. 5

Integrated Assessment
• Rubric for making a poster

Test Generator

Test Practice Transparencies TT1

PE **Section Assessment,** p. 26

Formal Assessment
• Section Quiz, p. 6

Integrated Assessment
• Rubric for writing a dialogue

Test Generator

Test Practice Transparencies TT2

RESOURCES FOR DIFFERENTIATING INSTRUCTION

Students Acquiring English/ESL

Reading Study Guide (Spanish and English), pp. 4–9

Access for Students Acquiring English Spanish Translations, pp. 1–6

Less Proficient Readers

Reading Study Guide (Spanish and English), pp. 4–9

TE **TE Activity**
• Synthesizing, p. 18

Gifted and Talented Students

TE **TE Activity**
• Making an Oral Report, p. 25

CROSS-CURRICULAR CONNECTIONS

Humanities
Markel, Michelle. *Cornhusk, Silk, and Wishbones: A Book of Dolls From Around the World.* New York: Houghton Mifflin, 2000. Museum-quality dolls from 26 cultures.

Literature
Koch, Kenneth. *Talking to the Sun: An Illustrated Anthology of Poems for Young People.* New York: Henry Holt, 1985. International collection illustrated with museum art.

Popular Culture
Braman, Arlette N. *Kids Around the World Cook!: The Best Foods and Recipes from Many Lands.* New York: John Wiley & Sons, 2000. Inclusive collection and fun facts.

Health
Ichord, Loretta. *Toothworms and Spider Juice: An Illustrated History of Dentistry.* Brookfield, CT: Millbrook Press, 2000. Dental details from many cultures and times.

Storring, Rod. *A Doctor's Life.* New York: NAL, 1998. Medicine from A.D. 50 to present.

Science/Math
D'Amico, Joan. *The Science Chef Travels Around the World: Fun Food Experiments and Recipes for Kids.* New York: John Wiley & Sons, 1996. Combines math and science with multicultural viewpoint.

Mathematics
Bruno, Leonard C. *Math and Mathematicians: The History of Math Discoveries Around the World.* Farmington Hills, MI: Gale Group, 1999. Multicultural context for mathematics.

Science
Branley, Franklyn. *Keeping Time: From the Beginning and into the 21st Century.* New York: Houghton Mifflin, 1993. Clear explanations of humanity's attempt to keep time.

Economics
Young, Robert. *Money.* Minneapolis, MN: Carolrhoda Books, 1998. History of money and types of economies.

ENRICHMENT ACTIVITIES

The following activities are especially suitable for classes following block schedules.

Teacher's Edition, pp. 19, 20, 25, 27
Pupil's Edition, pp. 21, 26

Geography Handbook, pp. 4–13
Interdisciplinary Challenge, pp. 22–23

Literature Connections, pp. 28–29
Outline Map Activities

INTEGRATED TECHNOLOGY

Go to **classzone.com** for lesson support and activities for Chapter 1.

BLOCK SCHEDULE LESSON PLAN OPTIONS: 90-MINUTE PERIOD

DAY 1

UNIT PREVIEW, pp. 14–15
Class Time 20 minutes

• **Discussion** Lead a class discussion about why people settle where they do, using Focus on Geography on PE p. 15. Encourage students to identify what needs people are meeting when they choose a location in which to settle.

GEOGRAPHY HANDBOOK, pp. 4–13
Class Time 35 minutes

• **Peer Teaching** Divide students into pairs and have them alternate quizzing each other about content on the Geography Handbook pages.

SECTION 1, pp. 17–21
Class Time 35 minutes

• **Making Connections** Have students reread Learning About the World, PE p. 18. Divide the class into five groups. Assign each group a field of social studies. Have each group develop one specific detail about the different grade levels in your school that is an example of the assigned social studies theme. Reconvene as a whole class for discussion.

DAY 2

SECTION 1, continued
Class Time 50 minutes

• **Applying Understanding** Write the five themes of geography on the chalkboard and review them as a class. Choose a country and have students write five questions about it, one question for each geography theme. Review and compare questions as a group.
Class Time 30 minutes

• **Clarifying Economics** Lead a discussion about economics, using the question prompts under Objective 3, on TE p. 18. Be sure that students understand the important terms and can identify examples of each.
Class Time 20 minutes

SECTION 2, pp. 24–26
Class Time 40 minutes

• **Reading Maps** Divide the class into seven groups. Assign each a culture region from the map Culture Regions of the World, PE p. 25. Have groups use the map to create a brief profile of their region. Each profile should include the region's size and location, its bordering regions, and one generalization. Have teams present their profiles, and discuss each concluding generalization as a class.

DAY 3

SECTION 2, continued
Class Time 20 minutes

• **Understanding Connections** Have students reread the section Culture Regions Change, PE p. 26. Ask students to share examples of items or events from their daily lives that are examples of interdependence upon other regions. Write their examples on the board.

CHAPTER 1 REVIEW AND ASSESSMENT, pp. 30–31
Class Time 70 minutes

• **Review** Have students work in teams to prepare a brief oral summary of the chapter by reviewing the Main Ideas and Why It Matters Now features in each section in Chapter 1. Have one student from each group deliver the summary.
Class Time 35 minutes

• **Assessment** Have students complete the Chapter 1 Assessment.
Class Time 35 minutes

TECHNOLOGY IN THE CLASSROOM

DIGGING FOR INFORMATION ON THE WEB

This type of activity asks students to dig through a few Web sites to answer specific questions. This exercise requires them to practice their reading and skimming skills, to pay attention to detail, and to be patient enough to look for the correct information. It can serve as a warm-up for larger Internet research projects. Students can do this activity individually or with partners. To make the project shorter, simply omit one or more questions.

ACTIVITY OUTLINE

Objective Students will answer eight questions about world cultures, based on information they find at specified Web sites.

Task Discuss the meaning of *culture*, and have students dig through the Web sites to find the answers to the eight questions listed below. As an option, have students choose one culture to research in more depth and write a two-page report on the computer about this culture.

Class Time 1–2 class periods (not including optional research project)

DIRECTIONS

1. Ask students what they think *culture* means, and write their ideas on the chalkboard. Explain that culture includes such things as customs, daily activities, language, religion, art, and music. Can they think of other things that are part of a person's culture? What are some elements of their own culture?

2. Have students go to the Web sites listed at **classzone.com** to find the answers to the following questions about world cultures. The answers are all available at the Web sites, but students will have to do some digging to find them.

   • What do Jewish children in Israel (and other parts of the world) do on Purim?

   • How do you play "sick cat," a Brazilian game?

   • Describe three traditions, stories, songs, or dances of the Tuareg people of the Sahara Desert.

   • What is Komba, and what is its importance to the Baka people of the African rain forest?

   • How do most teenagers in France get around town?

   • Why might you experience culture shock on a trip to Kathmandu, Nepal?

   • What is Talavera, a Mexican tradition?

3. Discuss students' answers as a group, and have them point out the places they have learned about on a world map.

CHAPTER 1 OBJECTIVE

Students will examine the fields of learning that contribute to social studies and develop an understanding of culture and culture traits.

FOCUS ON VISUALS

Interpreting the Photograph Direct students' attention to the photographs of children from all over the world. Read the caption aloud, and then ask students to explain how the photographs support the caption. Have students consider how the children are alike as well as how they are different.

Possible Responses Although their clothes and environments are very different, they are all children who appear to share friendships and smiles.

Extension Have students create a collage of class photos similar to the ones shown here to demonstrate the differences and similarities among classmates.

CRITICAL THINKING ACTIVITY

Recognizing Effects Prompt a discussion about how people adapt to where they live. Brainstorm a list of factors that affect people's lifestyles, such as climate and geography. Have students list these factors and make notes about the ways that people might adapt to each one.

Class Time 15 minutes

Welcome to the World

SECTION 1 The World at Your Fingertips

SECTION 2 Many Regions, Many Cultures

Region The peoples of the world live in an astonishing variety of ways.

14

Recommended Resources

BOOKS FOR THE TEACHER
Angeloni, Elvio. *Anthropology 01/02.* Guilford, CT: McGraw-Hill, 2001. Forty articles covering cultures, structures, and perspectives.
Geertz, Clifford. *The Interpretation of Cultures.* New York: Basic Books, 2000. What culture is, what role it plays in social life, and how to study it.

Mark, Joan T. *Margaret Mead: Coming of Age in America.* New York: Oxford University Press, 1999. Traces Mead's life and groundbreaking work.
Moehn, Heather. *World Holidays.* Danbury, CT: Franklin Watts, 2000. Alphabetical and chronological guide.

VIDEOS
People. New York: Lightyear Entertainment, 1995. Cultures around the world.

INTERNET
For more information about world cultures, visit **classzone.com**

FOCUS ON GEOGRAPHY

How have geographic features influenced settlement patterns?

Movement • People settle where they can most easily and comfortably meet their needs for clean water, food, work, communication, trade, and transportation. Before there were good roads, boats were the easiest way to travel or send and receive goods. As a result, people often settled near rivers, lakes, and oceans. They also often settled where the land was suitable for cultivation and the climate was comfortable. You will not find many cities in the frozen wastelands of Siberia.

What do you think?

♦ Why are there few settlements in the desert?

♦ Why is there often a city where two rivers meet?

FOCUS ON GEOGRAPHY

Objectives

• To help students identify the relationship between geography and the way people meet their needs

• To explain how geographic factors present global challenges

What Do You Think?

1. Make sure students know that a desert is a region so dry that relatively few animals and plants exist there. Then guide a discussion of why the lack of resources discourages settlement in most deserts.

2. Guide students to think about trade, transportation, communication, and other opportunities provided by rivers.

How have geographic features influenced settlement patterns?

Ask students to consider the immediate needs of people who settled in places before transportation and communication systems were established. Have them think about what they might have brought with them, what they would need to make a living, and how they would get food and water. Ask students to think about how people might have changed the land once they settled there.

MAKING GEOGRAPHIC CONNECTIONS

Ask students to make a list of geographic features that might have presented problems to settlers. Then ask them to list the specific problem next to each feature.

Implementing the National Geography Standards

Standard 5 Give examples of regions at different spatial scales

Objective To have students form a mental map of where their community is in the world

Class Time 15 minutes

Task Students list the regions they live in, going from the largest region (e.g., Earth) to the smallest region (e.g., their street). Show the class a map of the world. Have the students identify what hemisphere they live in. Then ask students to identify what continent, country,

state, city, and neighborhood they live in. Tell students to identify other regions to which their community belongs.

Evaluation Students should correctly order the regions by size.

BEFORE YOU READ

What Do You Know?

Prompt a discussion about the term *social studies*. Have students discuss the kinds of information they have learned in social studies classes in the past. Have small groups of students work together to come up with a definition of social studies. Then have groups share and compare their definitions, looking for common words and ideas. Compare their definitions with dictionary and encyclopedia entries.

What Do You Want to Know?

Write the headings *history, geography, economics, government,* and *culture* on the chalkboard. Have students take turns listing what they already know about the terms. Then ask what more they would need to know in order to write definitions for the terms. Suggest that students list questions that they would like the chapter to answer. Students should look for answers to their questions as they read and record facts they find particularly interesting.

READ AND TAKE NOTES

Reading Strategy: Categorizing Remind students that a chart is an excellent format for organizing information, such as words and their meanings. Have them read the terms listed in the chart. Then explain that they will find these **boldfaced** terms in the chapter. As students locate each one, have them write its definition and any other important information in the chart. Tell them that when the chart is completed, they will be able to use it as a study resource.

 In-depth Resources: Unit 1
• Guided Reading Worksheets, pp. 6–7

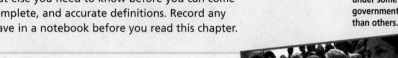
BEFORE YOU READ

▶▶ What Do You Know?

You live in the world, but how much do you know about it? The best way to find out is through social studies. *Social studies* is an umbrella term. It covers history, geography, economics, government, and culture. History, you probably know, is the study of the past. How clearly can you define the other terms? How do you think they can help you to learn about the world?

▶▶ What Do You Want to Know?

Think about what else you need to know before you can come up with clear, complete, and accurate definitions. Record any questions you have in a notebook before you read this chapter.

Region • Citizens have more rights under some governments than others. ▼

READ AND TAKE NOTES

Reading Strategy: Categorizing One way to make sense of information is to organize it in a chart. Writing your notes in a chart with categories can help you remember the most important parts of what you have read.

• Copy the chart below into your notebook.
• As you read the chapter, note the definition of each term listed on the chart.
• Write these definitions next to the appropriate heading.

Region •
Prepared for a flood, this house was built to suit its environment. ▲

Term	Definition
history	The study of the past with the help of written records
geography	The study of people, places, and the environment
economics	The study of the ways in which people produce and exchange goods
government	The people and groups of people that have the power to make laws and see that they are obeyed
culture	The beliefs, customs, and ways of living that a group of people share

---

Teaching Strategy

Reading the Chapter This is a thematic chapter that defines social studies and the five areas of learning that contribute to the field of social studies: geography, history, economics, government, and culture. Encourage students to use prior knowledge and the photographs in the chapter to help them understand how each area contributes to the study of the world and its cultures.

Integrated Assessment The Chapter Assessment on page 30 describes several activities that may be used for integrated assessment. You may wish to have students work on these activities during the course of the chapter and then present them at the end.

The World at Your Fingertips

TERMS & NAMES
history
geography
government
citizen
economics
scarcity
culture
culture trait

MAIN IDEA

Social studies includes information from five fields of learning to provide a well-rounded picture of the world and its peoples.

WHY IT MATTERS NOW

Understanding your world is essential if you are to be an informed citizen of a global society.

DATELINE

 EXTRA

SAN FRANCISCO, USA, JUNE 26, 1945

Fifty nations signed a charter today to establish a new organization called the United Nations. The organization will go into effect October 24.

The United Nations is a successor to the old League of Nations, founded after World War I to prevent another world war, which it failed to do.

The purpose of the new organization is to maintain peace and develop friendly relations among nations.

The member nations hope to cooperate to solve economic, social, cultural, and humanitarian problems and to promote respect for human rights and freedom.

Region • Flags of member countries fly in front of the United Nations headquarters in New York City. ▲

The Peoples of the World ❶

For centuries, people in different parts of the world have been trying to get along with one another, not always with success. Part of the problem is a lack of understanding of other people's ways of life. Certain advances in communication and transportation, such as the Internet and high-speed planes, have brought people closer together. So have increased international trade and immigration. Knowledge of other societies can be a key to understanding them.

Welcome to the World **17**

SECTION OBJECTIVES

1. To define social studies and identify the five fields of learning that it draws from
2. To identify the impact of geography and government on people
3. To explain economics and related terms
4. To define culture and culture traits

CRITICAL THINKING
• Drawing Conclusions, p. 19
• Clarifying, p. 20

FOCUS & MOTIVATE
WARM-UP

Identifying Problems Have students read <u>Dateline</u> and discuss the following questions to help them understand the United Nations.

1. What organization did the United Nations replace?
2. What are the purpose and goals of the United Nations?

INSTRUCT: Objective ❶

The Peoples of the World/ Learning About the World

• What is the key to understanding other societies? knowledge of the other societies
• What five fields of learning contribute to the field of social studies? geography, history, economics, government, culture

 In-depth Resources: Unit 1
• Guided Reading Worksheet, p. 6

Reading Study Guide
(Spanish and English), pp. 4–5

Program Resources

 In-depth Resources: Unit 1
• Guided Reading Worksheet, p. 6
• Reteaching Activity, p. 12

 Reading Study Guide
(Spanish and English), pp. 4–5

 Formal Assessment
• Section Quiz, p. 5

 Integrated Assessment
• Rubric for making a poster

 Outline Map Activities

Access for Students Acquiring English
• Guided Reading Worksheet, p. 1

 Technology Resources
classzone.com

TEST-TAKING RESOURCES
⚓ Strategies for Test Preparation
⚓ Test Practice Transparencies
🌐 Online Test Practice

INSTRUCT: Objective ❷

History and Geography/ Government

- What are the five themes of geography? location, region, place, movement, human-environment interaction

- Why do we use these different themes? They allow us to examine geography from different angles; each suggests different facts.

- What is the definition of government? people and groups in a society who have the authority to make laws and see they are carried out

Connections to Science

Almost any object can help us understand how people lived in the past. Evidence is organized by archaeologists into three basic types: artifacts, features, and ecofacts. Objects that were made by people and can be moved, like pottery and beads, are called artifacts. Houses, tombs, and large structures are called features. The natural objects found within artifacts or features are ecofacts; these include seeds and bones.

A VOICE FROM TODAY

David McCullough is a distinguished writer, teacher, and historian. He grew up believing that history is a lively subject. He communicates this belief to his readers. "I write to find out," he says. "There isn't anything in this world that isn't inherently interesting—if only someone will explain it to you…will frame it into a story."

Learning About the World ❶

Social studies is a way to learn about the world. It draws on information from five fields of learning—geography, history, economics, government, and culture. Each field looks at the world from a different angle. Consider the approaches you might use if you were starting at a new school. Figuring out how to get around would be learning your school's geography. Asking other students where they come from is learning their history. Making choices about which school supplies you can afford to buy is economics. Learning the school rules is learning about its government. Clubs, teams, styles of clothing, holidays, and even ways of saying things are part of the school's culture.

Place • The five fields of learning in social studies are well represented in daily life. ▲

History and Geography ❷

Knowing history and geography helps orient you in time and space. **History** is a record of the past. The people and events of the past shaped the world as it is today. Historians search for primary sources, such as newspapers, letters, journals, and other documents, to find out about past events.

Vocabulary

orient: to become familiar with a situation

A VOICE FROM TODAY

How can we know who we are and where we are going if we don't know anything about where we have come from and what we have been through, the courage shown, the costs paid, to be where we are?

David McCullough, Historian

The Five Themes of Geography **Geography** is the study of people, places, and the environment. Geography deals with the world in spatial terms. The study of geography focuses on five themes: location, region, place, movement, and human-environment interaction.

Connections to Science

Digging into the Past
Archaeologists are scientists who study artifacts to learn about people's culture and history. Artifacts include pots, tools, artworks, and even food remains. Using special techniques and tools, archaeologists carefully remove artifacts from underground or underwater. They use their knowledge about the place and people they are studying to figure out how the artifact was used.

Activity Options

Differentiating Instruction: Less Proficient Readers

Synthesizing To help students understand the terms *geography, history, economics, government,* and *culture,* draw a chart like the one shown at right. Define the meaning of each term, and then discuss how each one figures into people's daily lives. Have students copy the chart onto their own papers and complete it, showing how the five fields of social studies apply to their own lives.

Geography	name of hometown
History	where ancestors might have come from
Economics	facts about allowance or baby-sitting job
Government	rules at home
Culture	holidays, music we listen to

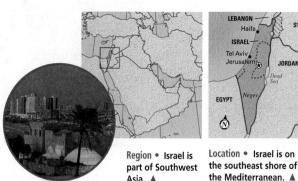

Human-Environment Interaction • Irrigation systems supply Israel's dry climate with water. ▼

Region • Israel is part of Southwest Asia. ▲

Location • Israel is on the southeast shore of the Mediterranean. ▲

Movement • Immigrants arrive in Israel. ▲

Place • **Israel has a dry climate in the south, and a wetter climate in the north, with prosperous farms and thriving cities.** ▲

Location tells where a place is. Several countries that have features in common form a region. Place considers an area's distinguishing characteristics. Movement is a study of the migrations of people, animals, and even plants. Human-environment interaction considers how people change and are changed by the natural features of Earth.

Government ❷

Every country has laws and a way to govern itself. Laws are the rules by which people live. **Government** is the people and groups within a society that have the authority to make laws, to make sure they are carried out, and to settle disagreements about them. The kind of government determines who has the authority to make the laws and see that they are carried out.

Limited and Unlimited Governments

In a limited government, everyone, including those in charge, must obey the laws. Some of the laws tell the government what it cannot do. Democracy is a form of limited government. In a democracy the people have the authority to make the laws, either directly or through their elected representatives. The governments of the United States, Mexico, and India are examples of democratic governments.

Rulers in an unlimited government can do whatever they want without regard to the law. Totalitarianism is a form of unlimited government. In a totalitarian government the people have no say. Rulers have total control.

Vocabulary

totalitarian government: a government in which the rulers have total control

---

CRITICAL THINKING ACTIVITY

Drawing Conclusions Review with students the characteristics of a limited government (everyone, including those in charge, must obey the laws) and an unlimited government (rulers do not have to obey the laws). Have students work in small groups to discuss why a country might have an unlimited government. Help them draw conclusions about the advantages and disadvantages of an unlimited government. Have groups share their ideas.

Class Time 15 minutes

FOCUS ON VISUALS

Interpreting Photographs and Maps
Have students study the maps and photographs that represent the themes of geography. Ask the following questions to help students understand how the maps and photographs relate to the themes. What nation is represented? What characteristics of Israel are seen in the left-hand photo? What does the middle photo show? What does it tell you about the climate and about how Israelis interact with the environment? What countries border Israel? Have students look at a map to find other countries in the region.

Possible Responses Israel is represented. Characteristics shown are a hot, dry climate, land on the sea, a modern city with ancient buildings. The middle photograph shows an irrigation system. The climate is dry, but Israelis have made it suitable for settlement. Lebanon, Syria, Jordan, and Egypt all border Israel. Other countries in the region include Saudi Arabia, Iraq, and Turkey.

Extension Have students write descriptions of maps and photographs that could represent the five themes as they pertain to your state.

Activity Options

Interdisciplinary Link: Art

Class Time One class period

Task Creating posters showing the five themes of geography

Purpose To understand the five themes of geography

Supplies Needed
• Poster board
• Glue
• Scissors
• Markers
• Old magazines

 ### Block Scheduling

Activity Review the five themes of geography. Explain that students will make collages of photographs that pertain to each of the five themes. Brainstorm the subject matter of photographs that could be used for each theme. For example, for the theme of economics, students might find photographs of factory workers or trains carrying goods. Display the finished posters.

MORE ABOUT...
Naturalization

Nearly half a million people were naturalized as citizens in the United States in 1998. Applicants for citizenship must be 18 years or older and be permanent residents for at least five years. They must also be able to speak, understand, read, and write simple English and pass a test about basic American history.

INSTRUCT: Objective ③

Economics/Kinds of Economies

- What are the three types of resources? natural, human, and capital
- What is the difference between a command economy and a market economy? command: government decides quantity and cost of product; market: individual businesses decide

MORE ABOUT...
Amartya Sen

After he won the Nobel Prize, Amartya Sen was asked why he was particularly interested in studying famine and its causes. Sen replied that he had seen the effects of famine in India in 1943, when close to 3 million people died of starvation. Sen was nine years old at the time and, he says, "very impressionable." His family was committed to social causes and gave what they could to anyone who asked for food.

CRITICAL THINKING ACTIVITY

Clarifying For students who may not understand the two economies, ask these questions:
- In what type of economy does the government decide how many videos to produce?
- In what type of economy do video producers decide how many videos will be produced?

Citizenship A <u>citizen</u> is a legal member of a country. Citizens have rights, such as the right to vote in elections, and duties, such as paying taxes. Being born in a country can make you a citizen. Another way is to move to a country, complete certain requirements, and take part in a naturalization ceremony.

Vocabulary
naturalization: the process of becoming a citizen

Economics ③

Looking at the long list of flavors at the ice cream store, you have a decision to make. You have only enough money for one cone. Will it be mint chip or bubble gum flavor? You will have to choose. <u>Economics</u> is the study of how people manage their resources by producing, exchanging, and using goods and services. Economics is about choice.

Some economists claim that people's desires are unlimited. Resources to satisfy these desires, however, are limited. These economists refer to the conflict between people's desires and their limited resources as <u>scarcity</u>.

Resources Economists identify three types of resources: natural, human, and capital. Natural resources are gifts of nature, such as forests, fertile soil, and water. Human resources are skills people have to produce goods and services. Capital resources are the things people make, such as machines and equipment, to produce goods and services.

Kinds of Economies ③

Blue jeans are a product. Who decides whether to make them and how many to make and what price to charge? In a command economy, the government decides. In a market economy, individual businesses decide, based on what they think consumers want.

Levels of Development Different countries and regions have different levels of economic development. In a country with a high level of development, most people are well educated, have good health, and earn decent salaries. Services such as clean running water, electricity, and transportation are plentiful. Technology is advanced, and businesses flourish.

Biography

Amartya Sen (b. 1933)
Amartya Sen (ah•MART•yah sen) was born in India. As a professor at Trinity College in Cambridge, England, he taught and studied economics. An important part of his research was to look at catastrophes, such as famine, that happen to the world's poorest people. By showing governments that food shortages are often caused by social and economic conditions, he hoped to prevent famines in the future. In 1998, Sen won the Nobel Prize in Economic Sciences for his research in welfare economics.

Movement •
One way people become American citizens is by participating in a naturalization ceremony. ▲

Reading Social Studies
A. Possible Answer
In a market economy, businesses make decisions about how much of a product to make and how much to charge. These decisions are made by the government in a command economy.

Reading Social Studies
A. Contrasting How does a market economy differ from a command economy?

Activity Options

Skillbuilder Mini-Lesson: Reading a Textbook | Block Scheduling

Explaining the Skill Explain to students that when they read a text book, they should look for important information and answers to specific questions.

Applying the Skill Have students scan a chapter in this textbook and use these strategies to find out what information it contains.

1. Look at the chapter opener to find out what is covered in the chapter.

2. Read the headings of each section and subsection in the chapter. These headings indicate what the section will cover.

3. Look for maps, graphs, tables, and photographs. Point out that these usually provide additional information that supports the text.

4. Scan the chapter for terms that are boldfaced, underlined, or italicized. These terms are vocabulary that is key to the subject matter.

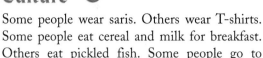

Vocabulary

literacy:
ability to read and write

life expectancy:
average number of years people live

A country with a low level of development is marked by few jobs in industry, poor services, and low literacy rates. Life expectancy is low. These countries are often called developing countries.

Culture ④

Some people wear saris. Others wear T-shirts. Some people eat cereal and milk for breakfast. Others eat pickled fish. Some people go to church on Sunday morning. Others kneel and pray to Allah five times a day. All these differences are expressions of **culture**. Culture consists of the beliefs, customs, laws, art, and ways of living that a group of people share.

Reading Social Studies

B. Recognizing Important Details
What are three characteristics that can define a culture?

Reading Social Studies
B. Possible Answer
Students should name any three of the following: beliefs, customs, laws, art, language, technology, tools, clothing, ways of living.

Religion is part of most cultures; so is a shared language. The ways people express themselves through music, dance, literature, and the visual arts are important parts of every culture; so are the technology and tools they use to accomplish various tasks. Each kind of food, clothing, or technology, each belief, language, or tool shared by a culture is called a **culture trait**. Taken together, the culture traits of a people shape their way of life.

Citizenship IN ACTION

High-tech for the Developing World Mae Jemison, below, is a former astronaut and the first African-American woman to orbit Earth. In 1993, she left the space program and set up the Jemison Institute for Advancing Technology in Developing Countries. This organization uses space program technology to help developing countries.

One project uses a satellite-based telecommunication system to improve health care in West Africa. Another project is an international science camp for students ages 12 to 16.

SECTION 1 ASSESSMENT

Terms & Names
1. Identify:
(a) history (b) geography (c) government (d) citizen
(e) economics (f) scarcity (g) culture (h) culture trait

Taking Notes
2. Use a chart like this one to list the five themes of geography and their characteristics.

Theme	Characteristics

Main Ideas
3. (a) What five areas of learning does social studies include?

(b) What are the three main kinds of resources, and how is each one defined?

(c) What is the difference between limited and unlimited government?

Critical Thinking
4. Making Inferences
Does the United States have a shared, or common, culture?

Think About
- what you eat and wear, where you live, how you spend your free time
- who else shares these activities with you

ACTIVITY -OPTION- Reread the section on citizenship. Make a **poster** showing the rights and responsibilities of a citizen.

Citizenship IN ACTION

As a medical student, Mae Jemison traveled to Cuba, Kenya, and Thailand to provide medical care. Although her first application to the astronaut program at NASA was not successful, she applied again and became one of 15 chosen astronauts. In 1988, she became the first female African-American astronaut in NASA.

INSTRUCT: Objective ④

Culture

- What shared factors make up a culture? beliefs, customs, laws, art, ways of living
- What is a culture trait? food, clothing, tools, technology, language, or belief shared by a culture

ASSESS & RETEACH

Reading Social Studies Have students fill in definitions in the chart on page 16.

Formal Assessment
- Section Quiz, p. 5

RETEACHING ACTIVITY

Pair students, and have one explain the importance of history and geography. Have the partner ask questions to clarify the explanation. Then have students switch roles to define government and economics.

In-depth Resources: Unit 1
- Reteaching Activity, p. 12

Access for Students Acquiring English
- Reteaching Activity, p. 5

Section 1 Assessment

1. Terms & Names
a. history, p. 18
b. geography, p. 18
c. government, p. 19
d. citizen, p. 20
e. economics, p. 20
f. scarcity, p. 20
g. culture, p. 21
h. culture trait, p. 21

2. Taking Notes

Location	where it is
Region	what it is similar to
Place	characteristics such as climate, soil, land use
Movement	who and what have come and gone
Human-environment interaction	how people have changed and been changed by the natural world

3. Main Ideas
a. Social studies includes geography, history, economics, government, and culture.
b. The three kinds of resources are natural (gifts of nature), human (skills people have), and capital (tools people make).
c. In a limited government, everyone must obey the laws; in an unlimited government, rulers do not have to obey the laws.

4. Critical Thinking
Students might mention the music they listen to, the food they eat, or the religion they practice.

ACTIVITY OPTION
 Integrated Assessment
- Rubric for making a poster

OBJECTIVE

Students work alone or in groups to create a programmed, interactive globe and related materials.

 Block Scheduling

PROCEDURE

Provide materials such as paper, tracing paper, poster board, and pencils. Have students form groups of four or five and divide the work among the groups. Then ask each group to plan a strategy for completing the challenge and assign tasks to each group member.

HISTORY/ECONOMICS CHALLENGE

Class Time 50 minutes

Students will need to do research in order to complete this challenge. Discuss with them possible sources of information and search terms for using the Internet.

Possible Solutions

Time lines should focus on your community and include

- a broad scope of major events starting with Native Americans and ending at the present.
- clear but brief explanations of the events.

The thematic maps should

- clearly show the products and industries important to your state and where they are located.

Investigate Your World

Suppose that someone has given you a globe as a gift. What a great present! Unlike a flat map, your globe gives you a more accurate view of the world. Best of all, this new globe is programmable. You can input new information about different features and places on Earth. In fact, the manufacturer has set up a contest—the Global Game—giving prizes for the best and most creative approaches to programming the globe. Good luck!

COOPERATIVE LEARNING On these pages are challenges you will meet in trying to win the Global Game. Working with a small group, choose which one you want to solve. Divide the work among group members. Look for helpful information in the Data File. Keep in mind that you will present your solution to the class.

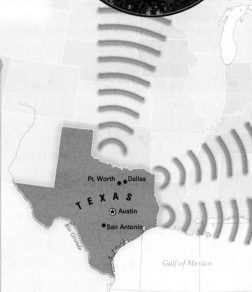

HISTORY/ECONOMICS CHALLENGE

". . . you want to know more about the world closer to home."
Now that your globe has shown you the worldwide picture, you want to know more about the world closer to home. How has geography influenced the history of your community? What features or resources brought settlers there? Choose one of these options. Look in the Data File for information.

ACTIVITIES
1. Make a time line of major events in the growth of your community. If possible, begin with the Native Americans who originally inhabited the area. Include the arrival of immigrants from various places.
2. Draw or trace an outline of your state. Then make a thematic map of its major products and industries. Use words or symbols (such as a cow, a factory, a computer) and create a map key to identify each product.

Standards for Evaluation

HISTORY/ECONOMICS CHALLENGE
Option 1 Time lines should
- highlight key events in your community's history.
- begin with Native Americans and end in the present.

Option 2 Thematic maps should
- show the location of major industries and products of your state.

LANGUAGE ARTS CHALLENGE
Option 1 The script should
- present key information about the geography and culture of the continent.
- be informative and appealing.

Option 2 The geography game should
- require use of a globe.
- be fun and challenging.

GEOGRAPHY CHALLENGE
Option 1 The list should
- focus on geographical records.
- include records for every continent.

Option 2 The collector's cards should
- be factually true.
- include information from all aspects of geography.

LANGUAGE ARTS CHALLENGE

". . . you are taken on an audio journey to new places."

Your new globe has built-in sensors activated by a laser wand. When you point the wand at a spot on the globe, you are taken on an audio journey to new places. The sound clip introduces you to a place's culture—the things that make it unique.

As part of the Global Game, the manufacturer is looking for new ways to present this information. What will you include in your approach? How can you add to the globe's popular appeal? Choose one of these options. Look in the Data File for help.

ACTIVITIES

1. Choose one continent and write a script about it for a seven-minute "audio journey." Remember to include information about geographic features as well as aspects of culture.
2. Design another geography game that the manufacturer can use to market its globe. The game should appeal to students of your age. Write a brief description of the game and its rules.

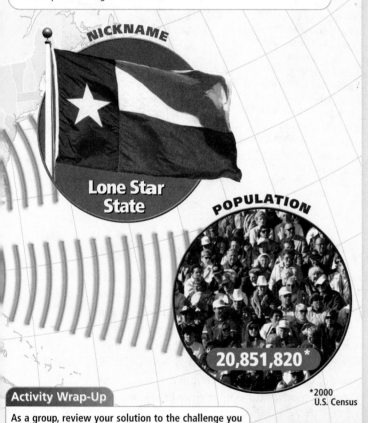

NICKNAME

Lone Star State

POPULATION

20,851,820*

*2000 U.S. Census

Activity Wrap-Up

As a group, review your solution to the challenge you selected. Then present your solution to the class.

WORLD STATISTICS

- **Circumference** at Equator: 24,902 mi.
- **Earth's speed** of orbit: 18.5 mi./sec.
- **Total area:** 197,000,000 sq. mi.; land area: 57,900,000 sq. mi.
- **Highest point:** 29,035 ft.— Mt. Everest.
- **Lowest point:** 35,800 ft. below sea level—Marianas Trench, Pacific Ocean.
- **Lowest point on land:** 1,312 ft. below sea level, Dead Sea, Israel and Jordan.

HIGHEST ELEVATIONS BY CONTINENT

- **Asia:** Mt. Everest, Nepal–Tibet, 29,035 ft.
- **South America:** Mt. Aconcagua, Argentina–Chile, 22,834 ft.
- **North America:** Mt. McKinley (Denali), Alaska, 20,320 ft.
- **Africa:** Mt. Kilimanjaro, Tanzania, 19,340 ft.
- **Europe:** Mt. Elbrus, Russia, 18,510 ft.
- **Antarctica:** Vinson Massif, 16,066 ft.
- **Western Europe:** Mont Blanc, France, 15,771 ft.
- **Australia:** Mt. Kosciusko, 7,310 ft.

SOME MAJOR RIVER SYSTEMS

- **Nile,** Africa: 4,160 mi.
- **Amazon,** South America: 4,080 mi.
- **Mississippi**–Missouri, North America (U.S.): 3,740 mi.
- **Chang Jiang** (Yangtze), China: 3,915 mi.
- **Yenisey,** Russia: 2,566 mi.
- **Plata,** South America: 3,030 mi.
- **Huang He** (Yellow), China: 3,010 mi.
- **Congo** (Zaire), Africa: 2,880 mi.

To learn more about Earth's geography, go to

RESEARCH LINKS
CLASSZONE.COM

LANGUAGE ARTS CHALLENGE

Class Time 50 minutes

For the "audio journey," students might consider background music unique to the continent. For the second option, have students use familiar games as models.

Possible Solutions

For the first option, the scripts will

- highlight the most important, unique features of the continent's geography and cultures.

Student games will

- include the use of the globe.
- have simple, easy-to-follow directions.

ALTERNATIVE CHALLENGE...

GEOGRAPHY CHALLENGE

On which continent do you find the longest river system? the highest mountain? the biggest rock? the tallest tree? On which continent are the most languages spoken? On which continent is the country with the most telephones per person? the fastest train? the tallest building? All of these are questions about Global Geography Records.

- Imagine that you can touch any continent on your programmable globe and hear about that continent's records. Use information from the Data File and research in other sources to list the records that you would hear for each continent.
- Create a set of collector's cards of Global Geography Records.

Activity Wrap-Up

To help students evaluate the creativity of their challenge solutions, have them make a grid with criteria like the one shown. Then have them rate each solution on a scale from 1 to 5.

• Originality	1	2	3	4	5
• Creativity	1	2	3	4	5
• Accuracy	1	2	3	4	5
• Overall effectiveness	1	2	3	4	5

Many Regions, Many Cultures

TERMS & NAMES
culture region
interdependence

SECTION OBJECTIVES

1. To identify a culture region
2. To explain how a culture region evolves

SKILLBUILDER
• Interpreting a Map, p. 25

CRITICAL THINKING
• Summarizing, pp. 25–26

FOCUS & MOTIVATE
WARM-UP

Analyzing Motives Have students read <u>Dateline</u>, and use questions such as the following to discuss the rebellion of Indian troops in 1857.

1. In what way did the British East India Company show a lack of respect for others' customs?
2. What might help groups of people to understand the customs of others?

INSTRUCT: Objective ❶

Different Places, Different Cultures

• What do people in culture regions share? beliefs, history, language
• What makes a region multicultural? when it contains other cultures in addition to the dominant culture
• How do culture regions change? They borrow from other cultures and come to depend on one another.

 In-depth Resources: Unit 1
• Guided Reading Worksheet, p. 7

 Reading Study Guide
(Spanish and English), pp. 6–7

MAIN IDEA

The world can be divided into regions according to culture.

WHY IT MATTERS NOW

Understanding other cultures can help you understand how people in other regions live and think.

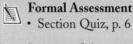 **DATELINE**

MEERUT, INDIA, MAY 10, 1857— Indian troops serving in the army of the British East India Company rebelled today. Reasons given for the revolt include anger at the way the company has been taking over Indian lands and a lack of respect for Indian customs. The immediate cause was the new Enfield rifles issued to the troops. To load them, soldiers have to bite off the ends of the cartridges.

Word quickly spread that the cartridges were greased with cow and pig fat. This was an insult to both Hindu and Muslim soldiers.

Hindus hold cows sacred and never kill them. Muslims believe the meat of pigs is unclean.

Place • The rebellion in Meerut spread to the city of Lucknow and left the Chutter Munzil Palace in ruins. ▲

Culture • Cows are sacred to Hindus in India. ▲

Different Places, Different Cultures ❶

Indian soldiers and British officials belonged to cultures with different beliefs. The British came from a region of the world where most people ate the meat of pigs and cows. The Indians lived in a region where most people did not. A **culture region** is an area of the world in which many people share similar beliefs, history, and languages. The people in a culture region may have religion, technology, and ways of earning a living in common as well. They may grow and eat similar foods, wear similar kinds of clothes, and build houses in similar styles.

24 CHAPTER 1

Program Resources

 In-depth Resources: Unit 1
• Guided Reading Worksheet, p. 7
• Reteaching Activity, p. 13

 Reading Study Guide
(Spanish and English), pp. 6–7

 Formal Assessment
• Section Quiz, p. 6

 Integrated Assessment
• Rubric for writing a dialogue

 Outline Map Activities

 Access for Students Acquiring English
• Guided Reading Worksheet, p. 2

 Technology Resources classzone.com

TEST-TAKING RESOURCES
⚓ Strategies for Test Preparation
⚓ Test Practice Transparencies
🖱 Online Test Practice

Culture Regions of the World

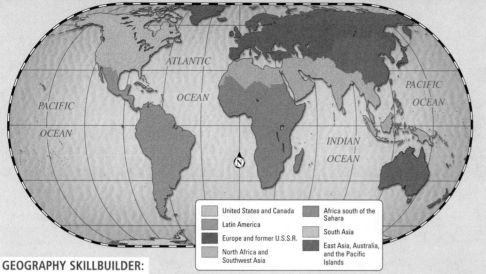

Map Legend:
- United States and Canada
- Latin America
- Europe and former U.S.S.R.
- North Africa and Southwest Asia
- Africa south of the Sahara
- South Asia
- East Asia, Australia, and the Pacific Islands

GEOGRAPHY SKILLBUILDER: Interpreting a Map

1. **Region** • How many culture regions are shown on this map?
2. **Location** • Name three culture regions in the Eastern Hemisphere.

The World's Culture Regions

The map above shows the major culture regions of the world. Latin America is one culture region. The Spanish and Portuguese languages help to tie its people together. So does its common history. Southwest Asia and North Africa is another culture region. Most countries in this region share a common desert climate and landscape. People have adapted to the desert in similar ways, thus creating a common culture. Islam, which is the major religion in this region, also helps shape a common culture.

Usually, not every person in a region belongs to the dominant, or mainstream, culture. Some regions are multicultural. For example, the United States and Canada contain other cultures besides the dominant one. Although most people in this region speak English, many people in eastern Canada speak French. Many people in the United States speak Spanish, especially in the Southwest. In both countries, Catholics, Protestants, Jews, Muslims, Buddhists, and members of other religions all flourish.

Children Invent Language In the late 1700s, most people in Hawaii spoke English or native Hawaiian. As people began immigrating to Hawaii to work on the sugar cane plantations, they brought their native languages with them: Japanese, Chinese, Korean, Spanish, and Portuguese.

At school, the children of these immigrants began speaking a form of English that was a blend of native Hawaiian, Pidgin English, Pidgin Hawaiian, and their native languages, especially Portuguese. Eventually, children began to learn this form of English as their native language. This was the beginning of Hawaii Creole English, and it soon became the language of the majority of Hawaiians.

Da kaet ste in da haus.

FOCUS ON VISUALS

Interpreting the Photographs Have students study the three photographs and draw conclusions about the cultures shown. Have students use the chart headings below to organize their ideas.

Where Live	Information from Photo	Conclusions About Culture

Have students find photographs in newspapers or magazines that reveal information about the culture shown. Ask students to share the photographs and discuss what aspects of culture are demonstrated in each.

CRITICAL THINKING ACTIVITY

Summarizing Have students work in pairs to make a list of ways their community is dependent on or affected by other cultures. Ask pairs to share lists and discuss similarities and differences among them.

Class Time 15 minutes

ASSESS & RETEACH

Reading Social Studies Have students add terms and definitions to the chart on page 16.

 Formal Assessment
• Section Quiz, p. 6

RETEACHING ACTIVITY

Divide the class into two groups. Have one group of students work together to explain cultural interdependence, and have the other group explain how cultures change.

 In-depth Resources: Unit 1
• Reteaching Activity, p. 13

 Access for Students Acquiring English
• Reteaching Activity, p. 6

Culture Regions Change For thousands of years, culture regions have changed and evolved as they have borrowed culture traits from one another. They have also come to depend upon each other economically. Decisions and events in one part of the world affect other parts. Advances in transportation and communication have increased this **interdependence**. When oil-producing nations in the Middle East raise the price of oil, for example, the price of gasoline at the neighborhood gas station is likely to rise. If there is an especially abundant banana crop in parts of Latin America, the price of bananas may drop at the local grocery store. More and more, people of different countries are becoming part of one world.

Region • Home life can differ greatly in different culture regions, sometimes depending on a region's climate or natural resources. ▲

SECTION 2 ASSESSMENT

Terms & Names

1. **Identify:** (a) culture region (b) interdependence

Taking Notes

2. Use a chart to list the major culture regions of the world.

Major Culture Regions of the World
1.
2.
3.
4.
5.
6.
7.

Main Ideas

3. (a) List at least three things people in a culture region may have in common.

   (b) Which continents have more than one culture region?

   (c) What is one cause of cultural change?

Critical Thinking

4. **Clarifying**

   Why might Brazilian coffee at your local supermarket suddenly cost more?

   Think About
   • price-setting
   • coffee supplies

ACTIVITY -OPTION- Write a **dialogue** between you and a visitor from another country in which you explain what makes the culture in your region different from others.

26 CHAPTER 1

Section 2 Assessment

1. Terms & Names
  a. culture region, p. 24
  b. interdependence, p. 26

2. Taking Notes

1. United States/Canada
2. Latin America
3. Europe
4. North Africa/Southwest Asia
5. Africa south of the Sahara
6. South Asia
7. East Asia/Australia/Pacific Islands

3. Main Ideas
  a. The people in a culture region may have religion, history, and language in common.
  b. North America, Africa, Europe, Asia
  c. One cause of cultural change is interdependence.

4. Critical Thinking
The coffee harvest may have been poor.

ACTIVITY OPTION

 Integrated Assessment
• Rubric for writing a dialogue

Reading a Time Zone Map

▶▶ Defining the Skill

A time zone map shows the 24 time zones of the world. The prime meridian runs through Greenwich (GREHN•ich), England. Each zone east of Greenwich is one hour later than the zone before. Each zone west of Greenwich is one hour earlier. The International Date Line runs through the Pacific Ocean. It is the location where each day begins. If it is Saturday to the east of the International Date Line, then it is Sunday to the west of it.

▶▶ Applying the Skill

Use the strategies listed below to help you find times and time differences on a time zone map.

How to Read a Time Zone Map

Strategy ❶ Read the title. It tells you what the map is intended to show.

Strategy ❷ Read the labels at the top of the map. They show the hours across the world when it is noon in Greenwich. The labels at the bottom show the number of hours earlier or later than the time in Greenwich.

Strategy ❸ Locate a place whose time you know. Locate the place where you want to know the time. Count the number of time zones between them. Then add or subtract that number of hours.

For example, if it is noon time on the west coast of Africa, you can see that it is 7:00 A.M. on the east coast of the United States. That is a difference of five hours.

❶ WORLD TIME ZONES

▶▶ Practicing the Skill

On the Internet, refer to http://www.worldtimezone.com/time24.htm. Choose three pairs of locations and compare the time zones for each pair.

SKILLBUILDER

Reading a Time Zone Map

Defining the Skill

Display a globe and point out your location. Ask students to note the time. Then point to a location in another time zone and ask students if they think the time is the same or different. Explain that the time changes by one hour as you move from one time zone to the next. Ask students to think about why it might be important to understand time differences in the world. Discuss information needed to plan a trip or make a long-distance call.

Applying the Skill

How to Read a Time Zone Map Point out the three strategies for reading a time zone map. Ask a volunteer to read the title and labels on the map. Explain that the labels on the top of the map show hours across the world in one-hour increments, and that the labels at the bottom show time differences.

Make a Chart

Discuss the information on the map with students. Ask questions such as: How many time zones are there? (24) What time is it on the East Coast of the United States when it is noon in London? (7 A.M.) What time is it on the West Coast of the United States when it is noon on the East Coast? (9 A.M.)

Practicing the Skill

Have students turn to page 25 and read the title of the map. Explain that since this map shows culture regions, the strategy for reading it is slightly different. Color is used to indicate each culture region. Name each continent; have students tell which culture region(s) can be found there.

   In-depth Resources: Unit 1
   • Skillbuilder Practice, p. 10

Career Connection: Cultural Geographer

Encourage students who enjoy reading the time zone map and thinking about differences in time around the world to find out about careers that analyze the relationship between people and their environment. For example, within the broad field of geography, some geographers study the cultural characteristics of different regions of the United States or the world. These geographers are called cultural geographers.

1. Suggest that small groups of students look for information about specific jobs that cultural geographers hold. Examples include a commu-nity or urban planner and a university professor. Have students explain how each job they identify relates to cultural geography.

2. With the different directions that cultural geography can take, what education is needed to become a cultural geographer? Help students learn what schooling cultural geographers get before embarking on their careers.

3. Have each group of students share an oral summary of its findings.

🅱 Block Scheduling

OBJECTIVE

Students analyze an ancient myth from China, which explains how a mountain range was formed from the body of a giant.

FOCUS & MOTIVATE

Making Inferences To help students understand the origin and purpose of this myth, have them study the illustrations and answer the following questions:

1. What predictions can you make about the story from the illustrations?
2. Using your imagination, what do you see in the mountain outline?

 Block Scheduling

MORE ABOUT...
"The Giant Kuafu Chases the Sun"

Chinese civilization dates back at least 7,000 years. The ancient Chinese developed agriculture and writing, used bronze, and raised silkworms to make silk. Though China was geographically isolated, silk trading became an international business by 100 B.C.

This creation myth dates back to at least 500 B.C. Even then, it might have been an old story, and it might have been told as story rather than as fact.

The Giant Kuafu Chases the Sun

FROM THE EARLIEST TIMES, people have created myths and legends to explain the natural world. Some stories explain why earthquakes occur or lightning strikes. Others tell how rivers, deserts, canyons, and other landforms came to be. This ancient Chinese myth, dating back at least 2,500 years, comes from the area of northern China where Chinese civilization first began. The myth explains how the province of Shaanxi got its mountains.

Shaanxi, also known as Shensi, is in northern China. The southern part of the province contains the high and rugged Qinling range, also called the Tsinling Mountains, where the average peak is 8,000 feet high and some are over 12,000 feet high.

Long ago, soon after time began, giants roamed the flat and fertile Earth. One of the largest, bravest, and fastest of them all was named Kuafu—and his strength knew no bounds.

Every day, Kuafu watched the sun rise in the east and set in the west. When night came, he became greatly saddened. He thought, "I do not like the darkness. All life falls into a silent slumber. If I could catch the sun, then I could keep night as bright as day. The plants could grow forever, and it would always be warm. I would never have to sleep again."

Activity Options

Differentiating Instruction: Less Proficient Readers

Building Language Skills Have students work in pairs or small groups, matching less proficient readers with more fluent readers. Have pairs take turns reading the story aloud together, noting and discussing any words that are unfamiliar or difficult to pronounce. Then ask students to review the story and note problems Kuafu has. Ask them to create a two-column chart with the heads *Problems* and *Solutions*. Students can list Kuafu's problems in the first column, and tell how each was solved in the second column. Have pairs check their work with other pairs.

The next day, Kuafu stretched his legs and started to race after the sun. He ran like the wind over several thousand miles without rest. Finally, he chased the sun to the Yu Valley where it came to rest every day but Kuafu was thirsty and very, very tired. His thirst grew, and soon it became overwhelming. He had never known a thirst like this, and his body seemed to be drying up like mud bricks in an oven.

Kuafu found the nearest stream and drank it dry. It was not enough. With a giant's stride, he quickly reached the mighty Yellow River. He drank it dry, but again, it was not enough. He continued toward the Great Sea—surely it held water enough to quench his thirst.

On his journey, he drank dry every well and every stream and every lake he came across. His thirst became over powering, and Kuafu fell to the ground before he reached the Sea. In a fit of anger, with a branch of a peach tree, he made a final swing at the sun. But before the branch reached the sun, Kuafu died of thirst.

The sun set in the Yu Valley, and night came. When the sun rose again, Kuafu's body had been transformed into a mountain range. The peach tree branch extended from his side and formed a peach tree grove. To this day, the peaches in this grove are sweet and moist, always ready to relieve the thirst of those who would choose to chase the sun.

Reading
THE LITERATURE

Before you read, examine the title. Why might the title character want to chase the sun? What abilities will he or she need to catch it?

Thinking About
THE LITERATURE

Contests involving the sun, as well as efforts to reach the sun, are common in the myths and legends of many societies. Why do you think stories about the sun are told in so many cultures?

Writing About
THE LITERATURE

Although Kuafu was not a real person, his myth has survived for thousands of years. Why? What does it teach about human behavior?

Further Reading

Legends of Landforms by Carole G. Vogel explores Native American legends about the origins of many places in the United States.

Why Snails Have Shells by Carolyn Han retells the folk tales of the Han people and other Chinese ethnic groups.

INSTRUCT

Reading the Literature
Possible Responses
Kuafu might chase the sun to catch it for heat or light. To succeed, Kuafu will need to be tall, fast, and heat-resistant.

Thinking About the Literature
Possible Responses
All people depend on the sun for light, heat, food, and survival. Ancient cultures could not understand the sun scientifically, so they made up stories to explain it and relate to it.

Writing About the Literature
Possible Responses
Students may suggest that this myth has survived because it is a clever explanation of mountains and peaches, relies on imagination, is humorous, and contains vivid language. They may say that Kuafu's character represents humans' desire to control their environment, or explain unknown aspects of nature.

MORE ABOUT...
How Mountains Form

Fold mountains form when the plates under Earth's crust collide, buckling the crust. Fault-block mountains form when the crust cracks and one side rises. Volcanoes and magma bulges also build mountains.

 World Literature

More to Think About

Making Personal Connections Ask students what this story explains. What other stories have they read that explain natural phenomena? Have students brainstorm a list of questions people might have about landforms or weather in your area. Have students come up with a myth and a scientific explanation for each question. This can be a class activity, or students can choose a question to address.

Vocabulary Activity List the news questions *Who? Where? When? Why? What? How?* on the chalkboard. Tell students to answer each question with information from the story. Then have them use their answers, in any order, to write a news flash for this headline: "New Mountain Range Forms."

TERMS & NAMES

1. history, p. 18
2. geography, p. 18
3. government, p. 19
4. citizen, p. 20
5. economics, p. 20
6. scarcity, p. 20
7. culture, p. 21
8. culture trait, p. 21
9. culture region, p. 24
10. interdependence, p. 26

REVIEW QUESTIONS

Possible Responses

1. The five themes of geography are history, geography, economics, government, and culture.
2. In a limited government, everyone, including those in charge, must obey the laws; in an unlimited government, the rulers do not have to obey the laws.
3. To become a citizen of a country, you are either born there or you move there, complete certain requirements, and then take part in a naturalization ceremony.
4. In a command economy, the government makes decisions about what is produced and the price of those goods. In a market economy, businesses make these decisions.
5. Characteristics of a culture include religion, language, customs, art, laws, and ways of living.
6. Answers may vary. For example, if a country decides to produce less of a good, that good will be more expensive in other countries.
7. Shared aspects of daily life might include clothing, food, language, and religious rituals.
8. Most people in the United States and Canada speak English, but some people in Canada speak French and some in the United States speak Spanish. Many religions are practiced in both countries.

TERMS & NAMES

Explain the significance of each of the following:

1. history
2. geography
3. government
4. citizen
5. economics
6. scarcity
7. culture
8. culture trait
9. culture region
10. interdependence

REVIEW QUESTIONS

The World at Your Fingertips *(pages 17–21)*

1. What are the five themes of geography?
2. What are the main differences between a limited and an unlimited government?
3. How can someone become a citizen of a country?
4. What is the difference between a command economy and a market economy?
5. What are some characteristics of a culture?

Many Regions, Many Cultures *(pages 24–26)*

6. How can decisions made in one part of the world affect people in another part of the world?
7. What aspects of daily life might people in the same culture region share?
8. What makes the United States and Canada a multicultural region?

CRITICAL THINKING

Remembering Definitions

1. Using your completed chart from Reading Social Studies, p. 16, tell how understanding the culture could help you make friends in a new country.

Making Inferences

2. Why might someone's life expectancy be low in a region with a low level of development?

Identifying Problems

3. If countries in the Middle East stopped producing oil, how might that affect the economy of the United States?

Visual Summary

1

The World at Your Fingertips

- History, geography, government, economics, and culture are five ways to understand Earth and its peoples.

United States and Canada
Latin America
Europe and former U.S.S.R.
North Africa and Southwest Asia
Africa south of the Sahara
South Asia
East Asia, Australia, and the Pacific Islands

2

Many Regions, Many Cultures

- People live, dress, and think differently in each of the world's culture regions.

CRITICAL THINKING: Possible Responses

1. Remembering Definitions

When you can identify the language someone speaks, what is valued in his or her culture, and what is shared between your cultures, you have a better chance of becoming friends.

2. Making Inferences

Life expectancy in a developing economy is low because of poor health care services, low literacy rates, lack of clean running water, and low salaries.

3. Identifying Problems

If the countries in the Middle East stopped producing oil, the cost of oil would go up. The increased cost of oil would affect transportation and production in the United States.

SOCIAL STUDIES SKILLBUILDER

SKILLBUILDER: Reading a Time Zone Map

1. If it is 2 P.M. in Houston, what time is it in Chicago?
2. What is the time difference between Los Angeles and New York City?

FOCUS ON GEOGRAPHY

1. **Human-Environment Interaction** • What needs determine where people settle?
2. **Place** • What geographic features made the location of this town a good place to settle?

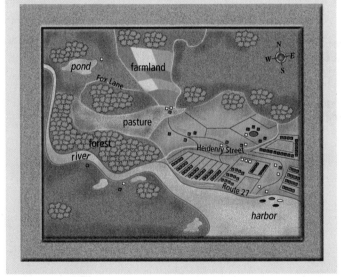

CHAPTER PROJECTS

Interdisciplinary Activity: Art

Making a Poster Research what kinds of clothing people wear in other parts of the world. Create a poster that shows the clothing, both modern and traditional, that different groups of people wear. Use photographs or drawings with captions that illustrate the types of clothes.

Cooperative Learning Activity

Setting Up a Peace Conference With a group of three to five students, set up a peace conference to help two warring groups make peace. Choose two specific groups and a specific issue that caused the hostility, such as harming a cow in a Hindu society.
• Take on the roles of intermediary and spokesperson for each group.
• See how understanding the other group's perspective helps you agree.
• Present your conference to the class as a skit.

INTERNET ACTIVITY

Use the Internet to research a culture, such as the people of Lebanon or Hong Kong. Find out what most people value, what jobs they have, what foods they eat, what governments they live under, and what difficulties they face.

Writing About Geography Write a report of your findings. List the Web sites you used to prepare your report.

For Internet links to support this activity, go to

 RESEARCH LINKS
CLASSZONE.COM

CHAPTER PROJECTS

Interdisciplinary Activity: Art

Making a Poster Discuss where students might find information about traditional and modern clothing, such as print and on-line reference sources, travel brochures, or museums. Encourage students to write captions for their illustrations.

Cooperative Learning Activity

Setting Up a Peace Conference Discuss the purpose of a peace conference and how one might be arranged. Then brainstorm some locations in the world where tension exists, such as the Middle East, Ireland, or India. Help students understand the sources of tension in a given region. Provide source materials such as books, magazine articles, or videos. Students might also find useful information through a Web search. Urge students to identify each group's vital interests in the conflict. Be sure that students understand the role of the intermediary as a neutral party.

Guide groups to focus on a single issue. Assign the roles of intermediary and spokesperson. Suggest that students role-play conferences before presenting them to the class.

INTERNET ACTIVITY

Discuss how students might find information about the culture of a country using the Internet. Brainstorm possible key words, Web sites, and search engines students might explore.

Discuss the other issues that students might find interesting, such as language, education, food, or the role of women in government.

Suggest that students make a chart listing the areas they are interested in exploring and then fill it in as they locate the information.

Skills Answers

Social Studies Skillbuilder
Possible Responses
1. 2 P.M.
2. 3 hours

Focus on Geography
Possible Responses
1. The needs that determine where people settle include the need for fresh water, a food supply, and good transportation.
2. Geographic features such as waterways, fertile land, and climate may have helped determine the location of this town.

The Geographer's World

	OVERVIEW	COPYMASTERS	INTEGRATED TECHNOLOGY
CHAPTER RESOURCES	Students will examine the five themes used to describe Earth, some of the tools geographers use, and how these themes and tools are used to help us understand people, places, and environments of the past and present.	**In-depth Resources: Unit 1** • Guided Reading Worksheets, pp. 14–15 • Skillbuilder Practice, p. 18 • Unit Atlas Activities, pp. 1–4 • Geography Workshop, pp. 22–23 **Reading Study Guide** (Spanish and English), pp. 10–15 **Outline Map Activities**	Power Presentations Electronic Teacher Tools Online Lesson Planner Chapter Summaries on CD Critical Thinking Transparencies CT3

	KEY IDEAS		
SECTION 1 The Five Themes of Geography pp. 35–40	• The five themes of geography are location, place, region, movement, and human-environment interaction. • Location can be described as absolute or relative. • A place is characterized by physical, political, or cultural features. A region is a group of places with common features. • Humans migrate to different places for various reasons, and adapt to and modify the world around them.	**In-depth Resources: Unit 1** • Guided Reading Worksheet, p. 14 • Reteaching Activity, p. 20 **Reading Study Guide** (Spanish and English), pp. 10–11	Map Transparencies MT5, 6, 7, 8, 9 classzone.com Chapter Summaries on CD
SECTION 2 The Geographer's Tools pp. 45–49	• Maps and globes provide similar information in different ways. • Geographers use charts and graphs to display and compare information.	**In-depth Resources: Unit 1** • Guided Reading Worksheet, p. 15 • Reteaching Activity, p. 21 **Reading Study Guide** (Spanish and English), pp. 12–13	Critical Thinking Transparencies CT4 Map Transparencies MT2, 3, 4, 8 classzone.com Chapter Summaries on CD

Audio

 CD-ROM

Copymaster

 Internet

Overhead Transparency

 Pupil's Edition

 Teacher's Edition

Video

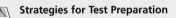
ASSESSMENT OPTIONS

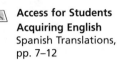
RESOURCES FOR DIFFERENTIATING INSTRUCTION

Chapter Assessment, pp. 50–51

Formal Assessment
• Chapter Tests: Forms A, B, C, pp. 21–32

Test Generator

Online Test Practice

Strategies for Test Preparation

Section Assessment, p. 40

Formal Assessment
• Section Quiz, p. 19

Integrated Assessment
• Rubric for writing a magazine advertisement

Test Generator

Test Practice Transparencies TT3

Section Assessment, p. 49

Formal Assessment
• Section Quiz, p. 20

Integrated Assessment
• Rubric for drawing a map

Test Generator

Test Practice Transparencies TT4

Students Acquiring English/ESL

Reading Study Guide
(Spanish and English), pp. 10–15

Access for Students Acquiring English
Spanish Translations, pp. 7–12

Less Proficient Readers

Reading Study Guide
(Spanish and English), pp. 10–15

TE Activity
• Illustrating a Region, p. 38

Gifted and Talented Students

TE Activity
• Designing an Illustrated Map, p. 47

CROSS-CURRICULAR CONNECTIONS

Literature
Creech, Sharon. *The Wanderer.* New York: HarperCollins, 2000. A sailing voyage from Connecticut across the Atlantic. Rich geographic detail.

Health
Smith, Carter. *Mapping Epidemics: A Historical Atlas of Disease.* New York: Franklin Watts, 2000. Thirty-two diseases and their geographical progressions.

Geography
Dorling, Kindersley. *The Ultimate Panoramic Atlas.* New York: DK Publishing, 1998. Each continent's land mass and sea features are exaggerated to give a 3-D effect.
Dash, Joan. *The Longitude Prize.* New York: Frances Foster Books, 2000. John Harrison spent forty years developing a machine to determine longitude at sea.

Science/Math
Lye, Keith. *Atlas in the Round: Our Planet As You've Never Seen It Before.* Philadelphia: Running Press, 1999. The spherical perspective corrects misleading aspects of flat maps.

Language Arts/Literature
Hopkins, Lee Bennett. *My America: A Poetry Atlas of the United States.* New York: Simon & Schuster, 2000. Unique concept, nicely rendered.

Science
Kerrod, Robin, and John Stidworthy. *Facts on File Wildlife Atlas.* New York: Facts on File, 1998. Full color photos, maps, and diagrams.

ENRICHMENT ACTIVITIES

The following activities are especially suitable for classes following block schedules.

Teacher's Edition, pp. 30, 36, 41, 47
Pupil's Edition, pp. 40, 49

Geography Handbook, pp. 4–13
Linking Past and Present, pp. 42–43

Technology: 2000, p. 44
Outline Map Activities

INTEGRATED TECHNOLOGY

Go to **classzone.com** for lesson support and activities for Chapter 2.

BLOCK SCHEDULE LESSON PLAN OPTIONS: 90-MINUTE PERIOD

DAY 1

CHAPTER PREVIEW, pp. 32–33
Class Time 20 minutes

- **Hypothesize** Use "What do you think?" questions in Focus on Geography on PE p. 33 to help students hypothesize about the uses of geography in exploring and understanding the world.

SECTION 1, pp. 35–40
Class Time 70 minutes

- **Summarizing** Have students write a brief description of a place they know well. Ask them to imagine they are describing it to someone who has never seen it. Write the five geography themes (location, place, region, movement, human-environment interaction) on the chalkboard. Have students share their descriptions, and ask them to decide into which geographical theme their description best fits. Review the themes as you discuss.
Class Time 30 minutes

- **Comparing** To compare the ideas of absolute location and relative location, have a student stand somewhere in the room. Ask students to describe his/her location first in an absolute way, then in a relative way. Have students explain the differences.
Class Time 10 minutes

- **Internet** Divide students into groups and have them visit **classzone.com** to learn more about Pangaea and changes in the locations of Earth's continents.
Class Time 30 minutes

DAY 2

SECTION 1, continued
Class Time 60 minutes

- **Reading a Map** Divide students into teams. Have them use the Rand McNally World Physical map on PE pp. A2–3 to find two location examples of each region shown in the Natural Regions of the World chart, on PE p. 38. Have groups present their examples to the class; they can point them out on a map.
Class Time 30 minutes

- **Analyzing Causes** Have students review the Human Migration map on PE p. 39. Lead a discussion about what natural features may have influenced or affected these movement patterns.
Class Time 10 minutes

- **Peer Review** To practice using longitude and latitude, ask students to choose a place in the world they would like to visit. Have students use the Skillbuilder on PE p. 41 to plot the longitude and latitude of their choice, keeping the location a secret. Then have students exchange coordinates, figure out the location, and check their answer with their partner.
Class Time 20 minutes

SECTION 2, pp. 45–49
Class Time 30 minutes

- **Making a Map** Review the concept of thematic maps, then ask students to make a thematic map of the school. They should clearly indicate the theme in the map's legend. Some possible themes: the locations of student activities, or the places where one can get food in the school.

DAY 3

SECTION 2, continued
Class Time 35 minutes

- **Cartographer** Have students use PE pp. 42–44 to review the skills cartographers use to construct maps. Encourage them to make an illustrated map of their town or neighborhood. Display the finished maps.

CHAPTER 2 REVIEW AND ASSESSMENT, pp. 50–51
Class Time 55 minutes

- **Review** Have students use the charts they created for Reading Social Studies on PE p. 34 to review the five geography themes.
Class Time 20 minutes

- **Assessment** Have students complete the Chapter 2 Assessment.
Class Time 35 minutes

TECHNOLOGY IN THE CLASSROOM

DESIGNING WEB SITES

Students can design their own Web sites to organize information and to share their knowledge with other students at school and around the world. By creating a Web site, students gain experience in organizing information in a nonlinear fashion and get a behind-the-scenes look at what goes into developing materials for the Internet. Their Web sites can be kept on the classroom computer, uploaded to the school district's server, or uploaded to the Internet for students at other schools to view. The Web site at **classzone.com** is a helpful resource for students to learn about designing their own Web pages.

ACTIVITY OUTLINE

Objective Students will design Web pages to teach other students about the Five Themes of Geography.

Task Have students work in groups to create a Web site that provides examples of the Five Themes of Geography and that teaches other students about each of the themes.

Class Time Three class periods

DIRECTIONS

1. Hold a class discussion reviewing the Five Themes of Geography, as discussed in Chapter 2. Ask students to provide examples to explain each theme, and ask them to describe the reasons why it is important to be familiar with the concepts covered by each of these themes. For example, why is it important to identify your location (Theme 1) or to understand the impact of migration and transportation (Theme 4)?

2. Divide the class into small groups of about four students each. Assign one of the Five Themes. It may be necessary to assign some themes to more than one group.

3. Ask groups to create Web pages that will teach students in their grade or the grade below them about their assigned theme. They will need to provide text and images to help students learn the concepts of the theme. For example, for place (Theme 2), they might provide a brief description of what *place* means and then create a Web page that shows pictures of the landscape and people in their home town. They could then ask the audience to think about the special characteristics of their own home and to compare and contrast those features to the things they see on the Web page.

4. Suggest that students use the following criteria for completing their Web pages:

   • They must provide a two- to four-sentence description of what their theme is about.

   • They must include at least one example of how this theme relates to things they already know about (e.g., their home town, transportation, world regions).

   • They must include at least one image, and they must cite the source of the image if they have taken it from a book or another Web site.

5. Help several students design an overall home page that will link to each group's Web page. This main home page should contain a list of the Five Themes. As an option, upload this page and each group's site onto the school district's server, and register it with a search engine.

CHAPTER 2 OBJECTIVE

Students will examine the five themes used to describe Earth, some of the tools geographers use, and how these themes and tools help us understand people, places, and environments of the past and present.

FOCUS ON VISUALS

Interpreting the Photograph Have students observe the perspective of Earth and some of Earth's features. Ask them to describe what they can tell about Earth from this photograph. Then ask how people on Earth might have responded on seeing this first photograph of Earth from the moon.

Possible Response It is a round ball, with possible landmasses and water. It is covered by clouds. People might have been surprised to see how little they could recognize.

Extension Provide students with a globe. Have them compare the features in the photograph with those on the globe.

CRITICAL THINKING ACTIVITY

Recognizing Effects Discuss with students how Earth can be seen as a whole system. Encourage students to point out the cloud cover, bodies of water, and visible landmasses in the photograph. Show them how the bodies of water and landmasses are connected on the globe. Have students suggest ways in which changes on one part of Earth might affect other parts.

Class Time 10 minutes

The Geographer's World

Place "Viewed from the distance of the moon," said scientist and writer Lewis Thomas, "the astonishing thing about the Earth . . . is that it is alive."

32

Recommended Resources

BOOKS FOR THE TEACHER
Elsom, Derek. *Planet Earth.* Detroit, MI: Macmillan Reference USA, 2000. Geography and geology.

The National Geographic Desk Reference: A Geographical Reference with Hundreds of Photographs, Maps, Charts, and Graphs.

Washington, D.C.: National Geographic Society, 1999. Mapmaking and evolution of Earth's people.

VIDEOS
Geography Tutor, Volume 2: Types of Maps and Map Projections. Venice, CA: TMW Media Group. Explanation of mapping Earth.

SOFTWARE
Planet Earth: Explore the Worlds Within. Library Video Company, 2000. Lands, habitats, peoples, and cultures of the world.

INTERNET
For more information about Earth, visit **classzone.com**.

How has new technology increased our knowledge of Earth?

Human-Environment Interaction • *Terra*, the Earth Observing System (EOS) satellite launched in 1999, helps scientists understand how Earth's lands, oceans, air, ice, and plant and animal life work together as a system. Scientists at the National Aeronautics and Space Administration (NASA) use sensors mounted on satellites to study Earth's air, land, and water.

Terra helps to answer such questions as: Which environmental changes result from natural causes? Which are caused by humans? Satellites like *Terra* also help scientists study natural disasters such as hurricanes, volcanic eruptions, and floods. Today, several countries are working together in the Earth Observing System program to gather information about climate and environmental change on Earth.

What do you think?

♦ How can *Terra* benefit people?

♦ Why do countries work together to study climate and environmental change?

33

FOCUS ON GEOGRAPHY

Objectives

• To recognize the importance of human-environment interaction

• To describe the tools that geographers use to learn about Earth's features

What Do You Think?

1. Encourage students to consider how scientists and governments might use the data collected by *Terra*. What changes might people make based on this data?

2. Point out that many of Earth's physical features cover a large region and encompass many countries.

How has new technology increased our knowledge of Earth?

Have students consider how data about Earth was collected before satellite technology. Point out that even with aerial photography only a limited area could be observed at any one time.

MAKING GEOGRAPHIC CONNECTIONS

Ask students to brainstorm a list of natural disasters, such as floods, earthquakes, hurricanes, tornadoes, and volcanic eruptions. Then have them suggest how technology might help track and predict these events.

Then ask students to brainstorm a list of other events on Earth's surface that scientists could use information from satellites to study. These events could include the loss of seashore or rain forests, the spread of oil from an oil-tanker spill, or the increase in traffic at night. Have them suggest how technology might help scientists understand these events.

Implementing the National Geography Standards

Standard 4 Identify and compare the physical characteristics of places

Objective To construct a chart comparing the physical characteristics of the local area with the physical characteristics of other places

Class Time 15 minutes

Task Bring pictures of different natural regions to class from magazines, photo collections, and so on. Have each student prepare a six-column chart identifying the soils, landforms, vegetation, wildlife, climate, and natural hazards of different places. Students should record on their charts the similarities and differences

between their local environment and the pictured environments.

Evaluation In their charts, students should identify at least one difference and one similarity between the local environment and each pictured environment.

BEFORE YOU READ

What Do You Know?

Ask students if they have ever given someone directions to their house. What kind of information do they use? If they had to give directions to the continent of North America, what would they say? Ask students to tell about what makes their neighborhood unique.

Ask students to pick a region in the United States that they have visited. Ask how the climate, landforms, and rainfall or other water resources differ from the region in which they live. Then ask what the region in which they live was like 100 years ago. How has it changed? What changes did humans make, and why? What changes are humans making today, and why?

What Do You Want to Know?

Have students work in pairs to generate questions about what they want to know about the field of geography and record the questions in their notebooks. Have students record the answers they find as they read this chapter. Students can compare their answers when they have completed the chapter.

READ AND TAKE NOTES

Reading Strategy: Identifying Main Ideas
Point out that each of the five themes is a major heading in Section 1. Explain that each heading is a main idea and that the text under each heading contains supporting details. Encourage students to find several supporting details for each main idea and expand their webs to include these details.

 In-depth Resources: Unit 1
• Guided Reading Worksheets, pp. 14–15

BEFORE YOU READ

▶▶ What Do You Know?

Do you know how to find important places in your town? Have you visited cities, towns, or rural areas and noticed what made these places special? Do you ever use terms like "up north" or "back east"? Have you ever moved from one neighborhood, town, or country to another? Do you know about the harmful effects of pollution on wildlife habitats? If you answered yes, then you know something about each of geography's five big themes—location, place, region, movement, and human-environment interaction.

▶▶ What Do You Want to Know?

Decide what more you want to learn about geography's five themes. Write your ideas, and any questions you may have, in your notebook before you read this chapter.

READ AND TAKE NOTES

Reading Strategy: Identifying Main Ideas One way to make sense of what you read is to look for main ideas and supporting details. Each paragraph, topic heading, and section in a chapter usually has a main idea. Supporting details help to explain the main idea. Use this spider map to write a main idea and its supporting details from this chapter.

• Copy the spider map in your notebook.
• As you read, look for information about the five themes of geography.
• Write a main idea in the center circle.
• Write details supporting the main idea in the other circles.

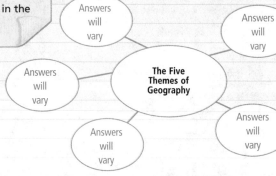

Place • **Physical and human characteristics reveal patterns in places.** ▲

Answers will vary

Answers will vary

Answers will vary

The Five Themes of Geography

Answers will vary

Answers will vary

Teaching Strategy

Reading the Chapter This is a thematic chapter focusing on the five themes of geography and on the variety of maps, globes, charts, and other tools used to depict information about Earth and human societies. Encourage students to focus on understanding the five themes and explaining how tools are used to describe and learn about Earth.

Integrated Assessment The Chapter Assessment on page 50 describes several activities for integrated assessment. You may wish to have students work on these activities during the course of the chapter and then present them at the end.

The Five Themes of Geography

TERMS & NAMES
absolute location
latitude
longitude
relative location
migrate

MAIN IDEA

The five themes of geography are location, place, region, movement, and human-environment interaction.

WHY IT MATTERS NOW

The five themes enable you to discuss and explain people, places, and environments of the past and present.

SECTION OBJECTIVES

1. To identify the five themes of geography
2. To describe the theme of location
3. To describe the themes of place and region and explain their relationship
4. To describe the movement of people in the world and how people interact with their environment

SKILLBUILDER
• Interpreting a Map, p. 36
• Interpreting a Chart, p. 38

CRITICAL THINKING
• Synthesizing, p. 37
• Drawing Conclusions, pp. 39, 48
• Recognizing Effects, p. 40

FOCUS & MOTIVATE
WARM-UP

Making Predictions Have students read <u>Dateline</u> and look at the map and a globe. Then discuss these questions.

1. According to Wegener's theory, what mountain chains in Africa and South America might once have been joined?

2. If Earth's crust moves, what might happen to the continents in the distant future?

INSTRUCT: Objective 1

The Five Themes

• Into what five themes is the study of geography divided? location, place, region, movement, human-environment interaction

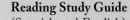
In-depth Resources: Unit 1
• Guided Reading Worksheet, p. 14

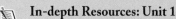
Reading Study Guide
(Spanish and English), pp. 10–11

DATELINE EXTRA

FRANKFURT, GERMANY, JANUARY 6, 1912

Scientist Alfred Wegener sent out shock waves today when he proposed a radical new hypothesis. The continents were once joined together as one huge landmass. In time, he suggests, pieces of this landmass broke away and drifted apart.

Wegener calls this supercontinent *Pangaea*. To support his theory, Wegener points out that the continents seem to fit together.

He notes, for example, that the east coast of South America fits snugly against the west coast of Africa. Mountain ranges continue across both continents as smoothly as the lines of print across torn pieces of a newspaper.

Other scientists reject Wegener's claim. They say that they know of no force strong enough to cause continents to move.

Movement • Seven continents were once one continent. ▲

Region • Alfred Wegener was born in Germany in 1880. ▲

The Five Themes 1

Eventually, the scientific community accepted Alfred Wegener's theory. Scientists discovered that giant slabs of Earth's surface, called tectonic plates, move, causing the continents to drift. This creates earthquakes, volcanoes, and mountains. Geographers study the processes that cause changes like these. To help you understand how geographers think about the world, consider geography's five themes—location, place, region, movement, and human-environment interaction.

Vocabulary

tectonic plates: huge slabs of Earth's surface

The Geographer's World **35**

Program Resources

In-depth Resources: Unit 1
• Guided Reading Worksheet, p. 14
• Reteaching Activity, p. 20

Reading Study Guide
(Spanish and English), pp. 10–11

Formal Assessment
• Section Quiz, p. 19

Integrated Assessment
• Rubric for writing an advertisement

Outline Map Activities

Access for Students Acquiring English
• Guided Reading Worksheet, p. 7

Technology Resources
classzone.com

TEST-TAKING RESOURCES
⚓ Strategies for Test Preparation
⚓ Test Practice Transparencies
💿 Online Test Practice

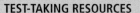
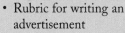

INSTRUCT: Objective ❷

Location

- How is absolute location determined? by using latitude and longitude lines
- How is relative location determined? by describing it in relation to other places

FOCUS ON VISUALS

Interpreting the Map Guide students to name each of the lines of latitude shown on the map. Then have them identify the cities of Australia that are located at latitude 35°S.

Possible Response Students should identify Canberra, Adelaide, and Albany.

Extension Have students use a map to locate their community or the closest city and identify the latitude at which their community is located.

The WORLD'S HERITAGE

In 1835, British naturalist Charles Darwin visited the Galápagos Islands. He was intrigued with the many variations in a type of bird—the finch—that he observed there. He noticed that some finches ate mainly plants, while others fed only on insects. The shapes of their bills varied depending on their diet. Their bills were adapted for grasping, biting, crushing, or probing. Darwin's observations in the Galápagos and elsewhere in South America helped him form the basis for his theory of natural selection. In part, the theory states that animals change over time to adapt to their specialized environments.

GEOGRAPHY SKILLBUILDER: Interpreting a Map

1. **Location** • What is the latitude of Adelaide?
2. **Location** • What island is almost entirely enclosed by the lines 40° and 45° south latitude and 145° and 150° east longitude?

The WORLD'S HERITAGE

The Galápagos Islands The Galápagos Islands are an archipelago, or group of islands, 600 miles off the coast of South America. These islands, which contain many forms of plant and animal life found nowhere else in the world, are a unique "living museum."

Scientists and tourists are fascinated by the islands' creatures, such as Galápagos hawks, land iguanas, waved albatrosses, and blue-footed boobies. The islands are also home to giant tortoises, which can weigh up to 650 pounds and can live to be 200 years old. One of the 11 subspecies of giant tortoises has only one member left. Lonesome George, shown below, is about 80 years old.

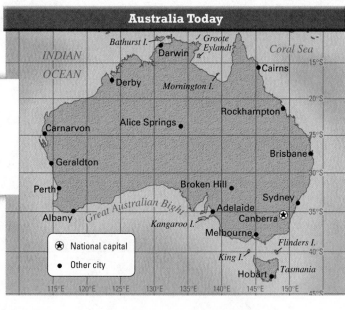

Australia Today

Location ❷

Often, the first thing you want to know about a place is where it is located in space. Geography helps you think about things spatially—where they are located and how they got there. Location allows you to discuss places in the world in terms everyone can understand.

Absolute Location If someone asks you where your school is, you might say, "At the corner of Fifth Street and Second Avenue." Ask a geographer where Melbourne, Australia, is located, and you may get the answer "38° south latitude, 145° east longitude." This is the absolute location of the city of Melbourne. **Absolute location** is the exact spot on Earth where a place can be found.

Using a system of imaginary lines drawn on its surface, geographers can locate any place on Earth. Lines that run parallel to the equator are called **latitude** lines. They measure distance north and south of the equator. Lines that run between the North and South Poles are called **longitude** lines. They measure distance east and west of the prime meridian.

Activity Options

Skillbuilder Mini-Lesson: Reading a Time Zone Map

Explaining the Skill Tell students that a time zone map shows 24 time zones. The day begins at the International Date Line, 180° longitude.

Applying the Skill Refer students to the Time Zone Map on page 27. Have them use the following strategies to read the map.

1. Read the title of the map to find out what it is about.

B Block Scheduling

2. Read the labels across the top of the map that show the hours across the world. Read the labels at the bottom of the map that show the time differences from the prime meridian.

3. Locate the time zone of your community. Compare your time with the time at the prime meridian.

Relative Location Another way to define the location of a place is to describe its relation to other places. You might say your school is "near the fire station" or "two blocks west of the pet store." If someone asks you where Canada is, you might say, "North of the United States." The location of one place in relation to other places is called its **relative location**.

Place • Thousands of years ago, this part of Southwest Asia, then called Mesopotamia, was green and fertile. Today, as you can see, this area is mostly desert. ▲

Place ❸

Another useful theme of geography is place. If you go to a new place, the first thing you want to know is what it is like. Is it crowded or is there a lot of open space? How is the climate? What language do people speak? Every place on Earth has a distinct group of physical features, such as its climate, landforms and bodies of water, and plant and animal life. Places can also have human characteristics, or features that human beings have created, such as cities and towns, governments, and cultural traditions.

Places Change If you could go back to the days when dinosaurs roamed Earth, you would see a world much different from the one you know. Much of Earth had a moist, warm climate, and the continents were not located where they are today. Rivers, forests, wetlands, glaciers, oceans—the physical features of Earth—continue to change. Some changes are dramatic, caused by erupting volcanoes, earthquakes, and hurricanes. Others happen slowly, such as the movement of glaciers or the formation of a delta.

Place • This satellite photo shows the Ganges River delta. It was formed from sediment and mud carried by the river to its mouth. ▼

Region ❸

Geographers group places into regions. A region is a group of places that have physical features or human characteristics, or both, in common. A geographer interested in languages, for example, might divide the world into language regions. All the countries where Spanish is the major language would form one Spanish-speaking language region. Geographers compare regions to understand the differences and similarities among them.

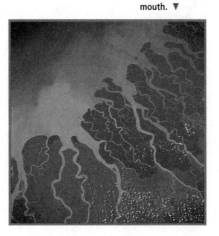

Place/Region

- What are some characteristics of place? climate, landforms, bodies of water, plant and animal life, cities, governments, and cultural traditions
- What causes places to change? change in climate, earthquakes, volcanic eruptions, hurricanes, movements of glaciers, and so on.
- What is a region? a group of places that have common physical features and/or human characteristics
- What is a natural region? a region that has its own unique combination of plant and animal life and climate

CRITICAL THINKING ACTIVITY

Synthesizing Have students work in pairs to complete a spider map about the place—the town, city, or neighborhood—where they live. Students can choose to make either a spider map about the physical features of their place or a spider map about the human characteristics of their place. Have pairs compare and discuss their spider maps.

Class Time 15 minutes

MORE ABOUT...
Geography

The word *geography* comes from two Greek words. *Geo-* means "earth" and *-graphy* means "writing," so geography means "writing about Earth." Geographers are involved in a huge range of activities. Some study information gleaned from satellites, while others study traffic flow in a community. Some focus on changes in the natural world, while others trace human movement and interaction with the planet.

Activity Options

Interdisciplinary Links: Language Arts/History

Class Time One class period

Task Writing a report on the 1980 eruption of Mount St. Helens

Purpose To learn about the effects of a volcanic eruption on the environment and humans

Supplies Needed
- Reference materials about the 1980 eruption of Mount St. Helens
- Pencils or pens
- Writing paper

Activity Remind students that a volcanic eruption can cause swift and dramatic changes to a place. Briefly discuss the 1980 eruption of Mount St. Helens. Then encourage them to focus their research on the effects the eruption had on the landscape and the people living in the area. Have students write brief reports and share selected information with the class.

INSTRUCT: Objective ④

Movement/Human-Environment Interaction

- What are some reasons that people migrate to other areas? to leave difficult circumstances; to find a better life
- What are some natural barriers to human movement? mountains, canyons, raging rivers
- How do humans and the environment interact? Humans depend on, adapt to, and modify the world around them. The environment and human society are shaped by each other.

FOCUS ON VISUALS

Interpreting the Chart Have students notice the relationship between the climate and plant life shown for each region. Ask them to identify the natural region in which they live and what kind of vegetation is in the area.

Possible Response If students have trouble identifying the natural region in which they live, have them identify the climate of their surroundings.

Extension Have students use an encyclopedia to find out more about one of these types of regions. Then have them describe a specific place on Earth that typifies that region.

Natural Regions of the World		
Region	**Climate**	**Plant Life**
Tropical Rain Forest	Hot and wet all year	Thick trees, broad leaves Trees stay green all year
Tropical Grassland	Hot all year Wet and dry seasons	Tall grasses Some trees
Mediterranean	Hot, dry summers Cool-to-mild winters	Open forests Some clumps of trees Many shrubs, herbs, grasses
Temperate Forest	Warm summers Cold-to-cool winters	Mixed forests; some trees lose leaves in winter, others stay green all year
Cool Forest	Cool-to-mild summers Long, cold winters	Mostly trees with needles; stay green all year; some trees lose leaves in winter
Cool Grassland	Warm summers Cool winters Drier than forest regions	Prairies: Tall, thick grass Higher lands: Shorter grass
Desert	Hot all year Very little rain	Sand or bare soil, few plants May have cactus, some grass and bushes
Tundra	Short, cool summers Long, cold winters Little rain or snow	Rolling plains: No trees Some patches of moss, short grass, flowering plants
Arctic	Very cold Covered in ice all year	None
High Mountain	Varies, depending on altitude	Varies, depending on altitude

SKILLBUILDER: Interpreting a Chart

1. **Region** • How are desert regions and tropical grasslands alike and how are they different?
2. **Region** • In which type of climate are trees most likely to stay green all year?

Skillbuilder Possible Answers

1. They are both hot all year. Deserts are mostly dry all year and have few plants. Tropical grasslands have dry and wet seasons and some plants.

2. tropical rain forest and temperate forest

Natural Regions The world can be divided into ten natural regions. A natural region has its own unique combination of plant and animal life and climate. Tropical rain forest regions are in Central and South America, Africa south of the Sahara, Southeast Asia, Australia, and the Pacific Islands. Where are desert regions located?

Region • The tundra is one of the ten natural regions of the world. ▲

Movement ④

People, goods, and ideas move from one place to another. So do animals, plants, and other physical features of Earth. Movement is the fourth geographic theme. The Internet is a good tool for the movement of ideas. Sometimes people move within a country. For example, vast numbers of people have migrated from farms to cities. **Migrate** means to move from one area to settle in another. You may have ancestors who immigrated to the United States—perhaps from Africa, Europe, Latin America, or Asia. When people emigrate, they take their ideas and customs with them. They may also adopt new ideas from their new home.

Reasons for Moving Migration is a result of push and pull factors. Problems in one place push people out. Advantages in another place pull people in. Poverty, overcrowding, lack of jobs and schooling, prejudice, war, and political oppression are push factors. Pull factors include a higher standard of living, employment and educational opportunities, rights, freedom, peace, and safety.

Reading Social Studies B. Possible Answer

Problems push people out of one place. The advantages of another place pull them in.

Vocabulary

immigrate: to move to an area

emigrate: to move away from an area

Reading Social Studies

B. Synthesizing How do push and pull factors work together?

Activity Options

Differentiating Instruction: Less Proficient Readers

Illustrating a Region To help students visualize what types of plants and animals might be found in the regions described in the chart, display photos depicting these features for some of the regions. Discuss the plants and animals they see, and have students choose one of the natural regions to illustrate. Ask them to draw illustrations of vegetation and animals that might be found in the region. Encourage students to label each illustration.

When students have completed their illustrations, have them present the drawings to the class and tell about what the drawings show and why they chose those particular plants and animals. After each student presents his or her drawing, ask the following questions: Would you like to live here? Why or why not? What would you have to do to live comfortably in this region?

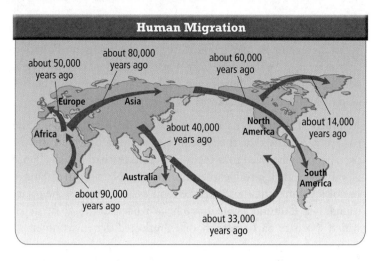

Human Migration

about 50,000 years ago

about 80,000 years ago

about 60,000 years ago

Europe

Asia

Africa

North America

about 14,000 years ago

about 40,000 years ago

Australia

about 90,000 years ago

South America

about 33,000 years ago

Movement • As you can see, people have been on the move for at least 90,000 years. ◄

Barriers to Movement Natural barriers, such as mountain ranges, canyons, and raging rivers, can make migration difficult. Oceans, lakes, navigable rivers, and flat land can make it easier. Modern forms of transportation have made it easier than ever for people to move back and forth between countries.

Human-Environment Interaction

Interaction between human beings and their environment is the fifth theme of geography. Human-environment interaction occurs because humans depend on, adapt to, and modify the world around them. Human society and the environment cannot be separated. Each shapes and is shaped by the other. Earth is a unified system.

Some places are the way they are because people have changed them. For example, if an area has a lot of open meadows, this may be because early settlers cleared the land for farming.

Citizenship IN ACTION

Saving Special Places Many of the most wonderful and special places on Earth may be destroyed or ruined over time unless they are protected. To prevent this, UNESCO (the United Nations Educational, Scientific, and Cultural Organization) set up the World Heritage Committee in 1972. This group identifies human-made and natural wonders all over the world and looks for ways to protect them for the benefit of the world community. So far, the list of World Heritage Sites numbers over 690. The Grand Canyon (see photograph at right), the Galápagos Islands, the Roman Coliseum, and the Pyramids of Giza are just a few of the places protected for future generations.

The Geographer's World **39**

CRITICAL THINKING ACTIVITY

Drawing Conclusions Have students make a chart that shows their family's interaction with the environment.

Depend On	Adapt To	Modify

Students should think of as many details as possible to list in each column, such as recycling, the food they eat, the clothing they wear, how they get around, and so on.

When students have completed their charts, have them work in small groups to compare the charts. Have students discuss the following questions: What actions are beneficial to Earth? What actions are not?

Citizenship IN ACTION

The natural heritage sites designated by the World Heritage Committee are places that show examples of Earth's geologic development or contain a record of ancient life. Dinosaur Provincial Park in the Canadian province of Alberta is one such place. Located in Alberta's badlands, the park holds many important dinosaur fossils. Fossils from more than 30 species of dinosaurs, some up to 75 million years old, have been found there.

Other natural sites are chosen because they are home to rare or endangered plants and animals or to a wide range of species. Everglades National Park at the southern tip of Florida is such a site. It has been called a "river of grass flowing imperceptibly" into the sea. The Everglades is home to many types of birds and reptiles, as well as to the endangered manatee.

Activity Options

Interdisciplinary Link: Science

Class Time One class period

Task Preparing a brochure describing unusual physical features of Yellowstone National Park

Purpose To identify unusual physical features of Yellowstone

Supplies Needed
• Reference materials, including Internet access, if possible
• Writing paper
• Pencils or pens

Activity Have small groups of students research the unusual physical features of Yellowstone. Then have each group choose a different feature, such as a geyser basin, lava formations, or thermal springs. Have groups write a section on their features for an informative brochure for visitors to Yellowstone. Encourage students to include information about how the feature was formed.

CRITICAL THINKING ACTIVITY

Recognizing Effects Review the ways in which the environment affects how people live. Choose one region from the chart on page 38 and work with students to complete a web. Write the name of the region in the center and topics such as food, clothing, and shelter in surrounding circles. Then have students add details about how people might adapt to that environment. For example, people who live near oceans might make fish an important part of their diet.

Class Time 15 minutes

ASSESS & RETEACH

Reading Social Studies Have students complete the web diagram on page 34.

 Formal Assessment
  • Section Quiz, p. 19

RETEACHING ACTIVITY

Have pairs of students create a three-column chart of the five themes of geography. Charts should include theme names, definitions, and examples.

 In-depth Resources: Unit 1
  • Reteaching Activity, p. 20

 Access for Students Acquiring English
  • Reteaching Activity, p. 11

Human changes may help or hurt the environment. Pollution is an example of a harmful effect. The environment can also harm people. For example, hurricanes wash away beaches and houses along the shore; earthquakes cause fire and destruction.

Adaptation Humans have often adapted their way of life to the natural resources that their local environment provided. In the past, people who lived near teeming oceans learned to fish. Those who lived near rich soil learned to farm. People built their homes out of local materials and ate the food easily grown in their surroundings. Cultural choices, such as what clothes to wear or which sports to participate in, often reflected the environment.

Because of technology, this close adaptation to the environment is not as common as it once was. Airplanes, for example, can quickly fly frozen fish from the coast to towns far inland. Even so, there are many more ice skaters in Canada and surfers in California than the other way around.

Interaction People and the environment continually interact. For example, when thousands of people in a city choose to use public transportation or ride bicycles rather than drive, less gasoline is burned. When less gasoline is burned, there is less air pollution. In other words, when the environment is healthy, the people who live in it are able to lead healthier lives.

SECTION 1 ASSESSMENT

Terms & Names

1. Identify: (a) absolute location (b) latitude (c) longitude (d) relative location (e) migrate

Taking Notes

2. Use a chart like this one to list and explain the five themes of geography.

Theme	Explanation

Main Ideas

3. (a) What physical processes can cause places to change over time?

(b) How do push and pull factors cause migration?

(c) What are some ways people have adapted to their environment?

Critical Thinking

4. **Making Inferences**

What factors make your part of the United States a region?

Think About

  • similar human geography
  • similar physical geography

ACTIVITY -OPTION- Write and illustrate a **magazine advertisement** to persuade people to move to a new place. Include several pull factors for the place you are advertising.

Section 1 Assessment

1. Terms & Names

  a. absolute location, p. 36
  b. latitude, p. 36
  c. longitude, p. 36
  d. relative location, p. 37
  e. migrate, p. 38

2. Taking Notes

Location	where place is located in space
Place	area with distinct group of physical features
Region	places with common physical/human characteristics
Movement	people, animals, plants, and ideas go from one place to another
Human-environment interaction	when humans depend on, adapt to, and modify the world around them

3. Main Ideas

  a. Volcanic eruptions, earthquakes, hurricanes, and glacial movement cause change.
  b. Difficult conditions push people to leave a place; the promise of better conditions pulls people to a new place.
  c. Adaptation may involve building homes from local material, learning new work skills, or eating locally grown food.

4. Critical Thinking

Students should describe human and physical characteristics that make up a region.

ACTIVITY OPTION

 Integrated Assessment
  • Rubric for writing an advertisement

Reading Latitude and Longitude

▶▶ Defining the Skill

To locate places, geographers use a global grid system (see the chart directly below). Imaginary lines of latitude, called parallels, circle the globe. The equator circles the middle of the globe at 0°. Parallels measure distance in degrees north and south of the equator.

Lines of longitude, called meridians, circle the globe from pole to pole. Meridians measure distance in degrees east and west of the prime meridian. The prime meridian is at 0°. It passes through Greenwich, England.

▶▶ Applying the Skill

The world map below shows lines of latitude and longitude. Use the strategies listed directly below to help you locate places on Earth.

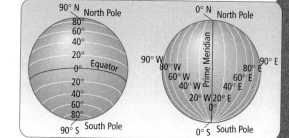

How to Read Latitude and Longitude

Strategy ❶ Place a finger on the place you want to locate. With a finger from your other hand, find the nearest parallel. Write down its number. Be sure to include north or south. (You may have to guesstimate the actual number.)

Strategy ❷ Keep your finger on the place you want to locate. Now find the nearest meridian. Write down its number. Be sure to include east or west. (You may have to guesstimate the actual number.)

Strategy ❸ If you know the longitude and latitude of a place and want to find it on a map, put one finger on the line of longitude and another on the line of latitude. Bring your fingers together until they meet.

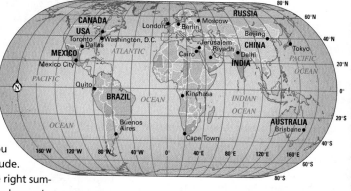

Write a Summary

Writing a summary will help you understand latitude and longitude. The paragraph below and to the right summarizes the information you have learned.

▶▶ Practicing the Skill

Turn to page 36 in Chapter 2, Section 1, "The Five Themes of Geography." Look at the map of Australia and write a paragraph summarizing how you located the city of Adelaide.

Use latitude and longitude to locate a place on a globe or map. Lines of latitude circle Earth. Lines of longitude run through the poles. The numbers of the lines at the place where two lines cross is the location of that place.

Reading Latitude and Longitude

Defining the Skill

Tell students that globes and world maps usually show longitude and latitude lines. Point out that if they know the longitude and latitude coordinates of a place, they can find the location of that place on any map or globe, whether for a classroom assignment or for planning a trip.

Applying the Skill

How to Read Latitude and Longitude
Suggest that students work through each strategy. Remind students that meridians indicate distance east or west of the prime meridian and are marked E or W. Point out that they must identify the north/south and east/west lines of longitude and latitude.

Write a Summary

Discuss the summary in detail with students before they begin to write. Encourage them to note the importance of identifying the longitude and latitude lines as accurately as they can.

Practicing the Skill

Have students locate two cities on the map and estimate their exact locations. If students need more practice, ask a group to determine the longitude and latitude for two cities. Then suggest the group give the coordinates to another group and ask them to identify the cities.

 In-depth Resources: Unit 1
• Skillbuilder Practice, p. 18

Career Connection: Ship Captain

Encourage students who enjoy reading longitude and latitude to learn about careers that use navigational skills. For example, a ship captain uses navigation to determine the ship's position and course on the open sea, the Great Lakes, or major rivers.

 **Block Scheduling**

1. Suggest that students find out how ship captains use longitude and latitude in their navigation. Encourage them to learn how changing technology is affecting navigation.

2. Help students find out what education and training they would need to embark on this career.

3. Have students present an oral summary of their findings to the class.

The Legacy of World Exploration

OBJECTIVE

Students learn about the development of navigational tools, the role they played in world exploration, and how these tools are used today.

FOCUS & MOTIVATE

Recognizing Important Details Ask students to study the pictures and read each paragraph. Then have them answer these questions:

1. How many years have people been using some form of a navigational tool?

2. Why might there have been an increase in navigational tool invention between the 1400s and the 1800s?

 Block Scheduling

MORE ABOUT...
Portolan Charts

Portolan charts were the first step toward renewed interest in mapmaking in Europe in the 1300s. One of the next important steps was the invention of the printing press. By the mid-1400s, maps were more widely available. Identical copies could be more easily and quickly produced by printing than by copying by hand.

MORE ABOUT...
Magnetic Compass

The magnetic compass works by responding to the natural magnetic fields on Earth. The compass needle is made of a magnetic material that points to where the magnetic fields come closest together— at the poles. Compasses are usually designed to point toward the north magnetic pole, but this changes as the magnetic fields shift over time. Explorers and sailors learn to compensate for this to increase the accuracy of their navigation.

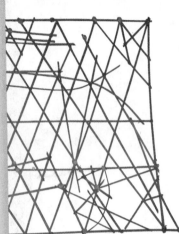

Early Pacific Navigation

More than 2,000 years ago, Polynesian sailors were among the first people to sail the Pacific Ocean. Without charts or instruments to help them find their way, these ancient navigators made sea charts from palm sticks tied together with coconut threads, using small shells to represent islands.

Magnetic Compass

In the 1100s, mariners of China and Europe independently discovered the magnetic compass. They discovered that an iron or steel needle touched by a lodestone, or piece of magnetic ore, tends to point roughly in a north-south direction. Today, surveyors and navigators consider the magnetic compass an essential tool for determining direction.

Portolan Charts

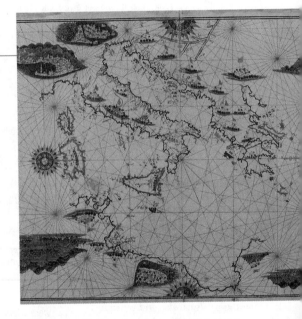

Portolan charts were first made in the 1300s in Italy and Spain. *Portolan* comes from an Italian word meaning "navigation instructions." These charts, which were actually rough maps, were based on accounts of medieval Europeans who sailed the Mediterranean and Black seas. Drawn on sheepskin, portolan charts show coastal features and main ports. The straight lines crisscrossing the charts represent the 32 directions of the mariner's compass.

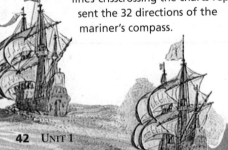

Activity Option

Interdisciplinary Link: Science/World History

Class Time 80 minutes

Task Researching and reporting changes in navigational technology throughout history

Supplies Needed

• Encyclopedia and other research materials about Portolan charts, magnetic compass, Global Positioning System, astrolabe, chronometer, and sextant

Activity Have students work in groups. Assign one of the six navigational tools listed above to each group and tell them to research the following: when the tool came into use; conditions of use (during daylight, in starlight, on wooden ships, etc.); when it went out of use (if it did); why it was replaced or dropped; and what it was replaced with. When they have completed their research, have each group present their findings. Discuss as a class.

Modern Electronic Navigation

In the 1970s, the U.S. Department of Defense developed the Global Positioning System (GPS). GPS allows people on land, at sea, or in the air to pinpoint their location or to track moving objects in any weather. A network of 24 satellites that orbit Earth beam down data to palm-sized receivers, aiding the military in maneuvers. Civilians use them for hiking or finding shorter travel routes.

Astrolabe

The astrolabe was first used in the 400s in Europe and the Islamic world. It is a flat, circular piece of either metal or wood. The edge of the circle is marked to show 360 degrees. Sailors used the astrolabe to measure the sun's and stars' angles above the horizon in order to determine their ships' positions at sea.

Chronometer

John Harrison worked for nearly half a century before he perfected, in 1762, a ship's clock that would revolutionize navigation. This tool, called a chronometer, enabled sailors for the first time to determine accurately a ship's longitude, or east-west position. The modern chronometer, which looks like a large, heavy watch, continues to help sailors find their ships' longitude.

Sextant

In the 1730s, the sextant replaced the astrolabe. This device measures the angle between the horizon and the sun, the moon, or a star and is used to calculate latitude, or north-south position. The sextant continues to be a basic navigational tool today.

Find Out More About It!

Study the text and photos on these pages to learn about world exploration. Then choose the item that interests you the most and research it in the library or on the Internet to learn more about it. Use the information you gather to write a short play that you and your classmates can perform.

RESEARCH LINKS
CLASSZONE.COM

INSTRUCT

- What did Portolan charts show?
- What navigational tool was discovered independently about the same time in two different places?
- What other technological tool does the most modern navigational tool rely on to work?

MORE ABOUT...
Modern Electronic Navigation

The Global Positioning System, or GPS, is a worldwide navigation system using radio signals broadcast by satellites. The United States Air Force operates the satellites, but the system has both military and civilian users.

GPS's 24 satellites, called Navstars, are arranged in six orbits of about 12,500 miles above Earth. When viewed from any point on Earth, there may be as many as eight satellites above the horizon.

GPS can be incredibly precise. While civilian GPS users can determine their location within 330 feet, a special technique called differential GPS can improve the accuracy to within 33 feet. Beyond those, a technique called carrier phase GPS can be accurate to within 0.4 inch!

Sextant

The sextant is an optical instrument used for both navigation and surveying. It has a graduated arc, a movable index arm, two mirrors, and a small telescope.

The sextant works according to an optical rule: If an object is seen by repeated reflection from two mirrors perpendicular to the same plane, the angular distance between the object and its image is double the angle between the surfaces of the mirrors. The sextant's index measures the angle between the mirrors, and this is doubled to give the angular distance of an object, such as the sun, above the horizon.

More to Think About

Making Personal Connections Ask students to think about how they might use any of these tools in their daily life. Under what conditions would they want or need which specific navigational device discussed here? Ask them to consider which tool might be best for use on a hike, a sailing trip, and a cross-country driving trip.

Vocabulary Activity Ask students to work in pairs and take turns quizzing each other on the definition of the six navigational tools described on this page. Have one student attempt to identify the name of the tool based on clues given by the other student. You could develop a reward system for the correct answer with the least number of clues.

A Map of Earth in 3-D

OBJECTIVES

1. To explain how technology has changed the way maps are made and used

2. To explain the usefulness of data collected from maps of Earth's surface

3. To use information from a photograph and captions to support the text

INSTRUCT

• How was radar used to produce 3-D images during the SRTM mission?

• How might maps of Earth's surface be useful to the general public?

 Block Scheduling

MORE ABOUT...

Gathering Information for Maps

Although photographs of Earth were taken from balloons in the 1800s, it was not until after World War I that they were routinely used in making maps. In the 1970s, the United States used satellites called Landsats to gather data. Much of this information is now collected by radar, which can penetrate obstructions in ways that photography cannot.

Connect to History

Strategic Thinking As a mapmaker in the 15th century, how might you have gathered data?

Connect to Today

Strategic Thinking How have photography and flight changed the way maps are made?

On February 11, 2000, the space shuttle *Endeavour* was launched into space on an 11-day mission to complete the most in-depth mapping project in history. The Shuttle Radar Topography Mission (SRTM) collected data on 80 percent of Earth's surface. This information was gathered by beaming radar waves at Earth and converting the echoes into images through a process known as interferometry (IHN•tuhr•fuh•RAHM•ih•tree).

With the aid of computers, the resulting information can be used to produce almost limitless numbers of three-dimensional (3-D) maps. These maps show the topography—rivers, forests, mountains, and valleys—of Earth's surface. It took one year to process the data into 3-D maps. These maps, the most accurate topographical maps ever, will help scientists to better study Earth's surface. The data will also be useful to the general public; for example, it can be used to find new locations for cellular-phone towers and to create maps for hikers.

The data collected on the 11-day SRTM mission can be used by many people—such as the military, the science community, and civic groups—and can be tailored to their needs.

The 200-foot mast is the longest structure used in space today.

Radar interferometry uses radar images taken from two different angles to produce a single 3-D image.

THINKING Critically

1. Drawing Conclusions How will new, sophisticated tools such as radar interferometry and computers change the study of Earth and the environment?

2. Making Predictions How will these topographical maps help the world?

Thinking Critically

1. Drawing Conclusions Possible Responses Scientists will be able to look at Earth in ways never available before. They will be able to see physical characteristics more clearly, and the data they receive will be more accurate. They will be able to study concepts such as population groupings and changes in climate.

2. Making Predictions Possible Responses The data from these maps will be available to a variety of groups all over the world, including scientists, the military, politicians, civic groups, industrialists, and the general public. Greater knowledge may help deal with environmental issues, military strategies, and overcrowding of cities.

The Geographer's Tools

SECTION 2

TERMS & NAMES
cartographer
thematic map
map projection

MAIN IDEA

Geographers use maps, globes, charts, graphs, and new technology to learn about and display the features of Earth.

WHY IT MATTERS NOW

Knowing how to use the tools of geography adds to your ability to understand the world.

SECTION OBJECTIVES

1. To explain the differences between maps and globes, and to identify types of maps and map projections
2. To describe how geographers use charts and graphs to display and compare information

SKILLBUILDER
• Interpreting a Map, pp. 47, 48
• Reading a Graph, p. 49

CRITICAL THINKING
• Comparing, p. 46

FOCUS & MOTIVATE
WARM-UP

Making Inferences Have students read Dateline and examine the map and the diagram of the map. Then discuss these questions.

1. Why might the Babylonians have had a distorted view of their surroundings?
2. Do you think this map could be used to determine relative or absolute location?

INSTRUCT: Objective 1

Maps and Globes

• How do maps and globes differ? globe—accurate, three-dimensional; maps—two-dimensional, not perfectly accurate

In-depth Resources: Unit 1
• Guided Reading Worksheet, p. 15

Reading Study Guide
(Spanish and English), pp. 12–13

DATELINE

BABYLONIA, ABOUT 600 B.C.— Palace officials today released the first map of the world seen in this area. As suspected, Babylon lies at the center of the world. The star-shaped map is drawn on a clay tablet disk about four inches high.

It shows the world surrounded by the Earthly Ocean, which we call the Bitter River. Seven outer regions are also shown as equal triangles rising up out of the oceans. One side of the tablet gives the names of the countries and cities in cuneiform. The other side describes the seven islands. Officials say the map will enable viewers to see the relation of these foreign places to Babylon.

Location • The Babylonian world map was drawn on a clay tablet. ▲

Location • This diagram shows the Babylonian world map translated into English. ▲

Maps and Globes 1

People have been drawing maps of their world for thousands of years. Geographers today have many tools, such as remote sensing and the Global Positioning System, to help them represent Earth. Increased knowledge and technology allows a **cartographer,** or mapmaker, to construct maps that give a much more detailed and accurate picture of the world. The "Linking Past and Present" and "Technology: 2000" features on pages 42–44 provide more information on modern mapmaking technology.

The Geographer's World **45**

Program Resources

In-depth Resources: Unit 1
• Guided Reading Worksheet, p. 15
• Reteaching Activity, p. 21

Reading Study Guide
(Spanish and English), pp. 12–13

Formal Assessment
• Section Quiz, p. 20

Integrated Assessment
• Rubric for making a map

Outline Map Activities

Access for Students Acquiring English
• Guided Reading Worksheet, p. 8

Technology Resources
classzone.com

TEST-TAKING RESOURCES
⚓ Strategies for Test Preparation
⚓ Test Practice Transparencies
🖱 Online Test Practice

CRITICAL THINKING ACTIVITY

Comparing Review the differences and similarities between maps and globes and the advantages and disadvantages of each. Have students decide if a map, a globe, or both would be the preferred tool for each of the following tasks: to convey a specific theme, to locate latitude and longitude, to take on a trip, to determine a continent's size in relation to another, and to find a route. Have students give reasons for their answers.

Class Time 15 minutes

Connections to Math

Eratosthenes used geometry to calculate the circumference of Earth. Geometry is also the basis for determining longitude lines. The Prime Meridian is an imaginary line drawn halfway around the center of Earth from pole to pole. Directly opposite the prime meridian is the longitude line designated 180°. The lines of longitude are numbered from 0° to 180° east or west. Combined, these lines equal 360°, which is the circumference of a circle.

FOCUS ON VISUALS

Interpreting the Map Have students study the map of Prince Edward Island. Ask what different kinds of information can be found on the map.

Possible Responses Information on the map includes cities, three types of highways, national parks, and the names of bodies of water.

Extension Have students name three other kinds of information that could be included on the map, such as camping areas or railways.

Location • Draw a picture on the entire surface of an orange and then peel the orange in one continuous piece. After you lay the peel flat, your image will be distorted. ◄

Differences Between Maps and Globes Both maps and globes represent Earth and its features. A globe is an accurate model of the world because it has three dimensions and can show its actual shape. Globes are difficult to carry around, however. Maps are more practical. They can be folded, carried, hung on a wall, or printed in a book or magazine. However, because maps show the world in only two dimensions, they are not perfectly accurate. Look at the pictures above to see why. When the orange peel is flattened out, the picture on the orange is distorted, or twisted out of shape. Cartographers have the same problem with maps.

Three Kinds of Maps General reference maps, which show natural and human-made features, are used to locate a place. **Thematic maps** focus on one specific idea or theme. The population map on page 48 is an example of a thematic map. Pilots and sailors use nautical maps to find their way through air and over water. A nautical map is sometimes called a chart.

Reading Social Studies

A. Clarifying Why does a globe represent Earth better than a map?

Reading Social Studies
A. Possible Response
Since Earth is round and a globe is round, a globe is a more accurate representation of Earth.

Location • A road map is a reference map that shows how to get from one place to another. ▼

Connections to Math

Measuring Earth In 230 B.C., the Greek scientist Eratosthenes (see page 42) used basic geometry to measure the circumference of Earth. Eratosthenes knew that at noon on June 21, the sun cast no shadow in the Egyptian city of Syene (now Aswan). (See the diagram below.) At the same time, the sun cast a shadow of 7°12′ in Alexandria, about 500 miles from Syene.

The circumference of a circle is 360°; 7°12′ is about 2 percent, or 1/50, of 360°. Therefore, he concluded, 500 miles must be about 2 percent of the distance around Earth, which at the equator would be about 25,000 miles.

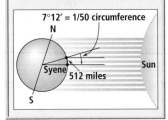

7°12′ = 1/50 circumference
N
Syene
512 miles
Sun
S

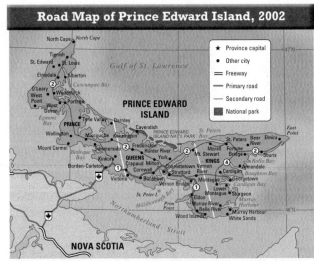

Road Map of Prince Edward Island, 2002

★ Province capital
● Other city
═ Freeway
— Primary road
— Secondary road
■ National park

PRINCE EDWARD ISLAND

NOVA SCOTIA

Activity Options

Differentiating Instruction: Students Acquiring English/ESL

Reading in Pairs Students may have difficulty with the details of this section. Pair fluent readers with students acquiring English, and have them read this section together, listing any difficult passages or concepts. When students have completed the section, have the pairs meet in groups to discuss and clarify the problem passages with one another. You may wish to help students clarify any remaining questions.

To help students understand the three kinds of maps, provide samples of each kind. Guide students as they study the maps. Point out what makes the map a general reference map, a reference map, or a nautical chart. Then have students make a chart that lists the three kinds of maps and describes the function and properties of each kind.

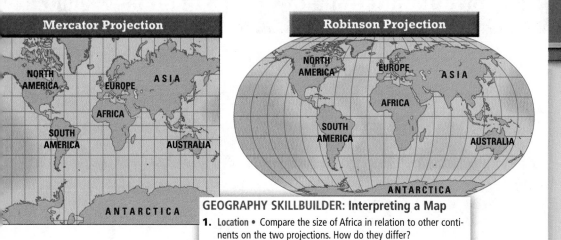

GEOGRAPHY SKILLBUILDER: Interpreting a Map

1. **Location** • Compare the size of Africa in relation to other continents on the two projections. How do they differ?
2. **Location** • What other differences do you notice between the Mercator projection and the Robinson projection?

Map Projections

The different ways of showing Earth's curved surface on a flat map are called **map projections**. All projections distort Earth, but different projections distort it in different ways. Some make places look bigger or smaller than they really are in relation to other places. Other projections distort shapes. For more than 400 years, the Mercator projection was most often shown on maps of the world. Recently, the Robinson projection has come into common use because it gives a fairer and more accurate picture of the world.

Reading Social Studies

B. Identifying Problems What are the main problems faced by cartographers?

Reading Social Studies
B. Possible Answer All map projections distort Earth.

Geography Skillbuilder Possible Answers

1. On Robinson, Africa appears larger in relation to Europe and Asia.

2. On Robinson, South America is larger in relation to North America; Europe is smaller in relation to Asia.

FOCUS ON VISUALS

Interpreting the Maps Encourage students to compare the size of all the continents shown on the maps on this page. Then ask what effect these two different maps might have on the way people think about the world and the importance of various parts of the world. For example, how might people think differently about the continents of Africa or South America using one or the other of these projections?

Possible Response Students may suggest that when a continent appears larger on a map projection, people might consider it to be more important in world affairs.

Extension Ask students to use an atlas to determine the number of square miles in two of the continents. Then have them compare the square mileage of the two continents with the Mercator projection of the same continents. Is the difference in size accurately depicted? Is it accurately depicted on the Robinson projection?

Spotlight on CULTURE

Mercator Map This map of the Arctic was drawn in 1595 by Gerardus Mercator (1512–1594), the famous mapmaker for whom the map projection was named. It is one of many old maps that are rare, beautiful, and important historical artifacts.

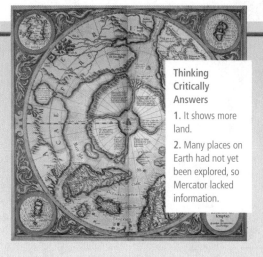

THINKING CRITICALLY

1. **Recognizing Important Details** Does Mercator's map show more land or more water?
2. **Identifying Problems** What types of problems might Mercator have faced when he created this map?

Thinking Critically Answers

1. It shows more land.

2. Many places on Earth had not yet been explored, so Mercator lacked information.

Spotlight on CULTURE

Old illustrated maps often bear labels in the Latin language. For example, the label shown here, *Mare Pacificum*, means "Pacific Ocean."

Mercator was born near Antwerp to German parents. His given name was Gerhard Krämer, but like many Renaissance scholars, he changed it to a Latin version, Gerardus Mercator.

The Geographer's World **47**

Activity Options

Differentiating Instruction: Gifted and Talented

Block Scheduling

Designing an Illustrated Map Discuss the illustrated map shown on this page. Have students identify some of the illustrations and how they relate to what was known and what was happening in world exploration at the time. You might provide other examples of illustrated maps, especially from before Mercator's time. Explain that illustrators often made up imaginary plants and animals for their maps.

Then have students trace a map of North and South America and the surrounding oceans. Have them label the map and illustrate it with pictures depicting conditions today. Ask them to consider what kinds of ships sail the oceans today and what the inhabitants of these continents look like. Have students display their work in class.

World Population and Life Expectancy, 2000

FOCUS ON VISUALS

Interpreting the Maps Guide students to name the continents with the densest and least dense populations. Guide them to name the continents where people can expect to live longest and where their lives are much shorter.

Possible Responses The continents with the densest populations are Asia and Europe, and Australia has the least dense. People live longer in North America, Europe, and Australia. People in Africa have the shortest lives.

Extension Have students find a population map for the United States. Have them compare the way the information is shown with the population map on this page. Ask them to identify the states with the densest and the least dense populations.

CRITICAL THINKING ACTIVITY

Drawing Conclusions Have students compare the two maps on this page. Have them look for areas with dense population and high life expectancy. Then have them look for areas with dense population and low life expectancy. What conclusions can they draw from making these comparisons, if any?

Class Time 15 minutes

MORE ABOUT...
Life Expectancy

Many factors determine the life expectancy of a population. These include education, health care, clean running water, low pollution, and employment.

Population

• = 500,000 people

Geography Skillbuilder Possible Answers

1. Asia; Australia
2. 75 years or more

Life Expectancy

Life Expectancy in Years, 2000

Less than 55
55–64
65–69
70–74
75 or more
No data

GEOGRAPHY SKILLBUILDER: Interpreting a Map
1. **Region** • Which continent has the largest population? the smallest?
2. **Region** • What is the life expectancy in most parts of North America?

48 CHAPTER 2

Activity Options

Interdisciplinary Links: Visual/Geography

Explaining the Skill Tell students that the population map uses dots to show the number of people and where they live. The life expectancy map uses color to show how long people in different regions of the world can expect to live.

Applying the Skill Have students use the following strategies to read the maps.

1. Read the titles of the maps to find out what they show.

2. Read the map key. The population map uses a dot to represent 500,000 people. Read the key of the life expectancy map to see what life expectancy each color represents.

3. Study each map. Where is the population densest? Where in the world can people expect to live longest?

Comparing Maps, Charts, and Graphs ❷

Along with maps, geographers use charts and graphs to display and compare information. The graphs on this page and the maps on page 48 contain related information about the world's population. Notice how each quickly and clearly presents facts that would otherwise take up many paragraphs of text.

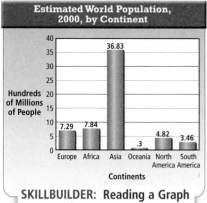

Estimated World Population, 2000, by Continent

SKILLBUILDER: Reading a Graph

1. How many people live in Europe?
2. Which continent has the smallest population?

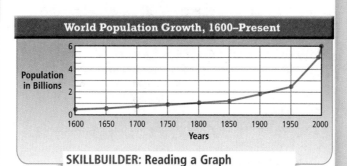

World Population Growth, 1600–Present

SKILLBUILDER: Reading a Graph

1. How many people lived in the world in 1900?
2. How much did the world's population increase between 1600 and 1900? between 1900 and 2000?

Skillbuilder Answers

1. 729 million
2. Oceania

1. 1.9 billion
2. 1.5 billion; 3.3 billion

SECTION ❷ ASSESSMENT

Terms & Names

1. **Identify:** (a) cartographer (b) thematic map (c) map projection

Taking Notes

2. Use a chart like this one to compare the advantages and disadvantages of maps and globes.

	Maps	Globes
Advantages		
Disadvantages		

Main Ideas

3. (a) What are the differences among the three main kinds of maps?

   (b) How have new tools and knowledge helped cartographers?

   (c) What kinds of information can be displayed in maps and graphs?

Critical Thinking

4. **Using Maps**

   What kind of map would show how many students are in each school in your district?

   Think About

   • the three kinds of maps
   • what information different kinds of population maps show

ACTIVITY -OPTION- Draw a **map** of the route you take to and from school or some other familiar destination. Include the names of streets, landmarks such as shops and other buildings, and any other useful information.

The Geographer's World **49**

Section ❷ Assessment

1. Terms & Names

a. cartographer, p. 45
b. thematic map, p. 46
c. map projection, p. 47

2. Taking Notes

	Maps	Globes
Advantages	portable; can show thematic material	show physical features accurately
Disadvantages	distort physical features	cannot be easily carried

3. Main Ideas

a. general reference maps: natural and human-made features; thematic maps: one specific idea; nautical maps: used for navigation
b. They allow cartographers to make more detailed and accurate maps.
c. facts, data, and statistics

4. Critical Thinking

Students may say a thematic map that shows population density.

ACTIVITY OPTION

 Integrated Assessment
   • Rubric for making a map

INSTRUCT: Objective ❷

Comparing Maps, Charts, and Graphs

• What is an advantage of using maps, charts, and graphs instead of text? They quickly and clearly present information.

FOCUS ON VISUALS

Interpreting the Graphs Guide students as they read the graphs. What information is along the x-axis and the y-axis? Be sure students understand that in the right-hand graph, the numbers are in billions, and in the left-hand graph, they are in hundreds of millions.

Possible Response Right graph: x-axis is years, y-axis is population; left graph: x-axis is continents, y-axis is population.

Extension Ask students to think of other information about population that could be displayed in charts.

ASSESS & RETEACH

Reading Social Studies Have students create a web diagram with a center circle labeled "Geographer's Tools." Then have them add details for each category.

 Formal Assessment
   • Section Quiz, p. 20

RETEACHING ACTIVITY

Have students list ways in which each of the geographer's tools might be used.

 In-depth Resources: Unit 1
   • Reteaching Activity, p. 21

 Access for Students Acquiring English
   • Reteaching Activity, p. 12

Teacher's Edition **49**

TERMS & NAMES

1. absolute location, p. 36
2. latitude, p. 36
3. longitude, p. 36
4. relative location, p. 37
5. cartographer, p. 45
6. thematic map, p. 46
7. map projection, p. 47
8. migrate, p. 38

REVIEW QUESTIONS

Possible Responses

1. Latitude and longitude are used to determine absolute location.
2. Relative location tells where a place is in relation to another place, whereas absolute location uses latitude and longitude.
3. Mountain ranges, canyons, and rivers made migration difficult in the past.
4. Because of technology, humans have not had to adapt as closely to their environments.
5. Because a globe is round like Earth, there is less distortion.
6. A pilot would use a nautical map to find his or her way through air and over water.
7. Modern technology has helped cartographers to be more detailed and accurate.
8. The Robinson projection more accurately shows the size of continents in relation to one another.

TERMS & NAMES

Explain the significance of each of the following:

1. absolute location
2. latitude
3. longitude
4. relative location
5. cartographer
6. thematic map
7. map projection
8. migrate

REVIEW QUESTIONS

The Five Themes of Geography *(pages 35–40)*

1. What system do geographers use to determine absolute location?
2. How is relative location different from absolute location?
3. What are some of the natural barriers that made migration difficult in the past?
4. How has technology changed the way humans adapt to their environment?

The Geographer's Tools *(pages 45–49)*

5. Why is a globe an accurate representation of the world?
6. Why would a pilot use a nautical map?
7. How has modern technology helped cartography?
8. Why do most modern cartographers prefer the Robinson projection to the Mercator projection?

CRITICAL THINKING

Drawing Conclusions

1. Using your completed spider map from Reading Social Studies, p. 34, draw a conclusion about which theme of geography is most useful in familiarizing you with an area of the world. Which details in your chart help you understand a country or region?

Contrasting

2. Maps and globes both represent Earth and its features. Contrast the advantages of a map with the advantages of a globe.

Clarifying

3. Why would the leaders of a country find a population density map of their country useful?

Visual Summary

The Five Themes of Geography *1*

- The five themes of geography are location, place, region, movement, and human-environment interaction.
- These themes are the keys to understanding the geography of the world.

The Geographer's Tools *2*

- Maps, globes, charts, graphs, and other tools are available to geographers to help them understand the features of Earth.
- Geographers use these tools to organize and explain Earth's features.

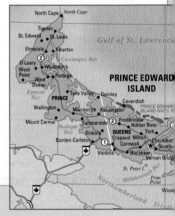

CRITICAL THINKING: Possible Responses

1. Drawing Conclusions

Answers may vary. Students might say that place is the most useful theme because it gives information about the climate, landforms, and bodies of water and tells about human characteristics such as cultural traditions. Accept any answer that students can justify.

2. Contrasting

Students may note that the advantages of a map are that it can be readily carried around and referred to, is easy to read, and can depict a small and specific area. The advantages of a globe are that it is a more accurate picture of the whole world, there is no distortion, and you can see parts of the world in relation to other parts.

3. Clarifying

Students may note that leaders could use population density maps to apportion natural resources where they are needed and to anticipate needs in the future.

SOCIAL STUDIES SKILLBUILDER

SKILLBUILDER: Reading Longitude and Latitude

A hurricane is expected to touch land briefly at latitude 34°N and longitude 79°W. It will move over the water and touch land again at latitude 30°N and longitude 82°W. Then it will move out over the sea.

1. Which state will feel the effects of the hurricane first?
2. Which state will be touched by the hurricane next?

FOCUS ON GEOGRAPHY

1. **Location** • What is special about a satellite view of Earth?
2. **Location** • How might scientists use satellite images such as this to help people?

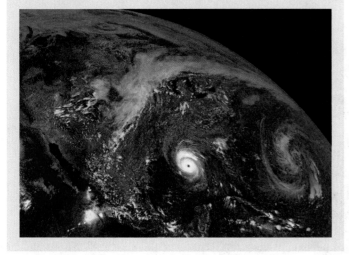

CHAPTER PROJECTS

Interdisciplinary Activity: Language Arts

Writing a Description Most people use relative location when they are giving directions. Write a paragraph describing the relative location of your home.

Cooperative Learning Activity

Describing Geography In a group of three to five students, choose a country and use the five themes of geography to describe it. Assign the themes to members of the group:

- Where is your country located?
- What are the physical and human characteristics of the place?
- How can you classify the region?
- What movement has occurred in the country?
- How have the people who live there adapted to the environment?

Gather your findings and present them to the class in the form of a book or on a poster board.

 INTERNET ACTIVITY

Use the Internet to research how technology can be used to study natural events. Focus on one natural event, like tropical rainfall or global warming, and look into how technology is helping us understand it.

Writing About Geography Write a report of your findings. Include information about the technology and how it is used. Make a prediction about the future uses of technology.

For Internet links to support this activity, go to

RESEARCH LINKS
CLASSZONE.COM

CHAPTER PROJECTS

Interdisciplinary Activity: Language Arts

Writing a Description Encourage students to describe the location of their homes in relation to another place, a reference point, or a landmark. Suggest they refer to other places or landmarks in their directions.

Cooperative Learning Activity

Describing Geography Remind students that their book or poster should describe the location, climate, and landforms of their country. Encourage them to describe the people who live there, the type of region, the patterns of human migration, and the inhabitants' unique patterns of adapting to their environment. Remind students that they can classify the region according to physical features, climate, or human characteristics. Provide time and space for students to display and explain their completed projects.

INTERNET ACTIVITY

Brainstorm with students possible key words they might explore, such as "global warming" and "technology." Point out that students' reports should have a main idea statement identifying the natural event and give details about the specific technology and how it is used. Suggest that students conclude with an explanation of how the technology might be used in the future.

Skills Answers

Social Studies Skillbuilder
Possible Responses

1. South Carolina will feel the effects of the hurricane first.
2. Florida will feel the effects of the hurricane next.

Focus on Geography
Possible Responses

1. Students might say that a satellite image is the only way to see so much area at one time, to see it from so high up, or to be above the clouds.
2. Students may say that scientists could use satellite images to warn people about possible bad weather or to locate areas of growing pollution.

UNIT 2

Europe, Russia, and the Independent Republics

Before You Read

Previewing Unit 2

Unit 2 explores European culture and society from its roots in ancient Greece and Rome to the many challenges facing the region today. It begins by identifying the major physical features of Europe that influenced human development. It then highlights the developments in European history that help explain the modern Europe we know today and concludes with information about Europe's role in the world.

Place Completed in A.D. 80, the Colosseum in Rome, Italy, held 50,000 spectators. There they watched battles between gladiators, among other contests. The Colosseum is the largest structure that survives from the Roman Empire.

52

Unit Level Activities

1. Create a Time Line

Hang a large sheet of mural paper on the wall. Draw a horizontal line along the bottom of the paper. Show students how to divide the time line by adding small vertical lines marking every hundred years between 800 B.C. and A.D. 2000. Have students write in the years. As students read the chapter, ask volunteers to write events on the time line and to illustrate the events.

2. Identify Locations on a Map

Hang a large map of Europe on the wall. Before you begin Chapter 3, ask students to identify any European countries they have visited. Have them use red pins to mark on the map all the countries they have visited. Then ask if any students have ancestors who came from Europe, and have them use blue pins to mark those countries on the map. As you read each chapter, ask volunteers to identify the region being studied and to put a yellow pin on the map.

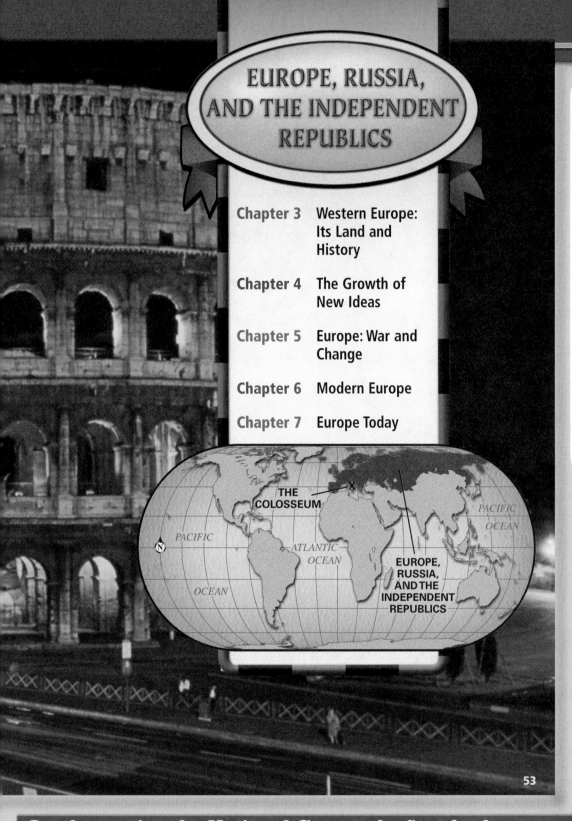

EUROPE, RUSSIA, AND THE INDEPENDENT REPUBLICS

THE COLOSSEUM

PACIFIC

PACIFIC OCEAN

N

ATLANTIC OCEAN

OCEAN

EUROPE, RUSSIA, AND THE INDEPENDENT REPUBLICS

53

FOCUS ON VISUALS

Interpreting the Photograph Direct students' attention to the photograph of the Colosseum and read the caption aloud. Ask students to use their imaginations to picture what the inside of this large building must have looked like when it was completed in A.D. 80. Then ask them to list some of the events they think might have been held there. Have them compare the structure and style of the Colosseum with buildings of similar size and function today. What style of building would they be likely to see today? What use would it be put to?

Possible Responses A building of this size today would be more sleek and modern; it would be used for sports events or concerts.

Extension Ask students to draw a plan of what they think the inside of the Colosseum looked like. Have them indicate seating, playing field, entrances, and exits.

Implementing the National Geography Standards

Standard 18 Describe the immigrant experience

Objective To role-play being immigrants who are adjusting to life in their new country

Class Time 20 minutes

Task Have students role-play being immigrants to a country in Europe. Encourage them to describe how it feels to be in that situation. Ask stu-

dents to explore the immigrants' perceptions of the new nation and of how to adjust to life in a different environment in order to appreciate the significance of people's beliefs, attitudes, and values in environmental adaptation.

Evaluation Students should mention the following cultural differences: language, religion, social customs, and cuisine.

UNIT 2

ATLAS
Europe, Russia, and the Independent Republics

ATLAS OBJECTIVES

1. Describe and locate physical features of Europe, Russia, and the Independent Republics

2. Examine maps and data concerning climate, landmass, and population of the region

3. Identify political features of Europe, Russia, and the Independent Republics

4. Analyze the population and examine a road map of Europe

5. Compare data on the countries of Europe, Russia, and the Independent Republics

FOCUS & MOTIVATE

Ask students how this physical map can help them understand the geography of Europe, Russia, and the Independent Republics of the former Soviet Union. Answers will vary, but students should understand the use of a physical map and the key that explains it.

INSTRUCT: Objective ❶

Physical Map of Europe, Russia, and the Independent Republics

• What mountains separate France and Spain?
Pyrenees

• The Aral Sea lies in what two countries?
Kazakhstan and Uzbekistan

• The Ural River drains into what body of water? Caspian Sea

 In-depth Resources: Unit 2
• Unit Atlas Activities, p. 1

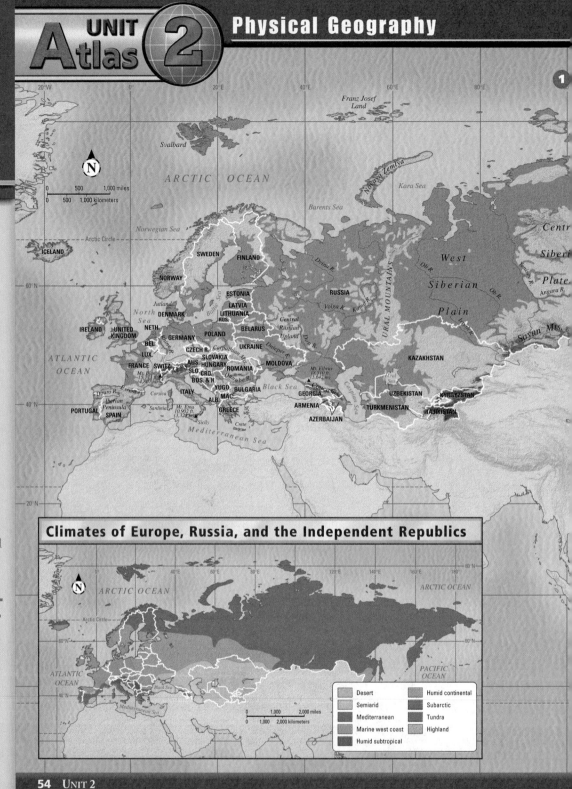

Physical Geography

UNIT Atlas 2

Climates of Europe, Russia, and the Independent Republics

Desert Humid continental
Semiarid Subarctic
Mediterranean Tundra
Marine west coast Highland
Humid subtropical

54 UNIT 2

Activity Options

Interdisciplinary Link: Math

Explaining the Skill Students will demonstrate an understanding of elevation and other features shown on a physical map, as well as the use of a compass rose and scale of miles.

Applying the Skill Ask students to plan a trip that will take them through any three high mountain ranges of Europe, Russia, and the

Block Scheduling

Independent Republics. Beginning with one mountain range, they should write a description of the route they take, the direction and distance they travel, and their elevation gains and losses as they travel from one range to the next. They should tell when they pass from one country to another and identify any major rivers they cross.

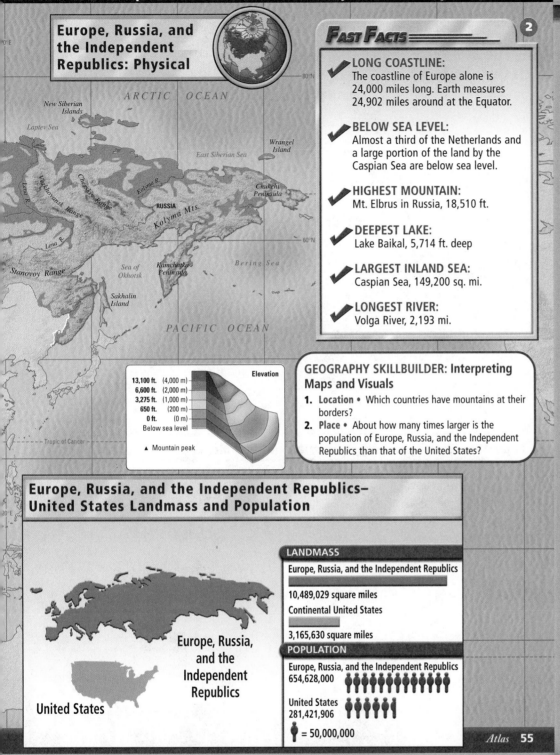

Europe, Russia, and the Independent Republics: Physical

FAST FACTS ❷

✔ **LONG COASTLINE:**
The coastline of Europe alone is 24,000 miles long. Earth measures 24,902 miles around at the Equator.

✔ **BELOW SEA LEVEL:**
Almost a third of the Netherlands and a large portion of the land by the Caspian Sea are below sea level.

✔ **HIGHEST MOUNTAIN:**
Mt. Elbrus in Russia, 18,510 ft.

✔ **DEEPEST LAKE:**
Lake Baikal, 5,714 ft. deep

✔ **LARGEST INLAND SEA:**
Caspian Sea, 149,200 sq. mi.

✔ **LONGEST RIVER:**
Volga River, 2,193 mi.

Elevation

13,100 ft.	(4,000 m)
6,600 ft.	(2,000 m)
3,275 ft.	(1,000 m)
650 ft.	(200 m)
0 ft.	(0 m)
Below sea level	

▲ Mountain peak

GEOGRAPHY SKILLBUILDER: Interpreting Maps and Visuals

1. **Location** • Which countries have mountains at their borders?
2. **Place** • About how many times larger is the population of Europe, Russia, and the Independent Republics than that of the United States?

Europe, Russia, and the Independent Republics– United States Landmass and Population

Europe, Russia, and the Independent Republics

United States

LANDMASS

Europe, Russia, and the Independent Republics
10,489,029 square miles

Continental United States
3,165,630 square miles

POPULATION

Europe, Russia, and the Independent Republics
654,628,000

United States
281,421,906

👤 = 50,000,000

INSTRUCT: Objective ❷

Climate of Europe, Russia, and the Independent Republics

• What kind of climate would you find east of the Caspian Sea? desert

Landmass

• About how many times larger are Europe, Russia, and the Independent Republics than the United States? about three and one-third times as large

Population

• What is the population of Europe, Russia, and the Independent Republics? 654,628,000 people

Fast Facts

• Is the coastline of Europe longer or shorter than the equator? By how much? shorter by 902 miles

MORE ABOUT...
Lake Baikal

At more than a mile deep, Lake Baikal is the deepest lake in the world. It is so deep that it holds more than 20 percent of the world's supply of fresh, unfrozen water. It is also an extremely old lake, dating back 25 million years. Many kinds of fish and other wildlife are found only in and around Lake Baikal.

Fast Facts

Urge students to begin their own Fast Facts file. They should add to it as they read the unit and by looking in sources such as almanacs and encyclopedias.

Geography Skillbuilder
Answers
1. Spain, France, Italy, Switzerland, Austria, Liechtenstein, Germany, Slovenia, Croatia, Bosnia and Herzegovina, Greece, Albania, Bulgaria, Romania, Russia, Kyrgyzstan
2. about two and one-third times

Country Profiles

The Netherlands The Netherlands is one of the world's smaller nations. It would be much smaller were it not for the hard work of generations of Dutch people. The North Sea, swamps, and lakes once covered more than 40 percent of the land. But the Netherlands is a crowded place, and the country has always needed more land for farms and people. The solution was simple: take the land from the sea. The Dutch would first build a dike around a section of sea or swamp and then drain it with pumps and canals. These new lands, called polders, are below the level of the sea. The Dutch must constantly battle with the sea to protect their land. Pumps run constantly to keep the polders dry. Once the pumps were powered by windmills. Today, electric pumps do the work. These polders are rich farmland. Dairy farming and dairy products are key components of the Netherlands economy.

INSTRUCT: Objective ❸

Political Map of Europe, Russia, and the Independent Republics

- What European countries border the Baltic Sea? Sweden, Finland, Russia, Estonia, Latvia, Lithuania, Poland, Germany, Denmark

- Approximately how far is Russia from its eastern to its most western border? about 5,000 miles

- What is the capital of Belarus? Minsk

MORE ABOUT...

The Caspian Sea

The Caspian Sea is the largest inland body of water in the world. It covers 149,200 square miles, an area larger than Japan and nearly five times the area of Lake Superior, the largest of the Great Lakes. Unlike Lake Superior, the Caspian Sea contains saltwater. In fact, it was once connected to the oceans by the Sea of Azov, the Black Sea, and the Mediterranean Sea. Because it is fed by freshwater rivers and is now isolated from the ocean, its salinity is only one-third that of the ocean.

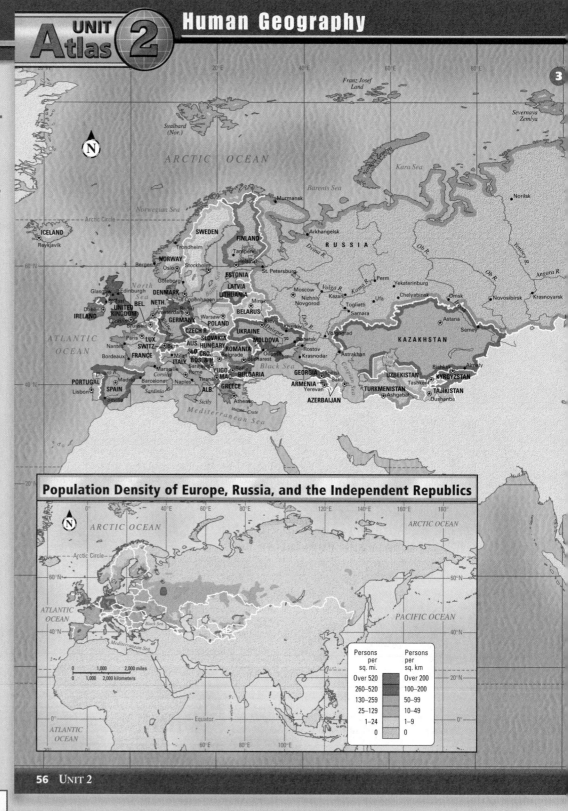

Activity Options

Interdisciplinary Link: Popular Culture

Class Time 20 minutes

Task Using a map scale and map to determine the actual size of countries

Purpose To use a map scale and map to learn about the size of

Europe, Russia, and the Independent Republics

Supplies Needed

- Paper and pencil
- Ruler

Activity Tell students that they represent a travel company and have been asked to test a new train route for tourists. They will begin in Madrid and visit many of the capitals of Europe, Russia, and the Independent Republics. From Madrid, they will go to Paris, Berlin, Vienna, Sarajevo, and Sofia. The train will swing north to Kiev and Moscow before turning south to Ashgabat in Turkmenistan. Have students calculate the number of miles they will travel. If the train travels 60 miles per hour, how long will the journey take?

Europe, Russia, and the Independent Republics: Political

New Siberian Islands

Laptev Sea

Wrangel Island

East Siberian Sea

Kolyma R.

RUSSIA

Lena R.

Yakutsk

Lena R.

Sea of Okhotsk

Bering Sea

Sakhalin Island

Petropavlovsk-Kamchatskiy

Khabarovsk

PACIFIC OCEAN

Vladivostok

Tropic of Cancer

	National boundary
★	National capital
•	Other city

0   500   1,000 miles
0   500   1,000 kilometers

FAST FACTS

✓ **SMALLEST COUNTRY IN THE WORLD:**
Vatican City, less than 0.2 sq. mi.

✓ **LARGEST COUNTRY IN THE WORLD:**
Russia, 6,592,800 sq. mi.

✓ **LONGEST ROAD TUNNEL:**
Oslo, Norway, 15.3 mi. long

✓ **OLDEST PAINTINGS:**
cave paintings near Verona, Italy, at 32,000 to 37,000 years of age

GEOGRAPHY SKILLBUILDER: Interpreting Maps and Visuals

1. **Location** • Name two countries that do not have seaports.
2. **Movement** • What route would you take to drive from Paris to Bern?

Road Map of Selected European Countries

Paris — A4, A4, N104, A11, A10, A5, Troyes, A31, A35, GERMANY, A5

Orléans — A6, A31, A38, Dijon, A36, A3, A1, A2

A10, FRANCE, A71, A5, Bern, SWITZERLAND, A12, A39, A1, Lausanne, A6, Geneva, A40, A72, Lyon, Chambéry, ITALY

0   25   50 miles
0   25   50 kilometers

★	National capital
•	Other city
—	Major road

Population Density and Road Map of Europe

- What is the population density near London, England? over 520 people per square mile
- What is the population density around Murmansk, Russia? between 1 and 24 people per square mile
- What would be the shortest route to take if you were driving from Troyes to Lyon, France? A31 to Dijon and N79 to Lyon

MORE ABOUT...
The Oldest Cave Paintings

Archaeologists have known about the Fumane Cave on a hill near Verona, Italy, for many years. Only recently, however, have they discovered that this cave may contain what may be the oldest cave paintings in the world. The paintings date back between 32,000 and 37,000 years. The images found are somewhat mysterious. They are painted in red on rock. One picture is of an animal, which may be a weasel or cat, with five legs. The other picture is of a human wearing a mask. The mask has horns, and archaeologists speculate that the picture may represent a wizard.

Fast Facts

Encourage students to continue adding details to their Fast Facts files as they do research and continue their reading.

Geography Skillbuilder
Possible Answers
1. include Switzerland, Czech Republic, Austria, Liechtenstein, Slovakia, Hungary, Macedonia, Belarus, Azerbaijan, Kazakhstan, Uzbekistan, Turkmenistan, Tajikistan, Kyrgyzstan.
2. A6 from Paris, A38 to Dijon, A36 to Basel, and 4 to Bern

Country Profiles

Vatican City Located on just 109 acres, Vatican City is the smallest independent nation in the world. It is the center of the Roman Catholic Church, and the Pope's home is located there. Vatican City is located in the middle of Rome on the bank of the Tiber River. In most ways, the city is completely independent. It has its own radio station, telephone and banking system, post office, gardens, and pharmacy. However, many essential supplies must be imported. These include food, water, gas, and electricity. Although Vatican City is a peaceful nation, it does require protection for the Pope and for its irreplaceable works of art. The need for protection is provided by Swiss Guards who have been on duty in the Vatican since 1506.

DATA FILE OBJECTIVE

1. Examine and compare data on Europe, Russia, and the Independent Republics

FOCUS & MOTIVATE

Which nation of Europe, Russia, and the Independent Republics has the highest rate of car ownership? Which has the highest birthrate? Tell students to scan the Data File to find the answers. car ownership: San Marino; highest birthrate: Uzbekistan Have students find these nations on the map on page 56.

INSTRUCT: Objective ⑤

Data File

• Which country has the fewest doctors per 100,000 people? Liechtenstein

• What is the official currency of Russia? ruble

• How does the life expectancy in Denmark compare with that of Uzbekistan? Denmark: 77 years; Uzbekistan: 69 years

 In-depth Resources: Unit 2
  • Data File Activities, p. 2

Country Flag	Country/Capital	Currency	Population (2001 estimate)	Life Expectancy (years)	Birthrate (per 1,000 pop.) (2000)
	Albania Tiranë	Lek	3,510,000	71	19
	Andorra Andorra la Vella	French Franc	68,000	83	11
	Armenia Yerevan	Dram	3,336,000	75	10
	Austria Vienna	Schilling/Euro*	8,151,000	78	10
	Azerbaijan Baku	Manat	7,771,000	70	15
	Belarus Minsk	Ruble	10,350,000	68	9
	Belgium Brussels	Franc/Euro*	10,259,000	78	11
	Bosnia-Herzegovina Sarajevo	Conv. Mark	3,922,000	73	.13
	Bulgaria Sofia	Lev	7,707,000	71	8
	Croatia Zagreb	Kuna	4,334,000	73	11
	Czech Republic Prague	Koruna	10,264,000	75	9
	Denmark Copenhagen	Danish Krone	5,353,000	77	12
	Estonia Tallinn	Kroon	1,423,000	70	8
	Finland Helsinki	Markka/Euro*	5,176,000	78	11
	France Paris	Franc/Euro*	59,551,000	79	13
	Georgia Tbilisi	Lavi	4,989,000	73	9
	Germany Berlin	Mark/Euro*	83,029,000	77	9

*On January 1, 2002, the euro became the common currency for 12 of the member nations of the European Union.

Activity Options

Multiple Learning Styles: Logical

Class Time 45 minutes

Task Determining relationships among data

Purpose To draw conclusions about countries in different parts of the region based on data

Activity Ask students to work in pairs and choose two countries from Europe, two Independent Republics formed from the former Soviet Union, and Russia. Have them create their own chart in which they compare life expectancy, infant mortality, numbers of doctors, and passenger cars per 1,000 people. Have students look for a relationship among these data. Then guide a class discussion. What conclusions have students drawn? What is the basis and reasoning for their conclusions?

DATA FILE

Infant Mortality (per 1,000 live births) (2000)	Doctors (per 100,000 pop.) (1990–1998)	Literacy Rate (percentage) (1991–1998)	Passenger Cars (per 1,000 pop.) (1996–1997)	Total Area (square miles)	Map (not to scale)
41.3	129	83	10 (1990)	11,100	
6.4	253	100	552	174	
41.0	316	98	2	11,506	
4.9	302	100	468	32,378	
83.0	360	99	36	33,436	
15.0	443	100	111	80,154	
5.6	395	99	434	11,787	
25.2	143	86	23	19,741	
14.9	345	98	202	42,822	
8.2	229	98	160	21,830	
4.6	303	99	428	30,448	
4.7	290	100	339	16,637	
13.0	297	99	294	17,413	
4.2	299	100	378	130,560	
4.8	303	99	437	212,934	
53.0	436	99	80	26,911	
4.7	350	100	504	137,830	

MORE ABOUT...
Quality of Life

The Soviet Union collapsed in 1991, and the wall dividing East and West Berlin was opened in 1989. Since then, data show that significant changes have occurred in the quality of life among people of the region. Record the following data on the chalkboard, and ask students to draw conclusions about changes that have occurred between Eastern and Western Europe following the breakup of the Soviet Union.

Germany

Life expectancy before 1991: 72

Life expectancy in 2000: 77

Cars per 1,000 people before 1991: 479

Cars per 1,000 people in 1997: 504

Poland

Life expectancy before 1991: 66

Life expectancy in 2000: 74

Cars per 1,000 people before 1991: 138

Cars per 1,000 people in 1997: 195

Slovenia

Life expectancy before 1991: 73

Life expectancy in 2000: 75

Cars per 1,000 people before 1991: 289

Cars per 1,000 people in 1997: 343

Activity Options

Differentiating Instruction: Gifted and Talented

Class Time Two class periods

Task Preparing a time line to depict the history of one republic

Purpose To learn about the history of the Independent Republics formed after the breakup of the Soviet Union

Supplies Needed
- Library and Internet resources
- Art supplies
- Computer

Activity Tell students that the Independent Republics formed after the collapse of the Soviet Union—nations such as Kazakhstan, Kyrgyzstan, Uzbekistan, and Tajikistan—have histories dating back thousands of years. Have students choose one country and explore its history. Ask them to prepare a time line to show major events. Then have them tell the story of these countries to the class.

MORE ABOUT...
Flags

Flags have special meanings to the people of the countries they fly over. Each color and symbol has a special meaning. The thirteen stars of the U.S. flag stand for the original states. The color white stands for innocence; red stands for valor; blue for vigilance and justice. Many Christian nations, such as Denmark and Switzerland, include a cross. Many Muslim nations, such as Turkmenistan, Azerbaijan, and Uzbekistan, include a crescent moon and star to symbolize life and peace. They may also use the colors black, green, red, and white to represent unity. The Star of David appears on Israel's flag.

Country Flag	Country/Capital	Currency	Population (2001 estimate)	Life Expectancy (years)	Birthrate (per 1,000 pop.) (2000)
	Greece Athens	Drachma/Euro*	10,624,000	78	10
	Hungary Budapest	Forint	10,106,000	71	9
	Iceland Reykjavik	Krona	278,000	80	15
	Ireland Dublin	Punt/Euro*	3,841,000	76	15
	Italy Rome	Lira/Euro*	57,680,000	78	9
	Kazakhstan Astana	Tenge	16,731,000	65	14
	Kyrgyzstan Bishkek	Som	4,753,000	67	22
	Latvia Riga	Lat	2,385,000	70	8
	Liechtenstein Vaduz	Franc/Euro*	33,000	73	14
	Lithuania Vilnius	Litas	3,611,000	72	10
	Luxembourg Luxembourg	Lux. Franc	443,000	77	13
	Macedonia Skopje	Denar	2,046,000	73	15
	Malta Valletta	Lira	395,000	77	12
	Moldova Chisinau	Leu	4,432,000	67	11
	Monaco Monaco	French Franc	32,000	79	20
	Netherlands Amsterdam	Guilder/Euro*	15,981,000	78	13
	Norway Oslo	Krone	4,503,000	79	13

*On January 1, 2002, the euro became the common currency for 12 of the member nations of the European Union.

Activity Options

Differentiating Instruction: Citizenship Activities

Class Time One class period

Task Creating a flag to represent a school or community

Purpose To think about the symbolism of flags

Supplies Needed
- Colored markers, pencils, or crayons
- Art paper

Activity Explain to students that they have been asked to create a flag to represent their school or community. Have them think about the most important ideas or qualities of their school or community. What makes it special? Why are they proud to live in their community? What do they hope their community can become? Then have them create symbols and assemble them into a flag that will represent their school or community. Have them draw the flags on art paper and display them in the room. Provide opportunities for them to explain the meaning of their flags.

DATA FILE

Infant Mortality (per 1,000 live births) (2000)	Doctors (per 100,000 pop.) (1990–1998)	Literacy Rate (percentage) (1991–1998)	Passenger Cars (per 1,000 pop.) (1996–1997)	Total Area (square miles)	Map (not to scale)
6.7	392	97	223	50,950	
8.9	357	99	222	35,919	
4.0	326	100	489	39,768	
6.2	219	100	292	27,135	
5.5	554	98	540	116,320	
59.0	353	99	61	1,048,300	
77.0	301	97	32	76,641	
16.0	282	100	174	24,595	
5.1	100	100	592 (1993)	62	
15.0	395	100	242	25,174	
5.0	272	100	515	999	
16.3	204	89	132	9,927	
5.3	261	91	321	124	
43.0	400 (1995)	99	46	13,012	
5.9	664	100	548	0.6	
5.0	251	100	372	16,033	
4.0	413	100	399	125,050	

MORE ABOUT...
Currency

Explain that some cultures did not have money. Instead, they traded for the things they wanted. Ask students to consider how convenient it might be to trade a cow for some cloth, especially if the owner of the cloth did not want a cow. People began using money because it has a definite value. If the cow is worth 50 dollars and the cloth is worth 20, what would you do? If you pay in money, the exchange is easy. You can also save the money; it will be worth as much next year as it is today. Of course, money itself is of no real value. The paper it is printed on or the metals it is made from have little real value. Their value comes from the agreement among people of a society that each coin or piece of currency has a certain value.

Activity Options

Multiple Learning Styles: Logical/Mathematical

Class Time 30 minutes

Task Creating a table to aid in estimating population density of six countries

Purpose To compare the population density of different countries

Activity Working independently, have students choose six countries from the Data File that have high populations. Then ask them to create a table with three columns and six rows. They should label the first column *country*, the second column *population*, and the third column *population density*. Have them fill out the first two columns with information from the Data File. Then have them turn to the population density map on page 56. Based on the map and on the key provided, have them estimate the population density of the six countries. Are they surprised at the results?

MORE ABOUT...
Census

Nations have been taking censuses for thousands of years. Ancient Rome was among the first. Its interest in people and property had mainly to do with taxation and military service. Modern census-taking for the purpose of learning about how people live, their longevity, how much they earn, and what they do, for example, began in the 17th century. The first census of an entire nation took place in Canada in 1665. Sweden followed in 1749, Italy in 1770, and the United States in 1790. Today, most industrialized nations conduct a census every five or ten years. Census-taking remains an uncertain science, however. People move around and are hard to find, so many do not get counted. In South America, the government sends helicopters to survey the rain forest, looking for homes. In some cities, thousands of people live on the street and may never be counted.

Country Flag	Country/Capital	Currency	Population (2001 estimate)	Life Expectancy (years)	Birthrate (per 1,000 pop.) (2000)
	Poland Warsaw	Zloty	38,634,000	74	10
	Portugal Lisbon	Escudo/Euro*	10,066,000	76	11
	Romania Bucharest	Leu	22,364,000	70	11
	Russia Moscow	Ruble	145,470,000	67	8
	San Marino San Marino	Italian Lira	27,000	80	11
	Slovakia Bratislava	Koruna	5,415,000	73	11
	Slovenia Ljubljana	Tolar	1,930,000	75	9
	Spain Madrid	Peseta/Euro*	40,038,000	78	9
	Sweden Stockholm	Krona	8,875,000	80	10
	Switzerland Bern	Franc	7,283,000	80	11
	Tajikistan Dushanbe	Ruble	6,579,000	68	21
	Turkmenistan Ashgabat	Manat	4,603,000	66	21
	Ukraine Kiev	Hryvnya	48,760,000	68	8
	United Kingdom London	Pound	59,648,000	77	12
	Uzbekistan Tashkent	Som	25,155,000	69	23
	Vatican City Vatican City	Vatican Lira/Italian Lira	870 (2000)	N/A	N/A
	Yugoslavia Belgrade	New Dinar	10,677,000	73	11

*On January 1, 2002, the euro became the common currency for 12 of the member nations of the European Union.

Activity Options
Multiple Learning Styles: Visual

Class Time One class period

Task Drawing an important building or monument

Purpose To learn about a capital city in Europe, Russia, or the Independent Republics

Supplies Needed
- Encyclopedia, Internet, or other information sources
- Art supplies

Activity Point out to students that a country's capital is always special. It has unique buildings for its leaders and monuments to recognize accomplishments of the people. Have students select one of the capital cities listed in the Data File and do research to learn about one important building or monument that makes the city special. Ask students to make a drawing of the building or monument. Have them share their drawings and tell what is important about the building or monument.

DATA FILE ⑤

Infant Mortality (per 1,000 live births) (2000)	Doctors (per 100,000 pop.) (1990–1998)	Literacy Rate (percentage) (1991–1998)	Passenger Cars (per 1,000 pop.) (1996–1997)	Total Area (square miles)	Map (not to scale)
8.9	236	99	195	124,807	
6.0	312	91	295	35,514	
20.5	184	98	106	92,042	
20.0	421	100	120	6,592,812	
8.8	252	99	955	23	
8.8	353	100	185	18,923	
5.2	228	99	343	7,819	
5.7	424	97	384	195,363	
3.5	311	100	417	173,730	
4.8	323	100	460	15,942	
117.0	201	99	31	55,251	
73.0	300 (1997)	98	N/A	188,455	
22.0	299	100	97	233,089	
5.7	164	100	434	94,548	
72.0	309	88	37	173,591	
N/A	N/A	100	N/A	0.17	
10.4	203	98	173	39,448	

GEOGRAPHY SKILLBUILDER: Interpreting a Chart
1. **Place •** Which country in the region has the highest life expectancy?
2. **Place •** How many fewer cars per thousand people does Greece have than Germany?

Atlas **63**

MORE ABOUT...
Life Expectancy

Life expectancy is a means of measuring how long people of a particular age can expect to live. Students should be aware that life expectancy is based on many factors, including health care, nutrition, physical condition, heredity, and occupation. Typically, more highly industrialized nations have higher life expectancies than poor countries. This may be because of a higher standard of living that permits better and more frequent health care, better food, and safer working conditions. It is also true that in most countries, women have a longer life expectancy than men.

Geography Skillbuilder
Answers
1. Andorra with a life expectancy of 83 years
2. 281 fewer cars per thousand people

Activity Options

Interdisciplinary Links: Science/Health

Class Time One class period

Task Researching and preparing a line graph showing changes in life expectancy

Purpose To learn how life expectancy has changed

Supplies Needed
• Library or Internet resources
• Pencil or pen
• Graph paper

Block Scheduling

Activity Have students do research to learn about life expectancy since 1900. Students might research life expectancy in the United States or in one of the other nations listed in the Data File. Have students plot their findings on a line graph. Invite them to share what they learn with the class.

Western Europe: Its Land and Early History

	OVERVIEW	COPYMASTERS	INTEGRATED TECHNOLOGY
UNIT ATLAS AND CHAPTER RESOURCES	The students will explore the geography of Europe, the lasting achievements of the ancient Greek and Roman civilizations, and developments in Europe during the medieval period.	**In-depth Resources: Unit 2** • Guided Reading Worksheets, pp. 3–6 • Skillbuilder Practice, p. 9 • Unit Atlas Activities, pp. 1–2 • Geography Workshop, pp. 61–62 **Reading Study Guide** (Spanish and English), pp. 16–25 **Outline Map Activities**	Power Presentations Electronic Teacher Tools Online Lesson Planner Chapter Summaries on CD Critical Thinking Transparencies CT5

	KEY IDEAS		
SECTION 1 A Land of Varied Riches pp. 67–71	• Geographical features of Europe contributed to the development of different cultures. • Europe's temperate climate benefits its agricultural and tourist industries. • The natural resources of Europe affect what it produces today.	**In-depth Resources: Unit 2** • Guided Reading Worksheet, p. 3 • Reteaching Activity, p. 11 **Reading Study Guide** (Spanish and English), pp. 16–17	Map Transparencies MT14, 15 classzone.com Chapter Summaries on CD
SECTION 2 Ancient Greece pp. 72–76	• Greek city-states differed in forms of government, but shared common beliefs and a way of life. • Democracy was first practiced in sixth-century Greece. • Greek culture spread across Europe through military conquests.	**In-depth Resources: Unit 2** • Guided Reading Worksheet, p. 4 • Reteaching Activity, p. 12 **Reading Study Guide** (Spanish and English), pp. 18–19	classzone.com Chapter Summaries on CD
SECTION 3 Ancient Rome pp. 78–83	• Rome became a republic in 509 B.C., but the lives of patricians and plebeians were very different. • The Roman Empire expanded under Julius Caesar and Augustus. • After initial persecution by the Romans, Christianity became the official religion of the Roman Empire.	**In-depth Resources: Unit 2** • Guided Reading Worksheet, p. 5 • Reteaching Activity, p. 13 **Reading Study Guide** (Spanish and English), pp. 20–21	Critical Thinking Transparencies CT6 classzone.com Chapter Summaries on CD
SECTION 4 Time of Change: The Middle Ages pp. 84–89	• The fall of the Roman Empire brought rapid decline to most of Europe. • The Roman Catholic Church was a central part of life in the Middle Ages. • Nobles and peasants benefited from feudalism and manorialism differently.	**In-depth Resources: Unit 2** • Guided Reading Worksheet, p. 6 • Reteaching Activity, p. 14 **Reading Study Guide** (Spanish and English), pp. 22–23	classzone.com Chapter Summaries on CD

KEY TO RESOURCES

 Audio

 Internet

 Teacher's Edition

CD-ROM

Overhead Transparency

Video

Copymaster

PE Pupil's Edition

ASSESSMENT OPTIONS

PE **Chapter Assessment,** pp. 90–91

Formal Assessment
• Chapter Tests: Forms A, B, C, pp. 37–48

Test Generator

Online Test Practice

Strategies for Test Preparation

PE **Section Assessment,** p. 71

Formal Assessment
• Section Quiz, p. 33

Integrated Assessment
• Rubric for writing a short story

Test Generator

Test Practice Transparencies TT5

PE **Section Assessment,** p. 76

Formal Assessment
• Section Quiz, p. 34

Integrated Assessment
• Rubric for presenting an oral report

Test Generator

Test Practice Transparencies TT6

PE **Section Assessment,** p. 83

Formal Assessment
• Section Quiz, p. 35

Integrated Assessment
• Rubric for creating a comparison chart

Test Generator

Test Practice Transparencies TT7

PE **Section Assessment,** p. 89

Formal Assessment
• Section Quiz, p. 36

Integrated Assessment
• Rubric for writing journal entries

Test Generator

Test Practice Transparencies TT8

 ## RESOURCES FOR DIFFERENTIATING INSTRUCTION

Students Acquiring English/ESL

Reading Study Guide (Spanish and English), pp. 16–25

Access for Students Acquiring English Spanish Translations, pp. 13–22

Less Proficient Readers

Reading Study Guide (Spanish and English), pp. 16–25

TE **TE Activities**
• Rereading, p. 68
• Understanding Key Concepts, p. 86

Gifted and Talented Students

TE **TE Activity**
• Researching a Historical Figure, p. 75

 ## CROSS-CURRICULAR CONNECTIONS

Humanities
Hart, Avery, and Paul Mantell. *Knights and Castles: 50 Hands-On Activities to Experience the Middle Ages.* Charlotte, VT: Williamson Publishing, 1998. Games, celebrations, food, and customs.

Stroud, Jonathan. *Ancient Rome: A Guide to the Glory of Imperial Rome.* New York: Kingfisher, 2000. Ancient Rome in a travel guide format.

Literature
Spires, Elizabeth. *I Am Arachne: Fifteen Greek and Roman Myths.* New York: Farrar, Straus & Giroux, 2001. First-person retellings.

Popular Culture
Connolly, Peter, and Hazel Dodge. *The Ancient City: Life in Classical Athens and Rome.* London: Oxford University Press, 2000. Detailed illustrations and descriptions.

Copeland, Tim. *Ancient Greece.* Cambridge, UK: Cambridge University Press, 1998. Uses the Olympic Games as a method of exploring the ancient world.

Science/Math
Nardo, Don. *Roman Roads and Aqueducts.* San Diego, CA: Lucent Books, 2001. Engineering feats of ancient Rome.

Language Arts/Literature
Cushman, Karen. *Catherine, Called Birdy.* New York: Harper, 1995. Spirited fictional diary of a young noblewoman in medieval England.

ENRICHMENT ACTIVITIES

The following activities are especially suitable for classes following block schedules.

Teacher's Edition, pp. 70, 75, 77, 81, 82, 87
Pupil's Edition, pp. 71, 76, 83, 89

Unit Atlas, pp. 54–63

Outline Map Activities

 ## INTEGRATED TECHNOLOGY

Go to **classzone.com** for lesson support and activities for Chapter 3.

BLOCK SCHEDULE LESSON PLAN OPTIONS: 90-MINUTE PERIOD

DAY 1

UNIT PREVIEW, pp. 52–53
Class Time 20 minutes

- **Discussion** Discuss the objective for Chapter 3 on TE p. 64.

UNIT ATLAS, pp. 54–63
Class Time 20 minutes

- **Small Groups** Divide the class into five groups and have each group answer the questions designated for each Unit Atlas objective.

SECTION 1, pp. 67–71
Class Time 50 minutes

- **Small Groups** Divide the class into three groups. Assign each group one of the following headings: "The Geography of Europe," "Climate," and "Natural Resources." Have students turn their headings into a question, then read to find out the answer to their question. Reconvene as a whole class to discuss the answers.
Class Time 30 minutes

- **Understanding Climate** Use the maps from the Activity Option on TE p. 69 to help students understand how landforms affect climate. Have students identify the location of the Alps and the Pyrenees and draw them on their maps. Ask students to use arrows to show the direction of the wind that blows southward from the Arctic Circle. Discuss with students the effects of the mountains on the region's climate.
Class Time 20 minutes

DAY 2

SECTION 2, pp. 72–76
Class Time 50 minutes

- **Small Groups** Divide students into groups of three to four. Have them skim the section for information on the achievements of the ancient Greeks and fill in the chart in the Section Assessment on PE p. 76. Review the chart with the class.
Class Time 25 minutes

- **Peer Teaching** After reading aloud Strange but True on TE p. 74, ask a panel of four students to debate the following question: Are Spartan virtues important in today's world? Have the rest of the class act as debate judges, deciding which speakers make the most convincing arguments.
Class Time 25 minutes

SECTION 3, pp. 78–83
Class Time 40 minutes

- **Creating a Time Line** Lead the class in creating a time line on the board that traces the development of ancient Rome from its early beginnings.
Class Time 20 minutes

- **Summarizing** Have students use the Terms & Names to write a summary of the section.
Class Time 20 minutes

DAY 3

SECTION 4, pp. 84–89
Class Time 35 minutes

- **Hypothesizing** Use the Critical Thinking Activity on TE p. 85 as a starting point to discuss why the church played such an important role in medieval life.
Class Time 10 minutes

- **Role-Playing** Have pairs of students create a pantomine depicting a feudal relationship. Ask for volunteers to perform their pantomine in front of the class. Have the rest of the class guess what social groups are being portrayed.
Class Time 25 minutes

CHAPTER 3 REVIEW AND ASSESSMENT, pp. 90–91
Class Time 55 minutes

- **Review** Divide students into pairs. Using the Visual Summary on PE p. 90, have students provide two supporting details for each statement.
Class Time 20 minutes

- **Assessment** Have students complete the Chapter 3 Assessment.
Class Time 35 minutes

TECHNOLOGY IN THE CLASSROOM

The Web lends itself to student research because of the availability of Web sites with valuable, up-to-date information, including text and pictures. However, the Web also contains many sites that are not up-to-date or that have irrelevant, erroneous, or inappropriate information. One way to ensure that students use appropriate Web sites is to have them look through a limited set of preselected sites. Students should be given a list of sites sponsored by organizations that are generally considered reliable, such as major news sources, television networks, nonprofit organizations, or museums. This will save a good deal of classroom time, and students will be less likely to contact sites that are inappropriate.

ACTIVITY OUTLINE

Objective Students will use the Internet to research daily life in ancient Greece and Rome. They will use a word processing program to create paragraphs describing what they have learned.

Task Ask students to visit Web sites to gather information about ancient Greek and Roman housing, clothing, food, family life, recreation, education, business and work, holidays, and religion. Have them discuss their findings and write paragraphs from the point of view of ancient Greeks and Romans. Suggest that they write additional paragraphs describing some of the things the Romans borrowed from the Greeks.

Class Time 2–3 class periods

DIRECTIONS

1. Ask students what they think it would have been like to live in ancient Greece and Rome. List their ideas, and discuss why the Romans might have borrowed some ideas from Greek culture.

2. Have students make charts with two columns, one labeled "Ancient Greece" and the other labeled "Ancient Rome."

3. Have students visit the Web sites at **classzone.com** to find out what life was like in ancient Greece and Rome. As they explore the sites, have them take notes on features of daily life such as housing, clothing, food, family life, recreation, education, business and work, holidays, and religion.

4. As a class discuss these questions:

   • What were the major similarities and differences between daily life in ancient Greece and Rome?

   • What did the Romans borrow from the Greeks?

5. Have students choose one aspect of daily life to focus on. Ask each student to assume the role of a person from ancient Greece, and use a word processing program to write a one-paragraph story describing this aspect of their life. Then have them write an additional one-paragraph story describing the same aspect of life from the point of view of a person from ancient Rome. If time permits, encourage students to illustrate their stories.

6. Finally, ask students to write a final paragraph in which they name an item, custom, or skill the Romans borrowed from the Greeks. They should include what this meant to each civilization.

CHAPTER 3 OBJECTIVE

Students will explore the geography of Europe, the lasting achievements of the ancient Greek and Roman civilizations, and developments in Europe during the medieval period.

FOCUS ON VISUALS

Interpreting the Photograph Have students look at the photograph of Segovia, Spain, and identify the castle and arches of the Roman aqueduct. Point out that the aqueduct probably was built in about A.D. 100, at least 1,000 years before the castle was built. This chapter focuses on the early history of Western Europe. What do these two structures show about that history?

Possible Responses They show that the history of Europe extends many centuries back in time, with different cultures following one another.

Extension Have students look up the word *aqueduct* in an encyclopedia to discover the original purpose of aqueducts and how they are used today.

CRITICAL THINKING ACTIVITY

Hypothesizing Prompt a discussion about why the history of Europe is so important to people in our country. Guide students to consider where many of our ancestors came from, where our language and many of our customs originated, how the political systems in our country and Europe are similar, and other ways in which our country is connected culturally and politically to Europe.

Class Time 10 minutes

CHAPTER
3

Western Europe: Its Land and Early History

SECTION 1   A Land of Varied Riches

SECTION 2   Ancient Greece

SECTION 3   Ancient Rome

SECTION 4   Time of Change: The Middle Ages

Region Many European cities show their history in their architecture. In Segovia, Spain, an ancient Roman aqueduct lies below the walls of a castle built in the Middle Ages.

64

Recommended Resources

BOOKS FOR THE TEACHER
Gies, Frances and Joseph. *Life in a Medieval City*. New York: HarperCollins, 1981. Authoritative resource with a companion volume, *Life in a Medieval Village*.
Rees, Rosemary. *The Ancient Romans*. Des Plaines, IL: Heinemann Library, 1999. Examination of social, economic, political, and cultural life.

VIDEOS
Ancient Greece. Wynnewood, PA: Schlessinger Media, 1998. Explore the mysteries of ancient Greece, including a visit to the Acropolis.

SOFTWARE
The Romans. Library Video Company, 1998. Construct a mosaic, view clothing, explore mythology, and more.

INTERNET
For more information about Europe, visit **classzone.com**.

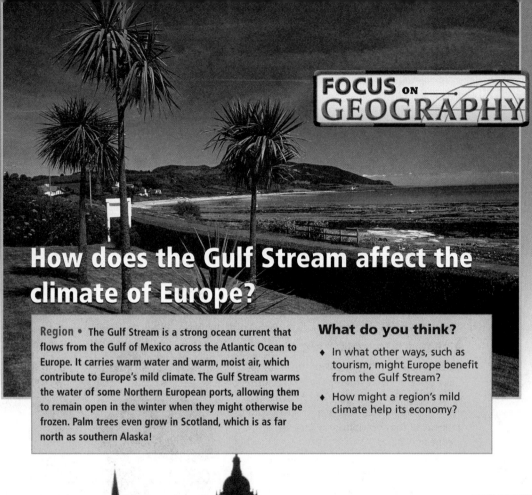

FOCUS ON GEOGRAPHY

How does the Gulf Stream affect the climate of Europe?

Region • The Gulf Stream is a strong ocean current that flows from the Gulf of Mexico across the Atlantic Ocean to Europe. It carries warm water and warm, moist air, which contribute to Europe's mild climate. The Gulf Stream warms the water of some Northern European ports, allowing them to remain open in the winter when they might otherwise be frozen. Palm trees even grow in Scotland, which is as far north as southern Alaska!

What do you think?

♦ In what other ways, such as tourism, might Europe benefit from the Gulf Stream?

♦ How might a region's mild climate help its economy?

65

FOCUS ON GEOGRAPHY

Objectives

• To help students understand how geography affects climate in Europe

• To show a relationship between climate and the economy

What Do You Think?

1. Point out that a moderate climate extends the season when people want to visit a country, sightsee, or take part in outdoor sports. Have them speculate whether it is easier for cultures to develop and prosper in a moderate climate rather than in one that is either extremely hot or frigid.

2. Students should understand that economy refers to both the goods and services produced in a region and how those goods are produced. Help students to recognize how climate affects the ability to raise crops and the ease with which people and goods move from one region to another.

How does the Gulf Stream affect the climate of Europe?

Help students understand that the Gulf Stream brings warm water from the Gulf of Mexico across the ocean, making Europe's climate milder than that of other places at the same latitude.

MAKING GEOGRAPHIC CONNECTIONS

Ask students to think about how climate affects people in Africa, Latin America, and Antarctica. Discuss how the lives of people living in these places might differ from those of people living in Europe because of climate.

Implementing the National Geography Standards

Standard 3 Describe and analyze the spatial arrangement of urban land-use patterns

Objective To build a scale model of the students' local community

Class Time 40 minutes

Task Invite students to work together to build a scale model of their community, indicating the commercial, residential, and industrial areas.

After the model is built, have each student refer to the model to write an explanation of the distribution of these three types of land use in the community.

Evaluation In their explanations of the three types of land use, students should mention local landforms and transportation routes.

BEFORE YOU READ

What Do You Know?

Poll students to see how many of them have ever been to Europe, have relatives from Europe, or are themselves European-born. Have them describe what they know about the Continent from visits, relatives, or personal experience. Ask whether they have seen any sports events on television that took place in Europe or read any books set in Europe. Have them describe their impressions of Europe from these sources. How might Europe differ from the United States?

What Do You Want to Know?

Suggest that students make a three-column chart with the headings *Ancient Greece, Ancient Rome,* and *Middle Ages.* Have them work in pairs to write what they want to know about each topic. After the students have taken notes, have volunteers read their notes aloud. Ask students to note on their charts any additional items that interest them about each topic. They can add to their charts as they read each section.

READ AND TAKE NOTES

Reading Strategy: Categorizing Categorizing facts and details in a meaningful way can help students identify similarities and differences across cultures and time periods. Point out that they might use this strategy to categorize other topics in the chapter.

 In-depth Resources: Unit 2
• Guided Reading Worksheets, pp. 3–6

BEFORE YOU READ

▶▶ *What Do You Know?*

Before you read the chapter, think about what you already know about Europe. What are some of its geographical features? What do you know about its early history? Have you ever read myths from ancient Greece or ancient Rome? Have you ever heard of Julius Caesar or Hercules? What do you know about knights and castles from the Middle Ages?

▶▶ *What Do You Want to Know?*

Decide what you want to know about these early periods of European history. Record your questions in your notebook before you read this chapter.

Region • Ancient Greece made important contributions in literature, philosophy, and architecture. ▼

READ AND TAKE NOTES

Reading Strategy: Categorizing One way to make sense of what you read is to categorize, or sort, information. Making a chart to categorize the information in this chapter will help you to understand the contributions made by early European cultures.

• Copy the chart below into your notebook.
• As you read, look for information relating to the categories of social structure, architecture, religion, and arts and sciences.
• Write your notes under the appropriate headings.

Region • The Middle Ages saw the rise of the Catholic Church and the growth of a middle class. ▲

Region • Ancient Rome made its mark in government, law, and engineering. ▲

Time Period	Social Structure	Architecture	Religion	Arts and Sciences
Ancient Greece	city-states, oligarchy, democracy, government participation limited to free, adult males	built temples atop the Acropolis, the Parthenon	shared religious beliefs within city-states, honored gods and goddesses through literature	myths, poems, plays, philosophy, architecture
Ancient Rome	republic, senate, patricians, plebeians, empire	public buildings, lighthouses	different religious beliefs, rise of Christianity	great literature, Aeneid
Middle Ages	no central government, feudalism, manorialism, growth of towns, guilds	castles	Catholicism, church became center of community, clash between government and church	the Bayeux Tapestry

---

Teaching Strategy

Reading the Chapter This is a thematic chapter that focuses on how the development of Europe's diverse cultures has been affected by geographic features and the contributions of the ancient Greeks and Romans, as well as how the events of the Middle Ages transformed Europe into a modern society. As students read about each period, encourage them to think about the system of government in place and about how much economic freedom individuals had.

Integrated Assessment The Chapter Assessment on page 91 describes several activities that can be used for integrated assessment. You may wish to have students work on these activities during the course of the chapter and then present them at the end.

SECTION 1

A Land of Varied Riches

TERMS & NAMES
Mediterranean Sea
peninsula
fjord
Ural Mountains
plain

MAIN IDEA

Europe is a continent with varied geographic features, abundant natural resources, and a climate that can support agriculture.

WHY IT MATTERS NOW

The development of Europe's diverse cultures has been shaped by the continent's diverse geography.

DATELINE
EXTRA

LONDON, ENGLAND, MAY 6, 1994

Rough waters have always made the English Channel, which separates England and France, difficult to cross. Now, however, you can make the trip under the water! Today, a tunnel nicknamed "the Chunnel" opens, allowing high-speed trains to travel between London and Paris in about three hours. The Chunnel—short for Channel Tunnel—was carved through chalky earth under the sea floor and took seven years to build. It is the largest European construction project of the 20th century.

Movement • Eurostar trains make the 31-mile trip under the English Channel in only 20 minutes. ▲

Chunnel

England

English Channel

France

Location • The Channel Tunnel connects England and France. ▲

The Geography of Europe ❶

Today, cars, airplanes, and trains are common forms of high-speed transportation across Europe. Before the 19th century, however, the fastest form of transportation was to travel by water—on top of it, rather than under it.

Western Europe: Its Land and Early History **67**

SECTION OBJECTIVES

1. To describe Europe's geography
2. To describe factors affecting Europe's climate
3. To explain how Europe's natural resources affect what it produces today

SKILLBUILDER
• Interpreting a Map, p. 71

CRITICAL THINKING
• Making Inferences, p. 68
• Generalizing, p. 69

FOCUS & MOTIVATE
WARM-UP

Making Inferences Have students read Dateline and encourage them to think about how transportation has changed since ancient times.

1. What are some advantages of the Chunnel?
2. How might improvements in transportation affect economic development?

INSTRUCT: Objective ❶

The Geography of Europe

• What are the distinctive features of Europe's geography? oceans, rivers, peninsulas, mountain ranges, central plain
• What geographical feature of Europe influenced the development of different cultures? Mountain ranges separated groups of people from one another as they settled.
• What is an important feature of the Great European Plain? rich farmland

 In-depth Resources: Unit 2
• Guided Reading Worksheet, p. 3

 Reading Study Guide
(Spanish and English), pp. 16–17

Program Resources

 In-depth Resources: Unit 2
• Guided Reading Worksheet, p. 3
• Reteaching Activity, p. 11

 Reading Study Guide
(Spanish and English), pp. 16–17

 Formal Assessment
• Section Quiz, p. 33

 Integrated Assessment
• Rubric for writing a story

 Outline Map Activities

 Access for Students Acquiring English
• Guided Reading Worksheet, p. 13

 Technology Resources
classzone.com

TEST-TAKING RESOURCES
↯ Strategies for Test Preparation
↯ Test Practice Transparencies
🌐 Online Test Practice

CRITICAL THINKING ACTIVITY

Making Inferences Using the map on page 71 or in the Unit Atlas, draw students' attention to the lengthy coastlines of many European countries. Ask them to infer how this access to water, plus the number of great inland rivers, might affect the history of nations and civilizations. Encourage them to consider such factors as trade, warfare and defense, ways of making a living, and the spread of skills and ideas.

Class Time 15 minutes

MORE ABOUT...
Peninsulas

Europe has sometimes been described as "a peninsula of peninsulas." Other peninsulas jutting into the Mediterranean Sea are the Italian Peninsula, the Balkan or Greek Peninsula, and Asia Minor (Turkey). The strategically located Crimean Peninsula, which extends into the Black Sea from southern Ukraine, is also historically important. The word *peninsula* comes from the Latin words for "almost" *(paene)* and "island" *(insula)*.

Reading Social Studies
A. Possible Answer
Before the 1800s, it was easier and quicker to travel by water than over land.

Waterways Look at the map of Europe on page 71. Water surrounds the continent to the north, south, and west. The southern coast of Europe borders the warm waters of the **Mediterranean Sea.** Europe also has many rivers. The highly traveled Rhine and Danube rivers are two of the most important. The Volga, which flows nearly 2,200 miles through western Russia, is the continent's longest. For hundreds of years, these and other waterways have been home to boats and barges carrying people and goods inland across great distances.

Landforms Several large **peninsulas,** or bodies of land surrounded by water on three sides, form the European continent. In Northern Europe, the Scandinavian Peninsula is home to Norway and Sweden. Along the jagged shoreline of this peninsula are beautiful fjords (fyawrdz). A **fjord** is a long, narrow, deep inlet of the sea located between steep cliffs. In Western Europe, the Iberian Peninsula includes Portugal and Spain. The Iberian Peninsula is separated from the rest of the continent by a mountain range called the Pyrenees (PEER·uh·neez). The entire continent of Europe, itself surrounded by water on three sides, is a giant peninsula.

Reading
Social Studies
A. Clarifying Why were waterways important for the movement of people and goods?

BACKGROUND

Europe can be divided into four areas: Western Europe, Northern Europe, Eastern Europe, and Russia and its neighboring countries.

Place • The Scandinavian Peninsula is the location of many spectacular fjords, such as this one in Norway. ▶

Activity Options

Differentiating Instruction: Less Proficient Readers

Rereading To ensure that less proficient readers are able to pick out important details from the text, ask them to reread the section on the geography of Europe. Then have them write answers to questions such as those in the next column.

• What sea forms the southern border of Europe?
• What is a fjord?
• What is a peninsula?
• What countries in Northern Europe are located on the Scandinavian Peninsula?

Place • The Alps remain snowcapped year-round. ▶

B. Clarifying
What natural landform separates Europe from Asia?

Reading Social Studies
B. Answer
the Ural Mountains

Mountain ranges, including the towering Alps, also stretch across much of the continent. Along Europe's eastern border, the **Ural Mountains** (YUR·uhl) divide the continent from Asia. The many mountain ranges of Europe separated groups of people from one another as they settled the land thousands of years ago. This is one of the reasons why different cultures developed across the continent.

The Great European Plain Not all of Europe is mountainous. A vast region called the Great European Plain stretches from the coast of France to the Ural Mountains. A **plain** is a large, flat area of land, usually without many trees. The Great European Plain is the location of some of the world's richest farmland. Ancient trading centers attracted many people to this area, which today includes some of the largest cities in Europe—Paris, Berlin, Warsaw, and Moscow.

Climate ❷

Although the Gulf Stream brings warm air and water to Europe, the winters are still severe in the mountains and in the far north. In some of these areas, cold winds blow southward from the Arctic Circle and make the average temperature fall below 0°F in January. The Alps and the Pyrenees, however, protect the European countries along the Mediterranean Sea from these chilling winds. In these warmer parts of southern Europe, the average temperature in January stays above 50°F.

Western Europe: Its Land and Early History **69**

INSTRUCT: Objective ❷

Climate

• What are the average January and July temperatures in southern Europe? January: above 50°F; July: about 80°F
• Why is the Mediterranean coast a popular vacation spot? has hot, dry summers

CRITICAL THINKING ACTIVITY

Generalizing Provide students with the average summer and winter temperatures for five cities in North America and five cities located at about the same latitudes in Europe. Then ask students to make generalizations concerning climate and latitude based on the data about the climates on the two continents.

Class Time 10 minutes

MORE ABOUT...
The Ural Mountains

Although the Urals mark the traditional boundary between Europe and Asia, they are relatively low-lying mountains. The rugged range stretches about 1,500 miles north-south across Russia, from Arctic tundra in the north to deserts north of the Caspian Sea in Kazakhstan. The highest peaks are in the north. The foothills of the range slope westward toward the Volga River. In the east, the land drops to the lowlands of western Siberia.

Activity Options

Multiple Learning Styles: Visual

Class Time 30 minutes

Task Identifying access to major oceans and seas

Purpose To explore the importance of a country's location in relation to a major sea or ocean

Supplies Needed
• Photocopies of a map of Europe showing current national boundaries and country names
• Colored pencils

Activity Distribute copies of the map of Europe. Have students use pencils of one color to identify countries on the Mediterranean Sea and pencils of another color to identify countries on the North Sea. Then have students use a third color to identify all remaining countries on the Atlantic Ocean. When they have finished, ask students to identify the countries that do not have ocean access.

Teacher's Edition **69**

INSTRUCT: Objective ❸

Natural Resources

- What are some of Europe's mineral resources? coal and iron ore
- What factors make Europe a good place to grow crops? rich soil, plentiful rainfall, moderate temperatures

FOCUS ON VISUALS

Interpreting the Photographs Have students examine the photographs and point out details that demonstrate the variety of resources and landforms in different regions of Western Europe. Ask them to identify the natural resources shown and explain how humans are using these different environments and interacting with them.

Possible Responses Forests, mountains, oceans, grazing land. The sheep are grazing on hillsides that are probably too steep to farm; factories use natural resources and energy.

Extension Ask students to collect photographs illustrating the geographical variety of Western Europe, using travel magazines, tour brochures, or posters. Have them write captions for the pictures, then arrange them as a bulletin board display.

The summers in the south are usually hot and dry, with an average July temperature around 80°F. This makes the Mediterranean coast a popular vacation spot. Elsewhere in Europe, in all but the coldest areas of the mountains and the far north, the average July temperature ranges from 50°F to 70°F.

Natural Resources ❸

Europe has a large variety of natural resources, including minerals. The rich coal deposits of Germany's Ruhr (roor) Valley region have helped to make that area one of the world's major industrial centers. Russia and Ukraine have large deposits of iron ore, which is used to make iron for automobiles and countless other products.

Region • Western Europe benefits from a varied landscape rich in natural resources. ▼

Activity Options

Interdisciplinary Link: Current Events

🅑 **Block Scheduling**

Class Time Two 30-minute sessions

Task Holding a roundtable discussion

Purpose To identify and report on current economic issues in Europe

Supplies Needed
- Writing paper
- Pencils or pens
- Current newspapers and newsmagazines
- Internet access

Activity Divide the class into six to eight small groups and ask each group to report on a different European nation. In the first session, have students research newspapers, newsmagazines, or the Internet for current news about their chosen country, focusing on resource-related issues, and write a short news item (one to two paragraphs). Next, ask one member from each group to present the news item in a roundtable discussion on "Europe Today." Have the other students discuss the presentations.

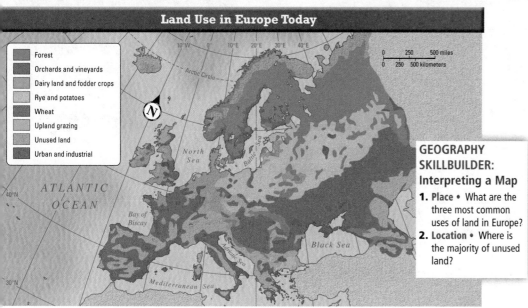

Land Use in Europe Today

Key:
- Forest
- Orchards and vineyards
- Dairy land and fodder crops
- Rye and potatoes
- Wheat
- Upland grazing
- Unused land
- Urban and industrial

GEOGRAPHY SKILLBUILDER: Interpreting a Map

1. **Place** • What are the three most common uses of land in Europe?
2. **Location** • Where is the majority of unused land?

Vocabulary

precipitation: moisture, including rain, snow, and hail, that falls to the ground

Europe also has rich soil and plentiful rainfall. The average precipitation for the Great European Plain, for example, is between 20 and 40 inches per year. The map above shows the agricultural uses of the land, highlighting the major crops. Notice that few parts of the continent are too cold or too hot and dry to support some form of agriculture. These characteristics have made Europe a world leader in crop production.

Geography Skillbuilder Answers

1. forests, growing wheat, growing rye and potatoes

2. in the far north and the mountains of Scandinavia

SECTION 1 ASSESSMENT

Terms & Names

1. **Identify:**
   (a) Mediterranean Sea
   (b) peninsula
   (c) fjord
   (d) Ural Mountains
   (e) plain

Taking Notes

2. Use a spider map like this one to list the different geographic features of Europe, and give a few specific examples of each.

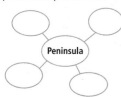

Peninsula

Main Ideas

3. (a) How does the Gulf Stream affect the climate of Europe?
   (b) What separates Europe from Asia?
   (c) How do waterways, such as rivers and seas, strengthen trade in Europe?

Critical Thinking

4. **Recognizing Effects**

   How did Europe's many mountain ranges affect its development?

   Think About
   - climate
   - trade and travel
   - the separation of groups of people

ACTIVITY -OPTION-
Reread the information about the Chunnel. Write a **short story** in which you imagine what it might have been like to work on the Chunnel's construction.

FOCUS ON VISUALS

Interpreting the Map Review with stdents the importance of using the key to get information from a thematic map like this one. Make sure they recognize the difference between the gray color that indicates unused land and the neutral shade indicating nosubject areas. Ask them to use the key to determine the most widely grown crop in this part of Europe.

Response wheat

Extension Have students use the map to determine the answers to these questions: Where are most vineyards located? on the Mediterranean coast What land use dominates Scandinavia? forests

ASSESS & RETEACH

Reading Social Studies Have students list several facts about landforms, waterways, climate, and natural resources of Europe.

 Formal Assessment
- Section Quiz, p. 33

RETEACHING ACTIVITIES

Divide the class into groups and assign each group one of the section topics. Ask each group to write a short summary of the topic. Have one member from each group read the summary aloud.

 In-depth Resources: Unit 2
- Reteaching Activity, p. 11

 Access for Students Acquiring English
- Reteaching Activity, p. 19

Section 1 Assessment

1. Terms & Names
a. Mediterranean Sea, p. 68
b. peninsula, p. 68
c. fjord, p. 68
d. Ural Mountains, p. 69
e. plain, p. 69

2. Taking Notes

Greece (Balkan) — Iberia — Peninsula — Italy — Scandinavia

3. Main Ideas
a. It carries warm water and warm, moist air across Europe, resulting in a relatively mild climate.
b. the Ural Mountains
c. They carry people and goods across great distances.

4. Critical Thinking

Mountains separated groups of people when they settled thousands of years ago, which partly explains why different cultures developed in different areas.

ACTIVITY OPTION

 Integrated Assessment
- Rubric for writing a story

SECTION OBJECTIVES

1. To describe the geography of Greece, the development of Greek city-states, and the birth of democracy in Greece

2. To describe the achievements of Greek culture and explain its spread and influence

SKILLBUILDER
• Interpreting a Map, p. 73

CRITICAL THINKING
• Analyzing Motives, p. 75

FOCUS & MOTIVATE
WARM-UP

Making Inferences Have students read Dateline and ask them to think about excavations in their own region.

1. What artifacts might be discovered underground in your region?

2. Why do you think these artifacts would be different from those found in Athens?

INSTRUCT: Objective ❶

The Land and Early History of Greece/Athens and Sparta

• How did geography influence the development of ancient Greece? Mountains separated city-states; people became skilled sailors and established colonies overseas.

• How were city-states alike and different? alike: common language, religious beliefs, way of life; different: laws, forms of government

• What kind of government did Athens have by the end of the sixth century? a democracy

 In-depth Resources: Unit 2
• Guided Reading Worksheet, p. 4

 Reading Study Guide
(Spanish and English), pp. 18–19

Ancient Greece

TERMS & NAMES
city-state
polis
Aegean Sea
oligarchy
Athens
philosopher
Aristotle
Alexander the Great

MAIN IDEA
The ancient Greeks developed a complex society, with remarkable achievements in the arts, sciences, and government.

WHY IT MATTERS NOW
The achievements of the ancient Greeks continue to influence culture, science, and politics in the world today.

DATELINE

ATHENS, GREECE, FEBRUARY 2, 1997— Five years after construction workers began building the new Athens subway, artifacts from ancient Greek civilization are still being discovered. When completed, the new subway will reduce traffic and air pollution in the capital. Historians and archaeologists, however, have been the first to benefit from this massive public works project.

Workers have discovered statues, coins, jewelry, and gravesites from ancient Greece. Recently, workers digging the foundation for a downtown Athens station found an ancient dog collar decorated with gemstones. Local officials have promised to create

Place • Building the subway in Athens led to spectacular discoveries of ancient artifacts. ▲

permanent displays of some artifacts in stations throughout the new subway system.

The Land and Early History of Greece ❶

The Greek Peninsula is mountainous, which made travel by land difficult for early settlers. Most of the rocky land also contains poor soil and few large trees, but settlers were able to cultivate the soil to grow olives and grapes. The greatest natural resource of the peninsula is the water that surrounds it. The ancient Greeks depended on these seas for fishing and trade, and they became excellent sailors.

Vocabulary

cultivate:
to prepare land for growing crops

Program Resources

 In-depth Resources: Unit 2
• Guided Reading Worksheet, p. 4
• Reteaching Activity, p. 12

 Reading Study Guide
(Spanish and English), pp. 18–19

 Formal Assessment
• Section Quiz, p. 34

 Integrated Assessment
• Rubric for presenting an oral report

 Outline Map Activities

 Access for Students Acquiring English
• Guided Reading Worksheet, p. 14

 Technology Resources
classzone.com

TEST-TAKING RESOURCES
⚓ Strategies for Test Preparation
⚓ Test Practice Transparencies
 Online Test Practice

The Formation of City-States As the ancient Greek population grew, people created city-states. A <u>city-state</u> included a central city, called a <u>polis,</u> and surrounding villages. Each ancient Greek city-state had its own laws and form of government. The city-states were united by a common language, shared religious beliefs, and a similar way of life.

The Growth of Colonies By the mid-eighth century B.C., the Greeks were leaving the peninsula in search of better land and greater opportunities for trade. During the next 200 years, they built dozens of communities on the islands and coastline of the <u>Aegean Sea</u> (ih·JEE·uhn). Some Greeks settled as far away as modern-day Spain and North Africa.

Once established, these distant Greek communities traded with each other and with those communities on the Greek Peninsula. This made a great variety of goods available to the ancient Greeks, including wheat for bread, timber for building boats, and iron ore for making strong tools and weapons.

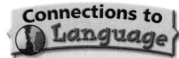

Connections to Language

Metropolis When ancient Greeks moved away from a large polis to a distant community, they referred to their former city-state as their "metropolis." In Greek, this means "mother-city." Today, we use the word *metropolis* to mean any large urban area, such as Los Angeles, London, Tokyo, or Athens, shown below.

Connections to Language

Many English words come from Greek. These include words that end in the suffix *-logy,* meaning "study of," and words that end in the suffix *-phobia,* meaning "fear of." Common English words using these suffixes include biology, geology, psychology, claustrophobia, xenophobia, and hydrophobia.

FOCUS ON VISUALS

Interpreting the Map Have students relate this area map to the map of Europe on page 71 or in the Unit Atlas. Have them point out the area of the Mediterranean Sea in which Greece is located. Ask them to recall what kind of landform these two land areas (Greece and Asia Minor) represent.

Response peninsula

Extension Have students use the map scale to estimate these distances: Athens to Sparta about 200 miles; Ionia to Ephesus about 80 miles; Athens to Crete about 380 miles.

Greek Colonization, 800 B.C.

Map legend:
- Greek colonization
- *Ionia* Historic city name
- Sparta Historic and current city name

GEOGRAPHY SKILLBUILDER: Interpreting a Map

1. **Place** • What was the value to the Greeks of controlling Byzantium?
2. **Location** • What was the southernmost Greek territory at this time?

Activity Options

Multiple Learning Styles: Visual/Linguistic

Class Time One hour

Task Creating museum brochures for Athens and Sparta

Purpose To reinforce the differences between Sparta and Athens through a visual learning experience

Supplies Needed
- Poster board or paper
- Markers or crayons
- Books with pictures of Athens and Sparta

Activity Divide the class into groups of five students. Assign Athens to half the groups and Sparta to the other half. Ask each group to design a museum brochure to inform visitors about the city-state. Encourage students to include information about the location of each state, the kind of government it has, and other details they learn through their research. Remind students that the brochures must be historically accurate. Allow time for brief presentations of the brochures to the class.

Strange but TRUE

From the minute he was born, a Spartan boy belonged to the state. At the age of seven, boys were assigned to military companies made up of 15 boys. Discipline in these units was strict. The boys took their meals in a public dining hall, where they ate with their unit. The bravest boy became the captain of the unit and was allowed to command and punish the other unit members. The young soldiers in training slept on beds made out of reeds, which they gathered themselves. Living conditions were tough, because Spartans valued endurance, and the rejection of luxuries denoted strength—all still considered "Spartan" virtues today.

INSTRUCT: Objective ❷

Learning and the Arts

- In what cultural fields did the ancient Greeks excel? literature, philosophy, architecture
- Who were usually the major characters in Greek poetry and tragic plays? gods and goddesses
- What were some of the topics that interested Socrates and other philosophers? friendship, knowledge, justice, government, human behavior
- How did Greek culture spread beyond Greece? through the expansion of the Greek empire under Alexander the Great, a military leader who conquered the Mediterranean and lands as far east as India during the fourth century B.C.

Strange but TRUE

Spartan Soldiers Sparta was the only city-state with a permanent army. At age seven, Spartan boys were sent by their families for military training. They had to remain in the army until they were 30 years old.

Individual Forms of Government Some ancient Greek city-states were oligarchies (AHL·ih·GAHR·kees). An **oligarchy** is a system in which a few powerful, wealthy individuals rule. The word *oligarchy* comes from an ancient Greek word meaning "rule by the few." Other city-states were ruled by a tyrant, a single person who took control of the government against the wishes of the community. Still other ancient Greek city-states developed an early form of democracy. The word *democracy* comes from an ancient Greek word meaning "rule by the people." In a democracy citizens, take part in the government.

Athens and Sparta ❶

Athens, centrally located on the Greek Peninsula, was one of the largest and most important ancient Greek city-states. By the end of the sixth century B.C., Athens had developed a democratic form of government. Athenian citizens took part in political debates and voted on laws, but not everyone who lived in Athens enjoyed these rights. Participation in government was limited to free, adult males whose fathers had been citizens of Athens. Women, slaves, and foreign residents could not be citizens and could not take part in government.

Athens's chief rival among the other Greek city-states was Sparta. Located in the southernmost part of the Greek Peninsula, Sparta was an oligarchy. It was ruled by two kings, who were supported by other officials. Sparta, like Athens, had a powerful army. Each city-state's army helped protect it from slave rebellions, guard against attack by rival city-states, and defend it from possible foreign invaders.

Learning and the Arts ❷

In 480 B.C., the Persians, who controlled a large empire to the east, tried to conquer the Greek Peninsula. Several Greek city-states, including Athens and Sparta, joined forces to defeat the Persians. In the years following this victory, the ancient Greeks made remarkable achievements in literature, learning, and architecture.

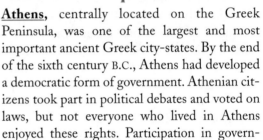

Reading Social Studies

A. Comparing Compare the three forms of government most common in ancient Greek city-states.

Reading Social Studies A. Answer A small group of wealthy men ruled an oligarchy; one ruler became a tyrant; citizens took part in ruling a democracy.

BACKGROUND After the defeat of Persia, Athens became the most powerful Greek city-state. The most important Athenian leader of the time was Pericles (PEHR·uh·kleez), who lived from c. 495 to 429 B.C.

Activity Options

Differentiating Instruction: Students Acquiring English/ESL

Using Section Vocabulary To ensure that students acquiring English understand the vocabulary terms used in this section, discuss as a group the words listed to the right. Discuss where and when students have seen these words in print sources or heard them on radio or television. Then ask students to write each word in a sentence.

- community
- united
- rival
- victory
- architecture

Literature To honor their gods and goddesses, the ancient Greeks created myths and wrote poems and plays. Some of the greatest Greek plays were written during the fifth century B.C. During that time, the playwrights Aeschylus (ES·kuh·luhs), Sophocles (SAHF·uh·kleez), and Euripides (yoo·RIP·uh·deez) wrote tragedies, which are serious plays that end unhappily. Many of these stories have been the basis for modern films and operas.

In addition to using the gods as characters, ancient Greek playwrights sometimes poked fun at important citizens, including generals and politicians. Aristophanes (ar·uh·STOF·uh·nees) was a popular writer of comedies of this type.

Philosophy Ancient Greece was the birthplace of some of the finest thinkers of the ancient world. Socrates (SOK·ruh·tees) was an important philosopher of the fifth century B.C. A **philosopher** studies and thinks about why the world is the way it is. Socrates studied and taught about friendship, knowledge, and justice. Another great philosopher, Plato (PLAY·toh), was a student of Socrates who studied and taught about human behavior, government, mathematics, and astronomy.

The ancient Greek philosopher Heraclitus (heh·ruh·KLY·tuhs) wrote the following lines.

Reading
Social Studies

B. Making Inferences Why do you think philosophers felt the need to teach?

Reading Social Studies
B. Possible Answer
They wanted to pass on their ideas, to share them.

> **A VOICE FROM ANCIENT GREECE**
>
> One cannot step twice into the same river, for the water into which you first stepped has flowed on.
>
> *Heraclitus*

Many people continue to study and write about the same philosophical questions that these, and other, ancient Greek philosophers explored.

The WORLD'S HERITAGE

Ancient Greek Architecture Ancient Greek builders created some of the world's most impressive works of architecture. They built several beautiful temples atop the Acropolis (uh·KRAH·puh·lis) in Athens, shown at right. The most famous of the temples is the Parthenon (PAHR·thuh·non).

In the United States and elsewhere, government buildings, such as courthouses and post offices, have been built similar in style to the Parthenon. This use of ancient architecture echoes the democratic ideals of ancient Greece.

Western Europe: Its Land and Early History **75**

The WORLD'S HERITAGE

The main part of the Parthenon was destroyed in 1687, after the Venetians attempted to conquer Athens. The 2,000-year-old building, which was being used as a powder house, exploded.

By the 19th century, Greece had become part of the Turkish Empire. In 1801, the Turkish government granted the British ambassador in Constantinople, Lord Elgin, permission to remove some of the most beautiful marble statues from the Acropolis. These statues included many sculptures from the Parthenon created under the direction of Phidias, the greatest Greek sculptor. Lord Elgin sold these statues, known as the Elgin Marbles, to the British government in 1816. Despite attempts by the Greek government to have the statues returned to Greece, they remain in the British Museum, in London.

A VOICE FROM ANCIENT GREECE

Ask a volunteer to read aloud the words of the philosopher Heraclitus. Explain that the message contains the philosopher's view that things in life continually change. Ask students to relate his message to situations in their own lives.

CRITICAL THINKING ACTIVITY

Analyzing Motives After students have discussed the quotation from Heraclitus and its meaning for them, ask them to take a broader look at the Greek philosophers and their influence. Ask them to suggest reasons that thinkers 2,500 years later are still puzzling over the same questions about the world and human behavior.

Class Time 15 minutes

Activity Options

Differentiating Instruction: Gifted and Talented

 Block Scheduling

Researching a Historical Figure Have students use library resources and the Internet to find information about famous Greek figures, such as Plato, Sophocles, Herodotus, Pericles, Hippocrates, or Alexander the Great. Encourage students not to attempt a complete biographical sketch but to focus on just one or two aspects of the historical figures they have chosen—for example, Herodotus's approach to history or Alexander's conquests. Ask students to write a two-page report focusing on those aspects and on how the person's achievements have influenced contemporary literature, history, or science.

Biography

Aristotle may have been the first philosopher to conduct organized scientific research. He analyzed the functions of parts of animals and wrote several treatises on the subject. He also wrote about literature, analyzing the plots, characters, and themes of classic Greek dramas.

ASSESS & RETEACH

Reading Social Studies Have students fill in the column on Greece in the chart on page 66.

 Formal Assessment
• Section Quiz, p. 34

RETEACHING ACTIVITIES

Ask students to work in groups of three to write a review of this section. Have one student summarize each heading. Then have students combine their work in a complete summary.

 In-depth Resources: Unit 2
• Reteaching Activity, p. 12

Access for Students Acquiring English
• Reteaching Activity, p. 20

 **Biography**

Aristotle At the age of 17, Aristotle (384–322 B.C.) began studying philosophy with Plato. After Plato died, Aristotle received his most important assignment—to teach Alexander, the teenage son of King Philip II of Macedonia.

After teaching Alexander, Aristotle returned to Athens. There he taught and wrote about poetry, government, and astronomy. He started a famous school called the Lyceum (lie•SEE•uhm). Aristotle also collected and studied plants and animals. The work of this brilliant philosopher continues to greatly influence scientists and philosophers today.

The Spread of Greek Culture The city-states of ancient Greece were constantly at war with one another. By the fourth century B.C., this fighting had weakened their ability to defend themselves against foreign invaders. In 338 B.C., King Philip II of Macedonia conquered the land. After Philip died, his son, Alexander—who had been taught by **Aristotle**—took control.

Alexander the Great was an excellent military leader, and his armies conquered vast new territories. As Alexander's empire expanded, Greek culture, language, and ideas were spread throughout the Mediterranean region and as far east as modern-day India. Upon Alexander's death, however, his leading generals fought for control of his territory and divided it among themselves. This marked the end of one of the great empires of the ancient world.

Region • In this mosaic Alexander the Great is shown riding into battle on his beloved horse, Bucephalus (byoo•SEF•ah•lus). ▲

SECTION ② ASSESSMENT

Terms & Names

1. **Identify:** (a) city-state (b) polis (c) Aegean Sea (d) oligarchy
   (e) Athens (f) philosopher (g) Aristotle (h) Alexander the Great

Taking Notes

2. Use a chart like this one to list and describe the ancient Greek achievements in government, literature, and architecture.

Government	Literature	Architecture

Main Ideas

3. (a) Why were the surrounding areas of water an important natural resource of the Greek Peninsula?

   (b) Which people were allowed to participate in the government of ancient Athens?

   (c) How did Alexander the Great help to spread Greek culture?

Critical Thinking

4. **Summarizing**

   Why was the fifth century B.C. a remarkable time in ancient Greek history?

   Think About
   ◆ warfare
   ◆ leaders
   ◆ literature and philosophy

ACTIVITY -OPTION- Reread the information about the individual forms of government common in ancient Greece. Present an **oral report** to the class that compares and contrasts two of the forms.

Section ② Assessment

1. Terms & Names
   a. city-state, p. 73
   b. polis, p. 73
   c. Aegean Sea, p. 73
   d. oligarchy, p. 74
   e. Athens, p. 74
   f. philosopher, p. 75
   g. Aristotle, p. 76
   h. Alexander the Great, p. 76

2. Taking Notes

Government	Literature	Architecture
formation of city-states, each with its own laws and form of government	tragedies (Aeschylus, Sophocles, and Euripides)	temples (Acropolis)
creation of democracy in Athens at the end of the sixth century B.C.	comedies (Aristophanes)	
	philosophy (Socrates, Plato, Aristotle, and Heraclitus)	

3. Main Ideas
   a. The oceans provided fish and facilitated trade.
   b. Free, adult males whose fathers had been citizens could participate.
   c. Alexander conquered vast territories, spreading Greek language and ideas.

4. Critical Thinking
   Democracy first developed at that time; many great playwrights, philosophers, architects, and artists lived during the fifth century B.C.

ACTIVITY OPTION

 Integrated Assessment
• Rubric for presenting an oral report

Making a Generalization

▶▶ Defining the Skill

To make generalizations means to make broad judgments based on information. When you make generalizations, you should gather information from several sources.

▶▶ Applying the Skill

The following three passages contain different information on the government of ancient Athens. Use the strategies listed below to make a generalization about Athenian government based on the passages.

How to Make a Generalization

Strategy ❶ Look for all the information that the sources have in common. These three sources all explain about Athenian government.

Strategy ❷ Form a generalization that describes ancient Athenian government in a way that all three sources would support. State your generalization in a sentence.

Make a Chart

Using a chart can help you make generalizations. The chart below shows how the information you just read can be used to generalize about the government of ancient Athens.

> ❶ Athenian citizens took part in political debates and voted on laws, but not everyone who lived in Athens enjoyed these rights. Participation in government was limited to free, adult males whose fathers had been citizens in Athens.
>
> —*World Cultures and Geography*
>
> In return for playing their parts as soldiers or sailors, ❶ ordinary Athenians insisted on controlling the government.
>
> —*Encyclopaedia Britannica*
>
> Unlike representative democracies or republics, in which one man is elected to speak for many, Athens was a true ❶ democracy: every citizen spoke for himself.
>
> —*Classical Greece*

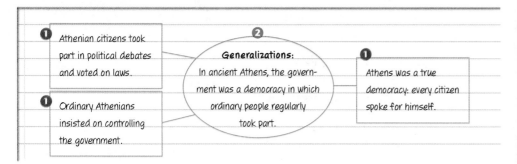

▶▶ Practicing the Skill

Turn to Chapter 3, Section 2, "Ancient Greece." Read the sections on literature and philosophy. Also read about ancient Greek writings in an encyclopedia, a library book, or on the Internet. Then make a chart like the one above to form a generalization about the importance of knowledge and learning to the ancient Greeks.

SKILLBUILDER

Making a Generalization
Defining the Skill

Explain to students that when they generalize, they draw conclusions based on information gathered from different sources. Ask students to think about real-life situations where being able to generalize might help them, such as estimating how much money they might need for a movie or deciding what clothing to take on a trip.

Applying the Skill

How to Make a Generalization Point out the two strategies for making a generalization and help students work through each. For example, ask students to read the three passages, and have a volunteer tell what information they all have in common. Ask students to think of a generalization about the Athenian government that would be supported by all three sources.

Make a Chart

Discuss the three passages and the point being made by each. Ask questions such as: How did Athenian citizens participate in government? What did ordinary Athenians expect in return for being soldiers or sailors? In what way was Athens a true democracy? Have volunteers read the completed chart aloud.

Practicing the Skill

Find information about Greek writers in several sources, and distribute copies to students. Also have them reread the suggested sections on literature and philosophy. Suggest that students make notes of main points on a chart like the one shown. Then ask them to make a generalization.

 In-depth Resources: Unit 2
• Skillbuilder Practice, p. 9

Career Connection: Weather Forecaster

Encourage students who enjoy making generalizations to learn about careers that utilize this skill. For example, students might choose to research the work of meteorologists, scientists who study the atmosphere. Many meteorologists are weather forecasters who bring together and analyze scientific data from many sources to make generalizations about what the weather will be like.

Block Scheduling

1. Help students find information about the many sources weather forecasters use: ground-weather stations, weather balloons, high-tech aircraft, radar, satellites, and computer models.

2. Help students determine the education required to work in this field.

3. Have students create a chart to explain the process of becoming a weather forecaster.

Ancient Rome

TERMS & NAMES
republic
Senate
patrician
plebeian
Julius Caesar
empire
Augustus
Constantine

SECTION OBJECTIVES

1. To describe the Roman Republic and the spread of Rome's power
2. To explain the establishment and influence of the Roman Empire
3. To identify reasons for the rise of Christianity

SKILLBUILDER
• Interpreting a Map, pp. 80, 81

CRITICAL THINKING
• Contrasting, p. 79
• Finding Causes, p. 82

FOCUS & MOTIVATE
WARM-UP

Making Inferences Have students read <u>Dateline</u>, examine the illustration, and discuss building roadways 2,000 years ago.

1. Why did Rome need a roadway system?
2. What types of traffic were common?

INSTRUCT: Objective ❶

The Beginnings of Ancient Rome/The Expansion of the Roman World

• In what way did the government of Rome change in 509 B.C.? It became a republic.

• What were the two groups of Roman citizens? wealthy patricians, workers called plebeians

• How did Rome win control of the western Mediterranean? by defeating Carthage

 In-depth Resources: Unit 2
• Guided Reading Worksheet, p. 5

 Reading Study Guide
(Spanish and English), pp. 20–21

MAIN IDEA	WHY IT MATTERS NOW
The ancient Romans made important contributions to government, law, and engineering.	The cultural achievements of the Romans continue to influence the art, architecture, and literature of today.

DATELINE
EXTRA

ROME, 295 B.C.

Yet another Roman road was completed today! Rome is famous for its vast network of roadways. Repairing old roads and adding new ones keeps Roman engineers busy. Construction is time-consuming because the lengthy roads, which are paved with large stones, must be carefully planned. However, the benefits are worth the effort.

The roads connect the great city to distant lands under Roman rule. These roadways also enable the army to move quickly. These days, it seems that almost all roads lead to Rome. In fact, when this massive undertaking is finished, Roman roads will stretch for tens of thousands of miles across the land.

Location • All roads lead to Rome—including the Via Appia (WEE•ah APP•ee•ah) shown here. ▲

The Beginnings of Ancient Rome ❶

Ancient Rome began as a group of villages located along the banks of the Tiber River in what is now Italy. There, early settlers herded sheep and grew wheat, olives, and grapes. Around 750 B.C., these villages united to form the city of Rome.

78 CHAPTER 3

Program Resources

 In-depth Resources: Unit 2
• Guided Reading Worksheet, p. 5
• Reteaching Activity, p. 13

 Reading Study Guide
(Spanish and English), pp. 20–21

 Formal Assessment
• Section Quiz, p. 35

 Integrated Assessment
• Rubric for creating a chart

 Outline Map Activities

Access for Students Acquiring English
• Guided Reading Worksheet, p. 14

Technology Resources
classzone.com

TEST-TAKING RESOURCES
⚑ Strategies for Test Preparation
⚑ Test Practice Transparencies
⚐ Online Test Practice

The Formation of the Roman Republic For more than 200 years, kings ruled Rome. Then, in 509 B.C., Rome became a republic. A **republic** is a nation in which power belongs to the citizens, who govern themselves through elected representatives.

The Senate The Roman **Senate** was an assembly of elected representatives. It was the single most powerful ruling body of the Roman Republic. Each year, the Senate selected two leaders, called consuls, to head the government and the military.

Patricians At first, most of the people elected to the Senate were patricians (puh·TRIHSH·uhns). In ancient Rome, a **patrician** was a member of a wealthy, landowning family who claimed to be able to trace its roots back to the founding of Rome. The patricians also controlled the law, since they were the only citizens who were allowed to be judges.

Plebeians An ordinary, working male citizen of ancient Rome—such as a farmer or craftsperson—was called a **plebeian** (plih·BEE·uhn). Plebeians had the right to vote, but they could not hold public office until 287 B.C., when they gained equality with patricians.

The Expansion of the Roman World ❶

Over hundreds of years, Rome grew into a mighty city. By the third century B.C., Rome ruled most of the Italian Peninsula. This gave Rome control of the central Mediterranean.

The city-state of Carthage, which ruled North Africa and southern Spain, controlled the western Mediterranean. To take control over this area as well, Rome fought Carthage and eventually won.

As Rome's population grew, its army also expanded in size and strength. Under the leadership of ambitious generals, Rome's highly trained soldiers set out to conquer new territories one by one.

Roman Law It may be hard to believe, but in the early Roman Republic, laws were not written down. Only the patrician judges knew what the laws were. This meant that judges usually ruled in favor of fellow patricians and against plebeians.

The plebeians grew tired of unfair treatment and demanded that the judges create a written code of laws that applied to all Roman citizens. This code, called the Law of the Twelve Tables, was written around 450 B.C. It formed the foundation of Roman law.

Strange but TRUE

The Twelve Tables refers to 12 sets of laws covering issues from treason to intermarriage between classes. These laws are important because they established the principle of a written legal code for Roman law. After the laws were passed, justice was no longer based solely on interpretation by judges.

By today's standards, the punishments set by the Twelve Tables seem harsh. Debtors could be bound in chains. Slanderers could be clubbed to death. Arsonists could be burned at the stake. Judges who accepted bribes could also be put to death.

CRITICAL THINKING ACTIVITY

Contrasting Work with students to identify ways in which the Roman Senate and the United States Senate differ. Ask them to think about who was eligible to hold office in each senate, how much power each body held, and how each body was related to the head of government and to the head of the military.

Ask a volunteer to record the comparison points in a two-column chart on the chalkboard. Then extend the discussion by asking students to compare the rights and responsibilities of citizens in ancient Rome with those of American citizens today. Ask them to explain the difference between a republic and a democracy and to suggest modern nations that are republics but not democracies.

Class Time 10 minutes

Activity Options

Interdisciplinary Link: Language Arts

Class Time 30 minutes

Task Identifying words with Latin roots

Purpose To demonstrate that many English words come from Latin

Supplies Needed
- Writing paper
- Pencils or pens
- Dictionaries

Activity Write the following Latin roots on the chalkboard: *aqua* (water), *audi* (hearing), *cent* (hundred), *creat* (make), *mare* (sea), *oct* (eight), *ped* (foot), *scrib/script* (write), *uni* (one), *vis* (see). Have students work in small groups to list as many words as they can for each root. After about 15 minutes, ask volunteers from each group to read the lists aloud.

INSTRUCT: Objective ❷

From Republic to Empire

- **Who was Julius Caesar?** a general who became dictator of Rome in the first century B.C.

- **In what way did Augustus carry on the work of his great-uncle Julius Caesar?** by continuing to expand the Roman Empire

- **What were some of the activities that took place during the Augustan Age?** The empire grew, public buildings and lighthouses were built, trade increased, and famous works of literature were written.

FOCUS ON VISUALS

Interpreting the Map Review the use of a map key with students, making sure they can relate the colors to the regions shown. Check their understanding by asking what areas Rome controlled by 241 B.C.

Response most of the Italian Peninsula, island of Sicily

Extension Point out that the names on this map are modern. The Romans sometimes used different names for these provinces. For example, Romans called Italy *Italia*. Ask students to suggest a modern English term that derives from the Roman name for Spain, *Hispania*. Hispanic Have interested students research the names of other provinces in the Roman Empire such as *Britannia* and show how they relate to modern European nations.

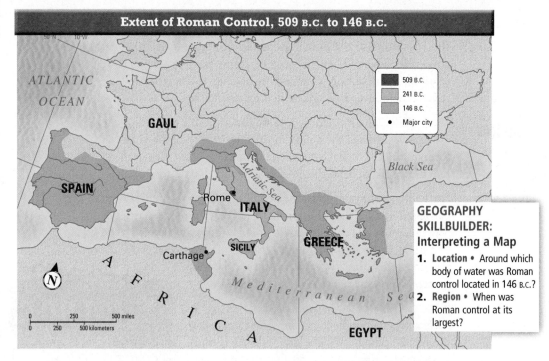

Extent of Roman Control, 509 B.C. to 146 B.C.

509 B.C.
241 B.C.
146 B.C.
• Major city

ATLANTIC OCEAN

GAUL

SPAIN

Rome ITALY

Carthage

SICILY

GREECE

AFRICA

Mediterranean Sea

Adriatic Sea

Black Sea

EGYPT

GEOGRAPHY SKILLBUILDER: Interpreting a Map

1. **Location** • Around which body of water was Roman control located in 146 B.C.?
2. **Region** • When was Roman control at its largest?

As Rome's control over its neighbors expanded, its culture and language continued to spread into Spain and Greece. By the end of the second century B.C., the Romans ruled most of the land surrounding the Mediterranean Sea. The ancient Romans even called the Mediterranean *mare nostrum* (MAH•ray NO•strum), which means "our sea."

Geography Skillbuilder Answers
1. Mediterranean Sea
2. in 146 B.C.

From Republic to Empire ❷

As the Roman Republic grew, its citizens became a more and more diverse group of people. Many Romans practiced different religions and followed different customs, but they were united by a common system of government and law. In the middle of the first century B.C., however, Rome's form of government changed.

The End of the Roman Republic **Julius Caesar,** a successful Roman general and famous speaker, was the governor of the territory called Gaul. By conquering nearby territories to expand the land under his control, he increased both his power and his reputation. The Roman Senate feared that Caesar might become too powerful, and they ordered him to resign. Caesar, however, had other ideas.

Region • Once in power, Julius Caesar had his likeness stamped on coins such as this one. ▼

BACKGROUND

Ancient Gaul included the lands that are modern-day France, Belgium, and parts of northern Italy.

80 CHAPTER 3

Activity Options

Multiple Learning Styles: Linguistic

Class Time 15 minutes

Task Identifying the origin of the terms *empire* and *emperor*

Purpose To trace the Latin roots of basic words used in the section

Supplies Needed
- Paper
- Pencils or pens
- Dictionaries

Activity Point out the heading "From Republic to Empire" on page 80 and the explanation of *empire* on page 81. Then ask students to use their dictionaries to determine the origins of the words *empire* and *emperor*. Suggest that they locate the dictionary entries and look in the first line of each entry to find information about the word's origin. When they have finished, ask volunteers to read their results aloud. Be sure that students understand that empire comes from the Latin word *imperium*, and emperor comes from the Latin word *imperator*.

Rather than resign, Caesar fought a long, fierce battle for control of the Roman Republic. In 45 B.C., he finally triumphed and returned to Rome. Caesar eventually became dictator of the Roman world. A dictator is a person who holds total control over a government. Caesar's rule marked the end of the Roman Republic.

The Beginning of the Roman Empire Julius Caesar had great plans to reorganize the way ancient Rome was governed, but his rule was cut short. On March 15, 44 B.C., a group of senators, angered by Caesar's plans and power, stabbed him to death on the floor of the Roman Senate. A civil war then erupted that lasted for several years.

In 27 B.C., Caesar's adopted son, Octavian, was named the first emperor of Rome. This marks the official beginning of the Roman Empire. An **empire** is a nation or group of territories ruled by a single, powerful leader, or emperor. As emperor, Octavian took the name **Augustus.**

The Augustan Age Augustus ruled the Roman Empire for more than 40 years. During this time, called the Augustan Age, the empire continued to expand. To help protect the enormous amount of land under his control, Augustus sent military forces along its borders, which now extended northward to the Rhine and Danube rivers.

Reading
Social Studies

A. Recognizing Important Details How many years separated the rules of Julius Caesar and Augustus?

Reading Social Studies
A. Answer
17 years (44–27 B.C.)

Region • Sculptures of Augustus were sent all over the Roman Empire to let people know what their leader looked like. ▲

Geography Skillbuilder Answers
1. Africa, Europe
2. Syria

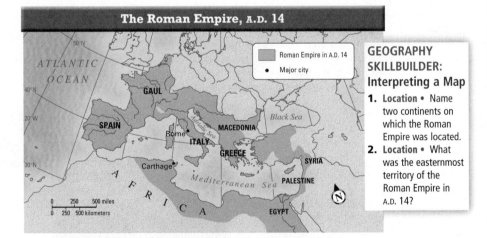

The Roman Empire, A.D. 14

Roman Empire in A.D. 14
• Major city

GEOGRAPHY SKILLBUILDER: Interpreting a Map

1. **Location** • Name two continents on which the Roman Empire was located.
2. **Location** • What was the easternmost territory of the Roman Empire in A.D. 14?

Western Europe: Its Land and Early History **81**

Spotlight on CULTURE

To supply water to the city of Rome, engineers built 11 major aqueducts in the period between 312 B.C. and A.D. 226. Aqueducts brought water from springs, lakes, and rivers in the hills around the city. Most of the Roman water system actually ran through underground channels, with only a relatively few miles carried across valleys on the spectacular stone arches that we now think of as "aqueducts."

Water flowed from the hills into distribution tanks. From there it traveled through pipes (of lead, tile, or stone) to different parts of the city. The best water was used for drinking and cooking, while some was only clean enough for watering gardens. Some very rich citizens had water piped directly into their private villas. Most people used water from public fountains that were located at 100-meter intervals throughout the city. Huge quantities of water also supplied the enormous bath complexes, such as the Baths of Caracalla.

CRITICAL THINKING ACTIVITY

Finding Causes Have students review the different stages in Rome's development to make sure that they understand the difference between the Roman Republic and the Roman Empire. Then ask them to identify the events that caused the end of the Roman Republic.

Class Time 10 minutes

Region • A diver holds an artifact from an ancient Roman shipwreck in the Mediterranean Sea. ▲

While the Roman army kept peace, architects and engineers built many new public buildings. Trade increased, with olive oil, wine, pottery, marble, and grain being shipped all across the Mediterranean. Lighthouses were constructed, too, to help ships find their way into port.

The Augustan Age was also a time of great Roman literature. One of the most famous works of the age is the *Aeneid* (ih·NEE·id). This long poem tells the story of Rome's founding. Augustus himself asked the famous poet Virgil to write it. This period of peace and cultural growth that Augustus created in the Roman Empire was called the "Pax Romana" (pahks roh·MAH·nah). The Pax Romana, or Roman Peace, lasted for 200 years.

Spotlight on CULTURE

Architecture Various inventions helped the Roman Empire grow and prosper. In addition to buildings and roads, Roman architects and engineers constructed water systems called aqueducts. Ancient aqueducts were raised tunnels that carried fresh water over long distances.

Built throughout the empire, aqueducts poured millions of gallons of water into Rome and other cities every day. They supplied clean water to private homes, fountains, and public baths. Today, some ancient Roman aqueducts still stand in France, Spain, and even on the outskirts of Rome itself.

THINKING CRITICALLY

1. **Analyzing Motives**
   Why did Romans want a way to transport water?

2. **Hypothesizing**
   Do you think the Roman Empire would have grown so large and prosperous without the aqueducts?

82 CHAPTER 3

Activity Options

Interdisciplinary Link: Art

Class Time One class period

Task Drawing a Roman structure

Purpose To familiarize students with the architecture of ancient Rome

Supplies Needed
• Drawing paper
• Colored pencils
• Illustrations/models of Roman architecture

Block Scheduling

Activity Display examples of Roman architecture and ask students to comment on what they see. Ask them where they think the materials came from, how the materials were transported to the site, who built the structures, and what they were used for. Then ask them to choose a Roman structure, such as the Colosseum, and draw it. Display the drawings. Ask students if they can identify any structures in the United States that have elements of Roman architecture.

The Rise of Christianity

Reading
Social Studies

B. Making Inferences How do you think the Roman Empire indirectly helped the spread of Christianity?

In the years following the death of Augustus in A.D. 14, a new religion from the Middle East began to take hold in the rest of the Mediterranean world: Christianity. At first, this religion became popular mainly in the eastern half of the Roman Empire. Many followers there preached about its teachings. Christianity spread along the transportation network constructed by the Romans. By the third century A.D., this religion had spread throughout the empire.

Most earlier Roman leaders had tolerated the different religions practiced throughout the empire. Christians, however, were viewed with suspicion and suffered persecution as early as A.D. 64. Roman leaders and people of other religions even blamed the Christians for natural disasters. Many Christians during this time were punished or killed for their beliefs.

Reading Social Studies
B. Possible Answer Roman roads and the stability of Roman laws let ideas spread throughout the empire.

Region • Constantine (died A.D. 337) was the first Christian emperor of Rome. ▼

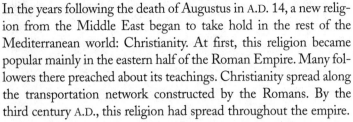

The First Christian Emperor

Things changed when **Constantine** became emperor of Rome in A.D. 306. In A.D. 312, before a battle, Constantine claimed to have had a vision of a cross in the sky. The emperor promised that if he won the battle, he would become a Christian. Constantine was victorious, and the next year he fulfilled his promise. Christianity became the official religion of the Roman Empire. Today, Christianity has nearly two billion followers worldwide.

SECTION 3 ASSESSMENT

Terms & Names

1. Identify:
   (a) republic
   (b) Senate
   (c) patrician
   (d) plebeian
   (e) Julius Caesar
   (f) empire
   (g) Augustus
   (h) Constantine

Taking Notes

2. Use a chart like this one to outline the achievements of ancient Rome's Augustan Age.

Achievement	Effects

Main Ideas

3. (a) On what waterway is the city of Rome located?

   (b) What helped to unite the many different citizens of the Roman Republic?

   (c) How did Christianity spread throughout the Roman Empire?

Critical Thinking

4. **Drawing Conclusions**

   Why was ancient Rome able to control most of the land surrounding the Mediterranean Sea?

   Think About

   ◆ the location of the Italian Peninsula

   ◆ Rome's army

   ◆ Rome's wars with Carthage

ACTIVITY -OPTION- Review the information about the beginnings of ancient Rome. Create a **chart** that compares the two important classes of Roman society: patricians and plebeians.

Western Europe: Its Land and Early History **83**

Section 3 Assessment

1. Terms & Names
a. republic, p. 79
b. Senate, p. 79
c. patrician, p. 79
d. plebeian, p. 79
e. Julius Caesar, p. 80
f. empire, p. 81
g. Augustus, p. 81
h. Constantine, p. 83

2. Taking Notes

Achievement	Effects
Literature	Virgil's *Aeneid*
Growth of empire	peace, cultural growth
Trade	olive oil, wine, pottery, grain shipped across Mediterranean
Engineering	lighthouses, aqueducts

3. Main Ideas
a. the Tiber River
b. a common system of government and law
c. At first, Christianity spread by means of the Roman transportation network; it spread more rapidly after Constantine converted in A.D. 312 and made it the official religion of Rome.

4. Critical Thinking
Rome was centrally located; its large, powerful army defeated its only regional rival for power, Carthage, in 146 B.C.

ACTIVITY OPTION

 Integrated Assessment
• Rubric for creating a chart

INSTRUCT: Objective

The Rise of Christianity/ The First Christian Emperor

• How did Roman attitudes toward Christians change over time? Romans at first were tolerant, then became suspicious of and persecuted Christians.

• How did Christianity come to be the official religion of the Roman Empire? Constantine, the Roman emperor, converted to Christianity.

ASSESS & RETEACH

Reading Social Studies Have students fill in the column on Rome in the chart on page 66.

Formal Assessment
• Section Quiz, p. 35

RETEACHING ACTIVITIES

With students, brainstorm ideas for newspaper articles based on events they learned about in this section. Have students work in groups to write a newspaper article about one of the events.

In-depth Resources: Unit 2
• Reteaching Activity, p. 13

Access for Students Acquiring English
• Reteaching Activity, p. 21

Teacher's Edition **83**

Time of Change: The Middle Ages

TERMS & NAMES
medieval
Charlemagne
feudalism
manorialism
guild
Magna Carta

SECTION OBJECTIVES

1. To describe Europe after the fall of the Roman Empire
2. To identify Charlemagne and describe the Church's role in the Middle Ages
3. To explain the relationships among people under feudalism and manorialism
4. To explain the changes that took place as towns developed and grew

CRITICAL THINKING

• Forming and Supporting Opinions, p. 85
• Recognizing Important Details, p. 87

FOCUS & MOTIVATE
WARM-UP

Drawing Conclusions Have students read <u>Dateline</u> and discuss the invasion of Rome.

1. How might the Visigoths have been able to overthrow the Roman government?
2. Why did invaders not attack the city earlier?

INSTRUCT: Objective ❶

Western Europe in Collapse

• What were the effects of the collapse of the Roman Empire? no central government, towns abandoned, unsafe travel, decreased trade
• What is the period between the end of ancient times and the beginning of the modern world called? Middle Ages or medieval era

 In-depth Resources: Unit 2
• Guided Reading Worksheet, p. 6

 Reading Study Guide
(Spanish and English), pp. 22–23

MAIN IDEA	WHY IT MATTERS NOW
The Middle Ages was a time of great change in Western Europe.	Some developments that occurred during the Middle Ages continue to affect life in Europe today.

DATELINE

ROME, A.D. 476—A Germanic tribe called the Visigoths has attacked our city of Rome and overthrown the emperor, Romulus Augustulus. The Roman army—no longer as large or as well organized as it was during the height of the empire—was unable to fight off the invaders.

After looting the great city, fierce bands of warriors and bandits have continued raiding towns and villages throughout Western Europe. They are stealing jewels and money, killing both people and animals, and even seizing control of entire territories. The Roman Empire seems to have breathed its last breath.

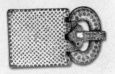

Region • Visigoth artifacts, like these saddle buckles, were found near Rome. ▲

Western Europe in Collapse ❶

As the Roman Empire collapsed in the fifth century, more and more people fled to the countryside to escape invaders from the north and east. Eventually, there was no central government to maintain roads, public buildings, or water systems. Most towns and cities in Western Europe shrank or were totally abandoned. Long-distance travel became unsafe, and trade less common.

84 CHAPTER 3

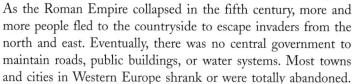

Program Resources

 In-depth Resources: Unit 2
• Guided Reading Worksheet, p. 6
• Reteaching Activity, p. 14

Reading Study Guide
(Spanish and English), pp. 22–23

 Formal Assessment
• Section Quiz, p. 36

 Integrated Assessment
• Rubric for writing a journal

Outline Map Activities

 Access for Students Acquiring English
• Guided Reading Worksheet, p. 16

Technology Resources
classzone.com

TEST-TAKING RESOURCES

↪ Strategies for Test Preparation
↪ Test Practice Transparencies
ⓘ Online Test Practice

Reading
Social Studies

A. Clarifying
Who provided
leadership during
the Middle Ages?

Reading Social
Studies
A. Answers
1. military leaders
and the Roman
Catholic Church

The Beginning of the Medieval Era The period of history between the fall of the Roman Empire and the beginning of the modern world is called the Middle Ages, or **medieval** (MEE·dee·EE·vuhl) era. During this time, many of the advances and inventions of the ancient world were lost. Without a strong central government, many Europeans turned to military leaders and the Roman Catholic Church for leadership and support.

Charlemagne and the Christian Church ❷

Among the most famous military leaders was the Germanic King Charlemagne (SHAR·lah·main). In the late 700s, **Charlemagne,** or Charles the Great, worked to bring political order to the northwestern fringes of what had been the Roman Empire. This great warrior not only fought to increase the size of his kingdom, he also worked to improve life for those who lived there.

A New Roman Emperor Eventually, news of Charlemagne's accomplishments spread to Rome. Although the old empire was gone, Rome was now the center of the Catholic Church. The Pope recognized that joining forces with Charlemagne might bring greater power to the Church.

In 800, the Pope crowned Charlemagne as the new Holy Roman Emperor. During Charlemagne's rule, education improved, the government became stronger, and Catholicism spread. But after Charlemagne's death, Western Europe was once again without a strong political leader.

Region •
Charlemagne
established
order and
supported
education and
culture for a
brief period
in the early
Middle Ages. ▲

The Role of the Church ❷

Throughout Western Europe in medieval times, each community was centered around a church. The church offered religious services, established orphanages, and helped care for the poor, sick, and elderly. They also hosted feasts, festivals, and other celebrations. As communities grew, their members often donated money and labor to build new and larger churches.

Monks and Nuns Some people chose to dedicate their lives to serving God and the Church. These religious people were called monks and nuns. Monks were men who devoted their time to praying, studying, and copying and decorating holy books by hand. Monks lived in communities called monasteries. Many monasteries became important centers of learning in medieval society.

Western Europe: Its Land and Early History **85**

INSTRUCT: Objective ③

Two Medieval Systems/ Medieval Ways of Life

- Who owned most of the land in Europe by the beginning of the Middle Ages? powerful nobles—lords, kings, high church officials
- Under feudalism, how were land and loyalty related? Nobles or rulers granted land to lesser nobles in exchange for political loyalty and help in war.
- What were the benefits of the manor system for the nobles and the peasants? nobles: food and labor; peasants: protection

Connections to History

Today we think of tapestries as works of art. During the Middle Ages, however, tapestries were used to make castle rooms easier to heat. The tapestries were woven to fit particular walls, on which they were hung using large rods. If the tapestry was moved to a different wall, it was cut to fit a smaller wall or to allow access to a door. This explains why tapestries seen in museums today may have different sections of different lengths.

Location • Convents and monasteries often were located in hard-to-reach areas. ▲

Women who served the Church were called nuns. In the Middle Ages, it was common for a woman to become a nun after her husband died. Nuns prayed, sewed, taught young girls, cared for the poor, and also copied and decorated books. They lived in secluded communities called convents.

Vocabulary

secluded: to be separate or hidden away

Two Medieval Systems ③

During the Middle Ages, almost all the land was owned by powerful nobles—lords, kings, and high church officials. The central government was not very strong. The nobles sometimes even controlled the king and constantly fought among themselves. To protect their lands and position, nobles developed a system known as feudalism.

The Feudal System <u>Feudalism</u> was a system of political ties in which the nobles, such as kings, gave out land to less powerful nobles, such as knights. In return for the land, the noble, called a vassal, made a vow to provide various services to the lord. The most important was to furnish his lord with knights, foot soldiers, and arms for battle.

The parcel of land granted to a vassal by his lord was called a fief (feef). The center of the lord's fief was the manor, which consisted of a large house or castle, surrounding farmland, villages, and a church. A fief might also include several other manors or castles belonging to the fief-owner's vassals.

Connections to History

The Bayeux Tapestry This famous work of art depicts the invasion of England by William the Conqueror in 1066. The Bayeux (BY•yeur) Tapestry is a series of scenes from the point of view of the invaders, who came from Normandy. Normandy is a part of what is now France. The work is an important source of information about not only the conquest of England, but also medieval armor, clothing, and other aspects of culture.

Although called a tapestry, the work is really an embroidered strip of linen about 230 feet long. It includes captions in Latin. The Bayeux Tapestry was probably made by nuns in England about 1092.

Activity Options

Differentiating Instruction: Less Proficient Readers

Understanding Key Concepts To help students understand the obligations and rewards of feudalism and manorialism, work with them to create a diagram like the one shown. As you create the diagram, be sure students understand that each group of people had responsibilities to other groups, and that each group benefited from the systems.

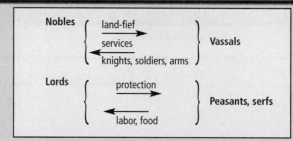

Manorialism On the manor, peasants lived and farmed, but they usually did not own the land they lived on. In exchange for their lord's protection, the peasants contributed their labor and a certain amount of the food they raised. Some peasants, known as serfs, actually belonged to the fief on which they lived. They were not slaves, but they were not free to leave the land without the permission of the lord. This system, in which the lord received food and work in exchange for his protection, is known as **manorialism.**

Place • Although castles were large, they were built for defense. Castles were usually located on high ground with a series of walls and towers. ▲

Medieval Ways of Life ❸

Medieval nobles had more power than the peasants. However, the difference in the standard of living between the very rich and the very poor was not as great as the difference today.

Castle Life The manor houses or castles may have been large, but they were built more for defense than for comfort. Thick stone walls and few windows made the rooms cold, damp, and dark. Fires added warmth but made the air smoky. Medieval noble families may have slept on feather mattresses, but lice and other pests were a constant annoyance. Most castles did not have indoor plumbing.

CRITICAL THINKING ACTIVITY

Recognizing Important Details Ask students to read the second sentence after the heading "Medieval Ways of Life." Then ask them to find details in the paragraphs that follow to show living conditions were difficult for both the rich and the poor in medieval Europe.

Class Time 5 minutes

MORE ABOUT...
Castles

Early medieval castles were built around a central mound (or motte), on which stood a wooden citadel. Within the castle's wooden walls was an open space, or bailey, where local people could gather for safety during wars. A moat around the walls gave still more protection. Later in the Middle Ages, castles were built of stone. As the picture on page 87 shows, the walls around the inner bailey contained a series of towers linked by a walkway along the top of the walls. Other buildings, including the central keep, stood within the walls. Also within the castle walls were wells to supply water.

Activity Options
Multiple Learning Styles: Linguistic

Block Scheduling

Class Time 30 minutes
Task Writing a dialogue between a lord and his serf
Purpose To understand the relationship between a lord and a serf and the responsibilities of and benefits for each

Supplies Needed
• Writing paper
• Pencils or pens

Activity Recall with students that under the manor system, lords protected peasants in return for labor and the food that the peasants raised. Invite students to work in pairs to write a dialogue between one lord and his serf. Suggest that they might focus on a discussion regarding problems or living conditions in the manor, or future plans. Remind them to keep in mind the social class gap between the two. Ask volunteers to read their dialogues aloud.

INSTRUCT: Objective ④

The Growth of Medieval Towns/The Late Middle Ages

- Why did people begin to move back into towns in the 11th century? Fewer people were needed on farms.
- What were the benefits of belonging to a guild? protected workers' rights, set wages and prices, settled disputes
- What were the conditions of the Magna Carta? limited power of king, gave nobles greater say

Connections to Economics

The rise of a middle class of merchants, skilled craftsworkers, and others began in the later Middle Ages, along with the growth of towns and trade. After the Industrial Revolution, in the 1800s and 1900s, the middle class grew rapidly in Western Europe. Today, most Western Europeans belong to the middle class. Nevertheless, a small group of very rich people controls an enormous percentage of the world's wealth. According to *Forbes* magazine, the world's 538 billionaires owned $1.72 trillion worth of assets in 2000—approximately 10 percent of total world production that year.

Peasant Life Peasants lived outside the castle walls in small dwellings, often with dirt floors and straw roofs. They owned little furniture and slept on straw mattresses. It was common for peasant families to keep their farm animals inside their homes.

Peasants often worked two or three days a week for their lord, harvesting crops and repairing roads and bridges. The rest of the week they farmed their own small plots. Many days were religious festivals during which no one worked.

Connections to Economics

The Middle Class In the early Middle Ages, only a small percentage of people in Western Europe were wealthy landowners. Most people worked on manor lands or at some sort of craft. However, those workers who found jobs in towns often were able to save money and build businesses. Eventually, their improved status led to the rise of a middle class.

Unlike nobles, the members of this new middle class did not live off the land they owned. They had to continuously earn money, as most people do today.

The Growth of Medieval Towns ④

By the middle of the 11th century, life was improving for many people in Western Europe. New farming methods increased the supply of food and shortened the time it took to harvest crops. Fewer farmers were needed, and workers began to leave the countryside in search of other opportunities. People moved back into towns or formed new ones that grew into booming centers of trade. The population increased, and more and more people owned property or started businesses.

Guilds As competition among local businesspeople grew, tradespeople and craftspeople created their own guilds, or business associations. Similar to modern trade unions, a **guild** protected workers' rights, set wages and prices, and settled disputes. Membership in a guild was also a common requirement for citizens who sought one of the few elective public offices.

The Late Middle Ages ④

Over time, the towns of the late Middle Ages grew in size, power, and wealth. The citizens of these towns began to establish local governments and to elect leaders.

Reading Social Studies
B. Possible Answer
to protect their businesses and crafts by joining with others

Reading
Social Studies
B. Analyzing Motives Why did people create guilds?

Activity Options

Skillbuilder Mini-Lesson: Reading a Time Line

Explaining the Skill Remind students that in a time line, dates and events are arranged in chronological order. Seeing events on a time line helps a reader see them in relation to one another as well as in order.

Applying the Skill Have students review the section on the Middle Ages and jot down important dates. Encourage them to include approximate dates, such as the 11th century, as well as exact dates, such as A.D. 476. Have students create time lines that begin with the fall of

Rome and end with the signing of the Magna Carta. Suggest that students illustrate the more interesting events listed on their time lines.

Extension Ask students to choose an event on their time line that they consider important. Then ask them to research the event and write a paragraph about it.

Governments Challenge the Church The Pope insisted that he had supreme authority over all the Christian lands. Kings and other government leaders, however, did not agree that the Pope was more powerful than they were. This is an issue that continues to be discussed today.

The Magna Carta The rulers of Western Europe also struggled for power with members of the nobility. In England, nobles rebelled against King John. In 1215, the nobles forced the English king to sign a document called the **Magna Carta** (MAG·nuh KAHR·tuh), or Great Charter. This document limited the king's power and gave the nobles a larger role in the government.

Region • High taxes and failures on the battlefield made King John one of the most hated kings of England. ▼

Region • The Magna Carta influenced the creators of the U.S. Constitution. ▲

SECTION 4 ASSESSMENT

Terms & Names

1. **Identify:**
   (a) medieval
   (b) Charlemagne
   (c) feudalism
   (d) manorialism
   (e) guild
   (f) Magna Carta

Taking Notes

2. Use a flow chart like this one to show how Europe changed over four time periods: A.D. 476, the 800s, the mid-1000s, and the 1200s.

   | 476 |
   | 800s |

Main Ideas

3. (a) Why is this era of European history called the Middle Ages?
   (b) Describe the role of the Church in medieval society.
   (c) How did manorialism help both nobles and peasants?

Critical Thinking

4. **Contrasting**
   How did life differ for nobles and peasants under feudalism?

   Think About
   • where they lived
   • what they ate
   • how they did their work

ACTIVITY -OPTION- Review the information about serfs. Write a series of short **journal entries** describing what a week in the life of a serf might have been like during the Middle Ages.

Section 4 Assessment

1. Terms & Names
   a. medieval, p. 85
   b. Charlemagne, p. 85
   c. feudalism, p. 86
   d. manorialism, p. 87
   e. guild, p. 88
   f. Magna Carta, p. 89

2. Taking Notes

| 476—collapse of Roman Empire |

| 800s—Charlemagne was emperor; government was stronger; Roman Catholicism spread. |

| mid-1000s—Farms prospered; towns and cities grew; guilds protected workers. |

| 1200s—Rulers struggled for power; nobles rebelled; Magna Carta limited the king's power. |

3. Main Ideas
   a. It falls between ancient times and the beginning of the modern era.
   b. Communities were built around a church, which held religious services and festivals. Monks and nuns taught children, cared for the sick and needy, and preserved books and learning.
   c. Nobles protected the peasants and were supported by the food and labor they provided.

4. Critical Thinking

peasants: few rights, owned little, depended on lord and worked hard to supply him with food and labor; nobles: housed and fed better, ran estates, often went to war

ACTIVITY OPTION

   Integrated Assessment
   • Rubric for writing a journal

MORE ABOUT...
The Magna Carta

The rights and protections of the Magna Carta originally benefited only the barons who forced King John to sign the document. They included trial by a jury of one's peers and the right to due process of law—which would prevent the king's arbitrarily seizing property or imprisoning a noble. Such legal limitations on a monarch were unprecedented. Over time, these rights were also extended to ordinary English people.

ASSESS & RETEACH

Reading Social Studies Have students complete the chart on page 66.

Formal Assessment
• Section Quiz, p. 36

RETEACHING ACTIVITIES

Have students work in small groups to identify the most important themes in this section. Then ask them to write a two- to three-sentence summary of each theme. Have a volunteer from each group read the group's summary.

In-depth Resources: Unit 2
• Reaching Activity, p. 14

Access for Students Acquiring English
• Reteaching Activity, p. 22

TERMS & NAMES

1. peninsula, p. 68
2. plain, p. 69
3. city-state, p. 73
4. Aegean Sea, p. 73
5. Athens, p. 74
6. republic, p. 79
7. empire, p. 81
8. Constantine, p. 83
9. feudalism, p. 86
10. Magna Carta, p. 89

REVIEW QUESTIONS

Possible Responses

1. Europe has a variety of waterways and land-forms, particularly peninsulas, mountains, and a central plain. It has a varied climate and abundant resources.
2. The Great European Plain has some of the richest farmland; trade with farmers attracted many people.
3. a common language, shared religious beliefs, similar way of life
4. They united to defeat the Persians.
5. Rome controlled most of the land surrounding the Mediterranean.
6. They feared he was too powerful, a threat to the republic.
7. There was no strong central government; the Church gave people a sense of purpose.
8. Technological advances in farming methods meant that fewer people were needed on farms. Many people left farms, moving to towns and starting businesses.

TERMS & NAMES

Explain the significance of each of the following:

1. peninsula
2. plain
3. city-state
4. Aegean Sea
5. Athens
6. republic
7. empire
8. Constantine
9. feudalism
10. Magna Carta

REVIEW QUESTIONS

A Land of Varied Riches *(pages 67–71)*
1. What is special about Europe's physical environment?
2. Why is the Great European Plain an important region?

Ancient Greece *(pages 72–76)*
3. What helped to unite the separate city-states of ancient Greece?
4. What caused the people of Athens to join forces with their rival city-state, Sparta, in 480 B.C.?

Ancient Rome *(pages 78–83)*
5. Why did the ancient Romans call the Mediterranean Sea "our sea"?
6. Why did the Roman Senate ask Julius Caesar to resign?

Time of Change: The Middle Ages *(pages 84–89)*
7. Why did the people turn to the Roman Catholic Church for leadership and support during the Middle Ages?
8. What contributed to the growth of towns during the Middle Ages?

CRITICAL THINKING

Recognizing Effects
1. Using your completed chart from Reading Social Studies, p. 66, identify changes in art, culture, religion, and social structure from the time of ancient Rome to the Middle Ages.

Hypothesizing
2. Many myths and plays of ancient Greece have been the basis for modern films and dramas. What does this indicate about these ancient stories and characters?

Analyzing Causes
3. How did the long, peaceful reign of Augustus help to promote architecture, literature, and art in the Roman Empire?

Visual Summary

 1 **A Land of Varied Riches**
- The rich natural resources and varied geography of Europe helped to shape its development.

2 **Ancient Greece**
- The ancient Greeks developed a complex society and system of government.
- The achievements of the ancient Greeks in architecture, literature, and philosophy had a lasting impact on the world.

 3 **Ancient Rome**
- Under strong leadership, ancient Rome experienced a time of great growth.
- Ancient Rome's contributions to government, engineering, and literature influenced Western culture.

 **4** **Time of Change: The Middle Ages**
- The social order and government of the Middle Ages transformed Europe into a modern society.

CRITICAL THINKING: Possible Responses

1. Recognizing Effects
Depending on their notes, students may trace the social/political changes from republic to empire to feudalism to the rise of the middle class; the change from worship of many gods to the supremacy of the Catholic Church; the decline in science, arts, and learning after the fall of Rome.

2. Hypothesizing
They dealt with universal themes that continue to appeal to people today.

3. Analyzing Causes
Augustus's long reign brought peace to the region, allowing creativity to flourish. Architects and engineers built many new buildings. The age was also a time of great literature.

SOCIAL STUDIES SKILLBUILDER

"Across the Roman Empire . . . [T]here were gods to protect the house, gods of healing, in fact gods of all aspects of life."
—*Ancient Rome*

"[The ancient Greeks] believed there were many gods and that those gods controlled the universe."
—*Greek Gods and Heroes*

"Each [Roman] home had a special niche or place for the household gods. Every aspect of nature had its particular spirit too."
—*The New Book of Knowledge*

SKILLBUILDER: Making a Generalization
1. What information do these passages have in common?
2. What generalization can you make from the passages?

FOCUS ON GEOGRAPHY

1. **Location** • What bodies of water does the Gulf Stream flow through on the way to Europe?
2. **Movement** • How might the Gulf Stream help transportation by sea?
3. **Location** • From looking at the map, what countries in Europe do you think are most directly affected by the Gulf Stream?

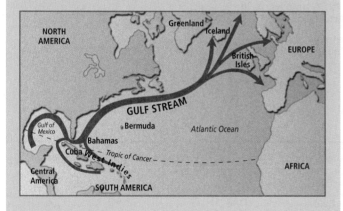

CHAPTER PROJECTS

Interdisciplinary Activity: Language Arts
Writing a Newspaper Report
Research the assassination of Julius Caesar by a group of Roman senators in 44 B.C. Write a front-page news article about the event. Include a headline and answers to the *who, what, where,* and *when* questions of good reporting.

Cooperative Learning Activity
Creating a Playbill With a group of two or three students, design and create a playbill, or program for the audience, for a Greek tragedy. Assign responsibilities for the playbill.
• Design a cover illustration.
• List and identify the characters.
• Provide information about the playwright.
• Include a brief summary of the story.

INTERNET ACTIVITY

Use the Internet to research the natural resources of Europe. Focus on one region, such as the Ruhr Valley, the Mediterranean Sea, or the independent republics of Eastern Europe. Identify the major natural resources and explain how they contributed to that region's development.

Presenting Your Findings Organize your research for a class presentation. Include a map that shows the region and its resources. Prepare a short oral report about how that region has developed in modern times. List the Web sites you used to prepare your report.

For Internet links to support this activity, go to

RESEARCH LINKS
CLASSZONE.COM

CHAPTER PROJECTS
Interdisciplinary Activity: Language Arts

Writing a Newspaper Report Recall with students that Caesar was assassinated by Roman senators who opposed his plans and his power.

Remind students that newspaper articles should report the facts in an impartial way. Brainstorm answers for the who, what, when, and where questions and guide students to include information such as the following: *who* (Caesar, born about 100 B.C., controlled vast armies, ruled Roman Empire); *what* (fatal stabbing by a group of Roman aristocrats led by Brutus and Gaius Cassius); *where* (Senate in Rome); *when* (March 15, 44 B.C.).

Ask students to write interesting headlines. Remind them to proofread.

Cooperative Learning Activity

Creating a Playbill Discuss the features of a playbill, a guide to a play. Point out that a playbill for a Greek tragedy should include a cover illustration that reflects the way actors dressed in ancient Greece, a list of characters, biographical information about the playwright, and a brief summary of the story. You might want to read a play with students, such as *The Trojan War* by Euripides.

INTERNET ACTIVITY

Discuss how students might find information about the natural resources of Europe using the Internet. Brainstorm ideas for keywords, Web sites, and search engines.

Suggest that students make a copy of their chosen map and include symbols and a key to identify the location of various types of natural resources. Encourage them to begin their oral reports with a main idea statement and then to add supporting details.

Skills Answers

Social Studies Skillbuilder
Possible Responses
1. All three passages mention the belief in ancient Greece and Rome in many gods who controlled every aspect of life.
2. People in ancient Greece and Rome worshiped many gods, whom they believed had power over the entire universe.

Focus on Geography
Possible Responses
1. the Gulf of Mexico and the Atlantic Ocean
2. It warms the water of Northern European ports, allowing the ports to remain open at times when they otherwise might be frozen. Ships move at faster speeds when they sail in the same direction as the Gulf Stream.
3. British Isles (England, Ireland, Scotland), France, northern Spain, Scandinavia, Iceland

The Growth of the Western World

	OVERVIEW	COPYMASTERS	INTEGRATED TECHNOLOGY
UNIT ATLAS AND CHAPTER RESOURCES	The students will explore the political and social changes that brought Europe from the Renaissance to the beginning of the modern era.	**In-depth Resources: Unit 2** • Guided Reading Worksheets, pp. 15–18 • Skillbuilder Practice, p. 21 • Unit Atlas Activities, pp. 1–2 • Geography Workshop, pp. 61–62 **Reading Study Guide** (Spanish and English), pp. 26–35 **Outline Map Activities**	Power Presentations Electronic Teacher Tools Online Lesson Planner Chapter Summaries on CD Critical Thinking Transparencies CT7
	KEY IDEAS		
SECTION 1 Renaissance Connections pp. 95–100	• The Renaissance was a new era of creativity and learning in Western Europe. • The Protestant Reformation led to changes in church practices and an increase in education for all people.	**In-depth Resources: Unit 2** • Guided Reading Worksheet, p. 15 • Reaching Activity, p. 23 **Reading Study Guide** (Spanish and English), pp. 26–27	classzone.com Chapter Summaries on CD
SECTION 2 Traders, Explorers, and Colonists pp. 101–105	• Europeans sought shorter trade routes to bring spices from Asia. • Explorers such as da Gama and Magellan discovered new routes and brought European influence to new lands. • European exploration led to imperialism, which brought hardship to African and Native American peoples.	**In-depth Resources: Unit 2** • Guided Reading Worksheet, p. 16 • Reaching Activity, p. 24 **Reading Study Guide** (Spanish and English), pp. 28–29	classzone.com Chapter Summaries on CD
SECTION 3 The Age of Revolution pp. 107–111	• The Industrial Revolution changed the way goods were produced and brought about the growth of cities and factories. • Capitalism is the private ownership of factories and businesses. • The French Revolution claimed thousands of lives before Napoleon gained control of France.	**In-depth Resources: Unit 2** • Guided Reading Worksheet, p. 17 • Reaching Activity, p. 25 **Reading Study Guide** (Spanish and English), pp. 30–31	Critical Thinking Transparencies CT8 classzone.com Chapter Summaries on CD
SECTION 4 The Russian Empire pp. 112–116	• The early czars held unlimited power and sought to minimize the influence of nobles. • Peter the Great and Catherine the Great helped make Russia a strong empire. • The Russian Revolution in 1917 overthrew the monarchy.	**In-depth Resources: Unit 2** • Guided Reading Worksheet, p. 18 • Reaching Activity, p. 26 **Reading Study Guide** (Spanish and English), pp. 32–33	classzone.com Chapter Summaries on CD

KEY TO RESOURCES

 Audio

 CD-ROM

Copymaster

 Internet

 Overhead Transparency

 Pupil's Edition

Teacher's Edition

Video

ASSESSMENT OPTIONS

 Chapter Assessment, pp. 118–119

Formal Assessment
• Chapter Tests: Forms A, B, C, pp. 53–64

Test Generator

Online Test Practice

Strategies for Test Preparation

Section Assessment, p. 100

Formal Assessment
• Section Quiz, p. 49

Integrated Assessment
• Rubric for writing a letter

Test Generator

Test Practice Transparencies TT9

Section Assessment, p. 105

Formal Assessment
• Section Quiz, p. 50

Integrated Assessment
• Rubric for writing a journal entry

Test Generator

Test Practice Transparencies TT10

Section Assessment, p. 111

Formal Assessment
• Section Quiz, p. 51

Integrated Assessment
• Rubric for writing a poem or lyrics

Test Generator

Test Practice Transparencies TT11

Section Assessment, p. 116

Formal Assessment
• Section Quiz, p. 52

Integrated Assessment
• Rubric for writing a summary

Test Generator

Test Practice Transparencies TT12

RESOURCES FOR DIFFERENTIATING INSTRUCTION

Students Acquiring English/ESL

Reading Study Guide (Spanish and English), pp. 26–35

Access for Students Acquiring English
Spanish Translations, pp. 23–32

TE Activities
• Prefixes, p. 96
• Understanding Multiple Meanings, p. 108

Less Proficient Readers

Reading Study Guide (Spanish and English), pp. 26–35

TE Activity
• Determining Cause and Effect, p. 115

Gifted and Talented Students

TE Activity
• Researching a Topic, p. 109

CROSS-CURRICULAR CONNECTIONS

Humanities

Lassieur, Allison. ***Leonardo da Vinci and the Renaissance in World History.*** Berkeley Heights, NJ: Enslow, 2000. Places da Vinci in the context of his world.

Murrell, Kathleen Berton. ***Eyewitness: Russia.*** New York: DK Publishing, 2000. From empire to today's federation.

Literature

Maynard, Christopher. ***The History News: Revolution.*** Cambridge, MA: Candlewick Press, 1999. Presents in fictional newspaper format facts relating to the French, American, Russian, and Chinese revolutions.

Science/Math

Sharth, Sharon. ***Way to Go!: Finding Your Way With a Compass.*** Pleasantville, NY: Reader's Digest, 2000. History, science, and activities using a compass.

History

Aaseng, Nathan. ***You Are the Explorer.*** Minneapolis: Oliver Press, 2000. Readers face the same dilemmas as explorers and must solve the problems.

Macaulay, David. ***Ship.*** Boston: Houghton Mifflin, 1993. Underwater archaeology uncovers caravels from the 15th century.

ENRICHMENT ACTIVITIES

The following activities are especially suitable for classes following block schedules.

Teacher's Edition, pp. 97, 98, 99, 103, 104, 106, 109, 113, 114
Pupil's Edition, pp. 100, 105, 111, 116

Unit Atlas, pp. 54–63

Technology: 1781, p. 117
Outline Map Activities

INTEGRATED TECHNOLOGY

Go to **classzone.com** for lesson support and activities for Chapter 4.

BLOCK SCHEDULE LESSON PLAN OPTIONS: 90-MINUTE PERIOD

DAY 1

CHAPTER PREVIEW, pp. 92–93
Class Time 20 minutes

- **Hypothesize** Use the "What do you think?" questions in Focus on Geography on PE p. 93 to help students hypothesize about the connection between trade and disease.

SECTION 1, pp. 95–100
Class Time 70 minutes

- **Identifying Cause and Effect** Working on their own, have students create a matching game of causes and effects of the Renaissance. Have students trade games and compete, then review and discuss as a class.
  Class Time 30 minutes

- **Discussion** Lead a discussion reviewing the reasons wealthy Renaissance patrons supported artists and scholars. Invite students to analyze the motives behind such support.
  Class Time 10 minutes

- **Forming and Supporting Opinions** Have students imagine they are living in Germany in 1530. Have each student create a logical written argument first in support of, and then in opposition to, translating the Latin Bible into German. Have students share their arguments when they finish.
  Class Time 30 minutes

DAY 2

SECTION 2, pp. 101–105
Class Time 50 minutes

- **Analyzing Motives** Have five students sit in a line across the classroom, and give the first student a pencil, saying it costs $.50. Tell students to "buy" and "sell" the pencil to the next in line, adding a $.20 profit for the seller each time. When the last student has "bought" the pencil, have students compare the first price ($.50) with the last price ($1.30). Point out that this is why European spice traders wanted to buy directly from Asia.
  Class Time 25 minutes

- **Calculating Mileage** Tell students that the Portuguese sailed east, around Africa, looking for the shortest route to Asia, while the Spanish sailed west, across the Atlantic. Have students predict which route they think is shorter. Ask students to use the scale on the globe to calculate mileage for each water route. Then have them use their calculations to verify their predictions.
  Class Time 25 minutes

SECTION 3, pp. 107–111
Class Time 40 minutes

- **Peer Competition** Divide the class into pairs. Assign each pair one of the Terms & Names for this section. Have pairs make up three questions that can be answered with the term or name. Have pairs take turns asking the class their questions.

DAY 3

SECTION 4, pp. 112–116
Class Time 35 minutes

- **Time Line** Have each student choose one important event or aspect of Russian history covered in this section and write it in large letters on a piece of paper. Holding their papers, have students stand up and organize themselves into a human time line. Discuss each event in order, identifying any missing events.

CHAPTER 4 REVIEW AND ASSESSMENT, pp. 118–119
Class Time 55 minutes

- **Review** Have students prepare a summary of the chapter by reviewing the Main Idea and Why It Matters Now features of each section in Chapter 4.
  Class Time 20 minutes

- **Assessment** Have students complete the Chapter 4 Assessment.
  Class Time 35 minutes

TECHNOLOGY IN THE CLASSROOM

VIEWING ART ON THE WEB

One advantage of the Internet is that it offers a variety of images that supplement textbook material. For example, the Internet offers excellent opportunities to view works of art from many periods and places, and in many styles. Students can view some of the world's most famous artworks from their classroom or computer lab.

ACTIVITY OUTLINE

Objective Students will view examples of pre-Renaissance and Renaissance art and compare and contrast these artworks in a document on the computer.

Task Ask students to visit Web sites to explore the differences between pre-Renaissance and Renaissance painting styles. Have them copy and paste one painting from each period into a document on the computer and write one-page reports comparing the two artworks.

Class Time Two class periods

DIRECTIONS

1. Have students reread Chapter 4. As a class or individually, have students list words that characterize the Renaissance.

2. Have students go through the first two Web sites at **classzone.com** to learn about artistic techniques that became common during the Renaissance. Ask them to take notes on the methods of painting that characterized the Renaissance and on how these methods differed from pre-Renaissance art. As an option, they may want to sketch some examples of linear perspective and other elements of Renaissance art.

3. Discuss students' findings as a class, making sure they understand that Renaissance art was characterized by attention to linear perspective, proportion, and careful observation of the subject.

4. Have students go to the third Web site at **classzone.com** to compare pre-Renaissance (Gothic and Byzantine) paintings with Renaissance paintings. Ask them to choose two paintings, one pre-Renaissance and one Renaissance, to compare and contrast.

5. Tell students to copy both paintings from the Web and paste them into a document on the computer. Ask them to label each painting with the URL where they found the painting, the name of the artist, the date, and the country.

6. Have students use a word processing program to write one-page reports comparing and contrasting these paintings. Encourage them to focus on the techniques employed in the Renaissance movement and to tell why the pre-Renaissance painting would have been considered outdated during the Renaissance.

CHAPTER 4 OBJECTIVE

Students will explore the political and social changes that brought Europe from the Renaissance to the beginning of the modern era.

FOCUS ON VISUALS

Interpreting the Photograph Have students look closely at the photograph. Ask them to identify the most distinguishing feature of the Cape of Saint Vincent. Then ask why they think Prince Henry's School of Navigation was located in this apparently desolate place.

Possible Responses There is water on both sides of the Cape of Saint Vincent. Its location made it a perfect spot from which to launch voyages of trade and exploration to the south.

Extension Have students make a list of the subjects that might have been taught at the School of Navigation.

CRITICAL THINKING ACTIVITY

Analyzing Motives Remind students that Portugal is a small country bordering Spain to the north and east. The Atlantic Ocean lies to the west and south. Display a world map and a map of Western Europe, and invite students to speculate about why Portugal became one of the greatest seafaring nations of the 15th and 16th centuries.

Class Time 15 minutes

The Growth of New Ideas

SECTION 1   Renaissance Connections

SECTION 2   Traders, Explorers, and Colonists

SECTION 3   The Age of Revolution

SECTION 4   The Russian Empire

92

Recommended Resources

BOOKS FOR THE TEACHER
Corrick, James A. *The Industrial Revolution.* San Diego, CA: Lucent Books, 1998. Overview of European and American Industrial Revolutions.
Fritz, Jean. *Around the World in a Hundred Years: From Henry the Navigator to Magellan.* New York:

Putnam & Grosset, 1998. Chronicles 15th-century European exploration.
Hosking, Geoffrey A. *Russia and the Russians: A History.* Cambridge, MA: Harvard University Press, 2001. Cultural history, ancient to modern.

SOFTWARE
Explorers of the New World. Cambridge, MA: Softkey. Journeys, findings, and results of exploration.

INTERNET
For more information about Europe and Russia, visit **classzone.com.**

How can trade spread disease?

FOCUS ON GEOGRAPHY

Movement • In 1347, an epidemic of bubonic plague (boo•BON•ik playg) hit Europe. This plague, also called the Black Death, started in Asia. Caravans and trading ships carried it to port cities on the Mediterranean Sea. The plague spread from Sicily to the Italian Peninsula and then to France, Spain, and England.

The Black Death was carried by fleas that infected both rats and humans. Rats did not die from the plague. Instead, they served as hosts, or carriers, for the disease. By 1349, the horrors of the epidemic reached Switzerland, Austria, and Hungary. Later, it even reached as far north and east as Scandinavia and Russia. Historians estimate that this plague killed one out of every three persons in Europe.

What do you think?

♦ Why might the plague have reached Italy before it spread to England?

♦ How do you think the Black Death might have affected the economy of Europe?

Place The Cape of Saint Vincent is at the southwest tip of Portugal, jutting into the Atlantic Ocean. This was the location of Prince Henry's School of Navigation, where Portuguese sailors learned ways to explore the oceans of the world.

93

FOCUS ON GEOGRAPHY

Objectives

• To help students understand the relationships among geography, trade, and economics

• To identify the physical and social impact of trade on communities

What Do You Think?

1. Make sure students understand the location of Sicily relative to the Italian mainland and England. Encourage them to compare the distances and to consider which route was likely to have more frequent trade contacts.

2. Ask students to think about what happens to an economy when there are fewer people to make and buy goods.

How can trade spread disease?

Ask students to develop a list of the different activities in trading. Lead them to understand that trade enables people to share and exchange food, goods, clothing, plants, animals, and ideas. Have students consider how these activities might transmit disease.

MAKING GEOGRAPHIC CONNECTIONS

Have students consider the recent spread of the West Nile virus. The virus, which came from Africa, recently has been found in birds along the East Coast of the United States. Ask students to describe how they think the speed of travel and the extent of human trade affect the spread of disease among people and animals.

Implementing the National Geography Standards

Standard 13 Explain why peoples sometimes engage in conflict to control Earth's surface

Objective To identify and list factors that contribute to conflicts between countries

Class Time 20 minutes

Task Ask each student to list two pairs of countries that have adjoining borders. Beneath each pair, students should indicate factors that might contribute to conflict between the countries, such as boundary disputes, dissimilar languages, competition for natural resources, and so on.

Evaluation Students should list at least three reasons for possible conflict between each pair of countries.

BEFORE YOU READ

What Do You Know?

Ask students to identify classroom items that are made in a factory, such as clothing, books, desks, and clocks. Lead students to conclude that almost all of the items we use in our everyday lives are mass-produced in a factory. Ask students to discuss what they know about factories and mass production, including why mass-produced items are less costly to make.

What Do You Want to Know?

Ask each student to copy the topic names from the Influences column in the chart to the right into their notebook. Have each student develop two questions about each topic that they would like answered. As students read the chapter, have them look for answers to these questions.

READ AND TAKE NOTES

Reading Strategy: Categorizing Explain to students that this chart will help them organize the main ideas of the chapter. Point out that there were many changes in this time period. Tell them that the completed chart will be an organized way to look at how those changes are connected. They may also find answers to many of their questions.

 In-depth Resources: Unit 2
• Guided Reading Worksheets, pp. 15–18

 READING SOCIAL STUDIES

BEFORE YOU READ

▶▶ What Do You Know?

Do you know who first sailed around the world? Do you know that Leonardo da Vinci drew plans for a helicopter 400 years before it was actually built? Think of other discoveries, inventions, events, and famous people. What do you think life was like for common people during this time? Think about movies you have seen, books you have read, and what you have learned in other classes about the Renaissance, the Industrial Revolution, and political revolutions in France, Russia, and the United States.

▶▶ What Do You Want to Know?

Decide what you know about changes in the West from the Renaissance into the 1800s. In your notebook, record what you hope to learn from this chapter.

READ AND TAKE NOTES

Reading Strategy: Categorizing One way to make sense of what you read is to categorize ideas. Categorizing means sorting information by certain traits, ideas, or characteristics. Use the chart below to categorize details about the topics covered in this chapter.

• Copy the chart into your notebook.
• As you read each section, look for information about ideas, people, and events.
• Record key details in each category.

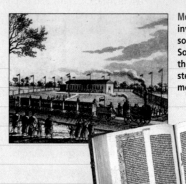

Movement • New tools inventions contributed social and political cha Some improvements i the astrolabe (above), steam engine (left), an movable type (below).

Influences	New Ideas	People/Achievements	Events/Effects
The Renaissance	emphasis on education, arts	trade, da Vinci, Shakespeare, printing press	new class of aristocrats, patrons
European Exploration and Conquest	desire to control trade routes	navigation, da Gama, Columbus, Magellan	imperialism, colonialism, slavery
Scientific and Industrial Revolutions	capitalism	locomotive, Galileo, telescope	factories, disease, pollution
Political Revolutions	political rights, equality, nationalism	French constitution, Napoleon	French Revolution, Reign of Terror
The Russian Empire	revolution, Western ideas	Ivan IV, Peter the Great, Catherine the Great, Nicholas II	expansion, Bloody Sunday, revolution

Teaching Strategy

Reading the Chapter This is a chronological chapter that covers periods in Europe from the 1400s to the early 1900s. These include the Renaissance, European exploration and trade, the Industrial Revolution, and the French and Russian Revolutions. The chapter identifies the ways in which these events are connected and explores the causes and effects of each. Encourage students to identify specific relationships among events.

Integrated Assessment The Chapter Assessment on pages 118–119 describes several activities that may be used for integrated assessment. You may wish to have students work on these activities during the course of the chapter and then present them at the end.

Renaissance Connections

TERMS & NAMES
Crusades
Renaissance
Florence
Leonardo da Vinci
William Shakespeare
Reformation
Martin Luther
Protestant

MAIN IDEA
The rebirth of art, literature, and ideas during the Renaissance changed European society.

WHY IT MATTERS NOW
Many accomplishments of the Renaissance are high points of Western culture and continue to inspire artists, writers, and thinkers of today.

SECTION OBJECTIVES
1. To explain the scope of Europe's Renaissance
2. To describe the growth of arts and learning in Europe during the Renaissance
3. To identify the religious conflicts that led to the Protestant Reformation
4. To describe the Reformation and Luther's work

SKILLBUILDER
• Interpreting a Map, p. 96

CRITICAL THINKING
• Summarizing, p. 96
• Analyzing Motives, p. 98
• Hypothesizing, p. 99

FOCUS & MOTIVATE
WARM-UP

Making Inferences Have students read <u>Dateline</u> and discuss these questions.
1. Why is this Crusade important to King Louis IX?
2. What long-term effect does the king hope to have on the lands around the Mediterranean?

INSTRUCT: Objective ❶

Europeans Encounter New Cultures/The Rebirth of Europe

• What was the Renaissance? When did it exist? a new era of creativity and learning in Western Europe; from the 14th to the 16th century

• What kinds of great works emerged during the Renaissance? paintings, large sculptures, impressive architecture, literature

 In-depth Resources: Unit 2
• Guided Reading Worksheet, p. 15

 Reading Study Guide
(Spanish and English), pp. 26–27

DATELINE (EXTRA)

PARIS, FRANCE, 1269

Paris is buzzing with activity as thousands of European soldiers assemble here. This is the starting-off point for the eighth Crusade, which has nearly a thousand miles to travel. King Louis IX of France, who is in command, is confident that his armies can restore European power over the Holy Land.

Since the Crusades began in 1096, the Christians have fought against the Muslims and founded four states in the eastern Mediterranean. European power has weakened since then. However, King Louis's army looks ready to recapture the lost territory for Christianity.

Movement • Crusaders will make their way toward the Holy Land. ▲

Europeans Encounter New Cultures ❶

BACKGROUND
The Holy Land of the eastern Mediterranean is important to Christians, Jews, and Muslims.

The **Crusades**—a series of military expeditions in the 11th, 12th, and 13th centuries by Western European Christians to reclaim control of the Holy Lands from the Muslims—had a great influence on life in Western Europe. The long distances traveled by the Crusaders opened up trade routes, connecting Western Europeans with people of southwestern Asia and North Africa. This increased contact also helped Europeans rediscover the ideas and achievements of the ancient Greeks and Romans.

The Growth of New Ideas **95**

Program Resources

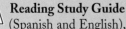 **In-depth Resources: Unit 2**
• Guided Reading Worksheet, p. 15
• Reteaching Activity, p. 23

 Reading Study Guide
(Spanish and English), pp. 26–27

 Formal Assessment
• Section Quiz, p. 49

 Integrated Assessment
• Rubric for writing a letter

 Outline Map Activities

 Access for Students Acquiring English
• Guided Reading Worksheet, p. 23

 Technology Resources
classzone.com

TEST-TAKING RESOURCES
🕭 Strategies for Test Preparation
🕭 Test Practice Transparencies
🕮 Online Test Practice

CRITICAL THINKING ACTIVITY

Summarizing Have students write a summary about what they have learned so far about the Renaissance. Remind students that a summary includes only the most important ideas about a topic. Have students work together to create a concept web on the chalkboard with the word *Renaissance* in the center. As they suggest main ideas, record their suggestions in the outer circles. Then ask each student to write a summary about the Renaissance, using the ideas in the web.

Class Time 15 minutes

FOCUS ON VISUALS

Analyzing the Photograph Point out the Duomo, the cathedral in the center of the photograph, and tell students that the construction of the cathedral's dome marks the beginning of Renaissance architecture. Studying in Rome, the architect Filippo Brunelleschi learned about the construction of columns and arches. He studied ancient Roman ruins and used the principles he discovered when designing the dome. The dome's diameter is 130 feet. Ask students why they think it might be difficult to build a dome of this size without internal or external support. Why is it unlikely that such a project would have succeeded or even been attempted before the Renaissance?

Possible Response The diameter of the dome is too large to be supported with columns. The design required a sophisticated understanding of mathematics and engineering—neither of which flourished during medieval times.

Extension Have students write a letter from Filippo Brunelleschi to a fellow architect about his design for the Duomo.

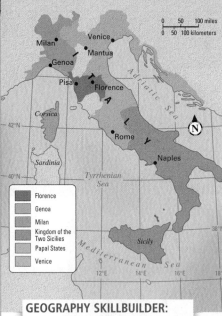

Italian City-States, c. 1350

Milan
Venice
Mantua
Genoa
Pisa
Florence
Corsica
Rome
Sardinia
Naples
Tyrrhenian Sea
Mediterranean Sea
Sicily
Adriatic Sea

0   50   100 miles
0   50   100 kilometers

Florence
Genoa
Milan
Kingdom of the Two Sicilies
Papal States
Venice

GEOGRAPHY SKILLBUILDER:
Interpreting a Map
1. **Location** • Which city-state does not have access to water?
2. **Location** • Which city-state was in the best position to trade by land and sea with Asia?

Over time, this interest in the ancient world sparked a new era of creativity and learning in Western Europe. This cultural era, which lasted from the 14th to the 16th century, is called the **Renaissance**.

The Rebirth of Europe ❶

The Renaissance began on the Italian Peninsula in the mid-14th century. During this time, many artists, architects, writers, and scholars created works of great importance. These included beautiful paintings, large sculptures, impressive buildings, and thought-provoking literature. As new ideas and achievements spread across the continent of Europe, they changed the way people viewed themselves and the world.

The Italian City-States In the 14th century, the Italian Peninsula was divided into many independent city-states. Some of these city-states, such as **Florence**, were bustling centers of banking, trade, and manufacturing.

Geography Skillbuilder Answers
1. Milan
2. Venice

Region • Florence, once a wealthy city-state, remains an important economic and cultural center. The Duomo, shown here, is a symbol of the city's Renaissance past. ▼

Activity Options

Differentiating Instruction: Students Acquiring English/ESL

Prefixes Students acquiring English may be confused about the meaning of the words *rebirth* and *rediscover*. Explain that the prefix *re–* means "again." Write the word equation *re–* + discover = rediscover (*discover again*) on the chalkboard. Then read aloud the heading "The Rebirth of Europe" on page 96. Ask students to explain in their own words what that heading means, focusing particularly on the word *rebirth*.

```
EQUATION

RE- + DISCOVER = REDISCOVER

DISCOVER AGAIN
```

Region • The wealthy merchants in Italy built large palaces, called palazzos, such as Florence's Palazzo Medici shown here. ▶

The wealthy businesspeople who lived in these city-states were members of a new class of aristocrats. Unlike the nobles of the feudal system, these aristocrats lived in cities, and their wealth came from money and goods rather than from the lands they owned.

A Changing View of the World Religion was important to people's daily life during the Renaissance, but many wealthy Europeans began to turn increased attention to the material comforts of life.

New wealth allowed aristocratic families to build large homes for themselves in the city centers, decorating them with luxurious objects. They ate expensive food and dressed in fine clothes and jewels, often acquired as a result of the expanded trade routes. Aristocrats also placed increased emphasis on education and the arts.

Learning and the Arts Flourish ❷

Wealthy citizens were proud of their city-states and often became generous patrons. A patron gave artists and scholars money and, sometimes, a place to live and work. They hired architects and designers to improve local churches, to design grand new buildings, and to create public sculptures and fountains. As one Italian city-state made additions and improvements, others competed to outdo it.

BACKGROUND

Some Renaissance architects, such as Filippo Brunelleschi (broo•nuh•LEHS•kee), studied the ruins of Roman buildings and modeled their new buildings after ancient designs.

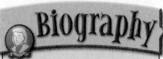

Biography

The Medici Family Among the most famous patrons of the Renaissance were the Medici (MEHD•uh•chee). They were a wealthy family of bankers and merchants. In fact, they were the most powerful leaders of Florence from the early 1400s until the 18th century.

Along with Lorenzo, pictured below, the Medici family included famous princes and dukes, two queens, and four popes. Throughout the 15th and 16th centuries, the Medici supported many artists, including Botticelli, Michelangelo, and Raphael. Today, Florence is still filled with important works of art made possible by the Medici.

The Growth of New Ideas **97**

Biography

Among the many famous members of the Medici family, three are especially noteworthy. Lorenzo Medici, grandson of the family founder, ruled Florence from 1469 until 1492. Under his leadership, Florence became one of Italy's most powerful cities.

Catherine Medici (1519–1589) was married to one French king, Henry II, and was the mother of three other French kings.

Marie Medici (1573–1642) was married to French king Henry IV. When he was assassinated in 1610, her eight-year-old son, Louis XIII, inherited the throne. Because of his youth, Marie ruled France as queen regent for seven years.

INSTRUCT: Objective ❷

Learning and the Arts Flourish/ The Northern Renaissance

- What did patrons do to improve their city-states? hired artists to beautify cities and scholars to increase their status
- How did art subjects change in the Renaissance? from solely religious subjects to a wider variety of subjects
- In addition to being an artist, what else was Leonardo da Vinci? He was an engineer, a scientist, and an inventor.
- What effect did Renaissance ideas have on Northern Europe? inspired artists and writers

Activity Options

Interdisciplinary Link: Art

Class Time One class period

Task Drawing an object, showing a light source

Purpose To understand one of the important changes in art that took place during the Renaissance

Supplies Needed
- Drawing paper
- Pencils
- Small objects to draw
- Information about Renaissance artist Giotto and copies of his drawings and paintings

Block Scheduling

Activity Explain that Giotto was among the first artists to show how light shines on an object in nature. He illuminated one side of an object and painted the opposite side in shadow. Place several small objects in a place where they will cast a shadow. Ask students to draw one object, showing the direction of the light source and the resulting shadows. Suggest students make realistic drawings.

CRITICAL THINKING ACTIVITY

Analyzing Motives Remind students that wealthy Renaissance patrons supported artists and scholars to improve and beautify their city-states. Invite students to analyze the motives behind such support. Lead students to consider various ways in which improving the appearance and status of their city-states would ultimately benefit these wealthy patrons, both socially and economically.

Class Time 15 minutes

Connections to Math

One Renaissance artist interested in perspective was Jacopo Bellini. He lived in Venice in the 1400s, and he used perspective to paint three-dimensional scenes on flat wooden panels. Most of his paintings, famous in his own time, have been lost. Today he is best known for his drawings, which range from simple sketches to more detailed compositions, all of which display his interest and skill in creating the illusion of space.

MORE ABOUT...
William Shakespeare

Many people consider William Shakespeare to be the greatest playwright who ever lived. In Shakespeare's time, attending plays in the afternoon was a popular form of entertainment for English people from all walks of life. Shakespeare wrote more than two dozen plays, including both comedies and tragedies. He also wrote many sonnets and other poems. Shakespeare's mastery of words, images, and rhythm was so great that his work is still among the most widely read in English, even though the language has changed a great deal in the nearly four centuries since his death. Today Shakespeare's plays are staged more often, and in more countries, than ever before.

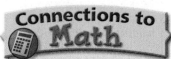

Culture •
Leonardo da Vinci completed the painting *La Belle Ferronniere* in 1495. ▲

As part of the competition to improve the appearance and status of their individual city-states, patrons wanted to attract the brightest and best-known scholars and poets of the time. Patrons believed that the contributions of these individuals would, in turn, add to the greatness of their city-states and attract more wealth.

The Visual Arts: New Subjects and Methods Most medieval art was based on religious subjects. Painters and sculptors of the early Renaissance created religious art too, but they also began to depict other subjects. Some made portraits for wealthy patrons. Others created works showing historical scenes or mythological stories.

Leonardo da Vinci One of the most famous artists and scientists of the Renaissance was **Leonardo da Vinci** (lee·uh·NAHR·doh duh VIN·chee) (1452–1519). Among his best-known paintings are the *Mona Lisa*, a portrait of a young woman with a mysterious smile, and *The Last Supper*. Da Vinci was more than just a talented painter, however.

Throughout his life, da Vinci observed the world around him. He studied the flow of water, the flight of birds, and the workings of the human body. Da Vinci, who became a skilled engineer, scientist, and inventor, filled notebooks with thousands of sketches of his discoveries and inventions. He even drew ideas for flying machines, parachutes, and submarines—hundreds of years before they were built.

The Northern Renaissance ❷

As the new Renaissance ideas about religion and art spread to Northern Europe, they inspired artists and writers working there. The Dutch scholar and philosopher Desiderius Erasmus (ih·RAZ·muhs) (1466–1536), for example, criticized the church for its wealth and poked fun at its officials. During the late 16th and early 17th centuries, another writer—the Englishman **William Shakespeare**—wrote a series of popular stage plays. Many of his works, including *Romeo and Juliet* and *Macbeth*, are still read and performed around the world.

Connections to Math

Perspective During the Renaissance, artists began to use a technique called linear perspective. Linear perspective is a system of using lines to create the illusion of depth and distance. In the drawing below, notice how the perspective lines move toward a single point in the distance, giving the picture depth.

Reading Social Studies

A. Contrasting How did the subject matter of Renaissance art differ from medieval art?

Reading Social Studies
A. Possible Answer It depicted more than religious subjects.

Activity Options

Skillbuilder Mini-Lesson: Making a Generalization

Explaining the Skill Remind students that making generalizations means to make broad judgments based on information gathered from several sources.

Applying the Skill Have students reread "Leonardo da Vinci" and use these strategies to begin to develop a generalization. Students will need to consult additional sources to complete the generalization.

🅱 Block Scheduling

1. Make a list of things Leonardo da Vinci studied. water, birds, body
2. Make a second list of the subjects he drew. people, buildings, machines, ideas for inventions
3. Use this information to write a generalization about da Vinci. Leonardo da Vinci had a wide range of interests.

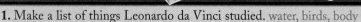

The Reformation 3

BACKGROUND

In 1516, the English writer Thomas More published a famous book called *Utopia*. It describes the author's idea of a perfect society. Today, the word "utopia" is used to describe any ideal place.

Roman Catholicism was still the most powerful religion in Western Europe. Some of the views of the northern Renaissance writers and scholars, however, were in conflict with the Roman Catholic Church. These new ideas would eventually lead to the **Reformation,** a 16th-century movement to change church practices.

Martin Luther The German monk **Martin Luther** (1483–1546) was one of the most important critics of the church. The wealth and corruption of many church officials disturbed him. Luther also spoke out against the church's policy of selling indulgences—the practice of forgiving sins in exchange for money.

In 1517, Luther wrote 95 theses, or statements of belief, attacking the sale of indulgences and other church practices. Copies were printed and handed out throughout Western Europe. After this, Luther was excommunicated, or cast out and no longer recognized as a member of a church, and went into hiding. While in hiding, he translated the Bible from Latin into German so that all literate, German-speaking people could read it. Under Luther's leadership, many Europeans began to challenge the practices of the Roman Catholic Church.

Thinking Critically Possible Answers

1. multiple copies, books made faster and more cheaply
2. monks or nuns

Spotlight on CULTURE

The Printing Press Until the Renaissance, each copy of a book had to be written by hand—usually by monks or nuns. A Renaissance invention, however, changed that forever. Around 1450, a German printer named Johannes Gutenberg (Yoh•HAN•es GOOT•en•burg) began to use a method of printing with movable type. This meant that multiple copies of books, such as this Bible, could be printed quickly and less expensively.

Although many Renaissance books dealt with religious subjects, printers also published plays, poetry, works of philosophy and science, and tales of travel and adventure. As greater numbers of books were published, more and more Europeans learned to read.

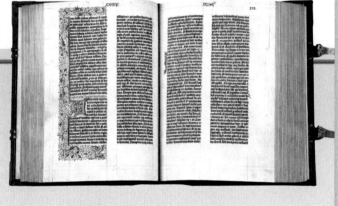

THINKING CRITICALLY

1. **Recognizing Effects**
   What were three effects of the invention of Gutenberg's printing press?

2. **Synthesizing**
   Before the printing press, who produced the books?

The Growth of New Ideas **99**

INSTRUCT: Objective 3

The Reformation

- What was the Reformation? a 16th-century movement to change church practices
- What were Martin Luther's criticisms of the Roman Catholic Church? wealth, corruption, selling indulgences

CRITICAL THINKING ACTIVITY

Hypothesizing Discuss with students why they think Martin Luther translated the Bible from Latin into German. Explain that at that time, Latin was a language used by priests but not understood by most people. Translating the Bible into German, the language of the people, meant that more people would have direct access to the Bible's ideas and would thus be less dependent on the authority of the church.

Class Time 15 minutes

Spotlight on CULTURE

Soon after Gutenberg created his first printing press, he began to improve his invention. The first method, which involved pressing by hand, did not produce evenly printed pages. Adding a large screw to the printing press solved the problem, and soon Gutenberg could print 300 pages a day. Within 50 years of Gutenberg's first efforts, there were more than 1,000 printing shops in Europe, and several million books had been printed.

Activity Options

Multiple Learning Styles: Logical

Class Time One class period

Task Using logical reasoning to support two opposing points of view

Purpose To create logical arguments to support and oppose

translating the Latin Bible into other languages

Supplies Needed
- Writing paper
- Pencils or pens

Block Scheduling

Activity Have students imagine they are living in Germany in 1530. They have learned that Martin Luther has translated the Latin Bible into German. Ask each student to create a logical written argument first to support, and then to oppose, this accomplishment. Remind students that their reasons on each side must make sense and support the main argument. Have students share their arguments when they finish.

INSTRUCT: Objective ❹

A Conflict over Religious Beliefs

• What were Martin Luther's followers called and why? Protestants; they protested against the church

• Why did Protestants push to expand education? so more people could read the Bible

ASSESS & RETEACH

Reading Social Studies Have students fill in the top row of the chart on page 94, "The Renaissance."

 Formal Assessment
• Section Quiz, p. 49

RETEACHING ACTIVITY

Have students work in small groups to create a five-question quiz about the section. Encourage students to write questions about the most important ideas and their supporting details. Then have groups exchange quizzes, answer questions, and return the quizzes to check their answers.

 In-depth Resources: Unit 2
• Reteaching Activity, p. 23

 Access for Students Acquiring English
• Reteaching Activity, p. 29

Reading Social Studies

B. Clarifying How did Protestants get their name?

Reading Social Studies
B. Possible Answer
They protested the intolerance of the church.

A Conflict over Religious Beliefs ❹

Luther's followers were called **Protestants** because they protested events at an assembly that ended the church's tolerance of their beliefs. Many people in Western Europe still supported the church, however. This conflict led to religious wars that ended in 1555. At that time, the Peace of Augsburg declared that German rulers could decide the official religion of their own state.

The Spread of Protestant Ideas By 1600, Protestantism had spread to England and the Scandinavian Peninsula. Protestants pushed to expand education for more Europeans. They did this because being able to read meant being able to study the Bible. They also encouraged translation of the Bible into the native language of each country.

The Counter Reformation The Roman Catholic Church responded to Protestantism by launching its own movement in the mid-16th century. As part of this movement, called the Counter Reformation, the church stopped selling indulgences. It also created a new religious order called the Society of Jesus, or the Jesuits. Jesuit missionaries and scholars worked to spread Catholic ideas across Europe, to Asia, and to the lands of the "new world" across the Atlantic Ocean.

Region • Martin Luther's writings and actions changed Christianity forever. ▲

SECTION ❶ ASSESSMENT

Terms & Names

1. Identify: (a) Crusades (b) Renaissance (c) Florence (d) Leonardo da Vinci
(e) William Shakespeare (f) Reformation (g) Martin Luther (h) Protestant

Taking Notes

2. Use a spider map like this one to chart the characteristics and accomplishments of the Renaissance.

Renaissance Accomplishments

Main Ideas

3. (a) Where and when did the Renaissance begin?

(b) In what ways were the wealthy Europeans of the Renaissance different from the wealthy Europeans of feudal times?

(c) What was the Counter Reformation?

Critical Thinking

4. Hypothesizing

Why do you think Protestantism spread so quickly in Northern Europe?

Think About

♦ new methods of printing

♦ the ideas of the northern Renaissance

♦ the work of Martin Luther

ACTIVITY -OPTION- Write a **letter** to an imagined patron asking for support to create a project—such as a public sculpture, park, fountain, or building—to beautify your community.

100 CHAPTER 4

Section ❶ Assessment

1. Terms & Names
a. Crusades, p. 95
b. Renaissance, p. 96
c. Florence, p. 96
d. Leonardo da Vinci, p. 98
e. William Shakespeare, p. 98
f. Reformation, p. 99
g. Martin Luther, p. 99
h. Protestant, p. 100

2. Taking Notes

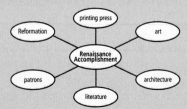
printing press — art
Reformation — Renaissance Accomplishment — architecture
patrons — literature

3. Main Ideas
a. The Renaissance began on the Italian Peninsula in the mid-14th century.
b. The wealth of Renaissance Europeans came from money and goods. The wealth of feudal Europeans came from land.
c. It was the Roman Catholic Church's response to its Protestant critics.

4. Critical Thinking

Possible Response The Protestants' support of widespread education and the translation of the Bible might have had great appeal to Northern Europeans.

ACTIVITY OPTION

 Integrated Assessment
• Rubric for writing a letter

Traders, Explorers, and Colonists

MAIN IDEA

European trade and exploration changed the lives of many people on both sides of the Atlantic.

WHY IT MATTERS NOW

Today, citizens of the Americas continue to feel the effects of European exploration and colonization.

TERMS & NAMES

Prince Henry the Navigator
Christopher Columbus
Ferdinand Magellan
circumnavigate
imperialism

SECTION OBJECTIVES

1. To recognize the importance of trade routes between Europe and Asia
2. To identify Portuguese explorers and routes
3. To identify Spanish and English explorers and routes
4. To describe the effect of European exploration on Africa and North and South America

SKILLBUILDER
• Interpreting a Map, pp. 102, 105

CRITICAL THINKING
• Summarizing, p. 104

FOCUS & MOTIVATE
WARM-UP

Drawing Conclusions Have students read Dateline and discuss these questions.

1. Why do you think Prince Henry invited people with different kinds of knowledge to his school?
2. What could you say about the maps, tools, and information available to early navigators?

INSTRUCT: Objective ❶

Trade Between Europe and Asia

• What item was in great demand in Europe? Why? spices; to preserve food and improve flavor
• Why did Europeans want a new route to Asia? land route was long, made spices expensive

In-depth Resources: Unit 2
• Guided Reading Worksheet, p. 16

Reading Study Guide
(Spanish and English), pp. 28–29

DATELINE

SAGRES, PORTUGAL, 1421—
Portugal's Prince Henry may not have journeyed to sea, but he has earned a well-deserved nickname: "The Navigator." He has organized expeditions of sailors to explore the west coast of Africa. Five years ago, Henry also founded a School of Navigation. It is here in Sagres, at Portugal's southwestern tip, which juts into the Atlantic Ocean.

Astronomers, geographers, and mathematicians gather here to study and teach new methods of traveling across the seas. They plan expeditions using the latest maps, tools, and information about the winds and currents of the Atlantic Ocean. Sometimes the scholars add to their knowledge by talking with sea captains about their voyages.

Movement • Prince Henry of Portugal founded the School of Navigation. ▲

Trade Between Europe and Asia ❶

For centuries before the Renaissance, European traders traveled back and forth across the Mediterranean. Merchants commonly journeyed from southern Europe to North Africa and to the eastern Mediterranean. Spices were one of the most important items traded at this time.

The Growth of New Ideas **101**

Program Resources

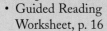

In-depth Resources: Unit 2
• Guided Reading Worksheet, p. 16
• Reteaching Activity, p. 24

Reading Study Guide
(Spanish and English), pp. 28–29

Formal Assessment
• Section Quiz, p. 50

Integrated Assessment
• Rubric for writing a journal entry

Outline Map Activities

Access for Students Acquiring English
• Guided Reading Worksheet, p. 24

Technology Resources
classzone.com

TEST-TAKING RESOURCES
↩ Strategies for Test Preparation
↩ Test Practice Transparencies
⬤ Online Test Practice

FOCUS ON VISUALS

Interpreting the Map Have students trace the routes of the Portuguese explorers shown on the map. Ask them why the explorers could not sail directly east through the Mediterranean Sea and into the Indian Ocean but instead had to take the longer, more hazardous route around the southern tip of Africa.

Possible Responses There was a small land barrier between the Mediterranean Sea and the Red Sea. The later construction of the Suez Canal made it possible to travel between the Mediterranean and Red seas.

Extension Have students imagine they are crew members on one of the Portuguese ships and write a letter home describing their experiences.

INSTRUCT: Objective ❷

Leaders in Exploration

- Why did Prince Henry send explorers down the coast of Africa? to find a shortcut to Asia
- Which Portuguese explorer first rounded the southern tip of Africa? Bartolomeu Dias
- What was the result of Vasco da Gama's expedition to India? Portugal controlled the sea route to Asia.

The Spice Trade Spices were in great demand by Europeans. Before refrigeration, meat and fish spoiled quickly. To help preserve food and to improve its flavor, people used spices such as pepper, cinnamon, nutmeg, and cloves. These spices came from Asia.

For centuries, Italian merchants from Genoa and Venice controlled the spice trade. They sailed to ports in the eastern Mediterranean, where they would purchase spices and other goods from traders who had traveled across Asia. The Italian merchants would then bring these goods back to Europe.

The Possibility of Great Wealth Transporting goods across these great distances was costly. Everyone along the way had to be paid and wanted to earn a profit. By the time the spices reached Europe, they had to be sold at extremely high prices.

European merchants knew that if they could trade directly with people in Asia, they could make enormous profits. In the 15th century, Europeans began to search for a new route to Asia.

Leaders in Exploration ❷

The small country of Portugal is at the westernmost part of the European continent. Portuguese sailors had navigated the waters of the Atlantic Ocean for centuries. As shown on the map below, they traveled down the west coast of Africa and as far west into the Atlantic as Madeira, the Azores, and the Canary Islands.

Exploring the African Coast In the early 1400s, Portugal's **Prince Henry the Navigator** decided to send explorers farther down the coast of Africa. He believed that if explorers could find a way around Africa, it might be a shortcut to Asia. Portuguese explorers returned home from these expeditions with gold dust, ivory, and more knowledge of navigation. By the time Henry died in 1460, the Portuguese had ventured around the great bulge of western Africa to present-day Sierra Leone.

Portuguese Explorers, 1400s

Dias 1487–1488
da Gama 1497–1498

Geography Skillbuilder Answers
1. da Gama
2. Africa

GEOGRAPHY SKILLBUILDER: Interpreting a Map
1. **Movement** • Which explorer reached Asia?
2. **Location** • Which continent was most explored by the Portuguese?

102 CHAPTER 4

Activity Options

Multiple Learning Styles: Interpersonal

Class Time 25 minutes
Task Demonstrating transactions along an "in-class" trade route
Purpose To understand why transporting goods across great distances makes them more costly

Supplies Needed
• Pencil

Activity Have five students sit in a line across the classroom. Give the first student a pencil and state that it costs $0.50. Instruct students to "buy" and "sell" the pencil to the next person in line, each time adding a $0.20 profit for the seller. Continue until the fifth and final student buys the pencil. Keep track of each transaction. Compare the first price ($0.50) and the last price ($1.30). Point out that this is the same process that drove up the cost of spices.

The Race Around Africa Bold Portuguese explorers continued to push farther down the African coast. Finally, in 1488, Bartolomeu Dias (bahr·TAHL·uh·myoo DEE·ahs) rounded the southern tip of Africa. The Portuguese named the tip the Cape of Good Hope.

Less than ten years later, Vasco da Gama (vas·KOH deh GAH·mah) led a sea expedition all the way to Asia. Da Gama and his crew traveled for 317 days and 13,500 miles before reaching the coast of India. They were the first Europeans to discover a sea route to Asia. Now, the riches of Asia could be brought directly to Europe. After setting up trading posts along the coast of the Indian Ocean, Portugal ruled these waterways.

Europe Enters a New Age ③

Portugal was not the only European country to understand that whoever controlled trade with Asia would have great power and wealth. Spain and England quickly entered the race to find a direct sea route of their own.

Christopher Columbus Some explorers believed that the shortest way to Asia was to sail west across the Atlantic Ocean. Queen Isabella of Spain agreed to fund an expedition across the Atlantic.

In August 1492, an Italian named **Christopher Columbus** and 90 crew members left Spain aboard three ships—the *Santa Maria,* the *Pinta,* and the *Niña.* The Atlantic Ocean proved to be wider than maps of the time suggested. On October 12, after weeks at sea, the crew spotted land. Although Columbus thought he had found Asia, they were off the coast of an island in the Caribbean. This was still a great distance from their spice-rich destination.

Ferdinand Magellan In 1519, Spain funded an expedition for the Portuguese explorer **Ferdinand Magellan** (muh·JEHL·uhn). Magellan left Spain with five ships and more than 200 sailors. As they traveled west, the crew battled violent storms and rough seas. Food was in short supply, and starving sailors ate rats and sawdust. Some died of disease.

Reading Social Studies

A. Recognizing Important Details What continent did Columbus reach, and where did he think he was?

Reading Social Studies
A. Answer
He reached the Caribbean, but he thought he had found Asia.

Connections to Science

New Ships In the early 15th century, Portuguese shipbuilders designed a sturdy ship called a caravel, pictured below. Built for exploration and trade, the caravel was small and had a narrow body. This helped the ship to cut through waves and to travel in shallow water.

The caravel also used a combination of square and triangular sails. These made sailing easier against strong, shifting winds.

Connections to Science

Caravels were used by the Portuguese and Spanish for both coastal and ocean journeys. The caravel was smaller and easier to maneuver than the other ship of the time, the galleon. Caravels varied in size and weight, depending on their purpose. For example, caravels used for coastal trading weighed approximately 10.2 metric tons, while caravels used for ocean expeditions weighed approximately 51 metric tons. Two of the three ships that Christopher Columbus used in his 1492 expedition were caravels—the *Niña* and the *Pinta.*

INSTRUCT: Objective ③

Europe Enters a New Age

- What lands did Christopher Columbus discover while searching for a route to Asia? the Caribbean Islands
- What did members of Magellan's crew accomplish that no one had ever done before? They circumnavigated the globe.
- What did the explorer John Cabot accomplish? In 1497, he sailed west from England, hoping to find Asia. Instead, he landed in present-day Newfoundland in Canada.
- Why did King Henry VII fund Cabot's voyage? He wanted a share in the riches of Asia, which Portugal and Spain had monopolized.

The Growth of New Ideas **103**

Activity Options

Interdisciplinary Links: Geography/Mathematics

Block Scheduling

Class Time 30 minutes

Task Calculating the mileage of two routes

Purpose To compare the distances of an eastward and westward sailing route from Spain to Asia

Supplies Needed
- World map or globe
- Calculators
- Paper
- Pens or pencils

Activity Point out to students that the Portuguese sailed east around Africa looking for the shortest route to Asia, while the Spanish sailed west, across the Atlantic and around South America. Have students study the map or globe and decide which route they think is shorter. Then have them use the scale on the map or globe to calculate two water routes from Spain to Asia: one traveling east, one traveling west.

MORE ABOUT...

Navigation

The first compasses were simple devices: pieces of magnetic iron, floating on straw or cork in a bowl of water. They were first used by Chinese and Mediterranean sailors around the year 1000 A.D. In the 1300s, compass makers began dividing the compass card into 32 different points of direction. Other improvements and continued experience enabled sailors to use compasses with increasing accuracy over time.

CRITICAL THINKING ACTIVITY

Summarizing At great expense of lives and time, Ferdinand Magellan's expedition was the first time human beings ever sailed all the way around the world. Have students summarize this undertaking by listing the obstacles the explorers faced. violent storms, rough seas, lack of food and fresh water, disease, hostile peoples, years at sea If students have trouble recalling the information, have them reread the information on pages 103–104. Ask them to imagine they are reporters in Spain who witnessed the return of the surviving members of Magellan's crew. Have them write and orally present a two-sentence "breaking news report" that summarizes the historic voyage.

Class Time 15 minutes

INSTRUCT: Objective ④

The Outcomes of Exploration

• What is imperialism? the practice of one country controlling the government and economy of another country

• What were some unexpected outcomes of European explorations for the people of Africa and North and South America? diseases, religious conversion, slavery

---

Movement • Sailors figured their ship's position with the astrolabe. It measured the position of the sun and stars in relation to the horizon. ▼

By the time Magellan and his ships reached the Philippines in Asia, the sailors had spent 18 long months at sea. Then, during a battle there, Magellan and several crew members were killed. The expedition returned to Spain after a three-year journey. Only one boat and 18 crew members succeeded. They had to **circumnavigate,** or sail completely around, the world.

John Cabot King Henry VII of England did not want Portugal and Spain to claim all the riches of Asia. He funded a voyage by Italian-born Giovanni Caboto, called John Cabot by the English, who believed that a northern route across the Atlantic Ocean might be a shortcut to Asia.

Aboard one small ship, Cabot and 18 crew members sailed west from England in May 1497. When they reached land the following month, Cabot thought they had found Asia. Most likely, they landed in present-day Newfoundland in Canada.

The Outcomes of Exploration ④

The kings and queens of Europe sent explorers in search of a direct trade route to Asia. These expeditions, however, turned out to have unexpected results.

A Clash of Cultures European countries founded many new colonies along the coastal areas of Africa and North and South America. This practice of one country controlling the government and economy of another country or territory is called **imperialism.** These conquered lands were already home to large, self-ruling populations. They had their own cultural traditions. After the arrival of the Europeans, the lives of these indigenous peoples would never be the same.

Religious Conversion The European monarchs were Christians. They had strong religious beliefs, and they sent missionaries and other religious officials to help convert conquered peoples to Christianity. The European rulers also hoped that these new converts would help Christianity overcome other powerful religions, especially Islam.

The Spread of Diseases Without knowing it, the European explorers and colonists carried diseases with them, including smallpox, malaria, and measles. These diseases were unknown in the Americas, and killed tens of thousands of people there.

Vocabulary

indigenous: born and living in a place, rather than having come from somewhere else

---

Reading **Social Studies**

B. Identifying Problems What were the main problems faced by Magellan and his crew?

Reading Social Studies
B. Possible Answers
storms, food shortages, disease

Activity Options

Interdisciplinary Link: Geography

Class Time One class period

Task Developing a board game based on alternative northern routes to Asia that John Cabot could have used

Purpose To develop creative ways to organize and express

information about sailing routes from England to Asia

Supplies Needed
• World map or globe
• Paper
• Pens or pencils
• Blank map outlines

Block Scheduling

Activity Have students find two or three alternative water routes that John Cabot could have used to reach Asia. Working in small groups, have students develop board games using those routes to get players from *Start* in England to *Finish* in Asia. Tell students that they must use actual waterways. They must decide where and how players move, create delays due to weather conditions, and determine rules for playing and winning. Have groups play each other's games.

Columbus, Cabot, and Magellan, 1492–1522

GEOGRAPHY SKILLBUILDER: Interpreting a Map
1. **Movement** • Which explorer traveled in the Pacific Islands?
2. **Location** • What continent did John Cabot reach?

←	Columbus 1492
←	Cabot 1497
←	Magellan 1519–1522

Slavery European explorations also led to an expanding slave trade. The Portuguese purchased West Coast African people to work as slaves back in Portugal, where the work force had been reduced by plague. In other colonized areas, such as Mexico and parts of South America, Europeans forced conquered peoples to work the land where they lived. For hundreds of years, Africans and conquered peoples of the Americas would be forced to work under horrible conditions.

Geography Skillbuilder Answers
1. Magellan
2. North America

SECTION 2 ASSESSMENT

Terms & Names

1. **Identify:** (a) Prince Henry the Navigator (b) Christopher Columbus (c) Ferdinand Magellan
   (d) circumnavigate (e) imperialism

Taking Notes

2. Use a chart like this one to compare characteristics of the voyages of Christopher Columbus and Vasco da Gama.

Columbus's Voyage	Da Gama's Voyage

Main Ideas

3. (a) Why were spices so important to Europeans?

   (b) Why did Europeans want to find a new route to Asia?

   (c) Name three ways in which European exploration affected the indigenous peoples of North and South America.

Critical Thinking

4. **Making Inferences**

   Why do you think the Portuguese became leaders of European exploration?

   Think About

   ◆ the location of Portugal

   ◆ early Portuguese voyages

   ◆ Prince Henry and his School of Navigation

ACTIVITY -OPTION- Reread the information about Magellan's voyage around the world. Write a **journal entry** describing the events of the voyage from the point of view of a crew member.

The Growth of New Ideas **105**

ASSESS & RETEACH

Reading Social Studies Have students fill in the second row of the chart on page 94, "European Exploration and Conquest."

 Formal Assessment
• Section Quiz, p. 50

RETEACHING ACTIVITY

Assign students different headings of the section to review. Ask each student to draw a picture or a cartoon that illustrates a main idea of the assigned reading. Tell them to write captions for their drawings. Arrange the drawings sequentially and use them to review the entire section.

 In-depth Resources: Unit 2
• Reteaching Activity, p. 24

Access for Students Acquiring English
• Reteaching Activity, p. 30

Section 2 Assessment

1. Terms & Names
a. Prince Henry the Navigator, p. 102
b. Christopher Columbus, p. 103
c. Ferdinand Magellan, p. 103
d. circumnavigate, p. 104
e. imperialism, p. 104

2. Taking Notes

Columbus's Voyage	da Gama's Voyage
Left in August 1492	Left about 5 years after Columbus
Three ships	Sailed east
Sailed west	Spotted land after 317 days at sea
Spotted land after weeks at sea	Made it to the coast of India
Made it to Caribbean Islands	

3. Main Ideas
a. Before refrigeration, spices preserved food and improved its flavor.
b. European merchants would make more money buying the spices directly.
c. European explorers brought new diseases, slavery, and religion.

4. Critical Thinking

Possible Response The Portuguese had been sailors and navigators for centuries. Also, Prince Henry's School of Navigation probably increased their chances of success.

ACTIVITY OPTION

 Integrated Assessment
• Rubric for writing a journal entry

SKILLBUILDER

Researching Topics on the Internet

Defining the Skill

Take a poll to discover how many students have used the Internet. Have students share the kinds of information they research on the Internet. Brainstorm real-life situations in which the Internet could provide useful information, such as planning a trip, finding directions, or learning information about a subject.

Applying the Skill

How to Research Topics on the Internet
Point out the three strategies for doing research on the Internet. Explain to students that they need to work through each strategy in order to fully understand and successfully use the Internet for research. Remind students that the Internet can provide access to a range of material not easily accessed in other ways. Impress upon them the importance of being a critical consumer.

Practicing the Skill

Have students work with partners to create a list of interesting topics about the Renaissance that they might want to explore further. Then they can come up with a list of keywords that they could use in their research. If students need additional practice, suggest a real-life topic they might research on the Internet. Examples include an interest or hobby, a current event, or directions to a given destination.

 In-depth Resources: Unit 2
• Skillbuilder Practice, p. 21

SKILLBUILDER

Researching Topics on the Internet

▶▶ Defining the Skill

The Internet is a computer network that connects libraries, museums, universities, government agencies, businesses, news organizations, and private individuals all over the world. Each location on the Internet has a home page with its own address, or URL (universal resource locator). With a computer connected to the Internet, you can reach the home pages of many organizations and services. The international collection of home pages, known as the World Wide Web, is an excellent source of up-to-date information about the regions and countries of the world.

▶▶ Applying the Skill

The Web page is the European Reading Room at the Library of Congress Web site. Use the strategies listed below to help you understand how to research topics on the Internet.

How to Research Topics on the Internet

Strategy ❶ Once on the Internet, go directly to the Web page. For example, type http://www.loc.gov/rr/european/extlinks.html in the box at the top of the Web browser and press ENTER. The Web page will appear on your screen.

Strategy ❷ Explore the European Reading Room links. Click any of the links to find more information about a subject. These links take you to other Web sites.

Strategy ❸ Always confirm information you have found on the Internet. The Web sites of universities, government agencies, museums, and trustworthy news organizations are more reliable than others. You can often find information about a site's creator by looking for copyright information or reviewing their home page.

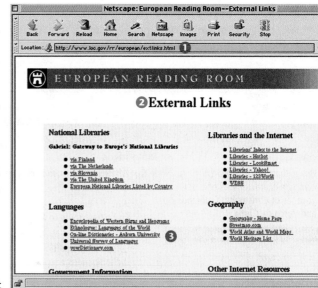

▶▶ Practicing the Skill

Turn to Chapter 4, Section 1, "Renaissance Connections." Read the section and make a list of topics you would like to research. Go to the Library of Congress European Reading Room at http://www.loc.gov/rr/european/extlinks.html. There you will find links that provide more information about topics in this section.

Career Connection: Reference Librarian

Encourage students who enjoy researching topics on the Internet to find out about careers that use this skill. Tell students that a reference librarian, for example, helps people locate information about a vast range of subjects.

1. Locate information about the typical tasks a reference librarian performs. Elicit from students that reference librarians must be able to

ⓑ Block Scheduling

find specific information on the Internet as well as in traditional reference books.

2. Help students find out what qualities and training a person needs in order to become a reference librarian.

3. Have students create a poster or other visual aid that summarizes their findings.

The Age of Revolution

SECTION 3

TERMS & NAMES
Scientific Revolution
Industrial Revolution
labor force
capitalism
French Revolution
Reign of Terror
Napoleon Bonaparte

MAIN IDEA

Scientific, industrial, and political revolutions transformed European society.

WHY IT MATTERS NOW

European revolutions in science, technology, and politics helped to create modern societies throughout the world.

DATELINE
EXTRA

LEIPZIG, GERMANY, APRIL 1839

A new era in German history has begun. The Leipzig-Dresden railway is open for business. Although short rail lines have been in service for a few years, this is the first long-distance railway in this part of Europe.

The steam locomotive that powers the German train was made in England. It is the latest improvement to

George Stephenson's "Rocket" train, which set a speed record of 30 mph in 1829. Already, this new form of transportation is changing Europe. The railroads are attracting many passengers and are also ideal for hauling goods. It seems that wherever new train stations are built, growth and prosperity soon follow.

Region • Leipzig's railway will now take passengers all the way to Dresden. ▲

Changes in Science and Industry ❶

The steam-powered locomotive was only one in a long line of technological improvements made in Europe since the 1600s. In fact, scientists and inventors made so many discoveries during these years that Europe experienced both a scientific and an industrial revolution. These periods of great change would help to create modern societies.

Vocabulary
revolution: a period of great change

The Growth of New Ideas **107**

SECTION OBJECTIVES

1. To describe the changes that occurred during the Scientific and Industrial Revolutions
2. To explain the effect of the Industrial Revolution on Europe's labor force
3. To identify the growth in citizens' rights and changes in government in France and England

SKILLBUILDER
• Interpreting a Chart, p. 109

CRITICAL THINKING
• Analyzing Motives, p. 111

FOCUS & MOTIVATE
WARM-UP

Making Inferences Have students read Dateline and discuss the following questions to help them understand how transportation changes affect an economy.

1. What might a long-rail service offer that a short-line service does not?
2. What other kinds of services and supplies will be needed around the new train stations?

INSTRUCT: Objective ❶

Changes in Science and Industry

• What were some inventions of the Scientific Revolution? telescope, microscope, classification systems
• What was the Industrial Revolution, and in what ways did it change workers' lives? a change in the way goods were produced; workers moved to cities to work in factories

In-depth Resources: Unit 2
• Guided Reading Worksheet, p. 17

Reading Study Guide
(Spanish and English), pp. 30–31

Program Resources

In-depth Resources: Unit 2
• Guided Reading Worksheet, p. 17
• Reteaching Activity, p. 25

Reading Study Guide
(Spanish and English), pp. 30–31

Formal Assessment
• Section Quiz, p. 51

Integrated Assessment
• Rubric for writing a poem

Outline Map Activities

Access for Students Acquiring English
• Guided Reading Worksheet, p. 25

Technology Resources
classzone.com

TEST-TAKING RESOURCES
➘ Strategies for Test Preparation
➘ Test Practice Transparencies
🌐 Online Test Practice

Teacher's Edition **107**

One of the leaders of the Renaissance's Scientific Revolution was Galileo. He emphasized two ideas: the importance of controlled experiments and the value of observation. He used these ideas in his own scientific research. For example, he tested the long-held belief, first established by Aristotle, that heavier objects fall to the ground faster than lighter ones. After dropping heavy objects and light objects from the same height, he observed that they landed at the same time. Controlled experimentation and careful observation had disproved an accepted belief and laid the groundwork for understanding basic physics.

INSTRUCT: Objective ❷

The Workshop of the World

- What is capitalism? a system in which factories and businesses are privately owned
- How were cities affected by industrialization? became dirtier, more crowded, polluted, and full of disease

MORE ABOUT...
The Industrial Revolution

The Industrial Revolution marked the beginning of modern technology, but it could not have taken place without coal miners, whose only tools were picks and shovels. The machines in the new factories required much more power than the traditional horses or water wheels could provide. One important new power source was the steam engine, which burned coal to heat water. Steam engines and many factory machines were made of iron, and smelting—the process of separating iron from ore—also required coal.

The Scientific Revolution In the 16th and 17th centuries, scientific discoveries changed the way Europeans looked at the world. This led to the **Scientific Revolution**.

In Italy, Galileo Galilei (gal·uh·LAY·oh gal·uh·LAY·ee) (1564–1642) studied the stars and planets using a new invention called the telescope. Later in Holland, Antoni van Leeuwenhoek (LAY·vun·hook) (1632–1723) used a microscope to explore an unknown world found in a drop of water. The Swedish botanist Carolus Linnaeus (lih·NEE·uhs) (1707–1778) even developed a system to name and classify all living things on Earth.

Culture •
In 1610, Galileo used his telescope to observe that Jupiter had moons. ▲

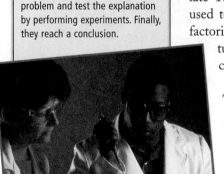

The Scientific Method During the Scientific Revolution, scientists began doing research in a new way, called the scientific method. This scientific method is still used by scientists today.

First, scientists identify a problem. Next, they collect data about the problem. Using this data, they develop an explanation for the problem and test the explanation by performing experiments. Finally, they reach a conclusion.

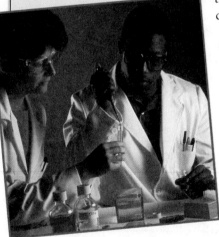

The Industrial Revolution Many inventions of the Scientific Revolution began to change the way people worked all across Europe. Machines performed jobs that once had been done by humans and animals. This brought about such great change that it led to a revolution in the way goods were produced: the **Industrial Revolution**.

Machines were grouped together to make products in large factories. Early factories were built in the countryside near streams and rivers so that they could be powered by water. By the late 1700s, however, new steam engines were used to power the machinery. More and more factories could now be built in cities. People, in turn, moved from the countryside to the cities in search of work.

The Workshop of the World ❷

The Industrial Revolution began in England in the late 1700s. The first English factories made textiles, or cloth. The steam-powered machines of the textile industry produced large amounts of goods quickly and cheaply. So many factories were built in England that the country earned the nickname "The Workshop of the World."

Reading Social Studies

A. Finding Causes How did the Scientific Revolution lead to the Industrial Revolution?

Reading Social Studies
A. Possible Answer
New inventions changed the way people worked.

Activity Options
Differentiating Instruction: Students Acquiring English/ESL

Understanding Multiple Meanings Point out the word *revolution* in the headings "The Scientific Revolution" and "The Industrial Revolution." Explain that the word *revolution* has several meanings. In this context, it means "major changes in ideas, materials, and methods."

Tell students that later in this section they will read about the French Revolution. Explain that *revolution* can also mean "the overthrow and replacement of a government." Ask students to use *revolution* in sentences, using both meanings of the word.

BACKGROUND

In the 1850s, laws were finally passed to help protect women and children from long hours and harsh working conditions.

Hard Work for Low Pay The Industrial Revolution created a need for workers, or a **labor force**, in cities. The workers who ran the textile machines made up part of this labor force. Most workers could earn more income in cities than on farms, but life could be hard. Factory laborers worked long hours and received low pay. In fact, many families often sent their children to work to help create more income.

In 1838, women and children made up more than 75 percent of all textile factory workers. Children as young as seven were forced to work 12 hours a day, six days a week.

The Spread of Industrialization

The textile industry in 18th-century England was one step in the development of an economic system called **capitalism.** In this system, factories and other businesses that make and sell goods are privately owned. Private business owners make decisions about what goods to produce. They sell these goods at a price that will earn a profit.

Industrialization spread from England to other countries, including Germany, France, Belgium, and the United States. Cities in these countries grew rapidly and became more crowded and dirtier. Diseases, such as cholera (KAHL·uh·ruh) and typhoid (TY·foyd) fever, spread. Smoke from factories blackened city skies, and pollution fouled the rivers.

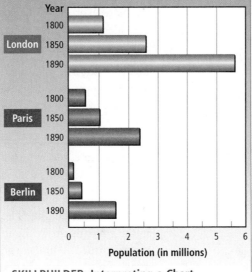

Population Growth in European Cities

SKILLBUILDER: Interpreting a Chart

1. Which city had the largest growth in population?
2. What was the population of Paris in 1890?

Skillbuilder Answers

1. London
2. about 2.3 million people

Place • Factories, like this one in Sheffield, England, were found throughout Western Europe by the mid-19th century. ▶

The Growth of New Ideas **109**

INSTRUCT: Objective ❸

The French Revolution

- What were some of the causes of the French Revolution? food shortages, hunger, heavy taxes, uncaring government
- What happened during the Reign of Terror? 17,000 people were executed for disagreeing with revolutionary leaders
- Who restored order to France? Napoleon Bonaparte

MORE ABOUT...
Marie Antoinette

Marie Antoinette was only a teenager when she became queen of France in 1774. She had little formal education and was bored by the affairs of the government. She soon became very unpopular with the French people, as she was quite unconcerned about their suffering and France's financial crisis. A popular but unsubstantiated story about her claims that she once asked a government official why the people were so angry. When he replied, "Because they have no bread," she answered, "Then let them eat cake." She did not understand that a large number of her subjects were too poor to afford either.

MORE ABOUT...
The Bastille

The Bastille held only seven prisoners when a mob stormed it on July 14, 1789. The rebels wanted the man in charge of the prison to turn over the weapons and ammunition that were stored there. His refusal to answer the demand so enraged the mob that it stormed and captured the prison. After they took over the government, the revolutionaries demolished the Bastille. July 14—Bastille Day—is a national holiday that the people of France celebrate with parades and fireworks.

The French Revolution ❸

Along with changes in science, technology, and the economy came new ideas about government. In the late 18th century, many ordinary citizens began to fight for more political rights.

Ripe for Political Change By the 1780s, the French government was deeply in debt because of bad investments and the costs of waging wars. Life was miserable for the common working people. Poor harvests combined with increased population had led to food shortages and hunger. People were forced to pay heavy taxes. At the same time, the French king, Louis XVI, and his queen, Marie Antoinette, continued to enjoy an expensive life at court, entertaining themselves and the French nobility.

Storming the Bastille The citizens of France demanded changes in the government, without success. Then, on July 14, 1789, angry mobs stormed a Paris prison called the Bastille (bah·STEEL). The attack on this prison, which reflected the royal family's power, became symbolic of the **French Revolution**.

Revolts spread from Paris to the countryside, and poor and angry workers burned the homes of the nobility. By 1791, France had a new constitution that made all French citizens equal under the law.

Reading Social Studies

B. Analyzing Motives Why did the French citizens demand a new government?

Region • The storming of the Bastille remains a symbol of the French Revolution. ▼

Activity Options

Interdisciplinary Link: Government

Class Time 20 minutes

Task Creating a list of questions that French citizens might have used to design a new government

Purpose To understand the role of government

Supplies Needed
- Paper
- Pens and pencils

Activity Point out to students that when the people of France overthrew the monarchy, they were faced with the task of creating a new government. Lead a discussion about the kinds of decisions a new government must make, such as how to raise money, how to make laws, and how to resolve conflicts. Have each student write a list of questions to be addressed by the framers of a new constitution.

The French Republic In 1792, France became a republic. King Louis XVI was found guilty of treason, or betraying one's country. In 1793, he and Marie Antoinette were sentenced to death. They were beheaded on the guillotine (GEE·yah·teen).

Still, France was not at peace. The new revolutionary leaders refused to tolerate any disagreement. Between 1793 and 1794, these new leaders executed 17,000 people. This period of bloodshed became known as the **Reign of Terror**.

Napoleon French leaders continued to struggle for power until 1799, when General **Napoleon Bonaparte** (nuh·POH·lee·uhn BOH·nuh·part) took control. The French Revolution and the disorder that followed were finally over.

However, the new sense of equality brought about by the Revolution stirred feelings of nationalism among the French. Nationalism is pride in and loyalty to one's nation. Soon, the citizens of other European nations began to fight for more political power. Slowly, they, too, won more rights.

Region • Napoleon Bonaparte crowned himself emperor of France in 1804. He led France to victory in what became known as the Napoleonic Wars. ▲

SECTION 3 ASSESSMENT

Terms & Names

1. Identify:
   (a) Scientific Revolution
   (b) Industrial Revolution
   (c) labor force
   (d) capitalism
   (e) French Revolution
   (f) Reign of Terror
   (g) Napoleon Bonaparte

Taking Notes

2. Use a chart like this one to list some of the scientific, industrial, and political changes that occurred during the Age of Revolutions.

Scientific Changes	Industrial Changes	Political Changes

Main Ideas

3. (a) Describe at least three inventions or discoveries of the Scientific Revolution.

   (b) How did the Industrial Revolution change the way people in Europe worked?

   (c) What changes occurred in France after the French Revolution?

Critical Thinking

4. **Recognizing Effects**
   How did industrialization change the cities to which it spread?

   Think About
   ◆ population
   ◆ diseases
   ◆ the environment

ACTIVITY -OPTION- Reread the section about the French Revolution. Write a **poem** or **lyrics** for a folk song that describe the events from the point of view of a common citizen or a member of the royal family.

The Growth of New Ideas **111**

Section 3 Assessment

1. Terms & Names
   a. Scientific Revolution, p. 108
   b. Industrial Revolution, p. 108
   c. labor force, p. 109
   d. capitalism, p. 109
   e. French Revolution, p. 110
   f. Reign of Terror, p. 111
   g. Napoleon Bonaparte, p. 111

2. Taking Notes

Scientific Changes	Industrial Changes	Political Changes
invented telescope, microscope	factories, labor force	French Revolution

3. Main Ideas
   a. Three inventions are telescopes, microscopes, and scientific method.
   b. More and more people worked in factories in cities.
   c. The French monarchy was overthrown and France became a republic with a new constitution.

4. Critical Thinking

   Possible Response Cities became crowded, polluted, and riddled with disease.

   ACTIVITY OPTION

    Integrated Assessment
   • Rubric for writing a poem

SECTION OBJECTIVES

1. To describe the impact of the early czars on the internal and external affairs of Russia

2. To explain the growth of Russia into a large empire under strong rulers

3. To explain problems of Russia's expansion

4. To identify causes of the Russian Revolution

SKILLBUILDER
• Interpreting a Map, p. 114

CRITICAL THINKING
• Recognizing Important Details, p. 114

FOCUS & MOTIVATE
WARM-UP

Drawing Conclusions Have students read <u>Dateline</u> and discuss the following questions to help them explore how the cathedral expresses Russia's growth and power.

1. What do the size and decorations of the Cathedral of St. Basil say about Russia's economy?

2. What does the addition of the Tatars' lands mean for Russia's future?

INSTRUCT: Objective ❶

Russia Rules Itself

• Who was the first czar of Russia after it broke free of the Mongols? Ivan IV, or Ivan the Terrible

• What is an unlimited government? a government in which a single ruler holds all the power

• Why were the early czars and nobles in conflict? Czars saw nobles as a threat to their control.

 In-depth Resources: Unit 2
• Guided Reading Worksheet, p. 18

 Reading Study Guide
(Spanish and English), pp. 32–33

The Russian Empire

TERMS & NAMES
czar
Ivan the Terrible
Peter the Great
Catherine the Great
Russian Revolution

MAIN IDEA

Strong leaders built Russia into a large empire, but the country's citizens had few rights and struggled with poverty.

WHY IT MATTERS NOW

Russia has had a great influence on world politics and is experiencing a period of great change.

MOSCOW, RUSSIA, 1560—Today, the most magnificent church in Moscow opened with a grand celebration. The Cathedral of St. Basil has ten domes—each one unique. The massive structure, built of bricks and white stone, is decorated with brilliant colors.

Ivan IV built this cathedral to celebrate his victory eight years ago over the Tatars (TAH•turz). These Turkish people who live in Central Asia have long threatened Russia's security.

The victory also added the lands of the Tatars, including their capital at Kazan, to our growing empire. Russians everywhere should be proud of Moscow's new church and of the victory it symbolizes.

Place • Ivan IV has honored a Russian victory over the Tatars with the construction of St. Basil's Cathedral. ▲

Ivan IV ▲

Russia Rules Itself ❶

Russia, geographically the world's largest nation, is located in both Europe and Asia. It takes up large parts of both continents, and both continents have helped shape its history.

Mongols from eastern Asia conquered Russia in the 13th century and ruled it for about 200 years. During the 15th century, Russia broke free of Mongol rule. At this time, the most important Russian city was Moscow, located in the west.

112 CHAPTER 4

Program Resources

 In-depth Resources: Unit 2
• Guided Reading Worksheet, p. 18
• Reteaching Activity, p. 26

 Reading Study Guide
(Spanish and English), pp. 32–33

 Formal Assessment
• Section Quiz, p. 52

 Integrated Assessment
• Rubric for writing a summary

 Outline Map Activities

Access for Students Acquiring English
• Guided Reading Worksheet, p. 26

Technology Resources
classzone.com

TEST-TAKING RESOURCES
↪ Strategies for Test Preparation
↪ Test Practice Transparencies
ⓘ Online Test Practice

The First Czars of Russia In 1547, a 16-year-old leader in Moscow was crowned the first **czar** (zahr), or emperor, of modern Russia. His official title was Ivan IV, but the people nicknamed him **Ivan the Terrible.** Ivan was known for his cruelty, especially toward those he viewed as Russia's enemies. During his rule of 37 years, the country was constantly at war.

During the reigns of Ivan the Terrible and the czars who followed him, Russia had an unlimited government. This is a form of government in which a single ruler holds all the power. The people have no say in how the country is run.

Conflicts at Home The first Russian czars were often in conflict with the Russian nobles, who possessed much land and wealth. The czars viewed the nobles as a threat to their control over the people. Ivan the Terrible ordered his soldiers to murder Russian nobles and church leaders who opposed him.

The poor farmers, or peasants, of Russia also suffered under the first czars. New laws forced the peasants to become serfs, who had to remain on the farms where they worked.

Region • Ivan the Terrible is said to have worn this fur-trimmed crown at his coronation in 1547. ▲

The Expansion of Russia ❷

In addition to strengthening their control over the Russian people, the czars wanted to gain new territory. Throughout the 17th and 18th centuries, rulers such as Peter the Great and Catherine the Great conquered neighboring lands.

A Window on the West An intelligent man with big ideas for his country, **Peter the Great** ruled Russia from 1682 to 1725. After defeating Sweden in war and winning land along the Baltic Sea, Peter built a port city called St. Petersburg. This city, which Peter saw as Russia's "window on the west," became the new capital.

One of Peter's goals was to have closer ties with Western Europe. He hoped to use the ideas and inventions of the Scientific Revolution to modernize and strengthen Russia. During his rule, Peter reformed the army and the government and built new schools. He even ordered Russians to dress like Europeans and to shave off their beards. Peter's reforms made Russia stronger, but they did not improve life for Russian peasants.

Movement • Peter the Great brought to Russia many of the improvements of the Scientific and Industrial Revolutions. ▲

The Growth of New Ideas **113**

CRITICAL THINKING ACTIVITY

Recognizing Important Details Help students identify important details about the reigns of Peter the Great and Catherine the Great. Work with students to create a spider map for each, recording important details around each ruler's name.

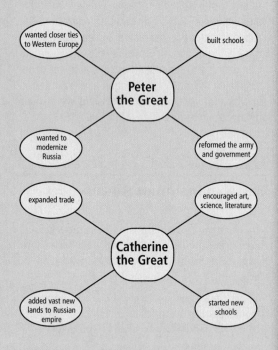

wanted closer ties to Western Europe

built schools

Peter the Great

wanted to modernize Russia

reformed the army and government

expanded trade

encouraged art, science, literature

Catherine the Great

added vast new lands to Russian empire

started new schools

INSTRUCT: Objective ❸

A Divided Russia

- Russia was divided into what two major classes in the 19th century? nobles, serfs
- Why did Alexander II's efforts to end serfdom fail? heavy taxes, poor land for farming
- What happened on Bloody Sunday? government troops shot protesting workers

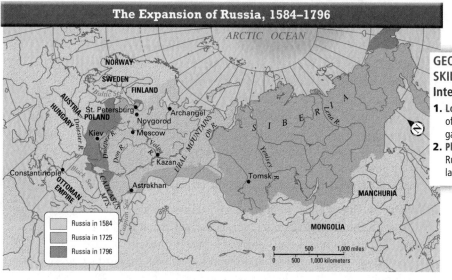

The Expansion of Russia, 1584–1796

Russia in 1584
Russia in 1725
Russia in 1796

0   500   1,000 miles
0   500   1,000 kilometers

GEOGRAPHY SKILLBUILDER:
Interpreting a Map

1. **Location •** What body of water did Russia gain access to in 1796
2. **Place •** When did Russia gain the most land?

Geography Skillbuilder Answers

1. Black Sea
2. between 1584 and 1725

A Great Empress **Catherine the Great** took control of Russia in 1762 and ruled until her death in 1796. Catherine added vast new lands to the empire, including the present-day countries of Ukraine (yoo·KRAYN) and Belarus (bel·uh·ROOS). Like Peter the Great, Catherine borrowed many ideas from Western Europe. She started new schools and encouraged art, science, and literature. Catherine also built new towns and expanded trade.

During Catherine's reign, Russia became one of Europe's most powerful nations. The lives of the peasants, however, remained miserable. Catherine thought about freeing them, but she knew the nobles would oppose her. When the peasants rebelled in the 1770s, Catherine crushed their uprising.

Movement •
Catherine the Great continued Peter the Great's practice of bringing the ideas of Western Europe to Russia. ▼

A Divided Russia ❸

In the 19th century, Russia remained a divided nation. Most people were poor peasants, and most of the wealth belonged to the nobles. This division would lead to conflict and eventually to a political revolution.

The Nobles Many Russian nobles sent their children to be educated in Germany and France. In fact, many noble families spoke French at home, speaking Russian only to their servants. The Western Europeans introduced many new ideas to the Russian nobles, among them the idea that a nation's government should reflect the wishes of its citizens.

BACKGROUND

Catherine the Great was born in Germany. She came to Russia at 15 to marry the heir to the throne, Peter III. He was a weak ruler, however, and Catherine, supported by the army and the people, overthrew him.

114 CHAPTER 4

Activity Options

Skillbuilder Mini-Lesson: Making a Generalization

ⓑ Block Scheduling

Explaining the Skill Remind students that to make a generalization, they must examine many sources of information about a topic and then draw a conclusion based on all the facts and evidence they have found.

Applying the Skill Have students reread the section entitled "A Great Empress" and use these strategies to support a given generalization. Write the following generalization on the board: "The lives of the Russian nobles were very different from the lives of the peasants." Ask students to reread

pages 114–115 and to make a list of information that specifically supports this generalization. Nobles owned land; sent their children to be educated in the west; did not speak Russian at home; were army officers or government officials. When they finish, brainstorm other reference sources where they might locate information to support this generalization.

Many Russian nobles were army officers or government officials. Most supported the czar and were proud of Russia's growing power. In 1825, one group of nobles tried to replace the government. Their attempt to gain more power failed.

The Serfs In the 19th century, the Russian serfs still had no land or money of their own. They worked on farms owned by others and received little help from the Russian government.

In 1861, Alexander II decided to end serfdom in Russia. He hoped that freeing the serfs would help his country compete with Western Europe. The serfs had to pay a heavy tax, though, and the land they were given was often not good for farming. Most former serfs felt that they had gained very little.

Bloody Sunday The serfs were not the only unhappy Russians. Many university students, artists, and writers believed that the government's treatment of the serfs was unfair. Some joined groups that tried to overthrow the government. In addition, workers in Russia's cities complained about low pay and poor working conditions.

In 1905, a group of workers marched to the royal palace in St. Petersburg with a list of demands. Government troops shot many of them. News of the events of this "Bloody Sunday" spread across Russia, making people even angrier with the government and czar.

Thinking Critically Possible Answers

1. They admired the culture of Western Europe and hoped it would strengthen and modernize Russia.

2. They hoped the public would admire and/or emulate the values and customs represented in the works of art.

Spotlight on CULTURE

The Hermitage is truly enormous. Its buildings run almost half a mile along the bank of the Neva River in the center of St. Petersburg, with almost 400 rooms and 3 million pieces of art.

The Hermitage was originally a royal residence known as the Winter Palace. When Catherine the Great moved into the Winter Palace in 1762, she brought her art collection with her. Two years later, she had a long, narrow building added to house her extensive collection. This addition was called the "Little Hermitage." Over the next hundred years, several other buildings were added.

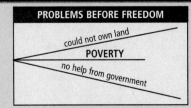

Spotlight on CULTURE

The Hermitage Museum One of the world's greatest and largest art museums is the Hermitage in St. Petersburg. It contains many famous works of art, including French, Spanish, and British paintings. Part of the collection is displayed in the former royal residence, the Winter Palace.

Both Peter the Great and Catherine the Great were collectors of European art. On a trip to Amsterdam in 1716, Peter bought paintings by the famous Dutch artist Rembrandt. Approximately 50 years later, Catherine purchased more than 200 works of art when she

visited Germany. These priceless royal collections became part of the Hermitage when it opened as a public museum in 1852.

THINKING CRITICALLY

1. **Analyzing Motives**
   Why did Peter the Great and Catherine the Great collect art from Western Europe?

2. **Making Inferences**
   Why do you think the works of art were displayed to the public in a museum?

Activity Options

Differentiating Instruction: Less Proficient Readers

Determining Cause and Effect Less proficient readers may need to review the reasons why the lives of Russian serfs did not improve after they gained their freedom. Have students create one cause-and-effect graphic organizer labeled "Problems Before Freedom" and one labeled "Problems After Freedom." Have students reread "The Serfs" on page 115 and fill in the organizer.

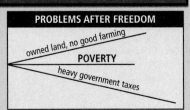

PROBLEMS BEFORE FREEDOM
could not own land
POVERTY
no help from government

PROBLEMS AFTER FREEDOM
owned land, no good farming
POVERTY
heavy government taxes

INSTRUCT: Objective ④

The End of the Russian Empire

- What problems led to the Russian Revolution in 1917? food shortages and worker strikes
- What happened to the Russian monarchy? It was overthrown.

ASSESS & RETEACH

Reading Social Studies Have students fill in the bottom line of the chart on page 94, "The Russian Empire."

 Formal Assessment
- Section Quiz, p. 52

RETEACHING ACTIVITY

Ask each student to choose one important event or aspect of Russian history that was discussed in this section and write it in large letters on a piece of paper. Holding their papers, have students stand up and organize themselves into a human time line. Have the class review and discuss, in order, each event represented on the time line. If necessary, have students identify missing events.

 In-depth Resources: Unit 2
- Reteaching Activity, p. 26

 Access for Students Acquiring English
- Reteaching Activity, p. 32

The End of the Russian Empire ④

In 1914, World War I began. Nicholas II—a quiet, shy man who did not want war—ruled Russia, but he failed to keep his country out of the battle. Russia, whose allies included the United Kingdom and France, suffered terrible losses fighting Germany and its allies.

During World War I, there were food shortages in the cities and workers went on strike. Russian revolutionaries organized the workers against the czar. Even the Russian army turned against their ruler, and in 1917, Nicholas was forced to give up power. This overturning of the Russian monarchy is known as the **Russian Revolution.**

Nicholas II and the royal family (the Romanovs) were imprisoned by the revolutionaries. On July 17, 1918, they were all shot to death. This execution ended more than 300 years of rule by the Romanov family and nearly 400 years of czarist rule.

Reading Social Studies

B. Analyzing Motives Why did Russian workers strike?

Reading Social Studies
B. Possible Answer
There were food shortages in the cities.

SECTION ④ ASSESSMENT

Terms & Names

1. Identify:
(a) czar
(b) Ivan the Terrible
(c) Peter the Great
(d) Catherine the Great
(e) Russian Revolution

Taking Notes

2. Use a chart like this one to describe three characteristics of czars of Russia.

Ivan the Terrible	Peter the Great	Catherine the Great	Nicholas II

Main Ideas

3. (a) What effects did an unlimited government have on Russian peasants?

(b) How did Peter the Great help reform Russia?

(c) Alexander II ended serfdom in 1861, but this did little to help the serfs. Why?

Critical Thinking

4. Finding Causes

What events led to the Russian Revolution?

Think About
- the life of the serfs
- Bloody Sunday
- the events of World War I

ACTIVITY -OPTION- Look at the map on page 114 that shows the expansion of Russia. Write a brief **summary** to describe how the Russian nation grew from the 1500s to 1800.

Section ④ Assessment

1. Terms & Names
a. czar, p. 113
b. Ivan the Terrible, p. 113
c. Peter the Great, p. 113
d. Catherine the Great, p. 114
e. Russian Revolution, p. 116

2. Taking Notes

Ivan the Terrible	Peter the Great	Catherine the Great	Nicholas II
Russia constantly at war	Closer ties with Western Europe	Added new lands to empire	Russia suffered terrible losses in WWI

3. Main Ideas
a. They had no say in how their country was run.
b. Peter the Great reformed the government and developed close ties to Western Europe.
c. They were heavily taxed and given poor land to farm.

4. Critical Thinking
Possible Response The unfair treatment of serfs, Bloody Sunday, and food shortages brought about by World War I all led to the Russian Revolution.

ACTIVITY OPTION

 Integrated Assessment
- Rubric for writing a summary

James Watt's Double-Action Steam Engine

Amid the excitement of the Industrial Revolution, James Watt (1736–1819), a Scottish inventor, patented a new steam engine. Steam power had been used for many years, but Watt's invention was an improved, double-action steam engine. This system, in which the steam pushes from both sides of the piston rather than from just one, enhanced efficiency and increased power. Watt's invention helped to advance manufacturing and transportation and influenced later inventions. Watt's double-action steam engine was one of the most important inventions of the Industrial Revolution.

How the Engine Works

Steam from the **boiler** enters the **piston cylinder**. The pressure of the steam pushes the **piston** to one side, moving the **piston rod**. When the piston reaches the end of the stroke, the **slide valve** shifts the steam to the other side of the piston, forcing it back and releasing the steam it compresses as exhaust.

❶ As water is converted to steam, its volume increases 1,600 percent.

❷ When the steam enters the piston cylinder, it forces the piston rod to one side.

❸ As the piston reaches the end of its stroke, the slide valve channels steam to the other side of the piston.

❹ The piston rod is pushed back, forcing the "old" steam out as exhaust.

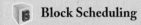

Key: | Steam | Exhaust

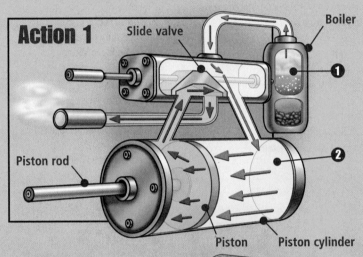

Action 1 — Slide valve, Boiler, Piston rod, Piston, Piston cylinder

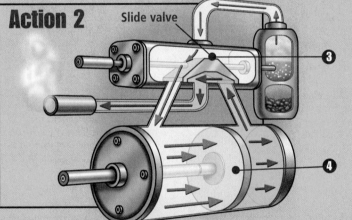

Action 2 — Slide valve

THINKING Critically

1. Drawing Conclusions
How did the steam engine help power the Industrial Revolution?

2. Recognizing Effects
How did Watt's steam engine change the lives of working people?

OBJECTIVES

1. To illustrate how the double-action steam engine works
2. To explain the great influence of the steam engine on industrial growth

INSTRUCT

- How did Watt's engine improve on others?
- What is the function of the boiler?

🅑 **Block Scheduling**

MORE ABOUT...
Rapid Industrial Growth

In 1783 Richard Arkwright adapted one of Watt's engines for a textile mill. Within 20 years, England and Scotland had 2,400 steam-powered looms. By 1857 some 250,000 were in operation. Imports of raw cotton increased six-fold from 1775 to 1790. Fabrics once spun by workers at home were mass produced in factories, greatly reducing costs. The price of cotton yarn in 1830 was about one-twentieth of its price in 1760.

Connect to History

Strategic Thinking How does the steam engine's history show the influence inventors have on each other?

Connect to Today

Strategic Thinking Why was the steam engine eventually replaced by electric and internal combustion engines?

Thinking Critically

1. Drawing Conclusions Possible Response The steam engine powered large, complex machines that made the Industrial Revolution possible. It also influenced later inventions that impacted on the revolution.

2. Recognizing Effects Possible Responses Steam power changed the way people worked. Early textile mills were powered by water from rivers and were located in the country. Many tasks, such as weaving, were done by hand. With the invention of the steam engine, people living in the country moved to towns and cities to find work in factories. Watt's invention also led to the development of railroads, which made transportation much faster and easier.

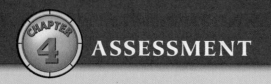

TERMS & NAMES

REVIEW QUESTIONS

Possible Responses

1. Before the Renaissance artists painted religious subjects; after the Renaissance they began to paint portraits, historical scenes, and mythological stories.
2. They were called Protestants because they protested against the Catholic Church.
3. Spices from Asia were transported over long distances. Each merchant along the trade route needed to make a profit.
4. They brought back gold dust, ivory, and an increased knowledge of navigation.
5. The Industrial Revolution began in England in the late 1700s.
6. National debt, food shortages, and heavy taxes led to the French Revolution.
7. Ivan the Terrible was known for his cruelty, especially against his enemies in other countries.
8. Catherine the Great started schools; encouraged art, science, and literature; built towns; and expanded trade.

CHAPTER 4 ASSESSMENT

TERMS & NAMES

Explain the significance of each of the following:

1. Renaissance
2. Leonardo da Vinci
3. Reformation
4. Ferdinand Magellan
5. circumnavigate
6. imperialism
7. Industrial Revolution
8. Napoleon Bonaparte
9. Peter the Great
10. Russian Revolution

REVIEW QUESTIONS

Renaissance Connections *(pages 95–100)*
1. How did the subjects chosen by artists change during the Renaissance?
2. Why were the followers of Martin Luther called Protestants?

Traders, Explorers, and Colonists *(pages 101–105)*
3. Why were spices from Asia so expensive when sold in Europe?
4. What did Portuguese explorers bring back from their expeditions to western Africa?

The Age of Revolutions *(pages 107–111)*
5. When and where did the Industrial Revolution begin?
6. What conditions in France during the 1780s led to the French Revolution?

The Russian Empire *(pages 112–116)*
7. How did Ivan the Terrible earn his nickname?
8. What ideas did Catherine the Great borrow from Western Europe?

CRITICAL THINKING

Finding Causes
1. Using your completed chart from Reading Social Studies, p. 94, list the events that led to the growth of cities during the Industrial Revolution.

Recognizing Effects
2. What were the effects of the Crusades on life in Western Europe?

Analyzing Causes
3. In 19th-century Russia, the lives of poor citizens were very different from those of wealthy citizens. How do you think this division led to political revolution?

Visual Summary

1 Renaissance Connections
- European society was transformed by the art, literature, and ideas of the Renaissance.
- The accomplishments of this period are an important part of Western culture.

2 Traders, Explorers, and Colonists
- People on both sides of the Atlantic were changed by the voyages of the European explorers.
- European exploration led to colonization and to the slave trade.

The Age of Revolution
- The Age of Revolution resulted in great changes in European society, industry, and politics.
- These changes were felt around the world.

4 The Russian Empire
- Many citizens of the Russian Empire were deprived of their rights.
- Today, Russia is a large nation experiencing great change.

CRITICAL THINKING: Possible Responses

1. Finding Causes

Early factories were built in the countryside near rivers that were used for power. During the Industrial Revolution, steam engines powered machines, so factories could be built in cities. People moved to cities in search of work.

2. Recognizing Effects

The Crusaders opened up trade routes that connected Western Europe with Asia and North Africa. This increased trade brought new ideas and products, and even new people, to Western Europe.

3. Analyzing Causes

The peasants were poor, and the wealth of the country belonged to the nobles. The nobles had opportunities for education and thus wielded power, while the peasants had no hope of bettering themselves. This inequality resulted in violence and the overthrow of the government.

SOCIAL STUDIES SKILLBUILDER

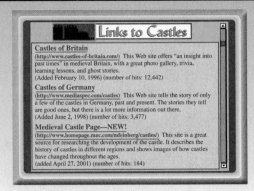

Links to Castles

Castles of Britain
(http://www.castles-of-britain.com/) This Web site offers "an insight into past times" in medieval Britain, with a great photo gallery, trivia, learning lessons, and ghost stories.
(Added February 10, 1996) (number of hits: 12,442)

Castles of Germany
(http://www.mediaspec.com/castles) This Web site tells the story of only a few of the castles in Germany, past and present. The stories they tell are good ones, but there is a lot more information out there.
(Added June 2, 1998) (number of hits: 3,477)

Medieval Castle Page—NEW!
(http://www.homepage.mac.com/mfeinberg/castles/) This site is a great source for researching the development of the castle. It describes the history of castles in different regions and shows images of how castles have changed throughout the ages.
(added April 27, 2001) (number of hits: 184)

SKILLBUILDER: Researching Topics on the Internet

1. What is the subject of this Web site?
2. Which site would you visit to learn about the history of castles?

FOCUS ON GEOGRAPHY

1. **Movement** • How might the path of the plague be related to trade routes?
2. **Place** • Why might the plague have reached Russia later than it reached the other countries in Europe?

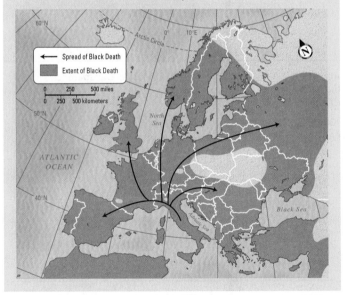

- Spread of Black Death
- Extent of Black Death

Interdisciplinary Activity: Science
Explaining an Invention Research one of the many scientific inventions of Leonardo da Vinci. Write a paragraph that explains how da Vinci came up with his idea and how it works. Find a copy of one of da Vinci's sketches or a photograph of a model, or make your own sketch to illustrate your paragraph.

Cooperative Learning Activity
Tracing a Voyage Work with three or four students to research and make a presentation about the voyage of Ferdinand Magellan, the first explorer to sail around the world.

- How many ships and sailors set out? Who helped finance the trip?
- Create a map of Magellan's route.
- Find details about the hardships the crew faced.
- Include information about what happened to Magellan.

INTERNET ACTIVITY

Use the Internet to research the Scientific Revolution. Focus on the discovery or invention of one great European scientist of the time, such as Galileo Galilei. How did the discovery help change daily life or add to people's knowledge of the world?

Presenting Your Findings Design a poster to explain your findings. Include a diagram or illustration that visually presents information about the scientific discovery. If appropriate, explain how the discovery or invention affects life today.

For Internet links to support this activity, go to

RESEARCH LINKS
CLASSZONE.COM

The Growth of New Ideas **119**

CHAPTER PROJECTS

Interdisciplinary Activity: Science

Explaining an Invention You might want to provide students with a list of Leonardo da Vinci's inventions as well as references they can use in their research. Ask students to try to answer the following questions.

- What gave him the idea for an invention?
- What did it do? How did it work?
- What modern machine or device is based on the same idea?

Show students examples of diagrams and discuss how they are a useful way to organize information. Suggest that they draw a diagram of the invention and then surround it with examples of how the invention affects life today.

Cooperative Learning Activity

Tracing a Voyage In advance, collect any materials that students might need, such as reference books, a world map, a globe, or an atlas. You might want to assign students the roles of researchers, illustrators, and presenters. Brainstorm interesting ways the groups could present their findings, such as making a videotape or transparencies, re-creating a diary or ship's log, or writing and performing a play.

INTERNET ACTIVITY

Discuss how students might find information about European scientists using the Internet. Brainstorm possible keywords, Web sites, and search engines that students might explore. To help them focus their research, you may want to write the framework for an outline on the chalkboard and have each student copy and complete it. Then have students write brief reports using the facts in their outlines.

Skills Answers

Social Studies Skillbuilder
Possible Responses
1. Castles
2. Castles of Britain, Germany, and medieval castles

Focus on Geography
Possible Responses
1. Traders carried the plague with them.
2. Traders reached Russia later.

Europe: War and Change

	OVERVIEW	COPYMASTERS	INTEGRATED TECHNOLOGY
UNIT ATLAS AND CHAPTER RESOURCES	Students will examine how the development of nationalism in Europe led to two world wars and a cold war during the 20th century.	**In-depth Resources: Unit 2** • Guided Reading Worksheets, pp. 27–29 • Skillbuilder Practice, p. 32 • Unit Atlas Activities, pp. 1–2 • Geography Workshop, pp. 61–62 **Reading Study Guide** (Spanish and English), pp. 36–43 **Outline Map Activities**	Power Presentations Electronic Teacher Tools Online Lesson Planner Chapter Summaries on CD Critical Thinking Transparencies CT9
SECTION 1 European Empires pp. 123–126	**KEY IDEAS** • Nationalism, colonialism, and empire building led to conflicts among European nations.	**In-depth Resources: Unit 2** • Guided Reading Worksheet, p. 27 • Reteaching Activity, p. 34 **Reading Study Guide** (Spanish and English), pp. 36–37	classzone.com Chapter Summaries on CD
SECTION 2 Europe at War pp. 127–132	• Countries join alliances to unite for a common cause, and for defense. • World War I brought many changes to the political makeup of Europe. • Hitler's aggression, including the invasion of Poland, led to World War II. • The Allies helped Western European nations rebuild after World War II.	**In-depth Resources: Unit 2** • Guided Reading Worksheet, p. 28 • Reteaching Activity, p. 35 **Reading Study Guide** (Spanish and English), pp. 38–39	Critical Thinking Transparencies CT10 classzone.com Chapter Summaries on CD
SECTION 3 The Soviet Union pp. 136–141	• The Iron Curtain served as a barrier between Eastern and Western Europe. • Joseph Stalin wielded dictatorial power over the Soviet Union and many Eastern European nations. • NATO and the Warsaw Pact nations would not trade or cooperate with each other during the Cold War.	**In-depth Resources: Unit 2** • Guided Reading Worksheet, p. 29 • Reteaching Activity, p. 36 **Reading Study Guide** (Spanish and English), pp. 40–41	classzone.com Chapter Summaries on CD

Audio
 CD-ROM
Copymaster

 Internet
Overhead Transparency
 Pupil's Edition

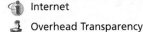 Teacher's Edition
Video

ASSESSMENT OPTIONS

Chapter Assessment, pp. 142–143

Formal Assessment
• Chapter Tests: Forms A, B, C, pp. 68–79

Test Generator

Online Test Practice

Strategies for Test Preparation

Section Assessment, p. 126

Formal Assessment
• Section Quiz, p. 65

Integrated Assessment
• Rubric for making an outline

Test Generator

Test Practice Transparencies TT13

Section Assessment, p. 132

Formal Assessment
• Section Quiz, p. 66

Integrated Assessment
• Rubric for writing a letter

Test Generator

Test Practice Transparencies TT14

Section Assessment, p. 141

Formal Assessment
• Section Quiz, p. 67

Integrated Assessment
• Rubric for writing a scene

Test Generator

Test Practice Transparencies TT15

RESOURCES FOR DIFFERENTIATING INSTRUCTION

Students Acquiring English/ESL

Reading Study Guide (Spanish and English), pp. 36–43

Access for Students Acquiring English Spanish Translations, pp. 33–40

TE Activity
• Base Words and Suffixes, p. 128

Less Proficient Readers

Reading Study Guide (Spanish and English), pp. 36–43

TE Activity
• Main Ideas and Details, p. 131

Gifted and Talented Students

TE Activities
• Debating, p. 130
• Reviewing a Movie, p. 140

CROSS-CURRICULAR CONNECTIONS

Humanities

Belloli, Andrea. *Exploring World Art.* Los Angeles: J. Paul Getty Museum, 1999. Places Western European art in a broad global context.

Moore, Reavis. *Native Artists of Europe.* Santa Fe, NM: Publishers Group West, 1994. Singer, painter, wood carver, potter, and musician from Western Europe.

Popular Culture

CultureGrams. *Volume I, The Americas and Europe: The Nations Around Us.* Salt Lake City: Millennial Star Network, 2000. Reports on seventy-four countries.

Steele, Philip. *Houses Through the Ages.* Mahwah, NJ: Troll Associates, 1994. From the caves of Stone Age hunters to modern apartment houses in Western Europe.

Science

Millard, Anne. *Street Through Time.* New York: DK Publishing, 1998. A European street from Stone Age path to 20th-century city street.

History

Burgan, Michael. *Belgium.* New York: Children's Press, 2000. Geography, plants, animals, history, economy, language, religions, culture, sports, arts, and people.

Costain, Meredith. *Welcome to the United Kingdom.* Broomall, PA: Chelsea House, 2000. Full overview with suggested activities.

ENRICHMENT ACTIVITIES

The following activities are especially suitable for classes following block schedules.

Teacher's Edition, pp. 124, 125, 129, 130, 133, 137, 139, 140
Pupil's Edition, pp. 126, 132, 141

Unit Atlas, pp. 54–63
Literature Connections, pp. 134–135

Outline Map Activities

INTEGRATED TECHNOLOGY

Go to **classzone.com** for lesson support and activities for Chapter 5.

BLOCK SCHEDULE LESSON PLAN OPTIONS: 90-MINUTE PERIOD

DAY 1

CHAPTER PREVIEW, pp. 120–121
Class Time 20 minutes

- **Small Groups** In small groups have students share the photo albums they made for Implementing the National Geography Standards on PE p. 121. Ask them to explain the significance of the images they chose. Exhibit student albums in the classroom.

SECTION 1, pp. 123–126
Class Time 70 minutes

- **Peer Teaching** Assign each student a partner and have the pairs do the Reteaching Activity on TE p. 126. Reconvene as a class and ask students to share their sentences.
Class Time 25 minutes

- **Map Reading** Use the map and the Geography Skillbuilder questions on PE p. 124 to lead students in identifying which Western European countries controlled which colonies.
Class Time 10 minutes

- **Cause and Effect** Use the Skillbuilder Mini-Lesson on TE p. 125 to guide a discussion about the causes and effects of colonialism.
Class Time 15 minutes

- **Internet** Extend students' background knowledge of the physical geography of Europe by visiting **classzone.com.**
Class Time 20 minutes

DAY 2

SECTION 2, pp. 127–132
Class Time 65 minutes

- **Peer Competition** Divide the class into pairs. Assign each pair one of the Terms & Names for this section. Have pairs make up five questions that can be answered with the term or name. Have groups take turns asking the class their questions. Give points for correct answers.
Class Time 20 minutes

- **Brainstorming** Lead the class to consider why a country might choose to remain neutral during a time of war. Record students' suggestions on the chalkboard.
Class Time 10 minutes

- **Interview** Have the class reread the biography of Anne Frank on PE p. 131. Ask students to imagine that they are newspaper reporters who have been assigned to interview Anne Frank while she is in hiding in Amsterdam. Have each student make a list of questions to ask about her life. Conduct the interview as a whole class.
Class Time 35 minutes

SECTION 3, pp. 136–141
Class Time 25 minutes

- **Discussion** Discuss the objectives for the section on TE p. 136.
Class Time 5 minutes

- **Peer Teaching** Have pairs of students review the Main Idea for the section on PE p. 136 and find three details to support it. Then have each pair list two additional important ideas and trade lists with another group to find details.
Class Time 10 minutes

- **Analyzing Issues** Use the Critical Thinking Activity on TE p. 137 to guide students in a discussion about how the Soviet Union became the strongest nation in Europe.
Class Time 10 minutes

DAY 3

SECTION 3, continued
Class Time 35 minutes

- **Political Cartoon** Review with students what they learned about political cartoons on PE p. 133. Have students reread "Joseph Stalin" in their texts. Then ask them to do Activity Options: Multiple Learning Styles on TE p. 138. When they have finished their cartoons, invite volunteers to share them with the rest of the class.

CHAPTER 5 REVIEW AND ASSESSMENT, pp. 142–143
Class Time 55 minutes

- **Review** Have students prepare a summary of the chapter, using the Terms & Names listed on the first page of each section.
Class Time 20 minutes

- **Assessment** Have students complete the Chapter 5 Assessment.
Class Time 35 minutes

TECHNOLOGY IN THE CLASSROOM

USING AND CREATING SOUNDS ON THE COMPUTER

Although we frequently think of computers and the Internet as visual media, they can also be very useful in storing and transmitting sounds. Students may already be accustomed to listening to music on the computer, but they may not have used computers to listen to other people speak or to record their own voices. The recent versions of most Internet browsers support audio, and most computers allow the user to record sounds, provided they have a microphone.

ACTIVITY OUTLINE

In this activity, students will listen to sound files in Real Audio format that describe the role of radio in England during World War II. Although recent versions of their Internet browsers should allow them to play the files automatically, it would be a good idea to check this feature before having students start this activity. Students will also need to use a microphone attached to the computer to create their own radio broadcasts.

Objective Students will listen to an on-line audio file and create their own audio files that will be organized into a multimedia presentation.

Task Have students listen to a description of the role radio played in England during World War II. Then have them create radio broadcasts that might have been heard at that time, and save them on the computer. Have them put their broadcasts together as a class multimedia presentation.

Class Time Three class periods

DIRECTIONS

1. Direct students to the Web site at **classzone.com** and select "Radio." Have them link to "Wartime Radio" and listen to British people discussing the role of radio in World War II. Students will need to listen carefully, and may even need to play the sound file several times. They can use the sliding navigator button in the Real Audio window to "rewind" the sound file so they can listen to all or part of it again.

2. As a class, discuss the role of radio during World War II. Discuss issues such as why radio was important, how radio was used, and why people liked the radio.

3. Divide the class into small groups and ask each group to pretend they lived in England during World War II. Have them prepare short (15–30 second) sound clips that might have been heard on the radio during that period.

4. Have students record their sound clips with a microphone, saving the sound files on the computer. Some students may want to try speaking with a British accent.

5. Have several students compile a page in a multimedia presentation program that will serve as the introductory page for students' sound files.

6. Groups can transfer their sound files to the folder containing the multimedia presentation so they can easily link from the introductory page to the sound files.

7. Have members of each group take turns creating links from the introductory page to their sound file. Play the presentation for the class so students can listen to other groups' broadcasts.

CHAPTER 5 OBJECTIVE

Students will examine how the development of nationalism in Europe led to two world wars and a cold war during the 20th century.

FOCUS ON VISUALS

Interpreting the Photograph Have students look at the nighttime photograph of Berlin and notice details that tell them something about the city today. Draw their attention to the contrasts between the ruined church, now a monument, and the modern skyscrapers. Ask them to point out specific features in the photograph that demonstrate Germany's recovery and prosperity.

Possible Responses brightly lit buildings, signs, and cafes, skyscraper office buildings, people on the sidewalk, busy traffic, construction scaffolding

Extension Have students write and illustrate a short guide to the sights of Berlin, using information from encyclopedias, tourist guides, and the Internet.

CRITICAL THINKING ACTIVITY

Hypothesizing Encourage a discussion on why a city might have been bombed even though it was not strictly a military target. Point out that such attacks are still the subject of debate many years after the war. Direct students' attention to the map of Europe and its major cities. Have students consider the long-term effects of such destruction.

Class Time 15 minutes

Europe: War and Change

SECTION 1   European Empires

SECTION 2   Europe at War

SECTION 3   The Soviet Union

EUROPE AND THE FORMER SOVIET UNION

PACIFIC OCEAN

ATLANTIC OCEAN

INDIAN OCEAN

PACIFIC OCEAN

Place Berlin's Kaiser Wilhelm Memorial Church remains semi-destroyed as a monument to World War II. Germany has since rebuilt its cities. It is once again an important part of Europe's economy, politics, and culture.

120

Recommended Resources

BOOKS FOR THE TEACHER
Map Packs Continents Series: Europe. Washington, D.C.: National Geographic Society, 1998. Sixty-five map transparencies with guide and suggested projects.
Mazower, Mark. *Dark Continent: Europe's Twentieth Century.* New York: Knopf, 1999. From World War I to the European Union.

Williams, Roger. *Insight Guide Continental Europe.* Maspeth, NY: Langenscheidt, 2000. History and culture of continental Europe.

VIDEOS
Europe: The Road to Unity. Washington, D.C.: National Geographic Society, 1993. The challenges in uniting citizens of diverse cultures and languages.

SOFTWARE
Great Museums of the World. Renton, WA: CounterTop Software, 1998. Electronic tours of the great European art museums.

INTERNET
For more information about Europe and the EU, visit **classzone.com.**

How has Europe's small landmass affected its history?

Place • The continent of Europe is home to more than 40 countries. Yet, it is approximately the same size as the United States. Since many European nations share borders with several other countries, Europeans often speak three or more languages. Across Europe, approximately 50 languages are spoken.

Europe is densely populated. In fact, the continent has almost three times as many people as the United States. So many people, living so close together, has sometimes led to competition and warfare over land and resources.

What do you think?

♦ How might the differences among Europeans cause conflict?

♦ How might the closeness of so many countries help to unite Europe?

121

BEFORE YOU READ

What Do You Know?

Ask students to describe movies they have seen or books they have read about Europe. Invite them to describe the topics of these movies or books. Then encourage students who have learned about World War I or World War II from these sources, or from museum or family visits, to share what they know about these events.

What Do You Want to Know?

Ask small groups of students to work together to make up questions about Europe in the 1900s and Europe today. Suggest that students record the questions in their notebooks, leaving space to write answers as they read the chapter.

READ AND TAKE NOTES

Reading Strategy: Analyzing Cause and Effect
Explain to students that many historians believe that if people understand the causes of certain events, it may be possible to prevent similar events from occurring again. Point out that when students have completed the causes/event/effects charts, they will be able to see the connections between causes and effects more clearly.

 In-depth Resources: Unit 2
• Guided Reading Worksheets, pp. 27–29

BEFORE YOU READ

▶▶ What Do You Know?

Do you know that during World War I, armies trained dogs to guard supplies and assist soldiers? What do you know about World War I and World War II? Have you ever seen a movie or read a book about either conflict? What do you hear in the news about current events in Europe? Think about how events in Europe in the past century might have contributed to life there today.

▶▶ What Do You Want to Know?

Decide what you know about Europe's history in the 1900s and what it is like there today. In your notebook, record what you hope to learn from this chapter.

Region • The image of the hammer and sickle became the symbol of the Soviet Union. ▲

READ AND TAKE NOTES

Reading Strategy: Analyzing Causes and Effects
Analyzing causes and effects is an essential skill for understanding what you read in social studies, because events are caused by other events or situations. This sequence is called a chain of events. Understanding which causes lead to which events is essential in understanding history and other areas of social studies. Use the chart below to show causes and effects discussed in Chapter 5.

• Copy the chart into your notebook.
• As you read, record causes and effects for each event.

Region • During World War I, armies trained do[gs] assist them. ▲

Causes	Event	Effects
domino effect of alliances	World War I	many deaths, poverty, homelessness, unemployment, shift in many European political boundaries
election of Hitler, fascism, Germany invades Poland	World War II	free governments established in Western Europe, NATO, Soviet Union occupies Eastern Europe
defeat of Germany, puppet governments throughout Eastern Europe	Growth of Soviet Union	Cold War, Stalin's five-year plans, collective farming, secret police

Teaching Strategy

Reading the Chapter This is a chronological chapter focusing on the causes and effects of wars that involved much of Europe during the 20th century. Encourage students to note the factors that led nations to war, as well as the events that happened as a result of war.

Integrated Assessment The Chapter Assessment on page 142 describes several activities for integrated assessment. You may wish to have students work on these activities during the course of the chapter and then present them at the end.

European Empires

SECTION 1

TERMS & NAMES
nationalism
colonialism
Austria-Hungary
dual monarchy

MAIN IDEA

The beginning of the 20th century was a time of change in Europe, as feelings of nationalism began to take hold.

WHY IT MATTERS NOW

Feelings of nationalism continue to lead to conflicts that change the map of Europe.

DATELINE EXTRA

NORWAY, SEPTEMBER 1905

It could have been war in the Scandinavian Peninsula. The armies of Norway and Sweden had begun preparations.

Instead, Sweden ended the crisis peacefully by granting Norway independence. Norway had been under Swedish control since 1814. Although Norway ran its own affairs within the country, Sweden set foreign policy and controlled

Norway's international shipping and trade.

Prince Charles of Denmark has been invited to become king of Norway. The Norwegians will vote to approve their new leader. If chosen, he will become King Haakon VII.

The king's role will be largely ceremonial. His chief task will be to help unite the newly independent people of Norway.

Region • Prince Charles of Denmark, pictured here with his family, hopes to become King Haakon VII of Norway.

The Spread of Nationalism ①

Norway's independence from Sweden was a sign of new ideas that were sweeping across Europe at the time. During the late 19th and early 20th centuries, **nationalism,** or strong pride in one's nation or ethnic group, influenced the feelings of many Europeans. An ethnic group includes people with similar languages and traditions, but who are not necessarily ruled by a common government.

Europe: War and Change **123**

SECTION OBJECTIVES

1. To explain how nationalism and colonialism led to conflicts among European nations in the early 20th century
2. To identify the dual monarchy of Austria-Hungary

SKILLBUILDER
• Interpreting a Map, pp. 124, 126

CRITICAL THINKING
• Recognizing Effects, p. 124
• Clarifying, p. 126

FOCUS & MOTIVATE
WARM-UP

Making Inferences Have students read <u>Dateline</u> and discuss how these two countries resolved a question that could have led to war.

1. Why do you think Swedish officials decided to grant Norway its independence peacefully?
2. What might this decision signify for future relations between the two countries?

INSTRUCT: Objective ①

The Spread of Nationalism

• What is nationalism? strong pride in one's nation or ethnic group
• Why were European powers interested in gaining colonies in Asia and Africa? They could obtain raw materials cheaply and turn them into manufactured goods.

 In-depth Resources: Unit 2
• Guided Reading Worksheet, p. 27

 Reading Study Guide
(Spanish and English), pp. 36–37

Program Resources

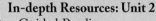 **In-depth Resources: Unit 2**
• Guided Reading Worksheet, p. 27
• Reteaching Activity, p. 34

 Reading Study Guide
(Spanish and English), pp. 36–37

 Formal Assessment
• Section Quiz, p. 65

 Integrated Assessment
• Rubric for making an outline

Outline Map Activity

 Access for Students Acquiring English
• Guided Reading Worksheet, p. 33

 Technology Resources
classzone.com

TEST-TAKING RESOURCES
 Strategies for Test Preparation
Test Practice Transparencies
Online Test Practice

CRITICAL THINKING ACTIVITY

Recognizing Effects Ask students to consider the relationship between the freedoms and rights that citizens have and the responsibilities they are willing to take on for their country. Encourage them to discuss how a medieval peasant might have felt when ordered to go to war by his lord, then compare that with the feelings of a citizen who has elected government leaders. If it seems appropriate, have students discuss their own feelings about nationalism, patriotism, and citizens' responsibilities.

Class Time 15 minutes

FOCUS ON VISUALS

Interpreting the Map Ask students to explain the map key by pointing out the colors that represent smaller colonial powers, such as Belgium and Denmark, and then locate those countries' possessions on the map. Have them discuss which countries were the dominant colonial powers in Asia and Africa in 1914, and why this might be so.

Possible Responses Great Britain (U.K.) and France in Asia and Africa; also in Africa, Germany. Those nations were the leading European powers.

Extension Remind students that some European nations also had possessions in South America and the Caribbean. Ask them to make a map showing those colonies. They should use different colors to represent each colonial nation's possessions and include a map key.

Constitutional Monarchies In part, the spread of nationalism was fueled by the fact that more Europeans than ever before could vote. For centuries, many monarchs had unlimited power. In country after country, however, citizens demanded the right to elect lawmakers who would limit their monarch's authority. This kind of government is called a constitutional monarchy. A constitutional monarchy not only has a king or queen, but also a ruling body of elected officials. The United Kingdom is one example of a constitutional monarchy.

By 1900, many countries in Western Europe had become constitutional monarchies. Citizens of these countries strongly supported the governments that they helped to elect. When one country threatened another, most citizens were willing to go to war to defend their homeland.

The Defense of Colonial Empires At the beginning of the 20th century, many Western European countries—including France, Italy, the United Kingdom, Germany, and even tiny Belgium—had colonies in Asia and Africa. Colonies supplied the raw materials that the ruling countries needed to produce goods in their factories back home. Asian and African colonies, sometimes larger than the ruling country, were also important markets for manufactured goods.

Reading
Social Studies

A. Contrasting
How does a constitutional monarchy differ from a democracy?

Reading Social Studies
A. Answers
A constitutional monarchy has a king or queen with limited power, and may or may not be a democracy.

Geography Skillbuilder Answers
1. United Kingdom
2. Africa

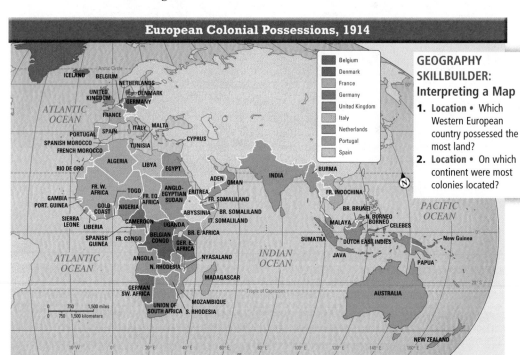

European Colonial Possessions, 1914

GEOGRAPHY SKILLBUILDER: Interpreting a Map

1. **Location** • Which Western European country possessed the most land?
2. **Location** • On which continent were most colonies located?

Activity Options

Interdisciplinary Link: Music

Class Time One class period

Task Listening to music that expresses nationalistic themes

Purpose To show how nationalism influenced the arts, including music, in the 19th and early 20th centuries

Supplies Needed
• CD or cassette player
• CDs or cassettes of music by composers such as Grieg, Dvorak, Smetana, Bartok, Liszt, Borodin, or Tchaikovsky
• Reference sources, including music encyclopedias

B Block Scheduling

Activity Explain that nationalism influenced many European composers to use folksongs and folk themes in their music (for example, Liszt's "Hungarian Rhapsodies"). Have students with an interest or background in classical music find short pieces by some of the composers listed and present them in class. Students should explain the composer's national background and the folk tradition or story that each piece represents.

Location • In 1914, the United Kingdom could truthfully state that the sun never set on the British Empire. ◄

During this period of **colonialism,** Western European nations spent much of their wealth on building strong armies and navies. Their military forces helped to defend borders at home as well as colonies in other parts of the world. Colonies were so important that the ruling countries sometimes fought one another for control of them. They also struggled to extend their territories.

FOCUS ON VISUALS

Interpreting the Illustration Ask students to study the details of this illustration praising the British Empire. Point out that the background represents the Union Jack, the flag of the United Kingdom. Ask them to identify the four territories shown and explain why the artist might have chosen them.

Possible Responses India, Australia, New Zealand, South Africa. They were the largest and most valuable British possessions.

Extension Have students use the map on page 124 to point out British possessions on a globe. Ask them to use the globe to demonstrate that "the sun never set on the British Empire."

The Ballets Russes Begun in Paris, France, in 1909, the Ballets Russes (bah•lay ROOSE) brought together artists from all across Europe. Under the direction of the famous Russian producer Sergey Diaghilev (DYAH•guh•lev), this dance company became both a critical and a commercial success.

Many talented dancers and choreographers, such as Nijinsky, worked for Diaghilev. In addition, famous composers—including Claude Debussy (duh•BYOO•see) and Igor Stravinsky—wrote music for performances. The Ballets Russes also attracted Pablo Picasso, Marc Chagall, and other great artists to design its sets. It continued until Diaghilev's death in 1929.

THINKING CRITICALLY

1. **Synthesizing**
   How did the Ballets Russes benefit the European art and theater communities?

2. **Clarifying**
   How did the Ballets Russes represent more than a collection of dancers, musicians, and artists?

Spotlight on CULTURE

The first choreographer of the Ballets Russes was Michel Fokine. Formerly with the St. Petersburg Ballet company, Fokine believed that a dancer could express a character's emotion and tell a story through his or her movements. Male dancers, such as Vaslav Nijinsky, were important soloists in Fokine's ballets. Among Fokine's well-known ballets are *Prince Igor* (1909), *The Firebird* (1910), and *Petrushka* (1911). He also created the famous solo, *The Dying Swan* (1905) for the ballerina Anna Pavlova. Fokine left Russia in 1918 and settled in New York City.

Europe: War and Change **125**

Activity Options

Skillbuilder Mini-Lesson: Identifying Causes and Effects

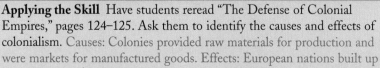 **Block Scheduling**

Explaining the Skill Discuss with students the importance of understanding what caused certain events in history. Explain that it is helpful when studying the history of Europe to understand how certain events led to other, often undesirable, events.

Applying the Skill Have students reread "The Defense of Colonial Empires," pages 124–125. Ask them to identify the causes and effects of colonialism. Causes: Colonies provided raw materials for production and were markets for manufactured goods. Effects: European nations built up armies and navies and fought one another for control of colonies.

FOCUS ON VISUALS

Interpreting the Map Have students notice the many countries crowded in this part of Europe. How might this cause problems?

Possible Response Countries would want more land for people and agriculture.

Extension Have students compare this map with a current atlas and list present-day countries once in Austria-Hungary.

CRITICAL THINKING ACTIVITY

Clarifying Ask students to consider why the countries of Eastern Europe were dependent on the countries of Western and Northern Europe. Guide them to recognize that these agricultural countries needed the manufactured goods produced in Western and Northern Europe.

Class Time 10 minutes

ASSESS & RETEACH

Reading Social Studies Have students create a cause-and-effect chart like the one on page 122 to show the causes and effects of nationalism and colonialism in Europe.

  Formal Assessment
  • Section Quiz, p. 65

RETEACHING ACTIVITY

Have students work in pairs to review the section and then write three sentences about the spread of nationalism in Europe.

  In-depth Resources: Unit 2
  • Reteaching Activity, p. 34

  Access for Students Acquiring English
  • Reteaching Activity, p. 38

GEOGRAPHY SKILLBUILDER: Interpreting a Map

1. **Location** • Name three countries that bordered Austria-Hungary.
2. **Region** • What was the capital of Austria-Hungary?

Austria-Hungary, 1900

Geography Skillbuilder Answers
1. (any three) Russia, Germany, Switzerland, Italy, Serbia, Romania
2. Vienna

Reading Social Studies
B. Possible Answers

Two nations would have different needs; they would include conflicting ethnic groups.

Reading
Social Studies

B. **Making Inferences** Why do you think governing a dual monarchy was difficult?

Austria-Hungary By the end of the 19th century, most nations of Western and Northern Europe had become industrialized. The majority of Eastern Europe, including Russia, remained agricultural. These Eastern European countries imported most of their manufactured goods from Western and Northern Europe.

The largest empire in Eastern Europe in 1900 was **Austria-Hungary.** The empire was a **dual monarchy**, in which one ruler governs two nations. As you can see in the map above, Austria-Hungary also included parts of many other present-day countries, including Romania, the Czech Republic, and portions of Poland.

SECTION 1 ASSESSMENT

Terms & Names

1. **Identify:**   (a) nationalism   (b) colonialism
                     (c) Austria-Hungary   (d) dual monarchy

Taking Notes

2. Look at the map on page 330 that shows European colonial territories. Use a chart like the one below to list the major colonial powers and their colonies.

Nation	Locations of Colonies

Main Ideas

3. (a) Identify one reason for the spread of nationalism in Europe.

   (b) Why did Western European nations spend much of their wealth on armies and navies?

   (c) How did the nations of Eastern Europe differ from those of Western and Northern Europe at the end of the 19th century?

Critical Thinking

4. **Drawing Conclusions**

   Why were their colonies so important to European nations?

   Think About

   • land and people
   • competition among nations
   • the production and sale of goods

 ACTIVITY -OPTION- Reread the information about the Ballets Russes. Write an **outline** of a story or book that might be a good choice for a ballet. Explain your choice.

Section 1 Assessment

1. Terms & Names
  a. nationalism, p. 123
  b. colonialism, p. 125
  c. Austria-Hungary, p. 126
  d. dual monarchy, p. 126

2. Taking Notes

Nation	Locations of Colonies
United Kingdom	Africa, India, Australia, New Zealand
France	West Africa, French Indochina
Germany	Africa
Belgium	Belgian Congo
Netherlands	Dutch East Indies

3. Main Ideas
  a. More Europeans could vote than in the past.
  b. They wanted to defend their borders at home, as well as their colonies.
  c. Western and Northern European nations were industrialized; most Eastern European nations remained agricultural.

4. Critical Thinking

Colonies provided raw materials and a market for manufactured goods; colonies helped make nations wealthier and stronger.

ACTIVITY OPTION

  Integrated Assessment
  • Rubric for making an outline

Europe at War

TERMS & NAMES
World War I
alliance
Adolf Hitler
fascism
Holocaust
World War II
NATO

MAIN IDEA

During the first half of the 20th century, European countries fought each other over land, wealth, and ideals.

WHY IT MATTERS NOW

The changes brought about by the two world wars continue to affect Europe today.

DATELINE

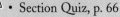

SARAJEVO, BOSNIA-HERZEGOVINA, JUNE 28, 1914—Today, Archduke of Austria-Hungary Franz Ferdinand and his wife, Duchess Sophie, were murdered as they drove through Sarajevo. A nineteen-year-old Serb, Gavrilo Princip, jumped on the Archduke's automobile and fired two shots. The first killed the Duchess. The second killed the Archduke, who was next in line to be emperor of Austria-Hungary.

The Serbians have protested against Austria-Hungary since 1908, when the empire took over Bosnia-Herzegovina (BOZ•nee•uh HAIR•tsuh•goh•VEE•nuh). Princip has been arrested.

Region • Archduke Franz Ferdinand and his wife, Duchess Sophie, were fatally shot in Sarajevo. ▲

• Gavrilo assassi-the future or of -Hungary 's wife. ▲

The World at War ❶

Because of the murder of Archduke Franz Ferdinand in 1914, the emperor of Austria-Hungary declared war on Serbia. When Russia sent troops to defend Serbia, Germany declared war on Russia. Russia supported Serbia because both Russians and Serbians share a similar ethnic background—they are both Slavic peoples. This was the beginning of **World War I.**

SECTION OBJECTIVES

1. To identify the issues that led to World War I
2. To describe Europe after World War I
3. To identify Germany's actions that led to World War II
4. To describe Europe after World War II

SKILLBUILDER
• Interpreting a Political Cartoon, p. 128
• Interpreting a Map, p. 129

FOCUS & MOTIVATE
WARM-UP

Making Inferences Have students read Dateline and think about causes and effects of the assassination.

1. What part might nationalism have played in inspiring the murder?
2. How do you think the nations of Europe reacted to this event?

INSTRUCT: Objective ❶

The World at War

• Why did Germany declare war on Russia? to support Austria after Russia sent help to Serbia
• Why would a country join an alliance? to unite for a common cause; to receive support if attacked

 In-depth Resources: Unit 2
• Guided Reading Worksheet, p. 28

 Reading Study Guide
(Spanish and English), pp. 38–39

Program Resources

 In-depth Resources: Unit 2
• Guided Reading Worksheet, p. 28
• Reteaching Activity, p. 35

 Reading Study Guide
(Spanish and English), pp. 38–39

 Formal Assessment
• Section Quiz, p. 66

 Integrated Assessment
• Rubric for writing a letter

 Outline Map Activities

 Access for Students Acquiring English
• Guided Reading Worksheet, p. 34

 Technology Resources
classzone.com

TEST-TAKING RESOURCES
🕭 Strategies for Test Preparation
🕭 Test Practice Transparencies
🕮 Online Test Practice

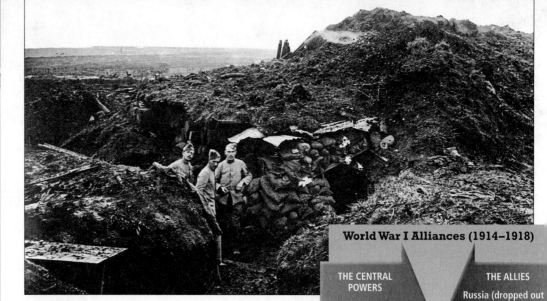

Place • World War I was primarily fought in trenches, which were dug by the armies for better defense. ▲

FOCUS ON VISUALS

Interpreting the Political Cartoon Ask students to give their first impressions of what this cartoon represents. Have them read the inscription on the pedestal and notice the weapons the figure is carrying or wearing. Then have them present their interpretations.

Possible Responses The figure looks not quite human but is probably a soldier. He is carrying a weapon with a bayonet and wearing a gas mask. Those new weapons are the kind of progress that the war represents.

Extension Ask students to sketch a cartoon that represents their opinion or attitude about a current political event or issue.

MORE ABOUT...
World War I Weaponry

Trench warfare was a terrifying way to fight, made worse by new weapons. Machine guns made it deadly to try to cross no man's land, the area between opposing lines of trenches. Other new weapons included long-range guns and poison gas. Later in the war, daring pilots took to the skies in small planes to take part in aerial dogfights.

World War I Alliances (1914–1918)

THE CENTRAL POWERS	THE ALLIES
Austria-Hungary Germany Turkey (Ottoman Empire) Bulgaria	Russia (dropped out in 1917) France United Kingdom Italy (joined 1915) United States (joined 1917)

World War I Alliances European rulers wanted other leaders to think twice before declaring war on their countries. To help defend themselves, several countries joined alliances (uh•LY•uhn•sez). An **alliance** is an agreement among people or nations to unite for a common cause. Each member of an alliance agrees to help the other members in case one of them is attacked.

When Germany joined the war to support Austria-Hungary, France came in on the side of Russia. Germany then invaded Belgium, which was neutral, to attack France. Because Great Britain had promised to protect Belgium, it, too, declared war on Germany. After German submarines sank four American merchant ships, the United States joined the side of Russia, France, and Great Britain.

The chart above shows the major powers on both sides of World War I. Italy had originally been allied with Germany and Austria-Hungary but joined the Allies after the war began. Russia dropped out of the war completely after the revolution in that country in 1917.

SKILLBUILDER:
Interpreting a Political Cartoon
1. What does the artist mean by naming the figure "Progress"?
2. Why is the man wearing a gas mask?

Reading **Social Studies**

A. Recognizing Important Details Why did Great Britain enter World War I?

Reading Social Studies
A. Answer
because Germany had invaded Belgium, an ally of Britain

Skillbuilder Answers
1. The artist is using "Progress" sarcastically, referring to the soldier's new weapons.

2. Poison gas was one of the weapons introduced in World War I.

Activity Options
Differentiating Instruction: Students Acquiring English/ESL

Base words and suffixes Write the words *ally* and *alliance* on the chalkboard. Explain that the word *alliance* was formed by adding the suffix *-ance* to the base word *ally*. Explain that an ally is "a person, group, or nation united with another." Review that an alliance is "an agreement to unite for a common cause." Have students practice using the words in sentences. You might want to provide models, such as "Great Britain was an ally of Belgium. Great Britain and Belgium formed an alliance."

ALLY

ALLIANCE = ALLY + ANCE

World War I was costly in terms of human life. When it was over, nearly 22 million civilians and soldiers on both sides were dead. The Allies had won, and Europe had been devastated.

Europe After World War I ②

More people were killed during World War I than during all the wars of the 19th century combined. Afterward, people in many countries on both sides of the costly war—and even those not directly involved—were poor, homeless, and without work.

The Allies blamed Germany for much of the killing and damage during the war. In 1919, Germany and the Allies signed the Treaty of Versailles (ver•SIGH).

Geography Skillbuilder Answers

1. Adriatic Sea

2. (any three) Poland, Romania, Austria, Hungary, Germany

Strange but TRUE

War Dogs During World War I, dogs were trained to guard ammunition, to detect mines, and to carry messages. Dogs even helped to search for the wounded.

War dogs saved many lives. They were especially helpful in forested areas and at night. These dogs are wearing protective masks to keep them safe from poison gas attacks.

GEOGRAPHY SKILLBUILDER: Interpreting a Map

Location • What body of water does the coast of Yugoslavia reach?

Location • Name three countries that border Czechoslovakia.

Europe After World War I

Europe: War and Change **129**

INSTRUCT: Objective ②

Europe After World War I

- What did the Treaty of Versailles require of Germany? to pay for damage done to Allied countries; to give up valuable territory
- How did the division of Austria-Hungary affect some ethnic groups in Eastern Europe? They became independent nations.

FOCUS ON VISUALS

Interpreting the Map Remind students that World War I brought the breakup of Austria-Hungary and the formation of several new nations. Have them look back at the map on page 126, then list the new nations that appear on this map of Europe.

Possible Responses Czechoslovakia, Yugoslavia, Poland, Albania. Austria and Hungary were separated. Romania and Italy gained territory.

Extension Have students draw a map of Yugoslavia after World War I, showing and labeling the smaller nations that were combined to create the new country.

Strange but TRUE

Animals other than dogs supported the war effort. The U.S. Army Signal Corps in World War I used more than 600 carrier pigeons in France. One of the bravest was called Cher Ami (SHER ah•MEE), meaning "dear friend." Cher Ami delivered 12 important messages in France. Even after being fatally wounded by enemy fire, he made it back to his own lines.

Activity Options

Interdisciplinary Link: Art

Class Time One class period

Task Designing a medal for heroic dogs

Purpose To combine form and function in the creation of a military-style decoration

Supplies Needed
- Drawing paper
- Pencils and markers
- Reference sources, including an encyclopedia

Block Scheduling

Activity Explain that the carrier pigeon Cher Ami earned a major French medal for service. Find and display illustrations of medals. Then ask students to design a medal to honor the service of a war dog that saved human lives. Encourage students to find examples of other designs on medals that they might incorporate into their own. Provide a bulletin board or other area for students to display their work.

Teacher's Edition **129**

INSTRUCT: Objective ❸

World War II

• Why did the majority of Germans support Hitler? They thought he would help Germany recover from World War I.

• What ideas do fascists support? strong central government, military dictatorship, racism, extreme nationalism

• What action by Germany brought about World War II? its invasion of Poland

• Which countries remained neutral? Denmark, Norway, Sweden, Switzerland

MORE ABOUT...

The Holocaust

Today, the German government continues to try to repair the damages and loss that so many families suffered. Throughout Europe, many sites connected to the Holocaust—including some of the former concentration camps—are permanent memorials to remind future generations of what happened.

Memorials to the Holocaust have also been built in many cities in the United States as well. The United States Holocaust Memorial Museum is located in Washington, D.C. The museum contains a three-floor exhibition that presents the history of the Holocaust through artifacts, photographs, films, and eyewitness reports.

The Treaty of Versailles demanded that Germany be punished by being forced to pay for the damage done to the Allied countries. Germany was also made to give up valuable territory.

A New Map of Europe Additional treaties during the following year also altered the political boundaries of many European countries. As the map on page 129 shows, Austria-Hungary was divided as a result of the war, becoming two separate countries. This allowed several Eastern European ethnic groups that had been part of Austria-Hungary to gain their independence.

World War II ❸

By the 1930s, Germany was still paying for the damage done to the Allied countries during World War I. The German economy was in ruins, and the Germans greatly wished to rebuild their own country. In 1933, citizens elected **Adolf Hitler** and the National Socialist, or Nazi, Party. The Nazi Party believed in fascism. **Fascism** (FASH·IHZ·uhm) is a philosophy that supports a strong, central government controlled by the military and led by a powerful dictator. People believed that this new leader would help Germany recover.

World War II Alliances (1939–1945)

THE AXIS POWERS
Germany
Italy
Japan

THE ALLIES
United Kingdom
France
(until June 1940)
Soviet Union
(formerly "Russia")
United States
(joined in 1941)

Hitler and the Nazi Party Fascists practiced an extreme form of patriotism and nationalism. Fascists also had racist beliefs.

In the 1930s, Hitler unjustly blamed the Jewish citizens of Germany, among other specific groups, for the country's problems. His Nazi followers seized Jewish property and began to send Jews, along with disabled people, political opponents, and others, to concentration camps. During this **Holocaust,** millions of people were deliberately killed, and others starved or died from disease.

In 1934, Hitler took command of the armed forces. Then, in 1939, Hitler's army invaded Poland. **World War II** had begun. By June 1940, Hitler's army had swept through Western Europe, conquering Belgium, the Netherlands, Luxembourg, France, Denmark, and Norway. A year later, Germany invaded the Soviet Union.

Reading Social Studies
B. Answers economic problems resentment at paying reparations

Reading Social Studies
B. Finding Causes What conditions led Germans to find hope in Adolf Hitler?

BACKGROUND
Like Germany, Italy was also ruled by a fascist dictator after World War I: Benito Mussolini (1883–1945).

Activity Options

Differentiating Instruction: Gifted and Talented

B Block Scheduling

Debating Examine the issue of neutrality in times of war. Divide students into groups, one group supporting neutrality and the other opposing it. Suggest that students examine issues such as a country's motives for remaining neutral; what is required from countries choosing neutrality; and/or whether other countries always truly recognize and observe this neutrality. Allow time for students to prepare their arguments.

WWII Alliances The chart on page 130 shows the major powers on both sides of World War II. As in World War I, the United States at first tried to stay out of the conflict but entered the war after Japan bombed U.S. military bases at Pearl Harbor in Hawaii on December 7, 1941.

Europe After World War II ④

World War II turned much of Europe into a battleground. By the end of the war, the United States, France, and the United Kingdom occupied Western Europe. The Soviet Union occupied Eastern Europe, including the eastern part of Germany.

Once peace was established, the western allies helped to set up free governments in Western Europe. In 1949, the countries of Western Europe joined Canada and the United States to form a defense alliance called **NATO** (NAY·toh). The members of this alliance, whose name stands for North Atlantic Treaty Organization, agreed to defend one another if they were attacked by the Soviet Union or any other country. Without a common enemy, political differences quickly separated the Soviet Union from Western Europe and the United States.

Place • The Kaiser Wilhelm Memorial Church in Berlin was nearly destroyed by Allied bombs. The ruins still stand today as a World War II monument. See pages 120–121. ▲

Europe: War and Change **131**

Biography

Anne Frank In July 1942, during World War II, Anne Frank and her family went into hiding in Amsterdam—a city in the Netherlands. The Frank family were Jewish and were afraid they would be sent to a concentration camp. Anne was only thirteen.

For two years, Anne, her father, mother, sister, and four other people lived in rooms in an attic. Their rooms were sealed off from the rest of the building. While in hiding, Anne kept a diary. Although the family was discovered and Anne died in a concentration camp, her diary was eventually published. Today, this famous book—translated into many languages and the basis for a play and a film—lives on.

INSTRUCT: Objective ④

Europe After World War II

• How did the Allies help Western European nations after the war? helped them set up free governments
• Why was NATO formed? to provide defense against attack by the Soviet Union or other countries

CRITICAL THINKING ACTIVITY

Recognizing Effects Explain to students that an occupied area is one in which a victorious army keeps its troops. For example, the United States and the United Kingdom occupied Western European countries after World War II. Have students brainstorm the positive and negative effects such a situation might have on the occupied country. Suggest that they consider freedom of movement within the country, economic factors, and national pride.

Class Time 15 minutes

Biography

Approximately 500,000 visitors each year line up at the entrance to the Anne Frank House, located in the center of Amsterdam. After watching an introductory video, visitors enter the "Secret Annex" through a revolving bookshelf that hides the entrance. There they can see the rooms occupied by Anne's family and the Van Daans for two years. Anne's original diary and a model of the annex during the occupation are on display in the house. The house serves as a reminder that nearly all of the Jewish people of Amsterdam were killed during World War II, and shows what life was like for those in hiding.

Activity Options

Differentiating Instruction: Less Proficient Readers

Class Time 30 minutes

Task Highlighting main ideas and details in text

Purpose To understand the relationship of main ideas and details

Supplies Needed
• Photocopies of pp. 130–131
• Colored highlighters

Activity Reread aloud the text under "World War II" and "Europe After World War II." Stop at the end of each subsection and work with students to identify the main idea. Tell them to highlight the main idea. Then work together to identify the important details that support the main ideas and highlight them in color. Continue the process until each subsection has been highlighted in a different color. Encourage students to use their colored copies as study guides.

FOCUS ON VISUALS

Interpreting the Map Have students compare the map of Europe after World War II with that on page 129 of the Continent after World War I. What major change do they notice?

Possible Response division of Germany into East and West

Extension Have students use the map to name the countries that border East and West Germany.

ASSESS & RETEACH

Reading Social Studies Have students fill in the first two rows of the chart on page 122.

 Formal Assessment
• Section Quiz, p. 66

RETEACHING ACTIVITY

Divide students into four groups. Ask each group to summarize the information under one of the headings in the section. When they have finished, have groups share their summaries with the other groups.

 In-depth Resources: Unit 2
• Reteaching Activity, p. 35

 Access for Students Acquiring English
• Reteaching Activity, p. 39

Europe After World War II

The Marshall Plan United States Secretary of State George C. Marshall created the Economic Cooperation Act of 1948, also known as the Marshall Plan. This plan offered U.S. aid—agricultural, industrial, and financial—to countries of Western Europe. The Marshall Plan greatly benefited war-torn Europe. It may also have prevented economic depression or political instability.

SECTION 2 ASSESSMENT

Terms & Names

1. **Identify:** (a) World War I (b) alliance (c) Adolf Hitler (d) fascism
   (e) Holocaust (f) World War II (g) NATO

Taking Notes

2. Use a Venn diagram like this one to compare the countries that were involved in World War I and World War II.

Involved in WWI Involved in Both Involved in WWII

Main Ideas

3. (a) What event set off World War I?
   (b) When did World War II begin and end? Which countries won?
   (c) What happened at the end of World War II?

Critical Thinking

4. **Making Inferences**
   How did World War I change Europe?

   Think About
   ◆ the destruction and many deaths
   ◆ the Treaty of Versailles
   ◆ Austria-Hungary

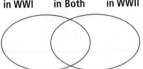 Look at the photographs in this section. Write a **letter** in which you describe what it might have been like to visit Europe just after World War I or World War II.

Section 2 Assessment

1. Terms & Names
a. World War I, p. 127
b. alliance, p. 128
c. Adolf Hitler, p. 130
d. fascism, p. 130
e. Holocaust, p. 130
f. World War II, p. 130
g. NATO, p. 131

2. Taking Notes

Involved in WWI:	Involved in Both World Wars:	Involved in WWII:
Austria-Hungary, Turkey, Bulgaria	Germany, Russia, France, United Kingdom, Italy, United States	Japan

3. Main Ideas
a. The assassination of the archduke and duchess of Austria set off WWI.
b. began: 1939; ended: 1945. The Allies [Great Britain (U.K.), United States, France, Soviet Union] won.
c. Western Allies occupied Western Europe; Soviet Union took control of Eastern Europe; Western powers formed NATO; Marshall Plan helped European economies rebuild.

4. Critical Thinking
Austria-Hungary was broken up; Eastern European ethnic groups became independent; Germany gave up territory.

ACTIVITY OPTION

 Integrated Assessment
• Rubric for writing a letter

Reading a Political Cartoon

▶▶ Defining the Skill

Political cartoons—also known as editorial cartoons—express an opinion about a serious subject. A political cartoonist uses symbols, familiar objects, and people to make his or her point quickly and visually. Sometimes the caption and words in the cartoon help to clarify the meaning. Although a cartoonist may use humor to make a point, political cartoons are not always funny.

▶▶ Applying the Skill

This political cartoon was created in the period between World War I and World War II. However, Europeans were already concerned about developments in Germany.

How to Read a Political Cartoon

Strategy ❶ Read the cartoon's title and any other words. For example, some cartoons have labels, captions, and thought balloons. Then study the cartoon as a whole.

Strategy ❷ If the cartoon has people in it, are they famous? Sometimes the cartoonist wants to comment on a famous person, such as a world leader. Look for symbols or details in the cartoon. For example, in this cartoon a German soldier is climbing out of the Versailles Treaty. Think about the relationships between the words and the images.

Strategy ❸ Summarize the cartoonist's message. What is the cartoonist's point of view about the subject? What does this cartoonist think was the cause of Hitler's rise to power?

❶ THE SOURCE

Make a Chart

A chart can help you to analyze the information in a political cartoon. Once you understand the cartoon's elements, you can summarize its meaning. Use a chart such as this one to help you organize the information.

Important Words	Hitler Party; Versailles Treaty
Important Symbols/Images	German soldier with "Hitler Party" on his helmet crawling out of the Versailles Treaty that officially ended World War I.
Summary ❸	The terms of the Versailles Treaty led to the rise of Hitler's party in Germany; Hitler's party, symbolized by a soldier, is war-like and threatens Europe.

▶▶ Practicing the Skill

Study the political cartoon in Chapter 5, Section 2, on page 128. Make a chart similar to the one above in which you list the important parts of the cartoon and write a summary of the cartoon's message.

SKILLBUILDER

Reading a Political Cartoon

Defining the Skill

Display several political cartoons or have students turn to the example in their text on page 128. Ask students to look for common features, such as the use of recognizable people, objects or symbols, and captions. Point out that political cartoons assume a certain knowledge about important events on the part of readers. Explain that they are also called editorial cartoons, meaning they express a point of view in the same way an editorial does.

Applying the Skill

How to Read a Political Cartoon Point out the strategies for reading a political cartoon and guide students in working through each one. Suggest that students note any significant words and identify any people or symbols they recognize. Remind students to look at the cartoon (text and drawing) as a whole.

Make a Chart

Guide students in completing a chart. Ask questions such as, What important words do you see? What does the appearance of the German soldier suggest? What might the cartoonist's purpose have been in drawing this cartoon?

Practicing the Skill

Have students work in pairs to complete a chart for the cartoon on page 128. If students need more practice with this skill, work with them to analyze a political cartoon from a current newspaper or newsmagazine.

In-depth Resources: Unit 2
• Skillbuilder Practice, p. 32

Activity Options

Career Connection: Political Cartoonist

Encourage students who enjoy reading political cartoons to find out about people who create them for a living. Tell students that most political cartoonists work for a single newspaper or magazine.

1. Suggest that students look for interviews with actual political cartoonists and articles about how they rose to their positions.

Block Scheduling

2. Help students learn what training and experience a person needs to become a political cartoonist.

3. Invite students to summarize in cartoon form what they have learned and to share their cartoon with the class.

OBJECTIVE

Students analyze an Irish folk tale in which Bláithín, the wife of folk hero Fíonn Mac Cumhail, saves her husband from a Scottish giant.

FOCUS & MOTIVATE

Drawing Conclusions To help students predict elements of this story, have them study the illustrations on pages 134–135 and answer the following questions:

1. What can you tell about the characters in this tale from the illustrations?

2. What might be special about the round cakes that are pictured?

 Block Scheduling

MORE ABOUT...

"Fíonn Mac Cumhail and the Giant's Causeway"

Celtic culture arose in Europe around 700 B.C. and flourished throughout Europe until the Romans conquered much of the region between 300 B.C. and A.D. 100. The only place where Celtic culture was preserved was Ireland, Scotland, Wales, and parts of England and France. The early Celts did not have a written language. However, during the Middle Ages the Celts adopted the Roman alphabet and became prolific writers. Many of their tales and legends have survived.

Fíonn Mac Cumhail and the Giant's Causeway[1]

FIONN MAC CUMHAIL, more commonly known as Finn MacCool, is a familiar figure in Irish folk tales. He first appears in the ancient Celtic tales known as the Fenian cycle. In the following story, retold by Una Leavy, Fionn is portrayed as a clever giant, hard at work with the Fianna, his band of Irish warriors. They begin to build a bridge from Ireland to Scotland, because, as the boastful Fionn says, "There are giants over there that I'm longing to conquer." Plans suddenly change, however, and Fionn must go home.

1. The Giant's Causeway, which takes its name from this legend, is a striking natural rock formation on the coast of Ireland.

2. The region of Ireland where Fionn and the Fianna are building their bridge to Scotland. It is the location of the actual Giant's Causeway.

Fíonn Mac Cumhail and the Fianna worked quickly on the bridge, splitting stones into splendid pillars and columns. Further and further they stretched out into the ocean. From time to time, there came a distant rumble. "Is it thunder?" asked the Fianna, but they went on working. Then one of their spies came ashore. "I've just been to Scotland!" he said. "There's a huge giant there called Fathach Mór. He's doing long jumps—you can hear the thumping. He has a magic little finger with the strength of ten men! He's in training for the long jump to Antrim."[2]

Fíonn's face paled. "The strength of ten men!" he thought. "I'll never fight him. He'll squash me into a pancake." But he could not admit that he was nervous, so he said to the Fianna, "I've just had a message from Bláithín, my wife. I must go home at once—you can all take a holiday."

He set off by himself and never did a man travel faster. Bláithín was surprised to see him. "And is the great causeway finished already?" she asked.

"No indeed," replied Fíonn.

"What's the matter?" Bláithín asked. So Fíonn told her.

"What will I do, Bláithín?" he asked. "There's the strength of ten men in his magic little finger. He'll squish me into a jelly!"

Bláithín laughed. "Just leave him to me. Stoke up the fire and fetch me the sack of flour. Then go outside and find nine flat stones." Fíonn did as he was told. Bláithín worked all night making ten oatcakes. In each she put a large flat stone, all except the last. This one she marked with her thumbprint. "Go and cut down some wood," she said. "You must make an enormous cradle."

Activity Options

Differentiating Instruction: Less Proficient Readers

Building Language Skills Have students work in small groups, each including less proficient readers and more fluent readers. Duplicate copies of the Literature Connection and give each student a copy of the folk tale. Assign character parts to the more proficient readers and sec-

tions of narrative text to less proficient readers. Suggest that all students highlight their speaking parts with a marker. Allow time for students to practice their parts and then have groups present the folk tale to the class.

Fionn worked all morning. The cradle was just finished when there was a mighty rumble and the dishes shook.

"It's him," squealed Fionn.

"Don't worry!" said Bláithín. "Put on this bonnet. Now into the cradle and leave me to do the talking."

"Does Fionn Mac Cumhail live here?" boomed a great voice above her.

"He does," said Bláithín, "though he's away at the moment. He's gone to capture the giant, Fathach Mór."

"I'm Fathach Mór!" bellowed the giant. "I've been searching for Fionn everywhere."

"Did you ever see Fionn?" she asked. "Sure you're only a baby compared with him. He'll be home shortly and you can see for yourself. But now that you're here, would you do me a favor? The well has run dry and Fionn was supposed to lift up the mountain this morning. There's spring water underneath it. Do you think you could get me some?"

"Of course," shouted the giant as he scooped out a hole in the mountain, the size of a crater.

Fionn shook with fear in the cradle and even Bláithín turned pale. But she thanked the giant and invited him in. "Though you and Fionn are enemies, you are still a guest," she said. "Have some fresh bread." And she put the oatcakes before him. Fathach Mór began to eat. Almost at once he gave a piercing yell and spat out two teeth.

"What kind of bread is this?" he screeched. "I've broken my teeth on it."

"How can you say such a thing?" asked Bláithín. "Even the child in the cradle eats them!" And she gave Fionn the cake with the thumbprint. Fathach looked at the cradle. "Whose child is that?" he asked in wonder.

"That's Fionn's son," said Bláithín.

"And how old is he?" he asked then.

"Just ten months," replied Bláithín.

"Can he talk?" asked the giant.

"Not yet, but you should hear him roar!" At once, Fionn began to yell.

"Quick, quick," cried Bláithín. "Let him suck your little finger. If Fionn comes home and hears him, he'll be in such a temper. With an anxious glance at the door, the giant gave Fionn his finger. Fionn bit off the giant's magic little finger. Screeching, the giant bolted from the house. Fionn leaped from the cradle in bib and bonnet and danced his Bláithín round the kitchen.

Reading
THE LITERATURE

Before reading this story, how did you expect Fionn Mac Cumhail to act? Did you expect him to be the hero of the story? Who is? How does this character solve the problem in the story? What skills are used to solve it?

Thinking About
THE LITERATURE

In many European myths and legends, the heroes are powerful and fearless. How does Fionn act in this story? What words does the author use to make clear Fionn's attitude toward the danger he faces? How does he differ from other legendary figures that you have read about?

Writing About
THE LITERATURE

Often, myths are created in order to answer questions about or explain mysteries in the world. This legend explains why the causeway was never finished. How might the story about Fionn be different if the causeway had been finished?

About the Author

Una Leavy, the author of *Irish Fairy Tales & Legends,* is an Irish writer who lives with her husband and children in County Mayo, Ireland.

Further Reading *The Names upon the Harp* by Marie Heaney recounts myths and legends of early Irish literature, including the stories about Fionn Mac Cumhail that make up the Fenian cycle.

INSTRUCT

Reading the Literature
Possible Responses

The title hints that Fíonn will be the hero, but when he gets scared, he goes to his wife, Bláithín, for help. Her cleverness and domestic skills enable them to outwit Fathach Mór by convincing him that Fíonn is their baby. When Fathach Mór lets Fíonn suck his magic finger, Fíonn bites it off.

Thinking About the Literature
Possible Responses

Fíonn's face paled; "He'll squash me . . ."; he was nervous; "What will I do, Bláithín? . . ."; he squealed; he shook with fear. Most legendary figures are strong and brave, but Fíonn is frightened and nervous.

Writing About the Literature
Possible Responses

Students' responses should explain how the causeway was finished. They might say that Fathach Mór finished it to get back to Scotland, or that Bláithín finished it herself.

MORE ABOUT...
Celtic Monuments

Made up of 40,000 separate stone columns, the Giant's Causeway juts out from the coast into the channel separating Scotland and Ireland. Some of its pillars are 82 feet high. It was formed 50 to 60 million years ago by inland lava flows that cooled when they reached the sea.

Though the Giant's Causeway is natural, the Celts left monuments throughout Ireland and Europe, including circular earthworks, terraced hillsides, burial mounds, and a huge horse carved into the ground in England.

World Literature

More to Think About

Making Personal Connections Brainstorm a list or web of folk tale characters students know. Include Fíonn Mac Cumhail and add characters from American folk tales, Native American tales, and folk tales from other lands. Then ask: Why do people tell these stories, even today? What do folk tales explain about a culture?

Vocabulary Activity Have students write lines from the story on index cards or slips of paper. Read or display the lines and see who can correctly match each line with its speaker.

SECTION OBJECTIVES

1. To explain the postwar division between the countries of Eastern and Western Europe
2. To describe the effects of the dictatorship of Joseph Stalin on the Soviet Union
3. To describe the climate of the Cold War

SKILLBUILDER
• Interpreting a Map, p. 138

CRITICAL THINKING
• Analyzing Issues, p. 137

FOCUS & MOTIVATE
WARM-UP

Recognizing Effects Have students read <u>Dateline</u> and discuss the Warsaw Pact.

1. Why would countries located between the Soviet Union and Western Europe be willing to have Soviet troops stationed there?
2. Why do you think Yugoslavia did not agree to sign the Warsaw Pact?

INSTRUCT: Objective ❶

East Against West

• In what way did the Iron Curtain serve as a barrier? kept people from traveling between the East and the West

• How did the Soviet Union control the Eastern European countries? through puppet governments, through force; people could be jailed for expressing anti-Soviet views

 In-depth Resources: Unit 2
• Guided Reading Worksheet, p. 29

 Reading Study Guide
(Spanish and English), pp. 40–41

SECTION **3** **The Soviet Union**

TERMS & NAMES
Iron Curtain
puppet government
one-party system
Joseph Stalin
collective farm
Warsaw Pact
Cold War

MAIN IDEA
After World War II, the Soviet Union was the most powerful country in Europe, but life for most Soviet citizens was difficult.

WHY IT MATTERS NOW
Russia, the former Soviet Union, remains powerful and is currently experiencing great change.

DATELINE · EXTRA

WARSAW, POLAND, MAY 14, 1955

Today, the Soviet Union and most Eastern European countries announced that they have signed the Warsaw Treaty of Friendship, Cooperation, and Mutual Assistance. The members of this alliance agree to offer military defense to one another for a period of 20 years.

Yugoslavia is the only country in Eastern Europe that did not sign the agreement.

The new treaty, also called the Warsaw Pact, allows the Soviet Union to keep troops in the countries that are located between the Soviet Union and Western Europe. The Warsaw Pact is a response to the formation of NATO, an alliance that Western European countries joined six years ago.

Region • Warsaw hosted Eastern European officials who signed a military alliance here in the Palace of Culture. ▲

East Against West ❶

After World War II, political differences divided the Soviet-controlled countries of Eastern Europe from those of Western Europe. These differences gave rise to an invisible wall known as the **Iron Curtain.** While there was no actual curtain, people of the East were restricted from traveling outside of their countries. Westerners who wished to visit the East also faced restrictions.

136 CHAPTER 5

Program Resources

 In-depth Resources: Unit 2
• Guided Reading Worksheet, p. 29
• Reteaching Activity, p. 36

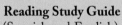 **Reading Study Guide**
(Spanish and English), pp. 40–41

 Formal Assessment
• Section Quiz, p. 67

Integrated Assessment
• Rubric for writing a scene

 Outline Map Activities

 Access for Students Acquiring English
• Guided Reading Worksheet, p. 35

Technology Resources
classzone.com

TEST-TAKING RESOURCES
⚓ Strategies for Test Preparation
⚓ Test Practice Transparencies
🕹 Online Test Practice

The Strongest Nation in Europe The Union of Soviet Socialist Republics, or USSR, was the official name of the Soviet Union. It included 15 republics, of which Russia was the largest. The Soviet Union entered World War II in 1941, when Germany invaded its borders. German troops destroyed much of the western Soviet Union and killed millions of people. This invasion brought the Soviet Union close to collapse. However, with the defeat of Germany, the Soviet Union rose to become the strongest nation in Europe.

Region • The hammer and sickle became the symbol of Soviet communism. The tools represent the unity of the peasants (sickle) with the workers (hammer). ▲

Vocabulary

establish: set up; create

Communism After World War II, the Soviet Union established Communist governments in Eastern Europe. The Soviets made sure—either by politics or by force—that these new Eastern European governments were loyal to the Soviet Union.

Soviet Control of Eastern Europe The Soviet Union controlled the countries of Eastern Europe through puppet governments. A **puppet government** is one that does what it is told by an outside force. In this case, the Eastern European governments followed orders from Soviet leaders in Moscow.

Reading Social Studies
A. Possible Answers
through fear and military force; by controlling elections

Reading
Social Studies

A. Making Inferences How do you think the Soviet Union enforced a one-party system in Eastern Europe?

Most Eastern Europeans did have the chance to vote, but they had only one political party to choose from: the Communist Party. All other parties were outlawed. This meant that there was only one candidate to choose from for each government position. This is an example of a **one-party system.** Soviet citizens could not complain about the government. In fact, they could be jailed for expressing any view that the Soviet leaders did not like.

Movement • The government-controlled factories in the Soviet Union did not produce enough of certain items. When goods that were often in short supply—such as bread and shoes—finally became available, people had to wait in long lines to buy them. ◄

Europe: War and Change **137**

MORE ABOUT...
The Iron Curtain
It was Britain's great wartime leader, Winston Churchill, who coined the term "Iron Curtain." On a visit to the United States in March 1946, he delivered an address in Fulton, Missouri. In that address, he warned Americans that "an iron curtain has descended across the Continent." Churchill was referring to the isolationism of the Soviet Union, which cut off the Soviet bloc—the Soviet Union and its Eastern European satellite countries—from the rest of the world.

CRITICAL THINKING ACTIVITY

Analyzing Issues Point out to students that at one point during World War II, the Soviet Union was on the verge of collapsing. However, at the end of the war, it was the strongest nation in Europe. To explain how this was possible, guide students to consider the size of the Soviet Union and its influence over Eastern European countries as well as the devastation suffered in the rest of the Continent.

Class Time 10 minutes

Activity Options

Multiple Learning Styles: Visual

Block Scheduling

Class Time One class period

Task Creating a political symbol

Purpose To understand how symbols are used to convey political messages and stir emotions

Supplies Needed
• Encyclopedia
• Paper
• Pencils, pens, markers

Activity Recall with students the political symbols they have seen in the text, such as the Soviet hammer and sickle. Point out that symbols can be a form of propaganda. They stir people's emotions. Have small groups of students create a political symbol to represent a current political concept in our country. Provide space for groups to display and explain their symbols and brief written descriptions.

INSTRUCT: Objective ❷

Joseph Stalin

- **Who was Joseph Stalin?** Communist leader of the Soviet Union during World War II

- **How did Stalin control agriculture in the Soviet Union?** through collective farms

- **In what way were the secret police important to Stalin's government?** arrested people whom Stalin did not trust and who did not support the government; sent them to Siberia

FOCUS ON VISUALS

Interpreting the Map Have students use the key to point out the area of the map showing the Soviet Union. Point out the vast extent of the country, especially the remote area of Siberia. Ask students to identify the oceans and seas that border Soviet territory on the north, south, east, and west. How might this access to the sea have influenced Russian and Soviet history?

Possible Responses North: Arctic Ocean; South: Black Sea; East: Pacific Ocean; West: Baltic Sea. Compared with its size, the Soviet Union had little seacoast in its European territory; this may have limited trade and economic development and prompted Russian and Soviet leaders to try to annex coastal territories.

Extension Have students compare this map with one of present-day Europe. Invite volunteers to point out differences and changes in national borders, both in the former Soviet Union and in the rest of Europe.

Region • Joseph Stalin ruled the Soviet Union from 1928 to 1953. ▲

Joseph Stalin ❷

Joseph Stalin (STAH·lin) (1879–1953) ruled the Soviet Union during World War II. Stalin took power after the death of Vladimir Lenin. Lenin was a Communist leader who had helped overthrow the czar and ruled the Soviet Union from 1917 until his death in 1924. The name Stalin is related to the Russian word for "steel." Stalin was greatly feared, and his rule was indeed as tough as steel. He controlled the government until his death.

The Five-Year Plans Under Stalin, the government controlled every aspect of Soviet life. Stalin hoped to strengthen the country with his five-year plans, which were sets of economic goals. For example, Stalin ordered many new factories to be built. The Soviet government decided where and what types of factories to build, how many goods to produce, and how to distribute them. These decisions were based on the Communist theory that this would benefit the most people.

Geography Skillbuilder Answers

1. East Germany, Poland, Czechoslovakia, Hungary, Romania, Bulgaria, Albania

2. East Germany

Region • The Soviet government managed the factories while citizens provided the actual labor. ◄

GEOGRAPHY SKILLBUILDER: Interpreting a Map

1. **Region** • Which countries are behind the Iron Curtain but not in the Soviet Union?
2. **Location** • What is the western-most country in the Warsaw Pact?

138 CHAPTER 5

Activity Options

Multiple Learning Styles: Visual

Class Time One hour

Task Creating a political cartoon about Stalin

Purpose To examine Stalin's policies and consider how people in democratic countries might have viewed them

Supplies Needed
- Textbook
- Drawing paper
- Pencils, pens, markers

Activity Review with students what they learned about political, or editorial, cartoons. Then have them reread the section "Joseph Stalin" in their textbooks. Ask students to create a political cartoon about Stalin and his policies that might have appeared in a newspaper in the United States. When they have finished their cartoons, invite volunteers to share them with the rest of the class.

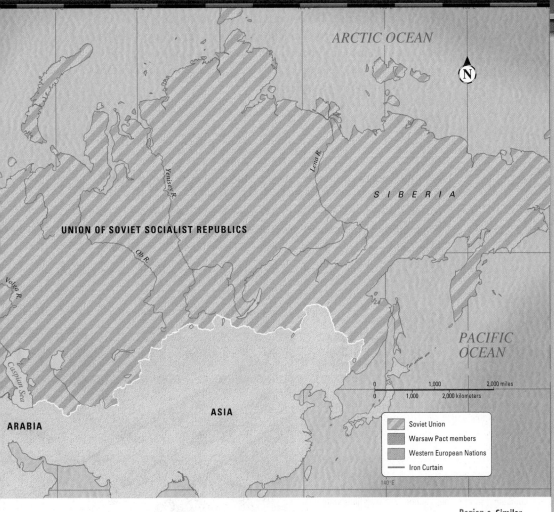

ARCTIC OCEAN

N

SIBERIA

UNION OF SOVIET SOCIALIST REPUBLICS

PACIFIC OCEAN

ASIA

ARABIA

| 0 | 1,000 | 2,000 miles |
| 0 | 1,000 | 2,000 kilometers |

Soviet Union

Warsaw Pact members

Western European Nations

Iron Curtain

140°E

MORE ABOUT...
The Soviet Union
Some facts about the Soviet Union:

- It was often just called Russia, because that was the dominant republic.
- It was the largest country in the world, extending about 6,800 miles (10,940 km) east to west and crossing 11 time zones.
- It was organized in 1922, mainly from Russia, Ukraine, and Belarus, eventually consisting of 15 republics.
- It was dissolved relatively peacefully in December 1991 and replaced by 15 independent states.

FOCUS ON VISUALS

Interpreting the Photographs Ask students to study the photographs of Soviet farm and factory workers and describe their impressions of the workers and their working conditions. Ask them to compare the farm workers with their ideas of an American farm in the 1930s or 1940s.

Possible Responses The farm workers are doing all the work by hand; they don't seem to have any farm machines. The workers in both pictures look very young.

Extension Have students look in history textbooks, popular histories, and other sources to find other photographs illustrating life in the Soviet Union from the 1930s through the 1950s.

Soviet Agriculture Stalin also hoped to strengthen the Soviet Union by controlling the country's agriculture. During the 1930s, peasants were forced to move to collective farms. A **collective farm** was government-owned and employed large numbers of workers. All the crops produced by the collective farms were distributed by the government. Sometimes farm workers did not receive enough food to feed themselves and their families.

Region • Similar to urban factory workers, Russian peasants labored on government-controlled collective farms. ▼

Activity Options

Interdisciplinary Links: Art/Language Arts

 Block Scheduling

Class Time One class period

Task Using persuasive writing techniques to create a propaganda poster

Purpose To understand how the employment of propaganda techniques can be used to manipulate the public

Supplies Needed
- Drawing paper
- Pens, markers

Activity Remind students that Joseph Stalin's government forced agricultural workers to join collective farms. Explain that the Communist government often employed propaganda posters to persuade workers that what they were doing was for the good of the country. Have students work in small groups to create propaganda posters. Brainstorm examples of persuasive words, phrases, and images that students might include in their posters.

INSTRUCT: Objective ❸

The Cold War

- What goal united the Soviet Union, the United States, and the United Kingdom from 1941 to 1945? the goal of defeating the Axis powers

- How was the Cold War different from World Wars I and II? NATO and the Warsaw Pact nations did not fight, but they would not trade or cooperate with each other either.

- What did the United States and its European allies fear? Soviet and Communist influence on other countries

- What did the Soviet Union fear from Western Europe? another invasion

Sergei Mikhailovich Eisenstein was born on January 23, 1898, in Riga, Latvia. In 1918, he joined the Red Army, where he worked as a poster designer. Shortly after, Eisenstein moved to Moscow and studied Japanese culture and language. It was this experience that influenced his new method of film editing known as montage. This method involves the grouping of unlike objects in such a way that they suggest a new meaning.

Thinking Critically Answers

1. Possible responses: He was responding to world events; he wanted to glorify Russian history and encourage patriotism.

2. He wanted to show that Germany was an ancient enemy of Russia but had been defeated before.

The Secret Police Stalin used his secret police to get rid of citizens he did not trust. The secret police arrested those who did not support the Soviet government. Suspects were transported to slave-labor camps in Siberia. Millions of men and women were sent to this remote and bitterly cold region of northeastern Russia. Many never returned home.

The Cold War ❸

From 1941 to 1945, the United Kingdom, the United States, and the Soviet Union shared a goal: to defeat the Axis Powers. They became allies to make that happen. Once the war ended, however, these countries no longer had a common enemy—and had little reason to work together. Most Western European countries were constitutional monarchies or democracies, and most Eastern European countries had Communist, largely Soviet-controlled, governments.

Soviet Film The Russian director Sergey Eisenstein (EYE•zen•stine) (1898–1948), bottom right, made only six movies, but they are among the most important works in film history. The silent film *Battleship Potemkin* (1925), whose poster is to the right, is one of Eisenstein's most famous. It is about a mutiny at sea. The director's use of close-ups and his method of combining short scenes changed the way films were made all over the world.

Just before the start of World War II, Eisenstein made the film *Alexander Nevsky* (1938). It tells the story of a historic battle that the Russians won against German-speaking invaders in the 1200s. This film became very popular during World War II, which it seemed to foreshadow.

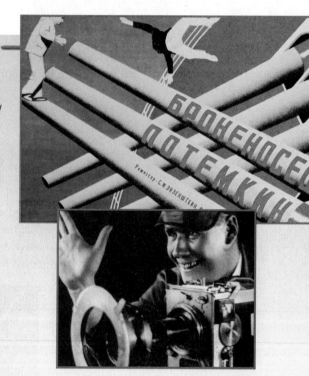

THINKING CRITICALLY

1. **Clarifying**
   What influenced Eisenstein to direct war films?

2. **Synthesizing**
   What did Eisenstein want to show about the relationship between Russians and Germans?

140 CHAPTER 5

Activity Options

Differentiating Instruction: Gifted and Talented

B Block Scheduling

Class Time One class period

Task Writing a review of a movie based on a historical event

Purpose To identify elements of a motion picture that appeal to feelings of patriotism and national pride

Supplies Needed
- Writing paper
- Pencils or pens

Activity Discuss any motion pictures that students have seen that had a historical background. Explain that most movie reviews assess films on such qualities as plot development, quality of performances, and special effects. Ask students to write a review of a movie that was based on an event in history. Encourage them to consider the features discussed, as well as the movie's appeal to feelings of patriotism and national pride. If possible, provide time for students to share their reviews and discuss their opinions.

Region • The Brandenberg Gate was a part of the Berlin Wall that separated East Berlin from West Berlin. ◄

Reading
Social Studies

B. Comparing Compare the Soviet Union's fears in the Cold War with those of the United States and Western Europe.

The members of NATO and the nations in the **Warsaw Pact**—the alliance of Eastern European countries behind the Iron Curtain—refused to trade or cooperate with each other. The countries never actually fought, so this period of political noncooperation is called the **Cold War.** Both sides in the Cold War were hesitant to start a war that would involve the use of newly developed nuclear weapons, which could cause destruction on a global scale.

The United States and Western Europe feared that the Soviet Union would influence other countries to become Communist. At the same time, the Soviet Union wanted to protect itself against invasion. This led the countries on either side of the Iron Curtain to view and treat each other as possible threats. The tense international situation caused by the Cold War would continue for almost 40 years.

SECTION ③ ASSESSMENT

Terms & Names

1. Identify:
   (a) Iron Curtain   **(b)** puppet government   **(c)** one-party system   **(d)** Joseph Stalin
   (e) collective farm   **(f)** Warsaw Pact   **(g)** Cold War

Taking Notes

2. Use a chart like this one to describe three elements of Joseph Stalin's rule of the Soviet Union.

Five-Year Plans	Agriculture	Secret Police

Main Ideas

3. (a) What happened to the Soviet Union during World War II?

(b) How did the governments of most Western and Eastern European countries differ?

(c) How did Joseph Stalin rule the Soviet Union?

Critical Thinking

4. Analyzing Motives

Why do you think the Soviet Union wanted to control the countries of Eastern Europe?

Think About

- the events of World War II
- the location of the Eastern European countries
- the governments of the Soviet Union and Western Europe

ACTIVITY -OPTION-
Reread the information about the secret police. Write a dramatic **scene** in which the main character is sent to a labor camp in Siberia.

Europe: War and Change **141**

MORE ABOUT...
The Brandenburg Gate
Built around 1790, the Brandenburg Gate was the symbol of the city of Berlin. It stands at the western end of the famous avenue, Unter den Linden. The gate was modeled after a famous Greek triumphal arch in Athens. The statue on the top represents a chariot drawn by four horses. The gate was badly damaged in World War II but restored in the late 1950s. After the Berlin Wall cut it off from West Berlin, the gate became a symbol of German reunification.

ASSESS & RETEACH

Reading Social Studies Have students complete the graphic organizer on page 122.

 Formal Assessment
- Section Quiz, p. 67

RETEACHING ACTIVITY

Have students work in groups to create five-question quizzes on the section. When they have finished, have groups exchange quizzes and answer the questions.

 In-depth Resources: Unit 2
- Reteaching Activity, p. 36

 Access for Students Acquiring English
- Reteaching Activity, p. 40

Section ③ Assessment

1. Terms & Names

  a. Iron Curtain, p. 136
  b. puppet government, p. 137
  c. one-party system, p. 137
  d. Joseph Stalin, p. 138
  e. collective farm, p. 139
  f. Warsaw Pact, p. 141
  g. Cold War, p. 141

2. Taking Notes

Five-Year Plans	Agriculture	Secret Police
Government-set economic goals	Controlled by government	Eliminated citizens Stalin didn't trust
Where to build factories	Peasants live on collective farms	Arrested those who did not support the government
What types of factories to build	Crops distributed by government	
How many goods to produce	Workers lack food	Sent suspects to labor camps
How to distribute goods		

3. Main Ideas

  a. invaded by Germany; widespread, severe destruction and millions of civilians killed

  b. Western Europe, mainly constitutional monarchies or democracies; Eastern Europe, Communist dictatorships

  c. used terror and repression to control people; controlled industry and agriculture to develop the economy

4. Critical Thinking

Soviets wanted a line of "buffer states" between themselves and Western Europe, to protect themselves against invasion.

ACTIVITY OPTION

 Integrated Assessment
- Rubric for writing a scene

Teacher's Edition **141**

TERMS & NAMES

1. nationalism, p. 123
2. colonialism, p. 125
3. World War I, p. 127
4. alliance, p. 128
5. World War II, p. 130
6. NATO, p. 131
7. Adolf Hitler, p. 130
8. Warsaw Pact, p. 141
9. Iron Curtain, p. 136
10. Cold War, p. 141

REVIEW QUESTIONS

Possible Reponses

1. The largest empire was Austria-Hungary.
2. Expanded armies protected their countries' borders and colonies.
3. Alliances provided help against outside attack.
4. It required Germany to pay for damages and give up valuable territory.
5. Poland
6. The Soviet Union installed puppet Communist governments that allowed only one, Communist Party candidate in elections.
7. It prevented travel and communication between Western and Eastern Europe.
8. Both had nuclear weapons that could have caused worldwide destruction.

CHAPTER 5
ASSESSMENT

TERMS & NAMES

Explain the significance of each of the following:

1. nationalism
2. colonialism
3. World War I
4. alliance
5. World War II
6. NATO
7. Adolf Hitler
8. Warsaw Pact
9. Iron Curtain
10. Cold War

REVIEW QUESTIONS

European Empires *(pages 123–126)*

1. What was the largest empire in Eastern Europe in 1900?
2. What is one reason why European nations built up their military?

Europe at War *(pages 127–132)*

3. Why did European countries join alliances?
4. What did the Treaty of Versailles require Germany to do?
5. What country did Germany invade to begin World War II?

The Soviet Union *(pages 136–141)*

6. Why did most Eastern European voters have only one political party to choose from?
7. How did the Iron Curtain affect the lives of Eastern Europeans?
8. Why were both sides in the Cold War hesitant to start a war?

CRITICAL THINKING

Identifying Problems

1. Using your completed chart from Reading Social Studies, p. 122, list some of the causes and effects of World Wars I and II.

Making Inferences

2. Why might a citizen who has helped elect a government be more willing to fight to defend it?

Hypothesizing

3. How do you think Soviet peasants felt about collective farms? Why?

Visual Summary

European Empires *1*

- In early-20th-century Europe, feelings of nationalism arose.
- Western European nations ruled colonial empires.

Europe at War *2*

- Due to a complex set of alliances, most of Europe was drawn into World War I.
- The Treaty of Versailles set the stage for an even more widespread conflict—World War II.

The Soviet Union *3*

- After World War II, the Soviet Union was very powerful.
- However, life was difficult for many Soviet citizens.

CRITICAL THINKING: Possible Responses

1. Identifying Problems

Causes of World War I: increasing nationalism; protests against power of Austria-Hungary; assassination of archduke of Austria; alliances bring in Russia and Germany, then other nations

Effects of World War I: destruction left many homeless; breakup of Austria-Hungary; independence for many ethnic groups

Causes of World War II: weakness of German economy; dictatorship of Adolf Hitler; German invasion of Poland

Effects of World War II: millions dead; occupation of Western Europe by Allies; occupation of Eastern Europe by Soviet Union

2. Making Inferences

A citizen might want to defend a government he or she voted for.

3. Hypothesizing

Farmers resented losing their own lands and animals, having to move to collectives, feeding people in cities while not having enough food for themselves.

SOCIAL STUDIES SKILLBUILDER

A Toast to Next Thanksgiving:
"Here's hoping we're not the bird!"

Dr. Seuss ©'41

SKILLBUILDER: Reading a Political Cartoon

1. Who is the subject of this cartoon?
2. What do you think the cartoonist, Dr. Seuss, was worried about?

FOCUS ON GEOGRAPHY

1. **Place** • Which areas of Europe are most densely populated?
2. **Place** • Which areas of Europe are least densely populated?
3. **Place** • Why do you think some areas are much more populated than others?

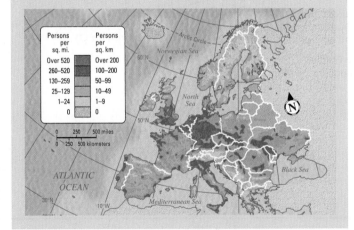

Persons per sq. mi.	Persons per sq. km
Over 520	Over 200
260–520	100–200
130–259	50–99
25–129	10–49
1–24	1–9
0	0

CHAPTER PROJECTS

Interdisciplinary Activity: Language Arts

Presenting an Oral Report
Research one of the European colonies in Asia or Africa. What was life like around 1900? Present your findings to the class in an oral report. Be sure to show the location of the colony on a map.

Cooperative Learning Activity

Designing a Monument In a group of three or four students, design a monument to commemorate an event in 20th-century Europe, such as a particular battle from World War I, the Holocaust, or World War II.

- Present background information about the event to the class.
- Display a drawing or a model of the monument.
- Show your suggested location for the memorial on a map.

INTERNET ACTIVITY

Use the Internet to research a European country that was not directly involved in World War I or World War II. Examples include Spain and Switzerland. What can you find out about that country's government and economy? What was life like there during the first half of the 20th century? How was the country affected by the wars?

Presenting Your Findings Write your findings in a report and include illustrations. List the Web sites that you used to prepare your report.

For Internet links to support this activity, go to

RESEARCH LINKS
CLASSZONE.COM

CHAPTER PROJECTS

Interdisciplinary Activity: Language Arts

Presenting an Oral Report Prepare a list of European countries and their colonies in Asia or Africa for students to choose from. Suggest that students use both print and on-line reference sources for their research. Have students take notes on life in their chosen colony during the 1900s, and then organize their notes into a brief oral presentation.

Cooperative Learning Activity

Designing a Monument Display photographs of a variety of monuments for students to observe, such as the Vietnam Veterans' Memorial in Washington, D.C. Discuss other monuments students have seen in your community or elsewhere. Groups should choose an event to commemorate, agree on a location for their monument, and then create a design. Encourage students to divide the responsibilities of researching, recording, designing, and presenting.

INTERNET ACTIVITY

Discuss how students might find information about a European country that was not directly involved in the world wars. Have them make lists of what they might want to find out about the countries in addition to the items suggested on page 143. Emphasize that as students do their research, they need to keep a log listing the information they get from each Web site.

Skills Answers

Social Studies Skillbuilder
Possible Answers
1. Hitler and Uncle Sam
2. that Hitler will "gobble up" the United States as he has much of Europe

Focus on Geography
Possible Answers
1. Central Germany, Netherlands, Belgium, coastal areas of France and Spain, Central and Southern England
2. mountainous regions and the Arctic
3. They have better land, more resources, water supplies, and other human needs.

Modern Europe

	OVERVIEW	COPYMASTERS	INTEGRATED TECHNOLOGY
UNIT ATLAS AND CHAPTER RESOURCES	Students will examine recent changes in modern Europe, including political, economic, and cultural aspects of life in Eastern Europe before and after the breakup of the Soviet Union. They will also look at the European Union and its activities.	**In-depth Resources: Unit 2** • Guided Reading Worksheets, pp. 37–39 • Skillbuilder Practice, p. 42 • Unit Atlas Activities, pp. 1–2 • Geography Workshop, pp. 61–62 **Reading Study Guide** (Spanish and English), pp. 44–51 **Outline Map Activities**	Power Presentations Electronic Teacher Tools Online Lesson Planner Chapter Summaries on CD Critical Thinking Transparencies CT11

	KEY IDEAS		
SECTION 1 Eastern Europe Under Communism pp. 147–152	• The Soviet Union attempted to create a national identity by controlling cultural and artistic expression. • The Soviets controlled factories, railroads, businesses, and other aspects of the economy. • Some Eastern European nations tried to change their Soviet-dominated governments and economies.	**In-depth Resources: Unit 2** • Guided Reading Worksheet, p. 37 • Reteaching Activity, p. 44 **Reading Study Guide** (Spanish and English), pp. 44–45	classzone.com Chapter Summaries on CD
SECTION 2 Eastern Europe and Russia pp. 154–160	• After the collapse of the Soviet Union in 1991, many Eastern European nations declared their independence. • Conflicts among ethnic groups led to war in the Balkan states. • Modern Russia enjoys many freedoms, but the free-market economy also poses difficulties.	**In-depth Resources: Unit 2** • Guided Reading Worksheet, p. 38 • Reteaching Activity, p. 45 **Reading Study Guide** (Spanish and English), pp. 46–47	classzone.com Chapter Summaries on CD
SECTION 3 The European Union pp. 161–165	• Many countries want to join the European Union to gain economic and political aid. However, they must first commit to certain improvements. • The European Union works to improve trade among member nations. • The European Union provides job training and protects citizens' rights in its culturally diverse member nations.	**In-depth Resources: Unit 2** • Guided Reading Worksheet, p. 39 • Reteaching Activity, p. 46 **Reading Study Guide** (Spanish and English), pp. 48–49	Critical Thinking Transparencies CT12 classzone.com Chapter Summaries on CD

Audio

 Internet

TE Teacher's Edition

CD-ROM

Overhead Transparency

Video

Copymaster

PE Pupil's Edition

ASSESSMENT OPTIONS

PE **Chapter Assessment**, pp. 168–169

Formal Assessment
- Chapter Tests: Forms A, B, C, pp. 83–94

Test Generator

Online Test Practice

Strategies for Test Preparation

PE **Section Assessment**, p. 152

Formal Assessment
- Section Quiz, p. 80

Integrated Assessment
- Rubric for writing a speech

Test Generator

Test Practice Transparencies TT16

PE **Section Assessment**, p. 160

Formal Assessment
- Section Quiz, p. 81

Integrated Assessment
- Rubric for writing a personal essay

Test Generator

Test Practice Transparencies TT17

PE **Section Assessment**, p. 165

Formal Assessment
- Section Quiz, p. 82

Integrated Assessment
- Rubric for writing a postcard or e-mail

Test Generator

Test Practice Transparencies TT18

RESOURCES FOR DIFFERENTIATING INSTRUCTION

Students Acquiring English/ESL

Reading Study Guide
(Spanish and English), pp. 44–51

Access for Students Acquiring English
Spanish Translations, pp. 41–48

TE **TE Activity**
- Borrowed Words, p. 155

Less Proficient Readers

Reading Study Guide
(Spanish and English), pp. 44–51

TE **TE Activities**
- Identifying Main Ideas and Details, p. 148
- Identifying Sequence, p. 157
- Setting a Purpose, p. 162

Gifted and Talented Students

TE **TE Activities**
- Comparing and Contrasting, p. 149
- Creating Crossword Puzzles, p. 158

CROSS-CURRICULAR CONNECTIONS

Humanities
Adler, Naomi. *Play Me a Story: Nine Tales About Musical Instruments.* Brookfield, CT: Millbrook Press, 1998. Folk tales linked to native instruments, including the Russian balalaika.

Literature
Riordan, James. *Russian Folk-Tales.* New York: Oxford University Press, 2000. Ten traditional folk tales.

Popular Culture
Carona, Laurel. *Life in Moscow.* San Diego: Lucent, 2001. Focuses on life after the fall of communism.
Toht, Patricia. *Daily Life in Ancient and Modern Moscow.* Minneapolis: Runestone Press, 2001. Nice overview of a tumultuous city history.

History
Burgan, Michael. *Cold War: The Collapse.* Austin, TX: Raintree Steck-Vaughn, 2001. Based on CNN's Cold War series, chronicles the final years of communism.

Economics
Thompson, Clifford, ed. *Russia & Eastern Europe.* New York: H. W. Wilson Co., 1998. Articles about post–Cold War economic conditions.

Science
Dommermuth-Costa, Carol. *Nikola Tesla: A Spark of Genius.* Minneapolis: Lerner Publications, 1994. Serbian-born scientist who pioneered work with alternating-current electricity.

ENRICHMENT ACTIVITIES

The following activities are especially suitable for classes following block schedules.

Teacher's Edition, pp. 150, 151, 153, 156, 158
Pupil's Edition, pp. 152, 160, 165

Unit Atlas, pp. 52–63
Literature Connections, pp. 166–167

Outline Map Activities

INTEGRATED TECHNOLOGY

Go to **classzone.com** for lesson support and activities for Chapter 6.

BLOCK SCHEDULE LESSON PLAN OPTIONS: 90-MINUTE PERIOD

DAY 1

CHAPTER PREVIEW, pp. 144–145
Class Time 30 minutes

- **Hypothesize** Use the "What do you think?" questions in Focus on Geography on PE p. 145 to help students hypothesize about the relationship between a country's economy and its natural resources.

SECTION 1, pp. 147–152
Class Time 60 minutes

- **Small Groups** On the chalkboard, list the section objectives from TE p. 147. Divide the class into three groups. Have each group select one objective and prepare a summary of the section based on it. Remind students that when they summarize, they should include the main ideas and the most important details in their own words. Reconvene as a whole class and have each group share its summary.
Class Time 35 minutes

- **Comparing** Use the Critical Thinking Activity on TE p. 148 to guide a discussion about the techniques used by the Soviet Union and the United States to create a national identity among their citizenry.
Class Time 15 minutes

- **Word Web** Have students work in pairs to organize important information about the Soviet economy using a word web.
Class Time 10 minutes

DAY 2

SECTION 2, pp. 154–160
Class Time 65 minutes

- **Internet** Extend students' background knowledge of the economies of Eastern Europe by visiting **classzone.com.**
Class Time 25 minutes

- **Venn Diagram** Divide the class into pairs. Use the Critical Thinking Activity on TE p. 158 to have groups create a Venn diagram comparing Soviet life before and after the breakup of the Soviet Union.
Class Time 25 minutes

- **Geography Skillbuilder** Use the questions in the Geography Skillbuilder on PE p. 159 to guide a discussion about Russia's natural resources.
Class Time 15 minutes

SECTION 3, pp. 161–165
Class Time 25 minutes

- **Analyzing Motives** Have students read Dateline on PE p. 161. Use the questions in Focus & Motivate on TE p. 161 to help students analyze the motives behind the creation of the European Union.
Class Time 10 minutes

- **Word Problems** Use the Activity Option on TE p. 163 to teach students about the relative value of the euro compared to the U.S. dollar. After you have created two or three word problems with the class, divide students into small groups. Have the groups create three work problems, and have the class solve them.
Class Time 15 minute

DAY 3

SECTION 3, continued
Class Time 35 minutes

- **Locating Places on a Map** Use the Activity Options on TE p. 164 to have students locate countries and cities in Western Europe.
Class Time 20 minutes

- **Summary** Have students write a short summary of the section using the Terms & Names on PE p. 165.
Class Time 15 minutes

CHAPTER 6 REVIEW AND ASSESSMENT, pp. 168–169
Class Time 55 minutes

- **Chapter Review** Divide students into pairs. Using the Visual Summary on PE p. 168, have students provide two supporting details for each statement.
Class Time 20 minutes

- **Assessment** Have students complete the Chapter 6 Assessment.
Class Time 35 minutes

TECHNOLOGY IN THE CLASSROOM

INTERNET RESEARCH

The Web is a valuable research tool, providing valuable, up-to-date information, including text and pictures. However, some sites should be screened before students do research on the Web, as many sites are not up to date or have erroneous or inappropriate information. Students should be given a list of sites sponsored by organizations that are generally considered reliable, such as major news sources, television networks, nonprofit organizations, or museums. This procedure will save class time and steer students in the right direction.

ACTIVITY OUTLINE

Objective Students will go to Web sites to find out about the Berlin Wall. Then they will use a word processing program to write several paragraphs about the significance of the wall.

Task Have students go to the Web sites and take notes on the Berlin Wall and its significance. Ask them to write paragraphs explaining the significance of the dismantling of the wall in the 1980s.

Class Time Two class periods

DIRECTIONS

1. As a class, discuss what students know about the Berlin Wall. Encourage volunteers to identify the location of Berlin and share what they know about why the wall was constructed.

2. Tell students that the Berlin Wall was torn down in 1989. This event is considered to be one of the most significant happenings of the 1980s. Ask them to find out more about the events surrounding the building and dismantling of the wall by going to the Web sites at **classzone.com.** Help students focus their research by suggesting that they create an outline with the following headings:

   • Why the wall was built

   • What the wall represented

   • What life was like in the East

   • What life was like in the West

   • Why the wall was taken down

   They should then take notes by adding important facts and details under each heading.

3. Have students use the information in their outlines to write one- or two-paragraph reports. Provide an opportunity for students to share what they have learned.

CHAPTER 6 OBJECTIVE

Students will examine recent changes in Europe, including political, economic, and cultural aspects of life in Eastern Europe before and after the breakup of the Soviet Union. They will also look at the European Union.

FOCUS ON VISUALS

Interpreting the Photograph Direct students' attention to the photograph of the locomotive and have them describe it. Have they seen trains like this before? If so, where? Discuss how it may be different from other trains they have seen. What conclusions might students draw about Europe based on this photograph?

Possible Responses Students' descriptions should indicate that the locomotive looks very modern. They may conclude that because the train is modern, the economies and technology of Eastern Europe are probably advanced as well.

Extension Ask students to research modern bullet trains. Challenge them to find out how fast bullet trains travel, where they are found, and why they are not more common.

CRITICAL THINKING ACTIVITY

Comparing Ask students to compare this passenger train with the trains they see where they live. Explain that people travel by train more frequently in Europe than in the United States. Ask students why this might be the case.

Class Time 5 minutes

Modern Europe

SECTION 1 Eastern Europe Under Communism

SECTION 2 Eastern Europe and Russia

SECTION 3 The European Union

Movement High-speed trains, like this one in France, make travel in Europe very convenient.

144

Recommended Resources

BOOKS FOR THE TEACHER

Kort, G. Michael. *The Handbook of the New Eastern Europe.* Brookfield, CT: Twenty-First Century Books, 2001.

Pinder, John. *The European Union: A Very Short Introduction.* New York: Oxford University Press, 2001. Compact and useful introduction.

Winters, Paul A., ed. *The Collapse of the Soviet Union.* San Diego: Greenhaven Press, 1999. Essays, articles, and interviews.

VIDEOS

People Power: The End of Soviet-Style Communism. Cambridge, MA: WGBH Public Television, 1999. Extensive coverage of Gorbachev and Yeltsin.

INTERNET

For more information about Eastern Europe and the European Union, visit **classzone.com.**

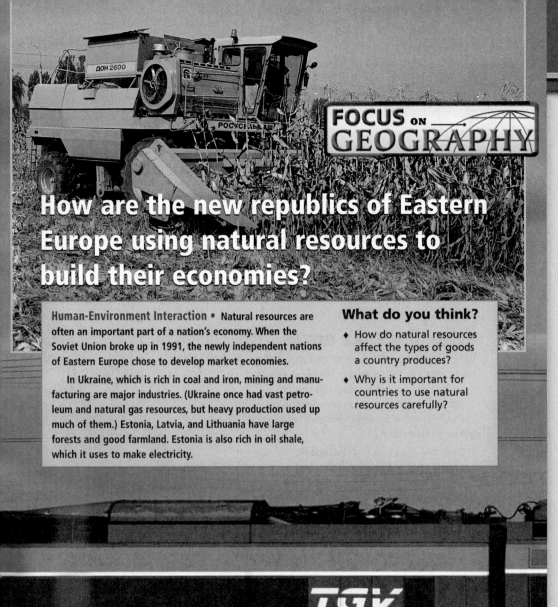

FOCUS ON GEOGRAPHY

How are the new republics of Eastern Europe using natural resources to build their economies?

Human-Environment Interaction • Natural resources are often an important part of a nation's economy. When the Soviet Union broke up in 1991, the newly independent nations of Eastern Europe chose to develop market economies.

In Ukraine, which is rich in coal and iron, mining and manufacturing are major industries. (Ukraine once had vast petroleum and natural gas resources, but heavy production used up much of them.) Estonia, Latvia, and Lithuania have large forests and good farmland. Estonia is also rich in oil shale, which it uses to make electricity.

What do you think?

- How do natural resources affect the types of goods a country produces?
- Why is it important for countries to use natural resources carefully?

145

FOCUS ON GEOGRAPHY

Objectives

- To identify the relationship between natural resources and economic development
- To recognize the importance of the wise use of natural resources

What Do You Think?

1. Remind students that natural resources are anything that occurs naturally in the environment, such as iron, coal, and trees. Ask students to discuss how different types of natural resources would affect the kinds of goods a nation produces.
2. Challenge students to discuss how depleting a natural resource would affect an economy based on that resource.

How are the new republics of Eastern Europe using natural resources to build their economies?

Have students consider how the people of Eastern Europe turned to the natural resources in their countries to develop individual economies. Do they think the availability of natural resources was taken into account when the Soviet Union divided into independent nations?

MAKING GEOGRAPHIC CONNECTIONS

Have students list natural resources that exist in their area. Then discuss how local industries and businesses use these resources. Invite them to speculate on how the local economy might be different if other natural resources were available.

Implementing the National Geography Standards

Standard 16 Develop and implement a personal plan to conserve water and recycle materials

Objective To create an environmental diary

Class Time 15 minutes

Task Have each student create an environmental diary by listing activities he or she can do to conserve water and recycle materials. Ask students to record the activities they were able to complete for at least a week. At the end of the week, have them speculate about how and why the list of activities might change within the next ten years.

Evaluation Students should list at least ten different activities. Students should complete at least five of the activities.

BEFORE YOU READ

What Do You Know?

Have students look at the Unit Atlas map and name the countries of Eastern Europe. Then ask them to recall information they have heard about any of these countries in the news or in a sports context. Ask students whether anyone in their family—themselves, family members, or ancestors—came from one of the countries in Eastern Europe or the former Soviet Union. Encourage them to share family stories about the culture, daily life, or history of the region.

What Do You Want to Know?

Suggest that students scan the chapter, looking at photographs and maps and reading heads and captions. As they preview the material, have them write questions in their notebooks that they would like answered.

READ AND TAKE NOTES

Reading Strategy: Comparing Explain to students that in this chapter they will be reading about various countries before and after a major change in their histories—the breakup of the Soviet Union. Tell students that their completed charts will provide a good tool for comparing the ways in which this event changed different aspects of life.

 In-depth Resources: Unit 2
• Guided Reading Worksheets, pp. 37–39

BEFORE YOU READ

▶▶ *What Do You Know?*

Before you read the chapter, think about what you already know about Europe. Do you have family, friends, or neighbors who were born in Europe? Have you read books, such as the Harry Potter series, that take place in Europe? Think about what you have seen or heard about Italy, England, France, or Germany in the news, during sporting events, and in your other classes.

▶▶ *What Do You Want to Know?*

Decide what you know about Europe today. Then, in your notebook, record what you hope to learn from this chapter.

Region • Euros are the most visible symbol of economic unity in Europe. ▲

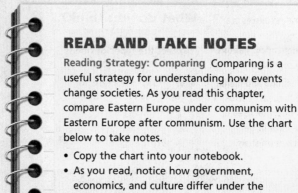

READ AND TAKE NOTES

Reading Strategy: Comparing Comparing is a useful strategy for understanding how events change societies. As you read this chapter, compare Eastern Europe under communism with Eastern Europe after communism. Use the chart below to take notes.

• Copy the chart into your notebook.
• As you read, notice how government, economics, and culture differ under the old and new systems.
• After you read each section, record key ideas on your chart.

Place • Some Christians in Ukraine dye Easter eggs brilliant colors. ▲

Aspect	Under Communism	After Communism
Government	government distributed propaganda, controlled economy, restricted cultural activities	greater freedom for citizens, democracy in many Eastern European countries
Economy	controlled by government, widespread poverty, private property seized	change to free-market economies in Eastern Europe, inflation, unemployment
Culture	many cultural celebrations outlawed, art censored, sports and space programs well funded	writers given greater freedom, freedom of religion, increased cultural freedom

146 CHAPTER 6

Teaching Strategy

Reading the Chapter This is a thematic chapter that examines the political, social, and economic events that have occurred in Eastern Europe since the 1950s. It then analyzes changes that have occurred following the breakup of the Soviet Union. Encourage students to pay particular attention to the effects of Soviet dominance on the countries of Eastern Europe and to the impact of those countries' sudden independence.

Integrated Assessment The Chapter Assessment on page 169 describes several activities for integrated assessment. You may wish to have students work on these activities during the course of the chapter and then present them at the end.

Eastern Europe Under Communism

TERMS & NAMES
propaganda
private property rights
Nikita Khrushchev
deposed
détente

MAIN IDEA
The Communist government of the Soviet Union controlled the lives of its citizens.

WHY IT MATTERS NOW
Today, many republics of the former Soviet Union have become independent nations.

DATELINE
EXTRA

THE KREMLIN, MOSCOW, APRIL 12, 1961

A 27-year-old Soviet pilot has become the first person to travel into space. Soviet officials proudly announced today that cosmonaut Yuri Gagarin had orbited Earth in 1 hour and 29 minutes.

His 4.75-ton spacecraft, *Vostok I*, flew at a maximum altitude of 187 miles above the planet. Its top speed was 18,000 miles per hour.

Gagarin graduated from the Soviet Air Force cadet school just four years ago. He is the son of a carpenter and began to study flying while in college. Gagarin's space flight puts the Soviet Union a giant step ahead of the United States in the space race.

Movement • Yuri Gagarin becomes the first human in space. ▶

Soviet Culture ❶

The Soviet space program of the 1950s and 1960s brought international attention to that country. Daily life for citizens of the Soviet Union and of the Eastern European countries under its control, however, was difficult. Most people were poor and had little, if any, say in their government.

Modern Europe **147**

SECTION OBJECTIVES

1. To describe the degree of control the Soviet Union had over its citizens
2. To describe the Soviet economy
3. To explain attempts to change Soviet-dominated governments and economies

SKILLBUILDER
• Interpreting a Map, p. 149

CRITICAL THINKING
• Comparing, p. 148
• Drawing Conclusions, p. 151

FOCUS & MOTIVATE
WARM-UP

Analyzing Motives Have students read <u>Dateline</u> and answer these questions.

1. Why did the United States and the Soviet Union compete to put people into space?
2. What might the Soviet Union have achieved by putting the first person into space?

INSTRUCT: Objective ❶

Soviet Culture

• Why did the Soviet government want to create a sense of national identity? to discourage ethnic groups from seeking independence
• What actions did the Soviet government take to try to establish a national identity? outlawed cultural celebrations, destroyed churches, prohibited use of native languages, controlled media and artistic expression

 In-depth Resources: Unit 2
• Guided Reading Worksheet, p. 37

 Reading Study Guide
(Spanish and English), pp. 44–45

Program Resources

 In-depth Resources: Unit 2
• Guided Reading Worksheet, p. 37
• Reteaching Activity, p. 44

 Reading Study Guide
(Spanish and English), pp. 44–45

 Formal Assessment
• Section Quiz, p. 80

Integrated Assessment
• Rubric for writing a speech

Outline Map Activities

 Access for Students Acquiring English
• Guided Reading Worksheet, p. 41

 Technology Resources
classzone.com

TEST-TAKING RESOURCES
 Strategies for Test Preparation
 Test Practice Transparencies
Online Test Practice

Strange but TRUE

Laika, a female dog, was part Siberian husky. She weighed about 13 pounds. The area that Laika traveled in was padded, and she had enough space to lie down and stand. She wore a harness and life support system. Before being recruited for the space program, Laika was a stray living on the streets of Moscow. American newspapers dubbed her "Muttnik."

Belka and Strelka were not alone on their journey into space. With them went 40 mice and 2 rats. Belka and Strelka returned to Earth after one day in orbit. Later, Strelka had six puppies, one of which was given to President John F. Kennedy.

CRITICAL THINKING ACTIVITY

Comparing Ask students to reread the two paragraphs under "Creating a National Identity." Discuss the ways the Soviet government went about creating a national identity. Then prompt a discussion about whether the government of the United States tries to do the same. Have students compare and contrast the ways each government tries or has tried to achieve this goal.

Class Time 15 minutes

Strange but TRUE

Space Dogs Four years before Yuri Gagarin blasted into space, a Russian dog orbited the planet. Her name was Laika (LIE•kuh), which means "Barker." Laika, pictured below, was launched into space on *Sputnik 2* in November 1957. The Soviets did not then have the ability to bring a spacecraft down safely, and Laika lived in space for only a few days.

In August 1960, however, the Russians sent two other dogs into space. Named Belka and Strelka, they were the first living creatures to go into space and return safely to Earth.

Creating a National Identity The Soviet government was fearful that some ethnic groups might want to break away from the Soviet Union. To keep this from happening, Soviet leaders tried to create a strong national identity. They wanted people in the republic of Latvia, for example, to think of themselves as Soviets, not as Latvians.

To help achieve its goals, the Soviet government created and distributed **propaganda** (proh•puh•GAN•duh), or material designed to spread certain beliefs. Soviet propaganda included pamphlets, posters, artwork, statues, songs, and films. It praised the Soviet Union, its leaders, and communism.

Soviet Control of Daily Life To prevent different ethnic groups from identifying with their individual cultures rather than with the Soviet Union, the Soviet government outlawed many cultural celebrations. It destroyed churches and other religious buildings and killed thousands of religious leaders. The members of many ethnic groups were not allowed to speak their native languages or celebrate certain holidays.

The Soviet government also controlled communications media, such as newspapers, books, and radio. This meant that most Soviet citizens could not learn much about other nations around the world.

Literature and the Arts The works of many writers, poets, and other artists who lived during the Soviet era often were banned or censored. Soviet artists were forced to join government-run unions. These unions told artists what kinds of works they could create. Artists who disobeyed were punished. Some were imprisoned or even killed.

Region • This statue, a form of propaganda, displays the Soviet belief in the unity of the worker (hammer) and the farmer (sickle). ▼

Activity Options

Differentiating Instruction: Less Proficient Readers

Identifying Main Ideas and Details Point out the headings "Creating a National Identity" and "Soviet Control of Daily Life." Explain to students that headings such as these identify main ideas. The paragraphs that follow provide details about the main ideas. On the chalkboard, draw a cluster diagram like the one shown here and guide students in completing it for "Soviet Control of Daily Life." Then have them work with a partner to develop a diagram for "Literature and the Arts."

Ethnic and Cultural Groups of the Soviet Union, c. 1950

ARCTIC OCEAN

RUSSIA
ESTONIA
LITHUANIA
LATVIA
BYELORUSSIA
MOLDAVIA
UKRAINE
RUSSIA
GEORGIA
ARMENIA
AZERBAIJAN
KAZAKHSTAN
UZBEKISTAN
TURKMENIA
KIRGHIZIA
TAJIKISTAN

Bering Sea

0   250   500 miles
0 250 500 kilometers

■ Caucasian peoples
■ Indo-European peoples
■ Uralic and Altaic peoples
■ Sparsely populated

GEOGRAPHY SKILLBUILDER: Interpreting a Map

1. **Place** • Where in the Soviet Union do most Uralic and Altaic people live?
2. **Region** • What is the most common ethnicity of the Soviet Union?

Geography Skillbuilder Answers

1. in the southeast, especially in Kazakhstan, Kirghizia, and Tadjikistan

2. Indo-European

Sports The leaders of the Soviet Union wanted their country to be seen as equal to, if not better than, other powerful nations. One way to achieve this goal was to become a strong competitor in the Olympics and in other international sports competitions.

The Soviet government supported its top athletes and provided for all their basic needs. It even hired and paid for the coaches and paid for all training. The hockey teams and gymnasts of the Soviet Union were among the best in the world.

The Soviet Economy ❷

In addition to controlling the governments of the Soviet Union and of those Eastern European countries under its influence, Soviet leaders also ran the economy. When the Soviets installed Communist governments in Eastern Europe after World War II, they promised to improve industry and to bring new wealth to be shared among all citizens. This did not happen.

Government Control Communism in the Soviet Union did not support **private property rights,** or the right of individuals to own land or an industry. The Soviets wanted all major industries to be owned by the government rather than by private citizens. So the government took over factories, railroads, and businesses.

Region • Romanian gymnasts, like Nadia Comaneci, won medals at the Olympics. ▼

Modern Europe **149**

INSTRUCT: Objective ❷

The Soviet Economy

• What major industries did the Soviet government take over? factories, railroads, businesses
• What was the Soviet government's role in production? decided what would be produced, how it would be produced, and who would get what was produced

FOCUS ON VISUALS

Interpreting the Map Have students read the title of the map and note that its time frame is about 1950. To avoid any confusion about the term "Caucasian," explain that in the context of ethnic groups, it refers only to certain peoples of the region called the Caucasus, between the Black and Caspian seas. Also ask students to notice the relationship between the ethnic term "Uralic" and the Ural Mountains, the traditional boundary between Europe and Asia, where some of these peoples still live. Have students point out the different ethnic groups that occupy the Caucasus. What might be the consequences of this mix?

Possible Responses Caucasian, Indo-European, Uralic, and Altaic. Many groups in a small area might result in ethnic conflicts.

Extension Suggest that interested students choose one of the regions shown on the map and learn more about its people, languages, geography, and history. They can prepare a short oral report for the class.

Activity Options

Differentiating Instruction: Gifted and Talented

Comparing and Contrasting Have students work in groups to find out how many medals the Soviet Union won in the winter and summer Olympic Games held from 1952 to 1992. Help them think of keywords to find this information on the Internet; results are also available in print sources. Explain that in the first years after the breakup of the Soviet Union, athletes from the former Soviet republics competed together as the Unified Team. (Later, each new nation sent its own athletes.)

Then have each group create a chart that compares the final medal standings of the United States and the Soviet Union for each of the Olympic years in which both countries competed. (There were boycotts in 1980 and 1984.) Have groups share their charts with the class.

INSTRUCT: Objective ❸

Attempts at Change

- **What characterized the era known as "The Thaw"?** Citizens had greater freedom; Khrushchev visited the United States.

- **What was the "Prague Spring"?** a period of improvement when the Soviet government loosened control over Czechoslovakia

- **After détente, what did the Soviet Union continue to spend most of its money on?** armed forces and nuclear weapons

Spotlight on CULTURE

Aleksandr Solzhenitsyn wrote several books about his experiences in the labor camps. The first was *One Day in the Life of Ivan Denisovich*, published in the Soviet Union in 1962. Nikita Khrushchev, who was promoting anti-Stalinist feelings, intervened personally to allow the book to be published. When Khrushchev was removed from office, Solzhenitsyn's writings were once again banned. *The Gulag Archipelago* was published in the West in 1973. It describes the cruel repression of the Soviet labor camps. Despite his treatment at home, Solzhenitsyn received recognition in other parts of the world. In 1970, he was awarded the Nobel Prize in Literature. However, he declined it because of threats that he would not be able to return to the Soviet Union if he went to Sweden to accept it.

Thinking Critically Answers

1. The government wanted citizens to think that things were wonderful in their country and that everyone was happy with the system.

2. Possible response: The U.S. government does not censor literature, but some local governments and libraries do.

The Soviet government decided what would be produced, how it would be produced, and who would get what was produced. These choices were made based on Soviet interests, not on the interests of the republics or of individuals. Communist countries of Eastern Europe were often unable to meet the needs—including bread, meat, and clothing—of their citizens.

Attempts at Change ❸

Starting in the 1950s, Eastern Europeans began to demand more goods of better quality. They also wanted changes in the government. In 1956, Hungary and Poland tried to free their governments and economies from Soviet control. But the Communist army put an end to these attempts at change.

Khrushchev From 1958 until 1964, **Nikita Khrushchev** (KROOSH•chev) ruled the Soviet Union. During this period, called "The Thaw," writers and other citizens began to have greater freedoms. Khrushchev even visited the United States in 1959, but the thaw in the Cold War did not last. In 1964, with the Soviet economy growing weaker, Khrushchev was **deposed,** or removed from power.

Spotlight on CULTURE

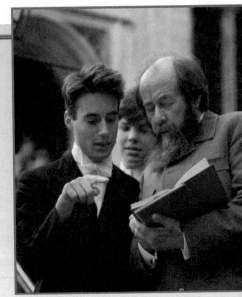

Solzhenitsyn In 1945, army officer Aleksandr Solzhenitsyn (sohl•zhuh•NEET•sin), far right, called the Soviet leader Joseph Stalin "the boss." For this, he was sentenced to eight years in slave-labor camps. Later, Solzhenitsyn wrote books about his experiences in those camps. He also wrote a letter against censorship. The government called him a traitor, and in 1969 it forced Solzhenitsyn to leave the writers' union. Five years later, Solzhenitsyn left the country.

Although Solzhenitsyn's works were banned, many Soviet citizens read them in secret. Copies of his and other banned books were passed from person to person across the nation. Through such writings, Soviet citizens learned many things that the government had tried to hide from them.

THINKING CRITICALLY

1. **Analyzing Motives** Why would the Soviet government stop people from reading Solzhenitsyn's books?

2. **Comparing** Compare the censorship of literature in the Soviet Union with censorship in the United States.

150 CHAPTER 6

Reading Social Studies

A. Clarifying Who benefited most from Soviet industry?

Reading Social Studies

A. Answer

The Soviet government, not its citizens, benefited.

Activity Options

Skillbuilder Mini-Lesson: Reading a Political Cartoon   ⬛ Block Scheduling

Explaining the Skill Remind students that political cartoons are created to express an opinion about a serious subject. They often use humor as well as symbols to make their point. They may have a title or caption.

Applying the Skill Challenge students to create political cartoons that express an opinion about the Soviet economy as seen through the eyes of Eastern Europeans during the 1950s and 1960s. Then have students use the following strategies as they share their cartoons in small groups.

1. Read the title and caption. Look at the cartoon as a whole.

2. Try to identify people in the cartoon. Look at how features or characteristics of the people may have been exaggerated. Look for details and symbols.

3. Summarize the cartoonist's message and point of view.

Reading
Social Studies

B. Recognizing Important Details How did the Soviet Union maintain control over other Eastern European nations?

Reading Social Studies
B. Answer

They used military force and economic pressure.

The Prague Spring In January 1968 in Czechoslovakia, Alexander Dubček (DOOB·chek) became the First Secretary of the Czechoslovak Communist Party. His attempts to lessen the Soviet Union's control over Czechoslovakia led to a period of improvement called the "Prague Spring." Czech citizens enjoyed greater freedoms, including more contact with Western Europe. In August of that year, however, the Soviet Union sent troops to force a return to strict Communist control. Dubček was later replaced, and Soviet controls were back in place.

Détente The member nations of NATO, which were concerned about starting an all-out war with the Soviet Union, were unable to stop the Soviet control of Eastern Europe. In the 1970s, however, leaders of the Soviet Union and the United States began to have more contact with each other. This led to a period of **détente** (day·TAHNT), or lessening tension, between the members of NATO and the Warsaw Pact nations.

Place • Nikita Khrushchev, the son of a miner and grandson of a peasant, lessened government control of Soviet citizens. ▲

Region • Citizens of Czechoslovakia protested Soviet control in 1968. ◄

151

MORE ABOUT...
Nikita Khrushchev

Joseph Stalin's death on March 5, 1953, left a void in the Communist leadership of the Soviet Union. At first, a group of leaders shared power. Gradually, Nikita Khrushchev (1894–1971) gained influence. In 1956, he delivered an address to the 20th Party Congress attacking Stalin and his policies. The "destalinization" of the Soviet Union had already begun, but now Khrushchev led it. Many legal procedures were revived, labor camps were closed, and the secret police became less powerful. By 1958, Khrushchev had gained complete power in the Soviet Union. He was a shrewd leader who sought peaceful coexistence with the West rather than confrontation.

CRITICAL THINKING ACTIVITY

Drawing Conclusions Have students study the photograph at the bottom of the page, which shows the violence that ended the "Prague Spring." Have them describe what they see happening in the photograph. Encourage them to identify details and emotions that the photo captures. Then ask them to discuss what message they think the photographer intended to convey about this event.

Class Time 10 minutes

Activity Options

Interdisciplinary Links: Language Arts/Writing

Class Time One class period

Task Writing a journal entry about life under Soviet rule

Purpose To develop an understanding of the points of view of citizens in Eastern Europe

Supplies Needed
• Writing paper
• Pens or pencils

Block Scheduling

Activity Encourage students to imagine that they are young people living in one of the nations under Soviet control in the 1960s, 1970s, or 1980s. Have them write a journal entry describing either the restrictions and problems of an ordinary day or the events of an upheaval such as the violent ending to the "Prague Spring."

ASSESS & RETEACH

Reading Social Studies Have students add notes to the first column of the chart on page 146.

 Formal Assessment
• Section Quiz, p. 80

RETEACHING ACTIVITY

Divide students into three groups and assign each group a heading in the section. Tell students to review the material under their assigned heading and then work together to create a short quiz. Have students orally quiz other groups.

 In-depth Resources: Unit 2
• Reteaching Activity, p. 44

 Access for Students Acquiring English
• Reteaching Activity, p. 46

Place • The old city of Dubrovnik is in Croatia, a part of the former Yugoslavia, which was a Communist country in Eastern Europe. ▶

Economic Crisis By the 1980s, economic conditions in the Soviet Union and in those countries under its control had still not improved. Even after détente, the Soviet government continued to spend most of its money on the armed forces and nuclear weapons. In addition, people who lived in the non-Russian republics of the Soviet Union now wanted more control over their own affairs. Many citizens began to reject the Soviet economic system, but the Soviet leaders refused to give up any of their power or control.

SECTION 1 ASSESSMENT

Terms & Names

1. **Identify:** (a) propaganda   (b) private property rights   (c) Nikita Khrushchev
   (d) deposed   (e) détente

Taking Notes

2. Use a chart like this one to list and describe major aspects of Soviet culture.

Aspects of Soviet Culture

Main Ideas

3. (a) Why did Soviet leaders try to create a strong national identity?

   (b) What began to happen in Eastern Europe in the 1950s?

   (c) Describe the significance of the "Prague Spring."

Critical Thinking

4. **Analyzing Motives**

   Why do you think the works of many writers, poets, and artists were banned or censored during the Soviet era?

   Think About

   • what Soviet citizens learned from Solzhenitsyn's works

   • the government's use of propaganda

   • what life was like for most Soviet citizens

 ACTIVITY -OPTION- Reread the information under "Literature and the Arts" and the Spotlight on Culture feature. Write a **speech** for or against censorship in the arts.

152 CHAPTER 6

Section 1 Assessment

1. Terms & Names
   a. propaganda, p. 148
   b. private property rights, p. 149
   c. Nikita Khrushchev, p. 150
   d. deposed, p. 150
   e. détente, p. 151

2. Taking Notes

Most people were poor.

Citizens had little say in government.

Officials suppressed ethnic identity.

Soviet propaganda praised Soviet Union.

3. Main Ideas
   a. They feared that ethnic groups might want to break away from the Soviet Union.
   b. People began trying to regain their independence from the Soviet Union.
   c. The Soviet Union loosened control over Czechoslovakia.

4. Critical Thinking

Possible Response The Soviet government feared that the truth about events and conditions in the Soviet Union might incite people to revolt.

ACTIVITY OPTION

 Integrated Assessment
• Rubric for writing a speech

Using an Electronic Card Catalog

▶▶ Defining the Skill

To find books, magazines, or other sources of information in a library, you may use an electronic card catalog. This catalog is a computerized search program on the Internet that lists every book, periodical, or other resource found in the library. You can search for resources in the catalog in four ways: by title, by author, by subject, and by keyword. Once you have typed in your search information, the catalog will give you a list of every resource that matches it. This is called bibliographic information. You can use an electronic card catalog to build a bibliography, or a list of books, on the topic you are researching.

▶▶ Applying the Skill

The screen below shows the results of an electronic search for information about the Danube River. To use the information on the screen, follow the strategies listed below.

How to Use an Electronic Card Catalog

Strategy ❶ To begin your search, choose Subject, Title, Author, or Keyword. The student doing this search chose "Subject" and then typed in "Danube River."

Strategy ❷ Based on your search, the catalog will give you a list of records that match that subject. You must then select one of the records to view the details about the resource. The catalog will then give you a screen like the one to the right. This detailed record lists the author, title, and information about where and when the resource was published, and by whom.

Strategy ❸ Locate the call number for the book. The call number indicates the section in the library where you will find the book. You can also find out if the book is available in the library you are using. If not, it may be available in another library in the network.

SEARCH REQUEST: Danube River

❶	Subject	Title	Author
	Find Options Locations Backup Startover Help		

❷ Lessner, Erwin Christian. The Danube; the dramatic history of the great river and the people touched by its flow. Westport, Conn.: Greenwood Press, 1961.

❷   AUTHOR: Lessner, Erwin Christian
    TITLE: The Danube; the dramatic history of the great river and the people touched by its flow

❷ PUBLISHED: Westport, Conn., Greenwood Press, 1961
   PAGING: 529 p.
   NOTES: Includes maps, bibliography
❸ CALL NO: 914.9603 L Book Available

▶▶ Practicing the Skill

Review the text in Chapter 6, Section 1 to find a topic that interests you, such as Yuri Gagarin. Use the Subject search on an electronic card catalog to find information about your topic. Make a bibliography about the subject. Organize your bibliography alphabetically by author. For each book you list, also include the title, city, publisher, and date of publication.

SKILLBUILDER

Using an Electronic Card Catalog

Defining the Skill

Tell students that many libraries today use an electronic card catalog, a computer program that keeps track of every book and other resource in the collection of a single library or a larger library system. (Some students may also be familiar with the older card catalog system, which consists of file drawers containing index cards.) Like older systems, an electronic card catalog indexes resources in four ways: Subject, Title, Author, and Keyword.

Applying the Skill

How to Use an Electronic Card Catalog If possible, use an actual electronic card catalog to take students through the strategies step by step. Remind them to follow these steps in order whenever they use an electronic card catalog. Library software systems may vary in the way they work. Students should follow any on-screen directions.

Write a Bibliography

Discuss the information shown on the screen, and help students identify which items they should include in a bibliography entry. Remind them to list entries alphabetically by the author's last name.

Practicing the Skill

Have students use the Subject search as suggested to create a bibliography about a topic in Section 1. If students need additional practice, suggest that they use an Author search to create a list of works by an author whose books they enjoy reading.

📝 **In-depth Resources: Unit 2**
• Skillbuilder Practice, p. 42

Career Connection: Database Programmer

Encourage students who enjoy using an electronic card catalog to research careers that involve creating and maintaining databases. Tell students that a database is a large collection of data that can be retrieved and searched quickly, usually using a computer. An electronic card catalog is one type of database.

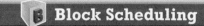

Block Scheduling

1. Suggest that students find out what other kinds of databases exist and what a database programmer does.

2. Help students learn about the aptitudes and education needed to become a database programmer.

3. Invite students to create a graphic organizer such as a flow chart to show what they have learned.

Eastern Europe and Russia

TERMS & NAMES
Mikhail Gorbachev
parliamentary republic
coalition government
ethnic cleansing
Duma

SECTION OBJECTIVES

1. To identify changes in Eastern Europe and Russia after the breakup of the Soviet Union
2. To describe the war in the Balkans
3. To describe modern Russia's culture, government, resources, industry, and economies

SKILLBUILDER
• Interpreting a Map, pp. 155, 157, 159

CRITICAL THINKING
• Summarizing, p. 156
• Comparing, p. 159

FOCUS & MOTIVATE
WARM-UP

Making Inferences Have students read <u>Dateline</u> and discuss these questions.

1. How do you think people reacted when Gorbachev began to remove troops from Eastern Europe?
2. What do you think were the effects of Gorbachev's changes?

INSTRUCT: Objective ❶

The Breakup of the Soviet Union/Modern Eastern Europe

• **What major change occurred in Eastern Europe during 1991?** Soviet republics and nations under Soviet control declared independence and set up new governments.

• **How are the economies of Eastern European countries changing?** from command economies to free-market economies

 In-depth Resources: Unit 2
• Guided Reading Worksheet, p. 38

 Reading Study Guide
(Spanish and English), pp. 46–47

MAIN IDEA

After the breakup of the Soviet Union, many former Soviet republics and countries of Eastern Europe became independent.

WHY IT MATTERS NOW

Nations once under Soviet rule are taking steps toward new economies and democratic governments.

DATELINE

THE KREMLIN, MOSCOW, 1988—To reduce military spending, the Soviet Union has begun removing large numbers of troops and arms from Eastern Europe. This latest news is just one of many changes in the Soviet government since Mikhail Gorbachev (GORE•buh•chawf) came to power three years ago.

Although Gorbachev believes in the ideals of the Soviet system, he thinks that change is necessary to help solve the country's economic and political problems. Since 1985, Gorbachev has reduced Cold War tensions with the United States. At home in the Soviet Union, he has allowed more political and economic freedom.

Region • Mikhail Gorbachev leads the Soviet Union toward a freer society. ▲

The Breakup of the Soviet Union ❶

Mikhail Gorbachev's reforms did not solve the problems of the Soviet Union. The economy continued to get worse. When Gorbachev did not force the countries of Eastern Europe to remain Communist, this further displeased many Communists.

Program Resources

 In-depth Resources: Unit 2
• Guided Reading Worksheet, p. 38
• Reteaching Activity, p. 45

 Reading Study Guide
(Spanish and English), pp. 46–47

 154 CHAPTER 6

 Formal Assessment
• Section Quiz, p. 81

Integrated Assessment
• Rubric for writing a personal essay

Outline Map Activities

 Access for Students Acquiring English
• Guided Reading Worksheet, p. 42

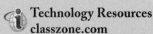 **Technology Resources**
classzone.com

TEST-TAKING RESOURCES
↪ Strategies for Test Preparation
↪ Test Practice Transparencies
⌨ Online Test Practice

coup d'état: the overthrow of a government, usually by a small group in a position of power; often shortened to "coup"

In 1991, a group of more traditional Soviet leaders tried to take over the Soviet government. Thousands of people opposed this coup d'état (koo•day•TAH), and the coup failed. Then, one by one, the Soviet republics declared independence. The Warsaw Pact was dissolved. By the end of 1991, the Soviet Union no longer existed. The huge country had become 15 different nations.

Modern Eastern Europe ❶

Each former Soviet republic set up its own non-Communist government. The countries of Eastern Europe that had been under Soviet control held democratic elections, and many wrote or revised their constitutions.

BACKGROUND

The Central Asian Soviet republics were mostly Muslim. These republics are now the countries of Kazakhstan, Turkmenistan, Uzbekistan, Kyrgyzstan, and Tajikistan.

In some countries, such as the Czech Republic, former Communists were banned from important government posts. In other countries, such as Bulgaria, the former Communists reorganized themselves into a new political party and have won elections. Many different ethnic groups also tried to create new states within a nation or to reestablish old states that had not existed in many years.

Parliamentary Republics Today, most of the countries of Eastern Europe are parliamentary republics. A **parliamentary republic** is a form of government led by the head of the political party with the most members in parliament. The head of government, usually a prime minister, proposes the programs that the government will undertake. Most of these countries also have a president who has ceremonial, rather than political, duties.

Geography
Skillbuilder
Answers

1. Estonia, Latvia, Belarus, Ukraine, Georgia, Azerbaijan, Kazakhstan; Poland and Lithuania border enclave on Baltic Sea

2. Slightly more than half are in Europe; the rest are in Central Asia.

FOCUS ON VISUALS

Interpreting the Map Explain to students that this map shows both the former republics that made up the Soviet Union and the Eastern European nations that were more or less under Soviet control. Have students trace the border of the former Soviet Union to make this distinction. Then ask students to name the former Soviet republics that do not border other European nations.

Possible Responses Georgia, Armenia, Azerbaijan, Kazakhstan, Uzbekistan, Turkmenistan, Kyrgyzstan, Tajikistan

Extension Have students choose one of the former Soviet republics and prepare a short illustrated report on its history and government since 1991, including a map and photographs if possible. Ask students to present their reports in class.

Former Soviet Republics and Warsaw Pact Members, 2001

GEOGRAPHY SKILLBUILDER: Interpreting a Map

1. **Location** • Which former Soviet republics and Warsaw Pact members border Russia?
2. **Region** • On which continent are most of these countries located?

Activity Options

Differentiating Instruction: Students Acquiring English/ESL

Borrowed Words Use the terms *détente* and *coup d'état* to introduce the idea that everyday English uses a number of words and terms taken directly from other languages. Encourage students to suggest words or terms from their own languages that they think would be useful to native English speakers. Then draw up a chart like this one and ask them to use their dictionaries to find out how the term is used in English.

esprit (French)	
savoir-faire (French)	
chic (French)	
gumbo (Bantu)	
machismo (Spanish)	
cliché (French)	

CRITICAL THINKING ACTIVITY

Summarizing Ask students to summarize the economic and social problems many Eastern European countries faced after they gained independence. As students identify information that should be included in a summary, have them record their ideas on a concept web. Then have students use the web to write a summary.

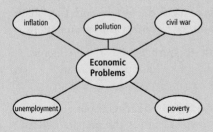

Class Time 15 minutes

Spotlight on CULTURE

In Ukraine, decorating Easter eggs is an art. The Easter eggs, which are called *pysanky*, are decorated using wax and dyes. It can take 15 or more hours to decorate a single egg. Every color and design has symbolic meaning. Red, for example, symbolizes love, and for centuries was the most important color for *pysanky*. Brown symbolizes Earth, and green represents spring, renewal, and freedom. The sun design, a circle with lines running out from the edges, symbolizes good fortune, while the flower stands for love and charity.

In some countries, small political parties have joined forces to work together to form a government. This is called a **coalition government.**

New Economies Under Soviet rule, Eastern Europe struggled economically and its people's freedoms were severely restricted. Although Eastern Europeans gained their freedom, they also faced problems such as inflation and unemployment.

Eastern Europe's countries are changing from command economies to free-market economies. Some countries, such as Slovakia, made this change slowly. Others, such as Poland, reformed their economic system and achieved economic success.

Many former Soviet republics, which did not quickly reform their economic systems, are in bad economic shape. Some of these nations are terribly poor. Struggles for power have led to violence and sometimes civil war. Pollution from the Soviet era threatens people's health. Still, some republics, including Ukraine, Latvia, Lithuania, and Estonia, are making progress as independent nations.

Defense After the breakup of the Soviet Union, Eastern European nations no longer looked to the Soviet government to defend them. Many wanted to become members of NATO. Belonging to NATO would help assure them of protection in case of invasion.

Reading Social Studies

A. Comparing Compare a command economy with a free-market economy.

Reading Social Studies A. Answer

In a command economy, the government owns land and industries, decides what and how much will be produced, and how it will be distributed. A free-market economy operates primarily through supply and demand.

Spotlight on CULTURE

Easter in Ukraine In Ukraine, most Christians belong to the Orthodox Church. These Ukrainians are known for the special way in which they celebrate the Easter holiday. They create beautiful Easter eggs, which are dyed bright colors and covered with intricate designs. These eggs are so beautiful that people around the world collect them.

Ukrainian families also bake a special bread for Easter. They decorate this bread with designs made from pieces of dough. Families bring the bread and other foods to church to be blessed on Easter. These foods then make up the family's holiday feast.

THINKING CRITICALLY

1. **Analyzing Issues**
   Why were Ukrainian Easter eggs not common during the Soviet era?

2. **Comparing**
   Compare how your family prepares for holidays with preparations made by Ukrainians in the Orthodox Church.

Activity Options

Multiple Learning Styles: Visual/Kinesthetic

Class Time One class period

Task Creating a poster promoting travel to an Eastern European country

Purpose To learn more about the countries of Eastern Europe

Supplies Needed
• Library or Internet resources
• Poster board
• Markers or crayons

Block Scheduling

Activity Explain that the countries of Eastern Europe are building modern tourist facilities and encouraging tourists to visit. Ask each student to choose a country from this region and learn more about it. Students should take notes on the country's physical geography, climate, and attractions. Then have them create posters promoting travel to their chosen countries. Tell them to create titles and slogans for their posters. Have them share their posters and what they have learned with their classmates.

In 1999, three new members joined NATO: Poland, Hungary, and the Czech Republic. In 2001, Bulgaria, Romania, Slovakia, Slovenia, and the Baltic States were also working to become NATO members.

Vocabulary

Baltic States: Estonia, Latvia, and Lithuania—former Soviet republics that are on the Baltic Sea

War in the Balkan Peninsula ❷

Since the late 1980s, much of Eastern Europe has been a place of turmoil and struggle. Yugoslavia, one of the countries located on Europe's Balkan Peninsula, has experienced terrible wars, extreme hardships, and great change.

Under Tito After World War II, Yugoslavia came under Marshal Tito's (TEE·toe) dictatorship. Tito controlled all the country's many different ethnic groups, which included Serbs, Croats, and Muslims. His rule continued until his death in 1980. Slobodan Milosevic (SLOW·boe·don muh·LOW·suh·vitch) became Yugoslavia's president in 1989, after years of political turmoil.

Milosevic Slobodan Milosevic, a Serb, wanted the Serbs to rule Yugoslavia. The Serbs in Bosnia began fighting the Croats and Muslims living there. The Bosnian Serbs murdered many Muslims so that Serbs would be in the majority. The Serbs called these killings of members of minority ethnic groups **ethnic cleansing.** Finally, NATO attacked the Bosnian Serbs and ended the war.

BACKGROUND

By 1991, Croatia, Slovenia, Macedonia, and Bosnia-Herzegovina had gained independence from Yugoslavia. Only Serbia and Montenegro were still part of the Yugoslavian federation.

Geography Skillbuilder Answers
1. Macedonia
2. Slovenia, Croatia, Bosnia-Herzegovina, Macedonia, and two autonomous provinces, plus two countries in federation

Connections to Science

Pollution Soviet leaders thought that industry would improve life for everyone. Developing industry was so important that the Soviet government did not worry about pollution. Few laws were passed to protect the environment.

In the 1970s and 1980s, there was not enough money to modernize industry or to reduce pollution. Some areas also could not afford proper sewage systems or recycling plants. Today, Eastern Europe has some of the worst pollution problems on the continent.

INSTRUCT: Objective ❷

War in the Balkan Peninsula

- What were the three major ethnic groups in Yugoslavia when Tito was dictator? Serbs, Croats, Muslims
- Why did Milosevic order ethnic cleansing? to kill minority ethnic groups so the Bosnian Serbs would be in the majority

Connections to Science

Since the fall of communism, environmental awareness has increased in Eastern Europe. Environmental organizations began to form in the 1980s. In 1990 the Regional Environmental Center for Central and Eastern Europe was formed. It is a not-for-profit organization devoted to solving environmental problems and encouraging public participation in environmental issues.

FOCUS ON VISUALS

Interpreting the Map Explain to students that the nation of Yugoslavia was formed after World War I as a federation of republics that brought together people of diverse ethnic and religious groups. Ask students to identify the countries that border the former Yugoslavia.

Response Austria, Hungary, Romania, Bulgaria, Greece, Albania, small part of Italy

Extension Have students research and report on the pre–World War I backgrounds of the republics of the former Yugoslavia.

The Balkan States, 1991 and 2001

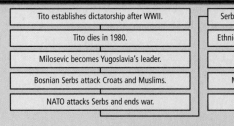

National boundaries, 2001
Yugoslavia, 1991
Autonomous province boundaries, 2001
★ National capital

AUSTRIA, HUNGARY, Slovenia, Croatia, Vojvodina, YUGOSLAVIA, Belgrade, ROMANIA, Bosnia and Herzegovina, Serbia, SAN MARINO, Adriatic Sea, ITALY, Montenegro, Kosovo, BULGARIA, Macedonia, ALBANIA, GREECE

GEOGRAPHY SKILLBUILDER: Interpreting a Map
1. **Location** • Which Balkan state borders Greece?
2. **Region** • How many countries developed from Yugoslavia?

Activity Options

Differentiating Instruction: Less Proficient Readers

Identifying Sequence Some students may have difficulty following the sequence of events in Yugoslavia that began with Tito's rise to power after World War II and ended with Milosevic's arrest for war crimes. To clarify these events, help students create a sequence chart like the one shown here. Then have students use the chart to review "War in the Balkan Peninsula."

Tito establishes dictatorship after WWII.
Tito dies in 1980.
Milosevic becomes Yugoslavia's leader.
Bosnian Serbs attack Croats and Muslims.
NATO attacks Serbs and ends war.

Serbs, Croats, Muslims sign peace treaty in 1995.
Ethnic cleansing is used against Albanians in 1999.
NATO again defeats Serbs.
Milosevic is removed from power in 2000.
Milosevic is arrested for war crimes.

INSTRUCT: Objective ③

Modern Russia

- What new freedoms do Russians have since the breakup of the Soviet Union? freedom to elect leaders and own property, freedom of speech and religion, end of censorship

- How has Russia's economy changed since the Soviet Union collapsed? developing a free-market economy; private property ownership; new businesses

- What difficulties have resulted from the free-market economy? uncontrolled high prices; economic inequality; crime

Before Communist rule, religion was very important in many Russians' lives. Most homes, even peasant cottages, had a special spot called the "beautiful corner"*(krasny ugol)* for an icon. One aftereffect of the breakup of the Soviet Union was a religious revival.

In 1995, the Serbs, Croats, and Muslims of Bosnia signed a peace treaty. In 1999, Milosevic began using ethnic cleansing against the Albanians in Kosovo, a region of Serbia. NATO launched an air war against Yugoslavia that ended with the defeat of the Serbs. In 2000, public protests led to Milosevic's removal. He was subsequently arrested and tried for war crimes by the United Nations.

Modern Russia

Life in Russia has improved since the breakup of the Soviet Union. Russian citizens can elect their own leaders. They enjoy more freedom of speech. New businesses have sprung up. And some Russians have become wealthy.

Unfortunately, Russia still faces serious problems. Many leaders are dishonest. The nation has been slow to reform its economic system. Most of the nation's new wealth has gone to a small number of people, so that many Russians remain poor. The crime rate has grown tremendously. The government has also fought a war against Chechnya (CHECH·nee·yah), a region of Russia that wants to become independent.

Russian Culture The fall of communism helped most Russians to follow their cultural practices more freely. Russians gained the freedom to practice the religion of their choice. They can also buy and read the great works of Russian literature that once were banned. At the beginning of the 21st century, writers and other artists also have far more freedom to express themselves.

New magazines and newspapers are being published. Even new history books are being written. For the first time in decades, these publications are telling more of the truth about the Soviet Union.

Russia's Government Russia has a democratic form of government. The president is elected by the people. The people also elect members of the **Duma** (DOO·muh), which is part of the legislature.

Russian Icons A special feature of Russian Orthodox churches are beautiful religious paintings called icons (EYE·kons). Russian icons usually depict biblical figures and scenes. They often decorate every corner of a church.

The greatest Russian icon painter was Andrei Rublev (AHN·dray ROO·blawf). He worked in the late 1300s and early 1400s. Rublev's paintings, one of which is shown below, are brightly colored and highlighted in gold. His work influenced many later painters, and today he is considered one of the world's great religious artists.

Reading Social Studies

B. Identifying Problems What are the main problems that face Russia today?

Reading Social Studies
B. Possible Answers
crime; dishonest officials; economic problems; small group of newly rich people, but many still poor

BACKGROUND

One of the most popular pastimes in Russia is the game of chess. In fact, many of the world's greatest chess players, such as Boris Spassky, have been Russian.

158 Chapter 6

Activity Options

Differentiating Instruction: Gifted and Talented

Crossword Puzzle Have students work in pairs to create crossword puzzles that include important terms from this section. Demonstrate how they can use graph paper to configure at least eight terms or names in a crossword-puzzle formation. Then have them write definitions for each term and number them as Across and Down clues. When students have finished, have them trade their puzzles with other classmates.

Block Scheduling

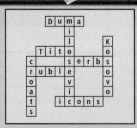

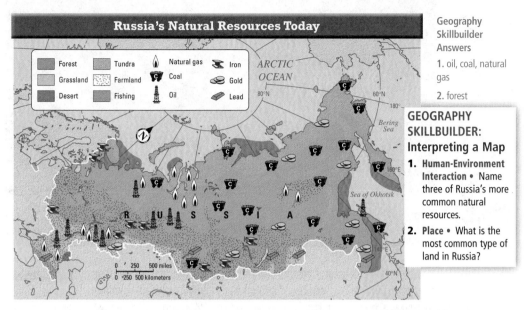

Russia's Natural Resources Today

Forest • Tundra • Natural gas • Iron
Grassland • Farmland • Coal • Gold
Desert • Fishing • Oil • Lead

ARCTIC OCEAN
Bering Sea
RUSSIA
Sea of Okhotsk

0 250 500 miles
0 250 500 kilometers

GEOGRAPHY SKILLBUILDER: Interpreting a Map

1. **Human-Environment Interaction** • Name three of Russia's more common natural resources.

2. **Place** • What is the most common type of land in Russia?

Democracy is still new to the Russian people. Some citizens are working to improve the system to reduce corruption and to ensure that everyone receives fair treatment. Even the thought of changing the government is new to most Russians. Under the Soviets, people had to accept things the way they were.

BACKGROUND

Russian highways are in poor condition. Also, many rivers and major ports are closed by ice in the winter. As a result, most Russian goods are transported by railroad.

Resources and Industry The map above shows Russia's major natural resources. The country is one of the world's largest producers of oil. Russia also contains the world's largest forests. Its trees are made into lumber, paper, and other wood products.

Russian factories produce steel from iron ore. Other factories use that steel to make tractors and other large machines. Since Russian ships can reach both the Pacific and Atlantic oceans, Russia also has a large fishing industry.

Economics Following the lead of Eastern European countries, Russia has been moving toward a free-market economy. Citizens can own land, and foreign companies are encouraged to do business in Russia. These changes have given many Russians more opportunities, but they have also brought difficulties.

Connections to Language

The Russian Language More than 150 million people speak Russian. It is related to other Slavic languages of Eastern Europe, including Polish, Serbian, and Bulgarian.

Russian is written using the Cyrillic (suh•RIL•ik) alphabet, which has 33 characters.

Many of the newly independent republics are now returning to the Latin alphabet, used to write English and most other languages of the Western world. The major powers in the world economy base their languages on the Latin alphabet, and clearer communication may improve the economies of these new countries.

Hello
Привет

Modern Europe **159**

FOCUS ON VISUALS

Interpreting the Map Go over the map key with students. Make sure that they notice the dotted areas showing "farmland" overlaying both forest and grassland areas. Ask them to point out the oceans in which there is fishing.

Response Arctic Ocean, Sea of Okhotsk

Extension Ask students to find and display photographs or paintings of Russian forests and steppe lands.

CRITICAL THINKING ACTIVITY

Comparing Ask students to compare the quality of life of Soviet citizens before and after the breakup of the Soviet Union. Create a Venn diagram to help make comparisons.

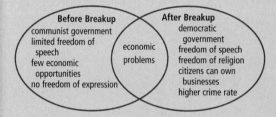

Before Breakup
communist government
limited freedom of speech
few economic opportunities
no freedom of expression

economic problems

After Breakup
democratic government
freedom of speech
freedom of religion
citizens can own businesses
higher crime rate

Class Time 15 minutes

Connections to Language

The Cyrillic alphabet was invented in the early 800s by followers of two missionaries, St. Cyril and St. Methodius, who traveled to Eastern Europe to convert the Slavs. The alphabet is based on Greek, but because the Slavic languages have more sounds than Greek, more letters were added. The first book written in Cyrillic was a translation of the Bible.

Activity Options

Interdisciplinary Link: Geography

Class Time One class period

Task Creating natural resource maps of Eastern European countries

Purpose To identify natural resources found in Eastern Europe

Supplies Needed
• Library or Internet resources
• Drawing paper
• Pencils or pens

Activity Have students study the map of Russia's natural resources. Then assign groups of students to create natural resource maps of the other independent countries of Eastern Europe. Suggest that groups delegate the responsibilities of researching and illustrating. Display the completed maps, and use them to compare and contrast the natural resources of countries throughout Eastern Europe.

ASSESS & RETEACH

Reading Social Studies Have students add notes to the second column of the chart on page 146.

 Formal Assessment
• Section Quiz, p. 81

RETEACHING ACTIVITY

Divide the class into groups of four, and assign a major heading from the section to each group. Ask students to work together to prepare an outline about the information presented in their assigned material. Then have a person from each group write the outline on the board. Use students' outlines to review the section.

 In-depth Resources: Unit 2
• Reteaching Activity, p. 45

 Access for Students Acquiring English
• Reteaching Activity, p. 47

Place • Forestry is a major industry in Russia. These harvested logs are being floated downriver to be processed. ▶

Prices are no longer controlled by the government. This means that companies can charge a price that is high enough for them to make a profit. At the beginning of the 21st century, however, people's wages have not risen as fast as prices. Many people cannot afford to buy new products.

Some Russians have done well in the new economy. On the other hand, people with less education and less access to power have not done as well. Also, today most new businesses and jobs are in the cities, which means that people in small towns have fewer job opportunities.

SECTION 2 ASSESSMENT

Terms & Names

1. Identify:
(a) Mikhail Gorbachev
(b) parliamentary republic
(c) coalition government
(d) ethnic cleansing
(e) Duma

Taking Notes	Main Ideas	Critical Thinking
2. Use a flow chart like this one to outline the changes in Eastern Europe and Russia from 1988 through 2000.	**3. (a)** What happened to the governments of the former Soviet republics after independence?	**4. Making Inferences** Why do you think many Eastern European countries would like to join NATO?

2. Use a flow chart like this one to outline the changes in Eastern Europe and Russia from 1988 through 2000.

1988:
↓
↓

3. (a) What happened to the governments of the former Soviet republics after independence?

(b) How have the economies of Eastern European countries changed now that those countries are free?

(c) In what ways has life in Russia improved since the breakup of the Soviet Union?

4. Making Inferences

Why do you think many Eastern European countries would like to join NATO?

Think About

♦ what happened to the Warsaw Pact
♦ the economies of Eastern Europe
♦ the relationship between Eastern Europe and Russia

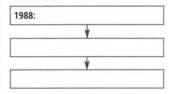 Reread the information in the Spotlight on Culture feature. Write a short, personal **essay** that describes a special family, school, neighborhood, or holiday celebration in which you participated.

160 CHAPTER 6

Section 2 Assessment

1. Terms & Names
a. Mikhail Gorbachev, p. 154
b. parliamentary republic, p. 155
c. coalition government, p. 156
d. ethnic cleansing, p. 157
e. Duma, p. 158

2. Taking Notes

1988	Soviet Union removes many troops and arms from Eastern Europe.
1991	Soviet republics declare independence; Yeltsin becomes first freely elected president of Russia.
1999	Some Eastern European countries join NATO.

3. Main Ideas
a. They set up their own non-Communist governments, mostly parliamentary republics, and held elections.
b. They changed from command economies to free-market economies.
c. People can elect their leaders; they have freedom of speech and religion; they can own land and businesses and travel freely; writers and artists have more freedom.

4. Critical Thinking
Possible Response They might want to join NATO because they are no longer defended by the Soviet Union. Many have weak economies and cannot afford a large military for self-defense.

ACTIVITY OPTION
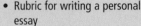 **Integrated Assessment**
• Rubric for writing a personal essay

The European Union

SECTION 3

TERMS & NAMES
European Union
currency
euro
tariff
standard of living
Court of Justice

MAIN IDEA
Europeans want to maintain a high quality of life for all citizens while preserving their unique cultures.

WHY IT MATTERS NOW
A prosperous and culturally diverse Europe provides goods and markets for the rest of the world.

DATELINE

Back Forward Stop Refresh Home

Address: [ ] go

WESTERN EUROPE, DECEMBER 2001—Starting next month, people in many Western European nations will begin trading their old bills and coins for euros—the new money of the European Union (EU). The design of the bills, below, is the same for all EU members.

The design of the euro coins, however, will be different. Individual countries are minting their own. As shown here, one side has a standard euro design. The other side has national symbols that relate to each country. In 1996, artists and sculptors from all over Europe entered a contest to design the coins. The winner was Luc Luycx (lewk lowx) from Belgium.

Region • Euros will reach the European market in January 2002. ▲

Western Europe Today ❶

Today, in Western Europe, all national leaders share their power with elected lawmakers. Citizens take part in government by voting and through membership in a variety of political parties. The Unit Atlas on pages 54–63 shows modern Europe.

Modern Europe **161**

SECTION OBJECTIVES

1. To identify the benefits of membership in the European Union
2. To describe the economies of European Union members
3. To describe the cultures of European Union members

CRITICAL THINKING
• Analyzing Issues, p. 162

FOCUS & MOTIVATE
WARM-UP

Analyzing Motives Have students read <u>Dateline</u> and answer questions about the euro.

1. Why might Western European nations decide to switch to a single currency?
2. Why do you think each country wants to mint its own coins?

INSTRUCT: Objective ❶

Western Europe Today

• What was the original goal of the European Union? to encourage trade
• Why do many former Communist countries want to join the European Union? to gain economic and political advantages
• What changes do Eastern European nations need to make to join the EU? economic, legal, and environmental improvements

📄 **In-depth Resources: Unit 2**
• Guided Reading Worksheet, p. 39

📄 **Reading Study Guide**
(Spanish and English), pp. 48–49

Program Resources

📄 **In-depth Resources: Unit 2**
• Guided Reading Worksheet, p. 39
• Reteaching Activity, p. 46

📄 **Reading Study Guide**
(Spanish and English), pp. 48–49

📄 **Formal Assessment**
• Section Quiz, p. 82

📄 **Integrated Assessment**
• Rubric for writing a postcard or e-mail

📄 **Outline Map Activities**

📄 **Access for Students Acquiring English**
• Guided Reading Worksheet, p. 43

🌐 **Technology Resources**
classzone.com

TEST-TAKING RESOURCES
✦ Strategies for Test Preparation
✦ Test Practice Transparencies
🌐 Online Test Practice

Teacher's Edition **161**

CRITICAL THINKING ACTIVITY

Analyzing Issues Point out to students that the current members of the EU want Eastern European countries to make economic, legal, and environmental improvements before admitting them to membership in the EU. Use the following questions to help students analyze this issue.

- What might happen if Eastern European countries joined the EU without improving their economies?
- How might environmental problems affect a nation's economy, as well as that of its neighbors?
- Why would it be helpful for all members of the EU to have similar legal systems?

Class Time 20 minutes

FOCUS ON VISUALS

Interpreting the Photograph Have individual students identify the countries on the Euro plaque, identifying each country by shape and by comparing its flag to the chart of EU members. Ask them to identify the EU members not included on the plaque and think of a reason for their absence.

Response Denmark, Greece, Sweden, United Kingdom; have not adopted the euro

Extension Have students research the flags of the five countries that have won initial EU approval (see Background, page 162).

Members of the European Union, 2001

Austria	
Belgium	
Denmark	
Finland	
France	
Germany	
Greece	
Ireland	
Italy	
Luxembourg	
Netherlands	
Portugal	
Spain	
Sweden	
United Kingdom	

The European Union Many countries of Western Europe belong to a group called the **European Union** (EU). At first, countries joined the EU to encourage trade. This economic group, however, is becoming a loose political union.

Many former Communist countries of Eastern Europe want to join the Union too. They know that membership will help them economically and politically. Eastern European countries, however, cannot automatically join the EU. Many must first make legal, economic, and environmental improvements. The EU has agreed to include them over time. With a possible membership of more than 20 nations by 2003, the EU may be the best hope for European peace and prosperity.

Regional Governments In Western Europe, each nation also has regional governments, similar to those of individual states in the United States. Regional governments are demanding—and receiving—greater power. As a result, many people in Western Europe enjoy increased self-rule and participation in the political process.

BACKGROUND

In 2001, the EU gave initial approval to the Czech Republic, Estonia, Hungary, Poland, and Slovenia to join in the near future.

Region • The headquarters of the European Central Bank is located in Frankfurt, Germany. ◄

Activity Options

Differentiating Instruction: Less Proficient Readers

Setting a Purpose To help students set a purpose for reading about the European Union, prepare a set of questions for students to use as a guide as they read the paragraphs under "The European Union" (page 162). Write the questions on the chalkboard, and read them aloud to students. When students have finished reading and answering the questions, review and discuss their answers as a group.

You might want to ask questions such as the following:
- Why did countries originally join the European Union?
- Why do former Communist countries want to join the EU?
- What must Eastern European countries do before they can join the EU?

EU Economies ❷

BACKGROUND
Some EU nations, including the United Kingdom and Denmark, have not agreed to give up their existing currency.

Traditionally, each European nation has had its own **currency,** or system of money. The EU is meant to make international trade much simpler. With more Europeans using the **euro,** the currency of the EU, currency no longer has to be exchanged every time a payment crosses a border.

Improved Trade To encourage trade, members have also done away with tariffs on the goods they trade with one another. A **tariff** is a duty or fee that must be paid on exported goods, making them more expensive. EU members have lifted border controls as well. This means that goods, services, and people flow freely among these member nations.

Another goal of the EU is to achieve economic equality among its members. To reach this goal, EU members are sharing their wealth. Poorer countries such as Ireland receive money to help them build businesses.

A Higher Standard of Living Member nations hope that increased trade and shared wealth will help give all citizens of the EU a high standard of living. A person's **standard of living,** or quality of life, is based on the availability of goods and services.

People who have a high standard of living have enough food and housing, good transportation and communications, and access to schools and health care. They also have a high rate of literacy, meaning that most adults are able to read.

Additional Benefits The members of the EU are helping the countries of Eastern Europe to raise their environmental standards. They are willing to pay up to 75 percent of the cost for a new waste treatment system in Romania, for example. The program includes recycling centers for paper, glass, and plastics. It will clean up and close old dumping grounds, which were leaking pollution into the ground water.

Reading Social Studies

A. Clarifying How would improved trade raise the standard of living?

Reading Social Studies
A. Possible Answer Trade can make more goods available and may create new jobs.

Connections to Economics

Tourism For many European nations, tourism is an important part of the economy. In fact, the continent represents about 60 percent of the world's tourist market. Visitors come to enjoy Europe's climate, historic sites, museums, and food.

Popular destinations include Spain, Italy, Austria, and the United Kingdom. France, below, is the most visited country in the world. In 1999, it hosted more than 73 million tourists.

INSTRUCT: Objective ❷

EU Economies

- What have members of the EU done to improve trade? done away with tariffs, lifted border controls, made development loans
- What steps did the EU take to improve the environment in Romania? new waste treatment system, including recycling centers and cleaning up old dumping grounds
- How is the EU improving the lives of people? tries to raise standards of living, provides job training, allows people to work in any member country, allows people to vote in local elections wherever they live, protects people's rights through a Court of Justice

Connections to Economics

Within the EU, travel and tourism account for about $1.4 billion in economic activity each year. This amounts to about 4.8 percent of the gross domestic product of the EU as a whole, and experts have predicted that tourism will increase by approximately 3.7 percent each year. Currently, travel and tourism provide more than 9 million jobs—nearly one of every 17 jobs in Europe.

Activity Options
Interdisciplinary Link: Math

Class Time 15 minutes
Task Converting euros to U.S. dollars
Purpose To learn about the relative value of the euro compared with the United States dollar

Supplies Needed
- Writing paper
- Pencils

Activity Explain to students that when Americans travel to Europe, they exchange, or trade, their U.S. money for euros. Explain that the exchange rate varies, but one euro is generally worth a little less than one U.S. dollar. Create word problems such as this one for students to solve.

- A European is traveling to America. She has 1,200 euros. If one euro is worth 90 cents, how many U.S. dollars will she get in exchange? ($1,080)

INSTRUCT: Objective ❸

Cultural Diversity

• What are some examples of cultural diversity among EU nations? different languages, unique foods, certain ways of doing business, special games and celebrations

• What conveniences do most major European cities offer? excellent public transportation, sidewalk cafés

MORE ABOUT...
European Languages

Much of Europe's rich cultural diversity is a result of its many languages—there are about 50 in all. Until recently, the use of many of these languages has been discouraged. The French Constitution, for example, declares that "the language of the country is French." Breton, Basque, Catalan, and other languages spoken in France have been ignored, and the specific dialect of French spoken in Paris has been recognized as the official language for the whole country. Other countries have likewise discouraged the use of minority languages. This is changing, however. In 1992, the Council of Europe adopted the European Charter for Regional or Minority Languages. The charter acknowledges the cultural value of Europe's regional languages and seeks to preserve them.

The EU also runs programs that train people for jobs. As citizens of a member nation, people are not limited to a job in their own country. They may work in any part of the EU. They can even vote in local elections wherever they live. In addition, the EU's **Court of Justice** protects the rights of all its citizens in whichever member country they live.

Cultural Diversity ❸

Although many European nations are part of the EU, they still have their own distinct cultural traditions. These traditions may include different languages, unique foods, certain ways of doing business, and even special games and celebrations. Many of these traditions developed over hundreds of years.

Some nations are a mix of several cultures. In Belgium, for example, Flemings live in the north and speak Dutch. Another major group, the Walloons, lives in the south. They speak French. A third group of German-speaking Belgians lives in the eastern part of the country. Many Belgian cities include people from all three groups.

City Life Many of the world's famous and exciting cities are located in Western Europe. London, Madrid, Paris, Amsterdam, and Rome are just a few of the major centers for the arts, business, and learning. These cities are centuries old, and Europeans work hard to preserve them.

Europeans also take pride in the conveniences that their cities offer. Most major urban areas have excellent public transportation, including subways, buses, and trains. Sidewalk cafés are also popular, where people come to meet friends, eat, and relax.

Reading Social Studies
B. Possible Answers
conflicting cultural traditions, national pride, economic inequality among members

Reading
Social Studies
B. Identifying Problems What are the main problems facing the European Union?

Region • Many Europeans center their social lives around urban sidewalk cafés, such as this one in Italy. ▼

Activity Options

Multiple Learning Styles: Visual/Spatial

Class Time 20 minutes

Task Locating countries and cities of Western Europe on a map

Purpose To learn where Western European countries and cities are located in relation to one another

Supplies Needed
• Map of Europe

Activity Read aloud the paragraphs under "Cultural Diversity." As you read about the various languages spoken in Belgium, ask students to locate the areas on the map. Then, as you read about London, Madrid, Paris, Amsterdam, and Rome, point out the cities and have students identify the country in which each city is located.

Region • The quaint European countryside is a popular tourist attraction. ▶

ASSESS & RETEACH

Reading Social Studies Have students add notes about EU membership to the second column of the chart on page 146, noting which countries are on their way to acceptance.

 Formal Assessment
• Section Quiz, p. 82

RETEACHING ACTIVITY

Assign a part of the section to each student. Ask each to create a cluster diagram to show the main ideas and supporting details for their assigned text. Then have students meet in groups and share their clusters. Encourage them to add details they may have overlooked as they study their classmates' work.

 In-depth Resources: Unit 2
• Reteaching Activity, p. 46

 Access for Students Acquiring English
• Reteaching Activity, p. 48

BACKGROUND

Many European families cannot make a living on a small farm. The government may offer support to such families, to help preserve the nation's rural culture.

Country Life European cities have much to offer, but the countryside is also popular—especially for vacationers. The Italian region of Tuscany (TUSK•uh•nee) and the French region of Provence (proh•VONSE) are two of the best-known examples of the many beautiful rural areas.

Small European villages may have only a café, a grocery store, a post office, a town square, and a collection of houses. Many families who live in such areas have been farming or raising animals on the same land for generations. Some even live in houses that their families have owned for hundreds of years.

SECTION 3 ASSESSMENT

Terms & Names

1. Identify:
   (a) European Union (EU) (b) currency (c) euro
   (d) tariff (e) standard of living (f) Court of Justice

Taking Notes

2. Use a chart like this one to compare aspects of city life and country life in Europe.

City Life	Country Life

Main Ideas

3. (a) Describe the importance of the new shared currency that is based on the euro.

   (b) Can any European country automatically join the EU? Why or why not?

   (c) List at least two benefits, other than a shared currency, for countries that are members of the EU.

Critical Thinking

4. **Synthesizing**

   Why may the EU be the best hope for European peace and prosperity?

   Think About
   • the number of member countries
   • the goals of the EU
   • modern European conflicts

ACTIVITY -OPTION- Choose one photograph from this section that shows a place in Europe. Write a **postcard** or **e-mail** to a friend or family member as if you were there. What sights and sounds will you describe?

Section 3 Assessment

1. Terms & Names
   a. European Union (EU), p. 162
   b. currency, p. 163
   c. euro, p. 163
   d. tariff, p. 163
   e. standard of living, p. 163
   f. Court of Justice, p. 164

2. Taking Notes

City Life	Country Life
many cafés, stores	beautiful scenery
excellent public transportation	many families farmed same land for generations

3. Main Ideas
   a. The euro makes trade among EU countries easier.
   b. No; they must meet certain economic, legal, and environmental conditions.
   c. economic assistance, improved trading opportunities, improved standard of living

4. Critical Thinking
   Possible Response The EU creates a common economic bond and goals to reduce conflicts among members.

   ACTIVITY OPTION

    Integrated Assessment
   • Rubric for writing a postcard or e-mail

The Legacy of Europe

OBJECTIVE

Students learn about the contributions of Europe to the world's languages, ideas, and inventions.

FOCUS & MOTIVATE

Making Inferences Ask students to study the pictures and read each paragraph. Then have them answer the following questions:

1. How might the printing press have changed other European technologies and inventions?

2. What do the stylistic similarities between the Agora and the White House suggest about the influence of Greek art on Roman art?

 Block Scheduling

MORE ABOUT...
Nitroglycerin

Along with his scientific and technological interests, Alfred Nobel wrote plays, novels, and poetry in his free time. He also traveled widely and spoke five languages. He became very wealthy from his work with explosives and decided that profits should reward human ingenuity. Nobel set up a fund of about $9 million in his will, and the interest from this fund is used for the Nobel Prizes—annual awards to those whose work benefits humanity. Today, they are the most honored prizes in the world.

Architecture

Roman architecture had a great deal of stylistic unity. For example, the Romans were the first to fully utilize the arch and the vault. The use of these reduced or eliminated the need for columns, and allowed the roof to rest completely on the outer walls. The Romans still used columns, but more as sculptural decoration.

Movable Type

Before Johann Gutenberg (1395–1468) invented the printing press in Germany, European monks copied books by hand. Movable type made it possible to print multiple copies of books quickly, allowing people access to them. The printing process advanced greatly in the 1930s. By the mid-1940s, printed works included complex illustrations and color. Today, people create text and images and print them directly from their computers.

Early printing pres

Nitroglycerin

For almost 20 years, Alfred Nobel (1833–1896), shown at left, worked on developing a way to safely contain and ignite nitroglycerin, a powerful explosive. Eventually, chemists and doctors realized that nitroglycerin widens blood vessels and can be used to treat patients with heart conditions. Given in tablet, patch, or oral-spray form, nitroglycerin has saved countless lives.

Architecture

The White House in Washington, D.C., is one of many buildings in the United States that have been influenced by Roman architecture. Roman buildings often featured vaulted domes, columns, and large interior spaces. This type of architecture has influenced other buildings in the United States, including many banks and courthouses.

Activity Option

Interdisciplinary Link: Government

Class Time 60 minutes

Task Preparing arguments, pro or con, about the effects of the printing press on government

Supplies Needed
• Information on the number of books available in Europe before, and after, the invention of the printing press

Activity Have students work in groups. Ask each group to imagine that they are advisors to a European king in the early 1400s. The king is considering the effects of a new invention, the printing press, on his rule. Each group should prepare a recommendation for the king, either to allow individual entrepreneurs to establish printing presses, or to outlaw this new invention as a dangerous idea. Remind each group to clearly state their reasons, pro or con, and to predict the effects the printing press will have on the king's government and his power.

Democracy

Around 500 B.C., several Greek city-states established democracies, replacing their single-ruler governments. The word *democracy* derives from two Greek words: *demos,* meaning "people," and *kratos,* meaning "power." Today, the idea of rule by the people is found around the world, from the United States to France to India.

The agora, or marketplace, of ancient Athens was often the scene of political activities. ▲

Yacht ▼

Robot ▶

Flamingo ▶

European Languages

Many words of different European languages have made their way into English. For example, the word *dinner* is actually French in origin. As English people traveled and settled around the world, they borrowed words from such European languages as German, Spanish, and Norwegian to use in their everyday communication. Examples of some of these words we use today are *kindergarten* (German), *dinner* (French), *yacht* (Dutch), *corridor* (Italian), *vanilla* (Spanish), *flamingo* (Portuguese), *robot* (Czech), and *ski* (Norwegian).

Find Out More About It!

Study the text and photos on these pages to learn about inventions, creations, and contributions that have come from Europe. Then choose the item that interests you the most and use the library or the Internet to learn more about it. Use the information you gather to create a poster celebrating the contribution.

RESEARCH LINKS
CLASSZONE.COM

INSTRUCT

- What architectural elements do the Agora and the White House share?
- Where was democracy first practiced in Europe?
- When was the printing press invented?

MORE ABOUT...
Democracy

Athens was the most powerful Greek city-state with a democratic government. All government officials in Athens were citizens chosen by lot. An Athenian citizen had to volunteer to participate in the political process. If the citizen chose to participate, he was eligible to be a member of either a jury or a council that ran the daily government.

MORE ABOUT...
European Languages

Today, English is the most widely spoken language in the world. This was not always true, however. In the 1500s, English was spoken by fewer than two million people, and all of them lived in the British Isles. Since then, because of various historical events, English has spread throughout the world. Today, English is the native language for roughly 400 million people. Another 100 million people speak English along with their native language. Additionally, some English is used by 200 million people.

With all these speakers, English is constantly growing and incorporating words from other languages. Today, the English vocabulary is larger than that of any other language. Examples of words incorporated from other languages include algebra from Arabic, fashion from French, piano from Italian, and canyon from Spanish.

More to Think About

Making Personal Connections Ask students to reread the section called "Architecture" and review the elements of Roman style: columns, domes, pediments, and arches. Ask them to identify any local buildings which show these elements of Roman influence. Have them bring in other examples from magazines and newspapers and create a display.

Vocabulary Activity Have students draw a visual expression of the title of each section. One example might be a drawing of the outline of Europe with several "heads" shown talking to represent "European Languages." Encourage students to be creative, but not deliberately tricky. Have them share their completed pictures with the class and discuss.

CHAPTER 6 ASSESSMENT

TERMS & NAMES

1. propaganda, p. 148
2. Nikita Khrushchev, p. 150
3. détente, p. 151
4. Mikhail Gorbachev, p. 154
5. ethnic cleansing, p. 157
6. Duma, p. 158
7. currency, p. 163
8. euro, p. 163
9. tariff, p. 163
10. standard of living, p. 163

REVIEW QUESTIONS

Possible Responses

1. The Soviets wanted to discourage ethnic identity so minorities would not seek independence.
2. The Soviet government controlled publications and the work of writers and artists, preventing people from learning about other nations.
3. through military force and economic control
4. A group of Soviet officials tried to undo Gorbachev's reforms, but public protest stopped them; republics in the Soviet Union declared their independence; the Soviet Union came to an end.
5. oil, coal, iron, lead, gold, natural gas
6. The EU unites 15 European countries in an economic and, increasingly, political union. It improves trade and reduces the possibility of conflicts among member countries.
7. no tariffs; free flow of goods, services, and people; political freedoms; job training; economic aid to poorer members; protection of rights by a Court of Justice
8. Paris, London, Madrid, Rome, Amsterdam

TERMS & NAMES

Explain the significance of each of the following:

1. propaganda
2. Nikita Khrushchev
3. détente
4. Mikhail Gorbachev
5. ethnic cleansing
6. Duma
7. currency
8. euro
9. tariff
10. standard of living

REVIEW QUESTIONS

The Soviet Union (pages 147–152)

1. Why did the Soviet government outlaw many cultural celebrations?
2. Explain why most Soviet citizens learned little about other nations around the world.
3. How did the Soviet Union maintain control over Eastern European countries?

Eastern Europe and Russia (pages 154–160)

4. How did the Soviet Union change during 1991?
5. List at least three of Russia's major natural resources.

The European Union (pages 161–165)

6. What is the importance of the European Union (EU)?
7. Name one benefit of being a member of the EU.
8. Identify at least three of Europe's major centers of the arts, business, and learning.

CRITICAL THINKING

Comparing

1. Using your completed chart from Reading Social Studies, p. 146, compare Eastern Europe under communism with Eastern Europe after communism.

Summarizing

2. Outline the changes to the Russian economy since the breakup of the Soviet Union.

Recognizing Important Details

3. What types of changes must Eastern European countries make in order to join the EU?

Visual Summary

1

The Soviet Union

- The Soviet Union's communist government controlled the lives of its citizens.
- Under Nikita Khrushchev, citizens began to have greater freedom.

2

Eastern Europe and Russia

- Today, independent nations once under Soviet rule are taking steps toward new economies and greater freedom.

3

The European Union

- Many European countries are members of an economic and political alliance called the European Union (EU).

CRITICAL THINKING: Possible Responses

1. Comparing

Under the Soviet Union, the governments of Eastern European countries were Communist; citizens' rights were strictly limited. The governments created in the 1990s were democratically elected and organized as parliamentary republics that protected the rights of citizens. Countries moved toward free-market economies.

2. Summarizing

The economy has changed from a command economy to a free-market economy. Now people can own land and have the right to start businesses. Foreign companies are encouraged to do business in Russia. The government no longer controls prices. Some people have grown wealthy; many remain poor, but standards of living have improved for many.

3. Recognizing Important Details

They must make environmental, legal, and economic improvements.

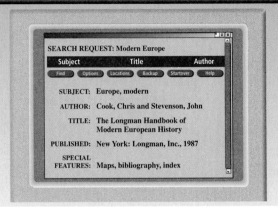

SEARCH REQUEST: Modern Europe

Subject	Title	Author

Find Options Locations Backup Startover Help

SUBJECT: Europe, modern

AUTHOR: Cook, Chris and Stevenson, John

TITLE: The Longman Handbook of Modern European History

PUBLISHED: New York: Longman, Inc., 1987

SPECIAL FEATURES: Maps, bibliography, index

SKILLBUILDER: Using an Electronic Card Catalog

1. Who wrote this book, and when was it published?
2. Will this book help you find other books related to the subject you researched?

FOCUS ON GEOGRAPHY

1. **Human-Environment Interaction** • Which nation or nations appear to have the largest amounts of farmland?
2. **Place** • Which nation or nations do not have coastal fishing resources?
3. **Place** • Which nation or nations appear to have the smallest amounts of forests?

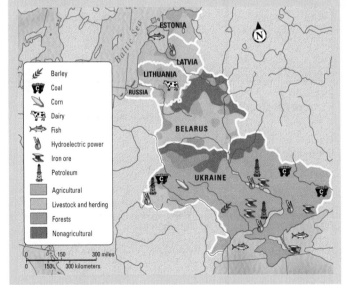

Barley
Coal
Corn
Dairy
Fish
Hydroelectric power
Iron ore
Petroleum
Agricultural
Livestock and herding
Forests
Nonagricultural

ESTONIA
LATVIA
LITHUANIA
RUSSIA
BELARUS
UKRAINE

Baltic Sea

0   150   300 miles
0   150   300 kilometers

CHAPTER PROJECTS

Interdisciplinary Activity: Math

Making an Inflation Chart This activity will help you to understand the effects of inflation on the economy. Look at a flier from a local grocery store. Write the names and prices of five food items in the first column of a chart. Then figure out and record what the prices would be for each item for the next two years.

- To find next year's price: multiply the original price by .03 (the rate of inflation). Add this to the original price.
- To find the following year's price: multiply next year's price by .03 (the rate of inflation). Add that to next year's price.

Cooperative Learning Activity

Creating a New Government Work in a group of three to five students to create a new class government and constitution.

- Assign each student a role in the new government, such as congressperson or president.
- Be sure to outline the responsibilities of each member.
- Write a brief constitution for your government. Include sections outlining basic rights, freedoms, and responsibilities of citizens.

 INTERNET ACTIVITY

Use the Internet to do research about the economy in Slovenia. Specifically look for information about the types of industries in Slovenia. What are its major imports and exports?

Writing About Economics Write a short report of your findings. Be sure to list the Web sites that you used to prepare your report.

For Internet links to support this activity, go to

 RESEARCH LINKS
CLASSZONE.COM

CHAPTER PROJECTS

Interdisciplinary Activity: Math

Making an Inflation Chart Before beginning this activity, have students ask their parents or other family members what the price of a quart of milk or a loaf of bread was 20 years ago. Then compare today's prices to what students' relatives once paid. Explain that inflation is a rise in prices caused by several economic factors, and that it varies from year to year. As a group, work out the future price of the first food listed on the chart. Then have students calculate the prices of the remaining foods and compare their answers.

Cooperative Learning Activity

Creating a New Government Before students begin writing their constitutions, review what they have learned about the newly formed governments of Eastern European countries after the breakup of the Soviet Union. List problems these new countries faced. Have students refer to their lists so their constitutions can address or avoid these problems.

INTERNET ACTIVITY

Discuss how students might locate information about Slovenia and its economy. Brainstorm possible keywords, Web sites, and search engines that students can use. You might have students create charts to help them organize and present the information they find. Demonstrate how to "bookmark" favorite Web sites so students have an ongoing record of helpful sites they have visited.

Skills Answers

Social Studies Skillbuilder
Possible Responses
1. Chris Cook and John Stevenson are the authors. It was published in 1987.
2. Yes; it includes a bibliography.

Focus on Geography
Possible Responses
1. Ukraine
2. Belarus
3. Estonia, Latvia, Lithuania, Russian enclave

Europe Today

	OVERVIEW	COPYMASTERS	INTEGRATED TECHNOLOGY
UNIT ATLAS AND CHAPTER RESOURCES	The students will learn about the government, economy, and culture of the United Kingdom, Sweden, France, Germany, and Poland.	**In-depth Resources: Unit 2** • Guided Reading Worksheets, pp. 47–51 • Skillbuilder Practice, p. 54 • Unit Atlas Activities, pp. 1–2 • Geography Workshop, pp. 61–62 **Reading Study Guide** (Spanish and English), pp. 52–63 **Outline Map Activities**	Power Presentations Electronic Teacher Tools Online Lesson Planner Chapter Summaries on CD Critical Thinking Transparencies CT13, 14
	KEY IDEAS		
SECTION 1 The United Kingdom pp. 173–174	• England, Scotland, Wales, and Northern Ireland make up the United Kingdom. • Trade is important to the British economy.	**In-depth Resources: Unit 2** • Guided Reading Worksheet, p. 47 • Reteaching Activity, p. 56 **Reading Study Guide** (Spanish and English), pp. 52–53	classzone.com Chapter Summaries on CD
SECTION 2 Sweden pp. 178–181	• Sweden's legislature, the Riksdag, makes the country's laws. • Outdoor recreation and the arts are popular in Sweden.	**In-depth Resources: Unit 2** • Guided Reading Worksheet, p. 48 • Reteaching Activity, p. 57 **Reading Study Guide** (Spanish and English), pp. 54–55	classzone.com Chapter Summaries on CD
SECTION 3 France pp. 184–187	• France's government and economy quickly recovered after World War II. • Nuclear power is the source of 75% of France's energy. • French culture centers around the capital city of Paris.	**In-depth Resources: Unit 2** • Guided Reading Worksheet, p. 49 • Reteaching Activity, p. 58 **Reading Study Guide** (Spanish and English), pp. 56–57	classzone.com Chapter Summaries on CD
SECTION 4 Germany pp. 188–191	• Both the division and the reunification of Germany presented many challenges. • Germany has a rich cultural heritage, especially in literature and music.	**In-depth Resources: Unit 2** • Guided Reading Worksheet, p. 50 • Reteaching Activity, p. 59 **Reading Study Guide** (Spanish and English), pp. 58–59	classzone.com Chapter Summaries on CD
SECTION 5 Poland pp. 194–197	• Solidarity, a workers' party, led the fight for political change in Poland. • Poland's constitution protects individual freedoms, including freedom of speech. • The Polish economy has struggled with the shift to a free-market system.	**In-depth Resources: Unit 2** • Guided Reading Worksheet, p. 51 • Reteaching Activity, p. 60 **Reading Study Guide** (Spanish and English), pp. 60–61	classzone.com Chapter Summaries on CD

KEY TO RESOURCES

 Audio

 CD-ROM

Copymaster

 Internet

 Overhead Transparency

Pupil's Edition

Teacher's Edition

 Video

ASSESSMENT OPTIONS

Chapter Assessment, pp. 198–199

Formal Assessment
• Chapter Tests: Forms A, B, C, pp. 100–111

Test Generator

Online Test Practice

Strategies for Test Preparation

Section Assessment, p. 177

Formal Assessment
• Section Quiz, p. 95

Integrated Assessment
• Rubric for writing a description

Test Generator

Test Practice Transparencies TT19

Section Assessment, p. 181

Formal Assessment
• Section Quiz, p. 96

Integrated Assessment
• Rubric for writing a description

Test Generator

Test Practice Transparencies TT20

Section Assessment, p. 187

Formal Assessment
• Section Quiz, p. 97

Integrated Assessment
• Rubric for drawing a portrait

Test Generator

Test Practice Transparencies TT21

Section Assessment, p. 191

Formal Assessment
• Section Quiz, p. 98

Integrated Assessment
• Rubric for writing a short story

Test Generator

Test Practice Transparencies TT22

Section Assessment, p. 197

Formal Assessment
• Section Quiz, p. 99

Integrated Assessment
• Rubric for writing a speech

Test Generator

Test Practice Transparencies TT23

RESOURCES FOR DIFFERENTIATING INSTRUCTION

Students Acquiring English/ESL

Reading Study Guide
(Spanish and English), pp. 52–63

Access for Students Acquiring English
Spanish Translations, pp. 49–60

TE Activities
• Prefixes, p. 190
• Identifying Sequence of Events, p. 195

Less Proficient Readers

Reading Study Guide
(Spanish and English), pp. 52–63

TE Activity
• Identifying Sequence of Events, p. 195

Gifted and Talented Students

TE Activity
• Forming and Supporting Opinions, p. 196

CROSS-CURRICULAR CONNECTIONS

Humanities
Lisandrelli, Elaine Slivinski. *Ignacy Jan Paderewski: Polish Pianist and Patriot.* Greensboro, NC: Morgan Reynolds, 1999. Portrait of a famous Polish hero.

Literature
Kuniczak, W. S., ed., *The Glass Mountain: Twenty-Eight Ancient Polish Folktales and Fables.* New York: Hippocrene Books, 1997. Literate anthology of rarely anthologized tales.

Banks, Lynne Reid. *Melusine: A Mystery.* New York: Avon Books, 1997. A teenage boy uncovers a mystery in the south of France.

Science
Linder, Greg. *Marie Curie: A Photo-Illustrated Biography.* Mankato, MN: Bridgestone Books, 1999. Polish scientist who discovered radium and won two Nobel Prizes.

History
Ayer, Eleanor H. *Poland: A Troubled Past, A New Start.* Tarrytown, NY: Benchmark Books, 1996. History, geography, daily life, culture, and customs.

Epler, Doris. *The Berlin Wall: How It Rose and Why It Fell.* Brookfield, CT: Millbrook Press, 1992. A history of the Wall, from its construction during the Cold War to its fall in 1989.

Lobel, Anita. *No Pretty Pictures: A Child of War.* New York: Avon Books, 2000. Life as a Polish Jew during WWII, and in Sweden for years after.

Popular Culture
Lalley, Linda. *The Volkswagen Beetle.* Mankato, MN: Riverfront Books, 1999. Traces the history, development, and design of this popular car.

Aronson, Marc. *Art Attack: A Short Cultural History of the Avant-Garde.* New York: Clarion Books, 1998. Traces the story of bohemians, radicals, hipsters, and hippies of the avant-garde movement begun in Paris.

ENRICHMENT ACTIVITIES

The following activities are especially suitable for classes following block schedules.

Teacher's Edition, pp. 174, 176, 179, 180, 186, 189, 192, 196

Pupil's Edition, pp. 177, 181, 187, 191, 197

Unit Atlas, pp. 54–63

Interdisciplinary Challenge, pp. 182–183

Outline Map Activities

INTEGRATED TECHNOLOGY

Go to **classzone.com** for lesson support and activities for Chapter 7.

BLOCK SCHEDULE LESSON PLAN OPTIONS: 90-MINUTE PERIOD

DAY 1

CHAPTER PREVIEW, pp. 170–171
Class Time 20 minutes

- **Hypothesize** Use the "What do you think?" questions in Focus On Geography on PE p. 171 to help students hypothesize about the challenges presented by environmental pollution.

SECTION 1, pp. 173–177
Class Time 40 minutes

- **Peer Competition** Divide the class into pairs. Assign each pair one of the Terms & Names for this section. Have pairs make up five questions that can be answered with the Term or Name. Have groups take turns asking the class their questions.
Class Time 20 minutes

- **Geography Skills** Help students use the map on PE p. 174 to identify the location of Great Britain, using latitude and longitude. Then divide the class into small groups. List the names of five cities on the map on the board and have groups identify their locations, using latitude and longitude.
Class Time 10 minutes

- **Brainstorming** Give students five minutes to list as many products as they can think of that the United States imports from the United Kingdom. Together as a class make a list on the board.
Class Time 10 minutes

SECTION 2, pp. 178–181
Class Time 30 minutes

- **Peer Teaching** Have pairs of students review the Main Idea for the section and find three details to support it. Then have each pair list two additional important ideas and trade lists with another group to find details.
Class Time 10 minutes

- **Section Assessment** Have students do the Section 2 Assessment.
Class Time 20 minutes

DAY 2

SECTION 3, pp. 184–187
Class Time 40 minutes

- **Small Groups** Divide the class into small groups. Assign each group one section objective on TE p. 184 to help them prepare a summary of this section. Remind students that when they summarize, they should include the main ideas and most important details in their own words. Reconvene as a whole class for discussion.

SECTION 4, pp. 188–191
Class Time 40 minutes

- **Decorating a Memorial** Use Focus & Motivate: Analyzing Motives on TE p. 188 to help the class imagine how Germans felt on the event of their reunification. Then divide the class into groups of two to three students and tell each group to plan and draw a sketch for a painting to decorate the Berlin Wall memorial. Have the class vote on which sketch they like best.

SECTION 5, pp. 193–197
Class Time 10 minutes

- **Comparing** Extend the Critical Thinking Activity on TE p. 195 by leading students in a discussion about the effects of guaranteeing even small ethnic groups a voice in government by reserving seats in parliament for them. Ask students if they think the United States would benefit by a similar arrangement.

DAY 3

SECTION 5, continued
Class Time 35 minutes

- **Creating a Chart** Divide the class into small groups. Have each group create a chart contrasting life in Poland before and after communism. Reconvene the class and have groups share their information for you to include in a master chart on the board.

CHAPTER 7 REVIEW AND ASSESSMENT, pp. 198–199
Class Time 55 minutes

- **Review** Have pairs of students review the information in the Visual Summary on p. 198 and find three details to support each statement.
Class Time 20 minutes

- **Assessment** Have students complete the Chapter 7 Assessment.
Class Time 35 minutes

TECHNOLOGY IN THE CLASSROOM

CHARTING AND GRAPHING DATA WITH A SPREADSHEET PROGRAM

Spreadsheet programs can be invaluable tools for analyzing and comparing data. Most spreadsheet programs allow the user to input numbers into rows and columns and to then create charts and graphs based on those numbers. These charts and graphs present the data in a visual manner that makes it easier to compare the data.

ACTIVITY OUTLINE

Objective Students will use a spreadsheet program to graph economic and social indicator numbers for Bosnia and Herzegovina, France, Germany, Poland, Sweden, the United Kingdom, and the United States. They will use a word processing program to write an analysis of the data.

Task Have students use an interactive Web site to generate economic and social data for these countries. Tell them to input this data into a spreadsheet and create column, bar, or line graphs to display the data. Have them conclude by writing paragraphs analyzing and explaining the graphs.

Class Time Two class periods

DIRECTIONS

1. Ask students to go to **classzone.com.** Have them click the boxes in the right-hand frame next to Bosnia and Herzegovina, France, Germany, Poland, Sweden, the United Kingdom, and the United States. Then have them click "Data Menu."

2. Ask students to select the following data fields: GDP per capita, life expectancy (women/men), illiteracy rate (total), and telephones.

3. Discuss the meanings of these four data fields, making sure students understand what each one measures. Ask them to explain what they think each type of data reveals about a country. For example, what does it mean for one country to have a lower life expectancy or GDP per capita than another country? Do students predict most of these countries will have figures that are higher than, lower than, or about the same as the United States? Why?

4. Have students click "View Info" to view the data. Ask them to look carefully at the chart and compare the data for the different countries. Why do they think Poland's figures are noticeably different? Explain that Bosnia and Herzegovina have recently been involved in a war. How do students think this fact might affect the data?

5. Assign each pair of students one of the categories: GDP per capita, life expectancy (women/men), or telephones. Have them enter the numbers for each country into a spreadsheet. The first (A) column should list the countries and the second (B) column should list the numbers.

6. Have students use the spreadsheet program's charting or graphing feature to create column, bar, or line graphs for the data they have entered. The charts should show the countries along the horizontal axis (x-axis) and the economic or social indicators up the vertical axis (y-axis).

7. Have students write paragraphs analyzing the data and hypothesizing reasons to explain it. In particular, they should explain why they think the data for several of the countries is similar to that of the United States. They should then explain why the data for two of the countries is significantly different.

CHAPTER 7 OBJECTIVE

Students will learn about the government, economy, and culture of the United Kingdom, Sweden, France, Germany, and Poland.

FOCUS ON VISUALS

Interpreting the Photograph Direct students' attention to the photograph of London's Piccadilly Circus. Ask students to identify both modern and historical elements in the scene. Tell students that the chapter describes Europe today, which is built on its long past. Which elements in the photograph show this connection?

Possible Responses Modern elements include shopping district and subway entrance. Historical elements include the old buildings and streets. Point out to students that the modern subway runs beneath the historical streets and the modern stores are located in the first floor of the old buildings.

Extension Have students work in groups, and assign each group a photograph of Stockholm, Paris, Berlin, or Warsaw. Ask the groups to identify and list both modern and historical elements.

CRITICAL THINKING ACTIVITY

Identifying Problems What problems may develop in a city trying to balance modern needs and methods with historical places, ideas, and customs? Direct students to look at the photograph again, and ask them to imagine what specific problems might have come up when the subway was being built in Piccadilly Circus.

Class Time 15 minutes

Europe Today

Place London's Piccadilly Circus is an intersection of major roads, with an Underground, or subway, stop at the center. Piccadilly Circus is a popular tourist attraction and shopping district.

170

Recommended Resources

BOOKS FOR THE TEACHER
Knab, Sophie Hodorowicz. *Polish Customs, Traditions, and Folklore.* New York: Hippocrene Books, 1993. Folklore resources are particularly good. Lord, Richard. *Germany.* Milwaukee: G. Stevens, 1999. Geography, history, and economics of unified Germany.

Zickgraf, Ralph. *Sweden (Major World Nations).* Philadelphia: Chelsea House Publishing, 1997. Overview of Sweden's history, government, and economy.

VIDEOS
Wondrous Kingdom: England, Scotland, and Ireland. Questar, 1999. One-hour guided tour.

INTERNET
For more information about modern Europe, visit **classzone.com.**

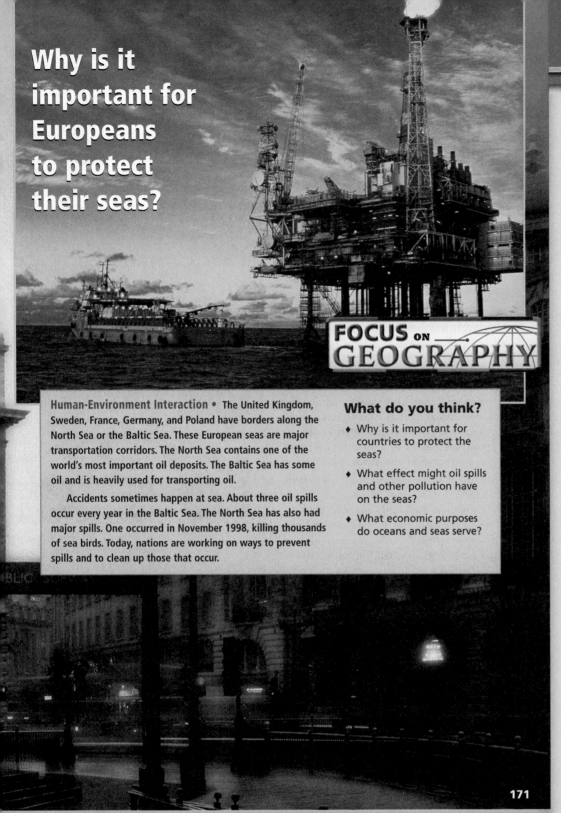

Why is it important for Europeans to protect their seas?

FOCUS ON GEOGRAPHY

Human-Environment Interaction • The United Kingdom, Sweden, France, Germany, and Poland have borders along the North Sea or the Baltic Sea. These European seas are major transportation corridors. The North Sea contains one of the world's most important oil deposits. The Baltic Sea has some oil and is heavily used for transporting oil.

Accidents sometimes happen at sea. About three oil spills occur every year in the Baltic Sea. The North Sea has also had major spills. One occurred in November 1998, killing thousands of sea birds. Today, nations are working on ways to prevent spills and to clean up those that occur.

What do you think?

♦ Why is it important for countries to protect the seas?

♦ What effect might oil spills and other pollution have on the seas?

♦ What economic purposes do oceans and seas serve?

171

FOCUS ON GEOGRAPHY

Objectives

• To help students recognize the risks to the environment caused by economic development

• To help students understand the relationship between economics and geography

What Do You Think?

1. Invite students to discuss what they like about seas and oceans. Ask why these bodies of water are important.

2. Guide a discussion of the effects of pollution on the sea. Ask how oil spills might affect humans and other animals.

3. Have students list the economic benefits countries get from the seas, such as food, recreation, and trade.

Why is it important for Europeans to protect their seas?

Have students consider the many things Europeans get from the sea. Guide them to understand that the seas provide many economic benefits, including oil reserves and transportation corridors.

MAKING GEOGRAPHIC CONNECTIONS

Have students discuss the importance of oceans and seas, as well as rivers, lakes, and streams, to the United States. Ask them why it is also important for us to protect our water resources.

Implementing the National Geography Standards

Standard 11 Draw some general conclusions about how transportation and communication innovations affect patterns of economic interaction

Objective To give a presentation about how a transportation or communication innovation will affect the economy

Class Time 40 minutes

Task Ask students to put together a presentation to explain to prospective clients how a new service will affect patterns of economic interaction. Have students pretend that they are developing one of the following services: refrigerated railroad cars, airfreight services,

telephone services, fax transmission services, or satellite-based communication systems.

Evaluation Students should use at least two drawings or charts to convey their ideas.

BEFORE YOU READ
What Do You Know?

Ask students to brainstorm one thing they associate with the European countries of Great Britain, Sweden, France, Germany, and Poland. Encourage them to think of products, ideas, people, or major events. Write their ideas on the board, and ask students to compare the items listed for each country. Are there more items for one country than others? How do the items themselves compare? Ask students to notice which country has the fewest items. Have students speculate about why the class knows the least about that country.

What Do You Want to Know?

Have each student make a chart with the headings What I Want to Know and What I Learned in their notebooks. Then ask students to work in pairs to develop questions they hope to have answered about the European countries covered in this chapter. They can record their questions in the first column of their chart, and, as they read the chapter, record the facts and ideas they learn in the second column.

READ AND TAKE NOTES

Reading Strategy: Comparing Explain to students that this chart compares five European countries in several ways. Point out that when it is completed, they will have a useful tool for understanding the differences and similarities of these countries.

 In-depth Resources: Unit 2
• Guided Reading Worksheets, pp. 47–51

BEFORE YOU READ
▶▶ What Do You Know?

Did you know that from the end of WW II until 1990, Germany was two separate countries and Poland was controlled by the Soviet Union? Do you have relatives or friends who come from the United Kingdom, Sweden, France, Germany, or Poland? Have you ever seen the Queen of England or the Pope, who is from Poland, on television? Have you heard of the Nobel Prize, which is awarded in Sweden? Think about what you have learned in other classes, what you have read, and what you have heard or seen in the news about these countries.

▶▶ What Do You Want to Know?

Consider what you know about the countries covered in Chapter 7. In your notebook, record what you hope to learn from this chapter.

Region • Sweden's Nobel Prize honors great achievements worldwide. ▲

READ AND TAKE NOTES

Reading Strategy: Comparing Comparing is a useful strategy for evaluating two or more similar subjects. Making comparisons also helps you to better understand what you have learned. Use the chart below to compare information about the United Kingdom, Sweden, France, Germany, and Poland.

• Copy the chart into your notebook.
• As you read, look for information for each category.
• Record details under the appropriate headings.

Movement • The German-made Volkswagen Beetle is the best-selling car ever. ▲

Country	Physical Geography	Government	Economy	Culture	Interesting Facts
United Kingdom	islands	constitutional monarchy	manufacturing, trade	music, literature	home of J. K. Rowling
Sweden	Scandinavian Peninsula	constitutional monarchy	engineering, communications	Nobel Prize	Workers get long vacations.
France	agricultural land	parliamentary republic	tourism	museums, literature	home to many artists
Germany	North and Baltic seas	democratic republic	rebuilt eastern part	music, literature	complex machinery
Poland	coast along Baltic Sea	parliamentary republic	free market	literature	publications sold tax-free

172 CHAPTER 7

Teaching Strategy

Reading the Chapter This is a thematic chapter focusing on the government structures, economies, unique cultures, and recent history of the United Kingdom, Sweden, France, Germany, and Poland. Ask students to compare and contrast each of these countries as they read. Encourage them to consider how history and geography help explain the similarities and differences.

Integrated Assessment The Chapter Assessment on page 199 describes several activities for integrated assessment. You may wish to have students work on these activities during the course of the chapter and then present them at the end.

The United Kingdom

SECTION 1

TERMS & NAMES
London
secede
Good Friday
  Accord
Charles Dickens

MAIN IDEA

The United Kingdom is a small nation in Western Europe with a history of colonization.

WHY IT MATTERS NOW

British economic, political, and cultural traditions have influenced nations around the world.

SECTION OBJECTIVES

1. To identify the four regions of the United Kingdom
2. To describe the cultural heritage of the United Kingdom
3. To explain the British economy

SKILLBUILDER
• Interpreting a Map, p. 174

CRITICAL THINKING
• Identifying Problems, p. 175

FOCUS & MOTIVATE
WARM-UP

Making Inferences Have students read <u>Dateline</u> and discuss British sports.

1. How are the British and Americans alike and different in their interest in soccer?
2. How would you describe British fans?

INSTRUCT: Objective ❶

A Kingdom of Four Political Regions

• What four regions make up the United Kingdom? Scotland, England, Wales, Northern Ireland
• Who actually leads the government in the United Kingdom? the prime minister

In-depth Resources: Unit 2
• Guided Reading Worksheet, p. 47

Reading Study Guide
(Spanish and English), pp. 52–53

DATELINE EXTRA

BARCELONA, SPAIN, MAY 30, 1999

They did it! Manchester United won the triple crown of soccer. The British fans here are going wild, and their excitement is easy to understand. Manchester United is only the third soccer team to win its league championship, cup titles, and the Champions League final.

Football, or "soccer" as Americans call it, is the world's most popular sport. The British invented a form of the game, called "mob football," in the 1300s. Back then, the playing field was the size of a small town, and there might have been as many as 500 players. A set of rules for the game was developed in 1863. Today, football is the national pastime in the United Kingdom.

Region • Manchester United celebrates after winning soccer's triple crown. ▲

A Kingdom of Four Political Regions ❶

The United Kingdom is a small island nation of Western Europe. Its culture has had an enormous impact on the world. The nation's official name is the United Kingdom of Great Britain and Northern Ireland. **London,** located in southeastern England, is the capital.

Vocabulary
Great Britain: the name for the island that contains Scotland, England, and Wales

---

Program Resources

In-depth Resources: Unit 2
• Guided Reading Worksheet, p. 47
• Reteaching Activity, p. 56

Reading Study Guide
(Spanish and English), pp. 52–53

Formal Assessment
• Section Quiz, p. 95

Integrated Assessment
• Rubric for writing a description

Outline Map Activities

Access for Students Acquiring English
• Guided Reading Worksheet, p. 49

Technology Resources
classzone.com

TEST-TAKING RESOURCES
⚓ Strategies for Test Preparation
⚓ Test Practice Transparencies
⚓ Online Test Practice

Vocabulary

monarchy:
government by
king or queen

FOCUS ON VISUALS

Interpreting the Map Instruct students to look at the map. Ask them what two bodies of water separate England from France. What main waterway lies between England and Ireland? What ocean lies to the north of the United Kingdom?

Responses English Channel, Strait of Dover; Irish Sea; North Atlantic Ocean

Extension Ask students to compare the size of the United Kingdom with their own state. They can use the scale of miles on this map to estimate the length and width of Britain. Have them turn to page 54 of the Unit Atlas and use the scale of miles to find the length and width of their state.

United Kingdom

England

Scotland

Wales

Northern Ireland

Four different political regions make up the United Kingdom: Scotland, England, Wales, and Northern Ireland (see the map below). The British monarchy has ruled over the four regions for hundreds of years.

National Government Today, the government of the United Kingdom is a constitutional monarchy. The British monarch is a symbol of power rather than an actual ruler. The power to govern belongs to Parliament, which is the national lawmaking body.

The British Parliament has two parts. The House of Lords is made up of nobles. Elected representatives make up the House of Commons. The House of Commons is the more powerful of the two houses.

The prime minister leads the government. He or she is usually the leader of the political party that wins the most seats in the House of Commons. The other political parties go into "opposition," which means their role is to question government policies.

Regional Government in Great Britain Recently, the national government of the United Kingdom has returned some self-rule to some regions of Great Britain. In the late 1990s, voters in Wales approved plans for their own assembly, or body of lawmakers. Also at this time, the Scots voted to create their own parliament. Both Wales's assembly and Scotland's parliament met for the first time in 1999.

Reading
Social Studies

A. Clarifying
Who is the head of government in the United Kingdom?

Reading Social Studies
A. Possible Answer
The prime minister is the head of government.

The United Kingdom Today

National boundary
Regional boundary
⊛ National capital
• Other city

GEOGRAPHY SKILLBUILDER:
Interpreting a Map

1. **Location** • Which region of the United Kingdom is on a different island?
2. **Location** • Which body of water separates the United Kingdom from France?

Geography Skillbuilder Answers
1. Northern Ireland
2. English Channel

174 CHAPTER 7

Activity Options

Multiple Learning Styles: Logical

Block Scheduling

Class Time 30 minutes

Task Creating a chart comparing and contrasting the governments of the United Kingdom and the United States

Purpose To understand

similarities and differences in the structures of governments

Supplies Needed
• Writing paper
• Pencils or pens
• Ruler

Activity Have students create a chart comparing the governments of the United States and the United Kingdom. Suggest that they compare the heads of government and the legislative bodies for both nations. They might add Sweden, France, Germany, and Poland as they read this chapter. Have students share their charts in class.

Governing Northern Ireland Throughout the 20th century, there were conflicts in Northern Ireland between Irish Catholic nationalists and Irish Protestants who supported the government of the United Kingdom. In fact, during the 1960s, many Irish Catholics wanted Northern Ireland to **secede,** or withdraw from, the United Kingdom. They hoped to unite Northern Ireland with the Republic of Ireland. Irish Protestants—a majority in the region—generally wanted to remain part of the United Kingdom.

In 1969, riots broke out, and the British government sent in troops to stop them. Violence between groups of Protestants and Catholics continued for almost 30 years. In 1998, representatives from both sides signed the **Good Friday Accord.** This agreement set up the Northern Ireland Assembly, which represents both Catholic and Protestant voters. For this government to succeed in Northern Ireland, however, the former enemies will need to work together.

CRITICAL THINKING ACTIVITY

Identifying Problems Have students work individually to list problems they identify in the discussion of Northern Ireland, including the information given as Background. Then ask them to discuss the following question: Why is it so difficult to govern Northern Ireland? List their responses on the chalkboard.

Class Time 10 minutes

The WORLD'S HERITAGE

The Houses of Parliament rest on the site of Westminster Palace, which was built in the 11th century by William II, the son of William the Conqueror. Only Westminster Hall, which was completed in 1097, survives from the original buildings. It has been in continuous use for more than 900 years. The clock, in contrast, is relatively new. It was installed in 1859. There are four clock faces, each 23 feet square. Each number is two feet high and each minute hand is 14 feet long. The clock is known for its extreme accuracy. The bell, Big Ben, came from the original Westminster Palace and was refurbished for installation with the clock.

The WORLD'S HERITAGE

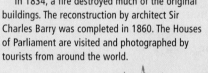

Parliament The Houses of Parliament have been used by the British government since 1547. The buildings are located in London, alongside the River Thames (tems). They include the House of Commons, the House of Lords, and Westminster Hall. One of the most famous parts of this complex is the clock tower. Commonly called "Big Ben," this is actually the name of the 13-ton bell inside the tower, not the tower itself.

In 1834, a fire destroyed much of the original buildings. The reconstruction by architect Sir Charles Barry was completed in 1860. The Houses of Parliament are visited and photographed by tourists from around the world.

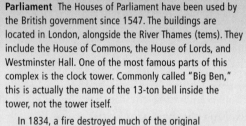

When Parliament is in session, the Union Jack flies from Victoria Tower.

House of Lords Chamber

Westminster Hall is more than 900 years old.

The clock tower that holds Big Ben is 316 feet high.

House of Commons Chamber

Activity Options

Interdisciplinary Link: Government

Class Time One class period

Task Writing arguments in support of and opposition to regional self-rule

Purpose To compare advantages and disadvantages of regional self-rule

Supplies Needed
• Writing paper
• Pens or pencils

Activity Guide a discussion to help students explore some advantages and disadvantages of regional self-rule. Encourage them to make comparisons with federal and state government in the United States. List their ideas on the board. Assign half the class to write a paragraph in support of regional self-rule, and assign the other half to write in opposition. Invite volunteers to read their paragraphs in class. Discuss.

Region • London's New Globe Theater is a replica of the 17th-century playhouse that originally hosted William Shakespeare's works. ◄

INSTRUCT: Objective ②

Cultural Heritage

- Why did the United Kingdom's culture spread to so many parts of the world? The United Kingdom was an imperial power with colonies around the world.

- Who are some important modern British musicians? Beatles, Rolling Stones, Elton John, Sting, Dido

- Who are some important British writers? William Shakespeare, Mary Shelley, Sir Arthur Conan Doyle, Charles Dickens, Virginia Woolf, George Orwell, C. S. Lewis, J. K. Rowling

MORE ABOUT...
Charles Dickens

Charles Dickens (1812–1870) is widely recognized as a major figure in English literature. As a child, he enjoyed reading adventure stories, fairy tales, and novels. In the 1820s, he became a newspaper reporter, covering Parliament debates and writing feature stories. Dickens's keen observation skills, understanding of humanity, and sense of humor contributed to his success as a writer. Some books by Dickens include *David Copperfield* and *Great Expectations.*

Cultural Heritage ②

The United Kingdom has a rich cultural heritage that includes the great Renaissance playwright William Shakespeare. With a long history as an imperial power, the nation has been exporting its culture around the world for hundreds of years. For example, India, Canada, and other former British colonies modeled their governments on the British parliamentary system. British culture has also set trends in sports, music, and literature.

Music British music influenced the early music of Canada and the United States, both former British colonies. One British tune long familiar to people in the United States is "God Save the Queen." You probably know it as "My Country, 'Tis of Thee." Several countries have put the words of their national anthems to this traditional British melody.

During the 1960s, many British musical groups—including the Beatles and the Rolling Stones—dominated music charts around the world. In later decades, other British singers, including Elton John, Sting, and Dido, became popular favorites.

Literature The best-known cultural export of the United Kingdom, aside from the English language itself, may be literature. In the 19th century, Mary Shelley dreamed up Frankenstein's monster, and Sir Arthur Conan Doyle first wrote about Sherlock Holmes. Another popular author of the time was **Charles Dickens** (1812–1870), who wrote *Oliver Twist* and *A Christmas Carol.*

Region • In the early 1960s, the Beatles became wildly popular, not only in the United Kingdom, but also around the world. ▼

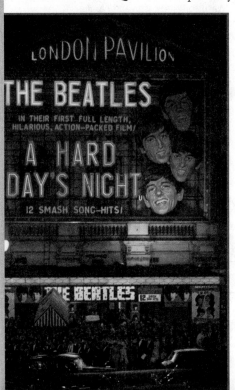

Activity Options

Skillbuilder Mini-Lesson: Using an Electronic Card Catalog   🅱 Block Scheduling

Explaining the Skill Remind students that books, magazines, and other library resources are listed in the library's electronic card catalog. These resources can be found by looking for the title, the author's name, or the subject.

Applying the Skill Assign individual students topics from the discussion of Britain's cultural heritage. Ask each to find library resources

for his or her topic, using the title, author's name, or subject catalogs. For example, one student might be assigned to find works about William Shakespeare. Another might be asked to find books written by Shakespeare. Have students make lists of their findings. In class discussion, ask them to summarize their discoveries about the use of the electronic card catalog.

Reading
Social Studies

B. Recognizing Important Details Why was the United Kingdom able to spread British culture across the world?

Reading Social Studies
B. Possible Answer

It has a long history as an imperial power.

Two gifted British writers of the 20th century are Virginia Woolf and George Orwell. Modern British authors have also given the world many popular stories for young people. They include C. S. Lewis, who wrote *The Chronicles of Narnia*, and J. K. Rowling, who created the Harry Potter books.

The British Economy

The United Kingdom is an important trading and financial center. Many British citizens also make their living in mining and manufacturing. Factories in the United Kingdom turn out a variety of products ranging from china to sports cars. The nation has plenty of coal, natural gas, and oil to fuel its factories, but it has few other natural resources.

The need for imported goods makes trade another major industry of the United Kingdom. The nation imports many raw materials used in manufacturing. It also imports food, because the farms of this nation produce only enough to feed about two-thirds of its large population.

Region • J. K. Rowling's Harry Potter books have captured the imaginations of children worldwide. ▲

SECTION 1 ASSESSMENT

Terms & Names

1. **Identify:**   (a) London   (b) secede
                (c) Good Friday Accord   (d) Charles Dickens

Taking Notes

2. Use a chart like this one to describe the major aspects of the United Kingdom's modern government, economy, and culture.

Modern United Kingdom	
Government	
Economy	
Culture	

Main Ideas

3. (a) Identify the four regions that make up the United Kingdom.

(b) What role does the British monarch play in the government of the modern United Kingdom?

(c) What impact has the culture of the United Kingdom had on its colonies and on other parts of the world?

Critical Thinking

4. **Analyzing Issues**

Why do you think the conflict in Northern Ireland is so difficult to resolve?

Think About

- differences in religious beliefs
- recent changes in British regional governments
- the long period of continued violence

 ACTIVITY -OPTION-   Reread the information about British football from the "Dateline" feature that opens the section. Write a **description** of a sport that interests you.

INSTRUCT: Objective ❸

The British Economy

- What natural resources are found in the United Kingdom? coal, natural gas, oil

- Why is trade an important industry of the United Kingdom? The country must import food and raw materials for manufacturing.

ASSESS & RETEACH

Reading Social Studies Have students add details from Section 1 to the chart on page 172.

 Formal Assessment
- Section Quiz, p. 95

RETEACHING ACTIVITY

Have pairs of students write one main-idea sentence for the discussion following each section heading. Then have students meet in groups to compare sentences and to decide on the best statement of each main idea.

 In-depth Resources: Unit 2
- Reteaching Activity, p. 56

Access for Students Acquiring English
- Reteaching Activity, p. 56

Section 1 Assessment

1. Terms & Names

a. London, p. 173
b. secede, p. 175
c. Good Friday Accord, p. 175
d. Charles Dickens, p. 176

2. Taking Notes

Modern United Kingdom	
Government	constitutional monarchy; Parliament governs; prime minister leads government
Economy	based on trade and finance; few natural resources; imports raw materials/food
Culture	cultural exports: English language, government, music, literature

3. Main Ideas

a. England, Wales, Scotland, Northern Ireland
b. The monarch is a symbol of power.
c. It has influenced language, government, music, and literature throughout the world.

4. Critical Thinking

People fear loss of religious freedom, distrust one another, and cannot forget past experiences.

ACTIVITY OPTION

 Integrated Assessment
- Rubric for writing a description

Sweden

TERMS & NAMES
Riksdag
ombudsman
armed neutrality
hydroelectricity
acid rain
skerry

SECTION OBJECTIVES

1. To identify governmental, economic, and environmental issues of Sweden

2. To describe Sweden's culture

SKILLBUILDER
• Interpreting a Map, p. 179

CRITICAL THINKING
• Analyzing Issues, p. 179
• Analyzing Causes, p. 180

FOCUS & MOTIVATE
WARM-UP

Drawing Conclusions After students read Dateline, discuss the Nobel Prize.

1. Why do you think Alfred Nobel established the Nobel Prize?

2. Why do you think the Nobel Prize has become so important?

INSTRUCT: Objective ❶

Sweden's Government/The Economy and the Environment

• What legislative body makes the laws of Sweden? Riksdag

• What environmental problems does Sweden face? safe sources for electrical power, acid rain

 In-depth Resources: Unit 2
• Guided Reading Worksheet, p. 48

 Reading Study Guide
(Spanish and English), pp. 54–55

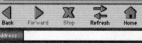

MAIN IDEA	WHY IT MATTERS NOW
Sweden offers its people a high standard of living, although it also faces environmental problems.	Modern Sweden is dealing with environmental issues that affect many countries around the world.

DATELINE

STOCKHOLM, SWEDEN, DECEMBER 4, 2001—This week in Stockholm, Sweden's capital, hundreds of past winners of the Nobel Prize gather to celebrate the centennial, or 100th anniversary, of this award. Concerts, lectures, and banquets lead up to the award ceremony in Stockholm City Hall on December 10.

The first Nobel Prize ceremony was held in Stockholm in 1901. Since then, awards in physics, chemistry, economics, medicine, literature, and peace have gone to more than 700 people, representing every inhabited continent. Besides achieving worldwide honor and fame, the winners receive a medal and a cash prize. The award was established at the request of Alfred Nobel (1833–1896), a Swedish chemist and millionaire who invented dynamite.

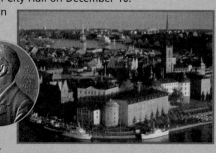

Place • Stockholm, Sweden, hosts events celebrating the 100th anniversary of the Nobel Prize. ▲

Sweden's Government ❶

Sweden is famous for the Nobel Prize, but it is also one of the most prosperous and beautiful countries in Europe. The Kingdom of Sweden shares the Scandinavian Peninsula with Norway in Northern Europe (see the map on page 179). The country is a constitutional monarchy, meaning that the Swedish monarch has only ceremonial powers. He or she cannot make laws. Instead, the people elect representatives to four-year terms in the Swedish parliament, called the **Riksdag** (RIHKS·dahg).

178 CHAPTER 7

Program Resources

 In-depth Resources: Unit 2
• Guided Reading Worksheet, p. 48
• Reteaching Activity, p. 57

 Reading Study Guide
(Spanish and English), pp. 54–55

 Formal Assessment
• Section Quiz, p. 96

Integrated Assessment
• Rubric for writing a description

 Outline Map Activities

 Access for Students Acquiring English
• Guided Reading Worksheet, p. 50

Technology Resources
classzone.com

TEST-TAKING RESOURCES
⚓ Strategies for Test Preparation
⚓ Test Practice Transparencies
🖱 Online Test Practice

The Riksdag The 349 members of the Riksdag nominate Sweden's prime minister. They also appoint ombudsmen. **Ombudsmen** are officials who protect citizens' rights and make sure that the Swedish courts and civil service follow the law.

Reading Social Studies
A. Possible Answer
Sweden tries not to form military alliances. It is a strong supporter of the United Nations.

Region • Women are active in Swedish government. ▶

Swedish citizens vote to determine how many members of each political party serve in the Riksdag. Before 1976, the Social Democratic Labour Party had been in power for nearly 44 years. Today, the Swedish government includes four other parties.

Foreign Policy Since World War I, Sweden's foreign policy has been one of **armed neutrality.** This means that in times of war, the country has its own military forces but does not take sides in other nations' conflicts.

Even during peacetime, the Swedish government tries not to form military alliances. Unless Sweden is directly attacked, it will not become involved in war. The country is a strong supporter of the United Nations.

Reading
Social Studies

A. Synthesizing How does Sweden's neutrality affect its foreign relations?

The Economy and the Environment ❶

Privately owned businesses and international trade are important to Sweden's economy. It exports many goods, including metals, minerals, and wood. Engineering and communications are major industries. The automobile industry also provides many jobs.

Geography Skillbuilder Answers
1. Norway
2. Stockholm

Sweden Today

National boundary
⊛ National capital
• Other city

100 miles
100 kilometers

Kiruna
Torneälven
Arctic Circle
Norwegian Sea
65°N
SCANDINAVIA
Umeälven
SWEDEN
Sundsvall
Ljusnan
FINLAND
Gulf of Bothnia
Falun
Gävle
NORWAY
N
60°N
Karlstad
Uppsala
Örebro
Stockholm
ESTONIA
Göteborg
Gotland
Visby
BALTIC SEA
Växjö
LATVIA
Halmstad
Kalmar
Öland
DENMARK
Helsingborg
Malmö
LITHUANIA

GEOGRAPHY SKILLBUILDER:
Interpreting a Map
1. **Location** • Which country shares the Scandinavian Peninsula with Sweden?
2. **Region** • What is the national capital of Sweden?

Europe Today **179**

The **Swedish Labor Force** After World War II, many Swedes left their towns and villages to find work in the large cities in the south. Today, more than 80 percent of the population lives in these urban areas. Much of Sweden's labor force is highly educated and enjoys a high standard of living.

Power Sources Hydroelectricity, or power generated by water, is the main source of electrical power in Sweden. Nuclear power is also widely used. The Swedish government is looking into other, safer sources of energy, which include solar- and wind-powered energy.

Acid Rain Sweden and its neighboring countries share similar environmental problems. One of the most severe problems is **acid rain.** Acid rain occurs when air pollutants come back to Earth in the form of precipitation. These pollutants may soon poison many trees throughout the region. Sweden and neighboring countries are working to clean up the environment by trying to control air pollutants produced by cars and factories.

Place • Many in Sweden's highly educated labor force work in the high-tech and engineering industries. ▲

Reading
Social Studies

B. Clarifying
What causes acid rain?

CRITICAL THINKING ACTIVITY

Analyzing Causes Guide a discussion of Sweden's sources of power. Ask students why the Swedish government is looking for power sources other than nuclear power. Discuss why solar- and wind-powered energy sources are being investigated. Students might suggest that such alternative sources of energy may be safer for the environment.

Class Time 10 minutes

INSTRUCT: Objective **2**

Daily Life and Culture

- In what way are Swedes a homogeneous people? Most are Caucasian, 90 percent are Lutherans, and most speak Swedish.

- What types of recreation are popular in Sweden? cross-country and downhill skiing, skating, ice hockey, ice fishing, hiking, camping, tennis, soccer, and outdoor performances

- In what areas has Sweden contributed to world culture? drama, literature, film

Region •
December 13 is
St. Lucia's Day,
one of Sweden's
most important
Christian
holidays. ▼

Daily Life and Culture **2**

Culturally and ethnically, Sweden is primarily a homogeneous country. Ninety percent of the population are native to Sweden and are members of the Lutheran Church of Sweden. The majority of people speak Swedish.

Since World War II, immigrants from Turkey, Greece, and other countries have brought some cultural diversity to Sweden's population. Today, about one in nine people living in Sweden is an immigrant or the child of an immigrant.

Recreation Workers in Sweden have many benefits, including long vacations. The Swedes love taking time to enjoy both winter and summer sports. Sweden, with its cold weather and many hills and mountains, is a great place for cross-country and downhill skiing. Skating, hockey, and ice fishing are also popular.

Vocabulary

homogeneous:
the same
throughout

Reading Social
Studies
B. Possible
Answer
air pollutants
returning to
Earth in the
form of rain

180 CHAPTER 7

Activity Options

Multiple Learning Styles: Visual

Class Time One class period

Task Creating a bulletin board display

Purpose To describe popular sports in Sweden

Supplies Needed
- Library or Internet resources
- Writing and drawing paper
- Pencils, pens, markers

B Block Scheduling

Activity Point out to students that the people of Sweden enjoy many sports throughout the year. Have students work in small groups and create a bulletin board display that describes these sports. Students should first do research. They should then plan a display that explains the sport, including equipment, rules, and so on. Their display should include diagrams, pictures, and other graphic organizers, as well as brief descriptions.

Place • Sweden's cold winters have made downhill and cross-country skiing popular. ▶

Many small islands, called **skerries,** dot the Swedish coast. In the summer, many people visit these islands to hike, camp, and fish. Tennis, soccer, and outdoor performances such as concerts are popular as well.

Contributions to World Culture Sweden is well-known for its contributions to drama, literature, and film. The late-19th-century and early 20th-century plays of August Strindberg are produced all over the world. Astrid Lindgren's children's books, including *Pippi Longstocking* (1945), still delight readers everywhere. Ingmar Bergman is famous for the many great films he directed.

SECTION ② ASSESSMENT

Terms & Names

1. Identify: (a) Riksdag   (b) ombudsman   (c) armed neutrality
          (d) hydroelectricity   (e) acid rain   (f) skerry

Taking Notes

2. Use a spider map like this one to outline the major aspects of Sweden's government, economy, and culture.

Government — Economy
Modern Sweden
Culture

Main Ideas

3. (a) On which European peninsula is Sweden located? What other country shares this peninsula?

(b) What happened to the Swedish labor force after World War II?

(c) How has immigration since World War II changed the population of Sweden?

Critical Thinking

4. Evaluating Decisions

What do you think might be the advantages and disadvantages of armed neutrality for Sweden?

Think About

- Sweden's location
- the damage and expense of war
- the benefits of alliances

ACTIVITY -OPTION-   Reread the "Dateline" feature at the beginning of this section. Write a short **description** of which category you would like to earn a Nobel Prize in and why.

Europe Today **181**

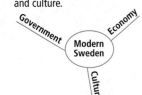

Teacher's Edition **181**

OBJECTIVE

Students work cooperatively to explore Florence at the time of the Renaissance.

PROCEDURE

In addition to the Data File, provide resources such as biographies, art books, documentary films, and magazine articles. Encourage students to divide the responsibilities of researching, writing, and presenting monologues. Some students may prefer to write journal entries individually. Give these students a chance to exchange solutions and offer constructive criticism.

 Block Scheduling

LANGUAGE ARTS CHALLENGE

Class Time 50 minutes

Suggest that students explore biographies and histories of the period. For the second option, journals or histories of daily life might be helpful. Invite volunteers to read their monologues and journal entries aloud.

Possible Solutions

Monologues should capture the key events in the figure's life and emphasize the figure's contributions. Presenters should bring the character to life. Journal entries should cover topics, such as guilds, the role of the apprentice, or the job description of the master, and include details of daily life.

Interdisciplinary Challenge

Spend a Day in Renaissance Florence

You are a traveler visiting Florence, Italy, in the year 1505. It is exciting to be here now. All over Europe, people have heard about the Renaissance, or cultural rebirth, that is taking place in this beautiful city. Artists, architects, writers, and scientists are turning out brilliant work. In the day you spend here, you want to learn about this new cultural movement. You want to be able to tell people at home about Renaissance Florence.

COOPERATIVE LEARNING On these pages are challenges you will encounter as you tour Renaissance Florence. Working with a small group, choose one of these challenges to solve. Divide the work among group members. Look for helpful information in the Data File. Keep in mind that you will present your solution to the class.

LANGUAGE ARTS CHALLENGE

"Florence is home to brilliant artists and writers."

Why did the Renaissance start here? Florence is home to brilliant artists and writers. Successful merchants and craftworkers, along with several powerful families, have made the city rich. Many wealthy people are patrons, or sponsors, of artists' work. You are curious about the people of Florence. Who are the leading figures? What is life like here? Choose one of these options to discover the answers. Use the Data File for help.

ACTIVITIES

1. Choose one major figure who lived in Florence during the Renaissance and research his or her life. Then write a short first-person monologue in which, speaking as that person, you describe your life and work.

2. Imagine you are an ordinary young Florentine living in 1505—for example, a goldsmith's apprentice. Write journal entries for a week in your life.

Standards for Evaluation

LANGUAGE ARTS CHALLENGE

Option 1 Monologues should
• highlight major events in the figure's life.
• explain the figure's significance.

Option 2 Journal entries should
• describe the roles of apprentice and master.
• capture details of life in Renaissance times.

SCIENCE CHALLENGE

Option 1 Diagrams should
• accurately reproduce the Duomo.
• show use of vaults and supporting walls.

Option 2 Interview questions should
• reflect Brunelleschi's contributions to architecture and Florence.

ARTS CHALLENGE

Option 1 Slide shows should
• include 5–6 major works of art.
• explain why they reflect the Renaissance.

Option 2 Maps should
• include major art sites in Florence.
• highlight works of art to be seen at those sites.

LANDMARKS OF RENAISSANCE FLORENCE

- Florence is built on both sides of the **Arno River**. Its population during the Renaissance was about 100,000. Most of the famous buildings are on the right bank. Besides its artists, Renaissance Florence was known for its craftworkers, such as goldsmiths and leatherworkers.

- The **Duomo** stands on the Piazza del Duomo, an open square. In 1418, Filippo Brunelleschi won a contest to build a dome over the unfinished church. He invented new methods and machines to build it. As in earlier domes, vaults or pointed arches support the dome. Brunelleschi added a circular support wall, called a drum, to build it higher.

- The **Ponte Vecchio** ("Old Bridge"), built in 1345, is one of several bridges across the Arno River. Shops, especially those of goldsmiths, line both sides of the bridge.

- The **Pitti Palace**, built in 1458, is on the left bank of the river.

MAJOR FIGURES OF THE RENAISSANCE

- **Filippo Brunelleschi** (1377–1446), architect of the Duomo and the Pitti Palace.

- **Dante** (1265–1321), poet, author of *Divine Comedy*. Dante pioneered the usage of everyday language, instead of Latin, in literature.

- **Isabella d'Este** (1474–1539), noblewoman and patron of many artists.

- **Leonardo da Vinci** (1452–1519), painter, sculptor, engineer, scientist.

- **Michelangelo** (1475–1564), sculptor, painter, architect; sculptor of *David* (1504).

- **Raphael** (1483–1520), painter and architect.

To learn more about Renaissance Florence, go to

RESEARCH LINKS
CLASSZONE.COM

SCIENCE CHALLENGE

"Its red-tiled dome soars above most other buildings."

The people of Florence are proud of their cathedral, known as the Duomo ("dome" in Italian). Its red-tiled dome soars above most other buildings. People say that its architect used new techniques to build the dome. What discoveries have Renaissance scientists made? How important is science in this cultural movement? Use one of these options to present information. Look in the Data File for help.

ACTIVITIES

1. Draw a cross-section diagram of the dome of the Duomo, designed by Filippo Brunelleschi. Be able to demonstrate how a dome like this is supported.
2. Prepare to interview Brunelleschi about his ideas and inventions. Research his life and work, and create a list of questions to ask him.

Activity Wrap-Up

As a group, review your solution to the challenge you selected. Then present your solution to the class.

Europe, Russia, and the Independent Republics **183**

SCIENCE CHALLENGE

Class Time 50 minutes

For both options, students will need outside reference sources. For the first option, provide students with poster board and rulers. Encourage students to display their diagrams.

Possible Solutions

The diagrams should emphasize the use of vaults and supporting walls. Interview questions should reflect an understanding of Brunelleschi's life and works and his contributions to the field of architecture.

ALTERNATIVE CHALLENGE…

ARTS CHALLENGE

Churches, palaces, and museums in Florence contain Renaissance paintings and sculptures. For example, the Uffizi Gallery houses da Vinci's *Adoration of the Magi* and Botticelli's *The Birth of Venus*. In the Accademia Gallery you can see Michelangelo's well-known sculpture *David*. In the Pitti Palace are paintings by Raphael and Rubens.

- Design a slide show of 5–6 slides of Renaissance works of art. Prepare a brief explanation of each work and its significance.

- Create a map for an "art tour" of Florence. Show key buildings and museums and include highlights of each visit.

Activity Wrap-Up

To help students evaluate their challenge solutions, have them make a grid with criteria like the one shown. Then have them rate each solution on a scale from 1 to 5, with 1 representing the lowest score and 5 the highest.

Originality	1	2	3	4	5
Creativity	1	2	3	4	5
Accuracy	1	2	3	4	5
Overall effectiveness	1	2	3	4	5

France

TERMS & NAMES
Charles de Gaulle
French Resistance
Jean Monnet
socialism
European Community
impressionism

SECTION OBJECTIVES

1. To describe the government of France's Fifth Republic
2. To describe France's economy
3. To explain France's contribution to world culture

SKILLBUILDER

• Interpreting a Map, p. 185
• Interpreting a Graph, p. 186

FOCUS & MOTIVATE
WARM-UP

Making Inferences Have students read <u>Dateline</u> and ask the following questions.

1. Why do you think the French Resistance was formed?
2. How do you think Parisians felt when they saw the French army enter the city?

INSTRUCT: Objective ❶

The Fifth Republic

• What contributions did Charles de Gaulle make to France during the war? led military as general and led the French in exile

• How is the government of the Fifth Republic organized? power split between president and parliament; parliament divided into Senate and National Assembly, with prime minister as head

 In-depth Resources: Unit 2
• Guided Reading Worksheet, p. 49

 Reading Study Guide
(Spanish and English), pp. 56–57

MAIN IDEA

France was ruined politically and economically by World War II but has since made a full recovery.

WHY IT MATTERS NOW

France is an important member of the European Union and continues to influence the world's economy and cultures.

DATELINE
EXTRA

PARIS, FRANCE, AUGUST 26, 1944

Paris is free! The church bells are still ringing from yesterday's celebrations. After four long years of German control, Paris finally has been liberated. General Charles de Gaulle returned from the United Kingdom yesterday and celebrated the liberation by leading a parade from the Arc de Triomphe to Notre Dame Cathedral.

The liberation of Paris is the result of a two-and-a-half-month advance of Allied forces from the beaches of Normandy in northern France. The French Resistance in Paris began disrupting the German occupiers on August 19, and yesterday, the French army entered Paris.

Region • The liberation of Paris is a significant symbolic victory for the Allies. ▲

Region • Charles de Gaulle is a hero to the French. ▲

The Fifth Republic ❶

During World War II, **Charles de Gaulle** (1890–1970) was a general in the French army. After Germany conquered France in 1940, de Gaulle fled to the United Kingdom. There, he became the leader of the French in exile and stayed in contact with the French Resistance. The **French Resistance** established communications for the Allied war effort, spied on German activity, and sometimes assassinated high-ranking German officers.

184 CHAPTER 7

Program Resources

 In-depth Resources: Unit 2
• Guided Reading Worksheet, p. 49
• Reteaching Activity, p. 58

 Reading Study Guide
(Spanish and English), pp. 56–57

 Formal Assessment
• Section Quiz, p. 97

 Integrated Assessment
• Rubric for drawing a portrait

 Outline Map Activities

Access for Students Acquiring English
• Guided Reading Worksheet, p. 51

Technology Resources
classzone.com

TEST-TAKING RESOURCES

↪ Strategies for Test Preparation
↪ Test Practice Transparencies
🖱 Online Test Practice

Map legend:
⊛ National capital
• Other city

Cities shown: UNITED KINGDOM, English Channel, Calais, Dunkerque, Lille, BELGIUM, LUXEMBOURG, Cherbourg, Le Havre, Amiens, Arras, Rouen, Reims, Metz, GERMANY, Caen, Seine, Paris, Nancy, Brest, Rennes, Le Mans, Chartres, Troyes, Strasbourg, Orléans, Mulhouse, Nantes, Tours, Dijon, Besançon, SWITZERLAND, Loire, Bourges, La Rochelle, Clermont-Ferrand, Vichy, Lyon, Limoges, St-Étienne, Grenoble, ITALY, Dordogne, Bordeaux, FRANCE, Garonne, Nîmes, Avignon, Nice, MONACO, Bayonne, Toulouse, Montpellier, Cannes, Lourdes, Narbonne, Toulon, Calvi, Carcassonne, Perpignan, Marseille, SPAIN, ANDORRA, Ajaccio, Bastia, Mediterranean Sea, Bay of Biscay, Rhône

Scale: 0 100 200 miles / 0 100 200 kilometers
45°N, 3°E, 6°E

GEOGRAPHY SKILLBUILDER:
Interpreting a Map
1. **Location** • Name three countries that border France.
2. **Location** • Which bodies of water does France have access to?

On December 21, 1958, Charles de Gaulle was elected president of France. He reorganized the French constitution and instituted the Fifth Republic of France.

The Government of the Fifth Republic France is a parliamentary republic. Governmental power is split between the president and parliament. The president is elected by the public to a seven-year term; beginning in 2002, the president will serve a five-year term. The president's primary responsibilities are to act as guardian of the constitution and to ensure proper functioning of other authorities.

Parliament has two parts: the Senate and the National Assembly. The president chooses a prime minister, who heads parliament and is largely responsible for the internal workings of the government. The French government is very active in the country's economy.

A Centralized Economy ❷

World War II left France poor and in need of rebuilding. The National Planning Board, established by **Jean Monnet** (mow•NAY) in 1946, launched a series of five-year plans to modernize France and set economic goals for the country.

Reading
Social Studies

A. Comparing
Compare the term and role of the president of France with the president of the United States.

Reading Social Studies
A. Possible Answer
United States: four-year terms, two-term maximum; France: seven-year terms, unlimited terms

Connections to History

Lascaux Cave Paintings On September 12, 1940, while hiking in the hills of Lascaux (lah•SKOE) near the town of Montignac in southern France, four teenage boys discovered ancient cave paintings. They found the caves after their dog fell in a hole in the ground.

Henri Breuil (broy), one of the first archaeologists on the scene, counted more than 600 images of horses (shown here), deer, and bison. The cave paintings are about 17,000 years old, making them some of the oldest works of art yet discovered.

INSTRUCT: Objective ❷

A Centralized Economy

• What was the result of France's five-year plan following the war? a mixed economy with both private ownership and the nationalization of some businesses and industries

• What was France's main source of power following the war, and what is it today? coal, oil, gas; nuclear energy

FOCUS ON VISUALS

Interpreting the Map France has at various times been at war with both Germany and Great Britain. Ask students to identify one physical feature between France and Great Britain that is not between France and Germany. How might this have affected each conflict?

Possible Responses A body of water, the English Channel, lies between France and Great Britain. This may have helped France defend against Great Britain more easily.

Extension Following World War I, France built a line of defense against German invasion along its eastern border, called the Maginot Line. Have students find out more about the Maginot Line.

Connections to History

When Lascaux was first discovered, the paintings were in perfect condition. The cave was first opened to public viewing in 1948. However, as many as 100,000 visitors a year and artificial lighting took its toll on the artwork, and the cave was closed to the public in 1963. A partial replica of the cave was opened in 1983. About 300,000 visit it annually.

Activity Options

Interdisciplinary Links: Government/History

Class Time One class period

Task Creating a chart on historical French governments

Purpose To learn about the various types of governments in France's history

Supplies Needed
• Reference materials related to French history
• Pencils or pens
• Paper

Activity Have students work in small groups to research the forms of government France has had in its history, beginning in the 15th century. Ask each group to create a chart that includes brief descriptions of each form of government and the time period in which each existed.

FOCUS ON VISUALS

Interpreting the Graph Ask students to determine if most countries on the graph get more than 50 percent of their power from nuclear energy or less than 50 percent. How many countries generate 20 percent or less of their power by nuclear energy? What percentage of the United States energy is generated by nuclear energy?

Possible Response Most countries get less than 50 percent of their power from nuclear energy; twelve countries; 20 percent

Extension Explain that controversy has surrounded the use of nuclear energy in the United States. Have students find out more about nuclear energy and list some of the advantages and disadvantages of its use.

INSTRUCT: Objective ❸

The Culture of Paris

• How has Paris contributed to world art? museums, home to leading school of fine arts, center of artistic activities and movements, such as impressionism

• Who are some important French literary figures? Marcel Proust, Albert Camus, Simone de Beauvoir

The result of these plans was a mixed economy, with both public and private sectors. The French government nationalized, or took over, major banks; insurance companies; the electric, coal, and steel industries; schools; universities; hospitals; railroads; airlines; and even an automobile company.

This nationalization of industry is a form of socialism. **Socialism** is an economic system in which some businesses and industries are controlled by the government. The government also provides many health and welfare benefits, such as health care, housing, and unemployment insurance. However, today the French government is slowly placing more of the economy under the control of private companies.

Energy The French economy grew rapidly after 1946, and the country's industry was powered mainly by coal, oil, and gas. When worldwide oil prices rose in the 1970s, the French economy suffered. In the 1980s, France turned to nuclear power so that its economy would be less dependent on oil. Today France draws 75 percent of its power from nuclear energy, a higher percentage than any other nation in the world.

Most famous for its wines, France also exports grains, automobiles, electrical machinery, and chemicals. Although only about 7 percent of the labor force works on farms, France exports more agricultural products than any other nation in the European Community.

The **European Community** is an association developed after World War II to promote economic unity among the countries of Western Europe. Its success gave rise to greater unity, both politically and economically, in the European Union.

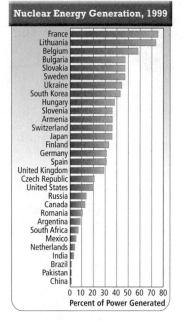

Nuclear Energy Generation, 1999

France, Lithuania, Belgium, Bulgaria, Slovakia, Sweden, Ukraine, South Korea, Hungary, Slovenia, Armenia, Switzerland, Japan, Finland, Germany, Spain, United Kingdom, Czech Republic, United States, Russia, Canada, Romania, Argentina, South Africa, Mexico, Netherlands, India, Brazil, Pakistan, China

0 10 20 30 40 50 60 70 80
Percent of Power Generated

Region • Nuclear power plants are a common sight in the French countryside. ▼

Reading Social Studies
B. Possible Answer
France wants to lessen its dependence upon oil.

Reading
Social Studies

B. Analyzing Motives Why does France produce a large amount of nuclear energy?

BACKGROUND

Tourism is a major industry in France. The country hosts more than 70 million visitors annually, making it the most visited country in the world.

The Culture of Paris ❸

Paris, the capital city of France, is famous for its contributions to world culture, most especially in the arts. Nicknamed "City of Light," Paris has long been an intellectual and artistic center.

Activity Options

Interdisciplinary Link: Art

Class Time One class period

Task Creating an Impressionist-style visual

Purpose To help students gain an understanding of Impressionist-style art

Supplies Needed
• Art books with examples of Impressionist paintings
• Colored pencils, pastels, or watercolor paints
• Drawing paper

⃝ Block Scheduling

Activity Display the copies of Impressionist art and discuss the style with students. Then invite students to select a subject from this chapter and create an Impressionist-style visual of it. Encourage students to use the medium with which they are most comfortable.

Edouard Manet (mah·NAY) (1832–1883) helped influence one of the most important art movements of modern times, impressionism. **Impressionism** is an art style that uses light to create an impression of a scene rather than a strictly realistic picture. Manet inspired such artists as Claude Monet (mow·NAY), Pierre Renoir (wren·WAR), and Paul Cézanne (say·ZAHN). This group of artists worked together in Paris and shared their thoughts and opinions of art.

Paris's Orsay Museum and the Louvre (loove) house two of the greatest collections of fine art in the world. The School of Fine Arts leads a tradition of education and art instruction that has produced artists such as Pierre Bonnard (bah·NAHR) (1867–1947) and Balthus (1908–2001).

Literature France has a rich tradition of literature as well. Marcel Proust, who wrote *Remembrance of Things Past*, was an influential writer in the early 20th century. Other significant writers include Albert Camus (kam·OO), who wrote *The Stranger*, and Simone de Beauvoir (bow·VWAR), author of *The Mandarins*.

Region • Monet and his family often modeled for Manet, as in this 1874 painting *Monet Working on His Boat in Argenteuil.* ▲

SECTION 3 ASSESSMENT

Terms & Names

1. Identify:
(a) Charles de Gaulle
(b) French Resistance
(c) Jean Monnet
(d) socialism
(e) European Community
(f) impressionism

Taking Notes

2. Use a chart like this one to list the major aspects of French government, economy, and culture.

	Major Aspects
Government	
Economy	
Culture	

Main Ideas

3. (a) What role does the French government play in the country's economy?

(b) What is France's primary source of power?

(c) Name three contributions of French culture to the world.

Critical Thinking

4. Clarifying

How was the liberation of Paris a symbolic victory?

Think About

♦ the actions of the French Resistance

♦ the cultural life of Paris

ACTIVITY -OPTION- Reread the text on Manet. Draw an impressionist **portrait** of a classmate, friend, or family member.

Section 3 Assessment

1. Terms and Names
a. Charles de Gaulle, p. 184
b. French Resistance, p. 184
c. Jean Monnet, p. 185
d. socialism, p. 186
e. European Community, p. 186
f. impressionism, p. 187

2. Taking Notes

	Major Aspects
Government	parliamentary republic; power split between president and parliament; parliament has two parts, Senate and National Assembly; prime minister heads parliament
Economy	mixed, with both public and private sectors; some industries nationalized
Culture	important center of painting and literature, birthplace of impressionism

3. Main Ideas
a. The French government controls the major banks; insurance companies; electric, coal, and steel industries; schools; universities; hospitals; railroads; airlines; and an automobile company.
b. Today France's primary source of power is nuclear energy.
c. French culture has contributed artists, museums, and writers.

4. Critical Thinking
Paris was the center of French cultural life, and freeing it from German control was a symbol of freeing France itself.

ACTIVITY OPTION

Integrated Assessment
• Rubric for drawing a portrait

ASSESS & RETEACH

Reading Social Studies Have students add details from Section 3 to the chart on page 172.

 Formal Assessment
• Section Quiz, p. 97

RETEACHING ACTIVITY

Work with students to develop an outline of this section on the chalkboard. Use the section heads as the main-idea headings; then ask students to identify details related to each one.

 In-depth Resources: Unit 2
• Reteaching Activity, p. 58

 Access for Students Acquiring English
• Reteaching Activity, p. 58

SECTION OBJECTIVES

1. To describe Germany as a divided, and then as a reunified, nation
2. To describe Germany's culture

SKILLBUILDER
• Interpreting a Map, p. 189

CRITICAL THINKING
• Hypothesizing, p. 189
• Recognizing Effects, p. 190

FOCUS & MOTIVATE
WARM-UP

Analyzing Motives Have students read Dateline and respond to these questions.

1. How would you feel if you were German, living in Berlin in October 1990?
2. Why was it important to save a part of the wall as a memorial?

INSTRUCT: Objective ❶

A Divided Germany/Reunified Germany

• **Why was West Germany able to achieve an economic miracle?** U.S. loans helped revitalize industry and the general economy.

 In-depth Resources: Unit 2
• Guided Reading Worksheet, p. 50

 Reading Study Guide
(Spanish and English), pp. 58–59

Germany

TERMS & NAMES
Berlin Wall
reunification
Ludwig van
  Beethoven
Rainer Maria Rilke

MAIN IDEA
Germany has overcome many obstacles to become both a unified and a modern nation.

WHY IT MATTERS NOW
Germany has helped to shape recent European history and contemporary Western culture.

DATELINE

BERLIN, GERMANY, OCTOBER 3, 1990—
It is just past midnight. Church bells are ringing, fireworks are exploding, bands are playing, and the streets are filled with celebrating Germans. At midnight, the treaty to reunite East and West Germany became official. Germany is whole once more!

Just a year ago, the Berlin Wall—a 103-mile-long barrier of concrete and barbed wire—still separated East and West Berlin. Constructed in 1961, the Wall kept East Germans from escaping from their Communist government to democratic West Germany. Then, in 1989, as the Communist government weakened, the Wall came down.

Location • Germans celebrate unification in front of the Reichstag, the seat of the federal government. ▲

Location • The largest remaining sections of the Berlin Wall, which stand up to 15 feet high, are covered with paintings and signatures. ▲

A Divided Germany ❶

Today, the reunified nation of Germany is one of the largest countries in Europe. When World War II ended in 1945, however, Germany was divided. U.S., French, and British soldiers occupied the new West German nation, and Soviet soldiers occupied the new East Germany.

Program Resources

 In-depth Resources: Unit 2
• Guided Reading Worksheet, p. 50
• Reteaching Activity, p. 59

 Reading Study Guide
(Spanish and English), pp. 58–59

 Formal Assessment
• Section Quiz, p. 98

Integrated Assessment
• Rubric for writing a story

 Outline Map Activities

Access for Students Acquiring English
• Guided Reading Worksheet, p. 52

 Technology Resources
classzone.com

TEST-TAKING RESOURCES
↪ Strategies for Test Preparation
↪ Test Practice Transparencies
🖱 Online Test Practice

West Germany The United States helped West Germany set up a democratic government. In part, the United States supported the new nation because it was located between the Communist countries of Eastern Europe and the rest of Western Europe.

With the help of U.S. loans, West Germany experienced a so-called economic miracle. In 20 years, it rebuilt its factories and became one of the world's richest nations. Its economy later became the driving force behind the European Union.

East Germany In contrast to West Germany, East Germany remained poor. Most East Germans saw West Germany, and Western Europe in general, as a place where people had better lives. East Germany's Communist government, however, discouraged contact between east and west.

By 1989, the Soviet Union's control of Eastern Europe was weakening. Hungary, a Soviet ally, relaxed control over its borders with Western Europe. East Germans began crossing the Hungarian border into Austria and eventually made their way into West Germany. After the **Berlin Wall** came down in 1989, more East Germans fled to West Germany.

Geography Skillbuilder Answers
1. Poland
2. West Germany

Germany Today

[Map of Germany showing North Sea, Baltic Sea, Denmark, Netherlands, Belgium, Luxembourg, France, Switzerland, Austria, Czech Republic, Poland, and cities including Hamburg, Bremen, Hanover, Berlin, Essen, Dortmund, Duisburg, Düsseldorf, Cologne, Bonn, Leipzig, Dresden, Frankfurt, Heidelberg, Stuttgart, Tübingen, Munich; rivers including Elbe, Weser, Rhine, Main, Danube, Neckar, Isar; features including Black Forest, Bavarian Forest, Mittelland Canal]

GEOGRAPHY SKILLBUILDER: Interpreting a Map

1. **Location** • Which country is nearest to Germany's national capital?
2. **Place** • Which was larger, East or West Germany?

Map legend:
- - - Former border of East and West Germany
— National boundary
✪ National capital
• Other city

0 25 50 miles
0 25 50 kilometers

INSTRUCT: Objective ②

German Culture

- Who are three of Germany's best-known composers? Johann Sebastian Bach, George Frederick Handel, Ludwig van Beethoven
- What two German writers have been awarded the Nobel Prize in Literature? Günter Grass, Thomas Mann

CRITICAL THINKING ACTIVITY

Recognizing Effects Remind students that culture is the literature, music, and art that a group of people enjoy. It is also the way the people do things, how they live, and what they value as a group. Ask students to name some of the cultural traditions of the United States. Then guide a discussion of why these traditions are important to people. Finally, talk about how cultural traditions may help to unite the people of East Germany and West Germany.

Class Time 15 minutes

🎭 Biography

Ludwig van Beethoven (1770–1827) began studying music as a child. By the time he was 11, he had become an assistant court organist. He published his own compositions at age 12. In his twenties, Beethoven had become renowned as a great pianist. He stopped performing in 1808, but he continued composing. When he died, 10,000 people attended his funeral.

Region • The new Volkswagen Beetle is typical of German car design, known for its simplicity and style. The first Volkswagen was designed by Ferdinand Porsche (POOR•sheh) in 1934. ▲

Reunified Germany ①

Since the 1990 **reunification,** or the reuniting of East and West Germany, the German government has spent billions of dollars rebuilding the eastern part of the country. The effort has included roads, factories, housing, and hospitals. The city of Berlin, once again the nation's capital, was also rebuilt. The newly reunified nation also restored the Reichstag (RIEKSH•tahg), where the Federal Assembly meets.

However, reunification has also caused tensions between "Ossies" (OSS•eez) and "Wessies" (VESS•eez). Many Ossies complain about the lack of jobs and the cost of housing. Many Wessies complain about paying taxes to rebuild the nation and to help support the former East Germans.

German Culture ②

Germany's rich cultural traditions may help to unite its people, who are especially proud of their music and literature. Germans are also famous for designing high-quality products, such as cars, electronic appliances, and other complex machinery.

Music Three of Germany's best-known composers are Johann Sebastian Bach (bahck) (1685–1750), George Frederick Handel (HAHN•duhl) (1685–1759), and **Ludwig van Beethoven** (LOOD•vig vahn BAY•toe•ven) (1770–1827). Their music is still performed and recorded all over the world. German composer Richard Wagner (VAG•nuhr) (1813–1883) wrote many operas, including a series based on German myths and legends known as the Ring Cycle.

🎭 Biography

Beethoven Perhaps the best-loved German composer is Ludwig van Beethoven. Beethoven began to lose his hearing when he was in his 20s. By the time he was 50, he was almost deaf.

Beethoven refused to let his deafness stop him from creating music, however. "I will grapple with Fate, it shall not overcome me," he wrote. In 1824, he finished his Ninth Symphony, which ends with a section containing the well-known "Ode to Joy." An orchestra played this same symphony at an open-air concert during the destruction of the Berlin Wall.

190 CHAPTER 7

Reading Social Studies
A. Clarifying Why did East Germany need to be rebuilt and not West Germany?

Vocabulary

Ossies: former East Germans

Wessies: former West Germans

Reading Social Studies
A. Possible Answer
Unlike West Germany, East Germany's economy was too poor to maintain roads and buildings.

Activity Options

Differentiating Instruction: Students Acquiring English/ESL

Prefixes Point out the word *reunified* in the first head on this page. Explain that this word is formed by combining the prefix *re-* with the base word *unified*. Remind students that they can often figure out the meaning of unfamiliar words if they know what the word parts mean. Here, *re-* means "again" and *unified* means "brought together." *Reunified,* therefore, means "brought together again."

Have students find other words on this page that are formed from the prefix *re-* (*reunification, reuniting, rebuilding, rebuilt, rebuild*). Have students define the words and restate the sentences in their own words.

Place •
Half-timber
architecture,
shown here,
is common
throughout
Germany. ▲

Literature One of the greatest writers in the German language was **Rainer Maria Rilke** (RIL·keh) (1875–1926). His poems, which are still admired and studied today, were a way for Rilke to communicate his feelings and experiences.

BACKGROUND

More than 100 million people around the world speak German.

Other important 20th-century German authors include Günter Grass (grahss) (b. 1927) and Thomas Mann (mahn) (1875–1955). Grass has written about the horrors of World War II, the setting for his novel *The Tin Drum*. Both writers were awarded the Nobel Prize in Literature—Mann in 1929 and Grass in 1999.

SECTION 4 ASSESSMENT

Terms & Names

1. **Identify:**
   (a) Berlin Wall   (b) reunification   (c) Ludwig van Beethoven
   (d) Rainer Maria Rilke

Taking Notes

2. Use a chart like this one to compare aspects of Germany before and after reunification.

Before Reunification	After Reunification

Main Ideas

3. (a) Describe the economic miracle that occurred in West Germany.

   (b) Why has there been tension between the Ossies and the Wessies?

   (c) On what projects has Germany spent billions of dollars since 1990?

Critical Thinking

4. **Synthesizing**

   What makes Germany an important European country?

   Think About
   - its location
   - its size
   - its role in modern history

ACTIVITY -OPTION- Reread the "Dateline" feature at the beginning of the section. Write a **short story** describing what it might have been like to celebrate the reunification of Germany in 1990.

Section 4 Assessment

1. Terms & Names
   a. Berlin Wall, p. 189
   b. reunification, p. 190
   c. Ludwig van Beethoven, p. 190
   d. Rainer Maria Rilke, p. 191

2. Taking Notes

Before Reunification	After Reunification
Germany divided	Germany unified
Occupation: West Germany by U.S.; East Germany by Soviet Union	No occupation
	East Germany being rebuilt
West Germany economic miracle; East Germany poor	Wall removed
Berlin divided by wall	People can move freely
People cannot move freely	

3. Main Ideas
   a. West Germany rebuilt its economy and became one of the world's richest nations.
   b. Ossies need jobs and housing; Wessies dislike supporting Ossies.
   c. Billions have been spent on rebuilding eastern Germany's roads, factories, housing, and hospitals.

4. Critical Thinking
   Germany is centrally located, large, and economically powerful, and is a political leader in Europe.

ACTIVITY OPTION

 Integrated Assessment
   • Rubric for writing a story

ASSESS & RETEACH

Reading Social Studies Have students add details to line 4 of the chart on page 172.

 Formal Assessment
   • Section Quiz, p. 98

RETEACHING ACTIVITY

Have small groups of students collaborate in writing a three- or four-sentence summary of the discussion under one of the section headings. Have groups share their summaries in class.

 In-depth Resources: Unit 2
   • Reteaching Activity, p. 59

 Access for Students Acquiring English
   • Reteaching Activity, p. 59

SKILLBUILDER

Making an Outline
Defining the Skill

Explain that making an outline is essential for writing a research report and is also a useful study skill. After studying the strategies, students might, for example, outline Chapter 7 in order to have a concise guide to main ideas and details that could be used for review.

Applying the Skill

How to Make an Outline Ask a volunteer to read the first strategy. Point out the Roman numerals used to designate each main idea. Continue to work through each strategy. Reinforce the need to follow each strategy.

Make an Outline

Review the outline of Marie Curie's biography. Point out the relationship between main ideas and supporting ideas. Ask questions such as, How does item C support the first main idea: Who was she? Then discuss details that add to the supporting ideas. Ask how they relate to the main ideas.

Practicing the Skill

Brainstorm topics from the chapter that students might outline. Have students who chose similar topics compare their outlines. If students need more practice, have them turn to the discussion of the divided Germany. Work together to create an outline of this material.

 In-depth Resources: Unit 2
• Skillbuilder Practice, p. 54

SKILLBUILDER

Making an Outline

▶▶ Defining the Skill

Before writing a research report, you must decide on your topic and then gather information about it. When you have all of the information you need, then you begin to organize it. One way of organizing your information before writing the report is to make an outline. An outline lists the main ideas in the order in which they will appear in the report. It also organizes the main ideas and supporting details according to their importance. The form of every outline is the same. Main ideas are listed on the left and labeled with capital Roman numerals. Supporting ideas are indented and labeled with capital letters. Supporting details are indented farther and labeled with numerals.

▶▶ Applying the Skill

The outline to the right is for a biography of Marie Curie, one of the great physicists of all time. Use the strategies listed below to help you learn how to make an outline.

How to Make an Outline

Strategy ① Read the main ideas of this report. They are labeled with capital Roman numerals. Each main idea will need at least one paragraph.

Strategy ② Read the supporting ideas for each main idea. These are labeled with capital letters. Notice that some of the main ideas require more supporting ideas than others.

Strategy ③ Read the supporting details that are included in this outline. These are labeled with numerals. The writer of this outline did not include the supporting details for some of the supporting ideas. It is not necessary to include every piece of information that you have. An outline is intended merely as a guide for you to follow as you write the report.

Strategy ④ A report can be organized in different ways. This biography is organized chronologically, that is, according to time. It starts with Curie's birth and ends with her legacy after death. The outline follows the order of events in her life. A report can be organized in other ways, such as comparing and contrasting or according to advantages and disadvantages. The outline should clearly reflect the way the report is organized.

① I. Who Was She?
  A. Polish-born physicist
② B. Birth and early life
  C. Schooling
    1. In secret in Poland (women were not allowed to ente
③   higher education)
    2. In France at the Sorbonne
④   a. license of physical sciences, 1893
      b. license of mathematical sciences, 1894
II. The Physicist
  A. Life and work with husband, Pierre Curie
    1. Discoveries
      a. polonium, summer 1898
      b. radium, fall 1898
    2. Nobel Prize in Physics, 1903
      a. shared with Henri Becquerel
      b. Marie was the first woman to ever be awarde
        a Nobel Prize
  B. Her own accomplishments
    1. Became the first female professor at the Sorbon
      a. took over Pierre's position after his death, 190
    2. Her research on radioactivity was published, 1910
    3. Nobel Prize in Chemistry, 1911

▶▶ Practicing the Skill

Look through Chapter 7 and find a topic that interests you. Gather information about that topic, and then write an outline for a report about that topic. Be sure to use the correct outline form.

Career Connection: Biographer   **B** Block Scheduling

Encourage students who enjoy making an outline to learn about careers in writing that use this skill. For example, biographers write about other people. Because much research goes into a biography, making an outline is important for a biographer.

1. Point out to students that a biographer usually chooses a subject who is interesting to her or him.

2. Suggest that students find out how a biographer researches a subject and organizes the findings.

3. Ask students to research the education and experience an aspiring biographer should obtain. Have students prepare an outline of their findings.

Poland

TERMS & NAMES

Solidarity
Lech Walesa
Czeslaw Milosz
censorship
dissident

MAIN IDEA

Poland has gone through the difficulties of establishing a new democratic government and a new economic system.

WHY IT MATTERS NOW

Poland is an excellent example of the success that has been achieved by the newly independent Eastern European nations.

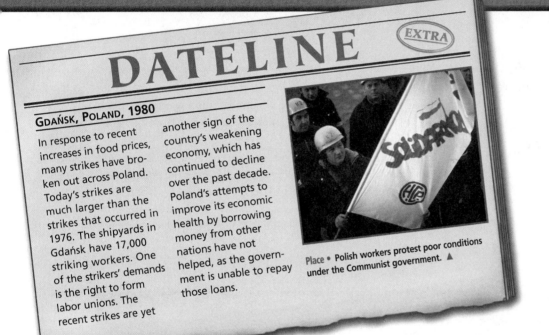

DATELINE

EXTRA

GDAŃSK, POLAND, 1980

In response to recent increases in food prices, many strikes have broken out across Poland. Today's strikes are much larger than the strikes that occurred in 1976. The shipyards in Gdańsk have 17,000 striking workers. One of the strikers' demands is the right to form labor unions. The recent strikes are yet another sign of the country's weakening economy, which has continued to decline over the past decade. Poland's attempts to improve its economic health by borrowing money from other nations have not helped, as the government is unable to repay those loans.

Place • Polish workers protest poor conditions under the Communist government. ▲

Political and Economic Struggles ❶

The strikes and riots of the 1970s and 1980s were not the first actions Polish citizens took against their government. In 1956, Polish workers had rioted to protest their low wages.

In fact, there have been political and economic struggles in Poland since World War II ended in 1945. At that time, Communists took over the government and set strict wage and price controls.

Europe Today **193**

SECTION OBJECTIVES

1. To explain Poland's political and economic struggles

2. To describe Poland's government and economy

3. To describe Poland's culture

SKILLBUILDER
• Interpreting a Map, p. 194

CRITICAL THINKING
• Drawing Conclusions, p. 194
• Comparing, p. 195

FOCUS & MOTIVATE
WARM-UP

Analyzing Motives After students read <u>Dateline</u>, discuss unions and strikes.

1. What conditions might prompt workers to strike?

2. What happens during a labor strike?

INSTRUCT: Objective ❶

Political and Economic Struggles

• Who led Poland's efforts toward political and economic change? workers, Solidarity movement

 In-depth Resources: Unit 2
• Guided Reading Worksheet, p. 51

 Reading Study Guide
(Spanish and English), pp. 60–61

Program Resources

 In-depth Resources: Unit 2
• Guided Reading Worksheet, p. 51
• Reteaching Activity, p. 60

 Reading Study Guide
(Spanish and English), pp. 60–61

 Formal Assessment
• Section Quiz, p. 99

 Integrated Assessment
• Rubric for writing a speech

 Outline Map Activities

 Access for Students Acquiring English
• Guided Reading Worksheet, p. 53

Technology Resources
classzone.com

TEST-TAKING RESOURCES
⌇ Strategies for Test Preparation
⌇ Test Practice Transparencies
⊕ Online Test Practice

Poland Today

FOCUS ON VISUALS

Interpreting the Map Ask students to look at the map and identify the capital of Poland. Where is the city of Gdańsk? What river flows into the Gulf of Gdańsk?

Responses Warsaw; Gdańsk is in north central Poland on the Gulf of Gdańsk; Vistula River

Extension Have students look at the cities shown on the map and at the scale of miles. Then ask them to create a chart showing the distance that each of the cities is from Poland's capital.

GEOGRAPHY SKILLBUILDER: Interpreting a Map

1. **Location** • Name a port city in Poland.
2. **Location** • How many different countries border Poland?

CRITICAL THINKING ACTIVITY

Drawing Conclusions Remind students that the Communist Party was originally organized to protect workers. Ask them why the Communist leaders of Poland now opposed Solidarity. What conclusions can they draw about the Communist Party's success?

Class Time 10 minutes

Geography Skillbuilder Answers
1. Gdańsk
2. seven

Solidarity In 1980, labor unions throughout Poland joined an organization called **Solidarity**. This trade union was led by **Lech Walesa** (LEK vuh·LESS·uh), an electrical worker from the shipyards of Gdańsk (geh·DAHNSK).

In the beginning, Solidarity's goals were to increase pay and improve working conditions. Before long, however, the organization set its sights on bigger goals. In late 1981, members of Solidarity were calling for free elections and an end to Communist rule. Even though Solidarity had about 10 million members, the government fought back. It suspended the organization, cracked down on protesters, and arrested thousands of members, including Walesa.

BACKGROUND

Poland's capital and largest city is Warsaw. The nation's citizens are called Poles.

Region • In 1980, Solidarity leader Lech Walesa gained the support of labor unions. Ten years later, he became Poland's president. ◄

Activity Options

Interdisciplinary Link: World History

Class Time 30 minutes

Task Creating a placard for a Solidarity strike

Purpose To identify and express ideas that motivated the Solidarity movement

Supplies Needed
• Art paper or poster board
• Markers

Activity Review the Solidarity movement with students, discussing its original goals and how those goals changed. Explain to students that during demonstrations and strikes, members of Solidarity would make placards, or posters, stating their demands or expressing their views. Ask students to work independently to create placards that Solidarity members might have displayed. Have students post their placards in the classroom.

Region • Poland's senate helps ensure that all the country's citizens have representation. ◄

A Free Poland ❷

In the late 1980s, economic conditions continued to worsen in Poland. The government asked Solidarity leaders to help them solve the country's economic difficulties. Finally, the Communists agreed to Solidarity's demand for free elections.

When the elections were held in 1989, many Solidarity candidates were elected, and the Communists lost power. In 1990, Lech Walesa became the president of a free Poland.

A New Constitution Today, Poland is a parliamentary republic. The country approved a new constitution in 1997. This constitution guarantees civil rights such as free speech. It also helps to balance the powers held by the president, the prime minister, and parliament.

Parliament Poland's parliament is made up of two houses. The upper house, or senate, has 100 members. The lower house, which has 460 members, chooses the prime minister. Usually, as in the United Kingdom, the prime minister is a member of the largest party or alliance of parties within parliament.

A number of seats in parliament are reserved for representatives of the small German and Ukrainian ethnic groups in Poland. In this way, all Polish citizens are ensured a voice in their government.

A Changing Economy ❷

Besides a new government, the Poles have also had to deal with a changing economy. In 1990, Poland's new democratic government quickly switched from a command economy to a free market economy. Prices were no longer controlled by the government, and trade suddenly faced international competition.

Europe Today **195**

Reading
Social Studies

A. Recognizing Important Details What led to free elections in Poland?

BACKGROUND

The Polish president, who is elected every five years, is the head of state.

Reading Social Studies
A. Possible Answer
The Communist government needed Solidarity's help to solve economic problems, and Solidarity demanded free elections.

INSTRUCT: Objective ❷

A Free Poland/A Changing Economy

• Why did Poland's government finally ask Solidarity for help? The economy had continued to worsen.

• How does Poland's new constitution help protect peoples' freedom? guarantees freedom of speech; balances powers of president, prime minister, and parliament so no one has too much power

• Why did Poland experience high unemployment following its switch to a free-market economy? Polish companies could not compete with high-quality foreign goods, and industries closed, so workers were laid off.

CRITICAL THINKING ACTIVITY

Comparing Review the discussion of Poland's new parliament. Then ask students to work independently to create Venn diagrams comparing Poland's new parliament with the United States Congress. Create a class diagram and have volunteers complete it with ideas from their own diagrams.

Class Time 15 minutes

Activity Options
Differentiating Instruction: Less Proficient Readers

Identifying Sequence of Events Discuss the events that occurred when Poland changed from a command economy to a free-market economy. Then have students work in small groups to create a sequence-of-events chart like the one shown. Tell them to add as many boxes as necessary to show events. Have groups share their charts in class.

| Change: command to free-market economy |
| Prices not controlled; international trade permitted |
| More goods for sale |
| Prices increase |

INSTRUCT: Objective ❸

Poland's Culture

- Why is Poland's literature filled with stories of national independence and kingdoms won and lost? It reflects Poland's history.

- How have the Polish government's actions toward the arts changed since Communist rule ended? Before communism, the government exercised censorship; now it supports and encourages the arts.

MORE ABOUT...
Czeslaw Milosz

Like that of many Polish writers, the work of Milosz remained unpublished in Poland for many years. When he won the Nobel Prize in 1980, however, the government suddenly recognized him. "My name was defrozen," he said. "The Polish public at large had not heard my name because of censorship." When Milosz visited Warsaw in 1981, he was a hero. People saw him as a symbol of freedom.

Inflation Although Polish shops were able to sell goods that had not been available before, prices rose quickly—by almost 80 percent. With this inflation, or a continual rise in prices, people's wages could not keep up with the cost of goods.

Many Polish companies, which could not compete with high-quality foreign goods, went out of business. This, in turn, resulted in high unemployment. As more and more people lost their jobs, Poland's overall standard of living fell.

Region • With Poland's economy on the rise, unemployment has decreased. ▲

An Improving Economy In time, new Polish businesses found success, giving more people work. Inflation started to drop. By 1999, inflation was down to around 7 percent. By 2000, Poland no longer needed the economic aid it had been receiving from the United States.

One way to measure the strength of a country's economy is to look at consumer spending. Between 1995 and 2000, Poles bought new cars at a high rate of half a million each year. Today, Poland has 2 million small and medium-sized businesses. The success of these small businesses is another sign of Poland's healthy economy.

Poland's Culture ❸

The history of Poland has been one of ups and downs. In the 1500s and 1600s, Poland was a large and powerful kingdom. By 1795, Russia, Prussia, and Austria had taken control of its land, and Poland ceased to exist as an independent country. Poland did not become a republic until 1918, after World War I. Throughout the centuries, however, Poland has had a rich culture.

Literature Polish literature is full of accounts of struggles for national independence and stories about glorious kingdoms won and lost by heroic patriots.

One of Poland's best-known writers of recent times is **Czeslaw Milosz** (CHEH·slawv MEE·lohsh) (b. 1911). Milosz published his first book of poems in the 1930s. After World War II, he worked as a diplomat in the United States and then France.

BACKGROUND

A famous Polish general and patriot, Thaddeus Kosciusko (TAHD·ee·oos kos·ee·US·koh), fought on the side of the colonists during the American Revolution.

Activity Options

Differentiating Instruction: Gifted and Talented

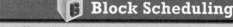 **Block Scheduling**

Forming and Supporting Opinions Tell students that many Polish writers resented the Communist government's censorship of their writing. Have students write speeches expressing their opinion of censorship. Tell them to consider these questions:

- Why is censorship a big issue for writers?

- How does censorship affect the citizens of a country?
- Why do some governments think it is necessary to control what people read?

Have students practice their speeches and deliver them in class.

Milosz, who became a professor at the University of California at Berkeley, won the Nobel Prize in Literature in 1980.

Reading
Social Studies

B. Analyzing Motives Why did the Communist government control the media?

Reading Social Studies
B. Possible Answer
It was trying to censor any criticism of government actions.

Censorship Under Communist rule, the Polish media were controlled by the government. The government decided what the media could and could not say. It outlawed any information that did not support and praise the accomplishments of communism. As a result of this **censorship**, many writers could not publish their works. Some of them became dissidents. A **dissident** is a person who openly disagrees with a government's policies.

Supporting the Arts In order to help Polish writers, the government now allows publications printed in Poland to be sold tax-free. To help Polish actors, screenwriters, and directors, movie theaters are repaid their costs for showing Polish movies. Public-sponsored television stations are supported not only by free-market advertising but also by fees the public pays to own television sets.

Place • In 1978, Poland's pride was greatly boosted when Polish-born John Paul II was elected pope. He was the first non-Italian to be elected pope in 456 years. ▲

SECTION 5 ASSESSMENT

Terms & Names

1. Identify: (a) Solidarity (b) Lech Walesa (c) Czeslaw Milosz
(d) censorship (e) dissident

Taking Notes

2. Use a chart like this one to compare and contrast one aspect of Poland with the same aspect of the United Kingdom, Sweden, France, or Germany.

Poland	Other Country

Main Ideas

3. (a) How did the Polish government respond to Solidarity's goals?

(b) What was the outcome of Poland's free election in the late 1980s?

(c) Describe the recent changes in the economy of Poland.

Critical Thinking

4. **Summarizing**
How would you describe what life was like in Poland before the changes of 1990?

Think About
 • strikes and riots
 • the Communist government
 • censorship

ACTIVITY -OPTION- Reread the information about Solidarity. Write a short **speech** that might have been given to gain support for the organization in the 1980s.

Europe Today **197**

ASSESS & RETEACH

Reading Social Studies Have students complete the chart on page 172.

 Formal Assessment
 • Section Quiz, p. 99

RETEACHING ACTIVITY

Ask each student to write one question about the content that follows each heading in the section. Then have students meet in small groups and take turns asking their questions and discussing the answers.

 In-depth Resources: Unit 2
 • Reteaching Activity, p. 60

 Access for Students Acquiring English
 • Reteaching Activity, p. 60

Section 5 Assessment

1. Terms & Names
  a. Solidarity, p. 194
  b. Lech Walesa, p. 194
  c. Czeslaw Milosz, p. 196
  d. censorship, p. 197
  e. dissident, p. 197

2. Taking Notes

Poland	Other Country
Formerly Communist	Sweden: never Communist
Parliamentary republic	Sweden: constitutional monarchy
Free-market economy	Sweden: free-market economy
Becoming economically prosperous	Sweden: prosperous economy

3. Main Ideas
  a. The government opposed Solidarity at first, and then asked for its help.
  b. Solidarity won; Communists lost power.
  c. Poland became a free-market economy, which resulted in inflation and unemployment. The economy is now improving.

4. Critical Thinking
Workers protested low wages; Solidarity organized strikes; the Communist government censored writers and media.

ACTIVITY OPTION
 Integrated Assessment
 • Rubric for writing a speech

TERMS & NAMES

1. London, p. 173
2. Good Friday Accord, p. 175
3. armed neutrality, p. 179
4. hydroelectricity, p. 180
5. Charles de Gaulle, p. 184
6. socialism, p. 186
7. Berlin Wall, p. 189
8. reunification, p. 190
9. censorship, p. 197
10. dissident, p. 197

REVIEW QUESTIONS

1. The House of Lords and the House of Commons form Parliament; the House of Commons is more powerful.
2. It has many people, little land, and few natural resources.
3. They make sure that the courts and civil service follow the law, and protect citizens' rights.
4. It has hills, mountains, and cold weather.
5. France's main source of energy is nuclear power.
6. Manet, Monet, Renoir, and Cézanne are Impressionist painters.
7. The U.S. government provided loans for rebuilding industry.
8. Bach, Handel, Beethoven, and Wagner are German composers.
9. He led Solidarity, which helped win Poland its freedom. He became free Poland's first president.
10. It protects civil rights and ensures a balance of power among the president, prime minister, and parliament.

TERMS & NAMES

Explain the significance of each of the following:

1. London
2. Good Friday Accord
3. armed neutrality
4. hydroelectricity
5. Charles de Gaulle
6. socialism
7. Berlin Wall
8. reunification
9. censorship
10. dissident

REVIEW QUESTIONS

The United Kingdom (pages 173–177)
1. What are the two houses that form the British Parliament? Which is more powerful?
2. Why is it necessary for the United Kingdom to import foods and other goods?

Sweden (pages 178–181)
3. What role do ombudsmen play in the Swedish government?
4. Why is Sweden an excellent place for skiing?

France (pages 184–187)
5. What is France's main source of energy?
6. Identify at least three Impressionist painters.

Germany (pages 188–191)
7. What role did the United States government play in West Germany after World War II?
8. Identify at least three famous German composers.

Poland (pages 193–197)
9. Why is Lech Walesa important to modern Poland?
10. Describe the new constitution that Poland approved in 1997.

CRITICAL THINKING

Comparing
1. Using your completed chart from Reading Social Studies, p. 172, compare the governments and economies of the United Kingdom, Sweden, France, Germany, and Poland.

Hypothesizing
2. One of Sweden's severe environmental problems is acid rain. Why might it be difficult for a country to solve this problem?

Making Inferences
3. Why do you think it was important to the United States that West Germany have a democratic government?

Visual Summary

The United Kingdom *1*
- British economic, political, and cultural traditions have influenced nations around the world.

2 **Sweden**
- Sweden offers its people a high standard of living.
- Sweden is dealing with environmental issues such as nuclear power and acid rain.

France
- France has made a speedy recovery from World War II.

Germany *4*
- Germany has overcome many obstacles to become a unified and modern nation.

Poland *5*
- Poland is an example of the success made possible by the recent independence of Eastern European nations.

CRITICAL THINKING: Possible Responses

1. Comparing
Great Britain and Sweden are constitutional monarchies. France and Poland are parliamentary republics. Germany, once split into Communist and democratic parts, is today democratic.

Great Britain and Sweden are free-trade economies. France has a mixed economy with public and private sectors. Poland has changed from a command economy to a free-market one.

2. Hypothesizing
Possible Answers Acid rain is caused by pollution from many countries. It's difficult to get all countries responsible to agree to reduce their polluting emissions. Also, the industries responsible may resist regulations that would reduce pollution.

3. Making Inferences
West Germany was a large, populous country that was historically highly industrialized. The United States realized West Germany would be powerful again and wanted it to be a democratic ally rather than a member of the Soviet-dominated East European bloc of nations.

SOCIAL STUDIES SKILLBUILDER

Jacques Cousteau (koo•STOW) (1910–1997) was the most famous undersea explorer of the 20th century. While serving in the French navy in 1943, Cousteau invented the Aqua-Lung, also known as scuba gear. *Scuba* stands for "self-contained underwater-breathing apparatus." Scuba gear allowed divers to more freely explore the depths of the oceans, which cover more than three-fifths of Earth's surface. Cousteau became a household name after he popularized underwater exploration through books, films, and a television series.

SKILLBUILDER: Making an Outline
Outline the text above.

FOCUS ON GEOGRAPHY

1. **Place** • How many airports does the map show in Germany? What cities are they located in or near?
2. **Movement** • Describe at least two possible routes that connect London and Stockholm.
3. **Place** • Which cities in Poland are located along major rail lines?

CHAPTER PROJECTS

Interdisciplinary Activity: Art
Preparing a Written Report Research the life and work of a well-known painter, sculptor, or other artist from the United Kingdom, Sweden, France, Germany, or Poland. Use your findings to write a short report. Be sure to include a description or a copy of at least one important work of art.

Cooperative Learning Activity
Researching a Festival In a group of three students, organize a classroom presentation about a festival or holiday that is celebrated in the United Kingdom, Sweden, France, Germany, or Poland. What is the importance of the festival? When is it celebrated? What kinds of activities or foods are associated with it?
- Research information about different festivals or holidays and select one that interests your group.
- Decide what form your presentation will take.
- Discuss how the festival compares with others that are familiar to you.

 INTERNET ACTIVITY

Use the Internet to research a major tourist site in the United Kingdom, Sweden, France, Germany, or Poland. Focus on one location, such as Edinburgh, Dublin, Stockholm, Paris, Munich, Heidelberg, or Warsaw. What special attractions or activities does that location offer to visitors?

Presenting Your Findings Write up your findings and include illustrations of the location. Be sure to list the Web sites you used to help you prepare your report.

For Internet links to support this activity, go to

RESEARCH LINKS
CLASSZONE.COM

CHAPTER PROJECTS
Interdisciplinary Activity: Art
Preparing a Written Report You might want to provide students with a list of artists to choose from, as well as a variety of reference materials for their research. Students' reports should be logically organized, include an introductory paragraph and a conclusion that summarizes the report, and include accurate source information.

Cooperative Learning Activity
Researching a Festival Encourage students in each group to assign roles of researcher, recorder, and presenter. Presentations should respond to the questions from the text; include specific, accurate information; and include photographs, drawings, models, or other visuals.

INTERNET ACTIVITY
Reports should be clearly and logically organized. They should begin with a statement that attracts the reader's interest. Paragraphs should be organized around main ideas that are supported by specific details. If possible, students should include photographs and other visuals that they download from the Internet.

Skills Answers

Social Studies Skillbuilder
Possible Responses
I. Who Was He?
  A. French-born undersea explorer
  B. Most famous undersea explorer of the 20th century
II. Accomplishments
  A. Inventor of Aqua-Lung
    1. Enabled divers to more freely explore ocean depths

    2. Scuba stands for "self-contained underwater breathing apparatus."
  B. Popularized underwater exploration through books, films, and a television series

Focus on Geography
Possible Responses
1. two; Frankfurt and Berlin
2. London and Stockholm are connected by air and shipping lines.
3. Krakow, Lodz, Warsaw, Gdansk, Wroclaw

UNIT 3

North Africa and Southwest Asia

Before You Read

Previewing Unit 3

Unit 3 begins with an overview of the geography
and important contributions of the ancient civilizations of Egypt and Mesopotamia, and the
rise of the three major religions of the region.
Then the focus of the unit shifts to the history
of the lands of Israel, Pakistan, and Turkey and
how this history has contributed to conflict in
the region today. Also examined in this unit is
the impact of oil production and the continuing
relationship between religion and political
unrest. The cultural contributions these countries
have made to the rest of the world are covered.

Place The Blue Mosque
was built in the 17th
century in Constantinople
(now Istanbul, Turkey).
On the land around the
mosque, there is a religious
school, a public bath,
souvenir shops, and a
kitchen to feed the poor.

200

Unit Level Activities

1. Make a Presentation

Have students work in small groups to find out more about the accomplishments and contributions of Ancient Mesopotamia and Ancient
Egypt. Suggest that each group take one accomplishment and find
out more about it. Have student groups present their information to
the class in the form of oral reports with visuals.

2. Conduct an Interview

Ask students to imagine that they are interviewing a visitor from one
of the countries in this unit for a local newspaper. They should work in
pairs to list questions about religion, culture, food, or the role of women,
and locate the answers in the chapters. Then have each pair of students
act out the interview situation with one student asking and the other
answering the questions.

NORTH AFRICA AND SOUTHWEST ASIA

THE BLUE MOSQUE

ATLANTIC

PACIFIC OCEAN

PACIFIC

OCEAN

NORTH AFRICA AND SOUTHWEST ASIA

OCEAN

201

FOCUS ON VISUALS

Interpreting the Photograph Conduct a class discussion about what students see in the photograph. Draw their attention to the shape of the mosque and the number of buildings on the land that surrounds it. Have a student volunteer read the caption aloud. In addition to being a religious center, what other services did the mosque provide for the people in the community? Ask students to think about what groups or organizations they are familiar with that provide similar services.

Possible Responses The mosque provided a school, a public bath, and a kitchen. A local church or community organization might also include a thrift shop or a homeless shelter or kitchen.

Extension Ask students to write the script for a tour guide to use while leading a group around the mosque and the outlying buildings.

Implementing the National Geography Standards

Standard 13 Identify the factors that contribute to conflict between countries

Objective To create a board game with the goal of solving conflicts that arise between countries

Class Time 45 minutes

Task Students work together to create a board game. The object of the game is to prevent war between countries. This should force the players to solve issues between countries such as economic competition for scarce resources, boundary disputes, cultural differences, and control of strategic locations. Have the class play the completed game.

Evaluation Students should identify at least six factors that contribute to international conflicts.

UNIT 3

ATLAS
North Africa and Southwest Asia

ATLAS OBJECTIVES

1. Locate physical features of North Africa and Southwest Asia

2. Analyze the precipitation of North Africa and Southwest Asia and compare the landmass and population of this region with the United States

3. Identify the political features of North Africa and Southwest Asia

4. Identify the religions and ethnic groups of North Africa and Southwest Asia

5. Compare data on the countries of North Africa and Southwest Asia

FOCUS & MOTIVATE

Ask students what they know about the countries of North Africa and Southwest Asia. Why do they think these regions are grouped together?

INSTRUCT: Objective ❶

Physical Map of North Africa and Southwest Asia

• What body of water separates Africa from Southwest Asia? Red Sea

• Into which body of water does the Nile River empty? Mediterranean Sea

• What is the highest mountain in Southwest Asia? Mount Damavand in Iran

 In-depth Resources: Unit 3
• Unit Atlas Activity, p. 1

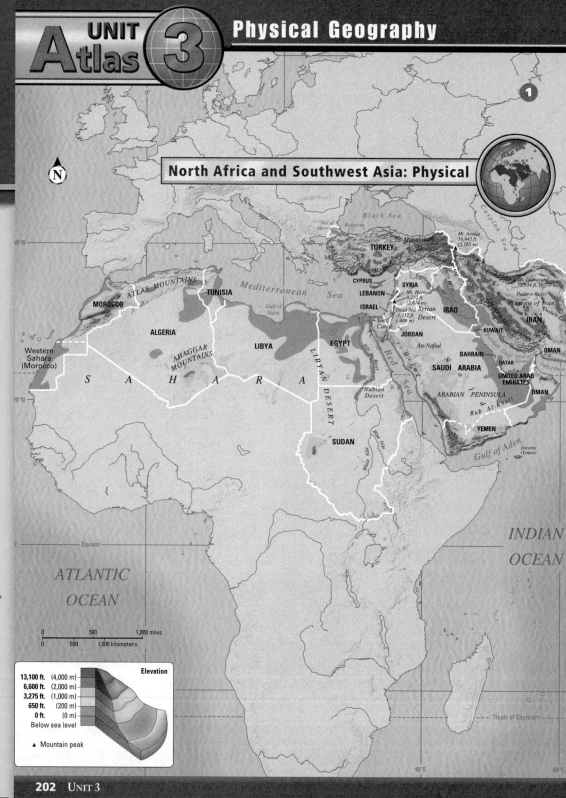

UNIT Atlas 3 — Physical Geography

North Africa and Southwest Asia: Physical

Elevation
13,100 ft. (4,000 m)
6,600 ft. (2,000 m)
3,275 ft. (1,000 m)
650 ft. (200 m)
0 ft. (0 m)
Below sea level

▲ Mountain peak

202 UNIT 3

Activity Options

Interdisciplinary Link: Math

Explaining the Skill Students will demonstrate an ability to read elevation changes and a scale of miles on a physical map.

Applying the Skill Point out that the Nile River is the longest river in the world. It begins near the Equator in the highlands of Burundi and flows north into the Mediterranean Sea. Have students draw a diagram of the river showing how it drops in elevation from its beginning to its

Ⓑ Block Scheduling

end. The diagrams should be according to scale. That is, students should measure on the map the distance the Nile flows at an elevation of 0 to 650 feet. Students might use colors to indicate elevation. They should also write on their diagrams the distances between changes in elevation. Have students meet in small groups to discuss their methods and compare their diagrams.

North Africa and Southwest Asia: Precipitation

②

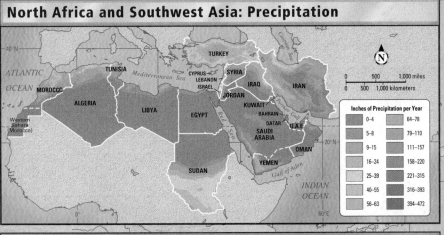

Inches of Precipitation per Year

0–4	64–78
5–8	79–110
9–15	111–157
16–24	158–220
25–39	221–315
40–55	316–393
56–63	394–472

Comparisons of Landmass and Population of the United States, North Africa, and Southwest Asia

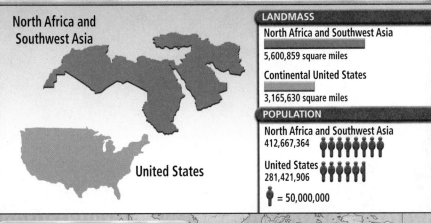

North Africa and Southwest Asia

United States

LANDMASS

North Africa and Southwest Asia

5,600,859 square miles

Continental United States

3,165,630 square miles

POPULATION

North Africa and Southwest Asia
412,667,364

United States
281,421,906

= 50,000,000

FAST FACTS

✓ **WORLD'S LONGEST RIVER:**
Nile, 4,132 mi.

✓ **WORLD'S LARGEST DESERT:**
Sahara, 3,350,000 sq. mi.

✓ **WORLD'S HIGHEST RECORDED TEMPERATURE:** 136°F at El Azizia, Libya, on September 13, 1922

✓ **WORLD'S LARGEST SUPPLY OF OIL:**
259 billion barrels of proven oil reserves in Saudi Arabia

✓ **DRIEST AREA IN THE WORLD:**
Nearly two-thirds of this region is desert.

GEOGRAPHY SKILLBUILDER: Interpreting Maps and Visuals

1. **Region** • Name three countries that get less than 10 inches of rain per year.
2. **Region** • Name the countries that border the Red Sea.

INSTRUCT: Objective ②

Precipitation of North Africa and Southwest Asia

• How much rain falls on most of this region? less than ten inches per year

Landmass

• How much larger is this region than the continental United States? about two and one-half million square miles

Population

• How many people live in the region? 412,667,364 people

Fast Facts

• What is the world's longest river? How long is it? Nile; 4,160 miles

MORE ABOUT...
The Nile River

The Nile has created some of the richest farmland in the world. It drains a large portion of Africa. Along the way, it gathers silt that it carries down to its delta. For thousands of years, the Nile would flood and deposit the silt, which enriched the ground and made crops flourish. In 1968, Egypt built the Aswan High Dam, which ended the flooding. Now the silt is trapped in the lake, and farmers must artificially fertilize their crops.

Fast Facts

Review the Fast Facts with students, and then direct them to create their own file of interesting details. Tell them to add facts as they read the unit and conduct research.

GEOGRAPHY SKILLBUILDER
Answers

1. Answers might include Morocco, Algeria, Libya, Egypt, and Saudi Arabia.
2. Libya, in north central Africa

Country Profiles

Sudan Sudan is Africa's largest country. Approximately half of the people are Arabs. They live mainly in the north. People of the southern part of Sudan are made up primarily of people of various black African ethnic groups. Arabic is the official language and is spoken by about half the people. Altogether, more than 100 languages are spoken. Not only is Sudan large, its geography is also extremely varied. Much of it is desert, some parts of which get as little as four inches of rain per year. But Sudan also has large plains, swamps, and the long valley of the Nile River. The southern part of Sudan is dominated by the Nile. The flood plain is vast and is covered with thick jungle. In the south, high mountain ranges form the borders with neighboring countries.

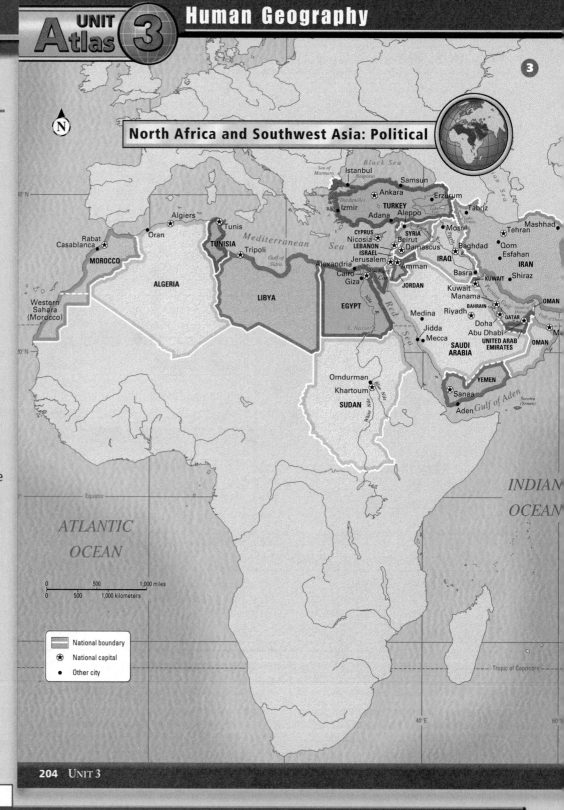

INSTRUCT: Objective ❸

Political Map of North Africa and Southwest Asia

- In what country do the Blue and White Nile rivers join? Sudan
- What is the capital of Libya? Tripoli
- What body of water lies between Saudi Arabia and Iran? Persian Gulf
- On what continents is Turkey located? Europe, Asia

MORE ABOUT...

The Sahara

The Sahara is a vast arid zone that occupies most of North Africa. It stretches from the Atlantic Ocean to the Red Sea, a distance of about 3,500 miles. It extends 1,200 miles from the Atlas Mountains to central Africa. The average rainfall is less than 4 inches per year. Sand dunes cover about 15 percent of the desert. Most of the rest is a rocky plateau covered with barren rock and gravel. There are some quite high mountains in the Sahara. Emi Koussi, part of the Tibesti massif in north Chad, reaches 11,000 feet. The name, Sahara, is from an Arabic word meaning "desert," so it is incorrect to say the Sahara Desert, which simply means "Desert Desert."

North Africa and Southwest Asia: Political

National boundary
⊛ National capital
• Other city

Activity Options

Interdisciplinary Link: Popular Culture

Class Time One class period

Task Researching and creating a poster to illustrate popular culture in a major city of the region

Purpose To learn about popular culture and daily lives of people

Supplies Needed
- Library or Internet resources
- Pencils or pens
- Art supplies

Activity Have students work in pairs to research the daily lives and culture of a major city of North Africa or Southwest Asia. Have them create a poster that illustrates the popular culture. The posters might be divided into parts to show the different extremes of culture that exist within a single city. Have students post their work and discuss the popular culture of the city they have chosen.

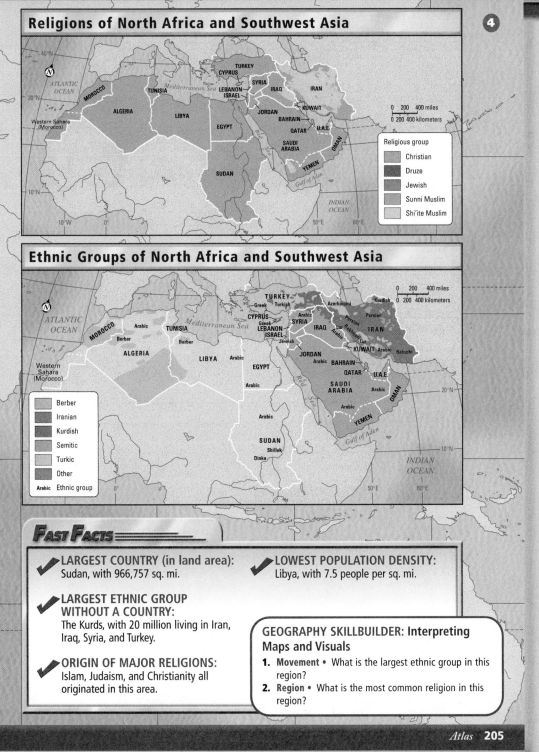

Religions of North Africa and Southwest Asia

Religious group
- Christian
- Druze
- Jewish
- Sunni Muslim
- Shi'ite Muslim

Ethnic Groups of North Africa and Southwest Asia

- Berber
- Iranian
- Kurdish
- Semitic
- Turkic
- Other

Arabic Ethnic group

FAST FACTS

✔ **LARGEST COUNTRY (in land area):**
Sudan, with 966,757 sq. mi.

✔ **LARGEST ETHNIC GROUP WITHOUT A COUNTRY:**
The Kurds, with 20 million living in Iran, Iraq, Syria, and Turkey.

✔ **ORIGIN OF MAJOR RELIGIONS:**
Islam, Judaism, and Christianity all originated in this area.

✔ **LOWEST POPULATION DENSITY:**
Libya, with 7.5 people per sq. mi.

GEOGRAPHY SKILLBUILDER: Interpreting Maps and Visuals

1. **Movement** • What is the largest ethnic group in this region?
2. **Region** • What is the most common religion in this region?

Atlas **205**

INSTRUCT: Objective ④

Religions of North Africa and Southwest Asia

- Which religious group occupies the greatest area of Southwest Asia? Sunni Muslim
- How much of North Africa is Sunni Muslim? almost all of it

Ethnic Groups

- Which part of North Africa is occupied by Arabs? the north and northeast portion

Fast Facts

- What is the largest city of North Africa and Southwest Asia? Cairo

MORE ABOUT...
The Kurds

Prior to World War I, the Kurds had their own country, Kurdistan. Following the war, their country was broken up as the victorious Allied powers tried to reconstruct the Middle East. The Kurds have struggled ever since to reclaim a national homeland. They remain the largest ethnic group in the world that lacks a homeland.

Fast Facts

Review the Fast Facts with students. Remind them to continue adding to their own files as they read the unit.

GEOGRAPHY SKILLBUILDER
Answers
1. Arab
2. Sunni Muslim

Country Profiles

Saudi Arabia Saudi Arabia is one of the wealthiest countries in the world, primarily because it possesses about one-quarter of the world's supply of petroleum. The United States depends upon Saudi oil. In 2000, about 17 percent of all U.S. oil imports came from Saudi Arabia. One drawback of Saudi Arabia's wealth in petroleum is that other aspects of its economy have been ignored. Revenue from oil makes up over 90 percent of the country's export income. Many of the workers who earn the most from Saudi oil—7.2 million in all—are foreigners working in the country. Saudi Arabia has recently issued a plan to reduce the number of foreign workers by 60 percent, providing more opportunities for Saudis.

DATA FILE OBJECTIVE

Examine and compare data on North Africa and Southwest Asia

FOCUS & MOTIVATE

Ask students which two countries in North Africa and Southwest Asia have the highest infant mortality rate. Which has the highest number of doctors per one thousand people? infant mortality: Sudan (69.2); doctors: Israel (385)

INSTRUCT: Objective 5

Data File

• Which country has the highest literacy rate? Israel (96)

• Which country has the highest life expectancy? Israel (79 years)

• Which of the countries in this region has the most cars per 1,000 people? Which has the fewest? most cars per 1,000 people: Lebanon (325); fewest cars: Sudan (1)

 In-depth Resources: Unit 3
• Data File Activity, p. 2

Country Flag	Country/Capital	Currency	Population (2001 estimate)	Life Expectancy (years)	Birthrate (per 1,000 pop.) (2000 estimate)
	Algeria Algiers	Dinar	31,736,000	70	23
	Bahrain Manama	Dinar	645,000	73	21
	Cyprus Nicosia	Pound	763,000	77	13
	Egypt Cairo	Pound	69,537,000	63	25
	Iran Tehran	Rial	66,129,000	70	18
	Iraq Baghdad	Dinar	23,332,000	67	35
	Israel Jerusalem	New Shekel	5,938,000	79	19
	Jordan Amman	Dinar	5,453,000	77	26
	Kuwait Kuwait	Dinar	2,042,000	76	22
	Lebanon Beirut	Pound	3,628,000	71	20
	Libya Tripoli	Dinar	5,241,000	75	28
	Morocco Rabat	Dirham	30,645,000	69	23
	Oman Muscat	Rial Omani	2,622,000	72	38
	Qatar Doha	Riyal	769,000	72	16
	Saudi Arabia Riyadh	Riyal	22,757,000	68	38
	Sudan Khartoum	Pound	36,080,000	57	39

206 UNIT 3

Activity Options

Cooperative Learning: Graphing Data

Class Time 30 minutes

Task Creating a double bar graph to make comparisons

Purpose To gather information from a chart and present it as a graph

Activity Have students work in pairs and together choose six countries from the Data File. Have them create a double bar graph that compares the birthrate and the infant mortality rate of each of the six countries.

You may wish to review how to construct a double bar graph with students. When students have completed their graphs, have them discuss their results in class. What conclusions can they draw?

5

DATA FILE

Infant Mortality (per 1,000 live births) (2000)	Doctors (per 100,000 pop.) (1992–1998)	Literacy Rate (percentage) (1995–2000)	Passenger Cars (per 1,000 pop.) (1996–1997)	Total Area (square miles)	Map (not to scale)
42.2	85	62	17	919,595	
14.0	100	85	242	268	
7.4	255	97	316	3,572	
65.7	202	51	20	385,230	
28.1	85	79	26	636,300	
62.4	55	58	32	167,975	
7.6	385	96	224	7,992	
32.1	166	87	40	34,342	
9.8	189	79	318	6,880	
29.4	210	92	325	3,950	
26.4	128	76	126	678,400	
37.0	46	44	39	274,461	
23.9	133	59	108	82,009	
16.4	126	79	151	4,416	
36.3	166	63	89	865,000	
69.2	9	46	1	966,757	

MORE ABOUT...
Berbers

The Berbers are an ancient people who occupied northwest Africa and the Sahara at least 5,000 years ago, long before the Arabs moved into the region. Today, about 15 million Berbers live in isolated groups throughout Morocco, Tunisia, Libya, Algeria, and Egypt. Most live in the mountains and desert. They speak a variety of dialects, and most are farmers and herders. After the Arabs moved into the land, most Berbers converted to Islam and follow Arabic cultural traditions.

Activity Options

Differentiating Instruction: Gifted and Talented

B Block Scheduling

Class Time Two class periods

Task Illustrating the history of the Sahara

Purpose To research the geologic history of the Sahara

Supplies Needed
- Library or Internet resources
- Pens or pencils

Activity Explain to students that the Sahara was not always a desert. Thousands of years ago, it supported many kinds of animal and plant life. Humans lived there then, and their lifestyles were much different than they are now. Have students research the history of the Sahara over the past 10,000 years. Encourage them to make drawings to illustrate what life might have been like 5,000 or 10,000 years ago.

Teacher's Edition **207**

MORE ABOUT...
The Arabian Nights

One of the most famous pieces of world literature is set in Southwest Asia. *The Thousand and One Nights,* which is also known as *The Arabian Nights,* is a collection of folk tales taken from Persia, Egypt, Arabia, India, and other countries in and around the region. The work was first written down in the 10th century in Arabic. It first appeared in English in the 1880s. Baghdad, which has been occupied since at least 4000 B.C., was the leading city in the ancient civilization of Mesopotamia. It is the setting for many of the tales in this story.

Country Flag	Country/Capital	Currency	Population (2001 estimate)	Life Expectancy (years)	Birthrate (per 1,000 pop.) (2000)
	Syria Damascus	Pound	16,729,000	68	31
	Tunisia Tunis	Dinar	9,705,000	74	17
	Turkey Ankara	Lira	66,494,000	71	19
	United Arab Emirates Abu Dhabi	Dirham	2,407,000	74	18
	Yemen Sanaa	Rial	18,078,000	60	43

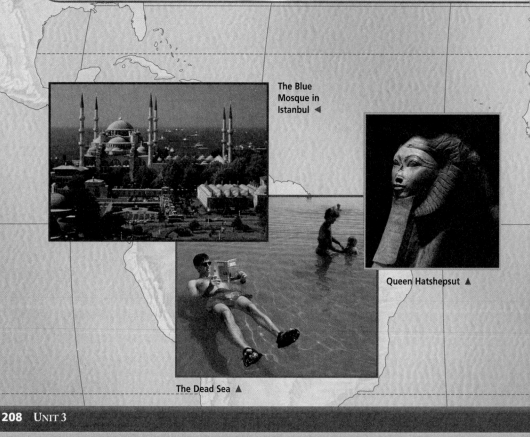

The Blue Mosque in Istanbul ◄

Queen Hatshepsut ▲

The Dead Sea ▲

Activity Options

Interdisciplinary Link: Literature

Class Time One class period

Task Learning a folk tale from North Africa or Southwest Asia and telling it to the class

Purpose To learn about the folk culture of people of the region

Supplies Needed

• Library or Internet resources

Block Scheduling

Activity Explain to students that most folk tales were created long ago and survived because people told them to each other, passing them down from generation to generation. Have students do research to find a folk tale from North Africa or Southwest Asia. Ask them to memorize the tale and then tell it to their classmates. Urge them to think how they can dramatize the tale by making changes in emphasis, using gestures, slowing down or speeding up their delivery, or pausing at critical points.

DATA FILE

Infant Mortality (per 1,000 live births) (2000)	Doctors (per 100,000 pop.) (1992–1998)	Literacy Rate (percentage) (1996–1998)	Passenger Cars (per 1,000 pop.) (1991–1998)	Total Area (square miles)	Map (not to scale)
35.2	144	79	9	71,498	
30.1	70	67	28	63,378	
33.3	121	82	53	300,948	
13.4	181	79	144	32,278	
67.4	23	43	15	203,796	

GEOGRAPHY SKILLBUILDER: Interpreting a Chart

1. **Region** • How much higher is Lebanon's literacy rate than Iran's?
2. **Region** • In general, how can a country's literacy rate be a predictor of its infant mortality rate in this region?

shadoof in Egypt ▼

Palestinians in Israel ▲

An oil well in Saudi Arabia ▲

MORE ABOUT...
Bahrain

Bahrain is the smallest of the countries of North Africa and Southwest Asia. It is made up of 30 islands in the Persian Gulf. Most of the land is desert, and the country was extremely poor until oil was discovered there in 1932. That discovery turned around the future of Bahrain. Today the people enjoy one of the highest standards of living in the region. The country's wealth enables the government to provide many services unavailable to poor nations. All children must attend primary school, which is free to all. Higher education is available as well. Medical care is also free. Invite students to compare the literacy rates, numbers of doctors, and other data of Bahrain with that of other countries of North Africa and Southwest Asia.

GEOGRAPHY SKILLBUILDER
Answers

1. Lebanon's literacy rate (92 percent) is 13 percent higher than that of Iran (79 percent).
2. In general, the higher the literacy rate, the lower the infant mortality rate.

Activity Options

Multiple Learning Styles: Logical/Mathematical

Class Time 40 minutes

Purpose To create a pie graph showing the relative populations of the countries of North Africa and Southwest Asia

Task Making a pie graph

Supplies Needed
- Paper
- Pencils
- Protractors
- Compasses

Activity Have students find the population of each country in North Africa and Southwest Asia and create a pie graph to represent the total population of the region. Next, have them determine the percentage of that total represented by each country and divide the pie graph into the proper proportions for each nation.

North Africa and Southwest Asia: Place and Times

	OVERVIEW	COPYMASTERS	INTEGRATED TECHNOLOGY
UNIT ATLAS AND CHAPTER RESOURCES	The students will examine ancient civilizations in the Nile River Valley and the Fertile Crescent and how three of the world's major religions developed there.	**In-depth Resources: Unit 3** • Guided Reading Worksheets, pp. 3–7 • Skillbuilder Practice, p. 10 • Unit Atlas Activities, pp. 1–2 • Geography Workshop, pp. 31–32 **Reading Study Guide** (Spanish and English), pp. 64–75 **Outline Map Activities**	Power Presentations Electronic Teacher Tools Online Lesson Planner Chapter Summaries on CD Critical Thinking Transparencies CT15

	KEY IDEAS		
SECTION 1 Physical Geography pp. 213–216	• The Nile, the Tigris, and the Euphrates rivers impacted ancient peoples' lives.	**In-depth Resources: Unit 3** • Guided Reading Worksheet, p. 3 • Reteaching Activity, p. 12 **Reading Study Guide** (Spanish and English), pp. 64–65	Map Transparencies MT18, 20 classzone.com Chapter Summaries on CD
SECTION 2 Ancient Mesopotamia and the Fertile Crescent pp. 217–221	• Mesopotamian city-states faced threats from invaders, a lack of water, and risky trade conditions. • The class system in Mesopotamia enforced strict social boundaries. • Scribes served an important function in Mesopotamian society.	**In-depth Resources: Unit 3** • Guided Reading Worksheet, p. 4 • Reteaching Activity, p. 13 **Reading Study Guide** (Spanish and English), pp. 66–67	classzone.com Chapter Summaries on CD
SECTION 3 Ancient Egypt pp. 223–227	• The Nile River made the soil fertile through annual floods, and also provided a route for trade. • The ancient Egyptians built pyramids where pharaohs could spend the afterlife.	**In-depth Resources: Unit 3** • Guided Reading Worksheet, p. 5 • Reteaching Activity, p. 14 **Reading Study Guide** (Spanish and English), pp. 68–69	Critical Thinking Transparencies CT16 classzone.com Chapter Summaries on CD
SECTION 4 Birthplace of Three Religions pp. 229–232	• Judaism, Christianity, and Islam all share common traits. • Judaism is a story of exile. • Christians believe that Jesus was the promised Messiah. • The Qur'an is the collection of God's revelations to Muhammad.	**In-depth Resources: Unit 3** • Guided Reading Worksheet, p. 6 • Reteaching Activity, p. 15 **Reading Study Guide** (Spanish and English), pp. 70–71	classzone.com Chapter Summaries on CD
SECTION 5 Islamic Empires pp. 235–237	• The Five Pillars of Islam are the five religious duties observed by Muslims. • Islamic ideas and culture were spread along trade routes during the Ottoman Empire.	**In-depth Resources: Unit 3** • Guided Reading Worksheet, p. 7 • Reteaching Activity, p. 16 **Reading Study Guide** (Spanish and English), pp. 72–73	classzone.com Chapter Summaries on CD

ASSESSMENT OPTIONS

PE **Chapter Assessment,** pp. 238–239

Formal Assessment
- Chapter Tests: Forms A, B, C, pp. 117–128

Test Generator

Online Test Practice

Strategies for Test Preparation

PE **Section Assessment,** p. 216

Formal Assessment
- Section Quiz, p. 112

Integrated Assessment
- Rubric for making a chart

Test Generator

Test Practice Transparencies TT24

PE **Section Assessment,** p. 221

Formal Assessment
- Section Quiz, p. 113

Integrated Assessment
- Rubric for designing a mural

Test Generator

Test Practice Transparencies TT25

PE **Section Assessment,** p. 227

Formal Assessment
- Section Quiz, p. 114

Integrated Assessment
- Rubric for writing a journal entry

Test Generator

Test Practice Transparencies TT26

PE **Section Assessment,** p. 232

Formal Assessment
- Section Quiz, p. 115

Integrated Assessment
- Rubric for writing a letter

Test Generator

Test Practice Transparencies TT27

PE **Section Assessment,** p. 237

Formal Assessment
- Section Quiz, p. 116

Integrated Assessment
- Rubric for creating an illustrated report

Test Generator

Test Practice Transparencies TT28

RESOURCES FOR DIFFERENTIATING INSTRUCTION

Students Acquiring English/ESL

Reading Study Guide
(Spanish and English), pp. 64–75

Access for Students Acquiring English
Spanish Translations, pp. 61–72

TE **TE Activity**
- Writing Sentences, p. 220

Less Proficient Readers

Reading Study Guide
(Spanish and English), pp. 64–75

TE **TE Activities**
- Identifying Details, p. 218
- Summarizing, p. 235

Gifted and Talented Students

TE **TE Activities**
- Discovering King Tut's Tomb, p. 225
- Researching a Report, p. 230

CROSS-CURRICULAR CONNECTIONS

Humanities
Hodge, Susie. *Ancient Egyptian Art.* Des Plaines, IL: Heinemann Interactive Library, 1998. Wall paintings, architecture, and sculpture.

Literature
Bower, Tamara. *The Shipwrecked Sailor: An Egyptian Tale with Hieroglyphs.* New York: Atheneum, 2000. An ancient tale told in hieroglyphs, modern Egyptian, and English.

Popular Culture
Nemet-Nejat, Karen Rhea. *Daily Life in Ancient Mesopotamia.* Westport, CT: Greenwood Press, 1998. From 3100 through 612 B.C.
Broida, Marian. *Ancient Egyptians and Their Neighbors: An Activity Guide.* Chicago: University of Chicago Press, 1999. Culture and customs of the Egyptians, Mesopotamians, Nubians, and Hittites.

Science/Math
Rumford, James. *Seeker of Knowledge: The Man Who Deciphered Egyptian Hieroglyphs.* Boston: Houghton Mifflin, 2000. Biography of Jean-Francois Champollion.
Woods, Geraldine. *Science in Ancient Egypt.* New York: Franklin Watts, 1998. Underscores scientific achievements.

Science
Kent, Peter. *Hidden Under the Ground: The World Beneath Your Feet.* New York: Dutton, 1998. Clues to ancient civilizations lie under the ground.
Tanaka, Shelly. *Secrets of the Mummies: Uncovering the Bodies of Ancient Egyptians.* New York: Hyperion, 1999. Archaeology and study of how bodies were mummified.

ENRICHMENT ACTIVITIES

The following activities are especially suitable for classes following block schedules.

Teacher's Edition, pp. 219, 222, 230, 231, 232, 236
Pupil's Edition, pp. 216, 221, 227, 232, 237

Unit Atlas, pp. 202–209
Technology: 6500 B.C., p. 228

Outline Map Activities

INTEGRATED TECHNOLOGY

Go to **classzone.com** for lesson support and activities for Chapter 8.

BLOCK SCHEDULE LESSON PLAN OPTIONS: 90-MINUTE PERIOD

DAY 1

UNIT PREVIEW, pp. 200–201
Class Time 20 minutes

UNIT ATLAS, pp. 202–209
Class Time 20 minutes

- **Small Groups** Divide the class into four groups and have each group answer Making Connections questions for one section of the Unit Atlas: Physical Geography, Human Geography, Regional Patterns, and Data File.

SECTION 1, pp. 213–216
Class Time 50 minutes

- **Conducting an Experiment** Use the Interdisciplinary Link: Science from TE p. 214 to teach students how soil is deposited along riverbanks as a result of flooding.
  Class Time 25 minutes

- **Internet** Extend students' background knowledge of the physical geography of North Africa and Southwest Asia by visiting **classzone.com.**
  Class Time 25 minutes

DAY 2

SECTION 2, pp. 217–221
Class Time 35 minutes

- **Peer Competition** Divide the class into pairs. Assign each pair one of the Terms & Names for this section. Have pairs make up five questions that can be answered with the term or name. Have groups take turns asking the class their questions.
  Class Time 20 minutes

- **Word Web** Divide the class into small groups. Have each group create a word web to display the differences among the various classes of people in ancient Mesopotamia. After each group has completed its web, have the entire class share their webs.
  Class Time 15 minutes

SECTION 3, pp. 223–227
Class Time 35 minutes

- **Creating Pictograms** Review the information about hieroglyphics on PE p. 225. Have students create nameplates, using pictograms they devise to represent themselves and their interests. Collect the nameplates and distribute them randomly to the class. Have students guess the identity of the person whose nameplate they have.
  Class Time 25 minutes

- **Brainstorming** Lead the class to consider how the Egyptians built the pyramids without using large equipment as we have today. Record students' suggestions on the chalkboard.
  Class Time 10 minutes

SECTION 4, pp. 229–232
Class Time 20 minutes

- **Making an Outline** Use the Skillbuilder Mini-Lesson from TE p. 231 to review with students the importance of organizing information in outline form.

DAY 3

SECTION 5, pp. 234–237
Class Time 35 minutes

- **Time Capsule** Remind students that Muslims translated and recorded important books and papers to preserve knowledge. Have students work in small groups to make a list of papers, objects, pictures, and so on that they would include in a time capsule. Students should share their lists with the class and combine them into one master list.
  Class Time 25 minutes

- **Peer Teaching** Have pairs of students review the Main Idea for the section on PE p. 234 and find three details to support it. Then have each pair list two additional important ideas and trade lists with another group to find details.
  Class Time 10 minutes

CHAPTER 8 REVIEW AND ASSESSMENT,
pp. 238–239
Class Time 55 minutes

- **Review** Have students use the charts they created for Reading Social Studies on PE p. 212 to review generalizations and supporting details about North Africa and Southwest Asia.
  Class Time 20 minutes

- **Assessment** Have students complete the Chapter 8 Assessment.
  Class Time 35 minutes

TECHNOLOGY IN THE CLASSROOM

MUSEUMS ON THE WEB

Most museums have their own Web sites that contain examples from their exhibits and collections. These sites are an excellent resource for students. Even if you teach in a large city, it is not always possible to coordinate a field trip to the museum. The Internet allows students to see exhibits from around the world as well as local museums.

ACTIVITY OUTLINE

Objective Students will visit Web sites and answer questions about daily life in ancient Egypt. They will create their own digital museum exhibits.

Task Have students go to the Web sites and answer the questions about what it was like to live in ancient Egypt. Ask them to choose three items that are particularly significant and create multimedia slides or Web pages showing and describing these items.

Class Time 2–3 class periods

DIRECTIONS

1. Discuss what students think daily life was like in ancient Egypt. They can provide examples from the textbook and from the things they have learned in class or elsewhere. Then ask them what they think can be learned about ancient Egyptian daily life from examining art and artifacts from this civilization.

2. Have students, individually or in small groups, go to the Web sites listed at **classzone.com** to find examples of ancient Egyptian art and artifacts that are now on display in museums. As they look at the exhibits, ask them to answer these questions:

   • What types of materials did the ancient Egyptians work with?

   • Which objects were probably used in everyday life (as opposed to being saved for special occasions or for the kings)?

   • What animals do you think the Egyptians had contact with? How do you think Egyptians felt about these animals?

   • Was religion important to the Egyptians? What types of religious objects did they make?

   • What conclusions can you draw from these exhibits about daily life in ancient Egypt?

3. Ask students to create an online museum exhibit to teach people about daily life in ancient Egypt. Because they have limited time and space, they must choose only three items to place in their exhibits. Have each group or individual choose three objects that they think would most effectively show modern-day people how the ancient Egyptians lived on a day-to-day basis.

4. Have students create multimedia slides or Web pages showcasing their three exhibit features. They should include images from the museum Web sites, making sure to credit the museums in small captions under the pictures. They should also provide a paragraph for each image, describing how that item relates to ancient Egyptian daily life and explaining why they have chosen to display this object in their exhibit.

CHAPTER 8 OBJECTIVE

Students will examine ancient civilizations in the Nile River valley and the Fertile Crescent, and how three of the world's major religions developed there.

FOCUS ON VISUALS

Interpreting the Photograph Have students look at the photograph of the Sahara and then locate North Africa on the inset map. Point out that this chapter focuses on the land and history of a region whose cultures have been shaped by lack of water. Ask them to give their first impressions of this place—the first words that come to mind to describe this vast, sandy stretch of land. How might people live in such an environment?

Possible Responses Empty, lonely, hot, dry, interesting, frightening, mysterious. Students may suggest images from movies and television such as people on camels, wearing loose robes.

Extension Ask students to write a short paragraph or poem describing their reactions to or impressions of the desert.

CRITICAL THINKING ACTIVITY

Hypothesizing Ask students what they know about the climate and physical geography of North Africa and Southwest Asia. Have them consider the kinds of economic activities they think took place in ancient times. Ask students to draw conclusions about how the region's geography might have affected the kinds of crops that people could grow and where they could live.

Class Time 20 minutes

CHAPTER
8

North Africa and Southwest Asia: Place and Times

SECTION 1   Physical Geography

SECTION 2   Ancient Mesopotamia and the Fertile Crescent

SECTION 3   Ancient Egypt

SECTION 4   Birthplace of Three Religions

SECTION 5   Muslim Empires

ATLANTIC
PACIFIC
OCEAN
PACIFIC
OCEAN
INDIAN
OCEAN
OCEAN
NORTH AFRICA AND SOUTHWEST ASIA

Region The Sahara stretches across much of North Africa.

210

Recommended Resources

BOOKS FOR THE TEACHER
Ancient Civilizations, 3000 B.C.–A.D. 500. Alexandria, VA: Time-Life Books, 1998. Sumer, Egypt, Nubia, Israel, and others.
George, Linda S. *The Golden Age of Islam.* New York: Benchmark Books, 1998. Eighth century to 13th century.

Reeves, Nicholas. *Ancient Egypt: The Great Discoveries.* New York: Thames & Hudson, 2000. A chronological view of the discoveries.

VIDEOS
The Pyramids of Egypt. New York: Ambrose Video, 1998. Construction and history.

SOFTWARE
Ancient Civilizations: Egypt and the Fertile Crescent. Washington, D.C.: National Geographic Society, 1995. Geography, culture, history, ancient treasures.

INTERNET
For more information about North Africa and Southwest Asia, visit **classzone.com**.

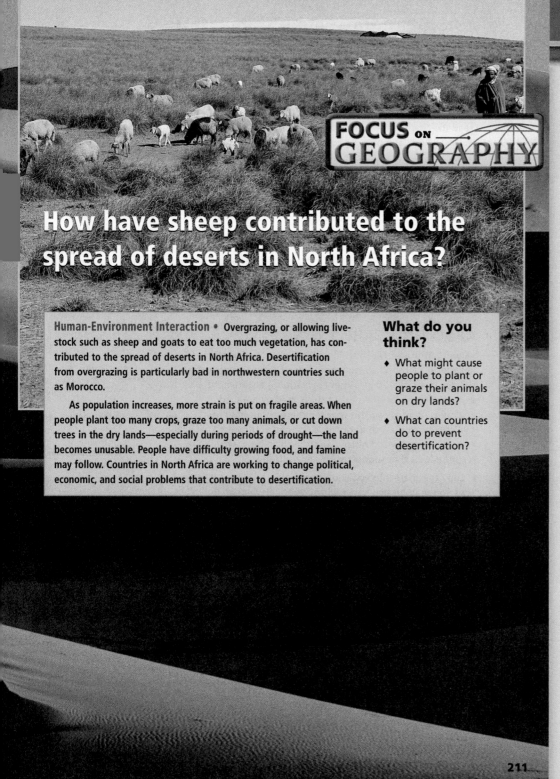

FOCUS ON GEOGRAPHY

How have sheep contributed to the spread of deserts in North Africa?

Human-Environment Interaction • Overgrazing, or allowing livestock such as sheep and goats to eat too much vegetation, has contributed to the spread of deserts in North Africa. Desertification from overgrazing is particularly bad in northwestern countries such as Morocco.

As population increases, more strain is put on fragile areas. When people plant too many crops, graze too many animals, or cut down trees in the dry lands—especially during periods of drought—the land becomes unusable. People have difficulty growing food, and famine may follow. Countries in North Africa are working to change political, economic, and social problems that contribute to desertification.

What do you think?

◆ What might cause people to plant or graze their animals on dry lands?

◆ What can countries do to prevent desertification?

211

FOCUS ON GEOGRAPHY

Objectives

• To help students understand the relationship between climate and natural resources

• To show students how human actions can affect the environment

What Do You Think?

1. Explain that very little rain falls in this region and that most of the land is dry. Guide students to understand that as the population increases land becomes more scarce. Therefore, land that was not originally chosen for planting or grazing must now be used.

2. Guide students to think about measures that countries can take to prevent desertification, such as planting trees, irrigating, providing food aid, and educating people about the dangers of overgrazing.

How have sheep contributed to the spread of deserts in North Africa?

Have students consider what they know about the eating habits of sheep. Tell students that sheep tend to overgraze grassy areas. Then have them discuss how such grazing might destroy an area that receives little rain. Ask them whether they think sheep are the only animals that have had this effect on North Africa.

MAKING GEOGRAPHIC CONNECTIONS

Have students identify parts of the United States that might have experienced similar cases of desertification due to overgrazing. Then ask them whether it would be likely for famines to occur in these areas, just as they have in parts of North Africa. Discuss their opinions.

Implementing the National Geography Standards

Standard 4 Explain how isolated communities have been changed by technology

Objective To write a script describing how technology is transforming a fictional small town in North Africa or Southwest Asia

Class Time 40 minutes

Task Have students write a script for a mini-documentary describing changes that have taken or are taking place because of technology in an isolated community in North Africa or Southwest Asia. Students should cover changes resulting from new highways, satellite dishes, and computers.

Evaluation The scripts should explain at least one direct consequence of the community's interactions with new technology.

BEFORE YOU READ

What Do You Know?

Invite students who come from, or have relatives who come from, North Africa or Southwest Asia to share what they know about the region. Ask if anyone in the class has read books, seen movies, or watched documentaries or news reports about the region. Have students describe what they learned from these sources.

What Do You Want to Know?

Suggest that students make a chart with the headings *What I Want to Know* and *What I Learned* in their notebooks. Ask them to record questions they hope to have answered or topics that they are curious about in the first column. As they read the chapter, have them record facts and ideas in the second column.

READ AND TAKE NOTES

Reading Strategy: Making Generalizations
Before students begin reading, have them practice making generalizations about the physical geography of the region where they live. First, make a generalization about the area and have students identify supporting details. Then ask them to make generalizations of their own.

 In-depth Resources: Unit 3
• Guided Reading Worksheets, pp. 3–7

BEFORE YOU READ

▶▶ What Do You Know?

Before you read the chapter, consider what you already know about North Africa and Southwest Asia. Look at a physical map of the region, and think about features, such as the Sahara. How might living in a desert affect the lives of people who live there? What do you know about the pyramids of ancient Egypt? Are you familiar with any of these sacred books—the Hebrew Scriptures, the Christian Bible, or the Qur'an of Islam? Many of the events in these books took place in this region. Try to imagine the changes that have occurred here in 5,000 years of human history.

▶▶ What Do You Want to Know?

Decide what you know about the physical features of the region and about ancient Mesopotamia, Egypt, and the Muslim Empires. In your notebook, record what you hope to learn from this chapter.

Place • Ziggurats were stepped towers on which temples were built in ancient Mesopotamia. ▲

READ AND TAKE NOTES

Reading Strategy: Making Generalizations Making generalizations is a useful strategy for understanding universal themes in social studies. A generalization is a statement expressed in general terms but supported by detailed evidence. As you read this chapter, think about how the civilizations that arose in North Africa and Southwest Asia influenced world history. Use the chart below to record details that support each generalization.

• Copy the chart into your notebook.
• As you read, notice how civilization has developed in this region.
• Beside each generalization, record some key details that support it.

Culture • The Qur'an is the sacred book of Islam. ▲

Generalizations	Supporting Details
1. Bodies of water provide resources for people in North Africa and Southwest Asia.	Rich farmland is around the Nile, the Tigris, and the Euphrates rivers. Over millions of years, the decomposition of sea life led to the valuable natural resource of oil.
2. Complex civilizations developed religions and laws in ancient Mesopotamia.	Sumerians organized the first city-states. These Mesopotamian city-states were centers of religious worship. Priests controlled religious life and economic life, and the king controlled political and military life.
3. An ancient Egyptian culture based on shared beliefs and goals left a monumental legacy.	The concept of an afterlife led Egyptians to build huge pyramids and other temples and monuments.
4. Three of the world's major religions began in Southwest Asia.	Judaism, Christianity, and Islam all began in Southwest Asia.
5. Islamic beliefs and achievements spread throughout the world.	After Muhammad died, caliphs ruled the Muslim community and created vast empires. Islamic beliefs were exchanged along trade routes. The Muslim Ottoman Empire controlled much of the region.

212 CHAPTER 8

Teaching Strategy

Reading the Chapter This is a thematic chapter focusing on the development of civilizations in the part of the world that was the birthplace of three major religions. Encourage students to think about the relationship between government and religion in this region. Ask them to think about how the region's physical geography and climate have affected its development.

Integrated Assessment The Chapter Assessment on page 239 describes several activities for integrated assessment. You may wish to have students work on these activities during the course of the chapter and then present them at the end.

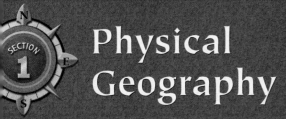

Physical Geography

TERMS & NAMES
fertile
hunter-gatherer
irrigation

MAIN IDEA

Water and the lack of it has shaped this region of flooding rivers, little rainfall, and surrounding seas.

WHY IT MATTERS NOW

Today the region enjoys the benefits of rich oil resources, but its people continue to struggle with problems of both dry land and flooding rivers.

SECTION OBJECTIVES

1. To describe how the Nile, the Tigris, and the Euphrates rivers have influenced life in the region
2. To explain how rivers and seas have shaped the region's economy and resources

SKILLBUILDER
• Interpreting a Map, p. 216

CRITICAL THINKING
• Clarifying, p. 214
• Drawing Conclusions, p. 215

FOCUS & MOTIVATE
WARM-UP

Drawing Conclusions Have students read Dateline and discuss the advantages and disadvantages of living near the Euphrates River.

1. Why do you think people in ancient Mesopotamia lived near the river, even though they knew it would flood every year?
2. What conclusions can you draw about the beliefs of the writer of the article?

INSTRUCT: Objective ❶

Rivers and Deserts/Three Rivers

• What are the three major rivers in this region? the Nile, the Tigris, the Euphrates
• Why did hunter-gatherers settle permanently in the Fertile Crescent? because they could raise animals and grow crops there
• How do rivers enrich the soil? Water overflows river banks and leaves behind rich soil.

 In-depth Resources: Unit 3
• Guided Reading Worksheet, p. 3

 Reading Study Guide
(Spanish and English), pp. 64–65

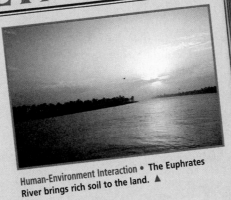

DATELINE ⬭EXTRA

MESOPOTAMIA, 3000 B.C.

Yesterday, the yearly spring flooding of the Euphrates River began. The river is high this year because of heavy rains. Farmers from nearby villages are afraid their homes will be lost. But they need the rich soil the swollen river brings. As soon as the river settles back in its bed, they can begin to plant.

It's like this every year. The gods tell the river to bring good soil, and the river obeys. To Mesopotamians, it means that life will go on.

Human-Environment Interaction • The Euphrates River brings rich soil to the land. ▲

Culture • Utu was one of the gods the Mesopotamians prayed to. ▲

Rivers and Deserts ❶

Water and the lack of it has shaped North Africa and Southwest Asia, a region where little rain falls. Seas of sand cover the deserts, which are dry all year. In these deserts, water is found only in oasis areas. Other areas have depended on the annual flooding of the rivers to make the soil **fertile**, or productive. Fertile soil provides the nutrients that plants need to grow.

North Africa and Southwest Asia: Place and Times **213**

Program Resources

 In-depth Resources: Unit 3
• Guided Reading Worksheet, p. 3
• Reteaching Activity, p. 12

 Reading Study Guide
(Spanish and English), pp. 64–65

 Formal Assessment
• Section Quiz, p. 112

 Integrated Assessment
• Rubric for making a chart

 Outline Map Activities

 Access for Students Acquiring English
• Guided Reading Worksheet, p. 61

 Technology Resources
classzone.com

TEST-TAKING RESOURCES
⬧ Strategies for Test Preparation
⬧ Test Practice Transparencies
⬤ Online Test Practice

The WORLD'S HERITAGE

The first plows were built thousands of years ago when early farmers simply broke off a forked branch from a tree and sharpened one prong to be used for turning the soil. Historians believe that people, not animals, pulled these very early plows. Later, some farmers used oxen to pull their plows. In some parts of the world, human beings, oxen, and camels still pull very primitive plows.

An American blacksmith named John Deere is credited with having made the first steel plow in 1837. The new plow was a boon to American farmers because the sticky soil of the prairies, which had clung to the cast-iron plows of the past, slid right off.

CRITICAL THINKING ACTIVITY

Clarifying To clarify how rivers enrich the soil, ask the following kinds of questions: What is the source of the water that causes the Nile to flood? What is the source of the water that causes the Tigris and Euphrates to flood? When the floodwaters recede, what is left behind?

To be sure students understand the process, have them use maps in the Unit Atlas to trace the routes of the rivers and their tributaries back to the mountains where they originate. The suggested activity (below) can help clarify the physical processes involved.

Class Time 5 minutes

Three Rivers ❶

Some of the ancient peoples who lived in North Africa and Southwest Asia benefited from three major rivers in the region—the Nile, the Tigris (TY·gris), and the Euphrates (yoo·FRAY·teez). The 4,000-mile-long Nile, the longest river in the world, flows from its source in east central Africa to the Mediterranean in northeast Egypt. The Tigris and Euphrates flow to the southeast from Turkey into the northern end of the Persian Gulf. (See the Unit Atlas map on page 202).

From Hunter-Gatherers to Farmers Thousands of years ago, **hunter-gatherers** roamed the east coast of the Mediterranean and the valleys formed from the rivers. These people found food by hunting, fishing, and gathering wild grains, fruits, and nuts. For 99 percent of the time human beings have been on Earth, they have been hunter-gatherers. Eventually, hunter-gatherers settled permanently in places where they could raise animals and grow crops. Some places where hunter-gatherers may have first become farmers are the valleys of the Nile, Tigris, and Euphrates rivers about 8,000 years ago.

The WORLD'S HERITAGE

The Plow No one knows who invented the plow, the farmer's most essential tool. The earliest plows were only sharpened sticks used to dig holes for planting.

Plows like the one shown below are still used in some parts of the world. Modern plows have more parts and are mechanized, but their function is the same.

handle

draft beam

How Rivers Enrich the Soil Most of the soil in the desert regions of North Africa and Southwest Asia is not good for farming. It contains a lot of salt or sand. Only the rivers make farming possible. In summer, when melted snow flowing from the Ethiopian mountains raises the level of the Nile, the river floods. Heavy spring and summer rains also cause the Nile to flood. When these flooding waters flow over the riverbanks, they leave behind fertile soil that has been carried from one area to another.

Snows also melt in the Turkish highlands, where the Tigris and Euphrates rivers begin. As a result, these rivers also flood yearly, bringing fertile soil into the river valleys.

Human-Environment Interaction • **Hunter-gatherers lived off the food they found in the natural world.** ▲

Reading Social Studies

A. Finding Causes Why might farming have begun in the valleys of the Nile, Tigris, and Euphrates rivers?

Reading Social Studies
A. Possible Answe
because there was a
natural water suppl
and good soil

214 CHAPTER 8

Activity Options

Interdisciplinary Link: Science

Class Time 20 minutes

Task Conducting an experiment that simulates flood conditions and soil movement

Purpose To teach students how soil is deposited along river banks as a result of flooding

Supplies Needed
- Small aluminum pie plate with small holes in bottom
- Large aluminum pie plate with small holes in bottom
- Soil and pebbles
- Water

Activity Fill the small pie plate with soil and pebbles and place it in the center of the larger one. Ask a student to pour water into the small plate until some soil flows from the small plate into the large one. After the water drains, have students make observations about how the water carried the soil from one place to another. Discuss how this experiment relates to flooding along the Nile and in Mesopotamia.

Human-Environment Interaction • This modern irrigation system is in the Draa Valley in Morocco. ▼

Human-Environment Interaction • For thousands of years farmers in the region have used simple irrigation tools, such as this shadoof, to water the land. ▲

Irrigation Few places in the region are close enough to the three major rivers to depend on them for deposits of fertile soil. Farmers in other areas have had to develop **irrigation** methods, or ways of bringing water to dry land.

Surrounding Waters ❷

The Mediterranean Sea, the Red Sea, and the Persian Gulf have shaped the climate, resources, and societies of the region. The Mediterranean is the largest body of water in the region. The mild climate of the lands around the Mediterranean attracted settlers. Early civilizations formed on its eastern shores.

Trade Routes Since ancient times, the Red Sea has been an important trade route. Goods and ideas that have traveled through the Red Sea have shaped the cultures that lie on either side of it. The Persian Gulf has also been an important trade route. Today, it draws the interest of the world because of its key position in the middle of oil-rich Southwest Asia.

Energy from an Ancient Sea Millions of years ago, a huge sea covered North Africa and Southwest Asia. When sea creatures died, their remains sank to the bottom.

Strange ?? but TRUE

The Dead Sea It's not actually a sea—it's a lake—and it's not completely dead—some bacteria can survive in its salty depths. The Dead Sea has an area of about 394 square miles. At 1,312 feet below sea level, it is the lowest point on Earth, and it is about ten times saltier than any ocean. Salt and minerals make the water so dense, you can easily float on it.

Surrounding Waters

- How did the region's seas affect its development? They served as trade routes.
- Why does the Persian Gulf attract worldwide interest today? because it is located in the middle of oil-rich Southwest Asia
- How is petroleum formed? by the action of heat and pressure from mud and sand on dead sea creatures over thousands of years

Strange ?? but TRUE

The water in the Dead Sea is lethal to fish and other ocean life. Fish that accidentally enter the sea from freshwater streams die instantly. Unlike fish, people can enjoy a dip in the sea without endangering their health. However, actually swimming in the sea is difficult because the high level of salt in the water makes bodies extremely buoyant. Therefore, instead of swimming, people bob like corks.

CRITICAL THINKING ACTIVITY

Drawing Conclusions The geography of North Africa and Southwest Asia presents both drawbacks and advantages. After students have read the paragraphs under "Surrounding Waters," ask them to draw conclusions about what made it possible for people to overcome the drawbacks and establish civilizations in this region.

Class Time 5 minutes

Activity Options
Multiple Learning Styles: Visual

Class Time 15 minutes

Task Locating the Mediterranean Sea, the Red Sea, and the Persian Gulf on a map

Purpose To understand how these bodies of water have affected the development of the region

Supplies Needed
- World map or map of region

Activity Read aloud the paragraphs under "Surrounding Waters." As you read the first paragraph, have a student locate the region and the bodies of water on the map. As you read the second paragraph, trace the trade routes mentioned and discuss where goods might have come from and what their destinations might have been.

FOCUS ON VISUALS

Interpreting the Maps Have students look at the three maps and ask them to explain what each of them shows. Point out that the two climate maps show different factors influencing climate. Ask them to use the vegetation map to locate the forest and grasslands mentioned in the paragraph "Turkey." What physical features may offset low rainfall?

Possible Responses Rivers allow forests to grow; winds from the Mediterranean Sea and Black Sea may bring moisture to the coastal land.

Extension Have students practice converting temperatures from Fahrenheit to Celsius, using this formula: °F − 32 × 5/9 = °C. If the temperature in Ankara is 68° Fahrenheit, what is it in Celsius? 20°C

ASSESS & RETEACH

Reading Social Studies Have students write supporting details about the physical geography of the region in the first item of the graphic organizer on page 212.

 Formal Assessment
• Section Quiz, p. 112

RETEACHING ACTIVITY

Ask pairs of students to work together to write a short quiz about the section. Then have each pair exchange quizzes with another pair of students.

 In-depth Resources: Unit 3
• Reteaching Activity, p. 12

 Access for Students Acquiring English
• Reteaching Activity, p. 68

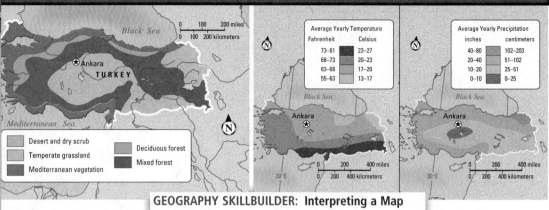

Turkey: Vegetation Map

Black Sea
★ Ankara
TURKEY
Mediterranean Sea

0   100   200 miles
0   100   200 kilometers

Desert and dry scrub
Temperate grassland
Mediterranean vegetation
Deciduous forest
Mixed forest

Turkey: Climate Map

Average Yearly Temperature
Fahrenheit	Celsius
73–81	23–27
68–73	20–23
63–68	17–20
55–63	13–17

Black Sea
Ankara ★

Average Yearly Precipitation
inches	centimeters
40–80	102–203
20–40	51–102
10–20	25–51
0–10	0–25

Black Sea
Ankara ★

0   200   400 miles
0   200   400 kilometers
30°E

GEOGRAPHY SKILLBUILDER: Interpreting a Map

1. **Place** • How does the amount of yearly precipitation affect the type of vegetation that grows?
2. **Location** • What is the average yearly temperature in Ankara?

Geography Skillbuilder Answers

1. the more rain and snow, the more grasslands and forests instead of deserts or dry shrubs
2. 63°–68° F

Over long periods of time, mud and sand and other materials were deposited on top of them. Heat and pressure from these materials changed the dead matter into petroleum, or oil.

Turkey Not all of North Africa and Southwest Asia is hot and dry. Turkey is cooler than the rest of the region and gets more rain. As a result, instead of deserts, Turkey has grasslands and even forest areas.

SECTION 1 ASSESSMENT

Terms & Names

1. **Identify:** (a) fertile (b) hunter-gatherer (c) irrigation

Taking Notes

2. Use a spider map like this one to map the importance of water in North Africa and Southwest Asia.

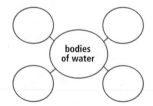

bodies of water

Main Ideas

3. (a) How did the area around the Persian Gulf come to be a rich source of petroleum?

(b) How did hunter-gatherers in North Africa and Southwest Asia become farmers?

(c) How did rivers in Southwest Asia enrich the soil?

Critical Thinking

4. **Analyzing Causes**

Why might the earliest farming communities have developed along the Nile, Tigris, and Euphrates rivers?

Think About

♦ needs of farmers
♦ annual flooding

ACTIVITY -OPTION- Make a **chart** of the major rivers and bodies of water discussed in this section and list the effects each has had on the region.

216 CHAPTER 8

Section 1 Assessment

1. Terms & Names
a. fertile, p. 213
b. hunter-gatherer, p. 214
c. irrigation, p. 215

2. Taking Notes

irrigation — soil enrichment — **Bodies of water** — trade — human needs

3. Main Ideas
a. Over time, heat and pressure from mud and sand turned the remains of dead sea organisms into petroleum.
b. They settled permanently in places where they could raise animals and grow crops.
c. Floodwaters carried rich soil and deposited it in the flood plain.

4. Critical Thinking
They developed there because the weather and the flooding of the river were predictable, allowing them to raise food in a single area.

ACTIVITY OPTION

 Integrated Assessment
• Rubric for making a chart

Ancient Mesopotamia and the Fertile Crescent

SECTION 2

TERMS & NAMES
Hammurabi
Fertile Crescent
Sumerian
ziggurat
class system
cuneiform
scribe

MAIN IDEA

Ancient Mesopotamia's complex civilization, based on city-states, developed a code of laws and a written language.

WHY IT MATTERS NOW

Mesopotamia's achievements led the way to the law codes and written languages in use today.

DATELINE

BABYLON, HAMMURABI'S EMPIRE, 1750 B.C.— Emperor Hammurabi has unveiled a huge black stone containing 282 laws given to him by the god Shamash. For one of the first times ever, a code of laws has been presented to the people of the empire.

According to the Code of Hammurabi, punishment for breaking the law will depend upon the status of the offender and the victim. Most serious crimes, such as murder, will be punished by death. If a house falls down on its owner, the builder of the house will be killed. If the owner's son is killed, then the builder's son will be killed as well. The idea is that a crime should be repaid with a similar punishment. Many of the laws can be boiled down to this statement: "An eye for an eye, a tooth for a tooth."

Culture • Emperor Hammurabi receives a code of laws from the god Shamash, patron of justice. ▲

The Mesopotamian City-State ❶

Hammurabi (hah·moo·RAH·bee), a famous emperor of ancient Mesopotamia, ruled from 1792 to 1750 B.C. (See the map on page 218.) Mesopotamia, which means "land between the rivers" in Greek, covers about the same area as modern Iraq, northeast Syria, and part of southeast Turkey. The region is sometimes called the **Fertile Crescent** because of its shape and fertile soil.

SECTION OBJECTIVES

1. To describe the physical surroundings, government, and struggles of Mesopotamian city-states
2. To explain the class system in Mesopotamia
3. To describe the role of scribes

SKILLBUILDER
• Interpreting a Map, p. 218

CRITICAL THINKING
• Making Inferences, p. 218
• Finding Causes, p. 219

FOCUS & MOTIVATE
WARM-UP

Evaluating Decisions Have students read Dateline and answer questions about the Code of Hammurabi.

1. Do you think the punishments set forth in the code made sense?
2. Do you think countries today should adopt a similar code? Why or why not?

INSTRUCT: Objective ❶

The Mesopotamian City-State

• Who were the first inhabitants of Mesopotamia? the Sumerians
• What were the three major challenges facing the Mesopotamian city-states? threat of invaders, lack of water, risky trade conditions
• What were the roles of priests and kings in the government of city-states? Priests controlled religious and economic life; kings controlled political and military life.

 In-depth Resources: Unit 3
• Guided Reading Worksheet, p. 4

Reading Study Guide
(Spanish and English), pp. 66–67

Program Resources

 In-depth Resources: Unit 3
• Guided Reading Worksheet, p. 4
• Reteaching Activity, p. 13

 Reading Study Guide
(Spanish and English),
pp. 66–67

 Formal Assessment
• Section Quiz, p. 113

 Integrated Assessment
• Rubric for designing a mural

 Outline Map Activities

 Access for Students Acquiring English
• Guided Reading Worksheet, p. 62

 Technology Resources
classzone.com

TEST-TAKING RESOURCES
⤴ Strategies for Test Preparation
⤴ Test Practice Transparencies
🖱 Online Test Practice

The Fertile Crescent

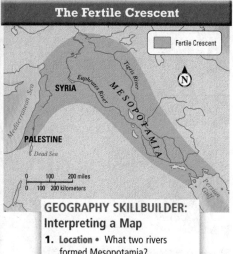

Fertile Crescent

SYRIA

Mediterranean Sea

Euphrates River

Tigris River

MESOPOTAMIA

PALESTINE

Dead Sea

N

Persian Gulf

0   100   200 miles
0   100   200 kilometers

GEOGRAPHY SKILLBUILDER:
Interpreting a Map

1. **Location** • What two rivers formed Mesopotamia?
2. **Place** • What does the map tell you about the importance of water in forming the Fertile Crescent?

Place • This is the gateway to a ziggurat built around 1250 B.C. ▼

City-States Around 3000 B.C., the **Sumerians,** the first inhabitants of the area, organized the first city-states. A city-state is made up of a city and the areas it controls. Three major challenges influenced the development of city-states. One was the threat of hostile invaders. To protect themselves, the Sumerians surrounded their cities with strong, high walls. The second challenge was lack of water. There was very little rainfall in the region. City-states built and maintained irrigation canals for local use.

The third challenge involved trade. The Sumerians lacked stones, metals, and timber for building and had to import these materials. The Sumerians wanted to export grain, dates, and cloth. But trade was risky. Traders often had to cope with bandits, pirates, and wild animals. Well-protected city-states would have helped traders feel more confident about doing business.

Government by Priests and Kings Mesopotamian city-states were centers of religious worship. The Sumerians believed in many gods. The most important gods, Enlil and Utu, controlled the rain and sun. Other gods, such as Inanna, Goddess of Love and War, cured diseases and helped kings fight wars. Each city-state built a temple to a specific god. The people believed this god was the city's special guardian. The temple was built on a pyramid-shaped tower called a **ziggurat.** From the winding terraces wrapped around the ziggurat, people could watch celebrations honoring their god.

Temple priests were the first governors of Mesopotamian city-states. When the city-states began to argue about land and water rights, leaders were elected to defend their interests. Later these rulers became kings. Each king chose who would rule after his death. From then on, the city-states were governed by two groups. The priests controlled religious and economic life, and the king controlled political and military life.

Reading
Social Studies

A. Recognizing Effects What were three effects of the founding of city-states?

Geography Skillbuilder Answers
1. Tigris and Euphrates rivers
2. The region is shaped by many rivers as well as the nearby Mediterranean Sea and Persian Gulf

From Kings to Emperors Occasionally, kings conquered other city-states. Sometimes these kings allowed the conquered cities to keep worshiping their own special gods. They let the ruling families and temple priests keep local control. Other kings built empires from the lands they had conquered. An empire is a group of countries under one ruler's control. These emperors demanded that the conquered people honor them as gods. Local rulers could no longer turn to their own gods for advice. Now they had to take orders directly from the emperor.

Reading
Social Studies

B. Analyzing Causes How did some kings become emperors?

Reading Social Studies
B. Possible Answer by conquering other cities and building an empire

The Class System ❷

Mesopotamia had a **class system**. This meant society was divided into different social groups. Each social group, or class, possessed certain rights and was protected by law. The most favored classes enjoyed more rights than anyone else.

The Three Classes Kings, priests, and wealthy property owners were at the top of the class system. The middle class included skilled workers, merchants, and farmers. Skilled workers specialized in one craft, such as making pottery or spinning thread. Merchants often sold goods brought from other Mesopotamian cities or from other countries. Farmers worked fields that belonged to the temple or the palace.

Many workers in Mesopotamia were enslaved. These people were at the bottom of the class system. Some had been captured in war. Others sold themselves and their families into slavery to pay off a debt. Once they paid the debt, their masters had to set them free. Even former slaves had some rights in Mesopotamian society.

Culture •
These necklaces, earrings, and headress were worn by a Sumerian queen. ▲

Place •
People in Mesopotamia raised animals, caught fish, raised crops, and traded goods. ▶

North Africa and Southwest Asia: Place and Times **219**

INSTRUCT: Objective ❸

A Culture Based on Writing

- In what ways was writing important to the Sumerians? sent business letters; kept records of history, religion, medicine, science; wrote literature and scientific works

- What writing system did the Sumerians use? wedge-shaped characters called cuneiform, inscribed on clay tablets

Spotlight on CULTURE

Europeans discovered the cuneiform writing of the Sumerians thousands of years after it was invented. At the start of the 17th century, Italian traveler and writer Pietro della Valle returned to Europe with examples of this writing. Two hundred years later, a German schoolmaster named George F. Grotefend deciphered the first four letters (D, A, R, and SH) of the name of the Persian King Darius.

In the late 1830s a British army officer named Henry Rawlinson discovered a carving and inscription on a steep cliff known as the Behistun, which stood on an old caravan route. Rawlinson studied the inscription for years. The message, placed there by Darius the Great, was in three languages: Old Persian, Babylonian, and Elamite. Since scholars could read Old Persian, the inscription provided a key to deciphering cuneiform.

Thinking Critically Possible Answers

1. Paper had not yet been invented; clay was plentiful.

2. Pictographs looked like what they represented; cuneiform used a symbol to represent a word.

A Culture Based on Writing ❸

The Sumerians developed one of the first systems of writing, called __cuneiform__ (KYOO•nee•uh•FAWRM). With this wedge-shaped writing, they kept lists and records. They sent business letters. They recorded their history, their religious beliefs, and their knowledge of medicine, mathematics, and astronomy. Few Sumerians actually learned to read and write. Schools trained __scribes__ to be society's record keepers and meet the different needs of the temple, the royal government, and the business world.

Educating Scribes Only the wealthy could afford to send their children to school. Most of these children were boys, but a few girls also studied at the schools—called tablet houses. Most scribes were children of government officials, priests, and wealthy merchants. Some were orphans who had been adopted by rich people and sent to school. The school day lasted from sunrise to sunset. There were about 600 different characters which students had to memorize. Students who misbehaved were punished by "the man in charge of the whip." Here is how one student scribe described his monthly school schedule:

Spotlight on CULTURE

The Development of Cuneiform The Sumerians created one of the world's first written languages more than 5,000 years ago. Cuneiform—which means "wedge-shaped"—developed from pictographs. Early pictographs looked like the object they represented, such as a fish or a bird. Sumerians used a pen made from a sharpened reed to draw pictographs in vertical rows on soft clay tablets. Over time, the pictograph forms became more simplified and people began to write in horizontal rows. Eventually the forms became wedge-shaped. Scribes began using a pen that created the wedge-shaped signs when it was pushed into the clay.

THINKING CRITICALLY

1. **Analyzing Information** Why do you think Sumerians wrote on clay tablets?

2. **Contrasting** What were the differences between early pictographs and cuneiform writing?

fish

| picture writing | cuneiform |

Activity Options

Differentiating Instruction: Students Acquiring English/ESL

Class Time 45 minutes

Task Writing sentences that include words with the same roots

Purpose To build students' vocabularies

Activity Write the word *scribe* on the board, and remind students that a scribe is a person who writes information. Explain that *scribe* is derived from the Latin word *scribere*, meaning "to write." List the following words on the board: *prescribe, script, scribble, describe,* and *manuscript.* Point out word parts that relate to *scribere* in each word; then discuss the words' meanings. Have students take turns using the words in original sentences.

A VOICE FROM SUMERIA

The reckoning of my monthly stay in the tablet house is (as follows):

My days of freedom are three per month.
Its festivals are three days per month.
Within it, twenty-four days per month
(is the time of) my living in the tablet house.
They are long days.

a student scribe

Scribes Played Many Roles Scribes did more than make lists, keep records, and write letters for their employers. Some wrote literary and scientific works of their own. Certain lullabies and love songs were written by women scribes. Traveling scribes from Mesopotamia shared their writings with people from neighboring countries.

Since few people in Mesopotamia could read, scribes read out loud to audiences. One favorite tale was about a flood that covered the earth. It is one of a collection of tales in a book called *Gilgamesh*, which relates the adventures of a semidivine hero.

Culture • The hero Gilgamesh was both a king and a god. ▲

SECTION 2 ASSESSMENT

Terms & Names

1. Identify: (a) Hammurabi (b) Fertile Crescent (c) Sumerian (d) ziggurat
   (e) class system (f) cuneiform (g) scribe

Taking Notes

2. Use a chart like this one to show how building city-states solved challenges faced by the Mesopotamians.

Challenge	Solution

Main Ideas

3. (a) Why do geographers refer to Mesopotamia as the Fertile Crescent?

   (b) How did some Mesopotamian kings become emperors?

   (c) How did scribes contribute to Mesopotamian civilization?

Critical Thinking

4. **Forming and Supporting Opinions**

   Are the laws set forth in Hammurabi's Code too harsh?

   Think About

   • the meaning of justice
   • the reasons for punishment
   • the role mercy plays in justice

ACTIVITY -OPTION- Design a **mural** of ancient Mesopotamia showing the roles and activities of typical citizens.

Section 2 Assessment

SKILLBUILDER

Comparing Climate and Vegetation Maps

Defining the Skill

Explain the purpose of climate maps and vegetation maps. Then have students brainstorm reasons why people might find these kinds of maps useful. Lead them to consider a variety of economic and recreational uses, such as farming, real estate development, and vacation planning.

Applying the Skill

How to Compare Climate and Vegetation Maps Guide students through each strategy. Ask questions about the map keys to be certain that students understand what is represented on each map. When students compare the two maps in Strategy 3, help them try to visualize one map overlaid on the other. This will help them to see how the information can be combined and then compared.

Make a Chart

Explain to students that using a chart to compare the information from the two maps will highlight the relationship between climate and vegetation and make the information easy to assess at a glance.

Practicing the Skill

Have students study the maps and the map keys. Ask students to identify the climates represented on the map of Turkey and list them in their charts. Then discuss the kinds of vegetation found in Turkey, and have students record them in their charts, next to the corresponding climate.

In-depth Resources: Unit 3
• Skillbuilder Practice, p. 10

SKILLBUILDER

Comparing Climate and Vegetation Maps

▶▶ Defining the Skill

A climate map shows the climate of a country or region. Climate has two important factors—average temperature and precipitation. A vegetation map shows what grows in the region. It shows, for example, whether the region has forests or deserts. The climate of a region influences its vegetation. The key shows what each map color means.

▶▶ Applying the Skill

The maps shown here are of the country of Morocco in northwestern Africa. The top map shows Morocco's climate and the bottom map shows its vegetation.

How to Compare Climate and Vegetation Maps

Strategy ❶ Look at the climate map. Read the key to see what types of climates are represented on the map. Then study the map to see where each of those climate types can be found in the country of Morocco.

Strategy ❷ Look at the vegetation map. Read the key, and then look at the map. What kind of vegetation is found in Morocco, and where?

Strategy ❸ Compare the maps. Look at the different climates and at the vegetation in those areas. What kind of vegetation grows where there is little rain? What kind grows where it rains some of the year?

Make a Chart

A chart can help you organize the information that you gain from comparing the two maps. The chart below lists the types of vegetation found in Morocco and the kind of climate that vegetation is located in.

Climate Map

Vegetation Map

❸

Climate	Vegetation
Desert	Desert
Semiarid	Semidesert
Semiarid and sub-tropical dry summer	Mediterranean evergreen forest/shrub

▶▶ Practicing the Skill

Turn to page 216 in Chapter 8, Section 1. Look at the climate map and the vegetation map found there. Create a chart to organize and analyze the information found in those two maps.

Career Connections: Botanist

Encourage students who enjoy comparing climate and vegetation maps to research careers that use this skill. For example, as factors such as rainfall and pollution change over time, botanists might create or use maps that reflect these changes.

1. Help students find information about different kinds of botanists. Point out that some do much outdoor field work, while others work in laboratories, classrooms, or museums.

Block Scheduling

2. Encourage students to learn about the educational requirements of this career.

3. Invite students to share their findings in booklet form.

Ancient Egypt

TERMS & NAMES

papyrus
pyramid
pharaoh
hieroglyphics
Re
Horus

MAIN IDEA

The civilization of the ancient Egyptians developed in response to both its desert environment and the flooding waters of the Nile River.

WHY IT MATTERS NOW

The ancient Egyptian civilization is a model of a well-organized society with limited natural resources.

SECTION OBJECTIVES

1. To explain the importance of the Nile River to ancient Egypt
2. To identify how and why pyramids were built
3. To describe the importance of religion in ancient Egypt

CRITICAL THINKING
• Identifying Problems, p. 224

FOCUS & MOTIVATE
WARM-UP

Making Inferences Have students read Dateline and answer questions about the temple construction.

1. What information in the article suggests that workers who built the temple were not enslaved?

2. Why was the temple built near the Nile?

INSTRUCT: Objective ❶

Ancient Egypt and the Nile

• Why was the Nile River so important to ancient Egyptian civilization? The Nile's yearly floods left silt that made the soil fertile. It also provided a route for trade and travel.

• What did ancient Egyptians do to manage the Nile? built canals, strengthened riverbanks

• How did the writing materials of the ancient Egyptians differ from that of the Mesopotamians? Egyptians wrote on papyrus; Mesopotamians wrote on clay tablets.

 In-depth Resources: Unit 3
• Guided Reading Worksheet, p. 5

 Reading Study Guide
(Spanish and English), pp. 68–69

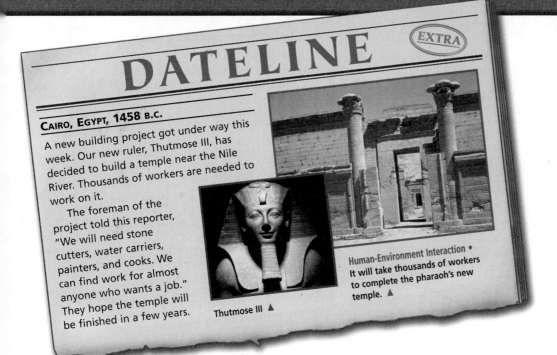

DATELINE
EXTRA

CAIRO, EGYPT, 1458 B.C.

A new building project got under way this week. Our new ruler, Thutmose III, has decided to build a temple near the Nile River. Thousands of workers are needed to work on it.

The foreman of the project told this reporter, "We will need stone cutters, water carriers, painters, and cooks. We can find work for almost anyone who wants a job." They hope the temple will be finished in a few years.

Thutmose III ▲

Human-Environment Interaction • It will take thousands of workers to complete the pharaoh's new temple. ▲

Ancient Egypt and the Nile ❶

Many of the temples and other monumental structures of ancient Egypt still stand. Without the Nile River, however, they probably would never have been built. As the Greek historian Herodotus (huh·RAHD·uh·tuhs) said approximately 2,500 years ago, Egyptian civilization was "the gift of the Nile."

Program Resources

 In-depth Resources: Unit 3
• Guided Reading Worksheet, p. 5
• Reteaching Activity, p. 14

 Reading Study Guide
(Spanish and English), pp. 68–69

 Formal Assessment
• Section Quiz, p. 114

 Integrated Assessment
• Rubric for writing a journal entry

 Outline Map Activities

Access for Students Acquiring English
• Guided Reading Worksheet, p. 63

 Technology Resources
classzone.com

TEST-TAKING RESOURCES

⌇ Strategies for Test Preparation
⌇ Test Practice Transparencies
ⓘ Online Test Practice

MORE ABOUT...

Papyrus

To create writing surfaces from papyrus reeds, the ancient Egyptians stripped away the hard outer fibers of the plant and cut the inner core into strips. They then soaked the strips in water to remove most of the sugar. To remove the water from the strips, they pounded the papyrus until it was completely dry. They then laid a second set of strips perpendicular to the first set. The remaining sugar in the papyrus made the strips adhere to each other. To complete the process, they polished the papyrus with a stone or block of wood.

Experts believe that papyrus was first made around 4000 B.C. Realizing how important it was, Egypt's rulers guarded the method by which it was made.

CRITICAL THINKING ACTIVITY

Identifying Problems Ask students to think about the two ancient writing materials—clay tablets and papyrus. Ask them the following questions: What problems might one encounter using papyrus as a writing material? What problems might be associated with clay tablets? Which material is probably more durable?

Class Time 10 minutes

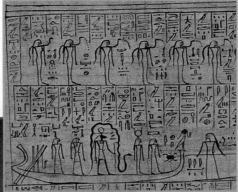

Human-Environment Interaction • **This page from the Book of the Dead was drawn on papyrus.** ◀

Place • **Papyrus reeds grow along the Nile River.** ▲

The River in the Sand Desert covers most of Egypt. The sands spread for hundreds of miles to the west and the south, discouraging outsiders from invading. The Nile River, which runs through the desert, is sometimes called "the river in the sand."

The Nile's yearly floods deposited tons of silt in the river valley. The deposits made the soil black and fertile. Every year, around October, the floodwaters began to retreat. Then the farmers planted their seeds. They harvested their crops during the months the Nile was at its lowest levels. The Egyptians knew the Nile would flood each year. But they could not predict how much it would flood or how high the water would rise. In years with very low floods, there might not be enough food. In years with very high floods, the waters would destroy fields and homes.

Taming the Nile The ancient Egyptians found ways to manage the unpredictable river. They built canals to carry water from the Nile to the parts of the land the flooding water did not reach. They strengthened the riverbanks to keep the river from overflowing.

Egyptian towns and cities were spread along the Nile River valley. The Nile made it possible for Egyptians living in distant places to come together. The Egyptians were expert boat builders. They built harbors and ports for large cargo boats. The Nile provided such good transportation that there were few roads in ancient Egypt. Because goods moved easily along the Nile, trade was very profitable.

The Nile's Gifts The ancient Egyptians used Nile mud to make pottery and bricks. They made a paperlike material called **papyrus** (peh·PYE·res) from the papyrus plant. This tall plant grew in marshes and swamps around the Nile. In fact, the English word *paper* comes from "papyrus." It was easier to write on papyrus than on the bulky clay tablets the Mesopotamians used.

Vocabulary

silt: particles of earth and rock that build up in rivers or streams

Reading **Social Studies**

A. Identifying Problems What problems did the Nile River cause Egyptian farmers?

Reading Social Studies
A. Answer
Flood levels were unpredictable.

224 CHAPTER 8

Activity Options

Interdisciplinary Link: Art

Class Time 30 minutes

Task Drawing pictographs to convey a message

Purpose To appreciate how ancient Egyptians communicated using pictographs

Supplies Needed
• Drawing paper
• Pencils or pens

Activity Hieroglyphics used picture symbols, or pictographs, to stand for both words and sounds. Have students look at the examples of hieroglyphics in this section and try to identify objects in the writing. Then write the following sentence on the board: The Egyptians knew the Nile would flood every year. Discuss how this information might be communicated by using only picture symbols. Then ask each student to select a sentence from this page and draw pictographs to convey the information.

Tutankhamen's Tomb

Place • In 1922, the tomb of Egyptian king Tutankhamen (toot·ahng·KHA·muhn) was found almost exactly as it had been left thousands of years before. Although his tomb may be the most famous, Tutankhamen was not buried in a pyramid. He was buried in an area now known as the Valley of the Tombs of the Kings. ◄

The Great Builders ❷

The Egyptians noticed that bodies buried in the sand on the edge of the desert resisted decay. It may have affected their beliefs in an afterlife. The concept of an afterlife played a central role in ancient Egyptian life and culture. It led the Egyptians to build huge **pyramids,** as well as many other temples and monuments.

Vocabulary

afterlife:
a life believed
to follow death

The Pyramids Pyramids are easily recognized by their shape. Four triangular sides on a rectangular base meet at a single point. The Egyptians built the pyramids for their kings, or **pharaohs** (FAIR·ohz). Each pyramid is a palace where an Egyptian king planned to spend the afterlife.

BACKGROUND

Nubia (NOO·bee·uh), a country to the south of Egypt, was a source of the gold the Egyptians used in their pyramids.

Materials and Labor To build the pyramids, the Egyptians used large blocks of stone. A single pyramid might contain 92 million cubic feet of stone, enough to fill a large sports stadium. The tips of pyramids were often capped with gold.

Building a pyramid was complicated. The pharaoh appointed a leader to organize the project. The leader and his staff used **hieroglyphics**—a writing system that uses pictographs to stand for words or sounds—to make lists of the workers and supplies they needed for the project.

Recording the Past The great statues and monuments of ancient Egypt have lasted thousands of years, but they will not last forever. They are threatened by pollution and other changes in the environment. Now a nonprofit group called INSIGHT (Institute for the Study and Implementation of Graphic Heritage Techniques) is using the latest technology, such as digital photography and laser scanning, to record Egypt's cultural heritage.

Working with archaeologists, INSIGHT volunteers record ancient tombs, temples, and statues before they fall apart or are destroyed. The results will be used for research and educational purposes.

North Africa and Southwest Asia: Place and Times **225**

FOCUS ON VISUALS

Interpreting the Illustration Ask students to study the drawing of one room in King Tut's tomb and point out its details.

Possible Responses coffin (sarcophagus), boxes for jewelry, furniture, wheels, wall paintings

Extension Have students research the discovery and opening of "King Tut's" tomb.

INSTRUCT: Objective ❷

The Great Builders

- Why did the ancient Egyptians build pyramids? to provide places for kings to spend the afterlife
- What is hieroglyphics? a writing system that uses pictographs to stand for words or sounds
- How did pharaohs get enough workers to build the pyramids? Every Egyptian family had to help with the project.

Citizenship IN ACTION

Some pollutants and changes to the environment that damage these ancient structures are subtle. For example, vibrations from increased traffic threaten architectural bases. Even breath from tourists dramatically raises the humidity within the monuments, causing plaster to crack and paintings to fade. Like INSIGHT volunteers, dedicated people are working to extensively photograph these ancient structures to create what they call a Virtual Heritage. Their hope is that by using virtual reality and the Internet, people will be able to explore ancient monuments without causing further damage.

Activity Options

Differentiating Instruction: Gifted and Talented

Discovering King Tut's Tomb Challenge students to research and write a brief dramatization (20–30 minutes) of the British archaeologist Howard Carter's discovery and entry into the tomb of the boy king Tutankhamen in 1922. Suggest that they refer to television documentaries or radio plays as models. Invite students to use their imagination for the style of their dramatic presentation. Working as a group, some students can research Carter's own account of the discovery; others can write the play script using his words. The main characters are Carter himself and Lord Carnarvon, sponsor of the expedition. To give more students a role in the production, parts can be written for other archaeologists and Egyptian workers at the dig. Allow class time for students to present their play.

Teacher's Edition **225**

INSTRUCT: Objective ❸

The Pharaoh and the Gods

• What beliefs did the ancient Egyptians have about their ruling pharaohs? The pharaoh was believed to be the living son of the sun god and was linked with the sky god. He was the main religious figure.

• How did ancient Egyptians prepare deceased loved ones for the afterlife? They treated their bodies with preservatives, or mummified them. They also filled their tombs with items they believed the deceased could use after death.

📝 **In-depth Resources: Unit 3**
• Guided Reading Worksheet, p. 5

 Biography

In addition to the ornate temples she had built, Hatshepsut ordered that a great memorial be constructed in her honor. She insisted on being represented as a man on all monuments that were built during her rule. Although these monuments were heavily damaged when Thutmose III attacked them after her death, they still preserve her fame.

The Rosetta Stone

The Rosetta stone was discovered by soldiers belonging to Napoleon's army, which invaded Egypt in 1798. The stone is inscribed with the same message in three languages: Greek, Egyptian hieroglyphics, and a cursive form of hieroglyphics known as demotic. The texts were translated—and the key to deciphering hieroglyphics thereby established—by Thomas Young, an Englishman, and Jean-Francois Champollion, a Frenchman. Today the 1,500-pound stone is displayed in the British Museum.

Biography

Hatshepsut (hat•SHEP•soot) was the first woman to rule Egypt. Like male pharaohs, she wore a tightly braided false beard.

Hatshepsut came to the throne around 1500 B.C., when her husband, the pharaoh Thutmose II, died. The throne passed to Thutmose III, Hatshepsut's stepson. Because he was a child, Hatshepsut acted as ruler. Even when he grew up, she refused to give him the throne. Instead, she had herself proclaimed pharaoh and ruled for 20 years.

She encouraged foreign trade and building projects, including a number of magnificent temples.

The Egyptians had no cutting tools or machines to get the stone they needed. Removing the stone and shaping it into blocks was very difficult work. The work was also dangerous. Every Egyptian family had to help with the project. They either worked as laborers or provided food for the workers.

The Pharaoh and the Gods ❸

Egyptians believed that the ruling pharaoh was the living son of the sun god, **Re** (RAY). The pharaoh was also linked with **Horus,** the sky god. The pharaoh was not only ancient Egypt's chief judge and commander-in-chief, he was also the chief religious figure. His religious example guided the common people in their daily lives and in their preparations for the afterlife.

Religion in Daily Life Temples were everywhere in ancient Egypt. Some were dedicated to major gods, like Re. Others were dedicated to local gods. Pharaohs had temples built in their honor so that people could worship them.

Ordinary citizens did not gather for prayer in the temples. Only priests carried out the temple rituals. Smaller buildings stood outside the temple grounds where common people could pray or leave offerings to the gods. Many private homes also contained small shrines where family members worshiped their gods and honored the spirits of dead family members.

Reading
Social Studies
B. Making Inferences How important was their religion to Egyptians?
Reading Social Studies
B. Possible Answer
It was part of their daily life.

Culture • Egyptian artists' drawings followed rules. Eyes and shoulders were drawn as if from the front, the rest of the body sideways. Important people were drawn larger than others. ▶

Activity Options

Multiple Learning Styles: Spatial

Class Time One class period
Task Creating a chart of gods and goddesses
Purpose To learn more about Egyptian gods and goddesses

Supplies Needed
• Chart paper
• Markers
• Reference sources

Activity Have students work together to research information about several Egyptian gods and goddesses. Have them record their findings in a chart.

God	Rules
Re	God of the sun and harvests
Isis	Goddess of mothers and wives
Thoth	God of wisdom and writing

Preparing for the Afterlife Average Egyptians were not buried in pyramids. They made careful preparations for the afterlife, however. Family members were responsible for burying their dead relatives and tending their spirits. Egyptians believed they could help the dead person live comfortably in the afterlife. They prevented bodies from decaying by treating them with preservatives, or mummifying them. The Egyptians filled tombs with items for the dead to use in the afterlife and they decorated the tombs with art. They also made regular offerings to honor the dead.

Culture • A mask covers this mummy's face. ▲

Culture • Osiris and Isis were the Egyptian god and goddess of the dead. ◄

MORE ABOUT...
Mummies
According to ancient texts, it took 70 days to complete a full mummifying treatment. First, embalmers removed the brain and most of the major organs from the body. Next, they filled the empty abdomen with linen pads or sawdust. They then used sodium carbonate to dry out the body's tissues. Once the tissues were dry, the embalmers wrapped the body in linen bandages and placed it in a coffin.

ASSESS & RETEACH

Reading Social Studies Have students write supporting details about ancient Egypt in the chart on page 212.

 Formal Assessment
• Section Quiz, p. 114

RETEACHING ACTIVITY

Have students work individually to create a section review. For each heading, have them write two or three sentences summarizing the material. Ask a few volunteers to read their summaries. Then have the rest of the class add any important points that may have been omitted.

 In-depth Resources: Unit 3
• Reteaching Activity, p. 14

 Access for Students Acquiring English
• Reteaching Activity, p. 70

SECTION ③ ASSESSMENT

Terms & Names

1. Identify:
  (a) papyrus   (b) pyramid   (c) pharaoh
  (d) hieroglyphics   (e) Re   (f) Horus

Taking Notes

2. Use a spider map like this one to record all the ways the Nile River benefited the ancient Egyptians.

(Nile River)

Main Ideas

3. (a) Why did the Egyptians build pyramids?

  (b) How did the use of hieroglyphics help Egyptian builders?

  (c) Why was the pharaoh so important to the Egyptians?

Critical Thinking

4. Summarizing

How did belief in an afterlife affect the culture of the ancient Egyptians?

Think About
  ♦ burial practices
  ♦ buildings

ACTIVITY -OPTION- Suppose that you are an ancient Egyptian. Write a **journal entry** about the daily work of an inhabitant of ancient Egypt.

Section ③ Assessment

1. Terms & Names
a. papyrus, p. 224
b. pyramid, p. 225
c. pharaoh, p. 225
d. hieroglyphics, p. 225
e. Re, p. 226
f. Horus, p. 226

2. Taking Notes

(fertile soil) (water for irrigation) (trade)
Nile River

3. Main Ideas
a. They built them to give pharaohs a place to spend their afterlife.
b. They used this system of writing to list workers and supplies.
c. They thought he was the son of the sun god, Re, and was linked to the sky god, Horus. He was also head of government, chief judge, military commander, and chief religious figure.

4. Critical Thinking

Egyptians took great care in preparing their loved ones for the afterlife and built pyramids and other monuments to house the pharaohs after death.

ACTIVITY OPTION

 Integrated Assessment
• Rubric for writing a journal entry

Technology: 3500 B.C.

OBJECTIVES

1. To explain how the wheel evolved over thousands of years

2. To explain the wide-ranging impact of the wheel

INSTRUCT

• How is a clay pot affected by spinning?

• What effect did the potter's wheel have on the way pottery was made?

• What effect did the potter's wheel have on trade?

 Block Scheduling

MORE ABOUT...
The Potter's Trade

Making containers from firm, fine-grained soil called clay is one of mankind's oldest skills. The earliest vessels were formed by hand or by pushing the clay into molds. A process called firing, which involved baking the vessels in ovens known as kilns, made the pots hard. Burnishing, painting, and applying a thin coating called slip made wares stronger and more attractive.

Connect to History

Strategic Thinking How do potsherds help archaeologists learn how a society evolved?

Connect to Today

Strategic Thinking How does the work of potters today differ from that of early potters?

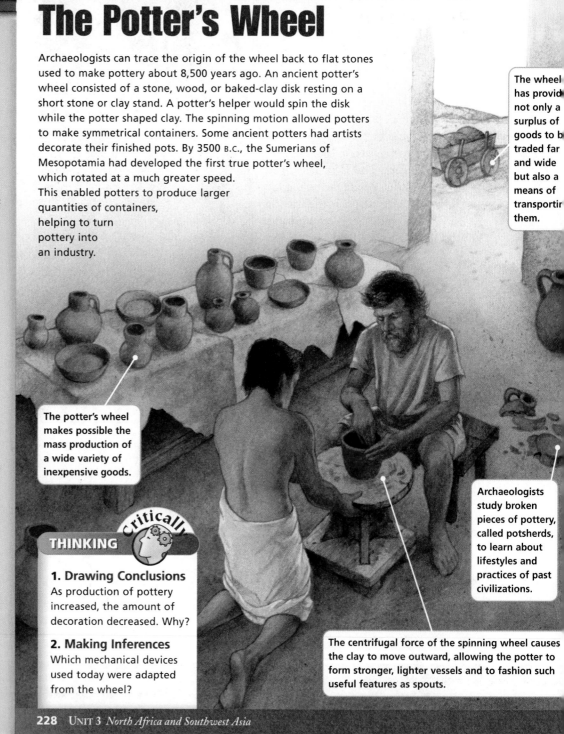

The Potter's Wheel

Archaeologists can trace the origin of the wheel back to flat stones used to make pottery about 8,500 years ago. An ancient potter's wheel consisted of a stone, wood, or baked-clay disk resting on a short stone or clay stand. A potter's helper would spin the disk while the potter shaped clay. The spinning motion allowed potters to make symmetrical containers. Some ancient potters had artists decorate their finished pots. By 3500 B.C., the Sumerians of Mesopotamia had developed the first true potter's wheel, which rotated at a much greater speed. This enabled potters to produce larger quantities of containers, helping to turn pottery into an industry.

The wheel has provid[ed] not only a surplus of goods to b[e] traded far and wide but also a means of transportin[g] them.

The potter's wheel makes possible the mass production of a wide variety of inexpensive goods.

Archaeologists study broken pieces of pottery, called potsherds, to learn about lifestyles and practices of past civilizations.

The centrifugal force of the spinning wheel causes the clay to move outward, allowing the potter to form stronger, lighter vessels and to fashion such useful features as spouts.

THINKING Critically

1. Drawing Conclusions
As production of pottery increased, the amount of decoration decreased. Why?

2. Making Inferences
Which mechanical devices used today were adapted from the wheel?

Thinking Critically

1. Drawing Conclusions Possible Response Potters may have used less decoration because of a shift in emphasis from the creative to the practical. As trading increased and the demand for pottery grew, potters became more interested in producing large numbers of inexpensive items than in creating small numbers of ornate, expensive ones.

2. Making Inferences Possible Response Virtually anything that uses rotating motion was adapted from the wheel, including pulleys, gears, record albums, CDs, tape-recorder reels, and merry-go-rounds.

Birthplace of Three Religions

TERMS & NAMES

Abraham
Judaism
Jesus
Christianity
Muhammad
Islam
Muslim
Qur'an

MAIN IDEA

Southwest Asia was the birthplace of Judaism, Christianity, and Islam.

WHY IT MATTERS NOW

Today, these three religions continue to attract believers and influence world events.

DATELINE

JERUSALEM, JUNE 10, 1967—The third war between Arab States and Israel ended today—after just six days of fighting. Israeli forces have gained control of Jerusalem's Old City, which has been in the hands of the Arabs since the first Arab-Israeli war in 1948.

The Old City includes sites sacred to three religions. Muslims revere the Dome of the Rock, built over the rock from which Muhammad made a night journey to heaven. The Wailing Wall, all that remains of the ancient Temple of Solomon, is sacred to the Jews. The Christian Church of the Holy Sepulcher marks the spot where Jesus Christ is believed to have been buried after his crucifixion.

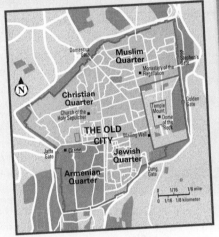

Location • This map of Jerusalem's Old City section shows the location of many sacred sites. ▲

Three Religions ❶

Jews, Christians, and Muslims have been fighting over Jerusalem and other areas of Southwest Asia for centuries. Each of these religious groups got its start in this region. All three religions share common traits. Each was first led by a single person and reveres a set of sacred writings. Each believes there is only one god, a belief called monotheism. The Sumerians and Egyptians believed in many gods, a belief called polytheism.

North Africa and Southwest Asia: Place and Times **229**

SECTION OBJECTIVES

1. To describe the origins of Judaism and how the religion changed over time
2. To describe Jesus' early life and teachings and the beginnings of Christianity
3. To describe how the divine revelations of Muhammad were collected in the Qur'an

SKILLBUILDER
• Interpreting a Map, p. 233

CRITICAL THINKING
• Clarifying, p. 230

FOCUS & MOTIVATE
WARM-UP

Recognizing Important Details Have students read <u>Dateline</u> and answer questions about the Arab-Israeli war.

1. What three sacred sites are located within Jerusalem's Old City?
2. What do you know about current events that helps you to understand that this third war did not resolve the dispute over this land?

INSTRUCT: Objective ❶

Three Religions/Abraham and the Origin of Judaism

• How do Judaism, Christianity, and Islam differ from the religions of the Sumerians and Egyptians? Jews, Christians, and Muslims believe in only one god, not many gods.
• What group of people drove the Jews into exile? Babylonians

 In-depth Resources: Unit 3
• Guided Reading Worksheet, p. 6

 Reading Study Guide
(Spanish and English), pp. 70–71

Program Resources

 In-depth Resources: Unit 3
• Guided Reading Worksheet, p. 6
• Reteaching Activity, p. 15

 Reading Study Guide
(Spanish and English), pp. 70–71

 Formal Assessment
• Section Quiz, p. 115

Integrated Assessment
• Rubric for writing a letter

 Outline Map Activities

 Access for Students Acquiring English
• Guided Reading Worksheet, p. 64

 Technology Resources
classzone.com

TEST-TAKING RESOURCES
↷ Strategies for Test Preparation
↷ Test Practice Transparencies
ⓘ Online Test Practice

230 CHAPTER 8

MORE ABOUT...
The Wailing Wall

The Wailing Wall, or Western Wall, is believed to be the remains of King Solomon's Temple. The Wailing Wall earned this name because the Jews have shed so many tears there. Jews often write prayers on tiny pieces of paper that they roll up and insert into the cracks of the wall. An Israeli Internet company currently prints out electronic messages from all over the world and places them in the wall.

CRITICAL THINKING ACTIVITY

Clarifying To clarify the sequence of Jewish exiles, write the following facts on the board in this mixed-up order. Have students read the facts and discuss the order in which they occurred.

Israel came under Roman control. Jews revolted against Rome, and Jerusalem was destroyed. (3)

Babylonians destroyed the First Temple in Jerusalem. Jews were exiled to Babylon. (1)

Persians took control of Mesopotamia. Cyrus allowed Jews to return to Jerusalem. (2)

Class Time: 10 minutes

INSTRUCT: Objective ❷

Jesus and the Birth of Christianity

- What story is told in the Gospels?
  the story of Jesus' life

- How does Christianity relate to Judaism?
  Christians believe that Jesus was the Messiah promised in Jewish scripture.

Movement • **Abraham led his household into the land of Canaan.** ▲

Place • **The Wailing Wall is all that remains of Solomon's Temple.** ▲

Abraham and the Origin of Judaism ❶

The Hebrew people were the first monotheists. They believed in a god they called Yahweh. According to the Hebrew scripture, Yahweh spoke to a man named **Abraham**. Abraham was from the city of Ur, in southeastern Mesopotamia. Yahweh told Abraham to leave his native land. Abraham obeyed and settled in Canaan, which is now in the land of Israel. Abraham's descendants are known as Jews, and their religious belief is called **Judaism**.

> **Vocabulary**
> scripture: sacred writing

How Judaism Adapted over Time The story of Judaism is the story of exile. In 586 B.C., the Babylonians from southern Mesopotamia destroyed the First Temple built by the Jews in Jerusalem. The Jews were exiled to Babylon. They continued to worship by praying and reading their holy texts.

> **Vocabulary**
> exile: forced removal from one's native country

About 50 years later, the Persians took control of Mesopotamia. The Persian ruler Cyrus allowed the Jews to return to Jerusalem and rebuild their Temple. Much later, the Jews came under Roman control. The Jews revolted against Rome in A.D. 66. Jerusalem and the Second Temple were destroyed in the struggle.

Although the Temple was never rebuilt, Judaism did not die out. Jewish teachers and religious leaders encouraged their people to replace worship in the Temple with prayer, study, and good deeds. For the next 1,800 years, most Jews lived outside Jerusalem. They hoped that Jerusalem might once again become the home of Judaism.

Jesus and the Birth of Christianity ❷

Sometime during the years 8 to 4 B.C., a Jewish boy named **Jesus** was born in Bethlehem, a small town in ancient Palestine. (See the map on page 233.) The story of his life is told in the four Gospels, part of the Christian scripture collected in the Bible. The first of the Gospels was written about 30 years after Jesus died.

Early Life According to the Gospels, Jesus grew up in Galilee, a region in northern Palestine. His father trained him to be a carpenter.

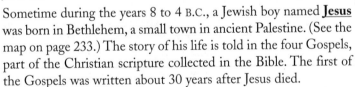

Activity Options

Differentiating Instruction: Gifted and Talented

Class Time One class period

Task Researching and writing a report on the conflict between Israel and the Palestinians

Purpose To show how current events are affected by events that took place thousands of years ago

Supplies Needed
- Library resources
- Current newspapers and magazines
- Internet access

🅱 Block Scheduling

Activity Have students research the ongoing conflict between Israel and the Palestinians. Ask them to find out who the Palestinians and Israelis are, what each side demands, what methods each side has used to put pressure on the other, and how each side has offered to end the conflict. Encourage students to accompany their reports with maps.

Culture • This famous painting, *The Last Supper* by Leonardo da Vinci, shows Jesus with his disciples shortly before his death. ◄

Vocabulary

baptize:
to purify and admit into a new way of life

disciple:
a follower of the teachings of another

When he was about 30, his cousin John the Baptist baptized him. For the next three years, he traveled around the countryside, preaching a religion of love and forgiveness and performing miracles. People flocked to hear his words. Disciples gathered around him.

The Jewish people believed that someday a Messiah, or savior, would come to lead them out of exile. Some people believed Jesus was the Messiah. He came to be called Christ, the Greek word for *messiah*. Those who believed in him and his teachings were called Christians.

Final Days Some government and religious leaders considered Jesus's teachings and his large following a threat to their own power. When Jesus came to Jerusalem to celebrate the Jewish feast of Passover, the authorities decided to get rid of him. Judas Iscariot, one of the 12 disciples who were closest to Jesus, betrayed him to the authorities. Jesus was arrested. After a brief trial, he was crucified and died. He was put into a tomb. After three days, according to his disciples, he was resurrected and later went up into heaven.

Vocabulary

crucify:
to put to death by fastening the hands and feet to a cross

resurrect:
to bring back to life

Beginnings of Christianity Jesus's disciples spread his teachings and their belief that he was the Messiah promised in Jewish scripture. From its roots in Judaism, a new religion developed called **Christianity**. It is based on the life and teachings of Jesus. Eventually, the new religion spread to other parts of the world. Today, only a small number of Christians live in Southwest Asia, the region where Christianity began. (See the Unit Atlas map on page 205.)

Place • Many Christians believe Jesus was buried at the site of the Church of the Holy Sepulcher in Jerusalem. ▼

Muhammad, the Prophet of Islam ❸

Less than 600 years after Christ's death, a third monotheistic religion arose in Southwest Asia. A man named **Muhammad** (mu·HAM·ihd) was born in Mecca (MEHK·uh) about A.D. 570.

FOCUS ON VISUALS

Interpreting the Painting Tell students that this is one of the most famous paintings in the world. Although it has been reproduced in many books and other forms, the original painting of *The Last Supper* is a fresco—a wall painting—in the refectory (dining hall) of a convent in Milan, Italy, painted by Leonardo da Vinci in 1495–97. Ask students to study the painting and point out its details. Which figure represents Jesus?

Possible Responses clothing styles, men's hair, food on the table; the central figure

Extension Have students look in art books and encyclopedias for examples of early Christian art from around the time when Jesus lived. Let students show the pictures in class.

INSTRUCT: Objective ❸

Muhammad, the Prophet of Islam

- Who was the founder of Islam? Muhammad
- According to the Islamic religion, who revealed the will of God to Muhammad? the angel Gabriel
- What is the Qur'an? the collection of God's revelations to Muhammad
- Why were the leaders of Mecca threatened by Muhammad's teachings? He criticized the wealthy and encouraged people to worship one God. His teachings threatened their traditions and businesses.

Activity Options

Skillbuilder Mini-Lesson: Making an Outline

Explaining the Skill Remind students that it is important to make an outline before writing a research report. Review proper outline format and notation.

Applying the Skill Have students use the outlining skills they learned in the previous chapter to create an outline for a report on the history of Judaism, Christianity, or Islam, following these steps:

Block Scheduling

1. Identify main topics and list them with Roman numerals.
2. Find important details that support each main topic and list them as A, B, C, and so on. Complete your outline with smaller details numbered 1, 2, 3.
3. Reread your outline and reorganize details if necessary.

ASSESS & RETEACH

Reading Social Studies Have students write supporting details about Judaism, Christianity, and Islam in the chart on page 212.

 Formal Assessment
• Section Quiz, p. 115

RETEACHING ACTIVITY

Assign students to small groups. Have each student write on individual strips of paper one fact he or she learned about each of the three religions, without naming the religion. For example, one fact might be "This religion was founded by Muhammad." Ask the groups to scramble their papers and place them in a pile. Then, within their groups, have students take turns drawing a paper from the pile, reading the fact aloud, and identifying the religion it refers to.

 In-depth Resources: Unit 3
• Reteaching Activity, p. 15

 Access for Students Acquiring English
• Reteaching Activity, p. 71

He is the founder of **Islam,** a religion whose followers believe there is one god and that Muhammad is his prophet. A believer in Islam is called a **Muslim.**

One day about A.D. 610, according to Muslim beliefs, when Muhammad was alone, he heard a voice commanding him: "Recite in the name of your Lord who created! He created man from that which clings. Recite; and thy Lord is Most Bountiful, He who has taught by the pen, taught man what he knew not."

Muhammad's Teachings Muhammad believed that the command came from the angel Gabriel, who was revealing to him the will of God. For the next 22 years, Gabriel continued to send revelations to Muhammad. Later, the revelations were collected into the **Qur'an** (keh·RAN), the sacred text of Islam. Muhammad told other people about the divine messages he received. He criticized the wealthy people of Mecca for turning their backs on the poor and needy. He encouraged them to reject their wicked ways and to worship the one true God.

The leaders of Mecca thought Muhammad's teachings threatened their traditions and businesses. Some plotted to kill him. In 622, Muhammad and a group of followers escaped to the nearby city of Medina (muh·DEE·nuh), where they were welcomed. Muslims date the beginning of their calendar from this important year in their history.

Place • The Sultan of Morocco donated this copy of the Qur'an to the city of Jerusalem. ▼

Vocabulary

prophet: a person who speaks through divine inspiration

Reading Social Studies
B. Possible Answer They all believed in only one god; they faced persecution and danger for their beliefs.

Reading **Social Studies**

B. Comparing What did the founders of Judaism, Christianity, and Islam have in common?

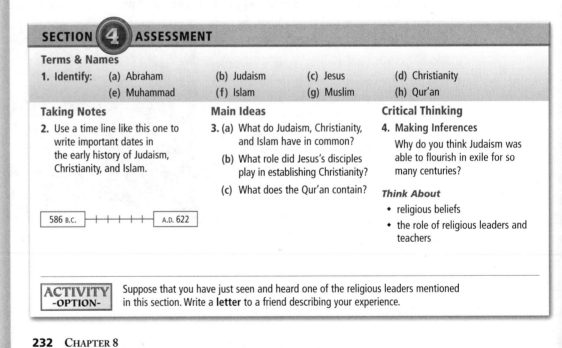

SECTION 4 ASSESSMENT

Terms & Names

1. **Identify:** (a) Abraham (b) Judaism (c) Jesus (d) Christianity
(e) Muhammad (f) Islam (g) Muslim (h) Qur'an

Taking Notes

2. Use a time line like this one to write important dates in the early history of Judaism, Christianity, and Islam.

586 B.C. ├─┼─┼─┼─┼─┤ A.D. 622

Main Ideas

3. (a) What do Judaism, Christianity, and Islam have in common?
(b) What role did Jesus's disciples play in establishing Christianity?
(c) What does the Qur'an contain?

Critical Thinking

4. **Making Inferences**
Why do you think Judaism was able to flourish in exile for so many centuries?

Think About
• religious beliefs
• the role of religious leaders and teachers

ACTIVITY -OPTION- Suppose that you have just seen and heard one of the religious leaders mentioned in this section. Write a **letter** to a friend describing your experience.

Section 4 Assessment

1. Terms & Names
a. Abraham, p. 230
b. Judaism, p. 230
c. Jesus, p. 230
d. Christianity, p. 231
e. Muhammad, p. 231
f. Islam, p. 232
g. Muslim, p. 232
h. Qur'an, p. 232

2. Taking Notes
Students' time lines should include these dates:
586 B.C.: Babylonians destroy First Temple
8–4 B.C.: Jesus born in Bethlehem
A.D. 66: Romans destroy Second Temple
A.D. 610: Muhammad receives revelation from God
A.D. 622: Muhammad welcomed in Medina

3. Main Ideas
a. They all believe in one god.
b. They spread his teachings and the belief that he was the Messiah.
c. It contains God's revelations to Muhammad, as told to him by Gabriel.

4. Critical Thinking
Students might say that Jewish teachers and religious leaders encouraged their followers to replace temple worship with individual prayer, study, and good deeds.

ACTIVITY OPTION

 Integrated Assessment
• Rubric for writing a letter

Holy Places of Three Religions

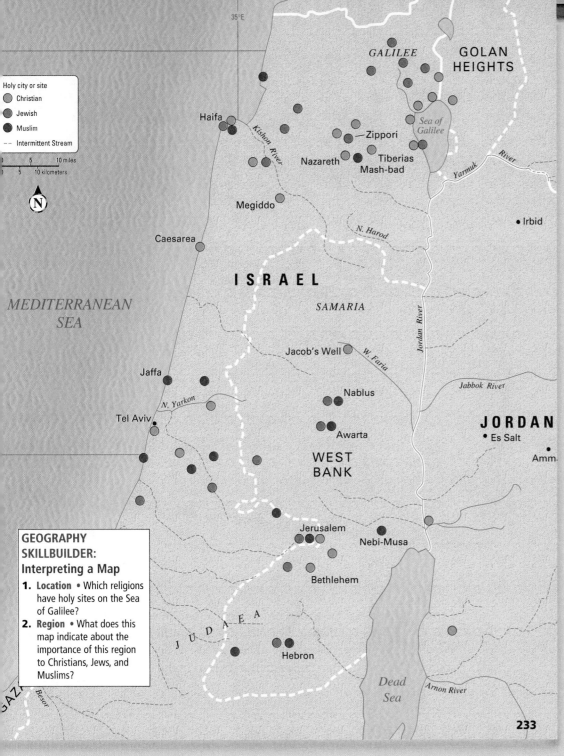

Holy city or site
- ○ Christian
- ● Jewish
- ● Muslim
- --- Intermittent Stream

0   5   10 miles
0   5   10 kilometers

N

GALILEE
GOLAN HEIGHTS

Haifa
Kishon River
Sea of Galilee
Zippori
Nazareth   Tiberias
Mash-bad
Yarmuk River

Megiddo
N. Harod
Irbid

Caesarea

ISRAEL

SAMARIA

MEDITERRANEAN SEA

Jordan River

Jacob's Well   W. Faria

Jaffa
N. Yarkon
Nablus
Jabbok River
Tel Aviv
Awarta

WEST BANK

JORDAN
Es Salt
Amm...

Jerusalem
Nebi-Musa

Bethlehem

JUDAEA

Hebron

Dead Sea
Arnon River

GAZ...
Besor

233

INTERPRETING A MAP
Holy Places of Three Religions, 2001

Ask students whether the names of any places on this map are familiar to them. Then have individual students use the map key to identify the places that are sacred to Jews, to Christians, and to Muslims. Tell students what areas along the Mediterranean Sea this map highlights. As needed, tell students why these religions all have holy sites in the same area. Ask them to look more closely at the map and answer the following questions:

- What two sites are holy to all three religions? Haifa, Jerusalem

- In what parts of the map are most of the Christian holy sites located? in the north, around the Sea of Galilee

- What river runs through the center of the map? Jordan River What two bodies of water does it connect? Sea of Galilee and Dead Sea

GEOGRAPHY SKILLBUILDER
Answers
1. Jewish and Christian
2. The number of holy places close together explains why all three religions compete for the region.

Activity Options

Interdisciplinary Link: Geography/Language Arts

Block Scheduling

Class Time One class period

Task Writing a two-page city guide

Purpose To identify interesting and important features of sites holy to various major religions

Supplies Needed
- Internet access and encyclopedia
- Pens or pencils
- Writing paper

Activity Have each student choose one of the major sites shown on the map and research its history and importance. Ask students to prepare a two-page guide to the site. One page should focus on its history as a place important to one or more religions. The second should give information on the modern city. Encourage students to include photocopies or printouts of illustrations as part of their guide.

Muslim Empires

TERMS & NAMES
Five Pillars of Islam
caliph
theocracy
Ottoman Empire
Constantinople
Suleiman I
Janissary
Sultan Mehmed VI

SECTION OBJECTIVES

1. To identify the Five Pillars of Islam and describe the spread of the religion
2. To describe the rise and strength of the Ottoman Empire
3. To explain the decline of the Ottoman Empire

CRITICAL THINKING
• Recognizing Important Details, p. 235

FOCUS & MOTIVATE
WARM-UP

Drawing Conclusions Have students read <u>Dateline</u> and answer questions about the event described.

1. What do you think a pilgrimage is?
2. Why do you think Muhammad felt it especially important to spread his beliefs at this time?

INSTRUCT: Objective ❶

The Five Pillars of Islam/ Muslim Empires

• What are the Five Pillars of Islam? belief in one god and that Muhammad is God's prophet, praying five times a day, giving to the poor, fasting during Ramadan, making a pilgrimage to Mecca

• What is a theocracy? a government ruled by a religious leader

• How were Islamic ideas and culture spread? through books and artwork exchanged along trade routes and through conquest

 In-depth Resources: Unit 3
• Guided Reading Worksheet, p. 7

 Reading Study Guide
(Spanish and English), pp. 72–73

MAIN IDEA

Islamic beliefs and culture spread throughout Southwest Asia and much of the world.

WHY IT MATTERS NOW

Islam, the world's second largest religion, influences society and governments in most Southwest Asian countries today.

DATELINE
EXTRA

MECCA, ARABIA, 9TH DAY OF DHUL HIIJAH, A.D. 622

The Prophet Muhammad today preached a sermon to 140,000 followers who have come to Mecca from all over Arabia on a pilgrimage. In his sermon, Muhammad reviewed all his teachings over the years. Many say it was the most important sermon he has ever preached. Some fear it may be his last.

He began by saying, "O People, lend me an attentive ear, for I know not whether after this year I shall ever be among you again." It is well-known that for the past few years the Prophet has been anxious to spread word of his religion wherever he can.

Place • Mecca is the holiest city in Islam. ▲

The Five Pillars of Islam ❶

The most important teachings of Muhammad are summed up in the **Five Pillars of Islam.** All members of the Muslim community believe in the central importance of these five religious duties. The Five Pillars of Islam unite Muslims around the world.

Program Resources

 In-depth Resources: Unit 3
• Guided Reading Worksheet, p. 7
• Reteaching Activity, p. 16

 Reading Study Guide
(Spanish and English), pp. 72–73

 Formal Assessment
• Section Quiz, p. 116

 Integrated Assessment
• Rubric for creating an illustrated report

Outline Map Activities

Access for Students Acquiring English
• Guided Reading Worksheet, p. 65

 Technology Resources
classzone.com

TEST-TAKING RESOURCES
↷ Strategies for Test Preparation
↷ Test Practice Transparencies
↻ Online Test Practice

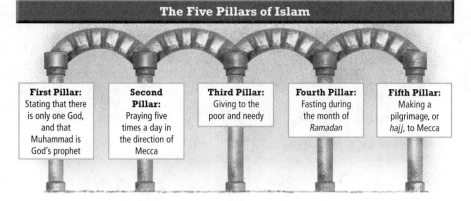

The Five Pillars of Islam

First Pillar: Stating that there is only one God, and that Muhammad is God's prophet

Second Pillar: Praying five times a day in the direction of Mecca

Third Pillar: Giving to the poor and needy

Fourth Pillar: Fasting during the month of *Ramadan*

Fifth Pillar: Making a pilgrimage, or *hajj*, to Mecca

Muslim Empires ❶

Muhammad died without choosing someone to continue his work. His close associates soon selected a **caliph** (KAY·lihf) to succeed him. The title of caliph was used by rulers of the Muslim community from 632 until 1924. The caliph's duty was to spread God's rule. In carrying out this task, the caliphs founded a new empire, the caliphate. The caliphate was a **theocracy** (thee·AHK·ruh·see), a government ruled by a religious leader.

Conquest, Trade, and Learning The caliphs created a vast trading system throughout their empires. Islamic ideas spread as books were exchanged along trade routes. Metalwork, pottery, and fabrics exposed other people to new and unique Muslim artwork.

In the early Middle Ages, Muslims collected and translated important books and papers in order to preserve knowledge. During the 1100s and 1200s, these ancient texts were translated from Arabic into Hebrew and Latin. European scholars could now study the knowledge of the ancient world. They could see how Islamic thinkers had further developed this knowledge.

Islam in Europe The caliphs conquered Christian Spain and introduced Islamic culture there. They had hoped to spread their influence elsewhere in Europe. In 732, however, that hope was dashed. Muslim armies trying to capture Tours, in what is now west-central France, were defeated by Charles Martel (sharl mar·TELL), Charlemagne's grandfather. By 1400, however, the Muslims had succeeded in conquering parts of Europe.

Reading
Social Studies

A. Analyzing Causes How did the caliphs' trading system lead to the spread of culture?

Reading Social Studies
A. Possible Answer Books, skills, and ideas were exchanged along trade routes.

MORE ABOUT...
Islam's Contribution to Learning

For about 700 years, Islamic scholars were among the leading thinkers of the world. During the Middle Ages, Islamic scientists, mathematicians, and doctors pushed forward the frontiers of knowledge.

Islamic scientists made important contributions to astronomy, meteorology, and physics. Arab mathematicians introduced the Arabic system of numerals, which dramatically reduced the time it took to make calculations.

Medicine also progressed in the Muslim empires. Every major city had a hospital, and doctors began to understand how the immune system and contagious diseases worked.

CRITICAL THINKING ACTIVITY

Recognizing Important Details Initiate a "round robin" of questions by asking a question about an important detail in this section, such as "Who used the title of caliph?" After a student answers your question, have him or her formulate a question about another detail and direct it to another student. Have the student who answers that question formulate another question, and so on. Continue until all important details have been reviewed.

Class Time 10 minutes

Activity Options

Differentiating Instruction: Less Proficient Readers

Summarizing To reinforce Section Objective 1, pair a less proficient reader with a more skilled reader. Ask the pairs to read the boldface main headings and the run-in subheadings on pages 234 and 235.

Student pairs should work together to think of one or more questions about each heading. For example, for the head "Muslim Empires," students might ask, "Where did Muslims establish empires? How were Muslim empires ruled? What kind of government did Muslim empires have?" For the subhead "Islam in Europe," students might ask, "How did Islam come to Europe?" At each heading, the members of each pair take turns reading the paragraph to each other, stopping to identify the answers to questions they wrote and summarize the information in the paragraph.

INSTRUCT: Objective ❷

The Ottoman Empire/ Slaves and Soldiers

- Where was the Ottoman Empire located? in modern-day Turkey and parts of North Africa, Southwest Asia, and Southeast Europe
- What were sultans? How did they show tolerance of other religions? rulers of the Ottoman Empire; allowed Christians and Jews to worship freely
- What did Suleiman I establish in his empire? a law code and system of justice
- Who were the Janissaries? a special group of soldiers that developed from a small force of slaves

MORE ABOUT...
Suleiman the Magnificent

Named after King Solomon, Suleiman I (1494?– 1566) is believed by many to have been the greatest Ottoman leader of all time. Many believe he achieved greater justice and harmony than any other Islamic leader. Europeans feared and respected this Ottoman sultan who conquered Rhodes, a large part of Greece, Hungary, and much of the Austrian Empire.

In addition to his role as lawmaker and conqueror, Suleiman launched a campaign to turn Constantinople into the greatest center of art, music, writing, and philosophy in the Islamic world. He both cultivated and practiced the arts, writing some of the most beautiful poetry of his time.

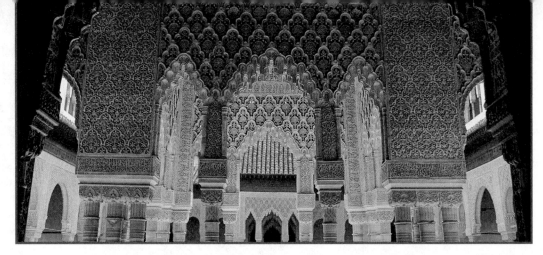

Culture • The influence of Islamic art left its mark in southern Spain, where Muslims built such works of art as the Alhambra, a magnificent palace. ▲

The Ottoman Empire ❷

The Muslim **Ottoman Empire** controlled what is now Turkey and parts of North Africa, Southwest Asia, and Southeast Europe. The Ottomans made **Constantinople**, called Istanbul in present-day Turkey, their capital city. The rulers of the Ottoman Empire were called sultans. The vast Ottoman Empire included people of different backgrounds. The sultans were tolerant of other religions. Christians and Jews could pay a tax that allowed them to worship as they pleased. Some achieved prominent positions in banking and business.

Region • Suleiman I was a 16th-century sultan of the Ottoman Empire. ▼

Suleiman, "The Magnificent" From 1520 to 1566, **Suleiman I** (SOO·lay·MAHN) ruled the Ottoman Empire. Christians called Suleiman "The Magnificent." Muslims called him "The Lawgiver." Suleiman published a code of laws that established a system of justice throughout his empire. Suleiman's chief architect, Sinan (SY·nihn), transformed Christian Constantinople into an Islamic capital. Sinan designed famous mosques in Istanbul and elsewhere in the Ottoman Empire. As long as Suleiman ruled the Ottoman Empire, it was the richest and most powerful empire in Europe and Southwest Asia.

Reading Social Studies

B. Forming and Supporting Opinions Do you think Suleiman I deserved to be called "The Magnificent"?

Reading Social Studies B. Possible Answer Yes, because he set up a justice system and made the empire rich and powerful.

Slaves and Soldiers ❷

Not everyone shared in the empire's wealth and glory. Many people were slaves, often prisoners from conquered nations. They served at court or in the homes of wealthy people. Many of the male slaves became soldiers.

Activity Options

Interdisciplinary Link: Math

Class Time One class period

Task Converting Arabic numbers to Roman numerals

Purpose To understand and appreciate the mathematical contributions made by Arabs

Supplies Needed
- Supermarket advertising fliers
- Pencils

ⓑ Block Scheduling

Activity Review Roman numerals (1=I, 5=V, 10=X, 50=L, 100=C, 500=D, 1,000=M) and how they can be used to represent numbers. Then distribute copies of supermarket fliers to pairs of students. Have them browse through the fliers and replace ten prices with equivalent Roman numerals. For example, 33 cents per pound would be XXXIII cents per pound. Emphasize to students the simplicity of the Arabic system.

The Janissaries A special group of soldiers loyal to the sultan, called **Janissaries,** developed in the late 1300s out of a small force of slaves. By the 1600s, they had become so powerful that even the sultans feared them. They refused to learn modern ways of fighting, however, and grew weak. In 1826, a group of Janissaries attacked the sultan. Forces loyal to the sultan fired on the attacking Janissaries, killing 6,000. The sultan then disbanded the force.

The Decline of the Ottoman Empire

Over the centuries, the Ottoman Empire grew weak. It fought wars constantly to hold on to its empire. By the 1800s, the empire came close to bankruptcy several times. It also had trouble competing in trade with industrialized Europe. **Sultan Mehmed V** fought on the losing side of World War I. After the war ended, the empire lost control of Arab lands. By 1924, the Ottoman Empire no longer existed. The modern country of Turkey had taken its place.

Culture • Three Janissaries (on the right) stand in front of their sultan. ▲

SECTION 5 ASSESSMENT

Terms & Names

1. **Identify:**
   (a) Five Pillars of Islam
   (b) caliph
   (c) theocracy
   (d) Ottoman Empire
   (e) Constantinople
   (f) Suleiman I
   (g) Janissary
   (h) Sultan Mehmed V

Taking Notes

2. Use a time line like this one to record major events in the spread of Islamic empires.

632 ├──┼──┼──┼──┤ 1924

Main Ideas

3. (a) How did the caliphs contribute to the growth of Islamic empires?

   (b) What regions of the world did the Ottoman Empire include?

   (c) What was Constantinople?

Critical Thinking

4. **Hypothesizing** How might the modern world be different if Muslim armies had won the battle of Tours?

Think About
  • cultural change
  • religious differences

ACTIVITY -OPTION- Create an illustrated **report** on the religious buildings of Judaism, Christianity, or Islam.

North Africa and Southwest Asia: Place and Times

INSTRUCT: Objective ❸

The Decline of the Ottoman Empire

• **What caused the Ottoman Empire to decline?** Too many wars weakened it and almost caused bankruptcy. It had trouble competing in trade with Europe.

• **What happened to the Ottoman Empire after World War I?** It lost control of Arab lands; by 1924 it no longer existed.

MORE ABOUT...
Istanbul

Istanbul is situated on both sides of the Bosporus, a narrow strait separating Europe from Asia. It is the only major city located on two continents.

ASSESS & RETEACH

Reading Social Studies Have students write supporting details about the Islamic empires in the chart on page 212.

 Formal Assessment
  • Section Quiz, p. 116

RETEACHING ACTIVITY

Organize the class into groups of five. Assign one of the section's visuals to each group member. Ask each student to write a paragraph about the significance of that visual to the section's main idea. Then have group members share their paragraphs with one another.

 In-depth Resources: Unit 3
  • Reteaching Activity, p. 16

Access for Students Acquiring English
  • Reteaching Activity, p. 72

Section 5 Assessment

1. Terms & Names
  a. Five Pillars of Islam, p. 234
  b. caliph, p. 235
  c. theocracy, p. 235
  d. Ottoman Empire, p. 236
  e. Constantinople, p. 236
  f. Suleiman I, p. 236
  g. Janissary, p. 237
  h. Sultan Mehmed V, p. 237

2. Taking Notes
  632: Title of caliph comes into use
  732: Muslim armies defeated at Tours
  1520: Suleiman I begins rule of Ottoman Empire
  1826: Janissaries attack sultan; sultan disbands force
  1924: Ottoman Empire ends

3. Main Ideas
  a. They established a vast trading system and conquered many countries.
  b. It included Turkey, parts of North Africa, Southwest Asia, and Southeast Europe.
  c. Constantinople was the capital of the Ottoman Empire.

4. Critical Thinking
  Answers will vary but should mention that many Europeans would probably be Muslims and speak Arabic, that art and architecture would be Islamic, and that laws might be Islamic laws.

ACTIVITY OPTION
   Integrated Assessment
    • Rubric for creating an illustrated report

ASSESSMENT

TERMS & NAMES

1. fertile, p. 213
2. irrigation, p. 215
3. Hammurabi, p. 217
4. Fertile Crescent, p. 217
5. pyramid, p. 225
6. hieroglyphics, p. 225
7. Re, p. 226
8. Muhammad, p. 231
9. caliph, p. 235
10. theocracy, p. 235

REVIEW QUESTIONS

Possible Responses

1. Annual flooding of the river deposits fertile soil and makes farming possible.
2. the Mediterranean Sea, the Red Sea, and the Persian Gulf
3. threat of invaders, lack of water, need for and risks of trade
4. highest class: kings, priests, and wealthy property owners; middle class: skilled workers, merchants, and farmers; lowest class: enslaved people
5. They constructed canals to control the river and use its waters for irrigation.
6. They believed the dead needed these items in the afterlife.
7. All three religions are monotheistic; they developed in the same region.
8. For Jews, it was the center of ancient Judaism and the site of the last Temple; for Christians, it is associated with events in Jesus' life; many believe that Jesus was buried there.
9. He established a law code and system of justice throughout his empire.
10. The empire waged costly wars; it could not compete with industrialized Europe; it was on the losing side in World War I.

ASSESSMENT

TERMS & NAMES

Explain the significance of each of the following:

1. fertile
2. irrigation
3. Hammurabi
4. Fertile Crescent
5. pyramid
6. hieroglyphics
7. Re
8. Muhammad
9. caliph
10. theocracy

REVIEW QUESTIONS

Physical Geography *(pages 213–216)*

1. What makes it possible to farm the desert near the Nile?
2. Name the three important bodies of water that helped to shape the region of North Africa and Southwest Asia.

Ancient Mesopotamia and the Fertile Crescent *(pages 217–221)*

3. What three problems faced the city-states of Mesopotamia?
4. List the three classes of people in Mesopotamia.

Ancient Egypt *(pages 223–227)*

5. Why did the ancient Egyptians build canals on the Nile?
6. Why did the ancient Egyptians fill their tombs with everyday items?

Birthplace of Three Religions *(pages 229–233)*

7. What do Judaism, Christianity, and Islam have in common?
8. Why is Jerusalem an important city for both Jews and Christians?

Muslim Empires *(pages 234–237)*

9. Why did the Muslims call Suleiman I "The Lawgiver"?
10. What caused the Ottoman Empire to grow weak?

CRITICAL THINKING

Comparing

1. Use the details in your completed chart from Reading Social Studies, p. 212, to compare the religion of ancient Egypt with the religion of Mesopotamia.

Evaluating Decisions

2. The nonprofit group INSIGHT is using technology to record Egypt's culture. (See page 431.) Based on the amount of work involved, do you think the work of INSIGHT is a good idea? Why or why not?

Making Inferences

3. The Greek historian Herodotus called Egypt "the gift of the Nile." What do you think he meant?

Visual Summary

1 Physical Geography

- The climate, resources, and soil conditions of North Africa and Southwest Asia are determined by the water and rainfall of the region.
- Dry land and flooding rivers still affect the region today.

2 Ancient Mesopotamia and the Fertile Crescent

- A complex civilization arose as Mesopotamia struggled with challenges.
- Early achievements in Mesopotamia led the way for later societies.

3 Ancient Egypt

- Environment influenced the development of civilization in ancient Egypt.
- The ancient Egyptians created a well organized and complex civilization.

4 Birthplace of Three Religions

- Three major world religions began in Southwest Asia.
- Judaism, Christianity, and Islam have a great deal in common.

5 Muslim Empires

- Islamic beliefs have spread through Southwest Asia and other parts of the world.
- These beliefs influence both society and government.

CRITICAL THINKING: Possible Responses

1. Comparing
Both Sumerians and Egyptians were polytheistic, meaning that they worshipped many gods. Only the Egyptians, however, believed that people could be related to gods. For instance, they believed that the pharaoh was the living son of the sun god.

2. Evaluating Decisions
Students may say that the work done by INSIGHT is very important because once ancient structures are destroyed, they are gone forever and humanity's link to that particular history is lost.

3. Making Inferences
He probably meant that the Nile made life possible there.

SOCIAL STUDIES SKILLBUILDER

Natural Vegetation in Algeria, Libya, and Egypt ▼

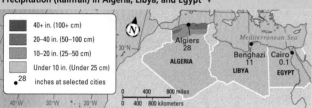

Desert and dry shrub
Temperate grassland
Mediterranean shrub
River valley and oasis

ALGERIA
LIBYA
EGYPT
Mediterranean Sea

0   400   800 miles
0   400   800 kilometers

Precipitation (Rainfall) in Algeria, Libya, and Egypt ▼

40+ in. (100+ cm)
20–40 in. (50–100 cm)
10–20 in. (25–50 cm)
Under 10 in. (Under 25 cm)
●28 inches at selected cities

Algiers 28
ALGERIA
Benghazi 11
LIBYA
Cairo 0.1
EGYPT
Mediterranean Sea

0   400   800 miles
0   400   800 kilometers

SKILLBUILDER: Comparing Precipitation/Climate and Vegetation Maps

1. What type of vegetation would you expect to find in these countries?
2. What does the precipitation map tell you about the availability of drinking water in these countries?
3. What relationship do you see between the two maps?

FOCUS ON GEOGRAPHY

1. **Region** • This map shows degrees of desertification in North Africa. What do you think the green areas represent?
2. **Human-Environment Interaction** • Which countries have lost the greatest amount of land to the desert?

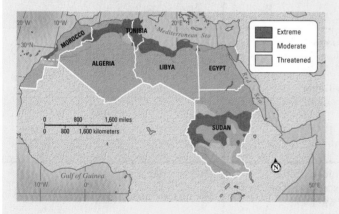

MOROCCO
TUNISIA
Mediterranean Sea
ALGERIA
LIBYA
EGYPT
Red Sea
SUDAN
Gulf of Guinea

Extreme
Moderate
Threatened

0   800   1,600 miles
0   800   1,600 kilometers

CHAPTER PROJECTS

Interdisciplinary Activity: Language Arts

Writing a Letter Imagine you are learning to be a scribe in Mesopotamia. Write a letter home to your parents describing your training and the responsibilities you will be taking on.

Cooperative Learning Activity

Writing a Documentary In a group of three to five students, plan a documentary about one of the female rulers of ancient Egypt. Choose a ruler, such as Hatshepsut, Nefertiti, or Cleopatra, and do research to find out when she ruled, how she came to power, and what she accomplished in her rule.

• Write the script for your documentary.
• Locate or create illustrations.
• Present your documentary to the class.

INTERNET ACTIVITY

Use the Internet to do research about hieroglyphics, the picture writing of the ancient Egyptians. Find out how many types of picture symbols there were, how they are organized, and the sounds, words, actions, or ideas they represented.

Making a Poster Create a poster that shows hieroglyphic symbols and what they represent and include an explanation. Try to create some simple sentences or signs to "translate." Report your finding to the class. List the Web sites you used to prepare your report.

For Internet links to support this activity, go to

RESEARCH LINKS
CLASSZONE.COM

CHAPTER PROJECTS

Interdisciplinary Activity: Language Arts

Writing a Letter Suggest that students review pages 220 and 221, which detail the education, responsibilities, and writing tasks taken on by scribes. Ask them to describe how they feel about these studies. Encourage them to write the letter in their very best handwriting, just as a scribe would have done.

Cooperative Learning Activity

Writing a Documentary Once students have decided on a topic, suggest that they divide the research assignment and have individuals in the group locate specific information and create illustrations about it. Then have students work cooperatively to assimilate the information and present the finished documentary to the class.

INTERNET ACTIVITY

Discuss how students might find information about hieroglyphics using the Internet. Brainstorm possible key words, Web sites, and search engines students might explore. Demonstrate how they can make use of bookmarks to easily return to the most useful sites. Suggest that students make a chart to organize the symbols and their meanings. Then they can use the information in the chart to create their posters.

Skills Answers

Social Studies Skillbuilder
Possible Answers
1. It would be mostly desert vegetation and shrub.
2. Drinking water is likely to be scarce here.
3. The level of rainfall is a major factor that determines what, if any, vegetation grows.

Focus on Geography
Possible Answers
1. desert or land that is not threatened
2. Sudan, Libya, Tunisia

North Africa and Southwest Asia Today

	OVERVIEW	COPYMASTERS	INTEGRATED TECHNOLOGY
UNIT ATLAS AND CHAPTER RESOURCES	Students will examine how geography and historical events have influenced the development of the governments, economies, and cultures of countries in North Africa and Southwest Asia.	**In-depth Resources: Unit 3** • Guided Reading Worksheets, pp. 17–21 • Skillbuilder Practice, p. 24 • Unit Atlas Activities, pp. 1–2 • Geography Workshop, pp. 31–32 **Reading Study Guide** (Spanish and English), pp. 76–87 **Outline Map Activities**	Power Presentations Electronic Teacher Tools Online Lesson Planner Chapter Summaries on CD Critical Thinking Transparencies CT17
SECTION 1 A Troubled Century pp. 243–247	**KEY IDEAS** • The United Nations tried to ease problems in Palestine by dividing it into two parts. • In recent years, the Iran-Iraq War and the Persian Gulf War brought further tension and destruction to the area.	**In-depth Resources: Unit 3** • Guided Reading Worksheet, p. 17 • Reteaching Activity, p. 26 **Reading Study Guide** (Spanish and English), pp. 76–77	classzone.com Chapter Summaries on CD
SECTION 2 Resources and Religion pp. 249–253	• Islam, Christianity, and Judaism are the dominant religions in the region. • Throughout the region, tensions between westernized leaders and fundamentalists, who believe in strict interpretation of religious law, have caused conflicts.	**In-depth Resources: Unit 3** • Guided Reading Worksheet, p. 18 • Reteaching Activity, p. 27 **Reading Study Guide** (Spanish and English), pp. 78–79	Critical Thinking Transparencies CT18 Map Transparencies MT19 classzone.com Chapter Summaries on CD
SECTION 3 Egypt Today pp. 256–261	• Egypt became a monarchy in 1922. • Much of Egypt is desert land; dams and irrigation provide water for agricultural needs. • Cairo has undergone many changes, as more people have moved to the city for education and employment.	**In-depth Resources: Unit 3** • Guided Reading Worksheet, p. 19 • Reteaching Activity, p. 28 **Reading Study Guide** (Spanish and English), pp. 80–81	classzone.com Chapter Summaries on CD
SECTION 4 Israel Today pp. 264–267	• Zionism is a Jewish movement to return to the homeland of Palestine. • Palestinian Arabs have less political power than Israeli Jews; some are refugees in the occupied Gaza Strip and West Bank.	**In-depth Resources: Unit 3** • Guided Reading Worksheet, p. 20 • Reteaching Activity, p. 29 **Reading Study Guide** (Spanish and English), pp. 82–83	classzone.com Chapter Summaries on CD
SECTION 5 Turkey Today pp. 270–273	• Mustafa Kemal, or Atatürk, was the founder of modern Turkey. • Modernization brought many changes to Turkey, and new opportunities for women. • Turkey supports NATO, and wishes to join the European Union.	**In-depth Resources: Unit 3** • Guided Reading Worksheet, p. 21 • Reteaching Activity, p. 30 **Reading Study Guide** (Spanish and English), pp. 84–85	classzone.com Chapter Summaries on CD

🔊	Audio	🌐	Internet	TE	Teacher's Edition
💿	CD-ROM	📊	Overhead Transparency	📹	Video
📄	Copymaster	PE	Pupil's Edition		

ASSESSMENT OPTIONS

PE **Chapter Assessment,** pp. 274–275

📄 **Formal Assessment**
• Chapter Tests: Forms A, B, C, pp. 134–145

💿 **Test Generator**

🌐 **Online Test Practice**

📄 **Strategies for Test Preparation**

PE **Section Assessment,** p. 247

📄 **Formal Assessment**
• Section Quiz, p. 129

📄 **Integrated Assessment**
• Rubric for tracing a map

💿 **Test Generator**

📊 **Test Practice Transparencies TT29**

PE **Section Assessment,** p. 253

📄 **Formal Assessment**
• Section Quiz, p. 130

📄 **Integrated Assessment**
• Rubric for making a poster

💿 **Test Generator**

📊 **Test Practice Transparencies TT30**

PE **Section Assessment,** p. 261

📄 **Formal Assessment**
• Section Quiz, p. 131

📄 **Integrated Assessment**
• Rubric for writing a letter

💿 **Test Generator**

📊 **Test Practice Transparencies TT31**

PE **Section Assessment,** p. 267

📄 **Formal Assessment**
• Section Quiz, p. 132

📄 **Integrated Assessment**
• Rubric for writing an interview

💿 **Test Generator**

📊 **Test Practice Transparencies TT32**

PE **Section Assessment,** p. 273

📄 **Formal Assessment**
• Section Quiz, p. 133

📄 **Integrated Assessment**
• Rubric for writing a dialogue

💿 **Test Generator**

📊 **Test Practice Transparencies TT33**

RESOURCES FOR DIFFERENTIATING INSTRUCTION

Students Acquiring English/ESL

📄 **Reading Study Guide**
(Spanish and English), pp. 76–87

📄 **Access for Students Acquiring English**
Spanish Translations, pp. 73–84

TE **TE Activity**
• Vocabulary, p. 259

Less Proficient Readers

📄 **Reading Study Guide**
(Spanish and English), pp. 76–87

TE **TE Activity**
• Sequencing, p. 245

Gifted and Talented Students

TE **TE Activities**
• Research, p. 252
• Examining Cultural Differences, p. 266

CROSS-CURRICULAR CONNECTIONS

Literature
Hickox, Rebecca. ***The Golden Sandal: A Middle Eastern Cinderella Story.*** New York: Holiday House, 1998. Based on an Iraqi folk tale.

Nye, Naomi Shihab, ed. ***The Space Between Our Footsteps: Poems and Paintings from the Middle East.*** New York: Simon & Schuster Books for Young Readers, 1998. Arabic, Hebrew, Turkish, and Persian poetry and art.

Popular Culture
Bator, Robert. ***Daily Life in Ancient and Modern Istanbul.*** Minneapolis, MN: Runestone Press, 2001. Development of the city.

Barghusen, Joan D. ***Daily Life in Ancient and Modern Cairo.*** Minneapolis, MN: Runestone Press, 2001. Development of the city.

Jerusalem and the Holy Land: Chronicles from National Geographic. Philadelphia: Chelsea House, 1999. Muslim village life, Jewish Passover, other interesting articles.

Geography
Pollard, Michael. ***The Nile.*** New York: Benchmark Books, 1998. Exploration, cultures, flooding, ecology.

Whitcraft, Melissa. ***The Tigris and Euphrates Rivers.*** New York: Franklin Watts, 1999. How the rivers affect human settlements in Turkey, Syria, and Iraq.

Science/Math
Stewart, Gail. ***The Suez Canal.*** San Diego: Lucent Books, 2001. How it was built and why it is important.

History
Harris, Nathaniel. ***Israel and the Arab Nations in Conflict.*** Austin, TX: Raintree Steck-Vaughn, 1999. Introduction to the conflict.

Williams, Mary, ed. ***The Middle East: Opposing Viewpoints.*** San Diego: Greenhaven Press, 2000. Articles, political cartoons, and provocative questions.

ENRICHMENT ACTIVITIES

The following activities are especially suitable for classes following block schedules.

Teacher's Edition, pp. 246, 250, 252, 258, 260, 265, 266, 271
Pupil's Edition, pp. 247, 253, 261, 267, 273

Unit Atlas, pp. 202–209
Interdisciplinary Challenge, pp. 254–255
Literature Connections, pp. 262–263

Linking Past and Present, pp. 268–269
Outline Map Activities

INTEGRATED TECHNOLOGY

Go to **classzone.com** for lesson support and activities for Chapter 9.

BLOCK SCHEDULE LESSON PLAN OPTIONS: 90-MINUTE PERIOD

DAY 1

CHAPTER PREVIEW, pp. 240–241
Class Time 20 minutes

- **Hypothesize** Use the "What do you think?" questions in Focus on Geography on PE p. 241 to help students hypothesize about how the importance of the Middle East might change as nations develop alternative sources of energy.

SECTION 1, pp. 243–247
Class Time 70 minutes

- **Small Groups** Divide the class into four groups. Have each group select one section objective on TE p. 243 to help them prepare a summary of this section. Remind students that when they summarize, they should include the main ideas and most important details in their own words. Reconvene as a whole class for discussion.
Class Time 35 minutes

- **Peer Competition** Divide the class into pairs. Assign each pair one of the Terms & Names for this section. Have pairs make up five questions that can be answered with the Term or Name. Have groups take turns asking the class their questions.
Class Time 35 minutes

DAY 2

SECTION 2, pp. 249–253
Class Time 35 minutes

- **Vocabulary** Write *OPEC, haji, Ramadan,* and *chadors* on individual index cards. Print enough cards so each student will have one. Ask students to draw a card, define the word, and explain the significance of that word. For discussion, have students form groups according to the cards they have chosen and discuss the significance of the word.

SECTION 3, pp. 256–261
Class Time 35 minutes

- **Travel Map** Have students create a map for a friend who is traveling to Egypt, Israel, or Turkey. Have them write a note to the friend telling why that map is important to have with them on their trip. Refer students to Geography Handbook PE pp. 8–11 to help them select a type of map.

SECTION 4, pp. 264–267
Class Time 20 minutes

- **Comparing** Have students use the research about a kibbutz in Multiple Learning Styles: Interpersonal TE p. 265 to compare life in a kibbutz with their own lives. Encourage students to use a graphic organizer to display the comparisons.

DAY 3

SECTION 5, pp. 270–273
Class Time 20 minutes

- **Debate** Use the Activity Option on TE p. 273 to have students prepare a debate between two Turks, one who welcomes Mustafa Kemal's changes and one who opposes them.

CHAPTER 9 REVIEW AND ASSESSMENT,
pp. 274–275
Class Time 70 minutes

- **Review** Have students work in small groups and use Main Ideas in each section opener to review the chapter.
Class Time 35 minutes

- **Assessment** Have students complete the Chapter 9 Assessment.
Class Time 35 minutes

TECHNOLOGY IN THE CLASSROOM

SATELLITE IMAGES ON THE WEB

The Internet is an excellent way to access and compare photographs and other images. The United States Geological Survey's Earthshots site provides satellite images of different parts of Earth. The images, which were taken over periods of three or four decades, allow students to see changes to the environment over time and are, thus, excellent classroom tools.

ACTIVITY OUTLINE

Objective Students will view satellite images of places in North Africa and Southwest Asia and take notes on the role of water in these locations. They will write paragraphs on the computer describing what they have seen, and they will draw future satellite images of these places.

Task Have students work in groups to analyze the changes to various parts of this region over time, as shown in the satellite images. Ask them to answer questions about the role of water in these changes. Have them write paragraphs explaining this role and draw pictures showing what a satellite image of the area might look like in ten years.

Class Time 2–3 class periods

DIRECTIONS

1. Students learned in Chapter 9 about the importance of oil to North Africa and Southwest Asia. Now ask them to consider the importance of water. In such an arid part of the world, how do they think people obtain water for drinking, irrigation, and other purposes? What happens as more people move into a desert area or develop more farms? How can farms be maintained in an arid climate? What happens to the environment as people use more and more water in a desert region?

2. Divide the class into small groups, and have each group go to the Earthshots Web site (link from **classzone.com**). If you have extra time, have students go to the first link ("First time readers: start at Garden City, Kansas"). This section will introduce them to the satellite images and explain how to "read" the images. If you do not have time for this introduction, provide the class with a brief overview of what satellite images are and what the colors mean (see the Garden City article).

3. Assign each group to one of the following places: Nile River Delta, Egypt; Elburz Mountains, Iran; Southern Mauritania; Riyadh, Saudi Arabia; Iraq-Kuwait. Ask students to look carefully at the images from different years and read the text to the right of the images.

4. As they look at the images, ask groups to take notes answering these questions: What changes shown in the images are related to water? What has caused these changes? What do you think the people in this area would say about their water supply? What do you think might happen here in the future? What might a satellite image taken here in ten years look like?

5. Have students write paragraphs on the computer describing the satellite images they have seen and the relationship between water and the changes shown in the images.

6. Have students draw pictures of the way they think a satellite image of the region they have studied might look in ten years.

CHAPTER 9 OBJECTIVE

Students will examine how geography and historical events have influenced the development of the governments, economies, and cultures of countries in North Africa and Southwest Asia.

FOCUS ON VISUALS

Interpreting the Photograph Direct students' attention to the photograph of the indoor bazaar. Ask them to read the caption, study the picture, and describe how shopping in such a market might compare with shopping in a mall near their homes.

Possible Response Prices in the markets are subject to bargaining, so making a purchase might take longer.

Extension Ask the students to write a brief passage describing a day in the life of one of the market's merchants.

CRITICAL THINKING ACTIVITY

Hypothesizing Direct students' attention to the world map inset on the page. Then prompt a discussion about why this region is considered strategically important by the United States, Europe, and other countries. Discuss the region's location between the Mediterranean Sea and the Arabian Sea and what significance that location has for trade in the region. Point out that geographical factors help oil-producing countries in the region control access to their oil.

Class Time 15 minutes

CHAPTER 9

North Africa and Southwest Asia Today

240

Recommended Resources

BOOKS FOR THE TEACHER
Cleveland, William. *A History of the Modern Middle East.* Boulder, CO: Westview Press, 1999. Concise overview.
Raymond, Andre. *Cairo.* Cambridge, MA: Harvard University Press, 2000. Compelling history of city.

Spencer, William. *Global Studies. The Middle East.* Guilford, CT: Dushkin/McGraw Hill, 2000. Essays and articles on each country.

VIDEOS
From Egypt to Israel. Chicago, IL: Questar, Inc., 1999. Tour of the area's many landmarks.

SOFTWARE
Nile: Passage to Egypt. Florence, KY: Discovery Channel, 1995. Navigate the river and learn about culture and history.

INTERNET
For more information about North Africa and Southwest Asia, visit **classzone.com**.

How have rich oil deposits affected Southwest Asia and the world?

FOCUS ON GEOGRAPHY

Human-Environment Interaction • Enormous amounts of petroleum, or oil, lie beneath the land surrounding the southern and eastern shores of the Mediterranean Sea, a region often called the Middle East. Experts believe the Middle East supplies about 40 percent of the world's oil. Other countries have come to depend on the oil produced here. The importance of providing energy resources for the planet has given the region great political and economic power. The governments of Middle Eastern nations try to control the price and amount of oil that is produced in their region.

What do you think?

◆ How are politics and economics related in the Middle East?

◆ How might the importance of this region change as nations develop alternative sources of energy?

Place A wealth of goods is sold in this vast indoor bazaar in Istanbul, Turkey.

Objectives

• To identify the relationships among geography, politics, and economics

• To explain the bargaining strength afforded by the presence of natural resources

What Do You Think?

1. Help students make a direct connection between politics and economics by asking how Middle Eastern countries could have an economic impact on countries whose political ideas conflict with theirs.

2. Guide students to think about how western countries could become less dependent on oil from the Middle East and how such a situation could affect countries within the region.

How have rich oil deposits affected Southwest Asia and the world?

Have students consider how much people depend on oil in their daily lives. Guide them to understand how their families use petroleum products in heating their homes or filling up their cars with gasoline. Remind students that the price of gas can affect such decisions as how people get to work or school, or whether or not families travel and take vacations.

MAKING GEOGRAPHIC CONNECTIONS

Ask students to identify natural resources that are plentiful in the part of the country where they live. Are any of these resources used to provide fuel or electricity? Guide students to consider potential alternative sources of energy.

Implementing the National Geography Standards

Standard 2 Draw sketch maps of different regions and compare them with atlas maps

Objective To draw a sketch map of North Africa and Southwest Asia

Class Time 20 minutes

Task With their textbooks closed, have students sketch a physical and political map of North Africa and Southwest Asia. When students have completed the maps, they should compare them with maps in the Unit Atlas to determine the accuracy of place location and knowledge. Students should write a paragraph explaining the discrepancies.

Evaluation Students should identify at least three discrepancies between their maps and the Unit Atlas maps, then make changes to their maps.

BEFORE YOU READ
What Do You Know?

Ask students to name some important cities and landmarks in North Africa and Southwest Asia. Remind them of some of the region's major rivers, such as the Nile and the Euphrates, and ask students to share any facts they know about them. Make sure students understand that several of the world's major religions have their roots in the Middle East, and ask students to name them. Ask why the region is considered by many people to be the "cradle of civilization."

What Do You Want to Know?

Have each student make a list of what he or she would like to know about North Africa and Southwest Asia. Then have them compare their lists in class. As they read the chapter, have students check off items from their lists.

READ AND TAKE NOTES

Reading Strategy: Identifying Problems and Solutions Explain to students that associating problems with their solutions will help them gain a better understanding of history. Point out the Resulting Problems column of the chart. Remind students that a solution can often create or highlight a new problem.

 In-depth Resources: Unit 3
- Guided Reading Worksheets, pp. 17–21

READING SOCIAL STUDIES

BEFORE YOU READ
▶▶ What Do You Know?

Before you read the chapter, consider what you know about North Africa and Southwest Asia today. You may know something about countries like Israel, Saudi Arabia, Iran, Egypt, Turkey, and Iraq from televised news reports about conflicts in this area. Think about the region's role as a major producer of oil. You, or people you know, may have been born in the region or may have lived or visited there. Review what you have learned about recent history and current events in this part of the world.

▶▶ What Do You Want to Know?

Decide what you want to know about contemporary North Africa and Southwest Asia. In your notebook, record what you hope to learn from this chapter.

Region • These girls live in Cairo, Egypt, the largest city in the region. ▼

READ AND TAKE NOTES

Reading Strategy: Identifying Problems and Solutions Recognizing problems and how they are solved will help you understand complicated issues you read about in social studies. Use the chart below to identify problems, solutions, and new problems discussed in Chapter 9.

- Copy the chart into your notebook.
- As you read, look for information related to each problem listed on the chart. Some issues are discussed more than once.
- Take notes on solutions that have been tried and problems that resulted.

Region • This sign is in three languages—Hebrew, Arabic, and English. ▲

Problems	Solutions	Resulting Problems
History of foreign influence	European control meant mandates.	Countries without mandates often had to fight for independence.
Changes in world markets	Oil-producing countries formed OPEC to decide price and amount of oil produced.	In 1973, OPEC placed an embargo on countries supporting Israel.
Severe water shortage	In 1956, Aswan Dam was built for crops and hydroelectric power.	Nile no longer deposits soil. Farmers use fertilizers, causing pollution.
Poverty in villages in Egypt	Peasants migrate to cities to find work and escape malnutrition and disease.	Cities become overcrowded and unemployment rises.
Lack of a homeland for Jews	The U.N. divided Palestine. Israel became independent; PLO.	Arabs did not accept plan; Arab-Israeli wars began.
Forced modernization in Turkey	Attatürk got rid of Islamic government and joined European Union.	EU fears that too many Turkish workers will relocate.

Teaching Strategy

Reading the Chapter This chapter focuses on the history, resources, and cultures of North Africa and Southwest Asia. The conflicts that dominate the region today have their roots in these elements. Encourage students to take notes as they read and to study the maps in the chapter carefully so that they can better understand this significant and complex region.

Integrated Assessment The Chapter Assessment on page 275 describes several activities that may be used for integrated assessment. You may wish to have students work on these activities during the course of the chapter and then present them at the end.

A Troubled Century

SECTION 1

TERMS & NAMES

mandate
Palestine
Arab-Israeli Wars
Kurd
Persian Gulf War

MAIN IDEA

Today's conflicts in North Africa and Southwest Asia have roots in the history of the region.

WHY IT MATTERS NOW

Regional conflicts affect the security and well-being of people around the world.

DATELINE EXTRA

SÈVRES, FRANCE, AUGUST 10, 1920

Turkey's Ottoman Empire, the "sick man of Europe" is dead at last. Today, Turkey agreed to surrender most of its territory to Great Britain and France. Revolts by Arab nationalists in recent years had weakened the once-great empire. Being on the losing side in the recent World War marked its end. Mesopotamia and Palestine will now be under British control. Syria, which includes Lebanon, goes to the French.

Region • European nations divided up the Ottoman Empire at the Sèvres conference. ▲

European Nations Take Over ➊

When World War I ended, the history of modern Southwest Asia and North Africa began. During the war, the Turkish Ottoman Empire had sided with Germany against Great Britain, France, and Russia. After the Ottoman Empire's defeat, most of its former territory was divided between Great Britain and France. The stage was set for major conflicts that still trouble the region today. (See the map on page 248.)

North Africa and Southwest Asia Today **243**

SECTION OBJECTIVES

1. To identify European control and subsequent independence in the region
2. To describe the political conflict over Palestine
3. To describe the conflicts caused by religious and ethnic differences among peoples in the region
4. To explain the causes and effects of the Iran-Iraq War and the Persian Gulf War

SKILLBUILDER
• Interpreting a Chart, p. 244
• Interpreting a Map, p. 245

FOCUS & MOTIVATE
WARM-UP

Making Inferences Have students read <u>Dateline</u> and discuss the following questions.

1. Why do you think the Ottoman Empire is referred to as the "sick man of Europe"?
2. What nations did the Ottoman Empire oppose in World War I?

INSTRUCT: Objective ➊

European Nations Take Over

• Who took over most of the Ottoman Empire after its defeat? Great Britain and France
• What is a mandate? a country placed under another power's control by international agreement

 In-depth Resources: Unit 3
• Guided Reading Worksheet, p. 17

 Reading Study Guide
(Spanish and English), pp. 76–77

Program Resources

 In-depth Resources: Unit 3
• Guided Reading Worksheet, p. 17
• Reteaching Activity, p. 26

 Reading Study Guide
(Spanish and English), pp. 76–77

 Formal Assessment
• Section Quiz, p. 129

 Integrated Assessment
• Rubric for tracing a map

 Outline Map Activities

 Access for Students Acquiring English
• Guided Reading Worksheet, p. 73

 Technology Resources
classzone.com

> **TEST-TAKING RESOURCES**
> ↪ Strategies for Test Preparation
> ↪ Test Practice Transparencies
> 🖱 Online Test Practice

Teacher's Edition **243**

FOCUS ON VISUALS

Interpreting the Chart Direct students' attention to the second column in the chart. Ask students which country controlled the most mandates. Then ask students to suggest why they think a country would want to have the most mandates in this region.

Possible Response Great Britain. It wanted colonies and mandates to provide raw materials for its factories and a strategic advantage in international relations.

Extension Point out to students that the chart does not include Palestine because the land that made up Palestine is now the state of Israel. Lead students in a discussion of what this exclusion might signify to Arab Palestinians and how they might feel about it.

INSTRUCT: Objective ❷

Conflict Over Palestine

- How did the United Nations attempt to solve the conflict between the Jews and Arabs in Palestine? Were they successful? It divided Palestine into two parts—one for the Jews and one for the Arabs. It was not successful. The Arabs rejected the plan.
- What is the PLO? When and why was it formed? The Palestine Liberation Organization. It was formed in 1964 to oppose Israel and create a Palestinian state.
- What happened in the region between 1964 and 1977? Israel won the third and fourth Arab-Israeli Wars; territory switched back and forth between the two countries.

Independence Days in Southwest Asia and North Africa

Country	Controlling Power	Taken Over	Achieved Independence
Algeria	France	1847	July 5, 1962
Bahrain	Great Britain	1880	August 15, 1971
Egypt	Great Britain	1882	February 28, 1922
Iraq	Great Britain	1920	October 3, 1932
Jordan	Great Britain	1921	May 25, 1946
Kuwait	Great Britain	1899	June 19, 1961
Lebanon	France	1920	November 22, 1943
Libya	Italy	1932	December 24, 1951
Morocco	France (1/3 under Spain)	1912	March 2, 1956 (April 1956 from Spain)
Oman	Portugal	late 1500s	1650
Qatar	Great Britain	1916	September 3, 1971
Sudan	Egypt/Great Britain	1898	January 1, 1956
Syria	France	1920	April 17, 1946
Tunisia	France	1881	March 20, 1956
United Arab Emirates	Great Britain	1952	December 2, 1971
Yemen	Great Britain	1882	1967 (South Yemen) May 22, 1990 (union of North and South Yemen)

**SKILLBUILDER:
Interpreting a Chart**

1. Which European nation controlled the most countries in the region?
2. In which century did most countries on the chart achieve independence?

A History of Foreign Control Europeans had been taking control of the region since before the 19th century. After World War I, this control often took the form of mandates. A **mandate** is a country placed under the control of another power by international agreement. The European powers promised to give their mandates independence by a certain date. Countries that were not mandates often had to fight for independence.

Skillbuilder Answers

1. Great Britain

2. 20th century

Conflict Over Palestine ❷

After World War I, Great Britain controlled **Palestine,** an Arab region that was also the land the Jews had lived in 2,000 years earlier. Starting in the late 1800s, Jews fleeing persecution in Eastern Europe had begun migrating there again. After World War II and the Holocaust, many Jews were left homeless and the number who wanted to migrate to Palestine increased.

Palestine, however, was already home to Arabs who had no desire to see their homeland become a Jewish state. Arabs in other countries backed them up. In 1947, Great Britain asked the United Nations to solve the problem. The United Nations divided Palestine—one part for Jews and another for Arabs. The Jews accepted the plan, but the Arabs did not. In May 1948, Jewish leaders declared Israel an independent state. Iraq, Syria, Egypt, Jordan, and Lebanon immediately declared war on Israel. The Israelis won the first of the **Arab-Israeli Wars.** (See the map on page 245.)

Reading Social Studies

A. Summarizing What was the main source of conflict between the Jews and Arabs in Palestine?

Reading Social Studies
A. Answer control of land

244 CHAPTER 9

Activity Options

Multiple Learning Styles: Visual/Interpersonal

Class Time 30 minutes

Task Tracing the movement of Jews and Palestinian Arabs to and from Palestine after World War II

Purpose To understand the relationship between geography and history in the region

Supplies Needed
- Blank outline map of the region
- Colored pens or pencils

Activity Have students work in pairs to trace the movements of Jews and Palestinians in the region after World War II. Have them draw arrows on the outline map from the various countries in Europe from which the Jews came to Palestine and also indicate on the map where Palestinians fled after the partition of Palestine. Have students write a summary of these events.

Changing Boundaries in Palestine, 1947–49

Jewish state
Arab state
International zone
1949 border of Israel

0 50 100 miles
0 50 100 kilometers

LEBANON
SYRIA
Haifa
Nazareth
Mediterranean Sea
Tel Aviv
WEST BANK
Jerusalem
Gaza
Dead Sea
ISRAEL
Suez Canal
EGYPT
TRANSJORDAN
SINAI PENINSULA
Red Sea
N

GEOGRAPHY SKILLBUILDER: Interpreting a Map

1. **Region** • What country occupied the Sinai Peninsula in 1967?

2. **Region** • What happened to Arab-owned states in the region in the first 20 years after Israel was founded?

The Arab-Israeli Wars, 1967 and 1973

Israel before 1967 war
Occupied by Israel 1967
Occupied by Israel 1973
Occupied by Egypt 1973

0 50 100 miles
0 50 100 kilometers

LEBANON
SYRIA
GOLAN HEIGHTS
Nazareth
Mediterranean Sea
WEST BANK
Port Said
Jerusalem
Gaza
Dead Sea
ISRAEL
JORDAN
Suez Canal
Suez
SINAI PENINSULA
EGYPT
Red Sea
N

Palestine Refugees About 700,000 Palestinian Arabs had to leave their homes. They became refugees living in other Arab countries. In 1964, some Palestinian people formed the Palestine Liberation Organization (PLO). The PLO's goal is the establishment of an independent Palestinian state.

Continuing Conflict In 1967 and 1973, Israel won the third and fourth of the Arab-Israeli Wars. Conflict continued even in peacetime. Over the years, territory passed back and forth between Israel and Arab countries. (See the map above.)

Attempts at Peace In 1979, Egypt became the first Arab country in the region to make peace with Israel. Leaders of Egypt and Israel discussed the Palestinians' wish for their own state. Ten years later, Palestinian Arabs rebelled in the territories controlled by Israel. Most countries around the world sided with the Palestinians. Finally, in 1993, Israel and the PLO signed an agreement. The PLO recognized Israel's right to exist. Israel returned land to the Palestinians. The next year, Israel and Jordan signed a peace treaty. In 2000, however, another Palestinian uprising broke out.

Sources of Conflict ❸

The conflict between Israel and the Arab countries is partly due to religious differences between Jews and Muslims. Religious conflicts between Christians and Muslims have erupted in Egypt, Lebanon, and Sudan. Conflicts also occur within religions.

Geography Skillbuilder Answers
1. Israel
2. Most were absorbed into Israel.

Interpreting the Map Ask students to read aloud the titles of the two maps and then calculate the time difference between the dates of the first map and the two events on the second. Ask them to relate the first map to the events they have read about. Then have students compare the maps and point out the major changes they observe. When did those changes occur?

Possible Responses Israel occupied the Sinai Peninsula and Golan Heights in the 1967 war; Israel's territory expanded; Transjordan was renamed Jordan.

Extension Ask students to point out the Suez Canal and suggest what control of the canal could mean to Egypt and to Israel.

INSTRUCT: Objective ❸

Sources of Conflict

- What are the two main sects of Islam? What is a major difference between them? Sunnis and Shi'ites. Shi'ites are more willing than Sunnis to accept religious leaders as political leaders.

- What are the ethnic differences that contribute to conflicts between Iran and Iraq? Iraqis are descendants of Arabs from the Arabian Peninsula. Most Iranians are Persian, with a different language and history.

- Why did Khomeini and his followers object to the shah's rule? They felt the shah had been westernizing the country.

Activity Options

Differentiating Instruction: Less Proficient Readers

Sequencing Some students may be confused about the chronology of events in Palestine and Israel. As a group, reread "Conflict Over Palestine." Work with students to create a time line like the one shown about events in the region. Display the time line on the chalkboard or bulletin board so students may refer to it.

1947	UN divided Palestine
1948	Israel declared an independent state First Arab-Israeli War won by Israel
1964	PLO formed
1967	Second Arab-Israeli War won by Israel
1973	Third Arab-Israeli War won by Israel
1977	Egypt sought peace with Israel
1993	Israel and the PLO signed agreement

INSTRUCT: Objective ❹

Recent Wars

- **What was the cause of the Iran-Iraq War?** Iraq, led by Saddam Hussein, invaded Iran in 1980 over a dispute about oil-rich territory.
- **What was the outcome of the war?** One million people died. There was no clear victory. Both countries signed a cease-fire agreement.
- **How did the Persian Gulf War begin?** Iraq invaded Kuwait in 1990.
- **What was the international response?** a trade embargo against Iraq; multinational missile and ground attacks that led to Iraq's surrender

MORE ABOUT...
Kurdish Culture

Traditionally, Kurds were nomads, herding sheep and goats in areas of Turkey, Iraq, and Iran. After World War I, the nations guarded their borders more closely, making it hard for Kurds to follow their flocks. Most Kurds were forced to exchange their traditional way of life for village life.

Region • Hebrew (top) is the official language of Israel. Arabic (bottom) is the language of many other countries in the region. ▼

Place • These Kurdish children live in Antalya, Turkey. ▼

Sunnis and Shi'ites Islam, for example, has two main sects, or groups—Sunnis (SUN·eez) and Shi'ites (SHEE·eyets). Most Muslims in the region are Sunni. In Iran, however, most people belong to the Shiah branch of Islam. Shi'ites are more willing than the Sunni to accept religious leaders as political leaders. This difference has contributed to conflict between the neighboring countries of Iran and Iraq. The most powerful Iraqis belong to the Sunni branch of Islam.

Conflict Between Ethnic Groups Trouble also occurs within and between countries when ethnic groups come into conflict. For example, like most people in the region, Iraqis are descendants of Arabs who spread out from the Arabian Peninsula in the 600s. Most Iranians, however, are Persian, people originally from Central Asia who have lived on the Iranian plateau for 3,000 years. Arabs and Persians have different histories and speak different languages. These differences contribute to conflicts between Iran and Iraq.

Nationalism Some ethnic groups want to have a country of their own instead of being part of a multi-ethnic nation. The **Kurds**, for example, are a mountain people who live in Armenia, Georgia, Iran, Iraq, Lebanon, Syria, and Turkey. Their independence movements have been defeated in Turkey, Iran, and Iraq. Many Kurds have died in these struggles.

Fundamentalism Muslim fundamentalists believe Islam should be strictly observed. In 1979, Shi'ite leader Ayatollah Khomeini (ah·yah·TOH·luh koh·MAY·nee) took over the government of Iran. Khomeini and his followers objected to the way the former shah, or ruler, had been westernizing the country. Khomeini's government passed laws forbidding the sale of alcohol and limiting the freedom of women. Such fundamentalist movements have also arisen in other countries in the region, often leading to battles between people who hold opposing points of view.

Recent Wars ❹

The neighboring countries of Iran and Iraq had long disputed who owned the oil-rich territory between them. In 1980, Iraq, led by its absolute ruler Saddam Hussein, invaded Iran.

246 CHAPTER 9

The Iran-Iraq War The war lasted eight years. As many as one million people died, including soldiers as young as 11 and 12. Neither side could gain a clear victory. In 1988, both countries finally signed a cease-fire agreement developed by the United Nations.

The Persian Gulf War In 1990, Iraq invaded the small oil-rich country of Kuwait. The United Nations imposed a trade embargo to prevent Iraq from importing goods or exporting oil. The embargo took away most of Iraq's income, but Hussein continued to fight. On January 16, 1991, the **Persian Gulf War** began when a multi-national armed force began missile attacks on Iraq, followed by a ground attack on February 24. One hundred hours later, Iraq surrendered. Iraq was out of Kuwait, but Saddam Hussein stayed in power. Both Kuwait and Iraq suffered widespread destruction in the war.

Human-Environment Interaction • Iraq devastated Kuwait when Iraq released oil into the Persian Gulf and torched Kuwait's oil fields. ▼

SECTION 1 ASSESSMENT

Terms & Names

1. **Identify:** (a) mandate (b) Palestine (c) Arab-Israeli Wars (d) Kurd (e) Persian Gulf War

Taking Notes

2. Use a time line like this one to write the dates of major wars in Southwest Asia and North Africa.

1948 |——|——|——|——| 1991

Main Ideas

3. (a) How have European nations contributed to turmoil in Southwest Asia and North Africa?

(b) In what ways has religion been a source of conflict in this region?

(c) What are some of the different ethnic groups in this region and how have they come into conflict?

Critical Thinking

4. **Forming and Supporting Opinions**

Do you think the United Nations should be more involved in settling conflicts in Southwest Asia and North Africa?

Think About

• the system of mandates

• conflict in the region

• the UN in the Persian Gulf War

ACTIVITY -OPTION- Trace a **map** of the countries of Southwest Asia and North Africa. Write each country's name and the year it achieved independence on the map.

FOCUS ON VISUALS

Interpreting the Photograph Have students study the photograph. Explain that in the six weeks of the Persian Gulf War, the multinational force lost about 300 troops; Iraqi casualties were estimated at 8,000 to 100,000. Ask students to discuss the effects of the war, including environmental damage done by oil-field fires and oil spills in the Gulf.

Possible Response The fires polluted the air, and the oil in the Gulf killed many birds, fish, and other creatures.

Extension Have students study a map of the region to see which neighboring countries and waterways might have been affected by the oil-field fires and oil spills.

ASSESS & RETEACH

Reading Social Studies Have students complete the first row of the chart on page 242.

 Formal Assessment
• Section Quiz, p. 129

RETEACHING ACTIVITY

Write the following categories on the chalkboard: Arab-Israeli Wars, Iran-Iraq War, Persian Gulf War. Work with students to identify the cause or causes of each conflict and the resolution of each. Encourage students to reread sections of the lesson to find this information.

 In-depth Resources: Unit 3
• Reteaching Activity, p. 26

 Access for Students Acquiring English
• Reteaching Activity, p. 80

Section 1 Assessment

1. Terms & Names

a. mandate, p. 244
b. Palestine, p. 244
c. Arab-Israeli Wars, p. 244
d. Kurd, p. 246
e. Persian Gulf War, p. 247

2. Taking Notes

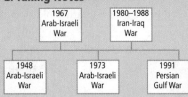

| 1967 Arab-Israeli War | 1980–1988 Iran-Iraq War |
| 1948 Arab-Israeli War | 1973 Arab-Israeli War | 1991 Persian Gulf War |

3. Main Ideas

a. divided territory once controlled by the Ottoman Empire

b. Conflicts have arisen between different religions (Muslims and Jews) and within a single religion (Sunni and Shi'ite Muslims).

c. Persians, Arabs, and Kurds; conflicts regarding history, language, culture

4. Critical Thinking

Possible Response The United Nations should be more involved because peace in those areas is beneficial to people around the world.

ACTIVITY OPTION

 Integrated Assessment
• Rubric for tracing a map

SKILLBUILDER

Reading a Historical Map

Defining the Skill

Explain that a historical map depicts a country or a region at a single moment in time. Some historical maps show patterns of exploration and migration, while others show how control of an area changes over time. Knowing how to read and interpret historical maps will help students better understand and remember what they read.

Applying the Skill

How to Read a Historical Map Guide students through the four strategies for reading a historical map. Ask a volunteer to read the title and the information in the map key. Discuss with the class why that information is important. Pay special attention to the dotted line in the map key, since it shows the original size of the Ottoman Empire. Ask a volunteer to interpret the different colors on the map and identify when the largest—and smallest—losses occurred.

Write a Summary

Be sure that students understand the main idea of the map. Ask them whether the map shows the Ottoman Empire growing or shrinking. Have students identify the original extent of the empire and discuss which modern countries were once part of it.

Practicing the Skill

Have students look at the map on page 245. Point out that, in contrast to the map of the Ottoman Empire, this map shows a relatively small geographical area. Ask students why they think an understanding of this map is important today. Ask questions such as, What countries border Palestine? Who controlled Jerusalem in 1949?

 In-depth Resources: Unit 3
• Skillbuilder Practice, p. 24

Reading a Historical Map

▶▶ Defining the Skill

Historical maps show an area of the world as it was in the past. Different historical maps contain different kinds of information. Some show trade routes or routes of exploration. Some show how an empire or nation has increased or decreased in size. Some show how political boundaries have changed over time. The map key tells what the symbols, lines, and colors on a historical map represent.

▶▶ Applying the Skill

The historical map below shows how the Ottoman Empire gradually collapsed. During the 15th and 16th centuries, the Ottoman Empire was one of the most powerful empires in the world. It lasted for more than 600 years, but by 1922 the empire was gone.

How to Read a Historical Map

Strategy ❶ Read the title to learn the time period that is shown on the map.

Strategy ❷ Read the key. Shown first on this key is a dotted line, which represents the boundary of the Ottoman Empire in 1807. Look at the map and find that boundary. As you follow the boundary, notice which bodies of water it touches and which continents it covers.

Strategy ❸ Look at each color on the key and the time period represented by that color. Then look for each color on the map. Some of the color regions are scattered. Be sure to locate all of them.

Strategy ❹ Read the map. Notice when different regions were lost to the Ottoman Empire. Some of these regions became independent; others fell under the rule of other nations.

Write a Summary

Writing a summary will help you gain a clearer understanding of the map. The paragraph to the right summarizes the information from this historical map.

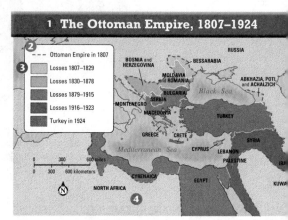

1 The Ottoman Empire, 1807–1924

❷ - - - Ottoman Empire in 1807
❸ Losses 1807–1829
  Losses 1830–1878
  Losses 1879–1915
  Losses 1916–1923
  Turkey in 1924

SUMMARY In 1807 the Ottoman Empire stretched from Bosnia and North Africa in the west to Kuwait in the east and from Russia in the north to Egypt in the south. Beginning in 1807, the area claimed by the Ottomans was gradually taken over by Greece, Austria-Hungary, Italy, and Great Britain.

▶▶ Practicing the Skill

Turn to page 245 in Chapter 9, Section 1. Look at the historical map entitled *Changing Boundaries in Palestine, 1947–49,* and then write a paragraph summarizing what you learned from it.

Career Connection: War Historian

Encourage students who enjoy reading historical maps to explore careers that use this skill. For example, a war historian uses many sources to learn about wars of the past. War historians both use and create historical maps in their research.

1. Suggest that students find out how war historians locate and use sources. Explain that people who participated in a recent war may still be living and can be interviewed. Wars that took place long ago must be studied by investigating old documents and other objects.

2. Help students find out what aptitudes and education a person needs to become a war historian.

3. Invite students to give an oral summary of their findings.

Resources and Religion

SECTION 2

TERMS & NAMES
OPEC
primary product
secondary product
petrochemical
hajj
Ramadan

MAIN IDEA

Oil resources are a powerful influence on the region's economies, and religion, especially Islam, is a powerful influence on its culture.

WHY IT MATTERS NOW

Peace in Southwest Asia and North Africa depends on prosperity and the ability of different religions to coexist.

DATELINE

KHUZISTAN PROVINCE, PERSIA (IRAN), 1908—A British company has just discovered oil here in Khuzistan. Both the British and the Persians expect it to bring their countries great wealth. The Shah of Iran (Persia) has given British businessman William Knox D'Arcy the rights to drill for oil here. D'Arcy plans to create the Anglo-Persian Oil Company and to begin exporting oil by 1912. The world's increasing dependence on oil for energy has led experts to predict that the value of oil will increase dramatically. The Middle East, they say, has the potential to become the greatest oil-producing area in the world.

Human-Environment Interaction • Workers lay an oil pipeline in the Khuzistan plain. ▶

Human-Environment Interaction • British businessman William Knox D'Arcy was the principal founder of the oil industry in Iran. ▲

The Importance of Oil ①

Oil was soon discovered in other countries of Southwest Asia and North Africa. Great Britain, France, the United States, and other western countries made agreements with the oil-rich nations to build and run companies to develop the oil fields. Today, nearly half the world's oil is found here, mainly in Saudi Arabia, Iran, Kuwait, and Iraq. Saudi Arabia, the world's largest oil-producing country, is also one of the largest oil exporters to the United States.

North Africa and Southwest Asia Today **249**

SECTION OBJECTIVES

1. To describe the relationship between oil and politics
2. To explain the role of religion in the region
3. To identify fundamentalist and western influences and the varying roles of women in Islamic countries
4. To describe the status of nomadic cultures

SKILLBUILDER
• Interpreting a Map, p. 250

CRITICAL THINKING
• Drawing Conclusions, p. 250

FOCUS & MOTIVATE
WARM-UP

Hypothesizing Have students read <u>Dateline</u> and answer the following questions.

1. Why were Europeans interested in oil-producing countries in the early 1900s?
2. Why do you think the Shah of Iran gave the rights to drill oil to a British businessman rather than to a Persian?

INSTRUCT: Objective ①

The Importance of Oil

• What countries produce nearly half of the world's oil? Saudi Arabia, Iran, Kuwait, Iraq
• How did OPEC inflate the price of gasoline in 1973? by placing an embargo on the export of oil to Israel-supporting nations
• What secondary products are produced from date palms? date syrup, palm leaf paper

 In-depth Resources: Unit 3
• Guided Reading Worksheet, p. 18

 Reading Study Guide
(Spanish and English), pp. 78–79

Program Resources

 In-depth Resources: Unit 3
• Guided Reading Worksheet, p. 18
• Reteaching Activity, p. 27

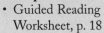 **Reading Study Guide**
(Spanish and English), pp. 78–79

 Formal Assessment
• Section Quiz, p. 130

 Integrated Assessment
• Rubric for making a poster

 Outline Map Activities

 Access for Students Acquiring English
• Guided Reading Worksheet, p. 74

 Technology Resources
classzone.com

TEST-TAKING RESOURCES
⤷ Strategies for Test Preparation
⤷ Test Practice Transparencies
① Online Test Practice

Human-Environment Interaction • OPEC's oil embargo in 1973 led to long lines at gas stations. ◄

FOCUS ON VISUALS

Interpreting the Photographs Direct students' attention to the photographs and then have them read the caption. Ask students to consider how the gasoline shortage led to an increased demand for cars with better gas mileage.

Possible Response Drivers were afraid that gas shortages would continue for years and that gas would soon be very expensive. Thus, they wanted cars that would travel more miles per gallon.

Extension Have students work in small groups to brainstorm examples of products whose prices rise as a result of a shortage, such as fresh fruits in winter and concert tickets. Ask students to list their ideas, then share them with the larger group.

CRITICAL THINKING ACTIVITY

Drawing Conclusions Ask students to explain what OPEC nations hoped to accomplish by placing an embargo on the export of oil to countries that supported Israel.

Class Time 10 minutes

Gaining Control After World War II, many nations in the region chose to nationalize, or have their governments take over the running of, their oil industries. In 1960, four of these countries—Iran, Iraq, Saudi Arabia, and Kuwait—joined with Venezuela, an oil-rich country in South America, to form the Organization of Petroleum Exporting Countries, or **OPEC**. OPEC would decide the price and amount of oil produced in each country each year. In a world dependent on oil as its major energy source, OPEC had a great deal of power. In 1973, OPEC placed an embargo on the export of oil to countries that supported Israel. As a result, the price of gasoline shot way up as its supply went down, leading to shortages.

Developing New Products Since the early 1900s, oil has been the most important **primary product,** or raw material, in Southwest Asia and North Africa. The countries of the region export mostly primary products. (See the map below.) Many countries have also developed **secondary products,** or goods manufactured from primary products. In Iraq, for example, date palms are an important primary product. From them, industries in Iraq manufacture date syrup, paper from palm leaves, and other secondary products.

Reading Social Studies

A. Analyzing Causes How did OPEC's oil embargo lead to a rise in the price of gasoline?

Reading Social Studies
A. Answer
When supplies of oil were cut, the price went up.

Geography Skillbuilder Answers
1. Egypt, Sudan, Turkey, Iran, Yemen
2. Iraq, Saudi Arabia, Algeria

Products of Southwest Asia and North Africa, 2000

GEOGRAPHY SKILLBUILDER: Interpreting a Map

1. **Human-Environment Interaction •** Which five countries produce cotton?
2. **Human-Environment Interaction •** Which three countries produce the greatest amount of oil?

Coal	Fish	Petroleum
Copper	Iron ore	Phosphate
Corn	Lead	Wheat
Cotton	Natural gas	

0 200 400 miles
0 200 400 kilometers

Activity Options

Interdisciplinary Links: Economics/Math

Class Time One class period

Task Graphing the average annual price of gasoline from 1970 to 2000

Purpose To understand that the price of an item or commodity fluctuates as supply and demand changes

Supplies Needed
• Reference materials, including Web sites
• Graph paper
• Pencils

B Block Scheduling

Activity Have each student work with a partner to find and graph the average price of a gallon of gasoline from 1970 to 2000. Tell students that they may decide to show intervals of years rather than every year on their graphs. When they have completed their graphs, ask each student to make up five math word problems, using the data on the graph. Then have students trade their word problems and solve them.

Oil Industries The oil-rich countries also use the oil to make secondary products. For over 30 years, Saudi Arabia and other Persian Gulf countries have been refining crude oil in modern refineries. They also make **petrochemicals** from crude oil and natural gas. Petrochemicals are used in the manufacture of cosmetics, plastics, synthetic materials, detergents, fertilizers, and many other products.

Religion in the Region ❷

BACKGROUND

The Israeli city of Haifa is the world center of the Bahai religion, which split off from Islam. Bahais believe in the equality of men and women and a universal God.

Islam is the dominant religion in the region, but not the only one. Jews and Christians have lived there for thousands of years. Most Jews in the region moved to Israel once it was created, but small communities of Jews remain in Turkey, Egypt, and Iran. Many Christians left after the breakup of the Ottoman Empire. Today the Copts of Egypt and the Maronites of Lebanon are the region's two largest Christian communities.

The Influence of Islam on Culture Every country in the region shows the influence of Islam. The Five Pillars of Islam (see page 235) are woven into the fabric of daily life. People stop to pray five times a day, no matter what they are doing—at home, in the streets, at school, at work. Radio and television stations air programs devoted to readings from the Qur'an many times a day. All Muslims try to go on a *hajj*, or pilgrimage to Mecca, once in a lifetime.

Place • During a *hajj*, the holy city of Mecca is packed with pilgrims. ▲

Ramadan During the ninth month of the Islamic year, called **Ramadan** (ram·uh·DAHN), Muslims fast from sunrise to sunset. Only the very young or sick or those on a journey are allowed to eat or drink during this time. During Ramadan, believers eat a light breakfast before dawn. Then they do not eat or drink again until dusk. The joyous *Id al-Fitr* (id uhl·FIT·uhr), the Feast of the Breaking of the Fast, ends Ramadan and lasts for several days.

The Muslim Calendar For Muslims, the calendar begins the year Muhammad fled to Medina, A.D. 622 according to the Western calendar. Each Islamic year has 12 months of about 29 days each, which makes the Islamic year about 11 days shorter than the Western year. Each day starts at sunset.

North Africa and Southwest Asia Today **251**

INSTRUCT: Objective ❷

Religion in the Region

- What is the dominant religion in North Africa and Southwest Asia? Islam
- How does Islam influence daily life in the region? People pray five times daily; the Qur'an is read on radio and television. All Muslims try to go on a pilgrimage to Mecca. During Ramadan, Muslims fast from sunrise to sunset.
- What event marked the beginning of the Islamic calendar? the year that Muhammad fled to Medina

FOCUS ON VISUALS

Interpreting the Photograph Direct students' attention to the photograph. Tell them that approximately 2 million people travel to Mecca on a *hajj* each year. Ask students how the observance of this solemn ritual might affect the culture of Islam.

Possible Response The pilgrimage promotes unity among Muslims who live in different places and belong to different sects.

Extension Ask students how this pilgrimage might affect the economy of Mecca.

MORE ABOUT...
Ramadan

The religious purpose of Ramadan is similar to that of the Jewish holiday of Yom Kippur. Both are periods of atonement, which involve acknowledging one's sins and restoring one's relationship with God. Both holidays are days of fasting and prayer.

Activity Options

Multiple Learning Styles: Visual/Spatial

Class Time 30 minutes

Task Analyzing the Muslim calendar

Purpose To compare the Western calendar with the Muslim calendar

Supplies Needed
- Western calendar
- Muslim calendar
- Chart paper
- Pencils

Activity Have students create a chart comparing the two calendars for this year. Encourage them to annotate both the Muslim and the Western calendars with notes about holidays and special events.

INSTRUCT: Objective ❸

Westernization vs. Traditional Culture/The Roles of Women/ Clothing and Culture

- What are some examples of westernization? fast-food restaurants, T-shirts, television, rap music, technological advances
- What restrictions do women face in some Islamic countries? limits on jobs, marriage rights, driving cars, mixing socially with men
- What is a *chador?* a floor-length cloak that covers everything but a woman's eyes

Persian carpet-making approached its artistic high point in the 15th century. Carpets at that time were produced only in palace workshops. Sheep were bred especially to produce fine wool for carpets, and plantations were operated to produce the best dyes. Designers and weavers of carpets could even win appointments to the royal court.

Westernization vs. Traditional Culture ❸

Many people in Southwest Asia and North Africa think western nations exert too much influence over their culture. Others are more open to westernization, adopting aspects of the way of life common in Europe and the United States. Fast-food restaurants, T-shirts, television, and rap music are examples of westernization. So are many technological advances in business, science, medicine, and agriculture. Some people in the region believe westernization will give them a higher standard of living and an easier, more exciting, more enjoyable way of life. For others, the loss of their traditional culture is too great a price to pay.

The Roles of Women ❸

Women in the region have different roles in society. In countries like Israel, Jordan, and Egypt, many women are well educated and hold important positions in business, politics, and the military. In some countries, however, religious beliefs limit the roles women can play. For example, Saudi Arabian women have fewer rights than do Saudi men. Women are not allowed to attend gatherings with men, and they are forbidden to drive cars. A Saudi woman may have only one husband, but a Saudi man is allowed by Islamic law to have up to four wives. Very few Saudi women work outside the home. Those that do usually teach in all girl schools or treat patients at maternity clinics.

Thinking Critically Answers
1. Carpets take a long time, great skill, and hand craftsmanship to produce.
2. They represent Iran's history; they have been part of the change from nomadic cultures to a country with major museums and public buildings.

Persian Carpets Persians—now called Iranians—have been making carpets for more than 2,500 years. The first Persian carpets were woven for nomads who needed protection from the cold. Brightly colored intricate designs made the carpets valuable for their beauty. Craftspeople spent months and even years carefully weaving dyed sheep's wool into artistic patterns. Today Persian carpets decorate palaces, important buildings, and museums.

THINKING CRITICALLY

1. **Drawing Conclusions**
   What do you think makes Persian carpets valuable?

2. **Summarizing**
   What role have Persian carpets played in Iranian culture?

252 CHAPTER 9

Activity Options

Differentiating Instruction: Gifted and Talented

🅱 Block Scheduling

Research Invite students to find out more about the city of Mecca, in Saudi Arabia. Have students work in pairs or small groups to locate information about the city's geography, history, economy, and architecture. Some may want to concentrate on the events and rituals surrounding the annual pilgrimages to Mecca.

Then challenge students to find different creative ways to share their information with the class. Possibilities include a multimedia presentation including a video and appropriate music; an on-the-spot news broadcast, a travel brochure, or a short dramatization.

Culture • **This woman is wearing a** *chador.* ▲

Clothing and Culture ❸

Clothing reveals much about the region's cultures. In Israel, for instance, some women and men dress in fashionable Western clothing. Orthodox Jewish women, however, wear more modest dress as their religious beliefs dictate. Orthodox men often wear black suits and hats and grow long ringlets of hair in front of their ears. In some Islamic countries, women wear *chadors,* floor-length cloaks that cover everything but the women's eyes. In Iran and Saudi Arabia, such clothing is not a choice; it's the law. Men, too, dress and grow facial hair as Islamic law demands.

A Disappearing Nomadic Culture ❹

Vocabulary

nomads: people with no fixed home who move about in search of food, water, and grazing land

Once nomads lived in the desert places of the region. Most nomads herded sheep from place to place in search of grazing lands. Other nomads escorted camel caravans of traders across the desert. Today, only one percent of the population is nomadic. Now trucks, not camels, cross the desert on paved roads. Droughts have decreased grazing lands. Governments encourage nomads to settle down. They have also made it more difficult for nomads from other countries to cross their borders.

SECTION ❷ ASSESSMENT

Terms & Names

1. **Identify:**
   (a) OPEC
   (e) *hajj*
   (b) primary product
   (f) Ramadan
   (c) secondary product
   (d) petrochemical

Taking Notes

2. Use a chart like this one to list major products in Southwest Asia and North Africa.

Primary Products	Secondary Products

Main Ideas

3. (a) How are oil resources important to Southwest Asia and North Africa?

   (b) How does Islam affect the culture of the region?

   (c) What is the status of women in most Islamic countries?

Critical Thinking

4. **Critical Thinking**
   What makes it difficult for nomadic peoples in Southwest Asia and North Africa to continue their traditional way of life?

   Think About
   ◆ modern technology
   ◆ climatic conditions
   ◆ government actions

ACTIVITY -OPTION- Make a **poster** showing crude oil and the products made from it. Label them as primary or secondary products.

MORE ABOUT...
Chadors

Women in Iranian cities often wear *chadors* over other clothing. A *chador*, which is usually black, is draped around the woman's body, across her shoulders, and over her head. Some women leave their faces exposed, but others leave only enough of an opening for their eyes. Women in the countryside seldom wear *chadors*. Instead, they wear loose blouses, black cotton trousers, and head scarves.

INSTRUCT: Objective ❹

A Disappearing Nomadic Culture

• How has life changed for nomadic peoples in the region? smaller population, fewer grazing lands, stricter national borders

ASSESS & RETEACH

Reading Social Studies Have students complete the second row of the chart on page 242.

 Formal Assessment
• Section Quiz, p. 130

RETEACHING ACTIVITY

Have students work in small groups to create a section review. Each group member can write a one- or two-sentence summary of the text for one section heading. Then have each student read his or her summary to the rest of the group.

 In-depth Resources: Unit 3
• Reaching Activity, p. 27

 Access for Students Acquiring English
• Reteaching Activity, p. 81

Section ❷ Assessment

1. Terms & Names
   a. OPEC, p. 250
   b. primary product, p. 250
   c. secondary product, p. 250
   d. petrochemical, p. 251
   e. *hajj*, p. 251
   f. Ramadan, p. 251

2. Taking Notes

Primary Product	Secondary Product
oil	refined oil, petrochemicals
date palms	date syrup, paper

3. Main Ideas
   a. Oil is the region's largest source of income.
   b. People pray five times a day. Radio and television stations broadcast readings from the Qur'an several times a day. Muslims try to make at least one pilgrimage to Mecca.
   c. Many women have few rights and are not allowed to work, to drive a car, or to attend gatherings with men.

4. Critical Thinking
   Possible Response Droughts have decreased grazing land, trucks have replaced camels for transportation, and international borders are harder to cross.

ACTIVITY OPTION
 Integrated Assessment
   • Rubric for making a poster

OBJECTIVE

Students work cooperatively and individually to explore one of the Seven Wonders of the Ancient World: the pyramids at Giza.

 Block Scheduling

PROCEDURE

Provide blocks of clay, paper, poster board, markers, and pencils. Have students form groups of three or four and divide the work among the group members. Students will use information from the Data File for the Math Challenge.

MATH CHALLENGE

Class Time 50 minutes

Students will draw the Great Pyramid of Khufu and then make a scale model of it. Be sure that they understand that a scale model is an exact replica, only much smaller. They will have to decide what measurement they will use to equal feet and then translate the measurements given in the Data File to the smaller measure.

Possible Solutions

The scale models of the Great Pyramid will use a scale such as an eighth of an inch to equal a foot. For the second option, the pyramid of Khafre is about 2 percent smaller than the Great Pyramid, and the pyramid of Menkure is about 55 percent smaller.

Interdisciplinary Challenge

Explain the Pyramids of Ancient Egypt

You are a tour guide and Egyptologist—an expert on ancient Egypt. Your specialty is the age of pyramid building, about 4,700 to 4,200 years ago (c. 2686–2160 B.C.). Pyramids, large and small, were built as tombs for the pharaohs of the Old Kingdom and members of their families. The most famous are the three pyramids at Giza, near Cairo, where you work. In the course of your work, tourists come to you with questions about the pyramids. You want to find interesting ways to share your knowledge with them.

COOPERATIVE LEARNING On these pages are challenges you will meet while dealing with visitors to the pyramids. Working with a small group, choose one challenge to solve. Divide the work among group members. Look for helpful information in the Data File. Keep in mind that you will present your solution to the class.

MATH CHALLENGE

". . . the Great Pyramid of Khufu was the world's tallest structure."

The three pyramids at Giza were built for Khufu, his son Khafre, and his grandson Menkure. For more than 4,300 years, the Great Pyramid of Khufu was the world's tallest structure. Khafre's pyramid is almost as big. How can you explain these huge structures to your visitors? Choose one of these options. Look in the Data File for information.

ACTIVITIES

1. Make an accurate drawing of the Great Pyramid of Khufu on graph paper, using the measurements given. Use blocks or clay to build a scale model.
2. How does the present height of the Great Pyramid compare with its original height? How does its height compare with the heights of the pyramids of Khafre and Menkure? Express your answers as percentages.

Standards for Evaluation

MATH CHALLENGE
Option 1 Scale models and drawings should
• be as accurate a representation as possible.
• explain importance of the figure.
Option 2 Answers should
• be accurate and show an understanding of the use of percentages.

ARTS CHALLENGE
Option 1 Drawings should
• be an accurate representation of the interior of a tomb, showing objects found there, such as jewelry and mummies.
Option 2 The scene sketches should
• show a narrative sequence of an archaeologist entering a pyramid.

LANGUAGE ARTS CHALLENGE
Option 1 The report should
• describe the varieties of work involved and an understanding of the materials and methods used.
Option 2 The daily log should
• creatively describe several days' labor on the pyramids.

THE PYRAMIDS OF EGYPT

- The pyramids at Giza were one of the **Seven Wonders of the Ancient World.** The oldest of all the wonders, they are the only ones that still stand today.

- Builders used mainly **limestone** and **granite blocks.** Originally, the pyramids were faced with smooth, white limestone. Vandals have stripped off most of this surface stone.

- Building the **Great Pyramid** took about 20 years. Ancient historians said that it took 100,000 workers. Archaeologists today, however, think that there were **20,000 to 30,000 workers.** The workers were probably not slaves, but farmers and villagers who worked in exchange for food and the chance to serve their god-king.

GREAT PYRAMID OF KHUFU

- Oldest and largest of pyramids at Giza, built about **4,500 years ago.**

- Square base: length of each side about **756 feet.**

- Original height: **481 feet;** now about 451 feet.

- Covers about **13 acres**—about seven city blocks.

- Contains about **2.3 million blocks** of stone, each weighing about 2.5 tons.

PYRAMID OF KHAFRE

- Square base: length of each side about **708 feet.**

- Original height: **471 feet.**

- Covers about **11.5 acres.**

PYRAMID OF MENKURE

- Square base: length of each side about **356.5 feet.**

- Original height: **218 feet.**

- Covers about **2.9 acres.**

To learn more about the pyramids, go to

RESEARCH LINKS
CLASSZONE.COM

ARTS CHALLENGE

ARTS CHALLENGE

"... what [is it] like to explore the interior of a pyramid?"

Most of what we know about ancient Egypt comes from hieroglyphics and artifacts found in tombs—jewelry, statues, cosmetics, mummies. Today, most pyramids are closed to outsiders. How can you give visitors an idea of what it is like to explore the interior of a pyramid? How can they have the same experience that an archaeologist has?

ACTIVITIES

1. Draw the interior of a tomb, including objects such as statues, jewelry, and mummies.

2. Sketch a series of scenes you would use in making a video about an archaeologist exploring the interior of a pyramid.

Activity Wrap-Up

As a group, review your solution to the challenge you selected. Then present your solution to the class.

ARTS CHALLENGE

Class Time 50 minutes

Provide students with outside sources showing the interior of a pyramid. Have students work in groups of three or four to outline the solution to the challenge. Then have them assign tasks to each group member.

Possible Solutions

The drawings will be an accurate representation of the inside of a pyramid or tomb, including objects found there, such as statues of animals, pottery, mummies, masks, and jewelry.

ALTERNATIVE CHALLENGE...

LANGUAGE ARTS CHALLENGE

The building of the pyramids involved many different jobs and used materials from as far as 500 miles away. Masons used copper chisels to carve the stone. The copper came from Sinai. The granite stones came from mines at Aswan. Laborers used papyrus twine to haul the giant stones up ramps built of mud, stone, and wood. Some of these supplies and building materials were transported to Giza on the Nile River. Imagine that you are the team leader for a group of workers.

- Write a short report that tells your boss about your team's work.

- Keep a daily log of the work that is accomplished by your team during a week.

Activity Wrap-Up

To help students evaluate the creativity and accuracy of their challenge solutions, have them make a grid with criteria like the one shown. Then have them rate each solution on a scale from 1 to 5.

Criteria					
• Originality	1	2	3	4	5
• Creativity	1	2	3	4	5
• Accuracy	1	2	3	4	5
• Overall effectiveness	1	2	3	4	5

Egypt Today

King Farouk
Gamal Abdel Nasser
Aswan High Dam
tradeoff
Anwar Sadat
Muslim Brotherhood
fellahin

SECTION OBJECTIVES

1. To trace foreign control, government changes, and major events in modern Egypt's history
2. To describe the land and people in Egypt
3. To describe Cairo, Egypt's capital city

SKILLBUILDER
• Interpreting a Map, p. 257, p. 259

CRITICAL THINKING
• Synthesizing, p. 261

FOCUS & MOTIVATE
WARM-UP

Drawing Conclusions Have students read Dateline and discuss the significance of the Suez Canal.

1. What was the motivation for building the Suez Canal?
2. Why might some Egyptians be unhappy about the opening of the canal?

INSTRUCT: Objective ❶

The Suez Canal/From Ancient to Modern Times

• Why did the Suez Canal come under British control? Egypt was bankrupt and sold its shares.
• How did Egypt's government change from the 1920s to the 1950s? became independent monarchy in 1922, became a republic in 1953
• How is the Aswan High Dam an example of a tradeoff? gives farmers a more dependable source of water but forces them to use artificial fertilizer

 In-depth Resources: Unit 3
• Guided Reading Worksheet, p. 19

 Reading Study Guide
(Spanish and English), pp. 80–81

MAIN IDEA
Egypt's modernization has brought progress and problems.

WHY IT MATTERS NOW
Egypt often sets the pace in the region for social and political change.

CAIRO, EGYPT, NOVEMBER 17, 1869
Today is a red-letter day for Egypt. The Suez Canal is open at last. Trade will surely increase now that ships can travel easily between the Mediterranean and Red seas. Not all Egyptians are happy about the canal, however.

More than ten years and 120,000 Egyptian lives have gone into building it. Egyptians wonder whether Egypt will benefit from the Suez Canal or whether Britain and France will continue to control the region. Only time will tell.

Place • Ships sail for the first time through the newly opened Suez Canal. ▲

Location • The Suez Canal connects the Mediterranean Sea and the Red Sea. ▲

The Suez Canal ❶

The Suez Canal was the grand project of Egyptian ruler Ismail Pasha (is•mah•EEL PAH•sha). He wanted it built to make Egypt the equal of Western nations. But the cost of the canal and other expensive projects drove Egypt into bankruptcy. Ismail had to sell Egypt's shares in the Suez Canal Company to the British government. From then until 1956, Great Britain had some control over Egypt.

256 CHAPTER 9

Program Resources

 In-depth Resources: Unit 3
• Guided Reading Worksheet, p. 19
• Reteaching Activity, p. 28

 Reading Study Guide
(Spanish and English), pp. 80–81

 Formal Assessment
• Section Quiz, p. 131

 Integrated Assessment
• Rubric for writing a letter

 Outline Map Activities

 Access for Students Acquiring English
• Guided Reading Worksheet, p. 75

 Technology Resources
classzone.com

TEST-TAKING RESOURCES
♻ Strategies for Test Preparation
♻ Test Practice Transparencies
ⓘ Online Test Practice

256 CHAPTER 9

From Ancient to Modern Times ①

Great Britain was not the first foreign power to rule Egypt after the time of the pharaohs. For 2,500 years, Egypt was under foreign influence. It was conquered in turn by Persians, Macedonians, and Romans. Arab Muslims from the Arabian peninsula invaded in A.D. 639–642. A military group called the Mamelukes (MAM·uh·looks) seized control in about 1250 and ruled until Ottoman troops invaded in 1517. From the late 1700s to the early 1900s, France and then Great Britain controlled much of Egypt. Britain gave up absolute control in 1922, and Egypt became a monarchy, a country ruled at first by King Fuad (fu·AHD), and after 1936 by his son, **King Farouk** (fuh·ROOK). Foreign policy, defense, and communications, however, remained under British control.

Place • Gamal Abdel Nasser was President of Egypt for 16 years. ▼

Nasser Takes Over An Egyptian Army officer, **Gamal Abdel Nasser,** resented the weakness of his government and the strong British influence on his country. In 1952, he and other officers overthrew King Farouk. The next year Egypt became a republic. Nasser was Egypt's leader from 1954 to 1970.

Controlling the Nile Nasser's most significant accomplishment was the construction of the **Aswan High Dam,** begun in 1956, to control the flooding of the Nile River. The dam gives Egyptian farmers a more dependable source of water for their crops and allows them to grow crops year round. It also gives Egypt more electrical power and has made fishing an important industry.

Human-Environment Interaction • The Aswan High Dam, opened in 1971, cost about $1 billion to build. ▼

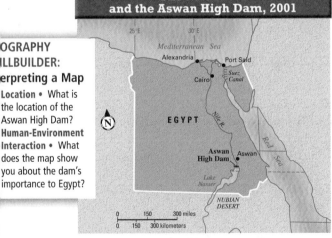

The Nile River and the Aswan High Dam, 2001

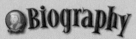

Biography

In 1942, during World War II, Anwar Sadat was imprisoned for plotting with the Germans to expel the British from Egypt. Sadat escaped from prison, and in 1950 he joined Nasser's successful effort to overthrow King Farouk. U.S. President Jimmy Carter brought Sadat and the Israeli prime minister Menachem Begin together to negotiate a treaty.

MORE ABOUT...
The Muslim Brotherhood

The Muslim Brotherhood was founded in 1928 and spread rapidly through Egypt, the Sudan and other parts of North Africa, Syria, Palestine, and Lebanon. Over the years, the group became more militant. Following a 1954 attempt to assassinate Nasser, six of the Brotherhood's leaders were executed for treason, many others went to prison, and the organization was suppressed. The organization's activities remained underground throughout the 1960s and 1970s but have again become visible and powerful in the Middle East.

Place • Egyptian women campaigned for the vote in Cairo in the 1920s. ▲

Biography

Anwar Sadat, 1918–1981
Anwar Sadat (below, left) took part in the 1952 seizure of the government of King Farouk. When President Nasser died in 1970, Vice President Sadat was elected President.

Sadat led Egypt to war with Israel in 1973. A few years later, however, he became the first Arab leader to seek peace between the two countries. He shared the 1978 Nobel Peace Prize with Israeli Prime Minister Menachem Begin (right, below). In 1979, Israel and Egypt signed a peace treaty. Muslim extremists objected to Sadat's peace treaty with Israel and his close ties with the United States. On October 6, 1981, extremists assassinated him.

Because of the dam, however, the river no longer deposits the rich soil from the south as it did during yearly flooding. Instead, over 100 million tons of earth settle behind the dam each year. Farmers now have to use artificial fertilizers which pollute the water. The Aswan High Dam is an example of a tradeoff. A **tradeoff** is an exchange of one benefit for another.

Rights for Women Women were active in the movement for Egyptian independence in the years from 1919 to 1922, yet were denied the vote. Although they gradually acquired the right to higher education, women were still subject to the Muslim Personal Status Law, which gave men far more rights in marriage. Women continued to demand their rights. In 1956, in Nasser's new government, they gained the right to vote and to run for office. A revised Muslim Personal Status Law in 1979 somewhat improved women's rights within the family. In 2000, Egypt passed a law making it easier for women to get a divorce.

A Search for Peace Egypt actively opposed Israel for many years. However, in 1979, led by President **Anwar Sadat,** Egypt became the first Arab state to sign a peace treaty with Israel. Egypt also led the region in opposing Iraq's 1990 invasion of Kuwait. Egypt has tried to settle arguments between Iraq and the United Nations. In the fall of 2000, President Hosni Mubarak met with other regional leaders to talk about how to end Israeli-Palestinian violence.

The Muslim Brotherhood Not everyone in Egypt values freedom and compromise. The **Muslim Brotherhood** is an extremist Muslim group which insists that Egypt be governed solely by Islamic law. The Brotherhood claims the Egyptian government is being untrue to the principles of Islam by working with Israel and the United States.

258 CHAPTER 9

GEOGRAPHY
SKILLBUILDER:
Interpreting a Map
• **Place** • What do you notice about the Nile River on each map?
• **Human-Environment Interaction** • What relationship do you notice between population and vegetation?

Population Distribution in Egypt, 1998

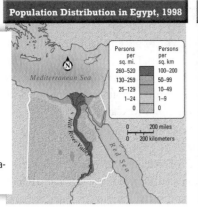

Persons per sq. mi.	Persons per sq. km
260–520	100–200
130–259	50–99
25–129	10–49
1–24	1–9
0	0

Mediterranean Sea

Nile River Valley

Red Sea

0   200 miles
0   200 kilometers

Vegetation in Egypt, 1998

	Desert
	Tropical desert shrub
	Swamp grass
	Salt flats

Mediterranean Sea

Red Sea

0   200 miles
0   200 kilometers

Geography
Skillbuilder
Answers

1. Conditions in the Nile Valley are very different from the surrounding area: denser population, more vegetation.

2. Population is denser where vegetation can grow.

The Land and the People ❷

Most of Egypt consists of desert lands where no one can live. Just about all of Egypt's 70 million people live in a narrow strip of land along either side of the Nile or in a few desert oases. Some live in big cities. Others farm the fields made fertile by the Nile.

Egyptian Cotton Cotton is a major primary product and agricultural export. Cotton-growing developed in Egypt during the 1860s when the Civil War in the United States disrupted cotton exports from southern states. Egypt produces some of the finest cotton in the world. It has also developed a textile industry that manufactures cotton yarns and cotton fabrics as secondary products.

Village Life More than half the population of Egypt lives in villages. Most villagers are **fellahin** (FEHL·uh·HEEN), or peasant farmers. The fellahin are some of the poorest Egyptians. Most rent land or work in their own fields. Many do not know how to read or write. Many fellahin children do not go to school.

Fellahin wear traditional Arab clothing. Men wear pants and loose-fitting, hooded gowns. Women wear long, flowing gowns. Like poor people in the cities, they eat a simple diet of bread and beans, which leads to malnutrition. Infectious diseases, such as tuberculosis, also afflict the fellahin. Only a lucky few are ever treated by doctors.

Reading
Social Studies

A. Identifying Problems What are the main problems the fellahin face?

Reading Social Studies
A. Possible Answers
lack of education and medical care, poor diet and living conditions

Human-Environment Interaction • **These fellahin raise sheep.** ▼

North Africa and Southwest Asia Today **259**

FOCUS ON VISUALS

Interpreting the Map Point out that the population density along the Nile is one of the highest in the world, with about 2,700 people per square mile. Ask how this might affect living conditions in the area.

Possible Response The area is overcrowded. Overcrowding is often accompanied by unemployment, poverty, and health problems.

Extension Have students research the population density and distribution in their own state and compare their results with the statistics for Egypt.

INSTRUCT: Objective ❷

The Land and the People

• What type of land covers much of Egypt? desert

• What is Egypt's most important primary product and agricultural export? cotton

• How would you describe the life of the fellahin? very poor, traditional way of life, little opportunity for schooling, poor diet, afflicted by disease, lack of medical care

MORE ABOUT...
Village Life

A typical Egyptian village features a mosque or a church and a primary school as well as a few shops and government service buildings. The houses have flat roofs made from dried date palm leaves, laid over rafters made from date palm logs. On their roofs, villagers store corn in small containers that protect the grain from rodents and insects. They also store dung cakes used for fuel. In hot weather, villagers sometimes sleep on the roofs.

Activity Options
Differentiating Instruction: Students Acquiring English/ESL

Vocabulary Write the terms *primary product* and *secondary product* on the board. Remind students that primary refers to "the first, or the original," and secondary refers to "not the first, not the original." Point out that cotton is the original, or primary, product. Cotton yarns and fabrics are made from cotton and therefore are secondary products. Brainstorm a list of other primary products and ask students to name possible secondary products for each.

Primary Product	Secondary Product
cotton	cotton thread, fabric
wood	paper, furniture
wool	yarn, wool fabric
cattle	beef, leather

INSTRUCT: Objective ③

Africa's Largest City/ The Region's Cultural Leader

- How has the city of Cairo changed through the years? Cairo once had gardens, trees, birds; now it is overcrowded and polluted.

- What types of jobs do poor Cairenes have, and where do they live? They work in factories or small shops and live in cemeteries, on roofs, or in poorly built apartment buildings.

- What types of jobs do wealthier Cairenes have? doctors, lawyers, teachers, factory managers, government officials

- In what ways has Egypt been a cultural leader? opened first modern school for girls in Arab world in 1829; requires all children to attend school; strong feminist movement; supports media and entertainment in print and broadcast

The WORLD'S HERITAGE

The sphinx is an important symbol in both Greek and Egyptian legends and art. A well-known sphinx of legend is the winged Sphinx of Thebes. According to legend, this sphinx struck terror in people by demanding the answer to a riddle, then devouring a man whenever a wrong answer was given. Legend also holds that if a man ever answered the riddle correctly, the sphinx would kill herself. Even today, the sphinx symbolizes wisdom.

Africa's Largest City ③

Life in Egyptian cities is different from life in rural areas. Cairo (KY·roh) is the capital of Egypt. The city's older inhabitants remember when the city had gardens, trees, and birds. Now those gardens have been paved over. The city is crowded and polluted, and the population continues to grow. Thousands of people leave Egypt's villages every year and come to Cairo looking for work. Instead, they find unemployment and overcrowding.

The total population of ancient Egypt was never more than four million people. Only about 5 percent of the population lived in cities. In 2000, the population of Cairo alone was more than 12 million. Cairo now has more people than any other African city.

Life in Cairo Cairo has both historic and modern sections. Many poor people live in the older sections. Some poor Cairenes live in cemeteries or on roofs. Others live in poorly built apartment buildings. Many have no steady work. Some are unskilled workers in factories. Others work in the city's small shops that sell jewelry and tourist souvenirs. Cairo's newer areas are along the west bank of the Nile. Most well-educated Cairenes live near the government buildings, foreign embassies, hotels, museums, and universities located there. They are doctors, lawyers, teachers, factory managers, and government officials.

Reading Social Studies

B. Analyzing Causes What is the main reason for Cairo's increase in population?

Reading Social Studies
B. Answer villagers looking for work in the city

The WORLD'S HERITAGE

The Pyramids and the Great Sphinx
The current residents of Cairo, Egypt, live in the shadows of some of the ancient world's most magnificent architecture—the pyramids and the Great Sphinx.

Egyptians built the pyramids as tombs for their kings more than 4,000 years ago. Near the pyramids, they also carved an enormous sphinx—a mythological creature with a lion's body and human head—out of natural rock. The head of the Great Sphinx is fashioned to look like King Khafre (c. 2575–c. 2465 B.C.).

Activity Options

Interdisciplinary Link: Language Arts

Class Time One class period

Task Writing a tourist presentation about Cairo

Purpose To familiarize students with important facts and features of ancient and modern Cairo

Supplies Needed
- Reference sources
- Paper
- Pencils or pens

Block Scheduling

Activity Divide the class into small groups. Have half of the groups research what the city of Cairo was like in ancient times and the other half research modern-day Cairo. Ask each group to write a presentation for tourists visiting Cairo. Then have one member of each group make a presentation to the class as if he or she were a tour guide.

Place • Cairo is a huge city crowded with buildings, cars, and millions of people. ▶

Place • These girls live in Cairo within sight of the Sphinx and pyramids of ancient Egypt. ▼

The Region's Cultural Leader ❸

Egypt has been the Arab world's cultural leader for over a century. It has led the region in education. In 1829, it opened the first modern school for girls in the Arab world. In the 1950s, it became the first Arab country to require that all children attend elementary school. It has also had a strong feminist movement for many years. Arabs throughout the region get much of their information and entertainment from Egyptian television, radio, movies, newspapers, and magazines.

SECTION ❸ ASSESSMENT

Terms & Names

1. Identify:
(a) King Farouk
(b) Gamal Abdel Nasser
(c) Aswan High Dam
(d) tradeoff
(e) Anwar Sadat
(f) Muslim Brotherhood
(g) fellahin

Taking Notes

2. Use a time line like this one to write the dates when control of Egypt changed hands.

639–642 ├──┼──┼──┼──┤ 1952

Main Ideas

3. (a) What were Nasser's major achievements?

(b) How have Egyptian women's rights improved over the last century?

(c) What has Egypt done to improve the search for peace in the region?

Critical Thinking

4. Evaluating Decisions

Do you think the building of the Aswan Dam was a worthwhile tradeoff?

Think About

♦ its value to farmers

♦ the consequences of pollution

ACTIVITY -OPTION- Write a **letter** telling about daily life as a young person in Cairo or in a farming village along the Nile.

Section ❸ Assessment

1. Terms & Names

a. King Farouk, p. 257
b. Gamal Abdel Nasser, p. 257
c. Aswan High Dam, p. 257
d. tradeoff, p. 258
e. Anwar Sadat, p. 258
f. Muslim Brotherhood, p. 258
g. fellahin, p. 259

2. Taking Notes

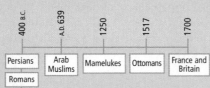

400 B.C. | A.D. 639 | 1250 | 1517 | 1700

Persians / Arab Muslims / Mamelukes / Ottomans / France and Britain
Romans
Macedonians

3. Main Ideas

a. Nasser reduced British influence over Egypt and promoted the building of the Aswan High Dam.
b. Women can vote, run for office, and attend school, and have more family rights.
c. Egypt signed a peace treaty with Israel in 1979, and opposed Iraq's invasion of Kuwait.

4. Critical Thinking

Students may say the dam was worthwhile because it allows year-round planting. Others may say that it created a need for the use of chemical pollutants.

ACTIVITY OPTION

 Integrated Assessment
• Rubric for writing a letter

CRITICAL THINKING ACTIVITY

Synthesizing Ask students to review the sections "From Ancient to Modern Times" and "The Region's Cultural Leader." Then have them briefly explain how Egypt has been a leader in terms of both social and political change.

Class Time 10 minutes

ASSESS & RETEACH

Reading Social Studies Have students add details to the third and fourth rows of the chart on page 242.

 Formal Assessment
• Section Quiz, p. 131

RETEACHING ACTIVITY

Have students work in groups to create a five-part outline of the section. Tell them to use the major, boldface headings as the headings for each part. They should add important facts and supporting details for each section.

 In-depth Resources: Unit 3
• Reteaching Activity, p. 28

Access for Students Acquiring English
• Reteaching Activity, p. 82

LITERATURE CONNECTIONS

OBJECTIVE

Students analyze a poem, in the form of an extended metaphor, that describes people weaving a cloth and creating a map for peace in Southwest Asia.

FOCUS & MOTIVATE

Making Inferences To help students prepare to understand this poem, have them study the illustrations on pages 262–263 and answer the following questions:

1. What do you notice about the people in the photos?

2. What might the thread represent?

 Block Scheduling

MORE ABOUT...
"Thread by Thread"

Into this poem about weaving, Bracha Serri weaves her dream of a future of conciliation, healing, and hope.

While the history of Southwest Asia is fraught with conflict and war, many people are working to foster communication and peace. Peace accords, though repeatedly broken, continue to be made. A project called "Seeds of Peace" brings students from Egypt, Israel, and neighboring countries to Maine to meet and live together at summer camp for a few weeks each year. Peace projects exist in many communities and countries.

Thread by Thread

OVER THE PAST 60 YEARS, wars in Southwest Asia have left a bitter legacy of anger, frustration, and despair. Despite continuing conflicts, however, many people in the region share a hope for peace. The author of this poem, Bracha Serri, believes that one day peace will be achieved.

> Thread by thread
> knot by knot
> like colonies of ants
> we weave a bridge
>
> Thread by thread
> piece by piece
> knitting embroidering
> sewing decorating
> thread by thread
> we weave
> the map of conciliation.[1]

1. Friendship.

Activity Option

Differentiating Instruction: Less Proficient Readers

Building Language Skills To increase understanding, preview the poem. Point out the margin note. Define words that may be unfamiliar and help students read the names in the poem. Explain that the poem is shaped by ideas, not sentences. Therefore, the poem does not contain capital letters and punctuation that readers might expect.

Have students work with partners, matching less proficient readers with more fluent readers. Duplicate copies of the Literature Connection and give a copy to each pair of students. Point out that the poem is broken into four sections. Have partners read each section, line-by-line, and stop at the end to paraphrase the ideas they have just read.

Rachel's is white
Yemima's purple
Amal's is green
Salima's rose-colored
thread by thread
we stitch together
torn hearts
bind the map of conciliation.

I pray for the life of Ami and Nitsi
you pray for Ilan, Shoshi and Itsik
and she prays
for Jehan, Asheraf and Fahed
with the same tear.
Word and another word
prayer and another prayer
and our heart is one
we embroider in hope
with the sisterhood of workers
a map of love
to tear down the borders . . .

Reading THE LITERATURE

What technique does the poet use to let the reader know that the "weavers" are people from different countries or ethnic backgrounds? Why is that important?

Thinking About THE LITERATURE

Why do you think this poem is called "Thread by Thread"? What do the threads represent? Who are the weavers and what are they making?

Writing About THE LITERATURE

Describe how you think the finished cloth would look. What size and shape would it be? What colors would it have in it? Where would it be placed or displayed?

About the Author

Bracha Serri, born in Yemen, grew up speaking Arabic. Later, her family moved to Israel. Serri has written, "I want my childhood spoken language, Arabic, to come together with my university education in linguistics. . . . I feel I have written my poems for women who do not have a voice, who can't speak up for themselves."

Further Reading *The Space Between Our Footsteps,* edited by Naomi Shihab Nye, contains poems by more than 100 poets and artists from 19 Southwest Asian countries.

263

INSTRUCT

Reading the Literature
Possible Responses
The poet puts in names from different cultures. People from different countries and ethnic backgrounds often have to work together to create peace.

Thinking About the Literature
Possible Responses
The title "Thread by Thread" gives the feeling that making way for peace is a long and steady task, just like weaving cloth. The threads represent people's lives or hopes. The weavers are people (women) who are making a new world of friendship and love.

Writing About the Literature
Possible Responses
Students might suggest that the cloth should be made in the shape of the Middle East, Southwest Asia, or the world. Perhaps it would include many colors, including those named in the poem: white, purple, green, and rose. They might suggest that it be hung in the United Nations Headquarters in New York.

MORE ABOUT...
Poetic Techniques

Discuss two techniques the author uses in this poem—repetition and symbolism. Point out some words that are repeated throughout the poem, such as thread, piece, pray, and explain that repetition emphasizes key ideas. Then explain that symbolism is the use of objects to represent ideas. Direct students' attention to the following uses of symbolism in this poem: thread, bridge = connection; map = world; heart = life, love.

 World Literature

More to Think About

Making Personal Connections Have students list specific ways that people can work for peace. Brainstorm actions that can be taken on several levels: the world, their country, their community, their school. Discuss what is already happening to promote peace on any of these levels. Ask students to name actions that require people to work together.

Vocabulary Activity Have students quote lines or images that catch their attention and explain why they are powerful. Some students may want to draw, paint, or sculpt a response and caption their work with quotes from the poem.

Israel Today

TERMS & NAMES

Zionism

kibbutz

Law of Return

Orthodox Jews

Rosh Hashanah

Yom Kippur

secular

SECTION OBJECTIVES

1. To identify Zionism as the movement for a Jewish homeland in Palestine

2. To describe the status of Palestinian Arabs and women in Israel

3. To explain the Law of Return

4. To describe the practice of Judaism in modern Israel

CRITICAL THINKING

• Analyzing Causes, p. 273

FOCUS AND MOTIVATE

WARM-UP

Making Inferences After students read <u>Dateline</u>, discuss the history of the conflict in Israel.

1. Why might Jews from around the world want to establish a Jewish homeland?

2. Why might Palestinian Arabs protest the movement?

INSTRUCT: Objective ❶

From Zionism to a Modern State

• What was Zionism? a Jewish movement to return to the homeland of Palestine

• What kinds of communities did early Jewish settlers establish in Palestine? cooperative farming villages called kibbutzim

• Why is drip irrigation an important technique? It does not waste water.

 In-depth Resources: Unit 3
• Guided Reading Worksheet, p. 20

 Reading Study Guide
(Spanish and English), pp. 82–83

MAIN IDEA

Israel's current problems are rooted in a long and complicated history.

WHY IT MATTERS NOW

Peace in the region depends on peace between Israelis and Palestinians.

DATELINE

TEL AVIV, PALESTINE, JULY 14, 1921— Newcomers from America arrived here today after a long and difficult trip. All have been active in the movement to establish a Jewish homeland in Palestine. Golda Mabovitz and her husband, Morris Myerson, born in Russia, hope to join a kibbutz. Riots in the port city of Jaffa delayed their arrival. Palestinian Arabs are protesting the immigration of Jews from America, Russia, and other countries who plan to settle in the land the Arabs consider their own.

Movement • Jewish immigrants from Europe arrive in Palestine. ▲

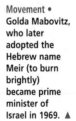

Movement • Golda Mabovitz, who later adopted the Hebrew name Meir (to burn brightly) became prime minister of Israel in 1969. ▲

From Zionism to a Modern State ❶

After A.D. 70, when the Romans destroyed the Temple in Jerusalem, Jews no longer had a country of their own. They lived scattered around the world, but still considered Palestine their homeland. <u>Zionism</u> was a Jewish movement that encouraged Jews to return to that homeland, which many called Zion. In the late 1800s, Jews began immigrating there and establishing colonies.

Program Resources

 In-depth Resources: Unit 3
• Guided Reading Worksheet, p. 20
• Reteaching Activity, p. 27

 Reading Study Guide
(Spanish and English), pp. 82–83

 Formal Assessment
• Section Quiz, p. 132

 Integrated Assessment
• Rubric for writing an interview

 Outline Map Activities

 Access for Students Acquiring English
• Guided Reading Worksheet, p. 76

 Technology Resources
classzone.com

TEST-TAKING RESOURCES

↷ Strategies for Test Preparation

↷ Test Practice Transparencies

⟳ Online Test Practice

Reading
Social Studies

A. Analyzing Motives What were the Jewish immigrants' main reasons for forming kibbutzim?

Reading Social Studies
A. Possible Answers
It gave them a chance to own land; they could share the pioneer spirit.

Life on a Kibbutz Many new arrivals came from Eastern Europe, where Jews were often denied the right to be landowners. Seizing the chance to own land, even in the desert, the newcomers formed communities called kibbutzim. A **kibbutz** (kih•BUTS; *kibbutzim* is the plural) is a farming village whose members own everything in common. Members share labor, income, and expenses. The people of the kibbutzim saw themselves as brave, hard-working pioneers.

A VOICE FROM ISRAEL

The kibbutz would break new ground, literally; it would make the parched earth bloom and beat back the attacks of marauders who sought to destroy our pioneering lives.

David Ben-Gurion

Kibbutzim Today About 270 kibbutzim still exist in Israel today. Some manufacture and sell products or welcome tourists. Others are still farming communities. Israel produces nearly all of its food. To improve the dry soil, Israelis practice drip irrigation. Tubes in the ground deliver the exact amount of water each plant needs.

The People of Israel ❷

Israel was established in 1948 as a Jewish state. Judaism is the state religion. Hebrew is the official language. Of its six million inhabitants, over 80 percent are Jews. The Declaration of the Establishment promised that Israel would treat all its inhabitants equally. Some Israelis feel their country has not always lived up to that promise.

Place •
A modern kibbutz sprawls over a desert landscape. ▲

Palestinian Arabs About 20 percent of the people in Israel are Palestinian Arabs. These Arab Israelis carry Israeli passports and vote. Arab politicians serve in Israel's government. However, Arab Israelis do not live as well as Jewish Israelis. Most do not have equal rights and opportunities in jobs, job training, higher education, and housing. In 1996, Arabs were elected to 11 of the 120 seats in the Knesset, the Israeli parliament, the most they had ever won. In October 2000, the Israeli government announced that it planned to spend a billion dollars on schools, housing, and new jobs for Arab Israelis.

North Africa and Southwest Asia Today **265**

A VOICE FROM ISRAEL
Ask a volunteer to read aloud the quote by David Ben-Gurion. Tell students that Ben-Gurion was the first prime minister of Israel after it gained independence in 1948. Point out the phrase "break new ground" and explain that Ben-Gurion uses the phrase both literally, as he states, and figuratively, meaning to forge into new territory. Ask students to identify words and phrases that capture his pioneering spirit, such as "parched earth bloom," "beat back attacks."

INSTRUCT: Objective ❷

The People of Israel

- **What is the population and ethnic makeup of Israel?** about 6 million; about 80 percent Jewish, 20 percent Palestinian Arabs
- **What is life like for the Palestinian Arabs?** less political power, fewer rights and opportunities; some refugees in the occupied Gaza Strip and West Bank
- **What opportunities do women have in Israel?** They can work outside home; child care is provided on kibbutzim; a woman was prime minister from 1969 to 1974.

MORE ABOUT...
Arabs

As Islam and the Arabic language have spread throughout the Middle East and beyond, the term *Arabs* has come to include people whose native language is Arabic. About three-quarters of the Arabs in Israel are Muslims; the others are Christians or Druze (a small sect).

Activity Options

Multiple Learning Styles: Interpersonal

 Block Scheduling

Class Time Two class periods

Task Gathering information in order to simulate a day on a kibbutz

Purpose To learn more about life on a kibbutz

Supplies Needed
- Reference books, Internet access, primary sources
- Writing paper
- Pens or pencils

Activity Have small groups of students do research about life on a kibbutz. In advance, try to locate primary sources written by kibbutz settlers. Encourage students to find out how people divide work responsibilities, choose leaders, and cooperate to achieve common goals. Then have each group assign its members roles in a kibbutz and act out part of a typical day.

Culture • Israeli women must serve in the military for two years; men must serve for three. ▲

FOCUS ON VISUALS

Interpreting the Photograph Have students look at the photograph of the soldier and read the caption. Ask them how requiring women to serve in the military might influence the role of women in Israeli politics and business.

Possible Response Women are more likely to consider themselves equals and to be treated as such.

Extension Have students write short stories about a woman soldier in the Israeli army.

INSTRUCT: Objective ❸

The Law of Return

• What does the Law of Return state? Any Jew can immigrate to Israel and become a citizen.

• Why did Jews from the USSR have difficulty finding jobs and housing in Israel? because 300,000 people arrived within a short time

• What helped Ethiopian Jews fit into Israeli society? They had useful skills, such as blacksmithing, weaving, and pottery-making.

Citizenship
🏛 IN ACTION

Human rights are the rights to which all people are entitled, regardless of where they live, what language they speak, or what their beliefs are. Most countries have laws to protect human rights, but not all countries enforce those laws effectively. International laws, developed primarily by the United Nations, help to ensure human rights when individual countries do not.

Some Palestinians are refugees from Israel who fled to the Gaza Strip and the West Bank after the 1948 Arab-Israeli War. (See the map on page 245.) Israel occupies these territories. Constant tension between Arabs and Israelis often leads to violence.

Women in Israel Even before Israel was a state, its women were encouraged to work outside the home. To free mothers from child-care duties, children on kibbutzim lived and slept in separate children's houses and visited their parents during evenings and weekends. An American-educated woman, Golda Meir (may•EER), was the prime minister of Israel from 1969 to 1974.

The Law of Return ❸

Since 1948, Israel has taken in nearly 3 million Jewish immigrants. The 1950 **Law of Return** states that Jews anywhere in the world can immigrate to Israel and become citizens.

Recent Immigrants In 1987, the USSR finally allowed Jews within its borders to emigrate. Within three years, 300,000 arrived in Israel. Many were skilled engineers and technicians. Because of their numbers, however, they had a hard time finding jobs and good housing.

In the 1980s, Israel began a policy of airlifting groups of Jews from countries such as Yemen, Albania, and Ethiopia and bringing them into Israel. Ethiopia's 38,000 Jews were airlifted between 1984 and 1999. These people had been so isolated they had thought they were the only Jews left in the world.

Reading Social Studies

B. Making Inferences Why might Jews in other countries want to emigrate to Israel?

Reading Social Studies
B. Possible Answers to escape prejudice, to be part of a Jewish state

Citizenship
👥 IN ACTION

B'Tselem Many Israelis are concerned about abuses of power by their own government. That was why the Israeli Center for Human Rights in the Occupied Territories, or B'Tselem, was founded in 1989. B'Tselem documents and reports human rights violations against the mostly Palestinian residents of Gaza and the West Bank. Such violations include housing discrimination, torture, killing, and the taking of land by Israeli security forces. B'Tselem believes that educating the public about these abuses is the best way to bring about change in Israeli policy in the Occupied Territories.

266 CHAPTER 9

Activity Options
Differentiating Instruction: Gifted and Talented

🄱 Block Scheduling

Examining Cultural Influences Challenge students to research the different places from which Jews have come to Israel, both in the past and in recent years. Suggest that students focus their research on European nations, Yemen, Ethiopia, the United States, or the Soviet Union. Ask them to list the places and to describe the contributions each group would bring to Israel.

To present their research, have students use a large-scale map that shows the United States and Europe (including at least part of Russia and Ukraine). Direct them to use their research in writing small informational captions about each country from which Jews have emigrated. Have them place their captions with push pins in the appropriate spots on the map.

Many had never used electricity or running water. Although poorly educated, they had useful skills such as blacksmithing, weaving, and pottery making that helped them fit into Israeli society.

Movement •
Jewish children from Ethiopia make a new home in Israel. ▲

Religion in Israel Today ④

Only about one in four of Israel's Jews strictly follows Jewish law. They are called **Orthodox Jews.** These Jews believe that Jewish law should help form government policy. Orthodox rabbis have official control over marriage, divorce, and burial. They also limit what Israeli Jews can do on the Sabbath and holidays. **Rosh Hashanah** (RAWSH huh•SHAW•nuh) is the Jewish New Year. **Yom Kippur** (YAWM KIHP•uhr) is the Day of Atonement, a day for fasting and reflecting on one's sins. It is the holiest day in the Jewish year. No government employee can work on these Jewish High Holy Days. No newspapers appear on either holiday. Most of Israel's Jews are **secular,** meaning that religious practices play a less important role in their lives. They are more interested in living a modern way of life. Many resent Orthodox control of daily life.

SECTION ④ ASSESSMENT

Terms & Names

1. Identify:
(a) Zionism
(b) kibbutz
(c) Law of Return
(d) Orthodox Jews
(e) Rosh Hashanah
(f) Yom Kippur
(g) secular

Taking Notes

2. Use a cause-and-effect chart like this one to write the reasons for Jewish immigration to Palestine.

Causes [ ] [ ] [ ]

↓ ↓ ↓

Effect | Jewish immigration to Palestine |

Main Ideas

3. (a) Why did early Jewish settlers in Israel establish kibbutzim?

(b) Why have Russian Jews faced problems fitting in to Israeli society?

(c) What are the major differences between Orthodox and secular Jews?

Critical Thinking

4. Forming and Supporting Opinions

How well do you think Israel has lived up to its promise to treat all its inhabitants equally?

Think About

♦ the treatment of Palestinian Arabs

♦ the treatment of women

♦ the treatment of immigrants

ACTIVITY -OPTION- Write an **interview** you might have with a new immigrant to Israel. Include information on where the immigrant comes from, the date and method of arrival, reasons for coming, and reactions to a new land.

Section ④ Assessment

1. Terms & Names
a. Zionism, p. 264
b. kibbutz, p. 265
c. Law of Return, p. 266
d. Orthodox Jews, p. 267
e. Rosh Hashanah, p. 267
f. Yom Kippur, p. 267
g. secular, p. 267

2. Taking Notes

| Loss of homeland | Persecution in other countries | Law of Return |

↓ ↓ ↓

| Jewish immigration to Palestine |

3. Main Ideas
a. Kibbutzim gave the immigrants the opportunity to own land.
b. So many Jews arrived in such a short time that jobs and housing were scarce.
c. Orthodox Jews observe religious laws strictly and believe that government policy should be based on these laws. Secular Jews observe the religious laws less strictly.

4. Critical Thinking

Students may say that at times Israel has not shown respect for the rights of Palestinian Arabs. All immigrants have been welcomed, but opportunity has varied for each.

ACTIVITY OPTION

Integrated Assessment
• Rubric for writing an interview

INSTRUCT: Objective ④

Religion in Israel Today

• What are the Jewish High Holy Days? Rosh Hashanah (Jewish New Year), Yom Kippur (Day of Atonement)

• How do Orthodox Jews differ from secular Jews? Orthodox Jews: follow Jewish law strictly and believe it should form government policy; secular: religious practices are less important; interested in living modern life

ASSESS & RETEACH

Reading Social Studies Have students fill in the fifth row of the chart on page 242.

Formal Assessment
• Section Quiz, p. 132

RETEACHING ACTIVITY

Have students work in teams to create a list of questions to help them review the section. Then have teams exchange questions and answer them.

In-depth Resources: Unit 3
• Reteaching Activity, p. 29

Access for Students Acquiring English
• Reteaching Activity, p. 83

Linking Past and Present

The Legacy of North Africa and Southwest Asia

OBJECTIVE

Students learn about the contributions of North Africa and Southwest Asia to specific tools, systems, and beliefs of today.

FOCUS & MOTIVATE

Making Inferences Ask students to study the pictures and read each paragraph. Then have them answer the following questions:

1. How might the invention of writing have affected the communication of the inventions of tools, such as the lever?

2. What did the use of a fork in Southwest Asia before the 1800s suggest about the user's status?

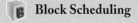 Block Scheduling

MORE ABOUT…
Religion

All three of the major religions that began in Southwest Asia believe that one city, Jerusalem, is a holy place. It is sacred to Jews because it was an ancient political and religious center. It is sacred to Christians because important events in the life of Jesus Christ took place there. It is sacred to Muslims because they believe the Prophet Muhammad ascended to heaven from there.

MORE ABOUT…
Writing

The Egyptians used hieroglyphics for more than 3,000 years and by the end of that time had developed more than 6,000 symbols. By the A.D. 300s, however, they replaced hieroglyphics with a simpler alphabet, and the ability to understand hieroglyphics was gradually lost. In the 1800s, a French scholar began deciphering the language. Today, much we know about ancient Egypt comes from translating Egyptian hieroglyphics.

Religion

Three major religions—Judaism, Christianity, and Islam—began in Southwest Asia. Judaism is based on the laws Moses received from God, which are written in the Torah. Christianity is based on the teachings of Jesus, which appear in the New Testament. Islam is based on the teachings of the prophet Muhammad and the sacred text called the Qur'an. The teachings and beliefs of Judaism, Christianity, and Islam spread east and south through Asia, north and west to Europe, south through Africa, and west to the Americas. All three religions share a belief in one God and encourage people to live a life of tolerance and peace.

Cosmetics

Archaeologists believe that cosmetics were used as early as 4000 B.C. Ancient Egyptians used plants and powdered minerals to make cosmetics. During and after the Renaissance, the use of cosmetics flourished in Europe, as both men and women made up their faces. Italy and France became cosmetic-manufacturing centers. By the 1900s, people of all social classes were using cosmetics. Since the 1930s, the cosmetic industry has developed into a big business.

Writing

About 5,500 years ago, Mesopotamians began to use what is considered the first developed system of writing. They made marks that represented words on wet clay tablets, some of which survive today. Two thousand years later, the Egyptians developed a sophisticated writing system, known as hieroglyphics, in which pictures were used to represent sounds and words. Today, people continue to communicate, not only by writing with pen and paper but also by using electronic mail.

Activity Options

Interdisciplinary Link: Language Arts

Class Time 60 minutes

Task Practicing writing and translating pictographs

Supplies Needed

• Information about, and samples of pictographs and Egyptian hieroglyphics

Activity Review the idea of the pictograph, or a drawing, to represent a word. Work as a class to create a pictograph for one of the paragraph titles in this feature. Have students work on their own to create one more for another title. Discuss the process. Then have students work on their own to write a three-sentence story in pictographs.

Have students exchange pictographs and translate them back into English. Ask for volunteers to read stories aloud to the class. Discuss the advantages and disadvantages of using pictographs for a written language.

anking

most 5,500 years ago, before the vention of coins or paper money, a rm of banking existed in ancient esopotamia. In Italy in the 1200s, bank- g took place on benches in the street. fact, the word *bank* comes from the alian word *banco,* which means ench." By the 1600s, customers of nks in England were using written afts, or checks, to make payments. odern banking is electronic. Though me people use written checks, many take advantage of auto- ated teller machines and telephone-banking systems to meet eir banking needs.

Find Out More About It!
Study the text and photos on these pages to learn about inventions, creations, and contributions that have come from North Africa and Southwest Asia. Then choose the item that interests you the most and, in a short essay, describe how your life would be different if it did not exist.

RESEARCH LINKS
CLASSZONE.COM

Lever

A lever is a rod or bar that pivots on a fulcrum, acting like a seesaw to help people perform work. Early people used levers to move and lift heavy rocks. In 1500 B.C., Egyptians used the shadoof— a lever with weights on one end and a bucket on the other—to lift water from rivers and canals into their fields. They also developed a balance scale based on the lever. Balance scales and wheelbarrows are examples of levers we use today.

Forks

Though the ancient Greeks first used kitchen forks for carving and serv- ing meat, it was not until the 800s that nobles in Southwest Asia used forks for dining. For the next 900 years, wealthy people continued to use forks for eating. Because the com- mon people believed forks were unnecessary and even odd, they con- tinued to use their hands, knives, and spoons for eating. Forks were not commonly used in the West until the 1800s.

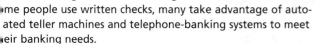

INSTRUCT

- What three major religions began in Southwest Asia?
- Where does the word *bank* come from?
- What did early people use levers for?

MORE ABOUT...
Banking

Before banking emerged in large Italian cities in the 1200s, the early Romans had developed an extended banking system to serve their large empire in Europe, Asia, and much of Africa. When the Roman Empire fell in the West, most of this banking system disappeared. It reappeared in Venice, Rome, Florence, and other Italian cities in the 1200s and gradually spread throughout Europe.

MORE ABOUT...
Lever

The lever is a highly efficient machine. Because it uses very little friction, it puts out as much work, or energy, as is used to power it. It is also one of six simple machines that all other machines, no matter how complex, are based on. The five other machines are the wheel and axle, the screw, the wedge, the pulley, and the inclined plane. Engineers develop complex and specialized machines by combining aspects of these simple machines.

More to Think About

Making Personal Connections Point out to students that writing is used in our lives every day to exchange information and tell stories. Ask students what their lives might be like without writing. In what ways would their daily lives be different? What would they have to do differ- ently? What would they not be able to do? Have students share specific examples.

Vocabulary Activity Identify and review important vocabulary words from this feature. List them on the chalkboard, and have students write sentences using each word. Tell students that the sentences should be written in ways that show the meanings of the words. Have students share their sentences with the class.

SECTION
5

Turkey Today

TERMS & NAMES

Mustafa Kemal

Grand National Assembly

Atatürk

Tansu Ciller

SECTION OBJECTIVES

1. To explain the influence of Mustafa Kemal on modern Turkey

2. To explain how modernization changed life in Turkey, especially for women

3. To identify civil rights issues in present-day Turkey

4. To describe Turkey's relationship with NATO and the European Union

CRITICAL THINKING

• Analyzing Causes, p. 273

FOCUS & MOTIVATE

WARM-UP

Making Inferences Have students read <u>Dateline</u> and discuss Turkish attitudes toward modernization.

1. What do you think the fez and the veil meant to the people who wore them?

2. How might some people be unhappy about changing the traditional Islamic way of life?

INSTRUCT: Objective ➊

Between Two Worlds/ A Powerful Ruler

• Who was Mustafa Kemal, and what was his vision for Turkey? The founder of modern Turkey; he wanted to adopt modern, "Western" ways and ideas in Turkey.

• What were the first changes Kemal made? organized legislature, replaced Arabic alphabet with the Western one, adopted Western calendar and styles of dress, closed religious schools

 In-depth Resources: Unit 3
• Guided Reading Worksheet, p. 21

 Reading Study Guide
(Spanish and English), pp. 84–85

MAIN IDEA

Turkey's culture blends modern European and traditional Islamic ways.

WHY IT MATTERS NOW

Turkey is an important military ally and trade partner of the United States and Europe.

DATELINE

ANKARA, TURKEY, NOVEMBER 25, 1925—No more fez. Turkish leader Mustafa Kemal has declared that Turkish men are no longer allowed to wear the fez, their traditional head covering.

According to the new Hat Law, hats are now the acceptable head covering for men. Muslim women are being strongly encouraged to give up the veil. These changes are in keeping with Kemal's drive to westernize Turkey. Many Turks are happy to see Turkey become more like Europe. Others are unhappy with this move away from the traditional Islamic way of life.

Culture • Turkish men are getting used to wearing hats. ▲

Culture • The fez will become a thing of the past. ▲

Between Two Worlds ➊

If you look at Turkey on the map on page 273, you will see that it is joined to Southwest Asia on the east and to Europe on the west. The question after World War I was: Would Turkey be like its Islamic neighbors and hold on to its traditions, or would it become more like the West? Its powerful new ruler, **Mustafa Kemal** (keh·MAHL), believed in westernization, by force if necessary.

Program Resources

 In-depth Resources: Unit 3
• Guided Reading Worksheet, p. 21
• Reteaching Activity, p. 30

 Reading Study Guide
(Spanish and English), pp. 84–85

 Formal Assessment
• Section Quiz, p. 133

Integrated Assessment
• Rubric for writing a dialogue

 Outline Map Activities

 Access for Students Acquiring English
• Guided Reading Worksheet, p. 77

 Technology Resources
classzone.com

TEST-TAKING RESOURCES

⌛ Strategies for Test Preparation

⌛ Test Practice Transparencies

🖱 Online Test Practice

A Powerful Ruler ❶

Mustafa Kemal was the founder of modern Turkey. He had been a Turkish officer and war hero for the Ottoman forces during World War I. The Ottomans had continued to rule Turkey even after the empire became weak. Turkey fought on the losing side during the war, which weakened it even more. In 1920, Great Britain occupied Turkey.

Place • **Mustafa Kemal Atatürk was the founder and first president of the Republic of Turkey (1923–38).** ▲

Mustafa Kemal Becomes Atatürk Kemal opposed Britain's action. He organized Turkey's first **Grand National Assembly,** or legislature. The assembly elected Kemal president. At his suggestion, the assembly officially adopted the name Turkey, the land of the Turkish people. In 1923, Kemal declared Turkey a republic and got rid of the old Islamic government the following year.

While Kemal was in the Ottoman army, he spent time in European cities. He admired the way of life he saw there. He believed adopting modern, "Western" ways and ideas would benefit Turkey. Over the next nine years, Kemal introduced his changes. The Western alphabet replaced the Arabic alphabet. The Western calendar replaced the Islamic calendar.

Before 1934, many Turks used only first names. In 1934, a new law required the use of last names. The National Assembly gave Kemal the name **Atatürk,** which means "Father of Turks."

Reading
Social Studies

A. Forming and Supporting Opinions Which of Mustafa Kemal's changes do you think had the greatest effect on Turkish life?

Reading Social Studies
A. Possible Answers establishing secular schools, starting new government

Changes Brought by Modernization ❷

For nearly 1,000 years, Islamic law had shaped Turkish life. Atatürk, however, believed in secular government. He closed all institutions that had been founded on Islamic law. He replaced religious schools with secular schools. Since people were used to having Islam play a major role in all aspects of their lives, many protested Atatürk's reforms.

Women in Turkey Turkish women benefited from Atatürk's reforms. He made it easier for women to divorce their husbands. Marriages could no longer be arranged by a woman's parents unless she agreed. Men were no longer able to have more than one wife at the same time.

Women could now also vote and run for office. In the mid-1930s, women were elected to the national parliament. The world's first woman supreme court justice was a Turk. For several years during the 1990s, a woman named **Tansu Ciller** was Turkey's prime minister.

Movement • In 1993, Prime Minister Tansu Ciller traveled from Turkey to the United States where she met with President Bill Clinton. ▼

INSTRUCT: Objective ❷

Changes Brought by Modernization

- What was the overall result of Atatürk's changes? to make Turkey a secular state, not run by Islamic law
- In what ways did women benefit from the reform movement? easier to get a divorce; arranged marriages required a woman's approval; men no longer could have multiple wives; women could vote and hold office

MORE ABOUT…
Tansu Ciller

When Tansu Ciller was elected as Turkey's first female prime minister, she became the first woman without a family political connection to head an Islamic country. Ciller, born to a prosperous Istanbul family, married at 17 and persuaded her husband to take her last name, which was practically unheard of in Turkey. She earned a degree in economics in Turkey, continued her education in the United States, and then returned to Turkey to teach. Ciller also became involved in the ruling political party in 1990 and was elected to Parliament the following year. Two years later, she became prime minister.

Activity Options

Interdisciplinary Link: Speech

Class Time One class period

Task Writing and presenting a speech Atatürk might have given

Purpose To learn about life in Turkey prior to Atatürk's rule, and understand his desire to modernize Turkey

Supplies Needed
- Reference materials about Turkey
- Writing paper
- Pens or pencils

Block Scheduling

Activity Have students research conditions in Turkey before Mustafa Kemal (Atatürk) instituted his reforms, and learn more about how Turkey changed after those reforms were in place. Divide the class into small groups and have each group write a "Declaration to the People" from Atatürk, defending his proposed changes. Have a volunteer from each group deliver the group's declaration to the class.

INSTRUCT: Objective ❸

Rights and Freedoms Today

- What rights are promised by the Turkish Constitution of 1982? freedom of religion, freedom of speech, freedom of the press, and other rights
- How has the Turkish government limited civil rights? censored the press, limited the rights of Kurdish people

INSTRUCT: Objective ❹

International Alliances

- Why was NATO formed? to keep the Soviet Union from attacking non-Communist countries
- What factors motivate Turkey to support the continued existence of NATO? protection of its borders; having a say in major decisions
- Why was the European Union reluctant to include Turkey? Too many Turkish workers might go to European countries for work.

Connections to Literature

The Greek army invaded Troy by hiding soldiers inside a huge wooden model of a horse that they presented to the Trojans as a gift. They claimed the horse was an offering to the goddess Athena that would protect Troy from invasions. The expression "Trojan horse" is still used to refer to something harmful that is disguised as something good, usually coming from an outside source.

Rights and Freedoms Today ❸

Turkey adopted its most recent constitution in 1982. The Turkish Constitution promises freedom of religion, freedom of speech, freedom of the press, and other rights. The government, however, does not always live up to these promises. It sometimes limits freedoms. Turkish journalists can be arrested for writing articles against the government. The government also bans some publications.

The Kurds The Kurds are a group of people who live in the mountainous regions of southeastern Turkey, Iraq, Iran, and Syria. They have been fighting for their own state since 1984. The Turkish government has made suspected Kurd fighters leave their homes. It limits the right to teach Kurdish in schools. It also limits the use of Kurdish in television and radio programs.

International Alliances ❹

Turkey and the United States are both members of the North Atlantic Treaty Organization (NATO). This alliance was formed in 1949 to keep the Soviet Union and its allies from attacking non-Communist countries in Western Europe. Turkey joined the alliance in 1952. When the Soviet Union fell apart in 1991, some NATO members felt the alliance was no longer necessary. Turkey disagreed because NATO membership helps protect its borders. Membership also gives Turkey a say in major decisions other members make.

Connections to Literature

Looking for Troy Two of the world's best-known epic poems tell about a long-ago war in the eastern Mediterranean. In the *Iliad*, Greeks besiege the city of Troy. Greek soldiers hide inside a giant wooden horse to trick the Trojans into opening the gates of the city. The photo at right shows a model of the Trojan Horse. In the *Odyssey*, the hero, Odysseus, has many adventures on his way home from the same war. Both poems may have been composed by the Greek poet Homer sometime around 800 B.C.

While many people thought the Trojan War was just a legend, Heinrich Schliemann, a German archaeologist, dreamed of finding the real Troy. In the 1870s, he began to dig at a site in northwestern Turkey. He found ruins of palaces and golden artifacts. In fact, Schliemann had found Troy—but not the city of the poems. Over centuries, people had built new cities on the ruins of older ones. Archaeologists think that the seventh city down on the site is the Troy of the *Iliad*. It was destroyed about 1250 B.C.

272 CHAPTER 9

Activity Options

Multiple Learning Styles: Visual/Spatial

Class Time One class period

Task Making a two-part mural showing contrasting scenes of life in Turkey before and after Atatürk's reforms

Purpose To illustrate the changes

that took place in everyday life in Turkey

Supplies Needed
- Poster paints or colored markers
- Poster paper or roll of kraft paper
- Reference materials on costumes

Activity Review with students the changes in dress and other aspects of daily life that Kemal Atatürk instituted during the 1920s. Ask them to illustrate one scene of a street or market in the early 1900s in which people wear traditional dress, signs are in Arabic, etc.; and another showing people in a street or market in Istanbul today (as in the photograph on pages 240–241).

EUROPE

Istanbul

Black Sea
Bosporus

Sea
of Marmara

TURKEY

Mediterranean Sea

ASIA

Joining the European Union Most of Turkey's trade is with Western Europe. In 1987, Turkey applied to join the European Union. The EU was reluctant to accept Turkey, partly because of the size of its population. There are not enough jobs in Turkey for all the people who want them. Two million Turks have gone to Germany to work. Millions more work in other European countries. Workers from EU countries are allowed to move freely within the region. European countries worried that membership in the EU would let more Turkish workers into their countries than they could handle.

Region •
The city of Istanbul is partly in Europe and partly in Asia. ▲

SECTION 5 ASSESSMENT

Terms & Names

1. Identify:
(a) Mustafa Kemal
(b) Grand National Assembly
(c) Atatürk
(d) Tansu Ciller

Taking Notes

2. Use a chart like this one to list changes made by Mustafa Kemal.

Old Ways	New Ways
1.	
2.	
3.	
4.	
5.	

Main Ideas

3. (a) How does Turkey limit the rights of the Kurds?

(b) How did Atatürk's reforms benefit women?

(c) Why does Turkey value its membership in NATO?

Critical Thinking

4. Analyzing Issues

How does the issue of unemployment affect Turkey's chances of joining the European Union?

Think About
• Turkey's population
• jobs in Europe

ACTIVITY -OPTION- Write a **dialogue** between two Turks, one who welcomes Mustafa Kemal's changes and one who opposes them.

North Africa and Southwest Asia Today **273**

CRITICAL THINKING ACTIVITY

Analyzing Causes Discuss the immigration of workers from developing countries to developed countries. Point out that large numbers of Mexicans enter the United States every year to find work. Ask students why they think so many Turks who immigrate to Europe are unable to find work in their own country.

Class Time 15 minutes

ASSESS & RETEACH

Reading Social Studies Have students complete the last row of the chart on page 242.

 Formal Assessment
• Section Quiz, p. 133

RETEACHING ACTIVITY

Have students work in pairs to create a matching activity for the section. Each student should write a numbered list of ten key terms and ideas and a lettered list of ten definitions and identifying phrases. Have students exchange activities and complete them.

In-depth Resources: Unit 3
• Reaching Activity, p. 30

Access for Students Acquiring English
• Reaching Activity, p. 84

Section 5 Assessment

1. Terms & Names

a. Mustafa Kemal, p. 270
b. Grand National Assembly, p. 271
c. Atatürk, p. 271
d. Tansu Ciller, p. 271

2. Taking Notes

Old Ways	New Ways
1. People wore fez and the veil.	"Western" style dress
2. Arabic alphabet	Western alphabet
3. Islamic calendar	Western calendar
4. Government based on Islamic law	Secular government
5. Difficult for women to divorce	Divorce easier for women

3. Main Ideas

a. limited use of Kurdish language; Kurds suspected of terrorism forced to leave their homes
b. easier for women to obtain divorces; women can vote, seek political office
c. NATO membership protects Turkey's borders; allows participation in major NATO decisions

4. Critical Thinking

Other EU countries fear that if they admit Turkey, large numbers of unemployed Turks will cross their borders in search of jobs.

ACTIVITY OPTION

Integrated Assessment
• Rubric for writing a dialogue

Teacher's Edition **273**

TERMS & NAMES

1. Arab-Israeli Wars, p. 244
2. OPEC, p. 250
3. primary product, p. 250
4. Aswan High Dam, p. 257
5. Anwar Sadat, p. 258
6. Zionism, p. 264
7. kibbutz, p. 265
8. Yom Kippur, p. 267
9. Mustafa Kemal, p. 270
10. Tansu Ciller, p. 271

REVIEW QUESTIONS

Possible Responses

1. The United Nations suggested dividing Palestine into two states.
2. Oil is the world's primary energy source, and the region produces nearly half of the supply.
3. People stop to pray five times a day, and radio and television air programs devoted to readings of the Qur'an.
4. France and Britain built the Suez Canal to create a trade route. The canal gave them control of the region's seas and rivers.
5. benefits: dependable water source for farmers, control of flooding to allow year-round crop production, more electrical power; drawbacks: no deposits of rich soil from flooding, forcing farmers to use artificial fertilizers that pollute the water
6. Most rural Egyptians are farmers, while Cairenes mainly work in factories.
7. They fight over land.
8. Many immigrants have arrived in a short time. Jobs and housing are in demand.
9. Men could no longer have more than one wife; it became easier to obtain a divorce, and women could vote and run for office.
10. Other EU countries fear that unemployed Turks will cross their borders to find jobs.

TERMS & NAMES

Explain the significance of each of the following:

1. Arab-Israeli Wars
2. OPEC
3. primary product
4. Aswan High Dam
5. Anwar Sadat
6. Zionism
7. kibbutz
8. Yom Kippur
9. Mustafa Kemal
10. Tansu Ciller

REVIEW QUESTIONS

A Troubled Century *(pages 243–247)*

1. What was the United Nations solution to the conflicting claims of Arabs and Zionists to Palestine?

Resources and Religion *(pages 249–253)*

2. Why is oil the most important resource in the region?
3. How does Islam influence the culture of the region?

Egypt Today *(pages 256–261)*

4. Why did France and Britain build the Suez Canal?
5. What are the main benefits and drawbacks of the Aswan Dam?
6. How is life in Egypt's rural areas different from life in Cairo?

Israel Today *(pages 264–267)*

7. Why do Jews and Arabs come into conflict in Israel?
8. Why has immigration caused problems in Israel today?

Turkey Today *(pages 270–273)*

9. What changes did Mustafa Kemal make in Turkey?
10. Why has Turkey had difficulty joining the European Union?

CRITICAL THINKING

Identifying Problems

1. Using your completed chart from Reading Social Studies, p. 242, list times when the solution to a problem in the region caused a new problem.

Analyzing Motives

2. Why have Muslim fundamentalists and others objected to westernization?

Comparing

3. Compare the progress of women's rights in modern-day Turkey to those of women in modern-day Saudi Arabia.

Visual Summary

1 A Troubled Century

- The conflicts of the past have contributed to problems today in North Africa and Southwest Asia.

2 Resources and Religion

- Oil and Islam are major factors in the region's economy and culture.

Egypt 3 Today

- Modernization has brought both benefits and problems to Egypt.

Israel Today

- Conflict continues because both Jews and Arabs claim the land of Israel.

5 Turkey Today

- Modern Turkey is the result of Mustafa Kemal's forcible westernization of a traditional Islamic culture.

CRITICAL THINKING: Possible Responses

1. Identifying Problems

Students may say that the solution to the water shortage in Egypt (dams), for example, caused conflicts over the control of the water. Other problems include the desire for a homeland for Jews after World War II or the push for modernization in Turkey.

2. Analyzing Motives

Muslim fundamentalists think that western nations exert too much influence over their culture.

3. Comparing

In Turkey, women have more personal and political freedom and have been elected to major political offices. In Saudi Arabia, women's political and social freedoms are restricted.

SOCIAL STUDIES SKILLBUILDER

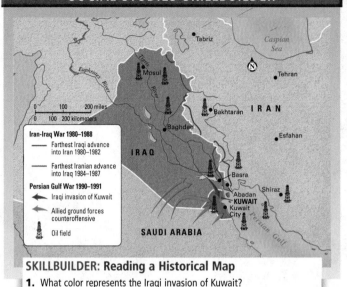

Iran-Iraq War 1980–1988
— Farthest Iraqi advance into Iran 1980–1982
— Farthest Iranian advance into Iraq 1984–1987

Persian Gulf War 1990–1991
← Iraqi invasion of Kuwait
← Allied ground forces counteroffensive
⛽ Oil field

SKILLBUILDER: Reading a Historical Map

1. What color represents the Iraqi invasion of Kuwait?
2. How are the boundaries of present-day borders shown?
3. Write a brief summary of the information in the map.

FOCUS ON GEOGRAPHY

1. **Location** • Where are most of the crude oil reserves in the region located?
2. **Region** • Name two countries with very little of this resource.
3. **Region** • How might this difference in oil reserves cause problems in the region?

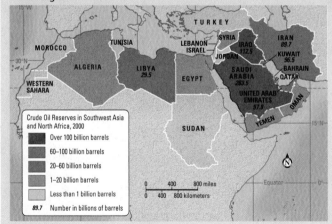

Crude Oil Reserves in Southwest Asia and North Africa, 2000
Over 100 billion barrels
60–100 billion barrels
20–60 billion barrels
1–20 billion barrels
Less than 1 billion barrels
89.7 Number in billions of barrels

Interdisciplinary Activity: Language Arts

Writing a Speech Imagine that you are a member of the United Nations involved in a debate about peace in Palestine. Write a short speech urging peace between the Israelis and the Palestinians. Review the history of the conflict and mention the rights of both sides. Suggest steps that the parties can take to achieve peace.

Cooperative Learning Activity

Make a Presentation In pairs, present information to the class about religious celebrations that involve fasting. Choose one celebration, such as Ramadan, Lent, or Yom Kippur, and research the celebration.
• Write a paragraph that explains the celebration.
• Arrange illustrations on a piece of poster board or overhead.
• Present your information to the class.

INTERNET ACTIVITY

Use the Internet to research one major city—Cairo, Istanbul, or Tel Aviv. Find out what a tourist would need to know before a visit. What language is spoken? What will the climate be? What historic sights would a tourist want to see?

Writing a Tourist Brochure Create a tourist brochure of your findings. Include a map or illustrations of the sights a tourist would expect to see. Include important information a tourist would need. List the Web sites you used to prepare your report.

For Internet links to support this activity, go to

RESEARCH LINKS
CLASSZONE.COM

North Africa and Southwest Asia Today **275**

CHAPTER PROJECTS

Interdisciplinary Activity: Language Arts

Writing a Speech Suggest that students consider how the Palestinians became dispersed and why the Jews want a homeland. Speeches should mention the tragedies of violence and the motives of both sides. They should make persuasive arguments for steps that can be taken to achieve peace.

Cooperative Learning Activity

Make a Presentation Students' presentations should include a one-paragraph explanation of the celebration and its significance, and illustrations that supply details and show participants in observance of the celebration.

🌐 INTERNET ACTIVITY

Discuss how students might find information about the cities of Cairo, Istanbul, or Tel Aviv using the Internet. Brainstorm possible keywords, Web sites, and search engines. Suggest that students make a chart in which they list the name of the city they have chosen as well as information about climate, languages spoken, and historic sites. They can use the information in their charts to write their brochures. When they have finished, ask students to exchange brochures with a classmate, read the brochures, and give feedback from the point of view of a tourist to the area.

Students should include a map or other interesting visuals to help a potential tourist prepare for a trip.

Skills Answers

Social Studies Skillbuilder
Possible Responses
1. blue
2. with white lines
3. The map shows the advances of Iraq into Iran from 1980 to 1982 and Iran's advances into Iraq from 1984 to 1987. Additionally, it illustrates the Iraqi invasion of Kuwait and the counteroffensive of Allied ground forces.

Focus on Geography
Possible Responses
1. in Saudi Arabia and Iraq
2. Turkey and Sudan
3. Students may say that since oil brings wealth and power to a nation, conflicts could arise among oil-rich and oil-poor nations.

UNIT 4

Africa South of the Sahara

Before You Read

Previewing Unit 4

Unit 4 covers the landforms, climates, and natural resources of the African countries south of the Sahara. Included is an exploration of the slave trade and the road to independence for the countries in this area. The focus of the unit shifts to the more specific histories, economies, and cultures of the countries in Western and Central Africa and then Eastern and Southern Africa. The unit highlights life in South Africa and Kenya today.

Place Elephants are one of many kinds of animals that inhabit the 5,700-square-mile Serengeti National Park in Tanzania, Africa. The Serengeti Plain is the last place in Africa where vast land-animal migrations take place.

276

Unit Level Activities

1. A Speech for Independence
Remind students that many of the countries in this unit were former colonies and that the independence they struggled to gain came with certain risks. Have students write a speech given by a freedom leader, urging people to take the risk and strive for independence. The speech should persuade the people to choose independence over colonization. Remind them to include the reasons why this is a good step, along with an honest assessment of the risks involved.

2. A Game of Jeopardy
Have students work in teams, with each team responsible for writing questions and answers for one of the countries in the unit. Students should write out questions about the history, geography, economy, and way of life of each country and use the information in the chapters for answers. When the unit is completed, use the questions for a class game similar to Jeopardy, with students choosing a country or topic and answering questions for their team.

AFRICA SOUTH OF THE SAHARA

ATLANTIC

PACIFIC OCEAN

N

PACIFIC OCEAN

INDIAN OCEAN

OCEAN

OCEAN

AFRICA SOUTH OF THE SAHARA

SERENGETI NATIONAL PARK

277

FOCUS ON VISUALS

Analyzing the Photograph Direct students' attention to the photograph of elephants migrating in Serengeti National Park. Be sure students read the caption and note that this park is the last place in Africa where migrations of large land animals can take place safely. Ask students to think about why the park is a safe place. What do they think occurred in other areas? What factors might have led to this situation? What steps can be taken to prevent further loss of land for migrating animals? What will be lost if nothing is done?

Possible Responses The land in the park has been protected; land in other places has been developed; it was needed for other things like farming or housing; land should be set aside and preserved; an important part of the natural world will be lost.

Extension Have students write letters to the local newspaper, urging that area lands be saved in a natural state. Remind them to include information about why this is important and suggestions about how this can be accomplished.

Implementing the National Geography Standards

Standard 9 Demonstrate an understanding of demographic concepts and explain how population characteristics differ from country to country

Objective To prepare a booklet on population patterns in selected African nations

Class Time 40 minutes

Task Have students prepare a booklet on population patterns in Eritrea, Liberia, Nigeria, Seychelles, and Zambia by analyzing the following information given in the Unit Atlas Data File: population, life expectancy, birthrate, infant mortality, doctors, and total area. The booklet should explain how population characteristics differ from country to country.

Evaluation Students should use graphs, maps, and written passages to compare population characteristics among countries.

UNIT 4

ATLAS
Africa South of the Sahara

ATLAS OBJECTIVES

1. Describe and locate key physical features of Africa south of the Sahara

2. Identify important mineral resources and compare the landmass and population of Africa south of the Sahara with those of the United States

3. Identify significant political features

4. Describe the population and languages in Africa south of the Sahara

FOCUS & MOTIVATE

Ask students to describe some of the physical features of Africa south of the Sahara. Students should identify mountainous areas, coastal regions, deserts, rivers, and lakes.

INSTRUCT: Objective ❶

Physical Map of Africa South of the Sahara

• What do the colors used on the map tell you? the elevation in feet and meters

• What mountains appear on the map? Mounts Kenya, Kilimanjaro, and Cameroon

• Into what body of water does the Niger River empty? Gulf of Guinea

• What major island lies off the east coast of Africa? Madagascar

 In-depth Resources: Unit 4
• Unit Atlas Activity, p. 1

UNIT Atlas 4   Physical Geography

Africa South of the Sahara: Physical

(Map of Africa showing physical features, including the Mediterranean Sea, Red Sea, Sahara, Sahel, countries such as Mauritania, Mali, Niger, Chad, Eritrea, Djibouti, Ethiopian Plateau, Ethiopia, Somalia, Cape Verde, Senegal, The Gambia, Guinea-Bissau, Guinea, Sierra Leone, Liberia, Burkina Faso, Côte d'Ivoire, Ghana, Togo, Benin, Nigeria, Cameroon, Equatorial Guinea, São Tomé and Príncipe, Gabon, Rep. of the Congo, Central African Republic, Democratic Republic of the Congo, Uganda, Kenya, Rwanda, Burundi, Tanzania, Seychelles, Angola, Zambia, Malawi, Mozambique, Comoros, Zimbabwe, Namibia, Botswana, Madagascar, South Africa, Lesotho, Swaziland. Physical features include Tibesti Mountains, L. Chad, Mt. Cameroon 13,451 ft. (4,100 m), Congo Basin, Mt. Kenya 17,058 ft. (5,199 m), Mt. Kilimanjaro 19,341 ft. (5,895 m), Great Rift Valley, L. Turkana, L. Victoria, Lake Tanganyika, Lake Nyasa, Katanga Plateau, Pemba Is., Zanzibar Is., Victoria Falls, Zambezi R., Kalahari Desert, Namib Desert, Limpopo R., Orange R., Karroo, Cape of Good Hope, Niger R., Benue R., Senegal R., Congo R., Ubangi R., Atlantic Ocean, Indian Ocean, Gulf of Guinea, Gulf of Aden, Mozambique Channel)

Elevation
13,100 ft.	(4,000 m)
6,600 ft.	(2,000 m)
3,275 ft.	(1,000 m)
650 ft.	(200 m)
0 ft.	(0 m)

Below sea level

▲ Mountain peak

Scale: 0   500   1,000 miles
0   500   1,000 kilometers

278 UNIT 4

Activity Options

Interdisciplinary Links: Math/Language Arts

Explaining the Skill Students will demonstrate an understanding of the use of a scale of miles, compass rose, and other data provided on a physical map.

Applying the Skill Provide each student with a piece of string about six inches long. Tell students to measure the map scale with their piece of string. They should then use the string to measure the length of the

Block Scheduling

longest rivers shown on the map of Africa south of the Sahara in order to determine which is the longest and its approximate length in miles and kilometers. Finally, have them write a description of the river, using the compass rose to indicate the direction it flows. They should include details from the map to indicate rivers that flow into it, as well as countries, cities, and other features near the river.

Resources of Africa South of the Sahara

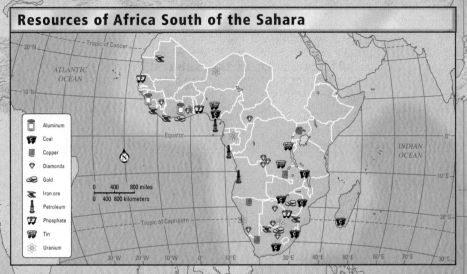

Map Legend:
- Aluminum
- Coal
- Copper
- Diamonds
- Gold
- Iron ore
- Petroleum
- Phosphate
- Tin
- Uranium

0   400   800 miles
0   400 800 kilometers

Africa South of the Sahara–U.S. Landmass and Population

LANDMASS

Africa South of the Sahara
8,389,419 square miles

Continental United States
3,165,630 square miles

POPULATION

Africa South of the Sahara
625,535,088

United States
281,421,906

👤 = 50,000,000

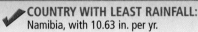

✓ **COUNTRY WITH LEAST RAINFALL:**
Namibia, with 10.63 in. per yr.

✓ **MOST DIAMONDS:**
Africa produces about 50 percent of the world's diamonds.

✓ **GOLD RESERVES:**
South Africa produces 495 tons of gold per year—about 30 percent of the world's total—and accounts for more than half of the world's known reserves.

GEOGRAPHY SKILLBUILDER: Interpreting Maps and Visuals
1. **Place** • Which country has the greatest number of mineral resources?
2. **Region** • Find Lesotho on the map on page 484. What are some issues that might arise due to its location?

INSTRUCT: Objective ❷

Mineral Resources of Africa South of the Sahara
• Which part of Africa south of the Sahara has rich deposits of oil? the central portion of the continent along the Atlantic coast

Landmass and Population
• About how many more people live in Africa south of the Sahara than live in the United States? more than twice as many

Fast Facts
• What is the highest mountain in Africa south of the Sahara? Mount Kilimanjaro

MORE ABOUT...
Diamonds
Diamonds are made of pure carbon, the same mineral that makes up coal, but what a difference! Diamonds are the hardest natural substance found on Earth. They are formed deep inside Earth and blown to the surface by volcanic eruptions. Diamonds are among the oldest substances on Earth. They may be 3 billion years old.

Fast Facts
Discuss the Fast Facts with students. Then encourage them to develop their own file of Fast Facts about Africa south of the Sahara. Good sources of information are almanacs, atlases, and encyclopedias.

GEOGRAPHY SKILLBUILDER
Answers
1. South Africa
2. South Africa completely surrounds Lesotho, making relations between the two countries important.

Country Profiles

Madagascar The nation of Madagascar comprises one large island and many small ones. It is located about 240 miles off the mainland of Africa. The large island, which is about twice the size of Arizona, is the fourth largest island in the world. Because of its isolation, many of the animals and plants of Madagascar are unique. Among them are lemurs, which are related to monkeys. The island also has tortoises, chameleons, butterflies, moths, and many types of plants that are found

nowhere else. Much of the island was originally covered in forest, but most has been cut over, leaving only remnants, mostly along the coast.

Madagascar was formerly a colony of France. It gained its independence in 1960 and today has a republican form of government. The nation has a population of about 16 million, 70 percent of whom live in poverty. The average per capita income is about $800 per year.

INSTRUCT: Objective ❸

Political Map of Africa South of the Sahara

- How does this map differ from the map on page 278? It shows capitals and major cities; the physical map shows elevations, mountains, and other physical features.

- What is the southernmost nation in Africa? South Africa

- What is the capital of Mali? Bamako

- Which countries are located on the equator? Gabon, Republic of the Congo, Democratic Republic of the Congo, Uganda, Kenya, Somalia

MORE ABOUT...

Liberia

Many European nations founded colonies in Africa. Liberia is the only one created by the United States. It began when a group of Americans decided to create a homeland for freed American slaves. They purchased land along the west coast of Africa, and in 1822, the first formerly enslaved African Americans began colonizing the land. The country was already occupied by 16 local ethnic groups, and the history of Liberia is a story of conflicts between the Americo-Liberians, who today make up 5 percent of the population, and the resident groups. In 1847, Liberia became the first African nation to declare its independence and set up a republican government.

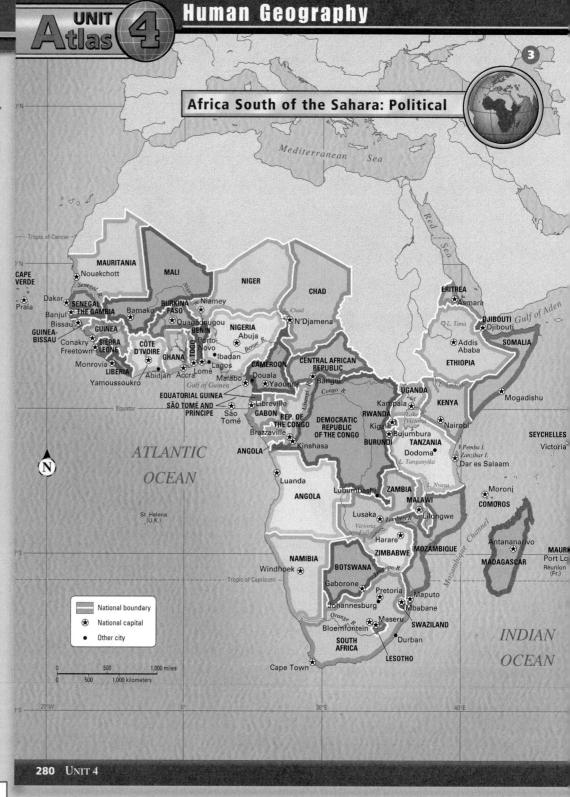

Africa South of the Sahara: Political

Legend:
- National boundary
- ⊛ National capital
- • Other city

Scale: 0 — 500 — 1,000 miles / 0 — 500 — 1,000 kilometers

Activity Options

Interdisciplinary Link: Current Events

Class Time Two class periods

Task Preparing a brief newscast about a current event in a country

Purpose To learn about current events in one African nation south of the Sahara.

Supplies Needed
- Internet resources
- Pencils or pens
- Writing paper

Activity Have students choose one of the nations shown on the map and use the Internet to do research about a current event in that country. Encourage students to consider political, environmental, population, economic, and other issues. Have students prepare a brief newscast and present it to the class.

④

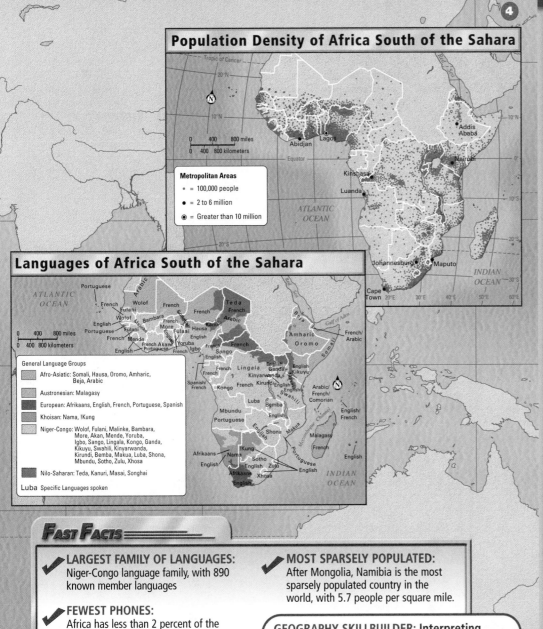

Population Density of Africa South of the Sahara

Tropic of Cancer

20°N

10°N

10°N

0   400   800 miles
0   400   800 kilometers

Abidjan   Lagos

Addis Ababá

Equator

Nairobi

Kinshasa

Metropolitan Areas

• = 100,000 people

● = 2 to 6 million

◉ = Greater than 10 million

Luanda

ATLANTIC OCEAN

10°S

20°S

Johannesburg   Maputo

INDIAN OCEAN   30°S

Cape Town   20°E   30°E   40°E   50°E   60°E

Languages of Africa South of the Sahara

ATLANTIC OCEAN

Portuguese

French   Wolof   French
Fulani
English   Wolof   Bambara   French   French   Teda   French
Portuguese   Fulani   More   French   Kanuri   Arabic
French   Mende   French Akan   Fulani   Hausa
English   Portuguese   Yoruba   English
Igbo   Sango   Amharic
French   English   Oromo   French/Arabic
French   Lingala   English   English
French   Kinyarwanda   Kikuyu   Somali
Spanish/French   Kongo   French   Kirundi   English   Arabic/French/Comorian
Luba   Bemba   Swahili
Mbundu   English   English/French
Portuguese   Shona   Makua   Malagasy
Afrikaans   Nama   English   French   English
English   IKung   Sotho   Zulu
Afrikaans   Xhosa   English   INDIAN OCEAN
English

0   400   800 miles
0   400   800 kilometers

General Language Groups

■ Afro-Asiatic: Somali, Hausa, Oromo, Amharic, Beja, Arabic

■ Austronesian: Malagasy

■ European: Afrikaans, English, French, Portuguese, Spanish

■ Khoisan: Nama, IKung

■ Niger-Congo: Wolof, Fulani, Malinke, Bambara, More, Akan, Mende, Yoruba, Igbo, Sango, Lingala, Kongo, Ganda, Kikuyu, Swahili, Kinyarwanda, Kirundi, Bemba, Makua, Luba, Shona, Mbundu, Sotho, Zulu, Xhosa

■ Nilo-Saharan: Teda, Kanuri, Masai, Songhai

Luba Specific Languages spoken

FAST FACTS

✓ **LARGEST FAMILY OF LANGUAGES:**
Niger-Congo language family, with 890 known member languages

✓ **FEWEST PHONES:**
Africa has less than 2 percent of the world's telephone lines. Most Africans have to travel two hours to find a phone. Eighty percent of the world's population has never placed a phone call. More people use the Internet in London than in all of Africa.

✓ **MOST SPARSELY POPULATED:**
After Mongolia, Namibia is the most sparsely populated country in the world, with 5.7 people per square mile.

GEOGRAPHY SKILLBUILDER: Interpreting Maps and Visuals

1. **Movement** • In which two countries is Afrikaans spoken?
2. **Place** • Name two countries that have low population densities.

Atlas **281**

INSTRUCT: Objective ④

Population of Africa South of the Sahara

• Which city has a population of more than 10 million people? Lagos

Languages of Africa South of the Sahara

• In what countries is the Khoisan language spoken? Namibia, Botswana, and parts of South Africa and Angola

Fast Facts

• How many languages make up the Niger-Congo language family? 890

MORE ABOUT...
African Languages

Many hundreds of languages are spoken in Africa. These belong to three main groups: European languages, African-Asian languages, and languages native to Africa. About 290 million people speak the African ethnic languages, and most of them live south of the Sahara. With so many languages, communication can be difficult. However, many Africans speak more than one language. In addition, certain languages, such as Swahili, Arabic, and Hausa, are spoken by large numbers of people. The most common European languages are English, French, Portuguese, and Afrikaans, a language developed by early Dutch settlers.

Fast Facts

Urge students to use atlases, almanacs, and other resources to build their Fast Facts files.

GEOGRAPHY SKILLBUILDER
Answers
1. South Africa, Namibia
2. Namibia, Botswana

Country Profiles

Ethiopia Ethiopia is one of the world's oldest countries. The Aksum Kingdom was established by A.D. 200, but tradition dates Ethiopian statehood to much earlier periods. Ethiopia is also unique in being the only African nation that was not at one time colonized, although it was occupied by Italian forces for five years, from 1936 to 1941. Some of the oldest human remains have been found in Ethiopia's Great Rift Valley. They date back about 2 million years. Ethiopians speak about 80 languages. Ethiopia is a large country, almost twice the size of Texas. Much of it is covered by a high plateau and mountains. The plateau extends over about two-thirds of the country. It has good farmland and receives about 40 inches of rain a year. However, droughts have periodically plagued Ethiopia, causing widespread starvation.

DATA FILE OBJECTIVE

Examine and compare data on Africa south of the Sahara

FOCUS & MOTIVATE

Direct students' attention to the Data File. Ask them which country in this region has the largest population. Which has the highest life expectancy? Nigeria with over 126 million people; Seychelles with an expectancy of 71 years

INSTRUCT: Objective 5

Data File

• Which country has the highest infant mortality rate? Sierra Leone

• Which has the most cars per 1,000 people? South Africa

• What is the official currency of Zambia? Kwacha

• What is the difference in the literacy rate of Uganda and Kenya? 16 percent (65 percent compared to 81 percent)

 In-depth Resources: Unit 4
• Data File Activity, p. 2

Country Flag	Country/Capital	Currency	Population (2001 estimate)	Life Expectancy (years)	Birthrate (per 1,000 pop.) (2000)
	Angola Luanda	Readjusted Kwanza	10,366,000	47	48
	Benin Porto-Novo	CFA Franc	6,591,000	50	45
	Botswana Gaborone	Pula	1,586,000	44	32
	Burkina Faso Ouagadougou	CFA Franc	12,272,000	47	47
	Burundi Bujumbura	Franc	6,224,000	47	42
	Cameroon Yaoundé	CFA Franc	15,803,000	55	37
	Cape Verde Praia	Escudo	405,000	68	37
	Central African Republic Bangui	CFA Franc	3,577,000	45	38
	Chad N'Djamena	CFA Franc	8,707,000	48	50
	Comoros Moroni	Franc	596,000	59	38
	Congo, Democratic Republic of the Kinshasa	Congolese Franc	53,625,000	49	48
	Congo, Republic of the Brazzaville	CFA Franc	2,894,000	48	40
	Côte d'Ivoire Yamoussoukro	CFA Franc	16,393,000	47	38
	Djibouti Djibouti	Djibouti Franc	461,000	48	39
	Equatorial Guinea Malabo	CFA Franc	486,000	50	41
	Eritrea Asmara	Birr	4,298,000	55	43
	Ethiopia Addis Ababa	Birr	65,892,000	46	45

Activity Options

Interdisciplinary Links: Science/Health

Class Time 20 minutes

Task Comparing data of two countries

Purpose To compare data from different countries and to draw conclusions based on the data

Supplies Needed
• Data File

Activity Have students work independently and choose any two countries listed in the Data File. Then ask them to compare the data for life expectancy, infant mortality, number of doctors, and literacy rate. Have them draw conclusions based on these comparisons. Prompt them by asking how the number of doctors might affect life expectancy and infant mortality. How might the literacy rate affect the health of people? Guide a class discussion of student conclusions.

5

DATA FILE

Infant Mortality (per 1,000 live births) (2000)	Doctors (per 100,000 pop.) (1997–1998)	Literacy Rate (percentage) (1996–1998)	Passenger Cars (per 1,000 pop.) (1991–1998)	Total Area (square miles)	Map (not to scale)
125.0	8	42	21	481,351	
93.9	6	38	6	43,483	
57.2	24	76	53	231,804	
105.3	3	22	3	105,869	
74.8	6	46	2	10,759	
77.0	7	74	7	183,591	
76.9	17	73	29	1,557	
96.7	4	44	3	240,534	
109.8	3	39	1	459,752	
77.3	7	59	18	719	
108.6	7	59	7	905,365	
108.6	25	78	10	132,047	
112.2	9	45	11	124,503	
115.0	14	62	31	8,958	
108.0	25	81	9	10,830	
81.8	3	52	2	10,830	
116.0	4	36	0.8	471,776	

MORE ABOUT...
Literacy

Only about half of all Africans can read and write. This number compares to three-fourths of the population worldwide. South of the Sahara, the literacy rate is even lower; more than half of adults are illiterate. African governments recognize the need for literacy and are building more schools, but there are many obstacles to improved literacy, such as a lack of books and trained teachers. Another obstacle is the lack of opportunities for many Africans to use the literacy they have gained. According to the United Nations Education, Scientific, and Cultural Organization (UNESCO), a successful literacy program must not only include education but also must provide opportunities that challenge people to use and develop their skills. These might include business opportunities, training in more advanced job skills, and greater responsibility in local government.

Activity Options
Multiple Learning Styles: Visual

Block Scheduling

Class Time 30 minutes

Task Creating a bar graph comparing life expectancy rates

Purpose To use information from the Data File to create a visual model

Supplies Needed
- Graph paper
- Pencil
- Ruler

Activity Point out to students that they can often use information provided on a chart to create graphs or other visual models. Explain that graphs are a visual representation of information and can make certain information easier to understand. Review bar graphs as necessary. Then have students work in pairs. They should choose six countries from Africa south of the Sahara and create a bar graph that compares the life expectancy of each. Have students meet in groups and compare their graphs.

Teacher's Edition **283**

MORE ABOUT...
Namibia

Namibia covers an area that is more than half the size of Alaska. However, it has a small population with an average of 5.7 people per square mile. Ninety percent of the population is of African descent and 7 percent is of European descent—chiefly Dutch, English, and German. Namibia's African population belongs to numerous ethnic groups. The largest of these is the Ovambo, which makes up more than half of the population.

Country Flag	Country/Capital	Currency	Population (2001 estimate)	Life Expectancy (years)	Birthrate (per 1,000 pop.) (2000)
	Gabon Libreville	CFA Franc	1,221,000	52	38
	Gambia, The Banjul	Dalasi	1,411,000	45	43
	Ghana Accra	Cedi	19,894,000	58	34
	Guinea Conakry	Franc	7,614,000	45	42
	Guinea-Bissau Bissau	CFA Franc	1,316,000	45	42
	Kenya Nairobi	Shilling	30,766,000	49	35
	Lesotho Maseru	Maloti	2,177,000	53	33
	Liberia Monrovia	Dollar	3,226,000	50	50
	Madagascar Antananarivo	Malagasy Franc	15,983,000	52	44
	Malawi Lilongwe	Kwacha	10,548,000	39	41
	Mali Bamako	CFA Franc	11,009,000	53	47
	Mauritania Nouakchott	Ouguiya	2,747,000	54	41
	Mauritius Port Louis	Rupee	1,190,000	70	17
	Mozambique Maputo	Metical	19,371,000	40	41
	Namibia Windhoek	Rand	1,798,000	46	36
	Niger Niamey	CFA Franc	10,355,000	41	54
	Nigeria Abuja	Naira	126,636,000	52	42

Activity Options

Interdisciplinary Link: Mathematics

Class Time 30 minutes

Task Finding population density of several countries

Purpose To compare the population density of various countries of Africa south of the Sahara

Supplies Needed
• Data File

Activity Explain to students that they can find the population density of a country by dividing the population by the square miles. You may wish to model the process on the chalkboard, using figures for the United States. Then ask students to work independently and choose three countries shown on the Data File. Have them use the data to determine population density. In class discussion, have students compare their results to see who has found the countries with the highest and lowest population density.

DATA FILE

Infant Mortality (per 1,000 live births) (2000)	Doctors (per 100,000 pop.) (1997–1998)	Literacy Rate (percentage) (1996–1998)	Passenger Cars (per 1,000 pop.) (1991–1998)	Total Area (square miles)	Map (not to scale)
87.0	19	63	21	103,346	
130.0	4	35	7	4,127	
56.2	6	69	5	92,100	
98.0	13	36	2	94,925	
130.0	17	37	3	13,948	
73.7	13	81	10	224,960	
84.5	5	82	3	11,720	
139.1	2	38	9	43,000	
96.3	11	65	4	226,658	
126.8	2	58	3	47,747	
122.5	5	38	3	478,764	
92.0	14	41	7	397,955	
19.4	85	84	61	790	
133.9	4	42	4	302,328	
68.3	30	81	38	318,000	
123.1	4	15	4	489,189	
77.2	19	61	5	356,669	

MORE ABOUT…
Infant Mortality

Infant mortality measures the number of children who die before age one. Some deaths occur because children are born prematurely or are too small. Other causes of infant mortality include lack of immunizations to protect against disease and inadequate health care, nutrition, and housing. Infant mortality is typically much higher in developing countries, such as many of those in Africa, and lower among more highly industrialized countries. Worldwide, the infant mortality rate is 80 deaths per 1,000 infants. Ask students to compare the number of doctors and the rate of infant mortality. What conclusions can they draw?

Activity Options

Interdisciplinary Link: Popular Culture

Class Time One class period

Task Creating a visual representation of information from the Data File

Purpose To create a drawing using Data File material for one country

Supplies Needed
- Encyclopedias, Internet access
- Pencils or pens
- Art supplies

 Block Scheduling

Activity Have students choose one of the countries and do research to learn about the culture of its people. They should limit their research to one or two topics, such as traditional dress, family structure, special foods, or festivals. Have students create a drawing depicting what they learn. They should meet in groups or as a class to display and explain their drawings.

MORE ABOUT...
AIDS

The population of African nations south of the Sahara is heavily affected by the frequency of AIDS in this region. The first known case of AIDS was in what is now the Democratic Republic of the Congo in 1959. Since then, the disease has swept around the world, but it infects the most people in Africa south of the Sahara. It has been estimated that 34.3 million people in the world have AIDS. Of these, 24.5 million are in Africa south of the Sahara. The consequences of the disease are vast. In Africa south of the Sahara, the disease has orphaned 12.1 million children. Life expectancy in the region is dropping. It has been estimated that life expectancy in the region will drop from 59 to 45 years by the year 2010. Even the economy is suffering. About 80 percent of the people dying are workers between 20 and 50 years old. The people of Botswana, Zimbabwe, Namibia, and Swaziland have suffered most from the disease.

Country Flag	Country/Capital	Currency	Population (2001 estimate)	Life Expectancy (years)	Birthrate (per 1,000 pop.) (2000)
	Rwanda Kigali	Franc	7,313,000	39	43
	São Tomé and Príncipe São Tomé	Dobra	165,000	64	43
	Senegal Dakar	CFA Franc	10,285,000	52	41
	Seychelles Victoria	Rupee	80,000	71	18
	Sierra Leone Freetown	Leone	5,427,000	45	47
	Somalia Mogadishu	Shilling	7,489,000	46	47
	South Africa, Pretoria/Cape Town/Bloemfontein	Rand	43,586,000	55	25
	Swaziland Mbabane	Lilangeni	1,104,000	38	41
	Tanzania Dar es Salaam	Shilling	36,232,000	53	42
	Togo Lomé	CFA Franc	5,153,000	49	42
	Uganda Kampala	Shilling	23,986,000	42	48
	Zambia Lusaka	Kwacha	9,770,000	37	42
	Zimbabwe Harare	Dollar	11,365,000	40	30

Activity Options

Differentiating Instruction: Less Proficient Readers

Class Time 30 minutes

Task Writing questions and answers regarding three countries

Purpose To use data to identify countries, and to find them on a map

Activity Have students work individually to write three statements and questions about three countries. Each should contain two pieces of information drawn from the Data File. For example: My capital is Lusaka, and we have about 16 cars per 1,000 people. What country am I? After students write their questions, have them meet in pairs and take turns asking and answering each other's questions. You might extend the project by having them locate each country on the political map on page 280.

5

DATA FILE

Infant Mortality (per 1,000 live births) (2000)	Doctors (per 100,000 pop.) (1997–1998)	Literacy Rate (percentage) (1996–1998)	Passenger Cars (per 1,000 pop.) (1991–1998)	Total Area (square miles)	Map (not to scale)
120.9	4	64	2	10,169	
50.8	47	73	30	372	
67.7	8	36	12	76,124	
8.5	132	84	85	178	
157.1	7	31	4	27,699	
125.8	4	24	2	246,200	
45.4	56	85	102	471,445	
107.7	15	78	29	6,705	
98.8	5	74	2	364,898	
79.7	8	55	17	21,853	
81.3	4	65	1	91,134	
109.0	7	76	16	290,585	
80.0	14	87	3	150,820	

GEOGRAPHY SKILLBUILDER: Interpreting a Chart

1. **Place** • How many more doctors does Cape Verde have than Burkina Faso?
2. **Place** • How much higher is Lesotho's literacy rate than Guinea's?

Atlas **287**

MORE ABOUT...
Small Countries of Africa

The two smallest countries of Africa south of the Sahara are Seychelles and São Tomé and Principe. Seychelles is made up of about 90 islands spread over 400,000 square miles of the Indian Ocean. The African mainland is about 1,000 miles away. The largest of the islands is Mahe. It has an area of just 59 square miles. Eighty-five percent of the people live there. São Tomé and Principe is an African nation made up of two large islands and several smaller ones. These islands lie about 200 miles west of Gabon in the Gulf of Guinea.

GEOGRAPHY SKILLBUILDER
Answers
1. 14 more doctors per 100,000 people
2. 46 percent higher, 82 percent compared with 36 percent

Activity Options
Interdisciplinary Link: History

Class Time One class period

Task Researching to learn about the names of an African country south of the Sahara

Purpose To learn how and why the names of countries have changed

Supplies Needed
- Paper
- Pencils or pens
- Encyclopedia or Internet access

Activity Point out that the names of most African nations have changed over time. Ask students to choose one country shown on the Data File and do research to learn about some of its previous names. Have them share their findings with the class.

Africa South of the Sahara: Geography and History

	OVERVIEW	COPYMASTERS	INTEGRATED TECHNOLOGY
UNIT ATLAS AND CHAPTER RESOURCES	The students will examine how geography and historical events have influenced the development of the governments, economies, and cultures of African countries south of the Sahara.	**In-depth Resources: Unit 4** • Guided Reading Worksheets, pp. 3–6 • Skillbuilder Practice, p. 9 • Unit Atlas Activities, pp. 1–2 • Geography Workshop, pp. 37–38 **Reading Study Guide** (Spanish and English), pp. 88–97 **Outline Map Activities**	Power Presentations Electronic Teacher Tools Online Lesson Planner Chapter Summaries on CD Critical Thinking Transparencies CT19
	KEY IDEAS		
SECTION 1 The Geography of Africa South of the Sahara pp. 291–295	• Africa south of the Sahara features both highlands and lowlands, as well as many rivers and lakes. • The major climate regions of Southern Africa are desert, semi-arid, tropical, and equatorial. • Africa south of the Sahara has renewable and nonrenewable resources.	**In-depth Resources: Unit 4** • Guided Reading Worksheet, p. 3 • Reteaching Activity, p. 11 **Reading Study Guide** (Spanish and English), pp. 88–89	classzone.com Chapter Summaries on CD
SECTION 2 African Cultures and Empires pp. 296–300	• The first humans, who lived in Africa millions of years ago, developed language, tools, and culture. • The Bantu were farmers who migrated throughout Southern Africa. • The development of trade networks in the region was influenced by the need for salt, the use of camels, and the interest in gold.	**In-depth Resources: Unit 4** • Guided Reading Worksheet, p. 4 • Reteaching Activity, p. 12 **Reading Study Guide** (Spanish and English), pp. 90–91	Critical Thinking Transparencies CT20 classzone.com Chapter Summaries on CD
SECTION 3 The Impact of Colonialism on African Life pp. 301–305	• The European slave trade in Africa resulted in the dissolution of family structures and communities. • Europeans colonized Africa to gain access to raw materials and natural resources. • Europeans did not value traditional African culture, and often created conflicts among ethnic groups.	**In-depth Resources: Unit 4** • Guided Reading Worksheet, p. 5 • Reteaching Activity, p. 13 **Reading Study Guide** (Spanish and English), pp. 92–93	classzone.com Chapter Summaries on CD
SECTION 4 The Road to Independence pp. 307–310	• Nationalism was the root of Africa's independence movement. • Nigeria became independent in 1960 but has struggled to survive amid political turmoil. • The South African apartheid system, which restricted the rights of non-whites, ended in 1990.	**In-depth Resources: Unit 4** • Guided Reading Worksheet, p. 6 • Reteaching Activity, p. 14 **Reading Study Guide** (Spanish and English), pp. 94–95	Map Transparencies MT23 classzone.com Chapter Summaries on CD

Audio

 CD-ROM

Copymaster

 Internet

Overhead Transparency

Pupil's Edition

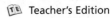 Teacher's Edition

Video

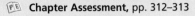
RESOURCES FOR DIFFERENTIATING INSTRUCTION

ASSESSMENT OPTIONS

Chapter Assessment, pp. 312–313

Formal Assessment
• Chapter Tests: Forms A, B, C, pp. 150–161

Test Generator

Online Test Practice

Strategies for Test Preparation

Section Assessment, p. 295

Formal Assessment
• Section Quiz, p. 146

Integrated Assessment
• Rubric for drawing a commemorative stamp

Test Generator

Test Practice Transparencies TT34

Section Assessment, p. 300

Formal Assessment
• Section Quiz, p. 147

Integrated Assessment
• Rubric for making a diorama

Test Generator

Test Practice Transparencies TT35

Section Assessment, p. 305

Formal Assessment
• Section Quiz, p. 148

Integrated Assessment
• Rubric for witing an opinion paper

Test Generator

Test Practice Transparencies TT36

Section Assessment, p. 310

Formal Assessment
• Section Quiz, p. 149

Integrated Assessment
• Rubric for designing a logo or writing a motto

Test Generator

Test Practice Transparencies TT37

Students Acquiring English/ESL

Reading Study Guide
(Spanish and English), pp. 88–97

Access for Students Acquiring English
Spanish Translations, pp. 85–94

TE Activity
• Discussing Diversity, p. 369

Less Proficient Readers

Reading Study Guide
(Spanish and English), pp. 88–97

TE Activities
• Rereading, p. 292
• Contrasting, p. 297

Gifted and Talented Students

TE Activity
• Atlantic Slave Trade, p. 302

CROSS-CURRICULAR CONNECTIONS

Literature
Mendlicott, Mary. *Tales from Africa.* New York: Larousse Kingfisher Chambers, 2000. Writers from 12 African countries retell traditional stories.

Popular Culture
MacDonald, Fiona. *Ancient African Town.* Danbury, CT: Watts, 1998. A 17th-century community based on Benin City of the Ebo Empire in Nigeria.
Prior, Jennifer. *The Games of Africa.* New York: HarperCollins, 1994. Five of the world's oldest and most exciting games from Africa.

Geography
Knight, Margy Burns. *Africa Is Not a Country.* Brookfield, CT: Millbrook, 2000. Distinctive customs of different areas.

History
Haskins, James. *African Beginnings.* New York: Lothrop, Lee, & Shepard, 1998. Geography and history reference book.
Myers, Walter Dean. *At Her Majesty's Request: An African Princess in Victorian England.* New York: Scholastic, 1999. Queen Victoria oversees the education of a rescued princess.
Worth, Richard. *Stanley and Livingstone and the Exploration of Africa in World History.* Berkeley Heights, NJ: Enslow Publishers, 2000. Traces the history of European colonialism on the African continent.

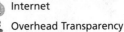
ENRICHMENT ACTIVITIES

The following activities are especially suitable for classes following block schedules.

Teacher's Edition, pp. 293, 294, 298, 299, 306

Pupil's Edition, pp. 295, 300, 305, 310
Unit Atlas, pp. 278–287

Technology: 1100, p. 311
Outline Map Activities

INTEGRATED TECHNOLOGY

Go to **classzone.com** for lesson support and activities for Chapter 10.

BLOCK SCHEDULE LESSON PLAN OPTIONS: 90-MINUTE PERIOD

DAY 1

UNIT PREVIEW, pp. 276–277
Class Time 10 minutes

• **Discussion** Discuss the Unit Introduction using the discussion prompts on TE pp. 276–277.

UNIT ATLAS, pp. 278–287
Class Time 30 minutes

• **Small Groups** Divide the class into four groups, and have each group answer the Making Connections questions for one section of the Unit Atlas: Physical Geography, Human Geography, Regional Patterns, or Data File.

SECTION 1, pp. 291–295
Class Time 50 minutes

• **Identifying Cause and Effect** Have students read Dateline. Use the questions in Focus & Motivate on TE p. 291 to guide students in a discussion about the causes and effects of desertification.
Class Time 10 minutes

• **Climate Map** Use Activity Options, Multiple Learning Styles: Visual/Kinesthetic on TE p. 294 to have students draw and illustrate a climate map of Africa south of the Sahara. When students have finished, collect and display their maps in the classroom.
Class Time 40 minutes

DAY 2

SECTION 2, pp. 296–300
Class Time 50 minutes

• **Discussion** Use the questions in Geography Skillbuilder on TE p. 297 to lead students in a discussion about the Bantu migration. Extend the discussion by asking students how the migration affected the character of Africa south of the Sahara.
Class Time 10 minutes

• **Class Encyclopedia** Have students use the encyclopedia articles they prepared in Interdisciplinary Link: Science on TE p. 298 to compile a class encyclopedia. Discuss the parts of the book that students will need to develop, such as front and back covers and a table of contents. Provide space to display the finished class encyclopedia.
Class Time 40 minutes

SECTION 3, pp. 301–305
Class Time 40 minutes

• **Peer Teaching** Assign the content under each heading in Section 3 to small groups of students. Each group is responsible for teaching the information to the class.

DAY 3

SECTION 4, pp. 307–310
Class Time 35 minutes

• **Peer Competition** Divide the class into pairs. Assign each pair one of the Terms & Names for this section. Have pairs make up five questions that can be answered with the term or name. Have groups take turns asking the class their questions.

CHAPTER 10 REVIEW AND ASSESSMENT, pp. 312–313
Class Time 55 minutes

• **Review** Have students use the charts they created for Reading Social Studies on PE p. 290 to review the causes and effects of events that shaped the history of Africa south of the Sahara.
Class Time 20 minutes

• **Assessment** Have students complete the Chapter 10 Assessment.
Class Time 35 minutes

TECHNOLOGY IN THE CLASSROOM

CREATING MAPS ON THE INTERNET

The Web site presented in this activity allows students to create their own maps by typing in the coordinates for the places they want to map and then simply clicking a button. By making maps on the Internet, students can practice their understanding of latitude and longitude as well as their ability to recognize the shapes and patterns of the places they are mapping. This activity will help them become more familiar with the shapes and locations of many African countries south of the Sahara.

ACTIVITY OUTLINE

Objective Students will create maps of African countries south of the Sahara and quiz their classmates, using the maps they have made.

Task Have students input latitude and longitude for eight African countries south of the Sahara to create maps of those countries. Have them create quizzes asking their classmates to input the coordinates and to figure out which countries they have mapped.

Class Time 2–3 class periods, depending on the number of computers and connection speed

DIRECTIONS

1. Ask a few students to point out the Sahara on a class wall map. Make sure students understand what is meant by Africa south of the Sahara.

2. Demonstrate how to create a map of the entire African continent at the **classzone.com** Web site. To do this, type in Africa's northernmost and southernmost latitudes (40° North, 36° South) and its easternmost and westernmost longitudes (56° East,19° West). Use negative numbers for latitudes south of the equator and longitudes west of the prime meridian. Then scroll to the bottom of the page and click "create map."

3. Divide the class into small groups, and have them create quizzes that will test their classmates' ability to recognize the countries of Africa south of the Sahara (or, optionally, the entire African continent). They should first choose eight countries in this region (fewer, if you have less time) and

use a world map or atlas to determine those countries' latitudes and longitudes. Then have students type the coordinates into the input form on the Web site and create the maps. If you have only one computer, have groups take turns and map only two or three countries.

4. Have students write the coordinates on a blank piece of paper and the countries on another page. Ask them to trade coordinate pages with another group.

5. Then ask the groups to take each other's quizzes, using the input form to create the maps. Ask them to refer to a map of Africa to figure out which countries they have mapped. They should write down the names of those countries. Ask them to double check their answers with the group that created the quiz.

CHAPTER 10 OBJECTIVE

Students will examine how geography and historical events—from antiquity to the slave trade, from colonialism to independence—have influenced the development of the governments, economies, and cultures of African countries south of the Sahara.

FOCUS ON VISUALS

Interpreting the Photograph Point out to students that there are many different styles of village architecture in Africa. Ask them to read the caption to determine what these houses are made of. Then ask: What do the building materials suggest about the climate and geography of the area?

Possible Response The materials—stone, mud, and thatch—suggest that the climate is dry and that not many trees grow in the area.

Extension Ask students to imagine what it would be like to live in a small village. Have them draw up some rules and regulations that might be important in such a community.

CRITICAL THINKING ACTIVITY

Hypothesizing Ask students why these dwellings might have been built in the cliffs. What advantages and disadvantages might their inhabitants have? Then ask students what kinds of dwellings people might build in the desert, rain forest, and mountain regions of Africa.

Class Time 10 minutes

SECTION 1 The Geography of Africa South of the Sahara

SECTION 2 African Cultures and Empires

SECTION 3 The Impact of Colonialism on African Life

SECTION 4 The Road to Independence

AFRICA SOUTH
OF THE SAHARA

288

Recommended Resources

BOOKS FOR THE TEACHER

Encyclopedia of African Peoples. New York: Facts on File, 2000. One thousand ethnic groups in Africa. Falola, Toyin, ed. *Africa. Volume 1, African History Before 1885*. Durham, NC: Carolina Academic Press, 2000. Kingdoms, civilizations, and the slave trade.

Stewart, John. *African States and Rulers*. Jefferson, NC: McFarland & Co., 1999. Political history of Africa.

VIDEO

Ancient Africa. Wynnewood, PA: Schlessinger Media, 1998. Great Zimbabwe in Southern Africa and the Swahili civilization in East Africa.

SOFTWARE

Microsoft Encarta Africana. Redmond, WA: Microsoft Corp., 1999. A comprehensive multimedia encyclopedia.

INTERNET

For more information about Africa south of the Sahara, visit **classzone.com**.

Who owns a country?

FOCUS ON GEOGRAPHY

Place • This 1892 drawing of a British imperialist illustrates the United Kingdom's claim on Africa. In the late 1800s, many European nations wanted to control a piece of the continent. By the early 1900s, all but two African nations were colonized by European powers. What did Africans think about this? Who owned Africa: the Africans or the European colonizers?

What do you think?

◆ Why do you think the artist drew the British man with his feet planted on Egypt and South Africa?

◆ What are the benefits and disadvantages of being a colony?

Place Most Africans live in villages, not in cities. The cliffside dwellings of the Tellem tribe are built above a Banani village in Mali.

289

FOCUS ON GEOGRAPHY

Objectives

- To locate major landforms and regions of Africa south of the Sahara
- To identify the main causes of the Atlantic slave trade
- To describe some of Africa's efforts to gain independence

What Do You Think?

1. Guide students to think about how the British regarded Africa. Lead a discussion about how the man's stance in the cartoon is both confident and arrogant.

2. Lead students to consider benefits such as military protection, and disadvantages such as lack of political power and loss of culture.

Who owns a country?

Have students study the cartoon and make observations about the man's appearance. Then ask them about the significance and purpose of the string that he has in his hands. Ask students why European nations would want a piece of Africa, considering the distance between Europe and Africa.

MAKING GEOGRAPHIC CONNECTIONS

Remind students that before the United States was a country, Great Britain controlled the original 13 colonies. Because they lived and worked in North America, the colonists believed that they should have a voice in their government. The British, on the other hand, needed the raw materials of the colonies and insisted on ownership and control. One major difference between the Americans and Africans, however, was that the Africans had lived in Africa for thousands of years. They did not begin as willing colonists who later sought to attain their independence.

Implementing the National Geography Standards

Standard 16 Discuss the relationship between a country's standard of living and its accessibility to resources

Objective To design a diagram depicting the relationship between standard of living and accessibility to resources

Class Time 30 minutes

Task Have each student design a diagram that explains the direct relationship between a country's standard of living and its accessibility to resources. It should illustrate such resources as foodstuffs, energy supplies, and materials from which consumer goods are manufactured.

Evaluation The diagram should show that easy access to resources usually means a higher standard of living and that the opposite usually means a lower standard of living.

BEFORE YOU READ
What Do You Know?

Have students take turns stating what they know about Africa. Encourage them to think about its geography, climate, wildlife, political systems, art, and culture. Ask students if they have heard of apartheid, and discuss what it means. Then point out that this chapter is specifically about Africa south of the Sahara. Ask students to share what they know about the Sahara and its location within Africa.

What Do You Want to Know?

Have each student make a list of what he or she would like to know about Africa, then have them compare their lists in class.

READ AND TAKE NOTES

Reading Strategy: Analyzing Causes and Effects Discuss the chart with students. Point out the processes identified in the chart and read them aloud. Explain that each process has a cause that explains why it occurred, and an effect that states what resulted from that process. Tell students to look for information about each process as they read and record facts about the causes and effects of each.

 In-depth Resources: Unit 4
• Guided Reading Worksheets, pp. 3–6

BEFORE YOU READ

▶▶ What Do You Know?

Africa south of the Sahara is a land rich in natural resources. Despite this, many countries in this part of Africa do not have strong economies. What do you know of Africa's early history? How did Europeans affect the development of this region? Reflect on what you have learned in other classes, what you have read, and what you have seen in movies or on television about the countries in Africa south of the Sahara.

▶▶ What Do You Want to Know?

Decide what you know about Africa south of the Sahara. In your notebook, record what you hope to learn from this chapter.

Place • Baule gold masks sometimes represent the face of an enemy killed in battle.

READ AND TAKE NOTES

Reading Strategy: Analyzing Causes and Effects
As you read about history, it is important to understand not only historical events, but also why the events happened (causes) and what resulted from the events (effects). Use the chart below to record the causes and effects of processes that shaped the history of Africa south of the Sahara.

• Copy the chart into your notebook.
• As you read, look for information about the geographic and human processes listed on the chart.
• Record the causes and effects of each process.

Culture • Traditional dances in Zambia are used for tribal ceremonies and entertainment. ▲

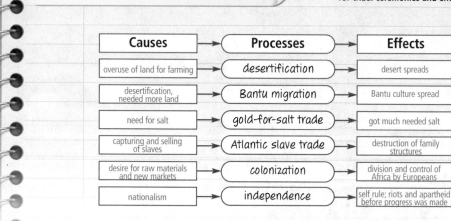

Causes	Processes	Effects
overuse of land for farming	desertification	desert spreads
desertification, needed more land	Bantu migration	Bantu culture spread
need for salt	gold-for-salt trade	got much needed salt
capturing and selling of slaves	Atlantic slave trade	destruction of family structures
desire for raw materials and new markets	colonization	division and control of Africa by Europeans
nationalism	independence	self rule; riots and apartheid before progress was made

Teaching Strategy

Reading the Chapter This chapter focuses on physical geography; the development of kingdoms, empires, and trade; colonization; and the struggle for independence in Africa south of the Sahara. Encourage students to use the visuals in each section to help them understand how the region's history and geography are reflected in daily life.

Integrated Assessment The Chapter Assessment on page 313 describes several activities that may be used for integrated assessment. You may wish to have students work on these activities during the course of the chapter and then present them at the end.

The Geography of Africa South of the Sahara

TERMS & NAMES

plateau
Great Rift Valley
Sahel
desertification
drought
savanna
nonrenewable resource
renewable resource

MAIN IDEA

Africa south of the Sahara is a region with dramatically different landforms and climates. This provides for a variety of natural resources.

WHY IT MATTERS NOW

Tourists come from all over the world to explore this region's natural landscapes.

SECTION OBJECTIVES

1. To identify landforms south of the Sahara
2. To describe the waterways of the region
3. To describe the four major climate regions
4. To identify nonrenewable and renewable resources

SKILLBUILDER
• Interpreting a Chart, p. 294

CRITICAL THINKING
• Comparing, p. 292
• Forming and Supporting Opinions, p. 294

FOCUS & MOTIVATE
WARM-UP

Identifying Cause and Effect Have students read <u>Dateline</u> and discuss these questions.

1. What do you think causes desertification? Are human or natural causes more to blame? Why?
2. How do you think the spread of the desert has affected families and villages in the region?

INSTRUCT: Objective ❶

The African Continent/Landforms of Africa South of the Sahara

• How did Africa become a continent? It was left after other continents broke away from Pangaea.
• What are Africa's two major land types? Where are they located? lowlands in the north and west, highlands in the south and east
• What is the Great Rift Valley? a long series of broad, steep-walled valleys

 In-depth Resources: Unit 4
• Guided Reading Worksheet, p. 3

 Reading Study Guide
(Spanish and English), pp. 88–89

DATELINE ⟨EXTRA⟩

BAMAKO, MALI, MARCH 8, 2000

Families in Mali are watching in despair as their farmland turns to sand. This problem—called desertification—is affecting many families in Africa. Experts have come to Mali for a United Nations–sponsored meeting to decide what can be done. In the past, efforts have focused on grand plans, such as planting thousands of trees to stop the advancing desert. When there was no money to water the trees, they died. Soon, the desert marched on.

Today's plans are more modest. One idea is to convince villagers to collect firewood from far away, leaving trees near

Human-Environment Interaction • This brushwood fence is an attempt to stabilize sand dunes and fight against the advance of the desert. ▲

the sand in place. Another idea is to change how people farm so that soil doesn't blow away. In these small ways, experts hope they can stop desertification.

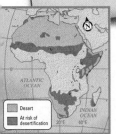

Desert
At risk of desertification

ATLANTIC OCEAN
INDIAN OCEAN
20° E   40° E

Region • More than half of Africa is desert or dry land. ▲

The African Continent ❶

The natural changes in Africa's lands, such as desertification, affect its people. Africa is roughly three times the size of the United States. About 225 million years ago, Africa was the center of Earth's only continent, called Pangaea (pan·JEE·uh). Pangaea began to break up into separate continents that drifted apart over many millions of years. The piece that became Africa stayed where it was. Africa's shape has changed very little over time.

Africa South of the Sahara: Geography and History **291**

Program Resources

 In-depth Resources: Unit 4
• Guided Reading Worksheet, p. 3
• Reteaching Activity, p. 11

 Reading Study Guide
(Spanish and English), pp. 88–89

 Formal Assessment
• Section Quiz, p. 146

 Integrated Assessment
• Rubric for drawing a commemorative stamp

 Outline Map Activities

 Access for Students Acquiring English
• Guided Reading Worksheet, p. 85

 Technology Resources
classzone.com

TEST-TAKING RESOURCES

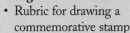 Strategies for Test Preparation
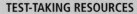 Test Practice Transparencies
Online Test Practice

CRITICAL THINKING ACTIVITY

Comparing Review the landforms and waterways described in the chapter and ask students to compare these with the landforms and waterways of the United States. You might draw a Venn diagram on the chalkboard and record students' responses in the appropriate areas of the diagram.

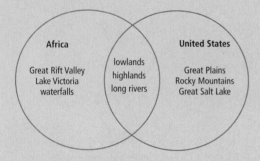

Africa
Great Rift Valley
Lake Victoria
waterfalls

lowlands
highlands
long rivers

United States
Great Plains
Rocky Mountains
Great Salt Lake

Class Time 15 minutes

MORE ABOUT...
Mount Kilimanjaro

Mount Kilimanjaro is an extinct volcano that has two peaks. It lies about 200 miles south of the equator on Tanzania's northern boundary. At 19,340 feet, Kibo is the highest point on the African continent. Year-round, this peak is covered with snow and ice almost 200 feet deep. The other peak, Mawenzi, has no glaciers. In fact, farmers grow coffee on its lower slopes.

Landforms of Africa South of the Sahara ❶

Africa has two major land types: lowlands and highlands. Locate the two regions on the Unit Atlas map on page 278. The lowlands are in the north and west, and the highlands are in the south and east. Several peaks rise out of the highlands of Kenya and Tanzania. The highest is Mount Kilimanjaro. The name *Kilimanjaro* comes from the Swahili (swah·HEE·lee) phrase *kilima njaro*, which means "shining mountain." From the sweltering rain forest below, Kilimanjaro looks as though it is shining in the sun. That's because its peak is snowcapped all year even though Kilimanjaro sits almost on the Equator.

Plateaus Look again at the Unit Atlas map on page 278. Most of Africa south of the Sahara—both highlands and lowlands—lies on a high plateau. A **plateau** is a raised area of relatively level land. The African plateau rises from coastal plains along much of the north and west coastlines. Steep cliffs line much of the southern and eastern coasts, rising sharply from the Atlantic and Indian oceans. The east side of the plateau is higher than the west, at about 5,000 feet above sea level. The western plateau averages about 1,500 feet above sea level.

Region • The Congo Basin is drained by the 2,900-mile-long Congo River (also called the Zaire River). ▼

Place • Mount Kenya, at 17,058 feet, is the second highest mountain in Africa. It is an extinct volcano. ▼

Region • The Great Rift Valley is nearly 4,000 miles long. It is 9,850 feet below sea level at its deepest point.

Activity Options

Differentiating Instruction: Less Proficient Readers

Rereading Students may have trouble visualizing the location of highlands, lowlands, and plateaus in Africa. Refer students to the map of Africa on page 278 and point out where these regions are located. Then have students reread page 292 and complete the following chart by filling in details about the geography of Africa south of the Sahara.

Highlands	Lowlands	Plateaus
in south and east peaks rise out of highlands of Kenya and Tanzania lie on high plateau	in north and west lie on high plateau	raised area of relatively low land east side of plateau higher than west

Rifts The tectonic plates on which Africa sits have been slowly pulling apart for 50 million years. The separation of the plates has been forming a series of broad, steep-walled valleys called rifts. The rifts make up the **Great Rift Valley,** which stretches from the Red Sea to Mozambique. Locate the valley on the Unit Atlas map on page 278. The Great Rift Valley will become larger and larger as East Africa pulls away from the rest of the continent. Eventually, East Africa may become an island. The island of Madagascar was formed in this way. Look again at the map on page 278 to find where Madagascar fit before it broke away.

Waterways of Africa South of the Sahara ❷

Reading
Social Studies

A. Summarizing What are some benefits provided by Africa's lakes and rivers?

Reading Social Studies
A. Possible Answer
by forming rifts and islands

Parts of the Great Rift Valley have filled with water to form huge lakes, such as Lake Tanganyika. Africa's largest lake, Lake Victoria, is pictured at the bottom of this page. It lies in a shallow basin between two rift valleys on the borders of Uganda, Kenya, and Tanzania. Lakes and rivers provide fresh water and fish. However, waterfalls and rapids make boat travel difficult.

Rivers Many of Africa's rivers have exceptional features. The Nile River, flowing northward out of the mountains of central Africa, is the world's longest river. The Okavango River crosses Angola, Namibia, and Botswana before emptying into marshes north of the Kalahari Desert. The Zambezi River features many powerful waterfalls, including Victoria Falls. The mist from these falls can be seen 25 miles away.

Place • Lake Victoria is the second largest freshwater lake in the world. It is the major source of the Nile River. ▼

Africa South of the Sahara: Geography and History **293**

INSTRUCT: Objective ❷

Waterways of Africa South of the Sahara

- What is Africa's largest lake? Lake Victoria
- What is unique about the Nile River? It is the world's longest river.
- What is the Okavango River's destination, and what happens to it there? the Kalahari Desert; it empties into marshes
- What famous waterfall is located on the Zambezi River? Victoria Falls

FOCUS ON VISUALS

Interpreting the Photograph Tell students that the Great Rift Valley is so big that astronauts can see it from the moon. Discuss how they think the Grand Canyon in Arizona compares with the Great Rift Valley. Then ask them if they think these two landforms were made the same way.

Possible Responses The Grand Canyon is much smaller than the Great Rift Valley. The Grand Canyon was formed as the Colorado River cut through layers of rock. The Great Rift Valley was formed when two continental plates pulled apart over the course of millions of years.

Extension Have students draw a scale model of the Great Rift Valley on acetate, then place it over a map of the continental United States drawn at the same scale in order to see how big the rift is.

Activity Options

Interdisciplinary Link: Language Arts

Block Scheduling

Class Time 30 minutes

Task Writing a poem about the Okavango River

Purpose To identify the course that the river follows and its final destination

Supplies Needed
- Maps of Africa showing the Okavango River
- Writing paper
- Pencils or pens

Activity Invite students to write poems that describe the Okavango River from its point of origin to its destination north of the Kalahari Desert. Encourage them to refer to maps to gain specific information about towns and geographic landforms along the way. Have them end their poems with a description of how the river eventually empties into marshes.

Africa's Deserts			
Desert	Area (sq. mi)	High Temp.	Annual Rainfall
Sahara	3,320,000	136°F	1" to 5"
Kalahari	360,000	115°F	<5" south; more northeast
Namib	52,000	over 100°F	0.5" to 2"

SKILLBUILDER: Reading a Chart
1. **Place** • Which desert is the largest?
2. **Place** • Which desert is the hottest?

INSTRUCT: Objective ③

Many Climates

- What are the major climate regions of Southern Africa? desert, semiarid, tropical, and equatorial

- What are the causes of desertification? lack of rain, overgrazing, and overuse for farming

- What are savannas, and where are they found? flat grasslands with scattered trees and shrubs; in both semiarid and tropical areas

- What is the climate of the equatorial region? tropical, with high temperatures year-round and rainfall of 50 to 60 inches per year

Citizenship
IN ACTION

A number of human rights organizations are working to alleviate the suffering in Africa. The United Nations, the Red Cross, and the Peace Corps are just a few of the many groups working to help African countries solve problems including hunger, epidemics, and violence.

CRITICAL THINKING ACTIVITY

Forming and Supporting Opinions Tell students that relatively few people live in the desert regions of Africa. Discuss some reasons this might be so. Ask them to form an opinion about life in the deserts and state at least two facts that would support that opinion.

Class Time 10 minutes

Citizenship
IN ACTION

Helping the Hungry Since 1977, a global volunteer organization called the Hunger Project has been working to end hunger in developing nations. In Africa, where poverty and hunger are widespread, the Hunger Project is sponsoring the African Woman Food Farmer Initiative.

So far, the program has loaned money to more than 14,000 women farmers like this one, in eight countries. The initiative has also provided health, nutrition, and literacy training for 9,000 more women in agriculture.

Many Climates ③

Four major climatic regions of Africa south of the Sahara are desert (arid), semiarid, tropical, and equatorial. The different temperatures and amounts of rainfall affect which plants and animals live in each region.

Desert and Semiarid Regions Desert climates are found in the Sahara to the north and the Namib (NAH•mihb) and Kalahari to the south. These areas have little rain, high temperatures, and few plants and animals. Around the desert areas are semiarid regions that also have high temperatures but have more rainfall than the deserts.

The **Sahel** (suh•HAYL) is a semiarid region south of the Sahara. This area is experiencing **desertification**—a process by which a desert spreads. **Drought,** or the lack of rain, is one cause of desertification. The lack of rain causes fewer plants to grow. Without plants, soil blows away, leaving a dry, barren landscape. Other causes are overgrazing and overuse of the land for farming. People in Africa and around the world are trying to stop this process because a lack of enough arable land contributes to the widespread hunger in many African countries.

Tropical and Equatorial Regions The tropical climate extends from the semiarid areas toward the Equator. There is a rainy season of up to six months, and the rest of the year is dry.

Savannas, found in both semiarid and tropical areas, are flat grasslands with scattered trees and shrubs. More than 4.5 million square miles of Africa are savannas. Many African animals, including lions, elephants, giraffes, and zebras, live on these grasslands.

The equatorial region has two rainy seasons and two brief dry seasons each year. Located at the Equator, this climate has high temperatures year-round and annual rainfall of 50 to 60 inches.

Skillbuilder Answers
1. Sahara
2. Sahara

Reading Social Studies

B. Analyzing Issues How does the great area of desert and semiarid land impact the lives of many Africans?

Reading Social Studies B. Possible Answer Because farming and grazing are difficult, there is a threat of widespread hunger.

Activity Options

Multiple Learning Styles: Visual/Kinesthetic

Class Time One class period
Task Creating a climate map for Africa south of the Sahara
Purpose To locate the different climate regions in relation to landforms and countries

Supplies Needed
- Outline map of Africa south of the Sahara
- Colored pencils

ⓑ Block Scheduling

Activity Review the locations and characteristics of the four climate regions. Then have students draw and label these climate regions on their maps. Next, have them write a brief description of each region. Encourage them to illustrate their maps with details from the text.

Rain forests with trees as tall as 195 feet grow here. Many animals, including the chimpanzee, gorilla, hippopotamus, and African gray parrot, live in the rain forest.

Resources of Africa South of the Sahara ④

Africa is rich in mineral resources, such as gold and diamonds, that form over hundreds of millions of years. Other plentiful minerals are copper, tin, chrome, nickel, and iron ore. **Nonrenewable resources,** such as copper and diamonds, cannot be replaced or can be replaced only over millions of years.

Renewable resources can be used and replaced over a relatively short time period. The renewable resources of this region include trees used to make wood products, cocoa beans, cashew nuts, peanuts, vanilla beans, coffee, bananas, rubber, sugar, and tea. Africa's natural wildlife and historic sites are important resources that draw tourists from all over the world.

The Fish That Did Not Die In 1938, off the coast of South Africa, some fishermen caught something surprising. The blue fish in their net was 5 feet long, weighed about 127 pounds, and had several rows of small, pointed teeth. The fishermen had never seen anything like it. Nor, according to scientists, should they have.

The fish, a coelacanth (see•luh•KANTH), was thought to have been extinct for 70 million years. Now here was proof that it wasn't. However, they aren't plentiful. It wasn't until 1952 that a second live coelacanth was found. Only a few hundred exist today.

SECTION ① ASSESSMENT

Terms & Names

1. Identify:
(a) plateau (b) Great Rift Valley (c) Sahel (d) desertification
(e) drought (f) savanna (g) nonrenewable resource (h) renewable resource

Taking Notes

2. Use a chart like this one to list some of this region's renewable and non-renewable resources.

Renewable Resources	Nonrenewable Resources

Main Ideas

3. (a) Describe the landforms and waterways of Africa.

(b) Describe four climatic regions of Africa south of the Sahara.

(c) Explain the differences between renewable and nonrenewable resources. Give examples of each.

Critical Thinking

4. **Using Maps**
Look at the map of Africa on page 280. Has the Great Rift Valley affected modern political boundaries in Africa? Explain your answer.

Think About
• the location of the Great Rift Valley
• current national borders in Africa

ACTIVITY -OPTION- Draw a **commemorative stamp** honoring a climatic region or landform in Africa south of the Sahara.

INSTRUCT: Objective ④

Resources of Africa South of the Sahara

• What is the difference between renewable and nonrenewable resources? Renewable ones can be used and replaced over a short period of time; nonrenewable resources cannot.

• What are some renewable resources in Southern Africa? trees, cocoa beans, cashews, peanuts, bananas

Local African fishermen call the fish *Kombessa*. The four lobed fins on the bottom of the coelacanth are like small legs, and the fish swims with a sort of walking motion.

ASSESS & RETEACH

Reading Social Studies Have students fill in the causes and effects of desertification on the chart on page 290.

 Formal Assessment
• Section Quiz, p. 146

RETEACHING ACTIVITY

Have pairs of students study a map of Africa south of the Sahara. Instruct them to take turns identifying major landforms, waterways, and climate regions.

 In-depth Resources: Unit 4
• Reteaching Activity, p. 11

Access for Students Acquiring English
• Reteaching Activity, p. 91

Section ① Assessment

1. Terms & Names
a. plateau, p. 292
b. Great Rift Valley, p. 293
c. Sahel, p. 294
d. desertification, p. 294
e. drought, p. 294
f. savanna, p. 294
g. nonrenewable resource, p. 295
h. renewable resource, p. 295

2. Taking Notes

Renewable Resources	Nonrenewable Resources
cocoa beans, peanuts, coffee, bananas, trees, cashew nuts, rubber, vanilla, sugar, tea	gold, diamonds, copper

3. Main Ideas
a. highlands; lowlands; high plateau; Great Rift Valley; lakes, rivers, waterfalls
b. desert, semiarid, tropical, equatorial
c. Renewable resources can be replaced relatively quickly; nonrenewable resources cannot.

4. Critical Thinking
Yes; the Great Rift Valley forms western edge of Ethiopia, Kenya, Uganda, Tanzania.

ACTIVITY OPTION

 Integrated Assessment
• Rubric for drawing a commemorative stamp

African Cultures and Empires

TERMS & NAMES
paleontologist
Bantu migration
Mansa Musa

SECTION OBJECTIVES

1. To relate information about early humans in Africa

2. To describe and analyze the Bantu migration

3. To explain how salt, camels, and gold influenced the development of trade networks in the region

4. To describe the rise and decline of the Mali Empire

SKILLBUILDER
• Interpreting a Map, p. 297

CRITICAL THINKING
• Recognizing Important Details, p. 299

FOCUS & MOTIVATE
WARM-UP

Hypothesizing Have students read <u>Dateline</u> and discuss the following questions.

1. Why might the Bantu have left their homelands in the north and migrated south?

2. Why did one group of Africans develop as hunters and another develop as farmers?

INSTRUCT: Objective ❶

The First Humans

• When did the first humans live in Africa?
millions of years ago

• What is known about the early humans in Africa? They were the first to develop language, tools, and culture.

 In-depth Resources: Unit 4
• Guided Reading Worksheet, p. 4

 Reading Study Guide
(Spanish and English), pp. 90–91

MAIN IDEA	WHY IT MATTERS NOW
Africa south of the Sahara has a rich and significant history.	Many scientists think Africa south of the Sahara is the cradle of the human race. The oldest fossil remains of humans have come from this region.

DATELINE

SOUTHERN AFRICA, A.D. 500—There is a group of newcomers in the area. They come from the north and speak languages unlike ours. Instead of hunting in the forests as we do, they raise animals for food. They plant grain in fields near their settlement.

The newcomers, who call themselves "Bantu," have sharp spears and blades made of a cold, dark metal. They use a short, sharp metal tool for digging—much better than our stone and wood tools. Many of our people have begun to trade goods for the newcomers' fine tools and pottery.

Movement • This woman is one of many Bantu who have settled in Southern Africa. ▲

The First Humans ❶

The roots of the Bantus can be traced back thousands of years. Fossil evidence shows that the first known humans lived in Africa several million years ago. **Paleontologists,** or scientists who study fossils, have discovered human remains in Kenya, South Africa, and other African nations. Fossilized human footprints 3.6 million years old have been found in Tanzania. It is now known that humans in Africa were the first to develop language, tools, and culture. Then, over tens of thousands of years, they migrated to other continents.

Program Resources

 In-depth Resources: Unit 4
• Guided Reading Worksheet, p. 4
• Reteaching Activity, p. 12

 Reading Study Guide
(Spanish and English), pp. 90–91

 Formal Assessment
• Section Quiz, p. 147

 Integrated Assessment
• Rubric for making a diorama

 Outline Map Activities

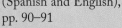 **Access for Students Acquiring English**
• Guided Reading Worksheet, p. 86

Technology Resources
classzone.com

TEST-TAKING RESOURCES
🔧 Strategies for Test Preparation
🔧 Test Practice Transparencies
💡 Online Test Practice

Early African Farmers ❷

The first humans lived in small groups. For food, they collected berries, plants, and nuts and hunted wild animals. As plants and animals became scarce in one place, the people moved on. During this time, a group known as Bantu lived in what is now Cameroon. Around 5,000 years ago, the Bantu became farmers instead of hunter-gatherers. They learned to grow grain and herd cattle, sheep, and other animals. Later, they learned how to work with iron to make tools and weapons.

On the Move The Bantu began to move to other parts of Africa around 1000 B.C. Perhaps the desert was spreading, or they needed more land for a growing population. For about 2,000 years, the Bantu gradually spread across the continent. Their great movement is called the **Bantu migration.** In their new homes, they learned to grow and use different plants. In some places, the native hunter-gatherers lived in separate villages or moved away, as did the Sans, or Bushmen. In other places, the Bantu and the local people, such as the Pygmies, intermarried. Over time, the Bantu culture became widespread throughout Africa. Today, many Africans speak Swahili, Zulu, and other Bantu languages.

Culture • These headdresses represent Tyi Wara—an antelope spirit who, according to Bantu mythology, taught the first people how to grow crops. ▲

**Reading Social Studies
A. Possible Answer**

It spread agriculture and new technology across Africa and led to the development of common languages for Africans.

**Reading
Social Studies**

A. Recognizing Effects How did the Bantu migration influence the character of Africa south of the Sahara?

GEOGRAPHY SKILLBUILDER:
Interpreting a Map

1. **Place** • Use the Unit Atlas map on page 280 and this map to name two countries in which the Bantu people lived c. 500 B.C.
2. **Region** • About how many miles from east to west did the area of the Bantu migration measure after A.D. 1000?

2,000 Years of Bantu Migration

Original Bantu Area

Equator

Congo River

Lake Victoria

INDIAN OCEAN

ATLANTIC OCEAN

N

- Bantu migration, c. 500 B.C.
- Bantu migration, date unknown (between 500 B.C. and A.D. 500)
- Bantu migration, after A.D. 500
- Bantu migration, after A.D. 1000

Lake Malawi

Zambezi River

Tropic of Capricorn

0   500   1,000 miles
0   500   1,000 kilometers

20°W   0°   40°E   60°

Geography Skillbuilder Answers

1. Democratic Republic of the Congo and Zambia

2. about 2,000 miles

Africa South of the Sahara: Geography and History **297**

INSTRUCT: Objective ❷
Early African Farmers

- How were the Bantu different from earlier groups of people in Africa? They were farmers instead of hunter-gatherers.

- Why do people think the Bantu migrated south? The desert was spreading; the population was growing.

- What happened to the Bantu culture as a result of this migration? It became widespread throughout Africa.

FOCUS ON VISUALS

Interpreting the Photograph Ask students if this headdress reminds them of other ceremonial headdresses and masks they have seen, and if they know of any holiday or ceremony in the United States that involves wearing costumes and masks. Ask them who they think might wear the headdress shown in the photograph.

Possible Responses Native Americans in North and South America also made and wore masks. So did various peoples of Europe and Asia. In the United States, costumes and masks are worn on Halloween and during Mardi Gras. A priest, a king, or a dancer might wear the headdress shown in the photograph.

Extension Have students make a mask or a headdress that symbolizes an important event in their lives.

Activity Options

Differentiating Instruction: Less Proficient Readers

Contrasting Some students may be confused about how the Bantu people differed from earlier humans in Africa. Help them construct a spider map for each group, then have students use the two maps to contrast the defining characteristics of the groups.

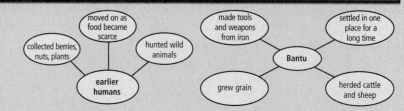

moved on as food became scarce

collected berries, nuts, plants

hunted wild animals

earlier humans

made tools and weapons from iron

settled in one place for a long time

Bantu

grew grain

herded cattle and sheep

Teacher's Edition **297**

INSTRUCT: Objective ❸

Trade Networks/An Empire Built by Trade

- What did people in Southern Africa trade for the salt they needed? gold, slaves, ivory, cola nuts

- How did camels change the nature of trade in Africa? Camels were well-equipped for travel across the desert, so traders could carry goods across the desert to North Africa.

- Why did people want to trade in North Africa? They could trade for goods from Europe and Asia.

- What two factors made Ghana such a wealthy empire? its location along the trade routes; the gold nuggets traders paid in tax

MORE ABOUT...
Camels

A large, thirsty camel can drink up to 53 gallons of water. Camels can go several months without water because they retain most of the water they carry. Unlike most animals that sweat to cool their bodies, camels sweat very little. The body temperature of camels can rise as much as 11 degrees on a hot day, then cool down at night. To fight off heat, they often press up against each other in groups, because their body temperatures may be lower than the air temperature.

Trade Networks ❸

Eventually, the Bantu built permanent villages. Trade routes began to develop between these communities across Africa.

The Salt Trade Salt was as precious to ancient Africans as gold and diamonds. People needed salt each day to stay alive. They also used it to preserve food. However, most of Africa south of the Sahara had no salt deposits. The closest source was in the Sahara, where giant salt slabs, some as heavy as 200 pounds, were mined. A vast trade network developed between the salt mines and the area south of the Sahara. To get salt, people in Southern Africa traded gold, slaves, ivory, and cola nuts.

Camels and Caravans African trade expanded even further when the Arabian camel was introduced to Africa in the A.D. 600s. Camels are well adapted for long treks across the desert. Using camels, salt traders could carry goods from the savannas and forests across the desert to Northern Africa. There they traded for goods from Europe and Asia, such as glass from Italy or cotton and spices from India. The desert trade was profitable but risky. Robbers lived in the desert. For protection, traders traveled together in caravans.

BACKGROUND

Salt cakes were used as currency in ancient Ethiopia.

Place •
Adapted to their desert environment, camels can drink up to 20 gallons of water in 10 minutes and store it in their bloodstream. ▼

Why Camels Are Well Adapted to Desert Travel

A double row of **long, curly eyelashes** keep sand out of eyes, and **bushy eyebrows** shield eyes from the sun.

Fur-lined ears filter out sand.

The fat-filled hump provides many days' worth of energy.

A large mouth, 34 sharp teeth, and a **tough mouth lining** enable the camel to eat thorn bushes.

Long, thin legs have powerful muscles; a camel can walk 25 miles in a day and carry 330 pounds of cargo.

Broad, flat feet don't sink into the sand.

Activity Options

Interdisciplinary Link: Science

Class Time 30 minutes

Task Writing an illustrated encyclopedia entry for an imaginary animal that would be well-suited to living in the desert

Purpose To understand ways in which animals adapt to their environments

Supplies Needed
- Drawing paper
- Writing paper
- Crayons and pencils

🅱 Block Scheduling

Activity Discuss how animals adapt to their environments, using polar bears, salamanders, and camels as examples. Then ask students to use their imaginations to draw pictures of animals that would be well-suited to hot desert conditions. After they have completed their pictures, have students write short encyclopedia articles that explain their imaginary animals' unique features and adaptations.

An Empire Built by Trade ❸

In the fourth century A.D., a kingdom called Ghana arose in the Niger River Valley. Ancient Ghana's location allowed it to control trade between Northern and Southern Africa. Traders had to pay a tax in gold nuggets to pass through the kingdom on their way to Europe and Southwest Asia. In addition, Ancient Ghana had many gold mines. Ghana had so much gold from these two sources that the kingdom was called the Land of Gold.

People eagerly traded gold for other precious items, such as salt. The merchants of Ghana also traded gold and slaves for cooking utensils, cloth, jewelry, copper, and weapons.

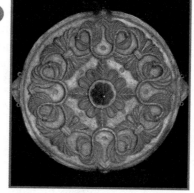

Human-Environment Interaction •
This 18th- or 19th-century gold jewelry from Ghana was probably worn by members of an Ashanti king's court. ▲

The Mali Empire ❹

Muslim armies began a war with Ghana in 1054. The fighting continued for many years and interfered with the trade upon which Ghana depended. This weakened the empire. By the 1200s, the people under Ghana's rule began to break away.

Mali Absorbs Ghana Around 1235, a Muslim leader named Sundiata united warring tribes. He then brought neighboring states under his rule to create the Mali Empire. In the year 1240, he took control of what was left of the Ghana Empire. The Mali Empire included most of the area that Ghana had ruled, along with lands to the east.

Culture • **This daughter of a Fanti chief continues a long tradition of Ghanian royalty by wearing gold jewelry and ornaments.** ▶

Africa South of the Sahara: Geography and History **299**

MORE ABOUT...

Mansa Musa

Mansa Musa was the grandnephew or grandson of the emperor Sundiata, who ruled Mali in the 13th century. In 1324–1325, when Mansa Musa made his famous pilgrimage to Mecca, 500 slaves marched before him carrying golden staffs. He brought along 100 camels, each bearing 300 pounds of gold. He spent so much gold in Cairo that he caused the price of gold there to fall and not recover for many years.

ASSESS & RETEACH

Reading Social Studies Have students fill in the boxes for "Bantu migration" and "gold-for-salt trade" in the chart on page 290.

 Formal Assessment
• Section Quiz, p. 147

RETEACHING ACTIVITY

Organize students into groups. Assign one section subhead to each student in the group. Have students summarize the material in their subsection. Members should then share their summaries with the rest of the group.

 In-depth Resources: Unit 4
• Reteaching Activity, p. 12

 Access for Students Acquiring English
• Reteaching Activity, p. 92

It controlled trade routes across the Sahara and from the south, as well as along the Niger River. Many rulers and people of Mali became Muslims but still continued to practice their traditional religions, too.

Mali's Golden Age <u>**Mansa Musa**</u> ruled Mali from about 1312 to 1332. Under his rule, Mali expanded and flourished. In 1324, he made a religious pilgrimage to Mecca in Arabia. During his journey, he persuaded Muslim scholars and artisans to return to Mali with him. Timbuktu, Mali's major city, became a cultural center. Architects built beautiful mosques in and around the city. Scholars brought their knowledge of Islamic law, astronomy, medicine, and mathematics. Universities in several West African cities became centers of Islamic education.

The Songhai Empire ④

Mali's power declined after Mansa Musa's death in 1337. Eventually, Mali was conquered by nearby Songhai. Like Mali and Ghana had in the past, Songhai controlled trade across the Sahara. It ruled neighboring states, and by the early 1500s was larger than Mali had been. Timbuktu again became a center of Muslim culture. In the early 1590s, a Moroccan army defeated the Songhai Empire.

Culture • Mansa (King) Musa spread interest in Mali as he traveled to Arabia. Tales of his wealth reached as far away as Europe. ▲

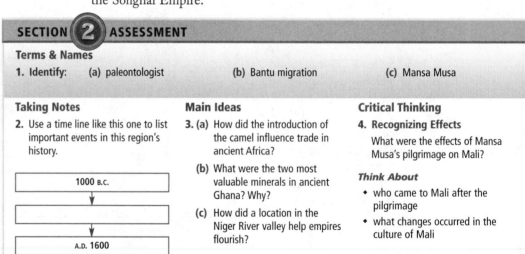

SECTION ② ASSESSMENT

Terms & Names

1. Identify: (a) paleontologist   (b) Bantu migration   (c) Mansa Musa

Taking Notes	**Main Ideas**	**Critical Thinking**
2. Use a time line like this one to list important events in this region's history.	**3. (a)** How did the introduction of the camel influence trade in ancient Africa?	**4. Recognizing Effects** What were the effects of Mansa Musa's pilgrimage on Mali?
▢ 1000 B.C. ↓ ▢ ↓ ▢ A.D. 1600	**(b)** What were the two most valuable minerals in ancient Ghana? Why? **(c)** How did a location in the Niger River valley help empires flourish?	***Think About*** ◆ who came to Mali after the pilgrimage ◆ what changes occurred in the culture of Mali

ACTIVITY -OPTION-   Make a **diorama** showing a camel caravan traveling through the Sahara, carrying salt to people in Southern Africa.

Section ② Assessment

1. Terms & Names
a. paleontologist, p. 296
b. Bantu migration, p. 297
c. Mansa Musa, p. 300

2. Taking Notes

Students might list any of the following dates:	
1000 B.C.	Bantus begin migration
A.D. 600s	camel introduced to Africa
1054	Muslim armies begin war with Ghana
1235	start of the Mali Empire
1312–1332	reign of Mansa Musa
1500s	rise of Songhai Empire
1590s	Moroccan army attacks Songhai; empire falls

3. Main Ideas
a. Camels expanded trade to North Africa because they could travel across the desert.
b. Gold and salt; Ghana taxed traders bringing salt to the South and gold to the North.
c. The Niger River valley was fertile and in a good position to control trade from North Africa and Europe to the rest of Africa.

4. Critical Thinking
Mansa Musa persuaded Muslim scholars and artisans to come to Mali. They brought knowledge of architecture, law, astronomy, medicine, and mathematics and built universities and beautiful mosques.

ACTIVITY OPTION

 Integrated Assessment
• Rubric for making a diorama

SECTION 3

The Impact of Colonialism on African Life

TERMS & NAMES
missionary
Hutu
Tutsi

AIN IDEA

he slave trade and colonialism estroyed traditional cultures nd social systems in Africa south f the Sahara.

WHY IT MATTERS NOW

Africa is still recovering from the effects of the slave trade and colonialism.

DATELINE

EXTRA

THE ROYAL PALACE, KONGO, JULY 6, 1526

King Affonso of Kongo has sent a letter to the king of Portugal, protesting the criminal behavior of Portuguese merchants and sailors in Kongo. Traders are kidnapping the young men of his kingdom to sell into slavery. They use European goods to bribe Kongolese to capture their own people. Even noblemen and the king's own relatives have been taken.

Affonso says that European ways are corrupting the Kongolese. Some of the king's courtiers believe the slave trade can bring Kongo a great deal of wealth. But the king's position remains firm.

Movement • Elmina is a slave-trading fortress through which the Portuguese move enslaved Africans. ▲

Movement • Enslaved Africans were forced to wear shackles like these. ▲

Africa Before the Europeans ❶

Before Europeans came, Africans had varied ways of life under different kinds of governments. Kings ruled great empires like Mali and Songhai. Some states had democratic rule. Some groups had no central government. Some Africans lived in great cities like Timbuktu, while others lived in small villages deep in the forests. Some were nomadic hunters, and some were skilled artists who sculpted masks and statues of wood, gold, or bronze.

SECTION OBJECTIVES

1. To explain the effects of European traders on the African slave trade
2. To describe European colonialism in Africa
3. To analyze the impact of colonial rule in Africa

SKILLBUILDER
- Interpreting a Map, p. 302

CRITICAL THINKING
- Synthesizing, p. 302
- Making Inferences, p. 305

FOCUS & MOTIVATE

WARM-UP

Making Inferences After students read Dateline, discuss these questions.

1. How do you think the king of Portugal will react when he receives King Affonso's letter?
2. Who is the greater threat to King Affonso and Portugal—the Portuguese or the Kongolese who have been bribed? Why?

INSTRUCT: Objective ❶

Africa Before the Europeans/ The Slave Trade

- What was life like in Africa before the Europeans came? varied governments, cities, villages, nomadic hunters, artists
- What were the effects of the European slave trade in Africa? Slaves died of diseases or starvation; communities were robbed of young men; family structures were destroyed.

In-depth Resources: Unit 4
- Guided Reading Worksheet, p. 5

Reading Study Guide
(Spanish and English), pp. 92–93

Program Resources

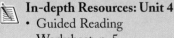

In-depth Resources: Unit 4
- Guided Reading Worksheet, p. 5
- Reteaching Activity, p. 13

Reading Study Guide
(Spanish and English), pp. 92–93

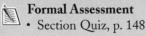

Formal Assessment
- Section Quiz, p. 148

Integrated Assessment
- Rubric for writing an opinion paper

Outline Map Activities

Access for Students Acquiring English
- Guided Reading Worksheet, p. 87

Technology Resources
classzone.com

TEST-TAKING RESOURCES
- Strategies for Test Preparation
- Test Practice Transparencies
- Online Test Practice

CRITICAL THINKING ACTIVITY

Synthesizing Point out that by 1808, it was illegal to bring slaves into the United States. Ask students when it became illegal to own slaves in the United States. Guide students to recall what they learned about 19th-century America and the causes, events, and effects of the Civil War. Have them explain how the American Civil War was one consequence of the slave trade in Africa.

Class Time 20 minutes

FOCUS ON VISUALS

Interpreting the Map Discuss the map with students, and have them identify the different areas to which enslaved Africans were taken. For example, many enslaved people from Africa were sent to the Spanish Americas, Brazil, and the British Caribbean. In fact, more slaves were sent to these regions than to British North America/ French Americas (the future United States). Ask students to identify the continents and the regions within them to which African slaves were sent. Which regions of Africa did slaves come from?

Possible Responses African slaves were sent to both North America and South America. They ended up in the eastern part of North America, all of Latin America, and eastern, western, and south-central South America. They came mainly from the west coast of Africa.

Extension Have students research the experience of African slaves in Brazil and the Spanish Americas and then write a report about what they have learned. Invite them to share their reports with the class.

The Slave Trade ❶

Slavery existed in Africa long before Europeans arrived. Rulers in Mali and Songhai had thousands of slaves who worked as servants, soldiers, and farm workers. Villages raided one another to take captives and sell them. Often, a slave could work to earn his or her freedom. In the 1400s, however, Europeans introduced a form of slavery that devastated African life and society.

From Africa to the Americas In the early 15th century, European traders began to sell slaves. They raided towns to capture unwilling Africans. Some Africans captured in wars were sold to European traders by other Africans. One estimate is that 10 to 12 million Africans were forced into slavery and sent to European colonies in North and South America from 1520 to 1860. Many more were captured but died of disease or starvation before arriving. About 1750, movements to stop the slave trade had begun. By 1808, the United States, the United Kingdom, and Denmark had made it illegal to bring in slaves from Africa. However, it would take longer for countries to make owning a slave illegal.

Impact on Africa In addition to the Africans captured and sold, many were killed during raids. About two-thirds of those taken were men between the ages of 18 and 30. Slave traders chose young, strong, healthy people, leaving few behind to lead families and villages. African cities and towns did not have enough workers. Family structures were destroyed.

Geography Skillbuilder Answers
1. the western part
2. (any three) British North America, British Caribbean, Spanish Americas, Brazil, French Americas

BACKGROUND
Conditions on slave ships were so bad that about 16 percent of slaves died during transport.

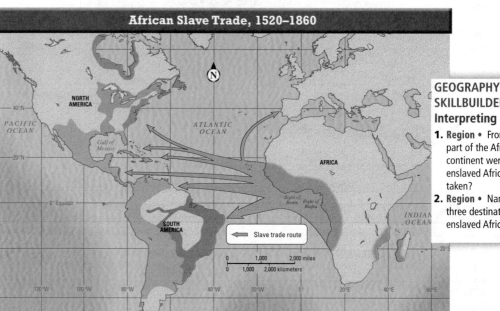

African Slave Trade, 1520–1860

Slave trade route

GEOGRAPHY SKILLBUILDER: Interpreting a Map
1. **Region** • From what part of the African continent were most enslaved Africans taken?
2. **Region** • Name three destinations of enslaved Africans.

Activity Options

Differentiating Instruction: Gifted and Talented

Encourage motivated students to learn more about the Atlantic slave trade. Have them read several narratives written by slaves about their capture in Africa and their transport across the Atlantic. Encourage them to explore the Internet in addition to more conventional resources to uncover these primary sources. Using these narratives as a foundation, have students write short stories in which two or more of these characters appear. If they wish, they may illustrate their stories with art from the period or their own drawings. Finally, have students share their stories with the class.

European Colonialism ❷

BACKGROUND

During the Industrial Revolution, inventions increased the speed of making goods. This created a need for more raw materials and markets.

When Europeans ended the slave trade, they did not lose interest in Africa. The Industrial Revolution had changed economies in Europe and the United States. Africa could supply both raw materials, such as minerals, and new markets for goods.

Explorers and Missionaries Europeans knew little about the interior of Africa, but many were curious. Scientists and explorers were interested in African wildlife and natural resources. European missionaries also traveled to Africa. A **missionary** is a person who goes to another country to do religious and social work. Missionaries wanted to convert Africans to Christianity and bring education and health care to Africa. Many also taught European ways of thinking, which often conflicted with, and destroyed, African traditions.

Competition for Africa In the 19th century, European nations began to compete for control of Africa. Each wanted the biggest or richest colonies and control of trade. To avoid wars over territory, European and U.S. leaders met in Berlin in 1884. There, and in later meetings, they discussed how to divide Africa. No Africans were consulted. Over the next 20 years, Belgium, France, the United Kingdom, Germany, Italy, Spain, Portugal, and the Ottoman Empire all established colonies in Africa. By 1912, only Ethiopia and Liberia remained independent.

A Wealth of Animals When European explorers came to Africa, they saw impressive sights—lions and cheetahs stalking zebras, elephants trumpeting messages to their young, giraffes delicately nibbling the tops of trees. Today, Tanzania's Serengeti National Park is where modern explorers watch animals in the wild—animals that most non-Africans have seen only in zoos.

The Serengeti is home to an astonishing variety of life. It is also the last place in Africa where huge migrations of animals take place. The sight of a million gnus, zebras, and gazelles moving majestically through the park is one of the wonders of the world.

INSTRUCT: Objective ❷

European Colonialism

- How did the Industrial Revolution promote interest in Africa? source of raw materials; a market for new goods
- What interested scientists and explorers about Africa? wildlife and natural resources
- Why did missionaries come to Africa? to convert Africans to Christianity; to bring education and health care to the people
- Why did European nations begin to compete for control of Africa? to get the biggest, richest colonies and to control trade
- Why did European and U.S. leaders meet in 1884, and what happened as a result of that meeting? to avoid wars over territory and discuss how to divide Africa; by 1912, many European countries as well as the Ottoman Empire had established colonies in Africa

The Serengeti is the site of one of the last great migratory systems still intact. Each May, when the rainy season ends, more than 1 million wildebeests travel from the Serengeti to the Masai Mara Park in Kenya in search of food and water. The wildebeests cover more than 1,500 miles on this journey. Their return trip to the Serengeti presents a variety of dangers to the animals. The wildebeests must cross the Mara River, where hundreds may drown in the swelling waters, or be attacked and eaten by crocodiles.

Activity Options

Skillbuilder Mini-Lesson: Reading Historical Maps

Explaining the Skill Remind students that maps can help them visualize and understand historical events.

Applying the Skill Have students reread "Competition for Africa" on page 303 and then turn to the map, European Colonies in Africa, 1912, on page 304. Ask pairs of students to determine which European country or countries gained the most control over Africa after the continent was divided by the European powers. Remind them that the map key will help them distinguish the countries. Have students use the map to explain their results.

INTERPRETING A MAP

European Colonies in Africa, 1912

Ask students what a political map shows. Point out the map key and discuss the different countries that had colonies in Africa in 1912. Also point out how many independent states there were in Africa at that time. Discuss why European countries wanted colonies in Africa. Ask students to use the map to answer the following questions:

- Which countries had African colonies along the Mediterranean Sea? Italy, France, the United Kingdom, and Spain

- Which countries were in possession of the many islands off the coast of Africa? Portugal, Spain, United Kingdom

- Egypt was a colony of which European nation? the United Kingdom

GEOGRAPHY SKILLBUILDER

Answers

1. British Empire
2. Ethiopia, Liberia

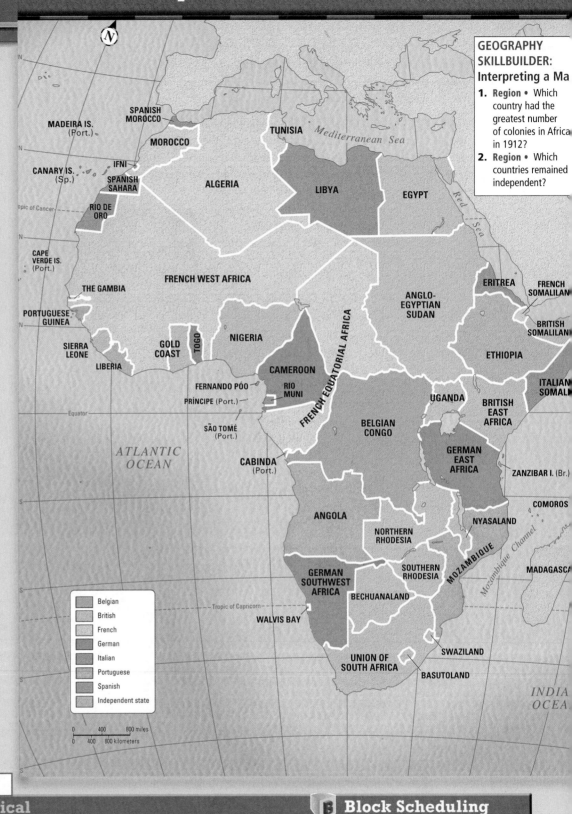

European Colonies in Africa, 1912

GEOGRAPHY SKILLBUILDER: Interpreting a Ma

1. **Region** • Which country had the greatest number of colonies in Africa in 1912?
2. **Region** • Which countries remained independent?

Map labels: SPANISH MOROCCO, MADEIRA IS. (Port.), MOROCCO, TUNISIA, Mediterranean Sea, CANARY IS. (Sp.), IFNI, SPANISH SAHARA, ALGERIA, LIBYA, EGYPT, Red Sea, Tropic of Cancer, RIO DE ORO, CAPE VERDE IS. (Port.), FRENCH WEST AFRICA, ANGLO-EGYPTIAN SUDAN, ERITREA, FRENCH SOMALILAN, THE GAMBIA, PORTUGUESE GUINEA, BRITISH SOMALILAN, SIERRA LEONE, GOLD COAST, TOGO, NIGERIA, FRENCH EQUATORIAL AFRICA, ETHIOPIA, LIBERIA, CAMEROON, FERNANDO PÓO, RIO MUNI, PRÍNCIPE (Port.), UGANDA, BRITISH EAST AFRICA, ITALIAN SOMAL, Equator, SÃO TOMÉ (Port.), BELGIAN CONGO, ATLANTIC OCEAN, CABINDA (Port.), GERMAN EAST AFRICA, ZANZIBAR I. (Br.), COMOROS, ANGOLA, NYASALAND, NORTHERN RHODESIA, MOZAMBIQUE, Mozambique Channel, MADAGASCA, GERMAN SOUTHWEST AFRICA, SOUTHERN RHODESIA, BECHUANALAND, Tropic of Capricorn, WALVIS BAY, UNION OF SOUTH AFRICA, SWAZILAND, BASUTOLAND, INDIA OCEA

Legend:
- Belgian
- British
- French
- German
- Italian
- Portuguese
- Spanish
- Independent state

Scale: 0 400 800 miles / 0 400 800 kilometers

Activity Options

Multiple Learning Styles: Logical

Class Time One class period

Task Creating a jigsaw puzzle

Purpose To gain a better understanding of the African continent and how modern political boundaries were developed

Supplies Needed
- Photocopies of the map on page 304
- Crayons or markers
- Scissors

B Block Scheduling

Activity Have students color individual countries on the photocopy of the map. Be sure that each color represents colonies of specific European nations. Each student should make his/her own map key. Make sure every student uses different colors to represent nations. Have students cut out each country on continental Africa, mix the pieces, and put them into an envelope. Have students trade puzzles and assemble them.

Impact of Colonial Rule ③

When Europeans divided Africa, most colonizers cared mainly about gold, diamonds, and other resources. The Europeans knew little about Africa's political and social systems. Many Europeans looked down on Africa's rich cultures and tried to make Africans more like Europeans.

Europeans also created conflicts among ethnic groups that had not existed before. For example, the Belgian rulers of Rwanda-Burundi insisted that everyone carry identity cards saying whether they were **Hutu,** the ethnic majority, or **Tutsi,** the minority that had ruled the Hutu. Many people did not know which of these they were. The Belgians decided that anyone who owned more than ten cows was Tutsi. The Tutsi got the best education and jobs. Soon the Hutu were resentful, and a violent conflict began. In 1994, the conflict between the Hutu and the Tutsi escalated into a brutal civil war. The Tutsi were victorious and formed a new government in Rwanda.

Movment • During and after the civil war, thousands of Tutsi were massacred, and thousands of Hutu refugees, such as these, were driven from their homeland. ▼

SECTION ③ ASSESSMENT

Terms & Names

1. **Identify:**　(a) missionary　　(b) Hutu　　(c) Tutsi

Taking Notes

2. Use a chart like this one to list the ways in which Europeans changed Africa, and the effects of the changes on African life.

Change	Effect

 ACTIVITY -OPTION-　Write an **opinion paper** explaining the negative effects of colonization.

Main Ideas

3. (a) How did Europeans change the institution of slavery in Africa?

(b) Why did European interest in Africa turn from the slave trade to colonization?

(c) How is the modern conflict between the Hutu and Tutsi a result of the actions of European rulers?

Critical Thinking

4. **Comparing**

How was the way of life of many Africans different after the arrival of Europeans?

Think About

* goals of missionaries and European countries
* history and traditions of ethnic peoples

Africa South of the Sahara: Geography and History **305**

INSTRUCT: Objective ③

Impact of Colonial Rule

* What was the European attitude toward African culture? disdain, superiority
* How did the Belgian rulers create conflict between ethnic groups in Rwanda-Burundi? gave Tutsi minority power over Hutu majority

CRITICAL THINKING ACTIVITY

Making Inferences Based on what they already know about colonizing powers, ask students why they think the Belgian rulers made the people of Rwanda-Burundi carry identity cards. Remind them that European countries hoped to profit from their colonies in Africa, and that to do so they needed to establish order and control.

Class Time 10 minutes

ASSESS & RETEACH

Reading Social Studies Have students record the causes and effects for "Atlantic slave trade" and "colonization" in the chart on page 290.

 Formal Assessment
* Section Quiz, p. 148

RETEACHING ACTIVITY

Have students work in pairs to create a time line of the events in this section.

 In-depth Resources: Unit 4
* Reteaching Activity, p. 13

 Access for Students Acquiring English
* Reteaching Activity, p. 93

Section ③ Assessment

1. Terms & Names

a. missionary, p. 303
b. Hutu, p. 305
c. Tutsi, p. 305

2. Taking Notes

Change	Effect
Took millions of slaves	Cities, towns lacked workers
Took young males	Family structures destroyed
Set boundaries without considering natural divisions	Created conflict between countries and ethnic groups

3. Main Ideas

a. Europeans did not allow slaves to buy their freedom; they did not treat them like human beings.
b. European nations needed raw materials and markets to fuel Industrial Revolution.
c. Belgian rulers forced people to define identity by ethnic background. People were treated differently, leading to conflict and civil war.

4. Critical Thinking

There were new ethnic conflicts; traditions were destroyed; many Africans converted to Christianity.

ACTIVITY OPTION

 Integrated Assessment
* Rubric for writing an opinion paper

Teacher's Edition **305**

SKILLBUILDER

Interpreting a Chart

Defining the Skill

Lead a discussion about why it is often preferable to display information in a chart. Point out that a chart allows a reader to make a quick visual comparison of facts and statistics. Discuss charts that students have used in science and other textbooks.

Applying the Skill

How to Interpret a Chart Explain that there are certain strategies for interpreting a chart. Ask a volunteer to state the main idea of the chart. Guide students in working through the remaining strategies. Ask questions requiring them to compare countries across columns and to use the data in a row.

Write a Summary

Discuss the information in the chart with the students. Ask questions such as, What is the population of Ghana? How many televisions are owned in Ghana? What is the ratio of people to televisions in Ghana? Then ask a volunteer to read aloud the summary provided.

Practicing the Skill

Ask volunteers to read their summaries aloud. For extra practice, work with students to summarize data from their science textbook in a chart.

 In-depth Resources: Unit 4
• Skillbuilder Practice, p. 9

SKILLBUILDER

Interpreting a Chart

▶▶ Defining the Skill

A chart organizes information in a visual form. The information is simplified or summarized and then arranged so that it is easy to read and understand.

▶▶ Applying the Skill

The chart below lists the population, number of radios, and number of televisions in several West African nations and the United States. Use the strategies listed below to help you interpret the chart.

How to Interpret a Chart

Strategy ❶ Read the title to learn the main idea of the chart.

Strategy ❷ Read the labels across the top and down the first column of the chart. The labels in the column list the countries represented in the chart. The labels across the top tell what information is provided for each country.

Strategy ❸ Study the information in the chart. Read down the columns to compare one country with another. Read across the rows to see the communications available in each country.

Strategy ❹ Summarize the information in the chart. The title helps you clarify the main idea of the chart.

❶ Communication in Western Africa and the United States, 2000

❷ Country	Population	Radios	Televisions
Benin	❸ 6.6 million	620,000	60,000
Ghana	❸ 19.9 million	4,400,000	1,730,000
Liberia	❸ 3.2 million	❸ 790,000	❸ 70,000
Mali	11 million	570,000	45,000
Niger	10.4 million	680,000	125,000
Nigeria	126.6 million	23,500,000	6,900,000
United States	284.5 million	575,000,000	219,000,000

❹ This chart compares the population, the number of radios, and the number of televisions in several West African nations and the United States. In the countries of Benin and Mali, there are very few radios and televisions compared to the number of people. For example, in Mali there is one television for every 244 people. In the United States, there is more than one radio per person. In Nigeria, there is one television for every 18 people.

Write a Summary

To gain a clear understanding of the information in this chart, write a summary. It is possible to produce other data from the information in this chart. To find out how many people there are for one television or radio in each nation, divide the population by the number of televisions or radios. The paragraph above summarizes the chart.

▶▶ Practicing the Skill

Turn to page 294 in Chapter 10. Study the chart titled "Africa's Deserts," and write a paragraph that summarizes the information in that chart.

Career Connection: Sociologist

Encourage students to think about situations where charts would be helpful in organizing information about different groups of people. Point out that individuals who are intrigued by gathering and organizing this kind of information might want to pursue careers as sociologists.

1. Discuss the chart displayed on this page. It shows that there are far fewer radios than people in each of the countries listed except the United States. In the United States, there are more than twice as

B Block Scheduling

many radios as people. A sociologist might try to determine what this says about the United States and other countries.

2. Help students understand that knowing the facts is just the first step. A sociologist uses facts as a springboard for creative thinking about cause and effect.

3. Tell students that sociologists are usually employed by universities, nonprofit organizations, and governments.

The Road to Independence

TERMS & NAMES
racism
diversity
apartheid

MAIN IDEA

During the 20th century, African nations gained independence from their colonial rulers.

WHY IT MATTERS NOW

Many independent nations in Africa are now struggling to form democratic governments.

DATELINE

NAIROBI, KENYA, DECEMBER 12, 1963— Thousands of Kenyans watched today as the British flag was lowered for the last time over the former colony. The new national flag of independent Kenya was raised in its place.

The new flag's stripes of black, red, and green stand for the country's people, their struggle for independence, and the country's rich resources. The center symbol is a Masai shield and spears.

To mark the change from British rule, Prince Philip of England attended the ceremony. All over Kenya, people cheered their new country, shouting "Uhuru!" the Swahili word for "freedom."

Place • Prince Philip and Kenya's Prime Minister Jomo Kenyatta attend the ceremony marking Kenya's independence. ▲

Culture • This flag is a symbol of Kenya's independence. ▲

Moving Toward Independence ❶

Colonial rule in Africa disrupted social systems and governments, and robbed Africa of resources. Many Africans objected, but they did not have enough power to act. During the 1920s and 1930s, colonial rulers sent a few Africans to attend universities in Europe and the United States. These educated young people started to dream of independence. Nationalism grew strong.

Africa South of the Sahara: Geography and History **307**

SECTION OBJECTIVES

1. To identify nationalism as the root of Africa's independence movement

2. To describe Nigeria's struggle for independence and survival since European colonialism

3. To explain the restrictions of South Africa's independence

SKILLBUILDER
• Interpreting a Map, p. 308

CRITICAL THINKING
• Making Inferences, p. 308

FOCUS & MOTIVATE
WARM-UP

Drawing Conclusions Have students read <u>Dateline</u> and discuss Kenya's independence.

1. How do you think Kenya's leaders chose the symbols for their new flag?

2. What do you think Prince Philip's presence at the ceremony represented?

INSTRUCT: Objective ❶

Moving Toward Independence/ Journey to Freedom

• What influenced the development of nationalism in Africa? Students sent to schools in Europe and the United States during the 1920s and 1930s dreamed of independence.

• What belief was expressed at the Pan-African congresses? that Africans were ready for independence and able to govern themselves

 In-depth Resources: Unit 4
• Guided Reading Worksheet, p. 6

 Reading Study Guide
(Spanish and English), pp. 94–95

Program Resources

 In-depth Resources: Unit 4
• Guided Reading Worksheet, p. 6
• Reteaching Activity, p. 14

 Reading Study Guide
(Spanish and English), pp. 94–95

 Formal Assessment
• Section Quiz, p. 149

 Integrated Assessment
• Rubric for designing a logo or writing a motto

 Outline Map Activities

 Access for Students Acquiring English
• Guided Reading Worksheet, p. 88

 Technology Resources
classzone.com

TEST-TAKING RESOURCES
⚓ Strategies for Test Preparation
⚓ Test Practice Transparencies
⚓ Online Test Practice

CRITICAL THINKING ACTIVITY

Making Inferences Ask students why they think the Europeans found their colonies in Africa expensive to maintain. Remind them that the government of a colony requires an extensive bureaucracy to oversee its affairs. Also remind them that many of these European countries had just spent large sums of money in two world wars and that they had heavy rebuilding costs.

Class Time 10 minutes

MORE ABOUT...
Kwame Nkrumah

Kwame Nkrumah was one of the most dynamic and effective leaders of modern, post-colonial Africa. He endured repeated imprisonment at the hands of the British before finally becoming president when Ghana became a republic in 1960. Nkrumah inspired other African leaders to fight for independence. He even urged other African colonies to become free and join with Ghana in a United States of Africa.

Unfortunately, Nkrumah became more and more dictatorial after he gained power. He had his critics arrested, and in 1964 he outlawed all political parties except for his own. He was overthrown by the army in 1966 and died in exile in Romania in 1972.

A VOICE FROM AFRICA

Ask students to read the quote from the 1945 Pan-African Congress and identify any words that indicate the participants' desire for change. Students might point out words such as determined, want, demand, education, or independence.

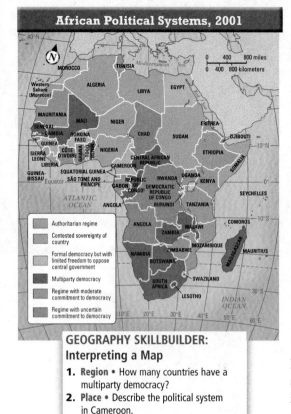

African Political Systems, 2001

Authoritarian regime

Contested sovereignty of country

Formal democracy but with limited freedom to oppose central government

Multiparty democracy

Regime with moderate commitment to democracy

Regime with uncertain commitment to democracy

GEOGRAPHY SKILLBUILDER:
Interpreting a Map

1. **Region** • How many countries have a multiparty democracy?
2. **Place** • Describe the political system in Cameroon.

Geography Skillbuilder Answers

1. 12

2. It is a formal democracy with little freedom to oppose government.

Reading Social Studies
A. Possible Answer
They reinforced the desire for self-rule.

Reading Social Studies

A. Analyzing Causes How did the two world wars and the Pan-African congresses affect the struggle for African independence?

Journey to Freedom ❶

European nations wanted to keep their colonies for their valuable resources although they were expensive to maintain. Many Europeans believed that Africans were unable to govern themselves. This attitude is an example of **racism,** the unfounded belief that one race is inferior to another race.

Pan-African Congresses Educated Africans believed they could govern themselves. African men had fought for the European Allies during World War I, and thousands had died. Ex-soldiers wanted self-rule. Pan-Africanism, an idea that people of African descent around the world should work together for their freedom, attracted more supporters. In 1919, the first Pan-African Congress was organized. Africans again fought in World War II. After this war, many felt that they now deserved independence.

A VOICE FROM AFRICA

...We are determined to be free. We want education. We want the right to earn a decent living; the right to express our thoughts and emotions, to adopt and create forms of beauty. We demand for Black Africa autonomy and independence....

The Pan-African Congress, 1945

At the fifth Pan-African Congress in 1945, there were 90 delegates; 26 were from all over Africa. Several were men who would become the political leaders of their countries, including Kwame Nkrumah of Ghana and Jomo Kenyatta of Kenya.

308 CHAPTER 10

Activity Options

Interdisciplinary Link: Citizenship

Forming Opinions Lead a discussion about the African contribution to the Allied victory in World War II and the rights and responsibilities of colonists during wartime. Explain that thousands of Africans lost their lives during World War II. Ask students how their participation in the war helped African people gain respect from citizens of the United States and other Allied nations.

Have students write letters to the Allied command in which they express their opinions regarding the involvement of the African soldiers in the war.

New African Countries ②

Between 1951 and 1980, most of the colonies in Africa south of the Sahara gained independence. For some countries, the path to nationhood was smooth. For others, it was not. Nigeria and South Africa had different experiences in achieving independence.

Nigeria: Diversity Brings Division ②

Before Nigeria gained independence from the United Kingdom in 1960, it had experienced a well-organized government, rich resources, and a strong economy under British rule. It was hoped that Nigeria's **diversity**—its many different cultures and viewpoints—would be a source of strength. Many Nigerians are Muslim, while others are Christian or follow traditional African religions. Nigerians speak more than 400 languages. However, instead of being a source of strength, this diversity caused problems.

Riots and War The slave trade and colonial rule had created hostility between the ethnic groups in Nigeria. Many Nigerian politicians focused on their ethnic group and not the whole country. Some leaders stole money and gave or took bribes.

Margin notes (left column)

Reading Social Studies
B. Possible Answers
Some Nigerian leaders were corrupt. They stole money and encouraged bribes. There was also tension among different ethnic groups.

Reading
Social Studies

B. Finding Causes What led to the 1966 rioting in Nigeria?

Margin notes (right of text column)

Thinking Critically Answers
1. Thanksgiving is also a harvest celebration.
2. Priests lead prayers for the yams.

Spotlight on CULTURE

Yam Festivals People celebrate what is precious to them. In Ghana, Nigeria, and Côte d'Ivoire, the yam is traditionally the most important crop. Among the Ibo people of Nigeria, a man's first prayer to God is for children. His second is for many yams.

Every year, people in these countries celebrate the harvest of the new yams with special dances and ceremonies. Côte d'Ivoire's King Kofti is shown at right accepting offerings at the Yam Festival. Yam paste is prepared in a large bowl.

Among the Aburi people of Ghana, a priest begins the festival by slicing and dropping three pieces from a yam. If the pieces fall skin-side down, the village will have good luck. If the slices fall cut-side down, trouble is ahead.

THINKING CRITICALLY

1. **Comparing** How is the American holiday Thanksgiving similar to the Yam Festival?

2. **Making Inferences** Why do you think a priest is involved with the Yam Festival in Ghana?

Africa South of the Sahara: Geography and History **309**

INSTRUCT: Objective ❸

Independence of South Africa

- When did South Africa gain independence? 1910

- How were nonwhites treated after independence? restricted in many ways, including right to vote

- What is apartheid? an official policy of racial segregation

- What was the outcome of the protests against apartheid? Apartheid ended in 1991.

ASSESS & RETEACH

Reading Social Studies Have students complete the chart on page 290.

 Formal Assessment
- Section Quiz, p. 149

RETEACHING ACTIVITY

Ask students to work in small groups to list the effects of colonialism and racism in Nigeria and South Africa. Have groups share and compare their lists.

 In-depth Resources: Unit 4
- Reaching Activity, p. 14

 Access for Students Acquiring English
- Reteaching Activity, p. 94

Place • **Signs such as these were common in South Africa during apartheid. Everything from businesses to bathrooms was segregated.** ▲

In 1966, deadly riots broke out, and many people were killed. The next year, people in the eastern part of Nigeria announced the formation of a separate country, Biafra. After three years of civil war between Biafran Nigerians and the Nigerian army, Biafra was defeated and rejoined Nigeria. Since then, military leaders have primarily ruled Nigeria.

❸

Independence of South Africa

The United Kingdom gave South Africa independence in 1910. This action did not bring freedom to most South Africans. Only white South Africans could vote, and many laws were passed to restrict nonwhites.

In 1948, an official policy of racial segregation known as **apartheid** (uh·PAHRT·HYT) was adopted. Apartheid strictly separated people by color. Many people resisted apartheid. Protesters held marches, went on strike, and sometimes became violent. Although many protesters were jailed or killed, they did make progress. In 1991, apartheid ended. In 1994, for the first time, all South African adults could vote.

BACKGROUND

The word *apartheid* is from the Afrikaans language. It means "apartness."

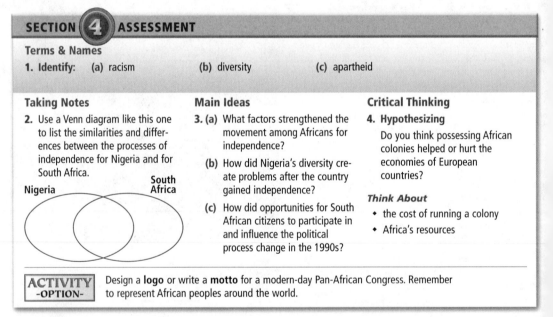

SECTION ❹ ASSESSMENT

Terms & Names

1. Identify: (a) racism (b) diversity (c) apartheid

Taking Notes

2. Use a Venn diagram like this one to list the similarities and differences between the processes of independence for Nigeria and for South Africa.

Nigeria ⬤⬤ South Africa

Main Ideas

3. (a) What factors strengthened the movement among Africans for independence?

(b) How did Nigeria's diversity create problems after the country gained independence?

(c) How did opportunities for South African citizens to participate in and influence the political process change in the 1990s?

Critical Thinking

4. **Hypothesizing**

Do you think possessing African colonies helped or hurt the economies of European countries?

Think About

- the cost of running a colony
- Africa's resources

ACTIVITY -OPTION- Design a **logo** or write a **motto** for a modern-day Pan-African Congress. Remember to represent African peoples around the world.

Section ❹ Assessment

1. Terms & Names
- **a.** racism, p. 308
- **b.** diversity, p. 309
- **c.** apartheid, p. 310

2. Taking Notes

Nigeria / former UK colonies / South Africa

independence in 1960s, riots and civil wars — former UK colonies — independence in 1910, racial segregation, currently peaceful

3. Main Ideas
- **a.** European education for some Africans, African soldiers in World Wars I and II, and the Pan-African congresses
- **b.** Hostility among ethnic groups led to corruption and violence.
- **c.** All South Africans, including non-whites, could now vote.

4. Critical Thinking

Students may note that possession of the colonies helped the European economies, as the colonies were a source of cheap labor and materials.

ACTIVITY OPTION

 Integrated Assessment
- Rubric for designing a logo or writing a motto

House of Stone

Scattered throughout the interior of southeastern Africa are hundreds of stone ruins archaeologists believe date to A.D. 1100–1500. The most spectacular, Great Zimbabwe, covers almost 1,800 acres. The word *zimbabwe* means "house of stone."

   For centuries Europeans wondered about the origins of this city. In the early 1900s, archaeologists proved that its builders were ancestors of the present-day Shona people. Artifacts from India, China, and Asia have been found at the site. They show that the area was a trade center for gold, ivory, cloth, beads, and ceramics. Trade in Great Zimbabwe was controlled by a few wealthy people.

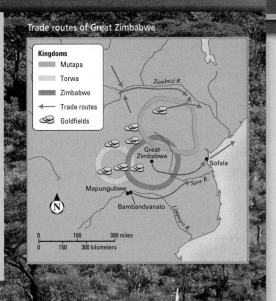

Trade routes of Great Zimbabwe

Kingdoms
- Mutapa
- Torwa
- Zimbabwe
- ← Trade routes
- Goldfields

Zambezi R.
Great Zimbabwe
Sofala
Mapungubwe
Save R.
Bambandyanalo
Limpopo R.
N

0   150   300 miles
0   150   300 kilometers

Builders used 900,000 granite slabs to create stone walls. The slabs were laid together without any type of mortar.

Natural weathering causes slabs of granite to break off hills in this area. Builders of Great Zimbabwe cut these slabs into smaller pieces and used them to create the stone walls.

Even though Great Zimbabwe has high walls and towers, archaeologists do not believe it was used as a fortress. Some archaeologists believe it was a religious center for the ancestors of the Shona.

THINKING Critically

1. Drawing Conclusions
The stone walls and towers of Great Zimbabwe were not built to protect the city. Why did its builders construct the walls and towers?

2. Making Inferences
How do trading networks of today differ from those of Great Zimbabwe?

OBJECTIVES

1. To explain how archaeologists learn about an ancient society
2. To explain how geography affects the development of a society

INSTRUCT

- How did the builders of Great Zimbabwe take advantage of natural resources?
- How did the location of the city affect its development?

   Block Scheduling

MORE ABOUT...
The Ruins at Great Zimbabwe

The site of Great Zimbabwe is divided into three areas. Atop a steep rise is the Hill Complex, which includes stone walls and the remains of earth and mud-brick buildings. The Great Enclosure has an outer wall measuring 820 feet around and up to 36 feet high. Inside the Valley Enclosure are the remains of approximately 50 households.

Connect to History

Strategic Thinking Why was Zimbabwe, once the home of 18,000 people, abandoned?

Connect to Today

Strategic Thinking What strategies and techniques do archaeologists use to learn about ancient societies and cultures?

Thinking Critically

1. Drawing Conclusions Possible Response The Shona may have built stone walls and towers to demonstrate the importance of the city's rulers. Archaeologists believe that at least some of the structures may have had religious significance.

2. Making Inferences Possible Response Modern technology has improved transportation and communication, making global trade possible. In addition to waterways and boats, motor vehicles, trains, air transport, and computer technology are used to trade a variety of items.

TERMS & NAMES

1. plateau, p. 292
2. Great Rift Valley, p. 293
3. Sahel, p. 294
4. desertification, p. 294
5. drought, p. 294
6. savanna, p. 294
7. Bantu migration, p. 297
8. Mansa Musa, p. 300
9. racism, p. 308
10. diversity, p. 309

REVIEW QUESTIONS

Possible Responses

1. Climatic regions include desert, semiarid, tropical, and equatorial.
2. Rift valleys are broad, steep-walled valleys, formed when Earth's plates pulled apart.
3. The Bantu migrated across Africa, bringing their knowledge of farming and their languages to other peoples.
4. Their location allowed them to control the trade routes across the desert, and they had rich supplies of gold to trade.
5. The slave trade depopulated villages and countries; it stole strong people who could have raised families and been leaders; it broke up family networks and other social ties.
6. They wanted control of trade and the largest or richest colonies.
7. The two world wars and the Pan-African congresses increased Africans' desire for independence.
8. Newly independent nations faced problems in economic development, violence, ethnic warfare, military rule, and racial discrimination.

ASSESSMENT

TERMS & NAMES

Explain the significance of each of the following:

1. plateau	2. Great Rift Valley	3. Sahel
6. savanna	7. Bantu migration	8. Mansa Musa

4. desertification 5. drought
9. racism 10. diversity

REVIEW QUESTIONS

The Geography of Africa South of the Sahara
(pages 291–295)
1. What climatic regions are found in Africa south of the Sahara?
2. What are rift valleys, and how are they formed?

African Cultures and Empires *(pages 296–300)*
3. How did Bantu culture spread through much of Africa?
4. How did kingdoms of Ghana, Mali, and Songhai become powerful?

The Impact of Colonialism on African Life *(pages 301–305)*
5. How did the European slave trade affect life in this region?
6. What factors did European countries consider while dividing up Africa?

The Road to Independence *(pages 307–310)*
7. What events increased the determination of Africans to gain independence from European rule?
8. What were some of the problems that accompanied independence in some African countries?

CRITICAL THINKING

Finding Causes
1. Using your completed chart from Reading Social Studies, p. 290, explain the causes and effects of desertification.

Analyzing Motives
2. Why were European nations so interested in establishing colonies in Africa?

Recognizing Effects
3. How did slave trade and colonialism in the past make it difficult for African leaders to build new, independent nations?

Visual Summary

1 The Geography of Africa South of the Sahara
- Africa south of the Sahara is a region of highlands and lowlands, with a variety of landforms and rich resources.

2 African Cultures and Empires
- Africa is the cradle of humankind.
- For over a thousand years (A.D. 400–1600), Africans built great empires based on trade.

3 The Impact of Colonialism on African Life
- Slave trade weakened African social systems by removing many healthy, young people from Africa.
- In the late 1800s, European nations divided Africa and established colonies, destroying existing governmental and social systems.

4 The Road to Independence
- In the late 20th century, most European colonies in Africa became independent nations.

CRITICAL THINKING: Possible Responses

1. Finding Causes
Overgrazing, overfarming, and a lack of rain cause desertification. Desertification makes land uninhabitable and useless for farming.

2. Analyzing Motives
They equated possession of colonies with power and importance. African colonies could supply cheap labor, rich resources, and markets for goods.

3. Recognizing Effects
The slave trade destroyed existing governments and social systems. Colonialism put government and legal systems in place that did not reflect African values and that robbed the continent of resources. Many Africans lacked education and experience in government.

SOCIAL STUDIES SKILLBUILDER

Major Lakes of Africa South of the Sahara

Name of Lake	Location	Area (sq. miles)	Length (miles)	Greatest Depth (feet)
Victoria	Tanzania, Uganda, Kenya	26,828	200	270
Tanganyika	Tanzania, Democratic Republic of the Congo, Zambia, Burundi	12,700	420	4,708
Nyasa	Malawi, Mozambique, Tanzania	11,600	360	2,316
Turkana (Rudolf)	Ethiopia	2,473	154	240

SKILLBUILDER: Interpreting a Chart

1. **Region** • What information does this chart present?
2. **Place** • Which lake is the largest in area? Which is the deepest?
3. **Place** • Which country has part of three major lakes within its borders? What are the lakes' names?

FOCUS ON GEOGRAPHY

Compare this map of Africa in 1886 with the map of Africa in 1912 on page 282.

1. Which two European countries had the most colonies in Africa?
2. What happened to African borders between 1886 and 1912?

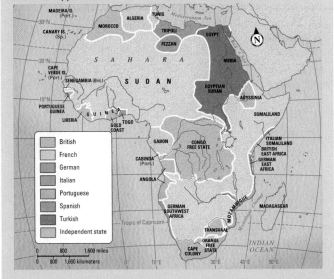

Legend:
- British
- French
- German
- Italian
- Portuguese
- Spanish
- Turkish
- Independent state

Interdisciplinary Activity: Science
Investigating a Process Africa's geological history makes it a major source of diamonds. Research and report on how diamonds are formed deep in the earth, how they are mined in Africa, and how different kinds of African diamonds are used. Use encyclopedias, science references, and other sources for your report. Include photographs or drawings if possible.

Cooperative Learning Activity
Creating an Art Display In a group of three to five classmates, gather photocopies, museum postcards, or magazine clippings showing art forms from at least four countries in Africa south of the Sahara. Each student in the group can choose a country. Organize your collection on the bulletin board around a map of Africa. Use string to connect each object to its country and label with the following information:

- The country where the art was created
- When the art was made
- How it was used

 INTERNET ACTIVITY

Use the Internet to research wildlife parks and refuges in Africa south of the Sahara. Where are they located? What are their goals? What problems do they face? **Writing About Geography** Prepare a written or oral report on one park. Discuss its climate and landforms, its animals, and the opportunities for visitors. Include information on how the country manages and protects its endangered wildlife.

For Internet links to support this activity, go to

RESEARCH LINKS
CLASSZONE.COM

313

CHAPTER PROJECTS

Interdisciplinary Activity: Science

Investigating a Process Suggest that students create an outline for their reports, focusing on how African diamonds are formed, mined, and used. Reports should be based on a variety of definitive reference sources and include photographs, illustrations, and other visuals.

Cooperative Learning Activity

Creating an Art Display Assign groups and have students choose countries to research. After students have collected the visuals, suggest that they share remaining responsibilities for creating the art displays. Encourage students to clearly label each item and to provide information about the country of origin, time period, and use of each item.

INTERNET ACTIVITY

Discuss how students might find information about Africa's wildlife parks and refuges. Brainstorm possible keywords and Web sites.

Suggest that students organize the data they collect in a chart, listing parks/refuges, locations, climate and landforms, animals, and so on. Students can use this information in their reports. Written reports should include concise introductory and concluding paragraphs. Provide time for students to present oral reports.

Skills Answers

Social Studies Skillbuilder
Possible Responses

1. This chart presents information about the area, length, depth, and location of Africa's large lakes.
2. Lake Victoria is the largest in area; Lake Tanganyika is the deepest.
3. Tanzania; Lake Victoria, Lake Tanganyika, Lake Nyasa

Focus on Geography
Possible Responses

1. France and the United Kingdom
2. They became more defined.

Western and Central Africa

	OVERVIEW	COPYMASTERS	INTEGRATED TECHNOLOGY
UNIT ATLAS AND CHAPTER RESOURCES	Students will examine the history, governments, economies, and culture of the countries of Western and Central Africa.	**In-depth Resources: Unit 4** • Guided Reading Worksheets, pp. 15–17 • Skillbuilder Practice, p. 20 • Unit Atlas Activities, pp. 1–2 • Geography Workshop, pp. 37–38 **Reading Study Guide** (Spanish and English), pp. 98–105 **Outline Map Activities**	Power Presentations Electronic Teacher Tools Online Lesson Planner Chapter Summaries on CD Critical Thinking Transparencies CT21

	KEY IDEAS		
SECTION 1 History and Political Change pp. 317–321	• European nations divided Africa along geographic borders to control its resources, ignoring traditional borders of ethnicity. • Mobuto Sese Seko tried to erase the effects of colonialism through radical means; his efforts led to civil war. • Kwame Nkrumah improved education and infrastructure in Ghana, but he eventually became a dictator.	**In-depth Resources: Unit 4** • Guided Reading Worksheet, p. 15 • Reteaching Activity, p. 22 **Reading Study Guide** (Spanish and English), pp. 98–99	classzone.com Chapter Summaries on CD
SECTION 2 Economies and Cultures pp. 324–328	• Economies in Western and Central Africa are changing, relying on agriculture for cash crops, rather than subsistence. • Mineral resources have brought wealth, but also conflict. • Many Western and Central Africans have moved from villages to large cities, where there are more opportunities, but greater strains on traditional family life.	**In-depth Resources: Unit 4** • Guided Reading Worksheet, p. 16 • Reteaching Activity, p. 23 **Reading Study Guide** (Spanish and English), pp. 100–101	classzone.com Chapter Summaries on CD
SECTION 3 Nigeria Today pp. 330–333	• The three main ethnic groups in Nigeria today are Yoruba, Igbo, and Hausa. • Nigeria gained independence from Britain in 1960, but ethnic tensions led to civil war soon after. • Nigerian artists and writers draw on traditional and modern sources for their work.	**In-depth Resources: Unit 4** • Guided Reading Worksheet, p. 17 • Reteaching Activity, p. 24 **Reading Study Guide** (Spanish and English), pp. 102–103	Critical Thinking Transparencies CT22 classzone.com Chapter Summaries on CD

- 🔊 Audio
- 💿 CD-ROM
- 📄 Copymaster
- 🌐 Internet
- 💡 Overhead Transparency
- 📄 Pupil's Edition
- TE Teacher's Edition
- 📹 Video

ASSESSMENT OPTIONS

PE **Chapter Assessment,** pp. 334–335

📄 **Formal Assessment**
- Chapter Tests: Forms A, B, C, pp. 165–176

💿 **Test Generator**

🌐 **Online Test Practice**

📄 **Strategies for Test Preparation**

PE **Section Assessment,** p. 321

📄 **Formal Assessment**
- Section Quiz, p. 162

📄 **Integrated Assessment**
- Rubric for designing a currency

💿 **Test Generator**

💡 **Test Practice Transparencies TT38**

PE **Section Assessment,** p. 328

📄 **Formal Assessment**
- Section Quiz, p. 163

📄 **Integrated Assessment**
- Rubric for making a poster

💿 **Test Generator**

💡 **Test Practice Transparencies TT39**

PE **Section Assessment,** p. 333

📄 **Formal Assessment**
- Section Quiz, p. 164

📄 **Integrated Assessment**
- Rubric for making a mask

💿 **Test Generator**

💡 **Test Practice Transparencies TT40**

RESOURCES FOR DIFFERENTIATING INSTRUCTION

Students Acquiring English/ESL

📄 **Reading Study Guide**
(Spanish and English),
pp. 98–105

📄 **Access for Students Acquiring English**
Spanish Translations,
pp. 95–102

Less Proficient Readers

📄 **Reading Study Guide**
(Spanish and English),
pp. 98–105

TE **TE Activity**
- Rereading, p. 327

Gifted and Talented Students

TE **TE Activities**
- Travel Packages, p. 326
- Researching, p. 331

CROSS-CURRICULAR CONNECTIONS

Humanities
Ahiagble, Gilbert Bobbo. *Master Weaver from Ghana.* Seattle, WA: Open Hand Publishing, 1998. Kente cloth techniques by a contemporary male weaver from Ghana.
Finley, Carol. *The Art of African Masks: Exploring Cultural Traditions.* Minneapolis, MN: Lerner Publishing, 1999. How this ancient custom reflects today's cultures.

Literature
Offodile, Buchi. *The Orphan Girl and Other Stories: West African Folktales.* New York: Interlink Books, 2001. Roots of the storytelling tradition in West Africa.

Popular Culture
Unobagha, Uzoamaka Chinyelu. *Off to the Sweet Shores of Africa and Other Talking Drum Rhymes.* San Francisco: Chronicle Books, 2000. Nigerian poet uses culture of her homeland to develop an original "Mother Goose" anthology.

Science/Math
Poynter, Margaret. *The Leakeys: Uncovering the Origins of Humankind.* Berkeley Heights, NJ: Enslow Publishers, 2001. Their search in Africa for the first man.

Mathematics
Zaslavsky, Claudia. *Count on Your Fingers African Style.* New York: Black Butterfly Books, 1999. Describes how finger counting is used in an African marketplace.

Science
Matthews, Tom. *Light Shining Through the Mist: A Photobiography of Dian Fossey.* Washington, D.C.: National Geographic Society, 1998. Fossey's work to save the mountain gorillas of Rwanda and the Congo.
Saign, Geoffrey. *The African Cats.* New York: Franklin Watts, 1999. Family tree, habitat, and future of ten species.

ENRICHMENT ACTIVITIES

The following activities are especially suitable for classes following block schedules.

Teacher's Edition, pp. 318, 320, 325, 326, 331
Pupil's Edition, pp. 321, 328, 333

Unit Atlas, pp. 278–287
Literature Connections, pp. 322–323

Outline Map Activities

INTEGRATED TECHNOLOGY

Go to **classzone.com** for lesson support and activities for Chapter 11.

BLOCK SCHEDULE LESSON PLAN OPTIONS: 90-MINUTE PERIOD

DAY 1

CHAPTER PREVIEW, pp. 314–315
Class Time 20 minutes

• **Hypothesize** Use the "What do you think?" questions in Focus on Geography on PE p. 315 to help students hypothesize about how Africa's waterways affect the region's ways of life.

SECTION 1, pp. 317–321
Class Time 70 minutes

• **Small Groups** Write the section objectives from TE p. 317 on the chalkboard. Divide the class into four groups. Have each group select one section to help them prepare a summary of this section. Remind students that when they summarize, they should include the main ideas and most important details in their own words. Reconvene as a whole class for discussion.
Class Time 35 minutes

• **Writing a Letter** Divide students into pairs. Have each pair write a letter, dated sometime in the year 1886, from an African leader in the Congo Basin to King Leopold II of Belgium, protesting the European agreement to divide Africa. Display the letters in the classroom.
Class Time 35 minutes

DAY 2

SECTION 2, pp. 324–328
Class Time 65 minutes

• **Peer Competition** Divide the class into pairs. Assign each pair one of the Terms & Names for this section. Have pairs make up five questions that can be answered with the term or name. Have groups take turns asking the class their questions.
Class Time 20 minutes

• **Interpreting a Chart** Have students complete the chart in the Section 2 Assessment on PE p. 328. Ask them to create a title for the chart. Use the Skillbuilder Mini-Lesson: Interpreting a Chart from TE p. 326 to review with students how to read and interpret information in a chart. Then have students exchange charts and summarize the information contained in them.
Class Time 25 minutes

• **Designing a Stool** Have students reread Spotlight on Culture on PE p. 327. Encourage students to sketch a design for their own school stool. Display student designs in the classroom.
Class Time 20 minutes

SECTION 3, pp. 330–333
Class Time 25 minutes

• **Word Web** Divide the class into small groups. Have each group create a word web to display the characteristics of Nigeria's three main ethnic groups: the Yoruba, the Igbo, and the Hausa. Provide time for the entire class to share their webs.
Class Time 15 minutes

• **Geography Skillbuilder** Use the questions in the Geography Skillbuilder on PE p. 331 to guide a discussion about Nigeria's ethnic groups. Extend the discussion by asking students how they think Nigeria is affected by its great diversity.
Class Time 10 minutes

DAY 3

SECTION 3, continued
Class Time 35 minutes

• **Main Idea** Have pairs of students review the Main Idea for each section and find three details to support each one. Then have each pair list two additional important ideas and trade lists with another group to find details.

CHAPTER 11 REVIEW AND ASSESSMENT, pp. 334–335
Class Time 55 minutes

• **Review** Have students use the charts they created for Reading Social Studies on PE p. 316 to review inferences about Western and Central Africa and key evidence that supports those inferences.
Class Time 20 minutes

• **Assessment** Have students complete the Chapter 11 Assessment.
Class Time 35 minutes

TECHNOLOGY IN THE CLASSROOM

If you are looking for information about the arts of a culture or country, the Internet is often the best place to go. Since it offers the multimedia features of images, videos, sound clips, and text, the Internet is an excellent place to see, hear, and read about a variety of art forms.

ACTIVITY OUTLINE

Objective Students will use the Internet to research traditional arts of Western Africa. They will create multimedia or Web pages promoting a Western African cultural center in their town.

Task Have students visit the Web sites to find examples of Western African art, music, dance, and folklore. Ask them to create advertisements for a Western African cultural center in their community, including examples they find on the Web.

Class Time 2–3 class periods

DIRECTIONS

1. Inform the class that Western Africa has a rich tradition of art, music, dance, and folklore. Students may have seen works of African art in museums.

2. Ask students to imagine that they have decided to open a Western African cultural center in their town to introduce their community to West African arts. The cultural center will contain examples of Western African art, music, dance, and folklore and will offer performances as well as exhibits.

3. Divide the class into small groups, with approximately four students each.

4. Have students visit the Web sites at **classzone.com** to see some of the things they might include in their cultural centers. Ask them to find examples of folk tales, traditional musical instruments, masks, wood carvings, textiles, and dances. They should choose at least two examples from each of these categories and, on paper, sketch the examples and write a one- or two-sentence description of what each one is and what it was used for. They may also choose to write a brief summary of a folk tale.

5. Ask each group to create one Web page or multimedia slide that could be used to advertise the new cultural center. These pages should include at least one example of Western African art, music (preferably including sound clips), dance, and folklore.

CHAPTER 11 OBJECTIVE

Students will examine the history, governments, economies, and cultures of the countries of Western and Central Africa.

FOCUS ON VISUALS

Interpreting the Photograph Have students closely study the photograph of the outdoor market. Ask them to list things they see in the photograph that they do not see in their own community.

Possible Responses Differences students might mention include: people carrying things on their heads, a baby carried in a scarf on its mother's back, thatched roofs, and pots for sale displayed on the ground.

Extension Have students imagine that they are children from the region shown in the photograph. They are visiting a mall in the United States for the first time. Have students list the things about the mall they would find remarkable.

CRITICAL THINKING ACTIVITY

Contrasting Prompt a discussion about how the marketplace in the photograph is different from stores and malls where students and their families shop. If students have been to farmers' markets, have them share their experiences and compare them with the outdoor market shown here.

Class Time 10 minutes

Western and Central Africa

SECTION 1 History and Political Change

SECTION 2 Economies and Cultures

SECTION 3 Nigeria Today

314

Recommended Resources

BOOKS FOR THE TEACHER

Achebe, Chinua. *Home and Exile.* New York: Oxford University Press, 2000. Nigerian exile discusses legacies of colonialism.

Falola, Toyin. *Culture and Customs of Nigeria.* Westport, CT: Greenwood Press, 2001. Overview of Nigerian culture.

Phillips, Tom, ed. *Africa: The Art of a Continent.* New York: Prestel, 1995. Stunning maps, images, and text show the range of African art through history.

The New African Poetry: An Anthology. Boulder, CO: Lynne Rienner Publishers, 2000. Works by more than 60 contemporary African poets, arranged by region.

VIDEOS

Travel the World by Train: Africa. Long Beach, CA: Pioneer Entertainment, 1999. Journey to Morocco, Tunisia, Egypt, Kenya, Uganda, and South Africa.

INTERNET

For more information about Western and Central Africa, visit **classzone.com**.

How can an entire town move across a country?

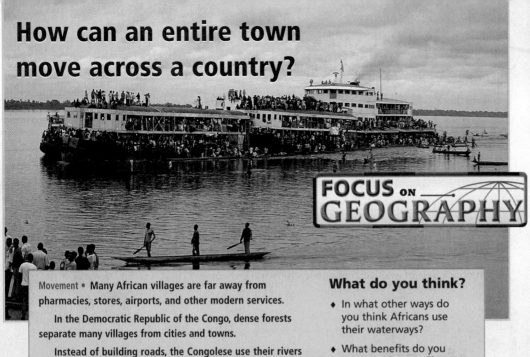

Movement • Many African villages are far away from pharmacies, stores, airports, and other modern services.

In the Democratic Republic of the Congo, dense forests separate many villages from cities and towns.

Instead of building roads, the Congolese use their rivers as highways. Great barges run up and down the Congo River, carrying thousands of people on each trip. These barges are moving towns, with clinics, churches, markets, restaurants, and more.

What do you think?

♦ In what other ways do you think Africans use their waterways?

♦ What benefits do you think the barge offers over airplane travel in the Democratic Republic of the Congo?

Place Most African towns and villages host daily or weekly outdoor markets. Many of the vendors live in the countryside and travel into town to sell their goods.

315

FOCUS ON GEOGRAPHY

Objectives

• To explain how rivers are used as transportation corridors

• To identify how geography affects a nation's economy

What Do You Think?

1. Guide students to consider ways Africans might use rivers and other waterways as sources of food, recreation, and power.

2. Prompt a discussion about the social aspects of barge travel. What kinds of social interaction occur on the barges? How important are the barges to people's lives?

How can an entire town move across a country?

Ask students to think about the various ways that the barges are like towns. Have them consider the number of passengers on the barge and the services provided for the people onboard.

MAKING GEOGRAPHIC CONNECTIONS

Have students discuss the importance of waterways in their region and in the entire United States. Do Americans use waterways in the same way as the people of the Democratic Republic of the Congo? Why or why not? Ask students to discuss the importance of waterways a century ago and what developments have caused a change in the use of waterways.

Implementing the National Geography Standards

Standard 5 Suggest criteria for and examples of formal, functional, and perceptual regions

Objective To create a map showing formal, functional, and perceptual regions in Africa

Class Time 30 minutes

Task Have students create criteria for formal, functional, and perceptual regions and then create a map locating those regions in Africa. Have students work in groups to create criteria for and examples of the three region types. The groups will share their criteria and then create a map showing Africa's regions.

Evaluation Maps should include at least one example of each region type.

BEFORE YOU READ

What Do You Know?

Have students look at the Unit Atlas map on pages 280–281 and the map on page 314. Ask them to name the countries and capital cities of the region. Then ask students to brainstorm information they have learned about the countries in this region.

What Do You Want to Know?

Have students list questions they would like answered about Western and Central Africa, leaving space for answers below each one. Have them use the five themes of geography as a guide to listing questions. As they read the chapter, they can write answers to their questions.

READ AND TAKE NOTES

Reading Strategy: Making Inferences Make sure students understand that their inferences should be based on information in the text, plus their own experience, reasoning, and knowledge. Direct students' attention to the chart. Tell them to read the statements in the first column and make an inference about each one. Urge students to use what they have learned in previous chapters and what they know from reading current events as they form inferences. Emphasize that inferences are not necessarily true or false but can be proven to be true or false. Then, as they read, have students look for evidence that confirms or changes each inference.

 In-depth Resources: Unit 4
• Guided Reading Worksheets, pp. 15–17

READING SOCIAL STUDIES

BEFORE YOU READ

▶▶ What Do You Know?

Western and Central African countries export many products to the United States, including gold and the cocao beans used to make chocolate. What else do you know about this region? Did you know that Liberia was founded by Americans? How did European colonialism affect the region? Reflect on what you have learned in other classes, what you read in Chapter 10, and what you have seen in the news about recent events in this area.

▶▶ What Do You Want to Know?

Decide what else you want to know about Western and Central Africa. In your notebook, record what you hope to learn from this chapter.

Culture • Cameroon's soccer team celebrated after winning the gold medal at the Olympic Games in 2000. ▼

READ AND TAKE NOTES

Reading Strategy: Making Inferences Making inferences is an important skill in reading social studies. Making inferences involves thinking beyond the text and interpreting the information you read. To make inferences, read carefully and use common sense and previous knowledge to make connections between ideas. Use the chart below to record inferences you can build on as you read.

• Copy the chart into your notebook.

• Read each statement. Use what you know to make inferences. Record your interpretations, connections, and ideas.

• As you read, record key evidence that confirms, changes, or builds on your inferences.

Culture • At one time only royalty in Ghana could wear this colorful Kente cloth. Today, it is popular among all Ghanaians. ▲

Statements	My Inferences	Key Evidence
European colonial powers divided Africa. Territories created by colonial powers became separate countries.	Students' inferences will vary. Ask volunteers to share their inferences, and discuss them as a class.	Students should select key evidence that supports their inferences.
In most African countries, governments are either too strong or too weak.		
Most countries of Western and Central Africa have a mix of different types of economies.		
Africa is culturally diverse. Before colonial rule, Africa had many different types of societies. There are some things that most of the peoples of Western and Central Africa have in common.		
Nigeria has more than 250 ethnic groups. Conflicts among these groups have sometimes led to civil war. This diversity has also led to a rich artistic and literary heritage.		

Teaching Strategy

Reading the Chapter This is a thematic chapter that focuses on the recent history of Western and Central Africa, beginning with the European colonialism of the nineteenth century. It then describes the current political and economic conditions of the region. Encourage students to pay particular attention to how colonialism affected the present political and economic conditions of the region.

Integrated Assessment The Chapter Assessment on page 334 describes several activities that may be used for integrated assessment. You may wish to have students work on these activities during the course of the chapter and then present them at the end.

History and Political Change

TERMS & NAMES

coup d'état

OAU

mediate

ECOWAS

MAIN IDEA

Since gaining independence, some of the countries of Western and Central Africa have had trouble establishing stable governments.

WHY IT MATTERS NOW

Unstable governments are the basis for many conflicts in Western and Central Africa.

SECTION OBJECTIVES

1. To describe how European nations divided Western and Central Africa
2. To examine the government of the Democratic Republic of the Congo
3. To examine the government of Ghana
4. To explain how the OAU and ECOWAS help developing nations in Africa

SKILLBUILDER

• Interpreting a Map, p. 318

CRITICAL THINKING

• Forming and Supporting Opinions, p. 319

FOCUS & MOTIVATE
WARM-UP

Hypothesizing Have students read <u>Dateline</u> and answer the following questions:

1. How does the cartoon support the article?
2. How might Africans have responded?

INSTRUCT: Objective ①

Dividing Western and Central Africa/New Maps of West Africa

• What was the European nations' goal in dividing Africa? to control its resources
• What factors were considered or ignored as Europeans divided Africa? Traditional borders between ethnic groups were ignored; geographic factors were used.
• What three nations acquired land in the Congo Basin? Belgium, France, Portugal

 In-depth Resources: Unit 4
• Guided Reading Worksheet, p. 15

 Reading Study Guide
(Spanish and English), pp. 98–99

DATELINE (EXTRA)

BERLIN, GERMANY, FEBRUARY 26, 1885

The competition for the riches of Africa has caused growing conflict. But today, the countries of Europe finally agreed on the rules for dividing up the African continent. The rules will enable the countries to claim land in Africa without going to war with one another.

When the powers of Europe take land in Africa, they must make sure that no other country has already claimed that land. Also, the agreement will allow open trade among the colonies. All countries will be able to freely move goods on the Congo River. At last, the takeover of Africa will be orderly.

Region • This political cartoon makes clear that European nations have been fighting for control of African lands and resources. ▲

Human-Environment Interaction • Explorers, such as Sir Henry Morton Stanley, have helped Europeans learn about Africa. Sir Henry is the first European to explore the entire Congo River. ▲

Dividing Western and Central Africa ①

European nations divided the African continent in the late 1800s. They were not thinking about creating new nations. Their goal was to control Africa's rich resources. To avoid war with one another, the European powers made trades. They traded one advantage—such as coastal land—for another.

Western and Central Africa **317**

Program Resources

 In-depth Resources: Unit 4
• Guided Reading Worksheet, p. 15
• Reteaching Activity, p. 22

 Reading Study Guide
(Spanish and English), pp. 98–99

 Formal Assessment
• Section Quiz, p. 162

 Integrated Assessment
• Rubric for drawing a model

 Outline Map Activities

 Access for Students Acquiring English
• Guided Reading Worksheet, p. 95

 Technology Resources
classzone.com

TEST-TAKING RESOURCES

↪ Strategies for Test Preparation
↪ Test Practice Transparencies
⊕ Online Test Practice

INSTRUCT: Objective ❷

Governments in Western and Central Africa/Government in the Democratic Republic of the Congo

- Why have many modern African nations had unstable governments? They lack ethnic and regional unity.

- How did Mobutu try to wipe out the effects of colonialism? changed name of country to Zaire, changed his name, made people wear African-style clothing and take African names, prohibited foreign music

- What was the result of the 1994 civil war in Congo? Mobutu's government was overthrown; name of the country was changed to the Democratic Republic of the Congo.

FOCUS ON VISUALS

Interpreting the Map Remind students that a basin is the land drained by a river. Ask students to name the countries that are part of the Congo Basin.

Possible Responses Countries in the Congo Basin include: Central African Republic, Cameroon, Gabon, the Republic of the Congo, and the Democratic Republic of the Congo.

Extension Have students use this map and one or more atlases to name the tributaries of the Congo River.

New Maps of West Africa ❶

When Europeans divided Africa, they ignored traditional borders between Africa's ethnic groups. They used other factors to draw new maps, such as the location of rivers or lakes.

Let's Make a Deal Look at The Gambia on the political map of Africa on page 280. The country is only 30 miles across at its widest point. How was a country with such strange borders formed? In 1816, the British bought an island at the mouth of the Gambia River. They used the island as a base to extend their control over the banks of the river. However, France claimed all the land around the river. When the Europeans drew borders in the late 1880s, the British kept The Gambia, with access to the river. In return, the French got more land for Senegal.

Dividing the Congo Basin European interest in a river affected borders in Central Africa too. The Congo River is the second-longest river in Africa. Belgium, France, and Portugal all wanted to claim the river and the lands around it. That rivalry was the main reason for the conference in Berlin that you read about on page 317. At the conference, the three nations agreed to divide the huge Congo Basin. King Leopold of Belgium took the land that is now the Democratic Republic of the Congo as his personal property. France possessed what is now the Republic of the Congo. Portugal controlled what is present-day Angola.

Governments in Western and Central Africa ❷

When African nations became independent, many of their colonial borders stayed the same. These borders split ethnic groups and regions that historically had been united, making it difficult for many modern African nations to establish stable governments.

Human-Environment Interaction • The Gambia's width was in large part determined by the firing range of the British gunboats that patrolled the Gambia River. ▲

Reading Social Studies

A. Analyzing Motives Why was controlling a river so important to the Europeans?

Reading Social Studies A. Possible Answer Control of a river meant control over commerce and greater ability to protect resources.

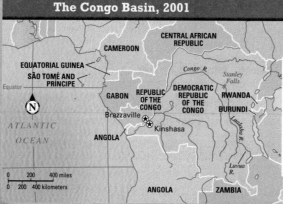

The Congo Basin, 2001

GEOGRAPHY SKILLBUILDER: Interpreting a Map

1. **Region** • What physical feature forms the border between the Republic of the Congo and the Democratic Republic of the Congo?
2. **Place** • What is the capital of the Republic of the Congo?

Geography Skillbuilder Answers

1. Congo River
2. Brazzaville

Activity Options

Interdisciplinary Links: Geography/Art

Class Time One class period

Task Creating jigsaw puzzles of Western and Central Africa

Purpose To identify the shape, size, and geographic features of individual countries of Western and Central Africa

Supplies Needed
- Drawing paper
- Pencils or markers
- Scissors

🅱 Block Scheduling

Activity Have students work in groups to draw a map of Western and Central Africa. Instruct them to label each country and add geographic features such as rivers. Then have students cut apart the individual countries to make puzzle pieces. Challenge students to think of two ways to categorize the puzzle pieces, such as by large and small countries or by coastal and landlocked countries. Have groups trade their puzzles and assemble them.

Since 1963, about 200 African governments have been ousted by coups d'état (koo day·TAH). A **coup d'état** is an overthrow of a government by force. Two of the many countries that have struggled to create stable democratic governments are the Democratic Republic of the Congo and Ghana.

Government in the Democratic Republic of the Congo ❷

In 1960, the former Belgian Congo gained independence, but a series of coups d'état toppled each established government. Five years later, an army general, Joseph Désiré Mobutu, took power. Mobutu tried to wipe out all traces of colonialism. He changed the name of the country to Zaire (ZEYE·eer) and his own name to Mobutu Sese Seko (SAY·say SAY·koh). He made people wear African-style clothing and take names that were African instead of Belgian.

Mobutu ruled as a dictator, calling the people of Zaire his "children." He allowed no criticism of his rule. At the same time, he built up a personal fortune by stealing government money intended for roads, schools, and hospitals.

Civil War A brutal civil war began in Zaire in 1994. It resulted in Laurent Désiré Kabila overthrowing Mobutu's government. Kabila changed the country's name to the Democratic Republic of the Congo. However, the country was not a true democracy, and civil war started again. Kabila was assassinated in 2001. His son, Joseph Kabila, replaced him as president.

Place • This banknote was printed in 1993, four years before Zaire became the Democratic Republic of the Congo. ▼

Government in Ghana ❸

In 1957, the British colony of Gold Coast became the first independent country in Africa south of the Sahara. The new nation took its name, Ghana, from a great ancient empire. The country's first leader was Kwame Nkrumah (uhn·KROO·muh). Nkrumah wanted to make Ghana modern. He built a new seaport, roads, and railroads to make shipping natural resources to factories and sending manufactured goods to stores easier and cheaper. Foreign trade improved. Ghana also became the first country in Africa south of the Sahara to have compulsory primary education.

Place • Kwame Nkrumah is shown here, at left, shortly after Ghana gained independence. ▼

Activity Options

Interdisciplinary Link: Citizenship

Patriotism Explain to students that Mobutu wanted people of his nation to reclaim their African heritage. He wanted to encourage patriotism and loyalty to their nation and continent. Point out that Americans show their patriotism when they fly the United States flag, sing the national anthem before baseball games, and attend fireworks displays on Independence Day. Challenge students to work in pairs and brainstorm a list of other ways to encourage people of the United States to show their patriotism and pride in their American heritage. Have pairs share their best three ideas in a class discussion. Be sure students consider songs that are unique to American patriotism and heritage. Discuss with students times in our nation's history when Americans have made special efforts to show their patriotism, for example, after the attacks on the World Trade Center.

Citizenship
IN ACTION

About 15,000 street children live in Accra, and the number is growing rapidly. Many of the children, between the ages of 10 and 18, were born in Accra, but others come from the surrounding countryside or from other parts of Africa. Poverty, abuse, and the breakdown of families are the major reasons the children live on the streets. Some were sent there to earn money to help support the family. Few of the children beg. Most earn money doing odd jobs. Boys shine shoes, push trucks, or collect trash, which they carry to the dumpsites. Some sell small items, such as chewing gum. Girls often sell oranges, ice water, and bread.

A VOICE FROM GHANA

Remind students that status quo means the existing state of affairs. Then ask students to identify times in our own country when people challenged the status quo, such as during Revolutionary times or during the civil rights movement of the 1960s.

MORE ABOUT...
Kofi Annan

Kofi Annan was born in Ghana in 1938 into a well-known family of chieftains of the Fante people. He studied in the United States and Switzerland and has spent most of his adult life working for the United Nations. Among his many important jobs in the UN, he worked to free hostages in Iraq and mediated among the nations involved in the war in Bosnia. He was named secretary-general of the United Nations in 1996—the first black African to hold that position. In 2001 Annan and the United Nations were awarded the Nobel Peace Prize. After winning the prize, he said, "The only true prize for them [the UN staff] and for us will be peace itself."

Place • This billboard in Accra, Ghana, showed Jerry John Rawlings (center) with the two candidates for the presidency in 2000. ▲

Military Rulers Although Nkrumah helped the new nation, he ruled as a dictator. He sent his opponents to prison. Some were tortured and killed. In 1966, the police and the army organized a coup d'état against Nkrumah. The coup d'état leaders freed political prisoners. They tried to help small businesses. Still, conditions in Ghana grew worse. People lost their jobs and did not have money for food. They went on strike to protest. When military leaders tried to take control, fighting began, and more coups d'état followed. In 1979, Jerry John Rawlings, a soldier, took power.

The Coming of Democracy In 1992, Rawlings allowed an election to take place. Ghana then became more democratic. A new constitution and parliament put limits on his power. In 2000, Rawlings became the first modern African military ruler to give up power peacefully. Elections brought in a new president. Today, Ghana is one of the most stable nations in Africa. In 1998, UN Secretary General Kofi Annan commented on Ghana's success.

A VOICE FROM GHANA

I grew up in Ghana at the time when we were fighting for independence, and so I saw lots of changes in my youth. I saw that it was possible to challenge the status quo and do something about it. And change did occur.

Kofi Annan, 1998

Reading Social Studies
C. Possible Answer
Answers will vary, but students may acknowledge that democracy requires a peaceful transfer of power.

Reading
Social Studies

C. Forming and Supporting Opinions What do you think of Rawlings's decision to give up power peacefully? Why might he have decided to do so?

Vocabulary
status quo: existing state of affairs

Citizenship
IN ACTION

Aid for Children In cities all over Africa, growing numbers of children can be found living on the streets. In Accra, Ghana, which has thousands of street children (shown at right), two local organizations are working to help them: Street Girls Aid (S.Aid) and Catholic Action for Street Children (CAS).

CAS provides places where children can wash, eat, rest, take classes, or simply play. For teenage mothers with children, S.Aid offers daycare so the mothers can work. Both groups provide health care and counseling to help children cope with the harshness of life on the streets.

320 CHAPTER 11

Activity Options

Multiple Learning Styles: Logical/Linguistic

B **Block Scheduling**

Class Time One class period
Task Writing a political speech
Purpose To analyze the actions of Ghana's political leaders

Supplies Needed
• Writing paper
• Pencils or pens
• Library or Internet resources (optional)

Activity Point out that Mobutu, Nkrumah, and even Jerry John Rawlings were controversial leaders. Each did good things for his country, but each used force and undemocratic actions to gain and maintain power. Have students imagine that they are writing a political speech to support or oppose one of these leaders. Have students plan, write, and practice their speeches, then deliver them to the class.

Region • In 2001, the OAU was being transformed into the African Union, whose new general secretary, Amara Essy, is shown here on the right. ▶

Nations Helping Nations ❹

Like Ghana, many African nations have had to struggle for peace and democracy. Some nations are working together to help one another. In 1963, the **OAU,** or the Organization of African Unity, was formed. The organization tries to promote unity among all Africans. For example, the OAU would like to establish a single currency for Africa. The OAU also mediates disputes between countries. To **mediate** means to help find a peaceful solution.

ECOWAS The nations of Western Africa also cooperate economically. **ECOWAS,** or the Economic Community of West African States, was formed in 1975. It works to improve trade within Western Africa and with countries outside the region. ECOWAS also has mediated disputes between countries in Western Africa and tried to end government corruption.

SECTION ① ASSESSMENT

Terms & Names
1. Identify: (a) coup d'état (b) OAU (c) mediate (d) ECOWAS

Taking Notes
2. Use a chart like this one to compare the governments of the Democratic Republic of the Congo and Ghana.

Democratic Republic of the Congo	Ghana

Main Ideas
3. (a) What was the impact of European colonization on the governments of modern Africa?

(b) What example was given in this section of a government with unlimited power? What example was given in this section of a government with limited power?

(c) How did Kwame Nkrumah influence Ghana?

Critical Thinking
4. Making Inferences

Why do you think it was important for the power of Jerry John Rawlings, the former president of Ghana, to be limited?

Think About

♦ other dictatorships around the world

♦ the progression of human rights

ACTIVITY -OPTION- Pretend you have been commissioned by the OAU to design a common currency for all of Africa. Draw a **model** or write a **description** of your design.

Nations Helping Nations

• What are some goals of the OAU? promote African unity, establish single currency for Africa, moderate disputes between countries

• What is the purpose of ECOWAS? improve trade, mediate disputes, end government corruption

ASSESS & RETEACH

Reading Social Studies Make sure that students have completed the top two rows of the chart they prepared on page 316.

 Formal Assessment
• Section Quiz, p. 162

RETEACHING ACTIVITY

Divide the class into five groups and assign each group a sub-section of the lesson, beginning with "New Maps of West Africa" on page 318. Ask students in each group to work together to create an outline of the main ideas and important details in their assigned sub-section. Then ask a student from each group to write the group's outline on the board. Use the five outlines to review the lesson.

 In-depth Resources: Unit 4
• Reteaching Activity, p. 22

 Access for Students Acquiring English
• Reteaching Activity, p. 100

Section ① Assessment

1. Terms & Names
a. coup d'état, p. 319
b. OAU, p. 321
c. mediate, p. 321
d. ECOWAS, p. 321

2. Taking Notes

Democratic Republic of the Congo	Ghana
not democratic	democratic
president not elected	president elected by people
country in civil war	stable government
president assassinated in 2001	peaceful change of leaders

3. Main Ideas
a. Nations formed from colonies lacked ethnic and regional unity.
b. unlimited power: Democratic Republic of the Congo; limited power: Ghana
c. He improved the economy and made primary education compulsory.

4. Critical Thinking
Possible Response Limiting his power prevented him from becoming a dictator and infringing on human rights.

ACTIVITY OPTION
 Integrated Assessment
• Rubric for drawing a model

Linking Past and Present

The Legacy of Africa South of the Sahara

Music

Music has always played an important role in the daily life of Africa south of the Sahara. Characteristic of the music are its complex rhythms. Hand clapping, drums, and iron bells produce different rhythmic patterns. Over the years, the music of Africa south of the Sahara has influenced music around the world. Jazz, a popular type of music that began in the early 1900s in the United States, is based on a combination of European harmonies and African rhythms.

Swahili Language

Swahili, also called Kiswahili, is a widespread language on the eastern coast of Africa. It evolved from the mixing of East African and Arab cultures. Swahili also includes words adapted from the English of British colonists, such as *penseli* (pencil), *basi* (bus), and *baiskeli* (bicycle). Today, it continues to be the language spoken in the business community and is one of the languages of Tanzania, Kenya, and Uganda.

Gold

For nearly 1,000 years, Africans s[o] of the Sahara have used their pri[z] possessions—gold and ivory—as signs of wealth and power. They have also traded these valuable materials for other commodities, such as glass, precious stones, and ceramics. Many European settlers came [to] South Africa to take part in the g[old] industry. Today, South Africa is th[e] continent's largest gold producer.

Find Out More About It!
Study the text and photos on these pages to learn about inventions, creations, and contributions that have come from Africa south of the Sahara. Then choose the item that interests you the most and use the library or the Internet to learn more about it. Use the information you gather to write a short essay about how what you researched relates to you.

RESEARCH LINKS
CLASSZONE.COM

Coffee

More than 1,000 years ago, coffee trees grew in Ethiopia. Coffee beans were first used as a food. In the 1400s, coffee as a beverage was popular in Arabia, Egypt, and Turkey. In the following centuries, it was introduced to Europe and to North America. Today, coffee comes in many varieties and blends and is served as a hot or a cold beverage. It is also used to flavor ice cream and other treats.

Sculpture

The earliest evidence of African sculpture outside of Egypt dates from around 500 B.C. in Nok, located in what is now Nigeria. Archaeologists have found baked-clay heads and figures made by the Nok people. In the 1400s, sculptures of kings and thrones were created to show respect for royalty. They also represented the wealth of a region. Today, many African sculptures continue to be based on traditional themes. Artists create sculptures for religious and social purposes as well as for the retail and tourist trade.

Africa South of the Sahara **323**

INSTRUCT

- What is the language of eastern Africa's business community?
- Where was coffee first grown?
- What are African sculptures used for today?

MORE ABOUT...
Coffee

First discovered in Ethiopia, coffee is now used by countries worldwide. It spread from Africa to the Middle East, then to Europe, and finally to North America. People in America began drinking coffee in the 1600s. People in South America began growing coffee in the 1700s. Today, people in the United States drink more coffee each year than people in any other country, while Brazil grows one-quarter of all the world's coffee. Coffee is also grown in Africa, Arabia, other South American countries, and even the United States, in Hawaii.

Sculpture

It was not until the 1900s that people outside of Africa became aware of African sculpture. When it did become known in Europe, it quickly became a major influence on Western art and artists. Artists, including Georges Braque (French), Henry Moore (English), and Pablo Picasso (Spanish), were drawn to African art's dramatic forms and creative designs. They were also interested in the way African sculpture did not work to create an accurate image of a subject, but used deliberately altered forms to make expressive, emotional pieces.

More to Think About

Making Personal Connections Ask students to bring in one example of African influence in some aspect of their daily lives. If they need ideas, have them reread the various features on pages 322–323. Encourage them to look at popular images, music, food, jewelry, art, and language. Have students share their examples and discuss.

Vocabulary Activity Have students work on their own to develop two questions for each section that can be answered using vocabulary words in the title or body of the section. Organize students into teams and have them take turns quizzing each other. Encourage students to write questions that are challenging but fair.

Economies and Cultures

SECTION 2

SECTION OBJECTIVES

1. To explain changes in the economies of Western and Central Africa

2. To describe the importance of African arts and mineral resources

3. To describe ways of life in Western and Central Africa

SKILLBUILDER
• Interpreting a Map, p. 326

CRITICAL THINKING
• Finding Causes, p. 328

FOCUS & MOTIVATE
WARM-UP

Making Inferences Have students read <u>Dateline</u> and discuss Cameroon's victory.

1. Why do you think the Olympic victory was important to people of Cameroon?

2. What effect might this victory have on how other nations view Cameroon?

INSTRUCT: Objective ❶

Economies of Western and Central Africa/Agriculture in Western and Central Africa

• How do subsistence and cash crops differ?
subsistence: crops grown for personal consumption; cash: crops grown only for sale

 In-depth Resources: Unit 4
• Guided Reading Worksheet, p. 16

 Reading Study Guide
(Spanish and English), pp. 100–101

MAIN IDEA	WHY IT MATTERS NOW
The economies in Western and Central Africa are mostly a mix of traditional and market economies.	Economic development is one of the keys to sustaining democracy in Africa.

◁ ▷ ✕ ⇄ ⌂
Back Forward Stop Refresh Home

Address: ▶go

DATELINE

YAOUNDE, CAMEROON, OCTOBER 1, 2000—
Thrilled by their soccer team's victory in the Summer Olympics in Sydney, the people of Cameroon spent today celebrating their first Olympic gold medal. In small villages and busy cities, they watched the victory on television, then ran cheering into the streets.

The people in this Central African country, like many Africans, love soccer. Cameroon's "Indomitable Lions," already the African champions, outscored the team from Spain 5–3. Four years ago, at the Olympics in Atlanta, Nigeria became the first African nation to win the gold for soccer.

Place • At the gold-medal game, the Lions grin proudly as thousands of Australian fans shout, "Cameroon! Cameroon!" to cheer them on. ▲

Culture • These gold medals are from the 2000 Olympic Games. ▲

Economies of Western and Central Africa ❶

Many Africans share not only a passion for soccer but also a common economic history. Most African countries once had traditional economies, which followed age-old trading customs. Colonial governments introduced market economies, in which goods were bought and sold. Government-controlled economies, or command economies, became common after independence. Today, most African countries again have market economies.

324 CHAPTER 11

Program Resources

 In-depth Resources: Unit 4
• Guided Reading Worksheet, p. 16
• Reteaching Activity, p. 23

 Reading Study Guide
(Spanish and English), pp. 100–101

 Formal Assessment
• Section Quiz, p. 163

 Integrated Assessment
• Rubric for making a poster

 Outline Map Activities

 Access for Students Acquiring English
• Guided Reading Worksheet, p. 96

Technology Resources
classzone.com

TEST-TAKING RESOURCES

⌇ Strategies for Test Preparation
⌇ Test Practice Transparencies
⌖ Online Test Practice

Agriculture in Western and Central Africa ❶

Most people in Western and Central Africa are farmers. Many practice **subsistence farming.** That is, they grow food, such as millet and sorghum, mainly to feed their own households. During the colonial era, European and African business owners started large plantations. They grew tropical crops—sugar cane, coffee, and cacao—for export. A crop grown only for sale is called a **cash crop.**

Edible Exports Have you eaten or used anything from Africa today? Chances are you have. Côte d'Ivoire (koht dee·VWAHR; formerly Ivory Coast) is the world's largest producer and exporter of cacao beans, which are used to make chocolate. Coastal West African countries also export coffee, bananas, pineapples, palm oil, peanuts, and kola nuts. Central African countries produce coffee, rubber, and cotton. These exports bring many African countries income for development, such as building roads and schools.

African Artisans ❷

Although the majority of people are farmers, some have other jobs. Some people craft items out of metal, leather, or wood. These workers make things such as iron hoes, leather shoes, and beautiful pieces of art. Other people are entertainers and musicians. Musicians act as the historians in some traditional African societies. Their skills and stories are passed down from generation to generation.

African Minerals ❷

Almost every type of mineral in the world can be found somewhere in Africa. Valuable minerals exported from Central and Western Africa include diamonds, gold, petroleum, manganese, and uranium. Many Africans earn their living by working in mines.

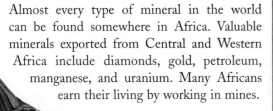

Culture • Kente cloth, exported from West Africa, has become popular in many non-African countries. ▼

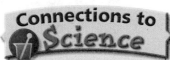

Connections to Science

Disappearing Tusks Ivory from African elephant tusks has been used to make items such as piano keys, jewelry, and billiard balls. Many elephants have been killed for their tusks, which you can see below. To protect elephants, ivory products were banned internationally in the 1980s. However, the demand for ivory is still so great that people continue to hunt elephants illegally for their tusks.

Because elephants born without tusks are not hunted, they live and reproduce. Often their offspring are tuskless. Biologists have noted that about 30 percent of African elephants are now tuskless—an impressive increase from 1 percent in the 1930s.

Western and Central Africa **325**

Connections to Science

Five hundred years ago, about 10 million elephants roamed Africa. By 1979 there were just 1.3 million, and today about 600,000 remain. Although loss of habitat contributes to the problem, at least as big a problem is poaching. More than a million elephants were killed by poachers between 1970 and 1989. Elephants can live up to 70 years in the wild, but few African elephants with tusks live that long.

INSTRUCT: Objective ❷

African Artisans/African Minerals

- What special role do musicians play? act as historians, pass down stories and skills through the generations
- What minerals are found in Africa? diamonds, gold, petroleum, manganese, uranium
- What are "conflict diamonds"? diamonds sold to buy weapons and finance wars

MORE ABOUT...
Storytelling in West Africa

In West Africa, storytelling has an important role in the upbringing of children even today. Through tales, fables, epics, and other types of stories, the history and values of the people are passed on. The storyteller, or griot, tells stories that recount the past or feature favorite characters, such as Brer Rabbit or Anansi, the spider. Many of these stories were carried by slaves to the Caribbean and the United States and are still told today. The Brer Rabbit stories are an example of stories that came from West Africa.

Activity Options

Interdisciplinary Link: Language Arts

Class Time One class period
Task Retelling an African folk tale
Purpose To become familiar with the folk literature of Africa

Supplies Needed
- Collections of African folk tales

Ⓑ Block Scheduling

Activity Remind students that folk tales are stories handed down from generation to generation within cultures. Discuss folk tales that students have read and remember. Next, invite small groups of students to find and read a traditional African folk tale. Then ask the students to read the folk tale as a group and practice retelling it. Finally, have one representative from each group retell their folk tale for the others.

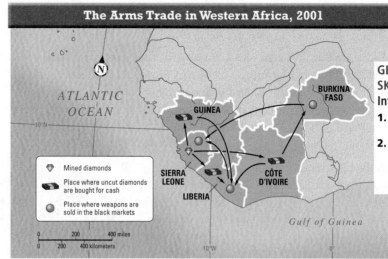

The Arms Trade in Western Africa, 2001

ATLANTIC OCEAN

GUINEA

BURKINA FASO

SIERRA LEONE

CÔTE D'IVOIRE

LIBERIA

Gulf of Guinea

◆ Mined diamonds

▬ Place where uncut diamonds are bought for cash

● Place where weapons are sold in the black markets

0   200   400 miles
0   200   400 kilometers

GEOGRAPHY SKILLBUILDER: Interpreting a Map

1. **Location** • Where are diamonds mined?
2. **Movement** • In Liberia, where does the money come from to buy weapons?

Diamonds for Weapons Africa's mineral wealth is sometimes used to help fund wars. During Angola's civil war, the government used income from oil exports to buy weapons, while rebel forces traded diamonds for guns. Diamonds have also been exported illegally to support brutal wars in Sierra Leone and the Democratic Republic of the Congo. In Sierra Leone, diamonds were smuggled out of the country in small envelopes and sold to buy weapons for rebel forces. World diamond markets are working to prevent the sale of "conflict diamonds."

Ways of Life in Western and Central Africa ❸

In Western and Central Africa, hundreds of different ethnic groups speak more than 1,000 languages. People practice many different religions, including Islam and Christianity. Most Africans live in small villages, but more Africans are moving to large, crowded cities, such as Lagos, Nigeria, or Accra, Ghana. City living has put strains on traditional African family life and culture.

Family Structure Society in Western and Central Africa is based on extended families that include children, parents, grandparents, and other close relatives such as aunts and cousins. Some ethnic groups trace ancestry through the mother's family; others, through the father's family. People share both work and free time with their family.

Place • Many African extended families live in compounds such as this one. In addition to living areas, there are storage buildings and an open space for community life. ◄

Social Status ③

In many African societies, older people have higher status and more influence than younger ones. For example, when men of the Igbo people in Nigeria gather for discussions, they sit in order of age. The eldest men are served food and drink first. In some African communities, each age group has different responsibilities. Men of the most senior rank settle legal disputes and police the village. Female elders punish behavior that harms women, such as unfair treatment by husbands.

Thinking Critically Possible Answers

1. symbolizes ancestors' support

2. The ancestor depicted was a woman.

Seats of Art In Central and Western Africa, artists—not carpenters—make the most valued piece of household furniture: the stool. The Ashanti of Ghana believe that a person's spirit flows into a stool each time the person sits on it. Because of this, each individual in a household has his or her own stool. Nobody else is allowed to sit on the stool.

Each stool is decorated with special carvings that indicate the person's social status. The stools of the Luba people living in the Democratic Republic of the Congo reflect the importance the Luba place on their ancestors. Like the one at the right, most Luba stools feature a carving of an important ancestor of the owner.

THINKING CRITICALLY

1. **Recognizing Important Details**
   What do you think is the symbolism of the carved person holding up the seat of the stool?

2. **Drawing Conclusions**
   Why do you think the artist made this figure a woman?

Western and Central Africa **327**

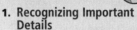

According to Ashanti myth, the first stool came from heaven and was given to the first Ashanti king. It was covered with gold. Later kings had their own stools, which were also often decorated with silver and gold. Elephants and leopards, symbols of the king's power or spirit, were often carved into the stools. These stools symbolized the king's authority. If he lost his people's confidence, the stool might be taken away.

Activity Options

Differentiating Instruction: Less Proficient Readers

Work with students to reread "Social Status." Discuss how older people are treated in Africa and why they are treated this way. Guide students to understand that, in Africa, the experience, wisdom, and seniority of older people is valued. Thus, they are respected and consulted in important matters. Then discuss how older people are treated in our society, encouraging students to note similarities and differences. You might have students use the chart on the right to organize their ideas.

The Role of Elders		
	Africa	United States
Family Life		
Community Life		

CRITICAL THINKING ACTIVITY

Finding Causes Invite students to discuss why the rite of passage of being recognized as an adult might be dying out. Then ask why having special skills gives some African young people higher status. Discuss the skills necessary in a changing world. Consider technology, the global market, and the shift to democracy. Why do the young Africans think the ability to speak a European language is valued?

Class Time 15 minutes

ASSESS & RETEACH

Reading Social Studies Have students add details to rows three and four of the chart on page 316.

  Formal Assessment
  • Section Quiz, p. 163

RETEACHING ACTIVITY

Have pairs of students write one main idea sentence and two supporting details for each heading in the section. Ask volunteers to share their ideas.

  In-depth Resources: Unit 4
  • Reteaching Activity, p. 23

  Access for Students Acquiring English
  • Reteaching Activity, p. 101

Culture • These young boys of the Ituri forest in the Congo dance in outfits made of straw and woven cords during a rite of passage. ▶

Because age is so important, a special ceremony, which is called a **rite of passage,** marks the transition from one stage of life to another. A major rite of passage occurs when young men and women are recognized as adults. However, this tradition is dying out in parts of Africa. Some younger people are gaining higher status because they have skills that are needed. For example, as people move to cities, educated youths who can speak a European language are highly valued.

SECTION **2** ASSESSMENT

Terms & Names

1. Identify: (a) subsistence farming   (b) cash crop   (c) rite of passage

Taking Notes

2. Use a chart like this one to list characteristics of this region's economy and way of life. How might the economy affect how people live?

Economy	Way of Life

Main Ideas

3. (a) What types of economies are present in Western and Central Africa?

(b) How is the use of Africa's mineral resources both beneficial and harmful to Africans?

(c) How is African family structure similar to and different from American family structure?

Critical Thinking

4. Drawing Conclusions

Do you think Africans will continue to have rites of passage in the future? Why or why not?

Think About

  ◆ how city life is affecting African societies

  ◆ other societies around the world

ACTIVITY -OPTION- Many Americans participate in rites of passage, such as baptisms, weddings, and funerals. Pretend you are studying American culture. Make a **poster** illustrating an American rite of passage.

Section **2** Assessment

1. Terms & Names
  a. subsistence farming, p. 325
  b. cash crop, p. 325
  c. rite of passage, p. 328

2. Taking Notes

Economy	Way of Life
market economies	many languages and religions
mostly agricultural	extended families
valuable minerals	smuggling, rebellions

3. Main Ideas
  a. traditional and market economies
  b. provide jobs and wealth, also finance violent conflicts
  c. Students may say that in both, people tend to live as family units. More Africans than Americans, however, live as extended family units.

4. Critical Thinking
  Students may say rites of passage may become less important as people move to cities and gain status in other ways.

ACTIVITY OPTION

  Integrated Assessment
  • Rubric for making a poster

Drawing Conclusions

▶▶ Defining the Skill

You are drawing conclusions when you read carefully, analyze what you read, and form an opinion based on facts about the subject. Often you must use your own common sense, your experiences, and your previous knowledge of a subject to draw a conclusion.

▶▶ Applying the Skill

The passage to the right is about the years following independence in the Democratic Republic of the Congo. Use the following strategies to help you draw conclusions based on the passage.

How to Draw Conclusions

Strategy ❶ Read the passage carefully. Pay attention to the statements that can be proved to be true.

Strategy ❷ Locate the facts in the passage and list them in a diagram. Use your common sense, your experiences, and your previous knowledge to understand how the facts relate to one another.

Strategy ❸ Apply your common sense, experiences, and previous knowledge to the new facts from the passage, and then write a conclusion based on your gathered evidence.

Make a Diagram

A diagram is a way of organizing facts. The diagram to the right shows how to organize the facts and inferences from the passage above and a conclusion that could be drawn from them.

▶▶ Practicing the Skill

Turn to pages 325–326 and reread the passage entitled "African Minerals." Make a diagram like the one to the right to draw conclusions from the passage.

In 1960, the country then known as the Belgian Congo gained independence. Five years later, Mobutu Sese Seko seized power and renamed the country Zaire. Mobutu ruled Zaire until 1997. ❶ Even though this country has some of the richest resources in Africa—copper, gold, and diamonds— Mobutu led the country into greater poverty. ❶ He put much of the country's money into his personal bank accounts. ❶ Mobutu ruled like a dictator, requiring men who worked in the government to dress like him and allowing only his political party to have any power.

❶ In 1997, Laurent Kabila led a rebel army into Zaire from the east and took over the government of Zaire. ❶ He immediately renamed the country the Democratic Republic of the Congo. Many people in Congo hoped that Kabila would work to improve life there, but instead, he led the country into war with neighboring nations. ❶ When Kabila seized power, Mobutu fled to Morocco, where he died in 1997. ❶ At the time of his death, there was no mention on radio or television in Congo that he died.

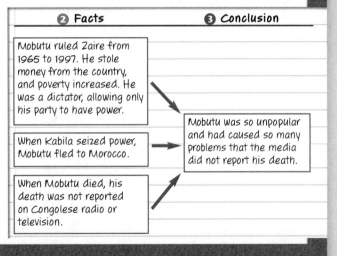

SKILLBUILDER

Drawing Conclusions

Defining the Skill

Explain to students that knowing how to draw conclusions helps them discover new ideas by putting pieces of information together. Emphasize that they will use this skill to discover new information when reading textbooks, doing research, listening to the evening news, watching a movie, or talking to friends.

Applying the Skill

How to Draw Conclusions Point out the three strategies for drawing conclusions. Stress that students will apply these strategies whenever they draw conclusions. If they follow the strategies in order, their conclusions will be valid and useful.

Make a Diagram

Review the diagram with students. Ask a volunteer how the three facts are related. Have students explain how their common sense, experiences, and knowledge will support this conclusion.

Practicing the Skill

Have students turn to the <u>Dateline</u> feature on page 330. Assign them to work in pairs and use the strategies to draw conclusions about the passage. Have students share their conclusions in class discussion.

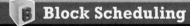 **In-depth Resources: Unit 4**
• Skillbuilder Practice, p. 20

Nigeria Today

TERMS & NAMES
Yoruba
Igbo
Hausa
Wole Soyinka

SECTION OBJECTIVES

1. To explain the history of the Nigerian people
2. To identify events that brought democracy to Nigeria
3. To describe the art and literature of Nigeria

SKILLBUILDER
• Interpreting a Map, p. 331

CRITICAL THINKING
• Recognizing Important Details, p. 331
• Analyzing Causes, p. 332

FOCUS & MOTIVATE
WARM-UP

Making Inferences After students read Dateline, discuss changes Nigerians will face.

1. How do you think the people might react to the new queen's proclamation?
2. In what ways do you think living conditions will change?

INSTRUCT: Objective ❶

A Look at Nigeria/History of Nigeria's People

• What are the three main ethnic groups in Nigeria today? Yoruba, Igbo, Hausa

 In-depth Resources: Unit 4
• Guided Reading Worksheet, p. 17

 Reading Study Guide
(Spanish and English), pp. 102–103

MAIN IDEA
Nigeria has a rich diversity of peoples and resources.

WHY IT MATTERS NOW
Nigeria's diversity has caused civil war, from which the country is currently recovering.

DATELINE

ZAZZUA, HAUSALAND, ANCIENT NIGERIA, 1566—The Queen is dead! Long live the Queen! This week the peaceful and prosperous reign of Queen Bakwa came to an end. Her daughter, Amina, was crowned queen. Unlike her peace-loving mother, Queen Amina is a warrior in the Zazzua cavalry.

At her crowning, she announced her intention to force other West African rulers to honor her and allow Hausa traders to travel safely through their lands. She also intends to build earthen defense walls around all of Zazzua's towns. She will begin her first military campaign in three months' time.

Place • These earthen defense walls are known as *ganuwar Amina*, or "Amina's walls." ▲

A Look at Nigeria ❶

Queen Amina's 16th-century military conquests helped make the present-day nation of Nigeria very diverse. Its land includes several types of environments, such as tropical rain forests, mangrove swamps, and savannas. Its people and cultures come from more than 250 ethnic groups. Nigeria has a long history and a rich artistic heritage. However, like other African countries, Nigeria faced violence on the way to becoming a modern democracy.

Program Resources

 In-depth Resources: Unit 4
• Guided Reading Worksheet, p. 17
• Reteaching Activity, p. 24

Reading Study Guide
(Spanish and English), pp. 102–103

 Formal Assessment
• Section Quiz, p. 164

Integrated Assessment
• Rubric for making a mask

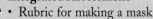 **Outline Map Activities**

 Access for Students Acquiring English
• Guided Reading Worksheet, p. 97

 Technology Resources
classzone.com

TEST-TAKING RESOURCES
⚓ Strategies for Test Preparation
⚓ Test Practice Transparencies
🖱 Online Test Practice

History of Nigeria's People ❶

The Nok people were one of the earliest known cultures in the land that is now Nigeria. By about 500 B.C., they occupied the central plateau. They were skilled in ironworking and weaving.

Today, about 60 percent of Nigerians belong to one of three major ethnic groups: the **Yoruba** (YAWR·uh·buh), the **Igbo**, and the **Hausa** (HOW•suh). The first Yoruba established their kingdom on the west bank of the Niger River. The Igbo were part of the Nri kingdom in the southeast, and the Hausa built cities in the northern savannas.

The Yoruba Most of the Yoruba today live in southwestern Nigeria. Before colonial rule, Yoruba society was organized around powerful city-states. Yoruba men grew yams, peanuts, millet, beans, and other crops on land around the cities. Artists and poets had great prestige in traditional Yoruba society. Yoruba women specialized in marketing and trade. Their businesses made some women wealthy and independent.

The Igbo For thousands of years, the Igbo have lived in the southeast region of Nigeria. Igbo villages are fairly democratic, with leaders being chosen rather than inheriting their position. They are known for their metalworking, weaving, and woodcarving. In British colonial times, many Igbo held jobs in business and government.

The Hausa The Hausa are the largest ethnic group in Nigeria. Almost all Hausa are Muslims. Most live in farming villages in northern Nigeria. Crafts such as leatherworking, weaving, and blacksmithing have been passed down through generations.

Culture • This sculpture was made by a Nok artist at least 1,500 years ago. ▲

Reading Social Studies
A. Possible Answer
Their locations have not changed.

Reading
Social Studies

A. Comparing How do the current locations of Nigeria's three ethnic groups compare with their original locations?

Culture • An Igbo woman paints a python on a house wall. ▲

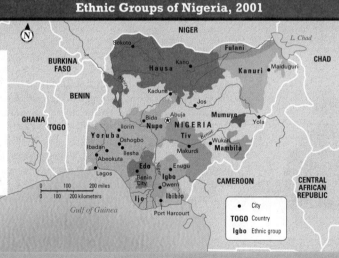

Ethnic Groups of Nigeria, 2001

GEOGRAPHY SKILLBUILDER:
Interpreting a Map
1. **Culture** • Which of Nigeria's ethnic groups covers the largest area?
2. **Location** • Which ethnic groups live alongside Lake Chad?

Geography Skillbuilder Answers
1. the Hausa
2. the Fulani and the Kanuri

INSTRUCT: Objective ❷

Becoming a Democracy/ Nigeria's Economy

- What European nation colonized Nigeria?
  United Kingdom
- When did Nigeria gain independence from Britain? 1960
- What was the cause of the war that raged in Nigeria from 1966 to 1970? The Igbo wanted to separate from Nigeria and set up the Republic of Biafra.
- What is Nigeria's main export? oil

CRITICAL THINKING ACTIVITY

Analyzing Causes Review with students what a civil war is. Then discuss the civil war in Nigeria. Ask why the Igbo declared independence and why the rest of Nigeria was unwilling to allow it.

Class Time 10 minutes

⊙Biography

Wole Soyinka's father was the headmaster of a Christian mission school in western Nigeria. Soyinka attended this school and later studied at Leeds University in England. Since then, Soyinka has promoted traditional African values and traditions in his literature and in his public and political actions. He was imprisoned for speaking out against the civil war and spent much of the next two years in solitary confinement. Later, he wrote about his experience in *The Man Died*.

Region • Cassava plants grow in Nigeria's tropical climate. Nigerians eat the cassava's starchy root, shown below. It must be prepared carefully, since it is poisonous if eaten raw. ▼

Becoming a Democracy ❷

In the 1800s, the United Kingdom colonized the northern and southern areas of what is now Nigeria. English became the common language. The two regions were united in 1914. In the 1920s, Nigerians began to work toward separating from British rule. Nigeria finally gained independence in 1960.

When oil was found in eastern Nigeria, the Igbo people there declared their independence. They set up the Republic of Biafra (bee•AF•ruh). Civil war raged from 1966 to 1970, causing a million deaths from fighting or starvation. After the war, military rulers took over. People had little freedom. Sometimes elections were held, but leaders often ignored the results. Finally, in May 1999, Nigeria had a free election. Former military ruler Olusegun Obasanjo was elected president.

Nigeria's Economy ❷

Nigeria has more than 123 million people— the largest population in Africa. More than half of Nigerians are farmers. Huge areas of the country have rubber, cacao, peanut, and palm oil plantations. The country has rich deposits of oil and natural gas. Oil is Nigeria's main export, supplying more than 90 percent of government income. Minerals, such as coal, iron ore, tin, lead, limestone, and zinc, are also important to the economy. Factories produce cars, cement, chemicals, clothing, and processed foods.

Reading
Social Studies

B. Recognizing Important Details What event prompted the Igbo people to declare independence from Nigeria?

Reading Social Studies
B. Possible Answer
the discovery of oil

⊙Biography

Wole Soyinka Wole Soyinka (WOH•leh shaw•YIHNG•kuh), a Yoruba man, was born in Abeokuta, Nigeria, in 1934. In 1986, Soyinka became the first black African to receive the Nobel Prize in literature. Soyinka (shown on the left) is best known for his plays, which combine African stories and European drama. He has also written novels, essays, and poetry. At the same time, he has been a voice for democracy, justice, and freedom of speech.

Soyinka's outspoken ideas got him into trouble with Nigeria's military rulers, and he was thrown into prison. After he was released, he left Nigeria. Soyinka lived in France and the United States for many years. He returned to Nigeria in 1998 to work for democratic reforms.

332 CHAPTER 11

Activity Options

Interdisciplinary Link: World History

Class Time One class period
Task Creating a time line of Nigeria's history
Purpose To learn about the history of Nigeria

Supplies Needed
- Library or Internet resources
- Paper
- Pencils or markers

Activity Divide students into small groups and assign each group a time period in Nigeria's history. Students in each group should use reference sources to learn about their assigned period. After they have listed key events and dates, they can create a time line for that time period. Students can assemble their group time lines into one complete time line to show the major events in Nigeria's history.

Nigerian Art and Literature 3

Nigeria's many cultures and ethnic groups have produced a rich mix of artistic styles. Yoruban artists have been making metal sculptures for about a thousand years. Yoruba also carve masks and figures out of wood. Decorated calabashes, or gourds, are another example of Nigerian art. Dried, hollow gourds are used as food containers or musical instruments. Baskets are made from local plants. Basket weavers turn practical containers into works of art.

Human-Environment Interaction • This decorated bowl was made from a calabash. ▲

Nigerians are also famous for their literature. Nigerian writers such as Amos Tutuola, Ben Okri, and **Wole Soyinka** have used folktale themes. Their novels and plays combine these themes with modern-day concerns such as human rights.

SECTION 3 ASSESSMENT

Terms & Names

1. Identify: (a) Yoruba   (b) Igbo   (c) Hausa   (d) Wole Soyinka

Taking Notes

2. Use a chart like this one to list the three major ethnic groups of Nigeria and give facts about each.

Group	Facts

Main Ideas

3. (a) How could a drought affect Nigeria's economy?

(b) How did the discovery of oil affect Nigeria after it gained independence?

(c) How are Nigeria's modern writers influenced by the past?

Critical Thinking

4. **Synthesizing**

What relationship exists between Nigerian society and history and its art and literature?

Think About

- what modern Nigerian artists and writers are concerned about
- how the past affects modern artists

ACTIVITY -OPTION- Make a **mask** inspired by Nigeria's history, economy, or peoples.

INSTRUCT: Objective 3

Nigerian Art and Literature

- What are some examples of Nigerian art? metal sculptures, wooden masks and figures, calabashes, and baskets
- What topics do Nigerian writers often explore? folklore, human rights

ASSESS & RETEACH

Reading Social Studies Have students complete the chart on page 316.

 Formal Assessment
- Section Quiz, p. 164

RETEACHING ACTIVITY

Have students work in small groups. Students should take turns reading a section heading, stating the main idea, and providing supporting details. Continue until all sections have been covered.

 In-depth Resources: Unit 4
- Reteaching Activity, p. 24

 Access for Students Acquiring English
- Reteaching Activity, p. 102

Section 3 Assessment

1. Terms & Names

a. Yoruba, p. 331
b. Igbo, p. 331
c. Hausa, p. 331
d. Wole Soyinka, p. 333

2. Taking Notes

Group	Facts
Hausa	northern Nigeria, largest ethnic group, mostly Muslim
Yoruba	southwestern Nigeria, high respect for artists and poets
Igbo	southeastern Nigeria, fairly democratic

3. Main Ideas

a. A drought could ruin crops that Nigerians grow for sale and consumption.
b. It resulted in a civil war.
c. They apply themes from folk tales to modern-day concerns.

4. Critical Thinking

Nigeria's artists and writers preserve its history and traditions in their work.

ACTIVITY OPTION

 Integrated Assessment
- Rubric for making a mask

Teacher's Edition **333**

ASSESSMENT

TERMS & NAMES

1. coup d'état, p. 319
2. mediate, p. 321
3. ECOWAS, p. 321
4. subsistence farming, p. 325
5. cash crop, p. 325
6. rite of passage, p. 328
7. Yoruba, p. 331
8. Igbo, p. 331
9. Hausa, p. 331
10. Wole Soyinka, p. 333

REVIEW QUESTIONS

Possible Responses

1. They wanted access to resources, such as gold and diamonds, rivers and seaports, and large areas of land.
2. Mobutu tried to make the Congo more African, suppressed all opposition, and took the country's money for his own use.
3. Positive: improved economy; new seaport, roads, railroads; compulsory primary education; Negative: dictatorship; imprisoned opponents
4. Most are farmers; many work in mining.
5. the extended family; it is breaking down as people move to cities
6. It has Africa's largest population.
7. Hausa: north; Yoruba: southwest; Igbo: southeast
8. Resources: oil, natural gas, coal, iron ore, rubber, cocoa, palm oil; Products: cars, cement, chemicals, clothing, processed foods

ASSESSMENT

TERMS & NAMES

Explain the significance of each of the following:

1. coup d'état
2. mediate
3. ECOWAS
4. subsistence farming
5. cash crop
6. rite of passage
7. Yoruba
8. Igbo
9. Hausa
10. Wole Soyinka

REVIEW QUESTIONS

History and Political Change *(pages 317–321)*

1. What factors influenced the way in which European nations divided Western and Central Africa?
2. Describe the rule of Mobutu Sese Seko in the Democratic Republic of the Congo.
3. What were some positive and negative aspects of Nkrumah's leadership of Ghana?

Economies and Cultures *(pages 324–328)*

4. How do most people in Western and Central Africa earn a living?
5. What is the basis of society in most African countries? How is this changing?

Nigeria Today *(pages 330–333)*

6. Where does Nigeria's population rank in Africa?
7. What are the three major ethnic groups in Nigeria? In what region does each live?
8. What are some important resources and products of Nigeria's economy?

CRITICAL THINKING

Recognizing Effects

1. Using your completed diagram from Reading Social Studies, p. 316, summarize one of your inferences and the evidence you based it on.

Drawing Conclusions

2. How would the establishment of plantations growing cash crops affect a society used to subsistence farming? Try to think of both positive and negative effects.

Analyzing Issues

3. How does their ethnic diversity both help and hurt modern African nations?

Visual Summary

1 History and Political Change

- Colonial rule upset traditional forms of government and natural boundaries, causing problems for modern countries in Western and Central Africa.
- Ethnic violence, corrupt officials, and military rule have made it hard for many countries to establish stable, democratic governments.

2 Economies and Cultures

- Most people in Western and Central Africa are subsistence farmers, but cash crops and minerals are also important in the economy.
- The extended family is the basis of society in Africa south of the Sahara.

3 Nigeria Today

- Nigeria has a large population, valuable resources, and a rich cultural history, but it has faced problems since gaining independence.
- The Hausa, Yoruba, and Igbo are the largest of Nigeria's more than 250 ethnic groups.

CRITICAL THINKING: Possible Responses

1. Recognizing Effects
Mineral resources attracted European colonists and large corporations to Africa; gave people work; and helped countries build roads, railroads, and seaports.

2. Drawing Conclusions
Economy would change from traditional to market; income from cash crops might improve people's standard of living; plantation farming might bring profits just to the owners; working on plantations might weaken families who are used to working together.

3. Analyzing Issues
Ethnic diversity provides rich cultural, literary, and artistic traditions, but it can lead to conflicts among ethnic groups.

SOCIAL STUDIES SKILLBUILDER

Endangered Animals in Western and Central Africa

Animal	Range	Reasons for Decline
Cheetah	Africa to India	Habitat destruction, fur trade
Gorilla	Central and Western Africa	Habitat destruction, capture of young, fur trade
Black Rhinoceros	Africa south of the Sahara	Habitat destruction, overhunting for horn
White Rhinoceros	Central Africa	Habitat destruction, overhunting for horn

SKILLBUILDER: Drawing Conclusions

1. What information does this chart present?
2. From this information, what can you conclude about how humans affect wild animals in Africa?

FOCUS ON GEOGRAPHY

1. **Movement** • In what direction would you travel on most of the roads and railroads in Liberia?
2. **Human-Environment Interaction** • Why do you think the roads follow the paths they do?
3. **Movement** • What forms of transportation are available for someone wishing to travel from Sulima, Sierra Leone, to Gbarnga, Liberia?

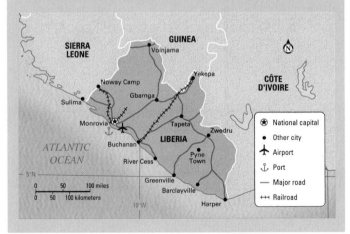

CHAPTER PROJECTS

Interdisciplinary Activity: Music
Exploring World Music Many musicians from Western and Central Africa, such as Youssou N'dour, have become internationally known. American jazz also grew out of African musical traditions. Learn more about an aspect of African music in a local music store or other music resource. Find and listen to music by one artist or in a certain style. Share your discoveries with the class.

Cooperative Learning Activity
Creating a Newspaper In a group of three to five classmates, write and produce a four-page newspaper, *Nigeria Today*, about current events in Nigeria. Write short articles about:
- Politics and economics
- Weather
- Human-interest stories
- Arts
- Sports
Find information and photographs on Web sites and in the library.

 INTERNET ACTIVITY

Choose a country in Western or Central Africa other than Nigeria and use the Internet to research it and prepare a country study. Include information about topics such as population, language, religion, type of government, ethnic groups, and important crops and products.

Writing About Geography Make a one-page chart or poster summarizing your findings. If possible, include a photograph from a Web site you used to prepare your display.

For Internet links to support this activity, go to

RESEARCH LINKS
CLASSZONE.COM

CHAPTER PROJECTS

Interdisciplinary Activity: Music
Exploring World Music Collect examples of African music on tape for students to listen to in their free time. Students' music presentations should demonstrate specific knowledge of an artist or musical style. Encourage students to share their personal reactions to the music.

Cooperative Learning Activity
Creating a Newspaper Suggest that students in each group meet to divide responsibilities of research, writing, and production. Finished newspapers should include articles on the given topics. Articles should feature appropriate, high-interest headlines and answer the questions Who? What? When? Where? Why? and How?

 INTERNET ACTIVITY

Suggest that students create a chart to use when taking notes and then present their findings in a chart or poster format. Charts and posters should have a title and appropriate labels and include specific details about the country. Students should provide accurate bibliographic information, including Web sites.

Skills Answers

Social Studies Skillbuilder
Possible Responses

1. The chart presents information on endangered animals in Western and Central Africa and reasons for their decline.
2. Human activity has resulted in many animals becoming endangered, through loss of habitat and poaching.

Focus on Geography
Possible Responses

1. Northeast/southwest
2. They probably follow landforms such as rivers.
3. Major road

Eastern and Southern Africa

	OVERVIEW	COPYMASTERS	INTEGRATED TECHNOLOGY
UNIT ATLAS AND CHAPTER RESOURCES	Students will examine the history and cultures of countries in Eastern and Southern Africa and analyze their effect on those countries' present-day governments and economies.	**In-depth Resources: Unit 4** • Guided Reading Worksheets, pp. 25–28 • Skillbuilder Practice, p. 31 • Unit Atlas Activities, pp. 1–2 • Geography Workshop, pp. 37–38 **Reading Study Guide** (Spanish and English), pp. 106–115 **Outline Map Activities**	Power Presentations Electronic Teacher Tools Online Lesson Planner Chapter Summaries on CD Critical Thinking Transparencies CT23
	KEY IDEAS		
SECTION 1 History and Governments pp. 339–343	• The empires of Zimbabwe and Mozambique traded precious metals for textiles, spices, silk, and porcelain. • African colonies became independent nations after World War II. Most were democracies, but some became dictatorships.	**In-depth Resources: Unit 4** • Guided Reading Worksheet, p. 25 • Reaching Activity, p. 33 **Reading Study Guide** (Spanish and English), pp. 106–107	classzone.com Chapter Summaries on CD
SECTION 2 Economies and Cultures pp. 346–350	• Drought and desertification have a negative impact on the agricultural economy of the region. • Southern Africa has mining and manufacturing jobs, which gives it more economic diversity than Eastern Africa. • Southern African music draws on a variety of other traditions.	**In-depth Resources: Unit 4** • Guided Reading Worksheet, p. 26 • Reaching Activity, p. 34 **Reading Study Guide** (Spanish and English), pp. 108–109	classzone.com Chapter Summaries on CD
SECTION 3 South Africa Today pp. 354–357	• The Dutch were the first European settlers of South Africa; their descendants were called Afrikaners. • The policy of apartheid wholly discriminated against nonwhites, and brought civil unrest to the country. • South Africa today is a diverse country, with eleven official languages.	**In-depth Resources: Unit 4** • Guided Reading Worksheet, p. 27 • Reaching Activity, p. 35 **Reading Study Guide** (Spanish and English), pp. 110–111	Critical Thinking Transparencies CT24 classzone.com Chapter Summaries on CD
SECTION 4 Kenya Today pp. 358–361	• Kenya has both desert areas and highlands with rich soil. • Prime Minister Moi ruled as a dictator until protests forced him to allow a multiparty system. • Kenya values ethnic diversity and education, and relies heavily on tourism in its economy.	**In-depth Resources: Unit 4** • Guided Reading Worksheet, p. 28 • Reaching Activity, p. 36 **Reading Study Guide** (Spanish and English), pp. 112–113	classzone.com Chapter Summaries on CD

KEY TO RESOURCES

🔊	Audio	🌐	Internet	TE	Teacher's Edition
💿	CD-ROM	⬇	Overhead Transparency	📹	Video
📄	Copymaster	PE	Pupil's Edition		

ASSESSMENT OPTIONS

PE **Chapter Assessment,** pp. 362–363

📄 **Formal Assessment**
• Chapter Tests: Forms A, B, C, pp. 181–192

💿 **Test Generator**

🌐 **Online Test Practice**

📄 **Strategies for Test Preparation**

PE **Section Assessment,** p. 343

📄 **Formal Assessment**
• Section Quiz, p. 177

📄 **Integrated Assessment**
• Rubric for writing a letter

💿 **Test Generator**

⬇ **Test Practice Transparencies TT41**

PE **Section Assessment,** p. 350

📄 **Formal Assessment**
• Section Quiz, p. 178

📄 **Integrated Assessment**
• Rubric for writing a letter

💿 **Test Generator**

⬇ **Test Practice Transparencies TT42**

PE **Section Assessment,** p. 357

📄 **Formal Assessment**
• Section Quiz, p. 179

📄 **Integrated Assessment**
• Rubric for creating a poster

💿 **Test Generator**

⬇ **Test Practice Transparencies TT43**

PE **Section Assessment,** p. 361

📄 **Formal Assessment**
• Section Quiz, p. 180

📄 **Integrated Assessment**
• Rubric for writing a postcard

💿 **Test Generator**

⬇ **Test Practice Transparencies TT44**

RESOURCES FOR DIFFERENTIATING INSTRUCTION

Students Acquiring English/ESL

📄 **Reading Study Guide** (Spanish and English), pp. 106–115

📄 **Access for Students Acquiring English** Spanish Translations, pp. 103–112

TE **TE Activity**
• Adjectives, p. 341

Less Proficient Readers

📄 **Reading Study Guide** (Spanish and English), pp. 106–115

TE **TE Activity**
• Creating a Graphic Organizer, p. 360

Gifted and Talented Students

TE **TE Activity**
• Researching, p. 347

CROSS-CURRICULAR CONNECTIONS

Literature
Lilly, Melinda. *Kwian and the Lazy Sun: A San Myth.* Vero Beach, FL: Rourke Press, 1998. Kwian throws a lazy villager into the sky, where he becomes the sun.
Naidoo, Beverley. *Journey to Jo'Burg: A South African Story.* New York: Harper Trophy, 1988. A brother and sister discover the pain of apartheid.
Wolfson, Margaret. *Marriage of the Rain Goddess: A South African Myth.* New York: Barefoot Books, 1999. Zulu myth about the joining of heaven and earth.

Popular Culture
Grimes, Nikki. *Is It Far to Zanzibar? Poems About Tanzania.* New York: HarperCollins, 2000. Culture illuminated by simple poems that incorporate Swahili words.

Geography
Oluonye, Mary N. *South Africa.* Minneapolis, MN: Carolrhoda Books, 1999. Climate, people, languages, history, society, economy, and culture.

Primary Sources
McKee, Tim, ed. *No More Strangers Now: Young Voices from a New South Africa.* New York: DK Ink, 1998. Twelve South African teens on life before and after apartheid.

Science
Lewin, Ted. *Elephant Quest.* New York: HarperCollins, 2000. Through the Moremi Wildlife Reserve in Botswana.

ENRICHMENT ACTIVITIES

The following activities are especially suitable for classes following block schedules.

Teacher's Edition, pp. 348, 351, 356
Pupil's Edition, pp. 343, 350, 357, 361

Unit Atlas, pp. 278–287
Interdisciplinary Challenge, pp. 344–345

Literature Connections, pp. 352–353
Outline Map Activities

INTEGRATED TECHNOLOGY

Go to **classzone.com** for lesson support and activities for Chapter 12.

BLOCK SCHEDULE LESSON PLAN OPTIONS: 90-MINUTE PERIOD

DAY 1

CHAPTER PREVIEW, pp. 336–337
Class Time 20 minutes

• **Hypothesize** Use the "What do you think?" questions in Focus on Geography on PE p. 337 to help students hypothesize about the effects of human interaction with the land.

SECTION 1, pp. 339–343
Class Time 70 minutes

• **Geography Skills** Use the suggestions for interpreting flow line maps on PE p. 11 of the Geography Skills Handbook to help students interpret the map on PE p. 340.
Class Time 10 minutes

• **Summary Chart** Lead the class in creating a four-column summary chart about the societies that developed in Eastern and Southern Africa. The headings for the four columns should be Aksum Empire, Shona Empire, Masai, and Zulu. Within each column, students should list important information from the text.
Class Time 30 minutes

• **Time Line** Divide students into pairs. Have them copy the time line you created on the board for Activity Options, Multiple Learning Styles: Mathematical/Logical on TE p. 340. Tell groups to add important dates under these headings: Other Eastern and Southern African Societies; African Independence; Government in Somalia; and Government in Rwanda. Students can use their completed time lines to review the section.
Class Time 30 minutes

DAY 2

SECTION 2, pp. 346–350
Class Time 45 minutes

• **Small Groups** Divide the class into four groups. Have each group select one section objective on TE p. 346 to help them prepare a summary of this section. Remind students that when they summarize, they should include the main ideas and most important details in their own words. Reconvene as a whole class for discussion.
Class Time 35 minutes

• **Skillbuilder** Use the questions in Skillbuilder: Interpreting a Chart on PE p. 348 to guide a discussion about Eastern and Southern Africa's economies.
Class Time 10 minutes

SECTION 3, pp. 354–357
Class Time 45 minutes

• **Peer Teaching** Have pairs of students review the Main Idea for the section on PE p. 354 and find three details to support it. Then have each pair list two additional important ideas and trade lists with another group to find details.
Class Time 10 minutes

• **Performing a Skit** Have groups perform the skits they wrote for Activity Options, Multiple Learning Styles: History/Drama on TE p. 356. Lead the class in a discussion based on the skits about how apartheid affected South Africans.
Class Time 35 minutes

DAY 3

SECTION 4, pp. 358–361
Class Time 35 minutes

• **Travel Poster** As an interesting way to review the section, have students work in pairs to create a travel poster to reflect Kenya today. Display student posters in the classroom.

CHAPTER 12 REVIEW AND ASSESSMENT, pp. 362–363
Class Time 55 minutes

• **Review** Have students prepare a summary of the chapter, using the Terms & Names listed on the first page of each section.
Class Time 20 minutes

• **Assessment** Have students complete the Chapter 12 Assessment.
Class Time 35 minutes

TECHNOLOGY IN THE CLASSROOM

USING THE INTERNET TO COMPARE AND CONTRAST INFORMATION

Some well-designed Web sites allow students to effectively compare and contrast information about topics, much as they would by using an encyclopedia but usually with more graphics and interactive features. This activity has students use the Web to compare and contrast information about several Eastern and Southern African countries.

ACTIVITY OUTLINE

Objective Students will complete a compare-and-contrast chart about the geography of Eastern and Southern Africa, using information from a Web site. They will conclude the activity by creating an essay and/or drawing pictures on the computer with text captions to show what they have learned.

Task Have students visit the Web site to gather information about the geographical similarities and differences among three regions of Eastern and Southern Africa. Have them prepare compare-and-contrast charts, highlight the similarities and differences, and create essays or pictures showing some of the facts on their charts.

Class Time Two class periods

DIRECTIONS

1. Review the Focus on Geography Section of Chapter 12, PE page 337, as a class. Ask students what they think might be some main differences between the climate, landscape, flora, and fauna of the different parts of this region. Have them list their ideas.

2. Have students go to the Web site listed at **classzone.com** and select "Explore the Regions." Then have them select "Explore the Regions with a Map Tool." When they see the map, ask them to scroll the mouse (without clicking) over the three regions in Eastern and Southern Africa (Great Lakes Region, Savanna, Southern Africa).

3. Have students make a four-column chart on a piece of paper or in a document on the computer. Ask them to label the second through fourth columns with the names of the three regions they have scrolled over.

4. Ask students to draw lines to create four rows in their charts. They should label the rows with these headings: topography, climate, animals, plants.

5. Have students go to each of the regions and select "Eco Info."

6. Ask students to fill in their charts with information they find at this Web site.

7. Have students use colored pencils, crayons, or highlighters to highlight in their charts the similarities among all three regions. Ask them to use a different color to highlight the things that are different among the regions.

8. Have students create three-paragraph essays on the computer, comparing and contrasting the geography of the three regions they have studied in this activity. Students may also draw pictures that show the similarities and differences among the regions, providing captions to explain what their pictures show.

CHAPTER 12 OBJECTIVE

Students will examine the history and cultures of countries in Eastern and Southern Africa and analyze their effects on those countries' present-day governments, economies, and societies.

FOCUS ON VISUALS

Interpreting the Photograph Have students study the photograph of the two Masai girls and identify what they are doing. Remind students that much of Africa south of the Sahara is savanna, the type of landscape shown in the photo. Explain that this chapter focuses on the past and present of this part of Africa. Ask them to suggest how this photograph represents Kenya's past and present.

Possible Responses The girls are wearing very traditional clothing; they are standing in a landscape with no cities or buildings visible, yet they are using a modern camera.

Extension Ask students to write an imaginary interview with the two Masai girls, in which they explain what they are doing with the long-range camera.

CRITICAL THINKING ACTIVITY

Making Inferences Ask students to locate the region shown on the inset map and notice its large north-south extent. What does this suggest about the variety of climates throughout the region? Ask them to recall what they have learned about African climates and landforms. From the information in the photograph, ask them to infer the climate and vegetation in this part of Kenya.

Class Time 10 minutes

Eastern and Southern Africa

SECTION 1 History and Governments

SECTION 2 Economies and Cultures

SECTION 3 South Africa Today

SECTION 4 Kenya Today

Culture Tradition meets modern technology as two Masai girls in Masai Mara National Reserve in Kenya peer through the viewfinder of a long-range camera.

EASTERN AND SOUTHERN AFRICA

336

Recommended Resources

BOOKS FOR THE TEACHER

Goodman, David. *Fault Lines: Journeys into the New South Africa.* Berkeley, CA: University of California Press, 1999. Post-apartheid South Africa.
Mandela, Nelson. *Long Walk to Freedom: The Autobiography of Nelson Mandela.* New York: Little

Brown, 1995. Written secretly while Mandela was imprisoned for 27 years on Robben Island.

VIDEOS

South Africa. New York: WNET, 1998. Native contemporary music enlivens this tour, which includes Robben Island.

SOFTWARE

Africa Trail. Minneapolis, MN: MECC, 1996. Interactive games and a wealth of information on the continent.

INTERNET

For more information about Eastern and Southern Africa, visit **classzone.com.**

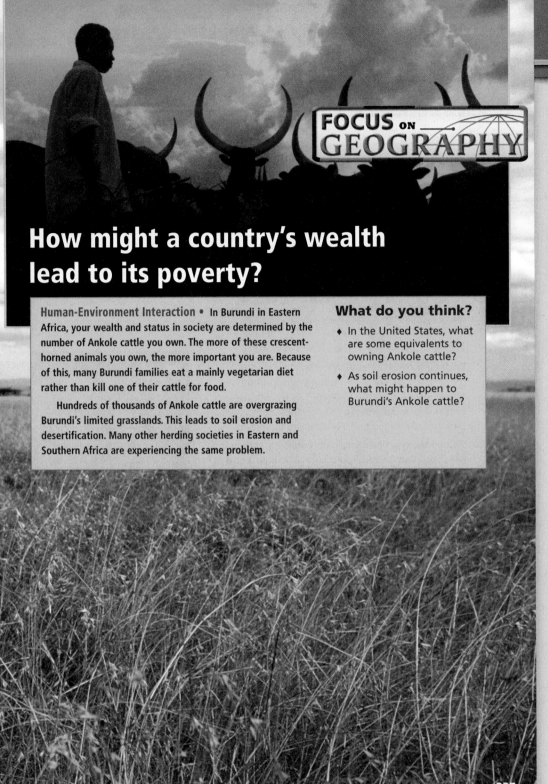

FOCUS ON GEOGRAPHY

How might a country's wealth lead to its poverty?

Human-Environment Interaction • In Burundi in Eastern Africa, your wealth and status in society are determined by the number of Ankole cattle you own. The more of these crescent-horned animals you own, the more important you are. Because of this, many Burundi families eat a mainly vegetarian diet rather than kill one of their cattle for food.

Hundreds of thousands of Ankole cattle are overgrazing Burundi's limited grasslands. This leads to soil erosion and desertification. Many other herding societies in Eastern and Southern Africa are experiencing the same problem.

What do you think?

♦ In the United States, what are some equivalents to owning Ankole cattle?

♦ As soil erosion continues, what might happen to Burundi's Ankole cattle?

337

FOCUS ON GEOGRAPHY

Objectives

• To help students identify the relationship between human activity and the environment

• To identify cultural factors that might limit economic development

What Do You Think?

1. Possible responses might be owning expensive cars, homes, or designer clothes.

2. The cattle might die from lack of food and water.

How might a country's wealth lead to its poverty?

To make sure that students understand this seemingly contradictory question, ask them to explain it in their own words, using the Ankole cattle as an example. Have them consider the factors that count as "wealth" in societies whose economies depend largely on agriculture or natural resources. How does overuse or other factors harm these sources of wealth? Then ask them to think about how the extraction of other kinds of natural resources, such as timber or minerals, can also impoverish a country.

MAKING GEOGRAPHIC CONNECTIONS

Prompt a discussion about ways in which natural disasters and human actions (such as floods or dam building) have disrupted agriculture in other places around the world, including the United States. Ask students to consider whether agricultural societies are more at risk than those with more industries and other kinds of economic activity.

Implementing the National Geography Standards

Standard 15 Speculate on the effects of undesirable changes in the physical environment on human activities

Objective To write a fictional journal from the point of view of an Ethiopian farmer

Class Time 30 minutes

Task Ask students to write a fictional journal from the point of view of an Ethiopian farmer describing how desertification and drought have affected the Ethiopian environment. The journal should describe how the farmer's activities have changed because of the changes in the environment. The journal should also suggest how the farmer's problems might be mitigated.

Evaluation The journal should list at least three activities the farmer has changed and two suggestions on how to solve or ease the farmer's problems.

BEFORE YOU READ

What Do You Know?

Write the following words and phrases on the chalkboard: *climate, social groups, apartheid, animals, diamonds.* Ask students to take turns stating how each of these topics relates to Eastern and Southern Africa. Encourage them to draw on knowledge gained from sources such as books, newspaper articles, movies, and previous chapters.

What Do You Want to Know?

Suggest that students make a chart with the headings *What I Want to Know* and *What I Learned.* Under the first heading, they can write questions they hope to have answered in this chapter. As they read, they can record information they learn.

READ AND TAKE NOTES

Reading Strategy: Predicting Explain to students that a chart like this will help them organize important factors of the past and present. Once they have completed it, they will have a tool that helps them link the past to the present and suggest certain outcomes in the future.

In-depth Resources: Unit 4
• Guided Reading Worksheets, pp. 25–28

BEFORE YOU READ

▶▶ What Do You Know?

Does your family own anything made of gold? If so, chances are that the gold came from Eastern or Southern Africa. What do you know about this region? What do you know about its people? What kinds of animals are found there? Recall what you read in Chapters 10 and 11, what you have learned in other classes, and what you have read or seen in the news about Kenya, South Africa, and the other countries of this region.

▶▶ What Do You Want to Know?

Decide what you know about Eastern and Southern Africa. In your notebook, record what you want to learn from this chapter.

Place • Mogadishu, the capital of Somalia, is one of many African cities devastated by civil war. ▲

READ AND TAKE NOTES

Reading Strategy: Predicting Predicting means using what you know to make an educated guess about what is going to happen. This is an important skill in social studies. Scholars look at the past and present to try to predict the future.

• Copy the chart into your notebook.
• As you read, record information about past and present situations in each category. If you find predictions about the future, record those also.
• After you read, review your information and use it to write your own predictions.

Place • Nairobi, Kenya, is a rapidly growing city with a population in 2000 of over 2 million. ▲

	Past	Present	Future
Government	colonization, many democracies overthrown by dictators	many nations turning toward democracy	Students' predictions will vary.
People	spread across Africa, farmers and herders	marriage and kinship changing	Students' predictions will vary.
Economy	trade developed	commercial fishing, agriculture	Students' predictions will vary.
Culture	spread of Christianity and Islam, zimbabwes	women's rights, many religions	Students' predictions will vary.
South Africa	colonization, apartheid	widespread poverty, strong economy	Students' predictions will vary.
Kenya	colonization, multiparty system emerged	ethnic diversity, education, agriculture, tourism	Students' predictions will vary.

Teaching Strategy

Reading the Chapter This is a thematic chapter that focuses first on the history of early kingdoms and societies in Eastern and Southern Africa, along with changes in government following independence from European colonial rule. It moves on to present-day African economies and cultures, followed by in-depth examinations of South Africa and Kenya.

Integrated Assessment The Chapter Assessment on page 363 describes several activities that may be used for Integrated Assessment. You may wish to have students work on these activities during the course of the chapter and then present them at the end.

History and Governments

TERMS & NAMES
Great Zimbabwe
Masai
Zulu

MAIN IDEA	WHY IT MATTERS NOW
There is a great diversity of cultural groups in Eastern and Southern Africa.	This diversity has contributed to several conflicts as different countries work to establish stable democratic governments.

DATELINE

EXTRA

HADAR, ETHIOPIA, NOVEMBER 1974

Three and a half million years ago, a humanlike being died beside a lake in Africa. This month, her remains were found by Don Johanson and Maurice Taieb.

After studying the skeleton, scientists determined that the female had been approximately three and a half feet tall, and she might have walked on two legs. Humans and their ancestors are the only known mammals that walk on two legs rather than four.

Discoveries such as this skeleton are very rare. One of the discoverers said, "They're even harder to find than diamonds, but they're the key to understanding human origins."

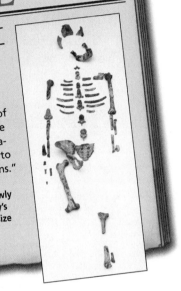

Place • Scientists named the newly discovered skeleton "Lucy." Lucy's brain was about one-third the size of a modern human brain. ▶

Early Humans in Eastern and Southern Africa ❶

The oldest fossils of human ancestors have been found in African sites ranging from Ethiopia to South Africa. Stone tools made 2.5 million years ago have also been found in Eastern Africa. Slowly, early humans spread across Africa before migrating to other continents. The humans that remained in Africa became farmers and herders.

Eastern and Southern Africa **339**

SECTION OBJECTIVES

1. To identify the great trade empires that developed in Eastern and Southern Africa
2. To describe the Masai and Zulu societies
3. To explain the establishment of independent nations
4. To describe the governments of Somalia and Rwanda

SKILLBUILDER
• Interpreting a Map, p. 340

CRITICAL THINKING
• Recognizing Important Details, p. 343

FOCUS & MOTIVATE
WARM-UP

Predicting Have students read <u>Dateline</u> and answer the following questions.

1. Why do you think scientists were excited about this discovery?
2. Why do you think humans' brains have grown in size since the time that Lucy lived?

INSTRUCT: Objective ❶

Early Humans in Eastern and Southern Africa/Early Eastern and Southern African Kingdoms

• What regions did the Aksum Empire trade with? Southern Africa, Arabia, Europe, India
• What kinds of goods did the empires of Zimbabwe and Mozambique trade in exchange for their precious metals? textiles, spices, silk, porcelain

 In-depth Resources: Unit 4
• Guided Reading Worksheet, p. 25

Reading Study Guide
(Spanish and English), pp. 106–107

Program Resources

 In-depth Resources: Unit 4
• Guided Reading Worksheet, p. 25
• Reteaching Activity, p. 33

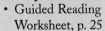 **Reading Study Guide**
(Spanish and English), pp. 106–107

 Formal Assessment
• Section Quiz, p. 177

 Integrated Assessment
• Rubric for writing a letter

 Outline Map Activities

 Access for Students Acquiring English
• Guided Reading Worksheet, p. 103

 Technology Resources
classzone.com

TEST-TAKING RESOURCES
↪ Strategies for Test Preparation
↪ Test Practice Transparencies
ⓘ Online Test Practice

Early Eastern and Southern African Kingdoms ❶

As the human population in Africa grew, societies became more complex. People began to trade with other regions. The income from trade helped build kingdoms.

The Aksum Empire Approximately 2,000 years ago, a great trading empire called Aksum (AHK•soom) developed in what is now Ethiopia. Find Aksum on the map below. Ships carried goods from Southern Africa, Arabia, Europe, and India to Aksum. About A.D. 350, King Ezana of Aksum became a Christian. Christianity spread throughout Ethiopia. When Islam came to Arabia, Aksum lost much of its trade because the Muslim Arabians preferred to trade with other Muslim nations.

Trade in Zimbabwe and Mozambique Around A.D. 700, trading empires arose in Southern Africa, in what are now Zimbabwe and Mozambique. These empires were rich in gold, copper, and iron. The mined metals were sent down the Zambezi River and then shipped across the Indian Ocean.

Human-Environment Interaction • Making stone tools is difficult. This symmetrical hand axe found in Tanzania had to be carefully chipped into shape. ▲

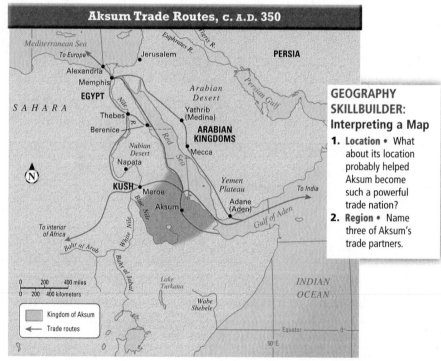

Aksum Trade Routes, c. A.D. 350

Geography Skillbuilder Answers

1. Its lands were along the Red Sea and the Blue Nile, so that it could ship goods to foreign ports and within the country.

2. Europe, India, Arabia, interior of Africa

GEOGRAPHY SKILLBUILDER: Interpreting a Map

1. **Location** • What about its location probably helped Aksum become such a powerful trade nation?
2. **Region** • Name three of Aksum's trade partners.

340 CHAPTER 12

The Africans traded their precious metals for textiles and spices from India, and silk and porcelain from China. Porcelain is a hard, white, glasslike material first made by the Chinese.

The Shona was one of the great trading empires of the lower Zambezi River from about 1100 to 1500. Its people created walled stone structures. These stone enclosures were called *zimbabwes* (zihm·BAB·wayz). The **Great Zimbabwe** is a spectacular stone ruin of a city made up of three parts. The Great Enclosure is the largest single ancient structure in Africa south of the Sahara. The Hill Complex, begun in 900, is the oldest section. The Valley Ruins include remnants of earthen and mud brick buildings. This city was abandoned in the 1400s. (See page 311 for more about the Great Zimbabwe.)

(See page 311 for more about the Great Zimbabwe.)

Other Eastern and Southern African Societies ❷

Eastern and Southern Africa had other societies besides the great trade kingdoms. Two of these societies were the Masai (mah·SY) and the Zulu (ZOO·loo).

The Masai and the Zulu The **Masai** once lived in nearly all of Kenya and about half of what is now Tanzania in Eastern Africa. They raised grazing animals, especially cattle. The Masai were nomads who moved from place to place so their animals would have fresh land to graze. Land generally belonged to the whole group, not to one person or family. In the 1800s, the Masai began fighting among themselves over water and grazing rights. Many Masai warriors died in these wars. Long periods without rain followed, during which many Masai cattle died. The Masai society was weakened by these events.

Place • A typical Masai village is set up in a circle. This layout helps the Masai defend their villages from attack. ▼

Floating Seeds Many sailors on trading vessels heading to and from the eastern coast of Africa saw huge seed pods floating on the ocean's surface. The seed pods were called *cocos de mer,* or coconuts of the sea.

It wasn't discovered until the late 1700s that the pods came from giant fan palm trees on the Seychelles Islands just north of Madagascar. The seeds of these trees are the largest in the world—some reaching 50 pounds in weight. It can take up to 10 years for a *coco de mer* to ripen.

INSTRUCT: Objective ❷

Other Eastern and Southern African Societies

- What were some characteristics of the Masai society? They raised grazing animals, were nomads, and owned land as a group.
- What events weakened the Masai society? wars, drought that killed their cattle
- How did Masai and Zulu lifestyles differ? The Masai were nomads; the Zulu lived in settled villages.
- What happened to the Masai when Europeans arrived? The Masai were forced to live on reserves.

Strange but TRUE

The uniqueness of the seeds of the giant fan palm has threatened its extinction. The palm grows only on the Seychelles Islands. Local residents gather the seeds in the wild to sell to tourists, thus limiting the number that can reproduce.

Activity Options

Differentiating Instruction: Students Acquiring English/ESL

Adjectives On the chalkboard, write the following phrases and underline the noun in each one:

grazing <u>animals</u>

glasslike <u>material</u>

mud brick <u>buildings</u>

giant palm <u>trees</u>

Cover the adjective in the first phrase as a volunteer reads aloud the underlined word. Ask students what images the word *animals* might suggest. Then uncover the adjective, and have another volunteer read aloud the entire phrase. Point out how the first word describes the noun that follows. Ask students what image they now have in mind. Follow a similar method to help students understand the other phrases.

INSTRUCT: Objective ❸

African Independence

- How did the end of World War II affect African colonies? European nations began to lose control of colonies; colonies became independent nations.

- What is the history of government in many African nations since they gained independence? Most established democracies, but some of those were overthrown by dictatorships; many have reverted to democracies.

INSTRUCT: Objective ❹

Government in Somalia/ Government in Rwanda

- How was Somalia governed from 1969 to 1991? by a dictator, Siad Barre

- How did women in Rwanda gain more rights? So many men were killed in civil wars that women had to take over as heads of households and were able to claim their constitutional rights.

The **Zulu** migrated to Southern Africa about 1,800 years ago. They have traditionally lived in settled villages, grown grains, and raised cattle. In 1815, a man named Shaka Zulu became chief of the Zulu. He led his people in a series of wars to expand Zulu territory. As the Zulu conquered other peoples, they made them Zulu as well. Shaka Zulu held unlimited power. Anyone who disagreed with him could be killed. Shaka's half-brother assassinated him in 1828.

European Colonization Soon after the death of Shaka Zulu, the Zulu began losing land to European settlers. The British and Germans then invaded Masai territory in the 1880s and 1890s. The Masai, weakened by war and drought, were no longer powerful. The Europeans quickly took the lands they wanted. The Masai were forced to live on reserves—small territories set aside for them. By the late 1800s, the United Kingdom, Germany, and France had claimed most of Eastern and Southern Africa.

Region • The Zulu, like this warrior chief, were members of a highly organized military society. ▲

African Independence ❸

World Wars I and II weakened Europe. After the wars, European nations began to lose control of their African colonies. This paved the way for the independence of African nations. Most of the countries of Eastern Africa, such as Kenya, Tanzania, Rwanda, and Burundi, became independent between 1960 and 1964. Most of the countries of Southern Africa achieved independence later. Almost all of the new African governments were democracies, but many of them were subsequently overthrown and became dictatorships. Today, many African nations are again turning toward democracy.

Reading Social Studies

A. Clarifying What events in Europe enabled African nations to gain their independence?

Place • These women and children in Mogadishu have struggled through years of brutal civil war in Somalia. ▼

Government in Somalia ❹

From 1969 to 1991, Somalia was governed by a dictator, Siad Barre (SEE·ahd BAH·reh), who had unlimited power. In the 1980s, more than 100 leading citizens published an open letter criticizing the government. An open letter is a letter that is published in a newspaper. In the United States it is legal to publish letters criticizing leaders. In Somalia it was not. Forty-five of those who signed the open letter were arrested.

Reading Social Studies

A. Answer World Wars I and II weakened the European colonial powers, so that they could no longer control their African colonies.

Activity Options

Interdisciplinary Link: World History

Class Time One class period

Task Researching statistics of present-day African countries

Purpose To understand the cultural diversity of Africa

Supplies Needed
- Reference sources such as almanacs, encyclopedias, and on-line resources
- Map of Africa
- Pencils and paper

Activity Explain to students that factors such as migrations and invasions have contributed to the cultural diversity of African countries. Have students work in groups to select several countries in Eastern and Southern Africa to research. Ask them to use a variety of resources to find statistics about the number of languages spoken in each country, ethnic groups represented, and the religions followed by the population. Encourage each group to present its findings in charts or graphs.

The arrests led to more protests. By 1990, fighting forced Barre to agree to reform his government. In 1991, he was driven from office. Since then, twelve clans have been fighting for control of the government.

Government in Rwanda

Reading Social Studies
B. Possible Answer
After men were killed in war, women took over households and gained property rights.

B. Analyzing Issues How did civil war in Rwanda lead to enforcement of women's rights?

Through much of the 1900s, Rwandan women could not own land, hold jobs, or participate in government. In 1991, a new constitution was passed. It gave women the right to own property and hold jobs. But the new laws were not enforced. Then, in 1994, a civil war began in Rwanda. So many men were killed that women began taking over as heads of households. Finally, as a result of the deadly wars, women were able to claim their constitutional rights. Since the conflict, more laws benefiting women have been passed. Today, not only can a Rwandan woman own property, but she can inherit property as well.

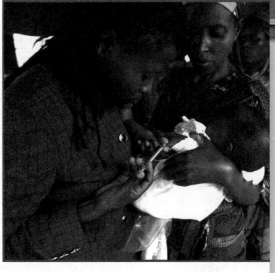

Place • Recently, Rwandan women have gained the right to own property and to work in fields such as medicine. ▲

SECTION 1 ASSESSMENT

Terms & Names

1. Identify: (a) Great Zimbabwe   (b) Masai   (c) Zulu

Taking Notes

2. Use a flow chart like this one to show the different societies that have flourished in Southern Africa.

The Aksum Empire
↓
↓

Main Ideas

3. (a) Explain how location helped build trade empires in ancient Ethiopia, Zimbabwe, and Mozambique.

(b) What factors contributed to the weakening of the Masai society?

(c) Describe how the lives of women in Rwanda have changed in recent years.

Critical Thinking

4. Clarifying

What led to the downfall of Siad Barre in Somalia?

Think About

- how Barre ruled Somalia
- the actions of the citizens

ACTIVITY -OPTION-   Imagine you are a Rwandan woman in 1992. Write an **open letter** criticizing the government for not enforcing your constitutional rights.

CRITICAL THINKING ACTIVITY

Recognizing Important Details Ask students to review the subsections that focus on governments in Somalia and Rwanda. Then invite them to identify the details that they feel are most important.

Class Time 10 minutes

ASSESS & RETEACH

Reading Social Studies Have students fill in the *Past* and *Present* columns for the first four categories in the chart on page 338.

 Formal Assessment
- Section Quiz, p. 177

RETEACHING ACTIVITY

Have students work in small groups to create a section review. Ask students to write one- or two-sentence summaries of each section. Then have each student share his or her summary with the group.

In-depth Resources: Unit 4
- Reaching Activity, p. 33

Access for Students Acquiring English
- Reteaching Activity, p. 109

Section 1 Assessment

1. Terms & Names
a. Great Zimbabwe, p. 341
b. Masai, p. 341
c. Zulu, p. 342

2. Taking Notes

The Aksum Empire
trading empires in Mozambique and Zimbabwe
Masai and Zulu

3. Main Ideas
a. They all had access to rivers and oceans, so they could ship goods and resources by water.
b. internal wars that killed many Masai, droughts that killed cattle
c. Since the 1991 constitution and later civil war, women can work and own and inherit property.

4. Critical Thinking
Barre, a dictator, arrested leading citizens who criticized his government; the protests that followed led first to reforms and then his ouster from office.

ACTIVITY OPTION

 Integrated Assessment
- Rubric for writing a letter

Discover the Source of the Nile

OBJECTIVE

Students work cooperatively and individually to explore the challenge of discovering the source of the Nile.

 Block Scheduling

PROCEDURE

Provide paper, pencils, and clay. Have students form groups of four or five and divide the work among the groups. Then have them plan a strategy for completing the challenge and assign tasks to each group member.

HEALTH CHALLENGE

Class Time 50 minutes

To help students as they research dangers and diseases, suggest they consider the following:

• diseases unique to the region
• dangerous animals of the region
• means for avoiding illness

Possible Solutions

Tropical diseases common to the region include sleeping sickness, river blindness, intestinal parasites, and elephantiasis. To avoid disease, travelers wear long-sleeved shirts, high boots, and hats, and they sleep under mosquito netting. They might carry quinine or snake bite medicine. Dangerous animals include cobras, puff adders, green mambas, lions, and rhinoceroses.

You are proud to be part of a daring expedition to the heart of Africa. The trip, which begins in 1856, is sponsored by the Royal Geographical Society. Its leaders are two of Britain's best-known explorers—John Hanning Speke and Richard Burton. They are chasing a legend—that there is a great lake in the heart of Africa that is the source of the Nile—and you are the newest member of their team.

COOPERATIVE LEARNING On these pages are challenges your expedition will face as you search for the source of the Nile. Working with a small group of other explorers, decide which one of these challenges you will solve. Divide the work among group members. Look for helpful information in the Data File. Keep in mind that you will present your solution to the class.

SCIENCE CHALLENGE

"The African rain forest is full of hazards, from warring tribes to malaria to deadly snakes."

Exploring Africa is dangerous, especially in the mid-1800s. The African rain forest is full of hazards, from warring tribes to malaria to deadly snakes. While your expedition is deep in the jungle, you and your companions must be your own doctors. How can you keep yourself and others in the expedition healthy? Choose one of these options. Use the Data File for help.

ACTIVITIES

1. Research dangers and diseases you may encounter in the rain forest. Make a list of the safety equipment and medicines you will pack for the expedition.

2. Write a short manual on tropical diseases common in East Africa.

Standards for Evaluation

HEALTH CHALLENGE

Option 1 Lists should
• include names of diseases and dangerous animals.
• include specific types of protective clothing, guns, medicines, and mosquito netting.

Option 2 Manuals should
• describe tropical diseases, the methods for avoiding them, and medicines used to cure them.

GEOGRAPHY CHALLENGE

Option 1 Large maps and presentation should
• show and describe the region explored and the route taken.

Option 2 The clay model should
• accurately represent the Nile and its source.

LANGUAGE ARTS CHALLENGE

Option 1 The news story should
• tell the who, what, where, when, why, and how of the discovery of the source of the Nile.

Option 2 The biography should
• give an accurate explanation of Speke's or Burton's contributions.

GEOGRAPHY CHALLENGE

". . . others are likely to challenge you."

Recently, Speke left the main expedition, and he now believes that he has found the Nile's source at Lake Ukerewe. He has renamed this huge lake Victoria, after the British queen. With him went a small group of people, and you are one of them. You are sure of your discoveries, but others are likely to challenge you. You need to demonstrate exactly how you found the source of the Nile. Choose one of these options. Use the Data File for help.

ACTIVITIES

1. Draw or trace a large map of East Africa that you can display on an easel. Make notes for a lecture-demonstration in which you will trace your route to show where the Nile begins.

2. Make a tabletop clay model of the lakes region of East Africa, including Lakes Victoria and Albert.

Activity Wrap-Up

As a group, review your solution to the challenge you selected. Then present your solution to the class.

DATA FILE

DISCOVERY TIME LINE

- February 1858: **Speke** and **Burton** are the first Europeans to reach Lake Tanganyika.

- July 1858: Speke breaks off from Burton, travels north, and finds and names **Lake Victoria**.

- 1860–1862: Speke and **James Grant** map Lake Victoria. Speke finds and names **Ripon Falls,** where the Nile flows out of the lake. The explorers start to follow the Nile but are stopped by local warfare.

- 1863: Speke passes on stories of another great lake to **Samuel W. Baker** and **Florence von Sass,** who find and name **Lake Albert.** It feeds into the White Nile.

AFRICA'S GREAT LAKES

- **Lake Victoria,** Uganda-Tanzania: area, 26,828 sq. mi.; length, 250 mi.; maximum depth, 270 ft.

- **Lake Tanganyika,** Tanzania-Congo: area, 12,700 sq. mi.; length, 420 mi.; maximum depth, 4,823 ft.

- **Lake Albert** (Mobuto), Congo-Uganda: area, 2,075 sq. mi.; length, 100 mi.; maximum depth, 168 ft.

- **Lake Turkana** (Rudolf), Kenya: area, 2,473 sq. mi.; length, 154 mi.; maximum depth, 240 ft.

EXPLORERS SEEKING THE SOURCE OF THE NILE

- **John Hanning Speke** (1827–1864): British soldier, discoverer of Lake Victoria.

- **Sir Richard Burton** (1821–1890): discoverer of Lake Tanganyika, looked for source of White Nile, also explored India and Arabia.

To learn more about Nile exploration, go to

RESEARCH LINKS
CLASSZONE.COM

Africa South of the Sahara **345**

GEOGRAPHY CHALLENGE

Class Time 50 minutes

Students should use tracing paper or an overhead projector as they prepare their maps. The Unit Atlas or another atlas could be used. For the clay model, students should use a relief map and photos of the region as sources.

Possible Solutions

The large map will show the region that was explored, Burton and Speke's route, Lake Victoria, and the Nile. The clay model will show the relationships of the lakes and the Nile.

ALTERNATIVE CHALLENGE...

LANGUAGE ARTS CHALLENGE

Burton and Speke had made a previous effort in 1855 to find the source of the Nile, but they were attacked and forced to return to England. Both men were intrepid explorers. Burton had traveled in Egypt and India. In disguise, he entered Mecca and Medina and later wrote of what he saw there. Speke had served in the British Army in India and Tibet. Both men added a great deal to the Western world's understanding of Africa and Asia. Imagine that you are a journalist.

• Write a news story telling about the discovery of the source of the Nile.

• Write a brief biography of either Speke or Burton, telling of his exploits.

Activity Wrap-Up

To help students evaluate their challenge solutions, have them answer the following questions.

• Is the solution accurate and thorough?

• Is the solution both informative and appealing?

• Does the solution reflect the importance of the subject matter?

• Is the solution presented in an original manner?

Economies and Cultures

TERMS & NAMES
pastoralism
overgrazing
kinship

SECTION OBJECTIVES

1. To describe the agricultural bases of the region's economy
2. To analyze Southern Africa's economy
3. To describe cultural aspects of Eastern and Southern Africa
4. To identify the religions followed in the region

SKILLBUILDER
• Interpreting a Map, p. 347
• Interpreting a Chart, p. 348

CRITICAL THINKING
• Using Maps, p. 347
• Comparing, p. 349

FOCUS & MOTIVATE
WARM-UP

Making Inferences Have students read <u>Dateline</u> and answer the following questions.

1. Do you think this drought ended in 1985?
2. What geographic factors might make Northern Ethiopia more prone to drought than Southern Ethiopia?

INSTRUCT: Objective ❶

Agriculture in Eastern and Southern Africa

• Why are there fewer places for nomads to graze their animals? Increased population took over land used for grazing.

• What did people do to upset the balance of life in Lake Victoria? introduced Nile perch

 In-depth Resources: Unit 4
• Guided Reading Worksheet, p. 26

 Reading Study Guide
(Spanish and English), pp. 108–109

MAIN IDEA	WHY IT MATTERS NOW
The economies of Eastern and Southern Africa are based primarily on agriculture.	Billions of dollars of U.S. aid goes to this region to boost its economy.

DATELINE

ETHIOPIA, 1985—Ethiopia has been experiencing a widespread famine for a year. In 1984, a drought hit Northern Ethiopia and other parts of Eastern Africa. Nearly all crops failed. Many nations sent food, but it was not enough. Almost one million Ethiopians have died of starvation.

The government has moved 600,000 people to Southern Ethiopia, where conditions are better. Another 100,000 went to Somalia, 10,000 to Djibouti, and 300,000 to Sudan. Currently, there is no end in sight to this tragedy.

Region • The drought has killed not only crops, but also many of Ethiopia's animals. ▲

Agriculture in Eastern and Southern Africa ❶

Agriculture is the primary industry of countries in Eastern and Southern Africa, even though drought is a serious problem. An exception is the area around Lake Victoria, which tends to get enough rain to support many different kinds of crops. People in this area grow bananas, strawberries, sweet potatoes, and yams. Cash crops such as coffee and cotton are grown in parts of Kenya, Rwanda, Burundi, and Uganda.

346 CHAPTER 12

Program Resources

 In-depth Resources: Unit 4
• Guided Reading Worksheet, p. 26
• Reteaching Activity, p. 34

Reading Study Guide
(Spanish and English), pp. 108–109

Formal Assessment
• Section Quiz, p. 178

Integrated Assessment
• Rubric for writing a letter

 Outline Map Activities

Access for Students Acquiring English
• Guided Reading Worksheet, p. 104

Technology Resources
classzone.com

TEST-TAKING RESOURCES
↪ Strategies for Test Preparation
↪ Test Practice Transparencies
ⓘ Online Test Practice

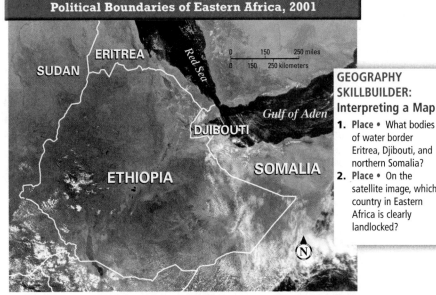

Political Boundaries of Eastern Africa, 2001

SUDAN
ERITREA
Red Sea
Gulf of Aden
DJIBOUTI
ETHIOPIA
SOMALIA

0   150   250 miles
0   150   250 kilometers

N

Geography Skillbuilder Answers

1. Red Sea and Gulf of Aden

2. Ethiopia

GEOGRAPHY SKILLBUILDER: Interpreting a Map

1. **Place** • What bodies of water border Eritrea, Djibouti, and northern Somalia?
2. **Place** • On the satellite image, which country in Eastern Africa is clearly landlocked?

Place • Tanzanian fishermen spread nets along the shore of Lake Victoria. This cichlid is one of the native fish threatened by the Nile perch in the lake. ▼

Place • Sorghum is a cereal grain plant native to Africa. It is a mainstay in the diets of 500 million people in more than 30 countries. ▲

Pastoralism In some areas of Africa, there is not enough rain to grow any crops. Somalia and most of Kenya receive less than 20 inches of rain each year. People survive by raising grazing animals, such as cattle, sheep, or goats. This way of life is called **pastoralism.** Many pastoralists are nomads. Today, because of Africa's increasing population, there are fewer places for nomads to graze their animals. As a result, the land is suffering from **overgrazing,** or the process in which animals graze grass faster than it can grow back. Overgrazing is a cause of desertification in Africa.

Fishing Africa's large lakes support commercial fishing. Lake Victoria was once home to almost 500 native species of fish. Most of these fish were too small to support a large fishing industry. The large Nile perch was then introduced into Lake Victoria. Since then, nearly all the native fish have disappeared. Today, commercial fishing of the Nile perch has brought many jobs to the area and provided an important export.

Eastern and Southern Africa **347**

FOCUS ON VISUALS

Interpreting the Map Make sure that students understand that this map is a satellite image with national boundaries superimposed on it. Explain that this region is often called the Horn of Africa. Ask them to study the image, point out features of the terrain such as mountains and large lakes, and then give a general description of the terrain as seen by satellite.

Possible Response Western Ethiopia is generally mountainous and rugged, with a chain of lakes lying in a valley. The east is a more level plain.

Extension Have students research Africa's Great Rift Valley and its landforms and then draw their own relief maps of the region.

CRITICAL THINKING ACTIVITY

Using Maps Tell students that quarrels over national boundaries have often been the causes of war. Explain that Eritrea was once a province of Ethiopia; since it won independence in 1993, the two countries have had several border wars. Have them use the satellite map image on page 347 to suggest reasons for conflict between Ethiopia and Eritrea. Why would Eritrea's independence make Djibouti important to Ethiopia?

Class Time 10 minutes

MORE ABOUT...
Lake Victoria

Lake Victoria is the largest lake in Africa and the second largest freshwater lake in the world. The only lake that is larger is Lake Superior, one of the Great Lakes in the United States.

Activity Options
Differentiating Instruction: Gifted and Talented

Researching Ideas Have these students brainstorm and research ideas for preventing or reducing the effects of overgrazing. Stress that the ideas should show consideration for the environment as well as for the cultural values of the people involved. Encourage students to use the Internet and other sources to locate similar plans that have already been suggested or put into use. Discuss keywords that might help them locate information, such as *overgrazing, Africa, animal husbandry,* and *desertification.*

INSTRUCT: Objective ❷

Africa's Economic Strength

- **Why is Southern Africa more economically diverse than Eastern Africa?** mining and manufacturing jobs

- **Which country has the strongest economy in the region?** South Africa

Spotlight on CULTURE

The influence of African drums crossed the ocean to the Western Hemisphere. The popular conga drum, used for dance music in South America, is an adaptation of African drums.

FOCUS ON VISUALS

Interpreting the Chart Have students read the title of the graph and then use the Unit Atlas map of Africa to locate each of the countries included, noting the great differences in size between them. Explain that the break in the horizontal scale indicates a gap in the amount of dollars being measured. Ask students to consider what kind of measurement might give a different picture of economies in various countries.

Possible Responses Students with some knowledge of economics may suggest that relating GDP to the number of people in the country (per capita GDP) would give a different picture, although many of these countries might still seem to be poor.

Extension Have students choose one of the smaller nations shown on the chart, such as Botswana; research its demographics and economy; and present a short overview of the country to the class.

Skillbuilder
Answers
1. largest: South Africa; smallest: Lesotho
2. Botswana

Reading Social Studies
A. Possible Answer
It is larger than the other countries, and it has mineral resources and manufacturing.

Thinking Critically Possible Answers
1. It is probably high because the players have important responsibilities.
2. A human messenger could be intercepted along the way, or killed after delivering a hostile message.

GDP of Southern African Nations, 2000

Botswana
Lesotho
Mozambique
South Africa
Zimbabwe

0 10 20 30 40 50 360 380
Billions of Dollars

SKILLBUILDER: Interpreting a Chart
1. Which of these countries had the largest GDP in 2000 the smallest?
2. Which country had a GDP about two times the size of Lesotho?

Africa's Economic Strength ❷

Eastern Africa is the poorest region on the continent. Countries in Southern Africa have more diverse economies than do those in Eastern Africa. This means people have more ways to earn a living. For example, several countries in Southern Africa are rich in mineral resources, so there are jobs in mining. South Africa and Zimbabwe also have many manufacturing jobs. South Africa has by far the strongest economy in the region. In 2000 it had a Gross Domestic Product, or GDP, of approximately $369 billion.

Reading
Social Studies

A. Analyzing Causes What contributes to South Africa's strong economy?

Spotlight on CULTURE

The Beat Goes On People have made and played drums since at least 6000 B.C. In many African cultures, drums are more than musical instruments. The Yoruba used drums that imitate the pitch and pattern of human speech to transmit messages over many miles. These "talking" drums would, for example, send the message to an unpopular king that his people wanted him to resign. In Uganda, kettledrums were used to symbolize the king's power and offer him protection. Sacrifices of cattle were regularly made to the drums to give them a life force.

THINKING CRITICALLY

1. **Making Inferences**
   What status do you think drum players hold in African society? Why?

2. **Analyzing Motives**
   Why do you think the Yoruba people would use drums instead of a human messenger to send messages to their king?

Activity Options

Interdisciplinary Link: Math

Class Time One class period

Task Expanding the GDP bar graph

Purpose To compare the GDPs of African nations with the GDP of Canada

Supplies Needed
- Almanac or on-line resources
- Graph paper
- Pencils

🄱 Block Scheduling

Activity Provide students with the following GDP information: Kenya: $45.6 billion, Uganda: $26.2 billion, Swaziland: $4.4 billion, Canada: $774.7 billion. Have students make an expanded graph that adds these countries to those shown in the graph on page 348. Suggest that they use larger intervals on the horizontal axis and add another break to accommodate Canada's GDP. Then ask each student to write two math word problems that can be answered by using the graph. Have students exchange and solve the problems.

Reading
Social Studies

B. Making Inferences Why do you think good transportation and communication will improve Southern Africa's economies?

Transportation and Communication The countries of Southern Africa work together to improve the economy of the region. This includes improving transportation and communication among countries. For example, the railway lines of Botswana, Namibia, Lesotho, South Africa, and Swaziland are linked. These lines carry goods from all areas of Southern Africa to major ports along the Atlantic and Indian coasts.

Cultures of Eastern and Southern Africa ❸

Marriage and kinship are changing in Eastern and Southern Africa as people move to cities. **Kinship** means family relationships. Economic activity brings people together; as they trade goods, they trade ideas. Their behavior and attitudes change as well.

BACKGROUND

The Tumbuka healers of Malawi use special songs and dances to diagnose and cure their patients' diseases.

Music in Eastern and Southern Africa In Eastern and Southern Africa, musical traditions of many different cultural groups come together. One characteristic of Southern African music is repetition. The Shona people of Zimbabwe make *mbira* (em·BEER·uh) music. *Mbira* music forms patterns of repetition using different voices or instruments. In Zulu choral music, individual voices singing different parts enter a song at various points in a continuous cycle. This creates a rich and varied pattern of sound. Another traditional way of making music is called *hocketing*. Groups of musicians play flutes or trumpets. Each musician plays one note. Then they rotate, or take turns, playing one note after another to create a continuous, freeform song.

Culture • Joseph Shabalala, founder of the South African vocal group Ladysmith Black Mambazo, performs with women dancers in traditional Zulu dress. ▼

INSTRUCT: Objective ❸

Cultures of Eastern and Southern Africa

- What is an important characteristic of Southern African music? repetition
- What is hocketing? a way of making music in which musicians take turns playing one note at a time
- What outside cultures have influenced new types of African music? European, West Asian, American

CRITICAL THINKING ACTIVITY

Comparing Music in Southern and Eastern Africa today incorporates influences from America, Europe, and Asia. Ask students to think about the kinds of music they like and the different influences on it, such as reggae from Jamaica. Ask them to compare the influences that other cultures have on American popular music with the ways that African music incorporates music from other cultures.

Class Time 15 minutes

Activity Options

Skillbuilder Mini-Lesson: Drawing Conclusions

Explaining the Skill Remind students that drawing conclusions while reading means using one's common sense, experiences, and previous knowledge along with information in the text to form an opinion.

Applying the Skill Draw students' attention to the last two sentences from the first paragraph of "Cultures of Eastern and Southern Africa." Then have them use these strategies to draw conclusions from the text.

1. Restate the main idea in your own words. People's behavior and attitudes change as they trade goods and ideas.

2. Use your common sense, experiences, and previous knowledge to link ideas. When people trade goods and ideas, they meet with people from other places. This contact helps change preconceived ideas and prejudices about people.

INSTRUCT: Objective 4

Religion in Eastern and Southern Africa

- What percentage of Southern and Eastern Africans practice a traditional African religion? 15 percent
- What is the focus of many traditional religions? worship of sky gods, ancestors, spirits of rivers and of Earth

Connections to History

There are two types of churches in Lalibela: four grottoes carved into mountain slopes and seven freestanding structures. The churches, some of which retain original murals painted on their walls, are still used for worship. In 1978, Lalibela was designated as a UNESCO World Heritage Site.

ASSESS & RETEACH

Reading Social Studies Have students add information to the chart on page 338.

Formal Assessment
- Section Quiz, p. 178

RETEACHING ACTIVITY

Have students work in small groups to create a section review of important concepts and vocabulary, along with their definitions.

In-depth Resources: Unit 4
- Reteaching Activity, p. 34

Access for Students Acquiring English
- Reteaching Activity, p. 110

Connections to History

Ancient Churches Ethiopia adopted Christianity in the 500s. In the 1200s, Emperor Lalibela of Ethiopia commissioned 11 churches to be built in the town of Roha. The town was later renamed after the emperor. All of the churches were carved from solid volcanic rock. A network of tunnels was built to connect the churches. Today, a community of approximately 1,000 monks presides over these ancient churches and the pilgrims who visit them.

Changing the Tune African musical traditions moved across North America, South America, and Europe because of the slave trade and European colonization. African musicians have added elements of European, West Asian, and American music to their own styles to create new types of music. *Jiti*, for example, is a type of Shona *mbira* music that follows the traditional *mbira* rhythms using an electric guitar.

Religion in Eastern and Southern Africa ④

Today, about 85 percent of Southern and Eastern Africans practice Islam or Christianity. Only 15 percent practice a traditional African religion. Many traditional African religions focus on the worship of sky gods, ancestors, or spirits of rivers and of Earth. However, like Islam and Christianity, African religions recognize one supreme creator. Many Africans practice a traditional African religion that is combined with another religion.

SECTION 2 ASSESSMENT

Terms & Names
1. **Identify:** (a) pastoralism   (b) overgrazing   (c) kinship

Taking Notes
2. Using a spider map like the one shown, fill in details that describe each type of economic activity. Add more lines as necessary.

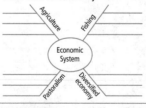

Agriculture   Fishing

Economic System

Pastoralism   Diversified economy

Main Ideas
3. (a) What geographic factors are responsible for the location of pastoralism in Eastern Africa?
   (b) How did cultural borrowing affect African music? How did it affect other types of music around the world?
   (c) What religious belief is common to all the major religions practiced by Africans?

Critical Thinking
4. **Recognizing Important Details** Describe unique characteristics of the music of some African peoples. What influence do they have in common?

Think About
- the variety of African music
- how Africans incorporate European, West Asian, and American music

ACTIVITY -OPTION- Imagine you have moved from a community of nomads in Kenya to South Africa. Write a **letter** describing what your life was like as a nomad and what kind of job you might find in your new home.

Section 2 Assessment

1. Terms & Names
a. pastoralism, p. 347
b. overgrazing, p. 347
c. kinship, p. 349

2. Taking Notes

Agriculture
primary industry; grow crops for food; cash crops

Pastoralism
overgrazing a cause of desertification

Economic System

Fishing
commercial fishing of Nile perch in Lake Victoria

Diversified economy
more in Southern Africa; mining; manufacturing

3. Main Ideas
a. There is not enough rain to grow crops; pastoralism is the only option.
b. African musicians created new music by borrowing elements from other cultures; their music spread worldwide.
c. All believe in one supreme creator.

4. Critical Thinking
Possible Responses Characteristics of African music are repetition, hocketing, and the use of drums; it incorporates influences from Europe, Asia, and America.

ACTIVITY OPTION

Integrated Assessment
- Rubric for writing a letter

Reading a Satellite Image

▶▶ Defining the Skill

A satellite image is a photograph taken from a satellite. Photographs taken from satellites can be of continents or neighborhoods. A satellite image of a large area shows water, land, and clouds. The color of the land indicates whether it is desert, forest, farmland, or mountains.

▶▶ Applying the Skill

This satellite image shows the continent of Africa. Use the strategies listed below to help you interpret the image.

How to Read a Satellite Image

Strategy ❶ Distinguish the land from the water. Water on a satellite image is blue or green. Notice the cloud formations, which appear as white on the image.

Strategy ❷ Look at the land. Areas that are desert are light tan. Mountainous areas are gray. Dark green areas show places where there is vegetation, or forests and farmland.

Strategy ❸ Compare the satellite image with the political map of Africa in the Unit Atlas on page 486. Use the chart below to match the regions on the satellite image as closely as possible with countries. Because of clouds, you cannot see the land in all parts of Africa.

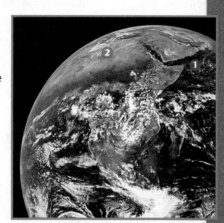

Make a Chart

A chart will help you organize the information found on the satellite image and on the political map of Africa.

Color on Satellite Map	Land Type	Countries
Light tan	Desert	Northern Africa
Orange	Semiarid	Sudan, Chad, Eastern Ethiopia, Namibia, Botswana
Dark green	Forest, farmland	Central Africa, Mozambique, Zimbabwe
Gray	Mountains	Ethiopia, Kenya

▶▶ Practicing the Skill

Turn to the satellite image shown on page 347. Compare that satellite image with the political map on page 280. Make a chart like the one shown above to organize the information found on the map and photo.

SKILLBUILDER

Reading a Satellite Image
Defining the Skill

Prompt a discussion about television weather forecasts that display satellite images. Discuss what the images show and the purpose they serve. Then ask students to name other features that a satellite image might reveal, such as mountains, rivers, and large bodies of water. Have them suggest what purposes satellite images might serve in addition to weather forecasting.

Applying the Skill

How to Read a Satellite Image Point out the three strategies for reading a satellite image, and guide students in working through each one. For example, have students distinguish water from land in the image by looking for areas that are blue or green. Then have them locate any tan, gray, and dark green areas and identify them as areas of desert, mountains, or vegetation. Finally, have them compare the image to the map of Africa on page 280 and match the regions not obscured by cloud cover.

Make a Chart

Point out to students that they will find it helpful to organize the information they gained from the satellite image in a chart.

Practicing the Skill

Ask students to find examples of satellite images in science textbooks and magazines and to make charts of the information they find there.

 In-depth Resources: Unit 4
• Skillbuilder Practice, p. 31

Career Connection: Ecologist

Encourage students who enjoy reading a satellite map to find out about careers that use this skill. For example, ecologists collect and interpret a variety of data to find out how environmental changes are affecting people, animals, and plants. Increasingly, ecologists use satellite maps to trace these changes.

 Block Scheduling

1. Help students find information about global positioning system (GPS) and geographic information system (GIS) technology, two satellite-based developments.

2. What academic courses does a person need to become an ecologist?

3. Invite students to share their findings on a large poster.

OBJECTIVE

Students analyze a poem describing vegetables, particularly yams, ripe for harvest on a farm in Nigeria.

FOCUS & MOTIVATE

Making Inferences To help students infer the setting and purpose of the poem, have them study the photographs on pages 352–353 and answer the following questions:

1. What do the photographs show?
2. What information do you think the poem will give you?

B Block Scheduling

MORE ABOUT...
"My Father's Farm"

While Nigeria once exported food, its economy became overly dependent on oil production, and population growth exceeded agricultural development. Nearly half of Nigerians live in poverty. Ethnic tensions, corruption, poor transportation systems, and periodic drought are serious problems. Nigeria recently became a democracy; it is working toward reform and self-sufficiency.

Nigeria has a rich literary tradition. Among its writers are Chinua Achebe, whose satirical historical novels include *Things Fall Apart* (1958), and Wole Soyinka, who won the Nobel Prize for Literature in 1986.

MY FATHER'S FARM

NIGERIA, with over 123 million people, has the largest population of any country in Africa. More than half of all Nigerians live in rural villages. In this selection, the Nigerian writer Isaac Olaleye vividly describes his father's farm in a small village called Erin in western Nigeria. In the language of the Yoruba people, *erin* means "laughter."

In the heart of a great tropical forest
In space and solitude
Lies my father's farm.
In the acres of solitude
Grow rows of yams,[1]
White like sugar,
Their vines, mounting stakes,
Are clothed in pea green.

*

In the acres of solitude grow:
Rows of yams
The color of vanilla ice cream,
Rows of yams
Smooth as eggshells,
Rows of yams,
Gray like blueberries,
Rows of yams,
Yellow like lemons, and
Rows of yams,
Smooth and creamy as butter.

1. Throughout southern Nigeria, roots—especially yams, taro, and cassava— are the main crops grown on small farms.

352 UNIT 4

Activity Options

Differentiating Instruction: Less Proficient Readers

Building Language Skills Have students work in pairs or small groups, matching less-proficient readers with more fluent readers. Duplicate copies of the Literature Connection and give each pair a copy and a highlighter. Write on the chalkboard: *Rows of yams.* Have pairs go through the poem and highlight this phrase. Tell them to highlight names of **other plants in the last verse.**

To aid understanding, preview the term *acres of solitude.* Explain that the poem compares crops grown on a Nigerian farm to foods readers will know. After students read the poem, have volunteers supply words from the poem to record on the chalkboard in two columns: **Farm Crops** and **Other Foods.** Alternatively, have each pair make a chart and check their work with another pair.

Their vines, all mounting stakes,
And their leaves glowing green—
Yellowish green to emerald.
All the colorful rows delight me.
On my father's farm,
Where it is quiet enough to hear
Bees and flies as they buzz and hum
Through another busy day.

❋

In the acres of solitude
Maize waves in the gentle wind.
Popondo beans hug one another.
Tomatoes sit on pumpkins.
The black-eyed peas climb the maize.
Sweet peas smother the okra
And while peppers flash
The color of danger,
White cotton balls
Laugh at them all.

Reading
THE LITERATURE

What techniques does the poet use to describe the variety and texture of the yams growing in the fields of his father's farm? How does the poet use language, particularly verbs, to give the vegetables human traits?

Thinking About
THE LITERATURE

At what time of year is this poem set? How can you tell? How might the images differ if the poem described the farm during another season of the year? during a drought?

Writing About
THE LITERATURE

In the second stanza of "My Father's Farm," the poet uses repetition and similes. Do these devices enhance the poem? In what ways?

About the Author

Isaac Olaleye (b. 1941) was born and grew up in Nigeria. In addition to the poetry collection in which this poem appears, he has written several books for young people about Nigeria. As an adult he lived for several years in England before settling in the United States.

Further Reading "My Father's Farm" is one of 15 poems by Isaac Olaleye in the book *The Distant Talking Drum*. These poems capture daily life in a Nigerian village by treating such topics as a market day, a tropical rainstorm, and village weavers.

INSTRUCT

Reading the Literature
Possible Responses

The poet uses repetition and comparison or simile to describe yams. Vines are "clothed" in green; plants wave, hug, sit, and laugh.

Thinking About the Literature
Possible Responses

The poem is set near harvest, shown by green vines, full rows, and ripe vegetables. Another season would show empty fields, seedlings, or flowers. In a drought, plants would be yellow, withered, or dead.

Writing About the Literature
Possible Responses

Students' responses should explain how repetition and simile enhance the second stanza, e.g., Repeating *rows of yams* reminds the reader that the stanza is about yams. The similes compare yams to more familiar things—vanilla ice cream, blueberries, etc.

MORE ABOUT...
Poetic Techniques

Have students find sensory images that appeal to sight, hearing, and touch. The last stanza uses personification, the technique of giving human qualities to things.

   World Literature

More to Think About

Making Personal Connections Ask students what they liked about this poem. Why did the poet write it? What places might they describe to give readers a glimpse of their country's bounty? Challenge them to use the form of the second stanza to describe a food product from their region of the United States.

Vocabulary Activity Students may work individually or together. Have them collect lines from the poem and add their own ideas to write a paragraph that describes a yam plant. Alternatively, students may make up questions that can be answered with lines from the poem. Have partners answer each other's questions, using quotes from the poem.

South Africa Today

TERMS & NAMES
veldt
Afrikaner
Boer
African National Congress
Nelson Mandela
sanction
Willem de Klerk

SECTION OBJECTIVES

1. To describe the geography of South Africa
2. To trace the history of colonization and settlement in South Africa
3. To describe the impact of apartheid on the country
4. To explain the challenges the South African government faces today

SKILLBUILDER
• Interpreting a Map, p. 356
• Interpreting a Chart, p. 356

CRITICAL THINKING
• Clarifying, p. 355

FOCUS & MOTIVATE
WARM-UP

Making Inferences Have students read Dateline and answer the following questions.

1. Why did Harrison not realize that he had made such a large discovery?
2. How do you think the discovery of gold changed Johannesburg?

INSTRUCT: Objective ❶

Geography of South Africa

• Where is South Africa located? at the southern tip of Africa
• What is the major geographical feature of South Africa? a plateau of flat grassland
• In what way are South Africa's seasons different from those in the U.S.? They are the opposite of the ones in the U.S.

 In-depth Resources: Unit 4
• Guided Reading Worksheet, p. 27

 Reading Study Guide
(Spanish and English), pp. 110–111

MAIN IDEA
South Africa is working to rebuild itself in the aftermath of apartheid.

WHY IT MATTERS NOW
Since the end of apartheid, South Africa has become a democracy.

DATELINE

EXTRA

WITWATERSRAND MAIN REEF, SOUTH AFRICA, 1896

Gold! Ten years ago, George Harrison, an Australian prospector, discovered gold in the Witwatersrand Main Reef. Most people, including Harrison, thought the find wasn't worth much. Harrison sold his claim for approximately $14. But many people were wrong.

The gold buried in the Witwatersrand is one of the biggest deposits in the world. Many expect these mines will soon produce 20 percent of the world's gold supply. Prospectors from all over the world are coming to the sleepy town of Johannesburg. Already, its population has passed 100,000.

Location • Johannesburg's growth is especially surprising considering that it is hundreds of miles from the nearest railroad, port, or major river. ▲

Place •
The discovery of gold nuggets has drawn many people to South Africa. ▲

Geography of South Africa ❶

Mineral-rich South Africa is located at the southern tip of Africa. The Witwatersrand, also called the Rand, remains the world's largest and richest gold field. It also contains diamonds, uranium, and platinum. Since South Africa is south of the Equator, winter is in July and summer is in January. Most of South Africa is on a plateau. Much of it is flat grassland called the **veldt** (vehlt), where farmers raise cattle, corn, fruit, potatoes, and wheat.

354 CHAPTER 12

Program Resources

 In-depth Resources: Unit 4
• Guided Reading Worksheet, p. 27
• Reteaching Activity, p. 35

 Reading Study Guide
(Spanish and English), pp. 110–111

 Formal Assessment
• Section Quiz, p. 179

 Integrated Assessment
• Rubric for creating a poster

 Outline Map Activities

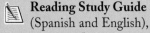 **Access for Students Acquiring English**
• Guided Reading Worksheet, p. 105

Technology Resources
classzone.com

TEST-TAKING RESOURCES
⌇ Strategies for Test Preparation
⌇ Test Practice Transparencies
ⓘ Online Test Practice

Place • The Dutch landed at Table Bay and later established Cape Town nearby. ◄

History of South Africa ❷

South Africa was home to Khoisan and Bantu peoples for more than 1,500 years. The Khoisan were herders and hunters, and the Bantu were farmers.

European Settlers In 1652, the Dutch founded the Cape Town colony. Their descendents, called **Afrikaners,** make up more than half of modern South Africa's white population. Over time, Dutch settlers left Cape Town to become pastoral farmers. Known as **Boers,** they developed their own culture and fought with Africans over land.

German, French, and British settlers followed the Dutch during the 1700s and 1800s. The Cape Town colony came under British control in the early 1800s. Africans resisted British efforts to force them out of the region. Thousands of Boers established two independent states in the 1850s and followed a policy of apartheid.

Wealth and War The discovery of diamonds and gold in the second half of the 19th century renewed European interest in the area. It also attracted prospectors and settlers from Australia, the United States, and Eastern Europe. Between 1899 and 1902, the British and the Boers fought each other in the South African War. Africans supported the British in hopes of gaining some equal rights. The British won and the Boer states came under British rule. Black protest organizations were formed when their situation did not improve.

Reading Social Studies
A. Possible Answers
availability of land, mineral wealth (gold, diamonds), colonial expansion

BACKGROUND
Cape Town later became the legislative capital of South Africa. The country also has an executive capital in Pretoria and a judicial capital in Bloemfontein.

Reading **Social Studies**

A. Analyzing Motives What drew Europeans to South Africa?

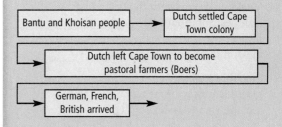

Eastern and Southern Africa **355**

INSTRUCT: Objective ❷

History of South Africa

- Who were the first European settlers in South Africa? What were their descendants called? the Dutch; Boers, and later Afrikaners
- Who gained control of the Cape Town colony in the early 1800s? the British
- Why did Africans support the British in their fight against the Boers? They hoped to gain equal rights.

CRITICAL THINKING ACTIVITY

Clarifying With student input, create a flow chart of the history of South Africa, from the Khoisan and Bantu people to British rule after the South African War. Use the completed flow chart to review and clarify information in the subsection.

Bantu and Khoisan people	→	Dutch settled Cape Town colony

→ Dutch left Cape Town to become pastoral farmers (Boers)

→ German, French, British arrived →

Class Time 10 minutes

Biography

Perhaps no words represent Nelson Mandela better than those he spoke at his inauguration: "Our daily deeds as ordinary South Africans must produce an actual South African reality that will reinforce humanity's belief in justice, strengthen its confidence in the nobility of the human soul, and sustain all our hopes for a glorious life for all."

Activity Options

Interdisciplinary Links: Government/Current Events
Ⓑ Block Scheduling

Class Time 30 minutes

Task Analyzing forms of nonviolent political protest

Purpose To identify methods of nonviolent protest and their effectiveness

Supplies Needed
- Chalkboard
- Current newspapers

Activity Point out that anti-apartheid protesters used both nonviolent and violent forms of protest. Write these forms of nonviolent protest on the chalkboard: *boycotts, strikes, rallies, protest songs, underground newspapers.* Ask students to discuss situations in which citizens might protest government actions and the methods that they might use. Have them give current examples if possible.

INSTRUCT: Objective ❸

A Nation of Apartheid

- In the Union of South Africa, in what ways were nonwhites discriminated against? where they could live and travel, their jobs, where they could attend school
- What was the goal of the African National Congress? to end apartheid
- What is a sanction? a measure taken by nations against a country violating international law

FOCUS ON VISUALS

Interpreting the Chart Have students compare the combined percentages of the nonwhite groups with the percentage of Europeans in South Africa. Ask them to suggest why and how this small group stayed the dominant group for so long.

Possible Responses The Europeans controlled resources and the government; they could retain power by force.

Extension Ask students to research recent elections in South Africa to find out what percentages of each group have participated in voting.

South Africans Today

Asian 2%
Mixed 9%
European 13%
Bantu 76%

**GEOGRAPHY SKILLBUILDER:
Interpreting a Chart**

1. **Place** • Which people make up more than three quarters of South Africa's population?
2. **Place** • Which group makes up only 2 percent of the South African people?

Geography Skillbuilder Possible Answers

1. Bantu
2. Asians

A Nation of Apartheid ❸

In 1910, the British colony became the Union of South Africa. Afrikaners retained a political voice in the new nation. Racial segregation or separation continued under several new laws. Nonwhites were discriminated against concerning where they could live and travel, what jobs they could hold, and whether they could attend school. Many were forced to leave their homes. Apartheid became the official policy of South Africa in 1948 under the rule of the Afrikaner Nationalist Party.

The African National Congress The ANC, or **African National Congress,** was a group of black Africans that opposed apartheid. When the government responded to their passive resistance during the 1950s with arrests and violence, the ANC became more aggressive in their protests. **Nelson Mandela** emerged as a leader of the ANC and the anti-apartheid movement. The fight continued for decades. Hundreds of demonstrators were killed, and thousands more were arrested.

Apartheid Ends Strikes had a negative impact on the economy and forced the government to change some of the apartheid laws in the 1970s and again in the 1980s. In 1985, the United States and Great Britain agreed to impose economic sanctions against South Africa. A **sanction** is a measure taken by nations against a country violating international law. **Willem de Klerk,** a white South African who opposed apartheid, became president in 1989. He helped to repeal many apartheid laws and to release from jail those who had worked to eliminate the policy.

Reading **Social Studies**

B. Recognizing Important Details What were the main ways in which apartheid affected the lives of black South Africans?

**Reading Social Studies
B. Possible Answer** imposed strict racia[l] segregation, limits o[n] housing, travel, jobs and education

Provinces of South Africa, 2001

- National capital
- ★ Provincial capital
- Provincial boundary

0   150   300 miles
0   150   300 kilometers

NORTHERN PROVINCE
Pietersburg ★
Mafikeng ★   ★ Pretoria   Nelspruit ★
NORTH-WEST   MPUMALANGA
GAUTENG   Johannesburg
Kimberley ★   FREE STATE   Ulundi ★
Bloemfontein ★   KWAZULU-NATAL
NORTHERN CAPE
EASTERN CAPE
ATLANTIC OCEAN   Bisho ★   INDIAN OCEAN
WESTERN CAPE
Cape Town ⊛

**GEOGRAPHY SKILLBUILDER:
Interpreting a Map**

1. **Place** • Name South Africa's three national capitals.
2. **Region** • How many provinces are there in South Africa?

Geography Skillbuilder Answers

1. Cape Town, Pretoria, Bloemfontein
2. nine

356 CHAPTER 12

Activity Options

Multiple Learning Styles: Visual/Interpersonal

Class Time 30 minutes

Task Explaining the origins of South Africa's non-Bantu ethnic groups and locating their original countries on a world map

Purpose To point out the mix of

cultures that make up present-day South Africa

Supplies Needed
- World map
- Reference sources on Asian and mixed population groups

🅱 Block Scheduling

Activity Divide students into groups representing each of the non-Bantu groups shown on the chart above. Have them research the national or ethnic origins of the Asian, Mixed, and European (mainly British and Dutch) populations of South Africa. Then have each group point out their countries of origin on the world map.

In 1993, a new constitution gave all adults the right to vote. Nelson Mandela was elected president, served one five-year term, and retired in 1999. Thabo Mbeki (em·BAY·kee) then became president.

A New Era for South Africa

BACKGROUND

At the beginning of the 21st century, South Africa was conducting a new movement called "transformation." Transformation aimed at making every aspect of South African society available to every citizen.

Today, the constitution of South Africa guarantees the same rights to everyone in South Africa. However, most black South Africans remain very poor. The government is working to provide better housing and to bring electricity and water to communities without them. South Africa continues to have the strongest economy in Southern Africa.

Cultures of South Africa Like its people, the cultures of South Africa are very diverse. For example, South Africa has 11 official languages. Although there are many official languages, English is understood by almost every South African because it is the language used in schools and universities. South African art and music are other examples of the country's diverse culture. Jazz and jive have combined with Zulu and Sotho rhythms to make a new, vibrant musical style.

Culture • South Africa's diverse cultures create a wide range of music and art. Zulu beadwork is one example. ▲

SECTION ③ ASSESSMENT

Terms & Names

1. **Identify:**
   (a) veldt
   (b) Afrikaner
   (c) Boer
   (d) African National Congress
   (e) Nelson Mandela
   (f) sanction
   (g) Willem de Klerk

Taking Notes

2. Use a chart like this one to list some of the reasons for conflicts between African and European groups during colonization.

European Group	Reason for Conflict

Main Ideas

3. (a) How have the veldt and the Witwatersrand contributed to South Africa's economy?

   (b) How did Nelson Mandela and the ANC influence South Africa's history?

   (c) How is apartheid related to South Africa's current political, social, and economic conditions?

Critical Thinking

4. **Recognizing Effects**

   What actions did South Africa and other nations take to change the policy of apartheid?

   Think About
   - the ANC's efforts
   - policies of the United States and Great Britain

ACTIVITY -OPTION-

Create a **poster** urging South Africans to vote. List several reasons why voting is important.

Section ③ Assessment

1. Terms & Names
a. veldt, p. 354
b. Afrikaner, p. 355
c. Boer, p. 355
d. African National Congress, p. 356
e. Nelson Mandela, p. 356
f. sanction, p. 356
g. Willem de Klerk, p. 356

2. Taking Notes

European Group	Reason for Conflict
Boers	Took African lands, policy of apartheid
British	Tried to force Africans out

3. Main Ideas
a. veldt: cattle and agriculture; Witwatersrand: gold, diamonds, uranium
b. The ANC, headed by Mandela, led the fight against apartheid, leading to changes in laws and a new constitution that gave all adults the vote.
c. Years of being segregated and denied jobs and education left black South Africans at a disadvantage; most are still poor.

4. Critical Thinking
The ANC led protests; outside nations imposed sanctions; South Africa then changed its laws and passed a new constitution.

ACTIVITY OPTION

Integrated Assessment
- Rubric for creating a poster

Teacher's Edition **357**

INSTRUCT: Objective ④

A New Era for South Africa

- How many official languages are there in South Africa? 11
- What are some examples of the diversity of South African culture? art and music

ASSESS & RETEACH

Reading Social Studies Have students add details to the "South Africa" row in the graphic organizer on page 538.

Formal Assessment
- Section Quiz, p. 179

RETEACHING ACTIVITY

Have students work in teams to prepare an outline for each subsection. Distribute copies of the outlines and use them to review the section.

In-depth Resources: Unit 4
- Reteaching Activity, p. 35

Access for Students Acquiring English
- Reteaching Activity, p. 111

Kenya Today

TERMS & NAMES
multiparty system
Swahili
harambee

SECTION OBJECTIVES

1. To describe the geography of Kenya
2. To identify the ancestors of modern Kenyans
3. To explain the evolution of Kenya's present-day government
4. To describe Kenya's ethnic groups, education policies, and economics

SKILLBUILDER
• Interpreting a Map, p. 359

CRITICAL THINKING
• Recognizing Important Details, p. 361

FOCUS & MOTIVATE
WARM-UP

Hypothesizing Have students read <u>Dateline</u> and answer the following questions.

1. Why do some people still kill rhinoceros even though they are endangered?
2. Why is it important to the governments of African countries that rhinos survive?

INSTRUCT: Objective ❶

Geography of Kenya

• Where do most Kenyans live? Why? in the highlands in the southwest; because there is rich soil and plenty of rain

• What is three-quarters of the land in Kenya like? dry plain

 In-depth Resources: Unit 4
• Guided Reading Worksheet, p. 28

 Reading Study Guide
(Spanish and English), pp. 112–113

MAIN IDEA

Kenya is a beautiful land that has rich natural resources.

WHY IT MATTERS NOW

In the future, Kenya may become the engine for economic growth in Eastern Africa.

Back Forward Stop Refresh Home

Address: ▸go

DATELINE

KENYA, 1999—The rhinoceros is an endangered species—at risk of becoming extinct. More than 90 percent of the world's rhinoceros have been killed for their horns. In Southwest Asia rhino horns are made into dagger handles. In parts of Asia powdered rhino horn is considered a powerful medicine.

A war on poaching—killing animals illegally— has meant fewer rhinoceros deaths in the 1990s. Many African countries want to make sure that rhinos and other endangered species will survive. Six of these countries, including Kenya, have formed a police force to stop poaching across their borders.

Human-Environment Interaction • Hunting was outlawed in Kenya in 1977. Today, people go on safaris only to observe animals, not to hunt them. ▲

Geography of Kenya ❶

Kenya, on Africa's east coast, lies directly on the Equator. Its national park system is home to many threatened species, including rhinoceros, elephants, and cheetahs. Most of Kenya's human population lives in the highlands in the southwest, where there is rich soil and plenty of rain. Nairobi, the capital and largest city, and Mount Kenya are found here. Kenya's coast has tropical beaches and rain forests. The remaining three-quarters of Kenya are covered by a plain that is too dry for farming. Kenyans who live here are herders.

358 CHAPTER 12

Program Resources

 In-depth Resources: Unit 4
• Guided Reading Worksheet, p. 28
• Reteaching Activity, p. 36

 Reading Study Guide
(Spanish and English), pp. 112–113

 Formal Assessment
• Section Quiz, p. 180

 Integrated Assessment
• Rubric for writing a postcard

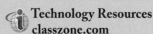 **Outline Map Activities**

 Access for Students Acquiring English
• Guided Reading Worksheet, p. 106

Technology Resources
classzone.com

TEST-TAKING RESOURCES

⮥ Strategies for Test Preparation
⮥ Test Practice Transparencies
🌐 Online Test Practice

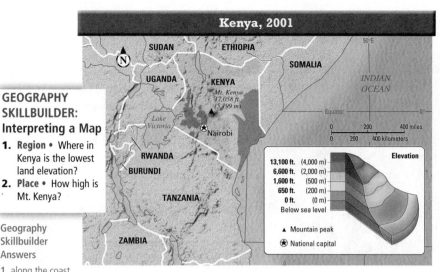

Kenya, 2001

SUDAN · ETHIOPIA · SOMALIA · UGANDA · KENYA · *Mt. Kenya 17,058 ft. (5,199 m)* · INDIAN OCEAN · Lake Victoria · ★Nairobi · RWANDA · BURUNDI · TANZANIA · ZAMBIA · Equator · 50°E · 0°

N

0   200   400 miles
0   200   400 kilometers

Elevation

13,100 ft.   (4,000 m)
6,600 ft.   (2,000 m)
1,600 ft.   (500 m)
650 ft.   (200 m)
0 ft.   (0 m)
Below sea level

▲ Mountain peak
⊛ National capital

GEOGRAPHY SKILLBUILDER: Interpreting a Map

1. **Region** • Where in Kenya is the lowest land elevation?
2. **Place** • How high is Mt. Kenya?

Geography Skillbuilder Answers

1. along the coast

2. 17,058 feet (5,199 m)

Culture • The Masai people migrated to Kenya a few thousand years ago. Masai warriors carried leather shields such as this one to help defend themselves and their animals from attack. ▼

Early History of Kenya ❷

The ancestors of modern Kenyans began arriving in Kenya approximately 3,000 years ago. They were farmers, herders, and hunters from other parts of Africa. Some were part of the Bantu migration. Others came from the northeast. Greek, Roman, and Arabian traders and sailors often visited Kenya's coast along the Indian Ocean. Arabs set up trading posts there about 1,200 years ago. Portuguese sailors arrived in the early 1500s and took control of these trading posts. In the late 1800s, Kenya became a British colony. It gained independence in 1963.

Government of Kenya ❸

Culture • Prime Minister Moi takes this baton, a symbol of his authority, to every public function he attends. ▼

Kenya's first prime minister, Jomo Kenyatta, ruled from 1963 until 1978, when he died in office. Vice President Daniel arap Moi then became prime minister. Moi's party was the only political party. By the early 1990s, however, many Kenyans became dissatisfied with this political system. One problem was that Moi gave special favors to people of his own ethnic group, the Kalenjin. After Kenyans held violent demonstrations in 1991, Moi agreed to allow a **multiparty system**. This meant that other parties could offer ideas for new laws and policies that might be different from Moi's ideas. Despite the change, Moi remained in power. Some people believe that Moi won the 1992 and 1997 elections through fraud.

Eastern and Southern Africa **359**

INSTRUCT: Objective ❷

Early History of Kenya

- Who were the earliest ancestors of modern Kenyans? farmers, herders, and hunters from other parts of Africa
- What groups of people traded along the coast of Kenya? Greeks, Romans, Arabs, and Portuguese

FOCUS ON VISUALS

Interpreting the Map If necessary, review the use of an elevation key. Then ask students to use the key to give a general description of the terrain and landforms of Kenya.

Possible Responses There are lowlands in the east along the coast, rising to highlands and Mount Kenya.

Extension Ask students to use the map to answer the following questions: In what countries is Lake Victoria located? Kenya, Tanzania, Uganda What ocean borders Kenya? Indian Ocean

INSTRUCT: Objective ❸

Government of Kenya

- What did Kenyans do to protest the political system under Moi? held violent demonstrations
- What was the result of these demonstrations? Moi agreed to allow a multiparty system.
- Did the government change? No, Moi remained in power, possibly through election fraud.

Activity Options

Interdisciplinary Links: Language Arts/Writing

Class Time 30 minutes

Task Writing an editorial

Purpose To understand the opposition to the political system under Prime Minister Moi

Supplies Needed
- Writing paper
- Pens or pencils
- Editorial section of newspaper

Activity Provide students with copies of editorials and have them read them to become familiar with their purpose and persuasive language. Then ask students to write editorials that might have been written by dissatisfied citizens of Kenya in 1991. In the editorials, have them voice their objections regarding Moi and the Kalenjin, state their opinions in support of a multiparty system, and try to persuade people to join political demonstrations.

Teacher's Edition **359**

INSTRUCT: Objective ④

The People of Kenya/Nairobi

- What is the largest ethnic group in Kenya? Kikuyu

- What is one indication of the value that Kenyans place on education? some have built schools where the government has not yet started them

- What industry brings the most money into Kenya's economy? tourism

- What are some problems faced by residents of Nairobi? unemployment, water shortages, power outages

MORE ABOUT...
The Masai

The Masai are well-known as tall warriors, famous for their use of weapons. Today, they are a large part of Kenya's nomad population. They move from place to place in search of grazing land and judge a person's wealth by the number of animals owned.

Culture • Most Kenyans wear Western clothing, but a few rural groups still dress in their traditional native clothing. ▲

The People of Kenya ④

Thirty to forty different ethnic groups live in Kenya today. The Kikuyu are the largest group, making up approximately 20 percent of the population. Other large ethnic groups include the Kalenjin, Kamba, Luhya, and Luo. Most groups have their own language. Many people also know Swahili (swah·HEE·lee) and use it to communicate with other groups. **Swahili** is a Bantu language that includes many Arabic words. Swahili and English are the official languages of Kenya.

Education Education is very important to Kenyans. About 80 percent of Kenya's children go to elementary school. Government-run elementary schools are free, but students must pay tuition to attend high school. Most parts of Kenya have government-run schools. However, Kenyans value education so much that some have built their own schools in places where the government has not started them yet. These schools are called *harambee* schools. *Harambee* means "pulling together" in Swahili.

How Kenyans Earn a Living About 80 percent of Kenyans work in agriculture. The most profitable cash crops are coffee and tea. Farmers also grow bananas, corn, pineapples, and sugar cane. Tourism brings the most money into Kenya's economy. More than 500,000 tourists visit Kenya each year. Tourists come to visit the national parks to see the antelope, buffalo, elephants, giraffes, lions, and other native animals. Kenya protects these animals as an important natural resource.

Human-Environment Interaction • One of Kenya's most famous tourist attractions are the flamingos of Lake Nakuru. Unfortunately, their population is declining because the lake is polluted. ◄

360 CHAPTER 12

Reading Social Studies

A. Drawing Conclusions Why do you think Swahili has Arabic influences?

**Reading Social Studies
A. Possible Answer**
Swahili incorporated words used by Arabic traders who built trading posts along the east coast of Africa.

BACKGROUND

The Masai Mara National Reserve in Kenya and the Serengeti National Park in Tanzania include a combined 6,345 square miles.

Activity Options
Differentiating Instruction: Less Proficient Readers

Graphic Organizers Some students may benefit from using a graphic organizer to review the material presented in the section. With students' help, create a spider map like the one shown for each subsection. Use the subsection headings as central ideas, and ask students to supply the details about each one. Encourage them to use the text to find and verify responses.

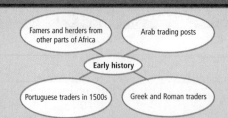

Nairobi

Nairobi is Kenya's capital. The city's name comes from a Masai word meaning "place of cool waters." With 2 million people, Nairobi is the biggest city in Eastern Africa. It has restaurants, bookstores, museums, and skyscrapers. Many foreign companies have offices in Nairobi. Every year, many Kenyans leave their rural homes to move to Nairobi. Not all of them find life in the city as easy as they had hoped. They are often unable to find work. Also, Nairobi suffers from water shortages and power outages. Despite these problems, many residents enjoy the big-city lifestyle that can be found in Nairobi.

Reading
Social Studies

B. Identifying Problems What are the main problems Kenyans face after they move to Nairobi?

Place • **Each month thousands of people move to Nairobi. The majority of newcomers are men. ▲**

Reading Social Studies
B. Possible Answers
unemployment, water shortages, power outages

SECTION ④ ASSESSMENT

Terms & Names

1. Identify: (a) multiparty system (b) Swahili (c) *harambee*

Taking Notes	**Main Ideas**	**Critical Thinking**
2. Use a time line like this one to document key events in Kenya's history.	**3.** (a) Why do most Kenyans live in the highlands?	**4. Synthesizing** What problems might be caused by the system of languages in Kenya?

Taking Notes

2. Use a time line like this one to document key events in Kenya's history.

> 1000 B.C., first Kenyans
> ↓
> A.D. 800s, first Arab trading posts
> ↓
> [ ]

Main Ideas

3. (a) Why do most Kenyans live in the highlands?

(b) Describe Kenya's government under Prime Minister Moi. How did it change in the 1990s?

(c) How does the educational system of Kenya compare with that of the United States?

Critical Thinking

4. Synthesizing
What problems might be caused by the system of languages in Kenya?

Think About
- the many ethnic groups
- the use of Swahili and English

ACTIVITY -OPTION- Imagine that you are on vacation in Kenya. Design a **postcard** to send home. Draw and write about some of the things you have seen on your visit.

Eastern and Southern Africa **361**

CRITICAL THINKING ACTIVITY

Recognizing Important Details Invite students to brainstorm a list of details about Nairobi from the photograph on page 361. After the list is complete, ask students if they were surprised by anything they learned from the photograph.

Class Time 10 minutes

ASSESS & RETEACH

Reading Social Studies Have students complete the graphic organizer on page 338.

 Formal Assessment
- Section Quiz, p. 180

RETEACHING ACTIVITY

Have students work in small groups to create outlines of the section. Assign each group one of the following aspects to outline: history, government, farming, tourism. Then ask groups to present their outlines to the rest of the class.

 In-depth Resources: Unit 4
- Reteaching Activity, p. 36

 Access for Students Acquiring English
- Reteaching Activity, p. 112

Section ④ Assessment

1. Terms & Names
a. multiparty system, p. 359
b. Swahili, p. 360
c. *harambee*, p. 360

2. Taking Notes

> 1500s: Portuguese sailors arrive
> │
> 1800s: becomes British colony
> │
> 1963: independence

3. Main Ideas
a. There is rich soil and rain there.
b. It was a single-party system. Then it became a multiparty system, though Moi stayed in power.
c. Elementary schools are free in both countries, but students in Kenya pay tuition for high school.

4. Critical Thinking
Many people have to communicate in a second language—Swahili or English—rather than in their native language, which could cause misunderstandings.

ACTIVITY OPTION

 Integrated Assessment
- Rubric for writing a postcard

Teacher's Edition **361**

TERMS & NAMES

1. Zulu, p. 342
2. pastoralism, p. 347
3. overgrazing, p. 347
4. kinship, p. 349
5. veldt, p. 354
6. Afrikaner, p. 355
7. Nelson Mandela, p. 356
8. sanction, p. 356
9. multiparty system, p. 359
10. *harambee*, p. 360

REVIEW QUESTIONS

1. Their societies were weakened by war and drought.
2. Somalia lost a dictator but now has 12 clans fighting for control of the government; Rwandan women gained jobs and more rights after many men were killed in civil wars.
3. There is not enough rainfall to support crops.
4. It has adopted some musical traditions from Europe, West Asia, and America.
5. Resources attracted colonizers who wanted to control them.
6. Nonwhites were discriminated against in housing, employment, and education.
7. Moi gave special favors to his ethnic group and allowed only one political party.
8. The largest city of Eastern Africa has restaurants, bookstores, museums, skyscrapers, and offices for many foreign businesses.

CHAPTER 12 ASSESSMENT

TERMS & NAMES

Explain the significance of each of the following:

1. Zulu
2. pastoralism
3. overgrazing
4. kinship
5. veldt
6. Afrikaner
7. Nelson Mandela
8. sanction
9. multiparty system
10. *harambee*

REVIEW QUESTIONS

History and Governments *(pages 339–343)*

1. Why did the Masai and Zulu lose control of their own lands?
2. Explain how civil war in the recent histories of Somalia and Rwanda caused changes in each country.

Economies and Cultures *(pages 346–350)*

3. Why do so many people of Eastern Africa live as nomadic pastoralists?
4. How has the music of Eastern Africa changed?

South Africa Today *(pages 354–357)*

5. How have South Africa's rich natural resources affected events in its history?
6. How did apartheid limit the lives of nonwhites in South Africa?

Kenya Today *(pages 358–361)*

7. Why did Kenyans become dissatisfied with the government of Daniel arap Moi?
8. Describe the city of Nairobi.

CRITICAL THINKING

Forming and Supporting Opinions

1. Use your completed chart from Reading Social Studies, p. 338, to list three predictions for Africa's future. Explain your predictions.

Comparing

2. Compare the leadership shown by Somalia's Siad Barre, Kenya's Daniel arap Moi, and South Africa's Willem de Klerk.

Making Inferences

3. The Nobel Peace Prize is awarded to people who have done the most to create peace in the world. What did Nelson Mandela do to earn this award?

Visual Summary

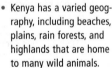

1 History and Governments

- The history of Eastern and Southern Africa spans millions of years and includes trading empires, European settlement, and independence.
- Nations of Eastern Africa have suffered under colonial governments and rulers with unlimited powers. They now are trying to achieve democracy and freedom.

2 Economies and Cultures

- Most Eastern and Southern African nations are poor due to lack of rainfall, but Southern Africa has a more diverse economy.
- Eastern and Southern Africa have rich cultural heritages.

3 South Africa Today

- South Africa was first settled 2,000 years ago and was later colonized by the Dutch, French, Germans, and British.
- South Africa has the largest economy in Africa south of the Sahara.

4 Kenya Today

- Kenya has a varied geography, including beaches, plains, rain forests, and highlands that are home to many wild animals.
- Education is very important to Kenyans.

CRITICAL THINKING: Possible Responses

1. Forming and Supporting Opinions

Government: There may be more civil wars as people protest current systems.

People: Women will gain more rights.

Economy: It will become more diversified and stronger as people receive more education.

Culture: There will be a greater mixing of new and old traditions.

South Africa: The equality of education will improve economic opportunities.

Kenya: The country will continue to protect its environment and attract tourists.

2. Comparing

Barre and Moi both abused their power. Unlike Barre, Moi remained in office but had to accept a multiparty system. De Klerk worked to end apartheid.

3. Making Inferences

He led the fight to end apartheid, an unjust system that created unrest in South Africa and alienated other countries.

SOCIAL STUDIES SKILLBUILDER

SKILLBUILDER: Reading a Satellite Image

1. **Place** • Locate Mount Kenya. Is it snow-covered? How can you tell?
2. **Region** • Describe the surrounding landforms.

FOCUS ON GEOGRAPHY

1. **Region** • What is the most common use of land in Southern Africa?
2. **Region** • What is most land used for in Eastern Africa?
3. **Region** • Use the Unit Atlas map on page 280 to identify two countries on this map in which nomadic herding is the main land use.

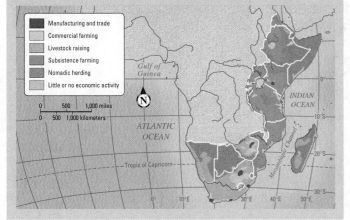

Legend:
- Manufacturing and trade
- Commercial farming
- Livestock raising
- Subsistence farming
- Nomadic herding
- Little or no economic activity

0   500   1,000 miles
0   500   1,000 kilometers

Gulf of Guinea
ATLANTIC OCEAN
INDIAN OCEAN
Mozambique Channel
Tropic of Capricorn
0°   10°E   30°E   40°E   50°E
0°   10°S   20°S   30°S

CHAPTER PROJECTS

Interdisciplinary Activity: Art

African Art Research the art produced by the Shona, Zulu, or another Eastern or Southern African group. Then choose a piece you especially like. Show it to your classmates, and tell what you like about it.

Cooperative Learning Activity

Create an African Collage Work in a group of two or three classmates. Make a collage about the daily lives and culture of one ethnic group living in Eastern or Southern Africa.

- Meet with your team and choose a group to research.
- Learn how and where the people live.
- Make pictures and write poems or sentences about your African group. As a team, make a collage of your work.

 INTERNET ACTIVITY

Use the Internet to learn more about the climate and vegetation of one region of Eastern or Southern Africa. Learn how climate and vegetation affect people's lives.

Writing About Geography Write a report of your findings. Create drawings, diagrams, or charts to show information. Include a list of Internet sites you used to gather information.

For Internet links to support this activity, go to

 **RESEARCH LINKS**
CLASSZONE.COM

CHAPTER PROJECTS

Interdisciplinary Activity: Art

African Art Collect library books about African art in advance, and make them available to students. You may wish to have students choose the art of different cultures so that the class sees a variety of art styles.

Cooperative Learning Activity

Create an African Collage With students, plan a series of checkpoints along the way to the final presentation. Plan to meet with each group to review its work at regular intervals. Create a chart that will allow you and the groups to assess their progress.

INTERNET ACTIVITY

Brainstorm with students a list of keywords they might use to find information about the climate and vegetation of the regions of Eastern or Southern Africa. Students should use only well-known sites, such as government databases, encyclopedias, and reliable on-line magazines. Remind students to keep a record of all the sources they use.

Skills Answers

Social Studies Skillbuilder
Possible Responses
1. Yes; its peak appears white in the satellite image.
2. mountainous, rugged, and dry

Focus on Geography
Possible Responses
1. nomadic herding and livestock raising
2. subsistence farming
3. Somalia and Botswana

Southern Asia

Before You Read

Previewing Unit 5

Unit 5 identifies the wide variety of physical geography, like mountains, plains, plateaus, and islands, that are present in the area. The influential social and cultural practices and the important religions that thrived in ancient India are also examined. Then the focus of the unit shifts to the history, government, economy, and culture of India and its neighbors in Southern Asia today.

Place The Grand Palace is the former residence of the king of Siam, the country now known as Thailand. The palace complex was constructed in 1782 in Bangkok, the national capital.

364

Unit Level Activities

1. Prepare a Summary

Tell students that this region is the birthplace of Hinduism and Buddhism. As they read, students should keep track of these religions throughout the history of the region up until modern times. After they have completed the unit, they should prepare a short summary of the beginnings, influences, and contributions of these religions, written for someone who is unfamiliar with them.

2. Plan a Magazine Feature

Have students take the role of a magazine photographer planning a feature story on India. Remind them that it is a region full of varied landscapes and resources. Will their photographs for the article be mostly the natural wonders of the country or objects made by humans? As they read the chapters, students should plan the article, noting the places they would photograph.

SOUTHERN ASIA

SOUTHERN ASIA

ATLANTIC

PACIFIC

PACIFIC OCEAN

OCEAN

THE GRAND PALACE

OCEAN

INDIAN OCEAN

365

FOCUS ON VISUALS

Interpreting the Photograph Ask students to describe the photograph of the Grand Palace, read the caption, and think about what they see. Why do they think the palace is so ornate? What does this say about the position of royalty in Siam? Ask students to think about current leaders' homes that they have seen in photographs or seen themselves. How do the homes compare with this palace? Would a country be likely to construct a building such as the Grand Palace in modern times? Why or why not?

Possible Responses The building is ornate because it was the home of royalty, and the royal family was valued in Siam. Buildings today would probably not be so fancy. Today a building might be impressive or large, but not as ornate. Architectural styles are simpler today.

Extension Have students write a postcard message from a visitor to the Grand Palace, describing how a tourist might react to the building.

Implementing the National Geography Standards

Standard 13 Identify and compare land uses that are frequently near or far apart from each other

Objective To prepare a report discussing land uses that are frequently near or far apart from each other

Class Time 40 minutes

Task Students use maps and telephone books to prepare a report identifying and comparing land uses that are frequently apart from each other. Some examples students should look for are residential areas and grocery stores, churches and bars, schools and nightclubs.

Evaluation Students should identify at least six examples.

UNIT 5

ATLAS
Southern Asia

ATLAS OBJECTIVES

1. Describe and locate physical features of southern Asia

2. Analyze data on the annual precipitation in southern Asia and compare landmass and population data of southern Asia and the United States

3. Identify political features of southern Asia

4. Analyze the distribution of religions and of population in southern Asia

5. Compare data about the countries of southern Asia

FOCUS & MOTIVATE

Ask students to describe the geography of southern Asia. Ask what physical maps can tell them about the region. Answers will vary, but students should mention mountain ranges, deserts, and rain forests. Physical maps give facts about landforms.

INSTRUCT: Objective ①

Physical Map of Southern Asia

• What do the colors on the map indicate?
elevation of the land

• Where is the highest region in southern Asia?
the Himalaya Mountains in northern India, Nepal, and Bhutan

• What body of water separates India, Pakistan, and Nepal from the rest of southern Asia? Bay of Bengal

 In-depth Resources: Unit 5
• Unit Atlas Activity, p. 1

Activity Options

Critical Thinking

Block Scheduling

Explaining the Skill Students will demonstrate their ability to use a map key to read elevation and changes in elevation on a physical map.

Applying the Skill Direct students to choose one of the larger countries in southern Asia. Then ask them to imagine that they are hiking across the country, either north to south or east to west. Have them use the mileage scale and the elevation key to aid them in writing a brief account of their imaginary journey. Students should describe the direc-

tion they walk and the elevation where their journeys begin. They should then describe the distance they travel before ascending or descending and how high they climb to the next height of elevation. Encourage student volunteers to read their accounts to the class.

Precipitation in Southern Asia

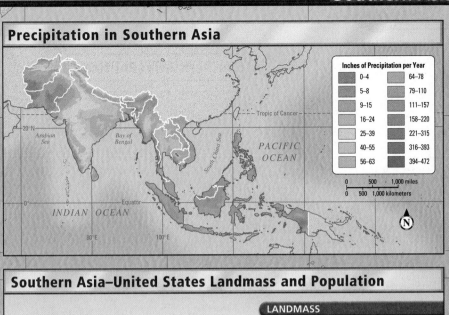

Inches of Precipitation per Year

0–4	64–78
5–8	79–110
9–15	111–157
16–24	158–220
25–39	221–315
40–55	316–393
56–63	394–472

Southern Asia–United States Landmass and Population

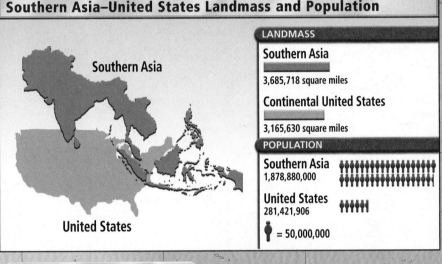

LANDMASS

Southern Asia
3,685,718 square miles

Continental United States
3,165,630 square miles

POPULATION

Southern Asia
1,878,880,000

United States
281,421,906

👤 = 50,000,000

FAST FACTS

✔ **MOST RAIN IN ONE MONTH:**
Meghalaya, India, July 1861, 366 in.

✔ **WORLD'S LARGEST RIVER DELTA:**
Ganges delta, Bangladesh

✔ **WORLD'S LARGEST ARCHIPELAGO:**
Indonesia, 3,231 mi., 17,000 islands

✔ **HUGE TSUNAMI:**
Java and Sumatra, 1883, 120-ft.-high wave

> **GEOGRAPHY SKILLBUILDER: Interpreting Maps and Visuals**
>
> 1. **Location** • What mountain range lies in the north of India?
> 2. **Place** • Which two rivers form the Ganges delta?

Atlas **367**

INSTRUCT: Objective ❷

Precipitation in Southern Asia

• What nations of southern Asia receive the most precipitation annually? Philippines, Indonesia

Landmass

• Approximately how much larger is southern Asia than the United States? about 500,000 square miles

Population

• Approximately how many more people live in southern Asia than in the United States? about 1.5 billion people

Fast Facts

• How many islands make up Indonesia? 17,000 islands

MORE ABOUT...
The Thar Desert

The Thar Desert in northwestern India covers 74,000 square miles. It receives less than ten inches of rain per year. Few people lived here before the irrigation projects begun in 1932 brought farmers into the area. The Thar also contains precious minerals, and India has nuclear power plants in the region.

Fast Facts

Direct students' attention to the Fast Facts. The tsunami that struck Java and Sumatra in 1883 was caused by a volcanic eruption. Have students find out more about the volcanic activity in the region, using almanacs and encyclopedias.

GEOGRAPHY SKILLBUILDER
Answers
1. Himalayas
2. Ganges and Brahmaputra

Country Profiles

Nepal Nepal has three very different regions. In the north are the Himalaya Mountains, a region with long, cold winters and short, mild summers. These mountains, the highest in the world, are covered with grasses and lichens at the highest altitudes. Below about 12,000 feet, forests cover the mountains. People herd sheep and yaks—longhaired oxen—in the mountains.

In the south is a region called the Tarai, with a tropical climate, and jungles and swamps, where crocodiles, elephants, deer, leopards, rhinoceros, and tigers live. The Tarai also has fertile farmland, where farmers grow rice, sugar cane, corn, and other crops.

Between the high Himalayas and the Tarai lie hills and valleys, where winters are cool, and farmers grow crops such as corn, rice, and wheat, and raise cattle, sheep, and goats.

INSTRUCT: Objective ❸

Political Map of Southern Asia

- What is the largest single country on this map? India
- What two countries lie to the west of India? Afghanistan and Pakistan
- What is the capital of the Philippines? Manila
- What nations border Thailand? Cambodia, Laos, Myanmar, Malaysia

MORE ABOUT...

The Spice Islands

Lying near the equator, the Moluccas are Indonesian islands. They were formerly known as the Spice Islands, a name given to them by early European traders. Portuguese traders first brought cloves from the islands in 1513, later establishing trading settlements there. The British explorer Sir Francis Drake visited the Spice Islands in 1579. By 1600 the Dutch, too, were trading for spices in the islands, and in 1605 the Dutch East India Company set up a trading settlement. The Dutch gained control of the islands, which eventually became part of the Netherlands East Indies, now the nation of Indonesia.

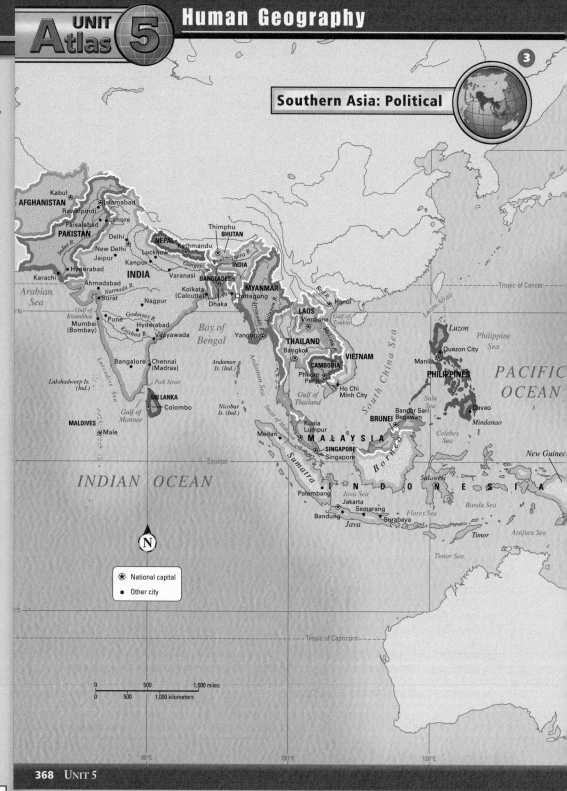

Southern Asia: Political

Activity Options

Interdisciplinary Link: Science

Class Time One class period

Task Creating a brochure of tea production

Purpose To learn how tea is produced

Supplies Needed
- Library or Internet resources
- Pencils or pens
- Writing paper
- Art supplies

Activity Tell students that India and Sri Lanka are two of the largest tea-producing nations in the world. Have students create brochures that describe how tea is grown and includes illustrations of tea leaves, tea plants, and of tea being cultivated. Urge students to make a bar graph comparing the quantities of tea produced in various countries. Encourage students to display their brochures in class.

Religions of Southern Asia

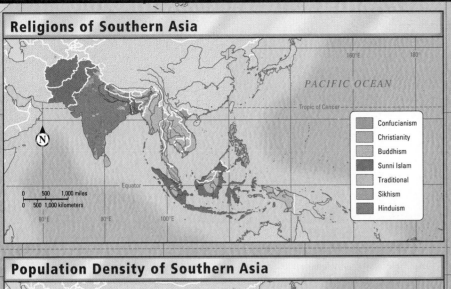

	Confucianism
	Christianity
	Buddhism
	Sunni Islam
	Traditional
	Sikhism
	Hinduism

Population Density of Southern Asia

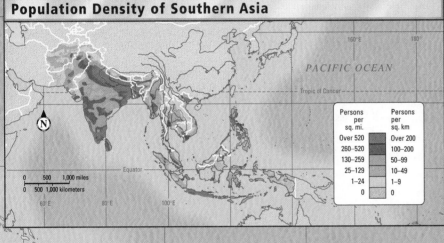

Persons per sq. mi.	Persons per sq. km
Over 520	Over 200
260–520	100–200
130–259	50–99
25–129	10–49
1–24	1–9
0	0

FAST FACTS

✓ **WORLD'S SECOND LARGEST COUNTRY POPULATION:**
India, 1,002,142,000 (2000)

✓ **WORLD'S TALLEST BUILDING:**
Petronas Towers, Kuala Lumpur, Malaysia, 1,483 ft.

✓ **WORLD'S LARGEST PRODUCER OF TEA:**
Assam, India, 1,700,000 lbs. per yr.

✓ **SINKING CITY:**
Bangkok, Thailand, sinking at about 3 in. per yr.

GEOGRAPHY SKILLBUILDER: Interpreting Maps and Visuals

1. **Region** • What country has the highest Hindu population?
2. **Place** • Which country shares borders with India and Afghanistan?

INSTRUCT: Objective ④

Religions of Southern Asia

• Islam is the dominant religion in which countries? Afghanistan, Bangladesh, the Maldives, Pakistan, Indonesia

Populations of Southern Asia

• What three nations of southern Asia have the densest population? India, Bangladesh, Sri Lanka

Fast Facts

• What is the population of India? 1,029,991,000

MORE ABOUT...
Sinking Bangkok

Bangkok, Thailand, is a coastal city of over 6 million people. It sits on the Chao Phraya River. The people use vast amounts of water, which they get from wells that tap underground water aquifers. As water is drained from these aquifers, the sand and clay in which the water was trapped condenses, and the city sinks. As the land sinks, the area is troubled with flooding, especially during the monsoon rains. With high tides and heavy rains, the Chao Phraya River rises, but because the land is so low, it empties slowly, causing great damage.

Fast Facts

Urge students to use almanacs, encyclopedias, and the Internet to find more facts about countries in southern Asia.

GEOGRAPHY SKILLBUILDER
Answers
1. India
2. Pakistan

Country Profiles

Afghanistan About 20 different ethnic groups live in Afghanistan. Although about 99 percent of Afghans practice Islam, most ethnic groups have a different culture and language. Members of these groups generally feel greater loyalty to their group than to the country of Afghanistan. The Pashtuns, who live mainly in the southeast, and the Tajiks, who live mainly in the central and northeastern regions, are the two largest ethnic groups, making up almost 75 percent of all Afghans.

Afghanistan has three main land regions. The northern plains are made of rolling hills and mountain plateaus. The people herd sheep and goats. The central highlands, which make up about two-thirds of the country, include the Hindu Kush Mountains. People live in high valleys among towering mountains. Some exceed 25,000 feet. To the southwest lies the southwestern lowlands, which is mainly desert or semidesert.

DATA FILE OBJECTIVE

Analyze and compare data on countries of southern Asia

FOCUS & MOTIVATE

Direct students' attention to the Data File. Help them focus on specific columns by asking the following questions: What nation has an infant mortality rate of 91 per 1,000 people? What nation has eight passenger cars per 1,000 people? Pakistan, Pakistan

INSTRUCT: Objective ⑤

Data File

• Which country has the largest population? India (1,029,991,000)

• Which country has the higher birthrate, Nepal or Bangladesh? Nepal (36 births per 1,000 people)

• Which country has the highest infant mortality rate? Afghanistan (149.8 per 1,000 live births)

• Which country has the lowest literacy rate? Afghanistan (32 percent literacy rate)

If students need help understanding the meaning of statistics on items such as doctors, birthrate, life expectancy, or other categories, explain and discuss these categories as students review the Data File.

 In-depth Resources: Unit 5
• Data File Activity, p. 2

Country Flag	Country/Capital	Currency	Population (2001) (estimate)	Life Expectancy (years) (2000)	Birthrate (per 1,000 pop.) (2000)
	Afghanistan Kabul	Afghani	26,813,000	46	43
	Bangladesh Dhaka	Taka	131,270,000	59	27
	Bhutan Thimphu	Ngultrum	2,049,000	66	40
	Brunei Bandar Seri Begawan	Dollar	344,000	71	25
	Cambodia Phnom Penh	Riel	12,492,000	56	38
	India New Delhi	Rupee	1,029,991,000	61	27
	Indonesia Jakarta	Rupiah	228,438,000	64	24
	Laos Vientiane	Kip	5,636,000	51	41
	Malaysia Kuala Lumpur	Ringgit	22,229,000	73	25
	Maldives Male	Rufiyaa	311,000	71	35
	Myanmar Yangon	Kyat	41,995,000	54	30
	Nepal Kathmandu	Rupee	25,284,000	57	36
	Pakistan Islamabad	Rupee	144,617,000	58	39
	Philippines Manila	Peso	82,842,000	67	29
	Singapore Singapore	Dollar	4,300,000	78	13

Activity Options

Critical Thinking: Comparing Data

Class Time One class period

Task Creating a bar graph to compare life expectancy and infant mortality

Purpose To gather information from a chart and present it in a bar graph in order to identify relationships

Activity Tell students that there is often a relationship between two or more categories of data. For example, countries with a high infant mortality rate often have a low rate of doctors per 1,000 or a low literacy rate. Have students choose five countries from the Data File and create a bar graph that shows the rate of life expectancy and the infant mortality rate for each. Then have students write a brief paragraph explaining how these two statistics seem to be related. Have students discuss their graphs and their conclusions in small groups.

DATA FILE

Infant Mortality (per 1,000 live births) (2000)	Doctors (per 100,000 pop.) (1992–1999)	Literacy Rate (percentage) (1996–1999)	Passenger Cars (per 1,000 pop.) (1996–1999)	Total Area (square miles)	Map (not to scale)
149.8	11	32	2	250,775	
82.2	20	40	1	55,126	
70.7	16	42 (1995)	1	16,000	
24.0	85	88	441	2,226	
80.8	30	65 (1993)	1.2	69,898	
72.0	48	56	4	1,195,063	
45.7	16	84	12	779,675	
104.0	24	57	1.7	91,428	
7.9	66	84	143	128,727	
27.0	40	96	3	115	
82.5	30	83	0.7	261,789	
78.5	4	39	N/A	54,362	
91.0	57	44	8	310,403	
35.3	123	95	9	115,651	
3.2	163	91	95	225	

MORE ABOUT...

Brunei

Although Brunei is one of the smallest countries of southern Asia, it is one of the wealthiest. The country's ruler, the Sultan of Brunei, is legendary for his fabulous wealth. Brunei's citizens have a high standard of living. The government provides Brunei citizens with free medical service and free education. Students can even attend foreign universities, for free! About half the workers are employed by the government. Brunei's wealth comes from its petroleum and natural gas reserves beneath the waters of its coast. Petroleum products account for nearly all the country's exports. However, the reserves are expected to run out in the early 2000s, which means that Brunei must work to develop other types of jobs.

Brunei's wealth affects some categories in the Data File. For example, because Brunei provides free education to all citizens, its literacy rate is 88 percent. The opportunity for education means that Brunei has one of the highest proportions of doctors per 100,000 in southern Asia—85 per 100,000. Only Singapore and the Philippines have more doctors per 100,000 people. Brunei also has more cars per 1,000 people (441) than any other country in southern Asia.

Activity Options

Interdisciplinary Links: Science/Health

Class Time 20 minutes

Task Determining number of doctors per country

Purpose To use information from the Data File to find the total number of doctors in selected countries

Activity Have students choose five countries from the Data File. Then have them figure out the total number of doctors in each of those countries. Explain that they can determine the number of doctors by first finding the total population for each country. They should then divide that number by 100,000 and then multiply the result by the number of doctors per 100,000. Have students discuss their findings in class. Suggest that students analyze what their findings might mean in terms of other services in the country, such as medical schools, hospitals, nurses, and so on.

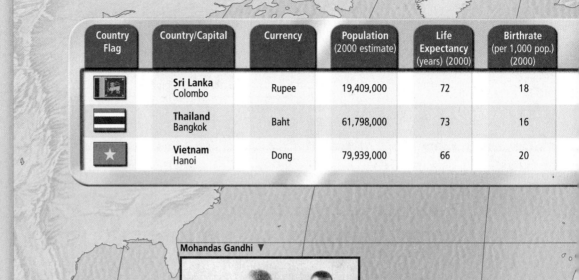

Country Flag	Country/Capital	Currency	Population (2000 estimate)	Life Expectancy (years) (2000)	Birthrate (per 1,000 pop.) (2000)
	Sri Lanka Colombo	Rupee	19,409,000	72	18
	Thailand Bangkok	Baht	61,798,000	73	16
	Vietnam Hanoi	Dong	79,939,000	66	20

MORE ABOUT...
Singapore

With a total area of 225 square miles and a population of over 4 million, Singapore is one of the most densely populated countries in the world. Singapore is an ethnically diverse country, with about 15 percent of the population Malay, 75 percent Chinese, and the rest Indians and Europeans. Singapore's four official languages are Chinese, English, Malay, and Tamil. Singapore has a literacy rate of 91 percent, one of the highest literacy rates in southern Asia.

The country of Singapore is made up of one large island, also called Singapore, and about 50 smaller islands. About half the islands are uninhabited. Most of Singapore's people live in the capital city—also called Singapore. The city of Singapore lies on the coast of the large island and is one of the world's most important port cities. The port of Singapore is a crossroads for ships sailing to China, Japan, and Australia. Many people work in the import and export business. Singapore is also an important financial center. This bustling economic activity makes Singapore one of the most prosperous countries in southern Asia.

Mohandas Gandhi ▼

The Shwezigon Pagoda, a Buddhist temple in Myanmar ▲

The Ganges River Valley ▲

Activity Options

Interdisciplinary Link: Mathematics

Class Time 30 minutes

Task Calculating population density

Purpose To compare population and total area of a selected country to determine the population density

Supplies Needed
• Paper
• Pencils or pens

Activity Tell students that population density can be calculated using total area and total population. Direct students to choose one of the countries from the Data File and divide the total population of the country by its total area. The dividend is the population density expressed as the average number of persons living on each square mile. Have students discuss their results. Ask what a high population density can tell them about a country.

⑤

DATA FILE

Infant Mortality (per 1,000 live births) (2000)	Doctors (per 100,000 pop.) (1992–1998)	Literacy Rate (percentage) (1996–1999)	Passenger Cars (per 1,000 pop.) (1996–1999)	Total Area (square miles)	Map (not to scale)
17.3	37	91	12	25,332	
22.4	24	94	25	198,455	
36.7	48	94	1	130,468	

GEOGRAPHY SKILLBUILDER: Interpreting a Chart

1. **Place** • How much lower is Singapore's birthrate than India's?
2. **Region** • How much higher is the literacy rate in the Philippines than in Laos?

Dancer in Rasa Lila drama in India ▼

Boys in Indonesia studying the Qur'an ▲

Central Highlands in Sri Lanka ▲

MORE ABOUT...
Passenger Cars

The number of passenger cars per 1,000 population is affected by several factors. One factor is the prosperity of the country and of individual citizens. For example, Afghanistan is one of the poorer countries of southern Asia. The number of passenger cars per 1,000 population is 2. The country of Brunei is one of the wealthiest nations of southern Asia. Its number of passenger cars per 1,000 is 441. On the other hand, Singapore is also one of the most prosperous countries of southern Asia, but its number of passenger cars per 1,000 is 95. In this case, most of Singapore's 4 million people live on its main island, which covers about 220 square miles. Most of the main island's inhabitants live in the city of Singapore. Many of Singapore's smaller islands are uninhabited, and much of the land is covered in rain forest. Consequently, it is not practical for large numbers of people to own passenger cars.

GEOGRAPHY SKILLBUILDER
Answers

1. India has a birthrate of 27; Singapore has a birthrate of 13; Singapore's birthrate is 14 per 1,000 lower than India's birthrate.
2. The literacy rate in the Philippines (95 percent) is 38 percent higher than the literacy rate of Laos (57 percent).

Activity Options

Interdisciplinary Link: Popular Culture

Class Time 30 minutes

Task Determining number of cars per country

Purpose To use information from the Data File to determine total number of cars in certain countries

Supplies Needed
• Paper
• Pencils or pens

B Block Scheduling

Activity Direct students to choose five countries and find the total number of passenger cars in each. First they should divide the population for each country by 1,000. Next, have them multiply that number by the number of passenger cars per 1,000. The result will be the total number of passenger cars. Have students discuss how passenger cars affect culture. Ask them to begin by considering how cars affect people in the United States.

Southern Asia: Place and Times

	OVERVIEW	COPYMASTERS	INTEGRATED TECHNOLOGY
UNIT ATLAS AND CHAPTER RESOURCES	Students will examine how geographic features have affected economic activity and the development of civilizations in Southern Asia, and how the cultures of ancient India and China have influenced the culture of Southeast Asia.	**In-depth Resources: Unit 5** • Guided Reading Worksheets, pp. 3–5 • Skillbuilder Practice, p. 8 • Unit Atlas Activities, pp. 1–2 • Geography Workshop, pp. 37–38 **Reading Study Guide** (Spanish and English), pp. 116–123 **Outline Map Activities**	Power Presentations Electronic Teacher Tools Online Lesson Planner Chapter Summaries on CD Critical Thinking Transparencies CT25
SECTION 1 Physical Geography pp. 377–383	**KEY IDEAS** • Southern Asia is made up of South Asia and Southeast Asia. • The Indochinese and Malay Peninsulas form mainland Southeast Asia; the archipelagos of Indonesia and the Philippines are also part of this region. • The monsoons are vital to South Asian agriculture; their timing and intensity determine the year's crop yield.	**In-depth Resources: Unit 5** • Guided Reading Worksheet, p. 3 • Reteaching Activity, p. 10 **Reading Study Guide** (Spanish and English), pp. 116–117	Critical Thinking Transparencies CT26 Map Transparencies MT28, 30 classzone.com Chapter Summaries on CD
SECTION 2 Ancient India pp. 385–390	• The Indus River Valley civilization thrived from 2500 to 1700 B.C. • The Aryans arrived from southern Russia around 1700 B.C.; they spoke different languages, and brought iron weapons to the region. • Hindus believe that a person's actions in one life influence his or her position in the next life. • The Gupta Dynasty was known as the Golden Age of India; science, art, and literature blossomed during this period.	**In-depth Resources: Unit 5** • Guided Reading Worksheet, p. 4 • Reteaching Activity, p. 11 **Reading Study Guide** (Spanish and English), pp. 118–119	classzone.com Chapter Summaries on CD
SECTION 3 Ancient Crossroads pp. 392–397	• Southeast Asia was a crossroads of trade, since it sat at the center of the trading routes of the South Pacific and Indian oceans. • Buddhist beliefs were spread through Southeast Asia by Buddha's followers. • Indian culture had great influence on the rest of Southeast Asia.	**In-depth Resources: Unit 5** • Guided Reading Worksheet, p. 5 • Reteaching Activity, p. 12 **Reading Study Guide** (Spanish and English), pp. 120–121	classzone.com Chapter Summaries on CD

Audio   Internet   TE Teacher's Edition

CD-ROM   Overhead Transparency   Video

Copymaster   PE Pupil's Edition

ASSESSMENT OPTIONS

PE **Chapter Assessment,** pp. 398–399

Formal Assessment
• Chapter Tests: Forms A, B, C, pp. 196–207

Test Generator

Online Test Practice

Strategies for Test Preparation

PE **Section Assessment,** p. 383

Formal Assessment
• Section Quiz, p. 193

Integrated Assessment
• Rubric for creating a map

Test Generator

Test Practice Transparencies TT45

PE **Section Assessment,** p. 390

Formal Assessment
• Section Quiz, p. 194

Integrated Assessment
• Rubric for writing a paragraph

Test Generator

Test Practice Transparencies TT46

PE **Section Assessment,** p. 397

Formal Assessment
• Section Quiz, p. 195

Integrated Assessment
• Rubric for writing a letter

Test Generator

Test Practice Transparencies TT47

RESOURCES FOR DIFFERENTIATING INSTRUCTION

Students Acquiring English/ESL

Reading Study Guide (Spanish and English), pp. 116–123

Access for Students Acquiring English Spanish Translations, pp. 113–120

TE **TE Activity**
• Categorizing, pp. 388, 396

Less Proficient Readers

Reading Study Guide (Spanish and English), pp. 116–123

TE **TE Activity**
• Create a Chart, p. 379

Gifted and Talented Students

TE **TE Activity**
• Analyzing the Noble Truths, p. 395

CROSS-CURRICULAR CONNECTIONS

Literature
Krishnaswami, Uma. *The Broken Tusk: Stories of the Hindu God Ganesha.* North Haven, CT: Linnet Books, 1996. Pantheon of Indian mythology.

Geography
Pollard, Michael. *The Ganges.* New York: Benchmark Books, 1998. Physical features, history, importance.

Science/Math
Moorcroft, Christine. *The Taj Mahal.* Austin, TX: Raintree Steck-Vaughn, 1998. Design, construction, and history.

Mathematics
Demi. *One Grain of Rice: A Mathematical Folktale.* New York: Scholastic, 1997. A clever girl tricks a selfish raja, using the doubling rule.

Science
Stewart, Melissa. *Science in Ancient India.* New York: F. Watts, 1999. Arabic numerals, ayurveda, basic chemistry and physics.

History
Ancient Civilizations, 3000 B.C.–A.D. 500. Alexandria, VA: Time-Life Books, 1998. People, culture, antiquities, and influences.
Rothfarb, Ed. *In the Land of the Taj Mahal: the World of the Fabulous Mughals.* New York: Henry Holt & Co., 1998. History and accomplishments of the Mogul dynasty.

ENRICHMENT ACTIVITIES

The following activities are especially suitable for classes following block schedules.

Teacher's Edition, pp. 381, 382, 386, 387, 391, 394, 397   **Unit Atlas,** pp. 366–373   **Outline Map Activities**

Pupil's Edition, pp. 383, 390, 397

INTEGRATED TECHNOLOGY

Go to **classzone.com** for lesson support and activities for Chapter 13.

BLOCK SCHEDULE LESSON PLAN OPTIONS: 90-MINUTE PERIOD

DAY 1

UNIT PREVIEW, pp. 364–365
Class Time 20 minutes

- **Discussion** Discuss the Unit Introduction, using the discussion prompts on TE pp. 364–365.

UNIT ATLAS, pp. 366–373
Class Time 20 minutes

- **Small Groups** Divide the class into four groups and have each group answer Making Connections questions for one section of the Unit Atlas: Physical Geography, Human Geography, Regional Patterns, and Regional Data File.

SECTION 1, pp. 377–383
Class Time 50 minutes

- **Peer Competition** Divide the class into pairs. Assign each pair one of the Terms & Names for this section. Have pairs make up two questions that can be answered with the Term or Name. Have groups take turns asking the class their questions.
Class Time 25 minutes

- **Internet** Extend students' background knowledge of the physical geography of Southern Asia by visiting **classzone.com.**
Class Time 25 minutes

DAY 2

SECTION 2, pp. 385–390
Class Time 55 minutes

- **Main Ideas** Assign each student one paragraph of this section to read silently. When students have finished, have them formulate the main idea of their paragraph in a single sentence. Beginning with the student who read the first paragraph and proceeding in order, have students say their sentences aloud.
Class Time 25 minutes

- **Discussion** Use the Reading Social Studies: Making Inferences questions on PE p. 386 to lead a discussion about the importance of water and fertile land for the development of civilization.
Class Time 10 minutes

- **Completing a Spider Map** Have students work in pairs to complete the spider map in the Section Assessment on PE p. 390. Then have students use the spider map to discuss the changes Aryans brought to ancient India.
Class Time 20 minutes

SECTION 3, pp. 392–397
Class Time 35 minutes

- **Small Groups** Divide the class into four groups. Have each group select one section objective on PE p. 392 to help them prepare a summary of this section. Remind students that when they summarize, they should include the main ideas and most important details in their own words. Reconvene as a whole class for discussion.

DAY 3

SECTION 3, continued
Class Time 35 minutes

- **Geography Skills** Review flow line maps with students on PE p. 11 of the Geography Skills Handbook. Divide students into pairs and tell them to make a flow line map to show the ideas and goods that came into and out of Southeast Asia. Reconvene as a whole class and discuss the maps.

CHAPTER 13 REVIEW AND ASSESSMENT, pp. 398–399
Class Time 55 minutes

- **Review** Have students prepare a summary of the chapter by reviewing the Main Idea and Why It Matters Now features of each section in Chapter 13.
Class Time 20 minutes

- **Assessment** Have students complete the Chapter 20 Assessment.
Class Time 35 minutes

TECHNOLOGY IN THE CLASSROOM

INTERNET RESEARCH

The World Wide Web lends itself well to student research because of the broad variety of topics and the convenience of search engines. Many Web sites contain valuable, up-to-date information; however, many sites are not current or have irrelevant, erroneous, or inappropriate information. One good way to keep students "on-task" and to ensure that they use appropriate Web sites is to have them look through a limited set of preselected sites. If you present students with a list of sites sponsored by organizations that are generally considered reliable, such as major news sources, nonprofit organizations, or museums, students can maximize on-line class time and will be less likely to access sites that are irrelevant or inappropriate.

ACTIVITY OUTLINE

Objective Students will visit Web sites and take notes on the Himalayas. They will create multimedia presentations or write reports demonstrating what they have learned.

Task Have students pretend they have just returned from the Himalayas and have participated in a specific activity (e.g., trekking). Have them research the Himalayas' geological history, cultures, environmental concerns, and the activity they have chosen. Then have students create multimedia presentations or written reports showing what they have done and learned on their virtual trip.

Class Time Three class periods (not including presentations to the class)

DIRECTIONS

1. Have students spend about 15 minutes browsing through the Web sites listed at **classzone.com.** Ask them to look for information on activities they might try if they visited the Himalayas.

2. Divide the class into small groups, and have each group choose an activity they might like to try if they were to visit the Himalayas. Examples of activities include trekking, mountain climbing, or simply spending time in a small village.

3. Have students imagine that they have just returned from completing this activity in the Himalayas and have been asked to give a slide show to a group of students and teachers, describing their experiences and providing an overview of the Himalayan region. Have them create multimedia presentations or write reports that contain the following components: an introduction to the geological history of the Himalayas, a description of the activity they chose to do on their trip, an overview of the cultures they have encountered on their trip, a description of some of the environmental problems facing this region. Students will need to return to the Web sites listed at **classzone.com** to take notes on the components of their presentations.

4. Provide time for students to share their presentations or reports with the class.

CHAPTER 13 OBJECTIVE

Students will examine how geographic features have affected economic activity and the development of civilizations in Southern Asia, and how the cultures of ancient India and China have influenced the culture of Southeast Asia.

FOCUS ON VISUALS

Interpreting the Photograph Direct students' attention to the photograph of Angkor Wat. Ask them to describe the architecture of the buildings. Point out that the buildings are temples. Discuss with students what they might expect to find inside.

Possible Responses The architecture is ornate, with many columns, levels, walkways, entrances, and carvings. Inside, one might expect an equally ornate style, perhaps with the interior divided into smaller areas rather than grand rooms. There also appears to be open-air areas inside the outer walls.

Extension Have students research Angkor Wat to verify what the inside looks like as well as to learn more about its history.

CRITICAL THINKING ACTIVITY

Comparing Ask students to identify churches, mosques, synagogues, and other houses of worship in your community. Then ask them to compare these structures to the temple complex at Angkor Wat. Have students brainstorm ways in which these places of worship are similar to, and different from, Angkor Wat.

Class Time 10 minutes

Southern Asia: Place and Times

SECTION 1 Physical Geography

SECTION 2 Ancient India

SECTION 3 Ancient Crossroads

Place The temple complex at Angkor Wat, Cambodia, is dedicated to the Hindu god Vishnu. Built in the 1100s, it covers almost one square mile.

374

Recommended Resources

BOOKS FOR THE TEACHER

Phillips, Charles. *The Eternal Cycle: Indian Myth.* Alexandria, VA: Time-Life Books, 2000. Hindu, Buddhist, and Jain mythology of India.
Tammita-Delgoda, Sinharaja. *A Traveller's History of India.* New York: Interlink Books, 1999. Covers the scope of India's history from earliest times.
Wolpert, Stanley A. *A New History of India.* New York: Oxford University Press, 1999. History and civilization of India.

VIDEOS

Ancient India. Wynnewood, PA: Library Video Company, 2000. Features an Indus Valley city of the Second Millennium B.C. and tours ancient Indian monuments.

INTERNET

For more information about Southern Asia, visit **classzone.com.**

FOCUS ON GEOGRAPHY

How did rivers contribute to the development of civilizations?

Human-Environment Interaction • The regular flooding of the Ganges River and other rivers during the rainy season deposits rich soil on the Northern Plains. This fertile soil has been farmed by the people of India for many centuries. A rich civilization known as the Gupta developed on these plains. The art, literature, philosophy, mathematics, and science developed during its golden age still influence the world.

What do you think?

♦ Why do complex civilizations depend on productive farmland?

♦ What might happen to a civilization if the climate changes and rivers dry up or change course?

FOCUS ON GEOGRAPHY

Objectives

• To explain how the geography of India influenced the development of the Gupta civilization

• To identify the geographic factors that made Southern Asia an economic and cultural crossroads

What Do You Think?

1. Guide students to identify the needs of a complex civilization, such as food and trade, and to explain how farming can help meet these needs.

2. Suggest that students think about what might happen to the farmland, farmers, and cities that rely on water if the rivers become unavailable.

How did rivers contribute to the development of civilizations?

Remind students that great civilizations developed in China and in Egypt along rivers. Ask them to think about how flooding rivers affect the fertility of the land around them.

MAKING GEOGRAPHIC CONNECTIONS

Ask students to look at maps and globes, and locate major cities around the world, such as Rome, London, Paris, Cairo, Moscow, Beijing, Montreal, and New York City. Have them identify the rivers on which these cities are located. Discuss the reasons many large cities are found on rivers or near the ocean.

Implementing the National Geography Standards

Standard 7 Relate the patterns of world agriculture to the physical processes that produce them

Objective To build a model of a river valley that annually floods

Class Time 45 minutes

Task Students work together to build a model of a river valley that is flooded annually. Students can use the Ganges, Nile, or Mississippi rivers for their model. Students should use their completed model to write a report about how annual flooding can distribute fertile soils needed for agriculture. They

should also hypothesize about how dams might affect the fertility of the valley.

Evaluation In their reports, students should explain that the flooding carries fresh, fertile soils, and that dams might stop the flooding and harm the agricultural output of the valley.

BEFORE YOU READ

What Do You Know?

Write India, Pakistan, Afghanistan, the Philippines, Indonesia, Cambodia, Vietnam, Thailand on the board. Ask students to tell what they know about each of these places, and record their ideas below the appropriate nation. Encourage students to mention aspects of geography, history, or culture. If students need prompting, suggest they consider what they know about: silk, elephants, tea, Buddha, curry, the Vietnam War, tigers, Gandhi, rice, and the spice trade.

What Do You Want to Know?

Suggest that students record questions that they would like to have answered about Southern Asia in their notebooks. Tell them to look for the answers to their questions as they read the chapter.

READ AND TAKE NOTES

Reading Strategy: Categorizing Tell students that categorizing ideas is an important reading strategy. By categorizing the information in this chapter, students will organize the details in such a way as to help them understand and remember what they read. Remind students to add details to the chart after they finish reading each section.

 In-depth Resources: Unit 5
  • Guided Reading Worksheets, pp. 3–5

BEFORE YOU READ

▶▶ What Do You Know?

Before you read the chapter, consider what you already know about Southern Asia. What stories have you read or heard about climbing the Himalayas, the highest mountains in the world? What do you know about explorers who have traveled the area's rain forests? What do you know about India? Have you read or heard about Hinduism or Buddhism, the major religions of Southern Asia? Reflect on what you have learned in other classes, what you have read, and what you may have seen in documentaries or news reports about the history of this region.

▶▶ What Do You Want to Know?

Decide what you know about Southern Asia. In your notebook, record what you hope to learn from this chapter.

Culture • Shiva is one of the Hindu gods worshiped in Southern Asia. ◀

Place • Mohenjo-Daro was once a thriving city in Southern Asia. ▼

READ AND TAKE NOTES

Reading Strategy: Categorizing   Categorizing is a useful strategy for organizing information you read about in social studies. Categorizing means sorting things or ideas into groups. Use the chart at the right to categorize information about the geographic and human factors that shaped the ancient history of Southern Asia.

• Copy the chart into your notebook.
• As you read, look for information about geographic features and human civilization.
• When you reach the end of a section, record key details next to the appropriate headings.
• Note that the geography of Southeast Asia is discussed in Section 1 and Section 3.

Factors	Impact of Geograph Contributions of Civilizations
South Asia	
Geography of Indian Subcontinent	Northern mountains, Ganges and Indus river valleys, Deccan Plateau
Indus River Civilization (about 2500–1700 B.C.)	cities of Harappa and Mohenjo-Daro, extensive irrigation by canals
Aryans (1700 B.C.)	iron tools, horses, influenced Hinduism, Sanskrit
Hinduism	Vedas, karma, reincarnation, caste system
Buddhism (500 B.C.)	arts and philosophy
Mauryan Dynasty (about 324–185 B.C.)	fine sculpture, sandstone carvings, first Indian empire
Gupta Dynasty (A.D. 320–500)	golden age of science, mathematics and the concept of zero, art
Southeast Asia	
Geography	archipelagoes; Indochinese and Malay peninsulas; volcanoes
Location	tropical climate between South Pacific and Indian oceans
Early Advances	bronze tools, sailing, grew yams and rice
Southeast Asian empires (6th century A.D.)	Khmer Empire, Pagan Kingdom

Teaching Strategy

Reading the Chapter This chapter describes the geography, cultural contributions, and development of civilizations in ancient India and in Southeast Asia. Encourage students to focus on how the geography of the region affected the development of civilizations and the diffusion of cultural traits from India across the region.

Integrated Assessment The Chapter Assessment on page 399 describes several activities for integrated assessment. You may wish to have students work on these activities during the course of the chapter and then present them at the end.

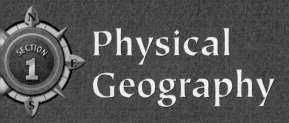

Physical Geography

 SECTION 1

TERMS & NAMES

subcontinent

Himalayas

Northern Plains

delta

sediment

Deccan Plateau

archipelago

monsoon

MAIN IDEA

Southern Asia's geography affects how the region's people live.

WHY IT MATTERS NOW

Studying the geography of Southern Asia will help you understand its history, economy, and customs.

DATELINE

EXTRA

NEPAL, SOUTHERN ASIA, MAY 29, 1953

Today, New Zealander Sir Edmund Hillary and Sherpa tribesman Tenzing Norgay became the first people to reach the top of Mount Everest in the Himalayas. Using oxygen canisters and boots and clothing with special insulation, the two men overcame the tremendous cold, high winds, and thin air to reach their goal. "We didn't know if it was humanly possible to reach the top of Mount Everest," said Hillary of their adventure. "And even using oxygen as we were, if we did get to the top, we weren't at all sure whether we wouldn't drop dead or something of that nature." Hillary and Tenzing survived and will go down in history as the first people to stand atop the highest mountain in the world.

Human-Environment Interaction • Tenzing Norgay (on the right) and Sir Edmund Hillary relax after their historic climb. ▲

The Variety of Southern Asia ①

The Unit Atlas maps on pages 366–367 show the great variety and contrasts in the geography of Southern Asia. There are the vast snow-capped mountain ranges, such as the Himalayas, and wet low-lying rain forests. Some people live in the mountains, while others live deep in the tropical rain forest or in the desert. Some places are dry, and others get plenty of water—some, in fact, get too much.

Southern Asia: Place and Times **377**

SECTION OBJECTIVES

1. To identify the two regions of Southern Asia
2. To identify the geographic regions of South Asia
3. To describe the mainland and islands of Southeast Asia
4. To explain the effects of the monsoons in South Asia

SKILLBUILDER
• Interpreting a Map, p. 378

CRITICAL THINKING
• Clarifying, p. 379
• Using Maps, p. 381

FOCUS & MOTIVATE
WARM-UP

Making Inferences Have students read <u>Dateline</u> and discuss the experience of climbing Mount Everest.

1. Why was Hillary accompanied by Tenzing Norgay, a native of the region?
2. Why do you think the climbers had to use oxygen?

INSTRUCT: Objective ①

The Variety of Southern Asia

• What are the two regions of Southern Asia? South Asia and Southeast Asia

• What countries are on the South Asian subcontinent? India, Bangladesh, Pakistan, Nepal, and Bhutan

 In-depth Resources: Unit 5
• Guided Reading Worksheet, p. 3

 Reading Study Guide
(Spanish and English), pp. 116–117

Program Resources

 In-depth Resources: Unit 5
• Guided Reading Worksheet, p. 3
• Reteaching Activity, p. 10

 Reading Study Guide
(Spanish and English), pp. 116–117

 Formal Assessment
• Section Quiz, p. 193

 Integrated Assessment
• Rubric for creating a map

 Outline Map Activities

 Access for Students Acquiring English
• Guided Reading Worksheet, p. 113

 Technology Resources
classzone.com

TEST-TAKING RESOURCES
⚓ Strategies for Test Preparation
⚓ Test Practice Transparencies
🌐 Online Test Practice

INSTRUCT: Objective ❷

Geographic Regions of South Asia

- What are the geographic regions of South Asia? the Northern Mountain Rim, the Northern Plains, the Deccan Plateau
- What mountain ranges make up the Northern Mountain Rim? the Hindu Kush, the Himalayas, and the Karakoram
- What two major river valleys are found in the Northern Plains? the Ganges and the Indus River valleys

FOCUS ON VISUALS

Interpreting the Map Have students compare the elevation of the Northern Mountain Rim, the Northern Plains, and the Deccan Plateau.

Possible Responses The Northern Mountain Rim ranges are the highest and the river valleys of the Northern Plains are the lowest. The Deccan Plateau is higher than the river valleys of the Northern Plains.

Extension Have students examine the map and then write a brief paragraph explaining why, historically, outsiders entered this region through Afghanistan.

Southern Asia is divided into two regions, South Asia and Southeast Asia. South Asia includes Afghanistan, Bangladesh, Bhutan, India, the Maldives, Nepal, Pakistan, and Sri Lanka (shree LAHNG•kuh). The South Asian subcontinent includes the countries of India, Pakistan, Bangladesh, Nepal, and Bhutan. A **subcontinent** is a large landmass that is part of a continent, but is geographically separate from it. India is the largest country on the subcontinent and in Southern Asia. It is the second most populous country in the world, next to China.

Geographic Regions of South Asia ❷

The subcontinent has three main geographic regions—the Northern Mountain Rim, the Northern Plains, and the Deccan (DEK•uhn) Plateau. Just off the coast are two island countries, Sri Lanka and the Maldives. Each of these regions has distinctive landforms and climate that affect how people live.

The Northern Mountain Rim The Northern Mountain Rim is made up of several mountain ranges. The Hindu Kush Mountains are located to the west and the **Himalayas** to the east. The Karakoram Mountains lie between the two, extending along the northern border of Pakistan. These mountains form a wall that separates the subcontinent from the rest of Asia.

Reading Social Studies
A. Possible Answer Since the mountains are essentially impassable, trade by water became more important.

GEOGRAPHY SKILLBUILDER: Interpreting a Map

1. **Location** • What is the highest mountain range in South Asia?
2. **Region** • How would you compare land elevations in Bangladesh with land elevations in Pakistan?

Geography Skillbuilder Answers

1. the Himalayas
2. They are about the same.

BACKGROUND
Geologists believe that the South Asian subcontinent was once part of the African continent. It broke away 200 million years ago. Forty million years ago, this subcontinent crashed into Asia and created the Himalayas.

Reading Social Studies

A. Making Inferences How might these mountains have made trade and travel by water important in ancient times?

Elevations of South Asia

Elevation
13,100 ft.	(4,000 m)
6,600 ft.	(2,000 m)
1,600 ft.	(500 m)
650 ft.	(200 m)
0 ft.	(0 m)
Below sea level

▲ Mountain peak

Activity Options

Interdisciplinary Links: Language Arts/Geography

Class Time One class period

Task Writing a report on the Himalayas

Purpose To learn how the Himalayas were formed, and how they have affected human activity in Asia

Supplies Needed
- Reference materials related to the Himalayas
- Pencils or pens
- Writing paper

Activity Tell students that the Himalayas are the highest mountains in the world, and their presence in the region has had a profound effect on the people. Have students find out more about the formation of the Himalayas as well as some of the myths, legends, or beliefs that surround them. Students should write and illustrate a brief report that addresses these issues. Invite students to share their reports.

However, there are some mountain passes that since ancient times have allowed travelers and invaders from Asia to get through the mountain barrier. The Khyber Pass, for example, connects the two modern-day countries of Pakistan and Afghanistan.

The Himalayas stretch for 1,500 miles across northern India and Nepal. They are 200 miles wide at some points, and many peaks are more than four and a half miles high. The tallest mountain in the world, Mount Everest, is almost five and a half miles high. This is taller than 23 Empire State Buildings stacked on top of one another. The terrain is rough in this region with few safe roads. It is also difficult to farm. As a result, fewer people live in this part of South Asia.

The Northern Plains The **Northern Plains** lie between the Himalayas and southern India. This region includes the Ganges (GAN·jeez) and Indus River valleys. The Ganges flows through Bangladesh and empties into the Bay of Bengal. The Indus River flows through Pakistan and empties into the Arabian Sea. The Indus and the Ganges rivers form large deltas where they empty into the sea. A **delta** is a triangular deposit of soil at the mouth of a river. The map on page 378 shows that the Ganges River delta is mostly within Bangladesh.

Human-Environment Interaction • **People in heavily populated Bangladesh crowd aboard a Ganges River ferryboat.** ▶

The Ganges River carries rich sediment from the Himalayas to the plains. **Sediment** includes minerals and debris that settle at the bottom of a river. During the rainy season, the Northern Plains flood, and the sediment from the Ganges River is deposited there. This makes the plains a fertile farming area.

Southern Asia: Place and Times **379**

MORE ABOUT...
The Khyber Pass

The Khyber Pass is one of the most strategically important passes in the world. The pass is 33 miles long, and at its narrowest point it is only ten feet wide. A portion of the pass widens into a valley dotted with villages and forts.

For more than 2,000 years the Khyber has witnessed invading armies passing through it and seen fierce battles for its control. The region has long been inhabited by the Pashtun people, who have fiercely resisted invasion and outside control. During the 19th century they engaged the British in several wars for control of the pass.

MORE ABOUT...
The Ganges River

The Ganges River is the holiest river of Hinduism. The Ganges is regarded as the path to heaven, and many Hindus make a pilgrimage to the river to die in its current. Ashes of loved ones are cast into the river as well, with the belief that the current will deliver the spirit to heaven. Every year, hundreds of thousands of Hindus travel to the Ganges to bathe in the waters.

CRITICAL THINKING ACTIVITY

Clarifying To help students understand the role of a flooding river in improving farmland, ask the following questions:

- What causes flooding?
- How is the current of a river different during a flood?
- What happens to the banks of a river during and after flooding?

Class Time 10 minutes

Activity Options

Differentiating Instruction: Less Proficient Readers

Create a Chart For those students who are having difficulty understanding the material in this section, create a chart on the board like the one shown. Have students copy the chart, adding the subheads within "Geographic Regions of South Asia" to the top row. Then, as they read, they can add important details to the appropriate column in the chart.

Northern Mountain Rim	Northern Plains	Deccan Plateau	Sri Lanka and the Maldive

CRITICAL THINKING ACTIVITY

Recognizing Effects Review with students the Focus on Geography feature on page 375. Then have them quickly review the material on pages 379–380. Ask students to identify the potential effects of a climate growing hotter and drier on a fertile river valley that was a center of civilization.

Class Time 15 minutes

MORE ABOUT...
Elephants

The elephant that is found in Southern Asia is the Asian elephant. While it was once found all over the region, a shrinking of habitat and poaching for ivory and skin have reduced its numbers so greatly that it is now endangered. The elephant has played an important role in Southern Asia. It is considered a symbol of power and peace and is equated with the Buddha. Because elephants carry as much as a ton, they have been used for logging. Before the 18th century, elephants had a military role. One Thai king had a force of 20,000 elephants he could take into battle. Mahouts, the elephant trainers, sometimes teach elephants sports, such as football, as well as dance steps. The elephant's grace and power, its refined sense of smell and hearing, and its gentle demeanor have endeared it to people all over the world.

Reading
Social Studies

B. Clarifying How could fertile soil lead to dense population?

Reading Social Studies
B. Possible Answer
Fertile soil allows farmers to produce surplus crops, which can feed workers in cities.

Because of the fertile soil, parts of the Northern Plains are densely populated. In Bangladesh, for example, more than 130 million people live in an area smaller than the state of Wisconsin. In ancient times, the Indus River valley was also fertile and densely populated. Today, however, the valley is mostly desert, and few people live in this hot, dry region.

The Deccan Plateau As you can see from the map on page 378, the **Deccan Plateau** makes up most of southern India. The plateau has mineral deposits, as well as forests where elephants roam. Mountains border the plateau to the east and west—the Eastern and Western Ghats (gahts). The Western Ghats are the higher peaks, reaching 8,000 feet at the southern tip of India. A coastal plain runs between the mountains and the oceans on both coasts. Along these coastal plains the soil is fertile and water is plentiful. In the interior part of the plateau, between the mountain ranges, the soil is not as rich. People do farm there but water supplies are unreliable and it is hot year round. Fewer people live on the Deccan Plateau than in the Northern Plains.

Sri Lanka and the Maldives The islands of Sri Lanka and the Maldives lie south and southwest of India. Sri Lanka is a picturesque, mountainous island, 23 miles off the southern tip of India. Parts of it receive a great deal of rain.

The Maldives is a country made up of more than 1,200 low, flat coral islands called atolls. People live on only about 300 of these islands. The Maldives stretch south for 400 miles. The highest elevation in the entire chain is just over six feet above sea level.

Place • An elephant gets its tusks washed at an elephant training camp in Mudumalai National Park. ▲

BACKGROUND

If scientists' predictions about global warming are accurate, sea levels could rise dramatically. The Maldives would then disappear, or nearly disappear, under the sea.

Place • The central highlands of Sri Lanka have mountains that reach over 7,000 feet and offer some spectacular scenery. ◄

Activity Options

Skillbuilder Mini-Lesson: Reading a Satellite Image

Explaining the Skill Remind students that the colors on a satellite map show water, clouds, and types of land. Review that water appears as blue or green; clouds as white; mountainous areas as gray; desert areas as light tan; semi-arid land as orange; and forests and farmland as dark green.

Applying the Skill Have students review "Geographic Regions of South Asia." Ask them to imagine that they are looking at a satellite photo of the Indian subcontinent, and then to answer these questions.

1. What color represents the northern rim of the subcontinent on the satellite photo?
2. What part of the Indian subcontinent would show as orange? Why?
3. What indicates where the land ends and the ocean begins?

Place • Mount Merapi, called the Fire Mountain, is the most active volcano in Indonesia. ◄

Regions and Nations of Southeast Asia ❸

Southeast Asia contains both a mainland region and many islands. The countries that make up Southeast Asia include Brunei, Cambodia, Indonesia, Laos, Malaysia, Myanmar (Burma), the Philippines, Singapore, Thailand, and Vietnam.

Mainland Southeast Asia The mainland lies on two peninsulas—the Indochinese Peninsula and the Malay Peninsula. The countries of mainland Southeast Asia are Cambodia, Laos, Myanmar, Thailand, Vietnam, and part of Malaysia. The Mekong River drains more than 313,000 square miles of this region. It starts in the highlands of the Plateau of Tibet and ends in the South China Sea. It flows through Laos, central Cambodia, and into Vietnam. This area is a major rice-producing region and is densely populated.

Islands of Southeast Asia The islands of Southeast Asia include Borneo, part of which belongs to the country of Malaysia, the island of Singapore, and the archipelagoes of Indonesia and the Philippines. An **archipelago** (AHR•kuh•PEHL•uh•GOH) is a group of islands.

Indonesia is the largest nation in Southeast Asia. It extends over an area about three times the size of Texas, and it has the fourth largest population in the world. Indonesia is made up of 17,000 islands that were formed by volcanoes.

Reading
Social Studies

C. Making Inferences How do you think the Mekong River contributes to growing crops in this region?

Reading Social Studies
C. Possible Answer
It enriches the soil with sediment and brings plenty of water.

Regions and Nations of Southeast Asia

• What two regions make up Southeast Asia? mainland region, many islands

• What two peninsulas form mainland Southeast Asia? Indochinese Peninsula and Malay Peninsula

• What nations form the mainland? Cambodia, Laos, Myanmar, Thailand, Vietnam, part of Malaysia

• Why are Indonesia and the Philippines referred to as archipelagoes? Both nations consist of a group of islands.

CRITICAL THINKING ACTIVITY

Using Maps Have students turn to the Unit 5 Atlas map on pages 366–367. Then ask the following questions:

• What is the capital of Cambodia? of Indonesia? of Laos? of Malaysia? of Myanmar? of the Philippines? of Thailand? of Vietnam?

• What body of water divides Singapore from the mainland?

• What bodies of water surround Indonesia?

• Through which countries does the Mekong River flow?

Class Time 15 minutes

Activity Options

Interdisciplinary Links: Current Events/Writing

Class Time One class period
Task Writing a newspaper article about events in Indonesia
Purpose To learn about the culture and government of Indonesia and its importance in the world

Supplies Needed
• Recent newspaper or magazine articles about social or political events in Indonesia
• Pens or pencils
• Writing paper

Block Scheduling

Activity Tell students that Indonesia is the fourth most populous nation on Earth, and that more than 85 percent of its people practice Islam. In recent years, Indonesia has suffered social unrest. Have students review the available material, and write a newspaper article about one event in or aspect of Indonesia today. Remind them that they should answer the questions who, what, when, where, and why in their articles.

INSTRUCT: Objective ❹

Climate and Monsoons

- How does the climate in Southeast Asia differ from that of the rest of Southern Asia? less variety, hot and rainy

- How is the timing of the monsoons important? too early: farmers don't have time to plant; too late: crops fail

- What are the effects of an extremely intense monsoon? severe flooding, crops ruined, property damaged, people injured

MORE ABOUT…

Krakatau

The only known eruption of Krakatau before 1883 was a moderate eruption in 1680. The 1883 eruption began on May 20, when clouds of ash shot 6 miles into the sky and explosions were heard as far away as 100 miles. By the end of May the eruption had calmed down, but it resumed on June 19. Then on August 26 the violent explosions began. Ash from the volcano spread over a 300,000 square mile area. Sailors on ships near the volcano could not see where they were going. The area was engulfed in darkness for two and a half days. Because of the eruption, all life on the island group was wiped out and did not reappear for five years.

More than 6,000 of these islands are inhabited. The islands have a tropical climate with a lot of rain, but the soil is not very fertile. Still, more than half the people of Indonesia are farmers.

The 7,100 islands of the Philippines cover an area about the size of the state of Arizona. Only 800 of these islands are inhabited. Nearly half of the Philippine people are farmers.

Climate and Monsoons ❹

Most of South Asia has three seasons—cool, hot, and rainy. The higher elevations are usually cooler. Much of India's weather is milder in the cool season. Sometimes frost forms on the Northern Plains. However, most of southern India is hot all year round.

Southeast Asia's climate has less variety. It is hot and rainy. Heavy seasonal winds and rains are common both to South Asia and Southeast Asia.

The Monsoon Cycle The period from June through September marks the coming of the monsoon winds and the rainy season. A **monsoon** is a seasonal wind that blows over the northern part of the Indian Ocean. From April through October, the monsoon blows from the southwest, building up moisture over the ocean and bringing heavy rains to South Asia and Southeast Asia. From November through March, the monsoon blows from the northeast.

South Asia and Southeast Asia have different monsoon cycles. In South Asia, heavy monsoon rains fall from June through October. November through February is mostly cool and dry. Because March through late May is hot and humid, the monsoon rains in June bring great relief. In India, school starts in June, after the rains begin. Children take their main vacation during the spring, when it is too hot to study. The monsoon rains reach as far north as the Himalayas. However, there is very little rain in most of western Pakistan.

Strange but TRUE

The World's Most Destructive Volcano Krakatau (krak•uh•TOW), a volcanic island between Java and Sumatra in Indonesia, is pretty quiet these days (see below). In 1883, however, it erupted with explosions so loud they were heard in Australia and Japan, thousands of miles away. Krakatau's volcanic eruption caused tidal waves that killed 36,000 people. The eruption blew nearly 5 cubic miles of rock into the air and spewed out volcanic ash at least 17 miles high, throwing the region into darkness for days. This ash, blown around Earth for two years, caused amazing sunsets worldwide.

Activity Options

Multiple Learning Styles: Logical/Spatial

 **Block Scheduling**

Class Time 30 minutes

Task Creating a diagram or table showing the seasons and monsoon cycles of South Asia and Southeast Asia

Purpose To graphically display the characteristics of the seasonal

cycles of South Asia and Southeast Asia

Supplies Needed
- Paper and pencils or markers

Activity Have students review the material in "Climate and Monsoons." Then ask them to design a graphic organizer showing the cycle of seasons and monsoons in this region. Suggest that they create a standard table of three columns and three rows to display the material. Or, if they choose, they can create a diagram using simple illustrations, captions, and arrows to explain the cycles. Provide space for students to display their work.

In Southeast Asia, there are two seasons. The summer monsoon lasts from April to September. During this time, there are heavy rains. The winter season from October through March is cool and dry.

Depending on Rain Agriculture depends on the timing of the monsoons. If the monsoons come too early, the farmers do not have time to plant their seeds. If the rains do not arrive or if they arrive too late, the crops fail. Sometimes the monsoons bring too much rain, resulting in severe flooding that ruins crops, damages property, and is dangerous to people.

Culture • **These women in India are celebrating Teej, a festival for welcoming the coming of the monsoons.** ▶

Reading
Social Studies

D. Compare and Contrast How does this cycle of hot, cool, and rainy seasons compare with the cycle of seasons where you live?

ASSESS & RETEACH

Reading Social Studies Tell students to add details to the Geography sections of the chart on page 376.

 Formal Assessment
• Section Quiz, p. 193

RETEACHING ACTIVITY

Have groups of students create an outline of the section. Suggest that they write the main headings and the subheadings from the section, and then add details under each heading.

 In-depth Resources: Unit 5
• Reteaching Activity, p. 10

 Access for Students Acquiring English
• Reteaching Activity, p. 118

SECTION 1 ASSESSMENT

Terms & Names

1. **Identify:**
   (a) subcontinent
   (b) Himalayas
   (c) Northern Plains
   (d) delta
   (e) sediment
   (f) Deccan Plateau
   (g) archipelago
   (h) monsoon

Taking Notes

2. Use a chart like this one to record important information about South Asia and Southeast Asia.

	South Asia	Southeast Asia
Countries		
Major Regions		
Major Rivers		
Monsoon Cycle		

Main Ideas

3. (a) Describe three distinctive regions of South Asia.

   (b) Where is the Mekong River? Which countries does it flow through?

   (c) Name two nations in Southeast Asia that are archipelagoes.

Critical Thinking

4. **Compare and Contrast**

   Compare the Northern Plains with the Deccan Plateau. How are they similar? How are they different?

   Think About
   ♦ location
   ♦ fertility of the soil and population density

ACTIVITY -OPTION-
Photocopy a **map** of Southeast Asia. Using highlighter markers, spotlight the places you have learned about in Section 1. Share your map with the class.

Southern Asia: Place and Times **383**

	South Asia	Southeast Asia
Countries	Afghanistan, Bangladesh, Bhutan, India, the Maldives, Sir Lanka, Nepal, Pakistan	Brunei, Cambodia, Indonesia, Laos, Malaysia, Myanmar (Burma), the Philippines, Singapore, Thailand, Vietnam
Major Regions	Northern Mountain Rim, Northern Plains, Deccan Plateau	Mainland, Islands
Major Rivers	Ganges, Indus	Mekong
Monsoon Cycle	rain: June–October; cool and dry: November–February; hot and humid: March–May	rain: April–September; cool and dry: October–March

Teacher's Edition **383**

FOCUS ON VISUALS

Interpreting the Map Have students study the map to orient themselves. Then ask what are the capital cities of India, Pakistan, Afghanistan, Nepal, Bhutan, Bangladesh, and Sri Lanka. Ask students to name the major rivers in each country and the body of water into which they flow. Have students measure the distance between Kathmandu and New Delhi and describe the natural features that would make a trip between those two cities difficult. Students may want to consult the map on page 378. Have students locate the islands that are ruled by India.

Possible Responses The capital cities are New Delhi (India), Islamabad (Pakistan), Kabul (Afghanistan), Kathmandu (Nepal), Thimphu (Bhutan), Dhaka (Bangladesh), Colombo (Sri Lanka). The Indus and the Narmada rivers flow into the Arabian Sea, the Godavari, Krishna, Ganges, and Brahmaputra rivers into the Bay of Bengal. The distance from Kathmandu to New Delhi is 500 miles and natural features include the Himalayas and the Ganges River and two tributaries. Islands ruled by India are Lakshadweep, Andaman, and Nicobar.

Extension Have students use the scale to create a chart showing distances between pairs of major cities in the region.

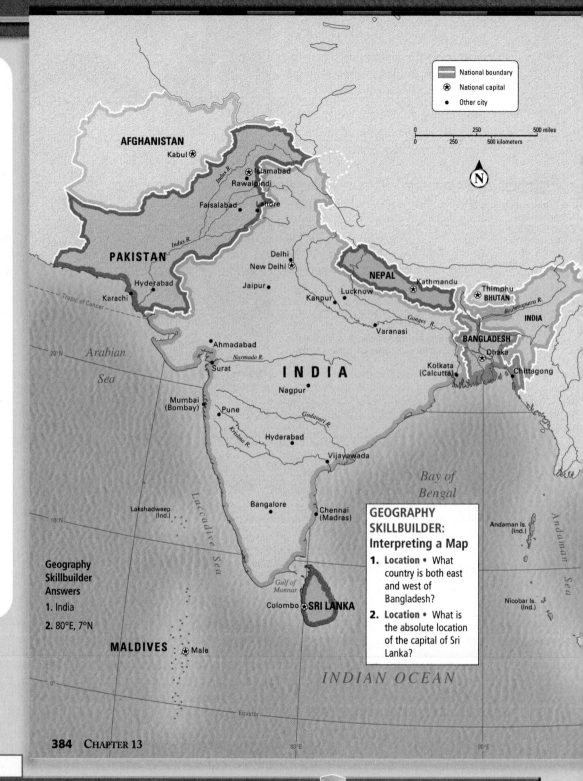

Geography
Skillbuilder
Answers
1. India
2. 80°E, 7°N

GEOGRAPHY SKILLBUILDER: Interpreting a Map

1. **Location** • What country is both east and west of Bangladesh?
2. **Location** • What is the absolute location of the capital of Sri Lanka?

384 CHAPTER 13

Activity Options

Multiple Learning Styles: Logical

Class Time One class period

Task Giving an oral presentation of a folk tale

Purpose To learn about the literature and culture of Southern Asia

Supplies Needed
• Folk tales from countries of Southern Asia

Block Scheduling

Activity Tell students that Southern Asia has a rich tradition of folk tales. Organize the class into small groups. Have each group choose a folk tale and read it aloud together. After groups have become familiar with their tales, invite representatives from each group to present the tale to the rest of the class.

Ancient India

SECTION 2

TERMS & NAMES
Mohenjo-Daro
Aryan
Sanskrit
Hinduism
Vedas
caste
Ashoka

MAIN IDEA

The people of ancient India established social and cultural practices that became widespread throughout the region.

WHY IT MATTERS NOW

The scientific and cultural contributions of ancient India affect our lives today.

DATELINE

MAURYAN EMPIRE 232 B.C.—The great Emperor Ashoka died yesterday. He was dearly loved by his people, and millions will mourn his death. Horrified by the suffering and bloodshed he saw at the battle of Kalinga in 262 B.C., Ashoka embraced the teachings of Buddhism.

From that point on, he put his beliefs into action and ruled his people without violence. Who can possibly step forward to take the place of our great leader?

Place • Three lion figures top this pillar at Sarnath, one of many pillars Ashoka had erected during his reign. ▲

The Indus River Valley Civilization ❶

Ashoka's empire was built on a civilization whose roots were more than 2,000 years old. Around 2500 B.C., a brilliant civilization developed in the Indus River valley. Sometimes called the Harappan civilization after one of its major cities, it flourished until about 1700 B.C. in an area that is mostly in present-day Pakistan. This civilization, which existed at the same time as ancient Egyptian civilization, stretched west to what is now Kabul, Afghanistan, and east to what is now Delhi, India. Its center was the rich farmland along the Indus River and its tributaries. The map on page 387 shows the extent of this civilization.

Southern Asia: Place and Times **385**

SECTION OBJECTIVES

1. To describe the early Indus River valley civilization
2. To analyze how the Aryans influenced South Asia
3. To explain Hinduism as both a religion and a way of life
4. To describe the accomplishments of the Maurya and Gupta Dynasties

SKILLBUILDER
• Interpreting a Map, pp. 387, 390

CRITICAL THINKING
• Summarizing, p. 388

FOCUS & MOTIVATE
WARM-UP

Making Inferences After students read Dateline, discuss the beliefs and influence of Emperor Ashoka.

1. Based on Ashoka's actions, what do you think Buddhism teaches?
2. What type of leader do you think the people are likely to support and follow?

INSTRUCT: Objective ❶

The Indus River Valley Civilization

• When did the Indus River valley civilization thrive? 2500–1700 B.C.

 In-depth Resources: Unit 5
• Guided Reading Worksheet, p. 4

 Reading Study Guide
(Spanish and English), pp. 118–119

Program Resources

 In-depth Resources: Unit 5
• Guided Reading Worksheet, p. 4
• Reteaching Activity, p. 11

 Reading Study Guide
(Spanish and English), pp. 118–119

 Formal Assessment
• Section Quiz, p. 194

 Integrated Assessment
• Rubric for writing a paragraph

 Outline Map Activities

 Access for Students Acquiring English
• Guided Reading Worksheet, p. 114

 Technology Resources
classzone.com

TEST-TAKING RESOURCES
⤵ Strategies for Test Preparation
⤵ Test Practice Transparencies
ⓘ Online Test Practice

Teacher's Edition **385**

INSTRUCT: Objective ❷

The Aryan Influence on South Asia

- When and from where did the Aryans arrive in South Asia? around 1700 B.C.; from southern Russia through the Hindu Kush mountains

- How were the Aryans different from the people of the Indus River valley? spoke different language; were nomads and herders; did not live in cities

- What new technology did the Aryans bring? iron plows and weapons; use of the horse

Although no one knows what the ancient people of the Indus River valley civilization called themselves, archaeologists named the city Mohenjo-Daro, which means "hill of the dead."

Objects found at Mohenjo-Daro include games, jewelry, toys, pottery, and kitchen utensils made of lead and silver. Clay statues of bulls and of female figures wearing elaborate headdresses were found, as well as weights and measures. The items were likely used in trade between the peoples of the Indus River valley and West Asia.

The civilization of the Indus River valley came to an end around 1700 B.C. No one knows for sure why the civilization ended. Some think the cause was a climate change—like a severe decrease in rainfall—while others think the urban centers were conquered and destroyed.

Hundreds of towns existed in the Indus River valley. There were two major cities: Harappa and **Mohenjo-Daro** (moh·HEHN·joh·DAHR·oh). Mohenjo-Daro was a large city with well-built homes and public buildings. Canals brought water from wells to farms outside the city walls.

The Aryan Influence on South Asia ❷

Around 1700 B.C., the **Aryans** (AIR·ee·uhnz) came to South Asia. These people migrated from southern Russia through passes in the Hindu Kush. The time of the Aryan arrival suggests that the Aryans played a role in the fall of the Harappan civilization, although there is no proof. Over time, the Aryan people and the people of the Indus River valley produced a new blend of culture in northern India.

A New People, a New Civilization The Aryans were different from the people of the Indus River valley. They spoke another language called **Sanskrit.**

Reading **Social Studies**

A. Making Inferences Why do you think this civilization developed in the Indus River valley rather than on the plains?

Reading Social Studies
A. Possible Answer The river valley was fertile; there was plenty of water.

Life in Mohenjo-Daro Mohenjo-Daro's streets were wide and laid out in a grid design. A thick brick wall with gateways surrounded the city. Houses were made of brick with stone foundations and had several rooms, a toilet, and a well. Drainage systems ran from the houses into brick-lined sewers.

The people of Mohenjo-Daro were skilled engineers and builders. They built a system of ditches and canals around the city to irrigate farms. A public bathhouse with a sunken courtyard was built on an artificial hill. A large building near the bathhouse might have been used as a storage area for grain or as a meeting hall.

Archaeologists have not yet been able to decode the writing of these people. Most of what is known about the city is based on what archaeologists have learned from digging in the ruins. Some of the artifacts they have found are shown at the right.

386

beads

painted pot

seal with bull

toy cart

Activity Options

Interdisciplinary Links: World History/Art

Class Time One class period

Task Creating a Mohenjo-Daro figurine

Purpose To appreciate the art of the Indus River valley civilization

Supplies Needed
- Images of terra cotta objects from Mohenjo-Daro and Harappa
- Modeling clay

ⓑ Block Scheduling

Activity Tell students that craft workers of Mohenjo-Daro and Harappa created many beautiful figurines from clay. Have students examine the images of clay objects from these two cities. Then ask them to create a clay figure similar in style to those pictured. After they have finished, have students explain their figure and what they think it represented in that civilization.

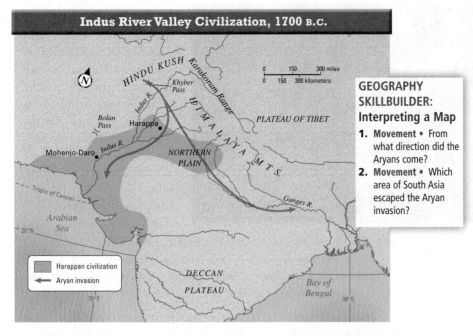

Indus River Valley Civilization, 1700 B.C.

HINDU KUSH
Karakoram Range
Khyber Pass
Bolan Pass
Harappa
Indus R.
Mohenjo-Daro
Indus R.
NORTHERN PLAIN
HIMALAYA MTS.
PLATEAU OF TIBET
Ganges R.
Tropic of Cancer
Arabian Sea
20°N
DECCAN PLATEAU
Bay of Bengal
70°E
90°E

0   150   300 miles
0   150   300 kilometers

Harappan civilization
Aryan invasion

GEOGRAPHY SKILLBUILDER:
Interpreting a Map
1. **Movement** • From what direction did the Aryans come?
2. **Movement** • Which area of South Asia escaped the Aryan invasion?

The Aryans had not settled in cities but were nomads and herders. Because the Aryans got their food and clothing from the animals they raised, they measured wealth by the number of cattle a person owned.

Geography Skillbuilder Answers

1. northwest
2. Deccan Plateau

New Technology The Aryans brought new technology, animals, and ideas with them to South Asia. Sometime after 1000 B.C., the Aryans discovered iron ore in the Ganges River valley. Iron plows improved agriculture, and with the Aryan adoption of some local ways—like growing rice—they began to settle in towns. The Aryans also developed new iron weapons. These weapons were stronger than those of the Harappan people. Improved weapons and the introduction of the horse enabled the Aryans to rule northern India.

Reading **Social Studies**

B. Drawing Conclusions How did the Aryans' use of iron help them settle and control India?

Reading Social Studies

B. Possible Answer

Iron plows made them more efficient farmers; iron weapons made them more powerful.

Hinduism—A Way of Life ❸

People of ancient India developed the religion of **Hinduism**, based on certain Aryan practices. Aryan priests chanted hymns in praise of their gods. For a long time, these hymns were passed down through oral tradition. Later, these hymns and other Aryan religious beliefs were written down and became part of the **Vedas** (VAY·duhz), or Books of Knowledge. The Vedas contain writings on prayers, hymns, religious rituals, and philosophy.

Southern Asia: Place and Times **387**

FOCUS ON VISUALS

Interpreting the Map Have students identify the mountain range and the mountain pass that the Aryan invaders crossed. Ask them why the Aryans followed this path.

Possible Responses They crossed the Hindu Kush mountains through the Khyber Pass. They may have followed this path because it provided the easiest route through the mountains and along the rich river valleys.

Extension Have students research some of the later invaders and create a map showing the path these invaders took. Have them attach a brief paragraph explaining who the invaders were and when they invaded.

INSTRUCT: Objective ❸

Hinduism—A Way of Life

- What do the Vedas contain and how did they develop? writings on prayers, hymns, religious rituals, and philosophy; brought by Aryans, passed down orally
- How do the Hindu beliefs of karma and reincarnation work together? person's actions in life directly influence status of next life
- How does the caste system affect an individual's life? determines a person's job, marriage partner, and friends

Activity Options

Multiple Learning Styles: Linguistic

Class Time One class period

Task Comparing Sanskrit words with English words

Purpose To learn more about the Sanskrit language and its relation to English

Supplies Needed
- Research materials showing English and Sanskrit cognates

 Block Scheduling

Activity Explain that because the ancient Aryans came from Europe, their language—Sanskrit—was related to the languages of Europe that form the basis of modern European languages. Have students research some Sanskrit words that have the same roots as some English words, such as mother, father, brother. Then have them create a chart showing these words.

Teacher's Edition **387**

MORE ABOUT...

Hinduism

The earliest Hindus believed that gods were present in nature. The gods they worshipped stood for powers in nature, such as the sun, moon, rain, and wind. Over time, some Hindus expanded their beliefs. They began to think of these gods and goddesses as part of one single spirit, which they called Brahman. All the many divinities that they worshipped were a part of this universal spirit of Brahman.

Hindus also believe that animals as well as humans have souls, and that gods take the form of animals. Monkeys, snakes, cows, and other animals are considered sacred.

CRITICAL THINKING ACTIVITY

Summarizing Have students use a graphic like the one below to show the Hindu caste system. Students may choose to research the caste system further and add to their charts.

The Hindu Caste System

Class Time 60 minutes

Culture • The god Vishnu is said to take ten forms, including a fish, a tortoise, and a boar. Here, he is half man and half lion. ▲

Karma and Reincarnation

The ideas of karma and reincarnation are central to Hinduism. Karma is the idea that a person's actions determine what will happen after his or her death. Reincarnation is the idea that after death a person's soul is reborn into a different body. Hindus believe that the cycle of birth, death, and rebirth occurs many times.

Each person's status in life is determined by his or her behavior in previous lives. A person who leads a virtuous life may be reborn as a wealthy or wise person. A person who lives an immoral life may be reborn as a poor or sick person.

The Caste System One of the main characteristics of Hinduism is the caste system. A **caste** is an inherited social class. Each person is born to a particular caste for his or her lifetime. Caste determines a person's job, marriage partner, and friends. The Hindu caste system was strongly influenced by the Aryan tribal social system, which was organized around the belief that people are not equal.

The Hindu caste system is based on four major classes—priests, warriors and princes, merchants and farmers, and laborers. Another group, once known as untouchables, has traditionally been considered inferior to the four major castes. Untouchables did the work that no one else wanted to do and were generally shunned by society. Today, the Hindu caste system is made up of thousands of castes and subcastes, but the four major castes are still the most important. The government and other groups are working to reduce the influence the caste system has on society.

Culture • The god Shiva may be represented in various forms. Here he is shown as the Lord of the Dance. ▶

BACKGROUND

Hindu worship many gods and goddesses. Most Hindu families have a shrine to a god or goddess set up in their homes.

Reading Social Studies
C. Possible Answer
People could be reborn into a higher caste if they live virtuously.

Reading Social Studies

C. Analyzing Issues How do the caste system and the idea of reincarnation work together?

Activity Options

Differentiating Instruction: Students Acquiring English/ESL

Categorizing To help students understand the concepts of karma and reincarnation, remind students that these two important ideas of Hinduism work together. Help students visualize these ideas by drawing a flow chart like the following on the chalkboard.

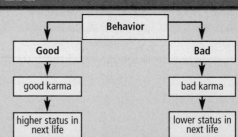

	Behavior	
Good		Bad
good karma		bad karma
higher status in next life		lower status in next life

The Maurya and Gupta Dynasties ❹

Two dynasties made important contributions to India. These dynasties were the Maurya and the Gupta. The contributions made by the people of these cultures still affect our lives today.

The Mauryan Empire The first Indian empire was called the Maurya (324–185 B.C.). It was founded by the descendants of the Aryans who moved eastward from the region of the Indus River valley civilization. One of its emperors, **Ashoka**, created a unified government. He built a palace of stone and religious monuments. The Mauryans were known for their fine sculpture and sandstone carvings.

The Golden Age and the Gupta Dynasty The Gupta Dynasty (A.D. 320–500) ruled during India's golden age in science, art, and literature. Most Gupta rulers were Hindus. However, both Hinduism and Buddhism were practiced throughout the empire at that time. Hindu and Buddhist beliefs inspired many artists. They created sculptures and paintings of Hindu gods and goddesses. Many temples were built that contained images of characters from Hindu mythology. Gupta architects hollowed out the solid stone of mountainside cliffs to create Buddhist temples. In the city of Ajanta, 30 Buddhist temples are carved into the side of a mountain.

Place • The Buddhist temples at Ajanta are carved into granite cliffs. The walls inside are covered with beautiful paintings. ▲

Biography

Ashoka Ashoka has been called one of the greatest emperors in world history. He ruled India's Mauryan Empire from 269 B.C. until his death in 232 B.C.

As a ruthless conqueror, Ashoka extended the Mauryan Empire over almost the entire subcontinent of South Asia. However, during one bloody battle, Ashoka became horrified at what he saw. He wrote, "150,000 persons were . . . carried away captive, 100,000 were [killed] and many times that number died." Ashoka vowed that this would be his last war, and he converted to the Buddhist religion.

He began to preach nonviolence and compassion for all living things and appointed "Officers of Righteousness" to relieve suffering among the people. Throughout the kingdom, the "principles for a just government" were carved in stone (shown at left) and displayed for all to see.

FOCUS ON VISUALS

Interpreting a Map Direct students' attention to the map of the Gupta Empire. Have them describe the natural boundaries of the empire. Then discuss which of these boundaries offered the greatest protection from outside invaders.

Possible Responses Natural boundaries are the Himalaya and Hindu Kush mountains and the Indus and Ganges rivers. The mountains offered the greatest protection because of their height and ruggedness.

Extension Have students research stories of exploration in the Himalayas and then share their research with the class.

ASSESS & RETEACH

Reading Social Studies Have students complete the South Asia portion of the chart on page 376.

 Formal Assessment
• Section Quiz, p. 194

RETEACHING ACTIVITY

Tell students to work with partners to create a chart showing the main ideas and supporting details of the section. Have them use each of the main headings of the section as a column heading in the chart. Under each column, they can list specific details.

 In-depth Resources: Unit 5
• Reteaching Activity, p. 11

 Access for Students Acquiring English
• Reteaching Activity, p. 119

Literature Sanskrit literature blossomed during the Gupta Dynasty. Kalidasa, who lived during the fifth century A.D., was the greatest poet and playwright of his age. His plays were used to teach moral principles and were filled with creativity and mystery.

Mathematics Gupta mathematicians made many important discoveries. They developed the concept of zero and the numerals that we use today. Centuries after the Gupta Empire fell, Europeans learned these numerals and the concept of zero from the Islamic civilizations of Southwest Asia. Europeans called this number system *Arabic*, the name still used today.

Geography Skillbuilder Answers
1. northernmost point of the Indus River; Hindu Kush
2. eastern part

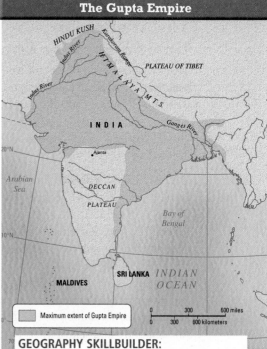

The Gupta Empire

Maximum extent of Gupta Empire

GEOGRAPHY SKILLBUILDER: Interpreting a Map
1. **Location** • How far north did the Gupta Empire reach?
2. **Movement** • In which part of the Deccan Plateau would you expect to find influences from the Gupta Empire?

SECTION 2 ASSESSMENT

Terms & Names

1. **Identify:**
   (a) Mohenjo-Daro
   (b) Aryan
   (c) Sanskrit
   (d) Hinduism
   (e) Vedas
   (f) caste
   (g) Ashoka

Taking Notes

2. Use a spider map like the one below to record information about changes the Aryans brought to ancient India.

Religion:
Language:
Aryans
Tools:
Weapons:
Animals:

Main Ideas

3. (a) Describe the city of Mohenjo-Daro.
   (b) Describe three aspects of Hinduism.
   (c) Why is the Gupta Dynasty considered a golden age in science, art, and literature?

Critical Thinking

4. **Analyze**
   Why do you think the originally nomadic Aryans settled in India?

   Think About
   ◆ where the Aryans came from and the geography of the subcontinent
   ◆ the civilization the Aryans encountered
   ◆ the discoveries the Aryans made in India

ACTIVITY -OPTION- Suppose you could go back in time to visit Mohenjo-Daro, the Mauryan Empire, or the Gupta Dynasty. Write a **paragraph** explaining which period you would visit and why.

Section 2 Assessment

1. Terms & Names
a. Mohenjo-Daro, p. 386
b. Aryan, p. 386
c. Sanskrit, p. 386
d. Hinduism, p. 387
e. Vedas, p. 387
f. caste, p. 388
g. Ashoka, p. 389

2. Taking Notes

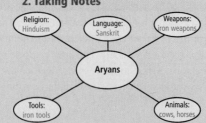

Religion: Hinduism
Language: Sanskrit
Weapons: iron weapons
Aryans
Tools: iron tools
Animals: cows, horses

3. Main Ideas
a. brick houses, toilets, sewers, wide streets; irrigation ditches and canals; public bathhouse and granary
b. set of gods; belief in karma and reincarnation; system of social classes
c. notable cultural advances

4. Critical Thinking
They might have been pushed out of their original homeland; crossed difficult mountain passes and were unable to go elsewhere; encountered an advanced civilization and rich, fertile land; discovered iron ore

ACTIVITY OPTION

 Integrated Assessment
• Rubric for writing a paragraph

390 CHAPTER 13

Reading an Elevation Map

▶▶ Defining the Skill

When you learn to read an elevation map, you will be able to tell how high above sea level the land in a region is. Land that is at sea level is at the same height, or level, as the sea. Land rises from that point. (In some inland areas, however, the land is actually below sea level.) The highest point above sea level on Earth is the peak of Mount Everest. It stands 29,028 feet above sea level. Elevation maps use color to show the height of the land. The key gives a color code for level of elevation. Usually, darker green areas are at or close to sea level. Light yellow or tan areas are the farthest above sea level.

▶▶ Applying the Skill

The elevation map at the right shows the country of Pakistan. Pakistan, a country in southern Asia, has its southern border on the Arabian Sea. Its northern border is in the Hindu Kush mountain range and the Karakoram range. Both ranges have mountain peaks higher than the highest peaks in the Rocky Mountains of the United States. Use the strategies below to help you read the elevation map.

How to Read an Elevation Map

Strategy ❶ Read the key. Notice how land closest to sea level is a dark green. Land that is farthest away from sea level is dark brown.

Strategy ❷ Look at the map. Find each of the elevation regions indicated on the key.

Strategy ❸ Find the two highest mountain peaks. Follow the flow of the Indus River. Find the mountain pass. A pass is an opening in the mountain range where people have made roads or laid railroad lines because it is the easiest place to get from one side of the range to the other.

Write a Summary

A summary will help you understand the information found in the elevation map. The paragraph to the right summarizes the information found in the map of Pakistan.

▶▶ Practicing the Skill

Turn to page 378 in Chapter 13, Section 1. Read the map, "Elevations of South Asia," and then write a paragraph summarizing the information found in that map.

Elevations of Pakistan

Elevation	
13,100 ft.	(4,000 m)
6,600 ft.	(2,000 m)
1,600 ft.	(500 m)
650 ft.	(200 m)
0 ft.	(0 m)
Below sea level	

The southern border of Pakistan is on the Arabian Sea. Land along that border is at sea level and then rises dramatically to the northern regions of Pakistan, where some of the highest peaks on Earth can be found. The Indus River flows from an area of over 2,000 feet through a region of less than 500 feet, until it reaches the sea. In the west of Pakistan are several mountain ranges that reach up to 5,000 feet. Pakistan is a country of great variety in elevation.

SKILLBUILDER

Reading an Elevation Map

Defining the Skill

Tell students that elevation maps show different land elevations of a given area or region. Explain that these maps enable hikers and cross-country skiers to determine the types of terrain they will cover, and calculate the distance they would have to climb from a given point to reach the summit of a hill or mountain.

Applying the Skill

How to Read an Elevation Map Tell students to look at each strategy carefully. Point out the importance of identifying the key and noting what each color represents.

Write a Summary

Discuss the summary shown on this page with students. Point out that the writer explains what part of the region rises and where in the region the elevations are highest and lowest. The writer also gives specific elevations for some points, and sums up the overall region.

Practicing the Skill

If students need additional practice, have them examine an elevation map of your state. Guide them to identify the colors on the key, find the regions on the map, and identify the highest and lowest points.

> **In-depth Resources: Unit 5**
> • Skillbuilder Practice, p. 8

Career Connection: Mountain-Climbing Guide

B Block Scheduling

Encourage students who enjoy reading elevation maps to find out about careers that use this skill. For example, guides on mountain-climbing expeditions lead small groups of people on trips to the summit of a mountain. Elevation maps provide them with crucial information.

1. Encourage students to think about how reading an elevation map could help guides anticipate the effects of high altitudes on their clients.

2. Ask what kinds of training and certification a person would need to become a guide.

3. Invite students to share what they learn using illustrations or photographs.

SECTION OBJECTIVES

1. To describe why Southeast Asia was a crossroads of trade and culture
2. To explain the teachings of Buddhism and the way it spread
3. To explain how Indian culture influenced Southeast Asia

SKILLBUILDER
• Interpreting a Map, pp. 393, 396

CRITICAL THINKING
• Analyzing Causes, p. 395

FOCUS & MOTIVATE
WARM-UP

Making Inferences Have students read <u>Dateline</u> and discuss the discovery of Angkor Wat.

1. Why do you think the ancient city went undiscovered for about 600 years?
2. Why do you think Henri Mouhot was so surprised when he found the ancient city?

INSTRUCT: Objective ❶

Crossroads of Culture

• Why was Southeast Asia a crossroads of trade? center of sea trading routes of South Pacific and Indian Ocean

 In-depth Resources: Unit 5
• Guided Reading Worksheet, p. 5

 Reading Study Guide
(Spanish and English), pp. 120–121

Ancient Crossroads

TERMS & NAMES
Buddhism
Siddhartha Gautama
Four Noble Truths
Eightfold Path
Khmer
Angkor Wat

MAIN IDEA

The culture of ancient Southeast Asia was heavily influenced by traders and travelers from China, India, and other countries.

WHY IT MATTERS NOW

The culture of modern Southeast Asia still reflects the influence of ancient Indian and Chinese cultures.

DATELINE — EXTRA

THE RAIN FORESTS OF CAMBODIA, 1861

In the rain forests of Southeast Asia, a young French explorer has made a startling discovery. He stumbled onto what appears to be one of the largest and most impressive archaeological discoveries in history. "We hacked our way through the dense [rain forest]," said Henri Mouhot. "Suddenly the huge stone towers of an ancient city, some of them 200 feet high, appeared before us." Experts believe this city may have been built by the Khmer people, who ruled a vast empire in the region about 600 years ago.

Place • Henri Mouhot has discovered the extraordinary lost city of Angkor. ▲

Crossroads of Culture ❶

The ancient city that Mouhot found was Angkor. It contains an impressive temple complex dating back to the time when the region was one of the crossroads of the ancient world. A crossroads is a place where people, goods, and ideas from many areas come together. In ancient times, travelers from India, China, and other countries came to Southeast Asian shores and made a lasting impression on the region.

Program Resources

 In-depth Resources: Unit 5
• Guided Reading Worksheet, p. 5
• Reteaching Activity, p. 12

 Reading Study Guide
(Spanish and English), pp. 120–121

 Formal Assessment
• Section Quiz, p. 195

 Integrated Assessment
• Rubric for writing a letter

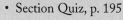 **Outline Map Activities**

 Access for Students Acquiring English
• Guided Reading Worksheet, p. 115

 Technology Resources
classzone.com

TEST-TAKING RESOURCES

↪ Strategies for Test Preparation
↪ Test Practice Transparencies
ℹ Online Test Practice

Trade Routes in Ancient Southern Asia

GEOGRAPHY SKILLBUILDER:
Interpreting a Map

1. **Movement** • About how many miles does the trade route from Borneo to India cover?
2. **Movement** • Why do you think so many routes are by sea rather than land?

Geography Skillbuilder Answers

1. about 3,750 miles

2. easier to travel by sea

Trade routes

BACKGROUND

Coastal traders used monsoon winds to sail their ships. They waited for favorable winds before sailing from India to Southeast Asia. When the winds shifted, the traders would sail back.

Reading Social Studies

A. Analyzing What effect did India have on Southeast Asia?

Reading Social Studies
A. Possible Answer India affected the art, architecture, and religion of Southeast Asia.

Early History Many important skills were developed in ancient Southeast Asia, including making tools from bronze, growing yams and rice, and sailing. In the past, historians thought that people from China or India brought these skills to the region. But now it seems clear that this knowledge was developed in Southeast Asia. Bronze Age items found in Thailand have been dated as far back as 3000 B.C. That is before bronze work was done in China. Eight to nine thousand years ago, rice was grown in Thailand. Yams and other roots were grown in Indonesia between 15,000 and 10,000 B.C. This is one of the earliest examples of agriculture ever found.

Trade and Travel Look at the map above. You can see that the central position of Southeast Asia made it a likely crossroads of trade for the area. Southeast Asia is in the center of the sea trading routes of the South Pacific and the Indian Ocean. Traders from India began to visit Southeast Asia around A.D. 100. Southeast Asian goods reached both India and China. From there, they traveled on to East Africa and Southwest Asia.

Southeast Asian trade goods included rice, tea, timber, and spices such as cloves, nutmeg, ginger, and pepper. Gold and other metals were also traded. Many ideas were shared as well. Religious ideas and knowledge spread. Skills such as farming and metalworking, as well as art forms and techniques, crossed to and from Southeast Asia.

Southern Asia: Place and Times **393**

FOCUS ON VISUALS

Interpreting the Map Have students trace the trade routes from India and China to Southeast Asia. Ask why most of the routes were over the sea. Then have students identify the route from India to Indonesia.

Possible Responses Students may say that that sea routes were the easiest, because they avoided barriers such as deserts and mountains. Traders from India would sail along the coastline of India, across the Bay of Bengal.

Extension Refer students to the Unit Atlas and have them locate major cities along the coasts of India, the Malay Peninsula, and Indonesia. Discuss how trade helped these cities develop.

MORE ABOUT...
Bronze Age

The term Bronze Age describes the period following the Stone Age, when people stopped using stone tools and weapons and began making bronze items. The Bronze Age arrived in different parts of the world at different times. The people of Sumer, in Mesopotamia, were the first to use bronze, beginning about 3500 B.C. China first began using bronze around 1700 B.C.

Bronze is an alloy made of copper and another metal, usually tin. It is harder than copper and easier to melt. It is also harder than iron and corrodes less easily. Interestingly, the Bronze Age was followed by the Iron Age.

Activity Options

Interdisciplinary Links: Geography/World History

Class Time One class period

Task Creating a map showing the Spice Islands and their major ports

Purpose To locate and learn more about the Spice Islands

Supplies Needed
- Materials about the Spice Islands and the spice trade from ancient times through the 19th century
- Writing paper
- Pencils or pens

Activity Tell students that spices from Southeast Asia were a major item of trade for nearly two thousand years. Organize students into groups and have them learn about the area of Southeast Asia that became known as the Spice Islands. Then have each group create a map showing the islands and the major ports. Maps should have a caption that describes an aspect of the Spice Islands.

INSTRUCT: Objective ❷

Buddhism in Southeast Asia

- Why did Gautama go off to seek the cause of human suffering? had visions of an old man, a sick man, a corpse, and a holy man
- How did Gautama achieve enlightenment? through meditation
- What are some important Buddhist teachings? the Four Noble Truths; the Eightfold Path
- How and where was Buddhism spread? by the Buddha's followers, through southern India, Sri Lanka, and Southeast Asia

MORE ABOUT...
The Buddha

Many stories exist telling of Siddhartha Gautama's life, but the historical facts are scant. The oldest and most popular of these stories tells of the Buddha's birth. When his mother was pregnant, she had a dream of a beautiful white elephant entering her womb from the side. A priest interpreted the dream to mean that the child would be a boy who would grow up to become either a monarch or a buddha. The Buddha was born in a park in Nepal, and Ashoka erected a pillar, which still stands, to mark the location. On the fifth day after his birth, 108 priests attended his name-giving ceremony. Siddhartha means "one whose aim is accomplished." The Buddha finally found enlightenment through meditation, not self-denial. Thereafter he began to teach people how to achieve freedom from suffering through a state of complete happiness and peace, called *nirvana*. The Buddha's teaching is called the *dharma*, which means "saving truth." The Buddha died when he was about 80 years old. His followers cremated his body and kept his bones as sacred relics. Many Buddhists today believe that these relics and the many images of the Buddha carry his power.

Influence of India Southeast Asia had a thriving culture of its own. However, it learned from and adopted customs from traders and travelers of other countries. Around A.D. 100, traders, Hindu priests, and Buddhist monks began to bring Indian culture to Southeast Asia, including art, architecture, and religion. These ideas were gradually adopted in the region.

Buddhism in Southeast Asia ❷

Buddhism came from the same religious roots as Hinduism. It began in India around 500 B.C., although Hinduism and Islam eventually became more important religions in India. The ideas of Buddhism, however, spread to East and Southeast Asia, where it is still strong today. It is one of the major religions of the world.

The Signs of the Buddha The founder of Buddhism was **Siddhartha Gautama** (sih·DAHR·tuh GAW·tuh·muh). He grew up as a wealthy prince and a member of the warrior class. Gautama lived in luxury in a palace with his wife and son.

One day, while out driving, he saw an old man. On other days, he saw a sick man, a corpse, and a holy man. Gautama interpreted these as signs to show him that life involves aging, sickness, and death. He believed that the holy man was a sign telling him to leave his family and seek the causes of human suffering.

For the next six years, Gautama was a wandering monk. He practiced self-denial and ate very little. However, he did not discover the cause of human suffering. One day, he decided to stop living a life of self-denial. He sat under a tree and began to meditate. Through meditation, Gautama gained enlightenment, or religious awakening. He now felt that he knew the reasons for human suffering and how to escape from it. News of his experience spread. People began to call him the Buddha, or the Enlightened One.

Buddhist Teachings The Buddha had once studied Hinduism. He was influenced by the Hindu beliefs in karma and reincarnation. These taught that life is a continuing cycle of death and rebirth. However, he did

Culture • According to legend, the Buddha was sitting under a bodhi tree when he received enlightenment and the inspiration for his religious teachings. ▼

Activity Options

Multiple Learning Styles: Visual

Class Time One class period

Task Creating a story board

Purpose To visualize the quest of the Buddha for enlightenment

Supplies Needed
- Drawing paper
- Colored pencils

Block Scheduling

Activity Direct students to review the material on this page. Then have them create a story board showing Siddhartha Gautama's search for enlightenment. The board should show frames of his four visions, his life as a wandering monk, and finally his realization of enlightenment. Have students display their boards in class.

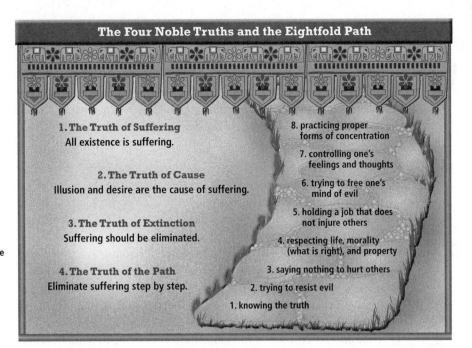

The Four Noble Truths and the Eightfold Path

1. **The Truth of Suffering**
All existence is suffering.

2. **The Truth of Cause**
Illusion and desire are the cause of suffering.

3. **The Truth of Extinction**
Suffering should be eliminated.

4. **The Truth of the Path**
Eliminate suffering step by step.

8. practicing proper forms of concentration

7. controlling one's feelings and thoughts

6. trying to free one's mind of evil

5. holding a job that does not injure others

4. respecting life, morality (what is right), and property

3. saying nothing to hurt others

2. trying to resist evil

1. knowing the truth

Culture • People in many parts of the world today still try to follow the teachings of the Buddha. ▶

not like the part of Hindu philosophy that was based on the Vedas, the ancient Aryan texts. In particular, he rejected the caste system and the role of priests.

The basic teachings of Buddhism are the **Four Noble Truths.** The first truth is that life is full of pain. The second truth is that suffering comes from the desire for possessions. The third truth explains that if people stop desiring these possessions, they will no longer suffer. The Buddha taught that the goal of life is to be free from desires and pain. Then one can progress to nirvana (nur·VAHN·uh), a state of happiness and peace.

The fourth truth says that people can escape suffering by following the Middle Way. The Middle Way is a set of guidelines called the **Eightfold Path.** These eight guidelines are as follows: right understanding, right purpose, right speech, right conduct, right means of livelihood, right effort, right awareness, and right meditation.

Reading
Social Studies

B. Making Inferences What challenges might a person face in trying to follow the Eightfold Path?

The Spread of Buddhism After the Buddha's death, his followers spread the new faith throughout southern India, Sri Lanka, and Southeast Asia. Buddhism also spread to Tibet, central Asia, China, Korea, and Japan. Buddhists organized schools and spiritual communities where monks and nuns could live and work.

Reading Social Studies

B. Possible Answer

Resisting the many temptations to say unkind things and keeping one's mind focused on good thoughts take a great deal of self-discipline.

Southern Asia: Place and Times **395**

MORE ABOUT...
Schools of Buddhism

As Buddhism spread, different schools developed. Theravada Buddhism is dominant in Thailand, Cambodia, Laos, Myanmar, and Sri Lanka. Theravada means "Way of the Elders." Theravada Buddhists focus on the Buddha as a historical figure and on the importance of the life of a monk.

Mahayana Buddhism is found mainly in East Asia. Followers believe that there are many Buddhas in heaven and many people on Earth who will become Buddhas. Mahayana Buddhism focuses on teaching how to achieve nirvana.

Zen Buddhism is practiced mainly in Japan, and focuses on the relationship between the master and the pupil. Zen also focuses on special practices that can lead to a state of enlightenment called *satori.* Mantrayana Buddhism is centered in the Himalayas, Japan, and Mongolia. Mantrayana means "sacred recitation vehicle." Mantrayana Buddhists also accept the teachings of Mahayana Buddhism, as well as the importance of a close relationship between the master, or *guru,* and his students.

CRITICAL THINKING ACTIVITY

Analyzing Causes Discuss with students the elements of Hinduism that Gautama kept and the elements he rejected. Then ask students to suggest why Buddhism may have been attractive to so many people.

Class Time 10 minutes

Activity Options

Differentiating Instruction: Gifted and Talented

Block Scheduling

Analyzing the Noble Truths Organize students into small groups. Challenge them to analyze the first three of the Four Noble Truths in a group discussion. When students have finished, invite them to present the results of their discussions to the class.

You might want to provide the following questions as a guide:

• Why might Gautama have believed "all existence is suffering"?
• What are the implications of this belief?
• Why might illusion and desire contribute to suffering?

INSTRUCT: Objective ❸

Indian Influence in Southeast Asia

- Upon what did the success of Southeast Asian empires frequently depend? the popularity of religious beliefs
- What factors contributed to the decline of the Khmer kingdom? the growth of Buddhism and decline of the number of Hindu followers
- What evidence of the influence of Indian Buddhism existed in Indonesia? large Buddhist temple, Borobudur

FOCUS ON VISUALS

Interpreting the Map Direct students to compare this map to the map on page 393. Ask students to point out and explain the similarities between the routes shown on these two maps.

Possible Responses The maps depict similar basic routes, which reach the same areas. Students should note that these religions were spread by people who followed the established trade routes.

Extension Have students find out more about the different schools of Buddhism and create a map like the one on this page. Students should use a color key to show where the various schools are dominant.

Indian Influence in Southeast Asia ❸

As the influence of India spread, new images and religious art became part of Southeast Asian culture. Historians can trace these images from one country to another. Empires were founded on the beliefs of Hinduism, Buddhism, and, later, Islam. The success of empires often depended on the ongoing popularity of these beliefs.

Empire of the Khmer In the sixth century A.D., the **Khmer** (KMAIR) people established a great kingdom in present-day Cambodia. This kingdom was Hindu and very much influenced by Indian culture. The Khmer built great Hindu temples, including the huge complex, **Angkor Wat**. The Khmer kingdom spread through much of Southeast Asia. Then, as Buddhism grew in influence, the number of Hindu followers declined, and the Khmer lost power. The Khmer retreated south to the area near the city of Phnom Penh.

Indian influence in the form of Buddhism was also felt in the island nations of Southeast Asia. In Indonesia, a huge Buddhist temple called Borobudur was built in the sixth century. The builders used about 2 million cubic feet of stone to build the temple. It is shaped like a pyramid, with three terraces, or levels, which contain relief carvings. At the center, the temple is 103 feet high.

Reading Social Studies
C. Possible Answer Students may suggest that traders as well as Buddhist monks and followers of Buddha spread Buddhism to other areas.

Geography Skillbuilder Answers
1. northeastern
2. Buddhism

Reading Social Studies
C. Making Inferences How do you think Buddhism spread to other areas?

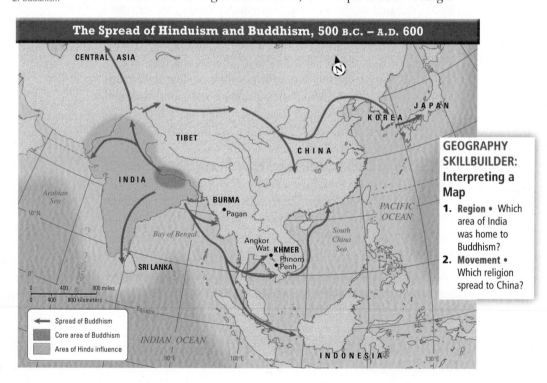

The Spread of Hinduism and Buddhism, 500 B.C. – A.D. 600

CENTRAL ASIA · TIBET · CHINA · INDIA · BURMA · Pagan · Bay of Bengal · Arabian Sea · 10° N · SRI LANKA · KOREA · JAPAN · PACIFIC OCEAN · South China Sea · Angkor Wat · KHMER · Phnom Penh · Equator · INDIAN OCEAN · INDONESIA · 90°E · 100°E · 130°E

0   400   800 miles
0   400   800 kilometers

→ Spread of Buddhism
■ Core area of Buddhism
■ Area of Hindu influence

GEOGRAPHY SKILLBUILDER: Interpreting a Map
1. **Region** • Which area of India was home to Buddhism?
2. **Movement** • Which religion spread to China?

396 CHAPTER 13

Activity Options

Differentiating Instruction: Students Acquiring English/ESL

Categorizing Students may have trouble tracing the Buddhist and Hindu influences from India. To help them clarify India's influence, work with them to create a spider map like the one to the right to show India's influence on religions of Southern Asia.

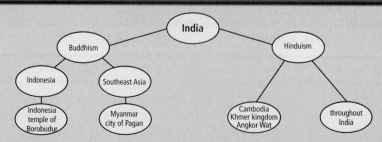

India — Buddhism — Indonesia (Indonesia temple of Borobudur), Southeast Asia (Myanmar city of Pagan); Hinduism — Cambodia Khmer kingdom Angkor Wat, throughout India

Place • The Ananda temple is located at Pagan, the old capital city of Myanmar, which was an important Buddhist center. ▲

Place • Borobudur is located in Indonesia on the large island of Java. The temple has three levels. Each represents a stage of spiritual perfection. ▲

Indian culture also spread to Myanmar. There, Buddhism was firmly in place by the fifth and sixth centuries. In the 11th century, the powerful king Anawrahta established a strong Buddhist kingdom in the capital city of Pagan. There were soon thousands of Buddhist temples and buildings in the kingdom. The most famous is the Ananda temple.

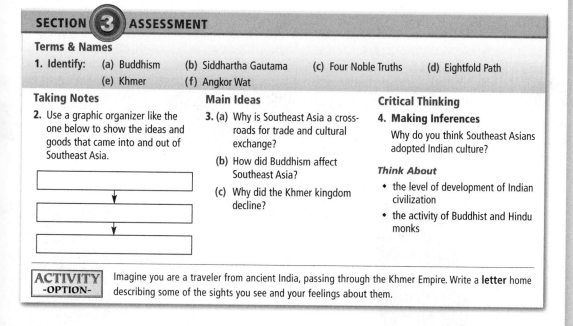

SECTION 3 ASSESSMENT

Terms & Names
1. Identify: (a) Buddhism (b) Siddhartha Gautama (c) Four Noble Truths (d) Eightfold Path
   (e) Khmer (f) Angkor Wat

Taking Notes
2. Use a graphic organizer like the one below to show the ideas and goods that came into and out of Southeast Asia.

Main Ideas
3. (a) Why is Southeast Asia a crossroads for trade and cultural exchange?
   (b) How did Buddhism affect Southeast Asia?
   (c) Why did the Khmer kingdom decline?

Critical Thinking
4. **Making Inferences**

   Why do you think Southeast Asians adopted Indian culture?

   Think About
   - the level of development of Indian civilization
   - the activity of Buddhist and Hindu monks

ACTIVITY -OPTION- Imagine you are a traveler from ancient India, passing through the Khmer Empire. Write a **letter** home describing some of the sights you see and your feelings about them.

Section 3 Assessment

1. Terms & Names
a. Buddhism, p. 394
b. Siddhartha Gautama, p. 394
c. Four Noble Truths, p. 395
d. Eightfold Path, p. 395
e. Khmer, p. 396
f. Angkor Wat, p. 396

2. Taking Notes
Buddhism, Hinduism, ideas of art and architecture came into Southeast Asia; bronze working, farming yams and rice, and sailing came out of Southeast Asia.

3. Main Ideas
a. in the center of the sea trading routes of the South Pacific and the Indian Ocean
b. displaced Hinduism as a religion; inspired many temples and other forms of architecture and art
c. Buddhism gained more influence than Hinduism.

4. Critical Thinking
Students might say Indian culture was highly developed and disseminated widely.

ACTIVITY OPTION

Integrated Assessment
• Rubric for writing a letter

MORE ABOUT...
King Anawrahta
Although King Anawrahta had conquered the Mon people in the south of what is now Myanmar, he was considered to be a religious man. He sent a ship full of treasures to the place where the Buddha achieved enlightenment in India, to restore the temple commemorating the site. In 1077, King Anawrahta was killed by a wild buffalo.

ASSESS & RETEACH

Reading Social Studies Have students complete the chart on page 376.

Formal Assessment
• Section Quiz, p. 195

RETEACHING ACTIVITY

Organize students into small groups. Have them create a chart to summarize what they learned about Buddhism and how it influenced Southeast Asia.

In-depth Resources: Unit 5
• Reteaching Activity, p. 12

Access for Students Acquiring English
• Reteaching Activity, p. 120

ASSESSMENT

TERMS & NAMES

1. subcontinent, p. 378
2. sediment, p. 379
3. archipelago, p. 381
4. monsoon, p. 382
5. Aryan, p. 386
6. Hinduism, p. 387
7. caste, p. 388
8. Buddhism, p. 394
9. Siddhartha Gautama, p. 394
10. Khmer, p. 396

REVIEW QUESTIONS

Possible Responses

1. Northern Mountain Rim, Northern Plains, and Deccan Plateau
2. The monsoons bring great amounts of rain, cause flooding, and ruin crops.
3. brought: horses, iron weapons and tools, and religion; learned: farming and living in cities
4. Hindus believe in karma, reincarnation, many gods, and a caste system.
5. during the Gupta Dynasty, from A.D. 320 to 500; art, architecture, literature, mathematics, and science
6. Early travelers brought the beliefs and practices of Hinduism and Buddhism.
7. similar: belief in cycle of life; different: rejection of caste system and role of priests
8. often foundation of culture and government, but empire's power depended on religion's influence

ASSESSMENT

TERMS & NAMES

Explain the significance of each of the following:

1. subcontinent
2. sediment
3. archipelago
4. monsoon
5. Aryan
6. Hinduism
7. caste
8. Buddhism
9. Siddhartha Gautama
10. Khmer

REVIEW QUESTIONS

Physical Geography *(pages 377–383)*
1. What are the three major geographical regions of South Asia?
2. How do the monsoons affect South Asia and Southeast Asia?

Ancient India *(pages 385–390)*
3. What did the Aryan people bring to the Indus Valley, and what did they learn from the civilization that was already in place?
4. What are the main beliefs and characteristics of Hinduism?
5. When did India's golden age occur, and what were its major contributions?

Ancient Crossroads *(pages 392–397)*
6. How did early travelers to Southeast Asia influence that region's culture?
7. How is Buddhism similar to and different from Hinduism?
8. How did Hindu and Buddhist beliefs affect the empires of Southeast Asia?

CRITICAL THINKING

Identifying Effects
1. Using your completed chart from Reading Social Studies, p. 376, write two or three sentences describing how Buddhism affected Southern Asia.

Making Inferences
2. If you were an archaeologist, what would you conclude about the people who inhabited Mohenjo-Daro, based on the evidence that currently exists?

Comparing and Contrasting
3. In what ways are Buddhism and Hinduism similar and different?

Visual Summary

1 Physical Geography
- The physical geography of South Asia and Southeast Asia includes mountains, plateaus, river deltas, and islands.
- Landforms and climate continue to influence where people settle and what they do for a living.

Ancient India 2

- Merging with the existing culture, the Aryan people influenced the development of social structure and religion in ancient India.
- Hinduism provided instruction for daily life as well as inspiration for artists and emperors.

3 Ancient Crossroads
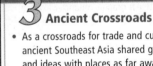
- As a crossroads for trade and culture, ancient Southeast Asia shared goods and ideas with places as far away as India, China, and Africa.
- Hinduism and Buddhism became the foundation of several powerful empires in Southeast Asia.

CRITICAL THINKING: Possible Responses

1. Identifying Effects
Students should mention changes in art, building of temples, and Buddhism's displacement of Hinduism.

2. Making Inferences
The people were quite advanced, with a large and well-planned city. They farmed, built canals, and dug wells.

3. Comparing and Contrasting
Buddhists and Hindus believe in karma and reincarnation. One characteristic of Hinduism is the caste system, but Buddhism rejects the idea of a caste system.

SOCIAL STUDIES SKILLBUILDER

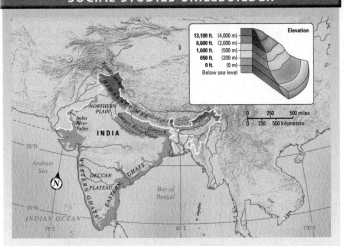

Elevation

13,100 ft.	(4,000 m)
6,600 ft.	(2,000 m)
1,600 ft.	(500 m)
650 ft.	(200 m)
0 ft.	(0 m)
Below sea level

SKILLBUILDER: Reading an Elevation Map

1. What kind of information does this map present?
2. What does the map illustrate about the geographic features of India?

FOCUS ON GEOGRAPHY

1. **Region** • From what mountain range does the river flow that nourished the first ancient Indian civilization?
2. **Movement** • What mountain range did ancient Aryan invaders of India cross?
3. **Location** • The Ganges River delta lies next to what body of water?

CHAPTER PROJECTS

Interdisciplinary Projects: Art

Making a Collage Research some of the visual arts of Southern Asia. Using encyclopedias, books, or the Internet, try to find as many examples as you can. Look for examples of costumes, jewelry, painting, sculpture, and architecture—in other words, the things that people of the region found beautiful or important. Use sketches or photocopies of these images to create a collage. Include a caption for each image.

Cooperative Learning Activity

Writing a Play In a group of three or four students, write a biographical sketch about one of the people in this chapter—perhaps Ashoka or Siddhartha Gautama. You might also invent a character, such as an Indian trader, a Buddhist monk, or a Gupta or Khmer emperor. Create a situation in which that person is trying to convince other people of his or her views and beliefs. One student might support those views and beliefs, and another student might disagree with them.

- Write a script for the play.
- Assign the roles of the central character, supporters, and critics.
- Perform the play for your class.

INTERNET ACTIVITY

Use the Internet to research floods in the Ganges River valley. Try to find information about floods that have been influenced by deforestation and soil erosion in Tibet.

Writing About Geography Write a report about what you have learned and present it to the class. List the Web sites you used to prepare your report.

For Internet links to support this activity, go to

RESEARCH LINKS
CLASSZONE.COM

CHAPTER PROJECTS

Interdisciplinary Projects: Art

Making a Collage Discuss Web sites and search terms students might use to research examples of visual art from Southern Asia. Students' collages should include a variety of art objects and contain items that are clearly products of the region. Encourage students to include identifying captions for each image. Captions should include details such as origin, date, and purpose.

Cooperative Learning Activity

Writing a Play Students' productions should have clearly identifiable characters, include clear statements of the views and beliefs of each character, and have characters who offer credible objections to the stated views and beliefs. Remind students to share responsibilities as they research, write, and perform the play.

INTERNET ACTIVITY

Students' reports should begin with a main idea statement identifying specific floods and provide details about the flood and its effects on the people of the area. Point out that if appropriate, students should explain how the flood was influenced by deforestation and soil erosion. Students might choose to address current or proposed projects for solving problems of deforestation and soil erosion. Encourage students to include illustrations or graphics in their reports.

Skills Answers

Social Studies Skillbuilder
Possible Responses
1. The map shows six categories of land elevations in India.
2. It shows that the Northern Mountain Rim has the highest elevation, that the Deccan Plateau's elevation is between 650 and 6,600 feet, and that the Northern Plain's elevation is between sea level and 1,600 feet.

Focus on Geography
Possible Responses
1. Himalayas
2. the Hindu Kush
3. Bay of Bengal

India and Its Neighbors

	OVERVIEW	COPYMASTERS	INTEGRATED TECHNOLOGY
UNIT ATLAS AND CHAPTER RESOURCES	Students will examine the history, government, economy, and culture of India and its neighboring countries.	**In-depth Resources: Unit 5** • Guided Reading Worksheets, pp. 13–17 • Skillbuilder Practice, p. 20 • Unit Atlas Activities, pp. 1–2 • Geography Workshop, pp. 37–38 **Reading Study Guide** (Spanish and English), pp. 124–135 **Outline Map Activities**	Power Presentations Electronic Teacher Tools Online Lesson Planner Chapter Summaries on CD Critical Thinking Transparencies CT27
SECTION 1 History pp. 403–407	**KEY IDEAS** • Arabs brought Islam to India and South Asia centuries ago. • The British set up factories and trading centers in India. • Leaders, such as Gandhi, led the movement for independence.	**In-depth Resources: Unit 5** • Guided Reading Worksheet, p. 13 • Reaching Activity, p. 22 **Reading Study Guide** (Spanish and English), pp. 124–125	classzone.com Chapter Summaries on CD
SECTION 2 Governments pp. 409–413	• Many types of governments exist in South Asia. • India's constitution protects freedom of speech and religion. • The panchayat, or village council, is the main governing body in India.	**In-depth Resources: Unit 5** • Guided Reading Worksheet, p. 14 • Reaching Activity, p. 23 **Reading Study Guide** (Spanish and English), pp. 126–127	Critical Thinking Transparencies CT28 classzone.com Chapter Summaries on CD
SECTION 3 Economies pp. 416–419	• South Asian countries are moving slowly from traditional to market economies. • The Green Revolution led not only to advances in agriculture, but also to greater pollution.	**In-depth Resources: Unit 5** • Guided Reading Worksheet, p. 15 • Reaching Activity, p. 24 **Reading Study Guide** (Spanish and English), pp. 128–129	Critical Thinking Transparencies CT28 classzone.com Chapter Summaries on CD
SECTION 4 The Culture of India pp. 420–423	• India has a rich cultural heritage, especially in literature and film. • Indians speak many languages, but most are from the Indo-Aryan family. • Family and religion are vital parts of daily life and culture in India.	**In-depth Resources: Unit 5** • Guided Reading Worksheet, p. 16 • Reaching Activity, p. 25 **Reading Study Guide** (Spanish and English), pp. 130–131	classzone.com Chapter Summaries on CD
SECTION 5 Pakistan pp. 425–429	• The Muslim League was formed to retain political power. • More than 20 languages are spoken in Pakistan; Urdu is the official language. • Pakistan faces conflicts with India over the region of Kashmir.	**In-depth Resources: Unit 5** • Guided Reading Worksheet, p. 17 • Reaching Activity, p. 26 **Reading Study Guide** (Spanish and English), pp. 132–133	classzone.com Chapter Summaries on CD

Audio   Internet   Teacher's Edition

CD-ROM   Overhead Transparency   Video

Copymaster   Pupil's Edition

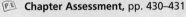

ASSESSMENT OPTIONS

Chapter Assessment, pp. 430–431

Formal Assessment
• Chapter Tests: Forms A, B, C, pp. 213–224

Test Generator

Online Test Practice

Strategies for Test Preparation

Section Assessment, p. 407

Formal Assessment
• Section Quiz, p. 208

Integrated Assessment
• Rubric for writing an article

Test Generator

Test Practice Transparencies TT48

Section Assessment, p. 413

Formal Assessment
• Section Quiz, p. 209

Integrated Assessment
• Rubric for summarizing a news story

Test Generator

Test Practice Transparencies TT49

Section Assessment, p. 419

Formal Assessment
• Section Quiz, p. 210

Integrated Assessment
• Rubric for writing a letter

Test Generator

Test Practice Transparencies TT50

Section Assessment, p. 423

Formal Assessment
• Section Quiz, p. 211

Integrated Assessment
• Rubric for developing a plot

Test Generator

Test Practice Transparencies TT51

Section Assessment, p. 429

Formal Assessment
• Section Quiz, p. 212

Integrated Assessment
• Rubric for drawing a political cartoon

Test Generator

Test Practice Transparencies TT52

RESOURCES FOR DIFFERENTIATING INSTRUCTION

Students Acquiring English/ESL

Reading Study Guide
(Spanish and English), pp. 124–135

Access for Students Acquiring English
Spanish Translations, pp. 121–132

TE Activity
• Building Vocabulary, p. 421

Less Proficient Readers

Reading Study Guide
(Spanish and English), pp. 124–135

TE Activity
• Sequencing Events, p. 404

Gifted and Talented Students

TE Activity
• Creating a Television Documentary, p. 406

CROSS-CURRICULAR CONNECTIONS

Literature
Arenson, Roberta. *Manu and the Talking Fish.* New York: Barefoot Books, 2000. Hindu version of the Great Flood.

Health
Parker, David L. *Stolen Dreams.* Minneapolis, MN: Lerner Publications, 1998. Child labor abuse in India, Pakistan, Bangladesh, and Nepal.

Geography
Coburn, Broughton. *Triumph on Everest: A Photobiography of Sir Edmund Hillary.* Washington, D.C.: National Geographic Society, 2000. Conquest of the world's highest mountain.

Language Arts/Literature
Aylward Whitesel, Cheryl. *Rebel: A Tibetan Odyssey.* New York: HarperCollins, 2000. Thunder is banished from his Tibetan village and sent to a monastery, where he continues to rebel.
Whelan, Gloria. *Homeless Bird.* New York: HarperCollins, 2000. National Book Award winner details life among the poor in modern India.

Science
Montgomery, Sy. *The Man-Eating Tigers of Sundarbans.* Boston: Houghton Mifflin, 2001. Easy-to-read examination of the ecosystem.

ENRICHMENT ACTIVITIES

The following activities are especially suitable for classes following block schedules.

Teacher's Edition, pp. 406, 410, 411, 412, 417, 418, 422, 424, 426, 427, 428
Pupil's Edition, pp. 407, 413, 419, 423, 429

Unit Atlas, pp. 366–373
Technology: 750 B.C., p. 408
Linking Past and Present, pp. 414–415

Outline Map Activities

INTEGRATED TECHNOLOGY

Go to **classzone.com** for lesson support and activities for Chapter 14.

BLOCK SCHEDULE LESSON PLAN OPTIONS: 90-MINUTE PERIOD

DAY 1

CHAPTER PREVIEW, pp. 400–401
Class Time 20 minutes

- **Hypothesize** Use the "What do you think?" questions on PE p. 401 to help students hypothesize about how population growth will affect life in South Asia.

SECTION 1, pp. 403–407
Class Time 70 minutes

- **Small Groups** Write the section objectives on TE p. 403 on the chalkboard. Divide the class into four groups. Have each group select one section objective to help them prepare a summary of this section. Remind students that when they summarize, they should include the main ideas and most important details using their own words. Reconvene as a whole class for discussion.
  Class Time 40 minutes

- **Internet** Extend students' background knowledge of South Asia by visiting **classzone.com.**
  Class Time 30 minutes

DAY 2

SECTION 2, pp. 409–413
Class Time 35 minutes

- **Travel Map** Have students create a map for a friend who is traveling to India. Have them write a note to the friend telling why that map is important to have available on the trip. Refer students to Geography Handbook, pp. 3–13, to help them select a type of map to create.

SECTION 3, pp. 416–419
Class Time 35 minutes

- **Vocabulary** Write *jute, information technology, Green Revolution, market economies,* and *traditional economies* on individual index cards. Print enough cards so each student will have one. Ask students to draw a card and define the word. For discussion, have students form groups according to the cards they have chosen, and discuss the significance of each word in terms of the content they are studying.

SECTION 4, pp. 420–423
Class Time 20 minutes

- **Peer Competition** Divide the class into pairs. Assign each pair one of the Terms & Names for this section. Have pairs make up five questions that can be answered with the term or name. Have groups take turns asking the class their questions.

DAY 3

SECTION 5, pp. 425–429
Class Time 35 minutes

- **Graphic Organizer** Have students use a Venn diagram and the Unit Atlas Data File on PE pp. 372–373 to compare the land areas of India and Pakistan. Provide time for students to present their comparisons to the class.

CHAPTER 14 REVIEW AND ASSESSMENT, pp. 430–431
Class Time 55 minutes

- **Review** Have students work in small groups and use Main Ideas in each section opener to review the chapter.
  Class Time 20 minutes

- **Assessment** Have students complete the Chapter 14 Assessment.
  Class Time 35 minutes

TECHNOLOGY IN THE CLASSROOM

SEARCHING AN ONLINE NEWS SOURCE

One significant advantage of using the Internet to obtain news is that many online news sources regularly update their information. Students can, therefore, search online news sources to get updates on current events or to learn more about recent events related to a region or topic discussed in their textbooks. The online news sources listed at **classzone.com** are three of many places to look for recent news articles online. You might want to have students search their local newspaper's Web site, but keep in mind that some newspaper Web sites require registration or a fee (the ones in this activity do not).

ACTIVITY OUTLINE

Objective Students will search an online news source to find out about recent issues involving India and Pakistan.

Task Have students enter keywords into an online news source's search engine to locate a recent article about India and Pakistan. Have them answer questions about their articles, share them with the class, and discuss what they have learned.

Class Time Two class periods

DIRECTIONS

1. Review the basic differences between India and Pakistan that students learned about in Chapter 14. What are the primary religions in these countries? Why did Pakistan become a separate country from India?

2. Make sure students can locate India and Pakistan on a map. Point out Kashmir, the region in the far northern part of India, and explain that India and Pakistan are fighting for control of this region.

3. Ask students to make charts with the headings "India" and "Pakistan."

4. Have students go to one or more of the online news sources listed at **classzone.com** and search for articles that discuss current issues in India and Pakistan, including issues that affect both countries. Sample search keywords include *India, Pakistan,* and *Kashmir.*

5. Have each student, or pairs of students, choose one article about India and Pakistan that has been written within the past year. Ask them to answer these questions: What is the title of the article? Who wrote the article? When was the article written? What is the article's main idea? What does the article say about India? What does the article say about Pakistan?

6. Have students present the main ideas of their articles to the class, and list these main ideas on the board.

7. Discuss the main ideas students have listed. What are the primary issues between India and Pakistan? What has been going on between these two countries during the last few years? What did the articles say about these countries' relations with the rest of the world, including the United States? What new things have students learned from these articles to supplement what they learned in their textbooks?

CHAPTER 14 OBJECTIVE

Students will examine the history, government, economy, and culture of India and its neighboring countries.

FOCUS ON VISUALS

Interpreting the Photograph Have students examine the photograph of people on the banks of the Ganges. Explain to students that the Ganges is sacred in Hinduism and that bathing in the river is an important ritual for Hindus. Ask students to point out details about the people and buildings in the scene and to describe their general impression of the scene and setting.

Possible Responses The scene looks very crowded and busy. People are standing in the water with their hands folded. There are old buildings like the tower at the left and modern buildings in the distance.

Extension Have students write and deliver a short "on-the-spot" news feature describing this scene.

CRITICAL THINKING ACTIVITY

Analyzing Causes Prompt a discussion about why people build new cities while still keeping reminders of an older way of life. Brainstorm a list of the benefits of both old and new elements. Ask students to think about what the reminders of the past might mean to people.

Class Time 10 minutes

CHAPTER

14

India and Its Neighbors

SECTION 1 History

SECTION 2 Governments

SECTION 3 Economies

SECTION 4 The Culture of India

SECTION 5 Pakistan

Place Bathers descend steps called ghats to reach the Ganges River. To Hindus, it is the holiest river in India.

400

Recommended Resources

BOOKS FOR THE TEACHER

Alter, Stephen. *Amritsar to Lahore: A Journey Across the India-Pakistan Border.* Philadelphia: University of Pennsylvania Press, 2000. A look at the conflict and the people caught up in the struggle.
Hutchings, Jane, ed. *Insight Guide: India.* Maspeth, NY: APA Publications, 2000. Insightful guide to the country.

VIDEOS

Freedom Now, 1947. Burlington, VT: WGBH Educational Foundation and the BBC. WGBH Boston Video (distributor), 1998. Historical footage and interviews.
Gandhi. Burbank, CA: Columbia TriStar Home Video, 1990. Academy Award–winning look at Gandhi's life.

SOFTWARE

Discover the Magic of India. Wynnewood, PA: Library Video Company, 1996. Narrated videos and slide shows.

INTERNET

For more information about India and its neighbors, visit **classzone.com**.

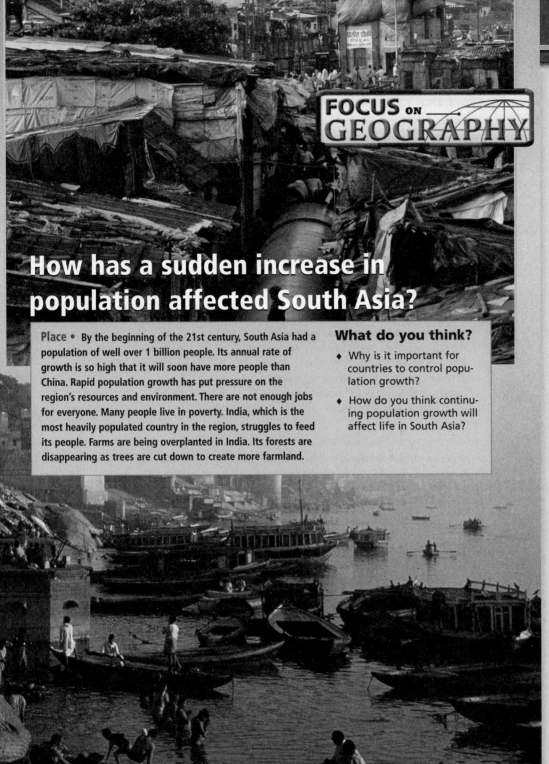

FOCUS ON GEOGRAPHY

How has a sudden increase in population affected South Asia?

Place • By the beginning of the 21st century, South Asia had a population of well over 1 billion people. Its annual rate of growth is so high that it will soon have more people than China. Rapid population growth has put pressure on the region's resources and environment. There are not enough jobs for everyone. Many people live in poverty. India, which is the most heavily populated country in the region, struggles to feed its people. Farms are being overplanted in India. Its forests are disappearing as trees are cut down to create more farmland.

What do you think?

♦ Why is it important for countries to control population growth?

♦ How do you think continuing population growth will affect life in South Asia?

401

BEFORE YOU READ
What Do You Know?

Explain that India and the countries that neighbor it are lands of varied geography and diverse cultures. Poll students about their knowledge of India and the rest of South Asia, including food, religions, cultures, and geography. Ask students who have eaten Indian food to describe it. Then ask them to share any stories, folktales, or movies they know that are set in India or other parts of South Asia.

What Do You Want to Know?

Suggest that students make a list of things about India that they are curious about. They should write these topics in a chart under the heading "What I Want to Know." As they read the chapter they should record facts and information about the subjects in a second column.

READ AND TAKE NOTES

Reading Strategy: Sequencing Putting events in sequential order means arranging them in a logical, useful order. Direct students' attention to the chart and discuss its structure. Point out that it covers the time periods before 1947 and after 1947, and that it includes India and Pakistan. By filling out the chart, students will have a complete time line for both countries.

 In-depth Resources: Unit 5
• Guided Reading Worksheets, pp. 13–17

BEFORE YOU READ

▶▶ What Do You Know?

Before you read the chapter, consider what you know about India and its neighbors. Who was Gandhi? Have you ever seen a Bengal tiger? How high is Mount Everest? What spices go into curry? Where do *The Jungle Books* take place? Reflect on what you read in Chapter 13 and what you have seen or heard in the news about India, Pakistan, and other countries in South Asia.

▶▶ What Do You Want to Know?

Decide what you know about India and its neighbors. In your notebook, record what you hope to learn from this chapter.

Place • **Farmers in Afghanistan still use traditional methods.** ▲

READ AND TAKE NOTES

Reading Strategy: Sequencing To sequence means to put events in the order in which they happened. Sequencing can help you understand how events lead to other events. Use the chart to the right to record key events in the histories of India and Pakistan and to note differences and similarities.

• Copy the chart into your notebook.

• As you read, look for dates and key events.

• In the top two boxes, record events and important details next to the dates.

• In the row of three boxes, record important details about India and Pakistan since 1947.

Before 1947
8th century A.D.—Muslims conquer northwestern India; 11th century A.D.—Turks attack northwestern India; 1526—Babur invades the south of India; 1600s—arrival of the British; 1900s—first ideas of independence

1947
India and Pakistan gain their independence from Britain, becoming two separate nations.

India	Both	Pakistan
mostly Hindu population, world's largest democracy, constitution in effect since 1950, slow changes in the caste social system	conflict over Kashmir, tests of nuclear weapons	mostly Muslim population, Islamic Republic, Bangladesh gains its independence in 1971

Place • **The sitar is a popular instrument in India.** ◀

Teaching Strategy

Reading the Chapter This is a thematic chapter that focuses on the history, government, economy, and culture of India and the countries that neighbor it. It includes information about ways that these countries affect one other and the way each country has dealt with modern-day conflicts. Encourage students to combine their prior knowledge, the visuals, and the text to help them acquire a better understanding of this region.

Integrated Assessment The Chapter Assessment on page 431 describes several activities that may be used for integrated assessment. You may wish to have students work on these activities during the course of the chapter and then present them at the end.

History

TERMS & NAMES
Mughal Empire
Indian National Congress
Muslim League
Mohandas Gandhi

MAIN IDEA

The movements of people and ideas through the nations of South Asia have produced a varied and exciting history.

WHY IT MATTERS NOW

Similarities and differences among these nations have led to both development and conflict.

SECTION OBJECTIVES

1. To describe the impact of Islam on India and the nations of South Asia
2. To trace the history of the Mughal Empire
3. To describe how the arrival of the British affected development of the area
4. To explain how the region gained independence

SKILLBUILDER
• Interpreting a Map, p. 405

CRITICAL THINKING
• Distinguishing Fact from Opinion, p. 405
• Analyzing Causes, p. 407

FOCUS & MOTIVATE
WARM-UP

Identifying Motives Have students read Dateline and answer the following questions:

1. Why do you think sailors were willing to take the risks involved in such a trip?
2. What might Indians have thought of the British ship's arrival?

INSTRUCT: Objective ❶

Islam Comes to India

• How and where did the religion of Islam first arrive in South Asia? Muslims from Arabia conquered the northwest region, which is now Pakistan and Afghanistan.

• How did Islam spread in India? Turkish Muslims established a kingdom; others came to India fleeing the Mongols.

 In-depth Resources: Unit 5
• Guided Reading Worksheet, p. 13

 Reading Study Guide
(Spanish and English), pp. 124–125

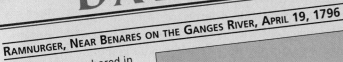

DATELINE
EXTRA

RAMNURGER, NEAR BENARES ON THE GANGES RIVER, APRIL 19, 1796

A British ship anchored in the river yesterday after sailing many months from England. Today, boatmen and British sailors outfitted in our native cotton dress have been working madly to load the ship. They hope to sail before the monsoon winds and storms begin. Hundreds of boxes of tea, spices, and cotton fabric will travel back to England.

Movement • Despite great risk, ships from Great Britain, France, and Portugal sail to India and other parts of South Asia to carry back valuable spices, tea, and other goods. ▲

Islam Comes to India ❶

The coast of India has been a site of trade for centuries. Arabs were trading along the coast of India a thousand years before the British arrived. Early in the eighth century A.D., Muslims from Arabia conquered northwest India. They converted many of the people of this region to their religion, Islam. Even today, the people of this region (what is now Afghanistan and Pakistan) are Muslim.

India and Its Neighbors **403**

Program Resources

 In-depth Resources: Unit 5
• Guided Reading Worksheet, p. 13
• Reteaching Activity, p. 22

 Reading Study Guide
(Spanish and English), pp. 124–125

 Formal Assessment
• Section Quiz, p. 208

 Integrated Assessment
• Rubric for writing an article

Outline Map Activities

 Access for Students Acquiring English
• Guided Reading Worksheet, p. 121

 Technology Resources classzone.com

TEST-TAKING RESOURCES
 Strategies for Test Preparation
Test Practice Transparencies
Online Test Practice

INSTRUCT: Objective ❷

The Mughal Empire

- Whose reign signaled the beginning of the Mughal Empire? Babur

- How did Akbar contribute to the Mughal Empire during his reign? He made India a place where Hindus and Muslims could live in peace; he also established a fair tax system and supported the arts.

- What caused the collapse of the Mughal Empire in 1707? the death of the last Mughal emperor

FOCUS ON VISUALS

Interpreting the Painting Point out the style of the Mughal painting and the artist's use of colorful patterns and design to give an impression of action and lively motion. Ask students to compare the painting with European or American works of art that they may be familiar with.

Possible Responses The painting is more like a poster than a realistic scene, especially the elephants' and horses' heads. Clothing and the animals' harnesses are very decorative and stylized.

Extension Have students use art reference books or Internet resources to find other examples of Mughal paintings and designs.

Location • The Hindu Kush Mountains in northern Pakistan helped to keep out invaders. ▲

Culture • Akbar, shown here crossing the Ganges, had his life story told in words and pictures in the *Akbarnama,* or *The Memoirs of Akbar.* ▼

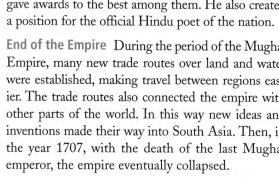

Turks and Mongols Beginning in the 11th century A.D., Turkish Muslims from what is now Afghanistan attacked northwest India, replacing the Arabs. By 1206, the Turkish kingdom stretched south to the Deccan Plateau. The region was ruled from the city of Delhi by a sultan. During this time, Mongols from Central Asia began spreading west and south. Because of the mountains in the northeastern part of South Asia, the Mongols never invaded the region. Many people who were threatened by the Mongols fled across the mountains into South Asia. These artists, teachers, government officials, and religious leaders brought with them their culture and learning.

The Mughal Empire ❷

In the year 1526, Babur (BAH·buhr), a Mughal (moo·GUL) ruler and a Muslim, invaded southward with his army. Eventually, his kingdom included northern India and land west into Afghanistan. Babur involved local leaders in his government and built trade routes, strengthening his rule. Babur's reign was the beginning of the great **Mughal Empire**.

Akbar, Mughal Emperor The third Mughal emperor, Akbar, was a strong and intelligent leader who was careful to include both Hindus and Muslims in his government. His policies made India a place where both Hindus and Muslims could live in peace. He taxed people according to the size and value of their land, which meant that poor farmers were not taxed as heavily as they had been before. Akbar was a strong supporter of the arts. He provided studios for painters and gave awards to the best among them. He also created a position for the official Hindu poet of the nation.

End of the Empire During the period of the Mughal Empire, many new trade routes over land and water were established, making travel between regions easier. The trade routes also connected the empire with other parts of the world. In this way new ideas and inventions made their way into South Asia. Then, in the year 1707, with the death of the last Mughal emperor, the empire eventually collapsed.

Vocabulary
sultan: emperor

Vocabulary
Mughal: Muslim Turks from what is now Turkistan

Reading Social Studies
A. Possible Answer Trade routes would result in a stronger economy, as well as increased interaction and new ideas.

Reading
Social Studies

A. Drawing Conclusions How would trade routes help to strengthen an empire?

Activity Options

Differentiating Instruction: Less Proficient Readers

Sequencing Events Some students may be better able to follow the sequence of events described if the events are organized in a flow chart. Draw a chart on the chalkboard and work with students to record the events that brought Muslims to India. Have students refer to the map on page 405 as you review the events.

Arab Muslims conquered northwest India in the 8th century A.D.

In A.D. 1001, Turkish Muslims attacked Arabs in northwest India.

By 1206, the Turkish kingdom stretched south to the Deccan.

Threatened by Mongol expansion, Muslims fled across the mountains into South Asia.

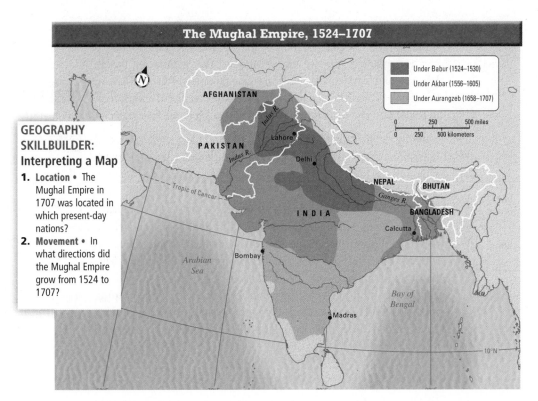

The Mughal Empire, 1524–1707

Under Babur (1524–1530)
Under Akbar (1556–1605)
Under Aurangzeb (1658–1707)

0   250   500 miles
0   250   500 kilometers

AFGHANISTAN

PAKISTAN

Indus R.

Lahore

Delhi

NEPAL   BHUTAN

Ganges R.

BANGLADESH

INDIA

Calcutta

Bombay

Arabian
Sea

Bay of
Bengal

Madras

Tropic of Cancer

10°N

GEOGRAPHY SKILLBUILDER:
Interpreting a Map

1. **Location •** The Mughal Empire in 1707 was located in which present-day nations?
2. **Movement •** In what directions did the Mughal Empire grow from 1524 to 1707?

Geography Skillbuilder Answers

1. India, parts of Pakistan and Afghanistan, most of Bangladesh, small areas of Nepal and Bhutan

2. mainly to the south and east, somewhat west

Arrival of the British ❸

In 1600, Queen Elizabeth I of England gave trade rights to the East India Company, an organization of English merchants, to trade in India and East and Southeast Asia. The Mughals agreed to let the British set up factories and trading centers. The East India Company shipped spices, tea, cotton, silk, indigo (used for dyeing), sugar, and saltpeter (used for gunpowder) to England. Gradually, the British increased their power. By 1818, after the Rajputs and other groups agreed to be ruled by the British, Great Britain's strength in the region was undeniable.

Movement • The British brought railroads to India, such as this steam train in Darjeeling, shown in 1930. ▼

India and Its Neighbors **405**

CRITICAL THINKING ACTIVITY

Distinguishing Fact from Opinion Remind students that a fact is information that can be proved. Ask students to reread the paragraph that describes the reign of Akbar and to identify facts about Akbar. Then ask them to formulate opinions about him or his reign.

Class Time 10 minutes

FOCUS ON VISUALS

Interpreting the Map Review the map key with students. Ask volunteers to point out the area of the expanding empire that each shade represents. Point out the names of the three emperors. Have them analyze which ruler oversaw the greatest expansion.

Possible Response The greatest expansion seems to have come in the reign of Akbar.

Extension Have students use the map to answer these questions: Which two river valleys were added in the reign of Akbar? Indus, Ganges What was the southernmost city in the empire? Madras

INSTRUCT: Objective ❸

Arrival of the British

• Why did the British want to set up factories and trading centers in India? so they could have access to spices, tea, cotton, silk, indigo, sugar, and saltpeter from India

• What technology did the British bring to the region? railroads, telegraphs, steamships, irrigation methods

• How did Indians respond to the British? Some interacted economically but maintained their traditions; some did not change their lives at all; others adopted English traditions and language.

Activity Options

Multiple Learning Styles: Spatial/Kinesthetic

Class Time 15 minutes

Task Analyzing the map of the Mughal Empire

Purpose To understand how the map indicates the growth of the Mughal Empire

Supplies Needed
• Map on page 405

Activity Direct students' attention to the map above. Read aloud the map's title, then discuss the purpose of the map. Ask students to use their fingers to trace the border of the Mughal Empire in 1524. Then have them trace the border that existed in 1707. Ask them whether the territory decreased or increased in size. Then ask map-specific questions to assess their understanding.

INSTRUCT: Objective ④

Independence

- What two groups were formed before the people of India began to think about independence? the Indian National Congress and the Muslim League
- What were Gandhi's hopes for India? All Indians would be treated equally; women would have the same freedoms as men; there would be peace between Hindus and Muslims.

Biography

When Gandhi was assassinated, the world agreed that one of the bravest and most inspirational leaders of the 20th century had been lost. Indian Prime Minister Jawaharlal Nehru mourned him with these words, "A light has gone out of our lives and there is darkness everywhere. . . ."

India's Neighbors and Great Britain In 1796, Great Britain took possession of the island nation of Sri Lanka, then called Ceylon, and the island nation of the Maldives. The nations of Nepal, Bhutan, and Afghanistan never became colonies of Great Britain, though the British tried to colonize Afghanistan. Nepal and Bhutan depended on their mountainous frontiers to keep out foreigners.

Making India British The British army and navy, merchants, and Christian missionaries came to India, bringing new technology for railroads, the telegraph, steamships, and new methods of irrigation. They also introduced the British legal system, with new laws regarding landownership, and made English the official language.

Indians responded to the British in different ways. Some chose to live just as they had before the British arrived. Others chose to interact economically with the British by working for and with them while maintaining their traditions. Still others studied the British traditions and adopted what seemed useful while keeping their own traditions. Among the higher castes, parents sent their children to British schools so that they could learn English and become successful.

Independence ④

In 1885, the **Indian National Congress** was formed to provide a forum where Indians could discuss their problems. Muslims formed the **Muslim League** in 1906. After World War I, Indians began to think of independence. They had a great leader in **Mohandas Gandhi.**

Reading Social Studies

B. Comparing Which changes brought by the British were cultural and which were technological?

Reading Social Studies
B. Possible Answers cultural: language, religion; technological: railroads, steamships, irrigation

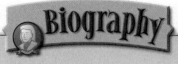

Biography

Mohandas Gandhi (GAHN•dee) Gandhi was born in India in 1869. He learned about discrimination when, as a young boy, he saw that no matter how wealthy and well educated Indians were, they were treated as second-class citizens by the British. Gandhi studied law in England and then spent the rest of his life working for justice for the Indian people.

He encouraged his followers to use nonviolence to resist the British and bring about social change. Gandhi believed that the forces of goodness and truth had powerful effects on people. As part of this belief, he went on hunger strikes and organized labor strikes and marches to force the British to grant India its independence.

The Indian people call Gandhi the *Mahatma,* which means "Great Soul." They honor him as the father of their nation. His ideas have influenced many people who have worked for justice around the world.

406 CHAPTER 14

Activity Options

Differentiating Instruction: Gifted and Talented   **B Block Scheduling**

Creating a Television Documentary Challenge students to plan and create a segment of a television documentary or newsmagazine on the life of Mohandas Gandhi. Have them decide on the roles they will play in the production: script writers, director, video producer, and reporters. Then ask them to use a variety of resources, including primary sources, to research Gandhi's life, his philosophy and commitment to nonviolence, and the effects of his ideas on other leaders around the world. Have them use their research to write a script, including real or imaginary interviews; create visuals; and present the program to the class.

Gandhi used nonviolence to impress upon the British the need for independence. He also wanted all Indians to be treated equally. He wanted women to have the same freedoms as men. He encouraged Hindus and Muslims to find peaceful ways to solve their problems. For example, to protest the British monopoly of salt, Gandhi led a 240-mile walk to the coast to gather sea salt.

Vocabulary

monopoly: The sale of a good by only one company

BACKGROUND

On the Unit Atlas Map on page 368, find India, Pakistan, and Bangladesh. Before independence, this entire region was India.

Eventually, Great Britain realized that it would have to leave India, but the Indian National Congress and the Muslim League disagreed about how the new government would be formed. Muslims were afraid of losing power because Hindus were the majority in India. The solution was to divide India into two separate countries, India for the Hindus and Pakistan for the Muslims. The two countries were formed and granted independence in 1947. Sri Lanka became independent in 1948, and the Maldives in 1965.

Movement • Gandhi led his countrymen to the coast at Dandi to protest the British sale of salt. ▲

SECTION 1 ASSESSMENT

Terms & Names

1. **Identify:**
   (a) Mughal Empire
   (b) Indian National Congress
   (c) Muslim League
   (d) Mohandas Gandhi

Taking Notes

2. Use a Venn diagram like the one below to compare and contrast the rule of the Mughals and the British in India.

Mughals   British

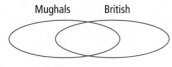

Main Ideas

3. (a) How did Islam reach India?
   (b) Name three achievements of the Mughal emperors.
   (c) Why did the British colonize India?

Critical Thinking

4. **Making Inferences**

   Do you think it was easier for rich Indians or poor Indians to live under British rule? Explain.

   Think About

   ◆ how Indians responded to British rule
   ◆ the opportunities for Indians of different castes

ACTIVITY -OPTION-   Imagine being a reporter for an Indian newspaper and attending a speech given by Gandhi. Write a **short article** reporting on the speech and giving your reaction to it.

India and Its Neighbors **407**

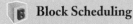
Qanats

Because much of their country has little or no rainfall, Iranians have relied on a system of collecting and transporting water that was developed more than 2,500 years ago. The ancient Iranians, known as Persians, dug 30-to-100-foot shafts at the feet of mountains to tap into the water table. They built underground tunnels called *qanats* (KAH•NAHTS) that followed the slope of the land. These *qanats* collect water that seeps into the ground from melting snow and from rivers and streams. Although they are expensive to build and difficult to maintain, the *qanats* carry water to villages as much as 50 miles away for drinking and irrigating fields. They supply more than 75 percent of Iran's water.

1 At the base of a mountain range, melting snow and rainwater collect underground on top of a layer of solid rock. The water table slopes downward farther and farther from the surface.

2 Workers dig a well as deep as 100 feet to reach the water table. This is called the mother well.

3 Shafts are dug at regular intervals so that villages can draw water and workers can maintain the tunnel.

4 Workers build a shaft and haul out soil. Then they use stone, soil, and existing mineral and salt deposits to line the tunnel.

THINKING Critically

1. Drawing Conclusions
What is a drawback of the *qanat* system?

2. Recognizing Effects
How would a drought affect the *qanat* system?

Thinking Critically

1. Drawing Conclusions Possible Response The *qanat* system depends on money and human labor to build and maintain it; without either, it could collapse.

2. Recognizing Effects Possible Response Lack of rain would cause rivers and streams to dry up. The *qanat* system could not function without its underground water supply.

Governments

TERMS & NAMES
Taliban
martial law
Dalit
Indira Gandhi
panchayat

MAIN IDEA

The countries of South Asia have different types of governments, but all face the challenges of economic growth and poverty.

WHY IT MATTERS NOW

As the nations of the world grow more and more connected, any individual nation's success becomes important to all.

DATELINE

NEW DELHI, INDIA, AUGUST 15, 1947—
Jawaharal Nehru, India's first prime minister, has today solemnly declared India a free and independent nation. At 8:30 A.M. the new government was sworn in. Prime Minister Nehru then unfurled India's flag, the Tricolor, which flew for the first time from the Council House against a free sky.

In February, the British government had announced its willingness to grant India its independence. On June 3, Lord Mountbatten, viceroy of India, took to the airwaves to explain the method by which power would be transferred from one government to another. Yesterday, the nation waited breathlessly for midnight to arrive. After 300 years of colonial rule, India has won her freedom at last.

Place • Indians celebrate independence in the streets of Calcutta and other cities and towns throughout India. ▲

South Asia's Governments ❶

Since independence, the nations of South Asia have chosen different forms of government. Some are republics. In a republic, the people elect leaders to represent them. Some countries, such as India, chose a parliamentary form of government. Others chose to be constitutional monarchies. In a constitutional monarchy, the king or queen serves a mostly ceremonial role, while the prime minister and cabinet actually run the government.

India and Its Neighbors **409**

SECTION OBJECTIVES

1. To identify the different types of governments that exist in South Asia

2. To describe how India's independence and constitution affected its people

3. To explain how a democratic government functions in India

CRITICAL THINKING
• Summarizing, p. 410
• Analyzing Causes, p. 412

FOCUS & MOTIVATE
WARM-UP

Making Inferences Have students read <u>Dateline</u> and answer these questions:

1. What group/groups of people do you think will benefit most from the new constitution?

2. Will the new constitution make as much difference for people in rural areas?

INSTRUCT: Objective ❶

South Asia's Governments

• What occurred in Afghanistan in 1979 that changed the country's type of government? invasion by the Soviet Union

• What types of government are represented in South Asia? republic, parliamentary system, constitutional monarchy

• What religion must Pakistan's prime minister and president follow? They must be Muslim.

 In-depth Resources: Unit 5
• Guided Reading Worksheet, p. 14

 Reading Study Guide
(Spanish and English), pp. 126–127

Program Resources

 In-depth Resources: Unit 5
• Guided Reading Worksheet, p. 14
• Reteaching Activity, p. 23

 Reading Study Guide
(Spanish and English), pp. 126–127

 Formal Assessment
• Section Quiz, p. 209

 Integrated Assessment
• Rubric for writing a summary

 Outline Map Activities

 Access for Students Acquiring English
• Guided Reading Worksheet, p. 122

 Technology Resources classzone.com

TEST-TAKING RESOURCES
↘ Strategies for Test Preparation
↘ Test Practice Transparencies
◉ Online Test Practice

CRITICAL THINKING ACTIVITY

Summarizing Prompt a discussion about how the governments of each of these South Asian countries has developed. Have students brainstorm factors that led to attempts to gain independence and the difficulties faced in the attempts. Record students' responses in a chart, and use it to summarize the development of these governments.

Afghanistan	attempted democracy, invaded by Soviets, Communist government overturned, Taliban took control
Bangladesh	gained independence from Pakistan in 1971, military has taken over government several times
Pakistan	martial law declared in 1958, military took control until 1988

Class Time 15 minutes

MORE ABOUT...
Bangladesh

Although the people of Bangladesh (called *Bangladeshis*) are mostly Muslim, they are culturally and ethnically different from Pakistanis. Most are Bengalis, a people whose ancestors probably migrated from countries to the east. Their language, which is Indo-Aryan, is also called Bengali. Much of this very crowded country lies on a huge delta formed by the Ganges and Brahmaputra rivers.

Afghanistan In 1964, a new constitution established a constitutional monarchy for Afghanistan. The monarchy collapsed in 1973 as the result of a coup. In 1979, the Soviet Union invaded Afghanistan and established a Communist government. A UN agreement forced Soviet troops to withdraw from Afghanistan in 1989, leaving behind an Afghani Communist government. This government was overturned and an Islamic republic was declared, but it did not have support from enough people and was too weak to maintain power.

A group of fundamentalist Muslims, the **Taliban,** took control of the government. Under the Taliban, people must follow strict rules. Women cannot go to school or hold jobs, nor can they go out in public without a male relative. Punishment for breaking rules includes being whipped or even executed.

The Taliban has been at war with opposing Muslim groups for many years. Although the Taliban has received help from a few other nations, such as Pakistan, most of the world has spoken out against the Taliban government. In 2001, the Taliban was accused of harboring terrorists responsible for the attacks on the United States made on September 11 of that year.

Bangladesh Bangladesh gained independence from Pakistan in 1971 and adopted its constitution in 1972. The constitution gives Bangladesh a parliamentary form of government, with a prime minister and a president. However, in 1975, and several times since, the military has taken over the government.

Culture • Bhutan is ruled by a king. This is King Jigme Singye Wangchuk (JIHG•may SING•yay WAHNG•chuk), in 1998. ▼

Bhutan For three centuries, Bhutan was ruled jointly by two types of leaders—one spiritual and the other political. In 1907, the spiritual ruler withdrew from public life, and since then Bhutan has had a king only. In 1953, an assembly was formed, which meets twice a year to pass laws. Then, in 1968, a Council of Ministers was created to advise the king. The king appoints ministers, but the assembly must approve them.

The Maldives In 1965, the Maldives gained independence from Great Britain and became a republic three years later. The Citizens' Council has 48 members, 40 elected by the people and 8 appointed by the president. The president also appoints the judges, who follow Islamic law in making their judgments.

Activity Options

Multiple Learning Styles: Visual

Class Time 30 minutes

Task Creating concept webs

Purpose To identify details about the governments of individual countries in South Asia

Supplies Needed
• Chalkboard and chalk

B Block Scheduling

Activity Work with students to create concept webs that identify details about the governments of Afghanistan, Bangladesh, the Maldives, Bhutan, Nepal, Pakistan, and Sri Lanka. Include details about the current forms of government, their histories, and any challenges the governments have faced. Use the completed webs to review the section.

Nepal For centuries, Nepal was ruled exclusively by kings. Prime ministers replaced kings as the country's ruling office. In 1962, Nepal became a constitutional monarchy and all political parties were banned. In the 1990s, the king allowed the formation of political parties. Soon, some had gained enough power to force a change in the government. The Nepalese wrote a new constitution and established a new parliamentary system.

Pakistan Pakistan gained independence from Great Britain in 1947. The constitution of 1947 gave Pakistan a parliamentary government. However, in 1958, **martial law** was declared. The military took control of the government and maintained power until 1988. Today, Pakistan is a republic, with a prime minister and a president, both of whom must be Muslim.

Reading
Social Studies

A. Recognizing Important Details What two attitudes do Pakistanis have about the role of Islam in their government?

Reading Social Studies
A. Possible Answer Some think Islam holds the nation together; others think that it has pulled people apart.

People in Pakistan have differing views about the role of Islam in the government. Some think Islam is what holds the people together as one nation. Others feel that Islam does not meet the needs of all the groups in the country and that it has actually pulled people apart.

Sri Lanka In 1948, Sri Lanka gained independence from Great Britain. Today, it is a democracy with a president as its leader. As in the United States, two political parties struggle for power in the government.

Culture • President Chandrika Kumaratunga (chan·DREE·kah kum·ruh·TUNG·ah), of Sri Lanka, opens the country's new Parliament in November 2000. ▲

The World's Largest Democracy ❷

India is the world's largest democracy. Approximately 370 million Indians voted in the 1999 elections. The country's official head of state is the president. However, India's prime minister actually runs the government.

Place • The prime minister of Pakistan works in the Offices of Government in Islamabad, the capital. ▶

INSTRUCT: Objective ❷

The World's Largest Democracy

- What two groups gained the most under India's new constitution? women and the poor
- What rights are protected in the Indian constitution? freedom of speech and religion, equal treatment under the law
- Who are the Dalits? people who were outside the caste system and considered lower than the lowest caste
- How did the new constitution help the Dalits? They can vote, have equal rights under the constitution, and have gained some political power.
- What rights have women in India gained since independence? right to vote, more opportunities in jobs and politics

FOCUS ON VISUALS

Interpreting the Photograph Explain to students that Islamabad was a planned capital city, built in the 1960s. Builders wanted to combine traditional Islamic architecture with modern design. Have them compare the buildings in the photograph with the Taj Mahal (page 420) and point out the traditional features.

Possible Responses Both are made of white marble or stone, with tall towers and small windows; there are long avenues of trees.

Extension Have students find out more about present-day Islamabad, such as the city's demographics and features, and write a brief guide for visitors.

Activity Options

Interdisciplinary Link: Math

Class Time One class period

Task Creating a bar graph that shows the number of voters in five democratic countries

Purpose To compare the number of voters in India with the number of voters in other large democracies

Supplies Needed
- Almanac
- Online reference sources (optional)
- Graph paper
- Pencils or markers

B Block Scheduling

Activity Working in small groups, students should conduct research to find the number of people who voted in recent national elections in five democratic countries around the world. When they have located the data, have them decide what scale to use and then create a bar graph that compares the number of voters in those countries with the number of voters in India.

India's constitution went into effect in 1950, protecting Indians from being treated unfairly. According to the constitution, all Indians are assured the same basic rights. These include the rights of free speech and religion, which are protected in the courts.

The Changing Caste System India's new constitution stated that even the lowest and poorest classes could vote. The poor are also represented in the government. Special programs reserve jobs for people of the lower castes and secure places for them in schools. The **Dalits** (formerly called "untouchables") have gained political power. They were outside the caste system and considered even lower than the lowest caste. Today, they vote for leaders, though more changes are needed to ensure the Dalits have equal rights in the government and the economy.

Culture • An Indian woman has her fing marked before votir in a 1999 election in Gujarat. ▲

Women in India After independence from Britain, Indian women gained many new rights. Finally, all women were granted the right to vote. It is now against the law in India to discriminate on the basis of gender.

Indian women began working at jobs that had been held only by men. Women became teachers and doctors. They were elected to public office. **Indira Gandhi** became India's first woman prime minister in 1966.

Village Life and Grass-roots Democracy ❸

Since ancient times, small rural Indian villages have governed themselves. Today they are governed by the *panchayat* system. A ***panchayat*** is a village council. India's constitution allows these councils to govern themselves. The *panchayat* collects taxes for maintaining schools and hospitals. It builds roads and digs wells for drinking water. The councils also take care of primary school education in India.

CRITICAL THINKING ACTIVITY

Analyzing Causes Ask students to think about why the caste system is changing in India after so many centuries. Prompt a discussion by asking questions such as the following: Why did this change take so long? What pressures might have been put on the government to correct this system? What type of system is likely to take the place of the caste system?

Class Time 10 minutes

The founder of the Jain religion was the son of a wealthy and powerful chief in Northeastern India. He was a persuasive preacher, and his followers called him *Mahavira*, the Great Hero, or *Jina*, the Conqueror. He believed that every living thing has a soul, and that killing any living thing is an evil.

INSTRUCT: Objective ❸

Village Life and Grassroots Democracy

- **What are the responsibilities of the *panchayat?*** to collect taxes for schools and hospitals, to build roads and dig wells, to monitor primary school education

- **What are the three levels of the *panchayat?*** The first level represents a village or a group of small villages. The second level is made up of chiefs from 100 villages. The third level represents an entire district.

- **What does the law say about women and *panchayats?*** One-third of *panchayat* representatives must be women.

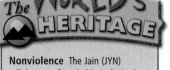

Nonviolence The Jain (JYN) religion was founded in India in the sixth century B.C. Its followers believe that people should never harm a living being, including the smallest insect. The Jain belief in nonviolence led to its use as a powerful political weapon.

Instead of leading an armed revolt, Gandhi used nonviolence as a tactic to drive the British out of India. The idea of nonviolence inspired American civil rights leader Martin Luther King, Jr. (shown at left below with his wife and Prime Minister Nehru). King used nonviolent methods, including marches and demonstrations, to fight against the discrimination of African Americans in the United States.

Activity Options

Interdisciplinary Link: Language Arts

Class Time One class period

Task Writing an editorial about nonviolence

Purpose To express an opinion about nonviolence

Supplies Needed
- Reference material on nonviolent ideas
- Newspaper editorials

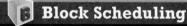

Block Scheduling

Activity Discuss with the class the ideas and techniques of persuasive writing. Have students examine newspaper editorials to find examples of the ways writers argue and support an opinion. Then ask students to write an editorial about the use of nonviolence as a method of change. Students may write their editorials from a historical perspective or a modern-day one.

Culture •
Traditionally, the *panchayat* meets under a banyan tree like this one. ▶

Reading Social Studies
B. Possible Answer
They build on each other. Each progressive level combines units of the previous level, representing more people and a larger area.

B. Contrasting
How are the three levels of *panchayats* different from one another?

Three Levels The *panchayat* works on three levels. The first level represents a village or a group of small villages. The second level is made up of *panchayat* chiefs from 100 villages. The third level represents an entire district. Some districts have as many as ten million people.

Today, there are over 3 million *panchayat* representatives in India. By law, one-third of them must be women. The constitution also makes room for the Dalits and other minorities to participate in the *panchayat* system.

SECTION 2 ASSESSMENT

Terms & Names

1. Identify: (a) Taliban   (b) martial law   (c) Dalit   (d) Indira Gandhi   (e) *panchayat*

Taking Notes

2. Use a chart like the one below to list the countries of South Asia and the features of their governments.

Country	Features of Government

Main Ideas

3. (a) Name three kinds of government found in South Asia.

   (b) What kind of government does India have?

   (c) Describe the responsibilities of the *panchayat*.

Critical Thinking

4. Synthesizing

How did India's 1950 constitution change the lives of women and members of the lower castes?

Think About

• the treatment of the lower castes and women before 1950

• what it means to live in a democracy

ACTIVITY -OPTION- Choose one of the following nations: Bhutan, Nepal, or Sri Lanka. Use the Internet to find a recent news story about it. **Summarize** the story for your class.

India and Its Neighbors **413**

Section 2 Assessment

1. Terms & Names
a. Taliban, p. 410
b. martial law, p. 411
c. Dalit, p. 412
d. Indira Gandhi, p. 412
e. *panchayat*, p. 412

2. Taking Notes

Country	Features of Government
India	parliamentary
Afghanistan	Islamic rule
Bangladesh	parliamentary
Bhutan	constitutional monarchy
The Maldives	republic
Nepal	constitutional monarchy
Pakistan	republic
Sri Lanka	republic

3. Main Ideas
a. Parliamentary systems, republics, and constitutional monarchies are found in South Asia.
b. India has a democratic parliamentary system.
c. The *panchayat* builds roads, digs wells for drinking water, oversees primary school education, and collects taxes for maintaining schools and hospitals.

4. Critical Thinking
Possible Response India's constitution changed life for women and members of the lower caste by granting equal treatment and the right to vote to all people.

ACTIVITY OPTION
 Integrated Assessment
• Rubric for writing a summary

Teacher's Edition **413**

ASSESS & RETEACH

Reading Social Studies Have students record key events in the development of the governments of India and Pakistan on the graphic organizer on page 402.

 Formal Assessment
• Section Quiz, p. 209

RETEACHING ACTIVITY

Have students work in small groups to create a section review. Have each student in the group describe the form of government in one of the countries covered in the section. Ask them to combine the descriptions into a review of the section.

 In-depth Resources: Unit 5
• Reteaching Activity, p. 23

 Access for Students Acquiring English
• Reteaching Activity, p. 129

OBJECTIVE

Students work cooperatively and individually to explore the challenge of leading a tour of the Ganges River.

 Block Scheduling

PROCEDURE

For the History Challenge and the first option of the Math Challenge have students form groups of four or five and divide the work among the groups. For the remaining challenges, students may work in pairs or individually.

HISTORY CHALLENGE

Class Time 50 minutes

To help students as they research the history of the Ganges River, suggest they:

• consult the text and seek outside sources.

• focus only on major events or key attractions.

Possible Solutions

Major historical events that students might include on the time line include: ancient civilizations, the Maurya and Gupta dynasties, the arrival of the Muslims and the Mongols, the Mughal Empire, the rule of the British, Gandhi and independence. The travel brochure should include sites of interest such as palaces, archeological digs, dams, temples, and other holy places.

Tour the Ganges River

You are a guide leading a group tour of the Ganges River in India and Bangladesh. Since ancient times, this great river has been central to Indian life and culture. The Ganges rises in an ice cave in the Himalayas and flows southeast across a wide plain into the Bay of Bengal. As it nears the coast, the river splits into many channels—the "Mouths of the Ganges"—which have built up a huge delta. You want your tour group to understand the river's importance over the centuries.

COOPERATIVE LEARNING On these pages are challenges you will encounter as you plan your tour of the Ganges. Working in a small group, choose one of these challenges. Divide the work among group members. Look in the Data File for helpful information. Keep in mind that you will present your solution to the class.

HISTORY CHALLENGE

"So much has happened in the Ganges region . . ."

To start your tour, give your group an overview of the Ganges and its place in history. So much has happened in the Ganges region; for centuries, cities and villages along the Ganges have been centers of trade, industry, and religion. How can you give your group a sense of place? What should the group learn from this trip? Choose one of these options. Use the Data File for help.

ACTIVITIES

1. Choose one city or region along the Ganges. Make a time line of major events that took place there, starting with its early history.
2. Design a travel brochure for a city in the Ganges Basin. Include a list of historical monuments and other attractions.

Standards for Evaluation

HISTORY CHALLENGE

Option 1 Time lines should
• include major historical events.
• accurately represent the events.

Option 2 Travel brochures should
• highlight the major sites of historical, religious, or artistic importance.

MATH CHALLENGE

Option 1 Itineraries should
• include sites with historical, artistic, or religious significance.
• allocate reasonable time for each visit.

Option 2 The answer:
• the trip will take just under 8 hours going at

11.5 miles an hour.

CIVICS CHALLENGE

Option 1 The editorial should
• emphasize the historical, religious, and environmental importance of the Ganges River.

Option 2 The letter should
• reflect the importance of a clean river.

MATH CHALLENGE

"... plan a travel schedule ... and keep to it."

Along the course of the Ganges are many historic cities and other attractions. One important part of a tour guide's job is to plan a travel schedule, or itinerary, and keep to it. Your trip is scheduled to take about four weeks. How will you plan your river journey? How will you divide your time? Choose one of these options to present information, using the map and the Data File for help.

ACTIVITIES

1. Prepare a four-week itinerary for the Ganges tour. List the places your group will visit and the time you will spend at each of them.

2. By riverboat, your trip from Kanpur to Allahabad—a distance of about 115 miles—takes about ten hours. After a stop for sightseeing, you leave Allahabad at 11:00 P.M. Your next stop is Varanasi, about 90 miles downriver. If you travel at the same speed as before, will you get to Varanasi in time for breakfast?

Brahmaputra

Brahmaputra

INDIA

BANGLADESH

Hugli

Mouths of the Ganges

Kolkata ●

Bay of Bengal

Activity Wrap-Up

As a group, review your solution to the challenge you selected. Then present your solution to the class.

DATA FILE

THE GANGES

- **Length:** 1,557 mi.
- Headwaters in Himalayas: **Alaknanda** and **Bhagirathi** are main streams; other tributaries enter along river's course.
- Ganges Basin is one of the most densely populated areas in the world.

Major Tributaries

- **Yamuna:** flows from Himalayas past Delhi and Agra.
- **Brahmaputra** (also called Jamuna): joins Ganges in Bangladesh to form delta.

Important Sites in the Ganges Basin

- **Patna:** center of Asoka's empire (third century B.C.).
- **Agra:** on Yamuna River, site of **Taj Mahal**; once capital of Mogul Empire.
- **Allahabad:** at junction of Yamuna and Ganges rivers; a holy place to Hindus.
- **Varanasi** (Benares): Hindu holy city; pilgrims come to bathe in the river.
- **Delhi/New Delhi:** on Yamuna River, India's capital city; once a Mogul capital.
- **Kolkata (Calcutta):** on Hugli River, major channel of the Ganges; was capital of British India, now capital of West Bengal.
- **Dhaka:** capital of Bangladesh.

INDIA

Population: 1.01 billion; population density: 799/sq. mi.; 28 percent urban.

Area: about 1.3 million sq. mi.

BANGLADESH

Population: 129.2 million; population density: 2,324/sq. mi.; 24 percent urban.

Area: 55,600 sq. mi.

To learn more about the Ganges River, go to

RESEARCH LINKS
CLASSZONE.COM

MATH CHALLENGE

Class time 50 minutes

Suggest that students use a simple map to indicate the places on the itinerary they would like to visit and then plan times based on their maps.

Possible Solution

An itinerary along the Ganges River might include some of the following locations: the glacier which is one source of the river, government buildings in Delhi, the holy bathing places in Allahabad and Varanasi, the Taj Mahal in Agra, remains of British Empire in Kolkata.

ALTERNATIVE CHALLENGE...
CIVICS CHALLENGE

The Ganges River basin is the home of more than 400 million people. All of these people and the industries that support their economy are the source of terrible pollution in the river. Chemicals from the leather industry, fertilizers, and pesticides from farms, and even untreated sewage are dumped into the river every day. Although efforts are being made to clean the river, they are not sufficient.

- Write an editorial explaining why the Ganges River should be cleaned.
- Write a letter to the Indian Ministry of Environment in support of efforts to clean the river.

Activity Wrap-Up

To help students evaluate their challenge solutions, have them make a grid with criteria like the one shown. Then have them rate each solution on a scale from 1 to 5, with 1 representing the lowest score and 5 the highest.

Attentiveness to historical/ religious/artistic significance	1	2	3	4	5
Creativity	1	2	3	4	5
Audience impact	1	2	3	4	5
Overall effectiveness	1	2	3	4	5

 Economies

SECTION OBJECTIVES

1. To describe economic development in South Asian countries

2. To analyze the role of the Green Revolution

SKILLBUILDER
• Interpreting a Map, p. 419

CRITICAL THINKING
• Identifying Problems, p. 417
• Analyzing Causes, p. 418

FOCUS & MOTIVATE
WARM-UP

Analyzing Effects Have students read <u>Dateline</u> and examine the photograph. Discuss the role of AID.

1. How might the strategy of making money available for small loans help the economy?

2. In what other ways might AID be important in rural areas?

INSTRUCT: Objective ❶

Developing Economies

• How do most people in South Asia make a living? traditional farming and herding

• How are the economies of Bhutan and Nepal similar? Both are isolated and accept financial help in order to modernize their economies.

• What is the wealthiest country in the region? Pakistan

 In-depth Resources: Unit 5
• Guided Reading Worksheet, p. 15

 Reading Study Guide
(Spanish and English), pp. 128–129

MAIN IDEA

The countries of South Asia have economies that have changed and grown in the last century.

WHY IT MATTERS NOW

As the economies of South Asia's countries grow, these nations have more influence on the economies of their neighbors.

DATELINE

MANTHINI, INDIA, JULY 1999—
In February, two people from the Association for India's Development (AID) came to our village. They talked to the women about saving money. Since then the women have saved 4,500 rupees.

Today, the people from AID returned. They talked to the women about making the money they saved available for loans. Other women can borrow money to start a new business or to improve a business. Everyone agrees that this new project will make our village a better place to live.

Place • Indian women learn how to improve their lives from AID. ▲

Developing Economies ❶

Organizations like AID are helping the developing nations of South Asia to move from traditional economies to market economies. Most people in South Asia live in rural areas. They have low incomes and literacy levels and depend on traditional farming methods to survive. They are farmers, shepherds, and herders.

416 CHAPTER 14

Program Resources

 In-depth Resources: Unit 5
• Guided Reading
  Worksheet, p. 15
• Reteaching Activity, p. 24

 Reading Study Guide
(Spanish and English),
pp. 128–129

 Formal Assessment
• Section Quiz, p. 210

Integrated Assessment
• Rubric for writing a letter

Outline Map Activities

 Access for Students Acquiring English
• Guided Reading
  Worksheet, p. 123

Technology Resources
classzone.com

TEST-TAKING RESOURCES
↪ Strategies for Test Preparation
↪ Test Practice Transparencies
ⓘ Online Test Practice

Human-Environment Interaction • This farmer in Afghanistan uses a plow and an ox, just as his ancestors did. ◄

Afghanistan In the 1960s and 1970s, Afghanistan worked to strengthen its economy. It built roads, dams, power plants, and factories. It provided education to more people and began irrigation projects. Then Afghanistan was invaded by the Soviet Union. The invasion was followed by civil war. Afghanistan has not returned to the improvement program of four decades ago. Today, Afghanistan is one of the poorest countries in the world. Most people work on farms, raising livestock. Only 12 percent of the land in Afghanistan is arable, and only half of that is cultivated in any year. Wheat is the chief crop, though cotton, fruits, and nuts are also grown.

Bangladesh Agriculture is a major part of the economy in Bangladesh. About three-fifths of the workers are farmers. The most important cash crops are rice, jute, and tea. Bangladesh supplies one-fifth of the world's **jute,** a fibrous plant used to make twine, bags, sacks, and burlap. Irrigation projects have reached many farms, but the monsoon rains bring floods and disaster to many farmers.

Bangladesh has almost no mineral resources, so its few industries are based on agricultural products, such as bamboo, which is made into paper at mills.

Bhutan and Nepal The economies of Bhutan and Nepal are similar. Until the 1950s and 1960s, both countries were largely isolated from the outside world. There were no highways or automobiles. Bhutan did not have a currency. People bartered for goods rather than using money. Since that time, with financial help from other countries and organizations, both countries have been working to modernize their economies. For example, they have built major roads allowing the transport of goods and people, especially tourists.

The Maldives The Maldives is one of the world's poorest nations. The majority of its workers fish or build or repair boats. Tourism has become an important industry as well. Nearly all the food people eat is imported, including rice, which is one of the main foods in people's diets.

India and Its Neighbors **417**

Reading Social Studies

A. Making Inferences How might the monsoon season affect a subsistence farmer?

Reading Social Studies
A. Possible Answer
The monsoon rains might flood the land and destroy a farmer's entire crop.

MORE ABOUT...
Jute

Jute is one of the least expensive natural fibers to produce and is second only to cotton in its variety of uses. Jute is used to make burlap sacks and cloth for wrapping bales. It can be woven into material for curtains, chair coverings, and carpets. The fibers of jute can also be blended with other fibers to make twine and rope.

CRITICAL THINKING ACTIVITY

Identifying Problems Ask students to imagine they are heading a development team for an organization such as AID in one of the countries in the region. Have them brainstorm to make a list of the major problems they will need to solve in order to help the country's economy, along with some possible answers. Encourage students to consider small-scale projects, such as micro-loans, as well as large-scale efforts.

Class Time 20 minutes

Activity Options

Interdisciplinary Link: Science

Class Time 30 minutes
Task Describing a monsoon
Purpose To learn about the causes, effects, locations, and features of monsoons

Supplies Needed
• Reference sources or Internet access
• Writing paper
• Pencils or pens

Block Scheduling

Activity Ask students to use the Internet or available reference sources to read about monsoons. Suggest that they focus their research on the causes of monsoons, effects of the heavy rains, locations of monsoons in the world, and special features of these storms. Ask students to take notes in the form of an outline and be prepared to share the data they have collected in a group discussion.

Teacher's Edition **417**

CRITICAL THINKING ACTIVITY

Analyzing Causes Ask students to review the information under the heading "Developing Economies" and think about the resources available to each country. Then discuss how the availability of resources affects the economy of each country. Encourage students to consider natural resources, geographic factors, work force, and so on.

Class Time 15 minutes

MORE ABOUT...
Sri Lanka

Sri Lanka is an island nation located off the southeast coast of India. Formerly known as Ceylon, Sri Lanka won its independence from Britain after World War II and changed its name in 1972. In the 19th century, the British government hired an agent in Brazil to gather seeds of wild rubber trees, which were then planted at Kew Gardens, near London. Seedlings from those plants were later taken to Sri Lanka and replanted in plantations, marking the start of a valuable world industry. Rubber continues to be an important product in Sri Lanka today.

INSTRUCT: Objective ②

The Green Revolution

• What were the effects of the Green Revolution? Farmers were introduced to more productive varieties of grains, pesticides, and new farming methods; they also learned how to handle surplus crops and how the use of chemicals damaged land and polluted rivers.

Human-Environment Interaction • **Many people in the Maldives earn a living by fishing.** ▲

Pakistan Pakistan is the richest country in South Asia. Half of its work force is employed in agriculture, forestry, and fishing. Pakistan is the third-largest exporter of rice in the world. Its important industries are fabric and clothing, sugar, paper, tobacco, and leather.

Sri Lanka Sri Lanka depends on agriculture and tourism. Its most important agricultural product is rice, followed by tea, rubber, and coconuts. Sri Lanka has not yet been able to benefit much economically from its many mineral resources.

India Although some regions of India have many valuable resources, millions of India's people are among the world's poorest. Most people work in agriculture. More than half of the farms are smaller than three acres. Farmers practice what is known as subsistence farming, which means they grow only enough food to live on. Rice and wheat are India's most important crops. Because many people do not eat meat, chickpeas and lentils are important sources of protein in the diet.

There is a growing information technology industry in India. **Information technology** includes computers, software, and the Internet. Since 1991, India's software exports have been doubling every year.

Human-Environment Interaction • **Village women plant rice, one of the chief crops in India. They carry the new rice shoots to the fields in flat baskets, which they then place on their backs as protection from the sun.** ▶

418 CHAPTER 14

Activity Options

Skillbuilder Mini-Lesson: Reading an Elevation Map   Block Scheduling

Explaining the Skill Remind students that an elevation map uses a key to show the elevation of land in relation to the level of the sea.

Applying the Skill In advance, choose an elevation map from the Unit Atlas. Have students use the following strategies to read the map:

1. Read the title of the map and identify the region shown on it.

2. Read the map key and identify the elevations each color shows.

3. Look at the labels on the map and identify the features shown.

4. Review the information and make a chart to show what you have learned.

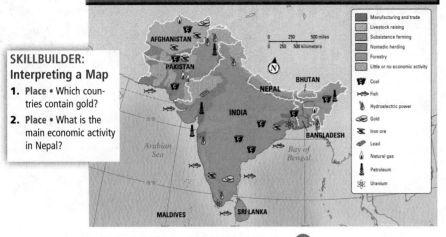

South Asia Economic Activities and Resources, 2000

Manufacturing and trade
Livestock raising
Subsistence farming
Nomadic herding
Forestry
Little or no economic activity

Coal
Fish
Hydroelectric power
Gold
Iron ore
Lead
Natural gas
Petroleum
Uranium

SKILLBUILDER:
Interpreting a Map
1. **Place** • Which countries contain gold?
2. **Place** • What is the main economic activity in Nepal?

The Green Revolution

Geography Skillbuilder Answers

1. Afghanistan, India

2. forestry

In the 1960s, the **Green Revolution** introduced farmers to varieties of grain that were more productive, the widespread use of pesticides, and different methods for farming. In India, farmers grew more rice and wheat than they needed. Much of this surplus was set aside in case of a poor growing season. Some was exported. The Green Revolution had some negative results too. The use of chemicals damaged the land and polluted rivers.

The cost of such new methods is too high for some small farmers. As a result, many farmers in South Asia still use old farming techniques despite their governments' efforts to introduce reform.

SECTION 3 ASSESSMENT

Terms & Names

1. **Identify:**   (a) jute   (b) information technology   (c) Green Revolution

Taking Notes

2. Use a chart like the one below to list the important economic activities of South Asian countries.

Country	Economic Activity

Main Ideas

3. (a) How do most people in the countries of South Asia make a living?

   (b) What new technology is becoming an important part of India's economy?

   (c) Why was the Green Revolution important in South Asia? What were its negative effects?

Critical Thinking

4. **Identifying Problems**

   What are the main problems faced by South Asian countries as they move from traditional economies to market economies?

   Think About
   - their natural resources
   - levels of economic development, including rates of poverty and literacy

ACTIVITY -OPTION- Choose a nation in South Asia. Imagine you are a government official applying to an international aid agency for help. Write a **letter** describing your economy and what it needs to develop further.

India and Its Neighbors **419**

Section 3 Assessment

1. Terms & Names

   a. jute, p. 417
   b. information technology, p. 418
   c. Green Revolution, p. 419

2. Taking Notes

Country	Economic Activity
Afghanistan	farming
Bangladesh	farming
Bhutan	tourism
Nepal	tourism
The Maldives	fishing, tourism
Pakistan	farming, fishing, industry
Sri Lanka	farming, tourism
India	farming, information technology, industry

3. Main Ideas

   a. Most people make a living by farming.
   b. information technology
   c. The Green Revolution was important because it helped farmers grow more crops. However, it also introduced the use of damaging chemicals.

4. Critical Thinking

   Possible Response Problems include the reliance on traditional farming, the inability to benefit from mineral resources, and the high illiteracy rate in rural areas.

   ACTIVITY OPTION

   📝 **Integrated Assessment**
   • Rubric for writing a letter

Teacher's Edition **419**

SECTION
4

The Culture of India

SECTION OBJECTIVES

1. To describe aspects of India's culture
2. To explore the variety of languages spoken in India
3. To explain the significance of religion and family in India

SKILLBUILDER
• Interpreting a Map, p. 421

FOCUS & MOTIVATE
WARM-UP

Making Inferences Have students read Dateline and discuss the importance of the Taj Mahal.

1. Why do you think the sight of the Taj Mahal brought the Shah to tears?
2. How do you think the Taj Mahal is thought of today?

INSTRUCT: Objective ❶

The Taj Mahal/ India and the Arts

• Why are the *Mahabharata* and the *Ramayana* so important? They have influenced all the arts; they tell about the growth of Hinduism.
• In what artistic industry do Indians lead the world? movies

 In-depth Resources: Unit 5
• Guided Reading Worksheet, p. 16

 Reading Study Guide
(Spanish and English), pp. 130–131

MAIN IDEA

India's rich cultural heritage has its roots in a long history and the influences of other cultures.

WHY IT MATTERS NOW

The languages, arts, and traditions of India, a country with over a billion people, have an international influence.

DATELINE

AGRA, NORTHERN INDIA, 1648
With tears in his eyes, Shah Jahan watched today as workers put the finishing touches on the Taj Mahal. The building is made of rare white marble and is decorated with semiprecious stones, such as lapis lazuli, crystal, and jade. The Taj Mahal is to be the tomb of Shah Jahan's wife, who died giving birth to their 14th child. "Some day, when I depart," Shah Jahan said, "we will lie here together forever."

Culture • The Taj Mahal has taken 20,000 workers 22 years to build. ▲

The Taj Mahal ❶

The Mughal emperor Shah Jahan built the **Taj Mahal** for his beloved wife, Mumtaz Mahal. This white marble building with its onion-shaped domes and thin towers is one of the finest examples of Islamic architecture in the world. Today, it is India's most famous building and a symbol of India's rich artistic heritage.

Program Resources

 In-depth Resources: Unit 5
• Guided Reading Worksheet, p. 16
• Reteaching Activity, p. 25

 Reading Study Guide
(Spanish and English), pp. 130–131

 Formal Assessment
• Section Quiz, p. 211

 Integrated Assessment
• Rubric for developing a plot

 Outline Map Activities

 Access for Students Acquiring English
• Guided Reading Worksheet, p. 124

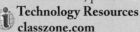 **Technology Resources**
classzone.com

┌─────────────────────────────────┐
│ **TEST-TAKING RESOURCES**   │
│ ➌ Strategies for Test Preparation │
│ ➌ Test Practice Transparencies   │
│ ⓘ Online Test Practice   │
└─────────────────────────────────┘

India and the Arts ❶

Literature Two great works of world literature come from India. One, the **Mahabharata** (MAH·huh·BAH·ruh·tuh), is an epic poem, which means that it tells a lengthy story, in a grand style, of one or more heroes. The *Ramayana* is another famous epic poem. Both the *Mahabharata* and the *Ramayana* have influenced painters, dancers, and other writers in India. Both are important because they tell about the growth of Hinduism.

Music and Film India has several styles of music, and each style is unique to a region of India. Music is played and sung in concerts, at parties, or in religious settings. Indians also love to see movies. India makes more films every year than any other country, including the United States. In rural areas, movie vans travel to villages to show films outdoors.

Culture • Long-necked stringed instruments, like the sitars (sih·TAHRS) shown here, are used to play North Indian classical music. ▲

The Languages of India ❷

The constitution of India now recognizes 18 official languages. However, Indians speak hundreds of other languages and dialects. A **dialect** is a regional variety of a language. Most languages in India come from one of two families: Indo-Aryan or Dravidian.

Geography Skillbuilder Answers

1. Andhra Pradesh, Karnataka, Tamil Nadu, Kerala, Goa

2. Hindi

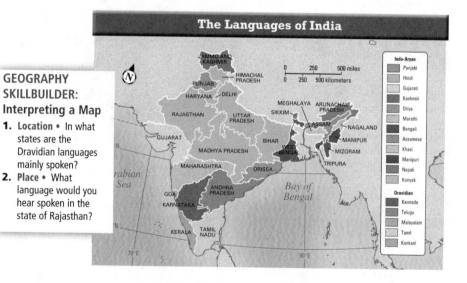

The Languages of India

Indo-Aryan
- Punjabi
- Hindi
- Gujarati
- Kashmiri
- Oriya
- Marathi
- Bengali
- Assamese
- Khasi
- Manipuri
- Nepali
- Konyak

Dravidian
- Kannada
- Telugu
- Malayalam
- Tamil
- Konkani

GEOGRAPHY SKILLBUILDER: Interpreting a Map

1. **Location** • In what states are the Dravidian languages mainly spoken?
2. **Place** • What language would you hear spoken in the state of Rajasthan?

India and Its Neighbors **421**

FOCUS

Interpre
understa
moderñ country or
Bangladesh, and the other nations
on the map on page 419. Ask individual students to locate spots on the map where each of the languages shown is spoken. Ask them to explain the geographical distribution of the two-language families. Which language is spoken most widely?

Possible Responses People who spoke Dravidian languages moved south as Indo-Aryan speakers moved into India. Hindi is most widely used.

Extension Have students find a chart showing the Indo-Aryan and Indo-European languages and trace the relationship between English and the languages of India.

INSTRUCT: Objective ❷

The Languages of India

- Which family of languages is spoken by the most people in India? Indo-Aryan

- Why has English become important in India? It was introduced by colonialism; it is the language of business, government, and science.

- Which people are more likely to speak English in India? people in business, government, and science

---

Activity Options

Differentiating Instruction: Students Acquiring English/ESL

Building Vocabulary Write the word *dialect* on the chalkboard and pronounce it. Have students read the first paragraph of "The Languages of India."

Guide students to use the context clues *regional* (relating to a particular area, especially a geographic one) and *variety* (lack of sameness; change) to help them understand the meaning of dialect.

Point out that several dialects of English are spoken in the United States. Discuss any dialects students might be familiar with from their region of the United States. Invite students to share examples of dialects in their native languages.

light on CULTURE

The *Mahabharata* is more than 100,000 verses long. The main tale is about the five royal Pandava brothers and their cousins, the Kauravas. Woven into that tale are many shorter episodes about the adventures of the Pandavas. This great Sanskrit epic was passed orally from generation to generation before it was eventually written down. It is still popular today.

INSTRUCT: Objective ❸

Religion in Daily Life/ The Family in India

- What religion do most people in India practice? Hinduism
- What is a dowry? money or property given by a bride's parents to her new husband and his family
- What foods are typical of an Indian meal? rice or flat bread, vegetables, beans or lentils

Reading Social Studies A. Possible Answers

Problems regarding community issues, playground and school situations, and one-on-one communication might all arise when neighbors speak different languages.

Thinking Critically Possible Answers

1. The poem was composed over an 800-year period.

2. Over time, different storytellers may have changed or exaggerated events in the stories.

The Indo-Aryan Language Family <u>**Indo-Aryan**</u> languages are related to the Indo-European language family, which comes from the ancient Aryan language Sanskrit and includes almost all European languages. Today, about three-fourths of the people in northern and central India speak Indo-Aryan languages.

The Dravidian Language Family About one-fourth of all Indians speak Dravidian languages. <u>**Dravidian**</u> was the language spoken centuries ago in India. As invaders moved into the north, the speakers of Dravidian moved south.

English English, which came to India with British colonialism, is spoken by less than 5 percent of the population. However, because it is the language of business, government, and science, English is important in India.

Religion in Daily Life ❸

Most people in India are Hindus. There are no rules dictating how Hinduism is practiced, nor is there one Hindu church. Many Hindus are vegetarians. Some Hindus perform daily rituals on behalf of their gods. The caste system, which is still in place in India, is less rigid than it once was.

Many Muslims who had been living in India moved to Pakistan and East Pakistan, now Bangladesh. Today, 14 percent of Indians are Muslim.

Reading Social Studies

A. Drawing Conclusions What problems might exist when neighbors speak different languages?

BACKGROUND

Look back to Chapters 8 and 13 to review what you read about Islam and Hinduism.

 **Spotlight on CULTURE**

The *Mahabharata* One of the greatest works of world literature comes from India. The epic poem the *Mahabharata* is the longest poem in the world. It was composed over a period of about 800 years, from about 400 B.C. to A.D. 400. The *Mahabharata* tells the story of two warring families, the five Pandava brothers (shown at right) and the Kauravas.

One famous section of the poem is called the *Bhagavad-Gita*. In this section, Arjuna, the leader of the Pandavas, receives good advice from his chariot driver, who is actually the god Krishna in disguise.

 THINKING CRITICALLY

1. **Clarifying** How do you know that more than one person must have created the *Mahabharata*?

2. **Making Inferences** What do you think might happen to the events in a story created like the *Mahabharata*?

Activity Options

Interdisciplinary Links: Language Arts/Drama

🅱 Block Scheduling

Class Time One class period

Task Reading aloud selected passages from the *Mahabharata*

Purpose To introduce students to an epic poem and familiarize them with some characters and events in the poem

Supplies Needed

- Copies of sections of the *Mahabharata*

Activity In advance, preview sections of the *Mahabharata* for readability and content; for example, the brothers' search for the castle of King Vaishravana. Make copies of chosen sections. Invite students to work in small groups to prepare and present an oral reading of one of the chosen sections. Ask students to distribute parts within their group and practice reading aloud before they read for the class.

The Family in India

Family is important to Indians. Often, several related families live together. Parents choose a bride or groom for their children from a family of the same caste. Parents may consider a potential mate's education, financial status, or even horoscope to help them make a decision.

Reading Social Studies

B. Analyzing Motives Why might parents want to arrange their child's marriage?

Parents prefer sons to daughters, partly because men have more power in this society. Women who have male children have greater influence in their families. These attitudes are beginning to change. Also, when a woman marries, her parents must provide a **dowry**, money or property given by a bride to her new husband and his family. This can be expensive, especially for rural families. As India modernizes, this practice, too, is beginning to change.

Family Meals A typical meal varies from region to region in India. In the south and east, a meal usually includes rice. In the north and northwest, people eat a flat bread called a *chapati* (chuh•PAH•tee). Along with rice or *chapatis*, a meal may include beans or lentils, some vegetables, and maybe yogurt. Chili peppers and other spices like cardamom, cinnamon, and cumin give the food extra flavor. Meat is rarely eaten, either because it is forbidden by religion or because it is so expensive.

Culture • A bride and groom circle a fire four times as part of a Hindu wedding ceremony. ▲

Reading Social Studies
B. Possible Answer
Parents might want to be sure that potential marriage partners are of the same caste educational or economic level.

Reading Social Studies Have students record information about the religions, languages, and cultures of India on the chart on page 402.

 Formal Assessment
• Section Quiz, p. 211

RETEACHING ACTIVITY

Divide the class into four groups and assign each group an aspect of India's culture. Have each group prepare a short oral report on that topic.

 In-depth Resources: Unit 5
• Reteaching Activity, p. 25

Access for Students Acquiring English
• Reteaching Activity, p. 131

SECTION 4 ASSESSMENT

Terms & Names

1. **Identify:**
   (a) Taj Mahal   (b) *Mahabharata*   (c) dialect   (d) Indo-Aryan
   (e) Dravidian   (f) dowry

Taking Notes

2. Use a spider map like the one below to list the unique traits of India's culture.

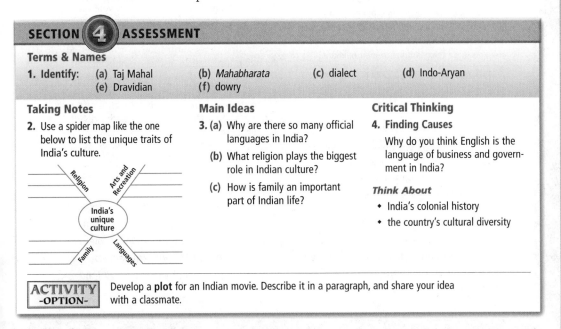

India's unique culture — Religion, Arts and Recreation, Languages, Family

Main Ideas

3. (a) Why are there so many official languages in India?

   (b) What religion plays the biggest role in Indian culture?

   (c) How is family an important part of Indian life?

Critical Thinking

4. **Finding Causes**

   Why do you think English is the language of business and government in India?

   Think About
   • India's colonial history
   • the country's cultural diversity

ACTIVITY -OPTION- Develop a **plot** for an Indian movie. Describe it in a paragraph, and share your idea with a classmate.

Section 4 Assessment

1. Terms & Names
  a. Taj Mahal, p. 420
  b. *Mahabharata*, p. 421
  c. dialect, p. 421
  d. Indo-Aryan, p. 422
  e. Dravidian, p. 422
  f. dowry, p. 423

2. Taking Notes

Family—traditional food, dowries; traditionally, males preferred

Languages—Indo-Aryan, Dravidian

India's unique culture

Arts and Recreation—music–sitar, literature–*Mahabharata*

Religion—Hindu, Muslim

3. Main Ideas
  a. There are so many languages because of the influence of many other cultures and countries.
  b. The Hindu religion plays the biggest role in Indian culture.
  c. Families live together and share meals, and parents choose potential spouses for their children.

4. Critical Thinking
Possible Response For many years, India was part of the British Empire, and English is spoken in the top private schools and universities.

ACTIVITY OPTION

 Integrated Assessment
• Rubric for developing a plot

SKILLBUILDER

Understanding Point of View

Defining the Skill

Ask students to think about their own opinions or beliefs on a particular topic such as school rules, acceptable sports behavior, or the environment. Then discuss how others might have a different point of view on the same subject. Lead the entire class in a discussion about the importance of trying to understand other points of view.

Applying the Skill

How to Understand Point of View Guide students through each strategy, making sure they understand the importance of looking for statements that reveal a personal point of view and clues about why an individual might have developed that point of view.

Write a Summary

Discuss the paragraph that summarizes the differing points of view held by Gandhi and Nehru. Ask students to identify the phrase that signals an opposing point of view. on the other hand

Practicing the Skill

Have students infer two points of view that farmers might have toward the Green Revolution, contrasting that of a poor, traditional farmer with that of a more progressive one. Still another point of view might come from environmentalists. Suggest that students who need further practice with the skills analyze the point of view of a newspaper editorial or a personal essay.

   In-depth Resources: Unit 5
   • Skillbuilder Practice, p. 20

SKILLBUILDER

Understanding Point of View

▶▶ Defining the Skill

The phrase *point of view* refers to the particular opinions or beliefs that a person holds. Education, religious beliefs, and life experiences all contribute to a person's point of view. Understanding point of view makes it possible to understand and explain a historical figure's opinions and actions.

▶▶ Applying the Skill

The passage to the right explains the differences and similarities between Mohandas Gandhi and Jawaharlal Nehru, who was the prime minister of India from 1947 until 1964. Use the strategies listed below to help you analyze their points of view.

How to Understand Point of View

Strategy ❶ Look for statements that reveal a person's point of view on a particular subject. Gandhi believed that government could not guarantee a person's rights. Nehru, on the other hand, had faith in the power of government.

Strategy ❷ Look for clues about why people hold the opinions they do. In these paragraphs you learn about Gandhi's and Nehru's childhoods, their educations, and their experiences as young men. How do these things influence their opinions?

Strategy ❸ Summarize the information given for each person that explains their opposing opinions.

Write a Summary

Writing a summary will help you understand differing points of view. The paragraph below and to the right summarizes the passage about Gandhi and Nehru.

▶▶ Practicing the Skill

Turn to page 419 in Section 3. Read "The Green Revolution." Then write a summary like the one on the right to understand the farmers' opposing points of view.

INDIAN INDEPENDENCE

Two of the men who led India in its struggle for independence from Great Britain, Mohandas Gandhi and Jawaharlal Nehru, had different ideas about how a fair and just society should be achieved.

❷ Gandhi grew up in a rural area of India, where he saw how difficult life was for many Indians. Through hard work and study he became a lawyer. Gandhi then lived in South Africa, a country that discriminated against people because of race. For 20 years he worked for the rights of Indian workers there. ❶ He saw how important it was for everyone in a country to have equal rights. At the same time, he did not trust that a government could provide people with those rights. He felt that each person individually had to seek ways to live in a fair and honorable manner.

❷ Nehru's father was a respected and wealthy lawyer, and Nehru had many privileges while growing up. Like Gandhi, Nehru went to England to study law. But when he finished his studies, he traveled around Europe, seeing other societies and learning about other governments. ❶ He came to believe that a government could be successful in granting its people equal rights and that it could do so by dividing up the land among all the people.

❸

Gandhi believed that government could not grant equal rights. He felt that each person, individually, could work for the good of the whole. Nehru, on the other hand, felt that government could grant equality by making sure that everyone had land.

Career Connections: Mediator

Encourage students who enjoy understanding different points of view to find out about careers that utilize this skill. For example, when people or groups are having a serious dispute, a mediator is a person who tries to help them solve their conflict. A mediator needs to understand all points of view in the conflict in order to do his or her job well.

 Block Scheduling

1. Suggest that students find out the specific tasks of mediators. Explain that mediators help people solve conflicts without favoring one side over the other.

2. What skills and training does a person need to become a mediator? Help students learn about the qualifications needed and certifications available for would-be mediators.

3. Invite students to share their findings in booklet form.

Pakistan

TERMS & NAMES
Mangla Dam
Tarbela Dam
Punjabi
Sindhi
Urdu

MAIN IDEA

Conflict between Muslims and Hindus in colonial times led to the creation of Pakistan.

WHY IT MATTERS NOW

Political and religious conflict continues to make this region unstable.

SECTION OBJECTIVES

1. To identify events and conflicts in Pakistan's history
2. To describe the four regions of Pakistan
3. To describe the languages and religion of Pakistan
4. To analyze current conflicts between India and Pakistan

SKILLBUILDER
• Interpreting a Map, p. 427

CRITICAL THINKING
• Distinguishing Fact from Opinion, p. 426
• Recognizing Effects, p. 428

FOCUS & MOTIVATE
WARM-UP

Making Inferences After students read Dateline, have them discuss these questions:

1. Why was the founding of a Muslim nation so important to Mohammed Ali Jinnah?
2. What changes might occur in Pakistan?

INSTRUCT: Objective ❶

History of Pakistan

• Where was Pakistan's oldest civilization? Indus River valley

• Before independence, what groups controlled the territory that is now Pakistan? Muslim kingdoms, Mughal Empire, Great Britain

• Why was the Muslim League formed? to give Muslims political power against Hindus

 In-depth Resources: Unit 5
• Guided Reading Worksheet, p. 16

 Reading Study Guide
(Spanish and English), pp. 132–133

DATELINE (EXTRA)

PAKISTAN, AUGUST 14, 1947

Today, as Pakistan becomes a new Muslim nation, Governor-General Mohammed Ali Jinnah celebrates quietly. The former leader of the Muslim League is dying of tuberculosis and lung cancer. "I have lived to see an independent and free Muslim nation," he says, eyes sparking fire. "It has been a long, hard fight, but it has been worth it."

Place • Mohammed Ali Jinnah was the leader of the Muslim League. ▶

History of Pakistan ❶

Great Britain granted independence to Pakistan and India on the same day. Both South Asian countries have a long and sometimes common history. The Indus River flows through eastern Pakistan, from the mountains in the north to the Arabian Sea. This river valley was the site of one of the world's oldest civilizations. Over time, invaders and immigrants crossed the Himalayas and the Hindu Kush Mountains to reach this fertile area.

India and Its Neighbors **425**

Program Resources

 In-depth Resources: Unit 5
• Guided Reading Worksheet, p. 17
• Reteaching Activity, p. 26

Reading Study Guide
(Spanish and English), pp. 132–133

 Formal Assessment
• Section Quiz, p. 212

 Integrated Assessment
• Rubric for drawing a political cartoon

 Outline Map Activities

 Access for Students Acquiring English
• Guided Reading Worksheet, p. 125

 Technology Resources
classzone.com

TEST-TAKING RESOURCES
⚓ Strategies for Test Preparation
⚓ Test Practice Transparencies
🕹 Online Test Practice

CRITICAL THINKING ACTIVITY

Distinguishing Fact from Opinion After students read "History of Pakistan," ask them to identify the following statements as examples of fact or opinion:

• Since A.D. 712, Muslim ideology and culture has existed in the region now known as Pakistan. fact

• Mohammed Ali Jinnah and the Muslim League supported the creation of an independent state. fact

• If the British had not set up trading posts in this region, the Hindus would not have gained control. opinion

Then ask students to take turns formulating statements about the material in the section. Challenge the rest of the class to identify the statements as either fact or opinion.

Class Time 10 minutes

Culture •
The city of Mohenjo-Daro thrived over 4,000 years ago in the Indus River valley. ◄

In A.D. 712, Arab Muslims brought Islam to the Indus Valley region. Then, around the year 1000, Muslims from Central Asia built their own kingdom in the Indus River valley. Lahore (luh·HAWR), today one of the biggest cities in Pakistan, was the capital of their kingdom and a major center of Muslim culture.

The British Influence In the 1600s, the British East India Company set up trading posts in India, which then included the region that is now Pakistan. When the Mughal Empire, which had been ruling India, grew weak in the 1700s, the company took control of India.

With British rule, the Muslims lost power in the government, and over time, the Hindus gained power. The Indian National Congress was controlled by Hindus, so Muslims formed the Muslim League in 1906 as a way of keeping some political power. As India moved closer to independence from Great Britain, the Muslim League, led by Mohammed Ali Jinnah, called for an independent Muslim state.

Pakistan Becomes a Nation Differences between Hindus and Muslims led to violence. Neither the British nor the Indian National Congress could find a way to settle the differences between the two groups. So on August 14, 1947, at the same time that India gained independence, Pakistan was declared a separate Muslim nation. Millions of Muslims living in India moved to Pakistan, and Hindus in Pakistan moved to India.

426 CHAPTER 14

Activity Options

Multiple Learning Styles: Visual

Block Scheduling

Class Time One class period

Task Creating a time line of events in Pakistan's history

Purpose To see the events in Pakistan's history in chronological order

Supplies Needed
• Textbook
• Unlined paper
• Pencils and markers

Activity Have students work with partners to create time lines of events in Pakistan's history. Review the features of a time line and remind students to work from left to right when adding dates and events. Suggest that students decide how many events they will include and plan how much space each entry will take before they begin to write. Encourage students to illustrate their time lines.

Pakistan Divides When Pakistan became a nation, it included two regions—East Pakistan and West Pakistan—separated from each other by 1,000 miles. This distance made Pakistan a difficult country to rule. Although most people of East and West Pakistan were Muslim, they had many differences. Many East Pakistanis were angry that West Pakistan was in charge of the government. War broke out between East and West Pakistan. When the war ended, over a million people had lost their lives. In 1971, East Pakistan became the country of Bangladesh.

The Land of Pakistan ②

Pakistan (once West Pakistan) is divided into four provinces: Baluchistan, North-West Frontier, Punjab, and Sindh. Most Pakistanis live in the northeast province of Punjab. Punjab is where the capital, Islamabad, is located.

Western and northern Pakistan are dry and mountainous, with few river valleys suitable for farming. The provinces of Sindh and Punjab are less mountainous, and although there is not much rain, the Indus River flows through them. About two-thirds of the people in Pakistan are farmers and herders who irrigate their land with water from the Indus River.

Pakistan, 2000

NORTHERN AREAS

NORTH-WEST FRONTIER

FEDERALLY ADMINISTERED TRIBAL AREAS

KASHMIR (disputed)

Islamabad ✪

AZAD KASHMIR

ISLAMABAD CAPITAL TERRITORY

Indus R.

Lahore •

PUNJAB

BALUCHISTAN

Indus R.

Indus R.

SINDH

Arabian Sea

Karachi •

| 0 | 100 | 200 miles |
| 0 | 100 | 200 kilometers |

✪ National capital
• Other city
▨ Province boundary

GEOGRAPHY SKILLBUILDER: Interpreting a Map

1. **Location** • In which province is Karachi located?
2. **Location** • Karachi is the most populous city in Pakistan. Why do you think that is?

Geography Skillbuilder Possible Answers

1. Sind

2. It is on the seacoast.

INSTRUCT: Objective 3

Language and Religion

• What are the most common of Pakistan's many languages? Punjabi and Sindhi

• Which people are more likely to speak the official language, Urdu? people who have gone to school or work in government

• In spite of other differences, what factor unites most Pakistanis? religion of Islam

CRITICAL THINKING ACTIVITY

Recognizing Effects Review the number of languages spoken in Pakistan. Then ask students to identify the problems that might result from this situation.

Class Time 15 minutes

River Power In 1967, Pakistan finished building the **Mangla Dam** on the Jhelum River in northeast Pakistan. The dam was built to control floodwaters and to provide hydroelectricity. In 1976, Pakistan opened one of the world's largest dams, the **Tarbela Dam**. Located on the Indus River, it is used for flood control and irrigation. In 1994, the Tarbela Dam began to produce hydroelectricity as well.

Connections to Technology

Drawbacks to Dams Dams can be useful for many things, such as irrigation and the production of electricity. Pakistan's Mangla Dam has stopped floods from destroying harvests (see below). Dams can also have negative effects. When a dam is built, hundreds of thousands of people may be forced to move because water that is held back by the dam covers nearby land and homes.

Fertile land can become unproductive because it becomes water-logged or because the salinity, or salt content, increases. Water has salt in it, and the salt stays behind in the soil. Over time, the salt content increases, and few plants will then grow in the soil. Wildlife suffers when rising waters disturb their natural habitats. In many countries, including Pakistan and India, there has been widespread opposition to dam building.

Language and Religion 3

Language divides the people of Pakistan, but the religion of Islam unites them. Each of Pakistan's four provinces has a unique culture with its own customs and languages.

Languages in Pakistan There are more than 20 languages spoken in Pakistan, of which **Punjabi** and **Sindhi** are the most common. Punjabi is spoken mostly in rural areas, and it is usually not written. **Urdu,** which is Pakistan's official language, is taught in schools. Students also learn their regional language. No single language is spoken by everyone in Pakistan, and in every province many different languages are spoken.

Movies made in Pakistan are usually in Punjabi or Urdu. The most popular newspapers are in Urdu, Sindhi, or English. This variety of languages has caused conflict among Pakistanis.

Culture • To read all the signs in Lahore, you would need to know several languages. ◄

428 CHAPTER 14

Religion in Pakistan The country's official name is the Islamic Republic of Pakistan. More than 97 percent of Pakistanis are Muslim. Public schools base their teaching on Islam. Except in the homes of the wealthy and educated, women follow the rules of purdah.

Vocabulary

purdah:
the practice of keeping women secluded

Modern Conflict in Pakistan

In 1947, when India and Pakistan became independent, each nation claimed the region of Kashmir. Find Kashmir on the map on page 427. This region is important to both nations because of its water resources. India and Pakistan have failed to reach an agreement about the future of Kashmir. Within South Asia, Hindus and Muslims have fought over whether Kashmir should join India or Pakistan or become independent.

Relations between Pakistan and India grew increasingly tense in 1998 when both nations tested nuclear weapons and then refused to sign a nuclear test-ban treaty. Since then, both nations have tested nuclear weapons and relations have not improved, though efforts continue to be made by Pakistan and India, with help from other nations.

Culture • **Benazir Bhutto became the leader of Pakistan in 1988. She was the first Muslim woman ever elected to lead an Islamic state.** ▲

SECTION 5 ASSESSMENT

Terms & Names

1. Identify: (a) Mangla Dam (b) Tarbela Dam (c) Punjabi
(d) Sindhi (e) Urdu

Taking Notes

2. Use a chart like the one below to outline the history of Pakistan from its earliest beginnings to its creation as a modern nation in 1947.

Event 1 → Event 2 → Event 3 →
Event 4 → Event 5 → Pakistan is declared a nation.

Main Ideas

3. (a) Why was Pakistan created in 1947?

(b) Why are rivers an important natural resource in Pakistan?

(c) What religion do most Pakistanis follow?

Critical Thinking

4. **Drawing Conclusions**

Why do you think it is important for India and Pakistan to solve the problem of Kashmir peacefully?

Think About

• the results of conflicts between India and Pakistan

• the reason relations between the two countries grew worse in 1998

ACTIVITY -OPTION- Draw a **political cartoon** that shows how the use of so many languages affects Pakistan.

INSTRUCT: Objective ❹

Modern Conflict in Pakistan

• Why is the region of Kashmir important to both India and Pakistan? because of its water resources

• What caused tensions between Pakistan and India to increase in 1998? nuclear weapons testing by both nations

ASSESS & RETEACH

Reading Social Studies Have students complete the chart on page 402.

 Formal Assessment
• Section Quiz, p. 212

RETEACHING ACTIVITY

Divide the class into small groups. Have students create charts in which they list details about the history, land, religion, languages, and modern conflicts in Pakistan.

 In-depth Resources: Unit 5
• Reteaching Activity, p. 25

Access for Students Acquiring English
• Reteaching Activity, p. 132

Section 5 Assessment

1. Terms & Names
a. Mangla Dam, p. 428
b. Tarbela Dam, p. 428
c. Punjabi, p. 428
d. Sindhi, p. 428
e. Urdu, p. 428

2. Taking Notes

A.D. 712 Muslims bring Islam to Indus valley → A.D. 1000 Muslims build kingdom in present-day location of Pakistan

1600s British East India Company sets up trading posts in India → 1700s British East India Company assumes control of India

1906 Muslims form Muslim League

3. Main Ideas
a. Muslims wanted their own country, independent from primarily Hindu India.
b. Rivers provide irrigation and hydroelectricity.
c. Most Pakistanis are Muslim.

4. Critical Thinking

Possible Response The two countries have had many conflicts in the past, but now that both have nuclear weapons, it is even more important to reach a peaceful or diplomatic solution.

ACTIVITY OPTION

 Integrated Assessment
• Rubric for drawing a political cartoon

TERMS & NAMES

1. Mughal Empire, p. 404
2. Mohandas Gandhi, p. 406
3. Indira Gandhi, p. 412
4. *panchayat*, p. 412
5. jute, p. 417
6. Green Revolution, p. 419
7. dialect, p. 421
8. dowry, p. 423
9. Mangla Dam, p. 428
10. Sindhi, p. 428

REVIEW QUESTIONS

Possible Responses

1. established trade between Great Britain and countries in East and Southeast Asia and ports on the coast of India, paved the way for British rule
2. encouraged nonviolent resistance as a means toward independence
3. parliamentary, constitutional monarchy, republic
4. the right to vote; freedom of speech and religion
5. changing from traditional to market economies
6. money and training are given to improve farming and irrigation techniques, build roads, support the information technology industry
7. eighteen official languages and many more dialects; Indo-Aryan languages come from the ancient Sanskrit brought by the Aryans to Northern India; Dravidian languages were spoken centuries ago in India
8. Related families often live together in the same household; marriages are made between families in the same caste.
9. formed to set Muslims apart from Hindus in India; led to establishment of Pakistan as a Muslim state
10. Indus River irrigates farmland and provides hydroelectricity.

ASSESSMENT

TERMS & NAMES

Explain the significance of each of the following:

1. Mughal Empire
2. Mohandas Gandhi
3. Indira Gandhi
4. *panchayat*
5. jute
6. Green Revolution
7. dialect
8. dowry
9. Mangla Dam
10. Sindhi

REVIEW QUESTIONS

History *(pages 403–407)*
1. How did the East India Company influence India's history?
2. What was Mohandas Gandhi's contribution to India's independence?

Governments *(pages 409–413)*
3. What kinds of governments do the nations of South Asia have?
4. What rights did India's 1950 constitution give some people?

Economies *(pages 416–419)*
5. How are the economies of South Asian nations changing?
6. What is being done to improve the economies of South Asia?

The Culture of India *(pages 420–423)*
7. What languages are spoken in India and why?
8. What role does family play in the lives of most Indians?

Pakistan *(pages 425–429)*
9. What was the Muslim League, and what did it accomplish?
10. How has Pakistan taken advantage of its natural resources?

CRITICAL THINKING

Sequencing Events
1. Using your completed chart from "Reading Social Studies," p. 402, explain why India's independence was inevitable.

Evaluating Decisions
2. Based on what you know about India-Pakistan relations since 1947, was the partition of Pakistan a good idea?

Forming and Supporting Opinions
3. What is your opinion of Gandhi's philosophy of nonviolence?

Visual Summary

History 1

- The early invasion of India by Muslims sowed the seeds of conflict that continues today.
- Britain's influence in the region lasted from the 17th century until Indian independence in 1947.

Governments 2
- Most South Asian countries are republics that became independent from British rule in the 20th century.

Economies 3
- The region's countries have traditional economies in which most people are farmers or market economies in which most people make money and buy what they need.

The Culture of India 4

- The diversity of cultures in India has its roots in a long history.
- Family plays an important role in the lives of most Indians.

Pakistan 5
- Pakistan is united by the common religion of Islam.
- Pakistan's history has been marked by conflict with other peoples in South Asia.

CRITICAL THINKING: Possible Responses

1. Sequencing Events
India had a long history of occupation and cultural mixing, ending with control by the British Empire. Conflicts between Hindus and Muslims led each to want to go their own way. Most world empires were weakened after World War I; Gandhi's leadership supplied the final step to independence.

2. Evaluating Decisions
Students may say that the partition was a good attempt, but that the two countries may always be at odds due to religious differences.

3. Forming and Supporting Opinions
Students may recognize the effectiveness of Gandhi's philosophy of nonviolence and support it. They should provide valid arguments for their opinion.

SOCIAL STUDIES SKILLBUILDER

"[A]dvance is certain when people are liberated and educated. . . . Conquest of illiteracy comes first."

John Kenneth Galbraith

Country	Literacy Rate	Gross Domestic Product (GDP) per capita
Sri Lanka	90 percent	$3,800
India	52 percent	$1,600
Afghanistan	32 percent	$800

SKILLBUILDER: Understanding Point of View

1. How does the table support the ideas expressed in the quotation?
2. If a different table showed you that Afghanistan's GDP per capita was $1,600, what might you conclude?

FOCUS ON GEOGRAPHY

1. **Location** • According to this population density map, which parts of India have the most people?
2. **Human-Environment Interaction** • What is likely to happen if India's population continues its rapid growth?

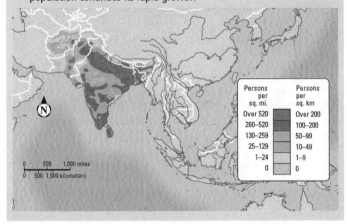

Persons per sq. mi.	Persons per sq. km
Over 520	Over 200
260–520	100–200
130–259	50–99
25–129	10–49
1–24	1–9
0	0

CHAPTER PROJECTS

Interdisciplinary Projects: Architecture

Making a Diorama Choose one of the buildings or cities described in the chapter. Find out more about it. Make a diorama showing the inside of the building or the layout of the city you have chosen.

Cooperative Learning Activity

Designing a Travel Brochure With a group of three to five students, design a travel brochure for someone who is visiting South Asia for the first time. Include details about the region's history, geography, governments, economies, and cultures.

- Take on the roles of editor, art director, and writers.
- Work on a rough draft of the text, a layout of the brochure, and ideas for photographs.
- Share your completed brochure with the class.

INTERNET ACTIVITY

Use the Internet to research the current leaders of India, Pakistan, and Afghanistan. These may be individuals or groups. Focus on their beliefs and their ideals—what they hope for their countries. Find a statement from each leader that you think best expresses beliefs and ideals.

Writing About Geography Write a report about what you have learned and present it to the class. Include a table showing the leaders of each country. List the Web sites you used to prepare your report.

For Internet links to support this activity, go to

 **RESEARCH LINKS**
CLASSZONE.COM

India and Its Neighbors **431**

CHAPTER PROJECTS

Interdisciplinary Projects: Architecture

Making a Diorama Suggest that students consider a traditional or a bird's-eye view for their dioramas. Complete projects should include significant features representative of the chosen building or city. Reports should "walk" the viewer through the site.

Cooperative Learning Activity

Designing a Travel Brochure Have students focus their brochures on one or two countries in the region. If possible, distribute examples of travel brochures for students to examine, and discuss features common to them. Completed brochures should be visually attractive and include information about the history, geography, government, economy, and culture of the chosen countries.

INTERNET ACTIVITY

Brainstorm possible search engines and Web sites that students might explore. Encourage students to focus their research on the leaders' beliefs and ideals.

Remind students that their reports should include a chart in which they list the name of each leader and statements describing his or her beliefs and hopes for the future.

Skills Answers

Social Studies Skillbuilder
Possible Responses

1. The countries with higher literacy rates have larger GDPs.
2. You might conclude that only a very high literacy rate, such as 90 percent, is effective in increasing economic development.

Focus On Geography
Possible Responses

1. The Ganges River valley, the seacoast
2. Greater population densities in marginal areas, more stress on resources and the environment

OBJECTIVE

Students analyze a selection that describes a sandstorm and its impact on a family living in Pakistan's Cholistan Desert.

FOCUS & MOTIVATE

Making Inferences To help students predict the setting and plot of the selection, have them study the art on pages 432–433 and answer the following questions:

1. What does the art indicate about where and when this story happens?

2. How might a sandstorm affect the people who live in the house?

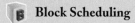 **Block Scheduling**

MORE ABOUT...
"The Sandstorm"

Pakistan's Cholistan Desert is part of the immense Thar Desert of India.

Most Pakistanis, like the family in this story, make a subsistence living as farmers or herders. Few rural children attend school. Rural homes tend to have two or three rooms. They are often made of clay or mud, with dirt floors that the people cover with straw mats. Most do not have plumbing or electric power, and water comes from a community well. Extended families often reside in the same house or village. The father is the head of the family.

The Sandstorm

IN *SHABANU: DAUGHTER OF THE WIND,* Suzanne Fisher Staples tells about 11-year-old Shabanu, the youngest child in a family of nomadic camel herders. Shabanu lives in the Cholistan Desert with her parents; her older sister, Phulan; her grandfather; and an aunt with two young children. She also has a camel named Mithoo and a pet dog named Sher Dil. In this hot and dry area of Pakistan, blinding sandstorms can strike without warning. When they do, they threaten the lives of the people who make the desert their home and of the camels they depend on for their livelihood.

One night Phulan shakes me awake in the middle of a deep sleep.

"Shabanu!" she shouts from such a great distance I can barely hear her.

She yanks the quilt away, and suddenly my skin is pierced by thousands of needles. The wind is howling around us. I can't see anything when I open my eyes, but I can tell by the sound and feel that it's a monstrous sandstorm, the kind few living things survive without protection. Phulan pulls me by the hand, but I yank away.

"Mithoo!" I stumble about the courtyard, tripping over huddled chickens, clay pots, and bundles of reeds that have broken away from the entrance. "Mithoo!"

Hands outstretched, I feel my way around the courtyard wall, where Mithoo normally sleeps. When I get to where the reeds were stacked on their stalks, lashed side by side and tied to cover the doorway, there is a gaping hole. Quickly I make my way around the courtyard again. Mithoo is gone.

1. A loose robe, worn by Islamic women, that covers the body and most of the face; also spelled *chador.*

2. A freshwater pond that serves as a water supply for desert nomads.

From SHABANU by Suzanne Fisher Staples, copyright © 1989 by Suzanne Fisher Staples. Used by permission of Alfred A. Knopf Children's Books, a division of Random House, Inc.

432 UNIT 5

Activity Option

Differentiating Instruction: Less Proficient Readers

Building Language Skills Have students work in pairs or small groups, matching less proficient readers with more fluent readers. Duplicate copies of the Literature Connection and give each pair a copy and a highlighter. Tell students that to understand this story, they must read the introduction. To help students follow the plot, tell them to highlight every detail about Mithoo as they read the introduction and the selection.

When students finish reading, have them review their highlighted sections and summarize what happens to Mithoo. Then ask what they recall about Sher Dil. Have them skim the introduction and the selection to find or confirm details about Sher Dil. They might use another color to highlight these details.

"You can't find him without a light and something to put over your eyes!" Phulan shouts, pulling on my arm. Together we drag the bed through the doorway. Mama struggles to close the window shutters and Phulan and I manage to push the door shut and wedge the bed against it. Dadi lights a candle and swears softly as the light fills the room. Grandfather and Sher Dil are missing too.

"Where can he have gone?" Mama gasps, her eyes bright with fear. Grandfather had been sound asleep, and the storm must have wakened him.

Dadi uses the candle to light the kerosene storm lantern and pulls the bed away from the door. Mama throws a shawl around his shoulders. He pulls it over his head and I follow him out to the courtyard, where *khar* shrubs, their shallow roots torn from the dry sand, tumble and hurl themselves against the walls.

With my *chadr*[1] over my face, I can open my eyes enough to see the haze of the lantern in Dadi's hand, the light reflecting from the dust in a tight circle around him.

Auntie has already closed up her house, and Dadi pounds on the door for several minutes before she opens it again and we slip inside.

"Have you seen Grandfather?" asks Dadi.

"And Mithoo and Sher Dil?" I shout.

She stands in the center of her house, mouth open and speechless, her hands raised helplessly. My cousins stand behind her skirt, their eyes wide. From between her feet Sher Dil's black nose glistens in the lamplight. But no Grandfather and no Mithoo.

"Come to our house," Dadi orders her, handing me the lantern. "I'll close up here. Shabanu, come back for me," he says, bending to light Auntie's storm lantern.

When I return, Dadi holds the light so we can see each other.

"Mithoo will be fine," he says, and I know it is a warning not to ask to look for him. "When the wind has died and it's light, we'll find him standing near a tree by the *toba*."[2]

Reading
THE LITERATURE

In this selection, the author draws on almost all of the five senses to help the reader understand what it might be like to live through a sandstorm. Find an example of how each sense is used to make the account more vivid.

Thinking About
THE LITERATURE

What role does nature play in the lives of Shabanu and her family? How does the author make clear the challenges of living in the Cholistan Desert?

Writing About
THE LITERATURE

In this story, Shabanu and her family work together to survive the sudden sandstorm. How do the members of the family help one another overcome the dangers of the storm?

About the Author

Suzanne Fisher Staples (b. 1945) has traveled widely as a reporter for a global news service. In 1979, she went to work in Southern Asia, covering such events as the civil war in Afghanistan. A 1985 trip to Pakistan, where she conducted a study of poor rural women, led her to write *Shabanu*. Staples currently lives in Florida.

Further Reading *The Land I Lost* by Huynh Quang Nhuong takes the reader to a tiny village in the central highlands of Vietnam, years before the Vietnam War. The book has won many awards, including selection as an ALA Notable Book.

INSTRUCT

Reading the Literature
Possible Responses

<u>Touch</u>: My skin is pierced by thousands of needles. <u>Hearing</u>: The wind is howling. <u>Sight</u>: I can't see anything; *khar* shrubs tumble and hurl themselves; haze of the lantern . . . light reflecting from the dust.

Thinking About the Literature
Possible Responses

Nature can cause disaster. People can get lost and die in a sandstorm. They may lose their livelihood if they lose their camel; they are trapped until the storm ends.

Writing About the Literature
Possible Responses

Students' responses should explain how characters help each other survive (e.g., Phulan and Shabanu move the bed against the door; Mama gives Dadi a shawl; they try to find Grandfather; they gather in one house; Dadi keeps Shabanu home).

MORE ABOUT...
Natural Disasters

Earthquakes and floods occur often in Pakistan. Bangladesh endures drought, cyclones, and flooding; in 1970, a cyclone caused a tsunami, killing 266,000 people.

 World Literature

More to Think About

Making Personal Connections Ask students what they learned about Pakistan from this story. Remind them of the story's limits: it is about one family in one part of Pakistan. Then ask students to think of an event in nature that can threaten people where you live. Have them use many senses to describe the event, creating either a web or a piece of shared writing.

Vocabulary Activity Students may work individually or together. Have them review the characters and decide who is worried about Mithoo, who is not, and why, using quotes from the story as evidence. Alternatively, students may read or write quotes from the story and have partners decide what sense is used in each quote.

Southeast Asia Today

	OVERVIEW	COPYMASTERS	INTEGRATED TECHNOLOGY
UNIT ATLAS AND CHAPTER RESOURCES	Students will examine how geography and historical events have shaped the governments, economies, and cultures of countries in Southern Asia.	**In-depth Resources: Unit 5** • Guided Reading Worksheets, pp. 27–30 • Skillbuilder Practice, p. 32 • Unit Atlas Activities, pp. 1–2 • Geography Workshop, pp. 37–38 **Reading Study Guide** (Spanish and English), pp. 136–143 **Outline Map Activities**	**Power Presentations** **Electronic Teacher Tools** **Online Lesson Planner** **Chapter Summaries on CD** **Critical Thinking Transparencies CT29**
SECTION 1 History and Governments pp. 437–441	**KEY IDEAS** • Southern Asian culture, especially in literature, religion, and government, was greatly influenced by India and China. • Europeans established colonies in the region in the 19th and 20th centuries. • After independence from the colonial powers, many Southern Asian nations faced military rule and other conflicts.	**In-depth Resources: Unit 5** • Guided Reading Worksheet, p. 27 • Reteaching Activity, p. 34 **Reading Study Guide** (Spanish and English), pp. 136–137	**Map Transparencies MT29** **classzone.com** **Chapter Summaries on CD**
SECTION 2 Economies and Cultures pp. 444–447	• Most Southern Asians live on farms; others work in factories producing clothing, fabric, or small electronics. • Southern Asian culture encompasses diverse languages, religions, and customs.	**In-depth Resources: Unit 5** • Guided Reading Worksheet, p. 28 • Reteaching Activity, p. 35 **Reading Study Guide** (Spanish and English), pp. 138–139	**Critical Thinking Transparencies CT30** **classzone.com** **Chapter Summaries on CD**
SECTION 3 Vietnam Today pp. 449–453	• Both China and France once ruled Vietnam, influencing its culture and daily life positively and negatively. • Ho Chi Minh led the independence movement against France. The U.S. opposed him, fearing the spread of communism. • Vietnam's economy suffered after the war, when the government restricted trade and many people fled the country	**In-depth Resources: Unit 5** • Guided Reading Worksheet, p. 29 • Reteaching Activity, p. 38 **Reading Study Guide** (Spanish and English), pp. 140–141	**classzone.com** **Chapter Summaries on CD**

KEY TO RESOURCES

🔊 Audio	🌐 Internet	TE Teacher's Edition
💿 CD-ROM	🔦 Overhead Transparency	📼 Video
📄 Copymaster	PE Pupil's Edition	

ASSESSMENT OPTIONS

PE **Chapter Assessment,** pp. 454–455

📄 **Formal Assessment**
• Chapter Tests: Forms A, B, C, pp. 228–339

💿 **Test Generator**

🌐 **Online Test Practice**

📄 **Strategies for Test Preparation**

PE **Section Assessment,** p. 441

📄 **Formal Assessment**
• Section Quiz, p. 225

📄 **Integrated Assessment**
• Rubric for making a chart

💿 **Test Generator**

🔦 **Test Practice Transparencies TT53**

PE **Section Assessment,** p. 447

📄 **Formal Assessment**
• Section Quiz, p. 226

📄 **Integrated Assessment**
• Rubric for tracing a map

💿 **Test Generator**

🔦 **Test Practice Transparencies TT54**

PE **Section Assessment,** p. 453

📄 **Formal Assessment**
• Section Quiz, p. 227

📄 **Integrated Assessment**
• Rubric for sharing an idea

💿 **Test Generator**

🔦 **Test Practice Transparencies TT55**

RESOURCES FOR DIFFERENTIATING INSTRUCTION

Students Acquiring English/ESL

📄 **Reading Study Guide** (Spanish and English), pp. 136–143

📄 **Access for Students Acquiring English** Spanish Translations, pp. 133–140

Less Proficient Readers

📄 **Reading Study Guide** (Spanish and English), pp. 136–143

TE **TE Activity**
• Creating a Flow Chart, p. 440

Gifted and Talented Students

TE **TE Activities**
• Creating Mandala Paintings, p. 438
• Researching, p. 445

CROSS-CURRICULAR CONNECTIONS

Humanities
Giles, Gail. *Breath of the Dragon.* New York: Bantam Doubleday Dell Books for Young Readers, 1998. A girl draws pictures to match her grandmother's tales of Thailand.

Literature
Shepard, Aaron. *The Crystal Heart: A Vietnamese Legend.* New York: Atheneum Books for Young Readers, 1998. A spoiled daughter learns the consequences of cruelty.

Popular Culture
Ferro, Jennifer. *Vietnamese Foods & Culture.* Vero Beach, FL: Rourke Press, 1999. Specific celebrations of Tet, Wandering Souls Day, and the Midautumn Festival.

Geography
Wee, Jessie. *Singapore.* Philadelphia: Chelsea House, 2000. The independent island republic.

Primary Sources
Huynh, Quang Nhuong. *Water Buffalo Days: Growing Up in Vietnam.* New York: HarperTrophy, 1999. Growing up in a village in the central highlands of Vietnam.

Language Arts/Literature
Glass, Tom. *Even a Little Is Something: Stories of Nong.* North Haven, CT: Linnet Books, 1997. Nong observes her village in Thailand transforming from rural to urban.

Science
Smith, Roland, and Michael J. Schmidt. *In the Forest with the Elephants.* San Diego: Harcourt Brace, 1998. Elephants are trained to help in the timber camps of Myanmar.

ENRICHMENT ACTIVITIES

The following activities are especially suitable for classes following block schedules.

Teacher's Edition, pp. 438, 446, 448, 452
Pupil's Edition, pp. 441, 447, 453

Unit Atlas, pp. 366–373
Interdisciplinary Challenge, pp. 442–443

Outline Map Activities

INTEGRATED TECHNOLOGY

Go to **classzone.com** for lesson support and activities for Chapter 15.

BLOCK SCHEDULE LESSON PLAN OPTIONS: 90-MINUTE PERIOD

DAY 1

CHAPTER PREVIEW, pp. 434–435
Class Time 20 minutes

- **Hypothesize** Use the "What do you think?" questions in Focus on Geography on PE p. 435 to help students hypothesize about how migration affected Southeast Asia's culture.

SECTION 1, pp. 437–441
Class Time 70 minutes

- **Geography Skills** Review the flow line maps on PE p. 11 with students. Divide the class into small groups, and have each group create a flow line map to show the movement of ideas and goods from China, India, Europe, and other countries to Southeast Asia.
Class Time 35 minutes

- **Brainstorming** Read aloud Citizenship in Action on TE p. 441 to the students after they have read the feature on PE p. 441. Lead the class to consider what personal qualities Aung San Suu Kyi needs to sustain her efforts to secure democracy in Myanmar in the face of the repressive military regime. Record students' suggestions on the chalkboard.
Class Time 15 minutes

- **Internet** Extend students' background knowledge of Southeast Asia by visiting **classzone.com.**
Class Time 20 minutes

DAY 2

SECTION 2, pp. 444–447
Class Time 60 minutes

- **Spider Map** Divide students into pairs, and have the groups create maps for each subsection. Students should use the subsection heads as central ideas. When students are finished, ask them to supply the details about each spider map as you write them on the chalkboard.
Class Time 35 minutes

- **Postcard** Tell students to imagine they are traveling through Southeast Asia on a vacation, and have them write a postcard to someone in the United States describing an activity or sight they saw there.
Class Time 15 minutes

- **Discussion** Use the Reading Social Studies Drawing Conclusions question on PE p. 436 to start a discussion about how geography affects the development of cultures.
Class Time 10 minutes

SECTION 3, pp. 449–453
Class Time 30 minutes

- **Writing Summaries** Have students use the time lines they created for Activity Options, Multiple Learning Styles: Spatial/Visual on TE p. 451 to write a summary of the conflict in Vietnam.

DAY 3

SECTION 3, continued
Class Time 35 minutes

- **Peer Competition** Divide the class into pairs. Assign each pair one of the Terms & Names on PE p. 449. Have pairs make up five questions that can be answered with the term or name. Have groups take turns asking the class their questions.

CHAPTER 15 REVIEW AND ASSESSMENT, pp. 454–455
Class Time 55 minutes

- **Review** Have students use the charts they created for Reading Social Studies on PE p. 436 to review facts and conclusions about Southeast Asia.
Class Time 20 minutes

- **Assessment** Have students complete the Chapter 15 Assessment.
Class Time 35 minutes

TECHNOLOGY IN THE CLASSROOM

ELECTRONIC FIELD TRIP

Electronic field trips are one of the most popular ways for students to use the Internet. Students generally visit a specified set of Web pages to see pictures of and read about places such as national parks or foreign countries. This type of field trip is often an excellent substitute for an actual field trip, which may be logistically impossible.

ACTIVITY OUTLINE

Objective Students will go to Web sites about Vietnam, take notes on specific things they see and read, and create multimedia presentations.

Task Have students visit Web sites to find out about cultural, historical, and geographical things they would see on a trip to Vietnam. Then ask them to create multimedia presentations on what they discovered on their trips.

Class Time 2–4 class periods

DIRECTIONS

1. Give each student a blank outline map of Vietnam (available at the first link at the **classzone.com** site). Ask them to label Ho Chi Minh City (Saigon), Hanoi, and Hue.

2. Inform the class that Vietnam has become a popular place to travel to and that many people travel through the country on trains or bicycles.

3. Have students take a virtual tour of Vietnam by going to the remaining Web sites listed at **classzone.com**. Have them visit at least ten places and label these spots on their maps. As they go on their tour, ask them to list at least one example of things they see in each of these categories: interesting scenery, Vietnamese food, a custom or activity that people in Vietnam practice differently from people in the United States, a custom or activity that is similar to one in the United States, agriculture, industry or manufacturing, a historical site, and religious practices.

4. Suggest that students create multimedia presentations that showcase the things they would see on a trip to Vietnam. Their presentations should include maps, photographs or drawings, and text. They can also provide links to Web sites that contain additional information about Vietnam.

5. Discuss the things students think they would like most and least about taking a real trip to Vietnam. What questions would they ask the people who live there? What things would they want to share about their own country? What would they most look forward to seeing?

CHAPTER 15 OBJECTIVE

Students will examine how geography and historical events have shaped the governments, economies, and cultures of countries in Southeast Asia.

FOCUS ON VISUALS

Interpreting the Photograph Direct students' attention to the photograph. Ask them what they observe about the land and the vegetation. Ask students what the photograph suggests about the region and its climate and resources.

Possible Response The climate is warm at least part of the year, and the region gets adequate rainfall to sustain plants; therefore the region probably has productive farms.

Extension Ask students to imagine themselves as newly arrived visitors to the place in the photograph. Have them write letters to someone at home about their first impressions and what they expect and hope to see.

CRITICAL THINKING ACTIVITY

Contrasting Lead a discussion about how the geography and climate of Southeast Asia are different from those of Western Europe. Ask students to contrast the photographs in this chapter with the photographs in Unit 2.

Class Time 10 minutes

Southeast Asia Today

SECTION 1   History and Governments

SECTION 2   Economies and Cultures

SECTION 3   Vietnam Today

Human-Environment Interaction
People harvest tea leaves in a field near Bao Loc, Vietnam. Tea growing began in Southeast Asia when the Dutch brought seeds to Java from Japan.

434

Recommended Resources

BOOKS FOR THE TEACHER
Suu Kyi, Aung San. *The Voice of Hope.* New York: Seven Stories Press, 1998. Dialogues on life with Alan Clements.
Somers Heidhues, Mary F. *Southeast Asia: A Concise History.* New York: Thames & Hudson, 2000. Southeast Asia as a crossroads.

Sponsel, Leslie, ed. *Endangered Peoples of Southeast and East Asia: Struggles to Survive and Thrive.* Westport, CT: Greenwood Press, 2000. Essays on indigenous people threatened by their current governments.

VIDEOS
North Thailand & Laos. Oakland, CA: Lonely Planet, 2000. From Bangkok to the Mekong.

INTERNET
For more information about Southeast Asia, visit **classzone.com.**

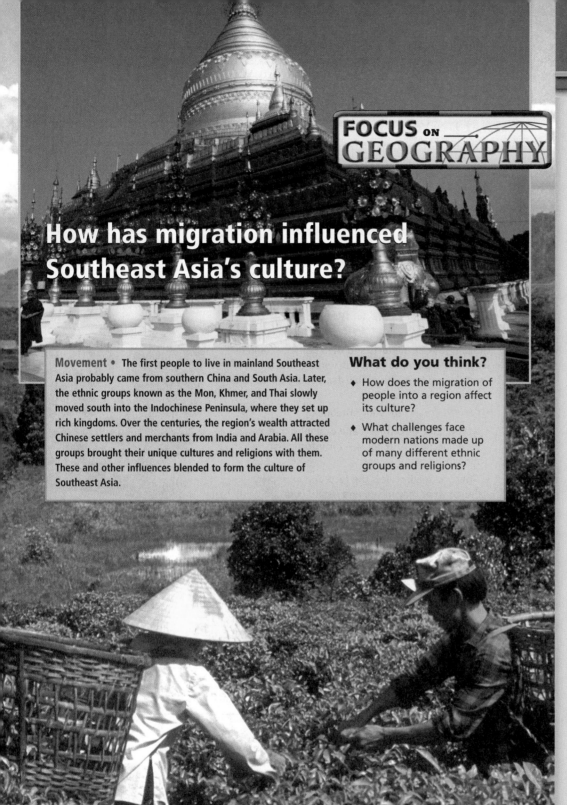

FOCUS ON GEOGRAPHY

How has migration influenced Southeast Asia's culture?

Movement • The first people to live in mainland Southeast Asia probably came from southern China and South Asia. Later, the ethnic groups known as the Mon, Khmer, and Thai slowly moved south into the Indochinese Peninsula, where they set up rich kingdoms. Over the centuries, the region's wealth attracted Chinese settlers and merchants from India and Arabia. All these groups brought their unique cultures and religions with them. These and other influences blended to form the culture of Southeast Asia.

What do you think?

♦ How does the migration of people into a region affect its culture?

♦ What challenges face modern nations made up of many different ethnic groups and religions?

FOCUS ON GEOGRAPHY

Objectives

• To help students identify settlement patterns

• To identify and discuss sources of economic wealth in Southeast Asia

What Do You Think?

1. Guide students in a discussion of how people assimilate into the culture of a region, while also keeping their own language and traditions.

2. Ask students to consider how the government of a country with many different ethnic groups might post traffic signs, issue licenses, and conduct other government activities that depend on language.

How has human migration influenced the culture of Southeast Asia?

Have students think about what elements contribute to one's culture, such as foods, religious celebrations, language, and dress. Then prompt a discussion about which of these cultural elements most easily blend with other cultures. Discuss the advantages and disadvantages to immigrants of safeguarding the unique elements of their culture.

MAKING GEOGRAPHIC CONNECTIONS

Ask the students what ethnic groups live in their area. Have large numbers of people moved there from other countries? From other states? Have students list the features that would attract people to their area from other areas, or problems that might cause them to move elsewhere.

Implementing the National Geography Standards

Standard 12 Design a city settlement pattern for a new city

Objective To conduct a class survey and use the results to design an ideal city settlement pattern

Class Time 35 minutes

Task Students conduct a survey of the class concerning students' wishes for a new city. Then they organize themselves into planning teams to design a city settlement pattern that incorporates most of their wishes. (Note: Before students conduct the survey, they should carefully consider what questions to ask to adequately assess people's wishes.)

Evaluation Each planning team should identify what city settlement type they designed and explain three ways the survey results influenced their plan.

BEFORE YOU READ
What Do You Know?

Ask students to name some important cities in Southern Asia. If they cannot think of any, name Saigon, Bangkok, Hanoi, and Manila, and ask if they have heard of them. Ask if any students have eaten Thai or Vietnamese food. If so, have the students tell about the meal and how it was different from their own cuisine. Ask if they have read books or seen movies about the war in Vietnam, or if they know anyone who served in the military during the war.

What Do You Want to Know?

Suggest that students look through the chapter and write questions based on the photographs, maps, charts, and headings. Have students compare their lists. As they read the chapter, have them write answers to their questions. If, after finishing the chapter, they still have unanswered questions, invite students to write these questions on the chalkboard. Lead a class discussion in an attempt to answer these questions.

READ AND TAKE NOTES

Reading Strategy: Drawing Conclusions Read aloud the questions in the first column of the chart. Tell students to look for facts and examples that answer each question. Then tell them to use that information, along with their common sense and experience, to draw conclusions about Southeast Asia.

 In-depth Resources: Unit 5
• Guided Reading Worksheets, pp. 27–29

BEFORE YOU READ
▶▶ What Do You Know?

Before you read the chapter, think about what you know about Southeast Asia. What countries make up this region? What do you know about the region's governments and economies? Have you ever seen a movie about the Vietnam War? What do you know about Vietnam today? Recall what you know from other classes, what you have read, and what you have seen on television.

▶▶ What Do You Want to Know?

In your notebook, record what you hope to learn from this chapter.

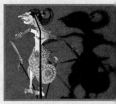

Culture • Puppets made from water buffalo hides are used in the ancient art of shadow theater. ▼

READ AND TAKE NOTES

Reading Strategy: Drawing Conclusions To draw conclusions, look at the facts and then use your common sense and experience to decide what the facts mean. Use the chart below to gather facts and draw conclusions about Southeast Asia.

• Copy the chart into your notebook.
• As you read, record facts and examples that answer each question. Look for specific information, as shown.
• After you read, review the facts and examples, decide what they mean, and record your conclusions.

Place • Singapore is a busy and wealthy city in Southeast Asia. ▲

	Facts/Examples	Conclusions
How are Southeast Asian nations linked to other countries?	China, U.S., Soviet Union, and France often controlled or influenced nations of Southeast Asia.	China, India, European nations, and others, as well as Communist ideology, have contributed to religion, economy, and politics.
What forms of government are in the region?	constitutional monarchies, republics, and communism	History, politics, and religion have shaped these governments.
What factors affect economies in Southeast Asia today?	agricultural, limited access to modern technology, farmers own small plots of land, slow communications, reliance on good weather	low productivity in farms, shift toward industry
What factors shape cultures in the region?	geography, such as natural barriers; religions, such as Islam, Buddhism, and Christianity; multiple languages	Differences of religion and language as well as geographic barriers create isolation and communication difficulties.
What are the effects of the Vietnam War?	3 million Vietnamese dead; 4 million wounded; north and south united as Socialist Republic of Vietnam	Because of the high level of poverty, Vietnam's Communist government opened its doors to investors.

Teaching Strategy

Reading the Chapter This is a thematic chapter that describes the history, governments, economies, and cultures of Southeast Asia. The final section focuses on Vietnam, particularly the Vietnam War and its aftermath. Encourage students to take notes as they read and to carefully study the photographs, maps, and charts in the chapter so that they can better understand this complex region.

Integrated Assessment The Chapter Assessment on page 456 describes several activities that may be used for integrated assessment. You may wish to have students work on these activities during the course of the chapter and then present their finished projects at the end.

History and Governments

TERMS & NAMES
mandala
military dictatorship
East Timor

MAIN IDEA	WHY IT MATTERS NOW
Southeast Asia has experienced a variety of cultural and governmental influences throughout its history.	The current governments of the nations of Southeast Asia are relatively new and unstable.

DATELINE
EXTRA

BURMA, 1274

Today, the famed traveler from Italy arrived. Marco Polo has come to Southeast Asia with his family. He is carrying important papers from a religious leader known as the Pope, but mostly he wants to see the land, the people, and the cultures. When he returns home, he plans to write a book about his adventures. Marco Polo marveled at our beautiful temples. He noted that they are "covered with gold, a full finger's breadth in thickness." Perhaps there is nothing quite so beautiful in Italy.

Culture • Marco Polo will return to Italy to share the wonders of the East. ▲

New Cultures in Southeast Asia ❶

Seven hundred years before Marco Polo's visit, Southeast Asia had come under the influence of two stronger, more advanced cultures: China and India. China made Vietnam part of its empire. Vietnam was not able to gain its independence until A.D. 939. India never ruled any part of Southeast Asia, but its culture spread throughout the region and had a lasting influence.

SECTION OBJECTIVES

1. To explain the influence of India and China on the cultures of Southeast Asia
2. To describe the effects of European colonialism on the region
3. To explain the effects of independence

SKILLBUILDER
• Interpreting a Map, p. 440

CRITICAL THINKING
• Contrasting, p. 440

FOCUS & MOTIVATE
WARM-UP

Hypothesizing Have students read Dateline and answer the following questions.

1. What impression might the gold temples have given Marco Polo about Southeast Asia?
2. How might Polo's description of what he saw in Southeast Asia have affected European leaders?

INSTRUCT: Objective ❶

New Cultures in Southeast Asia

• **How did India and China influence the region?** writing systems, literature, religions, ideas of government and social class
• **What were mandalas?** government systems whose rulers held power via trade and business
• **How did the mandalas change over time?** They developed into states, then into nations.

 In-depth Resources: Unit 5
• Guided Reading Worksheet, p. 27

Reading Study Guide
(Spanish and English), pp. 136–137

Program Resources

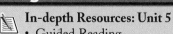 **In-depth Resources: Unit 5**
• Guided Reading Worksheet, p. 27
• Reteaching Activity, p. 34

 Reading Study Guide
(Spanish and English), pp. 136–137

Formal Assessment
• Section Quiz, p. 225

Integrated Assessment
• Rubric for making a chart

Outline Map Activities

Access for Students Acquiring English
• Guided Reading Worksheet, p. 133

 Technology Resources
classzone.com

TEST-TAKING RESOURCES
↴ Strategies for Test Preparation
↴ Test Practice Transparencies
🌐 Online Test Practice

FOCUS ON VISUALS

Interpreting the Picture Explain that people in Southeast Asia were designing and building ships and had well-developed navigational skills at least 4,000 years ago. Ask students how the region's use of ships might have influenced its relationship with the rest of the world.

Possible Responses Sailing would have enabled Southeast Asians to visit, trade with, and migrate to other parts of the world.

Extension Ask students to imagine themselves as ancient sailors living in Southeast Asia and write about the preparations for a journey they are about to make.

The WORLD'S HERITAGE

Invaders from Thailand had captured the city of Angkor and then abandoned it some 400 years before a French naturalist discovered its ruins in 1860. Soon after the discovery, French and Cambodian archaeologists began rebuilding Angkor Wat and other temples. One of the other temples is the Bayon, which has towers adorned by more than 200 gigantic stone faces. That temple was dedicated to Buddha and the king who reigned when it was built.

Influences of China and India New religions—Hinduism, Buddhism, and Confucianism—came to Southeast Asia from China and India. So did writing systems, literature, and ideas about government and social class. Indian ideas about government were especially important.

Southeast Asian Governments Instead of states or nations, Southeast Asia was made up of mandalas. A **mandala** (MUHN·duh·luh) had at its center a ruler who worked to gain support from others. The ruler used trade and business to influence others and maintain power. Mandalas varied. Some were larger than others, some depended on agriculture, and some had more advanced technology. The mandala system stayed in place in many parts of Southeast Asia until the 19th century. One ancient mandala, called Oc Eo, was located in southern Vietnam. Ships from this port carried goods to and from places as far away as Rome. Over time, the mandalas developed into states, and the people began to think of themselves as belonging to these states. Because of trade and communication, new ideas were exchanged among the peoples of the region and between the region and other parts of the world. Each state took what it wanted from these new ideas and developed into a unique nation.

Human-Environment Interaction • For centuries, Southeast Asians have been trading by sea in ships like this one in Jakarta, Indonesia. ▼

Reading Social Studies
A. Possible Answer
Gradually, the mandalas developed into states, and the people began to think of themselves as belonging to the states. Each state developed its own unique culture and eventually became a nation.

A. Summarizing How did nations develop out of mandalas?

The WORLD'S HERITAGE

Cambodia's Temple Treasures
Angkor (ANG·kawr) was an early civilization in northwestern Cambodia between the 9th and 14th centuries. Its capital, also called Angkor, contains temples that are among the world's greatest works of art and architecture.

One of these temples, Angkor Wat, is particularly splendid. It was built to honor the Hindu god Vishnu. This huge pyramid-shaped temple covers almost one square mile. Its stonework is covered with richly carved scenes from Hindu mythology. For centuries after the city and its magnificent temples were abandoned, jungle growth hid them until their rediscovery around 1860. Later, war kept admirers away. Today, efforts are under way to restore Angkor Wat as a world monument to Cambodian culture.

Activity Options

Differentiating Instruction: Gifted and Talented
B Block Scheduling

Activity Explain to students that mandala painting is an ancient Asian art form. The mandala is part of Buddhist and Hindu tradition and was brought to Southeast Asia from India and China. It is a sacred image used in meditation. Mandalas have been made on paper and cloth and formed out of bronze and stone. A mandala is always in the shape of a circle, with no beginning and no end, and is designed to draw the eye toward the center. Inside the circle there is often a square whose sides represent the cardinal directions.

Display transparencies of mandalas, and ask students why they think the same term is used to describe a kind of painting and a form of government in Southeast Asia. Have students create mandala paintings and display them in the classroom.

Culture • Today, most Indonesians, like these boys studying the Qur'an, are Muslims. ▲

New Religions Trade with other parts of the world also brought Christianity and Islam to Southeast Asia. In the ninth or tenth century, Muslim traders brought Islam to the region, especially to the islands of Sumatra and Java, part of what is now Indonesia. Islam spread gradually throughout the other islands of Indonesia and Malaya.

In the early 1500s, Christian missionaries came to Southeast Asia from Portugal, France, and Spain. The Spanish missionaries met with success in the Philippines, where there was no organized religion to combat, although each group of Filipinos had its own set of beliefs. Today, about 90 percent of Filipinos are Christians. However, in the rest of Southeast Asia, the missionaries were not as successful. Buddhist monks worked to keep the missionaries from making converts.

European Colonialism ❷

Europeans came to Southeast Asia as traders as well as missionaries. The Portuguese were the first to arrive, in 1509. The Spanish, the Dutch, the British, and the French all followed. These European traders came for wealth—spices, gems, and gold—not power. For the most part, the Europeans controlled port cities and nothing more for the first three centuries.

Southeast Asia Today **439**

Strange ?? *but* TRUE

Dragons of Komodo On Komodo (kuh•MO•do) Island and a few other islands in Indonesia lives one of Earth's most fearsome creatures. Its body is covered with scales, and its tail is long and powerful. It has sharp teeth, long claws, and a yellow tongue that flicks in and out. If this description makes you think of a storybook dragon, you are not alone.

Hundreds of years ago, Chinese fishermen thought the same thing when they called this creature a dragon. Komodo dragons are really lizards. In fact, they're the largest living lizards in the world. Some Komodo dragons grow more than 10 feet long and weigh as much as 200 pounds. They're so strong that they can overpower and eat deer, wild pigs, and water buffalo. They have even been known to attack people.

INSTRUCT: Objective ❷

European Colonialism

- When did Europeans first come to the region, and why did they come? in 1509; for wealth—spices, gems, gold
- When did Europeans establish colonies in the region? 19th and 20th centuries
- What countries were colonized by France and Britain? France—Cambodia, Laos, Vietnam; Britain—Burma, Malaysia, Singapore
- When did most countries gain independence? after 1945
- What did Europeans contribute to the region? chile peppers, coffee

MORE ABOUT...
European Colonialism

Starting in the early 1500s, the emerging countries of Portugal, Spain, the Netherlands, France, and England spread their institutions and cultures as they established colonies all over the world. The first European expeditions were made in galley ships with large numbers of rowers. As exploration grew in importance, the galleys were replaced by sailing ships that could carry more supplies and bring back more cargo from the colonies.

Strange ?? *but* TRUE

When Komodo dragons are first hatched, they live in trees. They later relocate to small caves that they burrow, sometimes as deep as 15 feet. Komodos will travel for miles from their home in search for food, and they rely on their sense of smell and sight to hunt for prey. Their yellow, forked tongue can reach one foot in length, and they use it to "smell" potential prey.

Activity Options

Interdisciplinary Link: Geography

Class Time 15 minutes

Task Analyzing the spread of religious ideas

Purpose To find the birthplace of Christianity and Islam on the globe, and then to visualize the spread of these religions

Supplies Needed
• Globe

Activity Remind students that Islam and Christianity both originated in Southwest Asia. Using a globe, ask volunteers to point out the cities of Jerusalem and Mecca. Then trace the various paths of the traders, colonizers, and missionaries, pointing out that these people brought their religious ideas with them and in many cases were successful in convincing local peoples to adopt their ideas.

FOCUS ON VISUALS

Interpreting the Map Direct the students' attention to the map key. Ask them to name the capitals of Myanmar, Vietnam, Thailand, Cambodia, Malaysia, Indonesia, and the Philippines.

Responses Yangon, Hanoi, Bangkok, Phnom Penh, Kuala Lumpur, Jakarta, and Manila, respectively

Extension Ask students to conduct research about one of the countries shown on the map. Ask each student to write five facts about the country that he or she chooses.

INSTRUCT: Objective ❸

After Independence

- After independence, which countries were taken over by military governments? Vietnam, Indonesia, Myanmar

- Which countries are republics? Indonesia, Philippines, Singapore

- What kind of government do Laos and Vietnam have? Communist

- What has happened in East Timor since 1975? East Timor declared independence in 1975; Indonesia took over; Indonesia is still trying to impose control.

CRITICAL THINKING ACTIVITY

Contrasting Ask students to contrast the region of Southeast Asia before and after World War II. You might want to create a chart on the board to help them organize their thoughts.

Class Time 10 minutes

Southeast Asia, 2001

PACIFIC OCEAN

Tropic of Cancer

20°N

MYANMAR · Hanoi

LAOS

Yangon · Vientiane

THAILAND · Bangkok

CAMBODIA

Phnom Penh · VIETNAM

Philippine Sea

Manila

PHILIPPINES

South China Sea

Andaman Sea

Gulf of Thailand

BRUNEI · Bandar Seri Begawan

Kuala Lumpur

Strait of Malacca

MALAYSIA

SINGAPORE · Singapore

Celebes Sea

Equator

I N D O N E S I A

Java Sea

Jakarta

Flores Sea

Banda Sea

INDIAN OCEAN

100°E

E. Timor (UN Admin.)

Arafura Sea

0   400   800 miles
0   400   800 kilometers

✴ National capital
▭ National boundary

GEOGRAPHY SKILLBUILDER:
Interpreting a Map
1. **Location •** What bodies of water surround Southeast Asia?
2. **Region •** What nations of Southeast Asia are found on the mainland?

Then, in the 19th and early 20th centuries, these European nations began to colonize the nations of Southeast Asia. The Philippines was under Spanish rule until 1898, when it came under the rule of the United States. Cambodia, Laos, and Vietnam were all ruled by France. The British ruled Burma, most of Malaysia, and Singapore, and the Dutch ruled Indonesia. Only Thailand never became a colony.

During World War II, the Japanese pushed out most Europeans from the region. When the war ended in 1945, Cambodia, Vietnam, Laos, Malaysia, and Indonesia fought for independence. The Philippines won independence peacefully.

Contributions of the Europeans The Spanish discovered the chile pepper in North America and brought it to Southeast Asia. Immediately, the chile pepper became a familiar part of the diet in Southeast Asia. Coffee came to the region with the Dutch. Today, coffee is an important crop in Indonesia, Laos, and Vietnam.

After Independence ❸

After gaining independence, many nations in Southeast Asia found themselves in turmoil. Political parties fought one another to gain power. In Vietnam, Myanmar, and Indonesia, the military eventually took control of the government. Over the next 20 years, the nations of Southeast Asia worked out their own unique government systems.

Culture • King Bhumidol Adulyadej (pu·mee·PAWL ah·dul·yah·DEHT) is the longest-reigning monarch in Thailand's history. His duties are mainly ceremonial. ▼

Geography Skillbuilder Answers

1. Indian Ocean, South China Sea, Philippine Sea, Celebes Sea, Arafura Sea, Flores Sea, Java Sea, Banda Sea, Andaman Sea, Gulf of Thailand, Strait of Malacca

2. Myanmar, Laos, Thailand, Cambodia, Vietnam; Malaysia is partly on the mainland, partly on an island.

Activity Options

Differentiating Instruction: Less Proficient Readers

The region's turbulent political history and the variety of governments that exist may confuse some students. Review the basic characteristics of constitutional monarchies, republics, Communist states, and military dictatorships. Ask students if they can remember examples of each type of government among the different countries they have studied. Encourage students to fill in a blank map of the region with the name of each country and the type of government it has.

To help students trace the change in government in some of the nations of Southeast Asia, have them create a flow chart like the one shown.

The Philippines

| Ruled by Spain | → | 1898, came under U.S. rule | → | 1945, gained independence, became republic |

Reading
Social Studies

B. Making Inferences How do you think the people of Myanmar might have felt about the overthrow of their elected government?

Reading Social Studies
B. Possible Answer

They were probably angry that their rights and choices had been taken away.

Governments Brunei, Malaysia, Cambodia, and Thailand are all constitutional monarchies. Indonesia, the Philippines, and Singapore are republics. Myanmar was also a republic, but in 1988, the military overthrew the government. Since then, it has been a **military dictatorship,** ruled by one man whose power comes from the army. Laos and Vietnam are both Communist states.

East Timor The island nation of **East Timor** declared its independence from Portugal in 1975. A month later, the neighboring country of Indonesia invaded and took over. The United Nations said the people of East Timor could decide their government for themselves. In 1999, they voted for independence.

However, Indonesia did not accept the people's ruling. The United Nations has accused the Indonesian army of killing and deporting people because of the vote. UN peacekeeping forces were stationed in East Timor. In August of 2001, East Timor held its first democratic elections.

Citizenship IN ACTION

Aung San Suu Kyi (AHNG•SAHN•SOO•CHEE) Suu Kyi was born in Burma, now called Myanmar, in 1945. In 1988, she became the leader of a new national movement against the brutal military dictatorship that controlled Myanmar. She and millions of followers used peaceful methods to protest human rights abuses and to demand a democratic government. The military killed thousands of protesters. Suu Kyi was put under house arrest. In 1991, she won the Nobel Peace Prize.

NATIONAL LEAGUE FOR DEMOCRACY

Citizenship IN ACTION

The National League for Democracy is led by Aung San Suu Kyi. In 1990, this party won four-fifths of the contested legislative seats, but the military government ignored the election results. Aung San Suu Kyi refused the military's offer to release her from house arrest if she promised to leave the country. In 1992, she donated $1.3 million of her Nobel Prize money for Burmese education and health. In 1995, she was released from house arrest. The military still controls Myanmar.

ASSESS & RETEACH

Reading Social Studies Have students answer the first and second questions of the chart on page 436.

 Formal Assessment
• Section Quiz, p. 225

RETEACHING ACTIVITY

Have students work in pairs to fill in a blank map of Southeast Asia. Then have them label countries and capital cities, and identify forms of government. Finally, have students use their completed maps to explain to their partners significant events discussed in this section.

 In-depth Resources: Unit 5
• Reteaching Activity, p. 34

 Access for Students Acquiring English
• Reteaching Activity, p. 138

SECTION 1 ASSESSMENT

Terms & Names
1. **Identify:** (a) mandala (b) military dictatorship (c) East Timor

Taking Notes
2. Use a cluster map like this one to take notes on ways the Chinese, Indian, European, and other cultures influenced Southeast Asian culture.

Main Ideas
3. (a) Who brought Islam and Christianity to Southeast Asia?
   (b) Why did European nations come to Southeast Asia?
   (c) How is the government of Thailand different from the government of the Philippines?

Critical Thinking
4. **Analyzing Causes**

   Why do you think many of the newly independent Southeast Asian nations came under the control of military dictators?

   Think About
   • the political and social confusion many countries find themselves in when their colonial rulers leave
   • the role of the military

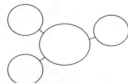 Make a **chart** showing the countries of Southeast Asia and each country's system of government.

Southeast Asia Today **441**

Section 1 Assessment

1. Terms & Names
   a. mandala, p. 438
   b. military dictatorship, p. 441
   c. East Timor, p. 441

2. Taking Notes

ideas about government

foods

religion

Chinese, Indian, European cultures

3. Main Ideas
   a. Islam: Muslim traders; Christianity: missionaries
   b. for spices, gems, and gold
   c. Thailand is a constitutional monarchy; the Philippines is a republic.

4. Critical Thinking

The region had no history of more democratic forms of government. The diversity of ethnic groups in some countries might also make it difficult for the populations to reach agreement.

ACTIVITY OPTION

 Integrated Assessment
• Rubric for making a chart

OBJECTIVE

Students learn about the contributions of Southern Asia to art, architecture, and culture throughout history.

FOCUS & MOTIVATE

Recognizing Important Details Ask students to study the pictures and read each paragraph. Have them answer the following questions:

1. How might the hand gestures shown in the photographs for Theater and Dance be important to the meaning of the dance?
2. Based on the photo of people gathering tea, is the production of tea in India highly mechanized?

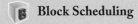 **Block Scheduling**

MORE ABOUT...
Architecture

The best-known pagodas are found in China, Japan, and Korea, where they are usually tall, ornate towers with many stories. Tibet and Southeast Asia each have different versions. While Tibet's tend to be bottle-shaped, Southeast Asia's pagodas are either shaped more like pyramids or cones. The design of the pagoda originated from an ancient Indian structure called a *stupa,* which was dome-shaped and constructed as a memorial.

Theater and Dance

One of India's most popular expressions of theater and dance can actually be found in its movies. India's motion-picture industry makes hundreds of films each year. These films include love stories, crime thrillers, and social dramas, but no matter what the story, all popular films feature song and dance sequences.

The Legacy of Southern Asia

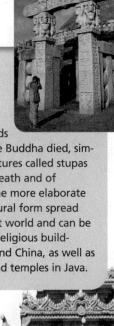

Architecture

Even before the rise of Buddhism in the 5th century B.C., people in India made burial mounds for their dead. When the Buddha died, similar mound-shaped structures called stupas became symbols of his death and of Buddhism. Stupas became more elaborate over time. This architectural form spread throughout the Buddhist world and can be found in the pagodas—religious buildings—of Korea, Japan, and China, as well as in shrines in Sri Lanka and temples in Java.

Theater and Dance

In ancient times, theater and classical dance productions were held in the temples and royal courts of India. Spectators watched dancers act out stories of Hindu gods and myths, especially from famous epics. The two most famous epics are the *Ramayana* (ruh•MAH•yuh•nuh) and the *Mahabharata* (MAH•huh•BAH•ruh•tuh). Folk dancing, another dance form, was popular in rural areas. Modern dance in Southern Asia includes elements of both classical and folk dancing.

442 UNIT 5

Activity Options

Interdisciplinary Links: Art/History

Class Time Two class periods

Task Comparing and contrasting the architectural style of pagodas in different parts of Southern Asia.

Supplies Needed
- Images of and information about Indian stupas
- Images of and information about Korean, Japanese, and Chinese pagodas, and shrines/temples in Sri Lanka and Java

Activity Have students work in groups. Give each group material about Indian stupas and material about pagodas from another Southern Asia culture. Have each group compare and contrast the Indian stupa architecture with the pagoda architecture of their assigned culture. What do the styles have in common? What is different? When they have finished, ask each group to report their findings.

Cities

One of the first cities in the world, Mohenjo-Daro, was built along the Indus River in what is now Pakistan. After archaeologists discovered the 4,000-year-old city in 1922, they spent years excavating its ruins. What they unearthed was a city laid out in a grid pattern, with streets, houses, assembly halls, storerooms, public baths, and a sewer system. Many modern cities are laid out in grids, and some cities in India have public baths similar to the ones found in Mohenjo-Daro.

Find Out More About It!

Study the text and photos on these pages to learn about inventions, creations, and contributions that have come from Southern Asia. Then choose the item that interests you the most and use the library or the Internet to research the subject and learn more about it. Use the information you gather to create a diorama to share with the class.

RESEARCH LINKS
CLASSZONE.COM

INSTRUCT

- In what present-day country is the ancient city of Mohenjo-Daro located?
- What stories did ancient Indian court dramas act out?
- Where has tea been grown for more than 3,000 years?

MORE ABOUT...
Cities

By about 2500 B.C. Mohenjo-Daro probably had more than 35,000 people. The Indus Valley had developed a system of agriculture that provided enough food for such large populations.

The city and other smaller valley settlements also traded with one another and outside groups. Standard-sized bricks and uniform weights and measures have been discovered throughout the valley. Traces of Indus Valley seals have also been found on items from Mesopotamia. It seems likely that the Indus people also traded with Southern India, Persia, and Central Asia.

No one knows why the Indus Valley civilization disappeared around 1700 B.C. Some scholars suggest that changing river paths or overuse of the riverbanks may have hurt the agriculture.

Black Tea

Though tea bushes were found growing wild in Assam, India, in the 1820s, it was not until the mid-1880s that India began to export tea. Workers used a process that turned green leaves to a brownish black color to produce a blend known as black tea. Though tea had been grown in China for more than 3,000 years, by 1888 England was importing more tea from Southern Asia than from China. Today, some of the best black teas come from India.

Sanskrit Language

Sanskrit, the oldest written language of India, was first brought to India around 1500 B.C. The language has distinctive sounds, as well as complex grammar rules. Some of India's modern languages—Hindi, Bengali, and Punjabi—are based on Sanskrit. Though by 100 B.C. Sanskrit was no longer being spoken, it is still used in many Hindu ceremonies and in scholarly works and teachings.

Black Tea

There are several steps to making black tea. First, the leaves are spread on shelves and air is blown over them to remove excess moisture. The leaves are then crushed between rollers to release their juices and placed in a fermenting room. There, under controlled humidity and temperature, the leaves change chemically and turn a coppery color. Lastly, the leaves are dried in ovens and turn brownish black.

Southern Asia **443**

More to Think About

Making Personal Connections Ask students to reread the section called "Cities." Ask them to identify modern parallels in their community to the parts of the ancient city of Mohenjo-Daro. What might be a local, modern equivalent of an assembly hall or storeroom? Is there a modern equivalent of the public bath? Discuss these points as a class.

Vocabulary Activity Ask students to write a fictional paragraph correctly combining words and phrases from the section inventively. You might give them a sample: *I drank black tea in the pagoda before seeing a performance of the Ramayana.* When they have finished, have them read their paragraphs aloud and discuss them.

Economies and Cultures

SECTION 2

TERMS & NAMES
developing nation
Bahasa Indonesian
pagoda
thatch
batik

SECTION OBJECTIVES

1. To describe agriculture and industry in Southeast Asia
2. To describe the diverse cultural characteristics of the region

SKILLBUILDER
• Interpreting a Chart, p. 445

CRITICAL THINKING
• Analyzing Issues, p. 445
• Making Inferences, p. 446

FOCUS & MOTIVATE
WARM-UP

Making Inferences Have students read <u>Dateline</u> and answer the following questions.

1. What trait of elephants is most celebrated by the people of Thailand?
2. What role do elephants play in Thailand?

INSTRUCT: Objective ❶

An Agricultural Economy

• Where do three-fourths of all Southeast Asians live? in rural areas, many of them on small farms

• What industries are most common? processing crops, making clothing and fabric, producing small electronics

• How is Singapore different from the rest of Southeast Asia? Most people live in the city. It is a rich nation. It exports more than half of the electronic goods it produces.

 In-depth Resources: Unit 5
• Guided Reading Worksheet, p. 28

 Reading Study Guide
(Spanish and English), pp. 138–139

MAIN IDEA	WHY IT MATTERS NOW
The economically and culturally unique nations of Southeast Asia trade with most of the world.	Southeast Asia's successes contribute to the strength of other economies.

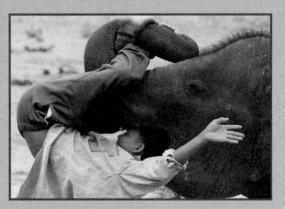

DATELINE

SURIN, THAILAND, NOVEMBER 17, 2001— One hundred elephants clashed today in a huge mock battle. Wooden weapons clattered and elephants trumpeted. Hundreds of tourists cheered during the Surin Elephant Round-Up. This yearly event reflects how important elephants have been to Thailand. Also featured was a tug of war with an elephant against men.

Place • A Thai man demonstrates his ease and skill with elephants. ▲

An Agricultural Economy ❶

Events such as elephant roundups take place in rural areas, where three-fourths of the people in Southeast Asia live, many of them on small farms where they grow rice to feed their families, not to sell for profit. Many nations of Southeast Asia are **developing nations**. They are working to improve their economies and to help people live safe, healthy, successful lives.

Program Resources

 In-depth Resources: Unit 5
• Guided Reading Worksheet, p. 28
• Reteaching Activity, p. 35

 Reading Study Guide
(Spanish and English), pp. 138–139

 Formal Assessment
• Section Quiz, p. 226

 Integrated Assessment
• Rubric for making a map

 Outline Map Activities

 Access for Students Acquiring English
• Guided Reading Worksheet, p. 134

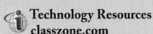 **Technology Resources** classzone.com

TEST-TAKING RESOURCES
🤿 Strategies for Test Preparation
🤿 Test Practice Transparencies
🎧 Online Test Practice

Small Farms and Factories The Green Revolution and irrigation have helped some farmers grow more food. But many others have small plots of land and cannot afford to buy fertilizers, chemicals, and modern equipment. They must rely on good weather and hard work for successful harvests.

Place • **The people of Singapore enjoy a high standard of living.** ▲

In the past 50 years, industry has become more important in Southeast Asia. Small factories that process crops, make clothing and fabric, and produce small electronic parts are the most common. Many people have moved into the larger cities looking for work.

Singapore The small country of Singapore is an exception in Southeast Asia. Virtually everyone lives in the city, also called Singapore. Though small in size, Singapore is one of the richest nations in the world and has one of the busiest ports. The production of electronic goods is its most important industry, and more than half of these goods are exported.

Skillbuilder: Reading a Chart

1. Singapore; many languages are necessary for its economy.

2. Many countries were French colonies.

The Cultures of Southeast Asia ❷

The people of Southeast Asia live in widely differing geographical regions. In rural communities, people's lives have not changed much in the past century. In the big cities, however, history and tradition stand side by side with modern architecture, automobiles, and fast-food restaurants.

Reading Social Studies
A. Possible Answer

Obstacles such as mountains, deserts, forests, or large bodies of water can isolate language groups.

Reading Social Studies

A. Drawing Conclusions
How can geography affect the languages of a nation?

Languages In Indonesia, the Philippines, and Myanmar, where communities are separated by water, dense forests, or mountains, people speak many languages. However, most people from Indonesia also speak **Bahasa Indonesian** (bah·HAH·suh), the national language. In places where there is a large Chinese population, dialects are spoken. Indians who live in parts of Southeast Asia speak Hindi or Tamil.

Languages of Southeast Asia, 2002

Country	Official Language	Other Languages Spoken
Brunei	Malay	English, Chinese
Cambodia	Khmer	French, English
Indonesia	Bahasa Indonesian	English, Dutch, Javanese, local dialects
Laos	Lao	French, English, local languages
Malaysia	Bahasa Malay	English, Chinese dialects, Tamil, Hindi, Telugu, Malayalam, Punjabi, Thai, local languages
Myanmar	Burmese	Local languages
Philippines	Filipino, English	Local languages
Singapore	Mandarin Chinese, Malay, Tamil, English	
Thailand	Thai	English, local languages and dialects
Vietnam	Vietnamese	Chinese, English, French, Khmer, local languages

SKILLBUILDER: Reading a Chart

1. Which country has the most official languages? Why do you think that is?
2. Why do you think French is spoken in several countries?

INSTRUCT: Objective ❷

The Cultures of Southeast Asia

- **Why are so many languages spoken in some countries?** People are separated by water, mountains, or forests.

- **Where are Buddhism, Islam, and Catholicism practiced in the region?** Buddhism—mainland; Islam—Indonesia, Philippines, Malaysia, Thailand; Catholicism—Vietnam, Philippines

- **What are common characteristics of Southeast Asian houses?** wood, bamboo, thatched roofs, some built on stilts

- **What is batik?** a process that uses wax and dye to make patterns on fabric

CRITICAL THINKING ACTIVITY

Analyzing Issues Ask students to consider how countries whose citizens speak, read, and write different languages should conduct elections. Discuss with students what they know about multilingual ballots in their community.

Class Time 15 minutes

FOCUS ON VISUALS

Reading a Chart Have students find the country where the most languages are spoken and discuss possible explanations for its multilingualism.

Answer Malaysia; Because it is an island nation that includes some land on the mainland, it was settled by different peoples who kept their languages or who developed new languages over time.

Extension Have students research one of the languages listed and report their findings to the class.

Activity Options

Differentiating Instruction: Gifted and Talented

Researching Challenge advanced students to do research about the major industries and products of Southeast Asia and then create a map or a chart illustrating what they have learned. If they are creating a map, remind them to invent symbols for the industries and products and to include a map key. If students create a chart, they might choose to organize information by country and by primary, secondary, tertiary, and quaternary industries. Have students prepare brief oral reports in which they use their maps or charts as references to discuss the industries of the region. In their reports, students might also discuss the historical and geographic influences on the industries, environmental concerns related to the industries, or both of these topics.

MORE ABOUT...
Pagodas

The best-known type of pagoda is found in China, Japan, and Korea. These pagodas are usually tall, ornate towers with many stories. Tibet and Southeast Asia each have different versions. While Tibet's tend to be bottle-shaped, Southeast Asia's pagodas are either shaped more like pyramids or cones. The design of the pagoda originated from an ancient Indian structure called a *stupa,* which was dome-shaped and constructed as a memorial.

CRITICAL THINKING ACTIVITY

Making Inferences Discuss with students the implications of living in a house on stilts. What difficulties does it pose? How would everyday life change during the monsoon season?

Class Time 10 minutes

Spotlight on CULTURE

An important part of any *wayang kulit* performance in Java or Bali is the accompaniment by a *gamelan* orchestra. This kind of orchestra consists of gongs and cymbals that are struck with mallets. A *gamelan* orchestra may also include a bowed stringed instrument called a *rebab* or a bamboo flute called a *suling.* The *gamelan* music establishes the mood and sets the rhythm for the puppets' movements.

Region • Buddhist temples are a common sight in Southeast Asia. ▶

Thinking Critically
Possible Answers
1. It indicates that people are very interested in ancient Hindu stories and like to use their imaginations.

2. The features on the puppets and the designs on the clothing are very intricate.

Religions A form of Buddhism is the most common religion in mainland Southeast Asia. Islam, brought by Muslims who came to Southeast Asia several centuries ago, is practiced in Malaysia, the Philippines, Thailand, and Indonesia. Spanish and Portuguese missionaries spread the Catholic faith, which is most important today in southern Vietnam and the Philippines. Protestantism and Hinduism are also practiced in the region.

Architecture Statues of the Buddha can be seen in temples all over Southeast Asia. Often the temples consist of one or more **pagodas,** or towers, built in many levels, with sculptures or carvings of Buddha on each level. Houses, built of wood or bamboo, have roofs made of **thatch,** or woven palm fronds. In areas where there is flooding from monsoons, houses are built on stilts.

Spotlight on CULTURE

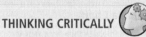

Wayang Kulit For over 1,000 years, shadow puppet theater has been a popular form of entertainment in Java, Bali, Thailand, and Cambodia. The most famous shadow theater is the Javanese *wayang kulit.* It tells ancient Hindu stories, such as the *Mahabharata.* To perform *wayang kulit,* the puppeteer sits behind a screen, moving the puppets (which are made from water buffalo hides) with rods connected to their bodies and arms. A light shines behind the puppets, casting shadows on the screen, and the audience sees only the shadows.

THINKING CRITICALLY

1. **Drawing Conclusions**
   What does the popularity of this art form tell you about Indonesian culture?

2. **Making Inferences**
   How can you tell from the design of these puppets that Javanese craftspeople are highly skilled?

446 CHAPTER 15

Activity Options

Multiple Learning Styles: Kinesthetic/Interpersonal   **Block Scheduling**

Class Time One hour

Task Creating a board game

Purpose To reinforce facts about Southeast Asia

Supplies Needed
• Poster board or cardboard
• Crayons or markers
• Index cards
• Dice
• Game pieces

Activity Have students work in small groups to create a board game about Southeast Asia. Have them think of a creative way to incorporate facts about the religion, economy, dance, architecture, language, music, dress, and theater of the region. Ask each group to create a game board and write directions for a game. Allow time for students to play one another's games.

Culture •
Weaving is an important part of Laotian culture. ▲

Culture • This Thai dance tells the story of the *Ramayana*. ▲

Dance Dancing is a popular art form in much of Southeast Asia. A dance might tell a story from history or the *Ramayana*, one of India's great epic poems. Dancers must train for years. They wear elaborate and beautiful costumes. The motions of their hands often tell the story.

Weaving Weavers in Southeast Asia use available resources. In the Philippines, fabrics are sometimes made of pineapple fiber. In Indonesia, weavers make cotton **batik** (buh·TEEK), using wax and dye to make intricate patterns on fabric. In Laos, they weave cotton and silk from fibers that are grown in Laos.

SECTION 2 ASSESSMENT

Terms & Names

1. Identify:
   (a) developing nation
   (b) Bahasa Indonesian
   (c) pagoda
   (d) thatch
   (e) batik

Taking Notes

2. Use a chart like this one to list important characteristics of the economies and cultures of Southeast Asia.

Economic Characteristics	Cultural Characteristics

Main Ideas

3. (a) Where do most of the people in Southeast Asia live?

   (b) How have the economies of Southeast Asia changed in the past 50 years?

   (c) What are the three main religions in Southeast Asia?

Critical Thinking

4. **Synthesizing**

   Why are so many languages spoken in Southeast Asia?

   Think About
   - the region's varied history and cultural influences
   - how geography contributes to the development of different ethnic groups and their languages

ACTIVITY -OPTION- Trace a **map** of Southeast Asia from the Unit Atlas on page 366. Draw arrows and write labels to show the paths of cultural influences.

Southeast Asia Today **447**

SKILLBUILDER

Distinguishing Fact from Opinion

Defining the Skill

Read aloud brief passages that contain both facts and opinions. Ask for volunteers to identify the facts and opinions. Remind students that only statements of fact can be verified. Statements of opinion often include words such as always, never, and should.

Applying the Skill

How to Distinguish Fact from Opinion
Point out the three strategies for distinguishing fact from opinion. Explain that in any given passage, as in the one here, there may be several facts and only one opinion. In other passages there may be several opinions and few if any facts. Point out that the one opinion in the passage is "it is very embarrassing." The rest of the information in the passage can be verified in sources such as encyclopedias, newspapers, and official Web sites.

Make a Chart

Discuss the chart, and ask students to add information from the passage. For each fact that is identified, discuss where the fact could be verified.

Practicing the Skill

Work with students to make a chart similar to the one shown here in order to evaluate the facts and opinions in the <u>Dateline</u> about Marco Polo on page 437. Point out that while Polo's arrival, the important papers he carried, and his plans can be considered facts, the last statement in the passage is the opinion of the writer.

 In-depth Resources: Unit 5
• Skillbuilder Practice, p. 32

Distinguishing Fact from Opinion

▶▶ Defining the Skill

A fact is a piece of information that can be proved to be true. Statements, statistics, and dates all may be facts. An opinion, on the other hand, is a belief, feeling, or judgment that is expressed by someone. An opinion cannot be proved to be true. Being able to distinguish fact from opinion is one part of critical thinking. It helps you know whether to trust an argument or to change your own opinion when someone is trying to influence you.

▶▶ Applying the Skill

The passage to the right tells about an unusual law in the country of Singapore. Use the strategies below to help you distinguish fact from opinion.

How to Distinguish Fact from Opinion

Strategy ❶ Look for facts, or information that can be proved to be true.

Strategy ❷ Look for statements that express a person's opinion, judgment, or feeling.

Strategy ❸ Think about how the facts in the passage could be checked for accuracy. Where might you look to see if they are true? Identify the facts and opinions expressed in the passage. List the facts and opinions in a chart. Also list where you could look to prove a fact.

A SINGAPORE LAW

❶ In 1992, Singapore began a program to stop littering. People caught tossing litter have to put on bright yellow vests and spend 12 hours sweeping up garbage. They may also be fined up to $2,940. And if they are caught several times, they have to attend a meeting where they learn about the costs of pollution. The punishment seems to be working. One woman who was sweeping garbage said, ❷ "Anyway, it is very embarrassing."

Make a Chart

The chart below lists some of the statements from the passage and shows whether they are facts or opinions.

Statement	❸ Can It Be Proved?	Fact or Opinion?
In 1992, Singapore began a program to stop littering.	Yes. Check a newspaper story or the laws in Singapore.	Fact
People caught littering have to sweep garbage for up to 12 hours.	Yes. Check a newspaper story or a magazine article.	Fact
"Anyway, it is very embarrassing."	No. This statement expresses a person's feelings.	Opinion

▶▶ Practicing the Skill

Turn to page 437 in Chapter 15, Section 1, and read the Dateline. Make a chart like the one above in which you list key statements and then determine whether they are facts or opinions.

Career Connection: Newspaper Columnist　　　　　🅱 **Block Scheduling**

Encourage students who enjoy distinguishing fact from opinion to find out about careers that use this skill. For example, newspaper columnists regularly express their opinions about facts that have recently been reported in the news. Columnists must make sure that readers understand which of their statements are facts and which are their opinions.

1. Help students find a variety of newspaper columns and discuss their topics. Explain that almost any topic can be appropriate for a newspaper column, but most columnists choose subjects that interest them or that are particularly timely.

2. Does a person need to be a journalist to become a newspaper columnist? Invite students to find out what education and experience are necessary to embark on this career. Ask students to share their findings in an oral summary.

Vietnam Today

TERMS & NAMES

Ho Chi Minh

Politburo

doi moi

supply and demand

Tet

MAIN IDEA

Vietnam has struggled for centuries to be a unified nation.

WHY IT MATTERS NOW

The United States and other countries have established new trade relations with a unified Vietnam.

DATELINE

SAIGON, SOUTH VIETNAM, APRIL 30, 1975—At last the war between North and South Vietnam is over. Saigon, the capital of South Vietnam, has fallen. Few thought this day would ever come. At this moment, North Vietnamese citizens and soldiers march victoriously toward Saigon.

Hundreds of South Vietnamese fought to climb aboard the last helicopters lifting Americans off the roof of the United States embassy. The thousands left behind worry about what will happen to them now.

Place • Helicopters evacuate Americans and some Vietnamese from defeated South Vietnam. ▲

A History of Struggle

The Vietnam War was only the latest in a series of wars and invasions that the people of Vietnam had endured. China ruled Vietnam for more than a millennium, until A.D. 939. During this time, the Chinese built roads and waterways. They introduced the use of metal plows, farm animals, and improved methods of irrigation. Though China strongly influenced life in Vietnam, the Vietnamese protected their own culture and traditions.

Southeast Asia Today **449**

SECTION OBJECTIVES

1. To explain Vietnam's history under the rule of the Chinese and French
2. To explain the causes of the Vietnam War and the United States' involvement
3. To identify Vietnam's current government and economy
4. To describe life in Vietnam today

SKILLBUILDER

• Interpreting a Map, p. 451

CRITICAL THINKING

• Analyzing Issues, p. 452

FOCUS & MOTIVATE
WARM-UP

Making Inferences Have students read <u>Dateline</u> and answer the following questions.

1. Who was winning the Vietnam War?
2. Why did the South Vietnamese worry about their future?

INSTRUCT: Objective ❶

A History of Struggle

• Who ruled Vietnam for more than a thousand years? China, until A.D. 939

• Why did Napoleon III invade Vietnam? to increase his empire and profit from trade

• How did the French presence influence daily life in Vietnam? higher prices of imported goods, no health care or education provided, land too expensive for the majority of farmers

 In-depth Resources: Unit 5
• Guided Reading Worksheet, p. 36

Reading Study Guide
(Spanish and English), pp. 140–141

Program Resources

 In-depth Resources: Unit 5
• Guided Reading Worksheet, p. 29
• Reteaching Activity, p. 36

Reading Study Guide
(Spanish and English), pp. 140–141

 Formal Assessment
• Section Quiz, p. 227

Integrated Assessment
• Rubric for creating ideas

 Outline Map Activities

 Access for Students Acquiring English
• Guided Reading Worksheet, p. 135

 Technology Resources
classzone.com

TEST-TAKING RESOURCES

↷ Strategies for Test Preparation
↷ Test Practice Transparencies
ⓘ Online Test Practice

INSTRUCT: Objective ❷

War

- **Who was Ho Chi Minh?** Communist leader of Vietnam's independence movement against the French

- **Why did the United States become involved in Vietnam?** to prevent the spread of communism in the region

- **What toll did the war take on the citizens of Vietnam?** 3 million died, 4 million wounded, half of the people left homeless

- **What happened when the war ended?** The country was reunited as the Socialist Republic of Vietnam. Many South Vietnamese fled to the United States and elsewhere.

MORE ABOUT...
Ho Chi Minh

Ho Chi Minh, who led the Vietnamese nationalist movement for almost 30 years, grew up in a rural village. His father was a scholar. Although Ho Chi Minh's family was poor, he was able to attend school as a teenager. After working as a schoolmaster, he became a cook on a French steamship. Later, he lived for several years in London and then France, where he worked at a variety of jobs. In France, Ho began working for the rights of Vietnamese under French colonial rule. In 1930, he helped to found the Indochinese Communist Party. Around the same time, a violent rebellion began in Vietnam. The French sentenced him to death, but he fled to safety in Moscow. He was one of the most powerful and influential leaders of the struggle against colonialism after World War II.

China invaded Vietnam again in 1407, but in 1428, after ten years of fighting, the Vietnamese were able to force out the Chinese. For a time, Vietnam enjoyed peace and prosperity. But during the 1500s and again in the 1600s, Vietnam was disrupted by civil wars. It has not enjoyed a long period of peace and growth like the one in the 1400s since.

French Rule In 1858, Napoleon III, the ruler of France, invaded Vietnam. He wanted to increase the size of his empire and benefit from more trade in Southeast Asia. Gradually, over the next 25 years, France took control of all of Vietnam, Cambodia, and Laos.

The French transported natural resources such as rice, coal, gems, and rubber out of Vietnam. They exported French goods to Vietnam, making the Vietnamese buy them at higher prices than they would have paid for goods made in neighboring countries. The French failed to bring health care and education to the people of Vietnam. Because of irrigation, there was more land to farm, but most farmers could not afford the land. During the first half of the 20th century, 3 percent of landowners in southern Vietnam owned 45 percent of the land. Peasants, who made up 70 percent of the landowners, owned only about 15 percent of the land.

Place • Ho Chi Minh was president of North Vietnam from 1954 to 1969. ▲

War ❷

Over time, the Vietnamese organized against the French. Some people, especially in northern Vietnam, also looked to China for help. **Ho Chi Minh** (HO CHEE MIN), who studied communism in the Soviet Union and China, became a leader in Vietnam's independence movement.

North and South Vietnam France tried to maintain its rule over Vietnam, but Ho Chi Minh and his government began fighting the French. He received support from the Communist government in China. The United States government, worried that communism would spread to Vietnam and other parts of the world, sent money and weapons to the French.

In 1954, an agreement was signed that again divided Vietnam into two parts: Communist North Vietnam and U.S.-supported South Vietnam. In South Vietnam, no government was able to rule successfully, and soon the Vietminh began looking for ways to overthrow South Vietnam's government and unite all of Vietnam as a Communist nation.

Reading Social Studies
A. Possible Answer They wanted to improve the quality of life for all Vietnamese, to fairly redistribute farmland, and to stop exporting necessary goods.

BACKGROUND
The organization that led Vietnam's independence movement was called the Vietminh.

Reading **Social Studies**
A. Analyzing Motives Why did the Vietnamese want to be independent from France?

Activity Options

Skillbuilder Mini-Lesson: Understanding Point of View

Explaining the Skill Explain to students that they can understand and explain historical figures' opinions and actions by analyzing their points of view.

Applying the Skill Have students reread the material about Ho Chi Minh and the U.S. intervention in Vietnam. Have them explain the opposing opinions held by the two sides in the war. To organize the information, have them create a diagram like the one shown here.

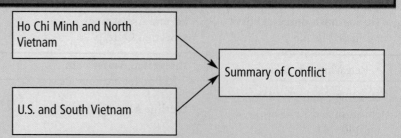

Ho Chi Minh and North Vietnam → Summary of Conflict

U.S. and South Vietnam → Summary of Conflict

Movement • Over 500,000 U.S. troops were in Vietnam in the late 1960s. ▼

Place • Many people in the United States protested the war in Vietnam. ▲

The United States Intervenes Not wanting South Vietnam to fall to communism, the United States provided it with military support. In 1965, the United States went a step further and began bombing North Vietnam. By 1973, however, opposition to the war by citizens in the United States led to the withdrawal of troops. North Vietnam overwhelmed South Vietnam, and the war ended in 1975. Three million Vietnamese died during the war, and four million were wounded. Bombs and chemical weapons destroyed much of Vietnam, leaving more than half the people homeless. The country reunited in 1976 as the Socialist Republic of Vietnam. Several hundred thousand South Vietnamese fled to the United States and other nations.

GEOGRAPHY SKILLBUILDER: Interpreting a Map

1. **Movement** • What body of water does the Red River flow into?
2. **Location** • Why might the capital city of Hanoi be located where it is?

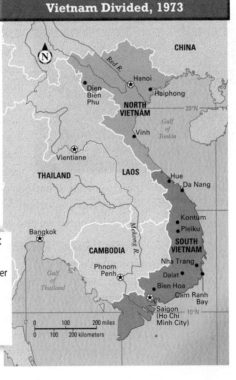

Vietnam Divided, 1973

CHINA
Red R.
Hanoi
Dien Bien Phu
Haiphong
NORTH VIETNAM
20°N
Gulf of Tonkin
Vinh
Vientiane
LAOS
THAILAND
Hue
Da Nang
Kontum
Pleiku
Bangkok
SOUTH VIETNAM
Nha Trang
CAMBODIA
Phnom Penh
Dalat
Mekong R.
Gulf of Thailand
Bien Hoa
Cam Ranh Bay
Saigon (Ho Chi Minh City)
10°N

0   100   200 miles
0   100   200 kilometers

Southeast Asia Today **451**

MORE ABOUT...
U.S. Intervention

Talks between the United States and North Vietnam began in 1968. In 1969, as antiwar protests spread throughout America, the United States began withdrawing troops from Vietnam. The United States continued to provide weapons, money, and other support for South Vietnam, but the number of American troops there fell from 540,000 in 1969 to 160,000 at the end of 1971. The peace talks broke down repeatedly. Finally, in 1973, North Vietnam, South Vietnam, and the United States reached an agreement that led to the withdrawal of nearly all American troops. By the time the war ended, more than 47,000 Americans had died fighting, another 11,000 had died of other causes while stationed in Southeast Asia, and 303,000 were wounded.

FOCUS ON VISUALS

Interpreting the Photograph Direct students' attention to the photograph of protesters and ask them to make observations about it. Prompt a discussion about the age range of the people in the photograph. Ask students why they think so many people in the United States protested the war.

Possible Response Many people were opposed to the United States' involvement in the war because they thought the United States should not decide the fate of South Vietnam.

Extension Have students go online to find primary sources that explain the point of view of protesters during the Vietnam War.

Activity Options
Multiple Learning Styles: Spatial/Visual

Class Time 30 minutes

Task Creating a time line

Purpose To understand the chronology of the conflict in Vietnam

Supplies Needed
• Paper
• Ruler
• Pens or pencils

Activity Have students create a time line of the conflict in Vietnam, beginning with the division of Vietnam in 1954. Tell students that they can design their time lines however they wish, but that they should make sure they communicate the information clearly. Encourage them to illustrate their time lines with maps, photographs, and art.

INSTRUCT: Objective ❸

Vietnam Today

- What kind of government does Vietnam have? Communist
- Why did Vietnam's economy suffer after the war? government restricted trade, many people lived in poverty, and many people left the country
- What is *doi moi?* "change for the new"; a policy that let farmers decide how to work state-controlled land and let business control prices
- What is the major crop in Vietnam? What are Vietnam's major industries? rice; food processing, silk production, and weaving

CRITICAL THINKING ACTIVITY

Analyzing Issues Remind students that the United States does not have trade or diplomatic relations with some countries. Discuss the advantages and disadvantages experienced by countries isolated from world markets and world opinion. Ask students why they think Vietnam took so long to open its borders to trade and diplomacy.

Class Time 15 minutes

MORE ABOUT...

Vietnam

Even though North Vietnam and South Vietnam are united today, the poor condition of the roads makes it difficult to travel from one to the other by land. Most of the land traffic is in a narrow area along the coast, where a railway connects Hanoi and Ho Chi Minh City.

Vietnam Today ❸

Vietnam is now a communist nation. People elect representatives to the National Assembly, which then chooses the prime minister. A group called the **Politburo** (PAHL·iht·BYUR·oh) heads the only political party, the Communist Party. The Communist Party and especially the Politburo have a major role in the government.

The Government and the Economy In a Communist nation, the government owns and runs industries and services. The government makes almost all decisions about the economy. After the Vietnam War, many people lived in poverty, while many educated people left the country. It was a difficult time for the new government. In an effort to improve the economy, the government restricted trade with other nations. Instead, this made the economic situation worse.

In 1986, the government began a policy called *doi moi* (dwa mwa), or "change for the new." Under *doi moi*, individuals gain more control of some industries. The state still owns the land, but farmers decide how to work it. Businesses can control prices, which rise and fall according to **supply and demand**. The price of a good goes up or down depending on how many people want it and how much of that good is available.

Place • People live in houseboats on the Saigon River in Ho Chi Minh City. ▲

Farming and Industry Most of the farmland in Vietnam is in the deltas of the Red and Mekong rivers. Almost four-fifths of the farmland is planted with rice, the main staple of the Vietnamese diet. There are also plantations for growing rubber, bananas, coffee, and tea. The most profitable industry in Vietnam is food processing. Seafood is frozen or canned and then exported to nations such as Japan, Germany, and the United States. Also important is silk, which is produced in Vietnam, woven into textiles, and exported around the world.

Opening Doors Perhaps the biggest boost to the Vietnamese economy occurred when Vietnam opened up trade with the rest of the world. Foreigners started businesses and invested in Vietnam, bringing money and modern technology with them.

In 1994, the United States began trading again with Vietnam. This is when the two nations reopened diplomatic relations. The governments now communicate and work together.

Reading Social Studies
B. Possible Answers
It took a long time for Vietnam to relax its restrictive trade policies; countries are most likely to form diplomatic relations when they form a good trade relationship.

B. Recognizing Effects Why might it have taken so long for diplomatic relations between Vietnam and the United States to be reopened?

452 CHAPTER 15

Activity Options

Interdisciplinary Link: Current Events

Class Time One class period
Task Create a display about Vietnam today
Purpose To learn more about life in Vietnam today

Supplies Needed
- Reference sources
- Internet access
- Mural paper or bulletin board space

ᴮ Block Scheduling

Activity Encourage students to use newspapers, magazines, and an Internet search engine to locate information about life in Vietnam today. You might want to assign students the task of finding information about the country's current economy, transportation, communication, and standard of living. Invite students to decide how to display the information they find most effectively.

Living in Vietnam

In the large cities of Vietnam, many people live in apartment buildings. One apartment may house children, their parents, and their grandparents. In the country, families live in stone houses in the north and in houses built of bamboo and wood in the warmer south. Many people do not have electricity or running water, and get their water from wells or creeks.

Culture • During the three days of Tet, people celebrate the New Year. ▲

Along the Mekong River, many people live in houseboats or in houses built on stilts to be safe from floods. In the mountains, people may live in longhouses (long, narrow buildings that hold up to 30 or 40 people). A fireplace in the middle of the house is used for cooking and warmth. A hole in the roof lets out the smoke.

Holidays The most important holiday is **Tet,** the Vietnamese New Year. This three-day festival includes parades, feasts, dances, and family gatherings. Tet marks the beginning of spring. People bring tree buds indoors to blossom. Fireworks light up the skies. Families feast on dried fruit, pickled vegetables, candy, and fish, duck, or meat in rice cakes. To start the New Year, people wear new clothes, pay debts, and settle old arguments. Children may receive gifts of money wrapped in red rice paper.

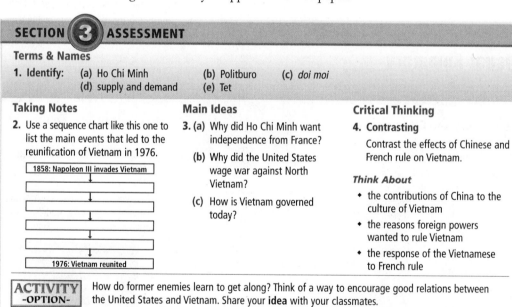

SECTION 3 ASSESSMENT

Terms & Names

1. Identify: (a) Ho Chi Minh   (b) Politburo   (c) *doi moi*
(d) supply and demand   (e) Tet

Taking Notes

2. Use a sequence chart like this one to list the main events that led to the reunification of Vietnam in 1976.

> 1858: Napoleon III invades Vietnam
> ↓
> ↓
> ↓
> ↓
> ↓
> 1976: Vietnam reunited

Main Ideas

3. (a) Why did Ho Chi Minh want independence from France?

(b) Why did the United States wage war against North Vietnam?

(c) How is Vietnam governed today?

Critical Thinking

4. Contrasting

Contrast the effects of Chinese and French rule on Vietnam.

Think About

- the contributions of China to the culture of Vietnam
- the reasons foreign powers wanted to rule Vietnam
- the response of the Vietnamese to French rule

ACTIVITY -OPTION-   How do former enemies learn to get along? Think of a way to encourage good relations between the United States and Vietnam. Share your **idea** with your classmates.

Living in Vietnam

- Where do city and country dwellers live in Vietnam? city: in apartment buildings; country: in stone or wooden houses, in houseboats, in houses on stilts, or in longhouses
- What is Vietnam's most important holiday? Tet, the New Year

ASSESS & RETEACH

Reading Social Studies Have students answer the question in the last row of the chart on page 436.

Formal Assessment
- Section Quiz, p. 227

RETEACHING ACTIVITY

Have students work in groups to outline the chapter. Have them use the section headings as headings in the outlines. Each heading should be followed by at least two subheadings or main ideas.

In-depth Resources: Unit 5
- Reteaching Activity, p. 36

Access for Students Acquiring English
- Reteaching Activity, p. 140

Section 3 Assessment

1. Terms & Names
- **a.** Ho Chi Minh, p. 450
- **b.** Politburo, p. 452
- **c.** *doi moi*, p. 452
- **d.** supply and demand, p. 452
- **e.** Tet, p. 453

2. Taking Notes

> 1954: Agreement divides Vietnam into North Vietnam and South Vietnam

> 1965: The United States intervenes against North Vietnam

> 1973: The U.S. withdraws troops from South Vietnam

3. Main Ideas
- **a.** The French were taking resources from Vietnam and demanding high prices for imported goods. There was inadequate health care and education.
- **b.** to prevent the spread of communism
- **c.** The people elect representatives to a National Assembly, which chooses the prime minister. The Communist Party is the only political party.

4. Critical Thinking

The Chinese built roads and waterways and improved agriculture. The French took resources and did not provide health care or education.

ACTIVITY OPTION

   Integrated Assessment
- Rubric for creating ideas

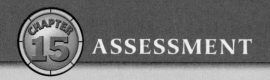

TERMS & NAMES

1. mandala, p. 438
2. military dictatorship, p. 441
3. East Timor, p. 441
4. Bahasa Indonesian, p. 445
5. batik, p. 447
6. Ho Chi Minh, p. 450
7. Politburo, p. 452
8. *doi moi*, p. 452
9. supply and demand, p. 452
10. Tet, p. 453

REVIEW QUESTIONS

Possible Responses

1. Southeast Asia adopted ideas of government and the religion of Hinduism from India. From China and India, Southeast Asia adopted Buddhism and writing systems.
2. Southeast Asians gained their independence and formed nations with different kinds of governments.
3. Most people in Southeast Asia make their living by farming.
4. People in Southeast Asia speak many different languages, practice different religions, have adapted to their physical environments in different ways, and create art and crafts unique to their region and ethnic group.
5. They wanted to free Vietnam from French rule.
6. The policies of *doi moi*, or "change for the new," and of open trade have contributed to Vietnam's economic growth.

ASSESSMENT

TERMS & NAMES

Explain the significance of each of the following:

1. mandala	2. military dictatorship	3. East Timor	4. Bahasa Indonesian	5. batik
6. Ho Chi Minh	7. Politburo	8. *doi moi*	9. supply and demand	10. Tet

REVIEW QUESTIONS

History and Governments *(pages 437–441)*

1. In what ways was the culture of Southeast Asia shaped by other cultures?
2. How did World War II and the end of colonialism affect Southeast Asia?

Economies and Cultures *(pages 444–447)*

3. How do most of the people in Southeast Asia make a living?
4. In what ways are people in Southeast Asia culturally different from one another?

Vietnam Today *(pages 449–453)*

5. Why were Ho Chi Minh and the Vietminh trying to overthrow the government of South Vietnam?
6. What two government policies contributed to Vietnam's growing economy?

CRITICAL THINKING

Drawing Conclusions

1. Using your completed chart from Reading Social Studies, p. 436, decide whether or not it is in the best interests of Southeast Asian countries to develop industries that will enable them to increase their international trade. List the facts and examples that support your conclusion.

Clarifying

2. Why do you think Southeast Asian nations were in political turmoil after the colonial powers withdrew?

Forming and Supporting Opinions

3. What personal qualities did Ho Chi Minh need to possess in order to lead Vietnam's independence movement?

Visual Summary

1 History and Governments

- India and China greatly influenced the culture of Southeast Asia.
- When European colonialism ended, Southeast Asian nations established their own governments including constitutional monarchies, republics, military dictatorships, and Communist states.

2 Economies and Cultures

- Most of the people in Southeast Asia make their living by farming, but industry is growing.
- Language, religion, and art in Southeast Asia are a blend of local and foreign influences.

Vietnam Today 3

- Vietnam struggled against France, China, the United States, and itself before being reunited as a single, independent country in 1976.
- Today Vietnam is a communist nation that encourages world trade, including trade with the United States.

CRITICAL THINKING: Possible Responses

1. Drawing Conclusions

Students may say that it is important for Southeast Asian countries to develop industries for the global market and point to the success of Singapore and Vietnam as examples.

2. Clarifying

Their colonial rulers left without setting up workable governments; Southeast Asians had not ruled themselves for many years and were not prepared to do so.

3. Forming and Supporting Opinions

Students may cite such qualities as charisma, commitment to his cause, courage, and determination.

SOCIAL STUDIES SKILLBUILDER

SKILLBUILDER: Distinguishing Fact from Opinion

In the 1960s, a military adviser to the President of the United States might have made the following statement:

> Vietnam borders two other Southeast Asian countries. If the North Vietnamese Communists win, all of Southeast Asia will fall to communism. To prevent that, we should support the South Vietnamese.

1. Look at the map and read the statement. Which part is factual? Which part is an opinion?
2. Based on the facts, do you agree with the opinion? Why or why not?

FOCUS ON GEOGRAPHY

1. **Movement** • From where did early invaders to Vietnam come?
2. **Place** • Which kingdom included much of present-day Myanmar?
3. **Location** • Why do you think China and India, but not Europe, had a great influence on Southeast Asia?

CHAPTER PROJECTS

Interdisciplinary Activity: Literature

Storytelling Find and memorize a folk tale from one of the Southeast Asian countries. Retell the story to your classmates. Be sure to remember all the important details and make it exciting for your listeners.

Cooperative Learning Activity

Creating a Newscast In a group of three to five students, create a television or radio newscast about a significant event in the chapter. For example, you might focus on the withdrawal of Europeans from Southeast Asia, the invasion of East Timor by Indonesia, or the Vietnam War.

- Take on the roles of director, writers, and anchors.
- Work on a rough draft of the report and practice delivering the news broadcast.
- Perform your final version of the news broadcast for the class.

INTERNET ACTIVITY

Use the Internet to research education in Southeast Asia. Choose one country and find out as much information as you can about how children are educated and what it's like to be a student in that country.

Writing About Geography Write a report about your findings. Include photographs and drawings to illustrate your information. List the Web sites you used to prepare your report.

For Internet links to support this activity, go to

RESEARCH LINKS
CLASSZONE.COM

Southeast Asia Today **455**

CHAPTER PROJECTS

Interdisciplinary Activity: Literature

Storytelling You might want to provide students with a list of sources to help them find the folk tales. Encourage students to include as many details as possible in their presentations and to make their presentations exciting by using gestures, facial expressions, sound effects, costumes, and props.

Cooperative Learning Activity

Creating a Newscast Once each group has selected a topic, briefly discuss the content and style of newscasts that students have seen on television or heard on the radio. Divide students into small groups and have them assign the roles of director, researchers, writers, and anchors. Remind them that the newscast they perform in class must be more polished than their written rough draft and initial practice sessions. Once the newscasts have been performed, encourage the other students to give constructive criticism, both of the content and of its delivery.

INTERNET ACTIVITY

Discuss how students might use the Internet to find information about education in a Southeast Asian country. Brainstorm possible key words, Web sites, and search engines, both for finding official data and for exploring individual opinions and personal experiences.

Suggest that students make a chart to record their information. They might want to create categories for the chart such as Literacy, Length of Schooling, and so on. Once they have gathered the information, they can use the information in their charts to write their reports. When they have finished, ask students to exchange reports with a classmate, read the reports, and note any remaining questions they might have.

Skills Answers

Social Studies Skillbuilder
Possible Responses

1. The quotation, with phrases like "all of Southeast Asia will eventually fall to communism" and "we should support," is an opinion. The map is factual because information on it can be checked in other places.
2. Students should give clear explanations about why they agree or do not agree with the opinion. They should refer to the map to support their ideas.

Focus on Geography
Possible Responses

1. China
2. pagan kingdom
3. China and India border Southeast Asia, which made Southeast Asia more accessible to rulers and traders living in those places.

UNIT 6

East Asia, Australia, and the Pacific Islands

Before You Read

Previewing Unit 6

Unit 6 explores the land and history of East Asia, Australia, and the Pacific Islands and the unique physical features and ancient cultures that define the area. Then the unit compares the changing governments, economies, and cultures of modern China and the other countries in East Asia. The focus of the unit turns to an examination of the histories and governments of Australia, New Zealand, and the Pacific Islands and the great diversity of cultures and economies that exists there today.

Place The Great Wall of China stretches for about 4,000 miles. Built to defend China from foreign invaders, the Great Wall was constructed in stages, from the 7th century B.C. to the 15th century A.D.

456

Unit Level Activities

1. Design a Travel Poster

Remind students that East Asia, Australia, and the Pacific Islands have many attractions for tourists. As they read the unit, have them look for places of particular interest. When they have completed the unit, they should design a travel poster that depicts the climate and scenery of one country. Remind students that their posters are meant to attract tourists to the area.

2. Writing a Letter

Remind the class that students in Australia and China participate in the same activities of school, sports, and friendships as they do. As they read, have students look for information about everyday life in one of these countries. After they have completed the unit, they should write a letter from a student to a student of similar age in another country. Suggest that they include details about climate, scenery, the type of the government, or the role of women in the country they have chosen.

EAST ASIA, AUSTRALIA, AND THE PACIFIC ISLANDS

FOCUS ON VISUALS

Analyzing the Photograph Have students look at the 4,000 mile expanse of the Great Wall in China. Ask them to think about why it was built. Have a student volunteer read the caption aloud. Then conduct a class discussion about the purpose of the wall. What kind of attacks do students think the wall was designed to protect against? Do they think is was successful in keeping out intruders? Do they know of any other cultures that built similar walls? Would they be likely to see something similar anywhere else in the world?

Possible Responses The wall was designed to protect against attacks on foot by people holding weapons. It was probably successful. Other cultures built forts or castles with a similar purpose. They are not likely to see anything this huge anywhere else in the world.

Extension Have students write a short paragraph describing the wall as it must look from space or from an airplane flying overhead.

457

Implementing the National Geography Standards

Standard 8 Identify flora and fauna of an ecosystem

Objective To create a diorama of an East Asian, Australian, or Pacific Islands ecosystem

Class Time 40 minutes

Task Have students work in groups to create a diorama illustrating an East Asian, Australian, or Pacific Islands ecosystem. Students can use the Internet or library references to choose and research which ecosystem they wish to depict. Students should write index cards explaining how elements in their ecosystems are both linked and independent.

Evaluation Each ecosystem diorama should illustrate at least three examples of linked elements and three examples of independent elements.

UNIT 6

ATLAS
East Asia, Australia, and the Pacific Islands

ATLAS OBJECTIVES

1. Locate physical features of East Asia, Australia, and the Pacific Islands

2. Describe the vegetation of East Asia, Australia, and the Pacific Islands and compare the landmass and population of this region with that of the U.S.

3. Identify political features of East Asia, Australia, and the Pacific Islands

4. Compare data about the countries of East Asia, Australia, and the Pacific Islands

FOCUS & MOTIVATE

Ask students what types of information maps and charts can convey about this region. Answers will vary. Maps and charts can give facts about landforms, bodies of water, national borders, population, and products and resources.

INSTRUCT: Objective ①

Physical Map of East Asia, Australia, and the Pacific Islands

• In what country do you find the highest elevations? China

• What ocean borders most of this region? Pacific Ocean

• What is the southernmost country of this region? New Zealand

 In-depth Resources: Unit 6
  • Unit Atlas Activity, p. 1

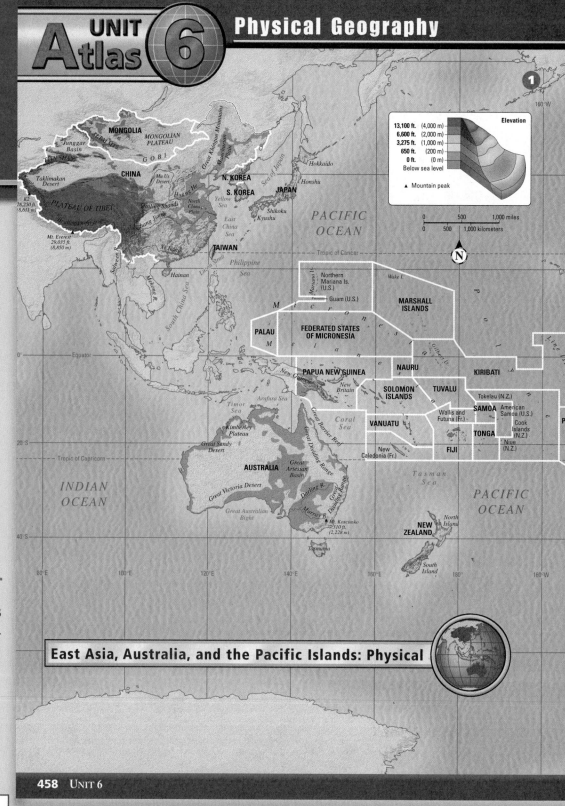

East Asia, Australia, and the Pacific Islands: Physical

Activity Options

Interdisciplinary Link: Mathematics

Block Scheduling

Explaining the Skill Students will demonstrate their ability to identify and compare elevations throughout a region, using a physical map.

Applying the Skill Direct students to create bar graphs showing the highest and lowest elevations for various parts of East Asia, Australia, and the Pacific Islands. On the vertical axis of the graph, have them mark the elevations shown in the map key on this page. On the horizon-

tal axis, have them write China, Australia, Melanesia, Micronesia, and Polynesia. Then have them identify the highest and lowest point in each region and draw two bars showing these elevations. Encourage students to use two different colored pencils when drawing the bars—one color for the highest and one color for the lowest elevation. Have students form small groups and compare their graphs.

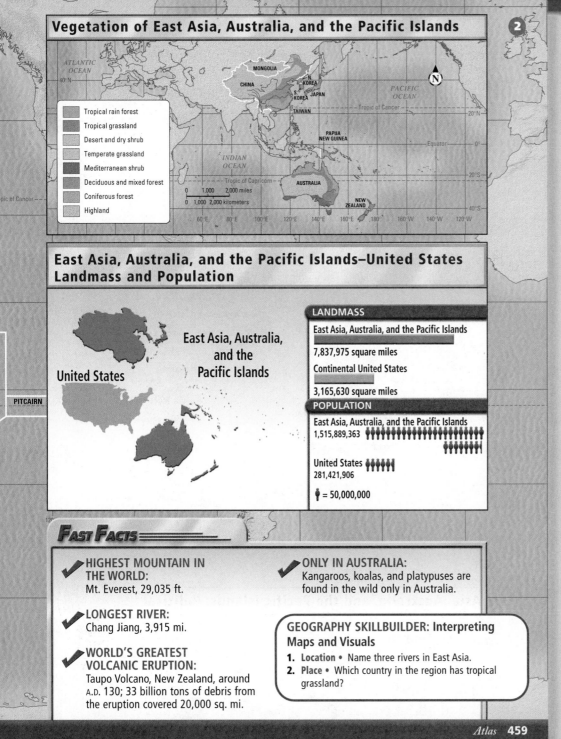

Vegetation of East Asia, Australia, and the Pacific Islands

Legend:
- Tropical rain forest
- Tropical grassland
- Desert and dry shrub
- Temperate grassland
- Mediterranean shrub
- Deciduous and mixed forest
- Coniferous forest
- Highland

East Asia, Australia, and the Pacific Islands—United States Landmass and Population

United States

East Asia, Australia, and the Pacific Islands

LANDMASS

East Asia, Australia, and the Pacific Islands
7,837,975 square miles

Continental United States
3,165,630 square miles

POPULATION

East Asia, Australia, and the Pacific Islands
1,515,889,363

United States
281,421,906

= 50,000,000

FAST FACTS

✓ **HIGHEST MOUNTAIN IN THE WORLD:**
Mt. Everest, 29,035 ft.

✓ **LONGEST RIVER:**
Chang Jiang, 3,915 mi.

✓ **WORLD'S GREATEST VOLCANIC ERUPTION:**
Taupo Volcano, New Zealand, around A.D. 130; 33 billion tons of debris from the eruption covered 20,000 sq. mi.

✓ **ONLY IN AUSTRALIA:**
Kangaroos, koalas, and platypuses are found in the wild only in Australia.

GEOGRAPHY SKILLBUILDER: Interpreting Maps and Visuals
1. **Location** • Name three rivers in East Asia.
2. **Place** • Which country in the region has tropical grassland?

Atlas **459**

INSTRUCT: Objective ②

Vegetation Map of East Asia, Australia, and the Pacific Islands

- What country is covered with dense vegetation? Papua New Guinea

Land Area

- About how much larger is this region than is the United States? about 4 million square miles

Population

- How many times larger is the population of this region than that of the United States? about 6 times larger

Fast Facts

- Where did the world's greatest volcanic eruption occur? New Zealand

MORE ABOUT...
Pidgin English

The people of Papua New Guinea speak over 700 languages. Today, they overcome that obstacle by using Pidgin English. Pidgin is a dialect based on English. It was created so that westerners could do business (*pidgin* is an altered pronunciation of the word *business*) with the people. In Pidgin English, English grammar and syntax are simplified, and the sounds have been altered. Examples include *bikos* (because) and *dispela* (this fellow).

Fast Facts

Direct students' attention to the Fast Facts. Urge them to build their own Fast Facts files using atlases, almanacs, and encyclopedias.

GEOGRAPHY SKILLBUILDER
Answers
1. Huang He (Yellow), Chang Jiang (Yangtze), Xi Jiang
2. Australia

Country Profiles

Republic of Nauru The country of Nauru is made up of a single eight-square-mile coral island about 2,400 miles northeast of Sydney, Australia. The central region of the island is a plateau of coral cliffs that is about 100 feet high. The plateau is formed from the mineral phosphate, which comes from bird droppings. The phosphate makes up about 70 percent of the island and is the center of Nauru's economy. The phosphate is mined and exported as fertilizer. This single export has made the Nauruans so wealthy that many choose not to work. Nauru imports nearly everything needed, including food and water. Nauru hires people from the outside to perform most of the manual labor needed on the island. Because phosphate deposits are expected to run out shortly, the government has invested much of the earnings in businesses outside the country, such as shipping lines, airlines, and real estate.

INSTRUCT: Objective 3

Political Map of East Asia, Australia, and the Pacific Islands

- What is the largest country in this region? China
- What two countries are on a peninsula? North Korea and South Korea
- What countries and island groups lie entirely in the Southern Hemisphere? Australia, New Zealand, Papua New Guinea, French Polynesia

MORE ABOUT…

Macao

The territory of Macao is made up of a peninsula extending into the South China Sea. It is connected by causeways to the islands of Taipa and Coloane. In December 1999 Macao officially became a special administrative region of China, but for centuries Portugal was a dominant influence in Macao. Today more than 90 percent of Macao's people are Chinese. People of Portuguese descent make up the rest of the population. Much of Macao's architecture is Portuguese, especially the churches, cathedrals, and colonial villas. Local radio stations broadcast in Portuguese, and a television station uses Portuguese and English.

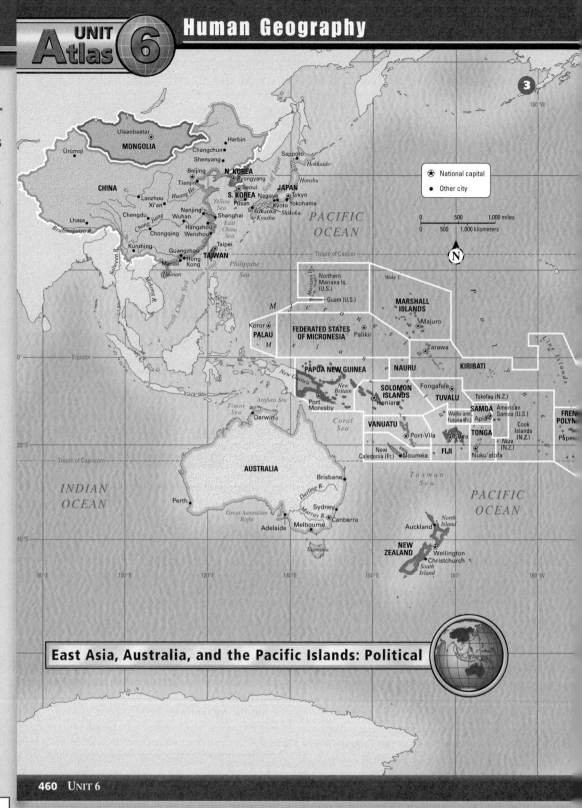

East Asia, Australia, and the Pacific Islands: Political

Activity Options

Interdisciplinary Link: History

Class Time One class period

Task Writing a travel narrative

Purpose To learn about the voyages of Captain James Cook

Supplies Needed
- Reference materials on Captain James Cook
- Writing paper
- Pens and pencils

Activity Tell students that the British explorer Captain James Cook made many voyages of discovery in the South Pacific. Have students read about some of Cook's voyages and what he discovered. Then have students imagine that they are passengers on Cook's ship. Have them write a brief narrative describing some part of the voyage or how Cook made one of his discoveries. Encourage student volunteers to read their narratives aloud in class.

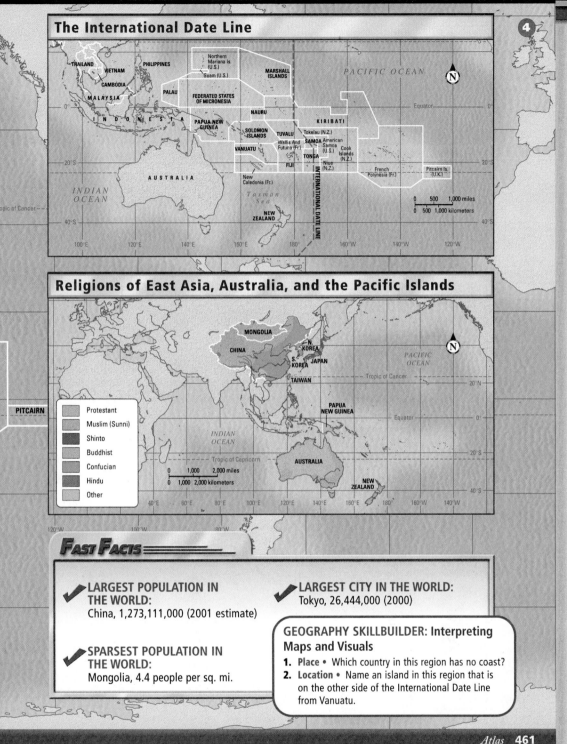

The International Date Line

Religions of East Asia, Australia, and the Pacific Islands

Protestant
Muslim (Sunni)
Shinto
Buddhist
Confucian
Hindu
Other

FAST FACTS

✓ **LARGEST POPULATION IN THE WORLD:**
China, 1,273,111,000 (2001 estimate)

✓ **SPARSEST POPULATION IN THE WORLD:**
Mongolia, 4.4 people per sq. mi.

✓ **LARGEST CITY IN THE WORLD:**
Tokyo, 26,444,000 (2000)

GEOGRAPHY SKILLBUILDER: Interpreting Maps and Visuals
1. **Place** • Which country in this region has no coast?
2. **Location** • Name an island in this region that is on the other side of the International Date Line from Vanuatu.

Atlas **461**

INSTRUCT: Objective ❹

International Date Line

• Is the date on the eastern side of the Date Line one day ahead or one day behind the date on the western side of the line? one day ahead

Religions of East Asia, Australia, and the Pacific Islands

• What are the dominant religions of Papua New Guinea, Australia, and China? Papua New Guinea: Christian and indigenous; Australia: Christian and indigenous; China: Confucianism

Fast Facts

• What is the average number of persons per square mile in the least populated country in the world? 4.4 persons

MORE ABOUT...
Dreamtime

The religion of the Australian Aborigines is based on a belief in the Dreamtime, or the Dreaming. Aborigines believe that during the Dreamtime, ancestral beings shaped the natural world, creating rivers, mountains, rocks, plants, and animals. According to the stories, these ancestral spirits still live today.

Fast Facts

Invite students to use these Fast Facts as a starting point to create their own fact file. Suggest that they use almanacs and atlases in their research.

GEOGRAPHY SKILLBUILDER
Answers
1. Mongolia
2. Cook Islands, French Polynesia, Pitcairn Islands

Country Profiles

Fiji Fiji is a country made up of about 330 islands in the Pacific Ocean, south of the equator. Two main islands make up most of the country: Viti Levu and Vanua Levu. Many of the other islands are tiny sand-covered coral reefs. Volcanoes formed most of the Fiji islands. The large islands are covered by tropical rain forests and grasslands, and have high volcanic peaks and fertile plains along the coast.

Native Fijians are Melanesian; they make up about half the population. The majority of native Fijians practice the Christian religion. About 45 percent of the population are descendants of people who came from India to work on Fiji sugar plantations between 1879 and 1916. Agriculture is the primary economic activity in Fiji, with most Fijians growing coconuts and sugar cane.

DATA FILE OBJECTIVE

Analyze and compare data on countries of East Asia, Australia, and the Pacific Islands

FOCUS & MOTIVATE

Direct students' attention to the Data File. Help them focus on individual columns in the chart by asking the following questions:

What column of data relates to a country's size? total area

What country has the largest area? China

What country has the smallest population? Tuvalu

INSTRUCT: Objective ⑤

Data File

• Which country has the lowest literacy rate? Vanuatu

• What currency is used in Kiribati? Australian dollar

• What is the approximate difference in population between North Korea and South Korea? South Korea has nearly 26 million more people than North Korea.

• Which country has the highest infant mortality rate, Australia or New Zealand? New Zealand, with 5.5 per 1,000 live births

  In-depth Resources: Unit 6
• Data File Activity, p. 2

Country Flag	Country/Capital	Currency	Population (2001 estimate)	Life Expectancy (years)	Birthrate (per 1,000 pop.) (2000 estimate)
	Australia Canberra	Australian Dollar	19,358,000	79	13
	China Beijing	Renminbi	1,273,111,000	71	15
	Fiji Suva	Dollar	844,000	67	22
	Japan Tokyo	Yen	126,772,000	80	9
	Kiribati Tawara	Australian Dollar	94,000	62	33
	Marshall Islands Majuro	U.S. Dollar	71,000	65	26
	Micronesia, Fed. States of Palikir	U.S. Dollar	135,000	66	33
	Mongolia Ulaanbaatar	Tugrik	2,655,000	63	20
	Nauru Yaren Administrative Center	Australian Dollar	12,000	61	19
	New Zealand Wellington	New Zealand Dollar	3,864,000	77	15
	North Korea Pyongyang	Won	21,968,000	70	21
	Palau Koror	U.S. Dollar	19,000	67	18
	Papua New Guinea Port Moresby	Kina	5,049,000	56	34
	Samoa Apia	Tala	179,000	68	31
	Solomon Islands Honiara	Dollar	480,000	71	37
	South Korea Seoul	Won	47,904,000	74	14
	Taiwan Taipei	New Taiwan Dollar	22,370,000	75	13

Activity Options

Interdisciplinary Link: Mathematics

Class Time One class period

Task Calculating a country's growth rate

Purpose To analyze vital statistics to identify population growth rate

Supplies Needed
• Almanacs or other references showing mortality statistics
• Writing paper
• Pencils or pens

Activity Tell students that they can calculate a country's growth rate by comparing birth and death statistics. Have students locate the birthrate per 1,000 for one country in the Data File. Then have them use reference sources to locate the death rate per 1,000 people for that country. Have students subtract the death rate from the birthrate. The result will tell them the growth rate. Have students share their findings in class.

DATA FILE

Infant Mortality (per 1,000 live births) (2000)	Doctors (per 100,000 pop.) (1994–1999)	Literacy Rate (percentage) (1996–1998)	Passenger Cars (per 1,000 pop.) (1996–1997)	Total Area (square miles)	Map (not to scale)
5.3	240.0	100	453	2,967,909	
31.4	161.7	82	4	3,704,427	
12.9	48.0	92	37	7,055	
3.5	193.2	99	367	143,619	
62.0	30.0	90	N/A	277	
30.5	42.0	93	N/A	70	
46.0	57.0	90	N/A	1,055	
34.1	243.3	83	8	604,247	
25.0	157.0	99	N/A	8.2	
5.5	217.0	100	391	103,736	
26.0	297.0	99	N/A	46,609	
19.2	110.0	98	N/A	191	
77.0	7.0	72	5	178,260	
25.0	34.0	98	7	1,209	
25.3	14.0	54	N/A	11,500	
11.0	136.1	98	2	38,022	
6.6	100.0	94	198	13,887	

MORE ABOUT...
Population Studies

The study of statistics related to human population is called demography. Demographers are concerned with the size, density, and distribution of populations, as well as with vital statistics such as births, marriages, and deaths. These statistics help government and business officials, as well as health providers, identify trends and predict future needs in society.

For centuries, marriages, baptisms, and deaths were recorded in local church registries. As early as the 17th century, an Englishman began studying these records and analyzing the birth and death rates.

In the 18th century, the life insurance business developed, and officials began to pay attention to the death rates. By the 19th century, official civil registries of births, deaths, and marriages took the place of church registries.

Today, many organizations are devoted to the study of demographics. The analysis of population statistics has become very sophisticated, but demographers must still rely on the accuracy of census takers and the registration of vital statistics.

Activity Options

Interdisciplinary Link: Mathematics

Class Time 30 minutes

Task Calculating doctor/patient ratio

Purpose To understand the significance of statistical information on doctors per 100,000

Supplies Needed
- Paper, pencils or pens
- Calculators (optional)

Activity Guide students through these calculations. First, have them choose one of the countries in the Data File. They should divide the population by 100,000 and then multiply that figure by the number of doctors per 100,000. This provides the total number of doctors. You might model the process by using figures for the United States. Have students discuss whether they think the number of doctors is adequate.

MORE ABOUT...
Polynesians

The settlers of the Pacific Islands came in waves, first to Melanesia and Micronesia, and later to Polynesia. The people of Polynesia are taller than people of the other groups and have lighter skin. Their hair may be straight or wavy. Inhabitants of some of the Polynesian islands—especially Hawaii, Tonga, and Samoa—are strong, large-boned people.

The people of Polynesia developed a distinct culture. One traditional and unique aspect of their culture was their approach to child rearing. In traditional Polynesian culture, the birth of a child was an important event, especially if the child was the firstborn son of a family of high status. Special traditions were followed to announce the birth to the community.

The new baby was usually welcomed into a large, warm family. Before he could walk, his primary care was turned over to other children of the family, such as brothers and sisters or cousins. He was carried around piggyback by an older sister or brother. When he learned to walk, he followed the other children around.

Polynesian children had especially warm, close ties with their grandparents, who passed on traditional lore and trained the children in technical crafts.

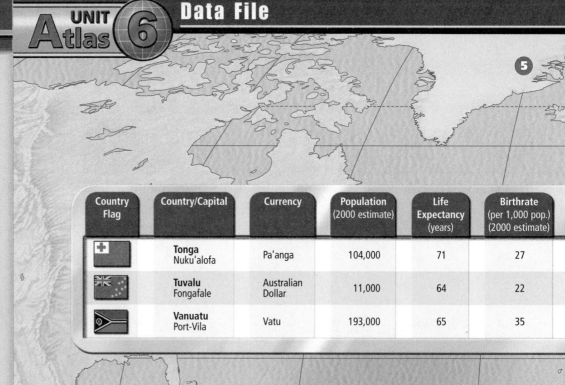

Country Flag	Country/Capital	Currency	Population (2000 estimate)	Life Expectancy (years)	Birthrate (per 1,000 pop.) (2000 estimate)
	Tonga Nuku'alofa	Pa'anga	104,000	71	27
	Tuvalu Fongafale	Australian Dollar	11,000	64	22
	Vanuatu Port-Vila	Vatu	193,000	65	35

An Aborigine artist ▼

Easter Island stone heads ▼

Celebration in Beijing ▼

Activity Options
Interdisciplinary Link: Mathematics

Class Time 30 minutes

Task Comparing population density

Purpose To calculate and compare the population density of two countries

Supplies Needed
• Paper
• Pencils or pens

Activity Explain that population density is determined by dividing the population of a country by its area. The result is the average number of people living in each square mile. Have students refer to the Data File and calculate the population density for China and Japan. Point out that Japan is more crowded than China, and yet the Japanese are more prosperous than are the people of China. Have students discuss why they think this is so.

DATA FILE

Infant Mortality (per 1,000 live births) (2000)	Doctors (per 100,000 pop.) (1994–1999)	Literacy Rate (percentage) (1996–1998)	Passenger Cars (per 1,000 pop.) (1996–1997)	Total Area (square miles)	Map (not to scale)
19.0	44	93	31	270	
24.8	30	95	N/A	9	
39.0	12	36	21	5,700	

GEOGRAPHY SKILLBUILDER: Interpreting a Chart

1. **Place** • How much lower is Vanuatu's literacy rate than New Zealand's?
2. **Place** • How much larger is Australia's population than Kiribati's?

Terraced rice fields in China ▼

A Chinese family ▼

A Shinto archway in Japan ▲

Atlas **465**

MORE ABOUT...
Birthrates

Birthrates are a way of measuring population change. They can be used to compare population information from year to year. The simplest kind of birthrate statistic is the crude birthrate, which gives the number of births for every 1,000 people. The death rate, or mortality rate, gives the number of deaths for every 1,000 people. When the birthrate is equal to the death rate, the condition is called zero population growth, meaning that theoretically the number of people remains constant.

The crude birthrate measures the number of births for every 1,000 people in the population, which includes people of all ages and sexes. Another way of measuring birthrate is the fertility rate, which measures the number of births to women of childbearing age in the population.

GEOGRAPHY SKILLBUILDER
Answers

1. New Zealand has 100% literacy, and Vanuatu has 36% literacy, which means that Vanuatu's rate is 64% lower than New Zealand's.
2. Australia's population is 19,358,000 while Kiribati's is 94,000, which means that Australia has 19,264,000 more people than Kiribati.

Activity Options

Interdisciplinary Instruction: Gifted and Talented

B **Block Scheduling**

Class Time One class period

Task Compiling statistics

Purpose To identify other important statistics

Supplies Needed
• Library and Internet resources
• Pens or pencils

Activity Divide the class into small groups. Have each group choose one country and brainstorm some statistics that would be useful in understanding more about that country. For example, students might want to know the number of bicycles or the average annual income. Urge students to choose two or three statistics and collaborate in locating the statistics for that country. Have each group compile their findings in a chart and share it with the class.

East Asia, Australia, and the Pacific Islands: Land and History

	OVERVIEW	COPYMASTERS	INTEGRATED TECHNOLOGY
UNIT ATLAS AND CHAPTER RESOURCES	Students will examine the geographic features of East Asia, Australia, and the Pacific Islands and how geography affects economic activity. Students will also examine the contributions of ancient China and ancient Japan and how China affected cultural developments in Japan.	**In-depth Resources: Unit 6** • Guided Reading Worksheets, pp. 3–5 • Skillbuilder Practice, p. 8 • Unit Atlas Activities, pp. 1–2 • Geography Workshop, pp. 35–36 **Reading Study Guide** (Spanish and English), pp. 144–151 **Outline Map Activities**	Power Presentations Electronic Teacher Tools Online Lesson Planner Chapter Summaries on CD Critical Thinking Transparencies CT31

	KEY IDEAS	COPYMASTERS	INTEGRATED TECHNOLOGY
SECTION 1 Physical Geography pp. 469–474	• East Asia consists of China, Japan, North Korea, South Korea, Mongolia, and Taiwan. • East Asia's physical geography includes high plateaus, deserts, coastal plains, and rivers. • Australia's landscape has remained largely unchanged for millions of years.	**In-depth Resources: Unit 6** • Guided Reading Worksheet, p. 3 • Reteaching Activity, p. 10 **Reading Study Guide** (Spanish and English), pp. 144–145	Map Transparencies MT33, 35 classzone.com Chapter Summaries on CD
SECTION 2 Ancient China pp. 475–490	• Dynasties, or families of rulers, ruled China for thousands of years. • Ancient Chinese contributions to world culture include the Tao and Buddhist religions, centralized government, and the manufacture of silk and porcelain.	**In-depth Resources: Unit 6** • Guided Reading Worksheet, p. 4 • Reteaching Activity, p. 11 **Reading Study Guide** (Spanish and English), pp. 146–147	Critical Thinking Transparencies CT32 classzone.com Chapter Summaries on CD
SECTION 3 Ancient Japan pp. 484–488	• China and Korea greatly influenced Japan's development. • The shogun held the most power in feudal Japan, while the emperor held a ceremonial role. • The Tokugawa shogun closed Japan to outsiders for fear of European influence and possible takeover.	**In-depth Resources: Unit 6** • Guided Reading Worksheet, p. 4 • Reteaching Activity, p. 12 **Reading Study Guide** (Spanish and English), pp. 148–149	classzone.com Chapter Summaries on CD

Audio   Internet   TE Teacher's Edition

 CD-ROM   Overhead Transparency   Video

Copymaster   PE Pupil's Edition

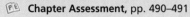
ASSESSMENT OPTIONS

RESOURCES FOR DIFFERENTIATING INSTRUCTION

PE **Chapter Assessment,** pp. 490–491

Formal Assessment
• Chapter Tests: Forms A, B, C, pp. 243–254

Test Generator

Online Test Practice

Strategies for Test Preparation

Students Acquiring English/ESL

Reading Study Guide (Spanish and English), pp. 144–151

Access for Students Acquiring English Spanish Translations, pp. 141–148

Less Proficient Readers

Reading Study Guide (Spanish and English), pp. 144–151

TE **TE Activities**
• Identifying Main Ideas and Details, p. 470
• Creating a Time Line, p. 476

Gifted and Talented Students

TE **TE Activity**
• Imagining Samurai Life, p. 487

PE **Section Assessment,** p. 474

Formal Assessment
• Section Quiz, p. 240

Integrated Assessment
• Rubric for making a diagram

Test Generator

Test Practice Transparencies TT56

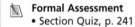
CROSS-CURRICULAR CONNECTIONS

Humanities
Ganeri, Anita. *Ancient China.* Mankato, MN: Thameside Press, 1999. Emphasizes legacies of the ancient Chinese.

Hamanaka, Sheila. *In Search of the Spirit: The Living National Treasures of Japan.* New York: HarperCollins, 1999. Crafts passed from ancient to modern times.

Literature
Chin, Charlie. *China's Bravest Girl: The Legend of Hua Mu Lan.* New York: Children's Press, 1997. Bilingual epic poem from fifth-century China.

Chen, Kerstin. *Lord of the Cranes.* New York: North-South, 2000. Chinese wisdom tale.

Popular Culture
MacDonald, Fiona. *Step into Ancient Japan.* New York: Lorenz Books, 1999. Fifteen projects related to Japanese civilization to 1600.

Geography
Pollard, Michael. *The Yangtze.* New York: Benchmark Books, 1998. How the river supports civilization and animal life.

Science/Math
Fisher, Leonard Everett. *The Great Wall of China.* New York: Aladdin, 1995. Classic and readable illustrated history.

Mathematics
Pilegard, Virginia. *The Warlord's Puzzle.* Gretna, LA: Pelican Press, 2000. Legend of how tangrams were discovered.

The Ancient Mystery of Tangrams. New York: Running Press, 2000. Geometric puzzles to reinforce *The Warlord's Puzzle.*

Science
Patent, Dorothy Hinshaw. *The Incredible Story of China's Buried Warriors.* New York: Benchmark Books, 2000. Archaeological find and history.

PE **Section Assessment,** p. 480

Formal Assessment
• Section Quiz, p. 241

Integrated Assessment
• Rubric for writing a journal entry

Test Generator

Test Practice Transparencies TT57

ENRICHMENT ACTIVITIES

The following activities are especially suitable for classes following block schedules.

Teacher's Edition, pp. 471, 478, 481, 486
Pupil's Edition, pp. 474, 480, 488

Unit Atlas, pp. 458–465
Literature Connections, pp. 482–483

Technology: 2009, p. 489
Outline Map Activities

PE **Section Assessment,** p. 488

Formal Assessment
• Section Quiz, p. 242

Integrated Assessment
• Rubric for writing a story

Test Generator

Test Practice Transparencies TT58

INTEGRATED TECHNOLOGY

Go to **classzone.com** for lesson support and activities for Chapter 16.

BLOCK SCHEDULE LESSON PLAN OPTIONS: 90-MINUTE PERIOD

DAY 1

UNIT PREVIEW, pp. 456–457
Class Time 10 minutes

• **Discussion** Discuss the Unit Introduction using the discussion prompts on TE pp. 456–457.

UNIT ATLAS, pp. 458–465
Class Time 30 minutes

• **Small Groups** Divide the class into four groups and have each group answer the Making Comparisons questions for one section of the Unit Atlas: Physical Geography, Human Geography, Regional Patterns, and Data File.

SECTION 1, pp. 469–474
Class Time 50 minutes

• **Outline Maps** In preparation for discussing Section 1, provide students with outline maps of China, Japan, the Koreas, and Australia. Have students fill in and label the major mountains, deserts, and rivers. If students need help completing the maps, have them refer to the Unit Atlas map on PE p. 458.
Class Time 40 minutes

• **Peer Teaching** Have pairs of students review the Main Idea for the section on PE p. 469 and find three details to support it. Then have each pair list two additional important ideas and trade lists with another group to find details.
Class Time 10 minutes

DAY 2

SECTION 2, pp. 475–480
Class Time 65 minutes

• **Creating a Time Line** Use Focus on Visuals: Interpreting the Chart on TE p. 476 to review the chart on PE p. 476 with the students. Then create a time line on the chalkboard to show the time period of each dynasty. Invite volunteers to add time periods and dynasties to the time line. Have students copy the time line on a piece of paper and add important events and achievements that occurred during each dynasty.
Class Time 40 minutes

• **Skillbuilder Practice** Use the Activity Options about distinguishing fact from opinion on TE p. 477 and the Skillbuilder Practice worksheet.
Class Time 25 minutes

SECTION 3, pp. 484–488
Class Time 25 minutes

• **Press Conference** Have a group of four students field questions about the history and culture of ancient Japan. The rest of the class should prepare questions to ask the group of four either as homework or in class.

DAY 3

SECTION 3, continued
Class Time 35 minutes

• **Pantomime** Divide students into small groups and give each group one of the Terms & Names from this section on a slip of paper. Tell students not to let anyone except members of their own group know what term or name they received. Instruct groups to communicate the meaning of their word using only body movements and facial expressions. Have the rest of the class guess what term or name is being represented.

CHAPTER 16 REVIEW AND ASSESSMENT, pp. 490–491
Class Time 55 minutes

• **Review** Have pairs of students review the information in the Visual Summary on PE p. 490 and find three details to support each statement.
Class Time 20 minutes

• **Assessment** Have students complete the Chapter 16 Assessment.
Class Time 35 minutes

TECHNOLOGY IN THE CLASSROOM

WEBQUEST

A WebQuest is a structured, inquiry-oriented activity that asks students to solve problems by using Web resources. Students are given a task and are asked to use the Web to help them complete the task, which usually involves drawing a conclusion or solving a problem for which there is no single correct answer. WebQuests can be very simple or highly complex. Below is a simple WebQuest to complement the material in Chapter 16. To learn more about WebQuests and how to design an official WebQuest, go to the WebQuest link at **classzone.com.**

ACTIVITY OUTLINE

Objective Students will visit Web sites and take notes on the Three Gorges Dam. They will write editorials describing their opinions of the Three Gorges Dam project.

Task Have students go to the Web sites and take notes on the pros and cons of the Three Gorges Dam project. Have them pretend to be journalists who have visited the Yangtze River region, and have them write editorials describing whether or not they think the dam should be built.

Class Time 2–3 class periods

DIRECTIONS

1. Have students read the section in Chapter 16 about the Three Gorges Dam. Ask them to summarize what they have learned about the dam in a class discussion. Make sure they can locate the Yangtze River on a map.

2. Ask students to pretend they are journalists who have the opportunity to visit China and learn more about the dam and its related controversies. The goal is to return to the United States and write an editorial in their local newspaper, explaining whether or not they think the dam is a good idea.

3. Have students visit the Web sites listed at **classzone.com** to learn more about the pros and cons of the Three Gorges Dam project. Have them take notes in charts, with the headings "Pro" and

"Con." In particular, they should look for information about the dam's projected role in energy production, flood control, and commerce; its impact on the people who live along the Yangtze; and its environmental impact. Their pro and con charts can also include information from Chapter 16.

4. Have students write their editorials, providing their opinions on whether or not the dam should be constructed. They should include specific examples from their research to support their arguments.

CHAPTER 16 OBJECTIVE

Students will examine the geographic features of East Asia, Australia, and the Pacific Islands and how geography affects economic activity. Students will also examine the contributions of ancient China and ancient Japan and the ways China affected cultural developments in Japan.

FOCUS ON VISUALS

Interpreting the Photograph Direct students' attention to the photograph of Ayers Rock, or Uluru. Encourage them to make observations about the rock and the land surrounding it. Then ask students to speculate as to whether this area supports a major population.

Possible Responses Students may suggest that the area around Ayers Rock appears to be desert; it probably would not support large numbers of people.

Extension Have students use print or electronic resources to find out more about Uluru, or Ayers Rock. Encourage them to find out the significance of the rock in native Aboriginal culture.

CRITICAL THINKING ACTIVITY

Comparing Tell students that Ayers Rock is a major tourist attraction in central Australia. Ask them to brainstorm a list of natural land formations in the United States that similarly attract large numbers of tourists from around the world.

Class Time 10 minutes

CHAPTER
16

East Asia, Australia, and the Pacific Islands: Land and History

SECTION 1   Physical Geography

SECTION 2   Ancient China

SECTION 3   Ancient Japan

Place Mount Uluru, also called Ayers Rock, stands out against the flat desert of Australia's Red Center, the vast interior part of Australia. Uluru is the largest single rock in the world.

466

Recommended Resources

BOOKS FOR THE TEACHER

Hall, John Whitney, ed. *The Cambridge History of Japan: Ancient Japan.* New York: Cambridge University Press, 1993. Definitive history and excellent resource.

Loewe, Michael, ed. *The Cambridge History of Ancient China: From the Origins of Civilization to*

221 B.C. New York: Cambridge University Press, 1999. Essays by experts.

Whitfield, Susan. *Life Along the Silk Road.* Berkeley, CA: University of California Press, 1999. The Silk Road, which linked Europe, India, and the Far East.

VIDEOS

Ancient China. Wynnewood, PA: Schlessinger Media, 1998. Nine early civilizations.

Mysteries of Asia, Volume 2. Secrets of the Great Wall. Seattle, WA: Unapix Home Entertainment, 2000. Learning Channel special on the civilization that built the Great Wall.

INTERNET

For more information about East Asia, Australia, and the Pacific Islands, visit **classzone.com**.

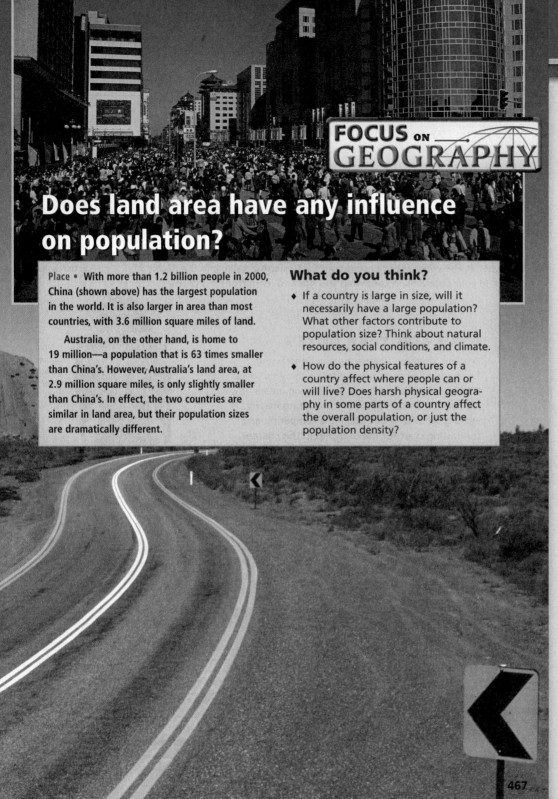

Does land area have any influence on population?

Place • With more than 1.2 billion people in 2000, China (shown above) has the largest population in the world. It is also larger in area than most countries, with 3.6 million square miles of land.

Australia, on the other hand, is home to 19 million—a population that is 63 times smaller than China's. However, Australia's land area, at 2.9 million square miles, is only slightly smaller than China's. In effect, the two countries are similar in land area, but their population sizes are dramatically different.

What do you think?

♦ If a country is large in size, will it necessarily have a large population? What other factors contribute to population size? Think about natural resources, social conditions, and climate.

♦ How do the physical features of a country affect where people can or will live? Does harsh physical geography in some parts of a country affect the overall population, or just the population density?

FOCUS ON GEOGRAPHY

FOCUS ON GEOGRAPHY

Objectives

• To discuss the relationship—or lack of relationship—between land area and population

• To identify factors that contribute to a large population

What Do You Think?

1. Encourage students to think about areas of the world that they know are heavily populated and those that are not. Have them consider what the heavily populated areas offer in terms of natural resources and climate.

2. Make sure that students understand the difference between overall population and population density. You may want to use Canada as an example of a country that has a low overall population and yet contains areas of high population density.

Does land area have any influence on population?

Have students work as a group to rank the continents according to their apparent sizes. Then have them discuss and rank the continents according to what they think their relative populations are. Have the class arrive at a consensus regarding the answer to the question. Ask a few students to use the Data File in the Unit Atlas or conduct on-line research to locate actual information about each continent's area and population.

MAKING GEOGRAPHIC CONNECTIONS

Ask students to study a population density map of the United States and identify specific areas that have a high population density. Then ask them to identify areas that they believe have a low population density. Guide a discussion about each of these kinds of regions and their natural resources, climate, and job opportunities.

Implementing the National Geography Standards

Standard 14 Identify, list, and evaluate the significance of major technological innovations that have been used to modify the physical environment

Objective To prepare a chart of technological innovations and their effects on the environment

Class Time 25 minutes

Task Have students construct a chart that lists major technological innovations in the first column and the innovations' effects on the physical environment in the second column. Students should use examples from both the past and the present. Help students start their chart with the following examples: the use of

fire by humans, work animals, steam power, and electricity.

Evaluation Including the provided examples, students should list at least ten major innovations and their effects.

BEFORE YOU READ
What Do You Know?

On the chalkboard, write the words *Australia, China, Japan.* Then have the class brainstorm words and phrases that they associate with each of these places. Write each suggestion on the board under the appropriate heading. Students might mention kangaroos and Sydney Harbor for Australia, martial arts and earthquakes for Japan, and silk and the Great Wall for China. Encourage students to mention geographic features as well as cultural features.

What Do You Want to Know?

Have students list several questions that they would like answered as they read about Australia, China, and Japan. Tell them to leave space under each question to record the answers as they find them.

READ AND TAKE NOTES

Reading Strategy: Comparing and Contrasting
Remind students to record only information about ancient Japan and ancient China that can be compared and contrasted. For example, point out that they might record that China covers a vast area with a wide variety of geographic features, while Japan is small and mostly mountainous.

 In-depth Resources: Unit 6
• Guided Reading Worksheets, pp. 3–5

BEFORE YOU READ

▶▶ *What Do You Know?*

Before you read the chapter, consider what you already know about East Asia, Australia, and the Pacific Islands. What are the geographic features of these areas? Have you seen a television program about the Ring of Fire or about Australia's Outback? You may have learned about ancient China and ancient Japan in other classes. Do you know who Confucius was or who the Japanese samurai warriors were? Do you know anyone who has visited the Great Wall of China, which is the world's longest wall?

▶▶ *What Do You Want to Know?*

Decide what else you want to know about East Asia, Australia, and the Pacific Islands. In your notebook, record what you hope to learn from this chapter.

Place • China's emperor lived in the Forbidden City, which still stands in the capital, Beijing. ◀

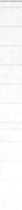

READ AND TAKE NOTES

Reading Strategy: Comparing and Contrasting
Comparing and contrasting places helps you understand more about each one. Comparing means looking for similarities, while contrasting means looking for differences. Making a comparing and contrasting chart for the countries in this chapter will help you better understand them.

• Copy the chart into your notebook.

• As you read the chapter, look for information about the geography and civilizations of ancient China and ancient Japan.

• Record key details under the appropriate headings in the chart.

Culture • Japanese warriors called samurai wore intricate suits of armor. ◀

	Ancient China	Ancient Japan
Geography	3.6 million square miles of diverse land	four main islands; 80 percent mountains; volcanoes and earthquakes
Government	series of dynasties	kingdoms—clans, feudalism, shogunate
Religion/Philosophy	Confucianism, Taoism, Buddhism	Shinto, Buddhism
Discoveries/Inventions	written language, porcelain, silk-making, gunpowder	innovations in bronze and metalwork
Trade/International Relations	Silk Road	isolationism with regard to the West

---

Teaching Strategy

Reading the Chapter This is a thematic chapter that begins with a description of the physical geography of East Asia, Australia, and the Pacific Islands. A study of the cultural contributions and the development of ancient China and Japan follows. Encourage students to focus on how the geography of the region affected the development of civilizations, as well as on how Chinese culture influenced cultural development in Japan.

Integrated Assessment The Chapter Assessment on page 491 describes several activities that may be used for integrated assessment. You may wish to have students work on these activities during the course of the chapter and then present them at the end.

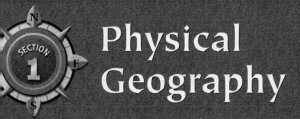
Physical Geography

TERMS & NAMES

Mount Everest

Mount Fuji

Ring of Fire

typhoon

outback

Great Barrier Reef

MAIN IDEA

The physical features of East Asia, Australia, and the Pacific Islands are the result of different geological processes.

WHY IT MATTERS NOW

Understanding these countries' physical features helps us to understand their political and economic roles in the world.

DATELINE EXTRA

YOKOHAMA, JAPAN, SEPTEMBER 1, 1923

Today, as thousands of people in Tokyo and in Yokohama were preparing to have lunch, a powerful earthquake struck. Walls bulged and buildings lurched as though made of cardboard.

Hundreds of thousands of houses completely collapsed, trapping unknown numbers of victims. The ground heaved and tossed, and in one area the earth was lifted 24 feet high. The massive uplifting of the ground caused thousands of landslides.

Some of the worst damage was caused by the fires that followed the quake. When the tremors began, people were cooking on stoves. Within minutes, kitchen fires sprang up throughout the cities. Many people who survived the quake died in the fires. As night falls, the entire city of Tokyo is in flames.

Human-Environment Interaction • It will take many people a long time to clean up the wreckage from the earthquake. ▲

The Lands of the Region ❶

Japan is one among many countries in the region of East Asia, Australia, and the Pacific Islands, which you can see on page 460 of the Unit Atlas. East Asia includes China, Japan, North Korea, South Korea, Mongolia, and Taiwan. Australia is an island, a nation, and a continent all its own, with New Zealand as a nearby neighbor. The thousands of Pacific Islands are grouped into three subregions—Melanesia, Micronesia, and Polynesia.

East Asia, Australia, and the Pacific Islands: Land and History **469**

SECTION OBJECTIVES

1. To identify the lands of the region and describe the physical geography of China

2. To describe the physical geography of Japan and the Koreas

3. To identify the physical features of Australia, New Zealand, and the Pacific Islands

SKILLBUILDER

• Interpreting a Map, p. 470, p. 472, p. 473

CRITICAL THINKING

• Distinguishing Fact from Opinion, p. 474

FOCUS & MOTIVATE
WARM-UP

Making Inferences Have students read Dateline and discuss these questions.

1. Do you think there was any warning before the earthquake struck?

2. What do you think people could do to help limit damage from future earthquakes?

INSTRUCT: Objective ❶

The Lands of the Region/China

• What countries make up the region known as East Asia? China, Japan, North Korea, South Korea, Mongolia, Taiwan

• Why is the Plateau of Tibet known as the roof of the world? It is the highest plateau on Earth.

• What physical features are typical of eastern China? plains and great rivers

• What two deserts are located in the north of China? Taklimakan, Gobi

 In-depth Resources: Unit 6
• Guided Reading Worksheet, p. 3

 Reading Study Guide
(Spanish and English), pp. 144–145

Program Resources

 In-depth Resources: Unit 6
• Guided Reading Worksheet, p. 3
• Reteaching Activity, p. 10

 Reading Study Guide
(Spanish and English), pp. 144–145

 Formal Assessment
• Section Quiz, p. 240

 Integrated Assessment
• Rubric for making a diagram

 Outline Map Activities

 Access for Students Acquiring English
• Guided Reading Worksheet, p. 141

 Technology Resources
classzone.com

TEST-TAKING RESOURCES

↳ Strategies for Test Preparation
↳ Test Practice Transparencies
◉ Online Test Practice

FOCUS ON VISUALS

Interpreting the Map Have students locate China's three great rivers and with their fingers trace the rivers' flow from the highlands toward the east. Ask students to identify what body of water each of the rivers empties into.

Possible Responses Huang He empties into Yellow Sea; Chang Jiang empties into East China Sea; Xi Jiang empties into South China Sea.

Extension Tell students that throughout China's early history, it has been relatively isolated from countries to its west. Ask students to examine the map and then write a brief paragraph explaining how geography contributed to China's isolation.

Region • The Himalayas loom in the distance beyond this family. ▲

China ❶

Look at the map below. Notice that the geography within China's boundaries varies greatly. Over much of China's area, mountains rise to great heights. Rivers and plains cover the eastern part of China. To the southwest, the land rises to high plateaus, and to the northwest, it stretches out in long, dry deserts.

China's Mountains Look again at the map. You can see that China's highest mountains are in the west. The Himalayas run along China's southwestern border, dividing China from Nepal. The highest peak in the Himalayas—and in the world—is **Mount Everest,** at 29,035 feet. Notice also the Plateau of Tibet. It spreads across one-fourth of China's land and is the highest plateau on Earth, earning it the nickname "roof of the world."

China's Great Rivers China's three great rivers are the Huang He (hwahng huh), the Chang Jiang (chahng jyahng), and the Xi Jiang (shee jyahng). They all start in the highlands and flow east. The southernmost is the Xi Jiang, as you can see on the map.

BACKGROUND

The Chang Jiang is known in the West as the Yangtze (yang•see).

Geography
Skillbuilder
Answers

1. the Himalayas
2. Hokkaido

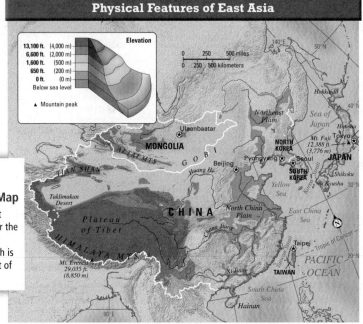

Physical Features of East Asia

Elevation
13,100 ft. (4,000 m)
6,600 ft. (2,000 m)
1,600 ft. (500 m)
650 ft. (200 m)
0 ft. (0 m)
Below sea level
▲ Mountain peak

0 250 500 miles
0 250 500 kilometers

GEOGRAPHY SKILLBUILDER: Interpreting a Map

1. **Location •** What mountains border the Plateau of Tibet?
2. **Location •** Which is the northernmost of Japan's islands?

Activity Options

Differentiating Instruction: Less Proficient Readers

Identifying Main Ideas and Details Some students may have difficulty remembering facts about China's physical features. Suggest they create a chart like the one shown here and record details as they read or reread the material.

Mountains	Rivers	Deserts
Himalayas—along southwestern border	Huang He, Chang Jiang, Xi Jiang	Taklimakan—sandy; has dust storms
Mount Everest— highest peak on Earth	All three flow east from highlands.	Gobi—rocky
Plateau of Tibet— highest plateau on Earth		

North of it, the Chang Jiang winds across China. At over 3,400 miles, this is China's longest river.

The northernmost river is the Huang He, or Yellow River. Its name comes from the color of the fine silt that covers the plains along parts of the river. You can see that the Huang He begins in the Plateau of Tibet. On its course east through the North China Plain, it often overflows. Because of the thousands of lives lost in its floods, the Chinese often call the river "China's Sorrow."

Vocabulary

silt: windblown material similar to clay

China's Deserts Two large deserts span China's northern lands. You can see on the map that the Taklimakan (TAH·kluh·muh·KAHN) covers northwestern China. With an east-west length of about 600 miles, it is one of the world's largest sandy deserts. During the spring, dust storms with the strength of hurricanes occur frequently, lifting the desert's dust as high as 13,000 feet in the air.

East of the Taklimakan, in central northern China, sprawls the Gobi (GOH·bee). In Mongolian, *gobi* means "waterless place." The Gobi's dryness is harsh, and so are its temperatures. In the summer, the Gobi's temperature can rise to 113°F. In the winter, it may get down to -40°F.

Place •
Much of the Gobi is made of rock rather than sand. ▲

Japan ❷

Japan is a country of islands that stretch for 1,500 miles across the Pacific Ocean. Look at the map on page 458 to see the four main islands—Hokkaido (hah·KY·doh), Honshu (HAHN·shoo), Shikoku (shee·KAW·koo), and Kyushu (kee·OO·shoo). Honshu is the largest, as well as the home of Japan's capital, Tokyo.

Japan sits atop two tectonic plates that often sink below a third plate. Because of this, Japan is more likely to have volcanic eruptions and earthquakes than are many places on Earth.

Mountains and Volcanoes Mountains cover more than 80 percent of Japan's land. Instead of forming ranges, these mountains are blocks separated by lowlands. This formation results from faults, or cracks in the rock, that cause the land either to lift up into a mountain or to drop down into lowlands. The largest stretch of lowlands is the Kanto Plain, where Tokyo lies.

Reading Social Studies
A. Possible Answers
The city is on the largest area of lowlands; the rest of the country is mountainous.

Reading Social Studies

A. Drawing Conclusions Why do you think the Japanese built Tokyo where they did?

East Asia, Australia, and the Pacific Islands: Land and History **471**

MORE ABOUT...
"China's Sorrow"

The worst flood of the Huang He took place in 1887, when the river flooded an area of approximately 50,000 square miles. The floodwaters carried so much silt that many villages were completely buried, killing nearly 1 million people.

The Taklimakan

The Taklimakan is a forbidding desert whose name means "who goes in, does not come out." This desert is the site of one of history's great mysteries. In the 1970s and 1980s, well-preserved ancient mummies—some 4,000 years old—were found buried throughout the desert. The great mystery about these mummies is that they have long reddish-blond hair and European features, unlike ancestors of modern Chinese people. Scientists speculate that thousands of years ago these people followed herds of animals from Eastern Europe, settling in the oases that ring the desert.

INSTRUCT: Objective ❷

Japan/The Koreas

• Why is Japan likely to have frequent volcanic eruptions and earthquakes? It sits atop two tectonic plates that often sink below another plate.

• What is the Ring of Fire? area of frequent volcanic and earthquake activity around the edges of the Pacific Ocean

• How do monsoons control Japan's climate? bring cold rain and snow to west in winter, warm rains to south and east in summer

• What are the major physical features of the Koreas? mountains, valleys, coastal plains, rivers

---

Activity Options

Interdisciplinary Links: Language Arts/Geography

ⓑ Block Scheduling

Class Time One class period

Task Writing a report about the Gobi or the Taklimakan Desert

Purpose To learn about the physical formations and the harsh conditions of these deserts

Supplies Needed
• Reference books or on-line resources
• Pencils or pens
• Writing paper

Activity Have students research one of the deserts. They should include information about one of these topics: physical characteristics, temperature extremes, animal and plant life, human interaction in the desert, or history or archaeology. Suggest that students take notes and outline their findings. Encourage students to include maps or illustrations in their reports.

MORE ABOUT...
Mount Fuji

The Japanese consider Mount Fuji to be a sacred mountain. Its name means "everlasting life." Even though Mount Fuji is considered to be an active volcano, the mountain is surrounded by temples and shrines. There are even shrines on the edge and the bottom of the crater. For centuries, climbing the mountain has been considered a religious pilgrimage. Today, as many as 100,000 people visit Mount Fuji during the climbing season between July 1 and August 26.

FOCUS ON VISUALS

Interpreting the Map Have students trace the Ring of Fire with their fingers. Then have them point out the volcanoes. Ask students to identify what continents the Ring of Fire touches. Why do they think the region is called the Ring of Fire?

Possible Responses The Ring of Fire touches Asia, South America, and North America. Students may suggest that the region is called the Ring of Fire because of the active volcanoes that frequently erupt in the region.

Extension Have students conduct research to find out more about volcanoes in the Ring of Fire. Students may research Mount Pinatubo in the Philippines, which erupted in 1991; El Chichon in Mexico, which erupted in 1982; or Krakatoa (Krakatau) in Indonesia, which erupted in 1883. Have them write a brief report describing one of the eruptions and how it affected the nearby population.

Japan's tallest mountain, **Mount Fuji,** is an active volcano. Volcanic eruptions are common in Japan, which is part of the **Ring of Fire**—an area of volcanic activity along the borders of the Pacific Ocean. This is where most of the world's earthquakes and volcanoes occur.

Earthquakes Japan records as many as 1,500 minor earthquakes each year. In 1923, a major earthquake hit Tokyo and its surrounding regions, which you read about on page 469. After 1923, Japan became a world leader in constructing buildings able to withstand the shock of frequent earthquakes.

Climate Japan's climate is largely controlled by monsoons. In the winter, the monsoons bring cold rain and snow to Japan's western coast. In the summer, they bring warm rains to the south and east. During the summer and early fall, storms called typhoons also occur often. A **typhoon** is a hurricane that occurs in the western Pacific.

The Koreas ❷

North and South Korea lie on the mountainous Korean Peninsula, which you can see on the map on page 470. North Korea is a land filled with mountains and valleys. Its major rivers, the Yalu and Tumen, mark the border with China. Its climate is temperate, with cold, dry winters and hot, humid summers.

Geography Skillbuilder Answers

1. Asia, South America, North America

2. no

GEOGRAPHY SKILLBUILDER: Interpreting a Map

1. **Location** • Which continents border the Ring of Fire?
2. **Place** • Is Mount Fuji the only volcano in Japan?

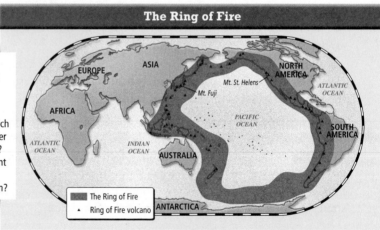

The Ring of Fire

▨ The Ring of Fire
▲ Ring of Fire volcano

Activity Options

Multiple Learning Styles: Visual/Logical

Class Time One class period

Task Creating a chart showing earthquake activity in East Asia or volcanic activity within the Ring of Fire

Purpose To learn about when and where earthquakes and

volcanoes have occurred over the centuries, and how they affected people in the region

Supplies Needed
• Reference books or on-line resources
• Paper
• Pencils

Activity Divide the class into two groups. Have one group research earthquakes in East Asia, and the other research volcanic activity within the Ring of Fire. Instruct each group to work together to create a chart like the one shown here. Display the charts and discuss the information.

Date	Name	Location	Details

Most of the rain each year falls between June and September, brought on by the monsoons of the Pacific. South Korea is a mix of rugged mountain ranges, coastal plains, and river valleys. Its main rivers are the Han, the Kum, and the Naktong.

Australia

Australia is one of the largest countries on Earth, though it is the smallest continent. Its landscape is unique in that it has not changed dramatically for more than 250 million years. In other continents, such as Europe and North America, major landscape changes have occurred even in just the past 25,000 years.

Flat and Dry Australia Look at the map below. Notice the Great Dividing Range that runs along Australia's eastern coast. This chain is the largest in Australia, but none of these mountains rise higher than 5,000 feet. To their west, vast plains extend across most of Australia. Australians call this huge stretch of interior land the **outback**.

Australia is the flattest continent on Earth, and it is also extremely dry. Deserts cover one-third of the country. The majority of people live along the northern and eastern coasts, where much of Australia's fresh water is found.

Place• Australia is home to many animals that are native only to that continent, such as the kangaroo. ▲

Physical Features of Australia

GEOGRAPHY SKILLBUILDER:
Interpreting a Map

1. **Region •** What type of physical feature covers much of western Australia?
2. **Location •** In which sea does the Great Barrier Reef lie?

Geography Skillbuilder Answers

1. deserts

2. Coral Sea

Elevation

13,100 ft.	(4,000 m)
6,600 ft.	(2,000 m)
1,600 ft.	(500 m)
650 ft.	(200 m)
0 ft.	(0 m)
Below sea level	

▲ Mountain peak
∨∨ Coral reef

0   400   800 miles
0   400   800 kilometers

INDIAN OCEAN

Timor Sea
Arafura Sea
Coral Sea
Gulf of Carpentaria
Cape York Peninsula
Great Barrier Reef
Kimberley Plateau
Tanami Desert
Great Sandy Desert
AUSTRALIA
Macdonnell Ranges
Gibson Desert
outback
▲ Uluru (Ayers Rock) 1,143 ft. (348 m)
Great Victoria Desert
Great Dividing Range
Grey Range
Nullarbor Plain
Darling Range
Darling R.
Lachlan R.
Murray R.
Great Australian Bight
Canberra
Tasmania
Tasman Sea

Tropic of Capricorn
20°S
40°S
100°E   120°E   140°E

CRITICAL THINKING ACTIVITY

Distinguishing Fact from Opinion Ask students to write two facts they learned about Australia, either from the section text or from research they have done for lesson activities. Then ask them to write two opinions about Australia. Have them label each statement as a fact or an opinion.

Class Time 10 minutes

ASSESS & RETEACH

Reading Social Studies Have students complete the top row of the graphic organizer on page 468.

   Formal Assessment
   • Section Quiz, p. 240

RETEACHING ACTIVITY

Provide students with the outline maps of China, Japan, the Koreas, and Australia. Have students fill in and label the major mountains, rivers, and deserts in these areas. If students need help completing the map, have them refer to the Unit Atlas maps on pages 458–461.

   In-depth Resources: Unit 6
   • Reteaching Activity, p. 10

   Access for Students Acquiring English
   • Reteaching Activity, p. 146

The Great Barrier Reef Off Australia's northeastern coast stretches the world's largest coral reef system, called the **Great Barrier Reef.** Made of more than 2,500 individual reefs and islands, the Great Barrier Reef extends 1,250 miles through the Pacific Ocean. Some of the reefs, called fringing reefs, run along coastlines. Others exist as far as 100 miles from shore. Over 400 species of coral and other ocean life call the reef home.

New Zealand and Other Pacific Islands

Thousands of islands dot the Pacific to the north and east of Australia. On the map on page 458 of the Unit Atlas, you can see that New Zealand's two main islands, which sit about 1,000 miles east of Australia, are among the largest. Most of the others are tiny in comparison.

The roughly 20,000 Pacific Islands are of three types: continental islands, high oceanic islands, and low oceanic islands. Continental islands, such as New Guinea (GIHN·ee) and New Zealand, are parts of Earth's crust that sit above the surface of the water. They often have active volcanoes, even though they were not formed by volcanic activity. High oceanic islands, such as Tahiti (tuh·HEE·tee), are mountainous islands formed by volcanic activity. Most of the Pacific Islands are low oceanic islands, which formed from coral reefs.

SECTION 1 ASSESSMENT

Terms & Names

1. **Identify:**   (a) Mount Everest   (b) Mount Fuji   (c) Ring of Fire
   (d) typhoon   (e) outback   (f) Great Barrier Reef

Taking Notes

2. Make a chart like this one to note the physical features in each region. You can list more features than the ones shown here.

Region	Rivers	Deserts
China		
Japan		
The Koreas		
Australia		
The Pacific Islands		

Main Ideas

3. (a) How is Japan affected by the three tectonic plates on which its islands rest?

(b) Why are some regions of Australia much more suitable for living than others? Which regions are suitable?

(c) What three types of islands exist in the Pacific?

Critical Thinking

4. **Drawing Conclusions**

Considering China's geographic features, which areas do you think have large populations? What about small populations?

Think About

♦ physical features that encourage population settlement

♦ physical features that would be hard to live in or near

ACTIVITY -OPTION-   Make a **diagram** that shows how high oceanic islands and low oceanic islands form.

Section 1 Assessment

1. Terms & Names
   a. Mount Everest, p. 470
   b. Mount Fuji, p. 472
   c. Ring of Fire, p. 472
   d. typhoon, p. 472
   e. outback, p. 473
   f. Great Barrier Reef, p. 474

2. Taking Notes

Region	Rivers	Deserts	Mountains
China	Huang He, Chang Jiang, Xi Jiang	Taklimakan, Gobi	
Japan			Mt. Fuji
The Koreas	Yalu, Tumen, Han, Kum, Naktong		
Australia		yes	
The Pacific Islands			volcanoes

3. Main Ideas
   a. Because of the plates' movement, Japan is more likely to have earthquakes and volcanoes than many places on Earth.
   b. Some regions have adequate water. Regions along the northern and eastern coasts are most livable.
   c. continental islands; high oceanic islands; low oceanic islands

4. Critical Thinking
Students may suggest that the plains and the coasts probably have the largest populations; the high mountains and the deserts probably have the smallest populations.

ACTIVITY OPTION

   Integrated Assessment
   • Rubric for making a diagram

SECTION
2

Ancient China

TERMS & NAMES
dynasty
Genghis Khan
Kublai Khan
Confucius
bureaucracy
Taoism
Lao Tzu

MAIN IDEA

The ancient Chinese developed a civilization that has lasted longer than any other on Earth.

WHY IT MATTERS NOW

China's very long and relatively stable existence has helped it to become one of the most powerful countries in the world.

DATELINE

THE IMPERIAL PALACE, CHINA, 2700 B.C.—Our 14-year-old Empress Si Ling-chi has made an amazing discovery. While walking in the palace gardens, she noticed that caterpillars, which just a few days before were eating mulberry tree leaves, had spun themselves into cocoons. These cocoons hung from branches, within easy reach of our empress, who plucked one and took it home to examine. When she dropped it into boiling water, it unraveled into a tangle of threads.

The empress immediately sent her maids to gather more cocoons. Soon she had enough thread for weaving, and she produced a shining fabric she called silk. Plans are now underway to begin manufacturing huge quantities of this wondrous fabric.

Human-Environment Interaction • Many Chinese women will work to twist the thin silk strands together to make thread thick enough for weaving. ▲

Foundations of Chinese Civilization ❶

Silk is just one of the many inventions for which the ancient Chinese are known. Over the course of thousands of years, the Chinese have built the longest-lasting culture in the world.

As early as 5000 B.C., Chinese people lived in the fertile river valley of the Huang He. Sometime in the 1700s B.C., their lives changed drastically when invaders, called the Shang (shahng), entered their valley. These invaders established China's first permanent, organized civilization.

East Asia, Australia, and the Pacific Islands: Land and History **475**

SECTION OBJECTIVES

1. To describe the origins of Chinese civilization and identify the dynasties that ruled China for thousands of years
2. To describe contributions of the ancient Chinese in the areas of religion, philosophy, arts, and technology
3. To identify the technological achievements made in ancient China

SKILLBUILDER

• Interpreting a Chart, p. 476
• Interpreting a Map, p. 479

CRITICAL THINKING

• Evaluating Decisions, p. 476

FOCUS & MOTIVATE
WARM-UP

Making Inferences Have students read Dateline and discuss the importance of silk.

1. Why do you think the Chinese planned to manufacture huge quantities of silk?
2. Why do you think people value silk?

INSTRUCT: Objective ❶

Foundations of Chinese Civilization

• Where and when did Chinese civilization begin? in the Huang He valley, in the 1700s B.C.
• What are dynasties? families of rulers
• What did the first Ming emperor accomplish? defeated the Mongols; unified China

 In-depth Resources: Unit 6
• Guided Reading Worksheet, p. 4

 Reading Study Guide
(Spanish and English), pp. 146–147

Program Resources

 In-depth Resources: Unit 6
• Guided Reading Worksheet, p. 4
• Reteaching Activity, p. 11

 Reading Study Guide
(Spanish and English),
pp. 146–147

 Formal Assessment
• Section Quiz, p. 241

 Integrated Assessment
• Rubric for writing a journal entry

 Outline Map Activities

 Access for Students Acquiring English
• Guided Reading Worksheet, p. 142

 Technology Resources
classzone.com

TEST-TAKING RESOURCES

↻ Strategies for Test Preparation
↻ Test Practice Transparencies
🖱 Online Test Practice

Teacher's Edition **475**

FOCUS ON VISUALS

Interpreting the Chart Review the notations for B.C. and A.D. on the chart. Ask which dynasties ruled for the longest time and which ruled for the shortest.

Response The Shang and Zhou ruled for the longest time; the Qin ruled for the shortest.

Extension Have pairs of students choose one dynasty and find three or four world events that happened during the same time period. Have students share their lists.

CRITICAL THINKING ACTIVITY

Evaluating Decisions Refer students to the discussion of the tomb of Shih Huang-ti. Ask them to evaluate the decision to excavate the tomb. Guide them to weigh possible objections to digging up a tomb against the knowledge that is gained by doing so.

Class Time 10 minutes

Strange but TRUE

The Emperor Shih Huang-ti came to the throne when he was 13 years old and immediately began building his tomb. The tomb is actually an underground city with copper-lined walls, a throne room, and a treasury of jewels and costly objects. The vaults contain life-size warriors and horses poised for battle. The clay army of Shih Huang-ti occupies three vaults.

For most of China's history since the Shang takeover, the country was ruled by **dynasties,** or families of rulers. Dynasties rose and fell in succession—some lasting only 15 years, others continuing for hundreds of years. Look at the chart to the right to learn the names and dates of each dynasty.

The Dynasties of China

Dynasty	Dates
Shang	1700s–1122 B.C.
Zhou	1122–221 B.C.
Qin	221–206 B.C.
Han	206 B.C.–A.D. 220
Sui	A.D. 581–618
Tang	A.D. 618–907
Song	A.D. 960–1279
Yuan	A.D. 1279–1368
Ming	A.D. 1368–1644
Qing	A.D. 1644–1911

SKILLBUILDER: Interpreting a Chart

1. Which dynasty ruled China in A.D. 1?
2. Which was the last dynasty to rule China?

Mongol Rule In the A.D. 1200s, China's greatest fear came to pass—foreign invaders conquered China. In 1211, the Mongols invaded China. They were led by **Genghis Khan** and later by his grandson **Kublai Khan.** In 1279, Kublai Khan conquered China's Song (sung) Dynasty. In its place, he founded the Yuan Dynasty. He also established a capital at Ta-tu.

The Ming Dynasty Warfare eventually broke out among the Mongol leaders, weakening the Yuan Dynasty significantly. The dynasty that took over was called the Ming. Because of his great military success, Ming founder Zhu Yuanzhang (joo yoo•ahn•jang) was called the Hongwu emperor—meaning "vast military power." In his battles, he won from the Mongols the Yunnan province. With this piece of land in his charge, he unified the region that is China today.

Skillbuilder Answers
1. Han
2. Qing

Reading Social Studies
A. Possible Answer
Foreign rulers might have a different language and customs; they might discriminate against native Chinese.

Reading Social Studies
A. Making Inferences How might life in China have changed when foreigners took over?

Strange but TRUE

The Tomb of Shih Huang-ti In 1974, farmers near Xi'an (shee•ahn) made a spectacular discovery. While digging a new well, their shovels hit some broken bits of pottery. Digging deeper, they found not water but a headless clay body. What they had uncovered was the tomb of China's Qin emperor Shih Huang-ti (shur•hwahng•dee)—filled with an army of about 8,000 life-sized clay soldiers and horses (shown at right).

The foot soldiers, charioteers, and archers were buried 22 centuries ago to guard the emperor in death just as his real soldiers had in life. Although the soldiers' heads and bodies are all similar, their eyes, ears, noses, lips, and hairstyles vary. Among the 8,000 soldiers, no two faces are the same.

476 CHAPTER 16

Activity Options

Differentiating Instruction: Less Proficient Readers

Creating a Time Line Some students may have difficulty understanding the organization of the data in the chart. You might want to create a time line to show the time period of each dynasty. Draw a horizontal line on the chalkboard, and mark 0 in the center. Explain that there was never a year "zero," but that in the Western calendar, dates with the notation B.C. ("Before Christ") are placed to the left of 0, numbering backwards from the largest number to the smallest. Time periods with the notation A.D. ("Anno Domini") are placed to the right, numbering from the smallest to the greatest number. Also point out that when the reign of a dynasty crosses the 0 marker (as the Han dynasty does), those dates must be added together. For practice, ask students to calculate the reign in years of various dynasties.

When the Hongwu emperor died, one of his grandsons took power, naming himself the Yongle emperor—meaning "eternal contentment." He is famous for rebuilding the Yuan capital, which he renamed Beijing (bay•jing). He ordered a huge palace complex to be constructed in the capital. This was called the Forbidden City because only the emperor, his family, and some of his officials could enter it.

Location •
The Forbidden City is the largest complex of buildings of its age in the world. ▲

The Ming Dynasty came to an end in 1644 at the hands of invaders from northeastern China, called the Manchu (MAN•choo). These attackers established China's last dynasty, the Qing (ching), which ruled China until 1911.

Religion and Philosophy ❷

China's dynasties are known for particular achievements—some military, some artistic, some technological, and some spiritual. Several of the world's most influential philosophies and religions arose during the thousands of years of Chinese history.

Confucianism Toward the end of the Zhou Dynasty, a man named Kongfuzi—later called **Confucius** (kuhn•FYOO•shuhs) by Europeans—developed a new philosophy. Confucius taught the importance of moral character and of individuals taking responsibility for the state of their society. He also taught that a ruler, like a good father, should take care of his people and be kind to them.

Reading Social Studies
B. Possible Answer
It was probably a good approach for the time but was not very democratic.

Reading
Social Studies

B. Forming and Supporting Opinions What do you think of Confucius' opinion of how a successful ruler should behave?

A VOICE FROM CHINA

If you are personally upright, things get done without any orders being given. If you are not personally upright, no one will obey even if you do give orders.

Confucius

The teachings of Confucius were not widely known during his lifetime. Only after his death did his students succeed in spreading his philosophy.

Religion and Philosophy

• How did the teachings of Confucius affect Chinese government? became official philosophy, brought the establishment of government departments staffed by well-trained Confucian civil servants

• What is the goal of a Taoist? to find harmony with the Tao and nature

• How did Buddhism come to China? through traders from India and other parts of Asia

A VOICE FROM CHINA

Have a volunteer read aloud the quote from Confucius. Discuss his vision of a good ruler. Guide students to understand that Confucius taught that a person who sets high standards for himself and leads by example is a good ruler.

MORE ABOUT...
Confucian Ideas

Confucius also defined social relationships, with the aim of creating a stable, structured society. In these relationships, the "superior" person was always expected to set a good example: ruler to subject, father to son, husband to wife, older brother or sister to younger sibling. The Confucian virtues included integrity, politeness and good manners, loyalty, and generosity.

Activity Options

Skillbuilder Mini-Lesson: Distinguishing Fact from Opinion

Explaining the Skill Remind students that a fact is information that can be proved true. An opinion is an idea or judgment. Although an opinion may seem valid, it cannot be verified or proved to be true.

Applying the Skill Have students reread "Confucianism" and use these strategies to identify the first sentence as a fact or an opinion.

1. Look for terms, dates, or statistics: Zhou Dynasty, Kong Fuzi, Confucius.

2. Decide whether the information can be checked and verified. If it can, it is a fact; if not, it is an opinion.

Have students formulate an opinion about a topic in the section.

INSTRUCT: Objective ③

Achievements of the Dynasties

• What significant achievements in science and technology were made in ancient China? silk thread and cloth, paper, porcelain (china), compass, writing system, construction projects

• Why was the Silk Road an important route? provided a trade route for carrying silk, porcelain, tea, and other goods that profited China

Connections to Technology

Gunpowder has had a dramatic impact on human affairs. Before the use of gunpowder, the weapons of war were limited to what warriors could carry. Individual weapons could not be too big or too heavy. With gunpowder, the power of weapons was no longer tied to the physical strength of the user.

Gunpowder also contributed to the end of the feudal system in Europe in the 1300s and 1400s. The center of feudal estates was the stone castle. Feudal lords relied on their stone castles and walls as protection from outside assault. However, stone walls could not stand up against cannons that fired heavy cannonballs.

The Impact of Confucianism In 121 B.C., the Han emperor Wudi established Confucianism as the official philosophy guiding the Chinese bureaucracy. **Bureaucracy** is the administration of a government through departments, called bureaus. The appointed officials that staff the bureaus are called bureaucrats. The Han called their bureaucracy the civil service and staffed it with scholars of Confucianism. The civil service gave the government capable officials and contributed to the stability of the culture.

Taoism The Zhou period also gave rise to **Taoism** (DOW· IHZ·uhm). This philosophy was developed in the 500s B.C. by **Lao Tzu** (low dzuh), who wrote the main Taoist book—the *Tao-te Ching* (DOW· day CHING). Lao Tzu described a force that guides the universe, though it cannot be seen or named. He called this force the *Tao*, which means "way of nature." The greatest achievement for any person, in Taoist belief, is to find harmony with the Tao and, therefore, with nature.

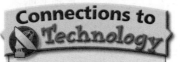

Connections to Technology

Gunpowder One Chinese invention had an explosive impact on the world—gunpowder. The Chinese had invented the first gunpowder, called black powder, by A.D. 1000. They used it originally not in guns (which were invented in Southwest Asia in the 1300s), but in fireworks used in warfare.

By the 1300s, people in the West were using gunpowder to power weapons, such as guns and the medieval Belgian cannon shown below. By the 1600s, Europeans also began using it for more peaceful tasks like mining and road construction.

Buddhism in China During the A.D. 200s, while the Han Dynasty was beginning to collapse, Buddhism made its way to China through traders from India and other areas in Asia. During the Tang Dynasty, Buddhist teachings of how to escape suffering appealed to many Chinese. However, Buddhism did not replace Confucianism or Taoism in China. The Chinese belief system today includes elements of all three philosophies.

Culture •
This statue shows Taoism's founder, Lao Tzu. ▲

Achievements of the Dynasties ③

China has also given the world some important inventions. Around 2700 B.C., the Chinese invented silk cloth and a new system of writing. In the first two centuries A.D., the Chinese invented paper and a type of pottery called porcelain. In the A.D. 1200s, Chinese navigators began using the compass. These inventions helped shape the civilizations of Asia and, through trade, Europe.

Silk The ancient Chinese were able to keep the secret of how to manufacture silk from foreigners for centuries, although others did eventually learn the Chinese method.

Activity Options

Interdisciplinary Links: Literature/Language Arts 🅱 Block Scheduling

Class Time One class period

Task Reading and analyzing a Taoist poem

Purpose To learn about the influence of Taoism on Chinese literature

Supplies Needed
• Books or copies of poems by Taoist Chinese poets

Activity Explain to students that poets influenced by Taoist ideas wrote poetry about the beauty of nature. Have small groups of students prepare a poetry reading and discussion. Encourage students to look for words, phrases, and images that reflect the beauty and harmony of nature. Have a member from each group read the poem aloud, and have other members summarize the group's discussion of the imagery and Taoist influence.

Reading Social Studies

C. Possible Answer Profits from trade were great enough to make the dangers worthwhile.

Reading Social Studies

C. Clarifying If the Silk Road was so dangerous, why did the Chinese continue to use it?

Vocabulary

kiln: high-temperature oven used to bake clay until it hardens

As long as no one else understood the process, however, China earned all the profits of the silk trade. Caravans carried the precious fabric for thousands of miles to cities in Europe and Southwest Asia, along a trade route named for the fabric—the Silk Road.

The Silk Road The first records of travel and trade along the Silk Road date to the Han Dynasty, around 114 B.C. On the map below, you can see the route of the 4,000-mile long Silk Road. Along it, the Chinese carried not only silk but also much-desired items such as porcelain, tea, incense, and spices. Travelers on the Silk Road faced many natural hazards—extreme heat, lack of water, sandstorms in the desert, and blizzards and altitude sickness in the mountains. Also, robbers lurked on the trade routes. Nevertheless, the Silk Road stayed in use until sea routes to Asia proved safer and until the Ming Dynasty decided to limit foreign trade.

Porcelain People often refer to fine pottery as china. The term actually refers to porcelain, a delicate but strong type of ceramic that the Chinese made from a kind of clay called kaolin (KAY·uh·lin). When fired in a kiln, the clay changes into a hard, glassy substance. As with silk, the Chinese kept the method for producing porcelain secret for many years after its invention during the Tang Dynasty.

Movement • Porcelain was an important trade item that the Chinese carried along the Silk Road. ▼

Geography Skillbuilder Answers

1. Luoyang
2. by sea routes across the Mediterranean Sea

The Route of the Ancient Silk Road

Silk Road
Sea route

GEOGRAPHY SKILLBUILDER: Interpreting a Map

1. **Location •** What city was at the easternmost point of the Silk Road?
2. **Movement •** How did goods travel to Rome from western points on the Silk Road?

The WORLD'S HERITAGE

To help defend against invaders, signal towers were built along the Great Wall. The towers were usually built on high points to insure that they could be seen. Soldiers used fire or lanterns to communicate during the night. During the day, they used smoke, banners, or clappers as signals.

ASSESS & RETEACH

Reading Social Studies Ask students to add information to the first column, "Ancient China," of the chart on page 468.

Formal Assessment
• Section Quiz, p. 241

RETEACHING ACTIVITY

Have students create an outline of the information in this section. Suggest that they use the main heads and subheads in the section as headings for their outlines and add details under each.

In-depth Resources: Unit 6
• Reteaching Activity, p. 11

Access for Students Acquiring English
• Reteaching Activity, p. 147

Culture • Chinese characters like these are drawn with brushes dipped in ink. ▲

Writing During the Shang Dynasty, the Chinese developed a written language. As in cuneiform, the Chinese system at first used pictograms to represent objects or ideas. Later, they simplified the pictograms into symbols, called characters, that do not look exactly like what they represent. About 50,000 characters exist in the Chinese written language. Most words are made up of compound graphs—two or more characters used together. Both the Japanese and Koreans use Chinese characters in their writing systems.

The Great Builders The ancient Chinese built large construction projects like the Great Wall. Many emperors ordered the building of canals. The most important of these was the Grand Canal, which allowed grain from fertile river valleys to be carried more easily to the cities. Construction began on the first segment of the canal in the 600s B.C. Today, it extends for more than 1,000 miles to connect the northern city of Beijing with the southern city of Hangzhou (hahng·joh).

The WORLD'S HERITAGE

The Longest Wall Stretching for about 4,000 miles across northern China, the Great Wall is the world's longest structure. Construction began in the 600s B.C. with a number of fortified walls to keep out invaders. Later, a series of emperors ordered the walls to be connected. In the 1400s, damaged sections were rebuilt and new portions were added, giving the Great Wall its present form.

Building the Great Wall required the labor of thousands of workers using pounded earth, bricks, and stones. When the wall was finished, over a million soldiers stood guard in its watchtowers. Today, tourists from around the world come to see the Great Wall, which symbolizes China's long history. (See photograph on pages 456–457.)

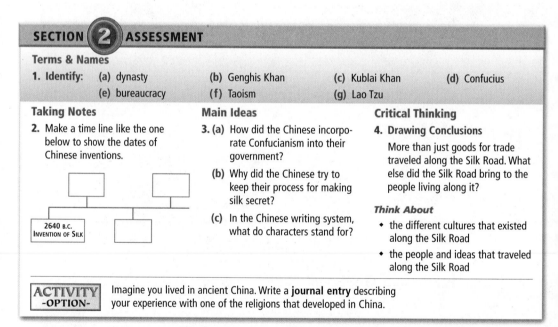

SECTION 2 ASSESSMENT

Terms & Names

1. Identify:
(a) dynasty
(b) Genghis Khan
(c) Kublai Khan
(d) Confucius
(e) bureaucracy
(f) Taoism
(g) Lao Tzu

Taking Notes

2. Make a time line like the one below to show the dates of Chinese inventions.

2640 B.C. INVENTION OF SILK

Main Ideas

3. (a) How did the Chinese incorporate Confucianism into their government?

(b) Why did the Chinese try to keep their process for making silk secret?

(c) In the Chinese writing system, what do characters stand for?

Critical Thinking

4. **Drawing Conclusions**

More than just goods for trade traveled along the Silk Road. What else did the Silk Road bring to the people living along it?

Think About

• the different cultures that existed along the Silk Road

• the people and ideas that traveled along the Silk Road

ACTIVITY -OPTION- Imagine you lived in ancient China. Write a **journal entry** describing your experience with one of the religions that developed in China.

Section 2 Assessment

1. Terms & Names
a. dynasty, p. 476
b. Genghis Khan, p. 476
c. Kublai Khan, p. 476
d. Confucius, p. 477
e. bureaucracy, p. 478
f. Taoism, p. 478
g. Lao Tzu, p. 478

2. Taking Notes

2500–2000 B.C., writing system

2500 B.C., silk

A.D. 1–200, paper

A.D. 1–200, porcelain

3. Main Ideas
a. Confucianism was the philosophy guiding Chinese bureaucracy; bureaucrats were Confucian scholars.
b. They wanted to dominate the market and receive the profits.
c. The characters stand for objects or ideas.

4. Critical Thinking
Travelers on the Silk Road also carried ideas, philosophies, and ways of doing things.

ACTIVITY OPTION

Integrated Assessment
• Rubric for writing a journal entry

Creating a Database

▶▶ Defining the Skill

A database is a collection of information, or data, that is organized so that you can find and retrieve information on a certain topic quickly and easily. Once you set up a database on the computer, you can search for specific information without going through the entire database. Learning how to use a database will help you to create your own.

▶▶ Applying the Skill

The screen below shows a database for the history of settlement in Melanesia. Use the strategies listed below to help you understand and use the database.

How to Create a Database

Strategy ❶ Read the title to identify the topic of the database. In this title, the most important words, or keywords, are "history," "settlement," and "Melanesia." These keywords were used to begin the research for this database.

Strategy ❷ Identify the kind of data you need to enter in your database. These will become the column headings of your database. In this case, the key words "country," "settlement," "colonization," and "independence" were chosen to focus the research.

Strategy ❸ Identify the entries included under each heading.

Strategy ❹ Use the database to help you find information quickly. For example, if this database were on a computer, you could search for "United Kingdom" to find out which of these countries were colonized by the United Kingdom.

❷ Country	First Settlement	Colonization	Independence
Fiji ❸	3,500 years ago	1874 by United Kingdom ❹	1970
New Caledonia	3,000 years ago	1853 by France	not independent
Papua New Guinea	50,000 years ago	1793 by United Kingdom 1828 by Holland 1885 by United Kingdom ❹ and Germany 1921 by Australia	1975
Solomon Islands	4,000 years ago	1886 by Germany and ❹ United Kingdom	1978
Vanuatu	3,300 years ago	1906 by United Kingdom ❹ and France	1980

❶ History of the Settlement of Melanesia   Cancel View   List View

▶▶ Practicing the Skill

Turn to page 475 in Chapter 16, Section 2, "Foundations of Chinese Civilization." Create a database about the dynasties of China. Use the information in the section to provide the data. Use a format like the one above for your database.

SKILLBUILDER

Creating a Database
Defining the Skill

Tell students that databases collect and organize information in one place so that the information can be accessed from one location quickly and easily. Databases can save them a great deal of time when doing research for classroom assignments.

Applying the Skill

How to Create a Database Tell students to work through each strategy one at a time. Point out that they need to clearly identify the keywords in the title. The keywords will be used for research and to identify what information the database covers.

Use the Database

Discuss the database shown on this page in detail with students. Encourage them to note the column headings. Ask them to tell what kind of information they will find in the database.

Practicing the Skill

Have students turn to the paragraphs on early Chinese dynasties, using keywords such as "dynasty" and "Chinese civilization" to create a database. If students need additional practice, have them use the information under the heading "Religion and Philosophy" on pages 477–478. Suggest that they create a database on Confucianism, Buddhism, and Taoism using the information in the section. They may later use the database for research reports.

In-depth Resources: Unit 6
• Skillbuilder Practice, p. 8

Career Connection: Anthropologist

Encourage students who enjoy creating a database to find out about careers that use this skill. For example, anthropologists are scientists who study and compare groups of people all over the world. As they collect information, they might enter it into a database for easy retrieval and comparison.

Block Scheduling

1. Explain that anthropology can be divided into subfields such as cultural anthropology or physical anthropology. Suggest that students find information about one of these subfields.

2. Help students learn about the education and experience a person needs to become an anthropologist.

3. Have students share their findings using a chart or other visual aid.

WAR WOUNDS

OBJECTIVE

Students analyze a story set in a refugee settlement during the Korean War that describes a girl's conflict over abandoning a beloved pet.

FOCUS & MOTIVATE

Making Inferences To help students predict the setting and conflicts in the story, have them study the illustrations and answer the following questions:

1. What do the airplane silhouettes indicate about the story?

2. What predictions can you make from the photograph of the dog?

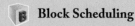 **Block Scheduling**

MORE ABOUT...

"War Wounds"

After World War II, Korea was divided along the 38th parallel. North Korea became Communist, supported by the Soviet Union, while the South became the Republic of Korea, supported by the United Nations and the United States.

In 1950, North Korean forces invaded the Republic of Korea. The U.N. and U.S. sent forces to aid South Korea, and Communist China entered the war to help North Korea. For three years, troops fought back and forth over the 38th parallel. In 1953, the war ended in a stalemate, and the two Koreas remained divided.

BASED VERY CLOSELY on the life of its author, Sook Nyul Choi, *Echoes of the White Giraffe* is the story of a 15-year-old Korean girl, Sookan. As the war between North Korea and South Korea rages, Sookan, her mother, and her younger brother, Inchun, are forced to flee their home in Seoul. They become separated from Sookan's father and older brothers. Sookan, her mother, and Inchun find shelter at a settlement for war refugees in Pusan, a city in southern Korea. There, Sookan slowly begins to make friends, including Junho, a boy who sings with her in a church choir.

"**I**s that a picture of your dog?" Junho asked, looking at the pencil sketch of Luxy that rested on top of the bookcase. "You must miss it very much. . . ."

"Oh that," I said, flustered and surprised. "Yes, that's my boxer, Luxy." I missed my dog, but I hadn't talked about her with anyone since we left Seoul. . . . I frequently thought of how Luxy used to wait eagerly at the top of the stone steps in front of our house for me to come home from school. Then, at night, she would sleep at the foot of my bed. But I never talked of Luxy, for I was afraid that people might think I was childish and insensitive to mourn the loss of my dog when so many people were dead or missing. Junho was different, though . . . sharing my sadness. . . . I stared at Luxy's picture, and I imagined how scared she must have felt when we all abandoned her. Suddenly the acrid[1] smell of bombs and sweeping fires filled my lungs, and the sound of sirens and planes flying low overhead buzzed in my ears. My mind raced back to that horrible day in late June when the dark airplanes roared through the skies and dropped a shower of dark, egg-shaped bombs from their bellies. . . . I shook my head and swallowed hard. . . .

"What is it, Sookan? What are you thinking about?" Junho said, looking very concerned.

"Oh, Junho, I was remembering the first bombing of Seoul. It was horrible. . . . All I could do was stand by the window and watch the bombs explode. Hyunchun, my third brother,

1. Harsh; foul.

Activity Option

Differentiating Instruction: Less Proficient Readers

Building Language Skills Have students work in pairs, matching less proficient readers with more fluent readers. Duplicate copies of the Literature Connection and give each pair a copy and two colored pencils. Have pairs reread the story and underline events, using one color to underline events that take place in the present and another color to underline events that happened in the past. Have volunteers read aloud the events and record them on the board in two columns, labeled Past and Present.

Then ask students to circle and discuss words that are unfamiliar or difficult to pronounce. Encourage fluent readers to help their partners by defining unfamiliar words or suggesting strategies for pronouncing difficult words.

came rushing into my room, shouting, '. . . Come on. Those planes will be right on top of us next. Let's go.' "

"Did you all get out safely?" Junho asked anxiously. . . .

"Oh, yes. We put thick blankets over our heads and joined the throngs of people headed up Namsan Mountain. We stayed up on the mountain all night and watched the bombs erupt into flames in the city below. . . . As we were sitting there, I realized my brother Jaechun was holding a large bundle in his arms, which he rocked back and forth like a baby. I instantly realized it was Luxy wrapped in that bundle. . . . It was a good thing that Luxy was bundled up to look like an infant, for other people on the mountain would have been afraid if they knew a dog was with them. They would have panicked, fearing that a dog would go crazy with the noise and the crowds and might bite them. . . .

"The bombing finally stopped at dawn and we began making our way back home. We found our house half bombed and smoldering. We were hungry, and exhausted, and didn't know what we would do next. We . . . started to unwrap poor Luxy. When we uncovered her, she gave such a loud, joyous bark. . . . She made us laugh and forget that we were sitting in the middle of a bombed city."

Junho's face brightened. . . . "Luxy was lucky to be so well loved and cared for."

"Well, . . . Things got worse. About six months after that, we had to leave Seoul. I left her all alone. I don't know what happened to her. . . . There were more bombs, and we had to run and follow the retreating South Korean and U.N. soldiers going south. . . . Mother, Inchun and I were separated from my father and my three older brothers. The three of us, along with thousands of other refugees, walked the whole day in the bitter cold snow to Inchon harbor. I was terribly cold and scared. . . . It was only once we were on the ship that I even thought of my Luxy. . . . I felt so guilty and ashamed that I never mentioned Luxy to Mother or to Inchun. . . .

". . . Each time I see a dog or hear a dog bark, I feel guilty that I did not love Luxy enough to save her; she, my dog, who depended on me. I had thought only of myself. . . ."

Junho listened intently. . . . "You couldn't have walked with her in that cold snow. She may still be alive in Seoul. You shouldn't feel bad."

How does the author show how much Sookan misses her pet? What are some of the reasons Sookan doesn't want to think or talk about her dog? Why does Sookan decide to share her feelings about her dog with Junho?

Thinking About
THE LITERATURE

How does the life of Sookan and her family change as a result of the war? Besides missing her pet, what other emotions does the loss of Luxy bring out in Sookan?

Writing About
THE LITERATURE

The title "War Wounds" has two meanings, one literal—the words mean exactly what they say—and the other figurative—the words have a symbolic meaning. What do you think are the literal and figurative meanings of the title of this selection?

About the Author

Sook Nyul Choi (b. 1937) was born in Pyongyang, Korea, and spent two and a half years as a refugee during the Korean War. She later emigrated to the United States, where she attended college and then taught school. She now lives in Cambridge, Massachusetts.

Further Reading The first book by Sook Nyul Choi was *Year of Impossible Goodbyes*. It is a moving fictionalized account of Choi's last months in Pyongyang under Japanese rule.

INSTRUCT

Reading the Literature
Possible Responses

Sookan has a sketch of Luxy, remembers a lot about her, and thinks of her when she sees or hears a dog. She feels childish and ashamed, but believes Junho understands her sadness.

Thinking About the Literature
Possible Responses

They had to flee from their home and city; their family is separated. Sookan feels guilty and ashamed that she did not "love Luxy enough to save her."

Writing About the Literature
Possible Responses

Students' responses should explain both literal and figurative meanings of the title. For example, literally, "war wounds" are injuries caused by battle. Figuratively, the words refer to the hurt Sookan suffers in losing her pet and blaming herself.

MORE ABOUT...
Historical Accounts

This story is from a book based on the author's own experiences. Discuss the distinctions among different genres, such as autobiography, fictionalized personal accounts, historical fiction, and nonfiction.

 World Literature

More to Think About

Making Personal Connections Ask students what they learned from this story. What is the value of writing about experiences like this? What is the value of reading about other peoples' experiences? Ask students to think of historical events they have experienced. What could they write about? What genre would they choose to tell their stories?

Vocabulary Activity Students may work individually or in groups. Have them make a chart with the headings Sookan, Junho, and Luxy. Tell them to review the story and list words that name emotions displayed by each character. Ask volunteers to read aloud the words they have found. Invite students to read aloud lines that explain why characters have each feeling.

Ancient Japan

TERMS & NAMES
Shinto
clan
Heian Age
The Tale of Genji
Zen
samurai
shogun

SECTION OBJECTIVES

1. To describe early Japan and the significant Chinese and Korean influences on its later development

2. To explain the development of the feudal system and Japan's decision to isolate itself

FOCUS & MOTIVATE
WARM-UP

Making Inferences After students read <u>Dateline</u>, discuss Japan's fateful survival.

1. Why do you think the people of Japan believed that the typhoon that destroyed the Mongol ships was sent by a divine power?

2. What effect do you think this event might have had on future foreign relations?

INSTRUCT: Objective ❶
Early Japan/Outside Influences

- What kind of governments ruled Japan before about A.D. 250? kingdoms organized around clans led by hereditary chiefs

- In what ways did Korea and China influence Japan? Korea: use of bronze, rice growing, and Buddhism; China: writing system, calendar, and centralized government

- How did the Heian Age influence Japanese culture? culture flourished; aristocrats lived in luxury, wrote diaries and novels; Zen Buddhism introduced

 In-depth Resources: Unit 6
 - Guided Reading Worksheet, p. 5

 Reading Study Guide
(Spanish and English), pp. 148–149

MAIN IDEA	WHY IT MATTERS NOW
For hundreds of years, Japan developed its unique culture with influence from only its closest neighbors, China and Korea.	Japan continues to follow an independent path in world affairs.

DATELINE
EXTRA

THE COAST OF JAPAN, A.D. 1281

Fifty-three days ago, our people were horrified to see a fleet of ships carrying 140,000 Mongol invaders approaching our shores. The Mongol emperor of China, Kublai Khan, sent the ships to conquer our country. Our brave samurai fought valiantly, but the Mongols had powerful crossbows and catapults that hurled terrifying missiles. Our warriors were near defeat.

Then, out of nowhere, a typhoon arose on the water. Mongol ships were smashed and sunk by the furious storm. Our people will always remember this *kamikaze*—the "divine wind"—that saved our country.

Culture • Japanese samurai prepare to battle the Mongols. ▲

Early Japan ❶

Long before the *kamikaze* (KAH•mih•KAH•zee) saved Japan from Mongol defeat, people inhabited its islands. From 10,000 to 300 B.C., hunters, gatherers, and skilled fishermen lived along Japan's eastern coast. Toward the end of this period, the Japanese began practicing a religion called **Shinto**, which means "the way of the gods." Shinto teaches that supernatural beings, called kami (KAH•mih), live in all objects and forces of nature.

Program Resources

 In-depth Resources: Unit 6
 - Guided Reading Worksheet, p. 5
 - Reteaching Activity, p. 12

 Reading Study Guide
(Spanish and English), pp. 148–149

 Formal Assessment
 - Section Quiz, p. 242

Integrated Assessment
 - Rubric for writing a short story

 Outline Map Activities

 Access for Students Acquiring English
 - Guided Reading Worksheet, p. 143

Technology Resources
classzone.com

TEST-TAKING RESOURCES
 ⤵ Strategies for Test Preparation
 ⤵ Test Practice Transparencies
 ⓘ Online Test Practice

The early Japanese lived in kingdoms organized around clans. A **clan** is a group of families who trace their descent from a common ancestor. Clans in Japan were each led by a chief who inherited the position. Around A.D. 250, the Yamato clan emerged as the most powerful, and it established a government that ruled Japan for hundreds of years.

Place • This gateway standing in the sea is the entrance to the Itsukushima Shrine, one of Japan's most famous places of Shinto worship. ▲

Outside Influences

Around the time that the Yamato clan took power, Japan began using new ideas and practices from its neighbors, Korea and China. From Korea, the Japanese gained knowledge of how to use bronze and iron technology to make tools and weapons, as well as how to grow an important crop—rice. Japanese religious life also changed significantly when the Koreans introduced Buddhism into Japan. This religion was one of many ideas and customs that originated in China and were brought to Japan by Koreans. In the A.D. 500s, China began to influence Japan's culture directly, as well.

Prince Shotoku At that time, Japanese rulers believed an understanding of Chinese civilization would help them gain political power in East Asia. Japan's Prince Shotoku Taishi (shoh·TOH·koo tay·EE·shee) became a Buddhist and a student of Chinese literature and culture. He established diplomatic relations with China and sent priests and students there to study its culture. Through this exchange, the Japanese adopted China's writing system, calendar, and system of centralized government.

The Heian Age In A.D. 794, the emperor Kammu built a new capital called Heian-kyo (HEY·ahn-KYOH). The period from that year to 1185 is called the **Heian Age** and is considered Japan's golden age. During this period, Japanese culture flourished. A bustling population of 100,000 made up of aristocrats, servants, and artisans lived in Heian-kyo.

Reading Social Studies
A. Possible Answer
Countries can learn valuable skills and new ideas by interacting with other countries.

Reading
Social Studies
A. Recognizing Effects What does Japan's experience with learning from its neighbors tell you about the importance of cultural exchange?

Vocabulary
artisan: craftsperson

Citizenship IN ACTION

Tokyo National Research Institute for Cultural Properties Keeping the rich cultural heritage of Japan alive is the mission of the Tokyo National Research Institute for Cultural Properties. The Institute's scientists, researchers, art historians, and other experts are dedicated to preserving Japan's art, artifacts, ancient monuments, and historic sites, such as Buddhist temples (see below).

In 1995, the Institute opened the Japan Center for International Cooperation in Conservation. The Japan Center works across national borders to help preserve ancient sites throughout the world.

MORE ABOUT...
State Shinto

Many Japanese people continued to practice Shinto, even after Buddhism was introduced. In 1868, the Japanese government established Shinto as the official state religion. This official religion was based on patriotism and was called State Shinto. It encouraged the worship of Japan's emperor as a divine being.

After World War II, the government abolished the official State Shinto. The emperor stated that he was not to be considered divine. Today, Japanese people continue to practice Shinto rituals, such as visiting shrines with offerings of food and prayers, asking for the blessing of the gods. Shinto priests often preside at weddings.

Citizenship IN ACTION

The National Research Institute of Cultural Properties trains people in restoring and preserving Japanese *urushi*, or lacquerware. The process of making lacquerware involves several steps. First, sap from the urushi tree in Japan is processed into lacquer. Then the lacquer is applied to very thin wood and polished to a high glaze. In a special process, gold and silver are inlaid in the lacquer to create a design and then covered with many coats of lacquer.

Activity Options

Interdisciplinary Link: Humanities

Identifying Cultural Heritage Sites and Artifacts Tell students that the United States also has many sites, monuments, and artifacts that people are working to preserve. Have groups of students brainstorm and create a list of sites that they think are important as part of our cultural heritage. After students complete their lists, create a class chart on the chalkboard, using the one shown as a model.

Prehistoric Sites	Historic Sites	Monuments	Art and Artifacts
Mesa Verde	Gettysburg	Lincoln Memorial	Liberty Bell

Culture • **In this illustration, Lady Murasaki sits under the moon, planning *The Tale of Genji*. ▲**

Members of the royal court lived in luxury and high style. Many aristocratic women wrote diaries, letters, and novels about life in the imperial court. Lady Murasaki Shikibu (MOO·rah· SAH·kee SHEE·kee·boo) wrote the world's first novel, called ***The Tale of Genji***. In the novel, Lady Murasaki described life at Heian-kyo's imperial court.

Zen Buddhism After first being established at the Heian-kyo court, Buddhism became a national religion. One branch of Buddhism, called **Zen**, was the most influential in Japan. Zen emphasizes that people can achieve enlightenment suddenly, rather than through many years of painful study. Zen teaches that to reach enlightenment, a person must focus intensely to understand certain concepts, called koans (KOH·ahnz). Koans are statements or questions that seem to make little sense. However, if someone concentrates very hard to understand one of them, then he or she might reach enlightenment.

Feudal Japan ❷

By the 1100s, the Heian-kyo aristocracy lost control of the country to powerful lords. The strongest lords enlisted warriors to fight rival lords. Japan began to develop a feudal system similar to that of medieval Europe, with the country divided into huge estates.

The Samurai While the aristocracy at the Heian-kyo court lived lavishly, disorder and violence spread throughout the rest of the country. Lords needed protection against outlaws and bandits. They relied on warriors called **samurai** (SAM·uh·RY) to protect their estates.

Vocabulary
imperial: relating to an empire or emperor

BACKGROUND
This is one of the most famous koans: "What is the sound of one hand clapping?"

Human-Environment Interaction • **Zen Buddhists take pride in creating peaceful gardens as settings for meditation. ▼**

Reading
Social Studies

B. Recognizing Important Details How did the use of samurai differ from the use of an army?

As with European knights, the samurai each pledged to serve a particular lord. They provided him with military and bureaucratic services. By law and privilege, samurai and their families became a distinct social class.

The Kamakura Shogunate During the 1100s, Japan was torn by a murderous war between two clans battling for power. After 30 years of fighting, the Minamoto clan claimed victory. In 1192 in Kamakura, the clan's leader, Yoritomo, established a new kind of warrior government called a shogunate (SHOH·guh·niht). He took on the role of **shogun**—or the emperor's chief general—and held most of the country's power.

In 1274 and again in 1281, the shoguns faced their greatest challenge—Kublai Khan attempted to invade and conquer Japan. On page 484, you read about the events of the second battle. The Kamakura shogunate defeated the Mongols, but at a great cost. The war drained the treasury, and the shogun was unable to pay the samurai. They turned back to individual lords for support, and many years of fighting among lords followed.

Tokugawa Shogunate

Finally, in the 1560s, the fighting began to settle down. The lord Tokugawa Ieyasu (toh·koo·GAH·wah ee·YAH·soo) defeated his rivals and became shogun in 1603. In that year, he moved the capital to Edo.

BACKGROUND

In a shogunate, the emperor and his court carried out merely ceremonial roles.

Reading Social Studies
B. Possible Answers
Samurai owed loyalty to a particular lord, unlike an army maintained by a government; *samurai* organized a fighting force when needed; they also did bureaucratic jobs.

Thinking Critically Possible Answers
1. The warrior was one of the highest-ranking samurai.
2. They wore tunics over armor on special occasions to add to the finery.

Fine Protection Samurai, who fought hand to hand against their enemies, wore finely made suits of armor and helmets for protection. Low-ranking samurai wore lightweight armor made of small metal panels. The highest-ranking samurai sported much fancier armor, such as the suit shown here. Made of iron panels that were laced or pinned together, it could also include panels of thick leather or linked pieces of metal called chain mail.

The armor was often intricately decorated. The entire suit could weigh as much as 40 pounds. At celebrations, to add to the finery, a samurai wore over his armor a long, loose tunic made of brightly dyed silk and embroidered with his family symbol.

THINKING CRITICALLY

1. **Drawing Conclusions** What does this suit of armor tell you about the rank of the warrior who wore it?
2. **Clarifying** For what purpose did samurai wear beautiful tunics over their armor?

MORE ABOUT...
Functions of Temples

With the rise of the Kamakura Shogunate and the samurai, the religious temples became the centers of learning and of culture. The temples, which originally had trained people destined to be monks, became essentially primary schools. The children of the warrior class, or samurai, were sent to the temples for their education. The most important subjects taught there were reading and writing, but the children were given spiritual instruction as well.

Spotlight on CULTURE

In addition to their distinctive clothing, the samurai had a unique system of values and code of honor. As warriors, the samurai valued military skills such as horsemanship and expertise with weapons. They also valued bravery and self-discipline. Loyalty and obedience to their lord was more important than life itself. If a samurai suffered defeat or dishonor, he often committed ritual suicide.

Activity Options

Differentiating Instruction: Gifted and Talented

Imagining Samurai Life Have students imagine that they are samurai warriors facing the Mongol invaders and watching the "divine wind" sink the invading ships. Have them refer to the <u>Dateline</u> feature, page 484. For more insight, suggest that students do further research into the samurai way of life and the samurai code, the "way of the warrior" (*bushido*), with its emphasis on honor.

Ask them to write a brief narrative describing their thoughts and feelings during the battle and afterward. Encourage them to include vivid descriptions and imaginative details to enliven their narratives. Have them display their narratives in class.

FOCUS ON VISUALS

Interpreting the Photograph Ask students to study the photograph of a busy Tokyo street and point out details that show what modern Tokyo is like.

Possible Responses signs in English as well as Japanese, many stores and advertising signs, crowds of hurrying people

Extension Have students write a short poem or personal essay comparing this photograph with that of the Zen garden on page 486.

ASSESS & RETEACH

Reading Social Studies Have students complete the column "Ancient Japan" in the chart on page 468.

Formal Assessment
• Section Quiz, p. 242

RETEACHING ACTIVITY

Ask students to create a time line recording the important events covered in this section. Have students write a brief explanatory sentence for each event.

In-depth Resources: Unit 6
• Reteaching Activity, p. 12

Access for Students Acquiring English
• Reteaching Activity, p. 148

Place • Today, Edo is called Tokyo and is still Japan's capital. ▲

The First Europeans in Japan In 1543, just before the Tokugawa Shogunate began, the first Europeans arrived in Japan. They brought firearms and other goods to trade for gold and silver. In 1549, Catholic missionaries arrived in Japan and began converting many Japanese. By 1614, 300,000 Japanese had become Catholics, including many peasants.

The Closing Door By the 1630s, Tokugawa Ieyasu was worried about foreigners in Japan. He got word that the Spanish had established a settlement in the Philippines. To avoid such a situation in Japan, he ordered all Christians to leave the country. He also declared that any Japanese who left the country would be put to death upon their return. He banned most European trade, finalizing his decision to free Japan of European influences. This situation continued for 200 years, during which Japan isolated itself from most outside contact.

SECTION 3 ASSESSMENT

Terms & Names

1. **Identify:** (a) Shinto   (b) clan   (c) Heian Age   (d) *The Tale of Genji*   (e) Zen   (f) samurai   (g) shogun

Taking Notes

2. Use a spider map like this one to list important facts about the development of Japan's culture.

Main Ideas

3. (a) How did the Chinese and the Koreans influence Japan's culture?

(b) What services did samurai provide, and to whom?

(c) Under the shogunates, who held more power—the emperor or the shogun?

Critical Thinking

4. **Evaluating Decisions**
Do you think Tokugawa Ieyasu was right to isolate Japan from European influence? Explain.

Think About
• the period before Tokugawa Ieyasu gained control of Japan
• European influence elsewhere
• effects of Japan's isolation

ACTIVITY -OPTION- Write a **short story** from the perspective of a samurai, a shogun, or a lord about life in feudal Japan.

488 CHAPTER 16

Section 3 Assessment

1. Terms & Names
a. Shinto, p. 484
b. clan, p. 485
c. Heian Age, p. 485
d. *The Tale of Genji*, p. 486
e. Zen, p. 486
f. samurai, p. 486
g. shogun, p. 487

2. Taking Notes

Tokugawa Shogunate and isolation

influenced by Korea and China

feudal Japan: samurai, shogun

Ancient Japan

3. Main Ideas
a. China: writing system, calendar, centralized government; Korea: use of bronze and iron technology, rice cultivation, Buddhism
b. Samurai provided lords with military and bureaucratic services.
c. The shogun was the ruler; the emperor had only a ceremonial role.

4. Critical Thinking
Students may say that it was right to isolate Japan, preventing influence or takeover. Others may say that it was not right because isolation might have let Japan fall behind in technological development.

ACTIVITY OPTION

Integrated Assessment
• Rubric for writing a short story

Technology: 2009

Three Gorges Dam

Rising in the Kunlun Mountains of Tibet, the Chang Jiang winds for more than 3,400 miles. It flows through some of China's most fertile agricultural land before emptying into the East China Sea at Shanghai. A stretch of the Chang Jiang known as the Three Gorges includes some of the world's most beautiful scenery. It is also an area rich in archaeological treasures dating back thousands of years. At this site, the Chinese government is building the world's largest dam. With an estimated completion date of 2009, the dam will help control floods and generate much-needed electricity. At the same time, however, construction of the dam will destroy archaeological sites and much of the region's natural beauty while forcing between 1 and 2 million people to relocate.

Three Gorges Dam Facts
Height: 600 ft. (181 m)
Width: 1.5 mi. (2.415 km)
Reservoir: 370 mi. (595.7 km) long
Cost: $25 billion
Workers: 40,000
Years to Complete: 17

CHINA

Area to be flooded
Three Gorges Dam
Sandouping
Wuhan
Chang Jiang (Yangtze R.)
Shanghai
Chongqing
Ling R.

A series of locks will enable ocean-going ships to travel as far as Chongqing, at the far end of the new reservoir. This is expected to greatly improve the economy of Chongqing.

The dam will control flooding. However, it may also affect fishing and create other environmental problems.

Water-driven turbines will generate as much electricity as 18 nuclear reactors. This hydroelectric power, one of the cleanest forms of energy, will reduce air pollution. That is important in China because the Chinese burn so much coal.

CHINA

When the Three Gorges reservoir is filled in 2009, it will be less than 1 mile wide but 370 miles long—about the distance from Los Angeles to San Francisco.

THINKING Critically

1. Analyzing Motives
How will the Three Gorges Dam benefit China? What are the drawbacks of the dam?

2. Recognizing Effects
The construction of the dam will cause the flooding of about 1,300 archaeological sites. How will this affect China's cultural heritage?

OBJECTIVES

1. To build awareness of what will be the world's largest dam, currently under construction in China
2. To explain the benefits of this project
3. To explain the drawbacks of this project

INSTRUCT

- When will the Three Gorges Dam be finished?
- List three facts about the Three Gorges Dam.
- What kind of energy does China rely on? Why does it want to explore other types of energy?

B **Block Scheduling**

MORE ABOUT...
Benefits/Drawbacks of Hydroelectric Power

Hydroelectric power, a very clean source of energy, helps reduce air pollution. This is important for China because they burn so much coal. Dams are a reliable, cheap source of power.

However, the reservoirs tend to fill up with silt (fine earth) from upstream. This gradually lowers the depth of water and reduces the volume held back by the dam, which in turn reduces the power of the hydroelectric turbines. When silt is held back by the dam, it also endangers fish and marine life.

Connect to History

Strategic Thinking Throughout history, what kinds of tasks have been made easier by harnessing the power of water?

Connect to Today

Strategic Thinking If you were in charge of planning a dam, what factors would you consider while deciding where to place the dam?

Thinking Critically

1. Analyzing Motives Possible Responses Benefits of the dam include flood control, electricity, reliable water supplies, recreation, and improved economy.

Drawbacks include: millions of people will need to relocate; cities, towns, and precious farmland will disappear; environmental problems will cost money to fix; part of China's link to its past will be destroyed with the flooding of historic sites.

2. Recognizing Effects Possible Response China will lose part of its culture when archaeological sites are destroyed. Archaeologists learn about past civilizations by studying artifacts, fossils, architecture, and drawings. Many of these will be lost forever.

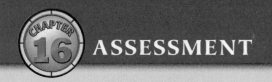
TERMS & NAMES

1. Mount Everest, p. 470
2. Ring of Fire, p. 472
3. outback, p. 473
4. dynasty, p. 476
5. Confucius, p. 477
6. bureaucracy, p. 478
7. clan, p. 485
8. *The Tale of Genji*, p. 486
9. Zen, p. 486
10. shogun, p. 487

REVIEW QUESTIONS

Possible Responses

1. It often flooded, destroyed villages, and took many lives.
2. the Ring of Fire region
3. It has not changed much in 250 million years.
4. Only the emperor, his family, and some of his officials could enter it.
5. silk, porcelain, paper, gunpowder, compass, writing system
6. Confucianism taught the importance of moral character and individual responsibility for society; Taoism taught harmony with nature; Buddhism taught how to understand suffering.
7. Korea: Buddhism, metalworking, and rice cultivation; China: system of writing and a calendar; Chinese art, literature, and centralized government
8. emperor: ceremonial role; lords: controlled estates and fought among themselves; samurai: warriors who served the lords
9. At first they traded with the Europeans, and many converted to Christianity. Later, the emperor isolated Japan from European contact.

CHAPTER 16 ASSESSMENT

TERMS & NAMES

Explain the significance of each of the following:

1. Mount Everest
2. Ring of Fire
3. outback
4. dynasty
5. Confucius
6. bureaucracy
7. clan
8. *The Tale of Genji*
9. Zen
10. shogun

REVIEW QUESTIONS

Physical Geography *(pages 469–474)*

1. Why do the Chinese often call the Huang He "China's Sorrow"?
2. Where do most of the world's earthquakes and volcanic eruptions occur?
3. How does Australia's landscape differ from that of the world's other continents?

Ancient China *(pages 475–480)*

4. How did the Forbidden City get its name?
5. What are some important inventions from China?
6. Describe the three philosophies that were popular in ancient China.

Ancient Japan *(pages 484–488)*

7. How did Japanese culture show influences from both China and Korea?
8. What roles did the emperors, the lords, and the samurai play in feudal Japan?
9. How did the Japanese respond to Europeans arriving in Japan?

CRITICAL THINKING

Comparing and Contrasting

1. Using your completed chart from Reading Social Studies, p. 468, describe important similarities and differences between ancient China and ancient Japan.

Making Inferences

2. How do you think China's dynasties helped establish and maintain a stable government?

Drawing Conclusions

3. Why did the shogun Tokugawa Ieyasu feel that isolating Japan from Europe was a good idea?

Visual Summary

Physical Geography *1*

- The physical geography of East Asia, Australia, and the Pacific Islands affects how and where people live and how and where civilizations developed.
- Japan and the Pacific Islands are particularly vulnerable to earthquakes and volcanic eruptions.

Ancient China *2*

- The ancient Chinese developed the longest-lasting civilization in history. It has existed for 4,000 years.
- Chinese civilization produced inventions and ideas that influenced both Asia and Europe.

Ancient Japan *3*

- Over hundreds of years, ancient Japan developed a unique culture that was influenced by only its nearest neighbors.
- Japan established a feudal system with lords and warriors. Eventually, the country established a central military government, which lasted into the 1800s.

CRITICAL THINKING: Possible Responses

1. Comparing and Contrasting

China's size and landforms differ from Japan's. Other differences include government and religion. Japan adopted many Chinese inventions and traded primarily with China, while China traded with the West.

2. Making Inferences

They provided an orderly succession of rulers, with power kept within one family line. The civil service provided educated officials who followed Confucian ideals.

3. Drawing Conclusions

The shogun probably felt he was protecting his country from possible attempts by Europeans to take over in Japan as they had in other parts of Asia.

SOCIAL STUDIES SKILLBUILDER

SKILLBUILDER: Creating a Database

1. What is the topic of the database? What title would you give it?
2. Under which column heading would you list information to show which Pacific Islands experience seasonal winds?

FOCUS ON GEOGRAPHY

1. **Region** • What is the population density in most of Australia?
2. **Region** • In what regions are Australia's major cities located?

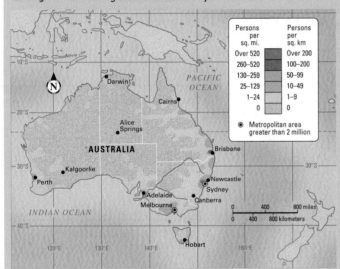

CHAPTER PROJECTS

Interdisciplinary Activity: Language Arts

Writing a Poem The ancient Japanese developed a type of poetry called tanka. A tanka is a 31-syllable poem with the theme of love, friendship, or nature. Research Japanese tanka. Then write your own tanka and illustrate it with images that reflect the poem's theme. You may also research Japanese art styles to use in your illustration.

Cooperative Learning Activity

Creating a Talk Show In a group of three to five classmates, create a talk show about travel on the Silk Road. Research the kinds of people and animals that traveled along the route, the terrain they passed through on the journey, the hazards they faced, and the cargo they carried.

• Take on the roles of talk-show host, travelers, and traders.
• Write a script for your roles.
• Conduct your talk show in front of the class.

 INTERNET ACTIVITY

Use the Internet to do research about a recent earthquake or volcanic eruption that occurred in the Ring of Fire. Focus on the event itself and how it affected the people in the area.
Writing About Geography Write a report of your findings. Include pictures showing the event or its aftermath. List the Web sites you used to prepare your report.

For Internet links to support this activity, go to

CLASSZONE.COM

CHAPTER PROJECTS

Interdisciplinary Activity: Language Arts

Writing a Poem If possible, obtain an example of a tanka and read it aloud to the class. Point out that students' tankas should have exactly 31 syllables and should have a theme such as some aspect of love, friendship, or nature. Encourage students to use vivid, colorful language and to include appropriate illustrations in the style of Japanese art.

Cooperative Learning Activity

Creating a Talk Show Discuss formats of talk shows students have seen. Suggest that students take the role of a host, who asks specific questions about travel on the Silk Road, or participants, who describe specific geography and natural hazards along the route. Encourage participants to address the topics listed and to represent a variety of people and experiences.

 INTERNET ACTIVITY

Remind students that their reports should begin with a main idea statement that identifies the specific earthquake or volcanic eruption and its location. Encourage them to include details about the event itself and to focus on specific details about how people in the area were affected.

Skills Answers

Social Studies Skillbuilder
Possible Responses
1. natural disasters; "Natural Disasters in Countries of the Western Pacific"
2. monsoons, typhoons

Focus on Geography
Possible Responses
1. 0
2. coastal regions

China and Its Neighbors

	OVERVIEW	COPYMASTERS	INTEGRATED TECHNOLOGY
UNIT ATLAS AND CHAPTER RESOURCES	Students will examine the government, economy, and culture of the countries in East Asia and the development of modern China and modern Japan.	**In-depth Resources: Unit 6** • Guided Reading Worksheets, pp. 13–17 • Skillbuilder Practice, p. 20 • Unit Atlas Activities, pp. 1–2 • Geography Workshop, pp. 35–36 **Reading Study Guide** (Spanish and English), pp. 152–163 **Outline Map Activities**	Power Presentations Electronic Teacher Tools Online Lesson Planner Chapter Summaries on CD Critical Thinking Transparencies CT33
SECTION 1 Establishing Modern China pp. 495–499	**KEY IDEAS** • Overpopulation, food shortages, and wars led to the downfall of the Qing dynasty. • Mao Zedong led the Communist Party in China, and increased government control drastically.	**In-depth Resources: Unit 6** • Guided Reading Worksheet, p. 12 • Reteaching Activity, p. 22 **Reading Study Guide** (Spanish and English), pp. 152–153	classzone.com Chapter Summaries on CD
SECTION 2 The Governments of East Asia pp. 502–505	• The Chinese Communist Party controls the government in China today. • The struggle for human rights is ongoing in China. • Conflicts in East Asia continue.	**In-depth Resources: Unit 6** • Guided Reading Worksheet, p. 13 • Reteaching Activity, p. 23 **Reading Study Guide** (Spanish and English), pp. 154–155	Critical Thinking Transparencies CT34 classzone.com Chapter Summaries on CD
SECTION 3 The Economies of East Asia pp. 506–509	• The Chinese government owns all financial institutions and sets both prices and production levels. • China and North Korea have similar government-run economic systems. The economies of Japan and South Korea have grown since the 1960s.	**In-depth Resources: Unit 6** • Guided Reading Worksheet, p. 14 • Reteaching Activity, p. 24 **Reading Study Guide** (Spanish and English), pp. 156–157	classzone.com Chapter Summaries on CD
SECTION 4 The Cultures of East Asia pp. 510–515	• Cultural exchange among East Asian countries has led to shared artistic ideas. • Ancient Chinese art forms include dance, opera, porcelain painting. • Communists repressed artistic freedom in China and North Korea.	**In-depth Resources: Unit 6** • Guided Reading Worksheet, p. 15 • Reteaching Activity, p. 25 **Reading Study Guide** (Spanish and English), pp. 158–159	Map Transparencies MT34 classzone.com Chapter Summaries on CD
SECTION 5 Establishing Modern Japan pp. 516–520	• During the Meiji Restoration, Japan became wealthy and powerful. • The Japanese worked hard to rebuild after World War II. • Japanese culture is largely homogenous; most people have common ancestors.	**In-depth Resources: Unit 6** • Guided Reading Worksheet, p. 16 • Reteaching Activity, p. 26 **Reading Study Guide** (Spanish and English), pp. 160–161	classzone.com Chapter Summaries on CD

Audio

 CD-ROM

Copymaster

Internet

Overhead Transparency

Pupil's Edition

TE Teacher's Edition

Video

ASSESSMENT OPTIONS

PE **Chapter Assessment,** pp. 522–523

Formal Assessment
• Chapter Tests: Forms A, B, C, pp. 260–271

Test Generator

Online Test Practice

Strategies for Test Preparation

PE **Section Assessment,** p. 499

Formal Assessment
• Section Quiz, p. 255

Integrated Assessment
• Rubric for creating a list of questions

Test Generator

Test Practice Transparencies TT83

PE **Section Assessment,** p. 505

Formal Assessment
• Section Quiz, p. 256

Integrated Assessment
• Rubric for writing a news story

Test Generator

Test Practice Transparencies TT84

PE **Section Assessment,** p. 509

Formal Assessment
• Section Quiz, p. 257

Integrated Assessment
• Rubric for making a chart

Test Generator

Test Practice Transparencies TT85

PE **Section Assessment,** p. 515

Formal Assessment
• Section Quiz, p. 258

Integrated Assessment
• Rubric for making a list

Test Generator

Test Practice Transparencies TT86

PE **Section Assessment,** p. 520

Formal Assessment
• Section Quiz, p. 259

Integrated Assessment
• Rubric for planning a schedule

Test Generator

Test Practice Transparencies TT87

RESOURCES FOR DIFFERENTIATING INSTRUCTION

Students Acquiring English/ESL

Reading Study Guide (Spanish and English), pp. 152–163

Access for Students Acquiring English Spanish Translations, pp. 149–160

TE **TE Activity**
• Identifying Suffixes, p. 496

Less Proficient Readers

Reading Study Guide (Spanish and English), pp. 152–163

TE **TE Activities**
• Finding Causes, p. 497
• Finding Main Ideas, pp. 508, 518

Gifted and Talented Students

TE **TE Activity**
• Interpreting the Sayings of Confucius, p. 511

CROSS-CURRICULAR CONNECTIONS

Humanities
Finley, Carol. *Art of Japan: Wood-Block Color Prints.* Minneapolis, MN: Lerner Publishing Group, 1998. History and contemporary samples.

Temko, Florence. *Traditional Crafts from China.* Minneapolis, MN: Lerner Publishing Group, 2001. Eight projects with background notes.

Literature
Fu, Shelley. *Ho Yi the Archer and Other Classic Chinese Tales.* North Haven, CT: Linnet Books, 2000. Retellings of seven classic Chinese folk tales.

Gollub, Matthew. *Cool Melons Turn to Frogs! The Life and Poems of Issa.* New York: Lee & Low, 1998. Haiku master poet, lovingly illustrated.

Popular Culture
Kimmel, Eric. *The Rooster's Antlers: A Story of the Chinese Zodiac.* New York: Holiday House, 1999. Engaging explanation of the Chinese Zodiac.

Geography
Dramer, Kim. *The Yellow River.* New York: Franklin Watts, 2001. History, geography, and environment of the Yellow River.

Language Arts/Literature
James, J. Alison. *The Drums of Noto Hanto.* New York: DK Publishing, 1999. Japanese villagers repel a warlord.

Wu, Priscilla. *The Abacus Contest: Stories from Taiwan and China.* Golden, CO: Fulcrum Press, 1996. Six short stories set in Taiwan.

ENRICHMENT ACTIVITIES

The following activities are especially suitable for classes following block schedules.

Teacher's Edition, pp. 498, 503, 504, 507, 512, 513, 514, 517, 521
Pupil's Edition, pp. 499, 505, 509, 515, 520

Unit Atlas, pp. 458–465
Literature Connections, pp. 500–501

Outline Map Activities

INTEGRATED TECHNOLOGY

Go to **classzone.com** for lesson support and activities for Chapter 17.

BLOCK SCHEDULE LESSON PLAN OPTIONS: 90-MINUTE PERIOD

DAY 1

CHAPTER PREVIEW, pp. 492–493
Class Time 20 minutes

• **Hypothesize** Use the "What do you think?" questions on PE p. 493 to help students hypothesize about how exchanging ideas affects a region's development.

SECTION 1, pp. 495–499
Class Time 70 minutes

• **Poster** Have students work in pairs to design a poster showing the events that led to the establishment of the People's Republic of China, beginning with the overthrow of the Qing Dynasty.

DAY 2

SECTION 2, pp. 502–505
Class Time 20 minutes

• **Organizing Information** As students reread the section, have them complete the chart in the Section 2 Assessment on PE p. 505.

SECTION 3, pp. 506–509
Class Time 30 minutes

• **Internet** Extend students' background knowledge of China by visiting **classzone.com.**

SECTION 4, pp. 510–515
Class Time 40 minutes

• **Making Outlines** Divide the class into small groups and assign each group one of the subsections in Section 4 to outline. Have the groups write their outlines on the board for the rest of the class to copy.

DAY 3

SECTION 5, pp. 516–520
Class Time 35 minutes

• **Small Groups** Divide the class into three groups. Have each group select one section objective on TE p. 516 to help them prepare a summary of this section. Remind students that when they summarize, they should include the main ideas and most important details in their own words. Reconvene as a whole class for discussion.

CHAPTER 17 REVIEW AND ASSESSMENT, pp. 522–523
Class Time 55 minutes

• **Review** Have students prepare a summary of the chapter, using the Terms & Names listed on the first page of each section.
Class Time 20 minutes

• **Assessment** Have students complete the Chapter 17 Assessment.
Class Time 35 minutes

TECHNOLOGY IN THE CLASSROOM

Graphic organizers can be extremely helpful when students are trying to gather information from a variety of sources, compare and contrast subject matter, or understand how certain topics are structured. Creating graphic organizers on the computer enables students to more easily manipulate, add, subtract, and change information than if they created their organizers on paper. Graphic organizers can be created in special software programs designed for that purpose or in the form of simple charts or tables in a word processing program.

ACTIVITY OUTLINE

Objective Students will go to Web sites describing life in Japan and enter their findings into a simple graphic organizer they create on the computer. They will write paragraphs based on the information they have put into their graphic organizers.

Task Have students visit the Web sites to learn about the daily lives of children in Japan. Then suggest that they input their findings into a graphic organizer created on the computer (either a table or a spider map). Have them conclude by writing paragraphs discussing the similarities and differences between life in Japan and life in the United States.

Class Time 2–3 class periods

DIRECTIONS

1. Ask students what they think it would be like to live in Japan. List their responses on the chalkboard.

2. Have students use the computer to make graphic organizers. The type of organizer they create will depend on the computer program they will be using, but two simple and effective examples would be tables (in this case with four columns for the four topics listed in step 3), or spider maps with four circles extending from a main-topic circle (the main topic would be "Life in Japan").

3. Either individually or in pairs, have students visit the Web sites listed at **classzone.com** to find out about life in Japan. As they go through the sites, ask them to look for information on the following aspects of Japanese children's lives: school, recreation (including arts, entertainment, and sports), holidays and festivals, and life at home. Have them input the information they find into their graphic organizers.

4. Suggest that students find items in their graphic organizers indicating how Japanese life is different from life in the United States. Ask them to use their computer program's font color tool to change the color of the text, or just have them underline those items that are differences. Have them highlight in a second color (or italicize) the similarities to life in the United States.

5. (optional step) Discuss students' findings as a class, and then have students return to their graphic organizers to add new information they have learned from this discussion.

6. Students should then write two to four paragraphs comparing and contrasting life in Japan with their own lives, using their graphic organizers as outlines.

7. Ask students to write closing paragraphs answering this question: Would you like to spend a year in Japan? Why or why not?

CHAPTER 17 OBJECTIVE

Students will examine the government, economy, and culture of the countries in East Asia and the development of modern China and modern Japan.

FOCUS ON VISUALS

Interpreting the Photograph Tell students that there are nearly 300 million bicycles in China. Most people, except for the very young and the very old, use them to get around. In Beijing, with a population of 13 million, there are 8 million bicycles. Often an entire family—father, mother, and baby—will ride on the same bicycle together. Ask students how they think China's environment, economy, and people might be different from those in other countries where bicycles are not as popular.

Possible Response A country where bicycles are very popular would probably have less air pollution from cars. The country would also be less dependent on oil, since gasoline for cars comes from oil. The people might be healthier since their method of transportation involves getting good exercise.

Extension Ask students to conduct a poll about bicycle use in their town or neighborhood. Have them prepare a chart or a graph based on the results of the poll.

CRITICAL THINKING ACTIVITY

Recognizing Effects Lead a discussion about the positive and negative effects that can result from cultural exchange. Ask students to give examples of each kind of effect.

Class Time 15 minutes

China and Its Neighbors

492

Recommended Resources

BOOKS FOR THE TEACHER
Collinwood, Dean, ed. *Global Studies: Japan and the Pacific Rim.* Guilford, CT: Dushkin/McGraw-Hill, 2000. Regional essays, country reports, world press articles, and an annotated list of Web sites.
Pascoe, Elaine. *The Pacific Rim: East Asia at the Dawn of a New Century.* Brookfield, CT:

Twenty-First Century Books, 1999. Close examination of Japan, China, Taiwan, and the Koreas.

VIDEO
Introducing East Asia. Huntsville, TX: Educational Video Network, 1998. Japan, Korea, and China: their commonalities and differences.

SOFTWARE
Chinese Shadow Puppet Theater. Wynnewood, PA: Library Video Company, 1999. Explains the role of puppetry in Chinese culture and gives students opportunities to develop their own puppets.

INTERNET
For more information about China and its neighbors, visit **classzone.com**.

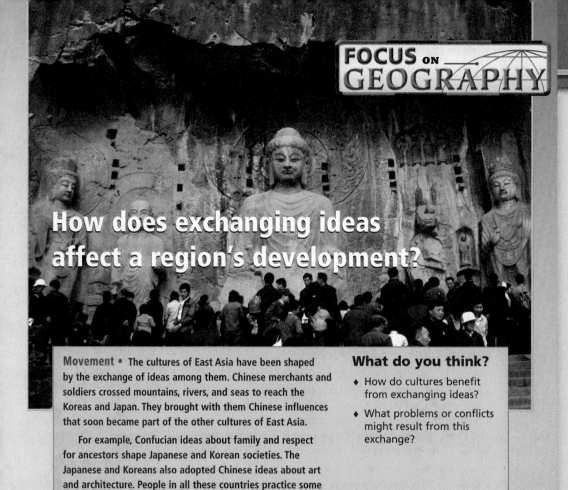

FOCUS ON GEOGRAPHY

How does exchanging ideas affect a region's development?

Movement • The cultures of East Asia have been shaped by the exchange of ideas among them. Chinese merchants and soldiers crossed mountains, rivers, and seas to reach the Koreas and Japan. They brought with them Chinese influences that soon became part of the other cultures of East Asia.

For example, Confucian ideas about family and respect for ancestors shape Japanese and Korean societies. The Japanese and Koreans also adopted Chinese ideas about art and architecture. People in all these countries practice some form of Buddhism. Also, in the past century, Western ideas about everything from government to clothes and music have influenced East Asian cultures.

What do you think?

♦ How do cultures benefit from exchanging ideas?

♦ What problems or conflicts might result from this exchange?

Place Millions of people in China use bicycles as their main form of transportation. This bicycle parking lot in Shanghai is filled to capacity.

BEFORE YOU READ
What Do You Know?

Ask students to share what they know about the culture, food, and art of China, Japan, and the other countries of East Asia. You might prompt discussion by mentioning topics such as types of Asian foods, martial arts, origami, and haiku. Ask them to identify aspects of Asian culture that have become part of life in the United States.

What Do You Want to Know?

Suggest that students think about aspects of Asian economy, religion, government, or culture that they would like to learn more about. Have them write a list of questions in their notebooks. As they read, they can look for and record answers.

READ AND TAKE NOTES

Reading Strategy: Making Predictions Suggest that students skim the chapter and note the headings, illustrations, maps, and captions. Then have them think about what they know about the topics listed in the chart. Explain that they can use what they know, and what they want to know, to make predictions about the material they will read. As they read, they can look for information to verify their predictions. After they read, students can use what they have learned to adjust or verify their predictions.

 In-depth Resources: Unit 6
• Guided Reading Worksheets, pp. 13–17

BEFORE YOU READ

▶▶ What Do You Know?

Before you read the chapter, consider what you already know about East Asia. Recall what you learned in Chapter 16 about ancient China and ancient Japan. Have you seen or tried the martial art tae kwon do? Do you know why sumo wrestlers are so honored in Japan? Reflect on what you have learned in other classes, what you have read in books or magazines, and what you have heard in the news about recent events in these countries.

▶▶ What Do You Want to Know?

Decide what else you want to know about East Asia. In your notebook, record what you hope to learn from this chapter.

Place • Many children in China take part in activities led by the Chinese Communist Party. ▲

READ AND TAKE NOTES

Reading Strategy: Making Predictions Making predictions is a helpful strategy for involving yourself in what you read. As you begin reading, reflect on what you already know about the subject. Then try to predict what will happen. After making your prediction, read further to see if your guess was correct. Use the following guidelines to make predictions about this chapter.

• Copy the chart into your notebook.

• Before you read, make predictions about what kinds of exchanges have taken place among the countries of East Asia and between those countries and the rest of the world. Organize these by category and record them in the second column of the chart.

• In the third column, list facts from the chapter that tell you whether your predictions were correct or incorrect.

Culture • Chinese-American actor Bruce Lee brought kung fu to Hollywood. ▼

Category	Predictions	Correct or Incorrect
Economy		
Religion	Students' predictions will vary but should reflect their prior knowledge.	Students' predictions should be compared to the text to determine accuracy.
Government		
Culture		

Teaching Strategy

Reading the Chapter This chapter focuses on the governments, economies, and cultures of China and its neighbors in East Asia. Encourage students to note ways in which cultural exchange has influenced the development of the nations in this region.

Integrated Assessment The Chapter Assessment on page 523 describes several activities for integrated assessment. You may wish to have students work on these activities during the course of the chapter and then present them at the end.

Establishing Modern China

TERMS & NAMES
Opium War
Taiping Rebellion
Boxer Rebellion
Sun Yat-sen
Chiang Kai-shek
Mao Zedong
Great Leap Forward
Cultural Revolution

MAIN IDEA

After the end of China's last dynasty and decades of conflict, a Communist government took control of China in 1949.

WHY IT MATTERS NOW

Because China is a large country with a huge population, its influence politically and economically is felt around the world.

DATELINE

EXTRA

THE FORBIDDEN CITY, BEIJING, CHINA, FEBRUARY 12, 1912

Word has just been received that Pu Yi, the six-year-old boy emperor, has given up China's throne. The Qing emperor, whose royal name is Xuantong, will probably be China's last emperor. Under a recent agreement, China will now be a republic led by a president. The age of dynasties has ended.

No one yet knows what will become of this last emperor, who once was called "The Son of Heaven." For the time being, he will be allowed to remain in the Imperial Palace of the Forbidden City. But his future, like China's, is uncertain.

Culture • Pu Yi is shown here, standing next to his father and brother. ▲

China's Last Dynasty ❶

In 1644, the Manchus established the Qing Dynasty—China's last and largest empire. The Qing drew both the southwestern region of Tibet and the island of Taiwan into China. However, by the mid-1800s, China's population had more than tripled, straining the country's ability to produce enough food. Shortages, famines, and wars overwhelmed Qing rulers, helping to bring their empire to an end.

China and Its Neighbors **495**

SECTION OBJECTIVES

1. To explain challenges that faced the Qing dynasty and led to its eventual downfall
2. To analyze and describe the rise of communism under Mao Zedong

SKILLBUILDER
• Interpreting a Map, p. 498

CRITICAL THINKING
• Hypothesizing, p. 496, p. 499
• Analyzing Causes, p. 496

FOCUS & MOTIVATE
WARM-UP

Making Inferences Have students read Dateline and discuss the end of Pu Yi's reign.

1. What did the end of Pu Yi's reign signify in China?
2. How do you think life in China might change under the new government?

INSTRUCT: Objective ❶

China's Last Dynasty

• What factors contributed to the downfall of the Qing Dynasty? overpopulation, food shortages, wars

📄 **In-depth Resources: Unit 6**
• Guided Reading Worksheet, p. 13

📄 **Reading Study Guide**
(Spanish and English), pp. 152–153

---

496 CHAPTER 17

MORE ABOUT…

Opium

Made from the juice of the opium poppy, opium is used as a base for a number of useful medicines. Since opium and the drugs made from it are highly addictive, their use must be restricted.

CRITICAL THINKING ACTIVITY

Hypothesizing Ask students to think about why Qing rulers tried to prohibit the sale of opium. Brainstorm a list of the reasons why they might have taken this action against the British. Then ask students to think about why the British would want to continue to import opium, and to consider the benefits to them. List students' ideas on the board.

Class Time 10 minutes

MORE ABOUT…

Boxers

The Boxers, or Righteous and Harmonious Fists, were united by a common hatred of outsiders. They were especially resentful of Western influences on the customs of their country. The Boxers were joined by many thousands of peasants and destitute vagrants who had been driven off their land by famine, flood, and drought.

CRITICAL THINKING ACTIVITY

Analyzing Causes Prompt a discussion about why the Boxers and their supporters might want to rid the country of all foreigners. Discuss why these foreigners were in China and what effect they had on its culture and economy.

Class Time 10 minutes

Place • This monument in Tiananmen Square shows the Chinese seizing the British opium in Canton. ▲

The Opium War The Qing rulers faced turmoil early on because of a drug called opium. They tried several times to prohibit the sale of opium in China but were not successful. In the late 1700s, the British began smuggling opium from India into China. They used opium, rather than money, to buy Chinese goods, which hurt China's economy.

In 1839, the Chinese government seized all the opium the British had stored in the Chinese port of Canton. The British responded with an attack, and the first **Opium War** began. Because Qing rule was weak, the British overpowered the Chinese. The Opium War ended in 1842 with the signing of the Treaty of Nanking. This treaty forced the Chinese to pay Great Britain money, hand over Hong Kong to British control, and allow British traders into more Chinese ports.

The Rise of Nationalism Angered by the Treaty of Nanking, peasants rebelled around China. The greatest revolt, the **Taiping Rebellion** (ty·PIHNG), raged for 14 years and took 20 million lives. Peasants demanded equality for women, the end of private property, and the division of surplus harvest among the neediest. The Chinese military, with help from other nations, finally crushed out the last of the rebellion in 1868.

In 1900, another rebel group, called the Boxers, rose up in the **Boxer Rebellion.** The Boxers hoped to defeat the Qing Dynasty and force all foreigners out of China. British, French, Russian, Japanese, and American troops joined together to defeat the Boxers, leaving China's government in turmoil.

A New Republic Many Western-educated Chinese wanted a new government. One ambitious leader, **Sun Yat-sen** (suhn yaht·sehn), had long hoped China would become a democracy. He founded the Chinese Nationalist Party, which in 1911 toppled the Qing Dynasty. The next year, China became a republic. Sun Yat-sen was named the first provisional president. For political reasons, he gave up the first presidency to Yuan Shigai (yoo·AHN shee·ky).

Reading
Social Studies

A. Recognizing Important Details Why would the Treaty of Nanking have angered the Chinese?
Reading Social Studies
A. Possible Answer
It gave the British more control over China.

BACKGROUND

The Boxers called themselves the "Righteous and Harmonious Fists." The British called this group the Boxers because they practiced a kind of boxing that they thought made them safe from bullets.

Activity Options

Differentiating Instruction: Students Acquiring English/ESL

Base Words and Suffixes Students may be confused about the meaning of the word *nationalism*. Explain that the base word *nation* means "an independent country," and the suffix *ism* means "the state or quality of." Nationalism means "an ardent belief in the importance of one's nation."

Guide students to understand how nationalism unites people. Ask,

• Who supported the rise of nationalism in China?

• What were they trying to accomplish?

• What were their reasons?

• Why might nationalism answer the needs of the country?

Ask students to identify and explain other words with the suffix *ism*, such as *heroism, patriotism,* or *communism*.

Over the next 16 years, China was in turmoil. Yuan struggled with rebels for power, and before and during World War I, China fought against Japan. During this time, the Nationalist Party gained more members. The Chinese Communist Party also formed. By the end of 1925, the Nationalist Party had about 200,000 members, and the Communist Party had about 10,000.

The Fight for Control In 1927, the two parties joined forces, and **Chiang Kai-shek** (chang ky·shehk), one of Sun Yat-sen's military commanders, became the leader of China. Soon, Chiang turned against the Communists, and the two parties began a long fight for power. In 1934, because the Nationalists seemed close to victory, the Communists retreated on what is known as the Long March. About 100,000 Communists marched more than 6,000 miles north to escape the Nationalist forces.

Chiang Kai-shek maintained control of China until 1949. During this time, the government improved transportation, provided education to more people, and encouraged industry. The lives of peasants and workers were not improved. Gradually many of these people turned to the Communist Party for help.

Culture • Chiang Kai-shek waved his hat at a celebration of the founding of the Nationalist Party. ▼

Communist Revolution ❷

By the end of the Long March, a leader emerged in the Communist Party— **Mao Zedong** (mow dzuh·dohng). When World War II began and Japan invaded China, Chiang Kai-shek turned to Mao and the Communist Red Army for help. At the end of the war in 1945, China's two parties again turned on each other. In 1949, the Communists defeated the Nationalists, forcing Chiang Kai-shek to flee to Taiwan. On October 1, Mao declared China a Communist state called the People's Republic of China.

Sun Yat-sen (1866–1925) Sun Yat-sen grew up in a poor farmer's family in northern China. In 1879, his older brother, who had been working in Hawaii, brought Sun to Honolulu. Sun learned about Western ways and became interested in Christianity. This troubled his brother, who sent him back to China after four years.

Sun studied medicine and became a doctor, but he had bigger ideas. He thought that China needed to move ahead, to leave some of its traditional ways behind and overcome the past political humiliations. After many struggles, Sun helped China to become a republic. Today, he is known as the Father of Modern China.

China and Its Neighbors **497**

Biography

Sun Yat-sen's efforts to help China become a republic were based on his Three Principles of the People: love of the fatherland, democracy, and the welfare of the people.

MORE ABOUT...
The Long March

For an entire year, Communist troops trekked through China's remote and poor areas, taking land from the wealthy and giving it to the poor. Many of the poor joined them. Eventually sickness, fatigue, and exposure took a toll on the troops. Only 20,000 men and women of the 100,000 who began the journey completed the Long March. The event proved that China's peasants and poor people would fight for the Communists if they were given guns and hope. And it taught the Communists that their power base would not be the educated classes living in cities, but the peasants.

INSTRUCT: Objective ❷

Communist Revolution/ Reform and Revolution

- Who emerged as a leader in China after the Long March? Mao Zedong

- What reforms were instituted by the Communists? redistribution of land, collective farms, industry under government control

- What was the goal of the Great Leap Forward? to speed up economic development

- Why was the Cultural Revolution launched? to remove opposition to the Communist Party

---

Activity Options

Differentiating Instruction: Less Proficient Readers

Finding Causes Review with students the idea that many factors led to the fight for control in China that resulted in the nation's becoming a Communist state. Have students reread "The Fight for Control" and "Communist Revolution," and create a list of these factors. Create a cause-and-effect chart like the one shown to record the events that led up to the revolution. Show an arrow from each event pointing to the effect.

| Chiang Kai-shek turns against the Communists |
| Communists retreat on the Long March |
| Many people turn to communism |
| Mao Zedong emerges as a leader |
| Communists defeat the Nationalists |

→ People's Republic of China, Communist state

MORE ABOUT...
Mao Zedong

The man who made China a Communist nation was born to a peasant family in the Hunan Province. Working in a library in Beijing, Mao was attracted to the ideas of communism. He witnessed the inequalities around him—hardworking peasants and farmers lived in poverty, while landlords who owned large tracts of land amassed great wealth. Mao's dream for China was said to be based on his belief that everyone should work together for the good of all people. His face became familiar throughout the world. People in China repeated his slogans and studied his writings.

MORE ABOUT...
The Cultural Revolution

During the Cultural Revolution, Mao Zedong gave the Red Guards complete power to root out what he called the Four Olds: old culture, old customs, old habits, and old thoughts. Young people were encouraged to challenge or even denounce their elders. They were also urged to attack any hint of new ideas, especially music, literature, and concepts such as economic freedom from the West. The Red Guards often used violent methods, including murdering anyone they believed to be disloyal to Mao. Over the course of a decade, thousands of people were executed, and many thousands more were threatened and beaten. Even today, many years after the Cultural Revolution, it is difficult for the Chinese to look back at this painful period.

The Long March, 1934

GEOGRAPHY SKILLBUILDER:
Interpreting a Ma

1. **Movement •** What river did the Communists cross o their march?
2. **Place •** Where did Long March end?

Geography Skillbuilder Answers
1. Chang Jiang
2. Yan'an

← Path of the Long March

Reform and Revolution ②

Mao Zedong became head of the Chinese Communist Party and China's government. The party set policy and the government carried it out, giving Chairman Mao nearly absolute power.

Chairman Mao's Reforms The Communists instituted many reforms. They seized land from the wealthy and gave it to the peasants. They also established a five-year plan that brought China's industry under government control. As in the Soviet Union, peasants combined their land into collective farms and worked together to grow food.

In 1958, Mao Zedong launched a program, called the **Great Leap Forward,** to speed up economic development. Collective farms became huge communes of 25,000 people. The communes grew crops, ran small industries, and provided education and health care for their members. In one year, this program shattered China's economy.

Reading Social Studies
B. Possible Answer
Perhaps he thought that large groups of people working together could be more productive.

Reading
Social Studies

B. Synthesizing How do you think Mao expected communes to help economic development?

Place • **This famous portrait of Mao Zedong hangs in Tiananmen Square.** ◄

498 CHAPTER 17

Activity Options
Multiple Learning Styles: Interpersonal

Class Time One class period

Task Evaluating the character of Mao Zedong in a group discussion

Purpose To learn about a former world leader and evaluate his goals and influence

Supplies Needed
• Reference materials about Mao Zedong, including excerpts from biographies

Block Scheduling

Activity Invite a group of students to read about Mao Zedong and discuss his philosophy, goals, and influence. Help each student choose a reference source, and allow time for students to read about Mao. Then guide students in a discussion of his power in China and the lasting effects of that power.

Poor agricultural production, droughts, and floods caused one of the worst famines in history. From 1958 to 1960, as many as 20 million people starved, while millions more died of disease. China then abandoned the Great Leap Forward, and Mao's influence wavered.

The Cultural Revolution After the Great Leap Forward, many people in government called for reform. Mao feared that they wanted to make China a capitalist country. In 1966, Mao launched a movement called the **Cultural Revolution,** which aimed to remove opposition to the Communist Party. Mao's new supporters were called the Red Guards. They sought out and punished people who spoke against Mao's principles or who had contact with Western people or ideas. China fell into chaos once again.

During this time, the economy weakened, and the government was unable to carry out many of its duties. Goods and services, such as health care and transportation, were not made available to the people. Many Chinese began calling for reform.

Culture • These Red Guards at a rally waved copies of the "Little Red Book," a collection of Mao's sayings. ▼

SECTION 1 ASSESSMENT

Terms & Names

1. **Identify:** (a) Opium War   (b) Taiping Rebellion   (c) Boxer Rebellion   (d) Sun Yat-sen
           (e) Chiang Kai-shek   (f) Mao Zedong   (g) Great Leap Forward   (h) Cultural Revolution

Taking Notes

2. Use a sequence map like this one to list the events that led to the establishment of the People's Republic of China.

[Sequence map: Overthrow of the Qing Dynasty → □ → □ ; People's Republic of China ← □ ← □]

Main Ideas

3. (a) Who fought in the Opium War, and why?

(b) What role did the Nationalist Party play in China?

(c) What reforms did Mao Zedong make?

Critical Thinking

4. **Recognizing Effects**

How do you think European actions in China contributed to feelings of discontent among China's peasants?

Think About

• European involvement in China during the 1900s

• the different goals of Europeans and the Chinese

ACTIVITY -OPTION- Imagine you are a journalist. Make a **list of questions** you would like to ask a person who lived during the Cultural Revolution.

China and Its Neighbors **499**

Section 1 Assessment

1. Terms & Names

a. Opium War, p. 496
b. Taiping Rebellion, p. 496
c. Boxer Rebellion, p. 496
d. Sun Yat-sen, p. 496
e. Chiang Kai-shek, p. 497
f. Mao Zedong, p. 497
g. Great Leap Forward, p. 498
h. Cultural Revolution, p. 499

2. Taking Notes

Event 1:	China in turmoil; Communist Party founded
Event 2:	Communists and Nationalists fight
Event 3:	Long March
Event 4:	Communists take over

3. Main Ideas

a. Great Britain and China; China seized Great Britain's illegal opium imports.
b. ruled in China from 1911 until 1949; provided better transportation and education; did little for the peasants or workers
c. land to peasants; a five-year plan for industry; collective farms; organized Cultural Revolution

4. Critical Thinking

Europeans fought against peasants in the Taiping and Boxer rebellions.

ACTIVITY OPTION

 Integrated Assessment

• Rubric for making a list of questions

Teacher's Edition **499**

CRITICAL THINKING ACTIVITY

Hypothesizing Lead a discussion about the Great Leap Forward and the Cultural Revolution. Ask students what they think might have happened if the Great Leap Forward had been successful. Would Mao have found it necessary to launch the Cultural Revolution? Would he have been so hostile to Western influences?

Class Time 15 minutes

ASSESS & RETEACH

Reading Social Studies Have students check their predictions about modern China in the chart on page 494. Have them verify or correct their predictions.

 Formal Assessment
• Section Quiz, p. 255

RETEACHING ACTIVITY

Have students work with partners to discuss the section. One partner can explain the steps that led to the end of China's dynasties and the beginnings of communism, while the other asks questions to clarify the explanation. Then have students switch roles to discuss the Communist Revolution and the reforms that followed.

 In-depth Resources: Unit 6
• Reteaching Activity, p. 22

 Access for Students Acquiring English
• Reteaching Activity, p. 156

Visit the Forbidden City

For centuries, only members of the emperor's household could pass through the gates of China's famous Forbidden City. Today, however, *you* are there to plan a TV feature about the palace complex. This collection of massive buildings with curving, golden-tiled roofs is actually a city within a city within a city. The Forbidden City is a square within the larger Imperial City, which is at the center of Beijing's Inner City district. The first things you see are huge buildings and broad, open squares. Stone carvings and fantastic animal figures decorate pillars and gateways.

COOPERATIVE LEARNING On these pages are challenges you will encounter as you visit the Forbidden City. Working with a small group, choose one of these challenges to meet. Divide the work among group members. You will find helpful information in the Data File. Keep in mind that you will present your solution to the class.

OBJECTIVE

Students work cooperatively to describe the Forbidden City of Beijing and the dynasties that inhabited it.

PROCEDURE

Provide reference sources about the Forbidden City and the art of the Ming Dynasty. Have students share the responsibilities of researcher, designer, artist, and presenter. Some students might want to work individually or with partners on the Language Arts Challenge. Suggest that they exchange their writing with partners and offer constructive criticism.

 Block Scheduling

ARTS CHALLENGE

Class Time 50 minutes

Encourage students to refer to the Data File, pictures from the chapter, and other reference sources, including books and magazines. Students might also consult home pages of museums for ideas.

Possible Solutions

Home page designs should be well-organized, accurate, informative, and attractive. Features might include carving, painting, and sculpture. Students' sketches might be of lions, turtles, or the phoenix. Captions for sketches should include details about the animal's symbolic significance.

ARTS CHALLENGE

". . . China's greatest artists used all their skills."

China's Ming emperors built the Forbidden City as the heart of their vast empire. To please the Ming and later Qing (Ch'ing) emperors, China's greatest artists used all their skills. They decorated palaces with elaborate statues and paintings. Many are animal figures, which are important symbols in Chinese mythology. What aspects of art and architecture do you want to include? How will you present them? Choose one of these options. Look for information in the Data File.

ACTIVITIES
1. Design a home page for a museum exhibit and virtual tour, focusing on the arts of the Ming Dynasty and the Forbidden City.
2. Sketch one of the fantastic animals used in Chinese art and architecture, such as the dragon. Research what it symbolizes and write a short caption for your drawing.

Standards for Evaluation

ARTS CHALLENGE

Option 1 Home pages should highlight
- the characteristics of Ming Dynasty art.
- major aspects of the Forbidden City.

Option 2 Sketches should
- include captions explaining the symbolic significance of the animal.

HISTORY CHALLENGE

Option 1 Maps should
- feature key buildings and terraces in the Forbidden City.
- include annotations explaining what occurred in the main locations.

Option 2 Time lines should
- include key events in chronological order.

LANGUAGE ARTS CHALLENGE

Options 1 and 2 Journals and letters should
- describe in detail some of the important sites in the Forbidden City.
- reflect the author's personal response.
- use information from the Data File and outside sources.

FORBIDDEN CITY

- Completed in **1420** by the **Yung-lo** emperor of the Ming dynasty, who moved the capital to Beijing. Buildings have been enlarged and rebuilt.

- Major buildings in Beijing's Outer City and Inner City are built along a straight, north-south, 1.7-mile axis. The axis passes across **Tiananmen Square** through large parks to the gates of the Forbidden City. The city is surrounded by a moat and a wall, with watchtowers at each corner.

- The **entrance** to the Forbidden City is through the **Meridian Gate**, which leads to marble bridges over the moat. On the other side of the bridges is a great open square that leads to the **Gate of Supreme Harmony.** Through the Gate of Supreme Harmony lie the three state halls of the Forbidden City.

- **Outer Court:** three great halls of state—the **Hall of Supreme Harmony,** the **Hall of Complete Harmony,** and the **Hall of Preserving Harmony**—stand one behind another on a high marble platform.

- **Inner Court:** palaces, courtyards, and pavilions where the emperor, his family, and the palace staff lived.

MING DYNASTY (1368–1644)

- **Restored Chinese rule** after conquest and rule by Mongols.

- Extended China's empire into **Korea, Mongolia,** and **Vietnam.**

QING (CH'ING) DYNASTY (1644–1911)

- **Last emperors** of China; dynasty established by Manchus.

- Dynasty troubled by wars and rebellions; **overthrown by revolution.**

To learn more about the Forbidden City, go to

RESEARCH LINKS
CLASSZONE.COM

HISTORY CHALLENGE

"... palaces and courtyards where the emperor's family ... lived."

As you approach the Forbidden City, you pass through three great state halls, one behind another on a marble platform. Official receptions and banquets were held here. Behind the halls are palaces and courtyards where the emperor's family and the men and women who served them lived. How can you show the importance of what took place within these walls? Use one of these options to present information. Look in the Data File for help.

ACTIVITIES

1. Make an annotated map of the Forbidden City. Include captions to explain the events that took place in major palaces and halls.

2. Make a time line of the Ming and Qing (Ch'ing) rulers who built and occupied the Forbidden City.

Activity Wrap-Up

As a group, review your solution to the challenge you selected. Then present your solution to the class.

HISTORY CHALLENGE

Class Time 50 minutes

Provide students with poster board, rulers, and colored pencils. Students will need additional resources, such as books or magazines, to make the maps and time lines.

Possible Solution

Students will make a general map of the city, showing only the major buildings and terraces. Time lines should show major developments and political disruptions of the two dynasties.

ALTERNATIVE CHALLENGE...

LANGUAGE ARTS CHALLENGE

For 500 years, almost no outsider was allowed inside the Forbidden City. The few individuals who did pass through the gates later wrote about their experiences. Among these were a missionary, a Russian representative, and a French novelist; all commented on the colors. The floors of the terraces are white, walls and columns are red, and the roofs are yellow. Imagine that you entered the Forbidden City before it was opened to the public.

- Write a journal entry detailing what you saw and how you felt as you toured the Forbidden City.

- Write a letter home describing your day inside the Forbidden City.

Activity Wrap-Up

To help students evaluate their challenge solutions, have them answer these questions:

- Is the solution accurate?
- Is the information presented in an organized, informative, and entertaining way?
- Does the solution cover the material as thoroughly as possible, given the available data?

SECTION 2

The Governments of East Asia

TERMS & NAMES
Deng Xiaoping
human rights
Tiananmen Square
Diet

SECTION OBJECTIVES

1. To describe China's current government
2. To explain the struggle to attain human rights
3. To describe the governments of China's neighbors in East Asia

SKILLBUILDER
• Interpreting a Map, p. 504

CRITICAL THINKING
• Analyzing Motives, p. 503
• Clarifying, p. 504

FOCUS & MOTIVATE
WARM-UP

Drawing Conclusions Have students read Dateline and discuss why the South Korean president won the Nobel Peace Prize.

1. Why do you think the prize committee chose President Kim Dae Jung to receive the award?
2. Why do you think the achievement of his goals is important to people around the world?

INSTRUCT: Objective ❶

Working Toward Change/ China's Government Today

• Who took control when Mao Zedong died? Deng Xiaoping

• Who has the real power of government in China today? Chinese Communist Party

 In-depth Resources: Unit 6
• Guided Reading Worksheet, p. 14

 Reading Study Guide
(Spanish and English), pp. 154–155

MAIN IDEA	WHY IT MATTERS NOW
The nations of China and North Korea have Communist governments. The other nations of East Asia are republics.	Many people in China and North Korea would like to see change in their governments and are turning to other nations for help.

DATELINE

SEOUL, SOUTH KOREA, DECEMBER 10, 2000— South Koreans are throwing a huge party today. President Kim Dae Jung has received the Nobel Peace Prize, a prize that is given annually to honor someone who has worked for peace.

Since 1947, when North and South Korea offically proclaimed themselves as separate nations, the relationship between the two countries has been tense. Just this year, for the first time, the presidents of North and South Korea met to discuss ways to reunite their divided countries. President Kim said that his goal was "to realize peace on the Korean peninsula, and to develop exchange [and] cooperation between both Koreas."

Culture • President Kim Dae Jung (on the right) received his Nobel Prize today in Oslo, Norway. ▲

Working Toward Change ❶

North Korea and China are Communist nations, and both have seen war and conflict in the past 50 years. Through efforts from within and from organizations and nations around the world, both nations are working to improve the lives of their people. They are also gradually becoming a part of the world market.

Program Resources

 In-depth Resources: Unit 6
• Guided Reading Worksheet, p. 14
• Reteaching Activity, p. 23

 Reading Study Guide
(Spanish and English), pp. 154–155

 Formal Assessment
• Section Quiz, p. 256

 Integrated Assessment
• Rubric for writing a news story

 Outline Map Activities

 Access for Students Acquiring English
• Guided Reading Worksheet, p. 150

 Technology Resources
classzone.com

TEST-TAKING RESOURCES

⬇ Strategies for Test Preparation
⬇ Test Practice Transparencies
🖱 Online Test Practice

China's Government Today ❶

When Mao Zedong died in 1976, the Cultural Revolution ended. Moderates who wanted to restore order and economic growth took power in 1977. Their leader was **Deng Xiaoping** (duhng show·pihng).

Under Deng, the Chinese government established diplomatic relations with the United States and increased trade with other countries. It also made reforms, such as allowing farmers to own land. It released many political prisoners and reduced the police force's power. However, the government was not willing to give up any of its basic control.

Place • The Chinese Communist Party sponsors activities for children, such as playing in a marching band. ▲

The Chinese Communist Party Officially, China's highest government authority is the National People's Congress. In practice, the Chinese Communist Party holds the real power. It controls what happens locally. The government allows only churches and temples that are closely linked to this party to operate.

The Fight for Human Rights ❷

Reading
Social Studies

A. Making Inferences What other rights would you include on a list of human rights?

**Reading Social Studies
A. Possible Answers**
freedom to travel, to study, to have access to good medical care

China's Communist government has a history of repressing criticism of its policies. Such actions often lead to the violation of **human rights,** which are rights to which every person is entitled. They include the freedom to say or write what you think, to worship as you believe, to be safe from physical harm and political persecution, and to have enough to eat.

Tiananmen Square In 1989, the Chinese military denied citizens a basic human right—freedom of speech—when it attacked protesters calling for democracy in **Tiananmen Square** (tyahn·ahn·mehn). For weeks, protesters occupied this 100-acre square in Beijing. Demonstrations soon occurred in other Chinese cities. The military killed hundreds and wounded thousands in their attempts to end the protests. As the events of 1989 unfolded, people around the world spoke up against the Chinese government. Since then, efforts have been made to help the people of China in their struggle for human rights.

China and Its Neighbors **503**

CRITICAL THINKING ACTIVITY

Analyzing Motives Prompt a discussion about why the Chinese government has taken steps to establish diplomatic relationships and increase trade with other countries. Ask what changes within China might have motivated leaders to do this, and what changes in the world might have prompted these steps. Have students brainstorm a list of benefits to China of having trade and diplomatic relationships with other countries.

Class Time 15 minutes

INSTRUCT: Objective ❷

The Fight for Human Rights

• What are some examples of basic human rights? freedom of expression and religion, freedom from fear, enough food

• What human right was denied to the protesters in Tiananmen Square? freedom of speech

MORE ABOUT...
Tiananmen Square

For weeks, the students in Tiananmen Square had been protesting the corruption of Communist officials as well as calling for democracy and greater equality among the people. The tragic climax to this protest came when Deng Xiaoping, the head of the government, ordered the army to break up the demonstration. On June 4, 1989, television viewers from around the world watched in shock as the events in Tiananmen Square unfolded. Hundreds of demonstrators were killed; as many as 30,000 were jailed.

Activity Options

Interdisciplinary Link: Civics

Class Time One class period

Task Reporting on the work of the United Nations to protect human rights around the world

Purpose To investigate the work of the United Nations regarding human rights violations

Supplies Needed
• Reference materials about United Nations human rights efforts

🄱 Block Scheduling

Activity Organize students into small groups. Have them use the available resources to learn about the work, beliefs, and ideas of the United Nations in the field of human rights protection. Ask them to find out how the United Nations investigates human rights conditions and decides how to respond to violations. Have each group present its findings in a panel discussion with the rest of the class.

INSTRUCT: Objective ❸

China's Neighbors

- What form of government exists in Japan? a constitutional monarchy with a parliamentary government

- What is the Diet? Japan's parliament

- Which nations took part in the creation of North and South Korea? the Soviet Union, the United States

- What form of government exists in Mongolia? republic

- What source of conflict exists between China and Taiwan? whether they will unify under one government

CRITICAL THINKING ACTIVITY

Clarifying Guide students to understand the differences between the governments of North and South Korea. Work with them to create a chart like the one shown to clarify how each government functions.

North Korea	South Korea
Communist dictatorship	democratic republic
Korean Workers' Party holds power	power divided among 3 branches of government
people have little freedom	people guarenteed freedom of the press and religion

Class Time 20 minutes

Culture • The protesters in Tiananmen Square included students, workers, and government employees. ▲ Geography Skillbuilder Answers

1. Cities often develop along waterways that provide means of transportation and trade.

2. The countries are located near each other, and probably trade frequently.

GEOGRAPHY SKILLBUILDER: Interpreting a Map

1. **Location •** Why do you think the capitals of North and South Korea are located on rivers?

2. **Movement •** Measure the distance between South Korea and Japan. What can you conclude about trade between these two nations?

China's Neighbors ❸

China's neighbors have different kinds of governments. Some are republics, while others are Communist.

Japan The United States occupied Japan after it was defeated in World War II. U.S. general Douglas MacArthur helped set up a constitutional monarchy with a parliamentary government and a separate judiciary. The parliament is called the **Diet,** and the House of Representatives holds most of the power. The Diet chooses the country's prime minister, who is then officially appointed by the emperor.

The constitution states that the emperor's position is symbolic. Thus the emperor has had limited power, though many people regard the emperor as partly divine. The constitution also gives the Japanese people rights and responsibilities similar to those of Americans.

North and South Korea Korea used to be one country, but it was divided after World War II. The Soviet Union helped set up a Communist dictatorship in the north, and the United States helped set up a democratic republic in the south. Each government thought it should govern the whole of the Korean Peninsula.

Reading Social Studies

B. Hypothesizing Why do you think Japan has an emperor, if the position is only symbolic?

Reading Social Studies B. Possible Answer The emperor is a symbol of tradition and continuity.

North and South Korea, 2001

★ National capital
• Other city

CHINA

Chongjin

NORTH KOREA

Sinuiju

Pyongyang ⊛   • Wonsan

Sea of Japan

Kaesong

Seoul ⊛

Inchon

SOUTH KOREA

Yellow   Sea

Taegu

Kwangju   • Pusan

JAPAN

0   50   100 miles
0   50 100 kilometers

132°E   134°E   136°E
42°N
40°N
38°N

122°E   124°E   128°E

Activity Options

Interdisciplinary Link: Language Arts

Class Time One class period

Task Writing an eyewitness news account of the events that took place at Tiananmen Square

Purpose To research the causes and events of June 4, 1989, in China and write an account

Supplies Needed

- News accounts of events at Tiananmen Square
- Writing paper
- Pens or pencils

Block Scheduling

Activity Review the events of Tiananmen Square and assist students in finding news accounts of the day. After students read the material, have them write an account for a newspaper reporting the event to the world. Remind students that since they are writing as an eyewitness to the event, they should use the pronouns *I, me,* and *my* in their accounts. Point out that they should answer the questions *who, what, when, where,* and *why* in their accounts.

In 1950, North Korea invaded South Korea. For three years the two fought the Korean War, but the borders did not change. In June of 2000, the two nations started talking about reuniting.

North Korea, or the Democratic People's Republic of Korea, is still a Communist state. Although there is a president and a cabinet, the Korean Workers' Party holds power. The people have little freedom, and the legislature—the Supreme People's Assembly—has little power.

South Korea, or the Republic of Korea, is a republic with a government similar to that of the United States. Power is divided among legislative, executive, and judiciary branches. People vote for the president as well as the legislature—the National Assembly. The government guarantees its citizens freedom of the press and of religion.

Mongolia One of the world's oldest countries, Mongolia was under either Chinese or Russian domination for years. It has been an independent republic since 1991 and has a constitution that guarantees its citizens certain basic rights. However, there is still a strong element of Communist party control in the government.

Taiwan Also a republic, Taiwan has a multiparty democratic system. For years it was a Chinese colony, but since 1949, the Chinese Nationalist government has been based there. The question of whether Taiwan and China will unify under one government has long caused conflict.

SECTION 2 ASSESSMENT

Terms & Names

1. Identify: (a) Deng Xiaoping   (b) human rights   (c) Tiananmen Square   (d) Diet

Taking Notes	Main Ideas	Critical Thinking
2. Use a chart like this one to list and compare the major characteristics of East Asia's governments.	**3. (a)** Who holds the power in China's government?	**4. Hypothesizing** Why do you think the Chinese government has taken actions that repress human rights?
	(b) Which East Asian countries have governments similar to China's?	
	(c) How do the governments of North Korea and South Korea differ?	***Think About*** ◆ China's political stance ◆ the goals of China's dissidents

Country	Characteristics of Government
China	
Japan	
North Korea	
South Korea	
Mongolia	
Taiwan	

ACTIVITY -OPTION- Write a **news story** that describes the events that helped establish the government of Japan, North Korea, or South Korea.

China and Its Neighbors **505**

FOCUS ON VISUALS

Interpreting the Map Have students look at the map and find the capitals of North and South Korea. Ask them how each city benefits from its location.

Possible Response Each capital city is located on a major river or rivers with access to the sea.

Extension Have students research either Seoul or Pyongyang and present reports to the class about these cities.

ASSESS & RETEACH

Reading Social Studies Ask students to check their predictions about the governments in East Asia on the chart on page 494. Have them verify or correct their predictions.

 Formal Assessment
• Section Quiz, p. 256

RETEACHING ACTIVITY

Organize students into five groups. Have the members of each group prepare a short presentation on the government of China, North Korea, South Korea, Mongolia, or Taiwan. Invite groups to make presentations and answer questions.

 In-depth Resources: Unit 6
• Reteaching Activity, p. 23

 Access for Students Acquiring English
• Reteaching Activity, p. 157

Section 2 Assessment

1. Terms & Names
a. Deng Xiaoping, p. 503
b. human rights, p. 503
c. Tiananmen Square, p. 503
d. Diet, p. 504

2. Taking Notes

China:	Communist dictators
Japan:	Constitutional monarchy with parliamentary government
South Korea:	Republic
Mongolia:	Republic with constitution
Taiwan:	Republic with multiparty system
North Korea:	Communist dictators

3. Main Ideas
a. the Communist Party
b. North Korea's government is similar to China's.
c. North Korea is a Communist dictatorship; legislature has little power. South Korea is a republic; citizens are guaranteed freedoms.

4. Critical Thinking
Students might say that the Chinese government is afraid of losing power if it allows people to dissent.

ACTIVITY OPTION

 Integrated Assessment
• Rubric for writing a news story

Teacher's Edition **505**

The Economies of East Asia

TERMS & NAMES
tungsten
antimony
textile
cooperative

SECTION OBJECTIVES

1. To describe the effects of communism on China's economy

2. To identify the types of economies that exist in other East Asian nations

SKILLBUILDER
• Interpreting a Map, p. 509

CRITICAL THINKING
• Clarifying, p. 507
• Drawing Conclusions, p. 508

FOCUS AND MOTIVATE
WARM-UP

Drawing Conclusions After students read <u>Dateline</u>, discuss the rebuilding of the Silk Road in Asia.

1. Why was the Silk Road important in the past?

2. Why do you think so many countries are interested in helping to rebuild it?

INSTRUCT: Objective ❶

Economies of the Region/ China's Economy

• What has made economic growth difficult for some countries in the region? wars, droughts, internal conflicts

• What role does the government play in the economy in China? owns all financial institutions; sets prices on goods; plans production

 In-depth Resources: Unit 6
• Guided Reading Worksheet, p. 15

 Reading Study Guide
(Spanish and English), pp. 156–157

MAIN IDEA	WHY IT MATTERS NOW
East Asian economies have changed, some drastically, since World War II.	As these economies grow stronger, they play a larger role in global markets and have a larger influence on the economies of other nations.

DATELINE

BAKU, AZERBAIJAN, SEPTEMBER 1998— The famous Silk Road is coming back to life. This remarkable path has fallen into disuse in the past few hundred years, except for a few hardy tourists who explore the old trade route.

Today, however, representatives from more than 30 countries are meeting to discuss rebuilding the trade routes that formed the Silk Road. Many countries and organizations, such as the United Nations, will give aid to the project. Railroads, highways, and ferries will be built or improved in an effort to increase trade among the nations along the road.

Human-Environment Interaction • This man is beginning repairs on a stretch of the Silk Road in China. ▲

Economies of the Region ❶

Since World War II, East Asia's countries have grown more active in the world market. Today, Japan has one of the strongest economies in the world. Consumers in the United States regularly purchase goods made in China, Japan, Taiwan, and South Korea. However, wars, droughts, and internal conflicts have made economic growth difficult for some countries, such as North Korea.

506 CHAPTER 17

Program Resources

 In-depth Resources: Unit 6
• Guided Reading Worksheet, p. 15
• Reteaching Activity, p. 24

 Reading Study Guide
(Spanish and English), pp. 156–157

 Formal Assessment
• Section Quiz, p. 257

Integrated Assessment
• Rubric for making a chart or a diagram

Outline Map Activities

 Access for Students Acquiring English
• Guided Reading Worksheet, p. 151

 Technology Resources
classzone.com

TEST-TAKING RESOURCES
↪ Strategies for Test Preparation
↪ Test Practice Transparencies
🌐 Online Test Practice

China's Economy ❶

Although this has begun to change, China's government controls most of its economy. It owns all financial institutions, such as banks, and the larger industrial firms. The government also sets the prices on goods and plans the quantity of goods each worker should produce.

Industry China has put a strong emphasis on improving its industry. It has become one of the world's largest producers of cotton cloth and of two metals—**tungsten** and **antimony**. The industries that have seen the most growth are machine building, metal production, and the making of chemical fertilizers and clothing.

Farming Many people in China live in the countryside and make a living by farming. They use traditional methods, such as plowing with oxen, rather than using farm machinery. Much of the land in China—in the deserts and mountainous regions—cannot be farmed. Nevertheless, China is the world's largest producer of rice. It is also a major source of wheat, corn, soybeans, peanuts, cotton, and tobacco.

Human-Environment Interaction • Much of China's rice is produced on terraced gardens like these. ▼

Human-Environment Interaction • Chinese villagers in Yunnan work in the rice terraces. ▲

China and Its Neighbors **507**

MORE ABOUT...
Hong Kong

Hong Kong is a center of finance, trade, and manufacturing. Once a part of the British Empire, the port was officially returned to China on July 1, 1997. The economy remains strong, in part, because the port has a free-trade policy and does not collect a tariff on imported goods.

CRITICAL THINKING ACTIVITY

Clarifying Explain that, like China, the U.S. government has at times imposed price controls and has controlled the production of certain industries. The difference, however, is that these governmental actions in the United States have been short-term solutions to glitches in what is primarily a market-driven economy.

Class Time 10 minutes

FOCUS ON VISUALS

Interpreting the Photographs Tell students that rice terraces are a series of flat steps going up a hillside. Each terrace is filled with shallow water in which the rice is planted by hand. Ask students why they think the terraces are necessary for some farmers.

Possible Response In mountainous or hilly regions, the terraces make it possible for water to be contained instead of running downhill; additionally, they prevent erosion.

Extension Have students write a poem from the point of view of a rice farmer in China.

Activity Options

Skillbuilder Mini-Lesson: Creating a Database

Block Scheduling

Explaining the Skill Remind students that organizing information in a database makes it easy to retrieve. Once you've set up a database on the computer, you can search for specific information quickly and easily.

Applying the Skill Have students follow these steps to create a database about the economies of East Asian countries.

1. Identify your topic and determine keywords for your research.
2. Identify the kind of data you will need to enter in your database.
3. Identify the entries included under each heading.
4. Use the database to find the information you need.

INSTRUCT: Objective ②

Other East Asian Economies

- How has Taiwan contributed to China's economy? by investing billions of dollars in mainland China
- How is North Korea's economy similar to China's? Government controls the economy in both countries.
- How has the economy of South Korea changed since the 1960s? government supported expansion, helped develop industry
- What are South Korea's major products? automobiles and electronics
- What role does the government play in Japan's economy? oversees and advises on all aspects of the economy
- How has Japan's economic development been similar to that of South Korea? grown significantly since early 1960s

CRITICAL THINKING ACTIVITY

Drawing Conclusions Ask students to consider the positive and negative aspects of cooperative farming. Encourage them to think about why cooperative farms might be especially useful in a large country with a large population, and why they might be more efficient than farms owned by individuals.

Class Time 10 minutes

Other East Asian Economies ②

Taiwan Taiwan has a growing market economy that relies heavily on manufacturing and foreign trade. Since 1988, Taiwanese businesses have invested billions of dollars in mainland China, significantly contributing to China's fast-growing economy.

North Korea Like China's, North Korea's government controls the economy. Also like China, North Korea has emphasized the growth of industry. Iron, steel, machinery, chemical, and textile production are the main industries in North Korea. A **textile** is a cloth manufactured by weaving or knitting.

Many people in North Korea are farmers. They work on large **cooperatives,** where some 300 families share the farming work. These farms have become more productive as improvements in irrigation, fertilizers, and equipment have been made.

For most of the 20th century, North Korea traded with other Communist nations. Since the fall of the Soviet Union, North Korea has opened its borders to investment and trade with other countries.

South Korea The economy of South Korea has changed dramatically since the early 1960s. At that time, it was a poor nation of subsistence farmers. Since then, however, the government has supported the expansion of the textile industry and the building of factories that make electronics, small appliances and equipment. The government also helped develop iron, steel, and chemical industries. Today, South Korea has one of the world's strongest economies. It is a major producer of automobiles and electronics and trades with many countries.

Japan The government of Japan does not control its economy in the way the governments of China and North Korea control theirs. However, it does oversee and advise all aspects of the economy, including trade, investment, banking, and production.

Like South Korea's, Japan's economy has grown significantly since the mid-20th century. Japan is a small nation with few natural resources and little farmland. Industry and a skilled, educated work force are vitally important to Japan's economy.

Place • This is one of many new ships manufactured by South Korea's shipbuilding industry. ▲

Reading Social Studies

A. Evaluating Decisions Do you think it makes sense for so many farmers to share their work?

Reading Social Studies
A. Possible Answer
Most students will probably say that cooperative farming makes sense.

Reading Social Studies
B. Possible Answer
There are fewer ups and downs than in a market economy.

Reading Social Studies

B. Synthesizing What is the benefit of having the government control the economy?

Activity Options

Differentiating Instruction: Less Proficient Readers

Finding Main Ideas Students may have difficulty understanding the differences between the economies of China and the other East Asian economies. Have them create web diagrams to list facts about the economy of each country. Remind them to write the name of each country in the center of the web, and to record details about the economy of that country on lines surrounding it.

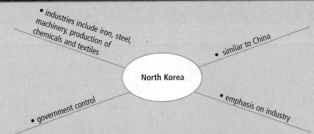

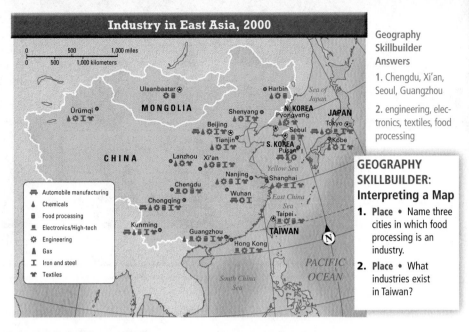

Industry in East Asia, 2000

Legend:
- Automobile manufacturing
- Chemicals
- Food processing
- Electronics/High-tech
- Engineering
- Gas
- Iron and steel
- Textiles

GEOGRAPHY SKILLBUILDER: Interpreting a Map

1. **Place** • Name three cities in which food processing is an industry.
2. **Place** • What industries exist in Taiwan?

The country imports the raw materials it needs and transforms them into goods for export. Ships, automobiles, steel, plastics, machinery, cameras, and electronics are Japan's major exports. The United States is Japan's biggest customer, although Japan also exports goods around the world. It is currently one of the world's largest economic powers.

SECTION 3 ASSESSMENT

Terms & Names

1. **Identify:**   (a) tungsten   (b) antimony   (c) textile   (d) cooperative

Taking Notes

2. Use a chart like this one to list important economic activities of the countries in East Asia.

Country	Important Economic Activities
China	
Taiwan	
North Korea	
South Korea	
Japan	

Main Ideas

3. (a) What role has China's government played in its economy?

(b) How does Japan's economy differ from those of China and North Korea?

(c) How have the economies of East Asia changed in recent years?

Critical Thinking

4. **Forming and Supporting Opinions**

How might the nearness of East Asia's small countries to China affect their economies?

Think About

- availability of resources
- possibilities of exchange among neighbors
- worldwide trade partners

ACTIVITY -OPTION-   Make a **chart** or **diagram** that illustrates the trade between Japan and the United States. What goods flow between these two countries?

The Cultures of East Asia

TERMS & NAMES
zither
haiku
Han

SECTION OBJECTIVES

1. To examine the effects of cultural exchange in East Asia

2. To describe current and traditional arts

3. To identify the effects of communism on the culture and the people

SKILLBUILDER
• Interpreting a Map, p. 512

CRITICAL THINKING
• Summarizing, p. 511
• Drawing Conclusions, p. 513
• Forming and Supporting an Opinion, p. 515

FOCUS & MOTIVATE
WARM-UP

Making Inferences Have students read Dateline and discuss the 2008 Olympics in Beijing.

1. In what way does being chosen to hold the 2008 Olympics signify a new era in China?

2. How might this event promote cultural exchange?

INSTRUCT: Objective ❶

Cultural Exchange/Exchange Within East Asia

• What has been the effect of cultural exchange on the East Asian countries? Countries have much in common.

 In-depth Resources: Unit 6
• Guided Reading Worksheet, p. 16

 Reading Study Guide
(Spanish and English), pp. 158–159

MAIN IDEA

The cultures of the nations of East Asia share much in common because of years of cultural exchange.

WHY IT MATTERS NOW

As East Asians are introduced to Western culture, they are careful not to forget their own cultural heritage.

DATELINE

BEIJING, CHINA, JULY 12, 2001—Today, Beijing won its bid to host the 2008 Summer Olympics. The announcement set off a celebration of fireworks, songs, and flag waving by thousands of people. One student shouted into a television camera, "Hello, world! We are the Chinese people!"

This is the first time that China, the world's most populous country, has been selected to host the Olympics. The historic decision begins a new era for the Chinese. They now feel recognized and accepted by the world community.

Culture • People gather in Beijing under fireworks to celebrate the news. ▶

Cultural Exchange ❶

Cultural exchange has occurred for centuries among the countries of East Asia. In recent decades, these countries have been influenced by Western culture as well. At the same time, aspects of East Asian cultures have spread outside the region. International events like the Olympics are sure to generate more awareness of the region around the world.

510 CHAPTER 17

Program Resources

 In-depth Resources: Unit 6
• Guided Reading Worksheet, p. 16
• Reteaching Activity, p. 25

 Reading Study Guide
(Spanish and English), pp. 158–159

 Formal Assessment
• Section Quiz, p. 258

 Integrated Assessment
• Rubric for making a list of questions

 Outline Map Activities

 Access for Students Acquiring English
• Guided Reading Worksheet, p. 152

 Technology Resources classzone.com

TEST-TAKING RESOURCES
⌁ Strategies for Test Preparation
⌁ Test Practice Transparencies
ⓘ Online Test Practice

Exchange Within East Asia ❶

East Asian cultures have much in common because of cultural exchange. Many of the shared aspects of culture originated in China, whose civilization has already existed for 4,000 years. For example, the Japanese and Koreans adapted the Chinese writing system to their own languages. The Japanese also adopted Chinese ideas about centralized government, urban planning, and painting techniques. Similarly, the Koreans picked up Chinese printing techniques and methods of government administration.

Place • This Buddhist temple in China stretches across a peaceful pond. ◄

Religion The religions of East Asia are strong indicators of cultural exchange within the region. Buddhism, for example, originated in India. The Chinese learned about the religion around 1,700 years ago. They then passed on their understanding of it to the Koreans, who later transmitted their knowledge to the Japanese. Some of the elements of Buddhism that the Japanese adopted were incorporated into their native Shinto religion. The Koreans and Japanese also developed interest in Confucianism. It, too, spread from China to their countries.

Reading Social Studies

A. Making Inferences By what means do you think the countries of East Asia passed their culture on to one another?

Reading Social Studies
A. Possible Answer
by trading with each other, by exploration and conquest

Practices Today Throughout East Asia, many people still practice Buddhism and Confucianism. They also practice other religions, such as Christianity and Taoism. The Communist government of North Korea discourages religious freedom. South Koreans, however, practice Buddhism and Christianity. Mongolians practice Tibetan Buddhism. Taiwan's dominant religion is based on Buddhism, Confucianism, and Taoism. Japan's two major religions are Zen Buddhism and Shinto.

Culture • Many Taoists practice tai chi, a form of exercise meant to relieve the body of stress and worry. ▼

Activity Options

Differentiating Instruction: Gifted and Talented

Interpreting the Sayings of Confucius Challenge interested students to research the sayings and teachings of Confucius, interpret them, and share them with the class. Students can make a list of the attitudes or beliefs that Confucius appears to be supporting and explain them to the group.

You might want to give students the following sayings as a starting point:

"Let there be no evil in your thoughts."

"When you know a thing, to recognize that you know it, and when you do not know a thing, to recognize that you do not know it. That is knowledge."

INTERPRETING A MAP

Cultural Exchange with East Asia Throughout History

Ask students what a thematic map shows. Discuss with students that this thematic map shows how different cultures came into contact with each other. Discuss what aspects of the students' cultures might have originated in East Asia. Ask students if there are other aspects of East Asian culture in the United States. Ask students to use the map to answer the following questions:

• Where did Buddhism originate? China

• What did China pass on to Japan? Buddhism, Confucianism, system of writing, system of government, painting styles, printmaking, literature

• What did the U.S. and Europe pass on to China, Japan, and Korea? music, clothing, democratic ideas, paintings, Christianity

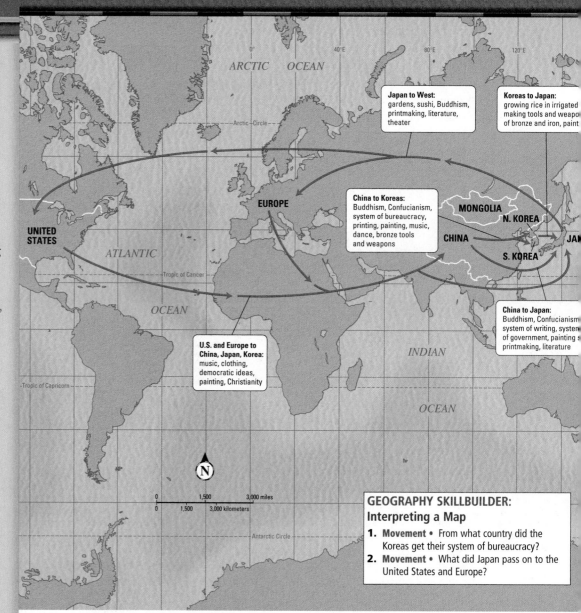

Japan to West: gardens, sushi, Buddhism, printmaking, literature, theater

Koreas to Japan: growing rice in irrigated making tools and weapo of bronze and iron, paint

China to Koreas: Buddhism, Confucianism, system of bureaucracy, printing, painting, music, dance, bronze tools and weapons

U.S. and Europe to China, Japan, Korea: music, clothing, democratic ideas, painting, Christianity

China to Japan: Buddhism, Confucianism system of writing, system of government, painting s printmaking, literature

GEOGRAPHY SKILLBUILDER:
Interpreting a Map

1. **Movement** • From what country did the Koreas get their system of bureaucracy?
2. **Movement** • What did Japan pass on to the United States and Europe?

Arts Past and Present

Like the religions, the art forms of East Asia's countries reflect cultural exchange. For example, similar methods of painting and making pottery are used throughout the region. However, each country also boasts unique artistic traditions.

Geography Skillbuilder Answers

1. China

2. gardens, haiku, sushi, Buddhism

512 CHAPTER 17

Activity Options

Multiple Learning Styles: Logical

🅱 Block Scheduling

Class Time One class period

Task Creating a trivia game show

Purpose To quiz students on the cultural exchanges between the East and West

Supplies Needed
• Pencils or pens
• Note cards

Activity On one side of the note cards, write questions derived from the map. Write the answers on the other side. For instance, Q: "In what country did the haiku originate?" A: "Japan." Divide the class into teams of three. You might choose one team to host the game, or you may prefer to host the game yourself.

Art in China Chinese art forms date back thousands of years. The art of bronze casting was developed around 1100 B.C. Music and dance are also ancient art forms in China. Many different kinds of instruments have been found in ancient tombs. Bells, flutes, drums, and a stringed instrument called a **zither** are all still played in China.

Fine porcelain dishes and vases are among China's greatest art treasures. The scenes, designs, and words that decorate them have also helped historians understand the cultural life of ancient China.

Today, theater is a popular art form in China. There are at least 300 forms of traditional opera in China. At the Beijing Opera, actors wear elaborate costumes to perform dramas based on Chinese stories, folklore, and history.

Reading Social Studies
B. Possible Answer
By contributing money, the Japanese government shows that the traditional arts are very important.

Reading
Social Studies

B. Clarifying What importance does the Japanese government give to traditional arts?

Art in Japan Buddhist ideas have influenced the arts in Japan. Artists consider simplicity, delicacy, and tradition to be important in their artwork. Painting, printing, dance, music, and theater all reflect these ideals. In literature, the **haiku** (HY·koo) is a world-famous form of Japanese poetry. Each haiku uses only 17 syllables. The goal of the form is to suggest, in a short description, much more than is stated. Many Japanese poets, such as Basho (1644–1694), have written haiku since the form was developed hundreds of years ago.

Some artists in Japan are working to preserve traditional crafts. Potters and weavers, in particular, receive money from the Japanese government so that they can continue their work and teach others. These artists are considered living treasures.

Culture • Bunraku puppetry is a famous Japanese art form. The puppets are nearly life-size. Each one is manipulated by three puppeteers, who control different parts of it. ▼

Bunraku Puppetry

Omodzukai
Chief Manipulator
• holds puppet
• moves puppet's head, body, and right hand

Ningyo
Bunraku puppet

Ashidzukai
Third Manipulator
• moves puppet's legs

Hidaridzukai
Second Manipulator
• moves puppet's left hand

MORE ABOUT...
Haiku
The haiku is a poetic form popular all over the world. In its original language, the first and third lines of a haiku have five syllables each, and the middle line has seven syllables. Haiku generally use familiar images and present them in a way that lets readers use their imaginations. Haiku often paint a picture of a brief moment in time. An example of a haiku follows.

An old silent pond...
A frog jumps into the pond
splash! Silence again.

CRITICAL THINKING ACTIVITY

Drawing Conclusions Ask students why the government of Japan allocates money to support the work of potters, weavers, and other artists who are working on traditional crafts. Have them consider why the Japanese government wants to preserve these crafts.

Class Time 10 minutes

MORE ABOUT...
Bunraku
Bunraku began in 1684, the creation of a traveling storyteller named Takemoto Gidayu. He had traveled for many years with puppeteers, providing the narrations and puppets' voices. Gidayu was joined by two other artists: Chikamatsu Monzaemon, the most famous playwright in Japanese history, and Takeda Isumo, a well-known theater owner. Bunraku is still popular in Japan today.

Activity Options

Multiple Learning Styles: Visual

Block Scheduling

Class Time One class period
Task Writing a haiku about a moment in time
Purpose To understand the haiku form and the way a haiku reflects a moment in time

Supplies Needed
• Samples of haiku
• Writing paper
• Pencils or pens

Activity Review the features of a haiku—a three-line poem with five syllables in the first line, seven in the second, and five in the third—and the type of moment most of them try to describe. Have students read and discuss examples of haiku. Then ask each student to write a haiku describing a moment. You might ask students to illustrate their haiku and assemble them in a class book.

INSTRUCT: Objective ③

Culture and Communism/
The Chinese People

- **What effect has communism had on artistic freedom in China and North Korea?** Communists repressed artistic freedom and damaged or destroyed works of art.

- **To what ethnic group do most of the people in China belong?** Han

- **How are elders and children treated in Chinese families?** the elders with respect, the children with a lot of attention

- **What steps has the government in China taken to slow population growth?** Married couples in urban areas can have only one child; couples in rural areas can have two.

Spotlight on CULTURE

As dawn breaks, the streets of China fill with people gathering to perform the traditional kung fu exercises. These exercises include boxing, weapon wielding, and different types of exercises that promote good health. The active aspect of kung fu exercises tendons, bones, and skin, and is based on the movements of animals such as tigers, panthers, monkeys, snakes, and cranes. The meditative aspect trains the spirit and the mind.

Culture and Communism

Communism has significantly affected some of East Asia's cultures. In North Korea and China, the Communists repressed artistic freedom. During the Cultural Revolution in China, artwork was frequently damaged or destroyed. Writers were forced to create propaganda instead of expressing their own ideas. Even Mao wrote poetry, but his poems only concerned Communist ideals. Playwrights and painters who created work that reflected Communist ideals were allowed to continue their work. Artists who used their art to criticize the government were punished.

In North Korea today, the government still controls the work of artists. The Chinese government has shown greater willingness to allow artists to pursue their own ideas.

The Chinese People

China contains about one-fifth of the world's population. Most people in China belong to an ethnic group called the **Han**. In addition, there are about 55 minority groups in China. Each has its own spoken language, and some also have their own written language. In school, students often speak their native language, and Mandarin Chinese is taught as the official language.

Reading Social Studies

C. Drawing Conclusions Why do you think the Communists worried about allowing artistic freedom?

Reading Social Studies
C. Possible Answer
Artistic freedom might lead to criticism of the government.

Spotlight on CULTURE

The Martial Arts The martial arts are a unique form of fighting. They originated in ancient East Asia but are now also practiced in other countries, such as the United States. Karate originated in Japan and involves striking and kicking with hands and feet. The Koreans practice a similar martial art called tae kwon do (ty kwahn doh). The Japanese also developed other forms, such as judo (JOO•doh) and aikido (EYE•kee•doh), that involve throwing or blocking an attack.

The Chinese call their fighting style kung fu, and for centuries, they shared it only with other Chinese. In the mid-1800s, however, Chinese laborers introduced their martial arts to the United States. In the 1960s, a young Chinese American, Bruce Lee (shown at right), began teaching kung fu's fantastic flying leaps and spin-kicks to Hollywood stars. He soon became an international action-movie star. Today, 4 million people in the United States take martial arts classes to exercise, learn self-defense, and enjoy the sport. As one of the most popular forms, tae kwon do became an official Olympic sport in 2000.

514 CHAPTER 17

Activity Options

Interdisciplinary Link: Language Arts

Class Time One class period

Task Writing an editorial about the decision to include tae kwon do as an Olympic event

Purpose To identify the pros and cons of the decision to include tae kwon do in the 2000 Olympics

Supplies Needed
- Samples of newspaper editorials
- Writing paper
- Pens or pencils

B Block Scheduling

Activity Display examples of editorials and discuss their features. Encourage students to read a few of the available editorials. Then ask students to consider the decision to include tae kwon do in the 2000 Olympics. Encourage students to form an opinion about this decision and to write an editorial that expresses their opinion. Remind them to include reasons supporting their opinions and to persuade others to adopt a similar opinion.

Changes to the Family The Chinese have traditionally lived in large, extended families. To slow down population growth, the Chinese government decreed in the 1980s that each married couple in a city may have only one child. Rural families may be allowed to have a second child, and families in ethnic minorities may have more than one child. Most Chinese households today are made up of small family units that may include the grandparents.

Family members in China depend on one another and follow traditional patterns. In a family, elders are greatly respected. Children, because there are so few, are given lots of attention. In the past, marriages were arranged by the parents, but that is no longer common. In present-day China, most parents work outside the home, so grandparents often care for the children.

Place • As is typical in China, this couple has only one child. ▲

SECTION 4 ASSESSMENT

Terms & Names

1. Identify: (a) zither (b) haiku (c) Han

Taking Notes

2. Use a diagram like this one to list aspects of culture that East Asian countries have exchanged with each other.

The Koreas

China ⟷ Japan

Main Ideas

3. (a) What is the goal of Japan's living treasures?

(b) How has the government affected religion and art in China and North Korea?

(c) What led the Chinese government to place restrictions on family size?

Critical Thinking

4. Drawing Conclusions

What factors do you think encourage cultural exchange?

Think About

- migration patterns
- geographic features
- speaking related languages

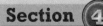 **ACTIVITY -OPTION-** Make a **list** of five questions that you would like to ask a Chinese teenager about his or her life.

China and Its Neighbors **515**

Section 4 Assessment

1. Terms & Names
  a. zither, p. 513
  b. haiku, p. 513
  c. Han, p. 514

2. Taking Notes

Koreas and China	Chinese writing, printing, Buddhism, Confucianism
Koreas and Japan	Buddhism
China and Japan	Chinese writing, painting, government, urban planning, Confucianism

3. Main Ideas

a. Their goal is to preserve traditional crafts in Japan.
b. Artistic freedom has been repressed. In China, writers and artists had to reflect Communist ideals. In North Korea, the government controls the work of artists and discourages religious practices.
c. The Chinese government restricted family size to limit population growth.

4. Critical Thinking

Students may say that geography, movement of people, similar languages, and shared experiences encourage cultural exchange.

ACTIVITY OPTION

 Integrated Assessment
  • Rubric for making a list of questions

Teacher's Edition **515**

CRITICAL THINKING ACTIVITY

Forming and Supporting an Opinion Ask students to offer opinions regarding China's approach to controlling population growth. Encourage students to consider the response of the Chinese people to the policy, the success of the approach, and the long-term effects of the policy.

Class Time 10 minutes

ASSESS & RETEACH

Reading Social Studies Have students check their predictions about the culture in East Asia in the chart on page 494. Encourage them to make necessary adjustments.

 Formal Assessment
  • Section Quiz, p. 258

RETEACHING ACTIVITY

Organize students into three groups. Have the first group conduct a panel discussion about the effects of cultural exchange within East Asia. Direct the second group to discuss art in China and Japan, and have the third discuss the effects on culture of Communist rule.

 In-depth Resources: Unit 6
  • Reteaching Activity, p. 25

 Access for Students Acquiring English
  • Reteaching Activity, p. 159

Establishing Modern Japan

SECTION 5

TERMS & NAMES
Meiji Restoration
Hiroshima
Nagasaki
homogeneous
Ainu

SECTION OBJECTIVES

1. To describe changes in Japan during the past century
2. To explain the rebuilding of Japan's economy after World War II
3. To identify unique aspects of Japanese culture

SKILLBUILDER
• Interpreting a Map, p. 519

CRITICAL THINKING
• Hypothesizing, p. 518
• Forming and Supporting Opinions, p. 519

FOCUS & MOTIVATE
WARM-UP

Making Inferences After students read Dateline, discuss Japan's new constitution.

1. Why was the timing of this event so important?
2. How do you think life in Japan will change?

INSTRUCT: Objective ❶
History

• **What changes occurred to industry and the economy during the Meiji Restoration?** Japan built industry, developed its economy, and became wealthy and powerful.

  In-depth Resources: Unit 6
• Guided Reading Worksheet, p. 17

Reading Study Guide
(Spanish and English), pp. 160–161

MAIN IDEA	WHY IT MATTERS NOW
After World War II, the Japanese built a modern industrial economy that is one of the largest in the world.	One challenge for Japan is to protect its unique identity even as it welcomes influences from the rest of the world.

DATELINE
EXTRA

TOKYO, JAPAN, MAY 3, 1947

Today, Japan celebrated its rebirth as a new nation. Less than two years after its surrender at the end of World War II, Japan has a Western-style constitution.

Emperor Hirohito conducted a solemn ceremony to celebrate the occasion. The government issued a pocket-sized pamphlet to every Japanese family. The new constitution is printed inside. It expresses the hopes of the Japanese for a peaceful future.

Culture • Emperor Hirohito stands before a crowd of 20,000 people celebrating the new constitution. ▲

History ❶

The people of Japan have seen remarkable changes in the past century, not just in their country's government, but also in its economy and its relations with the rest of the world. From the mid-1600s to the 1800s, Japan was a fairly isolated nation. It traded with China but was unaffected by the rest of the world.

516 CHAPTER 17

Program Resources

 In-depth Resources: Unit 6
• Guided Reading Worksheet, p. 17
• Reteaching Activity, p. 26

 Reading Study Guide
(Spanish and English), pp. 160–161

516 CHAPTER 17

 Formal Assessment
• Section Quiz, p. 259

 Integrated Assessment
• Rubric for planning a schedule

 Outline Map Activities

 Access for Students Acquiring English
• Guided Reading Worksheet, p. 153

 Technology Resources
classzone.com

TEST-TAKING RESOURCES

 Strategies for Test Preparation
↪ Test Practice Transparencies
ⓘ Online Test Practice

The Meiji Restoration Japan's location made it a convenient place for ships sailing from the United States to stop and replenish supplies of food and fuel. In 1853, American naval vessels commanded by Commodore Matthew C. Perry landed in Japan. Perry used a show of force to open Japan to Western contact, ending nearly 200 years of Japanese isolation.

In 1867, a group of samurai overthrew the ruling Tokugawa Shogunate and restored the emperor as head of government. The period that followed, from 1868 through 1911, became known as the **Meiji Restoration,** because the new emperor was called Meiji (MAY·jee). During this time, the Japanese people built modern industries and developed the economy. Japan became wealthy and powerful. Following a series of wars, Japan assumed control of Taiwan, Korea, and Manchuria.

Culture •
A Japanese artist painted this scene of Commodore Perry in Japan in 1853. ▲

Reading Social Studies

A. Summarizing What factors contributed to instability in Japan in the early 1900s?

Reading Social Studies
A. Possible Answer
war, earthquake, Great Depression

In the Early 1900s Japan, allied with the United States, Britain, and France, defeated Germany in World War I and thus was able to expand its holdings of ex-German colonies in the Pacific. The Great Kanto Earthquake in 1923 hurt Japan's economy, and like much of the world, Japan was affected by the Great Depression. During the 1930s, the military took control of Japan's government. In 1937, Japan invaded China and became involved in a long war there. Also at this time, Japan developed closer relations with Nazi Germany and Fascist Italy. As a result, the United States stopped selling oil to Japan. In 1941, Japan bombed the U.S. naval base at Pearl Harbor in Hawaii, bringing the United States into World War II.

World War II By 1942, the Japanese military had won many victories in East Asia and the South Pacific. But in June 1942, Japan lost the Battle of Midway; and in February 1943, it lost a battle on Guadalcanal Island. These defeats turned the tide of the war.

China and Its Neighbors **517**

MORE ABOUT...
Samurai Warriors

The samurai were local warriors whose leaders or generals were called shoguns. Their lives were dedicated to virtue and duty, and they lived by a code of honor called *bushido,* or the way of the warrior. They fought to keep order and protect their lords.

MORE ABOUT...
Pearl Harbor

It was the surprise attack by the Japanese on Pearl Harbor that forced the United States into World War II. A Japanese force of 33 ships arrived at night to a spot within 200 miles of the United States naval base there. On December 7, 1941, these carriers launched 360 airplanes against the Pacific fleet. Their targets were American battleships. Twenty-one ships and 300 planes were destroyed. More than 2,000 people were killed; many more were wounded.

MORE ABOUT...
Hiroshima

On August 6, 1945, the United States dropped a single atomic bomb on the city of Hiroshima. The bomb destroyed five square miles of the city; between 70,000 and 100,000 people were killed. Three days later a second bomb was dropped on the city of Nagasaki. The Japanese surrendered to the Allied forces in September.

Activity Options

Interdisciplinary Link: History

Class Time One class period

Task Presenting an oral, eyewitness account of the events at Pearl Harbor

Purpose To understand the significance of the events at Pearl Harbor and their impact on the world

Supplies Needed
• Reference materials about Pearl Harbor

B Block Scheduling

Activity Have students research the events of December 7, 1941. Encourage them to imagine themselves as eyewitnesses to the events. Then ask students to prepare a brief oral presentation about the events at Pearl Harbor that might have been aired on a radio program in the United States.

INSTRUCT: Objective ❷

Economy and Government

- Which Japanese values in particular contributed to the rebuilding effort after World War II? hard work, saving money
- What is the status of women in Japan's workforce today? About two-fifths of women work in temporary or part-time jobs; few women hold management positions.
- What kind of government exists now in Japan? a constitutional monarchy with a parliamentary government

CRITICAL THINKING ACTIVITY

Hypothesizing Remind students that Japan rose from a difficult position after World War II to become a major economic power. Ask students to think about how the values of hard work and saving money helped the rebuilding effort. Then lead a class discussion on how other aspects of life in Japan might be affected by these values.

Class Time 10 minutes

MORE ABOUT...
Women in Japan

Several factors contribute to the problems Japanese women face in the business world. One major factor is that Japanese women do not have the same access to business networks as their male colleagues. Because of gender roles, they are not free to entertain in traditional ways, and they have limited access to the corporate culture.

Place • **This scene of Nagasaki after the bombing shows only a few buildings still standing.** ▲

In 1945, the United States dropped atomic bombs on two Japanese cities—**Hiroshima** (heer•uh•SHEE•muh) and **Nagasaki** (nah•guh•SAH•kee). Emperor Hirohito then agreed to surrender, putting an end to the war.

Economy and Government ❷

After World War II, Japan's economy and government were in shambles. Its cities had been bombed. Many Japanese were homeless and without jobs.

Economy The Japanese values of hard work and saving money helped to rebuild the economy. The United States also gave Japan help through loans and advice. By the mid-1950s, Japanese industrial production matched its prewar levels. Today, Japan has one of the most powerful economies in the world.

Like the United States, Japan encourages free enterprise. This type of system can motivate people to develop new ideas as well as to expand their businesses with little government interference.

Women and the Economy Women's participation in the work force has grown since World War II. However, discrimination exists, and long-held ideas about women's roles as mother and housekeeper are changing very slowly. Approximately two-fifths of Japanese women hold jobs, but many of these jobs are temporary or part-time. Few women hold management positions.

Culture • **Many Japanese women, like this one, hold jobs in business and industry.** ▼

518 CHAPTER 17

Activity Options

Differentiating Instruction: Less Proficient Readers

Finding Main Ideas Students may have difficulty identifying the main ideas about the history, economy, and government of Japan. To help them identify the main ideas, have students create webs for each topic. Remind them to write the topic in the center of the web and to write the main points in the surrounding circles.

Government After World War II, the United States occupied Japan until 1952. It helped set up a new government. Under the new constitution, the rights and responsibilities of the Japanese are similar to those of Americans.

Today, Japan has a constitutional monarchy with a parliamentary government. The Diet is the highest law-making body in the country. Before 1945, Japan's emperor was the head of the government. He is now a symbolic head of state.

Culture ③

Japan's population is **homogeneous,** or largely the same. Most of its people are descended from the Mongolian people who settled Japan thousands of years ago. The exception is the approximately 15,000 Ainu (EYE·noo) people. Scholars believe that the **Ainu** came to Japan from Europe well before the other settlers arrived.

Social Behavior In Western culture, especially in the United States, people think of themselves first as individuals. In Japan, as in most of Asia, people think of themselves first as part of a group. Social behavior in Japan is governed by an idea the Japanese call *on* (ohn). This value is based on Confucian principles about proper relationships. The Japanese take the relationship between children and their elders particularly seriously. People always display respectful behavior toward their parents and elders. They also put the needs of their parents and elders before their own needs. Japanese people also seriously consider an elder's judgment when making important decisions.

Urban Living More than 90 percent of Japanese families live in urban areas. Many people live in apartment buildings, in part because there is not much space for single-family homes; because of this, owning a home is very expensive.

Geography Skillbuilder Answers

1. between 130 and 520 people

2. Hokkaido

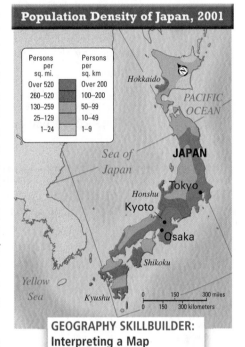

Population Density of Japan, 2001

Persons per sq. mi.	Persons per sq. km
Over 520	Over 200
260–520	100–200
130–259	50–99
25–129	10–49
1–24	1–9

Hokkaido

PACIFIC OCEAN

Sea of Japan

JAPAN

Honshu

Tokyo

Kyoto

Osaka

Shikoku

Yellow Sea

Kyushu

0   150   300 miles
0   150   300 kilometers

GEOGRAPHY SKILLBUILDER: Interpreting a Map

1. **Place •** How many people per square mile live on the islands of Kyushu and Shikoku?
2. **Place •** Which large island has regions with only 1 to 24 people per square mile?

Reading **Social Studies**

B. Forming and Supporting Opinions What is your opinion of putting the group ahead of the individual? What are the pros and cons of it?

Reading Social Studies B. Possible Answers

Responses will vary. Students should give pros and cons to support their answers.

Activity Options

Multiple Learning Styles: Visual/Tactile

Block Scheduling

Class Time One class period

Task Practicing the art of origami

Purpose To learn about and experience the Japanese art of paper folding

Supplies Needed
• Directions for origami
• Samples or illustrations of origami
• Paper for folding

Activity Display samples or illustrations of origami for students to observe. Then have pairs of students choose an image to create out of paper. Help students follow the directions for making their chosen image. Invite students to include their finished pieces in a classroom origami display.

MORE ABOUT...
Bonsai

The word *bonsai* means tray-planted. A bonsai gardener prunes and shapes a plant to create the illusion of a very old miniature tree. Bonsai can be made from evergreens, tropical plants, and deciduous shrubs. Most bonsai plants are started and grown in a container or tray. Bonsai range in height from only two inches to about three feet. The art of bonsai requires skill and patience, but plants can live for hundreds of years if they are tended carefully.

ASSESS & RETEACH

Reading Social Studies Have students verify or change their predictions regarding modern Japan in the graphic organizer on page 494.

 Formal Assessment
• Section Quiz, p. 259

RETEACHING ACTIVITY

Organize the class into three groups. Assign each group the topic of history, economy and government, or culture. Have groups summarize the information on their assigned topic and share their summaries with the class.

 In-depth Resources: Unit 6
• Reteaching Activity, p. 26

 Access for Students Acquiring English
• Reteaching Activity, p. 160

Culture • **Excited fans release balloons before a baseball game at the Fukoaka Dome on the island of Kyushu.** ▲

Many people commute to their jobs or to school. Most major cities have subway systems. During rush hour, these trains are packed with people traveling to and from work. High-speed commuter trains connect many of the big cities. The fastest trains reach speeds of 160 miles an hour. Railway tunnels also connect the islands. The world's first undersea railway tunnel was built to connect the islands of Kyushu and Honshu.

Cultural Exchange Some aspects of Japanese culture have gained popularity in the United States in recent years. These include the Japanese tea ceremony, sushi, and Japanese flower arranging. Japanese gardens, which stress simplicity in design, have been built in many parts of the world. Bonsai (bahn·SY)—the art of growing tiny, elegant plants and trees—has also gained popularity.

Two sports are wildly popular in Japan, both having come to Japan from other parts of the world. Baseball and soccer games draw enormous crowds. Today, several of Japan's top baseball players, such as Ichiro Suzuki, play on U.S. teams.

SECTION ⑤ ASSESSMENT

Terms & Names

1. Identify: (a) Meiji Restoration   (b) Hiroshima   (c) Nagasaki
(d) homogeneous   (e) Ainu

Taking Notes	Main Ideas	Critical Thinking
2. Use a sequence chart like this one to list the events leading to the growth of Japan's modern economy. 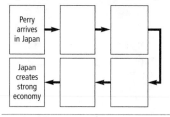	**3. (a)** How did World War II affect Japan's economy? **(b)** What effect has Confucianism had on the daily lives of the Japanese? **(c)** How has Japan been influenced by other cultures?	**4. Analyzing Causes** Why do you think Japan is such a densely populated country? ***Think About*** ◆ Japan's land area and geographic features ◆ social and cultural beliefs ◆ standard of living

ACTIVITY -OPTION- Plan the **schedule** of a Japanese Culture Day. Think about what activities you might have, what speakers you could invite, and what you would want participants to learn about Japan.

Section ⑤ Assessment

1. Terms & Names
a. Meiji Restoration, p. 517
b. Hiroshima, p. 518
c. Nagasaki, p. 518
d. homogeneous, p. 519
e. Ainu, p. 519

2. Taking Notes

Event 1:	Japan opened to Western contact
Event 2:	Meiji Restoration
Event 3:	Japanese worked hard, saved money
Event 4:	U.S. gave loans and advice

3. Main Ideas
a. Many people were homeless and jobless; the economy was in shambles.
b. The elderly are revered and their advice is sought; parents and elders come first.
c. many aspects of life influenced by China; government, economy, and sports influenced by Western values

4. Critical Thinking
Students may say that most of the people live in cities, where there is little space.

ACTIVITY OPTION

 Integrated Assessment
• Rubric for planning a schedule

Reading a Population Density Map

▶▶ Defining the Skill

A population density map allows you to compare the population densities of different regions. It shows how many people live in each square mile or square kilometer.

▶▶ Applying the Skill

The map below shows the population density of North Korea, South Korea, and Japan. Use the strategies listed below to help you read the map.

How to Read a Population Density Map

Strategy ❶ Read the map key. This key uses color to show population density. Areas with very dense population are purple. Areas with sparse population are pale yellow.

Strategy ❷ Look at the map. Find the areas on the map that are most densely populated. Then locate areas that are less densely populated.

Strategy ❸ Read the labels on the map. Notice that the major cities of these countries are in very densely populated areas. Look at the islands of Japan and notice which ones are the least populated.

Strategy ❹ Summarize the information given in the map. Use the key to help you remember which areas are more densely populated than others.

Write a Summary

Write a summary that will help you understand the information given in the map. The paragraph below and to the right summarizes the information from the map.

▶▶ Practicing the Skill

Turn to page 519 in Chapter 17, Section 5, "Culture." Look at the map entitled "Population Density of Japan, 2001" and write a paragraph summarizing what you learned from it.

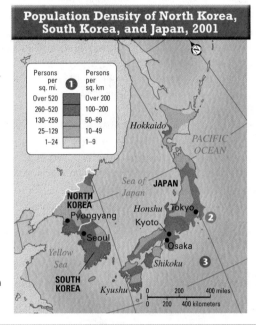

Population Density of North Korea, South Korea, and Japan, 2001

Persons per sq. mi.	❶	Persons per sq. km
Over 520		Over 200
260–520		100–200
130–259		50–99
25–129		10–49
1–24		1–9

❹   All three of these East Asian countries are densely populated. Japan is the most densely populated of the three. The areas around Japan's cities are more densely populated than those around the cities of the Koreas. In all three countries, the cities are in very densely populated areas, as would be expected. Of the larger islands of Japan, Hokkaido is the least populated. North Korea is slightly less populated than South Korea.

SKILLBUILDER

Reading a Population Density Map

Defining the Skill

Ask students to think about why it might be important to identify areas of heavy population. Lead a discussion about when this information could be useful. Elicit or point out issues such as allocation of funds and services, as well as planning to meet transportation and housing needs.

Applying the Skill

How to Read a Population Density Map
Point out the strategies for reading a population density map. Guide students through each step, and emphasize the importance of reading the map key and the labels. Have students locate densely populated areas and areas with less dense population on the map.

Write a Summary

Suggest that after students read the map, they take notes about the most and least densely populated areas of each country. Encourage them to make generalizations based on their notes.

Practicing the Skill

Have students use the strategies they practiced to summarize the map on page 519. If students need further practice, choose another population density map in this textbook and guide them in reading, interpreting, and summarizing the data on it.

In-depth Resources: Unit 6
• Skillbuilder Practice, p. 20

Career Connection: Census Researcher

Encourage students who enjoy reading a population distribution map to find out about careers that use this skill. For example, a census researcher is a person who may collect or analyze census data, including data about population distribution. A census researcher may both create and use population distribution maps and other kinds of maps.

 Block Scheduling

1. Suggest that students look for information about specific tasks that census researchers perform.

2. Help students find out what academic field is the best preparation for becoming a census researcher.

3. Have students share what they learn, using graphic organizers.

TERMS & NAMES

1. Sun Yat-sen, p. 496
2. Mao Zedong, p. 497
3. Cultural Revolution, p. 499
4. human rights, p. 503
5. Diet, p. 504
6. cooperative, p. 508
7. haiku, p. 513
8. Han, p. 514
9. homogeneous, p. 519
10. Ainu, p. 519

REVIEW QUESTIONS

Possible Responses

1. Taiping Rebellion, 1850 to 1864: Chinese peasants protested the Treaty of Nanking. Boxer Rebellion, 1900: Boxers tried to force all foreigners out of China.
2. The Communists defeated the National Party. Mao Zedong declared China a Communist state.
3. Deng Xiaoping came to power; he established relations and trade with other nations.
4. The government restricts the practices religion, free speech, and free expression.
5. the Communist Party
6. textiles, metals, steel, rice, cars, electronics, and chemicals
7. Japan and Korea adopted Chinese writing; Korea adopted Chinese printing techniques.
8. Artistic freedom was repressed; writers and artists were forced to express Communist ideals.
9. Modern industries were built and the economy developed. Japan became wealthy and powerful.
10. The Japanese have high regard for their elders, respect their needs, and value their advice.

ASSESSMENT

TERMS & NAMES

Explain the significance of each of the following:

1. Sun Yat-sen	2. Mao Zedong	3. Cultural Revolution	4. human rights	5. Diet
6. cooperative	7. haiku	8. Han	9. homogeneous	10. Ainu

REVIEW QUESTIONS

Establishing Modern China *(pages 495–499)*

1. Describe two rebellions under the Qing Dynasty.
2. What change did the Communists make in China in 1949?

The Governments of East Asia *(pages 502–505)*

3. What changes occurred in the Chinese government at the end of the Cultural Revolution?
4. How has the Chinese government repressed freedom?

The Economies of East Asia *(pages 506–509)*

5. Who controls China's economy?
6. What are some important East Asian products?

The Cultures of East Asia *(pages 510–515)*

7. Give two examples of cultural exchange in East Asia.
8. What changes did communism bring to the arts in China?

Establishing Modern Japan *(pages 516–520)*

9. What changes occurred during the Meiji Restoration?
10. How do the Japanese regard their elders?

CRITICAL THINKING

Hypothesizing

1. Using your completed chart from Reading Social Studies, p. 494, explain which of your predictions proved correct.

Drawing Conclusions

2. Why do you think Mao Zedong was successful in winning the civil war against the Nationalists?

Forming and Supporting Opinions

3. What is your opinion of the dissidents who demonstrated in Tiananmen Square? Should they have been more obedient to their government?

Visual Summary

1 Establishing Modern China

- The Nationalists toppled China's Qing Dynasty in 1911.
- Mao Zedong declared China Communist in 1949.

2 The Governments of East Asia

- China and North Korea are the only Communist countries in East Asia.
- China's government continues to repress people's freedom, but less so than in the past.

3 The Economies of East Asia

- Though they have faced challenges, East Asia's economies have grown strong.

4 The Cultures of East Asia

- Over the years, much cultural exchange has occurred in East Asia.
- Communism has changed Chinese culture, but traditions such as the arts still thrive.

5 Establishing Modern Japan

- After the devastating destruction of World War II, the Japanese rebuilt their economy to be one of the strongest in the world.

CRITICAL THINKING: Possible Responses

1. Hypothesizing

Some students may have predicted that the economies and governments are controlled by the Communists in China; others may have predicted that the Communists also control artistic and cultural freedom.

2. Drawing Conclusions

Students may say that Mao was successful because the Nationalists failed to improve the lives of workers and peasants.

3. Forming and Supporting Opinions

Students may say that the dissidents were simply expressing their right to free speech. Their actions presented risks to themselves, not to their government.

SOCIAL STUDIES SKILLBUILDER

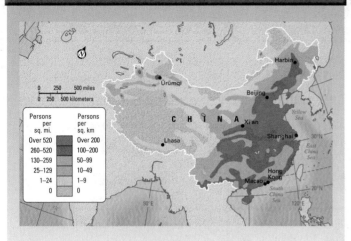

SKILLBUILDER: Reading a Population Density Map

1. Where are China's most densely populated areas?
2. Which areas are least populated? What might cause them to be so?

FOCUS ON GEOGRAPHY

1. **Location** • In what country did Buddhism originate?
2. **Movement** • From which countries did Buddhism spread to Japan?
3. **Movement** • When did Buddhism first spread to Korea?

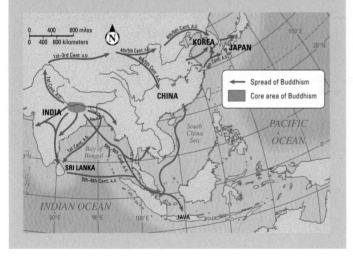

Interdisciplinary Activity: Mathematics

Creating a Graph The countries of East Asia have widely different standards of living. Look at the Regional Data File on pages 462–465 to find the gross domestic products for China, North Korea, South Korea, Taiwan, and Japan. Then determine each country's per capita GDP—or GDP per person—by dividing its total GDP by its total population. Create a bar graph showing the GDP and per capita GDP for these countries.

Cooperative Learning Activity

Creating an Oral Presentation Work in a group of three to five classmates to create a visual presentation about Japan's living treasures. Each group member should research and prepare a report on one treasure. The reports should include pictures of the art being practiced. As a group, give a presentation to the class.

 INTERNET ACTIVITY

Use the Internet to do research about the Long March. Find out details about the climate and terrain the marchers had to cross.

Writing About Geography Write a report of your findings, describing the climate and terrain along the route of the Long March. Explain what hardships the marchers probably faced due to these factors. List the Web sites you used to prepare your report.

For Internet links to support this activity, go to

RESEARCH LINKS
CLASSZONE.COM

CHAPTER PROJECTS

Interdisciplinary Activity: Mathematics

Creating a Graph You might want to look at the Data File as a group and have volunteers identify the GDP for the countries in the region. If appropriate, review the format and features of a bar graph. Students' bar graphs should show the GDP and per capita GDP for China, North Korea, South Korea, Taiwan, and Japan.

Cooperative Learning Activity

Creating an Oral Presentation Briefly discuss visual presentations in terms of content and style. Remind students that each group member should choose an art treasure to report on. Group presentations should include pictures of the art forms being practiced and represent the efforts of all group members.

INTERNET ACTIVITY

Brainstorm possible key words, Web sites, and search engines students might use to find out about the Long March. Students' reports should include details about the climate and terrain the marchers had to cross, and explain hardships the marchers faced due to these factors. Finally, students should list the Web sites they used to prepare their reports.

Skills Answers

Social Studies Skillbuilder
Possible Responses

1. China's most densely populated areas are in the southeast and northeast.
2. The least populated areas are in the west. The geography or climate might limit population.

Focus on Geography
Possible Responses

1. Buddhism originated in India.
2. From China and Korea
3. 4th and 5th centuries A.D.

Australia and the Pacific Islands

	OVERVIEW	COPYMASTERS	INTEGRATED TECHNOLOGY
UNIT ATLAS AND CHAPTER RESOURCES	Students will examine the various waves of people who settled Australia, New Zealand, and the Pacific Islands, and the governments and economies they established.	**In-depth Resources: Unit 6** • Guided Reading Worksheets, pp. 27–28 • Skillbuilder Practice, p. 31 • Unit Atlas Activities, pp. 1–2 • Geography Workshop, pp. 35–36 **Reading Study Guide** (Spanish and English), pp. 164–169 **Outline Map Activities**	Power Presentations Electronic Teacher Tools Online Lesson Planner Chapter Summaries on CD Critical Thinking Transparencies CT35

	KEY IDEAS	COPYMASTERS	INTEGRATED TECHNOLOGY
SECTION 1 History and Governments pp. 527–530	• The Maori and ancestors of the Aborigines were the first inhabitants of New Zealand and Australia, respectively. • Europeans came to the region in the 1500s seeking spices; colonization brought disease and slavery to the native peoples. • Many types of governments exist in the region; Australia and New Zealand maintain political ties to Great Britain.	**In-depth Resources: Unit 6** • Guided Reading Worksheet, p. 27 • Reteaching Activity, p. 33 **Reading Study Guide** (Spanish and English), pp. 164–165	Critical Thinking Transparencies CT36 classzone.com Chapter Summaries on CD
SECTION 2 Economies and Cultures pp. 531–534	• Australia's economy depends on service industries, mining, and farming. • Modernization has brought changes in transportation to the region, but traditional family structures and art forms are still influential.	**In-depth Resources: Unit 6** • Guided Reading Worksheet, p. 28 • Reteaching Activity, p. 34 **Reading Study Guide** (Spanish and English), pp. 166–167	classzone.com Chapter Summaries on CD

Audio

 Internet

Teacher's Edition

CD-ROM

 Overhead Transparency

Video

Copymaster

 Pupil's Edition

ASSESSMENT OPTIONS

Chapter Assessment, pp. 538–539

Formal Assessment
• Chapter Tests: Forms A, B, C, pp. 274–285

Test Generator

Online Test Practice

Strategies for Test Preparation

Section Assessment, p. 530

Formal Assessment
• Section Quiz, p. 272

Integrated Assessment
• Rubric for drawing and labeling a political map

Test Generator

Test Practice Transparencies TT64

Section Assessment, p. 534

Formal Assessment
• Section Quiz, p. 273

Integrated Assessment
• Rubric for writing an advertising slogan

Test Generator

Test Practice Transparencies TT65

 ## RESOURCES FOR DIFFERENTIATING INSTRUCTION

Students Acquiring English/ESL

Reading Study Guide (Spanish and English), pp. 164–169

Access for Students Acquiring English Spanish Translations, pp. 161–166

Less Proficient Readers

Reading Study Guide (Spanish and English), pp. 164–169

TE Activity
• Categorizing, p. 528

CROSS-CURRICULAR CONNECTIONS

Humanities
Finley, Carol. *Aboriginal Art of Australia: Exploring Cultural Traditions.* Minneapolis, MN: Lerner Publications, 1999. Involving text and clear photographs.

Literature
Flood, Bo, et al. *Pacific Island Legends: Tales from Micronesia, Melanesia, Polynesia, and Australia.* Honolulu, HI: Bess Press, 1999. Rich mixture of tales.

Morin, Paul. *Animal Dreaming: An Aboriginal Dreamtime Story.* San Diego: Silver Whistle/Harcourt, 1998. Animals in the dreamtime create a peaceful world.

Geography
Sammis, Fran. *Australia and the South Pacific.* New York: Benchmark Books, 1999. Geographical view of the region.

Language Arts/Literature
Honey, Elizabeth. *Fiddleback.* New York: Knopf, 2001. Camping trip adventure in modern Australia.

Sperry, Armstrong. *Call It Courage.* New York: Aladdin Books, 1990. Classic tale of Polynesia.

Science
Arnold, Caroline. *Australian Animals.* New York: HarperCollins, 2000. Diverse habitats of Australia.

Collard, Sneed B. *Lizard Island: Science and Scientists on Australia's Great Barrier Reef.* New York: Franklin Watts, 2000. Scientists protect the reef and its wildlife.

History
Ferry, Steven. *Australian Aborigines.* Mankato, MN: Smart Apple Media, 1999. Struggle to preserve their way of life.

 ## ENRICHMENT ACTIVITIES

The following activities are especially suitable for classes following block schedules.

Teacher's Edition, pp. 533, 535
Pupil's Edition, pp. 530, 534

Unit Atlas, pp. 458–455
Linking Past and Present, pp. 536–537

Outline Map Activities

INTEGRATED TECHNOLOGY

Go to **classzone.com** for lesson support and activities for Chapter 18.

BLOCK SCHEDULE LESSON PLAN OPTIONS: 90-MINUTE PERIOD

DAY 1

CHAPTER PREVIEW, pp. 524–525
Class Time 20 minutes

- **Discussion** Lead a class discussion using the "What do you think?" questions on PE p. 525. Then introduce the graphic organizer for the chapter found on PE p. 526.

SECTION 1, pp. 527–530
Class Time 70 minutes

- **Designing Artifacts** Have students reread Spotlight on Culture on PE p. 528. Lead a discussion about artifacts: what are considered artifacts, what form they might take, what they tell about people and cultures, and why they are important. Have students work in pairs to design an artifact that represents their culture. Provide time for students to share their products with the whole class.
  Class Time 40 minutes

- **Small Groups** Divide the class into four groups. Assign each group one of the following headings: history, culture, people, or government. Have students write everything they know about these four aspects of New Zealand. Reconvene as a whole class to create a master list on the board.
  Class Time 30 minutes

DAY 2

SECTION 1, continued
Class Time 25 minutes

- **Press Conference** To review the section, have the class conduct a press conference about New Zealand. Select a group of four students to field questions about the people, history, culture, and government of New Zealand. The rest of the class should prepare questions to ask the group.

SECTION 2, pp. 531–534
Class Time 65 minutes

- **Internet** Extend students' background knowledge of the diversity among economies and cultures of Australia by visiting **classzone.com.**
  Class Time 20 minutes

- **Mobiles** Have students work in pairs to make a mobile that portrays the history, government, economies, and cultures of Australia. Encourage students to label the pieces of the mobile with key ideas about each feature. Be sure that they understand that the mobiles must be balanced in order to be displayed in the classroom.
  Class Time 45 minutes

DAY 3

SECTION 2, continued
Class Time 35 minutes

- **Spider Map** Challenge students to use a spider map to display their answers to the question in Reading Social Studies on PE p. 533. Reconvene for a whole class discussion.

CHAPTER 18 REVIEW AND ASSESSMENT,
pp. 538–539
Class Time 55 minutes

- **Review** Have student pairs answer the Critical Thinking questions from the Chapter Assessment on PE p. 538. Then have them write an additional Critical Thinking question to pose to the class.
  Class Time 20 minutes

- **Assessment** Have students complete the Chapter 18 Assessment.
  Class Time 35 minutes

TECHNOLOGY IN THE CLASSROOM

WEBQUEST

A WebQuest is a structured, inquiry-oriented activity that asks students to solve problems by using Web resources. Students are given a task and are asked to use the Web to help them complete the task, which usually involves drawing a conclusion or solving a problem for which there is no one correct answer. Web-Quests can be very simple or highly complex. Below is a simple WebQuest to complement the material in Chapter 18. To learn more about WebQuests and how to design an official WebQuest, go to the WebQuest link at **classzone.com.**

ACTIVITY OUTLINE

Objective Students will conduct Web research to determine the pros and cons of living on a tropical Pacific island. They will write letters explaining their decision.

Task Have students use the specified Web sites to find out about the climate, geology, and natural resources of the South Pacific Islands. Have them write letters to friends explaining whether they would like to live on such an island, and why or why not.

Class Time Two class periods

DIRECTIONS

1. Ask students to describe their impressions of the South Pacific Islands. What comes to mind when they think of a tropical island?

2. Ask students to imagine that a friend has just made the comment, "I wish I could live on a tropical island in the South Pacific." Ask how they would respond.

3. Have students use the Web sites listed at **classzone.com** to gather information that will help them answer their friend's question. If there is time, have students search for additional sites. They should take notes on climate and weather patterns, geology and volcanic activity, and natural resources.

4. Take a class vote to see how many students would like to live on a South Pacific Island. Ask students to explain their answers. What would be the most desirable thing about living on an island in this region? What would be the least desirable?

5. Ask students to write letters to their friends describing the things they learned about the physical geography of the South Pacific Islands. They might want to insert pictures to illustrate their points. Ask them to conclude with a statement of whether they think they would like to live on an island in this region, including a discussion of the good and not-so-good things they might encounter.

CHAPTER 18 OBJECTIVE

Students will examine the various waves of people who settled Australia, New Zealand, and the Pacific Islands and the governments and economies they established.

FOCUS ON VISUALS

Interpreting the Photograph Have students look at the atlas on pages A14–15 and locate Wellington, New Zealand. Have students describe its location. Then have students tell what they notice about the place by looking at the photograph.

Possible Responses Location: Wellington is on a bay situated on the southern tip of the North Island. The bay feeds into Cook Strait, which connects the Tasman Sea with the Pacific Ocean. Place: The city lies on a bay, and mountains rise up on the city's limits. It is a modern city with many skyscrapers, a large marina, and neighborhoods built on the mountainsides.

Extension Have students research sites of interest to tourists visiting Wellington. Invite students to share their research with the class.

CRITICAL THINKING ACTIVITY

Making Inferences Prompt a discussion about human-environment interaction in Wellington, New Zealand, based on what can be inferred from the photograph. Urge students to draw on what they already know about city life, life near the ocean, and New Zealand. Have them consider such issues as construction, climate, pollution, traffic, wildlife, and vegetation.

Class Time 15 minutes

Australia, New Zealand, and the Pacific Islands

SECTION 1 History and Governments

SECTION 2 Economies and Cultures

Place Two islands make up New Zealand, whose capital, Wellington, encircles this harbor on North Island.

524

Recommended Resources

BOOKS FOR THE TEACHER
Denoon, Donald. *A History of Australia, New Zealand, and the Pacific.* Malden, MA: Blackwell Publishing, 2000. Comprehensive overview of the region.

Frost, Alan. *Voyage of the* Endeavour: *Captain Cook and the Discovery of the Pacific.* St. Leonards, NSW, Australia: Allen & Unwin, 1998. Early exploration.
Smith, Roff. *Australia: Journey Through a Timeless Land.* Washington, D.C.: National Geographic Society, 2000. From the outback to urban areas.

VIDEOS
Australia's Kangaroos. Washington, D.C.: National Geographic Society, 2000. Life cycle and habitat.
The Island Continent. Chicago, IL: Questar, 1999. Documentary.

INTERNET
For more information about Australia and the Pacific Islands, visit **classzone.com.**

How can people affect a region's environment?

FOCUS ON GEOGRAPHY

Human-Environment Interaction • When Europeans first came to Australia, New Zealand, and the Pacific Islands, the landscape had been largely unchanged for tens of thousands of years. In Australia and New Zealand, the settlers cleared the forests to provide land for farming and housing.

This human activity has had some unexpected consequences on the environment. In Australia, for example, more than 40 percent of the country's forests have been destroyed. Over-cultivation of this land has depleted the soil of valuable nutrients. Over-irrigation has resulted in too high a level of salt in the soil. As you can see above, very few plants are able to grow in salty soil.

What do you think?

♦ What do immigrants risk by changing an environment too quickly after settling in it?

♦ How might the people of Australia, New Zealand, and the Pacific Islands have benefited from the settlers balancing development with environmental concern?

525

FOCUS ON GEOGRAPHY

Objectives

- To identify how geography affected the settlement patterns of Australia and the Pacific Islands
- To explain the effects that settlement had on the environments of Australia and the Pacific Islands

What Do You Think?

1. Guide students to consider how decisions made quickly may result in problematic long-term effects.
2. Suggest that students consider the damage done to the environment by new settlers and how this damage might have been avoided.

How can people affect a region's environment?

Encourage students to think about changes settlers make to an environment on first arrival. What things do they need for survival? How does their use of resources affect the environment? How might their use of the land be positively or negatively impacted by the traditions they bring with them?

MAKING GEOGRAPHIC CONNECTIONS

Ask students to brainstorm a list of ways their community has changed in the last century. How has the population changed? How has the landscape been changed by humans? How have vegetation and wildlife been affected?

Implementing the National Geography Standards

Standard 2 Draw a world map from memory

Objective To sketch a world map without the aid of reference materials

Class Time 20 minutes

Task Each student draws a world map from memory, including country and region names.

When students complete their maps, have them use the Unit Atlas to check the accuracy of their maps. They should prepare a chart explaining why some countries are included and others are not. They should also use the chart to explain why some countries are too large and others are too small.

Evaluation The chart should list the reasons for at least five differences between the sketch map and the Unit Atlas map.

BEFORE YOU READ
What Do You Know?

Brainstorm with students a list of facts about Australia, New Zealand, and the Pacific Islands. To help them get started, ask: What animals are unique to Australia? What movies or television programs have you seen about this region? Have students look at the photograph of the Maori carving on this page and read the caption. Ask if they know anything else about the Maori and where they live.

What Do You Want to Know?

Remind students that most of the region they will be reading about is in the Southern Hemisphere. Have them make a list of things they would like to learn, and write each item on the chalkboard. Ask each student to review the list and write down in a notebook those items that interest him or her.

READ AND TAKE NOTES

Reading Strategy: Making Inferences Explain to students that they make inferences every day. Remind them that making inferences involves reading or listening to stated information, then using their own knowledge or past experiences to figure out what has not been stated. Encourage them to use the facts about Australia, New Zealand, and the Pacific Islands that they list in the chart and their prior knowledge or experiences about Hawaii to make inferences.

> **In-depth Resources: Unit 6**
> • Guided Reading Worksheets, pp. 27–28

BEFORE YOU READ
▶▶ **What Do You Know?**

Before you read the chapter, think about what you already know about Australia, New Zealand, and the Pacific Islands. What do you know about the history of these places? Have you read about the Aborigines or the Maori in other classes? Did you watch the 2000 Olympics when they were held in Australia? If you have been to this region, look back at your journal or photos and reflect on your experiences there.

▶▶ **What Do You Want to Know?**

Decide what else you want to know about this region. In your notebook, record what you hope to learn from this chapter.

Culture • Wood carvings like this are made by native people throughout New Zealand. ▲

READ AND TAKE NOTES

Reading Strategy: Making Inferences Making inferences means figuring out what a writer has suggested but not directly stated. It requires studying what is stated and using common sense and previous knowledge.

Use the chart below to gather facts about Australia, New Zealand, and the Pacific Islands. Then make inferences about Hawaii from them.

• Copy the chart in your notebook.
• As you read the chapter, record important facts about each place.
• After you read, review the facts and make inferences based on those facts.

Culture • Australian athlete Cathy Freeman lit the Olympic torch in the summer of 2000. ▲

	Place	Stated Facts	Inferences About Hawaii
Population	Australia	Aborigine, diverse	Southeast Asian influences
	New Zealand	Maori, European, Asian	
	Pacific Islands	Southeast Asian, European	
Government	Australia	commonwealth	United States
	New Zealand	commonwealth	
	Pacific Islands	self-rule, some ties to U.S., France	
Economy	Australia	farming, mining, tourism	tourism, agriculture
	New Zealand	farming, tourism	
	Pacific Islands	tourism, commercial agriculture	
Culture	Australia	Aboriginal art, diverse influences	strong traditions of other Pacific Islands
	New Zealand	Maori carvings	
	Pacific Islands	various traditons and art forms	

Teaching Strategy

Reading the Chapter This chapter describes the various waves of settlement of Australia, New Zealand, and the Pacific Islands. It also describes the governments and economies of the region. Encourage students to focus on the variety of cultures in the region and how the geography of the region affects the economies in different parts of the region.

Integrated Assessment The Chapter Assessment on page 539 describes several activities for integrated assessment. You may wish to have students work on these activities during the course of the chapter and then present them at the end.

History and Governments

TERMS & NAMES
Maori
Aborigine
Melanesia
Micronesia
Polynesia
Commonwealth of Nations

MAIN IDEA

The nations of this region were first settled by people from nearby and later colonized by European nations.

WHY IT MATTERS NOW

In many nations today, different groups struggle for their rights and for the opportunity to rule.

SECTION OBJECTIVES

1. To describe the history and first inhabitants of the region
2. To explain the European settlement of the region
3. To describe the governments of the region

SKILLBUILDER
• Interpreting a Map, p. 529

CRITICAL THINKING
• Drawing Conclusions, p. 528
• Contrasting, p. 530

FOCUS & MOTIVATE
WARM-UP

Drawing Conclusions Have students read <u>Dateline</u> and discuss the Maori citizens' situation.

1. Why do you think the Maori signed the treaty in 1840?
2. Why might the treaty have been unavailable to the public for so long?

INSTRUCT: Objective ❶

History of the Region

• Who were the original settlers of Australia? ancestors of the Aborigines
• Who were the original settlers of New Zealand? the Maori

 In-depth Resources: Unit 6
• Guided Reading Worksheet, p. 27

 Reading Study Guide (Spanish and English), pp. 164–165

DATELINE EXTRA

WAITANGI, NEW ZEALAND, 1940

One hundred years after it was signed, the Treaty of Waitangi can finally be seen by the public. On February 6, 1840, this historic treaty was signed by Lieutenant Governor William Hobson, several other Englishmen living in New Zealand, and about 45 Maori chiefs.

Long, heated arguments occurred between the English and the Maori chiefs about the treaty, which described how the British would rule New Zealand. The Maori chiefs were concerned that their people's rights would not be protected.

Many Maori today feel that the treaty has not been upheld and that their rights have not been protected. According to the treaty, lands, forests,

and fisheries owned by Maori would remain theirs. Today, however, Maori citizens own only 5 percent of New Zealand's land.

Culture • This painting shows William Hobson and a Maori chief signing the treaty in 1840. ▲

History of the Region ❶

Long before the British arrived in New Zealand, the country's first settlers—the **Maori** (MOW•ree)—lived there. In fact, people inhabited many of the islands in the Pacific and Indian oceans for thousands of years before any Europeans arrived. Today, we know this region as Australia, New Zealand, and the Pacific Islands.

Australia, New Zealand, and the Pacific Islands **527**

Program Resources

 In-depth Resources: Unit 6
• Guided Reading Worksheet, p. 27
• Reteaching Activity, p. 33

 Reading Study Guide (Spanish and English), pp. 164–165

 Formal Assessment
• Section Quiz, p. 272

Integrated Assessment
• Rubric for writing a dialogue

 Outline Map Activities

Access for Students Acquiring English
• Guided Reading Worksheet, p. 161

 Technology Resources classzone.com

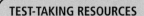
TEST-TAKING RESOURCES
↪ Strategies for Test Preparation
↪ Test Practice Transparencies
⊕ Online Test Practice

INSTRUCT: Objective 2

People of the Region

- What brought the Europeans to the Pacific in the 1500s? the search for spices
- Which nations established colonies in the Pacific Islands? Britain, France, Germany, Spain, United States, Japan
- How did European settlement affect the people of the region? brought smallpox and enslavement, Aborigines forced into interior of Australia, reduction of native populations

Spotlight on CULTURE

Many patterns in Maori carving come from mythology. A mythological character named Tangaroa, who was the guardian of the seas, invited a man to visit his home under the sea. The man was moved by the beautiful designs on Tangaroa's house and returned to land and began carving the same designs. The man also copied designs from the natural world around him.

In the past, carvings were done in whale bone and even human bone. Today, only bones from beached whales are used, but mostly, carvers use cow bones. The stone used is greenstone.

CRITICAL THINKING ACTIVITY

Drawing Conclusions Discuss with students how different languages and cultures developed as people settled islands farther west. Ask what might have contributed to the development. What characteristics of the different islands could have influenced the development of distinct cultures?

Class Time 15 minutes

Culture • This Aborigine artist displays one of the paintings on tree bark for which his people are famous. ▲

People of the Region 2

Australia's first inhabitants migrated there from Southeast Asia at least 40,000 years ago. Their descendants are called **Aborigines** (AB•uh•RIHJ•uh•neez). Settlers from Southeast Asia arrived in the Pacific Islands about 33,000 years ago. On the map on page 529, you can see the three regional groups of the Pacific— **Melanesia, Micronesia,** and **Polynesia.** Southeast Asians migrated first to Melanesia, then spread into Micronesia and finally Polynesia. About 1,000 years ago, Polynesians settled New Zealand. These settlers were the Maori.

Island Life Geography influenced which islands people settled. If an island had fresh water, wildlife, and vegetation, people settled there. If an island was too dry or too small, or lacked sources of food, it remained unpopulated.

Most of the early islanders fished or farmed. They also traded with nearby islanders. Because of the vast expanses of ocean, however, distinct languages and cultures developed over time.

Europeans in the Pacific In the 1500s, Europeans explored the Pacific for spices. In the 1600s and 1700s, missionaries and other settlers arrived. Some of them carried diseases, such as smallpox.

Spotlight on CULTURE

Maori Carvings The Maori have a long history of carving wood, stone, and bone. Many of the carvings are of human figures—either ancestors, gods, or characters from myths. Often, the carvings are found on items like canoes, weapons, and jewelry, though many also stand alone.

The most distinctive features of Maori carvings are the spiral patterns and seashells that decorate them, both of which you can see on the carvings shown here.

THINKING CRITICALLY

1. **Making Inferences** Think about the materials the Maori use in their carvings. How do you think these materials have helped to preserve their artwork?

2. **Hypothesizing** What do you think might be the inspiration for the spiral patterns that the Maori use on their carvings?

528 CHAPTER 18

Reading Social Studies

A. Using Maps
Look at the maps on pages 460 and 529. Why do you think Southeast Asians settled the islands in the order they did?

Reading Social Studies
A. Possible Answer
Since they traveled by boat they settled the nearer islands first.

Thinking Critically Possible Responses

1. Bone and stone do not decay easily. Wood and stone are continually available.

2. The Maori mimicked the spiral shapes of seashells, flowers, and other things in nature.

Activity Options

Differentiating Instruction: Less Proficient Readers

Categorizing To help students who are having difficulty reading and understanding this section, have them create a chart like the one shown. As they read the section, have them fill in the details about the three parts of the region.

	Australia	Melanesia/Micronesia/ Polynesia	New Zealand
Original settlers/dates			
European settlers/dates			
Reasons for settlement by Europeans			
Governments			

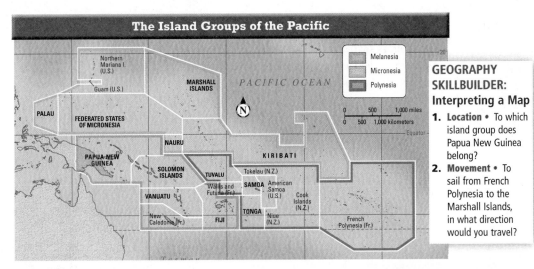

The Island Groups of the Pacific

Melanesia
Micronesia
Polynesia

GEOGRAPHY SKILLBUILDER: Interpreting a Map

1. **Location** • To which island group does Papua New Guinea belong?
2. **Movement** • To sail from French Polynesia to the Marshall Islands, in what direction would you travel?

FOCUS ON VISUALS

Interpreting the Map Have students use the map scale to determine the distance in miles between the Northern Mariana Islands and French Polynesia. Ask how much trade and cultural exchange they think could be carried on between these two locations.

Possible Responses The distance between the Marianas and French Polynesia is about 4,500 miles. This great distance probably made any kind of trade or cultural exchange difficult.

Extension Have students trace on an outline map the Pacific Islands and New Zealand. Have them draw lines on the map to show the paths of peoples as they moved from Southeast Asia, through the Pacific Islands, and finally to New Zealand.

Geography Skillbuilder Answers
1. Melanesia
2. northwest

Many of the native islanders died from these diseases. Some settlers also brought hardship upon the islanders by enslaving them.

Britain, France, Germany, Spain, the United States, and later Japan all established colonies in the Pacific. Since 1962, many islands have gained independence. Others are still colonies. For example, France governs New Caledonia, and the United States controls Guam.

Europeans in Australia and New Zealand In the 1700s, Great Britain sent many people to Australia. Some were convicts who labored on farms, and others were free colonists. By 1859, six British colonies made up Australia. In 1901, these colonies became states of the Commonwealth of Australia.

In the 1790s, New Zealand was settled by whale hunters and traders from Great Britain, the United States, and France, as well as European missionaries and colonists. In 1840, the Maori and the British signed the Treaty of Waitangi, which gave control of New Zealand to Britain. New Zealand did not become a self-governing country until 1907.

Mysterious Stone Statues Far out in the Pacific, along the slopes of Easter Island, stands a strange sight. Giant stone heads peer out across the landscape. Hundreds more lie knocked down all across the island.

The island's early inhabitants carved these statues (shown below), which weigh up to 90 tons, out of the side of a volcano. How they moved the statues many miles to their present locations, however, is a mystery that may never be solved.

Some of the giant stone statues of Easter Island are about 40 feet tall. The largest statue was never completed—its back is still attached to the stone of the quarry—but it stands about 68 feet tall.

Originally, the stone statues had topknots of red stone on their heads. The eye cavities of the statues were originally set with white coral shells and black stones. The statues always faced inland, in rows of up to a dozen.

Activity Options

Skillbuilder Mini-Lesson: Reading a Population Distribution Map

Explaining the Skill Remind students that they can use a population distribution map to determine the population density for different parts of a region. Review the features of a population distribution map, such as a color key that shows different densities or dots that represent numbers of people.

Applying the Skill In advance, make copies of a population distribution map of one or more countries in this region. Have students use the map to answer questions about population distribution and then make inferences based on this data.

INSTRUCT: Objective ❸

Governments

- What types of governments exist in this region? democracies, monarchies, rule by other countries
- How do Australia and New Zealand maintain their ties to Great Britain? by belonging to the Commonwealth of Nations and by having the British monarch as their ceremonial head of state

CRITICAL THINKING ACTIVITY

Contrasting Prompt a discussion with students about the United States and how it was once a British colony. Ask why the United States is not a part of the Commonwealth of Nations.

Class Time 10 minutes

ASSESS & RETEACH

Have students add details about population and government to the chart on page 526.

 Formal Assessment
- Section Quiz, p. 272

RETEACHING ACTIVITY

Have students work in small groups to create a quiz for this section. Groups should write two questions for the text under each heading. Have groups exchange questions and answer them.

 In-depth Resources: Unit 6
- Reteaching Activity, p. 33

 Access for Students Acquiring English
- Reteaching Activity, p. 165

Reading Social Studies
B. Possible Answers
Many died of disease brought by Europeans. Also, they were pushed into the less-hospitable interior and their numbers dwindled.

Impact of European Settlement When Europeans first came to Australia, as many as 750,000 Aborigines populated the continent. As more settlers arrived, Aborigines were forced into the country's interior. Today, only 1 percent of Australia's population is of Aborigine descent. Similarly, in New Zealand, only about 14 percent of the population today is of Maori descent.

Governments ❸

The governments of Australia, New Zealand, and the Pacific Island nations are quite varied. Some are democracies, some are monarchies, and some are ruled by other nations. Many countries have governments that resemble those of the nations that colonized them.

Australia and New Zealand Australia and New Zealand belong to the **Commonwealth of Nations.** This is a group of countries that were once British colonies and share a heritage of British law and government. Great Britain's monarch is their head of state but has no real power.

The Pacific Islands A few Pacific Islands still have official ties to various countries. For example, the United States is responsible for the defense of the Federated States of Micronesia, while the French Polynesians vote in French elections. Other islands rule themselves, such as Tonga, which is a constitutional monarchy.

Reading
Social Studies

B. Drawing Conclusions What factors could explain why Aborigines are now such a small minority in Australia?

Region • This photo shows a selection of flags from the Pacific Islands. ▼

SECTION ❶ ASSESSMENT

Terms & Names

1. **Identify:**
   (a) Maori
   (b) Aborigine
   (c) Melanesia
   (d) Micronesia
   (e) Polynesia
   (f) Commonwealth of Nations

Taking Notes

2. Use a chart like this one to list and compare important details of the history of Australia, New Zealand, and the Pacific Islands.

	Australia	New Zealand	Pacific Islands
Early Inhabitants			
European Settlement			
Government Today			

Main Ideas

3. (a) Where did the earliest settlers of Australia and the Pacific Islands come from?

   (b) List three reasons Europeans traveled to the region's islands.

   (c) What do the governments of Australia and New Zealand have in common?

Critical Thinking

4. **Summarizing**

   How did geography affect the region's settlement patterns?

   Think About
   - which islands the original settlers inhabited
   - how the arrival of Europeans affected native populations

ACTIVITY -OPTION- Imagine that you were a Maori inhabitant of New Zealand. Write a **dialogue** between you and one of the European settlers.

Section ❶ Assessment

1. Terms & Names
   a. Maori, p. 527
   b. Aborigine, p. 528
   c. Melanesia, p. 528
   d. Micronesia, p. 528
   e. Polynesia, p. 528
   f. Commonwealth of Nations, p. 530

2. Taking Notes

	Australia	New Zealand	Pacific Islands
Early Inhabitants	Aborigines	Maori	people from Southeast Asia
European Settlement	convicts, free colonists	whale hunters, traders, missionaries, colonists	missionaries, explorers
Government Today	British influence in law and government	British influence in law and government	official ties to other countries; self-rule (constitutional monarchy)

3. Main Ideas
   a. Southeast Asia
   b. trade, colonization, and missionary work
   c. belong to Commonwealth of Nations; British monarch is ceremonial head of state

4. Critical Thinking

Settlers chose islands with plentiful resources; European settlers pushed native inhabitants inland.

ACTIVITY OPTION

 Integrated Assessment
- Rubric for writing a dialogue

SECTION 2

Economies and Cultures

TERMS & NAMES

copra
matrilineal society
patrilineal society

MAIN IDEA

There is great diversity among the economies and cultures of the nations of the Pacific.

WHY IT MATTERS NOW

Modern communication and transportation have brought this once isolated region into closer contact with the rest of the world.

DATELINE

SYDNEY, AUSTRALIA, SEPTEMBER 15, 2000—
The cheers of more than 110,000 fans echoed through the new Olympic stadium. Athletes from all over the world marched into the stadium for the grand opening of the 2000 Summer Olympic Games. Around the world, an audience estimated to be in the billions watched the ceremonies broadcast on television.

The musical pageant of the opening ceremonies told the story of Australia. It began with the Aborigines' creation myths and continued through the establishment of the great coastal cities. The climax of the event occurred when Aborigine athlete Cathy Freeman carried the Olympic torch through the stadium and lit the cauldron of the Olympic flame.

Culture • Cathy Freeman won a silver medal in 1996 and hopes to win gold in the Sydney Olympics. ▲

Resources and Economies ❶

The economies of Australia, New Zealand, and the Pacific Islands have various foundations. On the one hand, tourists travel to the region to enjoy its beaches, mountains, fjords, and unusual plant and animal life. Thousands also came to Australia for the 2000 Summer Olympic Games. On the other hand, agriculture is the traditional base of the region's economies. Australia and New Zealand still depend more on farming than do most other developed countries.

Australia, New Zealand, and the Pacific Islands **531**

SECTION OBJECTIVES

1. To describe the economies of Australia, New Zealand, and the Pacific Islands

2. To explain how modernization has affected the cultures of the region

SKILLBUILDER
• Interpreting a Map, p. 532

CRITICAL THINKING
• Synthesizing, p. 533

FOCUS & MOTIVATE
WARM-UP

Making Inferences After students read <u>Dateline</u>, discuss the economic and cultural significance of Australia's Olympics.

1. Why do you think the officials chose an Aborigine athlete to light the torch?

2. How do you think the people who came for the Olympics helped the economy?

INSTRUCT: Objective ❶

Resources and Economies

• What are the main elements of Australia's economy? service industries, mining, farming

• Who are Australia's main trading partners? Japan, United States

 In-depth Resources: Unit 6
• Guided Reading Worksheet, p. 28

 Reading Study Guide
(Spanish and English), pp. 166–167

Program Resources

 In-depth Resources: Unit 6
• Guided Reading Worksheet, p. 28
• Reteaching Activity, p. 34

 Reading Study Guide
(Spanish and English), pp. 166–167

 Formal Assessment
• Section Quiz, p. 273

 Integrated Assessment
• Rubric for making a slogan

Outline Map Activities

 Access for Students Acquiring English
• Guided Reading Worksheet, p. 162

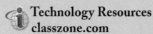 **Technology Resources**
classzone.com

TEST-TAKING RESOURCES
↪ Strategies for Test Preparation
↪ Test Practice Transparencies
🖥 Online Test Practice

Connections to

Technology

Tuvalu is made up of a group of nine coral atolls. Its total land area is only 26 square kilometers, about one-tenth the size of Washington, D.C. It has no natural source of fresh water—rainwater must be caught and stored. Tuvalu's main industries are fishing, tourism, and copra.

Because of its lack of resources, Tuvalu depends heavily on its income from the sale of its technology sources.

FOCUS ON VISUALS

Interpreting the Map Have students examine the variety of products shown on the map. Be sure students notice the difference between the symbols for zinc and bauxite. Ask them to identify the two main types of economic activity represented. Then ask where most cattle ranches are located.

Possible Responses Ranching and mining are the main types of economic activity represented. Most cattle ranches are located in the north central area.

Extension Explain to students that neither cattle nor sheep are native to Australia. Have students research when these animals were originally introduced and by whom. Students might also research what positive and/or negative effects cattle and sheep ranching have had on the Australian environment.

Connections to
Technology

TV in Tuvalu The Polynesian island nation Tuvalu (TOO·vuh·LOO) has poor soil and few natural resources. Its most valuable possession may be its Web address: ".tv." Television organizations hoped to use those letters in their own Web addresses.

In 1998, Tuvalu sold the rights for ".tv" to a Canadian company. The government has since used the money from the sale to make life better for the people of Tuvalu.

Pacific Island Economies Most Pacific Islanders fish, grow their own food, and build their own homes. However, some commercial agriculture does exist on the islands. **Copra** (KOH·pruh)—dried coconut meat—and coconut oil are important agricultural exports. Tourism also contributes significantly to the economies of some Pacific Islands, such as Tahiti.

Australia's Economy Australia has a strong market economy and relatively free trade with other nations, especially Japan. Service industries—including health care, tourism, news media, and transportation—provide nearly three-fourths of the country's jobs.

Australia's strong economy also depends on mining and farming. Australia is the world's leading producer of bauxite, lead, and zinc. It has also developed vast fields of natural gas. Wheat is Australia's most important cash crop, and about 80 percent of the harvest is exported. Sugar cane is also an important cash crop.

Trade During colonial times, Australia and New Zealand mostly traded with Great Britain. Today, Australia's main trading partners are Japan and the United States, while New Zealand's main trading partner is Australia.

Reading Social Studies
A. Possible Answer Factors might include: greater variety and supply of resources, more land for farms and ranches, better educated work force.

Reading Social Studies
A. Synthesizing List some factors that might have allowed Australia to have a stronger economy than the Pacific Islands have.

Geography Skillbuilder Answers
1. in the north central region
2. zinc, bauxite, lead, natural gas

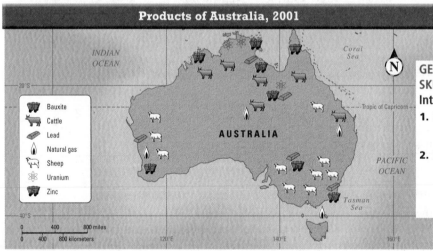

Products of Australia, 2001

Legend: Bauxite, Cattle, Lead, Natural gas, Sheep, Uranium, Zinc

GEOGRAPHY SKILLBUILDER: Interpreting a Map
1. **Location** • Where is most of the uranium in Australia found?
2. **Region** • Locate the sheep-ranching areas. What other products come from these areas?

Activity Options
Interdisciplinary Links: Language Arts/Art

Class Time One class period
Task Writing a report on Tahiti
Purpose To learn more about the geography and history of Tahiti

Supplies Needed
• Books or other reference materials related to Tahiti
• Pens or pencils
• Paper

Activity Tell students that Tahiti is known worldwide as a tropical paradise. It has captured the imagination of many artists and writers. Have students use reference materials to write a brief report in which they describe Tahiti and its attraction to artists and writers. Encourage them to illustrate their reports and/or include famous quotes about the island.

Asian countries are also playing a bigger role in New Zealand's economy. In 1983, Australia and New Zealand signed a free-trade agreement to boost the trade between them.

Reading Social Studies
B. Answer
The use of modern communication devices, electronic items, and so on could make life easier for the people.

B. Hypothesizing What else about Pacific Island life could modernization affect?

Cultures and Change ❷

Despite their remote locations, the islands of the region have attracted immigrants from around the world. Modernization and tradition both play strong roles in the region.

The Pacific Islands Modernization has affected life in some of the Pacific Islands. For example, modernization has clearly changed modes of transportation. For short trips, villagers take canoes just as they always have. However, for longer trips, they outfit canoes with modern outboard motors or travel by ship or airplane.

Tradition continues to be strong, especially in art forms and family structures. For example, matrilineal societies are less common than patrilineal societies, but they are still found in parts of the Pacific Islands, such as Papua New Guinea. In **matrilineal societies,** ancestry is traced through the mother's side of the family. In **patrilineal societies,** ancestry is traced through the father's side.

Place •
In Papua New Guinea, people still perform traditional dances. ▼

Charlie Perkins Charlie Perkins (shown above, center) grew up in Australia's outback near Alice Springs. Perkins was the first Aborigine in Australia to graduate from college. He also played professional soccer in England. However, he is best known for his struggle against discrimination.

In 1965, Perkins led "freedom rides" throughout Australia to teach people about equal rights for Aborigines. On these rides, he met with clubs and organizations to discuss discrimination. He also led activities such as taking Aborigine children swimming in pools where only white children were allowed to swim.

Perkins has been compared to Martin Luther King, Jr. When Perkins died in October 2000, Australia's prime minister said, "Charlie was a tireless fighter for the cause of his people."

Australia, New Zealand, and the Pacific Islands **533**

INSTRUCT: Objective ❷

Cultures and Change

• How do both modernization and tradition affect life in the Pacific Islands? modernization: modes of transportation; tradition: strong family structures, art forms

Biography

Charlie Perkins's work inspired an entire generation of Aborigine activists. His efforts helped gain citizenship for Aborigines, something that had been denied until the 1960s. According to his friend, advertising executive John Singleton, "If it hadn't been for the Charlie Perkins era, there wouldn't have been Cathy Freeman. . . . There wouldn't have been the opening ceremony of the Olympics." Perkins was one of the first people to take risks that made equal rights for Aborigines possible.

CRITICAL THINKING ACTIVITY

Synthesizing Have students reread <u>Dateline</u> on page 531 and the "Biography" feature on this page, and look at "A Voice From Australia" on page 534. Then discuss the following questions:

• Do you think Australia's diverse peoples live peacefully together? Why or why not?

• What did Cathy Freeman's appearance at the 2000 Olympics represent for Australia's Aborigine groups?

Class Time 15 minutes

Activity Options

Multiple Learning Styles: Visual/Logical/Mathematical　　　🅱 Block Scheduling

Class Time One class period

Task Creating a pie graph that shows the ethnic backgrounds of the people of New Zealand

Purpose To learn about the ethnic diversity of New Zealand

Supplies Needed
• Statistical information about the population of New Zealand
• Paper and pencils or markers

Activity Have students locate a pie graph in their math books and review the features of these graphs. Have students research statistical information about the ethnic backgrounds of the people of New Zealand. Then have them create a pie graph showing the percentage of the total population that each ethnic group represents. Suggest that students use a different color to indicate each ethnic group and label each section.

Teacher's Edition **533**

Immigrants to Australia

Immigrants have come to Australia in recognizable groups:

- 1788: first convicts arrived
- early 1800s: to encourage settlement, Britain gave immigrants free passage
- 1850: with the discovery of gold, immigrants came from Britain, China, and the United States
- 1850s: Irish came escaping the famine
- after WWII: displaced people came from Britain, Holland, Germany, and Italy
- 1960s: with growth of industry, unskilled labor came from Britain, Ireland, Italy, Greece, and Turkey
- since 1945: war refugees

A VOICE FROM AUSTRALIA

Have students read and discuss the quote. Ask them to describe Brewster's impression of Australia's diversity and to support their ideas with details from the quote. Ask if Brewster would make a similar comment about the United States.

ASSESS & RETEACH

Reading Social Studies Have students complete the chart on page 526.

 Formal Assessment
- Section Quiz, p. 273

RETEACHING ACTIVITY

Have pairs of students create a chart to summarize details about the economies and cultures of Australia, New Zealand, and the Pacific Islands.

 In-depth Resources: Unit 6
- Reteaching Activity, p. 34

 Access for Students Acquiring English
- Reteaching Activity, p. 166

Australia and New Zealand Australia has a diverse population. For example, people worship in mosques, churches, synagogues, and Buddhist temples. In the past 50 years, immigrants have come from many parts of the world, such as Cambodia, Laos, and Vietnam. Some of them came from places where there was war or other danger. In a memoir, writer Barbara Marie Brewster described her pleasant surprise at Australia's diversity.

> **A VOICE FROM AUSTRALIA**
>
> As we drove home, I was struck by the extraordinary mixture Australia represented. Here were two Americans, a German, a Hungarian, and a Malay girl from Brunei, and we'd been talking with an Englishman who was a Buddhist monk in a monastery in Australia, founded and funded by Thais and run by an Italian abbot. I liked it.
>
> **Barbara Marie Brewster**

In New Zealand, over half a million people are Maori. Most others are descendants of Scottish, English, Irish, and Welsh settlers. Many Asians also live in the cities, such as the capital, Wellington, and the largest city, Auckland.

SECTION 2 ASSESSMENT

Terms & Names
1. **Identify:** (a) copra (b) matrilineal society (c) patrilineal society

Taking Notes
2. Use a diagram like this one to organize the important economic activities of Australia, New Zealand, and the Pacific Islands.

Economic Activities		
Australia	New Zealand	Pacific Islands

Main Ideas
3. (a) How do the economies of the Pacific Islands and Australia benefit from the region's physical geography?
(b) How do Australia and New Zealand cooperate economically?
(c) What is the relationship between modernization and tradition in the Pacific Islands?

Critical Thinking
4. **Drawing Conclusions**
In what ways do you think Australia's ethnic diversity affects its culture and politics?

Think About
- the various ethnic groups in Australia and how long each has lived there
- how different ethnic groups contribute to diversity in other countries

 Make up an **advertising slogan** to promote tourism in Australia, the Pacific Islands, or New Zealand.

Section 2 Assessment

1. Terms & Names
a. copra, p. 532
b. matrilineal society, p. 533
c. patrilineal society, p. 533

2. Taking Notes

Economic Activities		
Australia	New Zealand	Pacific Islands
Service industries	Agriculture	Tourism
Mining		Agriculture
Agriculture		Fishing

3. Main Ideas
a. They rely on fishing, agriculture, and available minerals.
b. They have signed a free-trade agreement to increase trade between them.
c. Traditional practices can sometimes be altered by modernization, like placing a motor on a canoe.

4. Critical Thinking
Students may say that ethnic diversity promotes cultural understanding but can also cause political and social conflicts.

ACTIVITY OPTION
 Integrated Assessment
- Rubric for making a slogan

Using Primary Sources

▶▶ Defining the Skill

Primary sources are materials written by people who lived during historical events. They include letters, diaries, articles, videotapes, speeches, eyewitness accounts, and photographs. Secondary sources, such as social studies books, are materials designed to discuss or teach about an event. When you research a topic, look for useful primary sources. Include these in your writing if you want to illustrate or prove an important point.

▶▶ Applying the Skill

The passage to the right is an example of an essay about Captain James Cook's first voyage to the Pacific. Use the strategies listed below to help you determine when and how to use a primary source in your own writing.

How to Use Primary Sources

Strategy ❶ Choose a primary source that gives key information about your subject. Be sure that the material is from a primary source and not a secondary source.

Strategy ❷ Analyze the primary source and consider what the document was supposed to achieve and who would read it. Ask yourself how the primary source can help prove your point.

Strategy ❸ Quote the primary source exactly as it is written. Some primary sources, such as this letter, will have different language, spelling, capitalization, and punctuation than modern sources.

Make a Chart

Making a chart will help you determine when and how to use a primary source. The chart to the right explains the use of the primary source in the passage (above, right).

▶▶ Practicing the Skill

Turn to page 534 in Chapter 18, Section 2. Read the quotation from a primary source found there. Make a chart like the one above to determine how and why the primary source was used.

Captain James Cook made three trips from England to the South Pacific. The seeming purpose of his first trip in 1768 was to observe the movements of the planet Venus. ❶ As this letter from the king clearly shows, however, Britain's true purpose was to find and claim the southern continent:

❸ Whereas the making Discoverys of Countries hitherto unknown, and the Attaining a Knowledge of distant Parts ... will redound greatly to the Honour of this Nation as a Maritime Power, as well as to the Dignity of the Crown of Great Britain, and may tend greatly to the advancement of the Trade and Navigation thereof; ... You are therefore in Pursuance of His Majesty's Pleasure hereby requir'd and directed to put to Sea with the Bark you Command so soon as the Observation of the Transit of the Planet Venus shall be finished ....

Subject	Primary Source	Reason for Quoting the Primary Source
Captain Cook's first voyage to the South Pacific in 1768	The secret instructions given to Captain Cook	To prove that the true purpose of the voyage was different from the stated purpose

---

Determining When and How to Use Primary Sources

Defining the Skill

Ask students to tell which they would find more interesting and informative: an eye-witness report of an event in history, or an encyclopedia article about the topic. Explain that students might use primary sources to add validity to campaign speeches or in letters to the editor to reinforce an idea.

Applying the Skill

How to Use Primary Sources Have students read the first strategy and discuss where they could find a primary source about a subject. Have them read and consider the remaining strategies. Emphasize the importance of choosing a primary source that is appropriate to the purpose and that adds information or interest.

Make a Chart

Review the elements included in the chart. Ask the following questions: What is the subject of the essay? What primary source is used? Why did the writer include this primary source? Encourage students to note how the use of the primary source has enhanced the essay.

Practicing the Skill

Evaluate students' charts for the primary source on page 534. If students need additional practice, provide an article that includes quotes or other primary sources. Help them identify the subject, primary source, and reasons for including it.

 In-depth Resources: Unit 6
• Skillbuilder Practice, p. 31

Career Connection: Historian

Encourage students who enjoy determining when and how to use primary sources to find out about careers that employ this skill. For example, a historian is a professional who researches and analyzes the past. Historians usually specialize by studying a particular time period, a certain region or country, or a certain kind of history, such as political history. All historians use primary sources.

 Block Scheduling

1. Suggest that students find out about the kinds of primary sources historians use.

2. Help students learn what aptitudes and training a person should have in order to become a historian.

3. Invite students to share their findings on a "historian's panel."

1910 1920 1930 1940 1950 1960 1970   1700 1710 1720 1730 1740 1750 1760
1800 1810 1820 1830 1840 1850 1860
1890 1900 1910 1920 1930 1940 1950
1980 1990 2000

OBJECTIVE

Students learn about several inventions, creations, and contributions of East Asia, Australia, and the Pacific Islands and how they are used today.

FOCUS & MOTIVATE

Making Inferences Ask students to study the pictures and read each paragraph. Then have them answer the following questions:

1. What do images in Australian rock art have in common with images used in Japanese origami?

2. How have knowledge of martial arts and making boomerangs been passed through the years?

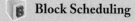 **Block Scheduling**

MORE ABOUT...
Soybeans

The ancient Chinese considered soybeans their most important crop. Today soybeans play a huge role in American life as well. Soybeans are used in making candy, ice cream, baking products, baby foods, cereals, and processed meats. They are also used to manufacture chemicals, cosmetics, and textiles. Soybean oil goes into candles, soaps and disinfectants, while soybean meal helps make fertilizers, fire extinguisher fluid, insect sprays, and paint.

MORE ABOUT...
Martial Arts

The most popular styles of Chinese martial arts are the Shaolin and t'ai chi chuan styles. Shaolin is made up of straight-line attacks and retreats, emphasizing strength and speed. T'ai chi chuan uses circular motions and intricate foot patterns and emphasizes gentle force and inner harmony.

The Legacy of East Asia, Australia, and the Pacific Islands

Australian Rock Art

There are thousands of sites in Australia where rocks are engraved and painted with silhouettes of humans and animals. Many of these rock-art sites have existed for almost 10,000 years. Every year, visitors tour these sites and learn about the early people of Australia.

Soybeans

Although the origin of the soybean plant is unknown, soybeans were being grown in China around 1200 B.C. They were introduced into the United States in 1804 and today are used as a vegetable and as a source of soymilk and tofu.

Martial Arts

Martial arts are forms of self-defense, many of them weaponless. In ancient times, people developed martial arts in China, India, and Tibet in the belief that they allowed peaceful energy, called *chi,* to flow through one's body. Today, people around the world practice martial arts for self-defense, sport, exercise, and spiritual development and as a means of reducing stress and lowering blood pressure.

536 UNIT 6

Activity Options
Interdisciplinary Link: Art

Class Time 60 minutes

Task Using an art activity to explore the ideas behind images used in Australian rock art

Supplies Needed
• Encyclopedia, art books, or other materials showing examples of Australian rock art
• Drawing paper

Activity Ask students to study the images used in Australian rock art. Point out that early Australians drew animals, people, and places that were important in their lives. Ask students to imagine they are decorating a rock art site today.

Have them identify three or four people, places, or animals important in their lives today, and draw these in a rock art style. When they finish, have them present their work to the class.

Find Out More About It!
Study the text and photos on these pages to learn about inventions, creations, and contributions that have come from East Asia, Australia, and the Pacific Islands. Then choose the item that interests you the most and do research in the library or on the Internet to learn more about it. Use the information you gather to write an article for your school or local newspaper that tells more about the contribution.

RESEARCH LINKS
CLASSZONE.COM

Origami

Origami, the art of folding paper into artistic objects, most likely originated from *gohei,* the art of folding cloth offerings in the Shinto religion of Japan. In origami, paper is folded to create figures of birds, animals, flowers, and people. Some origami figures actually have moving parts. Hundreds of books and courses on origami are available throughout the world.

Boomerangs

A boomerang is a curved, flat stick that is thrown either as a weapon or as a toy. Although boomerangs have been found in many parts of the world, they are most often associated with Australia and its native people, the Aborigines. Most Aboriginal boomerangs were "nonreturning"—that is, they did not return after they were thrown. A correctly thrown returning boomerang, on the other hand, will fly out, loop around, and return to the person who threw it. Returning boomerangs are used mainly for sport and as children's toys.

East Asia, Australia, and the Pacific Islands **537**

INSTRUCT

- How old are many of the Australian rock art sites?
- What figures are created by origami?
- Where did martial arts develop in ancient times?

MORE ABOUT...
Origami

While origami, like paper, originated in China, the art of paper folding has flourished in Japan. There are about 100 traditional origami figures, mostly natural forms such as birds, flowers, and fish. An abstract ceremonial form, called a *noshi,* is a pleated paper ornament attached to gifts. Most origami is folded from an uncut square of paper, most commonly six to ten inches square. The preferred paper is thin Japanese paper called washi, but foil-backed wrapping paper and heavy art paper are also used.

MORE ABOUT...
Boomerangs

Nonreturning boomerangs have played an important part in the Aborigine culture for many centuries. Because a spinning boomerang can hit a target with more force than a thrown rock, nonreturning boomerangs are useful weapons for hunting and fighting. A well-thrown nonreturning boomerang can travel about 650 feet.

Aborigines also use them as tools for skinning animals and digging holes, and as trading objects. Some Aborigines decorate boomerangs with carved or painted designs related to legends and traditions. These decorated boomerangs are treated with respect and used in religious ceremonies. The Aborigines also clap boomerangs together to provide rhythm for songs and chants.

More to Think About

Making Personal Connections Ask students to think about ways in which decorative and martial arts from East Asia and Australia have become part of American visual culture. Encourage them to think about movies, art exhibits, photography, and even advertisements. Ask students to bring to class one example of this influence from a magazine or newspaper.

Vocabulary Activity Remind students that *boomerang* is from a native Australian language. Have students work in groups, using a dictionary, to find the meanings of these other Australian native words: *billabong, dingo, kangaroo, budgerigar, koala, kookaburra, waddy,* and *wallaby.* Then have groups write a paragraph using at least five of these words correctly. Tell them the paragraph should be written so that the meaning of each word can be determined by its context. Have each group read its paragraph aloud, and discuss its meaning as a class.

TERMS & NAMES

1. Maori, p. 527
2. Aborigine, p. 528
3. Melanesia, p. 528
4. Micronesia, p. 528
5. Polynesia, p. 528
6. Commonwealth of Nations, p. 530
7. copra, p. 532
8. matrilineal society, p. 533
9. patrilineal society, p. 533

REVIEW QUESTIONS

Possible Responses

1. Australia was populated first.
2. Distinct languages and cultures developed.
3. With the European settlers came disease and a system of slavery.
4. They represent a small part of the population.
5. Two crops beneficial to the economy are copra and coconut oil.
6. Service industries provide the majority of jobs.
7. There are more patrilineal societies.
8. People use motorboats and airplanes for long-distance travel over water rather than traditional canoes, which are now used for short trips.

CHAPTER 18 ASSESSMENT

TERMS & NAMES

Explain the significance of each of the following:

1. Maori
2. Aborigine
3. Melanesia
4. Micronesia
5. Polynesia
6. Commonwealth of Nations
7. copra
8. matrilineal society
9. patrilineal society

REVIEW QUESTIONS

History and Governments *(pages 527–530)*

1. Which was populated first—Australia, New Zealand, or the Pacific Islands?
2. How did the isolation of the Pacific Islands from each other affect the languages and cultures that developed there?
3. Name two ways in which European settlers brought hardship to the Pacific Islands.
4. Do Aborigines and Maori represent large or small parts of their countries' populations?

Economies and Cultures *(pages 531–534)*

5. Name two crops that are beneficial to the economies of the Pacific Islands.
6. What type of industry provides the majority of jobs in Australia?
7. Which are there more of, matrilineal or patrilineal societies?
8. How has modern life transformed transportation in the Pacific Islands?

CRITICAL THINKING

Analyzing Motives

1. Using your completed chart from Reading Social Studies, p. 526, explain why you think Australia continues to attract immigrants from such a variety of cultures.

Drawing Conclusions

2. Why might the British have sent convicts to Australia to do labor?

Making Inferences

3. Why do you think Great Britain is no longer the main trading partner of Australia and New Zealand?

Visual Summary

History and Governments

1

- People from Southeast Asia settled Australia, New Zealand, and the Pacific Islands long before any Europeans arrived.
- Geographically isolated, these islands developed their own unique cultures.
- Europeans, Americans, and Japanese later colonized the region. The region now has many different forms of government.

Economies and Cultures

2

- Australia's economy is more developed than those of the Pacific Islands because it is richer in resources.
- Most Pacific Islands are self-sufficient, and traditional customs are practiced in some areas.
- The diverse populations of Australia and New Zealand are descended from early settlers, colonists, and immigrants.

538 CHAPTER 18

CRITICAL THINKING: Possible Responses

1. Analyzing Motives
From their completed charts, students may infer that Australia is a free society with a healthy economy and a diverse culture.

2. Drawing Conclusions
The British may have wanted to remove the convicts from their country and use them as laborers to help build the colony.

3. Making Inferences
Australia and New Zealand have both developed their own economies; they are located in the same region of the world; they are no longer colonies of Great Britain.

SOCIAL STUDIES SKILLBUILDER

Read the following quote by an Australian Aborigine who speaks only a little English. Then answer the questions that follow.

"First [white] people come to us, they started to run our life... quick.... First they should ask about fish, cave, Dreaming, but... they rush in. They make school... teach. Now Aborigine losing... everything."

SKILLBUILDER: Using Primary Sources

1. How could you use this primary source in an essay about the effect of European settlement on Australia's Aborigines?
2. Why might you include this primary source instead of a secondary source that summarizes the same facts and ideas?
3. What would you want your readers to think or feel as they read the quote?

FOCUS ON GEOGRAPHY

1. **Region** • Human activities can cause desertification. Why is such a vast region of Australia not at risk for this?
2. **Human-Environment Interaction** • Is there a lot of or a little land in Australia at low risk of desertification?
3. **Location** • Locate the regions of high or very high risk. Why might these regions be particularly at risk?

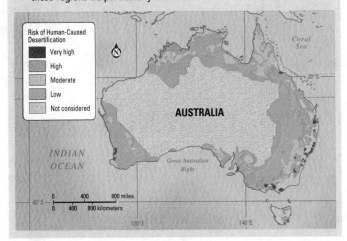

Risk of Human-Caused Desertification
- Very high
- High
- Moderate
- Low
- Not considered

AUSTRALIA
INDIAN OCEAN
Coral Sea
Great Australian Bight
20°S
40°S
120°E 140°E
0   400   800 miles
0   400   800 kilometers

CHAPTER PROJECTS

Interdisciplinary Activity: Ecology

Writing a Report The first Maori to arrive in New Zealand found an uninhabited land, with plants and animals they had never before encountered. Research these plants and animals, such as the moa. Then find out how the Maori changed the land. What new things did they bring? What animal faced extinction after their arrival? Write a report on your findings. Share your report with the class.

Cooperative Learning Activity

Creating an Illustrated Map The first settlers of Australia and the Pacific Islands came from Southeast Asia. In a group of three to five classmates, create an illustrated map with arrows showing the paths of migration. List the approximate dates of each migration. Illustrate the map with pictures or drawings of the people and items from their cultures. Divide the tasks of research, drawing, and writing among members of the group, assigning one or two members to each task.

 INTERNET ACTIVITY

Use the Internet to research Australia's Ayers Rock, which the Aborigines call Uluru. Focus on the appearance of the rock and its composition, and explain why it is so unusual.

Writing About Geography Write a report of your findings. If possible, include pictures of Ayers Rock. List the Web sites you used to prepare your report.

For Internet links to support this activity, go to

 **RESEARCH LINKS**
CLASSZONE.COM

CHAPTER PROJECTS
Interdisciplinary Activity: Ecology

Writing a Report Help students find print and Internet resources for their reports. Suggest that they use a chart or an outline to organize their notes. Reports should list specific plants and animals native to New Zealand as well as ones brought by the Maori, and clearly show how the Maori changed the environment of New Zealand.

Cooperative Learning Activity

Creating an Illustrated Map Students' maps should be accurate representations of the coasts of Southeast Asia, the Pacific Islands, Australia, and New Zealand. Students should use arrows to show the dispersion of people throughout the Pacific Islands and Australia. Dates of movement should be indicated. Encourage students to include illustrations of plants, animals, or other artifacts brought by various groups.

 INTERNET ACTIVITY

Reports on Ayers Rock should begin with a main-idea statement identifying specific elements about the rock and give details about the appearance and composition of the rock. Encourage students to give specific details about why the rock is unusual.

Skills Answers

Social Studies Skillbuilder
Possible Responses

1. It could be used to show the frustration of the Aborigines over the disregard for their values and loss of their culture.
2. It is more dramatic and evokes an emotional response.
3. Readers should recognize how upset the Aborigines were about white settlement and how harmful settlement was to the people and their culture.

Focus on Geography
Possible Responses

1. The region is already a desert and is not being farmed.
2. Little land is at low risk of desertification, since most land is desert or at high risk.
3. These regions are most likely where the highest intensity of farming occurs.

The War on Terrorism

 Reporter's Notes
By Kevin McCoy

NEW YORK—First came a deep rumble. Then a roar like a giant speeding train. But the sound came crashing from the sky, not along steel tracks. In an instant, a warm, sunny September morning at the World Trade Center in Lower Manhattan became a darkened moonscape of choking cement dust and swirling paper, wailing sirens and screaming victims.

"I heard the rumbling and I looked up, and one of the towers was coming down," said Sergeant Moises Cruz, a New York City police officer who ran for his life with other survivors of the most horrible terrorist attack in U.S. history. Lower Broadway, normally a bustling checkerboard of financial traders, government officials, businessmen and tourists, lay silenced under a three-inch carpet of gritty gray dust.

"I can't even describe it, it was so awful," said Wilbert, a 50-year-old elevator maintenance worker. "All I could do was run."

News reporters who covered the attacks knew instinctively this was the most significant story of a lifetime.

The twin towers of the World Trade Center in New York City, before (inset) and after the terrorist attacks of September 11, 2001

The Attack on America

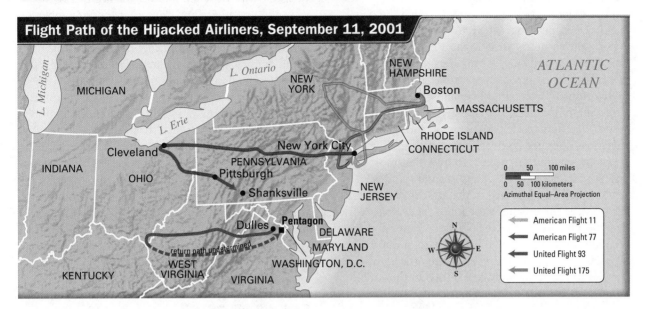

Flight Path of the Hijacked Airliners, September 11, 2001

American Flight 11
American Flight 77
United Flight 93
United Flight 175

McCoy's reporter's instincts were right. Before the day was over, there would be more than 3,000 victims of the most destructive act of terrorism in modern history. **Terrorism** is the calculated use of, or threatened use of, violence against individuals or property for the purpose of intimidating or causing fear for political or social ends.

The terrorist attacks on September 11 were aimed at well-known symbols of the economic and military power of the United States. But what they mainly destroyed was something Americans value much more—the lives of thousands of individual citizens.

UNIMAGINABLE HORROR

On the morning of September 11, 2001, many New Yorkers were heading for work or school when 19 Arab terrorists hijacked four airliners from East Coast airports. The first plane crashed into the upper floors of the north tower of the World Trade Center and exploded into flames. About 20 minutes later, the second plane sliced into the south tower.

Desks, chairs, paper—and people—blew out of the windows of the twin towers. People on the streets below watched in horror as more than a dozen workers on the upper floors jumped from the blazing buildings to their deaths. Other workers poured out of the towers to escape the fire.

Less than an hour after the twin towers were hit, the third hijacked plane rammed into the west side of the Pentagon in Arlington, Virginia. It tore a 75-foot gash in the five-sided, five-story building. That crash

site, too, immediately became engulfed in flames. Meanwhile, passengers on the fourth hijacked plane had used their cell phones and had heard about the other plane crashes. Some of the passengers rushed the hijackers and prevented them from striking their intended target, thought to be either the White House or the Capitol.

Because of these heroic efforts, the plane crashed not into a crowded building but into an empty field in Pennsylvania. No one will ever know how many lives the passengers saved as they gave up their own.

Recovery efforts continue on the collapsed section of the Pentagon's southwest side two days after the attack.

The Destruction The planes were loaded with fuel. They became destructive missiles when they crashed into the World Trade Center and the Pentagon. As one investigator noted, the hijackers "couldn't carry

The Attack on America **US3**

anything—other than an atom bomb—that could be as bad as what they were flying."

The explosions and fires so weakened the damaged skyscrapers that they crumbled to the ground less than two hours after impact. The fire and raining debris caused nearby buildings to collapse as well. Nine buildings in New York City's financial district completely or partially collapsed. Six others suffered major damage. The disaster area covered 16 acres. The damage at the Pentagon, though extensive, was confined to one wing of the building.

But it was the toll in human lives that most grieved Americans and others around the world. About 3,000 people died in the attacks. All passengers on the four planes were killed, as well as workers and visitors in the World Trade Center and the Pentagon. The dead included more than 300 New York City firefighters and 40 police officers who rushed to the scene and were buried in the rubble when the skyscrapers collapsed.

Grieving Families and Companies "Please tell the children I love them," said a father of three from the World Trade Center before the phone line went dead. From the burning towers and the hijacked planes, men and women used their last moments to call and to speak with their families for the last time.

In the first hours and days after the September 11 attacks, family members and friends of people in the World Trade Center frantically tried to find their loved ones. They checked hospitals and posted pictures of the missing on lampposts and walls. The thousands of people who escaped before the towers collapsed were reunited with their families. But only a few survivors were pulled from the wreckage of the buildings. For thousands of people, loved ones never returned home. Also, several businesses with offices in the towers lost large numbers of employees.

The horror of September 11 has haunted more than just the survivors and witnesses of the attacks, although they were the hardest hit. Millions of Americans watched the events on television shortly after they occurred. They, too, would have difficulty forgetting those horrifying images.

RESCUE EFFORTS

Amidst the brutal destruction at the World Trade Center, the courage, selflessness, and noble actions of New York City's firefighters, police officers, and rescue workers stood as a testament. Many of the first

Destruction in New York City

Destroyed
Severely Damaged

Millennium Hilton

TOWER 1   TOWER 2

WORLD TRADE CENTER

Bldg. 7   Bldg. 5

One Liberty Plaza

Bldg. 6

Bldg. 4   American Stock Exchange

WORLD FINANCIAL CENTER   Bldg. 3

3D model by Urban Data Solutions, Inc.

Bystanders view the twin towers of the World Trade Center shortly after impact (above). The destruction in New York City's financial district is illustrated in the infographic of "ground zero" to the right.

How the debris is removed

Truck staging area
Fifty-four city sanitation trucks, parked at 55th and West Side Highway, are dispatched along secure routes to the site to pick up any debris considered still sensitive by the FBI. Separate, privately owned trucks are picking up debris from ConEd and the Transit Authority.

Truck capacity:
6 tons or more

Total debris moved in one day:
6,000 to 10,000 tons

Hudson River

M A N H A T T A N

55th Street

Broadway

30th Street

14th Street

First Avenue

West Street

E. Houston Street

Warren Street

Hot Zone

Broadway

Rector Street

East River

Makeshift morgue where medical examiners inventory and catalog human remains for identification

1 Trucks are loaded at the site and driven to marine transfer stations, where debris is loaded onto barges.

2 The barges carry 600 tons of debris on each trip.

Staten Island

3 Trucks carrying the heaviest debris, such as steel beams, make the trip by flatbed trucks via the Battery Tunnel and across the Verrazano Narrows Bridge.

Screen Debris

Dirt filtered out

Tray

At the landfill site

4 Two piles are created. one that is considered debris...

5 ...and the other, which may yield more evidence. The workers have created a grid system on the ground; these truckloads are dumped into a checkerboard that is then sifted through in large, table-like trays with mesh-screen bottoms. FBI investigators are searching for clues, such as those that led to the cracking of the Oklahoma City bombing case when they found the Ryder truck axle with the vehicle identification number on it.

Sources: City of New York; Federal Emergency Management Agency; Caterpillar; Mueser Rutledge Consulting Engineers

Reporting by Debbie Howlett and Martha Moore, USA TODAY ®; graphic by Frank Pompa, Robert Ahrens, Adrienne Lewis and Dave Merrill, USA TODAY ®

firefighters at the scene disappeared into the burning buildings to help those inside and never came out again. Entire squads were lost. New York City Fire Department chaplain, Father Mychal Judge, was killed by falling debris just after giving the last rites of the Catholic Church to a firefighter at the scene.

Firefighters worked around the clock trying to find survivors in the wreckage. They had to contend with shifting rubble and smoky, ash-filled air. Medical workers from the area rushed to staff the city's trauma centers. But after the first wave of injured, there were few survivors to treat. One emergency medical technician said, "We were set up for any emergency. It was a great site, full of surgeons. But we were treating firemen and police who needed their eyes washed."

A flood of volunteers assisted rescue workers. Ironworkers helped cut through steel beams, while high school students helped provide water and food for the rescue workers. From around the country, people sent donations of blood, food, and money to New York City. The city kept functioning in the hours and days that followed the attack under the direction of its mayor, Rudy Giuliani.

The Cleanup After the first few days, the work at "ground zero," the World Trade Center disaster site, shifted to recovering bodies and removing the massive amount of debris. The twin towers alone contained more than 200,000 tons of steel, 425,000 cubic yards of concrete, and 14 acres of glass—an estimated 2 billion pounds.

SEARCH FOR TERRORISTS BEGINS

In the weeks that followed, the U.S. government organized a massive effort to identify those responsible for the attacks. Officials concluded that Osama bin Laden, a Saudi Arabian millionaire, directed the terrorists. He had been exiled from his native country because of suspected terrorist activities. Bin Laden was hiding in Afghanistan, protected there by the strict Islamic government known as the Taliban. The effort to bring him to justice would lead the United States to begin military action against Afghanistan in October, as the next section explains.

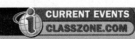

Thinking Critically | **CURRENT EVENTS** CLASSZONE.COM

- Why were the specific targets of the September attacks selected by the terrorists?
- What might cause individuals to use terrorist tactics to attempt to change situations they think are a problem?

Thinking Critically Answers
- They were symbols of American economic and military power.
- They feel that they are unable to change a situation through regular channels.

The Attack on America US5

Reporter's Notes
By Tim Friend

AFGHANISTAN— I entered Afghanistan from the north on an aging ferry boat at dusk on October 22. All I could see in the encroaching darkness were silhouettes of Northern Alliance fighters with Kalishnikov weapons slung loosely on their shoulders. My passport was stamped in a small mud hut under a dim lantern, then I was off to the village of Hoja Baddahuin, where the Northern Alliance had set up headquarters after the Taliban had taken over most of the country.

The United States had entered the war in Afghanistan after the terrorist attacks on September 11, 2001. Covering the war in Afghanistan has been the single most challenging experience of my career as a reporter at USA TODAY.

The most dangerous part of the experience was traveling through the front lines as I made my way to Kabul. My jeep had to cross minefields and the most narrow mountain roads imaginable. At Taloqan, the first city to be restored to the Northern Alliance, I wrote my stories while gunfire erupted outside my walled compound. I paid two men to stay inside with their machine guns and to answer the door should someone come knocking. Taliban fighters were still hiding out in houses just down the street. Through it all, I learned to stay calm by doing the best I could to ensure both my safety and the safety of my team, and to leave the rest to a healthy dose of faith.

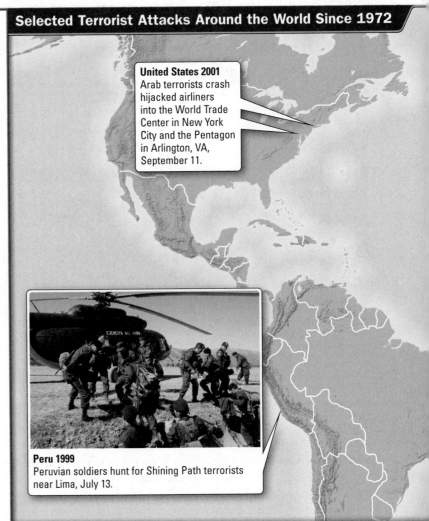

United States 2001
Arab terrorists crash hijacked airliners into the World Trade Center in New York City and the Pentagon in Arlington, VA, September 11.

Peru 1999
Peruvian soldiers hunt for Shining Path terrorists near Lima, July 13.

Hunting for the Terrorists

Terrorism is not new. Reporters like Tim Friend have been covering terrorist attacks across the globe for the last three decades. Throughout history, individuals, small groups, and governments have used terror tactics to try to achieve political or social goals—whether it be to bring down a government, eliminate opponents, or promote a cause.

In recent times, however, terrorism has become an international problem. Since the late 1960s, more than 14,000 terrorist attacks have occurred worldwide. International terrorist groups have carried out increasingly destructive, high-profile attacks to attract global attention. Many countries also face domestic terrorists who oppose their governments' policies or have special interests to promote.

The reasons for modern terrorism are many. The traditional motives, such as gaining independence, expelling foreigners, or changing society, still drive various terrorist groups around the world. These terrorists use violence to force concessions from their enemies, usually the governments in power. But other kinds of terrorists, driven by radical religious motives, began to emerge in the late 20th century.

The goal of these terrorists is the destruction of what they consider the forces of evil. This evil might be located in their own countries or in other parts of the world. These terrorists often threaten to use weapons of mass destruction, such as chemical, biological, or nuclear weapons, to kill their enemies.

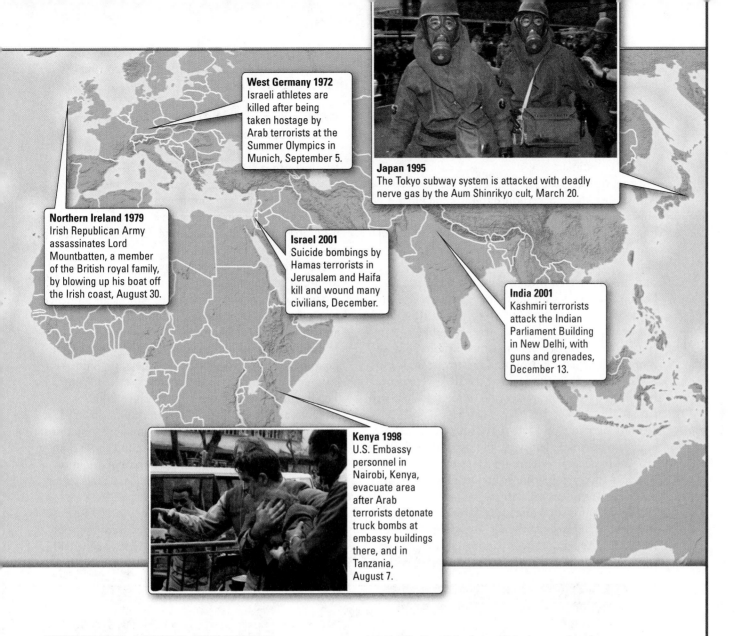

West Germany 1972
Israeli athletes are killed after being taken hostage by Arab terrorists at the Summer Olympics in Munich, September 5.

Japan 1995
The Tokyo subway system is attacked with deadly nerve gas by the Aum Shinrikyo cult, March 20.

Northern Ireland 1979
Irish Republican Army assassinates Lord Mountbatten, a member of the British royal family, by blowing up his boat off the Irish coast, August 30.

Israel 2001
Suicide bombings by Hamas terrorists in Jerusalem and Haifa kill and wound many civilians, December.

India 2001
Kashmiri terrorists attack the Indian Parliament Building in New Delhi, with guns and grenades, December 13.

Kenya 1998
U.S. Embassy personnel in Nairobi, Kenya, evacuate area after Arab terrorists detonate truck bombs at embassy buildings there, and in Tanzania, August 7.

TERRORISM AROUND THE WORLD

The problem of international terrorism first came to world attention in a shocking way during the 1972 Summer Olympic Games in Munich, Germany (then West Germany). Eight members of a Palestinian terrorist group called Black September killed two Israeli athletes and took nine others hostage. Five of the terrorists, all the hostages, and a police officer were later killed in a bloody gun battle. The attack became known as the Munich Massacre. Since then, few regions of the world have been spared from terrorist attacks.

The Middle East Like Black September, many terrorist organizations have their roots in the Israeli-Palestinian conflict over land in the Middle East.

("Middle East" is the political term for the geographic region of Southwest Asia.) Arab terrorist groups such as the Palestine Islamic Jihad, Hamas, and Hizballah have sought to prevent a peace settlement between Israel and the Palestinians. They want a homeland for the Palestinians on their own terms, with the most extreme among them denying Israel's right to exist. In a continual cycle of violence, the Israelis retaliate after each terrorist attack, and the terrorists attack again.

Among Muslims in the Middle East, the Israeli-Palestinian violence has bred widespread Arab anger at Israel—and at the United States for supporting Israel. For example, the Lebanese-based group Hizballah seeks to eliminate all non-Islamic influences in Muslim countries. It is thought to have been responsible for bombing the U.S. embassy and marine barracks in Beirut in 1983 and the U.S. embassy annex in Beirut in 1984.

In December 2001, terrorist attacks on Israeli civilians in Jerusalem and Haifa killed 27 people and wounded more than 200. Hamas claimed responsibility, and the Israelis responded with military strikes against Palestinian targets.

Israel then declared a "war on terrorism," patterned after the U.S. response to the September 11 attacks. Moderates in the region believe that the only long-term solution is a compromise between Israel and the Palestinians over the issue of land.

Europe Many countries in Europe—including Great Britain, Germany, and Italy—have been targets of domestic terrorists who oppose government policies. For example, for decades the Irish Republican Army engaged in terrorist attacks against Britain because it opposed British control of Northern Ireland. By 2001, however, the British and the IRA were peacefully negotiating for greater autonomy for Northern Ireland.

Both Germany and Italy have suffered terrorist attacks by extreme left-wing and right-wing domestic groups. In general, left-wing groups oppose capitalism, and right-wing groups support capitalism and oppose government regulation.

These groups sometimes join forces with other terrorist organizations when it suits their purposes. In 1975, for example, West Germany's Red Army Faction and Italy's Red Brigades cooperated with the Palestine Liberation Organization to kidnap officials at a meeting of the Organization of Petroleum Exporting Countries (OPEC) in Vienna, Austria.

South Asia and East Asia South Asia has become another hotbed of terrorism in recent years. Afghanistan became a haven for international terrorists after the extremist Muslim Taliban came to power in 1996. In that year, Osama bin Laden moved to Afghanistan and began using mountain hideouts in that country as a base of operations for his global network of Muslim terrorists known as al-Qaeda.

Muslim extremists from all over the world came to al-Qaeda training camps. Bin Laden and these other extremists were opposed to American influence in Muslim lands. Bin Laden called for terrorist attacks against Americans and U.S. allies.

Terrorist groups have arisen in East Asia, as well. Japanese terrorist groups include the Aum Shinrikyo (Supreme Truth Sect) and the Japanese Red Army. The Aum Shinrikyo (called Aleph since 2000) is a religious cult that wants to control Japan. In 1995, it released sarin, a deadly nerve gas, in subway stations in Tokyo. Twelve people were killed and more than 5,700 injured. This attack brought global attention to the threat of biological and chemical agents as terrorist weapons.

Africa Civil unrest and regional wars were the root causes of most terrorist activity in Africa at the end of the 20th century. But al-Qaeda cells operated in

International Terrorist Attacks

Total Attacks, 1981–2000

International Casualties of Terrorism, 1995–2000

	Africa	Asia	Euroasia	Latin America	Middle East	North America	Western Europe
1995	8	5369	29	46	445	0	287
1996	80	1507	20	18	1097	0	503
1997	28	344	27	11	480	7	17
1998	5379	635	12	195	68	0	405
1999	185	690	8	9	31	0	16
2000	102	898	103	20	69	0	4
Totals	5782	9713	199	299	2190	7	1232

Source: U.S. Department of State

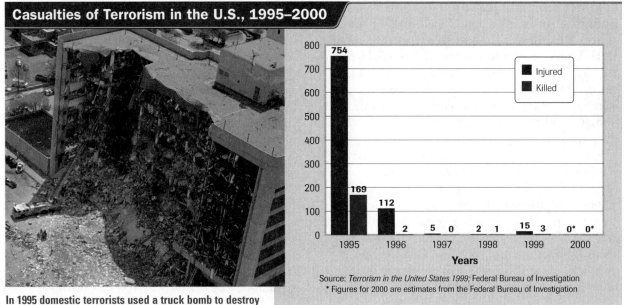

Casualties of Terrorism in the U.S., 1995–2000

Injured
Killed

Years	1995	1996	1997	1998	1999	2000
Injured	754	112	5	2	15	0*
Killed	169	2	0	1	3	0*

Source: *Terrorism in the United States 1999;* Federal Bureau of Investigation
* Figures for 2000 are estimates from the Federal Bureau of Investigation

In 1995 domestic terrorists used a truck bomb to destroy the Murrah Federal Building in Oklahoma City, Oklahoma.

many African countries, and several major attacks against U.S. personnel and facilities in Africa were linked to al-Qaeda.

For example, a 1993 attack on U.S. soldiers in Somalia killed 18. In 1998, bombings at the U.S. embassies in Kenya and Tanzania left 301 dead and more than 5,000 people injured. The United States responded to these attacks with missile strikes on suspected terrorist facilities in Afghanistan, and in Sudan where bin Laden was based from 1991 to 1996.

Latin America In 2000, more terrorist attacks occurred in Latin America than in any other region of the world. Terrorist activity was particularly heavy in Colombia, a country where powerful narcotics organizations have frequently turned to violence. The Revolutionary Armed Forces of Colombia (FARC) is a left-wing guerrilla group responsible for numerous bombings, hijackings, and kidnappings of Colombians and foreign citizens. It has attacked Colombian political, military, and economic targets, as well as those with American ties. FARC is linked to narcotics traffickers.

The region where the borders of Argentina, Brazil, and Paraguay meet has become a center of Islamic extremism and terrorist financing. The Israeli embassy in Buenos Aires, Argentina, was bombed in 1992, and another Israeli target was hit in 1994.

The United States Before September 11, the most destructive act of terrorism on American soil had been the 1995 truck bombing of the Murrah Federal Building in Oklahoma City, Oklahoma. That attack killed 168 people, but it was an act of domestic terrorism. It was carried out by an antigovernment extremist named Timothy McVeigh. Such domestic terrorists are motivated by the belief that the government has too much power to regulate people's lives.

The longest-lasting terrorist campaign by an individual in U.S. history was conducted by Theodore Kaczynski, who was known as the Unabomber. From 1978 to 1995, Kaczynski mailed bombs to business executives and scientists because he opposed the effects of modern technology on society. He killed 3 people and injured 23 others.

The attack on the World Trade Center on September 11 was not the first to have occurred there. A previous attack took place in 1993, when a van filled with explosives was detonated in the center's parking garage. Six people died and more than 1,000 were injured. The person responsible, Ramzi Yousef, was captured and imprisoned, but Osama bin Laden was suspected of being part of the plot. Another bin Laden-linked attack was the bombing of the destroyer USS *Cole* in Yemen in October 2000.

FINDING THOSE RESPONSIBLE

Immediately after the September 11 attacks, the Bush administration launched the largest criminal investigation in U.S. history. The FBI searched across the country—and the world—for clues to the identities of the suicide hijackers and those who aided them.

In an address to Congress and the nation, President George W. Bush pledged, "Whether we

The Attack on America US9

bring our enemies to justice or bring justice to our enemies, justice will be done." He called the terrorist attacks "acts of war" and declared that the United States would wage a war to end global terrorism. He vowed that as a part of that war, "We will pursue nations that provide aid or safe haven to terrorism. Every nation in every region now has a decision to make. Either you are with us, or you are with the terrorists."

Seven nations were on a U.S. government list of state sponsors of terrorism in 2001—Iran, Iraq, Syria, Libya, Cuba, North Korea, and Sudan. In addition, Afghanistan, Pakistan, Lebanon, and Yemen were considered major centers of terrorist activity. After the September 11 attacks, however, some of these countries, including Pakistan and Sudan, began to cooperate with the United States in hunting down those responsible.

The investigation into the September 11 attacks soon showed that top leaders in the al-Qaeda network were responsible for planning the attacks. The U.S. government then undertook a worldwide hunt for terrorists linked to al-Qaeda.

The United States built an international coalition, or alliance, to fight the war on terrorism. Canada, China, Great Britain, Pakistan, Russia, and many other nations joined the coalition. They agreed to share intelligence information, to arrest terrorists operating within their borders, and to seize the financial assets of terrorist groups. The coalition also gave support to U.S. military action in Afghanistan.

Great Britain took an especially active role in the coalition. One Londoner left a card at the U.S. embassy that reflected the surge of support that the United States received immediately after the devastating attacks: "Dear America, You supported us in two world wars. We stand with you now."

The War in Afghanistan

The U.S. government first focused its military response on Afghanistan, because that country was the home base of Osama bin Laden's al-Qaeda network. The strict Islamic regime that controlled most of Afghanistan—the Taliban—had harbored bin Laden and al-Qaeda since 1996. In return, bin Laden helped keep the Taliban in power by providing fighters in their civil war against the Northern Alliance, a coalition of anti-Taliban Afghan groups.

The United States demanded that the Taliban turn over bin Laden. After they refused, the United States began military action. The U.S. goals were to find bin Laden, to destroy al-Qaeda, and to end Taliban rule.

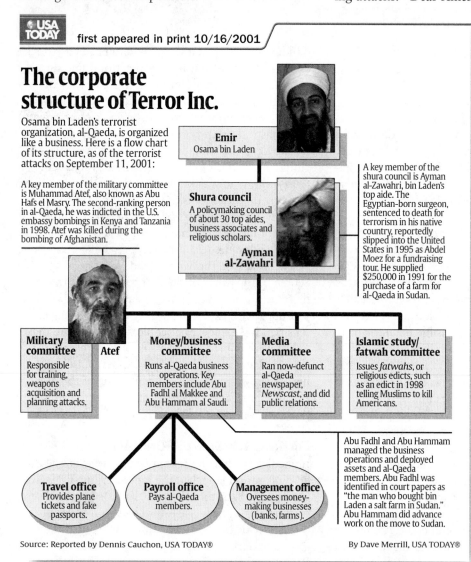

USA TODAY first appeared in print 10/16/2001

The corporate structure of Terror Inc.

Osama bin Laden's terrorist organization, al-Qaeda, is organized like a business. Here is a flow chart of its structure, as of the terrorist attacks on September 11, 2001:

A key member of the military committee is Muhammad Atef, also known as Abu Hafs el Masry. The second-ranking person in al-Qaeda, he was indicted in the U.S. embassy bombings in Kenya and Tanzania in 1998. Atef was killed during the bombing of Afghanistan.

Emir
Osama bin Laden

Shura council
A policymaking council of about 30 top aides, business associates and religious scholars.
Ayman al-Zawahri

A key member of the shura council is Ayman al-Zawahri, bin Laden's top aide. The Egyptian-born surgeon, sentenced to death for terrorism in his native country, reportedly slipped into the United States in 1995 as Abdel Moez for a fundraising tour. He supplied $250,000 in 1991 for the purchase of a farm for al-Qaeda in Sudan.

Atef

Military committee
Responsible for training, weapons acquisition and planning attacks.

Money/business committee
Runs al-Qaeda business operations. Key members include Abu Fadhl al Makkee and Abu Hammam al Saudi.

Media committee
Ran now-defunct al-Qaeda newspaper, *Newscast*, and did public relations.

Islamic study/ fatwah committee
Issues *fatwahs*, or religious edicts, such as an edict in 1998 telling Muslims to kill Americans.

Abu Fadhl and Abu Hammam managed the business operations and deployed assets and al-Qaeda members. Abu Fadhl was identified in court papers as "the man who bought bin Laden a salt farm in Sudan." Abu Hammam did advance work on the move to Sudan.

Travel office
Provides plane tickets and fake passports.

Payroll office
Pays al-Qaeda members.

Management office
Oversees money-making businesses (banks, farms).

Source: Reported by Dennis Cauchon, USA TODAY®

By Dave Merrill, USA TODAY®

Secretary of Defense Donald Rumsfeld
addresses U.S. troops in Afghanistan.

The War Against Terrorism, Afghanistan 2001

TURKMENISTAN

TAJIKISTAN

Mazar-e
Sharif
KONDOZ
TAKHAR
Feyzabad
JOWZJAN
BALKH
Konduz
BADAKHSHAN

Meymaneh
SAR-E-POL
Baghlan
BAGHLAN
Taloqan
FARYAB
SAMANGAN
KAPISA
LAGHMAN
BADGHIS
PARVAN
KONAR
KABUL

Herat
Bamian
BAMIAN
VARDAK
Kabul
Jalalabad
INDIA
HERAT
GHOWR
LOWGAR
NANGARHAR
Islamabad

AFGHANISTAN
PAKTIA

Shindand
FARAH
ORUZGAN
GHAZNI
Khowst

Farah
PAKTIKA

ZABOL
PAKISTAN

IRAN
NIMRUZ
HELMAND
Qandahar

QANDAHAR

Estimated area of Northern Alliance control

■ Suspected training camps/militia bases

◆ Taliban army bases

✈ Military and/or civilian airfields

--- Province boundaries

0   100   200 miles
0   100   200 kilometers
Conformal Conic Projection

In October 2001, the United States began bombing Taliban air defenses, airfields, and command centers, as well as al-Qaeda training camps. On the ground, the United States relied on anti-Taliban groups—first, the Northern Alliance and later, the Eastern Alliance—to do most of the fighting against the Taliban. These Afghan groups were assisted by U.S. air strikes against Taliban military positions and by a small number of U.S. special-forces troops and marines.

In December, the Taliban were driven from power, but the fight to destroy al-Qaeda continued. Meanwhile, the United Nations worked with the Northern Alliance and other Afghan groups to establish an interim government to replace the Taliban.

A number of nations in the antiterrorism coalition actively assisted the United States in Afghanistan, including Pakistan. The Pakistanis shared intelligence information and allowed the United States to stage military operations from their country.

Pakistan, a Muslim country, took a political risk by giving support to the United States. The Pakistani government's actions were opposed by groups within Pakistan who believed the antiterrorism campaign to be anti-Islamic.

The United States tried to make it clear to Muslim nations that the antiterrorism campaign was *not* anti-Islamic and that Americans respected the religion of Islam. For the United States, maintaining the support of moderate Muslim leaders was important to the long-term success of the war against terrorism—a war that in its next phase would target other nations that supported international terrorism.

Thinking Critically

CURRENT EVENTS
CLASSZONE.COM

- How will the graph on page US 8 change when the statistics for the year 2001 are added?

- What are some of the reasons for domestic terrorism in the various regions of the world?

The Attack on America   US11

Reporter's Notes

USA TODAY

By Blake Morrison

WASHINGTON, D.C.—A month after the September 11 terrorist hijackings, the pilot of US Airways Flight 62 stepped from the cockpit just before takeoff, an ax in his hand. "These are extraordinary times," he told passengers over the jet's public address system. The cabin quieted. Then he rattled off three scenarios in the event of a terrorist attack aboard the San Francisco-to-Charlotte flight.

"One, someone stands up and says 'bomb,' " the pilot said. "If they tell you that, it's a lie." Second, someone pretends to be an air marshal. "We don't have an armed marshal on this flight," he said, still holding the ax. Third, someone might threaten to release some sort of biological agent. Don't be afraid, he told passengers. Pilots would land the plane before any lasting harm could be done.

In any case, the pilot advised, passengers should not back down. "Throw your shoes at them. A couple of you get up and tackle him. Beat him. I don't care." As for the ax he was holding, standard on jets in case of emergency? It's kept in the cockpit, he said. "It's very sharp. I can shave with it. For anyone to try to break into this cockpit would be a very bad idea." Then the pilot paused. "Having said all this, I'd like you all to sit back, relax, and enjoy the trip." Some passengers chuckled. Almost everyone clapped.

The stunning announcement illustrates just how much flying changed in the wake of the September 11 terrorist attacks—and how quickly Americans have grown to accept the new reality.

The Impact on American Life

 USA TODAY first appeared in print 9/18/2001

Airport security tightens up

As the nation's 400 airports get back to business, passengers around the country are finding tighter security. Since the Sept. 11 hijacking of four U.S. airliners, the procedures from ticket counter to gate are stiffer. Airlines are recommending that passengers arrive between two and four hours early for flights. Security measures and wait times varied widely, according to USA TODAY® reporters.

Security
Passengers, and their families and friends, could all go to the gate. Keys, cell phones and change could be dropped into plastic dishes or cups to one side of the metal detectors. Hand-held sensors were used if metal still detected, or sometimes a manual pat-down.

Check in
Photo ID required. Ticket agent asks "Have your bags been in your possession since you packed them?"

Curb-side luggage check-in permitted

Carry-on
Bags are placed on a conveyor belt and contents displayed on a screen. Security employees are trained to spot suspicious objects.

Increased use of bomb-sniffing dogs. Dogs and police officers were highly visible at Newark International.

Before the Sept. 11 attack

No curb-side luggage check permitted.

After the attack

Before security checkpoint
Passengers asked to show tickets and photo IDs again.

Security
Only passengers beyond this point. Cell phones, keys, pagers and other loose objects have to be put on the conveyor belts, where they are screened, according to passengers at San Francisco and Chicago airports Monday. Knives and cutting tools prohibited. Overhead metal detectors are being used in addition to hand-held units. In Baltimore, some bags were checked for bomb dust.

Check in
Baggage checked randomly. Photo ID required. In some cases, passengers had to exchange e-tickets for paper tickets. Passengers still asked if they have had their bags in their possession since packing.

Sources: FAA; reporting by Jack Gruber, Debbie Howlett, Martin Kasindorf, USA TODAY®; and Reed Stacey

By Frank Pompa, USA TODAY®

After the September 11 attacks, many Americans reported feeling that everything had changed—that life would never be the same. Before, Americans had viewed war as something that happened in other countries. Now they felt vulnerable, and the threat of terrorism began to affect many aspects of American life—as the experience of those on Flight 62 showed.

THE AIRLINES AND THE ECONOMY

In the wake of the terrorist attacks, the Federal Aviation Administration (FAA) shut down all airports in the United States for the first time in the nation's history. They did so to prevent any other hijackings. When the airports reopened and flights resumed a few days later, the airlines had few passengers. Some people did not feel safe flying, and others did not want to face the delays caused by tighter airport security.

The number of passengers dropped 43 percent in the days after flights resumed. The airline industry lost an estimated $5 billion in September and cut more than 100,000 jobs to reduce their costs. Congress quickly passed a $15-billion-aid package to help the industry get through the crisis. After September, airline business partially recovered. But even months later, the passenger airfleet was still flying well below capacity.

Industries related to the airlines also suffered. Travel agents, hotels, resorts, and theme parks all lost business. Also hard hit was the insurance industry, which would have to pay billions in death and property loss claims due to the attacks.

The Impact on American Life   US13

The New York Stock Exchange and other stock markets closed after the attacks and did not reopen until the following Monday. The last time the New York exchange had shut down for more than three days was in 1914, at the start of World War I. After the stock markets reopened, the Dow Jones Industrial Average suffered its biggest weekly drop since the Great Depression—14.3 percent.

Over the next few weeks, the markets began to rebound, but the economy continued to decline. Consumers spent less, and unemployment rose. Experts believed that the attacks had only worsened an economic slowdown that had begun early in 2001. They agreed that the nation was in a recession.

THE ANTHRAX THREAT

Not long after September 11th, terrorism struck America again, but in a different form. Letters containing spores of a bacterium that causes the disease anthrax were sent to persons in the news media and to members of Congress in Washington, D.C.

Anthrax bacteria can cause illness when they come in contact with skin or when inhaled. The skin form of anthrax is usually not fatal. But if anthrax bacteria are inhaled, the poisons they produce can damage body tissues. If not treated quickly, inhalation anthrax can cause death.

The threat of biological warfare became real when letters containing the anthrax bacterium (right) were sent to some members of the U.S. Congress in Washington D.C. (below) and persons in the news media after the September 11 attacks.

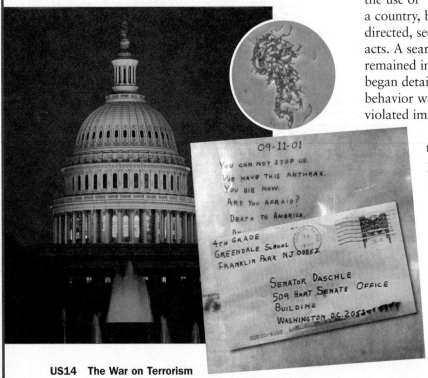

Five people who came in contact with spores from the tainted letters died of inhalation anthrax. Two were postal workers. Many others contracted the skin form of the disease. Thousands who were exposed to anthrax were treated with antibiotics.

The anthrax scare frightened many Americans. The U.S. Postal Service warned Americans to be suspicious of mail without return addresses or in strange packages and to wash their hands after handling mail. Many businesses began taking precautions.

Investigators did not immediately find a link between the anthrax letters and the September 11 attacks. Some experts believed that the anthrax letters might be the work of a lone terrorist rather than an organized group. The anthrax scare not only made Americans fearful of the mail but also of the threat of other biological or chemical weapons, such as the smallpox virus or the nerve gas sarin.

ANTITERRORISM MEASURES

The federal government warned Americans that additional terrorist attacks were likely. It then took actions to prevent such attacks. The Office of Homeland Security was created to coordinate national efforts against terrorism. Antiterrorism measures included a search for terrorists in the United States, the passage of an antiterrorism law, and the adoption of new aviation security regulations.

Searching for Terrorists The al-Qaeda network was able to carry out its terrorist attacks partly through the use of "sleepers." These are agents who move to a country, blend into a community, and then, when directed, secretly prepare for and carry out terrorist acts. A search to find any al-Qaeda terrorists who remained in the United States was started. Officials began detaining and questioning Arabs whose behavior was considered suspicious or who had violated immigration regulations.

Because the hijackers had been Arabs, the government held that the actions were justified. But some critics charged that detaining these men was unfair to the innocent and violated their civil rights. In one incident, Mohammed Irshaid, a Jordanian-born civil engineer who had lived in the United States for more than 20 years, was jailed for three weeks without being charged. His three children were American citizens. Although the incident humiliated him, he said that it "doesn't change my love of America."

President George W. Bush discusses the war against terrorism with advisers, including Vice President Dick Cheney (left) and Secretary of State Colin Powell (right).

More than three million Arab Americans live in the United States, and many were viewed with distrust by other Americans after the September 11 attacks. In one incident, three Arab Americans were taken off a plane when other passengers refused to fly with them. After questioning the men, officials allowed them to take a later flight.

Such incidents sparked debate about the need to respect civil rights while conducting searches for terrorists. The government argued that it was not unusual to curtail civil liberties during wartime in order to protect national security. This argument was also used to justify a proposal to try some terrorist suspects in military tribunals rather than in criminal courts.

Antiterrorism Law On October 26, 2001, President Bush signed into law an antiterrorism bill. The law allowed the government to

- detain foreigners suspected of terrorism for seven days without charging them with a crime
- tap all phones used by suspects and monitor their e-mail and Internet use
- make search warrants valid across states
- order U.S. banks to investigate sources of large foreign accounts
- prosecute terrorist crimes without any time restrictions or limitations

Again, critics warned that these measures would let the government infringe on people's civil rights.

Aviation Security The federal government also increased its involvement in aviation security. The Federal Aviation Administration ordered airlines to install bars on cockpit doors to prevent passengers from gaining control of planes, as the hijackers had done. Sky marshals were assigned to fly on planes; National Guard troops began patrolling airports.

In November 2001, a new aviation-security law made airport security the responsibility of the federal government. Previously, individual airports had been responsible. The law provided for a federal security force that would inspect passengers and carry-on bags. It also required the screening of checked baggage.

Airline and government officials debated these and other measures for making air travel more secure. Major concerns were long delays at airports and respect for passengers' privacy. It also became clear that public debate over security measures would continue as long as the United States fights terrorism and tries to balance national security with civil rights.

Thinking Critically Answers
- Some will say that civil rights always must be respected; others, that defeating terrorism is more important.
- Answers might include the continued fear of terrorism, the limitations on civil rights caused by increased security, or the economic costs of security measures.

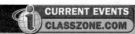

Thinking Critically

CURRENT EVENTS
CLASSZONE.COM

- Is it important for the U.S. government to respect people's civil rights as it wages a war against terrorism? Why or why not?
- What has been the greatest impact of terrorism on American life, aside from the tragic deaths caused by the September 11 attacks?

The Impact on American Life   US15

Glossary

A

Aborigine (AB•uh•RIHJ•uh•nee) *n.* one of Australia's first inhabitants or their descendents. (p. 528)

absolute location *n.* the exact spot on Earth where a place is found. (p. 36)

acid rain *n.* rain or snow that carries air pollutants to Earth. (p. 180)

Aegean (ih•JEE•uhn) **Sea** *n.* a branch of the Mediterranean Sea that is located between Greece and Turkey. (p. 73)

African National Congress (ANC) *n.* a group of black Africans opposed to apartheid. (p. 356)

Afrikaner *n.* a descendant of the Dutch settlers of South Africa. (p. 355)

Ainu (EYE•noo) *n.* the descendents of Japan's early settlers from Europe. (p. 519)

alliance (uh•LY•uhns) *n.* an agreement among people or nations to unite for a common cause and to help any alliance member that is attacked. (p. 128)

Angkor Wat *n.* a Hindu temple in Cambodia, built by the Khmer people. (p. 396)

antimony *n.* a type of metal. (p. 507)

apartheid (uh•PAHRT•HYT) *n.* an official policy of racial separation formerly practiced in South Africa. (p. 310)

Arab-Israeli Wars *n.* a series of wars between 1948 and 1973 that were fought between Israel and the Arab countries of Iraq, Syria, Egypt, Jordan, and Lebanon. (p. 244)

archipelago (AHR•kuh•PEHL•uh•GOH) *n.* a group of islands. (p. 381)

armed neutrality *n.* a policy by which a country maintains military forces but does not take sides in the conflicts of other nations. (p. 179)

Aryan (AIR•ee•uhn) *n.* a member of an ethnic group that migrated from what is now southern Russia through central Asia, settling in India. (p. 386)

Aswan High Dam *n.* a dam built in 1956 by the Egyptian leader Gamal Abdel Nasser to control the flooding of the Nile River. (p. 257)

Athens *n.* the capital of Greece and once one of the most important ancient Greek city-states. (p. 74)

Austria-Hungary *n.* in the 1900s, a dual monarchy in which the Hapsburg emperor ruled both Austria and Hungary. (p. 126)

B

Bahasa (bah•HAH•suh) **Indonesian** *n.* the national language of Indonesia. (p. 445)

Bantu migration *n.* the gradual spreading of the Bantu across Africa over 2,000 years. (p. 297)

batik (buh•TEEK) *n.* a method of dyeing fabric in which any parts of the fabric not intended to be dyed are covered with wax that is later removed. (p. 447)

Berlin Wall *n.* a wire-and-concrete wall that divided Germany's East Berlin and West Berlin from 1961 to 1989. (p. 189)

Boer *n.* one of a group of Dutch colonists in South Africa or one of their descendents. (p. 355)

Boxer Rebellion *n.* a rebellion led by a group called the Boxers in China in 1900. (p. 496)

Buddhism *n.* a religion founded by Siddhartha Gautama in India in the 500s B.C. (p. 394)

bureaucracy *n.* the administration of a government through departments called bureaus. (p. 478)

C

caliph (KAY•lihf) *n.* the title used by rulers of the Muslim community from 632 until 1924. (p. 235)

capitalism *n.* an economic system in which the factories and businesses that make and sell goods are privately owned and the owners make the decisions about what goods to produce. (p. 109)

cartographer *n.* a person who makes maps. (p. 45)

cash crop *n.* a crop grown for sale. (p. 325)

caste *n.* an inherited social class that separates people from other classes by birth, occupation, or wealth. (p. 388)

censorship *n.* the outlawing of materials that contain certain information. (p. 197)

Christianity *n.* a religion that developed out of Judaism and that is based on the life and teachings of Jesus. (p. 231)

circumnavigate *v.* to sail completely around. (p. 104)

citizen *n.* a legal member of a country. (p. 20)

city-state *n.* a central city and its surrounding villages, which together follow the same law, have one form of government, and share language, religious beliefs, and ways of life. (p. 73)

clan *n.* a group of families who trace their descent from a common ancestor. (p. 485)

class system *n.* a system in which society is divided into different social groups. (p. 219)

coalition government *n.* a government formed by political parties joining together. (p. 156)

Cold War *n.* after World War II, a period of political noncooperation between the members of NATO and the Warsaw Pact nations, during which these countries refused to trade or cooperate with each other. (p. 141)

collective farm *n.* a government-owned farm that employs large numbers of workers, often in Communist countries. (p. 139)

colonialism *n.* a system by which a country maintains colonies outside its borders. (p. 125)

Commonwealth of Nations *n.* a group of countries, including Australia and New Zealand, that were once British colonies and that share a heritage of British law and government. (p. 530)

Constantinople *n.* the capital of the Ottoman Empire, now called Istanbul. (p. 236)

cooperative *n.* a large farm on which hundreds of families work. (p. 508)

copra (KOH•pruh) *n.* dried coconut meat. (p. 532)

coup d'état (koo•day•TAH) *n.* an overthrow of a government by force. (p. 319)

Court of Justice *n.* the European Union court that protects the rights of all citizens in whichever of its member countries they live. (p. 164)

Crusades *n.* a series of military expeditions led by Western European Christians in the 11th, 12th, and 13th centuries to reclaim control of the Holy Lands from the Muslims. (p. 95)

Cultural Revolution *n.* a movement that Mao Zedong began in China in 1966 in an attempt to remove opposition to the Communist Party. (p. 499)

culture *n.* the beliefs, customs, laws, art, and ways of living that a group of people share. (p. 21)

culture region *n.* an area of the world in which many people share similar beliefs, history, and languages. (p. 24)

culture trait *n.* the food, clothing, technology, beliefs, language, and tools that the people of a culture share. (p. 21)

cuneiform (KYOO•nee•uh•FAWRM) *n.* a Sumerian system of writing, in which wedge-shaped symbols were used. (p. 220)

currency *n.* money used as a form of exchange. (p. 163)

czar (zahr) *n.* in Russia, an emperor. (p. 113)

D

Dalit *n.* a member of a group of people in India, formerly known as untouchables, who were outside the caste system, were considered lower than the lowest caste, and have gained some rights under India's new constitution. (p. 412)

Deccan Plateau *n.* a plateau that makes up most of southern India. (p. 380)

delta *n.* a triangular deposit of soil at the mouth of a river. (p. 379)

deposed *v.* removed from power. (p. 150)

desertification *n.* the process by which land that can be farmed or lived on turns into desert. (p. 294)

détente (day•TAHNT) *n.* a relaxing of tensions between nations. (p. 151)

developing nation *n.* a newly industrialized nation. (p. 444)

dialect *n.* a regional variety of a language. (p. 521)

Diet *n.* Japan's parliament. (p. 504)

dissident *n.* a person who openly disagrees with a government's policies. (p. 197)

diversity *n.* variety of cultures and viewpoints. (p. 309)

doi moi (doy moy) *n.* the name of a Vietnamese policy, meaning "change for the new." (p. 452)

dowry *n.* money or property given by a bride's family to her new husband and his family. (p. 423)

Dravidian *n.* an Indian language. (p. 422)

drought *n.* a long period of time without rain. (p. 294)

dual monarchy *n.* a form of government in which one ruler governs two nations. (p. 126)

Duma (DOO•muh) *n.* one of the two houses of the Russian legislature. (p. 158)

dynasty *n.* a family of rulers. (p. 476)

E

East Timor *n.* an island nation in Southeast Asia. (p. 441)

economics *n.* the study of how resources are managed in the production, exchange, and use of goods and services. (p. 20)

ECOWAS *n.* the Economic Community of West African States, formed in 1975 to improve trade within Western Africa and with countries outside the region. (p. 321)

Eightfold Path *n.* in Buddhism, a set of guidelines for how to escape suffering. (p. 395)

empire *n.* a nation or group of territories ruled by an emperor. (p. 81)

ethnic cleansing *n.* the organized killing of members of an ethnic group or groups. (p. 157)

euro *n.* the common unit of currency used by European Union countries. (p. 163)

European Community *n.* an association developed after World War II to promote economic unity among the countries of Western Europe. (p. 186)

European Union (EU) *n.* an economic and political grouping of countries in Western Europe. (p. 162)

F

fascism (FASH•IHZ•uhm) *n.* a political philosophy that promotes a strong, central government controlled by the military and led by a powerful dictator. (p. 130)

fellahin (FEHL•uh•HEEN) *n.* peasant farmers in Egypt. (p. 259)

fertile *adj.* rich in resources and nutrients. (p. 213)

Fertile Crescent *n.* a region consisting of what is now Iraq, northeast Syria, and part of southeast Turkey, shaped like a crescent and having fertile soil. (p. 217)

feudalism *n.* in medieval Europe, a political and economic system in which lords gave land to less powerful nobles, called vassals, in return for which the vassals agreed to provide various services to the lords. (p. 86)

Five Pillars of Islam *n.* in Islam, the most important teachings of Muhammad. (p. 234)

fjord (fyawrd) *n.* a long, narrow, deep inlet of the sea located between steep cliffs. (p. 68)

Florence *n.* a city in Italy that was a bustling center of banking, trade, and manufacturing during the 14th century. (p. 96)

Four Noble Truths *n.* the central teachings of Buddhism. (p. 395)

French Resistance *n.* an anti-German movement in France during World War II. (p. 184)

French Revolution *n.* a revolution that began on July 14, 1789, and that led to France's becoming a republic. (p. 110)

G

geography *n.* the study of people, places, and the environment. (p. 18)

Good Friday Accord *n.* an agreement signed in 1998 by Ireland's Protestants and Catholics that established the Northern Ireland Assembly to represent voters from both groups. (p. 175)

government *n.* the people and groups within a society that have the authority to make laws, to make sure they are carried out, and to settle disagreements about them. (p. 19)

Grand National Assembly *n.* Turkey's legislature. (p. 271)

Great Barrier Reef *n.* the world's largest coral reef system, located off Australia's northeastern coast. (p. 474)

Great Leap Forward *n.* a program that Mao Zedong began in China in 1958 to speed up economic development. (p. 498)

Great Rift Valley *n.* a series of broad, steep-walled valleys that stretch from the Red Sea to Mozambique. (p. 293)

Great Zimbabwe *n.* a stone city built by the Shona people, beginning in the A.D. 900s, in the area that is today Zimbabwe. (p. 341)

Green Revolution *n.* a movement that began in the late 1960s, through which genetically improved grains, pesticides, and new farming methods were introduced to farmers in developing nations. (p. 419)

guild *n.* a business association created by people working in the same industry to protect their common interests and maintain standards within the industry. (p. 88)

H

haiku (HY•koo) *n.* a Japanese form of poetry that contains only 17 syllables. (p. 513)

hajj *n.* a pilgrimage to Mecca that most Muslims try to make at least once in a lifetime (p. 251)

Han *n.* the majority ethnic group in China. (p. 514)

harambee *adj.* a Swahili term that means "pulling together" and that is used in reference to Kenyan schools built by Kenyan people rather than by the government. (p. 360)

Hausa (HOW•suh) *n.* the largest ethnic group in Nigeria. (p. 331)

Heian Age *n.* the golden age of Japanese culture, from 794 to 1185. (p. 485)

hieroglyphics *n.* a writing system in which pictures and symbols are used to represent words and sounds. (p. 225)

Himalayas *n.* a mountain range that stretches about 1,500 miles across South Asia. (p. 378)

Hinduism *n.* a religion developed in ancient India. (p. 387)

Hiroshima (HEER•uh•SHEE•muh) *n.* a Japanese city on which the United States dropped an atomic bomb in 1945. (p. 518)

history *n.* a record of the past. (p. 18)

Holocaust *n.* the organized killing of European Jews and others by the Nazis during World War II. (p. 130)

homogeneous *adj.* mostly the same. (p. 519)

human right *n.* a right to which every person is entitled. (p. 503)

hunter-gatherer *n.* a person who finds food by hunting, fishing, and gathering wild grains, fruits, and nuts. (p. 214)

Hutu *n.* the ethnic majority of Rwanda-Burundi. (p. 305)

hydroelectricity *n.* electrical power generated by water. (p. 180)

I

Igbo *n.* an ethnic group in southeastern Nigeria. (p. 331)

imperialism *n.* the practice of one country's controlling the government and economy of another country or territory. (p. 104)

impressionism *n.* a style of art that creates an impression of a scene rather than a strictly realistic picture. (p. 187)

Indian National Congress *n.* in India, a congress formed in 1885 to provide a forum for Indians to discuss their problems. (p. 406)

Indo-Aryan *adj.* related to the family of languages that includes all European and many Indian languages. (p. 422)

Industrial Revolution *n.* a period of change in the 18th century, during which goods began to be manufactured by power-driven machines. (p. 108)

information technology *n.* technology, including computers, software, and the Internet, that helps us process and use information. (p. 418)

interdependence *n.* the economic, political, and social dependence of culture regions on one another. (p. 26)

Iron Curtain *n.* a political barrier that isolated the peoples of Eastern Europe after World War II, restricting their ability to travel outside the region. (p. 136)

irrigation *n.* the process of bringing water to dry land. (p. 215)

Islam *n.* a religion that teaches that there is one god and that Muhammad is his prophet. (p. 232)

J

Janissary *n.* one of a group of soldiers loyal to the sultan of the Ottoman Empire. (p. 237)

Judaism *n.* the first monotheistic religion, which was founded by Abraham and whose followers are called Jews. (p. 230)

jute *n.* a fibrous plant used to make twine, bags, sacks, and burlap. (p. 417)

K

Khmer (KMAIR) *n.* an ancient ethnic group in Cambodia. (p. 396)

kibbutz (ki•Bo͞oTS) *n.* a Jewish farming village in Palestine (or present-day Israel) whose members own everything in common, sharing labor, income, and expenses. (p. 265)

kinship *n.* family relationships. (p. 349)

Kurd *n.* a member of a group of mountain people who live in Armenia, Georgia, Iran, Iraq, Lebanon, Syria, and Turkey. (p. 246)

L

labor force *n.* a pool of available workers. (p. 109)

latitude *n.* a measure of distance north or south of the equator. (p. 36)

Law of Return *n.* a law enacted in 1950 in Israel, granting Jews anywhere in the world permission to move to Israel and become citizens. (p. 266)

London *n.* the capital of England. (p. 173)

longitude *n.* a measure of distance east or west of a line called the prime meridian. (p. 36)

M

Magna Carta (MAG•nuh KAHR•tuh) *n.* a document signed by England's King John in 1215 that guaranteed English people basic rights. (p. 89)

Mahabharata (MAH•huh•BAH•ruh•tuh) *n.* an epic poem about the growth of Hinduism. (p. 421)

mandala (MUHN•duh•luh) *n.* in Southeast Asia, a political system in which a central ruler worked to gain support from others and used trade and business to influence others and maintain power. (p. 438)

mandate *n.* a country placed under the control of another power by international agreement. (p. 244)

Mangla Dam *n.* a dam built on the Jhelum River in northeast Pakistan to control floodwaters and to provide hydroelectricity. (p. 428)

manorialism *n.* a social system in which peasants worked on a lord's land and supplied him with food in exchange for his protection of them. (p. 87)

Maori (MOW•ree) *n.* the first inhabitants of New Zealand. (p. 527)

map projection *n.* one of the different ways of showing Earth's curved surface on a flat map. (p. 47)

martial law *n.* temporary military rule during a time of war or a time when the normal government has broken down. (p. 411)

Masai (mah•SY) *n.* an ethnic group in Africa. (p. 341)

matrilineal society *n.* a society in which ancestry is traced through the mother's side of the family. (p. 533)

mediate *v.* to help find a peaceful solution. (p. 321)

medieval (MEE•dee•EE•vuhl) *adj.* relating to the period of history between the fall of the Roman Empire and the beginning of the modern world, often dated from 476 to 1453. (p. 85)

Mediterranean Sea *n.* an inland sea that borders Europe, Southwest Asia, and Africa. (p. 68)

Meiji Restoration *n.* in Japan, the period from 1868 to 1911, during which the country was again ruled by an emperor after hundreds of years of military rule. (p. 517)

Melanesia *n.* one of three regional island groups into which the Pacific Islands are divided. (p. 528)

Micronesia *n.* one of three regional island groups into which the Pacific Islands are divided. (p. 528)

migrate *v.* to move from one area in order to settle in another. (p. 38)

military dictatorship *n.* a government ruled by a person in the military. (p. 441)

missionary *n.* a person who goes to another country to do religious and social work. (p. 303)

Mohenjo-Daro (moh•HEHN•joh•DAHR•oh) *n.* a large ancient city in the Indus River valley. (p. 386)

monsoon *n.* a seasonal wind that brings great amounts of rain. (p. 382)

Mount Everest *n.* the highest mountain peak in the world, located in the Himalayas on the border of China and Nepal. (p. 470)

Mount Fuji *n.* the tallest mountain and an active volcano in Japan. (p. 472)

Mughal Empire *n.* an empire, lasting from 1526 to 1707, that covered most of the subcontinent of India. (p. 404)

multiparty system *n.* a political system in which two or more parties exist. (p. 359)

Muslim *n.* a follower of the religion Islam. (p. 232)

Muslim Brotherhood *n.* a fundamentalist Muslim group that believes that Egypt should be governed solely by Islamic law in order to be true to the principles of Islam. (p. 258)

Muslim League *n.* a group formed by Muslims in India in 1906 to protect their rights. (p. 406)

N

Nagasaki (NAH•guh•SAH•kee) *n.* a Japanese city on which the United States dropped an atomic bomb in 1945. (p. 518)

nationalism *n.* strong pride in one's nation or ethnic group. (p. 123)

NATO (NAY•toh) *n.* the North Atlantic Treaty Organization, a defense alliance formed in 1949, with the countries of Western Europe, Canada, and the United States agreeing to defend one another if attacked. (p. 131)

nonrenewable resource *n.* a resource that cannot be replaced or that can be replaced only over millions of years. (p. 295)

Northern Plains *n.* plains that lie between the Himalaya Mountains and southern India. (p. 379)

O

OAU *n.* the Organization of African Unity, an organization formed in 1963 to promote unity among all Africans. (p. 321)

oligarchy (AHL•ih•GAHR•kee) *n.* a government in which a few powerful individuals rule. (p. 74)

ombudsman *n.* a Swedish official who protects citizens' rights and ensures that the courts and civil service follow the law. (p. 179)

one-party system *n.* a system in which there is only one political party and only one candidate to choose from for each government position. (p. 316)

OPEC *n.* the Organization of Petroleum Exporting Countries, which decides the price and amount of oil produced each year in Iraq, Iran, Saudi Arabia, Kuwait, Venezuela, and other countries. (p. 250)

Opium War *n.* a war over the trade of the drug opium, which was fought between the Chinese and the British from 1839 to 1842. (p. 496)

Orthodox Jew *n.* a Jew who strictly follows Jewish law. (p. 267)

Ottoman Empire *n.* a Muslim empire that lasted from the early 1400s until after World War I. (p. 236)

outback *n.* the vast, flat plain that extends across most of central Australia. (p. 473)

overgrazing *n.* a process in which animals graze grass faster than it can grow back. (p. 347)

P

pagoda *n.* a Buddhist tower built in many levels, with sculptures or carvings of Buddha on each level. (p. 446)

paleontologist *n.* a scientist who studies fossils. (p. 296)

Palestine *n.* a Southwest Asian region often called the Holy Land. (p. 244)

panchayat *n.* a village council in India. (p. 412)

papyrus (puh•PY•ruhs) *n.* a paperlike material made from a reed. (p. 224)

parliamentary republic *n.* a republic whose head of government, usually a prime minister, is the leader of the political party that has the most members in the parliament. (p. 155)

pastoralism *n.* a way of life in which people raise cattle, sheep, or goats as their primary economic activity. (p. 347)

patrician (puh•TRIHSH•uhn) *n.* in ancient Rome, a member of a wealthy, landowning family that claimed to be able to trace its roots back to the founding of Rome. (p. 79)

patrilineal society *n.* a society in which ancestry is traced through the father's side of the family. (p. 533)

peninsula *n.* a body of land surrounded by water on three sides. (p. 68)

Persian Gulf War *n.* a 1991 war between the United States and Iraq. (p. 247)

petrochemical *n.* a product made from petroleum or natural gas. (p. 251)

pharaoh (FAIR•oh) *n.* a king of ancient Egypt. (p. 225)

philosopher *n.* a person who studies and thinks about why the world is the way it is. (p. 75)

plain *n.* a large flat area of land that usually does not have many trees. (p. 69)

plateau *n.* a raised area of relatively level land. (p. 292)

plebeian (plih•BEE•uhn) *n.* a common citizen of ancient Rome. (p. 79)

polis *n.* the central city of a city-state. (p. 73)

Politburo (PAHL•iht•BYUR•oh) *n.* the group that heads a Communist party. (p. 452)

Polynesia *n.* one of three island groups into which the Pacific Islands are divided. (p. 528)

primary product *n.* a raw material used to manufacture other products. (p. 250)

private property rights *n.* the right of individuals to own land or industry. (p. 149)

propaganda (PRAHP•uh•GAN•duh) *n.* material designed to spread certain beliefs. (p. 148)

Protestant *n.* a member of a Christian church based on the principles of the Reformation. (p. 100)

Punjabi *n.* one of two most commonly spoken languages in Pakistan. (p. 428)

puppet government *n.* a government that is controlled by an outside force. (p. 137)

pyramid *n.* a structure with four triangular sides that rise from a rectangular base to meet at a point on top. (p. 225)

Q

Qur'an (kuh•RAN) *n.* the sacred text of Islam. (p. 232)

R

racism *n.* the belief that one race is inferior to another. (p. 308)

Ramadan (RAM•uh•DAHN) *n.* the ninth month of the Islamic year. (p. 251)

Reformation *n.* a 16th-century movement to change practices within the Roman Catholic Church. (p. 99)

Reign of Terror *n.* the period between 1793 and 1794 during which France's new leaders executed thousands of its citizens. (p. 111)

relative location *n.* the location of one place in relation to other places. (p. 37)

Renaissance *n.* an era of creativity and learning in Western Europe from the 14th century to the 16th century. (p. 96)

renewable resource *n.* a resource that can be used and replaced over a relatively short time period. (p. 295)

republic *n.* a form of government in which people rule through elected representatives. (p. 79)

reunification *n.* the uniting again of parts. (p. 190)

Riksdag (RIHKS•DAHG) *n.* Sweden's parliament. (p. 178)

Ring of Fire *n.* an area of volcanic activity along the borders of the Pacific Ocean. (p. 472)

rite of passage *n.* a special ceremony that marks the transition from one stage of life to another. (p. 328)

Rosh Hashanah (RAWSH huh•SHAW•nuh) *n.* the Jewish New Year. (p. 267)

Russian Revolution *n.* the 1917 revolution that removed the Russian monarchy from power after it had ruled for 400 years. (p. 116)

S

Sahel (suh•HAYL) *n.* a semiarid region south of the Sahara Desert. (p. 294)

samurai (SAM•uh•RY) *n.* a Japanese warrior who pledged to serve a particular lord and protect his estate. (p. 486)

sanction *n.* a penalty imposed upon a nation that is violating international law. (p. 356)

Sanskrit *n.* the classical language of India and Hinduism. (p. 386)

savanna *n.* a flat grassland in a tropical or subtropical region with scattered trees and shrubs. (p. 294)

scarcity *n.* a word economists use to describe the conflict between people's desires and limited resources. (p. 20)

Scientific Revolution *n.* a period of great scientific change and discovery during the 16th and 17th centuries. (p. 108)

scribe *n.* a professional record keeper or copier of documents. (p. 220)

secede *v.* to withdraw from a political union, such as a nation. (p. 175)

secondary product *n.* a product manufactured from raw materials. (p. 250)

secular *adj.* not specifically relating to religion. (p. 267)

sediment *n.* small fragments of rock or other materials that can be moved around by wind, water, or ice. (p. 379)

Senate *n.* the assembly of elected representatives that was the most powerful ruling body of the Roman Republic. (p. 79)

Shinto *n.* a Japanese religion that developed around 300 B.C. (p. 484)

shogun *n.* in feudal Japan, the emperor's chief general, who held most of the country's power. (p. 487)

Sindhi *n.* a language spoken in Pakistan. (p. 428)

skerry *n.* a small island. (p. 181)

socialism *n.* an economic system in which businesses and industries are owned collectively or by the government. (p. 186)

Solidarity *n.* a trade union in Poland that originally aimed to increase pay and improve working conditions and that later opposed Communism. (p. 194)

standard of living *n.* a measure of quality of life. (p. 163)

subcontinent *n.* a large landmass that is part of a continent but that has its own geographic identity. (p. 378)

subsistence farming *n.* a method of farming in which people grow food mainly to feed their households rather than to sell. (p. 325)

Sumerian *n.* one of the first inhabitants of Mesopotamia. (p. 218)

supply and demand *n.* an economic concept that states that the price of a good rises or falls depending on how many people want it (demand) and depending on how much of the good is available (supply). (p. 452)

Swahili (swah•HEE•lee) *n.* a Bantu language spoken in Africa. (p. 360)

T

Taiping (ty•PIHNG) **Rebellion** *n.* the greatest of the peasant revolts that occurred in China in response to the signing of the Treaty of Nanking. (p. 496)

Taj Mahal *n.* the most famous building in India, built by the Mughal emperor Shah Jahan in the A.D. 1640s. (p. 420)

Taliban *n.* a group of fundamentalist Muslims who took control of Afghanistan's government in 1996. (p. 410)

Taoism (DOW•ihz•uhm) *n.* a Chinese philosophy founded in the 200s B.C. by Lao Tzu. (p. 478)

Tarbela Dam *n.* a dam built on the Indus River to improve irrigation and flood control. (p. 428)

tariff *n.* a fee imposed by a government on imported or exported goods. (p. 163)

Tet *n.* the Vietnamese New Year. (p. 453)

textile *n.* cloth manufactured by weaving or knitting. (p. 508)

thatch *n.* woven palm fronds, reeds, or straw used to build roofs. (p. 446)

The Tale of Genji *n.* the world's first novel, written by Lady Muraskai Shikibu of Japan in the 11th century/ (p. 486)

thematic map *n.* a map that focuses on a specific idea or theme. (p. 46)

theocracy (thee•AHK•ruh•see) *n.* a government ruled by a religious leader. (p. 235)

Tiananmen (tyahn•ahn•mehn) **Square** *n.* a square in Beijing, China, where thousands of protesters gathered in demonstration and were injured or killed by the military in 1989. (p. 503)

tradeoff *n.* an exchange of one benefit for another. (p. 258)

tungsten *n.* a type of metal. (p. 507)

Tutsi *n.* the ethnic minority of Rwanda-Burundi. (p. 305)

typhoon *n.* a hurricane that occurs in the western Pacific Ocean. (p. 472)

U

Ural (YUR•uhl) **Mountains** *n.* a mountain range that divides Europe from Asia. (p. 69)

Urdu *n.* the official language of Pakistan. (p. 428)

V

Vedas (VAY•duhz) *n.* the Books of Knowledge of the ancient Aryans, which were the basis of Hinduism. (p. 387)

veldt (vehlt) *n.* the flat grassland of Southern Africa. (p. 354)

W

Warsaw Pact *n.* a treaty signed in 1955 that established an alliance among the Soviet Union, Albania, Bulgaria, Czechoslovakia, East Germany, Hungary, Poland, and Romania. (p. 141)

World War I *n.* a war fought from 1914 to 1918 between the Allies (Russia, France, the United Kingdom, Italy, and the United States) and the Central Powers (Austria-Hungary, Germany, Turkey, and Bulgaria). (p. 127)

World War II *n.* a war fought from 1939 to 1945 between the Axis powers (Germany Italy, and Japan) and the Allies (the United Kingdom, France, the Soviet Union, and the United States). (p. 130)

Y

Yom Kippur (YAWM KIHP•uhr) *n.* in Judaism, the Day of Atonement. (p. 267)

Yoruba (YAWR•uh•buh) *n.* an ethnic group in southwestern Nigeria. (p. 331)

Z

Zen *n.* a branch of Buddhism practiced in Japan, which emphasizes that people can achieve enlightenment suddenly. (p. 486)

ziggurat *n.* a Mesopotamian terraced pyramid in which each terrace is smaller than the one below it. (p. 218)

Zionism *n.* a movement that encouraged Jews to return to Palestine, the Jewish homeland, which many Jews call Zion. (p. 264)

zither *n.* a type of stringed instrument. (p. 513)

Zulu (ZOO•loo) *n.* an ethnic group in Africa. (p. 342)

Spanish Glossary

A

Aborigine (AB•uh•RIHJ•uh•nee) [aborigen australiano] *s.* los primeros pobladores de Australia o uno de sus descendientes. (pág. 528)

absolute location [ubicación absoluta] *s.* lugar exacto donde se halla un lugar en la Tierra. (pág. 36)

acid rain [lluvia ácida] *s.* lluvia o nieve que lleva sustancias contaminantes a la Tierra. (pág. 180)

Aegean (ih•JEE•uhn) **Sea** [mar Egeo] *s.* parte del Mar Mediterráneo ubicada entre Grecia y Turquía. (pág. 73)

African National Congress [Congreso Nacional Africano] *s.* grupo de africanos negros que se oponen al apartheid. (pág. 356)

Afrikaner [afrikander] *s.* descendiente de los primeros colonos holandeses en Sudáfrica. (pág. 355)

Ainu [ainu] *s.* descendientes de los primeros pobladores de Japón provenientes de Europa. (pág. 519)

alliance (uh•LY•uhns) [alianza] *s.* acuerdo de unión entre pueblos o naciones por una causa común y de ayuda mutua en caso de que uno sea atacado. (pág. 128)

Angkor Wat [Angkor Wat] *s.* templo hindú en Camboya construido por el pueblo khemer. (pág. 396)

antimony [antimonio] *s.* tipo de metal. (pág. 507)

apartheid (uh•PAHRT•HYT) [apartheid] *s.* política oficial de segregación racial que se llevó a cabo anteriormente en Sudáfrica. (pág. 310)

Arab-Israeli Wars [guerras árabe-israelíes] *s.* guerras del período comprendido entre 1948 y 1973, entre Israel y los países árabes de Irak, Siria, Egipto, Jordania y el Líbano. (pág. 244)

archipelago (AHR•kuh•PEHL•uh•GOH) [archipiélago] *s.* grupo de islas. (pág. 381)

armed neutrality [neutralidad armada] *s.* política mediante la cual un país mantiene fuerzas armadas pero no participa en conflictos de otras naciones. (pág. 179)

Aryan [ario] *s.* miembro de un grupo étnico que emigró de lo que hoy es el sur de Rusia y se estableció en la India, pasando por Asia central. (pág. 386)

Aswan High Dam [presa de Aswán] *s.* dique construido en 1956 por el líder egipcio Gamal Abdel Nasser con el fin de controlar las inundaciones del río Nilo. (pág. 257)

Athens [Atenas] *s.* capital de Grecia y una de las ciudades-estado más importantes de la antigua Grecia. (pág. 74)

Austria-Hungary [Austria-Hungría] *s.* monarquía dual mediante la cual a comienzos del siglo XX el emperador de la dinastía de los Hasburgo gobernó Austria y Hungría. (pág. 126)

B

Bahasa (bah•HAH•suh) **Indonesian** [bahasa indonesia] *s.* lengua nacional de Indonesia. (pág. 445)

Bantu migration [emigración bantú] *s.* difusión gradual de los bantú por África durante más de 2000 años. (pág. 297)

batik (buh•TEEK) [batik] *s.* método de teñido mediante el cual las partes de la tela que no se deben teñir son cubiertas con cera que luego se remueve. (pág. 447)

Berlin Wall [Muro de Berlín] *s.* pared de cemento y alambre que desde 1961 a 1989 dividía la parte este de Berlín de la parte oeste. (pág. 189)

Boer [boer] *s.* miembro de un grupo de colonos holandeses o sus descendientes establecidos en Sudáfrica. (pág. 355)

Boxer Rebellion [Rebelión Bóxer] *s.* rebelión llevada a cabo en 1900 por un grupo denominado Bóxer en la China. (pág. 496)

Buddhism [budismo] *s.* religión fundada por Siddhartha Gautama en la India en el siglo VI a. de C. (pág. 394)

bureaucracy [burocracia] *s.* administración de un gobierno que se divide en departamentos o ministerios. (pág. 478)

C

caliph (KAY•lihf) [califa] *s.* título que recibían los gobernantes de las sociedades musulmanas desde el año 632 hasta 1924. (pág. 235)

capitalism [capitalismo] *s.* sistema económico en el cual las empresas y comercios que fabrican y venden productos y mercancías son de propiedad privada; los dueños de dichas empresas y comercios deciden lo que desean producir y vender. (pág. 109)

cartographer [cartógrafo] *s.* persona que hace mapas. (pág. 45)

cash crop [cultivo industrial] *s.* cultivo que se produce para la venta. (pág. 325)

caste [casta] *s.* clase social heredada que separa a las personas de otras clases por motivos de nacimiento, ocupación o riqueza. (pág. 388)

censorship [censura] *s.* prohibición de materiales que contienen cierta información. (pág. 197)

Christianity [cristianaismo] *s.* religión derivada del judaísmo, basada en la vida y las enseñanzas de Jesús. (pág. 231)

circumnavigate [circunnavegar] *v.* dar la vuelta alrededor de algo en una nave. (pág. 104)

citizen [ciudadano] *s.* habitante legal de un país. (pág. 20)

city-state [ciudad estado] *s.* ciudad central y sus aldeas aledañas que acatan las mismas leyes, tienen una sola forma de gobierno y comparten una lengua, creencias religiosas y estilos de vida. (pág. 73)

clan [clan] *s.* grupo de personas con lazos familiares que tienen en común los mismos ancestros. (pág. 485)

class system [sistema de clases] *s.* sistema mediante el cual se divide la sociedad en diferentes grupos sociales. (pág. 219)

coalition government [gobierno de coalición] *s.* gobierno formado por la unión de partidos políticos. (pág. 156)

Cold War [Guerra Fría] *s.* período político posterior a la Segunda Guerra Mundial, caracterizado por la falta de cooperación y relaciones comerciales entre los países miembros de la OTAN y las naciones del Pacto de Varsovia. (pág. 141)

collective farm [granja colectiva] *s.* granja que pertenece al gobierno, que emplea a gran número de trabajadores generalmente en países comunistas. (pág. 139)

colonialism [colonialismo] *s.* sistema mediante el cual un país mantiene colonias en otras partes del mundo. (pág. 125)

Commonwealth of Nations [Mancomunidad Británica de Naciones] *s.* grupo de países, que incluye Australia y Nueva Zelandia, que fueron colonias británicas y que en la actualidad comparten la herencia británica en el campo jurídico y de gobierno. (pág. 530)

Constantinople [Constantinopla] *s.* capital de Turquía durante Del Imperio otomano, ahora llamada Estambul. (pág. 236)

cooperative [cooperativa] *s.* grande establecimiento agrícola donde trabajan centenares de familias. (pág. 508)

copra (KOH•pruh) [medula de coco] *s.* substancia seca que forma parte del coco de la palma. (pág. 532)

coup d'état (KOO day•TAH) [golpe de estado] *s.* acción de derrocar o hacer caer un gobierno por la fuerza. (pág. 319)

Court of Justice [Corte de Justicia] *s.* corte de la Unión Europea que protege los derechos de todos los ciudadanos, sea cual sea el país miembro donde vivan. (pág. 164)

Crusades [las cruzadas] *s.* serie de expediciones militares dirigidas por cristianos de Europa occidental en los siglos XI, XII y XIII, para apoderarse de nuevo de las Tierras Santas, en poder de los musulmanes. (pág. 95)

Cultural Revolution [Revolución Cultural proletaria] *s.* movimiento iniciado en 1966 por Mao Tse Tung en China, en un intento de eliminar la oposición del Partido Comunista. (pág. 499)

culture [cultura] *s.* conjunto de creencias, costumbres, leyes, formas artísticas y de vida compartidas por un grupo de personas. (pág. 21)

culture region [región cultural] *s.* territorio donde muchas personas comparten creencias, historia y lenguas similares. (pág. 24)

culture trait [característica culturale] *s.* alimento, vestimenta, tecnología, creencia, lengua u otro elemento compartido por un pueblo o cultura. (pág. 21)

cuneiform (KYOO•nee•uh•FAWRM) [escritura cuneiforme] *s.* sistema sumerio de escritura que usa símbolos con forma de cuña. (pág. 220)

currency [moneda] *s.* sistema que sirve para medir el valor de las cosas que se intercambian. (pág. 163)

czar (zahr) [zar] *s.* emperador ruso. (pág. 113)

D

Dalit [dalit] *s.* miembro de un grupo de personas en la India, también conocidas como los "intocables", fuera del sistema de castas y considerados por debajo de la casta inferior, que adquirieron algunos derechos bajo la nueva constitución de la India. (pág. 412)

Deccan Plateau [meseta de Dekán] *s.* meseta que ocupa casi todo el sur de la India. (pág. 380)

delta [delta] *s.* depósito de tierra de forma triangular en la boca de un río. (pág. 379)

deposed [depuesto] *v.* removido del poder. (pág. 150)

desertification [desertificación] *s.* proceso mediante el cual la tierra que antes podía cultivarse o era habitable se convierte en un desierto. (pág. 294)

détente (day•TAHNT) [distensión] *s.* disminución de la tensión entre países. (pág. 151)

developing nation [nación en vías de desarollo] *s.* nación recién industrializada. (pág. 444)

dialect [dialecto] *s.* forma regional de una lengua. (pág. 521)

Diet [Dieta] *s.* nombre que recibe el parlamento de Japón. (pág. 504)

dissident [disidente] *s.* persona que abiertamente muestra desacuerdo con la política de un gobierno. (pág. 197)

diversity [diversidad] *s.* variedad de culturas y puntos de vista. (pág. 309)

doi moi (doy moy) [doi moi] *s.* nombre que recibe una política de renovación y reforma llevada a cabo en Vietnam. (pág. 452)

dowry [dote] *s.* dinero o propiedad que entrega la familia de la novia a su futuro esposo y su familia. (pág. 423)

Dravidian [lengua drávida] *s.* lengua india. (pág. 422)

drought [sequía] *s.* período largo de falta de lluvia. (pág. 294)

dual monarchy [monarquía dual] *s.* gobierno en que un solo jefe gobierna dos naciones. (pág. 126)

Duma (DOO•muh) [Duma] *s.* una de las dos cámaras de la legislatura rusa. (pág. 158)

dynasty [dinastía] *s.* familia de soberanos. (pág. 476)

E

East Timor [Timor Oriental] *s.* nación situada en una isla en el sudeste asiático. (pág. 441)

economics [economía] *s.* estudio del uso de los recursos naturales y del modo de producción, intercambio y utilización de los productos, mercaderías y servicios. (pág. 20)

ECOWAS [CEDEAO, Comunidad Económica de los Estados de África Occidental] *s.* comunidad económica formada por los estados de África occidental en 1975 para mejorar el comercio en la región del África occidental y con países fuera de la región. (pág. 321)

Eightfold Path [Óctuple Sendero] *s.* conjunto de reglas en la religión budista que enseñan cómo escapar del sufrimiento. (pág. 395)

empire [imperio] *s.* nación o conjunto de territorios gobernados por un emperador. (pág. 81)

ethnic cleansing [limpieza étnica] *s.* matanza sistemática (genocidio) de uno o varios grupos étnicos que conforman una minoría. (pág. 157)

euro [euro] *s.* unidad monetaria de los países miembros de la Unión Europea. (pág. 163)

European Community [Comunidad Europea] *s.* asociación creada después de la Segunda Guerra Mundial para promover la unidad económica entre los países de Europa occidental. (pág. 186)

European Union [Unión Europea] *s.* asociación económica y política de países de Europa occidental. (pág. 162)

F

fascism (FASH•IHZ•uhm) [fascismo] *s.* filosofía que promueve un gobierno centralista fuerte, controlado por el ejército y dirigido por un dictador poderoso. (pág. 130)

fellahin (FEHL•uh•HEEN) [fellahín] *s.* nombre que recibe un agricultor en Egipto. (pág. 259)

fertile [fértil] *adj.* abundante en recursos y nutrientes. (pág. 213)

Fertile Crescent [Media Luna Fértil] *s.* región comprendida entre lo que hoy es Irak, el nordeste de Siria y parte del sudeste de Turquía, que tiene la forma de un creciente o medialuna y que posee tierras fértiles. (pág. 217)

feudalism [feudalismo] *s.* sistema político y económico de la Europa medieval en el que los señores feudales repartían tierras a miembros de la nobleza menos poderosos, llamados vasallos, quienes, a cambio de éstas, se comprometían a brindar varios servicios a los señores feudales. (pág. 86)

Five Pillars of Islam [los cinco pilares del Islam] *s.* las enseñanzas más importantes de Mahoma en la religión musulmana. (pág. 234)

fjord (fyawrd) [fiordo] *s.* entrada larga y estrecha del mar formada entre acantilados abruptos. (pág. 68)

Florence [Florencia] *s.* ciudad italiana que durante el siglo XIV mantuvo una dinámica actividad bancaria, comercial y manufacturera. (pág. 96)

Four Noble Truths [las cuatro nobles verdades] *s.* las enseñanzas más importantes del budismo. (pág. 395)

French Resistance [Resistencia francesa] *s.* en Francia, un movimiento antialemán durante la Segunda Guerra Mundial. (pág. 184)

French Revolution [Revolución francesa] *s.* revolución que comenzó el 14 de julio de 1789 y tuvo como resultado la conversión de Francia en una república. (pág. 110)

G

geography [geografía] *s.* estudio de los pueblos, lugares y el medio ambiente. (pág. 18)

Good Friday Accord [Acuerdo del Viernes Santo] *s.* acuerdo firmado por los protestantes y católicos de Irlanda del Norte que estableció la Asamblea de Irlanda del Norte, asamblea esta que representa a los votantes de ambos grupos. (pág. 175)

government [gobierno] *s.* los individuos y grupos en una sociedad que tienen la autoridad de crear leyes y hacerlas cumplir, y de resolver desacuerdos que puedan surgir con respecto a ellas. (pág. 19)

Grand National Assembly [Gran Asamblea Nacional] *s.* poder legislativo de Turquía. (pág. 271)

Great Barrier Reef [Gran Barrera de Arrecife/ Coral] *s.* arrecife de coral más grande del mundo, ubicado al noreste de la costa australiana. (pág. 474)

Great Leap Forward [Gran Salto Adelante] *s.* programa llevado a cabo por Mao Zedong en China en 1958 para acelerar el desarrollo económico. (pág. 498)

Great Rift Valley [Valle de la Gran Depresión] *s.* sucesión de extensos valles profundos que se extienden desde el Mar Rojo hasta Mozambique. (pág. 293)

Great Zimbabwe [Gran Zimbabue] *s.* ciudad en Zimbabue construida por los shona a principios del siglo X a. de C. y hecha de piedra. (pág. 341)

Green Revolution [revolución verde] *s.* movimiento que empezó a fines de la década de los 60 y que introdujo granos mejorados con ingeniería genética en la agricultura de naciones en vías de desarrollo. (pág. 419)

guild [gremio] *s.* asociación creada por personas que trabajan en una misma industria, con el fin de proteger sus intereses comunes y mantener ciertos criterios y principios aplicables a la industria. (pág. 88)

H

haiku (HY•koo) [haiku] *s.* forma de poesía japonesa que tiene sólo 17 sílabas. (pág. 513)

haj [haj] *s.* peregrinación a la Meca que la mayoría de los musulmanes intenta hacer por lo menos una vez en su vida. (pág. 251)

Han [han] *s.* etnia principal en China. (pág. 514)

harambee [harambee] *adj.* término en swahili que significa cooperar, que se usa para referirse a las escuelas construidas por los kenianos y no por el gobierno de Kenia. (pág. 360)

Hausa (HOW•suh) [hausa] *s.* etnia más numerosa en Nigeria. (pág. 331)

Heian Age [Período de Heian] *s.* época de oro de la cultura japonesa, desde 794 hasta 1185. (pág. 485)

hieroglyphics [jeroglíficos] *s.* sistema de escritura que utiliza dibujos y símbolos para representar palabras y sonidos. (pág. 225)

Himalayas [El Himalaya] *s.* cadena montañosa cuya extensión es de aproximadamente 1500 millas en el sur de Asia. (pág. 378)

Hinduism [hinduismo] *s.* religión desarrollada en la antigua India. (pág. 387)

Hiroshima (HEER•uh•SHEE•muh) [Hiroshima] *s.* ciudad japonesa en donde Estados Unidos arrojó una bomba atómica en 1945. (pág. 518)

history [historia] *s.* un registro de los acontecimientos del pasado. (pág. 18)

Holocuast [Holocausto] *s.* matanza sistemática (genocidio) de los judíos europeos y otros por el partido nazi durante la Segunda Guerra Mundial. (pág. 130)

homogeneous [homogéneo] *adj.* sin diferencias en la mayor parte. (pág. 519)

human right [derecho humano] *s.* derecho que pertenece a toda persona. (pág. 503)

hunter gatherer [cazador y recolector] *s.* persona que procura alimentos mediante la caza y la recolección de granos y frutas salvajes. (pág. 214)

Hutu [hutu] *s.* mayoría étnica de Rwanda-Burundi. (pág. 305)

hydroelectricity [electricidad hidráulica] *s.* energía eléctrica producida por el agua. (pág. 180)

I

Igbo [igbo] *s.* grupo étnico del sudeste de Nigeria. (pág. 331)

imperialism [imperialismo] *s.* práctica mediante la cual un país controla el gobierno y la economía de otro país o territorio. (pág. 104)

impressionism [impresionismo] *s.* estilo de arte que crea una impresión de algo en lugar de una obra con características concretas. (pág. 187)

Indian National Congress [Congreso Nacional Indio] *s.* congreso formado en 1885 en la India, donde los habitantes podían debatir sus problemas. (pág. 406)

Indo-Aryan [indoario] *adj.* que pertenece a la familia de lenguas que incluye a todas las lenguas europeas y muchas lenguas indias. (pág. 422)

Industrial Revolution [Revolución industrial] *s.* período de cambio en el siglo XVIII que dio lugar a la fabricación de productos por máquinas. (pág. 108)

information technology [tecnología informática] *s.* tecnología como computadoras, software y la Internet, que sirve para procesar y usar la información. (pág. 418)

interdependence [interdependencia] *s.* dependencia económica, política y social que mantienen las sociedades de diversas regiones culturales. (pág. 26)

Iron Curtain [Cortina de Hierro] *s.* barrera política que aisló los países de Europa del Este luego de la Segunda Guerra Mundial, limitando la capacidad de movimiento y tránsito fuera de esta región. (pág. 136)

irrigation [irrigación] *s.* proceso mediante el cual se riega el terreno seco. (pág. 215)

Islam [Islam] *s.* religión que enseña que hay un dios y que Mahoma es su profeta. (pág. 232)

J

Janissary [jenízaro] *s.* miembro del grupo de soldados leales al sultán del Imperio otomano. (pág. 237)

Judaism [judaísmo] *s.* primera religión monoteísta fundada por Abraham y cuyos seguidores se denominan judíos. (pág. 230)

jute [yute] *s.* planta fibrosa que se usa para hacer cordel, bolsas, sacos y arpillera. (pág. 417)

K

Khmer (KMAIR) [khmer] *s.* antigua etnia en Camboya. (pág. 396)

kibbutz (ki•BŏŏTS) [kibutz] *s.* pueblo o comunidad judía de agricultores en Palestina (o lo que hoy es Israel), cuyos miembros poseen todo en forma colectiva y comparten la labor agrícola, el ingreso y los gastos. (pág. 265)

kinship [parentesco] *s.* relación entre miembros de una familia. (pág. 349)

Kurd [kurdo] *s.* habitante que vive en las montañas de Armenia, Georgia, Irán, Irak, Líbano, Siria y Turquía. (pág. 246)

L

labor force [fuerza laboral] *s.* trabajadores disponibles. (pág. 109)

latitude [latitud] *s.* distancia norte-sur con relación al ecuador, de la superficie terrestre. (pág. 36)

Law of Return [Ley de Retorno] *s.* ley sancionada en 1950 mediante la cual se otorga permiso a los judíos de cualquier parte del mundo para inmigrar a Israel y convertirse en ciudadanos. (pág. 266)

London [Londres] *s.* capital de Inglaterra. (pág. 173)

longitude [longitud] *s.* distancia este-oeste de un punto de la Tierra, a partir de la línea inicial llamada primer meridiano (meridiano de Greenwich). (pág. 36)

M

Magna Carta (MAG•nuh KAHR•tuh) [Carta Magna] *s.* documento firmado por el rey Juan de Inglaterra en 1215 que garantizó los derechos básicos de las personas en ese país. (pág. 89)

Mahabharata (MAH•huh•BAH•ruh•tuh) [*Mahabharata*] *s.* poema épico sobre la expansión del hinduismo. (pág. 421)

mandala (MUHN•duh•luh) [mandala] *s.* sistema político en el sudeste de Asia en el que el gobernante con poder central intento obtener apoyo de otros y recurrío al comercio para ejercer influencia y mantener el poder. (pág. 438)

mandate [protectorado] *s.* país puesto bajo el control de otro por medio de un acuerdo internacional. (pág. 244)

Mangla Dam [presa Mangla] *s.* dique construido en el río Jhelum en el nordeste de Pakistán con el fin de controlar las aguas y proveer energía hidroeléctrica. (pág. 428)

manorialism [régimen señorial] *s.* sistema social en el que campesinos trabajan las tierras de un señor, a cambio de protección y seguridad. (pág. 87)

Maori (MOW•ree) [maorí] *s.* los primeros pobladores de Nueva Zelandia. (pág. 527)

map projection [proyección cartografía] *s.* una de las diversas maneras de mostrar la curvatura de la Tierra en una superficie plana. (pág. 47)

martial law [ley marcial] *s.* sistema temporal de gobierno militar durante tiempos de guerra o cuando el gobierno está en crisis. (pág. 411)

Masai (mah•SY) [masai] *s.* grupo étnico en África. (pág. 341)

matrilineal society [sociedad matrilineal] *s.* sociedad en la que sólo la línea materna se tiene en cuenta para determinar el árbol genealógico. (pág. 533)

mediate [mediar] *v.* ayudar en un conflicto para encontrar soluciones de paz. (pág. 321)

medieval (MEE•dee•EE•vuhl) [medieval] *adj.* que pertenece al período de la historia comprendido entre la caída del Imperio romano y el comienzo del mundo moderno, aproximadamente desde 476 a 1453. (pág. 85)

Mediterranean Sea [mar Mediterráneo] *s.* mar interno que bordea Europa, el sudoeste de Asia y África. (pág. 68)

Meiji Restoration [Restauración Meiji] *s.* período japonés comprendido entre 1868 y 1911 durante el cual Japón fue gobernado nuevamente por un emperador después de siglos de gobierno militar. (pág. 517)

Melanesia [Melanesia] *s.* uno de los tres grupos regionales de islas en el océano Pacífico. (pág. 528)

Micronesia [Micronesia] *s.* uno de los tres grupos regionales de islas en el océano Pacífico. (pág. 528)

migrate [migrar] *v.* irse de un área para establecerse en otra. (pág. 38)

military dictatorship [dictadura militar] *s.* gobierno de una persona militar. (pág. 441)

missionary [misionero] *s.* persona que va a otro país para transmitir enseñanzas religiosas y realizar obras de bien. (pág. 303)

Mohenjo-Daro (moh•HEHN•joh•DAHR•oh) [Mohenjo-Daro] *s.* ciudad antigua de gran tamaño ubicada en el valle del río Indo. (pág. 386)

monsoon [monzón] *s.* viento de estación que trae gran cantidad de lluvias. (pág. 382)

Mount Everest [monte Everest] *s.* pico más alto del Himalaya y en el mundo, ubicado en las fronteras de China y Nepal. (pág. 470)

Mount Fuji [monte Fuji] *s.* montaña más alta en Japón. (pág. 472)

Mughal Empire [Imperio mogol] *s.* imperio que duró de 1526 hasta 1707 y que comprendió la mayor parte del subcontinente de la India. (pág. 404)

multiparty system [sistema pluripartidista] *s.* sistema político en donde existe dos o más partidos. (pág. 359)

Muslim [musulmán] *s.* seguidor de la religión islámica. (pág. 232)

Muslim Brotherhood [Hermandad Musulmana] *s.* grupo musulmán fundamentalista que cree que Egipto debe ser gobernado solamente por la ley islámica para cumplir con los principios del Islam. (pág. 258)

Muslim League [Liga Musulmana] *s.* grupo formado por musulmanes en la India en 1906, establecido para proteger sus derechos. (pág. 406)

N

Nagasaki (NAH•guh•SAH•kee) [Nagasaki] *s.* ciudad japonesa en donde Estados Unidos arrojó una bomba atómica en 1945. (pág. 518)

nationalism [nacionalismo] *s.* intenso orgullo por el país o grupo étnico propio. (pág. 123)

NATO (NAY•toh) [OTAN, Organización del Tratado del Atlántico Norte] *s.* alianza de defensa que agrupa a los países de Europa occidental, Canadá y Estados Unidos, que acuerdan la defensa común en caso de ataque. (pág. 131)

nonrenewable resource [recurso no renovables] *s.* recurso que no se puede sustituir o que se puede sustituir sólo tras miles o millones de años. (pág. 295)

Northern Plains [Llanuras del a norte] *s.* llanuras que se extienden entre el sistema montañoso del Himalaya y el sur de la India. (pág. 379)

O

OAU [OUA, Organización de la Unidad Africana] *s.* organización formada en 1963 para promover la unidad entre todos los africanos. (pág. 321)

oligarchy (AHL•ih•GAHR•kee) [oligarquía] *s.* gobierno de sólo unos pocos individuos poderosos. (pág. 74)

ombudsman [defensor del pueblo] *s.* funcionario del gobierno sueco que protege los derechos de los ciudadanos y asegura que los tribunales y la administración pública cumplan con la ley. (pág. 179)

one-party system [sistema monopartidista] *s.* sistema donde sólo se puede votar por un partido político y por un candidato para cada puesto de gobierno. (pág. 316)

OPEC [OPEP, Organización de Países Exportadores de Petróleo] *s.* organización que determina el precio y la cantidad de petróleo que se deberá producir cada año en Irak, Irán, Arabia Saudita, Kuwait y Venezuela. (pág. 250)

Opium War [Guerra del Opio] *s.* guerra por el control del comercio del opio entre China y Gran Bretaña desde 1839 a 1842. (pág. 496)

Orthodox Jew [judío ortodoxo] *s.* judío que cumple estrictamente con la ley judía. (pág. 267)

Ottoman Empire [Imperio otomano] *s.* imperio musulmán, desde comienzos del siglo XV hasta la década de 1920. (pág. 236)

outback [llanura desértica] *s.* vasta superficie plana que se extiende por casi toda la zona central de Australia. (pág. 473)

overgrazing [pastoreo excesivo] *s.* proceso mediante el cual se lleva a pastar demasiado ganado sin permitir que la tierra recupere su vegetación. (pág. 347)

P

pagoda [pagoda] *s.* torre budista de muchos niveles, con esculturas o imágenes del Buda talladas en cada nivel. (pág. 446)

paleontologist [paleontólogo] *s.* científico que estudia los fósiles. (pág. 296)

Palestine [Palestina] *s.* región en el sudoeste de Asia, comúnmente llamada Tierra Santa. (pág. 244)

panchayat [panchayati] *s.* consejo rural en India. (pág. 412)

papyrus (puh•PY•ruhs) [papiro] *s.* material semejante al papel, hecho de un junco. (pág. 224)

parliamentary republic [república parlamentaria] *s.* república cuyo jefe de estado, en general un primer ministro, es el líder del partido político que tiene la mayoría de representantes en el parlamento. (pág. 155)

pastoralism [pastoreo] *s.* forma de subsistencia mediante la cría de ganado, ovejas o cabras. (pág. 347)

patrician (puh•TRIHSH•uhn) [patricio] *s.* miembro de familia adinerada y hacendada en la antigua Roma, que afirmaba que sus orígenes se remontan a la época de la fundación de Roma. (pág. 79)

patrilineal society [sociedad patrilineal] *s.* sociedad en las que sólo la línea paterna se tiene en cuenta para determinar el árbol genealógico. (pág. 533)

peninsula [península] *s.* territorio rodeado de agua en tres de sus lados. (pág. 68)

Persian Gulf War [Guerra del Golfo Pérsico] *s.* guerra entre Estados Unidos e Irak, en 1991. (pág. 247)

petrochemical [producto petroquímico] *s.* producto derivado del petróleo crudo y gas natural. (pág. 251)

pharaoh (FAIR•oh) [faraón] *s.* antiguo rey egipcio. (pág. 225)

philosopher [filósofo] *s.* persona que estudia y piensa sobre el mundo y su naturaleza. (pág. 75)

plain [llanura] *s.* superficie extensa y plana que suele no tener muchos árboles. (pág. 69)

plateau [meseta] *s.* área plana situada a cierta altura sobre el nivel del mar. (pág. 292)

plebeian (plih•BEE•uhn) [plebeyo] *s.* ciudadano corriente (sin título de nobleza) en la antigua Roma. (pág. 79)

polis [polis] *s.* ciudad central de una ciudad estado. (pág. 73)

Politburo (PAHL•iht•BYUR•oh) [Politburo] *s.* grupo que encabeza un partido comunista. (pág. 452)

Polynesia [Polinesia] *s.* uno de los tres grupos regionales de islas en océano Pacífico. (pág. 528)

primary product [producto primario] *s.* materia prima. (pág. 250)

private property rights [derechos de propiedad privada] *s.* derechos individuales de ser propietario de bienes raíces, campos o industrias. (pág. 149)

propaganda (PRAHP•uh•GAN•duh) [propaganda] *s.* material cuyo objetivo es difundir ciertas creencias. (pág. 148)

Protestant [protestante] *s.* miembro de una iglesia cristiana fundada de acuerdo a los principis de la Reforma. (pág. 100)

Punjabi [punjabí] *s.* lengua hablada en Pakistán. (pág. 428)

puppet government [gobierno títere] *s.* gobierno que hace lo que le indica un poder exterior. (pág. 137)

pyramid [pirámide] *s.* estructura con cuatro lados triangulares que se erige de una base rectangular y se junta con un vértice común en la parte superior. (pág. 225)

Q

Qur'an (kuh•RAN) [Corán] *s.* texto sagrado del Islam. (pág. 232)

R

racism [racismo] *s.* creencia de que una raza es inferior a otra. (pág. 308)

Ramadan (RAM•uh•DAHN) [Ramadán] *s.* noveno mes del año islámico. (pág. 251)

Reformation [Reforma] *s.* movimiento del siglo XVI que se propuso cambiar las prácticas de la Iglesia Católica. (pág. 99)

Reign of Terror [reino del Terror] *s.* período comprendido entre 1793 y 1794 durante el cual las nuevas autoridades en Francia ejecutaron miles de ciudadanos. (pág. 111)

relative location [ubicación relativa] *s.* ubicación de un lugar en relación con otros. (pág. 37)

Renaissance *s.* período de creatividad y de aprendizaje en Europa occidental entre los siglos XIV y XVI. (pág. 96)

renewable resource [recurso renovable] *s.* recurso que puede usarse y reemplazarse luego de un relativamente corto período. (pág. 295)

republic [república] *s.* forma de gobierno controlado por sus cuidadanos a través de representantes elegidos por los cuidadanos. (pág. 79)

reunification [reunificación] *s.* acción de unificar nuevamente las partes. (pág. 190)

Riksdag (RIHKS•DAHG) *s.* parlamento sueco. (pág. 178)

Ring of Fire [Cinturón de Fuego del Pacífico] *s.* área de actividad volcánica en el océano Pacífico. (pág. 472)

rite of passage [rito de paso] *s.* ceremonia especial que marca la transición de una etapa de la vida a otra. (pág. 328)

Rosh Hashanah (RAWSH huh•SHAW•nuh) [Rosh Hashana] *s.* año nuevo judío. (pág. 267)

Russian Revolution [Revolución rusa] *s.* revolución de 1917 que eliminó la monarquía rusa del poder luego de 400 años de vigencia. (pág. 116)

S

Sahel (suh•HAYL) [Sahel] *s.* región semiárida en el sur del Sahara. (pág. 294)

samurai (SAM•uh•RY) [samurai] *s.* guerrero japonés que mediante juramento presta servicio a un señor particular, protegiendo su propiedad. (pág. 486)

sanction [sanción] *s.* multas impuestas en un país que viola la ley internacional. (pág. 356)

Sanskrit [sánscrito] *s.* lengua clásica de la India y del hinduismo. (pág. 356)

savanna [sabana] *s.* llanura de regiones tropicales y subtropicales con escasos árboles y vegetación. (pág. 294)

scarcity [escasez] *s.* palabra usada por los economistas para describir el conflicto que existe entre el deseo de los seres humanos y los recursos limitados para satisfacerlo. (pág. 20)

Scientific Revolution [Revolución científica] *s.* período de grandes cambios científicos y descubrimientos durante los siglos XVI y XVII. (pág. 108)

scribe [escriba] *s.* profesional que se encarga de archivar o copiar documentos. (pág. 220)

secede [separarse] *v.* independizarse de una unidad política, como una nación. (pág. 175)

secondary product [producto secundario] *s.* producto manufacturado con materias primas. (pág. 250)

secular [secular] *adj.* no relacionado con ninguna religión. (pág. 267)

sediment [sedimento] *s.* pequeños fragmentos de roca que son movidos por el viento, el agua o el hielo. (pág. 379)

Senate [Senado] *s.* asamblea más poderosa de la República romana, cuyos representantes eran elegidos. (pág. 79)

Shinto [shinto] *s.* religión japonesa que se desarrolló alrededor de 300 a. de C. (pág. 484)

shogun [shogun] *s.* jefe militar del emperador japonés, en la época feudal, que ejercía el mayor poder. (pág. 487)

Sindhi [sindhi] *s.* lengua que se habla en Pakistán. (pág. 428) skerry [arrecife] *s.* islote. (pág. 181)

socialism [socialismo] *s.* sistema económico en donde algunos negocios e industrias le pertenecen a una cooperativa o al gobierno. (pág. 186)

Solidarity [Solidaridad] *s.* sindicato polaco cuya finalidad inicial fue aumentar el salario, mejorar las condiciones laborales de los trabajadores y luego oponerse al comunismo. (pág. 194)

standard of living [nivel de vida] *s.* forma de medir la calidad de vida. (pág. 163)

subcontinent [subcontinente] *s.* gran masa territorial que es parte de un continente pero que posee su propia identidad geográfica. (pág. 378)

subsistence farming [agricultura de subsistencia] *s.* método de agricultura mediante el cual los agricultores cultivan alimentos principalmente para alimentar a sus familias en vez de venderlos. (pág. 325)

Sumerian [sumerio] *s.* uno de los primeros pobladores de la Mesopotamia. (pág. 218)

supply and demand [oferta y demanda] *s.* concepto económico que establece que el precio de un producto sube o baja según la cantidad de personas que lo deseen (demanda) y según la disponibilidad del mismo (oferta). (pág. 452)

Swahili (swah•HEE•lee) [swahili] *s.* lengua bantú africana. (pág. 360)

T

Taiping (ty•PIHNG) Rebellion [rebelión Taiping] *s.* la mayor insurrección campesina que ocurrió en China a raíz de la firma del Tratado de Nanking. (pág. 496)

Taj Mahal [Taj Majal] *s.* la construcción más famosa de la India, construida por el emperador mogol Sha Jahan, en la década de 1640. (pág. 420)

Tale of Genji, The [*Cuento de Genji*] *s.* primera novela de la literatura universal, escrita por la japonesa Murasaki Shikibu en el siglo XI. (pág. 486)

Taliban [talibán] *s.* grupo musulmán fundamentalista que tomó el poder en Afganistán en 1996. (pág. 410)

Taoism (DOW•IHZ•uhm) [taoísmo] *s.* filosofía china fundada en el siglo III a. de C. por Lao Tzu. (pág. 478)

Tarbela Dam [presa de Tarbela] *s.* dique construido en el río Indo para el control de aguas e irrigación. (pág. 428)

tariff [arancel aduanero] *s.* tarifa o suma de dinero impuesto por el gobierno en productos que se importan o exportan. (pág. 163)

Tet [Tet] *s.* año nuevo vietnamita. (pág. 453)

textile [textil] *s.* material que se produce mediante el tejido de fibras. (pág. 508)

thatch [techo de paja] *s.* hojas de palmeras, cañas o paja que se usan para construir techos. (pág. 446)

thematic map [mapa temático] *s.* mapa que se centra en una idea o tema particular. (pág. 46)

theocracy (thee•AHK•ruh•see) [teocracia] *s.* gobierno encabezado por una autoridad religiosa. (pág. 235)

Tiananmen (tyahn•ahn•mehn) Square [Plaza de Tiananmen] *s.* plaza en Beijing, China, donde miles de manifestantes fueron heridos o matados por el ejército en 1989. (pág. 503)

tradeoff [contrapartida] *s.* la renuncia de ciertos beneficios a cambio de otros. (pág. 258)

tungsten [tungsteno] *s.* un metal. (pág. 507)

Tutsi [tutsi] *s.* etnia minoritaria en Rwanda-Burundi. (pág. 305)

typhoon [tifón] *s.* huracán muy frecuente del océano Pacífico occidental. (pág. 472)

Index

An *i* preceding a page reference in italics indicates that there is an illustration, and usually text information as well, on that page. An *m* or a *c* preceding an italic page reference indicates a map or a chart, as well as text information on that page.

Acknowledgments

Text Credits

Chapter 10, page 281: Quote by Herakleitos, translated by Guy Davenport, from *7 Greeks,* copyright © 1995 by Guy Davenport. Reprinted by Sales Territory: U.S./Canadian rights only.

Chapter 12, page 340: "The Giant's Causeway" from *Irish Fairy Tales and Legends* retold by Una Leavy. Copyright © 1996 by The Watts Publishing Group Ltd.

Chapter 15, page 427: Quote from *Everyday Life in Babylonia and Assyria* by H.W.F. Saggs. Copyright © 1965 by B. T. Batsford.

Chapter 16, page 468: "Thread by Thread" by Bracha Serri, translated by Shlomit Yaacobi and Nava Mizrahi, from *The Space Between Our Footsteps: Poems and Paintings from the Middle East,* selected by Naomi Shihab Nye. Copyright © 1998.

Chapter 19, page 558: Text copyright © 1995 by Isaac Olaleye from *The Distant Talking Drum: Poems from Nigeria* by Isaac Olaleye. Published by Wordsong/Boyds Mills Press, Inc. Reprinted by permission.

Chapter 23, page 683: Quote from Analects, page 57 from *The Essential Confucius,* translated by Thomas Cleary. Copyright © 1992 by Thomas Cleary. Reprinted by permission of HarperCollins Publishers Inc.

page 688: From *Echoes of the White Giraffe* by Sook Nyul Choi. Copyright © 1993 by Sook Nyul Choi. Reprinted by permission of Houghton Mifflin Company. All rights reserved.

Art Credits

Beverly Doyle 28; Ken Goldammer 12; Nenad Jakesevic 381, 404, 434, 614; Rich McMahon 44, 323; Gary Overacre 340; Matthew Pippin xvi, 420, 431, 460, 517, 550, 592, 706, 719. All other artwork created by Publicom, Inc.

Map Credits

This product contains proprietary property of **MAPQUEST.COM** Unauthorized use, including copying, of this product is expressly prohibited.

Photography Credits

Cover *Clockwise from top left* Copyright © Art Wolfe/Stone/GettyImages; Copyright © Superstock, Inc., Copyright © Bill Cardoni/Bruce Coleman, Inc.; Copyright © Stone/GettyImages; **ii–iii** Copyright © Stone/GettyImages; **ii** *top left* Copyright © Art Wolfe/Stone/GettyImages; *top right* Copyright © Superstock, Inc.; **iii** *top* Copyright © Bill Cardoni/Bruce Coleman, Inc.; **vi** *bottom* NASA; *children* See page 14 for full credits; **vii** *top left* Erich Lessing/Art Resource, New York; *bottom left* Dave Bartruff/Corbis; *bottom right* Hulton|Archive/Getty Images; *top* Erich Lessing/Art Resource, New York; *top right* Reunion des Musées Nationaux/ Art Resource, New York; *center right* Scott Gilchrist/Archivision.com; **viii** *top left* S. Bavister/Robert Harding Picture Library; *bottom left* John Noble/Corbis; *bottom* John Launois/Black Star Publishing/PictureQuest; *bottom right* AFP/Corbis; *top* Copyright © Brannhage/ Premium/Panoramic Images; **ix** *bottom left* Archivo Iconografico, S. A./ Corbis; *bottom* Copyright © IFA/Bruce Coleman; *top center* Carmen Redondo/Corbis; *top right* Ashmolean Museum, Oxford, England/The Bridgeman Art Library; **x** *top left* John Noble/ Corbis; *center left* Charles and Josette Lenars/Corbis; *bottom left* Copyright © Boyd Norton/The Image Works; *top right* Giraudon/Art Resource, New York; **xi** *center left* Brian A. Vikander/Corbis; *bottom* Wolfgang Kaehler/Corbis; *center right* Caroline Penn/Corbis; *top right* Paul Almasy/Corbis; **xii** *top* Reunion des Musées Nationaux/Art Resource, New York; *bottom* N. Blythe/ Robert Harding Picture Library; **xiii** *top* Quadrillion/Corbis; *center* James L. Amos/Corbis; *bottom* Eric Crichton/ Bruce Coleman/PictureQuest; *bottom right* Michael S. Yamashita/Corbis; **S12** Daniel Fitzpatrick/*St. Louis Post Dispatch,* © August 24, 1939; **S13** The Granger Collection/New York; **S26** Hulton|Archive/Getty Images; **S30** Victoria & Albert Museum, London/Art Resource, New York; **S32** Mary Evans Picture Library.

UNIT ONE

2–3 NASA; **4** *bottom right* NOAA; *left* Copyright © Owen Franken/Stock Boston; *top right* Science Museum/ Science and Society Picture Library, London.

Chapter 1

14 *top left* Brian A. Vikander/Corbis; *top center* Owen Franken/Corbis; *bottom left* Tim Thompson/Corbis; *center left* Kevin Schafer/Corbis; *bottom center* Maria Taglienti/The Image Bank/GettyImages; *center right* James A. Sugar/Corbis; *bottom right* Nicholas deVore III/Photographers Aspen/PictureQuest; *top right* Dean Conger/Corbis; **15** *top* John Callahan/Stone/GettyImages; *bottom left* The Purcell Team/Corbis; *center left* Helen Norman/Corbis; *center* Nik Wheeler/Corbis; *bottom center* Dennis Degnan/Corbis; *center right* Neil Rabinowitz/Corbis; *bottom right* Martin Rogers/Corbis; **16** *top* Jim West/Impact Visuals/PictureQuest; *bottom* K. Gilham/Robert Harding Picture

Library; **17** *top* Picture Finders/eStock Photography/PictureQuest; *bottom* The Military Picture Library/Corbis; **18** *bottom* Thomas Hoepker/Magnum/PictureQuest; *top* Copyright © Ellen Senisi/The Image Works; **19** *left* Oliver Benn/Stone/GettyImages; *right* Copyright © Alon Reininger/Contact Press Images; *center* Copyright © Alex Farnsworth/The Image Works; **20** *top right* Jim West/Impact Visuals/PictureQuest; *bottom left* Richard Drew/AP/ Wide World Photos; **21** NASA/Roger Ressmeyer/Corbis; **22** Joseph Sohm/Visions of America, LLC/PictureQuest; **23** *bottom* Joe Sohm, Chromosohm/Stock Connection/PictureQuest; *top* Scott Teven/Stock Connection/ PictureQuest; **24** *right* Hulton|Archive/Getty Images; *left* Lindsay Hebberd/Corbis; **26** *left* Dean Conger/Corbis; *right* K. Gilham/ Robert Harding Picture Library; *center* Chris Andrews Publications/Corbis; **30** *all* Picture Finders/eStock Photography/PictureQuest.

Chapter 2

32–33 Copyright © SuperStock; **33** *top* NASA; **34** *top* Christopher Morris/Black Star Publishing/PictureQuest; *bottom* David Muench/Stone/GettyImages; **35** *left* The Granger Collection, New York; **36** Schafer and Hill/Stone/ GettyImages; **37** *top* Christopher Morris/Black Star Publishing/PictureQuest; *bottom* World Perspectives/Stone/ GettyImages; **38** Copyright © Eastcott-Momatiuk/The Image Works; **39** David Muench/Stone/GettyImages; **42** *top left* Ethnic Art Institute of Micronesia; *top right* National Maritime Museum Picture Library, London; *bottom right* Royalty Free/Corbis; **43** *bottom* Austrian Archives/Corbis; **43** *center right, top* National Maritime Museum Picture Library, London; **43** *center left* Reproduced with permission of Garmin Corporation; **45** *right* The Granger Collection, New York; **47** The Newberry Library/The Granger Collection, New York; **50** David Muench/ Stone/GettyImages; **51** NASA.

UNIT TWO

52–53 Stuart Dee/The Image Bank/GettyImages.

Chapter 3

64–65 Copyright © James L. Stanfield/National Geographic Society Image Collection; **65** *top* Robert Harding Picture Library; **66** *top* Sef/Art Resource, New York; *bottom left, bottom right* Erich Lessing/Art Resource, New York; **67** Bill Ross/Corbis; **68** Arnulf Husmo/Stone/GettyImages; **69** Walter Bibikow/Index Stock Imagery/ PictureQuest; **70** *top left* Jonathan Blair/Corbis; *top right* Eye Ubiquitous/Corbis; *bottom* Johan Elzenga/Stone/ GettyImages; **72** *all* Greek Culture Ministry/AP/Wide World Photos; **73** HorreeZirkzee Produk/Corbis; **74** Foto Marburg/ Art Resource, New York; **75** Sef/Art Resource, New York; **76** *left* Nimatallah/Art Resource, New York; *right* Scala/ Art Resource, New York; **78** Copyright © Macduff Everton/The Image Works; **79** Erich Lessing/Art Resource, New York; **80** Giraudon/Art Resource, New York; **81** Erich Lessing/Art Resource, New York; **82** *top left* Jeff Rotman; *center* Scala/Art Resource, New York; *bottom right* O. Alamany and E. Vicens/Corbis; *bottom center* Bettmann/Corbis; **83** Erich Lessing/Art Resource, New York; **84** Art Resource, New York; **85** Reunion des Musées Nationaux/Art Resource, New York; **86** Catherine Karnow/Corbis; *spread* Musée de la Tapisserre, Bayoux, France/ The Bridgeman Art Library; **87** *top* Jose Fuste Raga/eStockPhotography/PictureQuest; **88** Erich Lessing/Art Resource, New York; **89** *right* Dept. of the Environment, London/The Bridgeman Art Library; *left* The Granger Collection, New York; **90** *top left* Sef/Art Resource, New York; *bottom* Erich Lessing/Art Resource, New York; *top right* Jose Fuste Raga/eStockPhotography/PictureQuest.

Chapter 4

92–93 Bruno Barbey/Magnum/PictureQuest; **93** *top* The Granger Collection, New York; *center* Leonard L. T. Phodes/Animals Animals; **94** *center* Mary Evans Picture Library; *top* Reunion des Musées Nationaux/Art Resource, New York; *bottom* The Pierpont Morgan Library/Art Resource, New York; **95** The Granger Collection, New York; **96** Alinari/Art Resource, New York; **97** *top* Scott Gilchrist/Archivision.com; *bottom* Palazzo Medici-Riccardi, Florence, Italy/The Bridgeman Art Library; **98** *bottom* Scala/Art Resource, New York; *top* Reunion des Musées Nationaux/Art Resource, New York; **99** The Pierpont Morgan Library/Art Resource, New York; **100** Corbis; **101** Giraudon/Art Resource, New York; **103** North Wind Pictures; **104** Reunion des Musées Nationaux/Art Resource, New York; **107** AKG London; **108** *center* Scala/Art Resource, New York; *top* NASA; *bottom* Copyright © Will & Deni McIntyre/Photo Researchers; **109** The Granger Collection, New York; **110** Hulton-Deutsch Collection/ Corbis; **111** Victoria & Albert Museum, London/Art Resource, New York; **112** *right* © Courtesy of the Estate of Ruskin Spear/Private Collection/Phillips, Fine Art Auctioneers, New York/The Bridgeman Art Library; *left* Giraudon/ Art Resource, New York; **113** *top* Scala/Art Resource, New York; *bottom* Roger Tidman/Corbis; **114** Erich Lessing/ Art Resource, New York; **115** Chuck Nacke/Woodfin Camp/PictureQuest; **116** Hulton-Deutsch Collection/Corbis; **118** *top left* North Wind Pictures; *bottom left* Alinari/Art Resource, New York; *bottom right* Hulton-Deutsch Collection/Corbis; *top right* © Courtesy of the Estate of Ruskin Spear/Private Collection/Phillips, Fine Art Auctioneers, New York/The Bridgeman Art Library; **119** The Library of Congress Website.

Chapter 5

120–121 Michael S. Yamashita/Corbis; 121 *top* Owen Franken/Corbis; 122 *top* Ralph White/Corbis; *bottom* Hulton|Archive/Getty Images; 123 Hulton|Archive/Getty Images; 125 *bottom* Hulton|Archive/Getty Images; *center* Gianni Dagli Orti/Corbis; *top* Mark Rykoff/Rykoff Collection/Corbis; 127 *right* Bettmann/Corbis; *left* Hulton|Archive/Getty Images; 128 *top* Hulton|Archive/Getty Images; *bottom* Art Young; 129 Hulton| Archive/ Getty Images; 131 *bottom* Hulton|Archive/Getty Images; *top* Hulton-Deutsch Collection/Corbis; 133 St. Louis Post Dispatch; 136 Paul Almasy/Corbis; 137 *bottom* Sovfoto/Eastfoto/PictureQuest; *top* Ralph White/ Corbis; 138 *bottom* Hulton|Archive/Getty Images; *top* Sovfoto/Eastfoto/PictureQuest; 139 Culver Pictures/ PictureQuest; 140 *bottom* Hulton|Archive/Getty Images; *center* The Kobal Collection; 141 Dave Bartruff/Corbis; 142 *right* Sovfoto/Eastfoto/PictureQuest; *left* Hulton|Archive/Getty Images; *center* Hulton-Deutsch Collection/Corbis; 143 Mandeville Special Collections at UCSD.

Chapter 6

144–145 Copyright © Brannhage/Premium/Panoramic Images; 145 *top* Sovfoto/Eastfoto; 146 *top* Premium Stock/Corbis; *bottom* Craig Aurness/Corbis; 147 Mark Rykoff/Corbis; 148 *left* NASA/AP/Wide World Photos; *right* Sovfoto/Eastfoto; 149 Copyright © Giuliano Bevilacqua/TimePix; 150 Bryn Colton/Corbis; 151 *top* Bettmann/ Corbis; *bottom* AP/Wide World Photos; 152 Bojan Brecelj/Corbis; 154 David and Peter Turnley/Corbis; 156 Craig Aurness/Corbis; 157 Copyright © Bios (F. Gilson)/Peter Arnold; 158 Scala/Art Resource, New York; 160 Sovfoto/ Eastfoto/PictureQuest; 161 *bottom* Hoa Qui/Index Stock Imagery/PictureQuest; *top* Premium Stock/Corbis; 162 AFP/Corbis; 163 Mike Mazzaschi/Stock Boston/PictureQuest; 164 S. Bavister/Robert Harding Picture Library; 165 Copyright © Malcolm S. Kirk/Peter Arnold; 166 *bottom* John Neubauer/Photo Edit/PictureQuest; *top right* Underwood & Underwood/Corbis; *top left* Bettmann/Corbis; 167 *top* Wolfgang Kaehler/Corbis; *left* Paul A. Souders/Corbis; *center* Roger Ressmeyer/Corbis; *bottom right* Academy of Natural Sciences of Philadelphia/ Corbis; 168 *left* Bettmann/Corbis; *right* Premium Stock/Corbis; *center* David and Peter Turnley/Corbis.

Chapter 7

170–171 Alan Thornton/Stone/GettyImages; 171 *top* Mark A. Leman/Stone/GettyImages; 172 *top* Ted Spiegel/ Corbis; *bottom* www.carpix.net; 173 *bottom right* Michael Neveux/Corbis; *center* AFP/Corbis; 176 *bottom* John Launois/Black Star Publishing/PictureQuest; *top* Copyright © Julian Nieman/Collections; 177 AFP/Corbis; 178 *right* Nik Wheeler/Corbis; *left* Ted Spiegel/Corbis; 179 Hans T. Dahlskog/Pressens Bild; 180 *bottom* AFP/Corbis; *top* Alex Farnsworth/The Image Works; 181 John Noble/Corbis; 182–183 Museo de Firenze Com'era, Florence, Italy/The Bridgeman Art Library; 184 *right* Bettmann/Corbis; *left* Corbis; 185 Bettmann/Corbis; 186 Robert Estall/Corbis; 187 Art Resource, New York; 188 *right* AFP/Corbis; *left* Thomas Hoepker/Magnum/PictureQuest; 190 *bottom center* Erich Lessing/Art Resource, New York; *top* www.carpix.net; *bottom right* Josef Karl Stieler/Archivo Iconografico, S. A./Corbis; 191 Carmen Redondo/Corbis; 193 Chuck Fishman/Contact Press Images/PictureQuest; 194 Bettmann/ Corbis; 195 Dennis Chamberlain/Black Star Publishing/PictureQuest; 196 Steven Weinberg/Stone/GettyImages; 197 Vittoriano Rastelli/Corbis; 198 *top left* Copyright © Alex Farnsworth/The Image Works; *top right* Thomas Hoepker/Magnum/PictureQuest; *bottom right* Bettmann/Corbis; *center* Corbis.

UNIT THREE

200–201 Copyright © IFA/Bruce Coleman; 208 *center* Richard T. Nowitz/Corbis; *right* Dagli Orti/Egyptian Museum Cairo/The Art Archive; 208 *left* Copyright © IFA/Bruce Coleman; 209 *left* Copyright © Floyd Norgaard/Ric Ergenbright Photography; *center* Copyright © Hubertus Kanus/Photo Researchers; *right* Copyright © ANAX/ IMAPRESS/The Image Works.

Chapter 8

210–211 Erv. Schowengerdt; 211 *top* Copyright © SuperStock; 212 *top* Roger Wood/Corbis; *bottom* Bojon Brecelj/Corbis; 213 *right* Copyright © Ingeborg Lippman/Peter Arnold; *left* Musée du Louvre, Paris/The Bridgeman Art Library; 215 *top right* Copyright © Robert Fried Photography; *top left* Copyright © Floyd Norgaard/Ric Ergenbright Photography; *bottom right* Richard T. Nowitz/Corbis; 217 Erich Lessing/Art Resource, New York; 218 Roger Wood/Corbis; 219 *bottom* Erich Lessing/Art Resource, New York; *top* Ancient Art and Architecture Collection, London; 220 *bottom right* Ashmolean Museum, Oxford, England/The Bridgeman Art Library; *center* Bettmann/Corbis; 221 Erich Lessing/Art Resource, New York; 223 *right* Dagli Orti/Egyptian Museum Cairo/The Art Archive; *left* Dagli Orti/Luxor Museum, Egypt/The Art Archive; 224 *center* Wolfgang Kaehler/Corbis; *top* Erich Lessing/Art Resource, New York; 225 Kevin Cain, Institute for Study and Intergration of Graphical Heritage Techniques, www.pelleas.org; 226 *left* Dagli Orti/Egyptian Museum Cairo/The Art Archive; 226 *right* Scala/Art Resource, New York; 227 *right* Charles Lenars/Corbis; *left* Philip De Bay/Historical Picture Archive/Corbis; 230 *top* The Jewish Museum, New York/Art Resource, New York; *bottom* Copyright © Fred Bruemmer/Peter Arnold; 231 *top* Scala/Art Resource, New York; *bottom* Carmen Redondo/Corbis; 232 Bojon Brecelj/Corbis; 234 Philip De Bay/Historical Picture Archive/Corbis; 236 *top* Copyright © Kevin Schafer/Peter Arnold; *bottom* Dagli Orti/Egyptian Museum Cairo/The Art Archive; 237 Mary Evans Picture Library; 238 *top left* Copyright © Robert Fried Photography; *top center* Erich Lessing/Art Resource, New York; *center* Erich Lessing/Art Resource, New York; *top right* Copyright © Fred Bruemmer/Peter Arnold; *bottom right* Philip De Bay/Historical Picture Archive/Corbis.

Chapter 9

240–241 Grant V. Faint/The Image Bank/GettyImages; **241** *top* Hubertus Kanus/Photo Researchers; **242** *top* Laura Zitc; *bottom* Chase Swift/Corbis; **243** Bettmann/Corbis; **246** *bottom* Copyright © Robert Fried Photography; *top* Chase Swift/Corbis; **247** Copyright © Tannenbaum/The Image Works; **249** *all* Hulton|Archive/Getty Images; **250** *right* Lambert/Hulton|Archive/Getty Images; *left* Copyright © Mark Antman/The Image Works; **251** Copyright © Kazuyoshi Nomachi/HAGA/The Image Works; **252** Chrisite and Apos's Images/Corbis; **253** Copyright © Margot Granitsas/The Image Works; **256** Bettmann/Corbis; **257** *top* Bettmann/Corbis; *bottom* Sean Saxton/Corbis; **258** *bottom* Corbis; *top* Bettmann/Corbis; **259** Copyright © O. Louis Mazzatenta/NGS Image Collection; **260** Copyright © Richard T. Nowitz; **261** *top* Robert Holmes; *center* Laura Zitc; **262–263** David and Peter Turnley/Corbis; Paul A. Souders/Corbis; Richard T. Nowitz/Corbis; Moshe Shai/Corbis; *all others* Cory Langley; **264** *right* Hulton|Archive/Getty Images; **264** *left* AP/Wide World Photos; **265** Copyright © Richard T. Nowitz; **266** *top* Copyright © Richard T. Nowitz; *bottom* Copyright © ANAX/IMAPRESS/The Image Works; **267** Rina Castelnuovo/PictureQuest; **268** *top* Robert Frerck/Woodfin Camp/PictureQuest; *bottom* Archivo Iconografico, S. A./Corbis; **269** *bottom* Copyright © Elan Sun Star/Index Stock; *center* Elio Ciol/Corbis; *top* David Young-Wolff/Photo Edit/PictureQuest; **270** *right* Culver Pictures; **271** *top* The Granger Collection, New York; *bottom* Copyright © Diana Walker/TimePix; **272** Ruggero Vanni/Corbis; **273** Adam Woolfitt/Corbis; **274** *top left* Copyright © Tannenbaum/The Image Works; *bottom left* Copyright © Kazuyoshi Nomachi/HAGA/The Image Works; *center* Sean Saxton/Corbis; *top right* Copyright © Richard T. Nowitz; *bottom right* Adam Woolfitt/Corbis.

UNIT FOUR

276–277 W. Perry Conway/Corbis.

Chapter 10

288–289 Copyright © Wolfgang Kaehhler; **289** *top* The Granger Collection, New York; **290** *top* Giraudon/Art Resource, New York; *bottom* Copyright © Syracuse Newspapers/The Image Works; **291** Copyright © Still Pictures (Schytte)/Peter Arnold; **292** *center left* Dave G. Houser/Corbis; *center right* John Noble/Corbis; **292–293** Corbis; **293** *bottom right* Peter Johnson/Corbis; **294** David and Peter Turnley/Corbis; **295** *left* D. Boone/Corbis; *right* Bettmann/Corbis; **296–297** Charles and Josette Lenars/Corbis; **298** Patrick Ward/Corbis; **299** *top* Werner Forman/Corbis; *bottom* Copyright © Bob Burch/Index Stock; **300** John Webb/The Art Archive; **301** *right* The Granger Collection, New York; *left* Adam Woolfitt/Corbis; **303** *left* Copyright © Boyd Norton/The Image Works; *right* Ann and Carl Purcell/Words and Pictures/PictureQuest; **305** Howard Davies/Corbis; **307** *right* Copyright © Marc and Evelyne Bernheim/Woodfin Camp; *left* Betty Press/Woodfin Camp/PictureQuest; **309** *all* Copyright © Gerald Buthaud; *bottom* Gerald Buthaud/Cosmos/Woodfin Camp; **310** Alon Reininger/Contact Press Images/PictureQuest; **311** I. Vanderharst/Robert Harding Picture Library; **312** *bottom left* Corbis; *bottom center* Copyright © Bob Burch/Index Stock; *top center* Adam Woolfitt/Corbis; *bottom right* Copyright © Marc and Evelyne Bernheim/Woodfin Camp.

Chapter 11

314–315 Jason Lauré; **315** *top* Copyright © Robert Caputo/Aurora; **316** *top* Reuters NewMedia Inc./Corbis; *bottom* Owen Franken/Corbis; **317** *bottom* Bettmann/Corbis; *top* The Granger Collection, New York; **318** Hulton|Archive/Getty Images; **319** *bottom* Copyright © Griffith J. Davis/TimePix; **320** *top* Copyright © Kwaku Sakyi-Addo/Reuters/TimePix; *bottom* Jason Lauré; **321** AFP/Corbis; **322** *right* Edward R. Degginger/Bruce Coleman/PictureQuest; *left* Tony Wilson-Bligh/Papilio/Corbis; **323** *top left* Kennan Ward/Corbis; *top center* Julian Calder/Corbis; **323** *bottom right* Werner Forman Archive/Art Resource, New York; **324** *right* Reuters NewMedia Inc./Corbis; *left* AFP/Corbis; **325** *left* Owen Franken/Corbis; *right* Steve Jackson/Black Star Publishing/PictureQuest; **327** *bottom* Bonhams, London/The Bridgeman Art Library; *top* Jose Azel/Aurora/PictureQuest; **328** Chris Barton; **330** Werner Forman Archive/Art Resource, New York; **331** *right* Margaret Courtney-Clarke/Corbis; *left* AFP/Corbis; **332** *bottom* AFP/Corbis; *top* Wolfgang Kaehler/Corbis; *center* Richard A. Cooke/Corbis; **333** Werner Forman/Archive/Art Resource, New York; **334** *left* Copyright © Kwaku Sakyi-Addo/Reuters/TimePix; *center* Jose Azel/Aurora/ PictureQuest; *right* AFP/Corbis.

Chapter 12

336–337 Jim Zuckerman/Corbis; **337** *top* The Durcell Team/Corbis; **338** *top* David and Peter Turnley/Corbis; *bottom* Thierry Geenen/Liaison/GettyImages; **339** Copyright © John Reader/Science Photo Library/Photo Researchers; **340** Courtesy, Kathy Schick & Nicholas Toth. Artwork by R. Freyman & N. Toth based on a drawing by Mary Leakey; **341** *right* Wolfgang Kaehler/Corbis; *left* Yann Arthus-Bertrand/Corbis; **342** *top* Bettmann/Corbis; *bottom* David and Peter Turnley/Corbis; **343** Copyright © Betty Press/Woodfin Camp/PictureQuest; **346** AFP/Corbis; **347** *left* Copyright © Grant Heilman/Grant Heilman Photography; *center right* Frank Lane Picture Agency/Corbis; *bottom right* Yann Arthus-Bertrand/Corbis; **348** David Samuel Robbins/Corbis; **349** Nubar Alexanian/Corbis; **350** Carmen Redondo/Corbis; **351** NASA; **352–353** Betty Press/Woodfin Camp/PictureQuest; **354** *bottom right* Lee Foster/Words and Pictures/ PictureQuest; *top* Reprinted from Photo-Publishing Co., *Photographs of South Africa* (Cape Town, 1894); **355** *bottom* AFP/Corbis; *top* The Granger Collection, New York; **357** Pictor International/PictureQuest; **358** Michele Burgess/Index Stock Imagery/PictureQuest; **359** *right* Corbis; *left* Copyright © William F. Campbell/TimePix; **3610** *top* Yann Arthus-Bertrand/Corbis; *bottom* Charles and Josette Lenars/Corbis; **361** Thierry Geenen/Liaison/GettyImages; **362** *top left* Courtesy, Kathy Schick & Nicholas Toth. Artwork by R. Freyman & N. Toth based on a drawing by Mary Leakey; *top right* AFP/Corbis; *bottom left* Nubar Alexanian/Corbis; *bottom right* Charles and Josette Lenars/Corbis; **363** NASA.

UNIT FIVE

364–365 John Lamb/Stone/GettyImages; **372** *left* Ann and Carl Purcell/PictureQuest; *center* Bettmann/Corbis; *right* Alison Wright/Corbis; **373** *center* James Strachan/Stone/GettyImages; *left* Lindsay Hebberd/Corbis; *right* AFP/Corbis.

Chapter 13

374–375 John Elk/Stone/GettyImages; **375** *top* Ann and Carl Purcell/PictureQuest; **376** *top* Reunion des Musées Nationaux/Art Resource, New York; *bottom* Corbis; **377** Hulton-Deutsch Collection/Corbis; **379** Copyright © RafiQur Rahman/Reuters/TimePix; **380** *bottom* James Strachan/Stone/GettyImages; *top* Ted Wood/Black Star Publishing/PictureQuest; **381** Paul Almasy/Corbis; **382** Charles O'Rear/Corbis; **383** Lindsay Hebberd/Corbis; **385** Sarnath, Uttar Pradesh, India/The Bridgeman Art Library; **386** *top center* Archivo Iconografico, S. A./Corbis; *top right* Paul Almasy/Corbis; *bottom center* Charles and Josette Lenars/Corbis; *bottom right* Corbis; **388** *all* Reunion des Musées Nationaux/Art Resource, New York; **389** *bottom* The Granger Collection, New York; *top* Chris Lisle/Corbis; **392** The Granger Collection, New York; **394** Jeremy Homer/Corbis; **397** *top right* Eye Ubiquitous/ Corbis; *all others* Charles and Josette Lenars/Corbis; **398** *center* The Granger Collection, New York; *right* Jeremy Homer/Corbis; *left* James Strachan/Stone/GettyImages.

Chapter 14

400–401 David Sutherland/Stone/GettyImages; **401** *top* Catherine Karnow/Corbis; **402** *top* Caroline Penn/Corbis; *bottom* Amma Clopet/Corbis; **403** Christie's Images, London/The Bridgeman Art Library; **404** *top* Ric Ergenbright/ Corbis; *bottom* Victoria & Albert Museum, London/The Bridgeman Art Library; **405** Hulton-Deutsch Collection/ Corbis; **406–407** Bettmann/Corbis; **409** Hulton|Archive/Getty Images; **410** Copyright © Robert Nickelsberg/ TimePix; **411** *bottom* Corbis; *top* Sena Vidanagama/AFP/Corbis; **412** *top* Sebastian D'Souza/AFP/Corbis; *bottom* Bettmann/Corbis; **413** Copyright © D. Banerjee/Dinodia Picture Agency; **414** *center* Lindsay Hebberd/Corbis; *top left* Baron/Hulton-Deutsch Collection/Corbis; *top right* Chris Lisle/Corbis; *bottom right* Richard Bickel/Corbis; **415** *center* Jeremy Homer/Corbis; *top* Diego Lezama Orezzoli/Corbis; *bottom* Victoria & Albert Museum, London/ The Bridgeman Art Library; **416** Courtesy of AID; **417** Caroline Penn/Corbis; **418** *top* Adam Woolfitt/Corbis; *bottom* Lindsay Hebberd/Corbis; **420** Cris Haigh/Stone/GettyImages; **421** Amma Clopet/Corbis; **422** Surya Temple, Somnath, Bombay, India/Dinodia Picture Agency, Bombay India/Bridgeman Art Library; **423** Earl & Nazima Kowall/Corbis; **425** Bettmann/Corbis; **426** Paul Almasy/Corbis; **428** *left* Bettmann/Corbis; **429** *right* Nik Wheeler/Corbis; *left* Saeed Khan/AFP/Corbis; **430** *bottom left* Bettmann/Corbis; *top left* Sebastian D'Souza/AFP/ Corbis; *top right* Earl & Nazima Kowall/Corbis; *center* Lindsay Hebberd/Corbis; *bottom right* Nik Wheeler/Corbis; **432** Ric Ergenbright/ Corbis; **433** Dave Bartruff/Corbis.

Chapter 15

434–435 Wolfgang Kaehler/Corbis; **435** *top* Alison Wright/Corbis; **436** *bottom* Ted Streshinsky/Photo 20-20/ PictureQuest; **436** *top* Copyright © Walter H. Hodge/Peter Arnold; **437** The British Library, London/The Bridgeman Art Library; **438** *left* Nik Wheeler/Corbis; *right* Copyright © TomPix/Peter Arnold; **439** *left* AFP/Corbis; *right* Copyright © Jose Azel/Woodfin Camp; **440** Hulton|Archive/Getty Images; **441** AFP/Corbis; **442** *bottom left* Brian A. Vikander/Corbis; *bottom right* David Samuel Robbins/Corbis; **443** Brian A. Vikander/Corbis; **444** Hulton| Archive/Getty Images; **445** Ted Streshinsky/Photo 20-20/PictureQuest; **446** *top* Pictor International/PictureQuest; *bottom* Copyright © Walter H. Hodge/Peter Arnold; **447** *right* Kevin R. Morris/Corbis; *left* Chris Rainier/Corbis; **449** Bettmann/Corbis; **450** Charles Bonnay/Black Star Publishing/PictureQuest; **451** *left* Bettmann/Corbis; *right* Dennis Brack/Black Star Publishing/PictureQuest; **452** Copyright © Dan Gair/Index Stock; **453** Hulton|Archive/ Getty Images; **454** *left* Hulton|Archive/Getty Images; *center* Chris Rainier/Corbis; *right* Hulton|Archive/Getty Images.

UNIT SIX

456–457 Copyright © Panoramic Images; **464** *left* Penny Tweedie/Corbis; *center* James L. Amos/Corbis; *right* Reuters NewMedia Inc./Corbis; **465** *left* Keren Su/Stone/GettyImages; *center* Copyright © Bill Lai/The Image Works; *right* Christopher Arnesen/Stone/GettyImages.

Chapter 16

466–467 Copyright © Eric Crichton/Bruce Coleman/PictureQuest; **467** *top* Liu Liqun/Corbis; **468** *bottom* Scala/Art Resource, New York; *top* Dallas and John Heaton/Corbis; **469** Bettmann/Corbis; **470** David Samuel Robbins/Corbis; **471** Dean Conger/Corbis; **472** Charles Rotkin/Corbis; **473** Michael S. Yamashita/Corbis; **475** Giraudon/Art Resource, New York; **476** Erich Lessing/Art Resource, New York; **477** Dallas and John Heaton/Corbis; **478** *right* Reunion des Musées Nationaux/Art Resource, New York; *left* NorthWind Pictures; **479** Reunion des Musées Nationaux/Art Resource, New York; **480** Reunion des Musées Nationaux/Art Resource, New York; **482–483** Corbis; **482** *bottom* Robert Pearcy/Animals Animals; *spread* Corbis; **484** Culver Pictures; **485** *top* Copyright © Bill Lai/The Image Works; *bottom* Craig Lovell/Corbis; **486** *top* Tsukioka Yoshitoshi/ Asian Art and Archaeology, Inc./*bottom* Michael S. Yamashita/Corbis; **487** Scala/Art Resource, New York; **488** N. Blythe/Robert Harding Picture Library; **490** *left* Charles Rotkin/Corbis; *center* Reunion des Musées Nationaux/Art Resource, New York; *right* Copyright © Bill Lai/The Image Works.

Chapter 17

492–493 Paul W. Liebhardt/Corbis; 493 *top* Wolfgang Kaehler/Corbis; 494 *bottom* Bettmann/Corbis; *top* Jay Dickman/Corbis; 495 Bettmann/Corbis; 496 Wolfgang Kaehler/Corbis; 497 *all* Bettmann/Corbis; 498 Roger Ressmeyer/Corbis; 499 Sovfoto/Eastfoto/PictureQuest; 500 John Wang/PhotoDisc/GettyImages; 502 AFP/Corbis; 503 Jay Dickman/Corbis; 504 David and Peter Turnley/Corbis; 506 David Samuel Robbins/Corbis; 507 *bottom left* Keren Su/Stone/GettyImages; *top* Travelpix/FPG/GettyImages; *bottom right* Yann Layma/Stone/GettyImages; 508 Vito Palmisano/Stone/GettyImages; 510 Reuters NewMedia Inc./Corbis; 511 *top* Brian A. Vikander/Corbis; *bottom* Vince Streano/Corbis; 514 Bettmann/Corbis; 515 Christopher Arnesen/Stone/GettyImages; 516 Bettmann/Corbis; 517 Courtesy of the U.S. Naval Academy Museum; 518 *top* Corbis; *bottom* Jed & Kaoru Share/Corbis; 520 Michael S. Yamashita/Corbis; 522 *bottom left* Roger Ressmeyer/Corbis; *bottom center* Jay Dickman/Corbis; *center* Keren Su/Stone/GettyImages; *top* Christopher Arnesen/Stone/GettyImages; *bottom right* Michael S. Yamashita/Corbis.

Chapter 18

524–525 Copyright © John Eastcott/YVA Momatiuk/The Image Works; 525 *top* Penny Tweedie/Corbis; 526 *top* Daniel Aubry; *bottom* Reuters NewMedia Inc./Corbis; 527 Alexander Turnbull Library, Wellington, N. Z./The Bridgeman Art Library; 528 *center* Daniel Aubry; *top* Penny Tweedie/Corbis; *bottom* Werner Forman/Corbis; 529 James L. Amos/Corbis; 530 Royalty Free/Corbis; 531 Reuters NewMedia Inc./Corbis; 533 *top* Penny Tweedie/Corbis; *bottom* Quadrillion/Corbis; 536 *bottom left* Galen Rowell/Corbis; *top right* Richard Hamilton Smith/Corbis; *top left* Penny Tweedie/Corbis; 537 *top* Walter Hodges/Corbis; *bottom* Scott Faulker/Corbis; *top center* Felicia Martinez/PhotoEdit/PictureQuest; 538 *left* James L. Amos/Corbis; *right* Quadrillion/Corbis.

The War on Terrorism

US2 Copyright © AFP/Corbis; *inset* Copyright © John Annerino/TimePix; US3 *top* MapQuest.com; *bottom* Susan Walsh/AP/Wide World Photos; US4 *left* AP/Wide World Photos; *right* MapQuest.com; US5 USA TODAY®; US6–US7 MapQuest.com; US6 *inset* Copyright © Reuters NewMedia Inc./Corbis; US7 *top inset* Katsumi Ksashara/AP/Wide World Photos; *bottom inset* Sayyid Azim/AP/Wide World Photos; US9 *left* AP/Wide World Photos; US10 USA TODAY®; *top inset* AP/Wide World Photos; *middle inset* Al-Jazeera/AP/Wide World Photos; *bottom inset* AP/Wide World Photos; US11 *top* Copyright © David Hume Kennerly/Corbis Sygma; *bottom* MapQuest.com; US12 Copyright © Jeff Christensen/Reuters/TimePix; *inset* Copyright © Greg Mathieson/MAI/TimePix; US13 USA TODAY®; US14 *left* Copyright © Digital Stock/Corbis; *top inset* Copyright © Kent Wood/Photo Researchers; *bottom* FBI/AP/Wide World Photos; *bottom inset* Justice Department/AP/Wide World Photos; US15 Copyright © Eric Draper/The White House/TimePix.

McDougal Littell Inc. has made every effort to locate the copyright holders for the images used in this book and to make full acknowledgment for their use. Omissions brought to our attention will be corrected in subsequent editions.